Collins

Collins
Spanish
Dictionary

this dictionary belongs
to Chrisyl Sarso
if lost please return
back if found
thank you xoxo

HarperCollins Publishers
Westerhill Road
Bishopbriggs
Glasgow
G64 2QT
Great Britain

Sixth Edition 2010

Previously published as
Collins Express Spanish Dictionary
© HarperCollins Publishers 2006

Based on Collins Gem Spanish Dictionary,
1982, 1989, 1993, 1998, 2001, 2004, 2006, 2009

Reprint 10 9 8 7 6 5 4 3 2 1 0

© William Collins Sons & Co. Ltd 1990
© HarperCollins Publishers 1995, 1999, 2002,
2006, 2010
© Collins Bartholomew Ltd 2005

ISBN 978-0-00-732498-9

Collins® is a registered trademark of
HarperCollins Publishers Limited

www.collinslanguage.com

A catalogue record for this book is available
from the British Library

Typeset by Wordcraft Ltd, Glasgow

Printed in Italy by
LEGO Spa, Lavis (Trento)

Acknowledgements

We would like to thank those authors and
publishers who kindly gave permission for
copyright material to be used in the Collins
Word Web. We would also like to thank Times
Newspapers Ltd for providing valuable data.

GENERAL EDITOR
Gaëlle Amiot-Cadey

CONTRIBUTORS
José Martín Galera
Wendy Lee
José María Ruiz Vaca
Cordelia Lilly

EDITORIAL COORDINATION
Maree Airlie
Joyce Littlejohn
Marianne Noble
Susanne Reichert

SERIES EDITOR
Rob Scriven

William Collins' dream of knowledge for all began with the publication of his first book in 1819. A self-educated mill worker, he not only enriched millions of lives, but also founded a flourishing publishing house. Today, staying true to this spirit, Collins books are packed with inspiration, innovation, and practical expertise. They place you at the centre of a world of possibility and give you exactly what you need to explore it.

Language is the key to this exploration, and at the heart of Collins Dictionaries, is language as it is really used. New words, phrases, and meanings spring up every day, and all of them are captured and analysed by the Collins Word Web. Constantly updated, and with over 2.5 billion entries, this living language resource is unique to our dictionaries.

Words are tools for life. And a Collins Dictionary makes them work for you.

Collins. Do more.

ÍNDICE

CONTENTS

marcas registradas

Las marcas que creemos que constituyen marcas registradas las denominamos como tales. Sin embargo, no debe considerarse que la presencia o la ausencia de esta designación tenga que ver con la situación legal de ninguna marca.

note on trademarks

Words which we have reason to believe constitute trademarks have been designated as such. However, neither the presence nor the absence of such designation should be regarded as affecting the legal status of any trademark.

INTRODUCCIÓN

Estamos muy satisfechos de que hayas decidido comprar este diccionario y esperamos que lo disfrutes y que te sirva de gran ayuda ya sea en el colegio, en el trabajo, en tus vacaciones o en casa.

Esta introducción pretende darte algunas indicaciones para ayudarte a sacar el mayor provecho de este diccionario; no sólo de su extenso vocabulario, sino de toda la información que te proporciona cada entrada. Esta te ayudará a leer y comprender – y también a comunicarte y a expresarte – en inglés moderno. Este diccionario comienza con una lista de abreviaturas utilizadas en el texto y con una ilustración de los sonidos representados por los símbolos fonéticos.

EL MANEJO DE TU DICCIONARIO

La amplia información que te ofrece este diccionario aparece presentada en distintas tipografías, con caracteres de diversos tamaños y con distintos símbolos, abreviaturas y paréntesis. Los apartados siguientes explican las reglas y símbolos utilizados.

ENTRADAS

Las palabras que consultas en el diccionario – las entradas – aparecen ordenades alfabéticamente y en color para una identificación más rápida. La palabra que aparece en la parte superior de cada página es la primera entrada (si aparece en la página izquierda) y la última entrada (si aparece en la página derecha) de la página en cuestión. La información sobre el uso o la forma de determinadas entradas aparece entre paréntesis, detrás de la transcripción fonética, y generalmente en forma abreviada y en cursiva

(p. ej.: (*fam*), (*Com*)). En algunos casos se ha considerado oportuno agrupar palabras de una misma familia (**nación, nacionalismo; accept, acceptance**) bajo una misma entrada que aparece en color.

Las expresiones de uso corriente en las que aparece una entrada se dan en negrita (p. ej.: **hurry:** [...] **to be in a ~**).

SÍMBOLOS FONÉTICOS

La transcripción fonética de cada entrada inglesa (que indica su pronunciación) aparece entre corchetes, inmediatamente después de la entrada (p. ej. **knife** [naif]). En las páginas xv-xviii encontrarás una lista de los símbolos fonéticos utilizados en este diccionario.

TRADUCCIONES

Las traducciones de las entradas aparecen en caracteres normales, y en los casos en los que existen significados o usos diferentes, éstos aparecen separados mediante un punto y coma. A menudo encontrarás también otras palabras en cursiva y entre paréntesis antes de las traducciones. Estas sugieren contextos en los que la entrada podría aparecer (p. ej.: **alto** (*persona*) o (*sonido*)) o proporcionan sinónimos (p. ej.: **mismo** (*semejante*)).

PALABRAS CLAVE

Particular relevancia reciben ciertas palabras inglesas y españolas que han sido consideradas palabras 'clave' en cada lengua. Estas pueden, por ejemplo, ser de utilización muy corriente o tener distintos usos (**de, haber; get, that**). La combinación de triángulos y números te permitirá distinguir las diferentes categorías gramaticales y los diferentes significados. Las indicaciones en cursiva y entre paréntesis proporcionan además importante información adicional.

FALSOS AMIGOS

Las palabras que se prestan a confusión al traducir han sido identificadas. En tales entradas existen unas notas que te ayudaran a evitar errores.

INFORMACIÓN GRAMATICAL

Las categorías gramaticales aparecen en forma abreviada y en cursiva después de la transcripción fonética de cada entrada (*vt, adv, conj*). También se indican la forma femenina y los plurales irregulares de los sustantivos del inglés (**child, -ren**).

We are delighted that you have decided to buy this Spanish dictionary and hope you will enjoy and benefit from using it at school, at home, on holiday or at work.

This introduction gives you a few tips on how to get the most out of your dictionary – not simply from its comprehensive wordlist but also from the information provided in each entry. This will help you to read and understand modern Spanish, as well as communicate and express yourself in the language. This dictionary begins by listing the abbreviations used in the text and illustrating the sounds shown by the phonetic symbols.

USING YOUR DICTIONARY

A wealth of information is presented in the dictionary, using various typefaces, sizes of type, symbols, abbreviations and brackets. The various conventions and symbols used are explained in the following sections.

HEADWORDS

The words you look up in a dictionary – 'headwords' – are listed alphabetically. They are printed in **colour** for rapid identification. The headwords appearing at the top of each page indicate the first (if it appears on a left-hand page) and last word (if it appears on a right-hand page) dealt with on the page in question.

Information about the usage or form of certain headwords is given in brackets after the phonetic spelling. This usually appears in abbreviated form and in italics (e.g. (*fam*), (*Com*)).

Where appropriate, words related to headwords are grouped in the same entry (**nación, nacionalismo; accept, acceptance**) and are also in colour. Common expressions in which the headword appears are shown in a different bold roman type (e.g. **cola:** [...] **hacer ~**).

PHONETIC SPELLINGS
The phonetic spelling of each headword (indicating its pronunciation) is given in square brackets immediately after the headword (e.g. **cohete** [ko^{1}ete]). A list of these symbols is given on pages xv-xviii.

TRANSLATIONS
Headword translations are given in ordinary type and, where more than one meaning or usage exists, these are separated by a semi-colon. You will often find other words in italics in brackets before the translations. These offer suggested contexts in which the headword might appear (e.g. **fare** (*on trains, buses*) or provide synonyms (e.g. **litter** (*rubbish*) o (*young animals*)). The gender of the Spanish translation also appears in italics immediately following the key element of the translation, except where this is a regular masculine singular noun ending in 'o', or a regular feminine noun ending in 'a'.

KEY WORDS
Special status is given to certain Spanish and English words which are considered as 'key' words in each language. They may, for example, occur very frequently or have several types of usage (e.g. **de, haber; get, that**). A combination of triangles and numbers helps you to distinguish different

parts of speech and different meanings. Further helpful information is provided in brackets and italics.

FALSE FRIENDS
Words which can be easily confused have been identified in the dictionary. Notes at such entries will help you to avoid these common translation pitfalls.

GRAMMATICAL INFORMATION
Parts of speech are given in abbreviated form in italics after the phonetic spellings of headwords (e.g. *vt, adv, conj*). Genders of Spanish nouns are indicated as follows: *nm* for a masculine and *nf* for a feminine noun. Feminine and irregular plural forms of nouns are also shown (**irlandés, esa; luz** (*pl* **luces**)).

abreviatura	ab(b)r	abbreviation
adjetivo, locución adjetiva	adj	adjective, adjectival phrase
administración	Admin	administration
adverbio, locución adverbial	adv	adverb, adverbial phrase
agricultura	Agr	agriculture
anatomía	Anat	anatomy
Argentina	Arg	Argentina
arquitectura	Arq, Arch	architecture
el automóvil	Aut(o)	the motor car and motoring
aviación, viajes aéreos	Aviac, Aviat	flying, air travel
biología	Bio(l)	biology
botánica, flores	Bot	botany
inglés británico	BRIT	British English
Centroamérica	CAM	Central America
química	Chem	chemistry
comercio, finanzas, banca	Com(m)	commerce, finance, banking
informática	Comput	computing
conjunción	conj	conjunction
construcción	Constr	building
compuesto	cpd	compound element
Cono Sur	CS	Southern Cone
cocina	Culin	cookery
economía	Econ	economics
eletricidad, electrónica	Elec	electricity, electronics
enseñanza, sistema escolar y universitario	Escol	schooling, schools and universities
España	ESP	Spain
especialmente	esp	especially
exclamación, interjección	excl	exclamation, interjection
femenino	f	feminine
lengua familiar (! vulgar)	fam(!)	colloquial usage (! particularly offensive)
ferrocarril	Ferro	railways
uso figurado	fig	figurative use
fotografía	Foto	photography
(verbo inglés) del cual la partícula es inseparable	fus	(phrasal verb) where the particle is inseparable
generalmente	gen	generally
geografía, geología	Geo	geography, geology
geometría	Geom	geometry

historia	*Hist*	history
uso familiar	*inf(!)*	colloquial usage
(! vulgar)		(! particularly offensive)
infinitivo	*infin*	infinitive
informática	*Inform*	computing
invariable	*inv*	invariable
irregular	*irreg*	irregular
lo jurídico	*Jur*	law
América Latina	LAM	Latin America
gramática, lingüística	*Ling*	grammar, linguistics
masculino	*m*	masculine
matemáticas	*Mat(h)*	mathematics
masculino/femenino	*m/f*	masculine/feminine
medicina	*Med*	medicine
México	MÉX, MEX	Mexico
lo militar, ejército	*Mil*	military matters
música	*Mús, Mus*	music
substantivo, nombre	*n*	noun
navegación, náutica	*Náut, Naut*	sailing, navigation
sustantivo numérico	*num*	numeral noun
complemento	*obj*	(grammatical) object
	o.s.	oneself
peyorativo	*pey, pej*	derogatory, pejorative
fotografía	*Phot*	photography
fisiología	*Physiol*	physiology
plural	*pl*	plural
política	*Pol*	politics
participio de pasado	*pp*	past participle
preposición	*prep*	preposition
pronombre	*pron*	pronoun
psicología, psiquiatría	*Psico, Psych*	psychology, psychiatry
tiempo pasado	*pt*	past tense
química	*Quím*	chemistry
ferrocarril	*Rail*	railways
religión	*Rel*	religion
Río de la Plata	RPL	River Plate
	sb	somebody
Cono Sur	SC	Southern Cone
enseñanza, sistema escolar	*Scol*	schooling, schools
y universitario		and universities
singular	*sg*	singular
España	SP	Spain
	sth	something

ABREVIATURAS

ABBREVIATIONS

sujeto	*su(b)j*	(grammatical) subject
subjuntivo	*subjun*	subjunctive
tauromaquia	*Taur*	bullfighting
también	*tb*	also
técnica, tecnología	*Tec(h)*	technical term, technology
telecomunicaciones	*Telec, Tel*	telecommunications
imprenta, tipografía	*Tip, Typ*	typography, printing
televisión	*TV*	television
universidad	*Univ*	university
inglés norteamericano	*US*	American English
verbo	*vb*	verb
verbo intransitivo	*vi*	intransitive verb
verbo pronominal	*vr*	reflexive verb
verbo transitivo	*vt*	transitive verb
zoología	*Zool*	zoology
marca registrada	®	registered trademark
indica un equivalente cultural	≈	introduces a cultural equivalent

SPANISH PRONUNCIATION

VOWELS

a	[a]	pata	not as long as *a* in f*a*r. When followed by a consonant in the same syllable (i.e. in a closed syllable), as in *a*mante, the *a* is short, as in b*a*t
e	[e]	me	like *e* in th*ey*. In a closed syllable, as in g*e*nte, the *e* is short as in p*e*t
i	[i]	pino	as in m*ea*n or mach*i*ne
o	[o]	lo	as in l*o*cal. In a closed syllable, as in c*o*ntrol, the *o* is short as in c*o*t
u	[u]	lunes	as in r*u*le. It is silent after q, and in g*ue*, g*ui*, unless marked g*üe*, g*üi* e.g. antig*üe*dad, when it is pronounced like *w* in *w*olf

SEMIVOWELS

i, y	[j]	bien hielo yunta	pronounced like *y* in *y*es
u	[w]	huevo fuento antigüedad	unstressed *u* between consonant and vowel is pronounced like *w* in *w*ell. See notes on *u* above.

DIPHTHONGS

ai, ay	[ai]	baile	as *i* in r*i*de
au	[au]	auto	as *ou* in sh*ou*t
ei, ey	[ei]	buey	as *ey* in gr*ey*
eu	[eu]	deuda	both elements pronounced independently [e] + [u]
oi, oy	[oi]	hoy	as *oy* in t*oy*

CONSONANTS

b	[b,β]	boda bomba labor	see notes on *v* below
c	[k]	caja	*c* before *a, o, u* is pronounced as in *c*at
ce, ci	[θe,θi]	cero cielo	*c* before *e* or *i* is pronounced as in *th*in
ch	[tʃ]	chiste	*ch* is pronounced as *ch* in *ch*air
d	[d,ð]	danés ciudad	at the beginning of a phrase or after *l* or *n*, *d* is pronounced as in English. In any other position it is pronounced like *th* in *th*e

g	[g, ɣ]	gafas paga	g before a, o or u is pronounced as in gap, if at the beginning of a phrase or after n. In other positions the sound is softened
ge, gi	[xe, xi]	gente girar	g before e or i is pronounced similar to ch in Scottish loch
h		haber	h is always silent in Spanish
j	[x]	jugar	j is pronounced similar to ch in Scottish loch
ll	[ʎ]	talle	ll is pronounced like the y in yet or the lli in million
ñ	[ʃ]	niño	ñ is pronounced like the ni in onion
q	[k]	que	q is pronounced as k in king
r, rr	[r, rr]	quitar garra	r is always pronounced in Spanish, unlike the silent r in dancer. rr is trilled, like a Scottish r
s	[s]	quizás isla	s is usually pronounced as in pass, but before b, d, g, l, m or n it is pronounced as in rose
v	[b, β]	vía	v is pronounced something like b. At the beginning of a phrase or after m or n it is pronounced as b in boy. In any other position the sound is softened
z	[θ]	tenaz	z is pronounced as th in thin

f, k, l, m, n, p, t and x are pronounced as in English.

STRESS

The rules of stress in Spanish are as follows:

(a)   when a word ends in a vowel or in n or s, the second last syllable is stressed:
patata, patatas; come, comen

(b)   when a word ends in a consonant other than n or s, the stress falls on the last syllable:
pared, hablar

(c)   when the rules set out in (a) and (b) are not applied, an acute accent appears over the stressed vowel:
común, geografía, inglés

In the phonetic transcription, the symbol [¹] precedes the syllable on which the stress falls.

LA PRONUNCIACIÓN INGLESA

VOCALES

		Ejemplo inglés	Explicación
[ɑ:]		father	Entre *a* de *padre* y *o* de *noche*
[ʌ]		but, come	*a* muy breve
[æ]		man, cat	Con los labios en la posición de *e* en *pena* y luego se pronuncia el sonido *a* parecido a la *a* de *carro*
[ə]		father, ago	Vocal neutra parecida a una *e* u *o* casi muda
[ə:]		bird, heard	Entre *e* abierta y *o* cerrada, sonido alargado
[ɛ]		get, bed	Como en *perro*
[ɪ]		it, big	Más breve que en *si*
[i:]		tea, see	Como en *fino*
[ɔ]		hot, wash	Como en *torre*
[ɔ:]		saw, all	Como en *por*
[u]		put, book	Sonido breve, más cerrado que *burro*
[u:]		too, you	Sonido largo, como en *uno*

DIPTONGOS

		Ejemplo inglés	Explicación
[aɪ]		fly, high	Como en *fraile*
[au]		how, house	Como en *pausa*
[ɛə]		there, bear	Casi como en *vea*, pero el sonido *a* se mezcla con el indistinto [ə]
[eɪ]		day, obey	*e* cerrada seguida por una *i* débil
[ɪə]		here, hear	Como en *manía*, mezclándose el sonido *a* con el indistinto [ə]
[əu]		go, note	[ə] seguido por una breve *u*
[əɪ]		boy, oil	Como en *voy*
[uə]		poor, sure	*u* bastante larga más el sonido indistinto [ə]

CONSONANTES

	Ejemplo inglés	Explicación
[b]	big, lobby	Como en tumban
[d]	mended	Como en conde, andar
[g]	go, get, big	Como en grande, gol
[dʒ]	gin, judge	Como en la *ll* andaluza y en Generalitat (*catalán*)
[ŋ]	sing	Como en vínculo
[h]	house, he	Como la jota hispanoamericana
[j]	young, yes	Como en ya
[k]	come, mock	Como en caña, Escocia
[r]	red, tread	Se pronuncia con la punta de la lengua hacia atrás y sin hacerla vibrar
[s]	sand, yes	Como en casa, sesión
[z]	rose, zebra	Como en desde, mismo
[ʃ]	she, machine	Como en chambre (*francés*), roxo (*portugués*)
[tʃ]	chin, rich	Como en chocolate
[v]	valley	Como *f*, pero se retiran los dientes superiores vibrándolos contra el labio inferior
[w]	water, which	Como la *u* de huevo, puede
[ʒ]	vision	Como en journal (*francés*)
[θ]	think, myth	Como en receta, zapato
[ð]	this, the	Como en hablado, verdad

f, l, m, n, p, t y x iguales que en español.

El signo [*] indica que la r final escrita apenas se pronuncia en inglés británico cuando la palabra siguiente empieza con vocal.
El signo [ˈ] indica la sílaba acentuada.

LOS NÚMEROS

NUMBERS

un, uno(a)	1	one
dos	2	two
tres	3	three
cuatro	4	four
cinco	5	five
seis	6	six
siete	7	seven
ocho	8	eight
nueve	9	nine
diez	10	ten
once	11	eleven
doce	12	twelve
trece	13	thirteen
catorce	14	fourteen
quince	15	fifteen
dieciséis	16	sixteen
diecisiete	17	seventeen
dieciocho	18	eighteen
diecinueve	19	nineteen
veinte	20	twenty
veintiuno	21	twenty-one
veintidós	22	twenty-two
treinta	30	thirty
cuarenta	40	forty
cincuenta	50	fifty
sesenta	60	sixty
setenta	70	seventy
ochenta	80	eighty
noventa	90	ninety
cien, ciento	100	a hundred, one hundred
ciento uno(a)	101	a hundred and one
doscientos(as)	200	two hundred
trescientos(as)	300	three hundred
cuatrocientos(as)	400	four hundred
quiniento(as)	500	five hundred
seiscientos(as)	600	six hundred
setecientos(as)	700	seven hundred
ochocientos(as)	800	eight hundred
novecientos(as)	900	nine hundred
mil	1000	a thousand
cinco mil	5000	five thousand
un millón	1000000	a million

LOS NÚMEROS

NUMBERS

primer, primero(a), 1°, 1er, (1ª, 1era)	first, 1st
segundo(a), 2° (2ª)	second, 2nd
tercer, tercero(a), 3° (3ª)	third, 3rd
cuarto(a), 4° (4ª)	fourth, 4th
quinto(a), 5° (5ª)	fifth, 5th
sexto(a), 6° (6ª)	sixth, 6th
séptimo(a)	seventh
octavo(a)	eighth
noveno(a)	ninth
décimo(a)	tenth
undécimo(a)	eleventh
duodécimo(a)	twelfth
decimotercio(a)	thirteenth
decimocuarto(a)	fourteenth
decimoquinto(a)	fifteenth
decimosexto(a)	sixteenth
decimoséptimo(a)	seventeenth
decimoctavo(a)	eighteenth
decimonoveno(a)	nineteenth
vigésimo(a)	twentieth
trigésimo(a)	thirtieth
centésimo(a)	hundredth
milésimo(a)	thousandth

NÚMEROS QUEBRADOS ETC

FRACTIONS ETC

un medio	a half
un tercio	a third
un cuarto	a quarter
un quinto	a fifth
cero coma cinco, 0,5	(nought) point five, 0.5
tres coma cuatro, 3,4	three point four, 3.4
diez por cien(to)	ten per cent
cien por cien	a hundred per cent

EJEMPLOS

EXAMPLES

va a llegar el 7 (de mayo)	he's arriving on the 7th (of May)
vive en el número 7	he lives at number 7
el capítulo/la página 7	chapter/page 7
llegó séptimo	he came in 7th

N.B. In Spanish the ordinal numbers from 1 to 10 are commonly used; from 11 to 20 rather less; above 21 they are rarely written and almost never heard in speech.

LA HORA

¿qué hora es?

es/son

medianoche, las doce (de la noche)
la una (de la madrugada)

la una y cinco
la una y diez
la una y cuarto *or* quince

la una y veinticinco

la una y media *or* treinta
las dos menos veinticinco, la una
    treinta y cinco
las dos menos veinte, la una cuarenta
las dos menos cuarto, la una cuarenta
    y cinco
las dos menos diez, la una cincuenta
mediodía, las doce (de la tarde)

la una (de la tarde)

las siete (de la tarde)

¿a qué hora?

a medianoche
a las siete

en veinte minutos
hace quince minutos

THE TIME

what time is it?

it's o it is

midnight, twelve p.m.
one o'clock (in the
    morning), one (a.m.)
five past one
ten past one
a quarter past one,
    one fifteen
twenty-five past one,
    one twenty-five
half-past one, one thirty
twenty-five to two,
    one thirty-five
twenty to two, one forty
a quarter to two,
    one forty-five
ten to two, one fifty
twelve o'clock, midday,
    noon
one o'clock (in the
    afternoon), one (p.m.)
seven o'clock (in the
    evening), seven (p.m.)

(at) what time?

at midnight
at seven o'clock

in twenty minutes
fifteen minutes ago

VERBOS IRREGULARES EN INGLÉS

PRESENTE	PASADO	PARTICIPIO	PRESENTE	PASADO	PARTICIPIO
arise	arose	arisen	dream	dreamed,	dreamed,
awake	awoke	awoken		dreamt	dreamt
be (am, is,	was, were	been	drink	drank	drunk
are; being)			drive	drove	driven
bear	bore	born(e)	dwell	dwelt	dwelt
beat	beat	beaten	eat	ate	eaten
become	became	become	fall	fell	fallen
begin	began	begun	feed	fed	fed
bend	bent	bent	feel	felt	felt
bet	bet,	bet,	fight	fought	fought
	betted	betted	find	found	found
bid (at auction,	bid	bid	flee	fled	fled
cards)			fling	flung	flung
bid (say)	bade	bidden	fly	flew	flown
bind	bound	bound	forbid	forbad(e)	forbidden
bite	bit	bitten	forecast	forecast	forecast
bleed	bled	bled	forget	forgot	forgotten
blow	blew	blown	forgive	forgave	forgiven
break	broke	broken	forsake	forsook	forsaken
breed	bred	bred	freeze	froze	frozen
bring	brought	brought	get	got	got,
build	built	built			(us) gotten
burn	burnt,	burnt,	give	gave	given
	burned	burned	go (goes)	went	gone
burst	burst	burst	grind	ground	ground
buy	bought	bought	grow	grew	grown
can	could	(been able)	hang	hung	hung
cast	cast	cast	hang (suspend)	hanged	hanged
catch	caught	caught	(execute)		
choose	chose	chosen	have	had	had
cling	clung	clung	hear	heard	heard
come	came	come	hide	hid	hidden
cost (be	cost	cost	hit	hit	hit
valued at)			hold	held	held
cost (work	costed	costed	hurt	hurt	hurt
out price of)			keep	kept	kept
creep	crept	crept	kneel	knelt,	knelt,
cut	cut	cut		kneeled	kneeled
deal	dealt	dealt	know	knew	known
dig	dug	dug	lay	laid	laid
do (does)	did	done	lead	led	led
draw	drew	drawn	lean	leant,	leant,

xxii

PRESENTE	PASADO	PARTICIPIO	PRESENTE	PASADO	PARTICIPIO
	leaned	leaned	shine	shone	shone
leap	leapt,	leapt,	shoot	shot	shot
	leaped	leaped	show	showed	shown
learn	learnt,	learnt,	shrink	shrank	shrunk
	learned	learned	shut	shut	shut
leave	left	left	sing	sang	sung
lend	lent	lent	sink	sank	sunk
let	let	let	sit	sat	sat
lie (lying)	lay	lain	slay	slew	slain
light	lit,	lit,	sleep	slept	slept
	lighted	lighted	slide	slid	slid
lose	lost	lost	sling	slung	slung
make	made	made	slit	slit	slit
may	might	–	smell	smelt,	smelt,
mean	meant	meant		smelled	smelled
meet	met	met	sow	sowed	sown,
mistake	mistook	mistaken			sowed
mow	mowed	mown,	speak	spoke	spoken
		mowed	speed	sped,	sped,
must	(had to)	(had to)		speeded	speeded
pay	paid	paid	spell	spelt,	spelt,
put	put	put		spelled	spelled
quit	quit,	quit,	spend	spent	spent
	quitted	quitted	spill	spilt,	spilt,
read	read	read		spilled	spilled
rid	rid	rid	spin	spun	spun
ride	rode	ridden	spit	spat	spat
ring	rang	rung	spoil	spoiled,	spoiled,
rise	rose	risen		spoilt	spoilt
run	ran	run	spread	spread	spread
saw	sawed	sawed,	spring	sprang	sprung
		sawn	stand	stood	stood
say	said	said	steal	stole	stolen
see	saw	seen	stick	stuck	stuck
seek	sought	sought	sting	stung	stung
sell	sold	sold	stink	stank	stunk
send	sent	sent	stride	strode	stridden
set	set	set	strike	struck	struck
sew	sewed	sewn	strive	strove	striven
shake	shook	shaken	swear	swore	sworn
shear	sheared	shorn,	sweep	swept	swept
		sheared	swell	swelled	swollen,
shed	shed	shed			swelled

PRESENTE	PASADO	PARTICIPIO	PRESENTE	PASADO	PARTICIPIO
swim	swam	swum	wear	wore	worn
swing	swung	swung	weave (on loom)	wove	woven
take	took	taken	weave (wind)	weaved	weaved
teach	taught	taught	wed	wedded, wed	wedded, wed
tear	tore	torn			
tell	told	told	weep	wept	wept
think	thought	thought	win	won	won
throw	threw	thrown	wind	wound	wound
thrust	thrust	thrust	wring	wrung	wrung
tread	trod	trodden	write	wrote	written
wake	woke, waked	woken, waked			

7 (*razón*): **a 30 céntimos el kilo** at 30 cents a kilo; **a más de 50 km/h** at more than 50 kms per hour

8 (*dativo*): **se lo di a él** I gave it to him; **vi al policía** I saw the policeman; **se lo compré a él** I bought it from him

9 (*tras ciertos verbos*): **voy a verle** I'm going to see him; **empezó a trabajar** he started working *o* to work

10 (+ *infin*): **al verlo, lo reconocí inmediatamente** when I saw him I recognized him at once; **el camino a recorrer** the distance we *etc* have to travel; **¡a callar!** keep quiet!; **¡a comer!** let's eat!

abad, esa [aˈβað, ˈðesa] *nm/f* abbot/abbess; **abadía** *nf* abbey

abajo [aˈβaxo] *adv* (*situación*) (down) below, underneath; (*en edificio*) downstairs; (*dirección*) down, downwards; **el piso de ~** the downstairs flat; **la parte de ~** the lower part; **¡~ el gobierno!** down with the government!; **cuesta/río ~** downhill/downstream; **de arriba ~** from top to bottom; **el ~ firmante** the undersigned; **más ~** lower *o* further down

abalanzarse [aβalanˈθarse] *vr*: **~ sobre** *o* **contra** to throw o.s. at

abanderado, -a [aβandeˈraðo] *nm/f* (*portaestandarte*) standard bearer; (*de un movimiento*) champion, leader; (*MÉX*: *linier*) linesman, assistant referee

abandonado, -a [aβandoˈnaðo, a] *adj* derelict; (*desatendido*) abandoned; (*desierto*) deserted; (*descuidado*) neglected

abandonar [aβandoˈnar] *vt* to leave; (*persona*) to abandon, desert; (*cosa*) to abandon, leave behind; (*descuidar*) to neglect; (*renunciar a*) to give up; (*Inform*) to quit; **abandonarse** *vr*: **~se a** to abandon o.s. to; **abandono** *nm* (*acto*) desertion, abandonment; (*estado*) abandon, neglect; (*renuncia*) withdrawal, retirement; **ganar por**

○ **PALABRA CLAVE**

a [a] (*a* + *el* = *al*) *prep* **1** (*dirección*) to; **fueron a Madrid/Grecia** they went to Madrid/Greece; **me voy a casa** I'm going home

2 (*distancia*): **está a 15 km de aquí** it's 15 kms from here

3 (*posición*): **estar a la mesa** to be at table; **al lado de** next to, beside; *V tb* **puerta**

4 (*tiempo*): **a las 10/a medianoche** at 10/midnight; **a la mañana siguiente** the following morning; **a los pocos días** after a few days; **estamos a 9 de julio** it's the ninth of July; **a los 24 años** at the age of 24; **al año/a la semana** a year/week later

5 (*manera*): **a la francesa** the French way; **a caballo** on horseback; **a oscuras** in the dark

6 (*medio, instrumento*): **a lápiz** in pencil; **a mano** by hand; **cocina a gas** gas stove

abandono to win by default

abanico [aβa'niko] *nm* fan; *(Náut)* derrick

abarcar [aβar'kar] *vt* to include, embrace; *(LAM: acaparar)* to monopolize

abarrotado, -a [aβarro'taðo, a] *adj* packed

abarrotar [aβarro'tar] *vt (local, estadio, teatro)* to fill, pack

abarrotero, -a [aβarro'tero, a] *(MÉX) nm/f* grocer; **abarrotes** *(MÉX) nmpl* groceries; **tienda de abarrotes** *(MÉX, CAM)* grocery store

abastecer [aβaste'θer] *vt:* **~ (de)** to supply (with); **abastecimiento** *nm* supply

abasto [a'βasto] *nm* supply; **no dar ~ a** to be unable to cope with

abatible [aβa'tiβle] *adj:* **asiento ~** tip-up seat; *(Auto)* reclining seat

abatido, -a [aβa'tiðo, a] *adj* dejected, downcast

abatir [aβa'tir] *vt (muro)* to demolish; *(pájaro)* to shoot o bring down; *(fig)* to depress

abdicar [aβði'kar] *vi* to abdicate

abdomen [aβ'ðomen] *nm* abdomen; **abdominales** *nmpl (tb:* **ejercicios abdominales)** sit-ups

abecedario [aβeθe'ðarjo] *nm* alphabet

abedul [aβe'ðul] *nm* birch

abeja [a'βexa] *nf* bee

abejorro [aβe'xorro] *nm* bumblebee

abertura [aβer'tura] *nf* = **apertura**

abeto [a'βeto] *nm* fir

abierto, -a [a'βjerto, a] *pp de* **abrir** ▷ *adj* open

abismal [aβis'mal] *adj (fig)* vast, enormous

abismo [a'βismo] *nm* abyss

ablandar [aβlan'dar] *vt* to soften; **ablandarse** *vr* to get softer

abocado, -a [a'βo'kaðo, a] *adj (vino)* smooth, pleasant

abochornar [aβotʃor'nar] *vt* to embarrass

abofetear [aβofete'ar] *vt* to slap (in the face)

abogado, -a [aβo'ɣaðo, a] *nm/f* lawyer; *(notario)* solicitor; *(en tribunal)* barrister *(BRIT)*, attorney *(US)*; **abogado defensor** defence lawyer o *(US)* attorney

abogar [aβo'ɣar] *vi:* **~ por** to plead for; *(fig)* to advocate

abolir [aβo'lir] *vt* to abolish; *(cancelar)* to cancel

abolladura [aβoʎa'ðura] *nf* dent

abollar [aβo'ʎar] *vt* to dent

abombarse [aβom'barse] *(LAM) vr* to go bad

abominable [aβomi'naβle] *adj* abominable

abonado, -a [aβo'naðo, a] *adj (deuda)* paid(-up) ▷ *nm/f* subscriber

abonar [aβo'nar] *vt (deuda)* to settle; *(terreno)* to fertilize; *(idea)* to endorse; **abonarse** *vr* to subscribe; **abono** *nm* payment; fertilizer; subscription

abordar [aβor'ðar] *vt (barco)* to board; *(asunto)* to broach

aborigen [aβo'rixen] *nmf* aborigine

aborrecer [aβorre'θer] *vt* to hate, loathe

abortar [aβor'tar] *vi (malparir)* to have a miscarriage; *(deliberadamente)* to have an abortion; **aborto** *nm* miscarriage; abortion

abovedado, -a [aβoβe'ðaðo, a] *adj* vaulted, domed

abrasar [aβra'sar] *vt* to burn (up); *(Agr)* to dry up, parch

abrazar [aβra'θar] *vt* to embrace, hug

abrazo [a'βraθo] *nm* embrace, hug; **un ~** *(en carta)* with best wishes

abrebotellas [aβreβo'teʎas] *nm inv* bottle opener

abrecartas [aβre'kartas] *nm inv* letter opener

abrelatas [aβre'latas] *nm inv* tin *(BRIT)* o can opener

abreviatura [aβreβja'tura] *nf* abbreviation

abridor [aβri'ðor] *nm* bottle opener;

(de latas) tin *(BRIT)* o can opener

abrigador, a [aβriɣaˈðor, a] *(MÉX)* adj warm

abrigar [aβriˈɣar] vt *(proteger)* to shelter; *(ropa)* to keep warm; *(fig)* to cherish

abrigo [aˈβriɣo] nm *(prenda)* coat, overcoat; *(lugar protegido)* shelter

abril [aˈβril] nm April

abrillantador [aβriʎantaˈðor] nm polish

abrillantar [aβriʎanˈtar] vt to polish

abrir [aˈβrir] vt to open (up) ▷ vi to open; **abrirse** vr to open (up); *(extenderse)* to open out; *(cielo)* to clear; **~se paso** to find o force a way through

abrochar [aβroˈtʃar] vt *(con botones)* to button (up); *(zapato, con broche)* to do up

abrupto, -a [aˈβrupto, a] adj abrupt; *(empinado)* steep

absoluto, -a [aβsoˈluto, a] adj absolute; **en ~** adv not at all

absolver [aβsolˈβer] vt to absolve; *(Jur)* to pardon; (: *acusado*) to acquit

absorbente [aβsorˈβente] adj absorbent; *(interesante)* absorbing

absorber [aβsorˈβer] vt to absorb; *(embeber)* to soak up

absorción [aβsorˈθjon] nf absorption; *(Com)* takeover

abstemio, -a [aβsˈtemjo, a] adj teetotal

abstención [aβstenˈθjon] nf abstention

abstenerse [aβsteˈnerse] vr: **~ (de)** to abstain o refrain (from)

abstinencia [aβstiˈnenθja] nf abstinence; *(ayuno)* fasting

abstracto, -a [aβsˈtrakto, a] adj abstract

abstraer [aβstraˈer] vt to abstract; **abstraerse** vr to be o become absorbed

abstraído, -a [aβstraˈiðo, a] adj absent-minded

absuelto [aβsˈwelto] pp de **absolver**

absurdo, -a [aβsˈurðo, a] adj absurd

abuchear [aβutʃeˈar] vt to boo

abuelo, -a [aˈβwelo, a] nm/f grandfather(-mother); **abuelos** nmpl grandparents

abultado, -a [aβulˈtaðo, a] adj bulky

abultar [aβulˈtar] vi to be bulky

abundancia [aβunˈdanθja] nf: **una ~ de** plenty of; **abundante** adj abundant, plentiful

abundar [aβunˈdar] vi to abound, be plentiful

aburrido, -a [aβuˈrriðo, a] adj *(hastiado)* bored; *(que aburre)* boring; **aburrimiento** nm boredom, tedium

aburrir [aβuˈrrir] vt to bore; **aburrirse** vr to be bored, get bored

abusado, -a [aβuˈsaðo, a] *(MÉX: fam)* adj *(astuto)* sharp, cunning ▷ excl: **¡~!** *(inv)* look out!, careful!

abusar [aβuˈsar] vi to go too far; **~ de** to abuse

abusivo, -a [aβuˈsiβo, a] adj *(precio)* exorbitant

abuso [aˈβuso] nm abuse

acá [aˈka] adv *(lugar)* here

acabado, -a [akaˈβaðo, a] adj finished, complete; *(perfecto)* perfect; *(agotado)* worn out; *(fig)* masterly ▷ nm finish

acabar [akaˈβar] vt *(llevar a su fin)* to finish, complete; *(consumir)* to use up; *(rematar)* to finish off ▷ vi to finish, end; **acabarse** vr to finish, stop; *(terminarse)* to be over; *(agotarse)* to run out; **~ con** to put an end to; **~ de llegar** to have just arrived; **~ por hacer** to end (up) by doing; **¡se acabó!** it's all over!, *(¡basta!)* that's enough!

acabóse [akaˈβose] nm: **esto es el ~** this is the last straw

academia [akaˈðemja] nf academy; **academia de idiomas** language school; **académico, -a** adj academic

acalorado, -a [akaloˈraðo, a] adj *(discusión)* heated

acampar [akamˈpar] vi to camp

acantilado [akantiˈlaðo] nm cliff

acaparar [akapaˈrar] vt to

monopolize; (*acumular*) to hoard

acariciar [akari'θjar] *vt* to caress; (*esperanza*) to cherish

acarrear [akarre'ar] *vt* to transport; (*fig*) to cause, result in

acaso [a'kaso] *adv* perhaps, maybe; **(por) si ~** (just) in case

acatar [aka'tar] *vt* to respect; (*ley*) obey

acatarrarse [akata'rrarse] *vr* to catch a cold

acceder [akθe'ðer] *vi*: **~ a** (*petición etc*) to agree to; (*tener acceso a*) to have access to; (*Inform*) to access

accesible [akθe'siβle] *adj* accessible

acceso [ak'θeso] *nm* access, entry; (*camino*) access, approach; (*Med*) attack, fit

accesorio, -a [akθe'sorjo, a] *adj, nm* accessory

accidentado, -a [akθiðen'taðo, a] *adj* uneven; (*montañoso*) hilly; (*azaroso*) eventful ▷ *nm/f* accident victim

accidental [akθiðen'tal] *adj* accidental

accidente [akθi'ðente] *nm* accident; **accidentes** *nmpl* (*de terreno*) unevenness *sg*; **accidente laboral** *o* **de trabajo/de tráfico** industrial/road *o* traffic accident

acción [ak'θjon] *nf* action; (*acto*) action, act; (*Com*) share; (*Jur*) action, lawsuit; **accionar** *vt* to work, operate; (*Inform*) to drive

accionista [akθjo'nista] *nmf* shareholder, stockholder

acebo [a'θeβo] *nm* holly; (*árbol*) holly tree

acechar [aθe'tʃar] *vt* to spy on; (*aguardar*) to lie in wait for; **acecho** *nm*: **estar al acecho (de)** to lie in wait (for)

aceite [a'θeite] *nm* oil; **aceite de girasol/oliva** olive/sunflower oil; **aceitera** *nf* oilcan; **aceitoso, -a** *adj* oily

aceituna [aθei'tuna] *nf* olive; **aceituna rellena** stuffed olive

acelerador [aθelera'ðor] *nm* accelerator

acelerar [aθele'rar] *vt* to accelerate

acelga [a'θelxa] *nf* chard, beet

acento [a'θento] *nm* accent; (*acentuación*) stress

acentuar [aθen'twar] *vt* to accent; to stress; (*fig*) to accentuate

acepción [aθep'θjon] *nf* meaning

aceptable [aθep'taβle] *adj* acceptable

aceptación [aθepta'θjon] *nf* acceptance; (*aprobación*) approval

aceptar [aθep'tar] *vt* to accept; (*aprobar*) to approve; **~ hacer algo** to agree to do sth

acequia [a'θekja] *nf* irrigation ditch

acera [a'θera] *nf* pavement (BRIT), sidewalk (US)

acerca [a'θerka]: **~ de** *prep* about, concerning

acercar [aθer'kar] *vt* to bring *o* move nearer; **acercarse** *vr* to approach, come near

acero [a'θero] *nm* steel

acérrimo, -a [a'θerrimo, a] *adj* (*partidario*) staunch; (*enemigo*) bitter

acertado, -a [aθer'taðo, a] *adj* correct; (*apropiado*) apt; (*sensato*) sensible

acertar [aθer'tar] *vt* (*blanco*) to hit; (*solución*) to get right; (*adivinar*) to guess ▷ *vi* to get it right, be right; **~ a** to manage to; **~ con** to happen *o* hit on

acertijo [aθer'tixo] *nm* riddle, puzzle

achacar [atʃa'kar] *vt* to attribute

achacoso, -a [atʃa'koso, a] *adj* sickly

achicar [atʃi'kar] *vt* to reduce; (*Náut*) to bale out

achicharrar [atʃitʃa'rrar] *vt* to scorch, burn

achichincle [atʃi'tʃinkle] (MÉX: *fam*) *nmf* minion

achicoria [atʃi'korja] *nf* chicory

achuras [a'tʃuras] (RPL) *nfpl* offal *sg*

acicate [aθi'kate] *nm* spur

acidez [aθi'ðeθ] *nf* acidity

ácido, -a ['aθiðo, a] *adj* sour, acid
▷ *nm* acid

acierto *etc* [a'θjerto] *vb* V **acertar**
▷ *nm* success; (*buen paso*) wise move;
(*solución*) solution; (*habilidad*) skill,
ability

acitronar [aθitro'nar] (*MÉX: fam*) *vt*
to brown

aclamar [akla'mar] *vt* to acclaim;
(*aplaudir*) to applaud

aclaración [aklara'θjon] *nf*
clarification, explanation

aclarar [akla'rar] *vt* to clarify,
explain; (*ropa*) to rinse ▷ *vi* to clear
up; **aclararse** *vr* (*explicarse*) to
understand; **~se la garganta** to clear
one's throat

aclimatación [aklimata'θjon] *nf*
acclimatization

aclimatar [aklima'tar] *vt* to
acclimatize; **aclimatarse** *vr* to
become acclimatized

acné [ak'ne] *nm* acne

acobardar [akoβar'ðar] *vt* to
intimidate

acogedor, a [akoxe'ðor, a] *adj*
welcoming; (*hospitalario*) hospitable

acoger [ako'xer] *vt* to welcome;
(*abrigar*) to shelter

acogida [ako'xiða] *nf* reception;
refuge

acomedido, -a [akome'ðiðo, a]
(*MÉX*) *adj* helpful, obliging

acometer [akome'ter] *vt* to attack;
(*emprender*) to undertake; **acometida**
nf attack, assault

acomodado, -a [akomo'ðaðo, a] *adj*
(*persona*) well-to-do

acomodador, a [akomoða'ðor, a]
nm/f usher(ette)

acomodar [akomo'ðar] *vt* to adjust;
(*alojar*) to accommodate; **acomodarse**
vr to conform; (*instalarse*) to install o.s.;
(*adaptarse*): **~se (a)** to adapt (to)

acompañar [akompa'ɲar] *vt* to
accompany; (*documentos*) to enclose

acondicionar [akondiθjo'nar] *vt* to
arrange, prepare; (*pelo*) to condition

aconsejar [akonse'xar] *vt* to advise,
counsel; **~ a algn hacer** *o* **que haga
algo** to advise sb to do sth

acontecer [akonte'θer] *vi* to happen,
occur; **acontecimiento** *nm* event

acopio [a'kopjo] *nm* store, stock

acoplar [ako'plar] *vt* to fit; (*Elec*) to
connect; (*vagones*) to couple

acorazado, -a [akora'θaðo, a]
adj armour-plated, armoured ▷ *nm*
battleship

acordar [akor'ðar] *vt* (*resolver*) to
agree, resolve; (*recordar*) to remind;
acordarse *vr* to agree; **~ hacer algo**
to agree to do sth; **~se (de algo)** to
remember (sth); **acorde** *adj* (*Mús*)
harmonious; **acorde con** (*medidas etc*)
in keeping with ▷ *nm* chord

acordeón [akorðe'on] *nm* accordion

acordonado, -a [akorðo'naðo, a]
adj (*calle*) cordoned-off

acorralar [akorra'lar] *vt* to round
up, corral

acortar [akor'tar] *vt* to shorten;
(*duración*) to cut short; (*cantidad*) to
reduce; **acortarse** *vr* to become
shorter

acosar [ako'sar] *vt* to pursue
relentlessly; (*fig*) to hound, pester;
acoso *nm* harassment; **acoso sexual**
sexual harassment

acostar [akos'tar] *vt* (*en cama*) to
put to bed; (*en suelo*) to lay down;
acostarse *vr* to go to bed; to lie down;
~se con algn to sleep with sb

acostumbrado, -a [akostum'braðo,
a] *adj* usual; **~ a** used to

acostumbrar [akostum'brar] *vt*: **~
a algn a algo** to get sb used to sth
▷ *vi*: **~ (a) hacer** to be in the habit of
doing; **acostumbrarse** *vr*: **~se a** to
get used to

acotación [akota'θjon] *nf* marginal
note; (*Geo*) elevation mark; (*de
límite*) boundary mark; (*Teatro*) stage
direction

acotamiento [akota'mjento] (*MÉX*)

nm hard shoulder (*BRIT*), berm (*US*)

acre ['akre] *adj* (*olor*) acrid; (*fig*) biting ▷ *nm* acre

acreditar [akreði'tar] *vt* (*garantizar*) to vouch for, guarantee; (*autorizar*) to authorize; (*dar prueba de*) to prove; (*Com: abonar*) to credit; (*embajador*) to accredit

acreedor, a [akree'ðor, a] *nm/f* creditor

acribillar [akriβi'ʎar] *vt*: **~ a balazos** to riddle with bullets

acróbata [a'kroβata] *nmf* acrobat

acta ['akta] *nf* certificate; (*de comisión*) minutes *pl*, record; **acta de matrimonio/nacimiento** (*MÉX*) marriage/birth certificate; **acta notarial** affidavit

actitud [akti'tuð] *nf* attitude; (*postura*) posture

activar [akti'βar] *vt* to activate; (*acelerar*) to speed up

actividad [aktiβi'ðað] *nf* activity

activo, -a [ak'tiβo, a] *adj* active; (*vivo*) lively ▷ *nm* (*Com*) assets *pl*

acto ['akto] *nm* act, action; (*ceremonia*) ceremony; (*Teatro*) act; **en el ~** immediately

actor [ak'tor] *nm* actor; (*Jur*) plaintiff ▷ *adj*: **parte ~a** prosecution

actriz [ak'triθ] *nf* actress

actuación [aktwa'θjon] *nf* action; (*comportamiento*) conduct, behaviour; (*Jur*) proceedings *pl*; (*desempeño*) performance

actual [ak'twal] *adj* present(-day), current

   No confundir **actual** con la palabra inglesa *actual*.

actualidad *nf* present; **actualidades** *nfpl* (*noticias*) news *sg*; **en la actualidad** at present; (*hoy día*) nowadays; **actualizar** [aktwali'θar] *vt* to update, modernize

actualmente [aktwal'mente] *adv* at present; (*hoy día*) nowadays

   No confundir **actualmente** con la palabra inglesa *actually*.

actuar [ak'twar] *vi* (*obrar*) to work, operate; (*actor*) to act, perform ▷ *vt* to work, operate; **~ de** to act as

acuarela [akwa'rela] *nf* watercolour

acuario [a'kwarjo] *nm* aquarium; (*Astrología*) **A~** Aquarius

acuático, -a [a'kwatiko, a] *adj* aquatic

acudir [aku'ðir] *vi* (*asistir*) to attend; (*ir*) to go; **~ a** (*fig*) to turn to; **~ a una cita** to keep an appointment; **~ en ayuda de** to go to the aid of

acuerdo *etc* [a'kwerðo] *vb* V **acordar** ▷ *nm* agreement; **¡de ~!** agreed!; **de ~ con** (*persona*) in agreement with; (*acción, documento*) in accordance with; **estar de ~** to be agreed, agree

acumular [akumu'lar] *vt* to accumulate, collect

acuñar [aku'nar] *vt* (*moneda*) to mint; (*frase*) to coin

acupuntura [akupun'tura] *nf* acupuncture

acurrucarse [akurru'karse] *vr* to crouch; (*ovillarse*) to curl up

acusación [akusa'θjon] *nf* accusation

acusar [aku'sar] *vt* to accuse; (*revelar*) to reveal; (*denunciar*) to denounce

acuse [a'kuse] *nm*: **~ de recibo** acknowledgement of receipt

acústica [a'kustika] *nf* acoustics *pl*

acústico, -a [a'kustiko, a] *adj* acoustic

adaptación [aðapta'θjon] *nf* adaptation

adaptador [aðapta'ðor] *nm* (*Elec*) adapter, adaptor; **adaptador universal** universal adapter *o* adaptor

adaptar [aðap'tar] *vt* to adapt; (*acomodar*) to fit

adecuado, -a [aðe'kwaðo, a] *adj* (*apto*) suitable; (*oportuno*) appropriate

a. de J.C. *abr* (= *antes de Jesucristo*) B.C.

adelantado, -a [aðelan'taðo, a] *adj* advanced; (*reloj*) fast; **pagar por ~** to pay in advance

adelantamiento [aðelanta'mjento]

nm (*Auto*) overtaking

adelantar [aðelan'tar] *vt* to move forward; (*avanzar*) to advance; (*acelerar*) to speed up; (*Auto*) to overtake ▷ *vi* to go forward, advance; **adelantarse** *vr* to go forward, advance

adelante [aðe'lante] *adv* forward(s), ahead ▷ *excl* come in!; **de hoy en ~** from now on; **más ~** later on; (*más allá*) further on

adelanto [aðe'lanto] *nm* advance; (*mejora*) improvement; (*progreso*) progress

adelgazar [aðelɣa'θar] *vt* to thin (down) ▷ *vi* to get thin; (*con régimen*) to slim down, lose weight

ademán [aðe'man] *nm* gesture; **ademanes** *nmpl* manners

además [aðe'mas] *adv* besides; (*por otra parte*) moreover; (*también*) also; **~ de** besides, in addition to

adentrarse [aðen'trarse] *vr*: **~ en** to go into, get inside; (*penetrar*) to penetrate (into)

adentro [a'ðentro] *adv* inside, in; **mar ~** out at sea; **tierra ~** inland

adepto, -a [a'ðepto, a] *nm/f* supporter

aderezar [aðere'θar] *vt* (*ensalada*) to dress; (*comida*) to season; **aderezo** *nm* dressing; seasoning

adeudar [aðeu'ðar] *vt* to owe

adherirse [aðe'rirse] *vr*: **~ a** to adhere to; (*partido*) to join

adhesión [aðe'sjon] *nf* adhesion; (*fig*) adherence

adicción [aðik'θjon] *nf* addiction

adición [aði'θjon] *nf* addition

adicto, -a [a'ðikto, a] *adj*: **~ a** addicted to; (*dedicado*) devoted to ▷ *nm/f* supporter, follower; (*toxicómano*) addict

adiestrar [aðjes'trar] *vt* to train, teach; (*conducir*) to guide, lead

adinerado, -a [aðine'raðo, a] *adj* wealthy

adiós [a'ðjos] *excl* (*para despedirse*) goodbye!, cheerio!; (*al pasar*) hello!

aditivo [aði'tiβo] *nm* additive

adivinanza [aðiβi'nanθa] *nf* riddle

adivinar [aðiβi'nar] *vt* to prophesy; (*conjeturar*) to guess; **adivino, -a** *nm/f* fortune-teller

adj *abr* (= *adjunto*) encl

adjetivo [aðxe'tiβo] *nm* adjective

adjudicar [aðxuði'kar] *vt* to award; **adjudicarse** *vr*: **~se algo** to appropriate sth

adjuntar [aðxun'tar] *vt* to attach, enclose; **adjunto, -a** *adj* attached, enclosed ▷ *nm/f* assistant

administración [aðministra'θjon] *nf* administration; (*dirección*) management; **administrador, a** *nm/f* administrator, manager(ess)

administrar [aðminis'trar] *vt* to administer; **administrativo, -a** *adj* administrative

admirable [aðmi'raβle] *adj* admirable

admiración [aðmira'θjon] *nf* admiration; (*asombro*) wonder; (*Ling*) exclamation mark

admirar [aðmi'rar] *vt* to admire; (*extrañar*) to surprise

admisible [aðmi'siβle] *adj* admissible

admisión [aðmi'sjon] *nf* admission; (*reconocimiento*) acceptance

admitir [aðmi'tir] *vt* to admit; (*aceptar*) to accept

adobar [aðo'βar] *vt* (*Culin*) to season

adobe [a'ðoβe] *nm* adobe, sun-dried brick

adolecer [aðole'θer] *vi*: **~ de** to suffer from

adolescente [aðoles'θente] *nmf* adolescent, teenager

adonde [a'ðonde] *conj* (to) where

adónde [a'ðonde] *adv* = **dónde**

adopción [aðop'θjon] *nf* adoption

adoptar [aðop'tar] *vt* to adopt

adoptivo, -a [aðop'tiβo, a] *adj* (*padres*) adoptive; (*hijo*) adopted

adoquín [aðo'kin] *nm* paving stone

adorar [aðo'rar] *vt* to adore

adornar [aðor'nar] *vt* to adorn
adorno [a'ðorno] *nm* ornament;
(*decoración*) decoration
adosado, -a [aðo'saðo, a] *adj*: **casa
adosada** semi-detached house
adosar [aðo'sar] (*MÉX*) *vt* (*adjuntar*) to
attach, enclose (*with a letter*)
adquiero *etc vb* V **adquirir**
adquirir [aðki'rir] *vt* to acquire,
obtain
adquisición [aðkisi'θjon] *nf*
acquisition
adrede [a'ðreðe] *adv* on purpose
ADSL *nm abr* ADSL
aduana [a'ðwana] *nf* customs *pl*
aduanero, -a [aðwa'nero, a] *adj*
customs *cpd* ▷ *nm/f* customs officer
adueñarse [aðwe'ɲarse] *vr*: **~ de** to
take possession of
adular [aðu'lar] *vt* to flatter
adulterar [aðulte'rar] *vt* to
adulterate
adulterio [aðul'terjo] *nm* adultery
adúltero, -a [a'ðultero, a] *adj*
adulterous ▷ *nm/f* adulterer/
adulteress
adulto, -a [a'ðulto, a] *adj, nm/f* adult
adverbio [að'βerβjo] *nm* adverb
adversario, -a [aðβer'sarjo, a] *nm/f*
adversary
adversidad [aðβersi'ðað] *nf*
adversity; (*contratiempo*) setback
adverso, -a [að'βerso, a] *adj* adverse
advertencia [aðβer'tenθja] *nf*
warning; (*prefacio*) preface, foreword
advertir [aðβer'tir] *vt* to notice;
(*avisar*): **~ a algn de** to warn sb
about o of
Adviento [að'βjento] *nm* Advent
advierto *etc vb* V **advertir**
aéreo, -a [a'ereo, a] *adj* aerial
aerobic [ae'roβik] *nm* aerobics *sg*;
aerobics (*MÉX*) *nmpl* aerobics *sg*
aerodeslizador [aeroðesliθa'ðor]
nm hovercraft
aeromozo, -a [aero'moθo, a] (*LAM*)
nm/f air steward(ess)
aeronáutica [aero'nautika] *nf*

aeronautics *sg*
aeronave [aero'naβe] *nm* spaceship
aeroplano [aero'plano] *nm*
aeroplane
aeropuerto [aero'pwerto] *nm*
airport
aerosol [aero'sol] *nm* aerosol
afamado, -a [afa'maðo, a] *adj*
famous
afán [a'fan] *nm* hard work; (*deseo*)
desire
afanador, a [afana'ðor, a] (*MÉX*)
nm/f (*de limpieza*) cleaner
afanar [afa'nar] *vt* to harass; (*fam*)
to pinch
afear [afe'ar] *vt* to disfigure
afección [afek'θjon] *nf* (*Med*) disease
afectado, -a [afek'taðo, a] *adj*
affected
afectar [afek'tar] *vt* to affect
afectísimo, -a [afek'tisimo, a] *adj*
affectionate; **suyo ~** yours truly
afectivo, -a [afek'tiβo, a] *adj*
(*problema etc*) emotional
afecto [a'fekto] *nm* affection; **tenerle
~ a algn** to be fond of sb
afectuoso, -a [afek'twoso, a] *adj*
affectionate
afeitar [afei'tar] *vt* to shave;
afeitarse *vr* to shave
afeminado, -a [afemi'naðo, a] *adj*
effeminate
Afganistán [afɣanis'tan] *nm*
Afghanistan
afianzar [afjan'θar] *vt* to strengthen;
to secure; **afianzarse** *vr* to become
established
afiche [a'fitʃe] (*RPL*) *nm* poster
afición [afi'θjon] *nf* fondness, liking;
la ~ the fans *pl*; **pinto por ~** I paint as
a hobby; **aficionado, -a** *adj* keen,
enthusiastic; (*no profesional*) amateur
▷ *nm/f* enthusiast, fan; amateur; **ser
aficionado a algo** to be very keen on
o fond of sth
aficionar [afiθjo'nar] *vt*: **~ a algn a
algo** to make sb like sth; **aficionarse**
vr: **~se a algo** to grow fond of sth

afilado, -a [afi'laðo, a] *adj* sharp

afilar [afi'lar] *vt* to sharpen

afiliarse [afi'ljarse] *vr* to affiliate

afín [a'fin] *adj* (*parecido*) similar; (*conexo*) related

afinar [afi'nar] *vt* (*Tec*) to refine; (*Mús*) to tune ▷ *vi* (*tocar*) to play in tune; (*cantar*) to sing in tune

afincarse [afin'karse] *vr* to settle

afinidad [afini'ðað] *nf* affinity; (*parentesco*) relationship; **por ~** by marriage

afirmación [afirma'θjon] *nf* affirmation

afirmar [afir'mar] *vt* to affirm, state; **afirmativo, -a** *adj* affirmative

afligir [afli'xir] *vt* to afflict; (*apenar*) to distress

aflojar [aflo'xar] *vt* to slacken; (*desatar*) to loosen, undo, (*relajar*) to relax ▷ *vi* (*tocar*) to drop; (*bajar*) to go down; **aflojarse** *vr* to relax

afluente [aflu'ente] *adj* flowing ▷ *nm* tributary

afmo, -a *abr* (= *afectísimo(a) suyo(a)*) Yours

afónico, -a [a'foniko, a] *adj*: **estar ~** to have a sore throat; to have lost one's voice

aforo [a'foro] *nm* (*de teatro etc*) capacity

afortunado, -a [afortu'naðo, a] *adj* fortunate, lucky

África ['afrika] *nf* Africa; **África del Sur** South Africa; **africano, -a** *adj*, *nm/f* African

afrontar [afron'tar] *vt* to confront; (*poner cara a cara*) to bring face to face

afrutado, -a [afru'taðo, a] *adj* fruity

after ['after] (*pl* **~s**) *nm* after-hours club; **afterhours** [after'aurs] *nm inv* = **after**

afuera [a'fwera] *adv* out, outside; **afueras** *nfpl* outskirts

agachar [aɣa'tʃar] *vt* to bend, bow; **agacharse** *vr* to stoop, bend

agalla [a'ɣaʎa] *nf* (*Zool*) gill; **tener ~s** (*fam*) to have guts

agarradera [aɣarra'ðera] (*MÉX*) *nf* handle

agarrado, -a [aɣa'rraðo, a] *adj* mean, stingy

agarrar [aɣa'rrar] *vt* to grasp, grab; (*LAM: tomar*) to take, catch; (*recoger*) to pick up ▷ *vi* (*planta*) to take root; **agarrarse** *vr* to hold on (tightly)

agencia [a'xenθja] *nf* agency; **agencia de viajes** travel agency; **agencia inmobiliaria** estate (*BRIT*) o real estate (*US*) agent's (office)

agenciarse [axen'θjarse] *vr* to obtain, procure

agenda [a'xenda] *nf* diary; **~ electronica** PDA

No confundir **agenda** con la palabra inglesa *agenda*.

agente [a'xente] *nmf* agent; (*tb: ~ de policía*) policeman/policewoman; **agente de seguros** insurance agent; **agente de tránsito** (*MÉX*) traffic cop; **agente inmobiliario** estate agent (*BRIT*), realtor (*US*)

ágil ['axil] *adj* agile, nimble; **agilidad** *nf* agility, nimbleness

agilizar [axili'θar] *vt* (*trámites*) to speed up

agiotista [axjo'tista] (*MÉX*) *nmf* (*usurero*) usurer

agitación [axita'θjon] *nf* (*de mano etc*) shaking, waving; (*de líquido etc*) stirring; (*fig*) agitation

agitado, -a [axi'aðo, a] *adj* hectic; (*viaje*) bumpy

agitar [axi'tar] *vt* to wave, shake; (*líquido*) to stir; (*fig*) to stir up, excite; **agitarse** *vr* to get excited; (*inquietarse*) to get worried o upset

aglomeración [aɣlomera'θjon] *nf* agglomeration; **aglomeración de gente/tráfico** mass of people/traffic jam

agnóstico, -a [aɣ'nostiko, a] *adj*, *nm/f* agnostic

agobiar [aɣo'βjar] *vt* to weigh down; (*oprimir*) to oppress; (*cargar*) to burden

agolparse [aɣol'parse] *vr* to crowd

together

agonía [aɣo'nia] nf death throes pl; (fig) agony, anguish

agonizante [aɣoni'θante] adj dying

agonizar [aɣoni'θar] vi to be dying

agosto [a'ɣosto] nm August

agotado, -a [aɣo'taðo, a] adj (persona) exhausted; (libros) out of print; (acabado) finished; (Com) sold out; **agotador, a** [aɣota'ðor, a] adj exhausting

agotamiento [aɣota'mjento] nm exhaustion

agotar [aɣo'tar] vt to exhaust; (consumir) to drain; (recursos) to use up, deplete; **agotarse** vr to be exhausted; (acabarse) to run out; (libro) to go out of print

agraciado, -a [aɣra'θjaðo, a] adj (atractivo) attractive; (en sorteo etc) lucky

agradable [aɣra'ðaβle] adj pleasant, nice

agradar [aɣra'ðar] vt: **él me agrada** I like him

agradecer [aɣraðe'θer] vt to thank; (favor etc) to be grateful for; **agradecido, -a** adj grateful; **¡muy agradecido!** thanks a lot!; **agradecimiento** nm thanks pl; gratitude

agradezco etc vb V **agradecer**

agrado [a'ɣraðo] nm: **ser de tu** etc ~ to be to your etc liking

agrandar [aɣran'dar] vt to enlarge; (fig) to exaggerate; **agrandarse** vr to get bigger

agrario, -a [a'ɣrarjo, a] adj agrarian, land cpd; (política) agricultural, farming

agravante [aɣra'βante] adj aggravating ▷ nm: **con el ~ de que ...** with the further difficulty that ...

agravar [aɣra'βar] vt (pesar sobre) to make heavier; (irritar) to aggravate; **agravarse** vr to worsen, get worse

agraviar [aɣra'βjar] vt to offend; (ser injusto con) to wrong

agredir [aɣre'ðir] vt to attack

agregado, -a [aɣre'ɣaðo, a] nm/f: **A~** ≈ teacher (who is not head of department) ▷ nm aggregate; (persona) attaché

agregar [aɣre'ɣar] vt to gather; (añadir) to add; (persona) to appoint

agresión [aɣre'sjon] nf aggression

agresivo, -a [aɣre'siβo, a] adj aggressive

agriar [a'ɣrjar] vt to (turn) sour

agrícola [a'ɣrikola] adj farming cpd, agricultural

agricultor, a [aɣrikul'tor, a] nm/f farmer

agricultura [aɣrikul'tura] nf agriculture, farming

agridulce [aɣri'ðulθe] adj bittersweet; (Culin) sweet and sour

agrietarse [aɣrje'tarse] vr to crack; (piel) to chap

agrio, -a ['aɣrjo, a] adj bitter

agrupación [aɣrupa'θjon] nf group; (acto) grouping

agrupar [aɣru'par] vt to group

agua ['aɣwa] nf water; (Náut) wake; (Arq) slope of a roof; **aguas** nfpl (de piedra) water sg, sparkle sg; (Med) water sg, urine sg; (Náut) waters; **agua bendita/destilada/potable** holy/distilled/drinking water; **agua caliente** hot water; **agua corriente** running water; **agua de colonia** eau de cologne; **agua mineral (con/sin gas)** (sparkling/still) mineral water; **agua oxigenada** hydrogen peroxide; **aguas abajo/arriba** downstream/ upstream; **aguas jurisdiccionales** territorial waters

aguacate [aɣwa'kate] nm avocado (pear)

aguacero [aɣwa'θero] nm (heavy) shower, downpour

aguado, -a [a'ɣwaðo, a] adj watery, watered down

aguafiestas [aɣwa'fjestas] nmf inv spoilsport, killjoy

aguamiel [aɣwa'mjel] (MÉX) nf fermented maguey o agave juice

aguanieve [aɣwa'njeβe] nf sleet

aguantar [aɣwan'tar] vt to bear, put up with; (sostener) to hold up ▷ vi to last; **aguantarse** vr to restrain o.s.; **aguante** nm (paciencia) patience; (resistencia) endurance

aguar [a'ɣwar] vt to water down

aguardar [aɣwar'ðar] vt to wait for

aguardiente [aɣwar'ðjente] nm brandy, liquor

aguarrás [aɣwa'rras] nm turpentine

aguaviva [aɣwa'biβa] (RPL) nf jellyfish

agudeza [aɣu'ðeθa] nf sharpness; (ingenio) wit

agudo, -a [a'ɣuðo, a] adj sharp; (voz) high-pitched, piercing; (dolor, enfermedad) acute

agüero [a'ɣwero] nm: **buen/mal ~** good/bad omen

aguijón [aɣi'xon] nm sting; (fig) spur

águila ['aɣila] nf eagle; (fig) genius

aguileño, -a [aɣi'leɲo, a] adj (nariz) aquiline; (rostro) sharp-featured

aguinaldo [aɣi'naldo] nm Christmas box

aguja [a'ɣuxa] nf needle; (de reloj) hand; (Arq) spire; (Tec) firing-pin; **agujas** nfpl (Zool) ribs; (Ferro) points

agujerear [aɣuxere'ar] vt to make holes in

agujero [aɣu'xero] nm hole

agujetas [aɣu'xetas] nfpl stitch sg; (rigidez) stiffness

ahí [a'i] adv there; **de ~ que** so that, with the result that; **~ llega** here he comes; **por ~** that way; (allá) over there; **200 o por ~** 200 or so

ahijado, -a [ai'xaðo, a] nm/f godson/daughter

ahogar [ao'ɣar] vt to drown; (asfixiar) to suffocate, smother; (fuego) to put out; **ahogarse** vr (en el agua) to drown; (por asfixia) to suffocate

ahogo [a'oɣo] nm breathlessness; (fig) financial difficulty

ahondar [aon'dar] vt to deepen, make deeper; (fig) to study thoroughly ▷ vi: **~ en** to study thoroughly

ahora [a'ora] adv now; (hace poco) a moment ago, just now; (dentro de poco) in a moment; **~ voy** I'm coming; **~ mismo** right now; **~ bien** now then; **por ~** for the present

ahorcar [aor'kar] vt to hang

ahorita [ao'rita] (fam) adv (LAM: en este momento) right now; (MÉX: hace poco) just now; (: dentro de poco) in a minute

ahorrar [ao'rrar] vt (dinero) to save; (esfuerzos) to save, avoid; **ahorro** nm (acto) saving; **ahorros** nmpl (dinero) savings

ahuecar [awe'kar] vt to hollow (out); (voz) to deepen; **ahuecarse** vr to give o.s. airs

ahumar [au'mar] vt to smoke, cure; (llenar de humo) to fill with smoke ▷ vi to smoke; **ahumarse** vr to fill with smoke

ahuyentar [aujen'tar] vt to drive off, frighten off; (fig) to dispel

aire ['aire] nm air; (viento) wind; (corriente) draught; (Mús) tune; **al ~ libre** in the open air; **aire aclimatizado/acondicionado** air conditioning; **airear** vt to air; **airearse** vr (persona) to go out for a breath of fresh air; **airoso, -a** adj windy; draughty; (fig) graceful

aislado, -a [ais'laðo, a] adj isolated; (incomunicado) cut-off; (Elec) insulated

aislar [ais'lar] vt to isolate; (Elec) to insulate

ajardinado, -a [axarði'naðo, a] adj landscaped

ajedrez [axe'ðreθ] nm chess

ajeno, -a [a'xeno, a] adj (que pertenece a otro) somebody else's; **~ a** foreign to

ajetreado, -a [axetre'aðo, a] adj busy

ajetreo [axe'treo] nm bustle

ají [a'xi] (cs) nm chil(l)i, red pepper; (salsa) chil(l)i sauce

ajillo [a'xiʎo] nm: **gambas al ~** garlic prawns

ajo ['axo] nm garlic

ajuar [a'xwar] nm household furnishings pl; (de novia) trousseau; (de niño) layette

ajustado, -a [axus'taðo, a] adj (tornillo) tight; (cálculo) right; (ropa) tight(-fitting); (resultado) close

ajustar [axus'tar] vt (adaptar) to adjust; (encajar) to fit; (Tec) to engage; (Imprenta) to make up; (apretar) to tighten; (concertar) to agree (on); (reconciliar) to reconcile; (cuentas, deudas) to settle ▷ vi to fit; **ajustarse** vr: **~se a** (precio etc) to be in keeping with, fit in with; **~ las cuentas a algn** to get even with sb

ajuste [a'xuste] nm adjustment; (Costura) fitting; (acuerdo) compromise; (de cuenta) settlement

al [al] = **a + el**; V **a**

ala ['ala] nf wing; (de sombrero) brim; winger; **ala delta** nf hang-glider

alabanza [ala'βanθa] nf praise

alabar [ala'βar] vt to praise

alacena [ala'θena] nf kitchen cupboard (BRIT) o closet (US)

alacrán [ala'kran] nm scorpion

alambrada [alam'braða] nf wire fence; (red) wire netting

alambre [a'lambre] nm wire; **alambre de púas** barbed wire

alameda [ala'meða] nf (plantío) poplar grove; (lugar de paseo) avenue, boulevard

álamo ['alamo] nm poplar

alarde [a'larðe] nm show, display; **hacer ~ de** to boast of

alardeador [alarɣa'ðor] nm (Elec) television lead

alargar [alar'ɣar] vt to lengthen, extend; (paso) to hasten; (brazo) to stretch out; (cuerda) to pay out; (conversación) to spin out; **alargarse** vr to get longer

alarma [a'larma] nf alarm; **alarma de incendios** fire alarm; **alarmar** vt to alarm; **alarmarse** to get alarmed; **alarmante** [alar'mante] adj alarming

alba ['alβa] nf dawn

albahaca [al'βaka] nf basil

Albania [al'βanja] nf Albania

albañil [alβa'ɲil] nm bricklayer; (cantero) mason

albarán [alβa'ran] nm (Com) delivery note, invoice

albaricoque [alβari'koke] nm apricot

albedrío [alβe'ðrio] nm: **libre ~** free will

alberca [al'βerka] nf reservoir; (MÉX: piscina) swimming pool

albergar [alβer'ɣar] vt to shelter

albergue etc [al'βerɣe] vb V **albergar** ▷ nm shelter, refuge; **albergue juvenil** youth hostel

albóndiga [al'βondiɣa] nf meatball

albornoz [alβor'noθ] nm (de los árabes) burnous; (para el baño) bathrobe

alborotar [alβoro'tar] vi to make a row ▷ vt to agitate, stir up; **alborotarse** vr to get excited; (mar) to get rough; **alboroto** nm row, uproar

álbum ['alβum] (pl **~s**, **~es**) nm album; **álbum de recortes** scrapbook

albur [al'βur] (MÉX) nm (juego de palabras) pun; (doble sentido) double entendre

alcachofa [alka'tʃofa] nf artichoke

alcalde, -esa [al'kalde, esa] nm/f mayor(ess)

alcaldía [alkal'dia] nf mayoralty; (lugar) mayor's office

alcance etc [al'kanθe] vb V **alcanzar** ▷ nm reach; (Com) adverse balance; **al ~ de algn** available to sb

alcancía [alkan'θia] (LAM) nf (para ahorrar) money box; (para colectas) collection box

alcantarilla [alkanta'riʎa] nf (de aguas cloacales) sewer; (en la calle) gutter

alcanzar [alkan'θar] vt (algo: con la mano, el pie) to reach; (alguien: en el camino etc) to catch up (with); (autobús) to catch; (bala) to hit, strike ▷ vi (ser

(*tienda*) confectioner's (shop)
confitura [konfiˈtura] *nf* jam
conflictivo, -a [konflikˈtiβo, a] *adj* (*asunto, propuesta*) controversial; (*país, situación*) troubled
conflicto [konˈflikto] *nm* conflict; (*fig*) clash
confluir [konˈflwir] *vi* (*ríos*) to meet; (*gente*) to gather
conformar [konforˈmar] *vt* to shape, fashion ▷ *vi* to agree; **conformarse** *vr* to conform; (*resignarse*) to resign o.s.; **~se con algo** to be happy with sth
conforme [konˈforme] *adj* (*correspondiente*): **~ con** in line with; (*de acuerdo*): **estar ~s (con algo)** to be in agreement (with sth) ▷ *adv* as ▷ *excl* agreed! ▷ *prep*: **~ a** in accordance with; **quedarse ~ (con algo)** to be satisfied (with sth)
confortable [konforˈtaβle] *adj* comfortable
confortar [konforˈtar] *vt* to comfort
confrontar [konfronˈtar] *vt* to confront; (*dos personas*) to bring face to face; (*cotejar*) to compare
confundir [konfunˈdir] *vt* (*equivocar*) to mistake, confuse; (*turbar*) to confuse; **confundirse** *vr* (*turbarse*) to get confused; (*equivocarse*) to make a mistake; (*mezclarse*) to mix
confusión [konfuˈsjon] *nf* confusion
confuso, -a [konˈfuso, a] *adj* confused
congelado, -a [konxeˈlaðo, a] *adj* frozen; **congelados** *nmpl* frozen food(s); **congelador** *nm* (*aparato*) freezer, deep freeze
congelar [konxeˈlar] *vt* to freeze; **congelarse** *vr* (*sangre, grasa*) to congeal
congeniar [konxeˈnjar] *vi* to get on (*BRIT*) o along (*US*) well
congestión [konxesˈtjon] *nf* congestion
congestionar [konxestjoˈnar] *vt* to congest

congraciarse [kongraˈθjarse] *vr* to ingratiate o.s.
congratular [kongratuˈlar] *vt* to congratulate
congregar [kongreˈɣar] *vt* to gather together; **congregarse** *vr* to gather together
congresista [kongreˈsista] *nmf* delegate, congressman/woman
congreso [konˈgreso] *nm* congress
conjetura [konxeˈtura] *nf* guess; **conjeturar** *vt* to guess
conjugar [konxuˈɣar] *vt* to combine, fit together; (*Ling*) to conjugate
conjunción [konxunˈθjon] *nf* conjunction
conjunto, -a [konˈxunto, a] *adj* joint, united ▷ *nm* whole; (*Mús*) band; **en ~** as a whole
conmemoración [konmemoraˈθjon] *nf* commemoration
conmemorar [konmemoˈrar] *vt* to commemorate
conmigo [konˈmiɣo] *pron* with me
conmoción [konmoˈθjon] *nf* shock; (*fig*) upheaval; **conmoción cerebral** (*Med*) concussion
conmovedor, a [konmoβeˈðor, a] *adj* touching, moving; (*emocionante*) exciting
conmover [konmoˈβer] *vt* to shake, disturb; (*fig*) to move
conmutador [konmutaˈðor] *nm* switch; (*LAM: centralita*) switchboard; (: *central*) telephone exchange
cono [ˈkono] *nm* cone; **Cono Sur** Southern Cone
conocedor, a [konoθeˈðor, a] *adj* expert, knowledgeable ▷ *nm/f* expert
conocer [konoˈθer] *vt* to know; (*por primera vez*) to meet, get to know; (*entender*) to know about; (*reconocer*) to recognize; **conocerse** *vr* (*una persona*) to know o.s.; (*dos personas*) to get to know each other; **~ a algn de vista** to know sb by sight
conocido, -a [konoˈθiðo, a] *adj*

(well-)known ▷ *nm/f* acquaintance

conocimiento [konoθi'mjento] *nm* knowledge; (*Med*) consciousness; **conocimientos** *nmpl* (*saber*) knowledge *sg*

conozco *etc vb* V **conocer**

conque ['konke] *conj* and so, so then

conquista [kon'kista] *nf* conquest; **conquistador, a** *adj* conquering ▷ *nm* conqueror; **conquistar** [konkis'tar] *vt* to conquer

consagrar [konsa'ɣrar] *vt* (*Rel*) to consecrate; (*fig*) to devote

consciente [kons'θjente] *adj* conscious

consecución [konseku'θjon] *nf* acquisition; (*de fin*) attainment

consecuencia [konse'kwenθja] *nf* consequence, outcome; (*coherencia*) consistency

consecuente [konse'kwente] *adj* consistent

consecutivo, -a [konseku'tiβo, a] *adj* consecutive

conseguir [konse'ɣir] *vt* to get, obtain; (*objetivo*) to attain

consejero, -a [konse'xero, a] *nm/f* adviser, consultant; (*Pol*) councillor

consejo [kon'sexo] *nm* advice; (*Pol*) council; **consejo de administración** (*Com*) board of directors; **consejo de guerra** court martial; **consejo de ministros** cabinet meeting

consenso [kon'senso] *nm* consensus

consentimiento [konsenti'mjento] *nm* consent

consentir [konsen'tir] *vt* (*permitir, tolerar*) to consent to; (*mimar*) to pamper, spoil; (*aguantar*) to put up with ▷ *vi* to agree, consent; **~ que algn haga algo** to allow sb to do sth

conserje [kon'serxe] *nm* caretaker; (*portero*) porter

conservación [konserβa'θjon] *nf* conservation; (*de alimentos, vida*) preservation

conservador, a [konserβa'ðor, a] *adj* (*Pol*) conservative ▷ *nm/f* conservative

conservante [konser'βante] *nm* preservative

conservar [konser'βar] *vt* to conserve, keep; (*alimentos, vida*) to preserve; **conservarse** *vr* to survive

conservas [kon'serβas] *nfpl* canned food(s) *pl*

conservatorio [konserβa'torjo] *nm* (*Mús*) conservatoire, conservatory

considerable [konsiðe'raβle] *adj* considerable

consideración [konsiðera'θjon] *nf* consideration; (*estimación*) respect

considerado, -a [konsiðe'raðo, a] *adj* (*atento*) considerate; (*respetado*) respected

considerar [konsiðe'rar] *vt* to consider

consigna [kon'siɣna] *nf* (*orden*) order, instruction; (*para equipajes*) left-luggage office

consigo *etc* [kon'siɣo] *vb* V **conseguir** ▷ *pron* (*m*) with him; (*f*) with her; (*Vd*) with you; (*reflexivo*) with o.s.

consiguiendo *etc vb* V **conseguir**

consiguiente [konsi'ɣjente] *adj* consequent; **por ~** and so, therefore, consequently

consistente [konsis'tente] *adj* consistent; (*sólido*) solid, firm; (*válido*) sound

consistir [konsis'tir] *vi*: **~ en** (*componerse de*) to consist of

consola [kon'sola] *nf* (*mueble*) console table; (*de videojuegos*) console

consolación [konsola'θjon] *nf* consolation

consolar [konso'lar] *vt* to console

consolidar [konsoli'ðar] *vt* to consolidate

consomé [konso'me] (*pl* **~s**) *nm* consommé, clear soup

consonante [konso'nante] *adj* consonant, harmonious ▷ *nf* consonant

consorcio [kon'sorθjo] *nm* consortium

conspiración [konspira'θjon] *nf* conspiracy

conspirar [konspi'rar] *vi* to conspire

constancia [kon'stanθja] *nf* constancy; **dejar ~ de** to put on record

constante [kons'tante] *adj, nf* constant

constar [kons'tar] *vi* (*evidenciarse*) to be clear *o* evident; **~ de** to consist of

constipado, -a [konsti'paðo, a] *adj:* **estar ~** to have a cold ▷ *nm* cold

No confundir **constipado** con la palabra inglesa *constipated*.

constitución [konstitu'θjon] *nf* constitution

constituir [konstitu'ir] *vt* (*formar, componer*) to constitute, make up; (*fundar, erigir, ordenar*) to constitute, establish

construcción [konstruk'θjon] *nf* construction, building

constructor, a [konstruk'tor, a] *nm/f* builder

construir [konstru'ir] *vt* to build, construct

construyendo *etc vb V* **construir**

consuelo [kon'swelo] *nm* consolation, solace

cónsul ['konsul] *nm* consul; **consulado** *nm* consulate

consulta [kon'sulta] *nf* consultation; (*Med*): **horas de ~** surgery hours; **consultar** [konsul'tar] *vt* to consult; **consultar algo con algn** to discuss sth with sb; **consultorio** [konsul'torjo] *nm* (*Med*) surgery

consumición [konsumi'θjon] *nf* consumption; (*bebida*) drink; (*comida*) food; **consumición mínima** cover charge

consumidor, a [konsumi'ðor, a] *nm/f* consumer

consumir [konsu'mir] *vt* to consume; **consumirse** *vr* to be consumed; (*persona*) to waste away

consumismo [konsu'mismo] *nm* consumerism

consumo [kon'sumo] *nm* consumption

contabilidad [kontaβili'ðað] *nf* accounting, book-keeping; (*profesión*) accountancy; **contable** *nmf* accountant

contactar [kontak'tar] *vi:* **~ con algn** to contact sb

contacto [kon'takto] *nm* contact; (*Auto*) ignition; **estar/ponerse en ~ con algn** to be/to get in touch with sb

contado, -a [kon'taðo, a] *adj:* **~s** (*escasos*) numbered, scarce, few ▷ *nm:* **pagar al ~** to pay (in) cash

contador [konta'ðor] *nm* (*ESP: aparato*) meter ▷ *nmf* (*LAM Com*) accountant

contagiar [konta'xjar] *vt* (*enfermedad*) to pass on, transmit; (*persona*) to infect; **contagiarse** *vr* to become infected

contagio [kon'taxjo] *nm* infection; **contagioso, -a** *adj* infectious; (*fig*) catching

contaminación [kontamina'θjon] *nf* contamination; (*polución*) pollution

contaminar [kontami'nar] *vt* to contaminate; (*aire, agua*) to pollute

contante [kon'tante] *adj:* **dinero ~ (y sonante)** cash

contar [kon'tar] *vt* (*páginas, dinero*) to count; (*anécdota, chiste etc*) to tell ▷ *vi* to count; **~ con** to rely on, count on

contemplar [kontem'plar] *vt* to contemplate; (*mirar*) to look at

contemporáneo, -a [kontempo'raneo, a] *adj, nm/f* contemporary

contenedor [kontene'ðor] *nm* container

contener [konte'ner] *vt* to contain, hold; (*retener*) to hold back, contain; **contenerse** *vr* to control *o* restrain o.s.

contenido, -a [konte'niðo, a] *adj* (*moderado*) restrained; (*risa etc*)

...ressed ▷ *nm* contents *pl*, content

...tentar [konten'tar] *vt* (*satisfacer*) ...satisfy; (*complacer*) to please; **...ontentarse** *vr* to be satisfied

...ontento, -a [kon'tento, a] *adj* (*alegre*) pleased; (*feliz*) happy

contestación [kontesta'θjon] *nf* answer, reply

contestador [kontesta'ðor] *nm* (*tb*: **~ automático**) answering machine

contestar [kontes'tar] *vt* to answer, reply; (*Jur*) to corroborate, confirm. No confundir **contestar** con la palabra inglesa *contest*.

contexto [kon'te(k)sto] *nm* context

contigo [kon'tixo] *pron* with you

contiguo, -a [kon'tixwo, a] *adj* adjacent, adjoining

continente [konti'nente] *adj*, *nm* continent

continuación [kontinwa'θjon] *nf* continuation; **a ~** then, next

continuar [konti'nwar] *vt* to continue, go on with ▷ *vi* to continue, go on; **~ hablando** to continue talking *o* to talk

continuidad [kontinwi'ðað] *nf* continuity

continuo, -a [kon'tinwo, a] *adj* (*sin interrupción*) continuous; (*acción perseverante*) continual

contorno [kon'torno] *nm* outline; (*Geo*) contour; **contornos** *nmpl* neighbourhood *sg*, surrounding area *sg*

contra ['kontra] *prep*, *adv* against ▷ *nm inv* con ▷ *nf*: **la C~** (*de Nicaragua*) the Contras *pl*

contraataque [kontraa'take] *nm* counter-attack

contrabajo [kontra'βaxo] *nm* double bass

contrabandista [kontraβan'dista] *nmf* smuggler

contrabando [kontra'βando] *nm* (*acción*) smuggling; (*mercancías*) contraband

contracción [kontrak'θjon] *nf* contraction

contracorriente [kontrako'rrjente] *nf* cross-current

contradecir [kontraðe'θir] *vt* to contradict

contradicción [kontraðik'θjon] *nf* contradiction

contradictorio, -a [kontraðik'torjo, a] *adj* contradictory

contraer [kontra'er] *vt* to contract; (*limitar*) to restrict; **contraerse** *vr* to contract; (*limitarse*) to limit o.s.

contraluz [kontra'luθ] *nm* view against the light

contrapartida [kontrapar'tiða] *nf*: **como ~ (de)** in return (for)

contrapelo [kontra'pelo]: **a ~** *adv* the wrong way

contrapeso [kontra'peso] *nm* counterweight

contraportada [kontrapor'taða] *nf* (*de revista*) back cover

contraproducente [kontraproðu'θente] *adj* counterproductive

contrario, -a [kon'trarjo, a] *adj* contrary; (*persona*) opposed; (*sentido, lado*) opposite ▷ *nm/f* enemy, adversary; (*Deporte*) opponent; **al** *o* **por el ~** on the contrary; **de lo ~** otherwise

contrarreloj [kontrarre'lo] *nf* (*tb*: **prueba ~**) time trial

contrarrestar [kontrarres'tar] *vt* to counteract

contrasentido [kontrasen'tiðo] *nm* (*contradicción*) contradiction

contraseña [kontra'seɲa] *nf* (*Inform*) password

contrastar [kontras'tar] *vt*, *vi* to contrast

contraste [kon'traste] *nm* contrast

contratar [kontra'tar] *vt firmar un acuerdo para*, to contract for; (*empleados, obreros*) to hire, engage

contratiempo [kontra'tjempo] *nm* setback

contratista [kontra'tista] *nmf* contractor

contrato [kon'trato] *nm* contract
contraventana [kontraβen'tana] *nf* shutter
contribución [kontriβu'θjon] *nf* (*municipal etc*) tax; (*ayuda*) contribution
contribuir [kontriβu'ir] *vt, vi* to contribute; (*Com*) to pay (in taxes)
contribuyente [kontriβu'jente] *nmf* (*Com*) taxpayer; (*que ayuda*) contributor
contrincante [kontrin'kante] *nmf* opponent
control [kon'trol] *nm* control; (*inspección*) inspection, check; **control de pasaportes** passport inspection; **controlador, a** *nm/f* controller; **controlador aéreo** air-traffic controller; **controlar** [kontro'lar] *vt* to control; (*inspeccionar*) to inspect, check
contundente [kontun'dente] *adj* (*instrumento*) blunt; (*argumento, derrota*) overwhelming
contusión [kontu'sjon] *nf* bruise
convalecencia [kombale'θenθja] *nf* convalescence
convalecer [kombale'θer] *vi* to convalesce, get better
convalidar [kombali'ðar] *vt* (*título*) to recognize
convencer [komben'θer] *vt* to convince; **~ a algn (de** o **para hacer algo)** to persuade sb (to do sth)
convención [komben'θjon] *nf* convention
conveniente [kombe'njente] *adj* suitable; (*útil*) useful
convenio [kom'benjo] *nm* agreement, treaty
convenir [kombe'nir] *vi* (*estar de acuerdo*) to agree; (*venir bien*) to suit, be suitable

> No confundir **convenir** con la palabra inglesa *convene*.

convento [kom'bento] *nm* convent
convenza *etc vb* V **convencer**
convergir [komber'xir] *vi* = **converger**
conversación [kombersa'θjon] *nf* conversation
conversar [komber'sar] *vi* to talk, converse
conversión [komber'sjon] *nf* conversion
convertir [komber'tir] *vt* to convert
convidar [kombi'ðar] *vt* to invite; **~ a algn a una cerveza** to buy sb a beer
convincente [kombin'θente] *adj* convincing
convite [kom'bite] *nm* invitation; (*banquete*) banquet
convivencia [kombi'βenθja] *nf* coexistence, living together
convivir [kombi'βir] *vi* to live together
convocar [kombo'kar] *vt* to summon, call (together)
convocatoria [komboka'torja] *nf* (*de oposiciones, elecciones*) notice; (*de huelga*) call
cónyuge ['konjuxe] *nmf* spouse
coñac [ko'ɲa(k)] (*pl* **~s**) *nm* cognac, brandy
coño ['koɲo] (*fam!*) *excl* (*enfado*) shit! (!); (*sorpresa*) bloody hell! (!)
cool [kul] *adj* (*fam*) cool
cooperación [koopera'θjon] *nf* cooperation
cooperar [koope'rar] *vi* to cooperate
cooperativa [koopera'tiβa] *nf* cooperative
coordinadora [koorðina'ðora] *nf* (*comité*) coordinating committee
coordinar [koorði'nar] *vt* to coordinate
copa ['kopa] *nf* cup; (*vaso*) glass; (*bebida*): **tomar una ~** (to have a) drink; (*de árbol*) top; (*de sombrero*) crown; **copas** *nfpl* (*Naipes*) ≈ hearts
copia ['kopja] *nf* copy; **copia de respaldo** o **seguridad** (*Inform*) back-up copy; **copiar** *vt* to copy
copla ['kopla] *nf* verse; (*canción*) (popular) song
copo ['kopo] *nm*: **~ de nieve** snowflake; **~s de maíz** cornflakes

coqueta [ko'keta] *adj* flirtatious, coquettish; **coquetear** *vi* to flirt

coraje [ko'raxe] *nm* courage; (*ánimo*) spirit; (*ira*) anger

coral [ko'ral] *adj* choral ▷ *nf* (*Mús*) choir ▷ *nm* (*Zool*) coral

coraza [ko'raθa] *nf* (*armadura*) armour; (*blindaje*) armour-plating

corazón [kora'θon] *nm* heart

corazonada [koraθo'naða] *nf* impulse; (*presentimiento*) hunch

corbata [kor'βata] *nf* tie

corchete [kor'tʃete] *nm* catch, clasp

corcho ['kortʃo] *nm* cork; (*Pesca*) float

cordel [kor'ðel] *nm* cord, line

cordero [kor'ðero] *nm* lamb

cordial [kor'ðjal] *adj* cordial

cordillera [korði'ʎera] *nf* range (of mountains)

Córdoba ['korðoβa] *n* Cordova

cordón [kor'ðon] *nm* (*cuerda*) cord, string; (*de zapatos*) lace; (*Mil etc*) cordon; **cordón umbilical** umbilical cord

cordura [kor'ðura] *nf*: **con ~** (*obrar, hablar*) sensibly

corneta [kor'neta] *nf* bugle

cornisa [kor'nisa] *nf* (*Arq*) cornice

coro ['koro] *nm* chorus; (*conjunto de cantores*) choir

corona [ko'rona] *nf* crown; (*de flores*) garland

coronel [koro'nel] *nm* colonel

coronilla [koro'niʎa] *nf* (*Anat*) crown (of the head)

corporal [korpo'ral] *adj* corporal, bodily

corpulento, -a [korpu'lento, a] *adj* (*persona*) heavily-built

corral [ko'rral] *nm* farmyard

correa [ko'rrea] *nf* strap; (*cinturón*) belt; (*de perro*) lead, leash; **correa del ventilador** (*Auto*) fan belt

corrección [korrek'θjon] *nf* correction; (*represión*) rebuke; **correccional** *nm* reformatory

correcto, -a [ko'rrekto, a] *adj* correct; (*persona*) well-mannered

corredizo, -a [korre'ðiθo, a] *adj* (*puerta etc*) sliding

corredor, a [korre'ðor, a] *nm* (*pasillo*) corridor; (*balcón corrido*) gallery; (*Com*) agent, broker ▷ *nm/f* (*Deporte*) runner

corregir [korre'xir] *vt* (*error*) to correct; **corregirse** *vr* to reform

correo [ko'rreo] *nm* post, mail; (*persona*) courier; **Correos** *nmpl* (*ESP*) Post Office *sg*; **correo aéreo** airmail; **correo basura** (*Inform*) spam; **correo electrónico** email, electronic mail; **correo web** webmail

correr [ko'rrer] *vt* to run; (*cortinas*) to draw; (*cerrojo*) to shoot ▷ *vi* to run; (*líquido*) to run, flow; **correrse** *vr* to slide, move; (*colores*) to run

correspondencia [korrespon'denθja] *nf* correspondence; (*Ferro*) connection

corresponder [korrespon'der] *vi* to correspond; (*convenir*) to be suitable; (*pertenecer*) to belong; (*concernir*) to concern; **corresponderse** *vr* (*por escrito*) to correspond; (*amarse*) to love one another

correspondiente [korrespon'djente] *adj* corresponding

corresponsal [korrespon'sal] *nmf* correspondent

corrida [ko'rriða] *nf* (*de toros*) bullfight

corrido, -a [ko'rriðo, a] *adj* (*avergonzado*) abashed; **un kilo ~** a good kilo

corriente [ko'rrjente] *adj* (*agua*) running; (*dinero etc*) current; (*común*) ordinary, normal ▷ *nf* current ▷ *nm* current month; **estar al ~ de** to be informed about; **corriente eléctrica** electric current

corrija *etc vb* V **corregir**

corro ['korro] *nm* ring, circle (of people)

corromper [korrom'per] *vt* (*madera*) to rot; (*fig*) to corrupt

corrosivo, -a [korro'siβo, a] *adj* corrosive

corrupción [korrup'θjon] *nf* rot,

decay; (fig) corruption

corsé [kor'se] nm corset

cortacésped [korta'θespeð] nm lawn mower

cortado, -a [kor'taðo, a] adj (gen) cut; (leche) sour; (tímido) shy; (avergonzado) embarrassed ▷ nm coffee (with a little milk)

cortafuegos [korta'fweɣos] nm inv (en el bosque) firebreak, fire lane (us); (Internet) firewall

cortalápices, cortalápiz [korta'lapiθes, korta'lapiθ] nm inv (pencil) sharpener

cortar [kor'tar] vt to cut; (suministro) to cut off; (un pasaje) to cut out ▷ vi to cut; **cortarse** vr (avergonzarse) to become embarrassed; (leche) to turn, curdle; **~se el pelo** to have one's hair cut

cortauñas [korta'uɲas] nm inv nail clippers pl

corte ['korte] nm cut, cutting; (de tela) piece, length ▷ nf: **las C~s** the Spanish Parliament; **corte de luz** power cut; **corte y confección** dressmaking

cortejo [kor'texo] nm entourage; **cortejo fúnebre** funeral procession

cortés [kor'tes] adj courteous, polite

cortesía [korte'sia] nf courtesy

corteza [kor'teθa] nf (de árbol) bark; (de pan) crust

cortijo [kor'tixo] (ESP) nm farm, farmhouse

cortina [kor'tina] nf curtain

corto, -a ['korto, a] adj (breve) short; (tímido) bashful; **~ de luces** not very bright; **~ de vista** short-sighted; **estar ~ de fondos** to be short of funds; **cortocircuito** nm short circuit; **cortometraje** nm (Cine) short

cosa ['kosa] nf thing; **~ de** about; **eso es ~ mía** that's my business

coscorrón [kosko'rron] nm bump on the head

cosecha [ko'setʃa] nf (Agr) harvest; (de vino) vintage; **cosechar** [kose'tʃar] vt to harvest, gather (in)

coser [ko'ser] vt to sew

cosmético, -a [kos'metiko, a] adj, nm cosmetic

cosquillas [kos'kiʎas] nfpl: **hacer ~** to tickle; **tener ~** to be ticklish

costa ['kosta] nf (Geo) coast; **a toda ~** at all costs; **Costa Brava** Costa Brava; **Costa Cantábrica** Cantabrian Coast; **Costa del Sol** Costa del Sol

costado [kos'taðo] nm side

costanera [kosta'nera] (cs) nf promenade, sea front

costar [kos'tar] vt (valer) to cost; **me cuesta hablarle** I find it hard to talk to him

Costa Rica [kosta'rika] nf Costa Rica; **costarricense** adj, nmf Costa Rican; **costarriqueño, -a** adj, nm/f Costa Rican

coste ['koste] nm = **costo**

costear [koste'ar] vt to pay for

costero, -a [kos'tero, a] adj (pueblecito, camino) coastal

costilla [kos'tiʎa] nf rib; (Culin) cutlet

costo ['kosto] nm cost, price; **costo de (la) vida** cost of living; **costoso, -a** adj costly, expensive

costra ['kostra] nf (corteza) crust; (Med) scab

costumbre [kos'tumbre] nf custom, habit; **como de ~** as usual

costura [kos'tura] nf sewing, needlework; (zurcido) seam

costurera [kostu'rera] nf dressmaker

costurero [kostu'rero] nm sewing box o case

cotidiano, -a [koti'ðjano, a] adj daily, day to day

cotilla [ko'tiʎa] (ESP: fam) nmf gossip; **cotillear** (ESP) vi to gossip; **cotilleo** (ESP) nm gossip(ing)

cotizar [koti'θar] vt (Com) to quote, price; **cotizarse** vr: **~se a** to sell at, fetch; (Bolsa) to stand at, be quoted at

coto ['koto] nm (terreno cercado) enclosure; (de caza) reserve

cotorra [ko'torra] nf parrot

coyote [ko'jote] *nm* coyote, prairie wolf

coz [koθ] *nf* kick

crack [krak] *nm* (*droga*) crack

cráneo ['kraneo] *nm* skull, cranium

cráter ['krater] *nm* crater

crayón [kra'jon] (*MÉX, RPL*) *nm* crayon, chalk

creación [krea'θjon] *nf* creation

creador, a [krea'ðor, a] *adj* creative ▷ *nm/f* creator

crear [kre'ar] *vt* to create, make

creativo, -a [krea'tiβo, a] *adj* creative

crecer [kre'θer] *vi* to grow; (*precio*) to rise

creces ['kreθes]: **con ~** *adv* amply, fully

crecido, -a [kre'θiðo, a] *adj* (*persona, planta*) full-grown; (*cantidad*) large

crecimiento [kreθi'mjento] *nm* growth; (*aumento*) increase

credencial [kreðen'θjal] *nf* (*LAM: tarjeta*) card; **credenciales** *nfpl* credentials; **credencial de socio** (*LAM*) membership card

crédito ['kreðito] *nm* credit

credo ['kreðo] *nm* creed

creencia [kre'enθja] *nf* belief

creer [kre'er] *vt, vi* to think, believe; **creerse** *vr* to believe o.s. (to be); **~ en** to believe in; **creo que sí/no** I think/don't think so; **¡ya lo creo!** I should think so!

creído, -a [kre'iðo, a] *adj* (*engreído*) conceited

crema ['krema] *nf* cream; **crema batida** (*LAM*) whipped cream; **crema pastelera** (confectioner's) custard

cremallera [krema'ʎera] *nf* zip (fastener)

crepe ['krepe] (*ESP*) *nf* pancake

cresta ['kresta] *nf* (*Geo, Zool*) crest

creyendo *etc vb* V **creer**

creyente [kre'jente] *nmf* believer

creyó *etc vb* V **creer**

crezco *etc vb* V **crecer**

cría *etc* ['kria] *vb* V **criar** ▷ *nf* (*de animales*) rearing, breeding; (*animal*) young; V *tb* **crío**

criadero [kria'ðero] *nm* (*Zool*) breeding place

criado, -a [kri'aðo, a] *nm* servant ▷ *nf* servant, maid

criador [kria'ðor] *nm* breeder

crianza [kri'anθa] *nf* rearing, breeding; (*fig*) breeding

criar [kri'ar] *vt* (*educar*) to bring up; (*producir*) to grow, produce; (*animales*) to breed

criatura [kria'tura] *nf* creature; (*niño*) baby, (small) child

cribar [kri'βar] *vt* to sieve

crimen ['krimen] *nm* crime

criminal [krimi'nal] *adj, nmf* criminal

crines ['krines] *nfpl* mane

crío, -a ['krio, a] (*fam*) *nm/f* (*niño*) kid

crisis ['krisis] *nf inv* crisis; **crisis nerviosa** nervous breakdown

crismas ['krismas] (*ESP*) *nm inv* Christmas card

cristal [kris'tal] *nm* crystal; (*de ventana*) glass, pane; (*lente*) lens; **cristalino, -a** *adj* crystalline; (*fig*) clear ▷ *nm* lens (of the eye)

cristianismo [kristja'nismo] *nm* Christianity

cristiano, -a [kris'tjano, a] *adj, nm/f* Christian

Cristo ['kristo] *nm* Christ; (*crucifijo*) crucifix

criterio [kri'terjo] *nm* criterion; (*juicio*) judgement

crítica ['kritika] *nf* criticism; V *tb* **crítico**

criticar [kriti'kar] *vt* to criticize

crítico, -a ['kritiko, a] *adj* critical ▷ *nm/f* critic

Croacia [kro'aθja] *nf* Croatia

croissan, croissant [krwa'san] *nm* croissant

cromo ['kromo] *nm* chrome

crónica ['kronika] *nf* chronicle, account

crónico, -a ['kroniko, a] *adj* chronic

cronómetro [kro'nometro] *nm* stopwatch

croqueta [kro'keta] nf croquette

cruce etc ['kruθe] vb V **cruzar** ▷ nm (para peatones) crossing; (de carreteras) crossroads

crucero [kru'θero] nm (viaje) cruise

crucificar [kruθifi'kar] vt to crucify

crucifijo [kruθi'fixo] nm crucifix

crucigrama [kruθi'ɣrama] nm crossword (puzzle)

cruda ['kruða] (MÉX, CAM: fam) nf hangover

crudo, -a ['kruðo, a] adj raw; (no maduro) unripe; (petróleo) crude; (rudo, cruel) cruel ▷ nm crude (oil)

cruel [krwel] adj cruel; **crueldad** nf cruelty

crujiente [kru'xjente] adj (galleta etc) crunchy

crujir [kru'xir] vi (madera etc) to creak; (dedos) to crack; (dientes) to grind; (nieve, arena) to crunch

cruz [kruθ] nf cross; (de moneda) tails sg; **cruz gamada** swastika

cruzada [kru'θaða] nf crusade

cruzado, -a [kru'θaðo, a] adj crossed ▷ nm crusader

cruzar [kru'θar] vt to cross; **cruzarse** vr (líneas etc) to cross; (personas) to pass each other

Cruz Roja nf Red Cross

cuaderno [kwa'ðerno] nm notebook; (de escuela) exercise book; (Náut) logbook

cuadra ['kwaðra] nf (caballeriza) stable; (LAM: entre calles) block

cuadrado, -a [kwa'ðraðo, a] adj square ▷ nm (Mat) square

cuadrar [kwa'ðrar] vt to square ▷ vi: ~ **con** to square with, tally with; **cuadrarse** vr (soldado) to stand to attention

cuadrilátero [kwaðri'latero] nm (Deporte) boxing ring; (Geom) quadrilateral

cuadrilla [kwa'ðriʎa] nf party, group

cuadro ['kwaðro] nm square; (Arte) painting; (Teatro) scene; (diagrama) chart; (Deporte, Med) team; **tela a**

~s checked (BRIT) o chequered (US) material

cuajar [kwa'xar] vt (leche) to curdle; (sangre) to congeal; (Culin) to set; **cuajarse** vr to curdle; to congeal; to set; (llenarse) to fill up

cuajo ['kwaxo] nm: **de ~** (arrancar) by the roots; (cortar) completely

cual [kwal] adv like, as ▷ pron: **el** etc **~** which; (persona sujeto) who; (: objeto) whom ▷ adj such as; **cada ~** each one; **déjalo tal ~** leave it just as it is

cuál [kwal] pron interr which (one)

cualesquier, a [kwales'kjer(a)] pl de **cualquier(a)**

cualidad [kwali'ðað] nf quality

cualquier [kwal'kjer] adj V **cualquiera**

cualquiera [kwal'kjera] (pl **cualesquiera**) adj (delante de nm y f **cualquier**) any ▷ pron anybody; **un coche ~ servirá** any car will do; **no es un hombre ~** he isn't just anybody; **cualquier día/libro** any day/book; **eso ~ lo sabe hacer** anybody can do that; **es un ~** he's a nobody

cuando ['kwando] adv when; (aún si) if, even if ▷ conj (puesto que) since ▷ prep: **yo, ~ niño ...** when I was a child ...; **~ no sea así** even if it is not so; **~ más** at (the) most; **~ menos** at least; **~ no** if not, otherwise; **de ~ en ~** from time to time

cuándo ['kwando] adv when; **¿desde ~?** since when?

cuantía [kwan'tia] nf extent

○ **PALABRA CLAVE**

cuanto, -a ['kwanto, a] adj **1** (todo): **tiene todo cuanto desea** he's got everything he wants; **le daremos cuantos ejemplares necesite** we'll give him as many copies as o all the copies he needs; **cuantos hombres la ven** all the men who see her

2 unos cuantos: había unos cuantos periodistas there were a few journalists

3 (+ *más*): **cuanto más vino bebes peor te sentirás** the more wine you drink the worse you'll feel

▷ *pron*: **tiene cuanto desea** he has everything he wants; **tome cuanto/cuantos quiera** take as much/many as you want

▷ *adv*: **en cuanto: en cuanto profesor** as a teacher; **en cuanto a mí** as for me; *V tb* **antes**

▷ *conj* **1 cuanto más gana menos gasta** the more he earns the less he spends; **cuanto más joven más confiado** the younger you are the more trusting you are

2 en cuanto: en cuanto llegue/llegué as soon as I arrive/arrived

cuánto, -a ['kwanto, a] *adj* (*exclamación*) what a lot of; (*interr*: *sg*) how much?; (: *pl*) how many? ▷ *pron, adv* how; (: *interr*: *sg*) how much?; (: *pl*) how many?; **¡cuánta gente!** what a lot of people!; **¿~ cuesta?** how much does it cost?; **¿a ~s estamos?** what's the date?

cuarenta [kwa'renta] *num* forty

cuarentena [kwaren'tena] *nf* quarantine

cuaresma [kwa'resma] *nf* Lent

cuarta ['kwarta] *nf* (*Mat*) quarter, fourth; (*palmo*) span

cuartel [kwar'tel] *nm* (*Mil*) barracks *pl*; **cuartel de bomberos** (*RPL*) fire station; **cuartel general** headquarters *pl*

cuarteto [kwar'teto] *nm* quartet

cuarto, -a ['kwarto, a] *adj* fourth ▷ *nm* (*Mat*) quarter, fourth; (*habitación*) room; **cuarto de baño** bathroom; **cuarto de estar** living room; **cuarto de hora** quarter (of an) hour; **cuarto de kilo** quarter kilo; **cuartos de final** quarter finals

cuatro ['kwatro] *num* four

Cuba ['kuβa] *nf* Cuba

cuba ['kuβa] *nf* cask, barrel

cubano, -a [ku'βano, a] *adj, nm/f* Cuban

cubata [ku'βata] *nm* (*fam*) large drink (*of rum and coke etc*)

cubeta [ku'βeta] (*ESP, MÉX*) *nf* (*balde*) bucket, tub

cúbico, -a ['kuβiko, a] *adj* cubic

cubierta [ku'βjerta] *nf* cover, covering; (*neumático*) tyre; (*Náut*) deck

cubierto, -a [ku'βjerto, a] *pp de* **cubrir** ▷ *adj* covered ▷ *nm* cover; (*lugar en la mesa*) place; **cubiertos** *nmpl* cutlery *sg*; **a ~** under cover

cubilete [kuβi'lete] *nm* (*en juegos*) cup

cubito [ku'βito] *nm* (*tb*: **~ de hielo**) ice-cube

cubo ['kuβo] *nm* (*Mat*) cube; (*ESP*: *balde*) bucket, tub; (*Tec*) drum; **cubo de (la) basura** dustbin (*BRIT*), trash can (*US*)

cubrir [ku'βrir] *vt* to cover; **cubrirse** *vr* (*cielo*) to become overcast

cucaracha [kuka'ratʃa] *nf* cockroach

cuchara [ku'tʃara] *nf* spoon; (*Tec*) scoop; **cucharada** *nf* spoonful; **cucharadita** *nf* teaspoonful

cucharilla [kutʃa'riʎa] *nf* teaspoon

cucharón [kutʃa'ron] *nm* ladle

cuchilla [ku'tʃiʎa] *nf* (large) knife; (*de arma blanca*) blade; **cuchilla de afeitar** razor blade

cuchillo [ku'tʃiʎo] *nm* knife

cuchitril [kutʃi'tril] *nm* hovel

cuclillas [ku'kliʎas] *nfpl*: **en ~** squatting

cuco, -a ['kuko, a] *adj* pretty; (*astuto*) sharp ▷ *nm* cuckoo

cucurucho [kuku'rutʃo] *nm* cornet

cueca ['kweka] *nf* Chilean national dance

cuello ['kweʎo] *nm* (*Anat*) neck; (*de vestido, camisa*) collar

cuenca ['kwenka] *nf* (*Anat*) eye socket; (*Geo*) bowl, deep valley

cuenco ['kwenko] *nm* bowl

cuenta *etc* ['kwenta] *vb* V **contar** ▷ *nf* (*cálculo*) count, counting; (*en* *café, restaurante*) bill (BRIT), check (US); (*Com*) account; (*de collar*) bead; **a fin de ~s** in the end; **caer en la ~** to catch on; **darse ~ de** to realize; **tener en ~** to bear in mind; **echar ~s** to take stock; **cuenta atrás** countdown; **cuenta corriente/de ahorros** current/savings account; **cuenta de correo (electrónica)** (*Inform*) email account; **cuentakilómetros** *nm inv* ≈ milometer; (*de velocidad*) speedometer

cuento *etc* ['kwento] *vb* V **contar** ▷ *nm* story; **cuento chino** tall story; **cuento de hadas** a fairy tale

cuerda ['kwerða] *nf* rope; (*fina*) string; (*de reloj*) spring; **dar ~ a un reloj** to wind up a clock; **cuerda floja** tightrope; **cuerdas vocales** vocal cords

cuerdo, -a ['kwerðo, a] *adj* sane; (*prudente*) wise, sensible

cuerno ['kwerno] *nm* horn

cuero ['kwero] *nm* leather; **en ~s** stark naked; **cuero cabelludo** scalp

cuerpo ['kwerpo] *nm* body

cuervo ['kwerβo] *nm* crow

cuesta *etc* ['kwesta] *vb* V **costar** ▷ *nf* slope; (*en camino etc*) hill; **~ arriba/abajo** uphill/downhill; **a ~s** on one's back

cueste *etc vb* V **costar**

cuestión [kwes'tjon] *nf* matter, question, issue

cuete ['kwete] *adj* (*MÉX: fam*) drunk ▷ *nm* (*LAM: cohete*) rocket; (*MÉX, RPL: fam: embriaguez*) drunkenness; (*MÉX: Culin*) steak

cueva ['kweβa] *nf* cave

cuidado [kwi'ðaðo] *nm* care, carefulness; (*preocupación*) care, worry ▷ *excl* careful!, look out!; **eso me tiene sin ~** I'm not worried about that

cuidadoso, -a [kwiða'ðoso, a] *adj* careful; (*preocupado*) anxious

cuidar [kwi'ðar] *vt* (*Med*) to care for; (*ocuparse de*) to take care of, look after ▷ *vi*: **~ de** to take care of, look after; **cuidarse** *vr* to look after o.s.; **~se de hacer algo** to take care to do sth

culata [ku'lata] *nf* (*de fusil*) butt

culebra [ku'leβra] *nf* snake

culebrón [kule'βron] (*fam*) *nm* (*TV*) soap(-opera)

culo ['kulo] *nm* bottom, backside; (*de vaso, botella*) bottom

culpa ['kulpa] *nf* fault; (*Jur*) guilt; **por ~ de** because of; **echar la ~ a algn** to blame sb for sth; **tener la ~ (de)** to be to blame (for); **culpable** *adj* guilty ▷ *nmf* culprit; **culpar** [kul'par] *vt* to blame; (*acusar*) to accuse

cultivar [kulti'βar] *vt* to cultivate

cultivo [kul'tiβo] *nm* (*acto*) cultivation; (*plantas*) crop

culto, -a ['kulto, a] *adj* (*que tiene cultura*) cultured, educated ▷ *nm* (*homenaje*) worship; (*religión*) cult

cultura [kul'tura] *nf* culture

culturismo [kultu'rismo] *nm* body-building

cumbia ['kumbja] *nf* popular *Colombian dance*

cumbre ['kumbre] *nf* summit, top

cumpleaños [kumple'aɲos] *nm inv* birthday

cumplido, -a [kum'pliðo, a] *adj* (*abundante*) plentiful; (*cortés*) courteous ▷ *nm* compliment; **visita de ~** courtesy call

cumplidor, a [kumpli'ðor, a] *adj* reliable

cumplimiento [kumpli'mjento] *nm* (*de un deber*) fulfilment; (*acabamiento*) completion

cumplir [kum'plir] *vt* (*orden*) to carry out, obey; (*promesa*) to carry out, fulfil; (*condena*) to serve ▷ *vi*: **~ con** (*deber*) to carry out, fulfil; **cumplirse** *vr* (*plazo*) to expire; **hoy cumple dieciocho años** he is eighteen today

cuna ['kuna] *nf* cradle, cot

cundir [kun'dir] *vi* (*noticia, rumor, pánico*) to spread; (*rendir*) to go a long way

cuneta [ku'neta] *nf* ditch

cuña ['kuɲa] *nf* wedge

cuñado, -a [ku'ɲaðo, a] *nm/f* brother-/sister-in-law

cuota ['kwota] *nf* (*parte proporcional*) share; (*cotización*) fee, dues *pl*

cupe *etc vb* V **caber**

cupiera *etc vb* V **caber**

cupo ['kupo] *vb* V **caber** ▷ *nm* quota

cupón [ku'pon] *nm* coupon

cúpula ['kupula] *nf* dome

cura ['kura] *nf* (*curación*) cure; (*método curativo*) treatment ▷ *nm* priest

curación [kura'θjon] *nf* cure; (*acción*) curing

curandero, -a [kuran'dero, a] *nm/f* quack

curar [ku'rar] *vt* (*Med: herida*) to treat, dress; (: *enfermo*) to cure; (*Culin*) to cure, salt; (*cuero*) to tan; **curarse** *vr* to get well, recover

curiosear [kurjose'ar] *vt* to glance at, look over ▷ *vi* to look round, wander round; (*explorar*) to poke about

curiosidad [kurjosi'ðað] *nf* curiosity

curioso, -a [ku'rjoso, a] *adj* curious ▷ *nm/f* bystander, onlooker

curita [ku'rita] (*LAM*) *nf* (sticking) plaster (*BRIT*), Bandaid® (*US*)

currante [ku'rrante] (*ESP: fam*) *nmf* worker

currar [ku'rrar] (*ESP: fam*) *vi* to work

currículo [ku'rrikulo] = **curriculum**

curriculum [ku'rrikulum] *nm* curriculum vitae

cursi ['kursi] (*fam*) *adj* affected

cursillo [kur'siʎo] *nm* short course

cursiva [kur'siβa] *nf* italics *pl*

curso ['kurso] *nm* course; **en ~** (*año*) current; (*proceso*) going on, under way

cursor [kur'sor] *nm* (*Inform*) cursor

curul [ku'rul] (*MÉX*) *nm* (*escaño*) seat

curva ['kurβa] *nf* curve, bend

custodia [kus'toðja] *nf* safekeeping; custody

cutis ['kutis] *nm inv* skin, complexion

cutre ['kutre] (*ESP: fam*) *adj* (*lugar*) grotty

cuyo, -a ['kujo, a] *pron* (*de quien*) whose; (*de que*) whose, of which; **en ~ caso** in which case

C.V. *abr* (= *caballos de vapor*) H.P.

D. *abr* (= *Don*) Esq

dado, -a ['daðo, a] *pp de* **dar** ▷ *nm* die; **dados** *nmpl* dice; **~ que** given that

daltónico, -a [dal'toniko, a] *adj* colour-blind

dama ['dama] *nf* (*gen*) lady; (*Ajedrez*) queen; **damas** *nfpl* (*juego*) draughts *sg*; **dama de honor** bridesmaid

damasco [da'masko] (*RPL*) *nm* apricot

danés, -esa [da'nes, esa] *adj* Danish ▷ *nm/f* Dane

dañar [da'ɲar] *vt* (*objeto*) to damage; (*persona*) to hurt; **dañarse** *vr* (*objeto*) to get damaged

dañino, -a [da'ɲino, a] *adj* harmful

daño ['daɲo] *nm* (*objeto*) damage; (*persona*) harm, injury; **~s y perjuicios** (*Jur*) damages; **hacer ~ a** to damage; (*persona*) to hurt, injure; **hacerse ~** to hurt o.s.

dañoso [da'ɲoso] *adj* harmful

○ **PALABRA CLAVE**

dar [dar] *vt* **1** (*gen*) to give; (*obra de*

teatro) to put on; (*film*) to show; (*fiesta*) to hold; **dar algo a algn** to give sb sth *o* sth to sb; **dar de beber a algn** to give sb a drink; **dar de comer** to feed

2 (*producir: intereses*) to yield; (*fruta*) to produce

3 (*locuciones + n*): **da gusto escucharle** it's a pleasure to listen to him; *V tb* **paseo**

4 (*+ n*: *= perífrasis de verbo*): **me da asco** it sickens me

5 (*considerar*): **dar algo por descontado/entendido** to take sth for granted/as read; **dar algo por concluido** to consider sth finished

6 (*hora*): **el reloj dio las 6** the clock struck 6 (o'clock)

7: **me da lo mismo** it's all the same to me; *V tb* **igual, más**

▷ *vi* **1 dar con: dimos con él dos horas más tarde** we came across him two hours later; **al final di con la solución** I eventually came up with the answer

2: **dar en** (*blanco, suelo*) to hit; **el sol me da en la cara** the sun is shining (right) on my face

3: **dar de sí** (*zapatos etc*) to stretch, give

darse *vr* **1**: **darse por vencido** to give up

2 (*ocurrir*): **se han dado muchos casos** there have been a lot of cases

3: **darse a: se ha dado a la bebida** he's taken to drinking

4: **se me dan bien/mal las ciencias** I'm good/bad at science

5: **dárselas de: se las da de experto** he fancies himself *o* poses as an expert

dardo [ˈdarðo] *nm* dart

dátil [ˈdatil] *nm* date

dato [ˈdato] *nm* fact, piece of information; **datos personales** personal details

dcha. *abr* (*= derecha*) r.h.

d. de C. *abr* (*= después de Cristo*) A.D.

○ **PALABRA CLAVE**

de [de] (*de + el = del*) *prep* **1** (*posesión*) of; **la casa de Isabel/mis padres** Isabel's/my parents' house; **es de ellos** it's theirs

2 (*origen, distancia, con números*) from; **soy de Gijón** I'm from Gijón; **de 8 a 20** from 8 to 20; **salir del cine** to go out *o* leave the cinema; **de 2 en 2** 2 by 2, 2 at a time

3 (*valor descriptivo*): **una copa de vino** a glass of wine; **la mesa de la cocina** the kitchen table; **un billete de 10 euros** a 10 euro note; **un niño de tres años** a three-year-old (child); **una máquina de coser** a sewing machine; **ir vestido de gris** to be dressed in grey; **la niña del vestido azul** the girl in the blue dress; **trabaja de profesora** she works as a teacher; **de lado** sideways; **de atrás/delante** rear/front

4 (*hora, tiempo*): **a las 8 de la mañana** at 8 o'clock in the morning; **de día/ noche** by day/night; **de hoy en ocho días** a week from now; **de niño era gordo** as a child he was fat

5 (*comparaciones*): **más/menos de cien personas** more/less than a hundred people; **el más caro de la tienda** the most expensive in the shop; **menos/más de lo pensado** less/more than expected

6 (*causa*): **del calor** from the heat

7 (*tema*) about; **clases de inglés** English classes; **¿sabes algo de él?** do you know anything about him?; **un libro de física** a physics book

8 (*adj + de + infin*): **fácil de entender** easy to understand

9 (*oraciones pasivas*): **fue respetado de todos** he was loved by all

10 (*condicional + infin*) if; **de ser posible** if possible; **de no terminarlo hoy** if I *etc* don't finish it today

dé [de] vb V **dar**

debajo [de'βaxo] adv underneath; **~ de** below, under; **por ~ de** beneath

debate [de'βate] nm debate; **debatir** vt to debate

deber [de'βer] nm duty ▷ vt to owe ▷ vi: **debe (de)** it must, it should; **deberes** nmpl (Escol) homework; **deberse vr: ~se a** to be owing o due to; **debo hacerlo** I must do it; **debe de ir** he should go

debido, -a [de'βiðo, a] adj proper, just; **~ a** due to, because of

débil ['deβil] adj (persona, carácter) weak; (luz) dim; **debilidad** nf weakness; dimness

debilitar [deβili'tar] vt to weaken; **debilitarse** vr to grow weak

débito ['deβito] nm debit; **débito bancario** (LAM) direct debit (BRIT) o billing (US)

debutar [deβu'tar] vi to make one's debut

década ['dekaða] nf decade

decadencia [deka'ðenθja] nf (estado) decadence; (proceso) decline, decay

decaído, -a [deka'iðo, a] adj: **estar ~** (abatido) to be down

decano, -a [de'kano, a] nm/f (de universidad etc) dean

decena [de'θena] nf: **una ~** ten (or so)

decente [de'θente] adj decent

decepción [deθep'θjon] nf disappointment

　No confundir **decepción** con la palabra inglesa deception.

decepcionar [deθepθjo'nar] vt to disappoint

decidir [deθi'ðir] vt, vi to decide; **decidirse** vr: **~se a** to make up one's mind to

décimo, -a ['deθimo, a] adj tenth ▷ nm tenth

decir [de'θir] vt to say; (contar) to tell; (hablar) to speak ▷ nm saying; **decirse** vr: **se dice que** it is said that; **es ~** that is (to say); **~ para sí** to say to o.s.;

querer ~ to mean; **¡dígame!** (Tel) hello!; (en tienda) can I help you?

decisión [deθi'sjon] nf (resolución) decision; (firmeza) decisiveness

decisivo, -a [deθi'siβo, a] adj decisive

declaración [deklara'θjon] nf (manifestación) statement; (de amor) declaration; **declaración fiscal** o **de la renta** income-tax return

declarar [dekla'rar] vt to declare ▷ vi to declare; (Jur) to testify; **declararse** vr to propose

decoración [dekora'θjon] nf decoration

decorado [deko'raðo] nm (Cine, Teatro) scenery, set

decorar [deko'rar] vt to decorate; **decorativo, -a** adj ornamental, decorative

decreto [de'kreto] nm decree

dedal [de'ðal] nm thimble

dedicación [deðika'θjon] nf dedication

dedicar [deði'kar] vt (libro) to dedicate; (tiempo, dinero) to devote; (palabras: decir, consagrar) to dedicate, devote; **dedicatoria** nf (de libro) dedication

dedo ['deðo] nm finger; **hacer ~** (fam) to hitch (a lift); **dedo anular** ring finger; **dedo corazón** middle finger; **dedo (del pie)** toe; **dedo gordo** (de la mano) thumb; (del pie) big toe; **dedo índice** index finger; **dedo meñique** little finger; **dedo pulgar** thumb

deducción [deðuk'θjon] nf deduction

deducir [deðu'θir] vt (concluir) to deduce, infer; (Com) to deduct

defecto [de'fekto] nm defect, flaw; **defectuoso, -a** adj defective, faulty

defender [defen'der] vt to defend; **defenderse** vr (desenvolverse) to get by

defensa [de'fensa] nf defence ▷ nm (Deporte) defender, back; **defensivo, -a** adj defensive; **a la defensiva** on the defensive

defensor, a [defen'sor, a] *adj*
defending ▷ *nm/f* (*abogado defensor*)
defending counsel; (*protector*)
protector
deficiencia [defi'θjenθja] *nf*
deficiency
deficiente [defi'θjente] *adj*
(*defectuoso*) defective; **~ en** lacking *o*
deficient in; **ser un ~ mental** to be
mentally handicapped
déficit ['defiθit] (*pl* **~s**) *nm* deficit
definición [defini'θjon] *nf* definition
definir [defi'nir] *vt* (*determinar*) to
determine, establish; (*decidir*) to define;
(*aclarar*) to clarify; **definitivo, -a** *adj*
definitive; **en definitiva** definitively;
(*en resumen*) in short
deformación [deforma'θjon] *nf*
(*alteración*) deformation; (*Radio etc*)
distortion
deformar [defor'mar] *vt* (*gen*) to
deform; **deformarse** *vr* to become
deformed; **deforme** *adj* (*informe*)
deformed; (*feo*) ugly; (*malhecho*)
misshapen
defraudar [defrau'ðar] *vt*
(*decepcionar*) to disappoint; (*estafar*)
to defraud
defunción [defun'θjon] *nf* death,
demise
degenerar [dexene'rar] *vi* to
degenerate
degradar [dexra'ðar] *vt* to debase,
degrade; **degradarse** *vr* to demean
o.s.
degustación [dexusta'θjon] *nf*
sampling, tasting
dejar [de'xar] *vt* to leave; (*permitir*)
to allow, let; (*abandonar*) to abandon,
forsake; (*beneficios*) to produce, yield
▷ *vi*: **~ de** (*parar*) to stop; (*no hacer*) to
fail to; **~ a un lado** to leave *o* set aside;
~ entrar/salir to let in/out; **~ pasar** to
let through
del [del] (=**de** + **el**) ∨ **de**
delantal [delan'tal] *nm* apron
delante [de'lante] *adv* in front;
(*enfrente*) opposite; (*adelante*) ahead; **~**
de in front of, before
delantera [delan'tera] *nf* (*de vestido,
casa etc*) front part; (*Deporte*) forward
line; **llevar la ~ (a algn)** to be ahead
(of sb)
delantero, -a [delan'tero, a] *adj*
front ▷ *nm* (*Deporte*) forward,
striker
delatar [dela'tar] *vt* to inform on
o against, betray; **delator, a** *nm/f*
informer
delegación [delexa'θjon] *nf* (*acción,
delegados*) delegation; (*Com: oficina*)
office, branch; **delegación de policía**
(*Méx*) police station
delegado, -a [dele'xaðo, a] *nm/f*
delegate; (*Com*) agent
delegar [dele'xar] *vt* to delegate
deletrear [deletre'ar] *vt* to spell (out)
delfín [del'fin] *nm* dolphin
delgado, -a [del'xaðo, a] *adj* thin;
(*persona*) slim, thin; (*tela etc*) light,
delicate
deliberar [deliβe'rar] *vt* to debate,
discuss
delicadeza [delika'ðeθa] *nf* (*gen*)
delicacy; (*refinamiento, sutileza*)
refinement
delicado, -a [deli'kaðo, a] *adj*
(*gen*) delicate; (*sensible*) sensitive;
(*quisquilloso*) touchy
delicia [de'liθja] *nf* delight
delicioso, -a [deli'θjoso, a] *adj*
(*gracioso*) delightful; (*exquisito*)
delicious
delimitar [delimi'tar] *vt* (*función,
responsabilidades*) to define
delincuencia [delin'kwenθja]
nf delinquency; **delincuente** *nmf*
delinquent; (*criminal*) criminal
delineante [deline'ante] *nmf*
draughtsman/woman
delirante [deli'rante] *adj* delirious
delirar [deli'rar] *vi* to be delirious,
rave
delirio [de'lirjo] *nm* (*Med*)
delirium; (*palabras insensatas*)
ravings *pl*

delito [de'lito] nm (gen) crime;
(infracción) offence

delta ['delta] nm delta

demacrado, -a [dema'krado, a]
adj: **estar ~** to look pale and drawn, be
wasted away

demanda [de'manda] nf (pedido,
Com) demand; (petición) request;
(Jur) action, lawsuit; **demandar**
[deman'dar] vt (gen) to demand; (Jur)
to sue, file a lawsuit against

demás [de'mas] adj: **los ~ niños** the
other o remaining children ▷ pron: **los/
las ~** the others, the rest (of them); **lo ~**
the rest (of it)

demasía [dema'sia] nf (exceso)
excess, surplus; **comer en ~** to eat
to excess

demasiado, -a [dema'sjaðo, a]
adj: **~ vino** too much wine ▷ adv (antes
de adj, adv) too; **~s libros** too many
books; **¡esto es ~!** that's the limit!;
hace ~ calor it's too hot; **~ despacio**
too slowly; **~s** too many

demencia [de'menθja] nf (locura)
madness

democracia [demo'kraθja] nf
democracy

demócrata [de'mokrata] nmf
democrat; **democrático, -a** adj
democratic

demoler [demo'ler] vt to demolish;
demolición nf demolition

demonio [de'monjo] nm devil;
demon; **¡~s!** hell!, damn!; **¿cómo ~s?**
how the hell?

demora [de'mora] nf delay

demos ['demos] vb V **dar**

demostración [demostra'θjon] nf
(Mat) proof; (de afecto) show,
display

demostrar [demos'trar] vt (probar)
to prove; (mostrar) to show; (manifestar)
to demonstrate

den [den] vb V **dar**

denegar [dene'ɣar] vt (rechazar) to
refuse; (Jur) to reject

denominación [denomina'θjon]

nf (acto) naming; **Denominación de
Origen** see note

⬤ **DENOMINACIÓN DE ORIGEN**
⬤
⬤ The **Denominación de Origen**,
⬤ abbreviated to **D.O.**, is a
⬤ prestigious classification awarded
⬤ to food products such as wines,
⬤ cheeses, sausages and hams
⬤ which meet the stringent quality
⬤ and production standards of the
⬤ designated region. **D.O.** labels
⬤ serve as a guarantee of quality.

densidad [densi'ðað] nf density; (fig)
thickness

denso, -a ['denso, a] adj dense;
(espeso, pastoso) thick; (fig) heavy

dentadura [denta'ðura] nf (set
of) teeth pl; **dentadura postiza** false
teeth pl

dentera [den'tera] nf (grima): **dar ~ a
algn** to set sb's teeth on edge

dentífrico, -a [den'tifriko, a] adj
dental ▷ nm toothpaste

dentista [den'tista] nmf dentist

dentro ['dentro] adv inside ▷ prep: **~
de** in, inside, within; **por ~** (on the)
inside; **mirar por ~** to look inside; **~ de
tres meses** within three months

denuncia [de'nunθja] nf (delación)
denunciation; (acusación) accusation;
(de accidente) report; **denunciar** vt to
report; (delatar) to inform on o against

departamento [departa'mento]
nm sección administrativa, department,
section; (LAM: apartamento) flat (BRIT),
apartment

depender [depen'der] vi: **~ de** to
depend on; **depende** it (all) depends

dependienta [depen'djenta] nf
saleswoman, shop assistant

dependiente [depen'djente] adj
dependent ▷ nm salesman, shop
assistant

depilar [depi'lar] vt (con cera) to wax;
(cejas) to pluck

deportar [depor'tar] vt to deport

deporte [de'porte] nm sport; **hacer ~** to play sports; **deportista** adj sports cpd ▷ nmf sportsman/woman; **deportivo, -a** adj (club, periódico) sports cpd ▷ nm sports car

depositar [deposi'tar] vt (dinero) to deposit; (mercancías) to put away, store; **depositarse** vr to settle

depósito [de'posito] nm (gen) deposit; (almacén) warehouse, store; (de agua, gasolina etc) tank; **depósito de cadáveres** mortuary

depredador, a [depreða'ðor, a] adj predatory ▷ nm predator

depresión [depre'sjon] nf depression; **depresión nerviosa** nervous breakdown

deprimido, -a [depri'miðo, a] adj depressed

deprimir [depri'mir] vt to depress; **deprimirse** vi (persona) to become depressed

deprisa [de'prisa] adv quickly, hurriedly

depurar [depu'rar] vt to purify; (purgar) to purge

derecha [de'retʃa] nf right(-hand) side; (Pol) right; **a la ~** (estar) on the right; (torcer etc) (to the) right

derecho, -a [de'retʃo, a] adj right, right-hand ▷ nm (privilegio) right; (lado) right(-hand) side; (leyes) law ▷ adv straight, directly; **siga todo ~** carry o (BRIT) go straight on; **derechos** nmpl (de aduana) duty sg; (de autor) royalties; **tener ~ a** to have a right to; **derechos de autor** royalties

deriva [de'riβa] nf: **ir** o **estar a la ~** to drift, be adrift

derivado [deri'βaðo] nm (Com) by-product

derivar [deri'βar] vt to derive; (desviar) to direct ▷ vi to derive, be derived; (Náut) to drift; **derivarse** vr to derive, be derived; to drift

derramamiento [derrama'mjento] nm (dispersión) spilling;

derramamiento de sangre bloodshed

derramar [derra'mar] vt to spill; (verter) to pour out; (esparcir) to scatter; **derramarse** vr to pour out

derrame [de'rrame] nm (de líquido) spilling; (de sangre) shedding; (de tubo etc) overflow; (pérdida) leakage; **derrame cerebral** brain haemorrhage

derredor [derre'ðor] adv: **al** o **en ~ de** around, about

derretir [derre'tir] vt (gen) to melt; (nieve) to thaw; **derretirse** vr to melt

derribar [derri'βar] vt to knock down; (construcción) to demolish; (persona, gobierno, político) to bring down

derrocar [derro'kar] vt (gobierno) to bring down, overthrow

derrochar [derro'tʃar] vt to squander; **derroche** nm (despilfarro) waste, squandering

derrota [de'rrota] nf (Náut) course; (Mil, Deporte etc) defeat, rout; **derrotar** vt (gen) to defeat; **derrotero** nm (rumbo) course

derrumbar [derrum'bar] vt (edificio) to knock down; **derrumbarse** vr to collapse

des etc vb V **dar**

desabrochar [desaβro'tʃar] vt (botónes, broches) to undo, unfasten; **desabrocharse** vr (ropa etc) to come undone

desacato [desa'kato] nm (falta de respeto) disrespect; (Jur) contempt

desacertado, -a [desaθer'taðo, a] adj (equivocado) mistaken; (inoportuno) unwise

desacierto [desa'θjerto] nm mistake, error

desaconsejar [desakonse'xar] vt to advise against

desacreditar [desakreði'tar] vt (desprestigiar) to discredit, bring into disrepute; (denigrar) to run down

desacuerdo [desa'kwerðo] nm disagreement, discord

desafiar [desa'fjar] vt (retar) to

desafilado | 86

challenge; (*enfrentarse a*) to defy
desafilado, -a [desafiˈlaðo, a]
adj blunt
desafinado, -a [desafiˈnaðo, a]
adj: **estar ~** to be out of tune
desafinar [desafiˈnar] *vi* (*al cantar*) to
be *o* go out of tune
desafío *etc* [desaˈfio] *vb* V **desafiar**
▷ *nm* (*reto*) challenge; (*combate*) duel;
(*resistencia*) defiance
desafortunado, -a
[desafortuˈnaðo, a] *adj* (*desgraciado*)
unfortunate, unlucky
desagradable [desaɣraˈðaβle]
adj (*fastidioso, enojoso*) unpleasant;
(*irritante*) disagreeable
desagradar [desaɣraˈðar] *vi*
(*disgustar*) to displease; (*molestar*) to
bother
desagradecido, -a [desaɣraðeˈθiðo,
a] *adj* ungrateful
desagrado [desaˈɣraðo] *nm*
(*disgusto*) displeasure; (*contrariedad*)
dissatisfaction
desagüe [desˈaɣwe] *nm* (*de un líquido*)
drainage; (*cañería*) drainpipe; (*salida*)
outlet, drain
desahogar [desaoˈɣar] *vt* (*aliviar*)
to ease, relieve; (*ira*) to vent;
desahogarse *vr* (*relajarse*) to relax;
(*desfogarse*) to let off steam
desahogo [desaˈoɣo] *nm* (*alivio*)
relief; (*comodidad*) comfort, ease
desahuciar [desauˈθjar] *vt* (*enfermo*)
to give up hope for; (*inquilino*) to evict
desairar [desaiˈrar] *vt* (*menospreciar*)
to slight, snub
desalentador, a [desalentaˈðor, a]
adj discouraging
desaliño [desaˈliɲo] *nm* slovenliness
desalmado, -a [desalˈmaðo, a] *adj*
(*cruel*) cruel, heartless
desalojar [desaloˈxar] *vt* (*expulsar,
echar*) to eject; (*abandonar*) to move out
of ▷ *vi* to move out
desamor [desaˈmor] *nm* (*frialdad*)
indifference; (*odio*) dislike
desamparado, -a [desampaˈraðo,

a] *adj* (*persona*) helpless;
(*lugar: expuesto*) exposed; (*desierto*)
deserted
desangrar [desanˈgrar] *vt* to bleed;
(*fig: persona*) to bleed dry; **desangrarse**
vr to lose a lot of blood
desanimado, -a [desaniˈmaðo,
a] *adj* (*persona*) downhearted;
(*espectáculo, fiesta*) dull
desanimar [desaniˈmar] *vt*
(*desalentar*) to discourage; (*deprimir*) to
depress; **desanimarse** *vr* to lose heart
desapacible [desapaˈθiβle] *adj* (*gen*)
unpleasant
desaparecer [desapareˈθer] *vi* (*gen*)
to disappear; (*el sol, la luz*) to vanish;
desaparecido, -a *adj* missing;
desaparición *nf* disappearance
desapercibido, -a [desaperθiˈβiðo,
a] *adj* (*desprevenido*) unprepared; **pasar
~** to go unnoticed
desaprensivo, -a [desaprenˈsiβo, a]
adj unscrupulous
desaprobar [desaproˈβar] *vt*
(*reprobar*) to disapprove of; (*condenar*) to
condemn; (*no consentir*) to reject
desaprovechado, -a
[desaproβeˈtʃaðo, a] *adj* (*oportunidad,
tiempo*) wasted; (*estudiante*) slack
desaprovechar [desaproβeˈtʃar]
vt to waste
desarmador [desarmaˈðor] (*MÉX*)
nm screwdriver
desarmar [desarˈmar] *vt* (*Mil, fig*) to
disarm; (*Tec*) to take apart, dismantle;
desarme *nm* disarmament
desarraigar [desarraiˈɣar] *vt* to
uproot; **desarraigo** *nm* uprooting
desarreglar [desarreˈɣlar] *vt*
(*desordenar*) to disarrange; (*trastocar*) to
upset, disturb
desarrollar [desarroˈʎar] *vt* (*gen*) to
develop; **desarrollarse** *vr* to develop;
(*ocurrir*) to take place; (*Foto*) to develop;
desarrollo *nm* development
desarticular [desartikuˈlar] *vt*
(*hueso*) to dislocate; (*objeto*) to take
apart; (*fig*) to break up

desasosegar [desasose'ɣar] vt
(*inquietar*) to disturb, make uneasy

desasosiego *etc* [desaso'sjeɣo] vb
V **desasosegar** ▷ nm (*intranquilidad*)
uneasiness, restlessness; (*ansiedad*)
anxiety

desastre [de'sastre] nm disaster;
desastroso, -a adj disastrous

desatar [desa'tar] vt (*nudo*) to untie;
(*paquete*) to undo; (*separar*) to detach;
desatarse vr (*zapatos*) to come
untied; (*tormenta*) to break

desatascar [desatas'kar] vt (*cañería*)
to unblock, clear

desatender [desaten'der] vt *no
prestar atención a*, to disregard;
(*abandonar*) to neglect

desatino [desa'tino] nm (*idiotez*)
foolishness, folly; (*error*) blunder

desatornillar [desatorni'ʎar] vt to
unscrew

desatrancar [desatran'kar] vt
(*puerta*) to unbolt; (*cañería*) to clear,
unblock

desautorizado, -a [desautori'θaðo,
a] adj unauthorized

desautorizar [desautori'θar]
vt (*oficial*) to deprive of authority;
(*informe*) to deny

desayunar [desaju'nar] vi to have
breakfast ▷ vt to have for breakfast;
desayuno nm breakfast

desazón [desa'θon] nf anxiety

desbarajuste [desβara'xuste] nm
confusion, disorder

desbaratar [desβara'tar] vt
(*deshacer, destruir*) to ruin

desbloquear [desβloke'ar] vt
(*negociaciónes, tráfico*) to get going
again; (*Com: cuenta*) to unfreeze

desbordar [desβor'ðar] vt
(*sobrepasar*) to go beyond; (*exceder*)
to exceed; **desbordarse** vr (*río*) to
overflow; (*entusiasmo*) to erupt

descabellado, -a [deskaβe'ʎaðo, a]
adj (*disparatado*) wild, crazy

descafeinado, -a [deskafei'naðo, a]
adj decaffeinated ▷ nm decaffeinated
coffee

descalabro [deska'laβro] nm blow;
(*desgracia*) misfortune

descalificar [deskalifi'kar] vt to
disqualify; (*desacreditar*) to discredit

descalzar [deskal'θar] vt (*zapato*) to
take off; **descalzo, -a** adj barefoot(ed)

descambiar [deskam'bjar] vt to
exchange

descaminado, -a [deskami'naðo,
a] adj (*equivocado*) on the wrong road;
(*fig*) misguided

descampado [deskam'paðo] nm
open space

descansado, -a [deskan'saðo, a] adj
(*gen*) rested; (*que tranquiliza*) restful

descansar [deskan'sar] vt (*gen*) to
rest ▷ vi to rest, have a rest; (*echarse*)
to lie down

descansillo [deskan'siʎo] nm (*de
escalera*) landing

descanso [des'kanso] nm (*reposo*)
rest; (*alivio*) relief; (*pausa*) break;
(*Deporte*) interval, half time

descapotable [deskapo'taβle] nm
(*tb:* **coche ~**) convertible

descarado, -a [deska'raðo, a] adj
shameless; (*insolente*) cheeky

descarga [des'karɣa] nf (*Arq, Elec,
Mil*) discharge; (*Náut*) unloading;
descargable [deskar'ɣaβle]
adj downloadable; **descargar**
[deskar'ɣar] vt to unload; (*golpe*) to
let fly; **descargarse** vr to unburden
o.s.; **descargarse algo de Internet** to
download sth from the Internet

descaro [des'karo] nm nerve

descarriar [deska'rrjar] vt
(*descaminar*) to misdirect; (*fig*) to lead
astray; **descarriarse** vr (*perderse*) to
lose one's way; (*separarse*) to stray;
(*pervertirse*) to err, go astray

descarrilamiento
[deskarrila'mjento] nm (*de tren*)
derailment

descarrilar [deskarri'lar] vi to be
derailed

descartar [deskar'tar] vt (*rechazar*)

to reject; (*eliminar*) to rule out;
descartarse *vr* (*Naipes*) to discard;
~se de to shirk

descendencia [desθen'denθja] *nf*
(*origen*) origin, descent; (*hijos*) offspring

descender [desθen'der] *vt*
(*bajar: escalera*) to go down ▷ *vi* to
descend; (*temperatura, nivel*) to fall,
drop; **~ de** to be descended from

descendiente [desθen'djente] *nmf*
descendant

descenso [des'θenso] *nm* descent;
(*de temperatura*) drop

descifrar [desθi'frar] *vt* to decipher;
(*mensaje*) to decode

descolgar [deskol'ɣar] *vt* (*bajar*)
to take down; (*teléfono*) to pick up;
descolgarse *vr* to let o.s. down

descolorido, -a [deskolo'riðo, a] *adj*
faded; (*pálido*) pale

descompasado, -a
[deskompa'saðo, a] *adj* (*sin
proporción*) out of all proportion;
(*excesivo*) excessive

descomponer [deskompo'ner] *vt*
(*desordenar*) to disarrange, disturb; (*Tec*)
to put out of order; (*dividir*) to break
down (into parts); (*fig*) to provoke;
descomponerse *vr* (*corromperse*) to
rot, decompose; (*LAM Tec*) to break
down

descomposición [deskomposi'θjon]
nf (*de un objeto*) breakdown; (*de fruta
etc*) decomposition; **descomposición
de vientre** (*ESP*) stomach upset,
diarrhoea

descompostura [deskompos'tura]
nf (*MÉX: avería*) breakdown, fault;
(*LAM: diarrea*) diarrhoea

descomprimir [deskompri'mir]
(*Internet*) to unzip

descompuesto, -a
[deskom'pwesto, a] *adj* (*corrompido*)
decomposed; (*roto*) broken

desconcertado, -a
[deskonθer'taðo, a] *adj* disconcerted,
bewildered

desconcertar [deskonθer'tar] *vt*

(*confundir*) to baffle; (*incomodar*) to
upset, put out; **desconcertarse** *vr*
(*turbarse*) to be upset

desconchado, -a [deskon'tʃaðo, a]
adj (*pintura*) peeling

desconcierto *etc* [deskon'θjerto] *vb*
V **desconcertar** ▷ *nm* (*gen*) disorder;
(*desorientación*) uncertainty; (*inquietud*)
uneasiness

desconectar [deskonek'tar] *vt* to
disconnect

desconfianza [deskon'fjanθa] *nf*
distrust

desconfiar [deskon'fjar] *vi* to be
distrustful; **~ de** to distrust, suspect

descongelar [deskonxe'lar] *vt* to
defrost; (*Com, Pol*) to unfreeze

descongestionar
[deskonxestjo'nar] *vt* (*cabeza, tráfico*)
to clear

desconocer [deskono'θer] *vt*
(*ignorar*) not to know, be ignorant of

desconocido, -a [deskono'θiðo, a]
adj unknown ▷ *nm/f* stranger

desconocimiento
[deskonoθi'mjento] *nm falta de
conocimientos*, ignorance

desconsiderado, -a
[deskonsiðe'raðo, a] *adj*
inconsiderate; (*insensible*) thoughtless

desconsuelo *etc* [deskon'swelo] *vb*
V **desconsolar** ▷ *nm* (*tristeza*) distress;
(*desesperación*) despair

descontado, -a [deskon'taðo, a]
adj: **dar por ~ (que)** to take (it) for
granted (that)

descontar [deskon'tar] *vt* (*deducir*)
to take away, deduct; (*rebajar*) to
discount

descontento, -a [deskon'tento, a]
adj dissatisfied ▷ *nm* dissatisfaction,
discontent

descorchar [deskor'tʃar] *vt* to
uncork

descorrer [desko'rrer] *vt* (*cortinas,
cerrojo*) to draw back

descortés [deskor'tes] *adj* (*mal
educado*) discourteous; (*grosero*) rude

descoser [desko'ser] vt to unstitch;
descoserse vr to come apart (at the seams)

descosido, -a [desko'siðo, a] adj (Costura) unstitched

descreído, -a [deskre'iðo, a] adj (incrédulo) incredulous; (falto de fe) unbelieving

descremado, -a [deskre'maðo, a] adj skimmed

describir [deskri'βir] vt to describe;
descripción [deskrip'θjon] nf description

descrito [des'krito] pp de **describir**

descuartizar [deskwarti'θar] vt (animal) to cut up

descubierto, -a [desku'βjerto, a] pp de **descubrir** ▷ adj uncovered, bare; (persona) bareheaded ▷ nm (bancario) overdraft; **al ~** in the open

descubrimiento [deskuβri'mjento] nm (hallazgo) discovery; (revelación) revelation

descubrir [desku'βrir] vt to discover, find; (inaugurar) to unveil; (vislumbrar) to detect; (revelar) to reveal, show; (destapar) to uncover; **descubrirse** vr to reveal o.s.; (quitarse sombrero) to take off one's hat; (confesar) to confess

descuento etc [des'kwento] vb V **descontar** ▷ nm discount

descuidado, -a [deskwi'ðaðo, a] adj (sin cuidado) careless; (desordenado) untidy; (olvidadizo) forgetful; (dejado) neglected, (desprevenido) unprepared

descuidar [deskwi'ðar] vt (dejar) to neglect; (olvidar) to overlook; **descuidarse** vr (distraerse) to be careless; (abandonarse) to let o.s. go; (desprevenirse) to drop one's guard; **¡descuida!** don't worry!; **descuido** nm (dejadez) carelessness; (olvido) negligence

○ **PALABRA CLAVE**

desde ['desðe] prep **1** (lugar) from;

desde Burgos hasta mi casa hay 30 km it's 30 km from Burgos to my house
2 (posición): **hablaba desde el balcón** she was speaking from the balcony
3 (tiempo: + adv, n): **desde ahora** from now on; **desde la boda** since the wedding; **desde niño** since I etc was a child; **desde 3 años atrás** since 3 years ago
4 (tiempo: + vb, fecha) since; for; **nos conocemos desde 1992/desde hace 20 años** we've known each other since 1992/for 20 years; **no le veo desde 1997/desde hace 5 años** I haven't seen him since 1997/for 5 years
5 (gama): **desde los más lujosos hasta los más económicos** from the most luxurious to the most reasonably priced
6: **desde luego (que no)** of course (not)
▷ conj: **desde que: desde que recuerdo** for as long as I can remember; **desde que llegó no ha salido** he hasn't been out since he arrived

desdén [des'ðen] nm scorn

desdeñar [desðe'ɲar] vt (despreciar) to scorn

desdicha [des'ðitʃa] nf (desgracia) misfortune; (infelicidad) unhappiness; **desdichado, -a** adj (sin suerte) unlucky; (infeliz) unhappy

desear [dese'ar] vt to want, desire, wish for

desechar [dese'tʃar] vt (basura) to throw o away; (ideas) to reject, discard; **desechos** nmpl rubbish sg, waste sg

desembalar [desemba'lar] vt to unpack

desembarazar [desembara'θar] vt (desocupar) to clear; (desenredar) to free; **desembarazarse** vr: **~se de** to free o.s. of, get rid of

desembarcar [desembar'kar] vt (mercancías etc) to unload ▷ vi to disembark

desembocadura [desemboka'ðura]
nf (*de río*) mouth; (*de calle*) opening

desembocar [desembo'kar] *vi* (*río*)
to flow into; (*fig*) to result in

desembolso [desem'bolso] *nm*
payment

desembrollar [desembro'ʎar]
vt (*madeja*) to unravel; (*asunto,
malentendido*) to sort out

desemejanza [deseme'xanθa] *nf*
dissimilarity

desempaquetar [desempake'tar]
vt (*regalo*) to unwrap; (*mercancía*) to
unpack

desempate [desem'pate] *nm* (*Fútbol*)
replay, play-off; (*Tenis*) tie-break(er)

desempeñar [desempe'ɲar] *vt*
(*cargo*) to hold; (*papel*) to perform; (*lo
empeñado*) to redeem; **~ un papel** (*fig*)
to play (a role)

desempleado, -a [desemple'aðo, a]
nm/f unemployed person; **desempleo**
nm unemployment

desencadenar [desenkaðe'nar]
vt to unchain; (*ira*) to unleash;
desencadenarse *vr* to break loose;
(*tormenta*) to burst; (*guerra*) to break out

desencajar [desenka'xar] *vt* (*hueso*)
to dislocate; (*mecanismo, pieza*) to
disconnect, disengage

desencanto [desen'kanto] *nm*
disillusionment

desenchufar [desentʃu'far] *vt* to
unplug

desenfadado, -a [desenfa'ðaðo,
a] *adj* (*desenvuelto*) uninhibited;
(*descarado*) forward; **desenfado** *nm*
(*libertad*) freedom; (*comportamiento*)
free and easy manner; (*descaro*)
forwardness

desenfocado, -a [desenfo'kaðo, a]
adj (*Foto*) out of focus

desenfreno [desen'freno] *nm*
wildness; (*de las pasiones*) lack of
self-control

desenganchar [desengan'tʃar] *vt*
(*gen*) to unhook; (*Ferro*) to uncouple

desengañar [desenga'ɲar] *vt* to
disillusion; **desengañarse** *vr* to
become disillusioned; **desengaño**
nm disillusionment; (*decepción*)
disappointment

desenlace [desen'laθe] *nm* outcome

desenmascarar [desenmaska'rar]
vt to unmask

desenredar [desenre'ðar] *vt* (*pelo*) to
untangle; (*problema*) to sort out

desenroscar [desenros'kar] *vt* to
unscrew

desentenderse [desenten'derse]
vr: **~ de** to pretend not to know about;
(*apartarse*) to have nothing to do with

desenterrar [desente'rrar] *vt* to
exhume; (*tesoro, fig*) to unearth, dig up

desentonar [desento'nar] *vi* (*Mús*)
to sing (*o* play) out of tune; (*color*)
to clash

desentrañar [desentra'ɲar] *vt*
(*misterio*) to unravel

desenvoltura [desenβol'tura]
nf ease

desenvolver [desenβol'βer] *vt*
(*paquete*) to unwrap; (*fig*) to develop;
desenvolverse *vr* (*desarrollarse*) to
unfold, develop; (*arreglárselas*) to cope

deseo [de'seo] *nm* desire, wish;
deseoso, -a *adj*: **estar deseoso de** to
be anxious to

desequilibrado, -a [desekili'βraðo,
a] *adj* unbalanced

desertar [deser'tar] *vi* to desert

desértico, -a [de'sertiko, a] *adj*
desert *cpd*

desesperación [desespera'θjon]
nf (*impaciencia*) desperation, despair;
(*irritación*) fury

desesperar [desespe'rar] *vt* to
drive to despair; (*exasperar*) to drive
to distraction ▷ *vi*: **~ de** to despair of;
desesperarse *vr* to despair, lose hope

desestabilizar [desestaβili'θar] *vt*
to destabilize

desestimar [desesti'mar] *vt*
(*menospreciar*) to have a low opinion of;
(*rechazar*) to reject

desfachatez [desfatʃa'teθ] nf (insolencia) impudence; (descaro) rudeness

desfalco [des'falko] nm embezzlement

desfallecer [desfaʎe'θer] vi (perder las fuerzas) to become weak; (desvanecerse) to faint

desfasado, -a [desfa'saðo, a] adj (anticuado) old-fashioned; **desfase** nm (diferencia) gap

desfavorable [desfaβo'raβle] adj unfavourable

desfigurar [desfixu'rar] vt (cara) to disfigure; (cuerpo) to deform

desfiladero [desfila'ðero] nm gorge

desfilar [desfi'lar] vi to parade; **desfile** nm procession; **desfile de modelos** fashion show

desgana [des'ɣana] nf (falta de apetito) loss of appetite; (apatía) unwillingness; **desganado, -a** adj: **estar desganado** (sin apetito) to have no appetite; (sin entusiasmo) to have lost interest

desgarrar [desɣa'rrar] vt to tear (up); (fig) to shatter; **desgarro** nm (en tela) tear; (aflicción) grief

desgastar [desɣas'tar] vt (deteriorar) to wear away o down; (estropear) to spoil; **desgastarse** vr to get worn out; **desgaste** nm wear (and tear)

desglosar [desɣlo'sar] vt (factura) to break down

desgracia [des'ɣraθja] nf misfortune; (accidente) accident; (vergüenza) disgrace; (contratiempo) setback; **por ~** unfortunately; **desgraciado, -a** [desɣra'θjaðo, a] adj (sin suerte) unlucky, unfortunate; (miserable) wretched; (infeliz) miserable

desgravar [desɣra'βar] vt (impuestos) to reduce the tax o duty on

desguace [des'ɣwaθe] (ESP) nm junkyard

deshabitado, -a [desaβi'taðo, a] adj uninhabited

deshacer [desa'θer] vt (casa) to break up; (Tec) to take apart; (enemigo) to defeat; (diluir) to melt; (contrato) to break; (intriga) to solve; **deshacerse** vr (disolverse) to melt; (despedazarse) to come apart o undone; **~se de** to get rid of; **~se en lágrimas** to burst into tears

deshecho, -a [des'etʃo, a] adj undone; (roto) smashed; (persona): **estar ~** to be shattered

desheredar [desere'ðar] vt to disinherit

deshidratar [desiðra'tar] vt to dehydrate

deshielo [des'jelo] nm thaw

deshonesto, -a [deso'nesto, a] adj indecent

deshonra [des'onra] nf (deshonor) dishonour; (vergüenza) shame

deshora [des'ora]: **a ~** adv at the wrong time

deshuesadero [deswesa'ðero] (MÉX) nm junkyard

deshuesar [deswe'sar] vt (carne) to bone; (fruta) to stone

desierto, -a [de'sjerto, a] adj (casa, calle, negocio) deserted ▷ nm desert

designar [desix'nar] vt (nombrar) to designate; (indicar) to fix

desigual [desi'ɣwal] adj (terreno) uneven; (lucha etc) unequal

desilusión [desilu'sjon] nf disillusionment; (decepción) disappointment; **desilusionar** vt to disillusion; to disappoint; **desilusionarse** vr to become disillusioned

desinfectar [desinfek'tar] vt to disinfect

desinflar [desin'flar] vt to deflate

desintegración [desinteɣra'θjon] nf disintegration

desinterés [desinte'res] nm (desgana) lack of interest; (altruismo) unselfishness

desintoxicarse [desintoksi'karse] vr (drogadicto) to undergo detoxification

desistir [desis'tir] vi (renunciar) to

stop, desist

desleal [desle'al] *adj* (*infiel*) disloyal;
(*Com: competencia*) unfair; **deslealtad**
nf disloyalty

desligar [desli'ɣar] *vt* (*desatar*) to
untie, undo; (*separar*) to separate;
desligarse *vr* (*de un compromiso*) to
extricate o.s.

desliz [des'liθ] *nm* (*fig*) lapse; **deslizar**
vt to slip, slide

deslumbrar [deslum'brar] *vt* to
dazzle

desmadrarse [desma'ðrarse]
(*fam*) *vr* (*descontrolarse*) to run wild;
(*divertirse*) to let one's hair down;
desmadre *nm* (*desorganización*)
chaos; (*jaleo*) commotion

desmán [des'man] *nm* (*exceso*)
outrage; (*abuso de poder*) abuse

desmantelar [desmante'lar] *vt*
(*deshacer*) to dismantle; (*casa*) to strip

desmaquillador [desmakiʎa'ðor]
nm make-up remover

desmayar [desma'jar] *vi* to lose
heart; **desmayarse** *vr* (*Med*) to
faint; **desmayo** *nm* (*Med: acto*) faint;
(*: estado*) unconsciousness

desmemoriado, -a
[desmemo'rjado, a] *adj* forgetful

desmentir [desmen'tir] *vt*
(*contradecir*) to contradict; (*refutar*)
to deny

desmenuzar [desmenu'θar] *vt*
(*deshacer*) to crumble; (*carne*) to chop;
(*examinar*) to examine closely

desmesurado, -a [desmesu'rado, a]
adj disproportionate

desmontable [desmon'taβle]
adj (*que se quita: pieza*) detachable;
(*plegable*) collapsible, folding

desmontar [desmon'tar] *vt*
(*deshacer*) to dismantle; (*tierra*) to level
▷ *vi* to dismount

desmoralizar [desmorali'θar] *vt* to
demoralize

desmoronar [desmoro'nar] *vt* to
wear away, erode; **desmoronarse** *vr*
(*edificio, dique*) to collapse; (*economía*)

to decline

desnatado, -a [desna'tado, a] *adj*
skimmed

desnivel [desni'βel] *nm* (*de terreno*)
unevenness

desnudar [desnu'ðar] *vt* (*desvestir*) to
undress; (*despojar*) to strip; **desnudarse**
vr (*desvestirse*) to get undressed;
desnudo, -a *adj* naked ▷ *nm/f* nude;
desnudo de devoid o bereft of

desnutrición [desnutri'θjon] *nf*
malnutrition; **desnutrido, -a** *adj*
undernourished

desobedecer [desoβeðe'θer] *vt*,
vi to disobey; **desobediencia** *nf*
disobedience

desocupado, -a [desoku'paðo,
a] *adj* at leisure; (*desempleado*)
unemployed; (*deshabitado*) empty,
vacant

desodorante [desoðo'rante] *nm*
deodorant

desolación [desola'θjon] *nf* (*de lugar*)
desolation; (*fig*) grief

desolar [deso'lar] *vt* to ruin, lay
waste

desorbitado, -a [desorβi'taðo,
a] *adj* (*excesivo: ambición*) boundless;
(*deseos*) excessive; (*: precio*) exorbitant

desorden [des'orðen] *nm* confusion;
(*político*) disorder, unrest

desorganización
[desorɣaniθa'θjon] *nf* (*de persona*)
disorganization; (*en empresa, oficina*)
disorder, chaos

desorientar [desorjen'tar] *vt*
(*extraviar*) to mislead; (*confundir,
desconcertar*) to confuse; **desorientarse**
vr (*perderse*) to lose one's way

despabilado, -a [despaβi'laðo,
a] *adj* (*despierto*) wide-awake; (*fig*)
alert, sharp

despachar [despa'tʃar] *vt* (*negocio*) to
do, complete; (*enviar*) to send, dispatch;
(*vender*) to sell, deal in; (*billete*) to issue;
(*mandar ir*) to send away

despacho [des'patʃo] *nm* (*oficina*)
office; (*de paquetes*) dispatch; (*venta*)

sale; (*comunicación*) message; **~ de billetes** o **boletos** (LAM) booking office

despacio [des'paθjo] *adv* slowly

desparpajo [despar'paxo] *nm* self-confidence; (*pey*) nerve

desparramar [desparra'mar] *vt* (*esparcir*) to scatter; (*líquido*) to spill

despecho [des'petʃo] *nm* spite

despectivo, -a [despek'tiβo, a] *adj* (*despreciativo*) derogatory; (*Ling*) pejorative

despedida [despe'ðiða] *nf* (*adiós*) farewell; (*de obrero*) sacking

despedir [despe'ðir] *vt* (*visita*) to see off, show out; (*empleado*) to dismiss; (*inquilino*) to evict; (*objeto*) to hurl; (*olor etc*) to give out o off; **despedirse** *vr*: **~se de** to say goodbye to

despegar [despe'ɣar] *vt* to unstick ▷ *vi* (*avión*) to take off; **despegarse** *vr* to come loose, come unstuck; **despego** *nm* detachment

despegue *etc* [des'peɣe] *vb* V **despegar** ▷ *nm* takeoff

despeinado, -a [despei'naðo, a] *adj* dishevelled, unkempt

despejado, -a [despe'xaðo, a] *adj* (*lugar*) clear, free; (*cielo*) clear; (*persona*) wide-awake, bright

despejar [despe'xar] *vt* (*gen*) to clear; (*misterio*) to clear up ▷ *vi* (*el tiempo*) to clear; **despejarse** *vr* (*tiempo, cielo*) to clear (up); (*misterio*) to become clearer; (*cabeza*) to clear

despensa [des'pensa] *nf* larder

despeñarse [despe'ɲarse] *vr* to hurl o.s. down; (*coche*) to tumble over

desperdicio [desper'ðiθjo] *nm* (*despilfarro*) squandering; **desperdicios** *nmpl* (*basura*) rubbish *sg* (BRIT), garbage *sg* (US); (*residuos*) waste *sg*

desperezarse [despere'θarse] *vr* to stretch

desperfecto [desper'fekto] *nm* (*deterioro*) slight damage; (*defecto*) flaw, imperfection

despertador [desperta'ðor] *nm* alarm clock

despertar [desper'tar] *nm* awakening ▷ *vt* (*persona*) to wake up; (*recuerdos*) to revive; (*sentimiento*) to arouse ▷ *vi* to awaken, wake up; **despertarse** *vr* to awaken, wake up

despido *etc* [des'piðo] *vb* V **despedir** ▷ *nm* dismissal, sacking

despierto, -a *etc* [des'pjerto, a] *vb* V **despertar** ▷ *adj* awake; (*fig*) sharp, alert

despilfarro [despil'farro] *nm* (*derroche*) squandering; (*lujo desmedido*) extravagance

despistar [despis'tar] *vt* to throw off the track o scent; (*confundir*) to mislead, confuse; **despistarse** *vr* to take the wrong road; (*confundirse*) to become confused

despiste [des'piste] *nm* absent-mindedness; **un ~** a mistake o slip

desplazamiento [desplaθa'mjento] *nm* displacement

desplazar [despla'θar] *vt* to move; (*Náut*) to displace; (*Inform*) to scroll; (*fig*) to oust; **desplazarse** *vr* (*persona*) to travel

desplegar [desple'ɣar] *vt* (*tela, papel*) to unfold, open out; (*bandera*) to unfurl; **despliegue** *etc* [des'pleɣe] *vb* V **desplegar** ▷ *nm* display

desplomarse [desplo'marse] *vr* (*edificio, gobierno, persona*) to collapse

desplumar [desplu'mar] *vt* (*ave*) to pluck; (*fam: estafar*) to fleece

despoblado, -a [despo'βlaðo, a] *adj* (*sin habitantes*) uninhabited

despojar [despo'xar] *vt* (*alguien: de sus bienes*) to divest of, deprive of; (*casa*) to strip, leave bare; (*alguien: de su cargo*) to strip of

despojo [des'poxo] *nm* (*acto*) plundering; (*objetos*) plunder, loot; **despojos** *nmpl* (*de ave, res*) offal *sg*

desposado, -a [despo'saðo, a] *adj*, *nm/f* newly-wed

despreciar [despre'θjar] *vt* (*desdeñar*) to despise, scorn; (*afrentar*) to slight; **desprecio** *nm* scorn, contempt; slight

desprender [despren'der] *vt*
(*broche*) to unfasten; (*olor*) to give off;
desprenderse *vr* (*botón: caerse*) to fall
off; (*broche*) to come unfastened; (*olor*,
perfume) to be given off; **~se de algo
que ...** to draw from sth that ...

desprendimiento
[desprendi'mjento] *nm* (*gen*)
loosening; (*generosidad*)
disinterestedness; (*de tierra, rocas*)
landslide; **desprendimiento de retina**
detachment of the retina

despreocupado, -a
[despreoku'paðo, a] *adj* (*sin
preocupación*) unworried, nonchalant;
(*negligente*) careless

despreocuparse [despreoku'parse]
vr not to worry; **~ de** to have no
interest in

desprestigiar [despresti'xjar] *vt*
(*criticar*) to run down; (*desacreditar*) to
discredit

desprevenido, -a [despreβe'niðo,
a] *adj* (*no preparado*) unprepared,
unready

desproporcionado, -a
[despropor0jo'naðo, a] *adj*
disproportionate, out of proportion

desprovisto, -a [despro'βisto, a]
adj: **~ de** devoid of

después [des'pwes] *adv* afterwards,
later; (*próximo paso*) next; **~ de comer**
after lunch; **un año ~** a year later; **~ se
debatió el tema** next the matter was
discussed; **~ de corregido el texto**
after the text had been corrected; **~ de
todo** after all

desquiciado, -a [deski'θjaðo, a]
adj deranged

destacar [desta'kar] *vt* to
emphasize, point up; (*Mil*) to detach,
detail ▷ *vi* (*resaltarse*) to stand
out; (*persona*) to be outstanding *o*
exceptional; **destacarse** *vr* to stand
out; to be outstanding *o* exceptional

destajo [des'taxo] *nm*: **trabajar a ~** to
do piecework

destapar [desta'par] *vt* (*botella*)

to open; (*cacerola*) to take the lid off;
(*descubrir*) to uncover; **destaparse** *vr*
(*revelarse*) to reveal one's true character

destartalado, -a [destarta'laðo,
a] *adj* (*desordenado*) untidy; (*ruinoso*)
tumbledown

destello [des'teʎo] *nm* (*de estrella*)
twinkle; (*de faro*) signal light

destemplado, -a [destem'plaðo, a]
adj (*Mús*) out of tune; (*voz*) harsh; (*Med*)
out of sorts; (*tiempo*) unpleasant, nasty

desteñir [deste'ɲir] *vt* to fade ▷ *vi* to
fade; **desteñirse** *vr* to fade; **esta tela
no destiñe** this fabric will not run

desternillarse [desterni'ʎarse] *vr*: **~
de risa** to split one's sides laughing

desterrar [deste'rrar] *vt* (*exiliar*) to
exile; (*fig*) to banish, dismiss

destiempo [des'tjempo]: **a ~** *adv*
out of turn

destierro *etc* [des'tjerro] *vb* V
desterrar ▷ *nm* exile

destilar [desti'lar] *vt* to distil;
destilería *nf* distillery

destinar [desti'nar] *vt* (*funcionario*)
to appoint, assign; (*fondos*): **~ (a)** to set
aside (for)

destinatario, -a [destina'tarjo, a]
nm/f addressee

destino [des'tino] *nm* (*suerte*)
destiny; (*de avión, viajero*) destination;
con ~ a Londres (*barco*) (bound) for
London; (*avión, carta*) to London

destituir [destitu'ir] *vt* to dismiss

destornillador [destorniʎa'ðor] *nm*
screwdriver

destornillar [destorni'ʎar] *vt*
(*tornillo*) to unscrew; **destornillarse** *vr*
to unscrew

destreza [des'treθa] *nf* (*habilidad*)
skill; (*maña*) dexterity

destrozar [destro'θar] *vt* (*romper*) to
smash, break (up); (*estropear*) to ruin;
(*nervios*) to shatter

destrozo [des'troθo] *nm* (*acción*)
destruction; (*desastre*) smashing;
destrozos *nmpl* (*pedazos*) pieces;
(*daños*) havoc *sg*

destrucción [destruk'θjon] *nf*
destruction

destruir [destru'ir] *vt* to destroy

desuso [des'uso] *nm* disuse; **caer en
~** to become obsolete

desvalijar [desβali'xar] *vt* (*persona*)
to rob; (*casa, tienda*) to burgle; (*coche*)
to break into

desván [des'βan] *nm* attic

desvanecer [desβane'θer] *vt*
(*disipar*) to dispel; (*borrar*) to blur;
desvanecerse *vr* (*humo etc*) to vanish,
disappear; (*color*) to fade; (*recuerdo,
sonido*) to fade away; (*Med*) to pass out;
(*duda*) to be dispelled

desvariar [desβa'rjar] *vi* (*enfermo*) to
be delirious

desvelar [desβe'lar] *vt* to keep
awake; **desvelarse** *vr* (*no poder dormir*)
to stay awake; (*preocuparse*) to be
vigilant o watchful

desventaja [desβen'taxa] *nf*
disadvantage

desvergonzado, -a
[desβerɣon'θaðo, a] *adj* shameless

desvestir [desβes'tir] *vt* to undress;
desvestirse *vr* to undress

desviación [desβja'θjon] *nf*
deviation; (*Auto*) diversion, detour

desviar [des'βjar] *vt* to turn aside;
(*río*) to alter the course of; (*navío*)
to divert, re-route; (*conversación*) to
sidetrack; **desviarse** *vr* (*apartarse del
camino*) to turn aside; (: *barco*) to go
off course

desvío *etc* [des'βio] *vb* V **desviar**
▷ *nm* (*desviación*) detour, diversion; (*fig*)
indifference

desvivirse [desβi'βirse] *vr*: **~ por**
(*anhelar*) to long for, crave for; (*hacer lo
posible por*) to do one's utmost for

detallar [deta'ʎar] *vt* to detail

detalle [de'taʎe] *nm* detail; (*gesto*)
gesture, token; **al ~** in detail; (*Com*)
retail

detallista [deta'ʎista] *nmf* (*Com*)
retailer

detective [detek'tiβe] *nmf* detective;

detective privado private detective

detención [deten'θjon] *nf* (*arresto*)
arrest; (*prisión*) detention

detener [dete'ner] *vt* (*gen*) to
stop; (*Jur*) to arrest; (*objeto*) to keep;
detenerse *vr* to stop; (*demorarse*): **~se
en** to delay over, linger over

detenidamente [deteniða'mente]
adv (*minuciosamente*) carefully;
(*extensamente*) at great length

detenido, -a [dete'niðo, a] *adj*
(*arrestado*) under arrest ▷ *nm/f* person
under arrest, prisoner

detenimiento [deteni'mjento]
nm: **con ~** thoroughly; (*observar,
considerar*) carefully

detergente [deter'xente] *nm*
detergent

deteriorar [deterjo'rar] *vt* to
spoil, damage; **deteriorarse** *vr*
to deteriorate; **deterioro** *nm*
deterioration

determinación [determina'θjon]
nf (*empeño*) determination; (*decisión*)
decision; **determinado, -a** *adj*
specific

determinar [determi'nar] *vt* (*plazo*)
to fix; (*precio*) to settle; **determinarse**
vr to decide

detestar [detes'tar] *vt* to detest

detractor, a [detrak'tor, a] *nm/f*
slanderer, libeller

detrás [de'tras] *adv* (*tb*: **por ~**)
behind; (*atrás*) at the back; **~ de** behind

detrimento [detri'mento] *nm*: **en ~
de** to the detriment of

deuda ['deuða] *nf* debt; **deuda
exterior/pública** foreign/national
debt

devaluación [deβalwa'θjon] *nf*
devaluation

devastar [deβas'tar] *vt* (*destruir*) to
devastate

deveras [de'βeras] (*MÉX*) *nf inv*: **un
amigo de (a) ~** a true o real friend

devoción [deβo'θjon] *nf* devotion

devolución [deβolu'θjon] *nf* (*reenvío*)
return, sending back; (*reembolso*)

repayment; (*Jur*) devolution

devolver [deβol'βer] *vt* to return; (*lo extraviado, lo prestado*) to give back; (*carta al correo*) to send back; (*Com*) to repay, refund ▷ *vi* (*vomitar*) to be sick

devorar [deβo'rar] *vt* to devour

devoto, -a [de'βoto, a] *adj* devout ▷ *nm/f* admirer

devuelto *pp de* **devolver**

devuelva *etc vb* V **devolver**

di *etc vb* V **dar; decir**

día ['dia] *nm* day; **¿qué ~ es?** what's the date?; **estar/poner al ~** to be/keep up to date; **el ~ de hoy/de mañana** today/tomorrow; **al ~ siguiente** (on) the following day; **vivir al ~** to live from hand to mouth; **de ~** by day, in daylight; **en pleno ~** in full daylight; **Día de la Independencia** Independence Day; **Día de los Muertos** (*MÉX*) All Souls' Day; **Día de Reyes** Epiphany; **día feriado** (*LAM*) holiday; **día festivo** (*ESP*) holiday; **día lectivo** teaching day; **día libre** day off

diabetes [dia'βetes] *nf* diabetes

diablo ['djaβlo] *nm* devil; **diablura** *nf* prank

diadema [dja'ðema] *nf* tiara

diafragma [dja'fraɣma] *nm* diaphragm

diagnóstico [diaɣ'nostiko] *nm* = **diagnosis**

diagonal [djaɣo'nal] *adj* diagonal

diagrama [dja'ɣrama] *nm* diagram

dial [djal] *nm* dial

dialecto [dja'lekto] *nm* dialect

dialogar [djalo'ɣar] *vi*: **~ con** (*Pol*) to hold talks with

diálogo ['djaloɣo] *nm* dialogue

diamante [dja'mante] *nm* diamond

diana ['djana] *nf* (*Mil*) reveille; (*de blanco*) centre, bull's-eye

diapositiva [djaposi'tiβa] *nf* (*Foto*) slide, transparency

diario, -a ['djarjo, a] *adj* daily ▷ *nm* newspaper; **a ~** daily; **de ~** everyday

diarrea [dja'rrea] *nf* diarrhoea

dibujar [diβu'xar] *vt* to draw,

sketch; **dibujo** *nm* drawing; **dibujos animados** cartoons

diccionario [dikθjo'narjo] *nm* dictionary

dice *etc vb* V **decir**

dicho, -a ['ditʃo, a] *pp de* **decir** ▷ *adj*: **en ~s países** in the aforementioned countries ▷ *nm* saying

dichoso, -a [di'tʃoso, a] *adj* happy

diciembre [di'θjembre] *nm* December

dictado [dik'taðo] *nm* dictation

dictador [dikta'ðor] *nm* dictator; **dictadura** *nf* dictatorship

dictar [dik'tar] *vt* (*carta*) to dictate; (*Jur: sentencia*) to pronounce; (*decreto*) to issue; (*LAM: clase*) to give

didáctico, -a [di'ðaktiko, a] *adj* educational

diecinueve [djeθi'nweβe] *num* nineteen

dieciocho [djeθi'otʃo] *num* eighteen

dieciséis [djeθi'seis] *num* sixteen

diecisiete [djeθi'sjete] *num* seventeen

diente ['djente] *nm* (*Anat, Tec*) tooth; (*Zool*) fang; (: *de elefante*) tusk; (*de ajo*) clove

diera *etc vb* V **dar**

diesel ['disel] *adj*: **motor ~** diesel engine

diestro, -a ['djestro, a] *adj* (*derecho*) right; (*hábil*) skilful

dieta ['djeta] *nf* diet; **estar a ~** to be on a diet

diez [djeθ] *num* ten

diferencia [dife'renθja] *nf* difference; **a ~ de** unlike; **diferenciar** *vt* to differentiate between ▷ *vi* to differ; **diferenciarse** *vr* to differ, be different; (*distinguirse*) to distinguish o.s.

diferente [dife'rente] *adj* different

diferido [dife'riðo] *nm*: **en ~** (*TV etc*) recorded

difícil [di'fiθil] *adj* difficult

dificultad [difikul'taθ] *nf* difficulty;

(*problema*) trouble

dificultar [difikul'tar] *vt* (*complicar*) to complicate, make difficult; (*estorbar*) to obstruct

difundir [difun'dir] *vt* (*calor, luz*) to diffuse; (*Radio, TV*) to broadcast; **~ una noticia** to spread a piece of news; **difundirse** *vr* to spread (out)

difunto, -a [di'funto, a] *adj* dead, deceased ▷ *nm/f* deceased (person)

difusión [difu'sjon] *nf* (*Radio, TV*) broadcasting

diga *etc vb* V **decir**

digerir [dixe'rir] *vt* to digest; (*fig*) to absorb; **digestión** *nf* digestion; **digestivo, -a** *adj* digestive

digital [dixi'tal] *adj* digital

dignarse [dix'narse] *vr* to deign to

dignidad [dixni'ðað] *nf* dignity

digno, -a [dix'no, a] *adj* worthy

digo *etc vb* V **decir**

dije *etc vb* V **decir**

dilatar [dila'tar] *vt* (*cuerpo*) to dilate; (*prolongar*) to prolong

dilema [di'lema] *nm* dilemma

diluir [dilu'ir] *vt* to dilute

diluvio [di'luβjo] *nm* deluge, flood

dimensión [dimen'sjon] *nf* dimension

diminuto, -a [dimi'nuto, a] *adj* tiny, diminutive

dimitir [dimi'tir] *vi* to resign

dimos *vb* V **dar**

Dinamarca [dina'marka] *nf* Denmark

dinámico, -a [ði'namiko, a] *adj* dynamic

dinamita [dina'mita] *nf* dynamite

dínamo ['dinamo] *nf* dynamo

dineral [dine'ral] *nm* large sum of money, fortune

dinero [di'nero] *nm* money; **dinero en efectivo** *o* **metálico** cash; **dinero suelto** (loose) change

dio *vb* V **dar**

dios [djos] *nm* god; **¡D~ mío!** (oh,) my God!; **¡por D~!** for heaven's sake!; **diosa** ['djosa] *nf* goddess

diploma [di'ploma] *nm* diploma

diplomacia [diplo'maθja] *nf* diplomacy; (*fig*) tact

diplomado, -a [diplo'maðo, a] *adj* qualified

diplomático, -a [diplo'matiko, a] *adj* diplomatic ▷ *nm/f* diplomat

diputación [diputa'θjon] *nf* (*tb:* **~ provincial**) ≈ county council

diputado, -a [dipu'taðo, a] *nm/f* delegate; (*Pol*) ≈ member of parliament (*BRIT*), ≈ representative (*US*)

dique ['dike] *nm* dyke

diré *etc vb* V **decir**

dirección [direk'θjon] *nf* direction; (*señas*) address; (*Auto*) steering; (*gerencia*) management; (*Pol*) leadership; **dirección única/ prohibida** one-way street/no entry

direccional [direkθjo'nal] (*MÉX*) *nf* (*Auto*) indicator

directa [di'rekta] *nf* (*Auto*) top gear

directiva [direk'tiβa] *nf* (*tb:* **junta ~**) board of directors

directo, -a [di'rekto, a] *adj* direct; (*Radio, TV*) live; **transmitir en ~** to broadcast live

director, a [direk'tor, a] *adj* leading ▷ *nm/f* director; (*Escol*) head(teacher) (*BRIT*), principal (*US*); (*gerente*) manager/ess; (*Prensa*) editor; **director de cine** film director; **director general** managing director

directorio [direk'torjo] (*MÉX*) *nm* (*telefónico*) phone book

dirigente [diri'xente] *nmf* (*Pol*) leader

dirigir [diri'xir] *vt* to direct; (*carta*) to address; (*obra de teatro, film*) to direct; (*Mús*) to conduct; (*negocio*) to manage; **dirigirse** *vr:* **~se a** to go towards, make one's way towards; (*hablar con*) to speak to

dirija *etc vb* V **dirigir**

disciplina [disθi'plina] *nf* discipline

discípulo, -a [dis'θipulo, a] *nm/f* disciple

Discman® ['diskman] *nm*

Discman®

disco ['disko] nm disc; (Deporte) discus; (Tel) dial; (Auto: semáforo) light; (Mús) record; **disco compacto/de larga duración** compact disc/long-playing record; **disco de freno** brake disc; **disco flexible/duro** o **rígido** (Inform) floppy/hard disk

disconforme [diskon'forme] adj differing; **estar ~ (con)** to be in disagreement (with)

discordia [dis'korðja] nf discord

discoteca [disko'teka] nf disco(theque)

discreción [diskre'θjon] nf discretion; (reserva) prudence; **comer a ~** to eat as much as one wishes

discreto, -a [dis'kreto, a] adj discreet

discriminación [diskrimina'θjon] nf discrimination

disculpa [dis'kulpa] nf excuse; (pedir perdón) apology; **pedir ~s a/por** to apologize to/for; **disculpar** vt to excuse, pardon; **disculparse** vr to excuse o.s.; to apologize

discurso [dis'kurso] nm speech

discusión [disku'sjon] nf (diálogo) discussion; (riña) argument

discutir [disku'tir] vt (debatir) to discuss; (pelear) to argue about; (contradecir) to argue against ▷ vi (debatir) to discuss; (pelearse) to argue

disecar [dise'kar] vt (conservar: animal) to stuff; (: planta) to dry

diseñar [dise'ɲar] vt, vi to design

diseño [di'seɲo] nm design

disfraz [dis'fraθ] nm (máscara) disguise; (excusa) pretext; **disfrazar** vt to disguise; **disfrazarse** vr: **disfrazarse de** to disguise o.s. as

disfrutar [disfru'tar] vt to enjoy ▷ vi to enjoy o.s.; **~ de** to enjoy, possess

disgustar [disɣus'tar] vt (no gustar) to displease; (contrariar, enojar) to annoy, upset; **disgustarse** vr (enfadarse) to get upset; (dos personas)

to fall out

┃ No confundir **disgustar** con la palabra inglesa disgust.

disgusto [dis'ɣusto] nm (contrariedad) annoyance; (tristeza) grief; (riña) quarrel

disimular [disimu'lar] vt (ocultar) to hide, conceal ▷ vi to dissemble

diskette [dis'ket] nm (Inform) diskette, floppy disk

dislocarse [dislo'karse] vr (articulación) to sprain, dislocate

disminución [disminu'θjon] nf decrease, reduction

disminuido, -a [disminu'iðo, a] nm/f: **~ mental/físico** mentally/physically handicapped person

disminuir [disminu'ir] vt to decrease, diminish

disolver [disol'βer] vt (gen) to dissolve; **disolverse** vr to dissolve; (Com) to go into liquidation

dispar [dis'par] adj different

disparar [dispa'rar] vt, vi to shoot, fire

disparate [dispa'rate] nm (tontería) foolish remark; (error) blunder; **decir ~s** to talk nonsense

disparo [dis'paro] nm shot

dispersar [disper'sar] vt to disperse; **dispersarse** vr to scatter

disponer [dispo'ner] vt (arreglar) to arrange; (ordenar) to put in order; (preparar) to prepare, get ready ▷ vi: **~ de** to have, own; **disponerse** vr: **~se a** o **para hacer** to prepare to do

disponible [dispo'niβle] adj available

disposición [disposi'θjon] nf arrangement, disposition; (voluntad) willingness; (Inform) layout; **a su ~** at your service

dispositivo [disposi'tiβo] nm device, mechanism

dispuesto, -a [dis'pwesto, a] pp de **disponer** ▷ adj (arreglado) arranged; (preparado) disposed

disputar [dispu'tar] vt (carrera) to compete in

disquete [dis'kete] *nm* floppy disk, diskette

distancia [dis'tanθja] *nf* distance; **distanciar** [distan'θjar] *vt* to space out; **distanciarse** *vr* to become estranged; **distante** [dis'tante] *adj* distant

diste *vb* V **dar**

disteis *vb* V **dar**

distinción [distin'θjon] *nf* distinction; (*elegancia*) elegance; (*honor*) honour

distinguido, -a [distin'giðo, a] *adj* distinguished

distinguir [distin'gir] *vt* to distinguish; (*escoger*) to single out; **distinguirse** *vr* to be distinguished

distintivo [distin'tiβo] *nm* badge; (*fig*) characteristic

distinto, -a [dis'tinto, a] *adj* different; (*claro*) clear

distracción [distrak'θjon] *nf* distraction; (*pasatiempo*) hobby, pastime; (*olvido*) absent-mindedness, distraction

distraer [distra'er] *vt* (*atención*) to distract; (*divertir*) to amuse; (*fondos*) to embezzle; **distraerse** *vr* (*entretenerse*) to amuse o.s.; (*perder la concentración*) to allow one's attention to wander

distraído, -a [distra'iðo, a] *adj* (*gen*) absent-minded; (*entretenido*) amusing

distribuidor, a [distriβui'ðor, a] *nm/f* distributor; **distribuidora** *nf* (*Com*) dealer, agent; (*Cine*) distributor

distribuir [distriβu'ir] *vt* to distribute

distrito [dis'trito] *nm* (*sector, territorio*) region; (*barrio*) district; **Distrito Federal** (*MÉX*) Federal District; **distrito postal** postal district

disturbio [dis'turβjo] *nm* disturbance; (*desorden*) riot

disuadir [diswa'ðir] *vt* to dissuade

disuelto [di'swelto] *pp de* **disolver**

DIU *nm abr* (= *dispositivo intrauterino*) IUD

diurno, -a ['djurno, a] *adj* day *cpd*

divagar [diβa'ɣar] *vi* (*desviarse*) to digress

diván [di'βan] *nm* divan

diversidad [diβersi'ðað] *nf* diversity, variety

diversión [diβer'sjon] *nf* (*gen*) entertainment; (*actividad*) hobby, pastime

diverso, -a [di'βerso, a] *adj* diverse; **~s libros** several books; **diversos** *nmpl* sundries

divertido, -a [diβer'tiðo, a] *adj* (*chiste etc*) amusing; (*fiesta etc*) enjoyable

divertir [diβer'tir] *vt* (*entretener, recrear*) to amuse; **divertirse** *vr* (*pasarlo bien*) to have a good time; (*distraerse*) to amuse o.s.

dividendos [diβi'ðendos] *nmpl* (*Com*) dividends

dividir [diβi'ðir] *vt* (*gen*) to divide; (*distribuir*) to distribute, share out

divierta *etc vb* V **divertir**

divino, -a [di'βino, a] *adj* divine

divirtiendo *etc vb* V **divertir**

divisa [di'βisa] *nf* (*emblema*) emblem, badge; **divisas** *nfpl* foreign exchange *sg*

divisar [diβi'sar] *vt* to make out, distinguish

división [diβi'sjon] *nf* (*gen*) division; (*de partido*) split; (*de país*) partition

divorciar [diβor'θjar] *vt* to divorce; **divorciarse** *vr* to get divorced; **divorcio** *nm* divorce

divulgar [diβul'ɣar] *vt* (*ideas*) to spread; (*secreto*) to divulge

DNI (*ESP*) *nm abr* (= *Documento Nacional de Identidad*) national identity card

Dña. *abr* (=*doña*) Mrs

do [do] *nm* (*Mús*) do, C

dobladillo [doβla'ðiλo] *nm* (*de vestido*) hem; (*de pantalón: vuelta*) turn-up (BRIT), cuff (US)

doblar [do'βlar] *vt* to double; (*papel*) to fold; (*caño*) to bend; (*la esquina*) to turn, go round; (*film*) to dub ▷ *vi* to turn; (*campana*) to toll; **doblarse** *vr* (*plegarse*) to fold (up), crease; (*encorvarse*) to bend; **~ a la derecha/izquierda** to turn right/left

doble ['doβle] *adj* double; (*de dos aspectos*) dual; (*fig*) two-faced ▷ *nm* double ▷ *nmf* (*Teatro*) double, stand-in; **dobles** *nmpl* (*Deporte*) doubles *sg*; **con ~ sentido** with a double meaning

doce ['doθe] *num* twelve; **docena** *nf* dozen

docente [do'θente] *adj*: **centro/personal ~** teaching establishment/staff

dócil ['doθil] *adj* (*pasivo*) docile; (*obediente*) obedient

doctor, a [dok'tor, a] *nm/f* doctor

doctorado [dokto'raðo] *nm* doctorate

doctrina [dok'trina] *nf* doctrine, teaching

documentación [dokumenta'θjon] *nf* documentation, papers *pl*

documental [dokumen'tal] *adj, nm* documentary

documento [doku'mento] *nm* (*certificado*) document; **documento adjunto** (*Inform*) attachment; **documento nacional de identidad** identity card

dólar ['dolar] *nm* dollar

doler [do'ler] *vt, vi* to hurt; (*fig*) to grieve; **dolerse** *vr* (*de su situación*) to grieve, feel sorry; (*de las desgracias ajenas*) to sympathize; **me duele el brazo** my arm hurts

dolor [do'lor] *nm* pain; (*fig*) grief, sorrow; **dolor de cabeza/estómago/muelas** headache/stomachache/toothache

domar [do'mar] *vt* to tame

domesticar [domesti'kar] *vt* = **domar**

doméstico, -a [do'mestiko, a] *adj* (*vida, servicio*) home; (*tareas*) household; (*animal*) tame, pet

domicilio [domi'θiljo] *nm* home; **servicio a ~** home delivery service; **sin ~ fijo** of no fixed abode; **domicilio particular** private residence

dominante [domi'nante] *adj* dominant; (*persona*) domineering

dominar [domi'nar] *vt* (*gen*) to dominate; (*idiomas*) to be fluent in ▷ *vi* to dominate, prevail

domingo [do'mingo] *nm* Sunday; **Domingo de Ramos/Resurrección** Palm/Easter Sunday

dominio [do'minjo] *nm* (*tierras*) domain; (*autoridad*) power, authority; (*de las pasiones*) grip, hold; (*de idiomas*) command

don [don] *nm* (*talento*) gift; **~ Juan Gómez** Mr Juan Gómez, Juan Gómez Esq (BRIT)

- **DON/DOÑA**
-
- The term **don/doña** often
- abbreviated to **D./Dña** is placed
- before the first name as a mark
- of respect to an older or more
- senior person – eg Don Diego,
- Doña Inés. Although becoming
- rarer in Spain it is still used
- with names and surnames on
- official documents and formal
- correspondence – eg "Sr. D. Pedro
- Rodríguez Hernández", "Sra. Dña.
- Inés Rodríguez Hernández".

dona ['dona] (*MÉX*) *nf* doughnut, donut (US)

donar [do'nar] *vt* to donate

donativo [dona'tiβo] *nm* donation

donde ['donde] *adv* where ▷ *prep*: **el coche está allí ~ el farol** the car is over there by the lamppost *o* where the

·lamppost is; **en ~** where, in which

dónde ['donde] *adv* where?; **¿a ~ vas?** where are you going (to)?; **¿de ~ vienes?** where have you been?; **¿por ~?** where?, whereabouts?

dondequiera [donde'kjera] *adv* anywhere; **por ~** everywhere, all over the place ▷ *conj*: **~ que** wherever

donut® [do'nut] (*ESP*) *nm* doughnut, donut (*US*)

doña ['doɲa] *nf*: **~ Alicia** Alicia; **~ Victoria Benito** Mrs Victoria Benito

dorado, -a [do'raðo, a] *adj* (*color*) golden; (*Tec*) gilt

dormir [dor'mir] *vt*: **~ la siesta** to have an afternoon nap ▷ *vi* to sleep; **dormirse** *vr* to fall asleep

dormitorio [dormi'torjo] *nm* bedroom

dorsal [dor'sal] *nm* (*Deporte*) number

dorso ['dorso] *nm* (*de mano*) back; (*de hoja*) other side

dos [dos] *num* two

dosis ['dosis] *nf inv* dose, dosage

dotado, -a [do'taðo, a] *adj* gifted; **~ de** endowed with

dotar [do'tar] *vt* to endow; **dote** *nf* dowry; **dotes** *nfpl* (*talentos*) gifts

doy [doj] *vb* V **dar**

drama ['drama] *nm* drama; **dramaturgo** [drama'turxo] *nm* dramatist, playwright

drástico, -a ['drastiko, a] *adj* drastic

drenaje [dre'naxe] *nm* drainage

droga ['droxa] *nf* drug; **drogadicto, -a** [droxa'ðikto, a] *nm/f* drug addict

drogarse [dro'xarse] *vr* to take drugs

droguería [droxe'ria] *nf* hardware shop (*BRIT*) o store (*US*)

ducha ['dutʃa] *nf* (*baño*) shower; (*Med*) douche; **ducharse** *vr* to take a shower

duda ['duða] *nf* doubt; **no cabe ~** there is no doubt about it; **dudar** *vt, vi* to doubt; **dudoso, -a** [du'ðoso, a] *adj* (*incierto*) hesitant; (*sospechoso*) doubtful

duela *etc vb* V **doler**

duelo ['dwelo] *vb* V **doler** ▷ *nm* (*combate*) duel; (*luto*) mourning

duende ['dwende] *nm* imp, goblin

dueño, -a ['dweɲo, a] *nm/f* (*propietario*) owner; (*de pensión, taberna*) landlord/lady; (*empresario*) employer

duermo *etc vb* V **dormir**

dulce ['dulθe] *adj* sweet ▷ *adv* gently, softly ▷ *nm* sweet

dulcería [dulθe'ria] (*LAM*) *nf* confectioner's (shop)

dulzura [dul'θura] *nf* sweetness; (*ternura*) gentleness

dúo ['duo] *nm* duet

duplicar [dupli'kar] *vt* (*hacer el doble de*) to duplicate

duque ['duke] *nm* duke; **duquesa** *nf* duchess

durable [dura'βle] *adj* durable

duración [dura'θjon] *nf* (*de película, disco etc*) length; (*de pila etc*) life; (*curso: de acontecimientos etc*) duration

duradero, -a [dura'ðero, a] *adj* (*tela etc*) hard-wearing; (*fe, paz*) lasting

durante [du'rante] *prep* during

durar [du'rar] *vi* to last; (*recuerdo*) to remain

durazno [du'raθno] (*LAM*) *nm* (*fruta*) peach; (*árbol*) peach tree

durex ['dureks] (*MÉX, ARG*) *nm* (*tira adhesiva*) Sellotape® (*BRIT*), Scotch tape® (*US*)

dureza [du'reθa] *nf* (*calidad*) hardness

duro, -a ['duro, a] *adj* hard; (*carácter*) tough ▷ *adv* hard ▷ *nm* (*moneda*) five-peseta coin o piece

DVD *nm abr* (= *disco de vídeo digital*) DVD

e

ecological, environmental ▷ *nmf* environmentalist

economía [ekono'mia] *nf* (*sistema*) economy; (*carrera*) economics

económico, -a [eko'nomiko, a] *adj* (*barato*) cheap, economical; (*ahorrativo*) thrifty; (*Com: año etc*) financial; (*: situación*) economic

economista [ekono'mista] *nmf* economist

Ecuador [ekwa'ðor] *nm* Ecuador; **ecuador** *nm* (*Geo*) equator

ecuatoriano, -a [ekwato'rjano, a] *adj, nm/f* Ecuadorian

ecuestre [e'kwestre] *adj* equestrian

edad [e'ðað] *nf* age; **¿qué ~ tienes?** how old are you?; **tiene ocho años de ~** he's eight (years old); **de ~ mediana/ avanzada** middle-aged/advanced in years; **la E~ Media** the Middle Ages

edición [eði'θjon] *nf* (*acto*) publication; (*ejemplar*) edition

edificar [eðifi'kar] *vt, vi* to build

edificio [eði'fiθjo] *nm* building; (*fig*) edifice, structure

Edimburgo [eðim'burɣo] *nm* Edinburgh

editar [eði'tar] *vt* (*publicar*) to publish; (*preparar textos*) to edit

editor, a [eði'tor, a] *nm/f* (*que publica*) publisher; (*redactor*) editor ▷ *adj* publishing *cpd*; **editorial** *adj* editorial ▷ *nm* leading article, editorial; **casa editorial** publisher

edredón [eðre'ðon] *nm* duvet

educación [eðuka'θjon] *nf* education; (*crianza*) upbringing; (*modales*) (good) manners *pl*

educado, -a [eðu'kaðo, a] *adj*: **bien/ mal ~** well/badly behaved

educar [eðu'kar] *vt* to educate; (*criar*) to bring up; (*voz*) to train

EE. UU. *nmpl abr* (= *Estados Unidos*) US(A)

efectivamente [efectiβa'mente] *adv* (*como respuesta*) exactly, precisely; (*verdaderamente*) really; (*de hecho*) in fact

efectivo, -a [efek'tiβo, a] *adj*

E *abr* (= *este*) E

e [e] *conj* and

ébano ['eβano] *nm* ebony

ebrio, -a ['eβrjo, a] *adj* drunk

ebullición [eβuʎi'θjon] *nf* boiling

echar [e'tʃar] *vt* to throw; (*agua, vino*) to pour (out); (*empleado: despedir*) to fire, sack; (*hojas*) to sprout; (*cartas*) to post; (*humo*) to emit, give out ▷ *vi*: **~ a correr** to run off; **~ una mirada** to give a look; **~ sangre** to bleed; **echarse** *vr* to lie down; **~ llave a** to lock (up); **~ abajo** (*gobierno*) to overthrow; (*edificio*) to demolish; **~ mano a** to lay hands on; **~ una mano a algn** (*ayudar*) to give sb a hand; **~ de menos** to miss; **~se atrás** (*fig*) to back out

eclesiástico, -a [ekle'sjastiko, a] *adj* ecclesiastical

eco ['eko] *nm* echo; **tener ~** to catch on

ecología [ekolo'ɣia] *nf* ecology; **ecológico, -a** *adj* (*producto, método*) environmentally-friendly; (*agricultura*) organic; **ecologista** *adj*

effective; (*real*) actual, real ▷ *nm*: **pagar en ~** to pay (in) cash; **hacer ~ un cheque** to cash a cheque

efecto [e'fekto] *nm* effect, result; **efectos** *nmpl* (*efectos personales*) effects; (*bienes*) goods; (*Com*) assets; **en ~** in fact; (*respuesta*) exactly, indeed; **efecto invernadero** greenhouse effect; **efectos especiales/ secundarios/sonoros** special/side/ sound effects

efectuar [efek'twar] *vt* to carry out; (*viaje*) to make

eficacia [efi'kaθja] *nf* (*de persona*) efficiency; (*de medicamento etc*) effectiveness

eficaz [efi'kaθ] *adj* (*persona*) efficient; (*acción*) effective

eficiente [efi'θjente] *adj* efficient

egipcio, -a [e'xipθjo, a] *adj, nm/f* Egyptian

Egipto [e'xipto] *nm* Egypt

egoísmo [exo'ismo] *nm* egoism

egoísta [exo'ista] *adj* egoistical, selfish ▷ *nmf* egoist

Eire ['eire] *nm* Eire

ej. *abr* (= *ejemplo*) eg

eje ['exe] *nm* (*Geo, Mat*) axis; (*de rueda*) axle; (*de máquina*) shaft, spindle

ejecución [exeku'θjon] *nf* execution; (*cumplimiento*) fulfilment; (*Mús*) performance; (*Jur: embargo de deudor*) attachment

ejecutar [exeku'tar] *vt* to execute, carry out; (*matar*) to execute; (*cumplir*) to fulfil; (*Mús*) to perform; (*Jur: embargar*) to attach, distrain (on)

ejecutivo, -a [exeku'tiβo, a] *adj* executive; **el (poder) ~** the executive (power)

ejemplar [exem'plar] *adj* exemplary ▷ *nm* example; (*Zool*) specimen; (*de libro*) copy; (*de periódico*) number, issue

ejemplo [e'xemplo] *nm* example; **por ~** for example

ejercer [exer'θer] *vt* to exercise; (*influencia*) to exert; (*un oficio*) to practise ▷ *vi* (*practicar*): **~ (de)** to

practise (as)

ejercicio [exer'θiθjo] *nm* exercise; (*período*) tenure; **hacer ~** to take exercise; **ejercicio comercial** financial year

ejército [e'xerθito] *nm* army; **entrar en el ~** to join the army, join up; **ejército del aire/de tierra** Air Force/Army

ejote [e'xote] (*MÉX*) *nm* green bean

○ **PALABRA CLAVE**

el [el] (*f* **la**, *pl* **los, las,** *neutro* **lo**) *art def* **1** the; **el libro/la mesa/los estudiantes** the book/table/students

2 (*con n abstracto: no se traduce*): **el amor/la juventud** love/youth

3 (*posesión: se traduce a menudo por adj posesivo*): **romperse el brazo** to break one's arm; **levantó la mano** he put his hand up; **se puso el sombrero** she put her hat on

4 (*valor descriptivo*): **tener la boca grande/los ojos azules** to have a big mouth/blue eyes

5 (*con días*) on; **me iré el viernes** I'll leave on Friday; **los domingos suelo ir a nadar** on Sundays I generally go swimming

6 (*lo +adj*): **lo difícil/caro** what is difficult/expensive; (*cuán*): **no se da cuenta de lo pesado que es** he doesn't realise how boring he is

▷ *pron demos* **1**: **mi libro y el de usted** my book and yours; **las de Pepe son mejores** Pepe's are better; **no la(s) blanca(s) sino la(s) gris(es)** not the white one(s) but the grey one(s)

2: **lo de: lo de ayer** what happened yesterday; **lo de las facturas** that business about the invoices

▷ *pron relativo* **1** (*indef*): **el que: el (los) que quiera(n) que se vaya(n)** anyone who wants to can leave; **llévese el que más le guste** take the one you like best

2 (*def*): **el que: el que compré ayer** the one I bought yesterday; **los que se van**

those who leave

3: **lo que**: **lo que pienso yo/más me gusta** what I think/like most

▷ *conj*: **el que**: **el que lo diga** the fact that he says so; **el que sea tan vago me molesta** his being so lazy bothers me

▷ *excl*: **¡el susto que me diste!** what a fright you gave me!

▷ *pron personal* **1** (*persona*: *m*) him; (: *f*) her; (: *pl*) them; **lo/las veo** I can see him/them

2 (*animal, cosa*: *sg*) it; (: *pl*) them; **lo** (*o* **la**) **veo** I can see it; **los** (*o* **las**) **veo** I can see them

3 (*como sustituto de frase*): **lo: no lo sabía** I didn't know; **ya lo entiendo** I understand now

él [el] *pron* (*persona*) he; (*cosa*) it; (*después de prep*: *persona*) him; (: *cosa*) it; **de ~** his

elaborar [elaβo'rar] *vt* (*producto*) to make, manufacture; (*preparar*) to prepare; (*madera, metal etc*) to work; (*proyecto etc*) to work on *o* out

elástico, -a [e'lastiko, a] *adj* elastic; (*flexible*) flexible ▷ *nm* elastic; (*un elástico*) elastic band

elección [elek'θjon] *nf* election; (*selección*) choice, selection; **elecciones generales** general election *sg*

electorado [elekto'raðo] *nm* electorate, voters *pl*

electricidad [elektriθi'ðað] *nf* electricity

electricista [elektri'θista] *nmf* electrician

eléctrico, -a [e'lektriko, a] *adj* electric

electro... [elektro] *prefijo* electro...; **electrocardiograma** *nm* electrocardiogram; **electrocutar** *vt* to electrocute; **electrodo** *nm* electrode; **electrodomésticos** *nmpl* (electrical) household appliances

electrónica [elek'tronika] *nf* electronics *sg*

electrónico, -a [elek'troniko, a] *adj* electronic

electrotren [elektro'tren] *nm* express electric train

elefante [ele'fante] *nm* elephant

elegancia [ele'ɣanθja] *nf* elegance, grace; (*estilo*) stylishness

elegante [ele'ɣante] *adj* elegant, graceful; (*estiloso*) stylish, fashionable

elegir [ele'xir] *vt* (*escoger*) to choose, select; (*optar*) to opt for; (*presidente*) to elect

elemental [elemen'tal] *adj* (*claro, obvio*) elementary; (*fundamental*) elemental, fundamental

elemento [ele'mento] *nm* element; (*fig*) ingredient; **elementos** *nmpl* elements, rudiments

elevación [eleβa'θjon] *nf* elevation; (*acto*) raising, lifting; (*de precios*) rise; (*Geo etc*) height, altitude

elevado [ele'βaðo] *adj* high

elevar [ele'βar] *vt* to raise, lift (up); (*precio*) to put up; **elevarse** *vr* (*edificio*) to rise; (*precios*) to go up

eligiendo *etc vb* ∨ **elegir**

elija *etc vb* ∨ **elegir**

eliminar [elimi'nar] *vt* to eliminate, remove

eliminatoria [elimina'torja] *nf* heat, preliminary (round)

élite ['elite] *nf* elite

ella ['eʎa] *pron* (*persona*) she; (*cosa*) it; (*después de prep*: *persona*) her; (: *cosa*) it; **de ~** hers

ellas ['eʎas] *pron* (*personas y cosas*) they; (*después de prep*) them; **de ~** theirs

ello ['eʎo] *pron* it

ellos ['eʎos] *pron* they; (*después de prep*) them; **de ~** theirs

elogiar [elo'xjar] *vt* to praise; **elogio** *nm* praise

elote [e'lote] (*MÉX*) *nm* corn on the cob

eludir [elu'ðir] *vt* to avoid

email [i'mel] *nm* email; (*dirección*) email address; **mandar un ~ a algn** to email sb, send sb an email

embajada [emba'xaða] *nf* embassy

embajador, a [embaxa'ðor, a] nm/f
ambassador/ambassadress
embalar [emba'lar] vt to parcel,
wrap (up); **embalarse** vr to go fast
embalse [em'balse] nm (presa) dam;
(lago) reservoir
embarazada [embara'θaða] adj
pregnant ▷ nf pregnant woman
▌ No confunda **embarazada** con la
palabra inglesa *embarrassed*.
embarazo [emba'raθo] nm (de mujer)
pregnancy; (impedimento) obstacle,
obstruction; (timidez) embarrassment;
embarazoso, -a adj awkward,
embarrassing
embarcación [embarka'θjon] nf
(barco) boat, craft; (acto) embarkation,
boarding
embarcadero [embarka'ðero] nm
pier, landing stage
embarcar [embar'kar] vt
(cargamento) to ship, stow; (persona) to
embark, put on board; **embarcarse** vr
to embark, go on board
embargar [embar'xar] vt (Jur) to
seize, impound
embargo [em'barxo] nm (Jur)
seizure; (Com, Pol) embargo
embargue etc vb V **embargar**
embarque etc [em'barke] vb V
embarcar ▷ nm shipment, loading
embellecer [embeʎe'θer] vt to
embellish, beautify
embestida [embes'tiða] nf attack,
onslaught; (carga) charge
embestir [embes'tir] vt to attack,
assault; to charge, attack ▷ vi to
attack
emblema [em'blema] nm emblem
embobado, -a [embo'βaðo, a] adj
(atontado) stunned, bewildered
embolia [em'bolja] nf (Med) clot
émbolo ['embolo] nm (Auto) piston
emborrachar [emborra'tʃar]
vt to make drunk, intoxicate;
emborracharse vr to get drunk
emboscada [embos'kaða] nf ambush
embotar [embo'tar] vt to blunt, dull

embotellamiento
[emboteʎa'mjento] nm (Auto)
traffic jam
embotellar [embote'ʎar] vt to bottle
embrague [em'braxe] nm (tb: **pedal
de ~**) clutch
embrión [em'brjon] nm embryo
embrollo [em'broʎo] nm (enredo)
muddle, confusion; (aprieto) fix, jam
embrujado, -a [embru'xado, a] adj
bewitched; **casa embrujada** haunted
house
embrutecer [embrute'θer] vt
(atontar) to stupefy
embudo [em'buðo] nm funnel
embuste [em'buste] nm (mentira)
lie; **embustero, -a** adj lying, deceitful
▷ nm/f (mentiroso) liar
embutido [embu'tiðo] nm (Culin)
sausage; (Tec) inlay
emergencia [emer'xenθja] nf
emergency; (surgimiento) emergence
emerger [emer'xer] vi to emerge,
appear
emigración [emixra'θjon] nf
emigration; (de pájaros) migration
emigrar [emi'xrar] vi (personas) to
emigrate; (pájaros) to migrate
eminente [emi'nente] adj eminent,
distinguished; (elevado) high
emisión [emi'sjon] nf (acto)
emission; (Com etc) issue; (Radio,
TV: acto) broadcasting; (: programa)
broadcast, programme (BRIT), program
(US)
emisora [emi'sora] nf radio o
broadcasting station
emitir [emi'tir] vt (olor etc) to emit,
give off; (moneda etc) to issue; (opinión)
to express; (Radio) to broadcast
emoción [emo'θjon] nf emotion;
(excitación) excitement; (sentimiento)
feeling
emocionante [emoθjo'nante] adj
(excitante) exciting, thrilling
emocionar [emoθjo'nar] vt (excitar)
to excite, thrill; (conmover) to move,
touch; (impresionar) to impress

emoticón [emoti'kon], **emoticono** [emoti'kono] nm smiley

emotivo, -a [emo'tiβo, a] adj emotional

empacho [em'patʃo] nm (Med) indigestion; (fig) embarrassment

empalagoso, -a [empala'ɣoso, a] adj cloying; (fig) tiresome

empalmar [empal'mar] vt to join, connect ▷ vi (dos caminos) to meet, join; **empalme** nm joint, connection; junction; (de trenes) connection

empanada [empa'naða] nf pie, pasty

empañarse [empa'ɲarse] vr (cristales etc) to steam up

empapar [empa'par] vt (mojar) to soak, saturate; (absorber) to soak up, absorb; **empaparse** vr: ~**se de** to soak up

empapelar [empape'lar] vt (paredes) to paper

empaquetar [empake'tar] vt to pack, parcel up

empastar [empas'tar] vt (embadurnar) to paste; (diente) to fill

empaste [em'paste] nm (de diente) filling

empatar [empa'tar] vi to draw, tie; ~**on a dos** they drew two-all; **empate** nm draw, tie

empecé etc vb V **empezar**

empedernido, -a [empeðer'niðo, a] adj hard, heartless; (fumador) inveterate

empeine [em'peine] nm (de pie, zapato) instep

empeñado, -a [empe'ɲaðo, a] adj (persona) determined; (objeto) pawned

empeñar [empe'ɲar] vt (objeto) to pawn, pledge; (persona) to compel; **empeñarse** vr (endeudarse) to get into debt; ~**se en** to be set on, be determined to

empeño [em'peɲo] nm (determinación, insistencia) determination, insistence; **casa de ~s** pawnshop

empeorar [empeo'rar] vt to make worse, worsen ▷ vi to get worse, deteriorate

empezar [empe'θar] vt, vi to begin, start

empiece etc vb V **empezar**

empiezo etc vb V **empezar**

emplasto [em'plasto] nm (Med) plaster

emplazar [empla'θar] vt (ubicar) to site, place, locate; (Jur) to summons; (convocar) to summon

empleado, -a [emple'aðo, a] nm/f (gen) employee; (de banco etc) clerk

emplear [emple'ar] vt (usar) to use, employ; (dar trabajo a) to employ; **emplearse** vr (conseguir trabajo) to be employed; (ocuparse) to occupy o.s.

empleo [em'pleo] nm (puesto) job; (puestos: colectivamente) employment; (uso) use, employment

empollar [empo'ʎar] (ESP: fam) vt, vi to swot (up); **empollón, -ona** (ESP: fam) nm/f swot

emporio [em'porjo] (LAM) nm (gran almacén) department store

empotrado, -a [empo'traðo, a] adj (armario etc) built-in

emprendedor, a [emprende'ðor, a] adj enterprising

emprender [empren'der] vt (empezar) to begin, embark on; (acometer) to tackle, take on

empresa [em'presa] nf (de espíritu etc) enterprise; (Com) company, firm; **empresariales** nfpl business studies; **empresario, -a** nm/f (Com) businessman(-woman)

empujar [empu'xar] vt to push, shove

empujón [empu'xon] nm push, shove

empuñar [empu'ɲar] vt (asir) to grasp, take (firm) hold of

○ **PALABRA CLAVE**

en [en] prep **1** (posición) in; (: sobre) on;

está en el cajón it's in the drawer; **en Argentina/La Paz** in Argentina/La Paz; **en la oficina/el colegio** at the office/school; **está en el suelo/quinto piso** it's on the floor/the fifth floor **2** (*dirección*) into; **entró en el aula** she went into the classroom; **meter algo en el bolso** to put sth into one's bag **3** (*tiempo*) in; on; **en 1605/3 semanas/ invierno** in 1605/3 weeks/winter; **en (el mes de) enero** in (the month of) January; **en aquella ocasión/época** on that occasion/at that time **4** (*precio*) for; **lo vendió en 20 dólares** he sold it for 20 dollars **5** (*diferencia*) by; **reducir/aumentar en una tercera parte/un 20 por ciento** to reduce/increase by a third/20 per cent **6** (*manera*): **en avión/autobús** by plane/bus; **escrito en inglés** written in English **7** (*después de vb que indica gastar etc*) on; **han cobrado demasiado en dietas** they've charged too much to expenses; **se le va la mitad del sueldo en comida** he spends half his salary on food **8** (*tema, ocupación*): **experto en la materia** expert on the subject; **trabaja en la construcción** he works in the building industry **9** (*adj + en + infin*): **lento en reaccionar** slow to react

enaguas [e'naɣwas] *nfpl* petticoat *sg*, underskirt *sg*

enajenación [enaxena'θjon] *nf* (*Psico: tb: ~ mental*) mental derangement

enamorado, -a [enamo'raðo, a] *adj* in love ▷ *nm/f* lover; **estar ~ (de)** to be in love (with)

enamorar [enamo'rar] *vt* to win the love of; **enamorarse** *vr*: **~se de algn** to fall in love with sb

enano, -a [e'nano, a] *adj* tiny ▷ *nm/f* dwarf

encabezamiento [enkaβeθa'mjento] *nm* (*de carta*) heading; (*de periódico*) headline

encabezar [enkaβe'θar] *vt* (*movimiento, revolución*) to lead, head; (*lista*) to head, be at the top of; (*carta*) to put a heading to

encadenar [enkaðe'nar] *vt* to chain (together); (*poner grilletes a*) to shackle

encajar [enka'xar] *vt* (*ajustar*): **~ (en)** to fit (into); (*fam: golpe*) to take ▷ *vi* to fit (well); (*fig: corresponder a*) to match

encaje [en'kaxe] *nm* (*labor*) lace

encallar [enka'ʎar] *vi* (*Náut*) to run aground

encaminar [enkami'nar] *vt* to direct, send

encantado, -a [enkan'taðo, a] *adj* (*hechizado*) bewitched; (*muy contento*) delighted; **¡~!** how do you do, pleased to meet you

encantador, a [enkanta'ðor, a] *adj* charming, lovely ▷ *nm/f* magician, enchanter/enchantress

encantar [enkan'tar] *vt* (*agradar*) to charm, delight; (*hechizar*) to bewitch, cast a spell on; **me encanta eso** I love that; **encanto** *nm* (*hechizo*) spell, charm; (*fig*) charm, delight

encarcelar [enkarθe'lar] *vt* to imprison, jail

encarecer [enkare'θer] *vt* to put up the price of; **encarecerse** *vr* to get dearer

encargado, -a [enkar'ɣaðo, a] *adj* in charge ▷ *nm/f* agent, representative; (*responsable*) person in charge

encargar [enkar'ɣar] *vt* to entrust; (*recomendar*) to urge, recommend; **encargarse** *vr*: **~se de** to look after, take charge of; **~ algo a algn** to put sb in charge of sth; **~ a algn que haga algo** to ask sb to do sth

encargo [en'karɣo] *nm* (*tarea*) assignment, job; (*responsabilidad*) responsibility; (*Com*) order

encariñarse [enkari'narse] *vr*: **~ con**

to grow fond of, get attached to

encarnación [enkarna'θjon] nf
incarnation, embodiment

encarrilar [enkarri'lar] vt (tren) to
put back on the rails; (fig) to correct,
put on the right track

encasillar [enkasi'ʎar] vt (fig) to
pigeonhole; (actor) to typecast

encendedor [enθende'ðor] nm
lighter

encender [enθen'der] vt (con
fuego) to light; (luz, radio) to put on,
switch on; (avivar: pasión) to inflame;
encenderse vr to catch fire; (excitarse)
to get excited; (de cólera) to flare up; (el
rostro) to blush

encendido [enθen'diðo] nm (Auto)
ignition

encerado [enθe'raðo] nm (Escol)
blackboard

encerrar [enθe'rrar] vt (confinar) to
shut in, shut up; (comprender, incluir) to
include, contain

encharcado, -a [entʃar'kaðo, a] adj
(terreno) flooded

encharcarse [entʃar'karse] vr to
get flooded

enchufado, -a [entʃu'faðo, a] (fam)
nm/f well-connected person

enchufar [entʃu'far] vt (Elec) to
plug in; (Tec) to connect, fit together;
enchufe nm (Elec: clavija) plug; (: toma)
socket; (do dos tubos) joint, connection;
(fam: influencia) contact, connection;
(: puesto) cushy job

encía [en'θia] nf gum

encienda etc vb V **encender**

encierro etc [en'θjerro] vb V **encerrar**
▷ nm shutting in, shutting up;
(calabozo) prison

encima [en'θima] adv (sobre) above,
over; (además) besides; **~ de** (en) on,
on top of; (sobre) above, over; (además
de) besides, on top of; **por ~ de** over;
¿llevas dinero ~? have you (got) any
money on you?; **se me vino ~** it took
me by surprise

encina [en'θina] nf holm oak

encinta [en'θinta] adj pregnant

enclenque [en'klenke] adj weak,
sickly

encoger [enko'xer] vt to shrink,
contract; **encogerse** vr to shrink,
contract; (fig) to cringe; **~se de
hombros** to shrug one's shoulders

encomendar [enkomen'dar] vt to
entrust, commend; **encomendarse**
vr: **~se a** to put one's trust in

encomienda etc [enko'mjenda]
vb V **encomendar** ▷ nf (encargo)
charge, commission; (elogio) tribute;
encomienda postal (LAM) package

encontrar [enkon'trar] vt (hallar)
to find; (inesperadamente) to meet, run
into; **encontrarse** vr to meet (each
other); (situarse) to be (situated); **~se
con** to meet; **~se bien (de salud)** to
feel well

encrucijada [enkruθi'xaða] nf
crossroads sg

encuadernación
[enkwaðerna'θjon] nf binding

encuadrar [enkwa'ðrar] vt (retrato)
to frame; (ajustar) to fit, insert;
(contener) to contain

encubrir [enku'βrir] vt (ocultar) to
hide, conceal; (criminal) to harbour,
shelter

encuentro etc [en'kwentro] vb V
encontrar ▷ nm (de personas) meeting;
(Auto etc) collision, crash; (Deporte)
match, game; (Mil) encounter

encuerado, -a (MÉX) [enkwe'raðo,
a] adj nude, naked

encuesta [en'kwesta] nf inquiry,
investigation; (sondeo) (public)
opinion poll

encumbrar [enkum'brar] vt
(persona) to exalt

endeble [en'deβle] adj (persona)
weak; (argumento, excusa, persona) weak

endemoniado, -a [endemo'njaðo,
a] adj possessed (of the devil);
(travieso) devilish

enderezar [endere'θar] vt (poner
derecho) to straighten (out);

(: *verticalmente*) to set upright;
(*situación*) to straighten o sort out;
(*dirigir*) to direct; **enderezarse** vr
(*persona sentada*) to straighten up

endeudarse [endeu'ðarse] vr to
get into debt

endiablado, -a [endja'βlaðo, a]
adj devilish, diabolical; (*travieso*)
mischievous

endilgar [endil'xar] (*fam*) vt: **~le algo
a algn** to lumber sb with sth

endiñar [endi'ɲar] (*ESP: fam*) vt
(*bofetón*) to land, belt

endosar [endo'sar] vt (*cheque etc*)
to endorse

endulzar [endul'θar] vt to sweeten;
(*suavizar*) to soften

endurecer [endure'θer] vt to
harden; **endurecerse** vr to harden,
grow hard

enema [e'nema] nm (*Med*) enema

enemigo, -a [ene'mixo, a] *adj*
enemy, hostile ▷ nm/f enemy

enemistad [enemis'tað] nf enmity

enemistar [enemis'tar] vt to make
enemies of, cause a rift between;
enemistarse vr to become enemies;
(*amigos*) to fall out

energía [ener'xia] nf (*vigor*) energy,
drive; (*empuje*) push; (*Tec, Elec*) energy,
power; **energía eólica** wind power;
energía solar solar energy o power

enérgico, -a [e'nerxiko, a] *adj* (*gen*)
energetic; (*voz, modales*) forceful

energúmeno, -a [ener'xumeno, a]
(*fam*) nm/f (*fig*) madman(-woman)

enero [e'nero] nm January

enfadado, -a [enfa'ðaðo, a] *adj*
angry, annoyed

enfadar [enfa'ðar] vt to anger,
annoy; **enfadarse** vr to get angry o
annoyed

enfado [en'faðo] nm (*enojo*) anger,
annoyance; (*disgusto*) trouble, bother

énfasis ['enfasis] nm emphasis,
stress

enfático, -a [en'fatiko, a] *adj*
emphatic

enfermar [enfer'mar] vt to make ill
▷ vi to fall ill, be taken ill

enfermedad [enferme'ðað] nf
illness; **enfermedad venérea** venereal
disease

enfermera [enfer'mera] nf nurse

enfermería [enferme'ria] nf
infirmary; (*de colegio etc*) sick bay

enfermero [enfer'mero] nm (male)
nurse

enfermizo, -a [enfer'miθo, a]
adj (*persona*) sickly, unhealthy; (*fig*)
unhealthy

enfermo, -a [en'fermo, a] *adj* ill,
sick ▷ nm/f invalid, sick person; (*en
hospital*) patient; **caer** o **ponerse ~**
to fall ill

enfocar [enfo'kar] vt (*foto etc*) to
focus; (*problema etc*) to approach

enfoque *etc* [en'foke] vb V **enfocar**
▷ nm focus

enfrentar [enfren'tar] vt (*peligro*)
to face (up to), confront; (*oponer*)
to bring face to face; **enfrentarse** vr (*dos
personas*) to face o confront each other;
(*Deporte: dos equipos*) to meet; **~se a** o
con to face up to, confront

enfrente [en'frente] *adv* opposite;
la casa de ~ the house opposite, the
house across the street; **~ de** opposite,
facing

enfriamiento [enfria'mjento] nm
chilling, refrigeration; (*Med*) cold, chill

enfriar [enfri'ar] vt (*alimentos*) to
cool, chill; (*algo caliente*) to cool down;
enfriarse vr to cool down; (*Med*) to
catch a chill; (*amistad*) to cool

enfurecer [enfure'θer] vt to enrage,
madden; **enfurecerse** vr to become
furious, fly into a rage; (*mar*) to get
rough

enganchar [engan'tʃar] vt to
hook; (*dos vagones*) to hitch up; (*Tec*)
to couple, connect; (*Mil*) to recruit;
engancharse vr (*Mil*) to enlist, join up

enganche [en'gantʃe] nm hook;
(*ESP Tec*) coupling, connection; (*acto*)
hooking (up); (*Mil*) recruitment,

enlistment; (*MÉX: depósito*) deposit

engañar [enga'ɲar] *vt* to deceive; (*estafar*) to cheat, swindle; **engañarse** *vr* (*equivocarse*) to be wrong; (*disimular la verdad*) to deceive o.s.

engaño [en'gaɲo] *nm* deceit; (*estafa*) trick, swindle; (*error*) mistake, misunderstanding; (*ilusión*) delusion; **engañoso, -a** *adj* (*tramposo*) crooked; (*mentiroso*) dishonest, deceitful; (*aspecto*) deceptive; (*consejo*) misleading

engatusar [engatu'sar] (*fam*) *vt* to coax

engendro [en'xendro] *nm* (*Bio*) foetus; (*fig*) monstrosity

englobar [englo'βar] *vt* to include, comprise

engordar [engor'ðar] *vt* to fatten ▷ *vi* to get fat, put on weight

engorroso, -a [engo'rroso, a] *adj* bothersome, trying

engranaje [engra'naxe] *nm* (*Auto*) gear

engrasar [engra'sar] *vt* (*Tec: poner grasa*) to grease; (: *lubricar*) to lubricate, oil; (*manchar*) to make greasy

engreído, -a [engre'iðo, a] *adj* vain, conceited

enhebrar [ene'βrar] *vt* to thread

enhorabuena [enora'βwena] *excl*: ¡~! congratulations! ▷ *nf*: **dar la ~ a** to congratulate

enigma [e'niɣma] *nm* enigma; (*problema*) puzzle; (*misterio*) mystery

enjambre [en'xambre] *nm* swarm

enjaular [enxau'lar] *vt* to (put in a) cage; (*fam*) to jail, lock up

enjuagar [enxwa'ɣar] *vt* (*ropa*) to rinse (out)

enjuague *etc* [en'xwaɣe] *vb* V **enjuagar** ▷ *nm* (*Med*) mouthwash; (*de ropa*) rinse, rinsing

enjugar [enxu'ɣar] *vt* to wipe (off); (*lágrimas*) to dry; (*déficit*) to wipe out

enlace [en'laθe] *nm* link, connection; (*relación*) relationship; (*tb: ~ matrimonial*) marriage; (*de carretera,*

trenes) connection; **enlace sindical** shop steward

enlatado, -a [enla'taðo, a] *adj* (*alimentos, productos*) tinned, canned

enlazar [enla'θar] *vt* (*unir con lazos*) to bind together; (*atar*) to tie; (*conectar*) to link, connect; (*LAM: caballo*) to lasso

enloquecer [enloke'θer] *vt* to drive mad ▷ *vi* to go mad

enmarañar [enmara'ɲar] *vt* (*enredar*) to tangle (up), entangle; (*complicar*) to complicate; (*confundir*) to confuse

enmarcar [enmar'kar] *vt* (*cuadro*) to frame

enmascarar [enmaska'rar] *vt* to mask; **enmascararse** *vr* to put on a mask

enmendar [enmen'dar] *vt* to emend, correct; (*constitución etc*) to amend; (*comportamiento*) to reform; **enmendarse** *vr* to reform, mend one's ways; **enmienda** *nf* correction; amendment; reform

enmudecer [enmuðe'θer] *vi* (*perder el habla*) to fall silent; (*guardar silencio*) to remain silent

ennoblecer [ennoβle'θer] *vt* to ennoble

enojado, -a [eno'xaðo, a] (*LAM*) *adj* angry

enojar [eno'xar] *vt* (*encolerizar*) to anger; (*disgustar*) to annoy, upset; **enojarse** *vr* to get angry; to get annoyed

enojo [e'noxo] *nm* (*cólera*) anger; (*irritación*) annoyance

enorme [e'norme] *adj* enormous, huge; (*fig*) monstrous

enredadera [enreða'ðera] *nf* (*Bot*) creeper, climbing plant

enredar [enre'ðar] *vt* (*cables, hilos etc*) to tangle (up), entangle; (*situación*) to complicate, confuse; (*meter cizaña*) to sow discord among *o* between; (*implicar*) to embroil, implicate; **enredarse** *vr* to get entangled, get tangled (up); (*situación*) to get complicated; (*persona*) to get embroiled; (*LAM: fam*) to meddle

enredo [en'reðo] *nm* (*maraña*) tangle; (*confusión*) mix-up, confusion; (*intriga*) intrigue

enriquecer [enrike'θer] *vt* to make rich, enrich; **enriquecerse** *vr* to get rich

enrojecer [enroxe'θer] *vt* to redden ▷ *vi* (*persona*) to blush; **enrojecerse** *vr* to blush

enrollar [enro'ʎar] *vt* to roll (up), wind (up)

ensalada [ensa'laða] *nf* salad; **ensaladilla (rusa)** *nf* Russian salad

ensanchar [ensan'tʃar] *vt* (*hacer más ancho*) to widen; (*agrandar*) to enlarge, expand; (*Costura*) to let out; **ensancharse** *vr* to get wider, expand

ensayar [ensa'jar] *vt* to test, try (out); (*Teatro*) to rehearse

ensayo [en'sajo] *nm* test, trial; (*Quím*) experiment; (*Teatro*) rehearsal; (*Deporte*) try; (*Escol, Literatura*) essay

enseguida [ense'ɣiða] *adv* at once, right away

ensenada [ense'naða] *nf* inlet, cove

enseñanza [ense'ɲanθa] *nf* (*educación*) education; (*acción*) teaching; (*doctrina*) teaching, doctrine; **enseñanza (de) primaria/secundaria** elementary/secondary education

enseñar [ense'ɲar] *vt* (*educar*) to teach; (*mostrar, señalar*) to show

enseres [en'seres] *nmpl* belongings

ensuciar [ensu'θjar] *vt* (*manchar*) to dirty, soil; (*fig*) to defile; **ensuciarse** *vr* to get dirty; (*bebé*) to dirty one's nappy

entablar [enta'βlar] *vt* (*recubrir*) to board (up); (*Ajedrez, Damas*) to set up; (*conversación*) to strike up; (*Jur*) to file ▷ *vi* to draw

ente ['ente] *nm* (*organización*) body, organization; (*fam: persona*) odd character

entender [enten'der] *vt* (*comprender*) to understand; (*darse cuenta*) to realize ▷ *vi* to understand; (*creer*) to think,

believe; **entenderse** *vr* (*comprenderse*) to be understood; (*ponerse de acuerdo*) to agree, reach an agreement; **~ de** to know all about; **~ algo de** to know a little about; **~ en** to deal with, have to do with; **~ mal** to misunderstand; **~se con algn** (*llevarse bien*) to get on o along with sb; **~se mal** (*dos personas*) to get on badly

entendido, -a [enten'diðo, a] *adj* (*comprendido*) understood; (*hábil*) skilled; (*inteligente*) knowledgeable ▷ *nm/f* (*experto*) expert ▷ *excl* agreed!; **entendimiento** *nm* (*comprensión*) understanding; (*inteligencia*) mind, intellect; (*juicio*) judgement

enterado, -a [ente'raðo, a] *adj* well-informed; **estar ~ de** to know about, be aware of

enteramente [entera'mente] *adv* entirely, completely

enterar [ente'rar] *vt* (*informar*) to inform, tell; **enterarse** *vr* to find out, get to know

enterito [ente'rito] (*RPL*) *nm* boiler suit (*BRIT*), overalls (*US*)

entero, -a [en'tero, a] *adj* (*total*) whole, entire; (*fig: honesto*) honest; (*: firme*) firm, resolute ▷ *nm* (*Com: punto*) point

enterrar [ente'rrar] *vt* to bury

entidad [enti'ðað] *nf* (*empresa*) firm, company; (*organismo*) body; (*sociedad*) society; (*Filosofía*) entity

entiendo *etc vb* V **entender**

entierro [en'tjerro] *nm* (*acción*) burial; (*funeral*) funeral

entonación [entona'θjon] *nf* (*Ling*) intonation

entonar [ento'nar] *vt* (*canción*) to intone; (*colores*) to tone; (*Med*) to tone up ▷ *vi* to be in tune

entonces [en'tonθes] *adv* then, at that time; **desde ~** since then; **en aquel ~** at that time; **(pues) ~** and so

entornar [entor'nar] *vt* (*puerta, ventana*) to half-close, leave ajar; (*los ojos*) to screw up

entorno [en'torno] nm setting, environment; **~ de redes** (*Inform*) network environment

entorpecer [entorpe'θer] vt (*entendimiento*) to dull; (*impedir*) to obstruct, hinder; (: *tránsito*) to slow down, delay

entrada [en'traða] nf (*acción*) entry, access; (*sitio*) entrance, way in; (*Inform*) input; (*Com*) receipts pl, takings pl; (*Culin*) starter; (*Deporte*) innings sg; (*Teatro*) house, audience; (*billete*) ticket; **~s y salidas** (*Com*) income and expenditure; **de ~** from the outset; **entrada de aire** (*Tec*) air intake o inlet

entrado, -a [en'traðo, a] adj: **~ en años** elderly; **una vez ~ el verano** in the summer(time), when summer comes

entramparse [entram'parse] vr to get into debt

entrante [en'trante] adj next, coming; **mes/año ~** next month/year; **entrantes** nmpl starters

entraña [en'traɲa] nf (*fig: centro*) heart, core; (*raíz*) root; **entrañas** nfpl (*Anat*) entrails; (*fig*) heart sg; **entrañable** adj close, intimate; **entrañar** vt to entail

entrar [en'trar] vt (*introducir*) to bring in; (*Inform*) to input ▷ vi (*meterse*) to go in, come in, enter; (*comenzar*): **~ diciendo** to begin by saying; **hacer ~** to show in; **me entró sed/sueño** I started to feel thirsty/sleepy; **no me entra** I can't get the hang of it

entre ['entre] prep (*dos*) between; (*más de dos*) among(st)

entreabrir [entrea'βrir] vt to half-open, open halfway

entrecejo [entre'θexo] nm: **fruncir el ~** to frown

entredicho [entre'ðitʃo] nm (*Jur*) injunction; **poner en ~** to cast doubt on; **estar en ~** to be in doubt

entrega [en'trexa] nf (*de mercancías*) delivery; (*de novela etc*) instalment; **entregar** [entre'xar] vt (*dar*) to hand (over), deliver; **entregarse** vr (*rendirse*) to surrender, give in, submit; (*dedicarse*) to devote o.s.

entremeses [entre'meses] nmpl hors d'œuvres

entremeter [entreme'ter] vt to insert, put in; **entremeterse** vr to meddle, interfere; **entremetido, -a** adj meddling, interfering

entremezclar [entremeθ'klar] vt to intermingle; **entremezclarse** vr to intermingle

entrenador, a [entrena'ðor, a] nm/f trainer, coach

entrenarse [entre'narse] vr to train

entrepierna [entre'pjerna] nf crotch

entresuelo [entre'swelo] nm mezzanine

entretanto [entre'tanto] adv meanwhile, meantime

entretecho [entre'tetʃo] (cs) nm attic

entretejer [entrete'xer] vt to interweave

entretener [entrete'ner] vt (*divertir*) to entertain, amuse; (*detener*) to hold up, delay; **entretenerse** vr (*divertirse*) to amuse o.s.; (*retrasarse*) to delay, linger; **entretenido, -a** adj entertaining, amusing; **entretenimiento** nm entertainment, amusement

entrever [entre'βer] vt to glimpse, catch a glimpse of

entrevista [entre'βista] nf interview; **entrevistar** vt to interview; **entrevistarse** vr to have an interview

entristecer [entriste'θer] vt to sadden, grieve; **entristecerse** vr to grow sad

entrometerse [entrome'terse] vr: **~ (en)** to interfere (in o with)

entumecer [entume'θer] vt to numb, benumb; **entumecerse** vr (*por el frío*) to go o become numb

enturbiar [entur'βjar] vt (*el agua*)

to make cloudy; (fig) to confuse;
enturbiarse vr (oscurecerse) to become
cloudy; (fig) to get confused, become
obscure

entusiasmar [entusjas'mar] vt to
excite, fill with enthusiasm; (gustar
mucho) to delight; **entusiasmarse**
vr: **~se con** o **por** to get enthusiastic o
excited about

entusiasmo [entu'sjasmo] nm
enthusiasm; (excitación) excitement

entusiasta [entu'sjasta] adj
enthusiastic ▷ nmf enthusiast

enumerar [enume'rar] vt to
enumerate

envainar [embai'nar] vt to sheathe

envalentonar [embalento'nar] vt
to give courage to; **envalentonarse** vr
(pey: jactarse) to boast, brag

envasar [emba'sar] vt (empaquetar)
to pack, wrap; (enfrascar) to bottle;
(enlatar) to can; (embolsar) to pocket

envase [em'base] nm (en paquete)
packing, wrapping; (en botella)
bottling; (en lata) canning; (recipiente)
container; (paquete) package; (botella)
bottle; (lata) tin (BRIT), can

envejecer [embexe'θer] vt to make
old, age ▷ vi (volverse viejo) to grow old;
(parecer viejo) to age

envenenar [embene'nar] vt to
poison; (fig) to embitter

envergadura [emberɣa'ðura] nf
(fig) scope, compass

enviar [em'bjar] vt to send; **~ un
mensaje a algn** (por movil) to text sb, to
send sb a text message

enviciarse [embi'θjarse] vr: **~ (con)**
to get addicted (to)

envidia [em'biðja] nf envy; **tener
~ a** to envy, be jealous of; **envidiar**
vt to envy

envío [em'bio] nm (acción) sending;
(de mercancías) consignment; (de dinero)
remittance

enviudar [embju'ðar] vi to be
widowed

envoltura [embol'tura] nf (cobertura)

cover; (embalaje) wrapper, wrapping;
envoltorio nm package

envolver [embol'βer] vt to wrap (up);
(cubrir) to cover; (enemigo) to surround;
(implicar) to involve, implicate

envuelto [em'bwelto] pp de
envolver

enyesar [enje'sar] vt (pared) to
plaster; (Med) to put in plaster

enzarzarse [enθar'θarse] vr: **~ en**
(pelea) to get mixed up in; (disputa) to
get involved in

épica ['epika] nf epic

epidemia [epi'ðemja] nf epidemic

epilepsia [epi'lepsja] nf epilepsy

episodio [epi'soðjo] nm episode

época ['epoka] nf period, time; (Hist)
age, epoch; **hacer ~** to be epoch-
making

equilibrar [ekili'βrar] vt to balance;
equilibrio nm balance, equilibrium;
mantener/perder el equilibrio to
keep/lose one's balance; **equilibrista**
nmf (funámbulo) tightrope walker;
(acróbata) acrobat

equipaje [eki'paxe] nm luggage;
(avíos): **hacer el ~** to pack; **equipaje de
mano** hand luggage

equipar [eki'par] vt (proveer) to equip

equipararse [ekipa'rarse] vr: **~ con**
to be on a level with

equipo [e'kipo] nm (conjunto de
cosas) equipment; (Deporte) team; (de
obreros) shift; **~ de música/de hi-fi**
music centre

equis ['ekis] nf inv (the letter) X

equitación [ekita'θjon] nf horse
riding

equivalente [ekiβa'lente] adj, nm
equivalent

equivaler [ekiβa'ler] vi to be
equivalent o equal

equivocación [ekiβoka'θjon] nf
mistake, error

equivocado, -a [ekiβo'kaðo, a] adj
wrong, mistaken

equivocarse [ekiβo'karse] vr to be
wrong, make a mistake; **~ de camino**

to take the wrong road

era ['era] *vb* V **ser** ▷*nf* era, age

erais *vb* V **ser**

éramos *vb* V **ser**

eran *vb* V **ser**

eras *vb* V **ser**

erección [erek'θjon] *nf* erection

eres *vb* V **ser**

erigir [eri'xir] *vt* to erect, build;
erigirse *vr*: ~**se en** to set o.s. up as

erizo [e'riθo] *nm* (*Zool*) hedgehog;
erizo de mar sea-urchin

ermita [er'mita] *nf* hermitage;
ermitaño, -a [ermi'taɲo, a] *nm/f*
hermit

erosión [ero'sjon] *nf* erosion

erosionar [erosjo'nar] *vt* to erode

erótico, -a [e'rotiko, a] *adj* erotic;
erotismo *nm* eroticism

errante [e'rrante] *adj* wandering,
errant

erróneo, -a [e'rroneo, a] *adj*
(*equivocado*) wrong, mistaken

error [e'rror] *nm* error, mistake;
(*Inform*) bug; **error de imprenta**
misprint

eructar [eruk'tar] *vt* to belch, burp

erudito, -a [eru'ðito, a] *adj* erudite,
learned

erupción [erup'θjon] *nf* eruption;
(*Med*) rash

es *vb* V **ser**

esa ['esa] (*pl* ~**s**) *adj demos* V **ese**

ésa ['esa] (*pl* ~**s**) *pron* V **ése**

esbelto, -a [es'βelto, a] *adj* slim,
slender

esbozo [es'βoθo] *nm* sketch, outline

escabeche [eska'βetʃe] *nm* brine; (*de
aceitunas etc*) pickle; **en ~** pickled

escabullirse [eskaβu'ʎirse] *vr* to slip
away, to clear out

escafandra [eska'fandra] *nf* (*buzo*)
diving suit; (*escafandra espacial*)
space suit

escala [es'kala] *nf* (*proporción, Mús*)
scale; (*de mano*) ladder; (*Aviac*) stopover;
hacer ~ en to stop o call in at

escalafón [eskala'fon] *nm* (*escala de*

salarios) salary scale, wage scale

escalar [eska'lar] *vt* to climb, scale

escalera [eska'lera] *nf* stairs *pl*,
staircase; (*escala*) ladder; (*Naipes*) run;
escalera de caracol spiral staircase;
escalera de incendios fire escape;
escalera mecánica escalator

escalfar [eskal'far] *vt* (*huevos*) to
poach

escalinata [eskali'nata] *nf* staircase

escalofriante [eskalo'frjante] *adj*
chilling

escalofrío [eskalo'frio] *nm* (*Med*)
chill; **escalofríos** *nmpl* (*fig*) shivers

escalón [eska'lon] *nm* step, stair; (*de
escalera*) rung

escalope [eska'lope] *nm* (*Culin*)
escalope

escama [es'kama] *nf* (*de pez,
serpiente*) scale; (*de jabón*) flake; (*fig*)
resentment

escampar [eskam'par] *vb impers* to
stop raining

escandalizar [eskandali'θar] *vt* to
scandalize, shock; **escandalizarse**
vr to be shocked; (*ofenderse*) to be
offended

escándalo [es'kandalo] *nm* scandal;
(*alboroto, tumulto*) row, uproar;
escandaloso, -a *adj* scandalous,
shocking

escandinavo, -a [eskandi'naβo, a]
adj, nm/f Scandinavian

escanear [eskane'ar] *vt* to scan

escaño [es'kaɲo] *nm* bench; (*Pol*) seat

escapar [eska'par] *vi* (*gen*) to escape,
run away; (*Deporte*) to break away;
escaparse *vr* to escape, get away;
(*agua, gas*) to leak (out)

escaparate [eskapa'rate] *nm* shop
window; **ir de ~s** to go window-
shopping

escape [es'kape] *nm* (*de agua, gas*)
leak; (*de motor*) exhaust

escarabajo [eskara'βaxo] *nm* beetle

escaramuza [eskara'muθa] *nf*
skirmish

escarbar [eskar'βar] *vt* (*tierra*) to

scratch

escarceos [eskar'θeos] nmpl: **en mis ~ con la política ...** in my dealings with politics ...; **escarceos amorosos** love affairs

escarcha [es'kartʃa] nf frost; **escarchado, -a** [eskar'tʃaðo, a] adj (Culin: fruta) crystallized

escarlatina [eskarla'tina] nf scarlet fever

escarmentar [eskarmen'tar] vt to punish severely ▷ vi to learn one's lesson

escarmiento etc [eskar'mjento] vb V **escarmentar** ▷ nm (ejemplo) lesson; (castigo) punishment

escarola [eska'rola] nf endive

escarpado, -a [eskar'paðo, a] adj (pendiente) sheer, steep; (rocas) craggy

escasear [eskase'ar] vi to be scarce

escasez [eska'seθ] nf (falta) shortage, scarcity; (pobreza) poverty

escaso, -a [es'kaso, a] adj (poco) scarce; (raro) rare; (ralo) thin, sparse; (limitado) limited

escatimar [eskati'mar] vt to skimp (on), be sparing with

escayola [eska'jola] nf plaster

escena [es'θena] nf scene; **escenario** [esθe'narjo] nm (Teatro) stage; (Cine) set; (fig) scene

▌ No confundir **escenario** con la palabra inglesa scenery.

escenografía nf set design

escéptico, -a [es'θeptiko, a] adj sceptical ▷ nm/f sceptic

esclarecer [esklare'θer] vt (misterio, problema) to shed light on

esclavitud [esklaβi'tuð] nf slavery

esclavizar [esklaβi'θar] vt to enslave

esclavo, -a [es'klaβo, a] nm/f slave

escoba [es'koβa] nf broom; **escobilla** nf brush

escocer [esko'θer] vi to burn, sting; **escocerse** vr to chafe, get chafed

escocés, -esa [esko'θes, esa] adj Scottish ▷ nm/f Scotsman(-woman), Scot

Escocia [es'koθja] nf Scotland

escoger [esko'xer] vt to choose, pick, select; **escogido, -a** adj chosen, selected

escolar [esko'lar] adj school cpd ▷ nmf schoolboy(-girl), pupil

escollo [es'koʎo] nm (obstáculo) pitfall

escolta [es'kolta] nf escort; **escoltar** vt to escort

escombros [es'kombros] nmpl (basura) rubbish sg; (restos) debris sg

esconder [eskon'der] vt to hide, conceal; **esconderse** vr to hide; **escondidas** (LAM) nfpl: **a escondidas** secretly; **escondite** nm hiding place; (ESP: juego) hide-and-seek; **escondrijo** nm hiding place, hideout

escopeta [esko'peta] nf shotgun

escoria [es'korja] nf (de alto horno) slag; (fig) scum, dregs pl

Escorpio [es'korpjo] nm Scorpio

escorpión [eskor'pjon] nm scorpion

escotado, -a [esko'taðo, a] adj low-cut

escote [es'kote] nm (de vestido) low neck; **pagar a ~** to share the expenses

escotilla [esko'tiʎa] nf (Náut) hatch(way)

escozor [esko'θor] nm (dolor) sting(ing)

escríbible [eskri'βiβle] adj writable

escribir [eskri'βir] vt, vi to write; **~ a máquina** to type; **¿cómo se escribe?** how do you spell it?

escrito, -a [es'krito, a] pp de **escribir** ▷ nm (documento) document; (manuscrito) text, manuscript; **por ~** in writing

escritor, a [eskri'tor, a] nm/f writer

escritorio [eskri'torjo] nm desk

escritura [eskri'tura] nf (acción) writing; (caligrafía) (hand)writing; (Jur: documento) deed

escrúpulo [es'krupulo] nm scruple; (minuciosidad) scrupulousness; **escrupuloso, -a** adj scrupulous

escrutinio [eskru'tinjo] nm (examen atento) scrutiny; (Pol: recuento de votos) count(ing)

escuadra [es'kwaðra] *nf* (*Mil etc*) squad; (*Náut*) squadron; (*flota: de coches etc*) fleet; **escuadrilla** *nf* (*de aviones*) squadron; (*LAM: de obreros*) gang

escuadrón [eskwa'ðron] *nm* squadron

escuálido, -a [es'kwaliðo, a] *adj* skinny, scraggy; (*sucio*) squalid

escuchar [esku'tʃar] *vt* to listen to ▷ *vi* to listen

escudo [es'kuðo] *nm* shield

escuela [es'kwela] *nf* school; **escuela de artes y oficios** (*ESP*) ≈ technical college; **escuela de choferes** (*LAM*) driving school; **escuela de manejo** (*MÉX*) driving school

escueto, -a [es'kweto, a] *adj* plain; (*estilo*) simple

escuincle, -a [es'kwinkle, a] (*MÉX: fam*) *nm/f* kid

esculpir [eskul'pir] *vt* to sculpt; (*grabar*) to engrave; (*tallar*) to carve; **escultor, a** *nm/f* sculptor(-tress); **escultura** *nf* sculpture

escupidera [eskupi'ðera] *nf* spittoon

escupir [esku'pir] *vt*, *vi* to spit (out)

escurreplatos [eskurre'platos] (*ESP*) *nm inv* draining board (*BRIT*), drainboard (*US*)

escurridero [eskurri'ðero] (*LAM*) *nm* draining board (*BRIT*), drainboard (*US*)

escurridizo, -a [eskurri'ðiθo, a] *adj* slippery

escurridor [eskurri'ðor] *nm* colander

escurrir [esku'rrir] *vt* (*ropa*) to wring out; (*verduras, platos*) to drain ▷ *vi* (*líquidos*) to drip; **escurrirse** *vr* (*secarse*) to drain; (*resbalarse*) to slip, slide; (*escaparse*) to slip away

ese ['ese] (*f* **esa**, *pl* **esos, esas**) *adj demos* (*sg*) that; (*pl*) those

ése ['ese] (*f* **ésa**, *pl* **ésos, ésas**) *pron* (*sg*) that (one); (*pl*) those (ones); **~ ... éste ...** the former ... the latter ...; **no me vengas con ésas** don't give me any

more of that nonsense

esencia [e'senθja] *nf* essence; **esencial** *adj* essential

esfera [es'fera] *nf* sphere; (*de reloj*) face; **esférico, -a** *adj* spherical

esforzarse [esfor'θarse] *vr* to exert o.s., make an effort

esfuerzo *etc* [es'fwerθo] *vb* V **esforzarse** ▷ *nm* effort

esfumarse [esfu'marse] *vr* (*apoyo, esperanzas*) to fade away

esgrima [es'ɣrima] *nf* fencing

esguince [es'ɣinθe] *nm* (*Med*) sprain

eslabón [esla'βon] *nm* link

eslip [ez'lip] *nm* pants *pl* (*BRIT*), briefs *pl*

eslovaco, -a [eslo'βako, a] *adj, nm/f* Slovak, Slovakian ▷ *nm* (*Ling*) Slovak, Slovakian

Eslovaquia [eslo'βakja] *nf* Slovakia

esmalte [es'malte] *nm* enamel; **esmalte de uñas** nail varnish *o* polish

esmeralda [esme'ralda] *nf* emerald

esmerarse [esme'rarse] *vr* (*aplicarse*) to take great pains, exercise great care; (*afanarse*) to work hard

esmero [es'mero] *nm* (great) care

esnob [es'nob] (*pl* **~s**) *adj* (*persona*) snobbish ▷ *nmf* snob

eso ['eso] *pron* that, that thing *o* matter; **~ de su coche** that business about his car; **~ de ir al cine** all that about going to the cinema; **a ~ de las cinco** at about five o'clock; **en ~** thereupon, at that point; **~ es** that's it; **¡~ sí que es vida!** now that is really living!; **por ~ te lo dije** that's why I told you; **y ~ que llovía** in spite of the fact it was raining

esos *adj demos* V **ese**

ésos *pron* V **ése**

espabilar *etc* [espaβi'lar] = **despabilar** *etc*

espacial [espa'θjal] *adj* (*del espacio*) space *cpd*

espaciar [espa'θjar] *vt* to space (out)

espacio [es'paθjo] *nm* space; (*Mús*) interval; (*Radio, TV*) programme (*BRIT*), program (US); **el ~** space; **espacio aéreo/exterior** air/outer space; **espacioso, -a** adj spacious, roomy

espada [es'paða] nf sword; **espadas** nfpl (Naipes) spades

espaguetis [espa'ɣetis] nmpl spaghetti sg

espalda [es'palda] nf (gen) back; **espaldas** nfpl (hombros) shoulders; **a ~s de algn** behind sb's back; **estar de ~s** to have one's back turned; **tenderse de ~s** to lie (down) on one's back; **volver la ~ a algn** to cold-shoulder sb

espantajo [espan'taxo] nm = **espantapájaros**

espantapájaros [espanta'paxaros] nm inv scarecrow

espantar [espan'tar] vt (asustar) to frighten, scare; (ahuyentar) to frighten off; (asombrar) to horrify, appal; **espantarse** vr to get frightened o scared; to be appalled

espanto [es'panto] nm (susto) fright; (terror) terror; (asombro) astonishment; **espantoso, -a** adj frightening, terrifying; astonishing

España [es'paɲa] nf Spain; **español, a** adj Spanish ⊳ nm/f Spaniard ⊳ nm (Ling) Spanish

esparadrapo [espara'ðrapo] nm (sticking) plaster (BRIT), adhesive tape (US)

esparcir [espar'θir] vt to spread; (diseminar) to scatter; **esparcirse** vr to spread (out), to scatter; (divertirse) to enjoy o.s.

espárrago [es'parraxo] nm asparagus

esparto [es'parto] nm esparto (grass)

espasmo [es'pasmo] nm spasm

espátula [es'patula] nf spatula

especia [es'peθja] nf spice

especial [espe'θjal] adj special; **especialidad** nf speciality (BRIT), specialty (US)

especie [es'peθje] nf (Bio) species; (clase) kind, sort; **en ~** in kind

especificar [espeθifi'kar] vt to specify; **específico, -a** adj specific

espécimen [es'peθimen] (pl **especímenes**) nm specimen

espectáculo [espek'takulo] nm (gen) spectacle; (Teatro etc) show

espectador, a [espekta'ðor, a] nm/f spectator

especular [espeku'lar] vt, vi to speculate

espejismo [espe'xismo] nm mirage

espejo [es'pexo] nm mirror; **(espejo) retrovisor** rear-view mirror

espeluznante [espeluθ'nante] adj horrifying, hair-raising

espera [es'pera] nf (pausa, intervalo) wait; (Jur: plazo) respite; **en ~ de** waiting for; (con expectativa) expecting

esperanza [espe'ranθa] nf (confianza) hope; (expectativa) expectation; **hay pocas ~s de que venga** there is little prospect of his coming; **esperanza de vida** life expectancy

esperar [espe'rar] vt (aguardar) to wait for; (tener expectativa de) to expect; (desear) to hope for ⊳ vi to wait; to expect; to hope; **hacer ~ a algn** to keep sb waiting; **~ un bebé** to be expecting (a baby)

esperma [es'perma] nf sperm

espeso, -a [es'peso, a] adj thick; **espesor** nm thickness

espía [es'pia] nmf spy; **espiar** vt (observar) to spy on

espiga [es'piɣa] nf (Bot: de trigo etc) ear

espigón [espi'ɣon] nm (Bot) ear; (Náut) breakwater

espina [es'pina] nf thorn; (de pez) bone; **espina dorsal** (Anat) spine

espinaca [espi'naka] nf spinach

espinazo [espi'naθo] nm spine, backbone

espinilla [espi'niʎa] nf (Anat: tibia) shin(bone); (grano) blackhead

espinoso, -a [espi'noso, a] adj (planta) thorny, prickly; (asunto) difficult

espionaje [espjo'naxe] *nm* spying,
espionage

espiral [espi'ral] *adj*, *nf* spiral

espirar [espi'rar] *vt* to breathe out,
exhale

espiritista [espiri'tista] *adj*, *nmf*
spiritualist

espíritu [es'piritu] *nm* spirit;
Espíritu Santo Holy Ghost *o* Spirit;
espiritual *adj* spiritual

espléndido, -a [es'plendiðo, a] *adj*
(*magnífico*) magnificent, splendid;
(*generoso*) generous

esplendor [esplen'dor] *nm*
splendour

espolvorear [espolβore'ar] *vt* to
dust, sprinkle

esponja [es'ponxa] *nf* sponge; (*fig*)
sponger; **esponjoso, -a** *adj* spongy

espontaneidad [espontanei'ðað]
nf spontaneity; **espontáneo, -a** *adj*
spontaneous

esposa [es'posa] *nf* wife; **esposas**
nfpl handcuffs; **esposar** *vt* to
handcuff

esposo [es'poso] *nm* husband

espray [es'prai] *nm* spray

espuela [es'pwela] *nf* spur

espuma [es'puma] *nf* foam; (*de
cerveza*) froth, head; (*de jabón*) lather;
espuma de afeitar shaving foam;
espumadera *nf* (*utensilio*) skimmer;
espumoso, -a *adj* frothy, foamy; (*vino*)
sparkling

esqueleto [eske'leto] *nm* skeleton

esquema [es'kema] *nm* (*diagrama*)
diagram; (*dibujo*) plan; (*Filosofía*)
schema

esquí [es'ki] (*pl* **~s**) *nm* (*objeto*) ski;
(*Deporte*) skiing; **esquí acuático** water-
skiing; **esquiar** *vi* to ski

esquilar [eski'lar] *vt* to shear

esquimal [eski'mal] *adj*, *nmf* Eskimo

esquina [es'kina] *nf* corner;
esquinazo [eski'naθo] *nm*: **dar
esquinazo a algn** to give sb the slip

esquirol [eski'rol] (*ESP*) *nm*
strikebreaker, scab

esquivar [eski'βar] *vt* to avoid

esta ['esta] *adj demos* V **este²**

está *vb* V **estar**

ésta *pron* V **éste**

estabilidad [estaβili'ðað] *nf*
stability; **estable** *adj* stable

establecer [estaβle'θer] *vt* to
establish; **establecerse** *vr* to
establish o.s.; (*echar raíces*) to settle
(down); **establecimiento** *nm*
establishment

establo [es'taβlo] *nm* (*Agr*) stable

estaca [es'taka] *nf* stake, post; (*de
tienda de campaña*) peg

estacada [esta'kaða] *nf* (*cerca*) fence,
fencing; (*palenque*) stockade

estación [esta'θjon] *nf* station;
(*del año*) season; **estación balnearia**
seaside resort; **estación de autobuses**
bus station; **estación de servicio**
service station

estacionamiento
[estaθjona'mjento] *nm* (*Auto*)
parking; (*Mil*) stationing

estacionar [estaθjo'nar] *vt* (*Auto*) to
park; (*Mil*) to station

estadía [esta'ðia] (*LAM*) *nf* stay

estadio [es'taðjo] *nm* (*fase*) stage,
phase; (*Deporte*) stadium

estadista [esta'ðista] *nm* (*Pol*)
statesman; (*Mat*) statistician

estadística [esta'ðistika] *nf* figure,
statistic; (*ciencia*) statistics *sg*

estado [es'taðo] *nm* (*Pol: condición*)
state; **estar en ~** to be pregnant;
estado civil marital status; **estado
de ánimo** state of mind; **estado de
cuenta** bank statement; **estado de
sitio** state of siege; **estado mayor**
staff; **Estados Unidos** United States
(of America)

estadounidense [estaðouni'ðense]
adj United States *cpd*, American ▷ *nmf*
American

estafa [es'tafa] *nf* swindle, trick;
estafar *vt* to swindle, defraud

estáis *vb* V **estar**

estallar [esta'ʎar] *vi* to burst; (*bomba*)

to explode, go off; (*epidemia, guerra, rebelión*) to break out; **~ en llanto** to burst into tears; **estallido** *nm* explosion; (*fig*) outbreak

estampa [es'tampa] *nf* print, engraving; **estampado, -a** [estam'paðo, a] *adj* printed ▷ *nm* (*impresión: acción*) printing; (: *efecto*) print; (*marca*) stamping

estampar [estam'par] *vt* (*imprimir*) to print; (*marcar*) to stamp; (*metal*) to engrave; (*poner sello en*) to stamp; (*fig*) to stamp, imprint

estampida [estam'piða] *nf* stampede

estampido [estam'piðo] *nm* bang, report

estampilla [estam'piʎa] (*LAM*) *nf* (postage) stamp

están *vb* V **estar**

estancado, -a [estan'kaðo, a] *adj* stagnant

estancar [estan'kar] *vt* (*aguas*) to hold up, hold back; (*Com*) to monopolize; (*fig*) to block, hold up; **estancarse** *vr* to stagnate

estancia [es'tanθja] *nf* (*ESP, MÉX: permanencia*) stay; (*sala*) room; (*RPL: de ganado*) farm, ranch; **estanciero** (*RPL*) *nm* farmer, rancher

estanco, -a [es'tanko, a] *adj* watertight ▷ *nm* tobacconist's (shop), cigar store (*US*)

⬤ **ESTANCO**

⬤
⬤ Cigarettes, tobacco, postage
⬤ stamps and official forms are all
⬤ sold under state monopoly in
⬤ shops called **estancos**. Although
⬤ tobacco products can also be
⬤ bought in bars and quioscos they
⬤ are generally more expensive.

estándar [es'tandar] *adj, nm* standard

estandarte [estan'darte] *nm* banner, standard

estanque [es'tanke] *nm* (*lago*) pool, pond; (*Agr*) reservoir

estanquero, -a [estan'kero, a] *nm/f* tobacconist

estante [es'tante] *nm* (*armario*) rack, stand; (*biblioteca*) bookcase; (*anaquel*) shelf; **estantería** *nf* shelving, shelves *pl*

○ **PALABRA CLAVE**

estar [es'tar] *vi* **1** (*posición*) to be; **está en la plaza** it's in the square; **¿está Juan?** is Juan in?; **estamos a 30 km de Junín** we're 30 kms from Junín

2 (*+ adj: estado*) to be; **estar enfermo** to be ill; **está muy elegante** he's looking very smart; **¿cómo estás?** how are you keeping?

3 (*+ gerundio*) to be; **estoy leyendo** I'm reading

4 (*uso pasivo*): **está condenado a muerte** he's been condemned to death; **está envasado en ...** it's packed in ...

5 (*con fechas*): **¿a cuántos estamos?** what's the date today?; **estamos a 5 de mayo** it's the 5th of May

6 (*locuciones*): **¿estamos?** (*¿de acuerdo?*) okay?; (*¿listo?*) ready?

7: **estar de: estar de vacaciones/ viaje** to be on holiday/away o on a trip; **está de camarero** he's working as a waiter

8: **estar para: está para salir** he's about to leave; **no estoy para bromas** I'm not in the mood for jokes

9: **estar por** (*propuesta etc*) to be in favour of; (*persona etc*) to support, side with; **está por limpiar** it still has to be cleaned

10: **estar sin: estar sin dinero** to have no money; **está sin terminar** it isn't finished yet

estarse *vr*: **se estuvo en la cama toda la tarde** he stayed in bed all afternoon

estas ['estas] adj demos V **este²**

éstas pron V **éste**

estatal [esta'tal] adj state cpd

estático, -a [es'tatiko, a] adj static

estatua [es'tatwa] nf statue

estatura [esta'tura] nf stature, height

este¹ ['este] nm east

este² ['este] (f **esta**, pl **estos, estas**) adj demos (sg) this; (pl) these

esté etc vb V **estar**

éste ['este] (f **ésta**, pl **éstos, éstas**) pron (sg) this (one); (pl) these (ones); **ése ... ~ ...** the former ... the latter ...

estén etc vb V **estar**

estepa [es'tepa] nf (Geo) steppe

estera [es'tera] nf mat(ting)

estéreo [es'tereo] adj inv, nm stereo; **estereotipo** nm stereotype

estéril [es'teril] adj sterile, barren; (fig) vain, futile; **esterilizar** vt to sterilize

esterlina [ester'lina] adj: **libra ~** pound sterling

estés etc vb V **estar**

estética [es'tetika] nf aesthetics sg

estético, -a [es'tetiko, a] adj aesthetic

estiércol [es'tjerkol] nm dung, manure

estigma [es'tiɣma] nm stigma

estilo [es'tilo] nm style; (Tec) stylus; (Natación) stroke; **algo por el ~** something along those lines

estima [es'tima] nf esteem, respect; **estimación** [estima'θjon] nf (evaluación) estimation; (aprecio, afecto) esteem, regard; **estimado, a** adj esteemed; **E~ señor** Dear Sir

estimar [esti'mar] vt (evaluar) to estimate; (valorar) to value; (apreciar) to esteem, respect; (pensar, considerar) to think, reckon

estimulante [estimu'lante] adj stimulating ▷ nm stimulant

estimular [estimu'lar] vt to stimulate; (excitar) to excite

estímulo [es'timulo] nm stimulus; (ánimo) encouragement

estirar [esti'rar] vt to stretch; (dinero, suma etc) to stretch out; **estirarse** vr to stretch

estirón [esti'ron] nm pull, tug; (crecimiento) spurt, sudden growth; **dar o pegar un ~** (fam: niño) to shoot up (inf)

estirpe [es'tirpe] nf stock, lineage

estival [esti'βal] adj summer cpd

esto ['esto] pron this, this thing o matter; **~ de la boda** this business about the wedding

Estocolmo [esto'kolmo] nm Stockholm

estofado [esto'faðo] nm stew

estómago [es'tomaxo] nm stomach; **tener ~** to be thick-skinned

estorbar [estor'βar] vt to hinder, obstruct; (molestar) to bother, disturb ▷ vi to be in the way; **estorbo** nm (molestia) bother, nuisance; (obstáculo) hindrance, obstacle

estornudar [estornu'ðar] vi to sneeze

estos ['estos] adj demos V **este²**

éstos pron V **éste**

estoy vb V **estar**

estrado [es'traðo] nm platform

estrafalario, -a [estrafa'larjo, a] adj odd, eccentric

estrago [es'traxo] nm ruin, destruction; **hacer ~s en** to wreak havoc among

estragón [estra'xon] nm tarragon

estrambótico, -a [estram'botiko, a] adj (persona) eccentric; (peinado, ropa) outlandish

estrangular [estrangu'lar] vt (persona) to strangle; (Med) to strangulate

estratagema [estrata'xema] nf (Mil) stratagem; (astucia) cunning

estrategia [estra'texja] nf strategy; **estratégico, -a** adj strategic

estrato [es'trato] nm stratum, layer

estrechar [estre'tʃar] vt (reducir) to narrow; (Costura) to take in; (abrazar) to hug, embrace; **estrecharse** vr (reducirse) to narrow, grow narrow;

(*abrazarse*) to embrace; **~ la mano** to shake hands

estrechez [estre'tʃeθ] *nf* narrowness; (*de ropa*) tightness; **estrecheces** *nfpl* (*dificultades económicas*) financial difficulties

estrecho, -a [es'tretʃo, a] *adj* narrow; (*apretado*) tight; (*íntimo*) close, intimate; (*miserable*) mean ▷ *nm* strait; **~ de miras** narrow-minded

estrella [es'treʎa] *nf* star; **estrella de mar** (*Zool*) starfish; **estrella fugaz** shooting star

estrellar [estre'ʎar] *vt* (*hacer añicos*) to smash (to pieces); (*huevos*) to fry; **estrellarse** *vr* to smash; (*chocarse*) to crash; (*fracasar*) to fail

estremecer [estreme'θer] *vt* to shake; **estremecerse** *vr* to shake, tremble

estrenar [estre'nar] *vt* (*vestido*) to wear for the first time; (*casa*) to move into; (*película, obra de teatro*) to première; **estrenarse** *vr* (*persona*) to make one's début; **estreno** *nm* (*Cine etc*) première

estreñido, -a [estre'ɲiðo, a] *adj* constipated

estreñimiento [estreɲi'mjento] *nm* constipation

estrepitoso, -a [estrepi'toso, a] *adj* noisy; (*fiesta*) rowdy

estrés [es'tres] *nm* stress

estría [es'tria] *nf* groove

estribar [estri'βar] *vi*: **~ en** to lie on

estribillo [estri'βiʎo] *nm* (*Literatura*) refrain; (*Mús*) chorus

estribo [es'triβo] *nm* (*de jinete*) stirrup; (*de coche, tren*) step; (*de puente*) support; (*Geo*) spur; **perder los ~s** to fly off the handle

estribor [estri'βor] *nm* (*Náut*) starboard

estricto, -a [es'trikto, a] *adj* (*riguroso*) strict; (*severo*) severe

estridente [estri'ðente] *adj* (*color*) loud; (*voz*) raucous

estropajo [estro'paxo] *nm* scourer

estropear [estrope'ar] *vt* to spoil; (*dañar*) to damage; **estropearse** *vr* (*objeto*) to get damaged; (*persona, piel*) to be ruined

estructura [estruk'tura] *nf* structure

estrujar [estru'xar] *vt* (*apretar*) to squeeze; (*aplastar*) to crush; (*fig*) to drain, bleed

estuario [es'twarjo] *nm* estuary

estuche [es'tutʃe] *nm* box, case

estudiante [estu'ðjante] *nmf* student; **estudiantil** *adj* student *cpd*

estudiar [estu'ðjar] *vt* to study

estudio [es'tuðjo] *nm* study; (*Cine, Arte, Radio*) studio; **estudios** *nmpl* studies; (*erudición*) learning *sg*; **estudioso, -a** *adj* studious

estufa [es'tufa] *nf* heater, fire

estupefaciente [estupefa'θjente] *nm* drug, narcotic

estupefacto, -a [estupe'fakto, a] *adj* speechless, thunderstruck

estupendo, -a [estu'pendo, a] *adj* wonderful, terrific; (*fam*) great; **¡~!** that's great!, fantastic!

estupidez [estupi'ðeθ] *nf* (*torpeza*) stupidity; (*acto*) stupid thing (to do)

estúpido, -a [es'tupiðo, a] *adj* stupid, silly

estuve *etc vb* V **estar**

ETA ['eta] (*ESP*) *nf abr* (= *Euskadi ta Askatasuna*) ETA

etapa [e'tapa] *nf* (*de viaje*) stage; (*Deporte*) leg; (*parada*) stopping place; (*fase*) stage, phase

etarra [e'tarra] *nmf* member of ETA

etc. *abr* (= *etcétera*) etc

etcétera [et'θetera] *adv* etcetera

eternidad [eterni'ðað] *nf* eternity; **eterno, -a** *adj* eternal, everlasting

ética ['etika] *nf* ethics *pl*

ético, -a ['etiko, a] *adj* ethical

etiqueta [eti'keta] *nf* (*modales*) etiquette; (*rótulo*) label, tag

Eucaristía [eukaris'tia] *nf* Eucharist

euforia [eu'forja] *nf* euphoria

euro ['euro] *nm* (*moneda*) euro

eurodiputado, -a [eurodipu'taðo, a] nm/f Euro MP, MEP

Europa [eu'ropa] nf Europe; **europeo, -a** adj, nm/f European

Euskadi [eus'kaði] nm the Basque Country o Provinces pl

euskera [eus'kera] nm (Ling) Basque

evacuación [eβakwa'θjon] nf evacuation

evacuar [eβa'kwar] vt to evacuate

evadir [eβa'ðir] vt to evade, avoid; **evadirse** vr to escape

evaluar [eβa'lwar] vt to evaluate

evangelio [eβan'xeljo] nm gospel

evaporar [eβapo'rar] vt to evaporate; **evaporarse** vr to vanish

evasión [eβa'sjon] nf escape, flight; (fig) evasion; **evasión de capitales** flight of capital

evasiva [eβa'siβa] nf (pretexto) excuse

evento [e'βento] nm event

eventual [eβen'twal] adj possible, conditional (upon circumstances); (trabajador) casual, temporary

▌No confundir **eventual** con la palabra inglesa eventual.

evidencia [eβi'ðenθja] nf evidence, proof

evidente [eβi'ðente] adj obvious, clear, evident

evitar [eβi'tar] vt (evadir) to avoid; (impedir) to prevent; **~ hacer algo** to avoid doing sth

evocar [eβo'kar] vt to evoke, call forth

evolución [eβolu'θjon] nf (desarrollo) evolution, development; (cambio) change; (Mil) manoeuvre; **evolucionar** vi to evolve; to manoeuvre

ex [eks] adj ex-; **el ~ ministro** the former minister, the ex-minister

exactitud [eksakti'tuð] nf exactness; (precisión) accuracy; (puntualidad) punctuality; **exacto, -a** adj exact; accurate; punctual; **¡exacto!** exactly!

exageración [eksaxera'θjon] nf exaggeration

exagerar [eksaxe'rar] vt, vi to exaggerate

exaltar [eksal'tar] vt to exalt, glorify; **exaltarse** vr (excitarse) to get excited o worked up

examen [ek'samen] nm examination; **examen de conducir** driving test; **examen de ingreso** entrance examination

examinar [eksami'nar] vt to examine; **examinarse** vr to be examined, take an examination

excavadora [ekskaβa'ðora] nf excavator

excavar [ekska'βar] vt to excavate

excedencia [eksθe'ðenθja] nf: **estar en ~** to be on leave; **pedir o solicitar la ~** to ask for leave

excedente [eksθe'ðente] adj, nm excess, surplus

exceder [eksθe'ðer] vt to exceed, surpass; **excederse** vr (extralimitarse) to go too far

excelencia [eksθe'lenθja] nf excellence; **su E~** his Excellency; **excelente** adj excellent

excéntrico, -a [eks'θentriko, a] adj, nm/f eccentric

excepción [eksθep'θjon] nf exception; **a ~ de** with the exception of, except for; **excepcional** adj exceptional

excepto [eks'θepto] adv excepting, except (for)

exceptuar [eksθep'twar] vt to except, exclude

excesivo, -a [eksθe'siβo, a] adj excessive

exceso [eks'θeso] nm (gen) excess; (Com) surplus; **exceso de equipaje/peso** excess luggage/weight; **exceso de velocidad** speeding

excitado, -a [eksθi'taðo, a] adj excited; (emociones) aroused

excitar [eksθi'tar] vt to excite; (incitar) to urge; **excitarse** vr to get excited

exclamación [eksklama'θjon] nf

exclamation

exclamar [ekskla'mar] vi to exclaim

excluir [eksklu'ir] vt to exclude; (dejar fuera) to shut out; (descartar) to reject

exclusiva [eksklu'siβa] nf (Prensa) exclusive, scoop; (Com) sole right

exclusivo, -a [eksklu'siβo, a] adj exclusive; **derecho ~** sole o exclusive right

Excmo. abr = **excelentísmo**

excomulgar [ekskomul'ɣar] vt (Rel) to excommunicate

excomunión [ekskomu'njon] nf excommunication

excursión [ekskur'sjon] nf excursion, outing; **excursionista** nmf (turista) sightseer

excusa [eks'kusa] nf excuse; (disculpa) apology; **excusar** [eksku'sar] vt to excuse

exhaustivo, -a [eksaus'tiβo, a] adj (análisis) thorough; (estudio) exhaustive

exhausto, -a [ek'sausto, a] adj exhausted

exhibición [eksiβi'θjon] nf exhibition, display, show

exhibir [eksi'βir] vt to exhibit, display, show

exigencia [eksi'xenθja] nf demand, requirement; **exigente** adj demanding

exigir [eksi'xir] vt (gen) to demand, require; **~ el pago** to demand payment

exiliado, -a [eksi'ljaðo, a] adj exiled ▷ nm/f exile

exilio [ek'siljo] nm exile

eximir [eksi'mir] vt to exempt

existencia [eksis'tenθja] nf existence; **existencias** nfpl stock(s) pl

existir [eksis'tir] vi to exist, be

éxito ['eksito] nm (triunfo) success; (Mús etc) hit; **tener ~** to be successful

  No confundir **éxito** con la palabra inglesa exit.

exorbitante [eksorβi'tante] adj (precio) exorbitant; (cantidad) excessive

exótico, -a [ek'sotiko, a] adj exotic

expandir [ekspan'dir] vt to expand

expansión [ekspan'sjon] nf expansion

expansivo, -a [ekspan'siβo, a] adj: **onda expansiva** shock wave

expatriarse [ekspa'trjarse] vr to emigrate; (Pol) to go into exile

expectativa [ekspekta'tiβa] nf (espera) expectation; (perspectiva) prospect

expedición [ekspeði'θjon] nf (excursión) expedition

expediente [ekspe'ðjente] nm expedient; (Jur: procedimento) action, proceedings pl; (: papeles) dossier, file, record

expedir [ekspe'ðir] vt (despachar) to send, forward; (pasaporte) to issue

expensas [eks'pensas] nfpl: **a ~ de** at the expense of

experiencia [ekspe'rjenθja] nf experience

experimentado, -a [eksperimen'taðo, a] adj experienced

experimentar [eksperimen'tar] vt (en laboratorio) to experiment with; (probar) to test, try out; (notar, observar) to experience; (deterioro, pérdida) to suffer; **experimento** nm experiment

experto, -a [eks'perto, a] adj expert, skilled ▷ nm/f expert

expirar [ekspi'rar] vi to expire

explanada [eskpla'naða] nf (llano) plain

explayarse [ekspla'jarse] vr (en discurso) to speak at length; **~ con algn** to confide in sb

explicación [eksplika'θjon] nf explanation

explicar [ekspli'kar] vt to explain; **explicarse** vr to explain (o.s.)

explícito, -a [eks'pliθito, a] adj explicit

explique etc vb V **explicar**

explorador, a [eksplora'ðor, a] nm/f (pionero) explorer; (Mil) scout ▷ nm (Med) probe; (Tec) (radar) scanner

explorar [eksplo'rar] vt to explore; (Med) to probe; (radar) to scan

explosión [eksplo'sjon] *nf*
explosion; **explosivo, -a** *adj* explosive

explotación [eksplota'θjon] *nf*
exploitation; (*de planta etc*) running

explotar [eksplo'tar] *vt* to exploit to
run, operate ▷ *vi* to explode

exponer [ekspo'ner] *vt* to expose;
(*cuadro*) to display; (*vida*) to risk;
(*idea*) to explain; **exponerse** *vr:* **~se
a (hacer) algo** to run the risk of
(doing) sth

exportación [eksporta'θjon] *nf*
(*acción*) export; (*mercancías*) exports *pl*

exportar [ekspor'tar] *vt* to export

exposición [eksposi'θjon] *nf* (*gen*)
exposure; (*de arte*) show, exhibition;
(*explicación*) explanation; (*declaración*)
account, statement

expresamente [ekspresa'mente]
adv (*decir*) clearly; (*a propósito*) expressly

expresar [ekspre'sar] *vt* to express;
expresión *nf* expression

expresivo, -a [ekspre'siβo, a] *adj*
(*persona, gesto, palabras*) expressive;
(*cariñoso*) affectionate

expreso, -a [eks'preso, a] *pp de*
expresar ▷ *adj* (*explícito*) express;
(*claro*) specific, clear; (*tren*) fast
▷ *adv:* **enviar ~** to send by express
(delivery)

express [eks'pres] (*LAM*) *adv:* **enviar
algo ~** to send sth special delivery

exprimidor [eksprimi'ðor] *nm*
squeezer

exprimir [ekspri'mir] *vt* (*fruta*) to
squeeze; (*zumo*) to squeeze out

expuesto, -a [eks'pwesto, a] *pp de*
exponer ▷ *adj* exposed; (*cuadro etc*) on
show, on display

expulsar [ekspul'sar] *vt* (*echar*) to
eject, throw out; (*alumno*) to expel;
(*despedir*) to sack, fire; (*Deporte*) to
send off; **expulsión** *nf* expulsion;
sending-off

exquisito, -a [ekski'sito, a] *adj*
exquisite; (*comida*) delicious

éxtasis ['ekstasis] *nm* ecstasy

extender [eksten'der] *vt* to extend;

(*los brazos*) to stretch out, hold out;
(*mapa, tela*) to spread (out), open (out);
(*mantequilla*) to spread; (*certificado*)
to issue; (*cheque, recibo*) to make out;
(*documento*) to draw up; **extenderse**
vr (*gen*) to extend; (*persona: en el suelo*)
to stretch out; (*epidemia*) to spread;
extendido, -a *adj* (*abierto*) spread out,
open; (*brazos*) outstretched; (*costumbre*)
widespread

extensión [eksten'sjon] *nf* (*de
terreno, mar*) expanse, stretch;
(*de tiempo*) length, duration; (*Tel*)
extension; **en toda la ~ de la palabra**
in every sense of the word

extenso, -a [eks'tenso, a] *adj*
extensive

exterior [ekste'rjor] *adj* (*de fuera*)
external; (*afuera*) outside, exterior;
(*apariencia*) outward; (*deuda, relaciones*)
foreign ▷ *nm* (*gen*) exterior, outside;
(*aspecto*) outward appearance;
(*Deporte*) wing(er); (*países extranjeros*)
abroad; **en el ~** abroad; **al ~** outwardly,
on the surface

exterminar [ekstermi'nar] *vt* to
exterminate

externo, -a [eks'terno, a] *adj*
(*exterior*) external, outside; (*superficial*)
outward ▷ *nm/f* day pupil

extinguir [ekstin'gir] *vt* (*fuego*) to
extinguish, put out; (*raza, población*) to
wipe out; **extinguirse** *vr* (*fuego*) to go
out; (*Bio*) to die out, become extinct

extintor [ekstin'tor] *nm* (fire)
extinguisher

extirpar [ekstir'par] *vt* (*Med*) to
remove (surgically)

extra ['ekstra] *adj inv* (*tiempo*) extra;
(*chocolate, vino*) good-quality ▷ *nmf*
extra ▷ *nm* extra; (*bono*) bonus

extracción [ekstrak'θjon] *nf*
extraction; (*en lotería*) draw

extracto [eks'trakto] *nm* extract

extradición [ekstraði'θjon] *nf*
extradition

extraer [ekstra'er] *vt* to extract,
take out

extraescolar [ekstraesko'lar]
adj: **actividad ~** extracurricular activity

extranjero, -a [ekstran'xero, a] adj
foreign ▷ nm/f foreigner ▷ nm foreign
countries pl: **en el ~** abroad

No confundir **extranjero** con la
palabra inglesa *stranger*.

extrañar [ekstra'ɲar] vt (sorprender)
to find strange o odd; (echar de menos) to
miss; **extrañarse** vr (sorprenderse) to
be amazed, be surprised; **me extraña**
I'm surprised

extraño, -a [eks'traɲo, a] adj
(extranjero) foreign; (raro, sorprendente)
strange, odd

extraordinario, -a
[ekstraordi'narjo, a] adj
extraordinary; (edición, número) special
▷ nm (de periódico) special edition;
horas extraordinarias overtime sg

extrarradio [ekstra'rradjo] nm
suburbs

extravagante [ekstraβa'ɣante]
adj (excéntrico) eccentric; (estrafalario)
outlandish

extraviado, -a [ekstra'βjaðo, a] adj
lost, missing

extraviar [ekstra'βjar] vt
(persona: desorientar) to mislead,
misdirect; (perder) to lose, misplace;
extraviarse vr to lose one's way,
get lost

extremar [ekstre'mar] vt to carry
to extremes

extremaunción [ekstremaun'θjon]
nf extreme unction

extremidad [ekstremi'ðað] nf
(punta) extremity; **extremidades** nfpl
(Anat) extremities

extremo, -a [eks'tremo, a] adj
extreme; (último) last ▷ nm end; (límite,
grado sumo) extreme; **en último ~** as
a last resort

extrovertido, -a [ekstroβer'tiðo, a]
adj, nm/f extrovert

exuberante [eksuβe'rante] adj
exuberant; (fig) luxuriant, lush

eyacular [ejaku'lar] vt, vi to
ejaculate
o lose one's way, get lost

extremar [ekstre'mar] vt to carry
to extremes

extremaunción [ekstremaun'θjon]
nf extreme unction

extremidad [ekstremi'ðað] nf
(punta) extremity; **extremidades** nfpl
(Anat) extremities

extremo, -a [eks'tremo, a] adj
extreme; (último) last ▷ nm end; (límite,
grado sumo) extreme; **en último ~** as
a last resort

extrovertido, -a [ekstroβer'tiðo, a]
adj, nm/f extrovert

exuberante [eksuβe'rante] adj
exuberant; (fig) luxuriant, lush

eyacular [ejaku'lar] vt, vi to
ejaculate

e

f

fa [fa] *nm* (*Mús*) fa, F
fabada [fa'βaða] *nf* bean and sausage stew
fábrica ['faβrika] *nf* factory; **marca de ~** trademark; **precio de ~** factory price

> No confundir **fábrica** con la palabra inglesa *fabric*.

fabricación [faβrika'θjon] *nf* (*manufactura*) manufacture; (*producción*) production; **de ~ casera** home-made; **fabricación en serie** mass manufacture
fabricante [faβri'kante] *nmf* manufacturer
fabricar [faβri'kar] *vt* (*manufacturar*) to manufacture, make; (*construir*) to build; (*cuento*) to fabricate, devise
fábula ['faβula] *nf* (*cuento*) fable; (*chisme*) rumour; (*mentira*) fib
fabuloso, -a [faβu'loso, a] *adj* (*oportunidad, tiempo*) fabulous, great
facción [fak'θjon] *nf* (*Pol*) faction; **facciones** *nfpl* (*de rostro*) features
faceta [fa'θeta] *nf* facet

facha ['fatʃa] (*fam*) *nf* (*aspecto*) look; (*cara*) face
fachada [fa'tʃaða] *nf* (*Arq*) façade, front
fácil ['faθil] *adj* (*simple*) easy; (*probable*) likely
facilidad [faθili'ðað] *nf* (*capacidad*) ease; (*sencillez*) simplicity; (*de palabra*) fluency; **facilidades** *nfpl* facilities; **facilidades de pago** credit facilities
facilitar [faθili'tar] *vt* (*hacer fácil*) to make easy; (*proporcionar*) to provide
factor [fak'tor] *nm* factor
factura [fak'tura] *nf* (*cuenta*) bill; **facturación** *nf* (*de equipaje*) check-in; **facturar** *vt* (*Com*) to invoice, charge for; (*equipaje*) to check in
facultad [fakul'tað] *nf* (*aptitud, Escol etc*) faculty; (*poder*) power
faena [fa'ena] *nf* (*trabajo*) work; (*quehacer*) task, job
faisán [fai'san] *nm* pheasant
faja ['faxa] *nf* (*para la cintura*) sash; (*de mujer*) corset; (*de tierra*) strip
fajo ['faxo] *nm* (*de papeles*) bundle; (*de billetes*) wad
falda ['falda] *nf* (*prenda de vestir*) skirt; **falda pantalón** culottes *pl*, split skirt
falla ['faʎa] *nf* (*defecto*) fault, flaw; **falla humana** (*LAM*) human error
fallar [fa'ʎar] *vt* (*Jur*) to pronounce sentence on ▷ *vi* (*memoria*) to fail; (*motor*) to miss
Fallas ['faʎas] *nfpl* *Valencian celebration of the feast of St Joseph*

● **FALLAS**
●
●
● In the week of 19 March (the feast
● of San José), Valencia honours its
● patron saint with a spectacular
● fiesta called **Las Fallas**. The **Fallas**
● are huge papier-mâché, cardboard
● and wooden sculptures which
● are built by competing teams
● throughout the year. They depict
● politicians and well-known public
● figures and are thrown onto

● bonfires and set alight once a jury
● has judged them – only the best
● sculpture escapes the flames.

fallecer [faʎe'θer] vi to pass away, die; **fallecimiento** nm decease, demise

fallido, -a [fa'ʎiðo, a] adj (gen) frustrated, unsuccessful

fallo ['faʎo] nm (Jur) verdict, ruling; (fracaso) failure; **fallo cardíaco** heart failure; **fallo humano** (ESP) human error

falsificar [falsifi'kar] vt (firma etc) to forge; (moneda) to counterfeit

falso, -a ['falso, a] adj false; (documento, moneda etc) fake; **en ~** falsely

falta ['falta] nf (defecto) fault, flaw; (privación) lack, want; (ausencia) absence; (carencia) shortage; (equivocación) mistake; (Deporte) foul; **echar en ~** to miss; **hacer ~ hacer algo** to be necessary to do sth; **me hace ~ una pluma** I need a pen; **falta de educación** bad manners pl; **falta de ortografía** spelling mistake

faltar [fal'tar] vi (escasear) to be lacking, be wanting; (ausentarse) to be absent, be missing; **faltan 2 horas para llegar** there are 2 hours to go till arrival; **~ al respeto a algn** to be disrespectful to sb; **¡no faltaba más!** (no hay de qué) don't mention it

fama ['fama] nf (renombre) fame; (reputación) reputation

familia [fa'milja] nf family; **familia numerosa** large family; **familia política** in-laws pl

familiar [fami'ljar] adj (relativo a la familia) family cpd; (conocido, informal) familiar ▷ nm relative, relation

famoso, -a [fa'moso, a] adj (renombrado) famous

fan [fan] (pl ~s) nmf fan

fanático, -a [fa'natiko, a] adj fanatical ▷ nm/f fanatic; (Cine, Deporte) fan

fanfarrón, -ona [fanfa'rron, ona] adj boastful

fango ['fango] nm mud

fantasía [fanta'sia] nf fantasy, imagination; **joyas de ~** imitation jewellery sg

fantasma [fan'tasma] nm (espectro) ghost, apparition; (fanfarrón) show-off

fantástico, -a [fan'tastiko, a] adj fantastic

farmacéutico, -a [farma'θeutiko, a] adj pharmaceutical ▷ nm/f chemist (BRIT), pharmacist

farmacia [far'maθja] nf chemist's (shop) (BRIT), pharmacy; **farmacia de guardia** all-night chemist

fármaco ['farmako] nm drug

faro ['faro] nm (Náut: torre) lighthouse; (Auto) headlamp; **faros antiniebla** fog lamps; **faros delanteros/traseros** headlights/rear lights

farol [fa'rol] nm lantern, lamp

farola [fa'rola] nf street lamp (BRIT) o light (US)

farra ['farra] (LAM: fam) nf party; **ir de ~** to go on a binge

farsa ['farsa] nf (gen) farce

farsante [far'sante] nmf fraud, fake

fascículo [fas'θikulo] nm (de revista) part, instalment

fascinar [fasθi'nar] vt (gen) to fascinate

fascismo [fas'θismo] nm fascism; **fascista** adj, nmf fascist

fase ['fase] nf phase

fashion ['faʃon] adj (fam) trendy

fastidiar [fasti'ðjar] vt (molestar) to annoy, bother; (estropear) to spoil; **fastidiarse** vr: **¡que se fastidie!** (fam) he'll just have to put up with it!

fastidio [fas'tiðjo] nm (molestia) annoyance; **fastidioso, -a** adj (molesto) annoying

fatal [fa'tal] adj (gen) fatal; (desgraciado) ill-fated; (fam: malo, pésimo) awful; **fatalidad** nf (destino) fate; (mala suerte) misfortune

fatiga [fa'tixa] *nf* (*cansancio*) fatigue, weariness

fatigar [fati'xar] *vt* to tire, weary

fatigoso, -a [fati'xoso, a] *adj* (*cansador*) tiring

fauna ['fauna] *nf* fauna

favor [fa'βor] *nm* favour; **estar a ~ de** to be in favour of; **haga el ~ de ...** would you be so good as to ..., kindly ...; **por ~** please; **favorable** *adj* favourable

favorecer [faβore'θer] *vt* to favour; (*vestido etc*) to become, flatter; **este peinado le favorece** this hairstyle suits him

favorito, -a [faβo'rito, a] *adj, nm/f* favourite

fax [faks] *nm inv* fax; **mandar por ~ to fax**

fe [fe] *nf* (*Rel*) faith; (*documento*) certificate; **actuar con buena/mala ~** to act in good/bad faith

febrero [fe'βrero] *nm* February

fecha ['fetʃa] *nf* date; **con ~ adelantada** postdated; **en ~ próxima** soon; **hasta la ~** to date, so far; **poner ~** to date; **fecha de caducidad** (*de producto alimenticio*) sell-by date; (*de contrato etc*) expiry date; **fecha de nacimiento** date of birth; **fecha límite** *o* **tope** deadline

fecundo, -a [fe'kundo, a] *adj* (*fértil*) fertile; (*fig*) prolific; (*productivo*) productive

federación [feðera'θjon] *nf* federation

felicidad [feliθi'ðað] *nf* happiness; **¡~es!** (*deseos*) best wishes, congratulations!; (*en cumpleaños*) happy birthday!

felicitación [feliθita'θjon] *nf* (*tarjeta*) greeting(s) card

felicitar [feliθi'tar] *vt* to congratulate

feliz [fe'liθ] *adj* happy

felpudo [fel'puðo] *nm* doormat

femenino, -a [feme'nino, a] *adj, nm* feminine

feminista [femi'nista] *adj, nmf* feminist

fenómeno [fe'nomeno] *nm* phenomenon; (*fig*) freak, accident ▷ *adj* great ▷ *excl* great!, marvellous!; **fenomenal** *adj* = **fenómeno**

feo, -a ['feo, a] *adj* (*gen*) ugly; (*desagradable*) bad, nasty

féretro ['feretro] *nm* (*ataúd*) coffin; (*sarcófago*) bier

feria ['ferja] *nf* (*gen*) fair; (*descanso*) holiday, rest day; (*MÉX: cambio*) small *o* loose change; (*CS: mercado*) village market

feriado [fe'rjaðo] (*LAM*) *nm* holiday

fermentar [fermen'tar] *vi* to ferment

feroz [fe'roθ] *adj* (*cruel*) cruel; (*salvaje*) fierce

férreo, -a ['ferreo, a] *adj* iron

ferretería [ferrete'ria] *nf* (*tienda*) ironmonger's (shop) (*BRIT*), hardware store (*US*); **ferretero** [ferre'tero] *nm* ironmonger

ferrocarril [ferroka'rril] *nm* railway

ferroviario, -a [ferro'βjarjo, a] *adj* rail *cpd*

ferry ['ferri] (*pl* **~s** *o* **ferries**) *nm* ferry

fértil ['fertil] *adj* (*productivo*) fertile; (*rico*) rich; **fertilidad** *nf* (*gen*) fertility; (*productividad*) fruitfulness

fervor [fer'βor] *nm* fervour

festejar [feste'xar] *vt* (*celebrar*) to celebrate

festejo [fes'texo] *nm* celebration; **festejos** *nmpl* (*fiestas*) festivals

festín [fes'tin] *nm* feast, banquet

festival [festi'βal] *nm* festival

festividad [festiβi'ðað] *nf* festivity

festivo, -a [fes'tiβo, a] *adj* (*de fiesta*) festive; (*Cine, Literatura*) humorous; **día ~** holiday

feto ['feto] *nm* foetus

fiable ['fjaβle] *adj* (*persona*) trustworthy; (*máquina*) reliable

fiambre ['fjambre] *nm* cold meat

fiambrera [fjam'brera] *nf* (*para almuerzo*) lunch box

fianza ['fjanθa] *nf* surety;

(Jur): **libertad bajo ~** release on bail

fiar [fi'ar] vt (salir garante de) to guarantee; (vender a crédito) to sell on credit ▷ vi to trust; **fiarse** vr to trust (in), rely on; **~ a** (secreto) to confide (to); **~se de algn** to rely on sb

fibra ['fiβra] nf fibre; **fibra óptica** optical fibre

ficción [fik'θjon] nf fiction

ficha ['fitʃa] nf (Tel) token; (en juegos) counter, marker; (tarjeta) (index) card; **fichaje** nm (Deporte) signing; **fichar** vt (archivar) to file, index; (Deporte) to sign; **estar fichado** to have a record; **fichero** nm box file; (Inform) file

ficticio, -a [fik'tiθjo, a] adj (imaginario) fictitious; (falso) fabricated

fidelidad [fiðeli'ðað] nf (lealtad) fidelity, loyalty; **alta ~** high fidelity, hi-fi

fideos [fi'ðeos] nmpl noodles

fiebre ['fjeβre] nf (Med) fever; (fig) fever, excitement; **tener ~** to have a temperature; **fiebre aftosa** foot-and-mouth disease

fiel [fjel] adj (leal) faithful, loyal; (fiable) reliable; (exacto) accurate, faithful ▷ nm: **los ~es** the faithful

fieltro ['fjeltro] nm felt

fiera ['fjera] nf (animal feroz) wild animal o beast; (fig) dragon; V tb **fiero**

fiero, -a ['fjero, a] adj (cruel) cruel; (feroz) fierce; (duro) harsh

fierro ['fjerro] (LAM) nm (hierro) iron

fiesta ['fjesta] nf party; (de pueblo) festival; (vacaciones: tb: **~s**) holiday sg; **fiesta mayor** annual festival; **fiesta patria** (LAM) independence day

● **FIESTAS**

● **Fiestas** can be official public holidays or holidays set by each autonomous region, many of which coincide with religious festivals. There are also many **fiestas** all over Spain for a local patron saint or the Virgin Mary.

● These often last several days and can include religious processions, carnival parades, bullfights and dancing.

figura [fi'ɣura] nf (gen) figure; (forma, imagen) shape, form; (Naipes) face card

figurar [fiɣu'rar] vt (representar) to represent; (fingir) to figure ▷ vi to figure; **figurarse** vr (imaginarse) to imagine; (suponer) to suppose

fijador [fixa'ðor] nm (Foto etc) fixative; (de pelo) gel

fijar [fi'xar] vt (gen) to fix; (estampilla) to affix, stick (on); **fijarse** vr: **~se en** to notice

fijo, -a ['fixo, a] adj (gen) fixed; (firme) firm; (permanente) permanent ▷ adv: **mirar ~** to stare

fila ['fila] nf row; (Mil) rank; **ponerse en ~** to line up, get into line; **fila india** single file

filatelia [fila'telja] nf philately, stamp collecting

filete [fi'lete] nm (de carne) fillet steak; (de pescado) fillet

filiación [filja'θjon] nf (Pol) affiliation

filial [fi'ljal] adj filial ▷ nf subsidiary

Filipinas [fili'pinas] nfpl: **las (Islas) ~** the Philippines; **filipino, -a** adj, nm/f Philippine

filmar [fil'mar] vt to film, shoot

filo ['filo] nm (gen) edge; **sacar ~ a** to sharpen; **al ~ del mediodía** at about midday; **de doble ~** double-edged

filología [filolo'xia] nf philology; **filología inglesa** (Univ) English Studies

filón [fi'lon] nm (Minería) vein, lode; (fig) goldmine

filosofía [filoso'fia] nf philosophy; **filósofo, -a** nm/f philosopher

filtrar [fil'trar] vt, vi to filter, strain; **filtrarse** vr to filter; **filtro** nm (Tec, utensilio) filter

fin [fin] nm end; (objetivo) aim, purpose; **al ~ y al cabo** when all's said and done; **a ~ de** in order to; **por ~**

finally; **en ~** in short; **fin de semana** weekend

final [fi'nal] *adj* final ▷ *nm* end, conclusion ▷ *nf* final; **al ~** in the end; **a ~es de** at the end of; **finalidad** *nf* (*propósito*) purpose, intention; **finalista** *nmf* finalist; **finalizar** *vt* to end, finish; (*Inform*) to log out *o* off ▷ *vi* to end, come to an end

financiar [finan'θjar] *vt* to finance; **financiero, -a** *adj* financial ▷ *nm/f* financier

finca ['finka] *nf* (*casa de campo*) country house; (*ESP: bien inmueble*) property, land; (*LAM: granja*) farm

finde ['finde] *nm abr* (*fam: fin de semana*) weekend

fingir [fin'xir] *vt* (*simular*) to simulate, feign ▷ *vi* (*aparentar*) to pretend

finlandés, -esa [finlan'des, esa] *adj* Finnish ▷ *nm/f* Finn ▷ *nm* (*Ling*) Finnish

Finlandia [fin'landja] *nf* Finland

fino, -a ['fino, a] *adj* fine; (*delgado*) slender; (*de buenas maneras*) polite, refined; (*jerez*) fino, dry

firma ['firma] *nf* signature; (*Com*) firm, company

firmamento [firma'mento] *nm* firmament

firmar [fir'mar] *vt* to sign

firme ['firme] *adj* firm; (*estable*) stable; (*sólido*) solid; (*constante*) steady; (*decidido*) resolute ▷ *nm* road (surface); **firmeza** *nf* firmness; (*constancia*) steadiness; (*solidez*) solidity

fiscal [fis'kal] *adj* fiscal ▷ *nmf* public prosecutor; **año ~** tax *o* fiscal year

fisgonear [fisxone'ar] *vt* to poke one's nose into ▷ *vi* to pry, spy

física ['fisika] *nf* physics *sg*; V *tb* **físico**

físico, -a ['fisiko, a] *adj* physical ▷ *nm* physique ▷ *nm/f* physicist

fisura [fi'sura] *nf* crack; (*Med*) fracture

flác(c)ido, -a ['fla(k)θiðo, a] *adj* flabby

flaco, -a ['flako, a] *adj* (*muy delgado*) skinny, thin; (*débil*) weak, feeble

flagrante [fla'xrante] *adj* flagrant

flama ['flama] (*MÉX*) *nf* flame; **flamable** (*MÉX*) *adj* flammable

flamante [fla'mante] (*fam*) *adj* brilliant; (*nuevo*) brand-new

flamenco, -a [fla'menko, a] *adj* (*de Flandes*) Flemish; (*baile, música*) flamenco ▷ *nm* (*baile, música*) flamenco; (*Zool*) flamingo

flamingo [fla'mingo] (*MÉX*) *nm* flamingo

flan [flan] *nm* creme caramel

No confundir **flan** con la palabra inglesa *flan*.

flash [flaʃ] (*pl ~ o ~es*) *nm* (*Foto*) flash

flauta ['flauta] *nf* (*Mús*) flute

flecha ['fletʃa] *nf* arrow

flechazo [fle'tʃaθo] *nm* love at first sight

fleco ['fleko] *nm* fringe

flema ['flema] *nm* phlegm

flequillo [fle'kiʎo] *nm* (*pelo*) fringe

flexible [flek'siβle] *adj* flexible

flexión [flek'sjon] *nf* press-up

flexo ['flekso] *nm* adjustable table-lamp

flirtear [flirte'ar] *vi* to flirt

flojera [flo'xera] (*LAM: fam*) *nf*: **me da ~** I can't be bothered

flojo, -a ['floxo, a] *adj* (*gen*) loose; (*sin fuerzas*) limp; (*débil*) weak

flor [flor] *nf* flower; **a ~ de** on the surface of; **flora** *nf* flora; **florecer** *vi* (*Bot*) to flower, bloom; (*fig*) to flourish; **florería** (*LAM*) *nf* florist's (shop); **florero** *nm* vase; **floristería** *nf* florist's (shop)

flota ['flota] *nf* fleet

flotador [flota'ðor] *nm* (*gen*) float; (*para nadar*) rubber ring

flotar [flo'tar] *vi* (*gen*) to float; **flote** *nm*: **a flote** afloat; **salir a flote** (*fig*) to get back on one's feet

fluidez [flui'ðeθ] *nf* fluidity; (*fig*) fluency

fluido, -a ['fluiðo, a] *adj, nm* fluid

fluir [flu'ir] *vi* to flow

flujo ['fluxo] *nm* flow; **flujo y reflujo**

ebb and flow

flúor ['fluor] nm fluoride

fluorescente [flwores'θente] adj fluorescent ▷ nm fluorescent light

fluvial [fluβi'al] adj (navegación, cuenca) fluvial, river cpd

fobia ['fobja] nf phobia; **fobia a las alturas** fear of heights

foca ['foka] nf seal

foco ['foko] nm focus; (Elec) floodlight; (MÉX: bombilla) (light) bulb

fofo, -a ['fofo, a] adj soft, spongy; (carnes) flabby

fogata [fo'ɣata] nf bonfire

fogón [fo'ɣon] nm (de cocina) ring, burner

folio ['foljo] nm folio, page

follaje [fo'ʎaxe] nm foliage

folleto [fo'ʎeto] nm (Pol) pamphlet

follón [fo'ʎon] (ESP: fam) nm (lío) mess; (conmoción) fuss; **armar un ~** to kick up a row

fomentar [fomen'tar] vt (Med) to foment

fonda ['fonda] nf inn

fondo ['fondo] nm (de mar) bottom; (de coche, sala) back; (Arte etc) background; (reserva) fund; **fondos** nmpl funds, resources; **una investigación a ~** a thorough investigation; **en el ~** at bottom, deep down

fonobuzón [fonoβu'θon] nm voice mail

fontanería [fontane'ria] nf plumbing; **fontanero, -a** nm/f plumber

footing ['futin] nm jogging; **hacer ~** to jog, go jogging

forastero, -a [foras'tero, a] nm/f stranger

forcejear [forθexe'ar] vi (luchar) to struggle

forense [fo'rense] nmf pathologist

forma ['forma] nf (figura) form, shape; (Med) fitness; (método) way, means; **las ~s** the conventions; **estar en ~** to be fit; **de ~ que ...** so that ...; **de**

todas ~s in any case

formación [forma'θjon] nf (gen) formation; (educación) education; **formación profesional** vocational training

formal [for'mal] adj (gen) formal; (fig: serio) serious; (: de fiar) reliable; **formalidad** nf formality; seriousness; **formalizar** vt (situación) to put in order, regularize; **formalizarse** vr (situación) to be put in order, be regularized

formar [for'mar] vt (componer) to form, shape; (constituir) to make up, constitute; (Escol) to train, educate; **formarse** vr (Escol) to be trained, educated; (cobrar forma) to form, take form; (desarrollarse) to develop

formatear [formate'ar] vt to format

formato [for'mato] nm format

formidable [formi'ðaβle] adj (temible) formidable; (estupendo) tremendous

fórmula ['formula] nf formula

formulario [formu'larjo] nm form

fornido, -a [for'niðo, a] adj well-built

foro ['foro] nm (Pol, Inform etc) forum

forrar [fo'rrar] vt (abrigo) to line; (libro) to cover; **forro** nm (de cuaderno) cover; (Costura) lining; (de sillón) upholstery; **forro polar** fleece

fortalecer [fortale'θer] vt to strengthen

fortaleza [forta'leθa] nf (Mil) fortress, stronghold; (fuerza) strength; (determinación) resolution

fortuito, -a [for'twito, a] adj accidental

fortuna [for'tuna] nf (suerte) fortune, (good) luck; (riqueza) fortune, wealth

forzar [for'θar] vt (puerta) to force (open); (compeler) to compel

forzoso, -a [for'θoso, a] adj necessary

fosa ['fosa] nf (sepultura) grave; (en tierra) pit; **fosas nasales** nostrils

fósforo ['fosforo] nm (Quím)

phosphorus; (*cerilla*) match

fósil ['fosil] *nm* fossil

foso ['foso] *nm* ditch; (*Teatro*) pit; (*Auto*) inspection pit

foto ['foto] *nf* photo, snap(shot); **sacar una ~** to take a photo o picture; **foto (de) carné** passport(-size) photo

fotocopia [foto'kopja] *nf* photocopy; **fotocopiadora** *nf* photocopier; **fotocopiar** *vt* to photocopy

fotografía [fotoɣra'fia] *nf* (*Arte*) photography; (*una fotografía*) photograph; **fotografiar** *vt* to photograph

fotógrafo, -a [fo'toɣrafo, a] *nm/f* photographer

fotomatón [fotoma'ton] *nm* photo booth

FP (*ESP*) *nf abr* (= *Formación Profesional*) vocational courses for 14- to 18-year-olds

fracasar [fraka'sar] *vi* (*gen*) to fail

fracaso [fra'kaso] *nm* failure

fracción [frak'θjon] *nf* fraction

fractura [frak'tura] *nf* fracture, break

fragancia [fra'ɣanθja] *nf* (*olor*) fragrance, perfume

frágil ['fraxil] *adj* (*débil*) fragile; (*Com*) breakable

fragmento [fraɣ'mento] *nm* (*pedazo*) fragment

fraile ['fraile] *nm* (*Rel*) friar; (: *monje*) monk

frambuesa [fram'bwesa] *nf* raspberry

francés, -esa [fran'θes, esa] *adj* French ▷ *nm/f* Frenchman(-woman) ▷ *nm* (*Ling*) French

Francia ['franθja] *nf* France

franco, -a ['franko, a] *adj* (*cándido*) frank, open; (*Com: exento*) free ▷ *nm* (*moneda*) franc

francotirador, a [frankotira'ðor, a] *nm/f* sniper

franela [fra'nela] *nf* flannel

franja ['franxa] *nf* fringe

franquear [franke'ar] *vt* (*camino*) to clear; (*carta, paquete postal*) to frank,

stamp; (*obstáculo*) to overcome

franqueo [fran'keo] *nm* postage

franqueza [fran'keθa] *nf* (*candor*) frankness

frasco ['frasko] *nm* bottle, flask

frase ['frase] *nf* sentence; **frase hecha** set phrase; (*pey*) stock phrase

fraterno, -a [fra'terno, a] *adj* brotherly, fraternal

fraude ['frauðe] *nm* (*cualidad*) dishonesty; (*acto*) fraud

frazada [fra'saða] (*LAM*) *nf* blanket

frecuencia [fre'kwenθja] *nf* frequency; **con ~** frequently, often

frecuentar [frekwen'tar] *vt* to frequent

frecuente [fre'kwente] *adj* (*gen*) frequent

fregadero [freɣa'ðero] *nm* (kitchen) sink

fregar [fre'ɣar] *vt* (*frotar*) to scrub; (*platos*) to wash (up); (*LAM: fam: fastidiar*) to annoy; (: *malograr*) to screw up

fregona [fre'ɣona] *nf* mop

freír [fre'ir] *vt* to fry

frenar [fre'nar] *vt* to brake; (*fig*) to check

frenazo [fre'naθo] *nm*: **dar un ~** to brake sharply

frenesí [frene'si] *nm* frenzy

freno ['freno] *nm* (*Tec, Auto*) brake; (*de cabalgadura*) bit; (*fig*) check; **freno de mano** handbrake

frente ['frente] *nm* (*Arq, Pol*) front; (*de objeto*) front part ▷ *nf* forehead, brow; **~ a** in front of; (*en situación opuesta de*) opposite; **al ~ de** (*fig*) at the head of; **chocar de ~** to crash head-on; **hacer ~ a** to face up to

fresa ['fresa] (*ESP*) *nf* strawberry

fresco, -a ['fresko, a] *adj* (*nuevo*) fresh; (*frío*) cool; (*descarado*) cheeky ▷ *nm* (*aire*) fresh air; (*Arte*) fresco; (*LAM: jugo*) fruit drink ▷ *nm/f* (*fam*): **ser un ~** to have a nerve; **tomar el ~** to get some fresh air; **frescura** *nf* freshness; (*descaro*) cheek, nerve

frialdad [frial'daθ] *nf* (*gen*) coldness;

(*indiferencia*) indifference

frigidez [friˈxiˈðeθ] *nf* frigidity

frigo [ˈfriɣo] *nm* fridge

frigorífico [friɣoˈrifiko] *nm* refrigerator

frijol [friˈxol] *nm* kidney bean

frío, -a *etc* [ˈfrio, a] *vb* V **freír** ▷ *adj* cold; (*indiferente*) indifferent ▷ *nm* cold; indifference; **hace ~** it's cold; **tener ~** to be cold

frito, -a [ˈfrito, a] *adj* fried; **me trae ~ ese hombre** I'm sick and tired of that man; **fritos** *nmpl* fried food

frívolo, -a [ˈfriβolo, a] *adj* frivolous

frontal [fronˈtal] *adj* frontal; **choque ~** head-on collision

frontera [fronˈtera] *nf* frontier; **fronterizo, -a** *adj* frontier *cpd*; (*contiguo*) bordering

frontón [fronˈton] *nm* (*Deporte: cancha*) pelota court; (: *juego*) pelota

frotar [froˈtar] *vt* to rub, **frotarse** *vr.* **~se las manos** to rub one's hands

fructífero, -a [frukˈtifero, a] *adj* fruitful

fruncir [frunˈθir] *vt* to pucker; (*Costura*) to pleat; **~ el ceño** to knit one's brow

frustrar [frusˈtrar] *vt* to frustrate

fruta [ˈfruta] *nf* fruit; **frutería** *nf* fruit shop; **frutero, -a** *adj* fruit *cpd* ▷ *nm/f* fruiterer ▷ *nm* fruit bowl

frutilla [fruˈtiʎa] (*cs*) *nf* strawberry

fruto [ˈfruto] *nm* fruit; (*fig: resultado*) result; (: *beneficio*) benefit; **frutos secos** nuts and dried fruit *pl*

fucsia [ˈfuksja] *nf* fuchsia

fue [fwe] *vb* V **ser; ir**

fuego [ˈfweɣo] *nm* (*gen*) fire; **a ~ lento** on a low heat; **¿tienes ~?** have you (got) a light?; **fuego amigo** friendly fire; **fuegos artificiales** fireworks

fuente [ˈfwente] *nf* fountain; (*manantial: fig*) spring; (*origen*) source; (*plato*) large dish

fuera *etc* [ˈfwera] *vb* V **ser; ir** ▷ *adv* out(side); (*en otra parte*) away; (*excepto, salvo*) except, save ▷ *prep*: **~ de** outside;

(*fig*) besides; **~ de sí** beside o.s.; **por ~** (on the) outside

fuera-borda [fweraˈβorða] *nm* speedboat

fuerte [ˈfwerte] *adj* strong; (*golpe*) hard; (*ruido*) loud; (*comida*) rich; (*lluvia*) heavy; (*dolor*) intense ▷ *adv* strongly; hard; loud(ly); **ser ~ en** to be good at

fuerza *etc* [ˈfwerθa] *vb* V **forzar** ▷ *nf* (*fortaleza*) strength; (*Tec, Elec*) power; (*coacción*) force; (*Mil, Pol*) force; **a ~ de** by dint of; **cobrar ~s** to recover one's strength; **tener ~s para** to have the strength to; **a la ~** forcibly, by force; **por ~** of necessity; **fuerza de voluntad** willpower; **fuerzas aéreas** air force *sg*; **fuerzas armadas** armed forces

fuga [ˈfuɣa] *nf* (*huida*) flight, escape; (*de gas etc*) leak

fugarse [fuˈɣarse] *vr* to flee, escape

fugaz [fuˈɣaθ] *adj* fleeting

fugitivo, a [fuxiˈtiβo, a] *adj*, *nm/f* fugitive

fui [fwi] *vb* V **ser; ir**

fulano, -a [fuˈlano, a] *nm/f* so-and-so, what's-his-name/what's-her-name

fulminante [fulmiˈnante] *adj* (*fig: mirada*) fierce; (*Med: enfermedad, ataque*) sudden; (*fam: éxito, golpe*) sudden

fumador, a [fumaˈðor, a] *nm/f* smoker

fumar [fuˈmar] *vt*, *vi* to smoke; **~ en pipa** to smoke a pipe

función [funˈθjon] *nf* function; (*en trabajo*) duties *pl*; (*espectáculo*) show; **entrar en funciones** to take up one's duties

funcionar [funθjoˈnar] *vi* (*gen*) to function; (*máquina*) to work; **"no funciona"** "out of order"

funcionario, -a [funθjoˈnarjo, a] *nm/f* civil servant

funda [ˈfunda] *nf* (*gen*) cover; (*de almohada*) pillowcase

fundación [fundaˈθjon] *nf* foundation

fundamental [fundamenˈtal] *adj*

fundamental, basic
fundamento [funda'mento] *nm*
(*base*) foundation
fundar [fun'dar] *vt* to found;
  fundarse *vr*: **~se en** to be founded on
fundición [fundi'θjon] *nf* fusing;
(*fábrica*) foundry
fundir [fun'dir] *vt* (*gen*) to fuse;
(*metal*) to smelt, melt down; (*nieve
etc*) to melt; (*Com*) to merge; (*estatua*)
to cast; **fundirse** *vr* (*colores etc*) to
merge, blend; (*unirse*) to fuse together;
(*Elec: fusible, lámpara etc*) to fuse, blow;
(*nieve etc*) to melt
fúnebre ['funeβre] *adj* funeral *cpd*,
funereal
funeral [fune'ral] *nm* funeral;
  funeraria *nf* undertaker's
funicular [funiku'lar] *nm* (*tren*)
funicular; (*teleférico*) cable car
furgón [fur'xon] *nm* wagon;
  furgoneta *nf* (*Auto, Com*) (transit) van
(*BRIT*), pick-up (truck) (*US*)
furia ['furja] *nf* (*ira*) fury; (*violencia*)
violence; **furioso, -a** *adj* (*iracundo*)
furious; (*violento*) violent
furtivo, -a [fur'tiβo, a] *adj* furtive
  ▷ *nm* poacher
fusible [fu'siβle] *nm* fuse
fusil [fu'sil] *nm* rifle; **fusilar** *vt* to
shoot
fusión [fu'sjon] *nf* (*gen*) melting;
(*unión*) fusion; (*Com*) merger
fútbol ['futβol] *nm* football (*BRIT*),
soccer (*US*); **fútbol americano**
American football (*BRIT*), football
(*US*); **fútbol sala** indoor football (*BRIT*)
o soccer (*US*); **futbolín** *nm* table
football; **futbolista** *nmf* footballer
futuro, -a [fu'turo, a] *adj, nm* future

g

gabardina [gaβar'ðina] *nf* raincoat,
gabardine
gabinete [gaβi'nete] *nm* (*Pol*)
cabinet; (*estudio*) study; (*de abogados
etc*) office
gachas ['gatʃas] *nfpl* porridge *sg*
gafas ['gafas] *nfpl* glasses; **gafas de
sol** sunglasses
gafe ['gafe] (*ESP*) *nmf* jinx
gaita ['gaita] *nf* bagpipes *pl*
gajes ['gaxes] *nmpl*: **~ del oficio**
occupational hazards
gajo ['gaxo] *nm* (*de naranja*) segment
gala ['gala] *nf* (*traje de etiqueta*) full
dress; **galas** *nfpl* (*ropa*) finery *sg*; **estar
de ~** to be in one's best clothes; **hacer
~ de** to display
galápago [ga'lapaxo] *nm* (*Zool*)
turtle
galardón [galar'ðon] *nm* award,
prize
galaxia [ga'laksja] *nf* galaxy
galera [ga'lera] *nf* (*nave*) galley; (*carro*)
wagon; (*Imprenta*) galley
galería [gale'ria] *nf* (*gen*) gallery;

(*balcón*) veranda(h); (*pasillo*) corridor; **galería comercial** shopping mall

Gales ['gales] *nm* (*tb:* **País de ~**) Wales; **galés, -esa** *adj* Welsh ▷ *nm/f* Welshman(-woman) ▷ *nm* (*Ling*) Welsh

galgo, -a ['galɣo, a] *nm/f* greyhound

gallego, -a [ga'ʎeɣo, a] *adj, nm/f* Galician

galleta [ga'ʎeta] *nf* biscuit (*BRIT*), cookie (*US*)

gallina [ga'ʎina] *nf* hen ▷ *nmf* (*fam: cobarde*) chicken; **gallinero** *nm* henhouse; (*Teatro*) top gallery

gallo ['gaʎo] *nm* cock, rooster

galopar [galo'par] *vi* to gallop

gama ['gama] *nf* (*fig*) range

gamba ['gamba] *nf* prawn (*BRIT*), shrimp (*US*)

gamberro, -a [gam'berro, a] (*ESP*) *nm/f* hooligan, lout

gamuza [ga'muθa] *nf* chamois

gana ['gana] *nf* (*deseo*) desire, wish; (*apetito*) appetite; (*voluntad*) will; (*añoranza*) longing; **de buena ~** willingly; **de mala ~** reluctantly; **me da ~s de** I feel like, I want to; **no me da la ~** I don't feel like it; **tener ~s de** to feel like

ganadería [ganaðe'ria] *nf* (*ganado*) livestock; (*ganado vacuno*) cattle *pl*; (*cría, comercio*) cattle raising

ganadero, -a [gana'ðero, a] (*ESP*) *nm/f* (*hacendado*) rancher

ganado [ga'naðo] *nm* livestock; **ganado porcino** pigs *pl*

ganador, a [gana'ðor, a] *adj* winning ▷ *nm/f* winner

ganancia [ga'nanθja] *nf* (*lo ganado*) gain; (*aumento*) increase; (*beneficio*) profit; **ganancias** *nfpl* (*ingresos*) earnings; (*beneficios*) profit *sg*, winnings

ganar [ga'nar] *vt* (*obtener*) to get, obtain; (*sacar ventaja*) to gain; (*salario etc*) to earn; (*Deporte, premio*) to win; (*derrotar a*) to beat; (*alcanzar*) to reach ▷ *vi* (*Deporte*) to win; **ganarse** *vr*: **~se**

la vida to earn one's living

ganchillo [gan'tʃiʎo] *nm* crochet

gancho ['gantʃo] *nm* (*gen*) hook; (*colgador*) hanger

gandul, a [gan'dul, a] *adj, nm/f* good-for-nothing, layabout

ganga ['ganga] *nf* bargain

gangrena [gan'grena] *nf* gangrene

ganso, -a ['ganso, a] *nm/f* (*Zool*) goose; (*fam*) idiot

ganzúa [gan'θua] *nf* skeleton key

garabato [gara'βato] *nm* (*escritura*) scrawl, scribble

garaje [ga'raxe] *nm* garage; **garajista** [gara'xista] *nmf* mechanic

garantía [garan'tia] *nf* guarantee

garantizar [garanti'θar] *vt* to guarantee

garbanzo [gar'βanθo] *nm* chickpea (*BRIT*), garbanzo (*US*)

garfio ['garfjo] *nm* grappling iron

garganta [gar'ɣanta] *nf* (*Anat*) throat; (*de botella*) neck; **gargantilla** *nf* necklace

gárgaras ['garɣaras] *nfpl*: **hacer ~** to gargle

gargarear [garɣare'ar] (*LAM*) *vi* to gargle

garita [ga'rita] *nf* cabin, hut; (*Mil*) sentry box

garra ['garra] *nf* (*de gato, Tec*) claw; (*de ave*) talon; (*fam: mano*) hand, paw

garrafa [ga'rrafa] *nf* carafe, decanter

garrapata [garra'pata] *nf* tick

gas [gas] *nm* gas; **gases lacrimógenos** tear gas *sq*

gasa ['gasa] *nf* gauze

gaseosa [gase'osa] *nf* lemonade

gaseoso, -a [gase'oso, a] *adj* gassy, fizzy

gasoil [ga'soil] *nm* diesel (oil)

gasóleo [ga'soleo] *nm* = **gasoil**

gasolina [gaso'lina] *nf* petrol (*BRIT*), gas(oline) (*US*); **gasolinera** *nf* petrol (*BRIT*) o gas (*US*) station

gastado, -a [gas'taðo, a] *adj* (*dinero*) spent; (*ropa*) worn out; (*usado: frase etc*) trite

gastar [gas'tar] vt (dinero, tiempo) to spend; (fuerzas) to use up; (desperdiciar) to waste; (llevar) to wear; **gastarse** vr to wear out; (estropearse) to waste; **~ en** to spend on; **~ bromas** to crack jokes; **¿qué número gastas?** what size (shoe) do you take?

gasto ['gasto] nm (desembolso) expenditure, spending; (consumo, uso) use; **gastos** nmpl (desembolsos) expenses; (cargos) charges, costs

gastronomía [gastrono'mia] nf gastronomy

gatear [gate'ar] vi (andar a gatas) to go on all fours

gatillo [ga'tiʎo] nm (de arma de fuego) trigger; (de dentista) forceps

gato, -a ['gato, a] nm/f cat ▷ nm (Tec) jack; **andar a gatas** to go on all fours

gaucho ['gautʃo] nm gaucho

⬤ **GAUCHO**
⬤
⬤ **Gauchos** are the herdsmen or
⬤ riders of the Southern Cone plains.
⬤ Although popularly associated
⬤ with Argentine folklore, **gauchos**
⬤ belong equally to the cattle-
⬤ raising areas of Southern Brazil
⬤ and Uruguay. **Gauchos'** traditions
⬤ and clothing reflect their mixed
⬤ ancestry and cultural roots. Their
⬤ baggy trousers are Arabic in
⬤ origin, while the horse and guitar
⬤ are inherited from the Spanish
⬤ conquistadors; the poncho, maté
⬤ and **boleadoras** (strips of leather
⬤ weighted at either end with
⬤ stones) form part of the Indian
⬤ tradition.

gaviota [ga'βjota] nf seagull

gay [ge] adj inv, nm gay, homosexual

gazpacho [gaθ'patʃo] nm gazpacho

gel [xel] nm: **~ de baño/ducha** bath/shower gel

gelatina [xela'tina] nf jelly; (polvos etc) gelatine

gema ['xema] nf gem

gemelo, -a [xe'melo, a] adj, nm/f twin; **gemelos** nmpl (de camisa) cufflinks; (prismáticos) field glasses, binoculars

gemido [xe'miðo] nm (quejido) moan, groan; (aullido) howl

Géminis ['xeminis] nm Gemini

gemir [xe'mir] vi (quejarse) to moan, groan; (aullar) to howl

generación [xenera'θjon] nf generation

general [xene'ral] adj general ▷ nm general; **por lo** o **en ~** in general; **Generalitat** nf Catalan parliament; **generalizar** vt to generalize; **generalizarse** vr to become generalized, spread

generar [xene'rar] vt to generate

género ['xenero] nm (clase) kind, sort; (tipo) type; (Bio) genus; (Ling) gender; (Com) material; **género humano** human race

generosidad [xenerosi'ðað] nf generosity; **generoso, -a** adj generous

genial [xe'njal] adj inspired; (idea) brilliant; (estupendo) wonderful

genio ['xenjo] nm (carácter) nature, disposition; (humor) temper; (facultad creadora) genius; **de mal ~** bad-tempered

genital [xeni'tal] adj genital; **genitales** nmpl genitals

genoma [xe'noma] nm genome

gente ['xente] nf (personas) people pl; (parientes) relatives pl

gentil [xen'til] adj (elegante) graceful; (encantador) charming

▍ No confundir **gentil** con la palabra inglesa gentle.

genuino, -a [xe'nwino, a] adj genuine

geografía [xeoxra'fia] nf geography

geología [xeolo'xia] nf geology

geometría [xeome'tria] nf geometry

gerente [xe'rente] nmf (supervisor)

manager; (*jefe*) director

geriatría [xeria'tria] *nf* (*Med*) geriatrics *sg*

germen ['xermen] *nm* germ

gesticular [xestiku'lar] *vi* to gesticulate; (*hacer muecas*) to grimace; **gesticulación** *nf* gesticulation; (*mueca*) grimace

gestión [xes'tjon] *nf* management; (*diligencia, acción*) negotiation

gesto ['xesto] *nm* (*mueca*) grimace; (*ademán*) gesture

Gibraltar [xiβral'tar] *nm* Gibraltar; **gibraltareño, -a** *adj, nm/f* Gibraltarian

gigante [xi'ɣante] *adj, nmf* giant; **gigantesco, -a** *adj* gigantic

gilipollas [xili'poʎas] (*fam*) *adj inv* daft ▷ *nmf inv* wally

gimnasia [xim'nasja] *nf* gymnastics *pl*; **gimnasio** *nm* gymnasium; **gimnasta** *nmf* gymnast; **gimnástica** [xim'nastika] *nf inv* gymnastics *sg*

ginebra [xi'neβra] *nf* gin

ginecólogo, -a [xine'koloɣo, a] *nm/f* gynaecologist

gira ['xira] *nf* tour, trip

girar [xi'rar] *vt* (*dar la vuelta*) to turn (around); (: *rápidamente*) to spin; (*Com: giro postal*) to draw; (: *letra de cambio*) to issue ▷ *vi* to turn (round); (*rápido*) to spin

girasol [xira'sol] *nm* sunflower

giratorio, -a [xira'torjo, a] *adj* revolving

giro ['xiro] *nm* (*movimiento*) turn, revolution; (*Ling*) expression; (*Com*) draft; **giro bancario/postal** bank draft/money order

gis [xis] (*MÉX*) *nm* chalk

gitano, -a [xi'tano, a] *adj, nm/f* gypsy

glacial [gla'θjal] *adj* icy, freezing

glaciar [gla'θjar] *nm* glacier

glándula ['glandula] *nf* gland

global [glo'βal] *adj* global; **globalización** *nf* globalization

globo ['gloβo] *nm* (*esfera*) globe,

sphere; (*aerostato, juguete*) ba...

glóbulo ['gloβulo] *nm* globul... corpuscle

gloria ['glorja] *nf* glory

glorieta [glo'rjeta] *nf* (*de jardín*) bower, arbour; (*plazoleta*) roundabou... (*BRIT*), traffic circle (*US*)

glorioso, -a [glo'rjoso, a] *adj* glorious

glotón, -ona [glo'ton, ona] *adj* gluttonous, greedy ▷ *nm/f* glutton

glucosa [glu'kosa] *nf* glucose

gobernador, a [goβerna'ðor, a] *adj* governing ▷ *nm/f* governor; **gobernante** *adj* governing

gobernar [goβer'nar] *vt* (*dirigir*) to guide, direct; (*Pol*) to rule, govern ▷ *vi* to govern; (*Náut*) to steer

gobierno etc [go'βjerno] *vb* V **gobernar** ▷ *nm* (*Pol*) government; (*dirección*) guidance, direction; (*Náut*) steering

goce etc ['goθe] *vb* V **gozar** ▷ *nm* enjoyment

gol [gol] *nm* goal

golf [golf] *nm* golf

golfa ['golfa] (*fam!*) *nf* (*mujer*) slut, whore

golfo, -a ['golfo, a] *nm* (*Geo*) gulf ▷ *nm/f* (*fam: niño*) urchin; (*gamberro*) lout

golondrina [golon'drina] *nf* swallow

golosina [golo'sina] *nf* (*dulce*) sweet; **goloso, -a** *adj* sweet-toothed

golpe ['golpe] *nm* blow; (*de puño*) punch; (*de mano*) smack; (*de remo*) stroke; (*fig: choque*) clash; **no dar ~** to be bone idle; **de un ~** with one blow; **de ~** suddenly; **golpe (de estado)** coup (d'état); **golpear** *vt, vi* to strike, knock; (*asestar*) to beat; (*de puño*) to punch; (*golpetear*) to tap

goma ['goma] *nf* (*caucho*) rubber; (*elástico*) elastic; (*una goma*) elastic band; **goma de borrar** eraser, rubber (*BRIT*); **goma espuma** foam rubber

gomina [go'mina] *nf* hair gel

g

...mita] (RPL) nf rubber

...a ['gorðo, a] adj (gen) fat; ...normous; **el (premio) ~** (en ...) first prize

...a [go'rila] nm gorilla

...ra ['gorra] nf cap; (de bebé) bonnet; ...militar) bearskin; **entrar de ~** (fam) to gatecrash; **ir de ~** to sponge

gorrión [go'rrjon] nm sparrow

gorro ['gorro] nm (gen) cap; (de bebé, mujer) bonnet

gorrón, -ona [go'rron, ona] nm/f scrounger; **gorronear** (fam) vi to scrounge

gota ['gota] nf (gen) drop; (de sudor) bead; (Med) gout; **gotear** vi to drip; (lloviznar) to drizzle; **gotera** nf leak

gozar [go'θar] vi to enjoy o.s.; **~ de** (disfrutar) to enjoy; (poseer) to possess

gr. abr (= gramo, gramos) g

grabación [graβa'θjon] nf recording

grabado [gra'βaðo] nm print, engraving

grabadora [graβa'ðora] nf tape-recorder; **grabadora de CD/DVD** CD/DVD writer

grabar [gra'βar] vt to engrave; (discos, cintas) to record

gracia ['graθja] nf (encanto) grace, gracefulness; (humor) humour, wit; **¡(muchas) ~s!** thanks (very much)!; **~s a** thanks to; **dar las ~s a algn por algo** to thank sb for sth; **tener ~** (chiste etc) to be funny; **no me hace ~** I am not keen; **gracioso, -a** adj (divertido) funny, amusing; (cómico) comical ▷ nm/f (Teatro) comic character

grada ['graða] nf (de escalera) step; (de anfiteatro) tier, row; **gradas** nfpl (Deporte: de estadio) terraces

grado ['graðo] nm degree; (de aceite, vino) grade; (grada) step; (Mil) rank; **de buen ~** willingly; **grado centígrado/Fahrenheit** degree centigrade/Fahrenheit

graduación [graðwa'θjon] nf (del alcohol) proof, strength; (Escol)

graduation; (Mil) rank

gradual [gra'ðwal] adj gradual

graduar [gra'ðwar] vt (gen) to graduate; (Mil) to commission; **graduarse** vr to graduate; **~se la vista** to have one's eyes tested

gráfica ['grafika] nf graph

gráfico, -a ['grafiko, a] adj graphic ▷ nm diagram; **gráficos** nmpl (Inform) graphics

grajo ['graxo] nm rook

gramática [gra'matika] nf grammar

gramo ['gramo] nm gramme (BRIT), gram (US)

gran [gran] adj V **grande**

grana ['grana] nf (color, tela) scarlet

granada [gra'naða] nf pomegranate; (Mil) grenade

granate [gra'nate] adj deep red

Gran Bretaña [-bre'tapa] nf Great Britain

grande ['grande] (antes de nmsg **gran**) adj (de tamaño) big, large; (alto) tall; (distinguido) great; (impresionante) grand ▷ nm grandee

granel [gra'nel]: **a ~** adv (Com) in bulk

granero [gra'nero] nm granary, barn

granito [gra'nito] nm (Agr) small grain; (roca) granite

granizado [grani'θaðo] nm iced drink

granizar [grani'θar] vi to hail; **granizo** nm hail

granja ['granxa] nf (gen) farm; **granjero, -a** nm/f farmer

grano ['grano] nm grain; (semilla) seed; (de café) bean; (Med) pimple, spot

granuja [gra'nuxa] nmf rogue; (golfillo) urchin

grapa ['grapa] nf staple; (Tec) clamp; **grapadora** nf stapler

grasa ['grasa] nf (gen) grease; (de cocinar) fat, lard; (sebo) suet; (mugre) filth; **grasiento, -a** adj greasy; (de aceite) oily; **graso, -a** adj (leche, queso, carne) fatty; (pelo, piel) greasy

gratinar [grati'nar] vt to cook au gratin

gratis ['gratis] adv free

grato, -a ['grato, a] adj (agradable) pleasant, agreeable

gratuito, -a [gra'twito, a] adj (gratis) free; (sin razón) gratuitous

grave ['graβe] adj heavy; (serio) grave, serious; **gravedad** nf gravity

Grecia ['greθja] nf Greece

gremio ['gremjo] nm trade, industry

griego, -a ['grjeɣo, a] adj, nm/f Greek

grieta ['grjeta] nf crack

grifo ['grifo] (ESP) nm tap (BRIT), faucet (US)

grillo ['griʎo] nm (Zool) cricket

gripa ['gripa] (MÉX) nf flu, influenza

gripe ['gripe] nf flu, influenza; **gripe aviar** bird flu

gris [gris] adj (color) grey

gritar [gri'tar] vt, vi to shout, yell; **grito** nm shout, yell; (de horror) scream

grosella [gro'seʎa] nf (red)currant

grosero, -a [gro'sero, a] adj (poco cortés) rude, bad-mannered; (ordinario) vulgar, crude

grosor [gro'sor] nm thickness

grúa ['grua] nf (Tec) crane; (de petróleo) derrick

grueso, -a ['grweso, a] adj thick; (persona) stout ▷ nm bulk; **el ~ de** the bulk of

grulla ['gruʎa] nf crane

grumo ['grumo] nm clot, lump

gruñido [gru'ɲiðo] nm grunt; (de persona) grumble

gruñir [gru'ɲir] vi (animal) to growl; (persona) to grumble

grupo ['grupo] nm group; (Tec) unit, set; **grupo de presión** pressure group; **grupo sanguíneo** blood group

gruta ['gruta] nf grotto

guacho, -a ['gwatʃo, a] (CS) nm/f homeless child

guajolote [gwaxo'lote] (MÉX) nm turkey

guante ['gwante] nm glove; **guantes de goma** rubber gloves; **guantera** nf glove compartment

guapo, -a ['gwapo, a] adj good-

looking, attractive; (elegante) s▪

guarda ['gwarða] nmf (persona) guard, keeper ▷ nf (acto) guarding; (custodia) custody; **guarda jurado** (armed) security guard; **guardabarre** nm inv mudguard (BRIT), fender (US);

guardabosques nm inv gamekeeper;

guardacostas nm inv coastguard vessel ▷ nmf guardian, protector;

guardaespaldas nmf inv bodyguard;

guardameta nmf goalkeeper;

guardar vt (gen) to keep; (vigilar) to guard, watch over; (dinero: ahorrar) to save; **guardarse** vr (preservarse) to protect o.s.; (evitar) to avoid; **guardar cama** to stay in bed; **guardarropa** nm (armario) wardrobe; (en establecimiento público) cloakroom

guardería [gwarðe'ria] nf nursery

guardia ['gwarðja] nf (Mil) guard; (cuidado) care, custody ▷ nmf guard; (policía) policeman(-woman); **estar de ~** to be on guard; **montar ~** to mount guard; **Guardia Civil** Civil Guard

guardián, -ana [gwar'ðjan, ana] nm/f (gen) guardian, keeper

guarida [gwa'riða] nf (de animal) den, lair; (refugio) refuge

guarnición [gwarni'θjon] nf (de vestimenta) trimming; (de piedra) mount; (Culin) garnish; (arneses) harness; (Mil) garrison

guarro, -a ['ɣwarro, a] nm/f pig

guasa ['gwasa] nf joke; **guasón, -ona** adj (bromista) joking ▷ nm/f wit; joker

Guatemala [gwate'mala] nf Guatemala

guay [gwai] (fam) adj super, great

güero, -a ['gwero, a] (MÉX) adj blond(e)

guerra ['gerra] nf war; **dar ~** to annoy; **guerra civil** civil war; **guerra fría** cold war; **guerrero, -a** adj fighting; (carácter) warlike ▷ nm/f warrior

guerrilla [ge'rriʎa] nf guerrilla warfare; (tropas) guerrilla band o group

guía etc ['gia] vb V **guiar** ▷ nmf

...guide; (nf: libro) guidebook; **...efónica** telephone directory; **...urística** tourist guide
... [gi'ar] vt to guide, direct; (Auto) ...teer; **guiarse** vr: **~se por** to be ...ided by
guinda ['ginda] nf morello cherry
guindilla [gin'diʎa] nf chilli pepper
guiñar [gi'ɲar] vt to wink
guión [gi'on] nm (Ling) hyphen, dash; (Cine) script; **guionista** nmf scriptwriter
guiri ['giri] (ESP: fam, pey) nmf foreigner
guirnalda [gir'nalda] nf garland
guisado [gi'saðo] nm stew
guisante [gi'sante] nm pea
guisar [gi'sar] vt, vi to cook; **guiso** nm cooked dish
guitarra [gi'tarra] nf guitar
gula ['gula] nf gluttony, greed
gusano [gu'sano] nm worm; (lombriz) earthworm
gustar [gus'tar] vt to taste, sample ▷ vi to please, be pleasing; **~ de algo** to like o enjoy sth; **me gustan las uvas** I like grapes; **le gusta nadar** she likes o enjoys swimming
gusto ['gusto] nm (sentido, sabor) taste; (placer) pleasure; **tiene ~ a menta** it tastes of mint; **tener buen ~** to have good taste; **coger el** o **tomar ~ a algo** to take a liking to sth; **sentirse a ~** to feel at ease; **mucho ~ (en conocerle)** pleased to meet you; **el ~ es mío** the pleasure is mine; **con ~** willingly, gladly

ha vb V **haber**
haba ['aβa] nf bean
Habana [a'βana] nf: **la ~** Havana
habano [a'βano] nm Havana cigar
habéis vb V **haber**

⭕ **PALABRA CLAVE**

haber [a'βer] vb aux **1** (tiempos compuestos) to have; **había comido** I had eaten; **antes/después de haberlo visto** before seeing/after seeing o having seen it
2: **¡haberlo dicho antes!** you should have said so before!
3: **haber de: he de hacerlo** I have to do it; **ha de llegar mañana** it should arrive tomorrow
▷ vb impers **1** (existencia: sg) there is; (: pl) there are; **hay un hermano/dos hermanos** there is one brother/there are two brothers; **¿cuánto hay de aquí a Sucre?** how far is it from here to Sucre?
2 (obligación): **hay que hacer algo**

something must be done; **hay que apuntarlo para acordarse** you have to write it down to remember
3: **¡hay que ver!** well I never!
4: **¡no hay de** o **por** (LAM) **qué!** don't mention it!, not at all!
5: **¿qué hay?** (*¿qué pasa?*) what's up?, what's the matter?; (*¿qué tal?*) how's it going?
▷ vt: **he aquí unas sugerencias** here are some suggestions; **no hay cintas blancas pero sí las hay rojas** there aren't any white ribbons but there are some red ones
▷ nm (*en cuenta*) credit side; **haberes** nmpl assets; **¿cuánto tengo en el haber?** how much do I have in my account?; **tiene varias novelas en su haber** he has several novels to his credit
haberse vr: **habérselas con algn** to have it out with sb

habichuela [aβi'tʃwela] nf kidney bean
hábil ['aβil] adj (*listo*) clever, smart; (*capaz*) fit, capable; (*experto*) expert; **día ~** working day; **habilidad** nf skill, ability
habitación [aβita'θjon] nf (*cuarto*) room; (Bio: *morada*) habitat; **habitación doble** o **de matrimonio** double room; **habitación individual** o **sencilla** single room
habitante [aβi'tante] nmf inhabitant
habitar [aβi'tar] vt (*residir en*) to inhabit; (*ocupar*) to occupy ▷ vi to live
hábito ['aβito] nm habit
habitual [aβi'twal] adj usual
habituar [aβi'twar] vt to accustom; **habituarse** vr: **~se a** to get used to
habla ['aβla] nf (*capacidad de hablar*) speech; (*idioma*) language; (*dialecto*) dialect; **perder el ~** to become speechless; **de ~ francesa** French-speaking; **estar al ~** to be in contact; (Tel) to be on the line; **¡González al ~!** (Tel) González speaking!
hablador, a [aβla'ðor, a] adj

talkative ▷ nm/f chatterbox
habladuría [aβlaðu'ria] nf rum~
habladurías nfpl gossip sg
hablante [a'βlante] adj speaking
▷ nmf speaker
hablar [a'βlar] vt to speak, talk ▷ vi to speak; **hablarse** vr to speak to each other; **~ con** to speak to; **~ de** to speak of o about; **¡ni ~!** it's out of the question!; **"se habla inglés"** "English spoken here"
habré etc [a'βre] vb V **haber**
hacendado [aθen'daðo] (LAM) nm rancher, farmer
hacendoso, -a [aθen'doso, a] adj industrious

○ **PALABRA CLAVE**

hacer [a'θer] vt **1** (*fabricar, producir*) to make; (*construir*) to build; **hacer una película/un ruido** to make a film/noise; **el guisado lo hice yo** I made o cooked the stew
2 (*ejecutar: trabajo etc*) to do; **hacer la colada** to do the washing; **hacer la comida** to do the cooking; **¿qué haces?** what are you doing?; **hacer el malo** o **el papel del malo** (Teatro) to play the villain
3 (*estudios, algunos deportes*) to do; **hacer español/económicas** to do o study Spanish/economics; **hacer yoga/gimnasia** to do yoga/go to gym
4 (*transformar, incidir en*): **esto lo hará más difícil** this will make it more difficult; **salir te hará sentir mejor** going out will make you feel better
5 (*cálculo*): **2 y 2 hacen 4** 2 and 2 make 4; **éste hace 100** this one makes 100
6 (+ *sub*): **esto hará que ganemos** this will make us win; **harás que no quiera venir** you'll stop him wanting to come
7 (*como sustituto de vb*) to do; **él bebió y yo hice lo mismo** he drank and I did likewise
8 **no hace más que criticar** all he does is criticize

n-aux (*directo*): **hacer** +*infin*: **les** ... **enir** I made o had them come; ... **r trabajar a los demás** to get ... ers to work

... **vi 1 haz como que no lo sabes** act ...s if you don't know

2 (*ser apropiado*): **si os hace** if it's alright with you

3 hacer de: hacer de Otelo to play Othello

▷ *vb impers* **1 hace calor/frío** it's hot/cold; V *tb* **bueno, sol, tiempo**

2 (*tiempo*): **hace 3 años** 3 years ago; **hace un mes que voy/no voy** I've been going/I haven't been for a month

3 ¿cómo has hecho para llegar tan rápido? how did you manage to get here so quickly?

hacerse *vr* **1** (*volverse*) to become; **se hicieron amigos** they became friends

2 (*acostumbrarse*): **hacerse a** to get used to

3 se hace con huevos y leche it's made out of eggs and milk; **eso no se hace** that's not done

4 (*obtener*): **hacerse de** o **con algo** to get hold of sth

5 (*fingirse*): **hacerse el sueco** to turn a deaf ear

hacha ['atʃa] *nf* axe; (*antorcha*) torch
hachís [a'tʃis] *nm* hashish
hacia ['aθja] *prep* (*en dirección de*) towards; (*cerca de*) near; (*actitud*) towards; **~ adelante/atrás** forwards/backwards; **~ arriba/abajo** up(wards)/down(wards); **~ mediodía/las cinco** about noon/five
hacienda [a'θjenda] *nf* (*propiedad*) property; (*finca*) farm; (*LAM*: *rancho*) ranch; **(Ministerio de) H~** Exchequer (*BRIT*), Treasury Department (*US*); **hacienda pública** public finance
hada ['aða] *nf* fairy
hago *etc vb* V **hacer**
Haití [ai'ti] *nm* Haiti
halagar [ala'ɣar] *vt* to flatter
halago [a'laɣo] *nm* flattery

halcón [al'kon] *nm* falcon, hawk
hallar [a'ʎar] *vt* (*gen*) to find; (*descubrir*) to discover; (*toparse con*) to run into; **hallarse** *vr* to be (situated)
halterofilia [altero'filja] *nf* weightlifting
hamaca [a'maka] *nf* hammock
hambre ['ambre] *nf* hunger; (*plaga*) famine; (*deseo*) longing; **tener ~** to be hungry; **¡me muero de ~!** I'm starving!;
hambriento, -a *adj* hungry, starving
hamburguesa [ambur'ɣesa] *nf* hamburger; **hamburguesería** *nf* burger bar
hámster ['amster] *nm* hamster
han *vb* V **haber**
harapos [a'rapos] *nmpl* rags
haré *vb* V **hacer**
harina [a'rina] *nf* flour; **harina de maíz** cornflour (*BRIT*), cornstarch (*US*); **harina de trigo** wheat flour
hartar [ar'tar] *vt* to satiate, glut; (*fig*) to tire, sicken; **hartarse** *vr* (*de comida*) to fill o.s., gorge o.s.; (*cansarse*): **~se (de)** to get fed up (with); **harto, -a** *adj* (*lleno*) full; (*cansado*) fed up ▷ *adv* (*bastante*) enough; (*muy*) very; **estar harto de hacer algo/de algn** to be fed up of doing sth/with sb
has *vb* V **haber**
hasta ['asta] *adv* even ▷ *prep* (*alcanzando a*) as far as; up to; down to; (*de tiempo: a tal hora*) till, until; (*antes de*) before ▷ *conj*: **~ que ...** until; **~ luego/el sábado** see you soon/on Saturday; **~ ahora** (*al despedirse*) see you in a minute; **~ pronto** see you soon
hay *vb* V **haber**
Haya ['aja] *nf*: **la ~** The Hague
haya *etc* ['aja] *vb* V **haber** ▷ *nf* beech tree
haz [aθ] *vb* V **hacer** ▷ *nm* (*de luz*) beam
hazaña [a'θaɲa] *nf* feat, exploit
hazmerreír [aθmerre'ir] *nm inv* laughing stock
he *vb* V **haber**
hebilla [e'βiʎa] *nf* buckle, clasp

hebra ['eβra] nf thread; (Bot: fibra) fibre, grain

hebreo, -a [e'βreo, a] adj, nm/f Hebrew ▷ nm (Ling) Hebrew

hechizar [etʃi'θar] vt to cast a spell on, bewitch

hechizo [e'tʃiθo] nm witchcraft, magic; (acto de magía) spell, charm

hecho, -a ['etʃo, a] pp de **hacer** ▷ adj (carne) done; (Costura) ready-to-wear ▷ nm deed, act; (dato) fact; (cuestión) matter; (suceso) event ▷ excl agreed!, done!; **de ~** in fact, as a matter of fact; **el ~ es que ...** the fact is that ...; **¡bien ~!** well done!

hechura [e'tʃura] nf (forma) form, shape; (de persona) build

hectárea [ek'tarea] nf hectare

helada [e'laða] nf frost

heladera [ela'ðera] (LAM) nf (refrigerador) refrigerator

helado, -a [e'laðo, a] adj frozen; (glacial) icy; (fig) chilly, cold ▷ nm ice cream

helar [e'lar] vt to freeze, ice (up); (dejar atónito) to amaze; (desalentar) to discourage ▷ vi to freeze; **helarse** vr to freeze

helecho [e'letʃo] nm fern

hélice ['eliθe] nf (Tec) propeller

helicóptero [eli'koptero] nm helicopter

hembra ['embra] nf (Bot, Zool) female; (mujer) woman; (Tec) nut

hemorragia [emo'rraxja] nf haemorrhage

hemorroides [emo'rroiðes] nfpl haemorrhoids, piles

hemos vb V **haber**

heno ['eno] nm hay

heredar [ere'ðar] vt to inherit; **heredero, -a** nm/f heir(ess)

hereje [e'rexe] nm/f heretic

herencia [e'renθja] nf inheritance

herida [e'riða] nf wound, injury; V tb **herido**

herido, -a [e'riðo, a] adj injured, wounded ▷ nm/f casualty

herir [e'rir] vt to wound, injure; (fig) to offend

hermanación [ermana'θjon] nf (of towns) twinning

hermanado [erma'naðo] adj (town) twinned

hermanastro, -a [erma'nastro, a] nm/f stepbrother/sister

hermandad [erman'dað] nf brotherhood

hermano, -a [er'mano, a] nm/f brother/sister; **hermano(-a) gemelo(-a)**, twin brother/sister; **hermano(-a) político(-a)**, brother-in-law/sister-in-law

hermético, -a [er'metiko, a] adj hermetic; (fig) watertight

hermoso, -a [er'moso, a] adj beautiful, lovely; (estupendo) splendid; (guapo) handsome; **hermosura** nf beauty

hernia ['ernja] nf hernia; **hernia discal** slipped disc

héroe ['eroe] nm hero

heroína [ero'ina] nf (mujer) heroine; (droga) heroin

herradura [erra'ðura] nf horseshoe

herramienta [erra'mjenta] nf tool

herrero [e'rrero] nm blacksmith

hervidero [erβi'ðero] nm (fig) swarm; (Pol etc) hotbed

hervir [er'βir] vi to boil; (burbujear) to bubble; **~ a fuego lento** to simmer, **hervor** nm boiling; (fig) ardour, fervour

heterosexual [eterosek'swal] adj heterosexual

hice etc vb V **hacer**

hidratante [iðra'tante] adj: **crema ~** moisturizing cream, moisturizer; **hidratar** vt (piel) to moisturize; **hidrato** nm hydrate; **hidratos de carbono** carbohydrates

hidráulico, -a [i'ðrauliko, a] adj hydraulic

hidro... [iðro] prefijo hydro..., water-...; **hidrodeslizador** nm hovercraft; **hidroeléctrico, -a**

h

...dj hydroelectric; **hidrógeno** nm
..ydrogen

hiedra ['jeðra] nf ivy

hiel [jel] nf gall, bile; (fig) bitterness

hiela etc vb V **helar**

hielo ['jelo] nm (gen) ice; (escarcha)
frost; (fig) coldness, reserve

hiena ['jena] nf hyena

hierba ['jerβa] nf (pasto) grass; (Culin,
Med: planta) herb; **mala ~** weed; (fig)
evil influence; **hierbabuena** nf mint

hierro ['jerro] nm (metal) iron; (objeto)
iron object

hígado ['ixaðo] nm liver

higiene [i'xjene] nf hygiene;
higiénico, -a adj hygienic

higo ['ixo] nm fig; **higo seco** dried fig;
higuera nf fig tree

hijastro, -a [i'xastro, a] nm/f
stepson/daughter

hijo, -a ['ixo, a] nm/f son/daughter,
child; **hijos** nmpl children, sons and
daughters; **hijo adoptivo** adopted
child; **hijo de papá/mamá** daddy's/
mummy's boy; **hijo de puta** (fam!)
bastard (!), son of a bitch (!); **hijo/a
político/a** son-/daughter-in-law; **hijo
único** only child

hilera [i'lera] nf row, file

hilo ['ilo] nm thread; (Bot) fibre; (metal)
wire; (de agua) trickle, thin stream

hilvanar [ilβa'nar] vt (Costura)
to tack (BRIT), baste (US); (fig) to do
hurriedly

himno ['imno] nm hymn; **himno
nacional** national anthem

hincapié [inka'pje] nm: **hacer ~ en**
to emphasize

hincar [in'kar] vt to drive (in),
thrust (in)

hincha ['intʃa] (fam) nmf fan

hinchado, -a [in'tʃaðo, a] adj (gen)
swollen; (persona) pompous

hinchar [in'tʃar] vt (gen) to swell;
(inflar) to blow up, inflate; (fig) to
exaggerate; **hincharse** vr (inflarse) to
swell up; (fam: de comer) to stuff o.s.;
hinchazón nf (Med) swelling; (altivez)

arrogance

hinojo [i'noxo] nm fennel

hipermercado [ipermer'kaðo] nm
hypermarket, superstore

hípico, -a ['ipiko, a] adj horse cpd

hipnotismo [ipno'tismo] nm
hypnotism; **hipnotizar** vt to
hypnotize

hipo ['ipo] nm hiccups pl

hipocresía [ipokre'sia] nf hypocrisy;
hipócrita adj hypocritical ▷ nmf
hypocrite

hipódromo [i'poðromo] nm
racetrack

hipopótamo [ipo'potamo] nm
hippopotamus

hipoteca [ipo'teka] nf mortgage

hipótesis [i'potesis] nf inv
hypothesis

hispánico, -a [is'paniko, a] adj
Hispanic

hispano, -a [is'pano, a] adj
Hispanic, Spanish, Hispano- ▷ nm/f
Spaniard; **Hispanoamérica** nf Latin
America; **hispanoamericano, -a** adj,
nm/f Latin American

histeria [is'terja] nf hysteria

historia [is'torja] nf history; (cuento)
story, tale; **historias** nfpl (chismes)
gossip sg; **dejarse de ~s** to come to
the point; **pasar a la ~** to go down
in history; **historiador, a** nm/f
historian; **historial** nm (profesional)
curriculum vitae, C.V.; (Med) case
history; **histórico, -a** adj historical;
(memorable) historic

historieta [isto'rjeta] nf tale,
anecdote; (dibujos) comic strip

hito ['ito] nm (fig) landmark

hizo vb V **hacer**

hocico [o'θiko] nm snout

hockey ['xokei] nm hockey; **hockey
sobre hielo/patines** ice/roller hockey

hogar [o'xar] nm fireplace, hearth;
(casa) home; (vida familiar) home life;
hogareño, -a adj home cpd; (persona)
home-loving

hoguera [o'xera] nf (gen) bonfire

hoja ['oxa] nf (gen) leaf; (de flor) petal; (de papel) sheet; (página) page; **hoja de afeitar** (LAM) razor blade; **hoja de solicitud** application form; **hoja electrónica** o **de cálculo** spreadsheet; **hoja informativa** leaflet, handout

hojalata [oxa'lata] nf tin(plate)

hojaldre [o'xaldre] nm (Culin) puff pastry

hojear [oxe'ar] vt to leaf through, turn the pages of

hojuela [o'xwela] (MÉX) nf flake

hola ['ola] excl hello!

holá [o'la] (RPL) excl hello!

Holanda [o'landa] nf Holland; **holandés, -esa** adj Dutch ▷ nm/f Dutchman(-woman) ▷ nm (Ling) Dutch

holgado, -a [ol'xaðo, a] adj (ropa) loose, baggy; (rico) comfortable

holgar [ol'xar] vi (descansar) to rest; (sobrar) to be superfluous

holgazán, -ana [olxa'ðan, ana] adj idle, lazy ▷ nm/f loafer

hollín [o'λin] nm soot

hombre ['ombre] nm (gen) man; (raza humana): **el ~** man(kind) ▷ excl: **¡sí ~!** (claro) of course!; (para énfasis) man, old boy; **hombre de negocios** businessman; **hombre de pro** honest man; **hombre-rana** frogman

hombrera [om'brera] nf shoulder strap

hombro ['ombro] nm shoulder

homenaje [ome'naxe] nm (gen) homage; (tributo) tribute

homicida [omi'θiða] adj homicidal ▷ nmf murderer; **homicidio** nm murder, homicide

homologar [omolo'ðar] vt (Com: productos, tamaños) to standardize

homólogo, -a [o'moloxo, a] nm/f: **su** etc **~** his etc counterpart o opposite number

homosexual [omosek'swal] adj, nmf homosexual

honda ['onda] (CS) nf catapult

hondo, -a ['ondo, a] adj deep; **lo ~** the depth(s) pl, the bottom; **hondonada** nf hollow, depression; (cañón) ravine

Honduras [on'duras] nf Honduras

hondureño, -a [ondu'reɲo, a] adj, nm/f Honduran

honestidad [onesti'ðað] nf purity, chastity; (decencia) decency; **honesto, -a** adj chaste; decent; honest; (justo) just

hongo ['ongo] nm (Bot: gen) fungus; (: comestible) mushroom; (: venenoso) toadstool

honor [o'nor] nm (gen) honour; **en ~ a la verdad** to be fair; **honorable** adj honourable

honorario, -a [ono'rarjo, a] adj honorary; **honorarios** nmpl fees

honra ['onra] nf (gen) honour; (renombre) good name; **honradez** nf honesty; (de persona) integrity; **honrado, -a** adj honest, upright; **honrar** [on'rar] vt to honour

hora ['ora] nf (una hora) hour; (tiempo) time; **¿qué ~ es?** what time is it?; **¿a qué ~?** at what time?; **media ~** half an hour; **a la ~ de recreo** at playtime, **a primera ~** first thing (in the morning); **a última ~** at the last moment; **a altas ~s** in the small hours; **¡a buena ~!** about time too!; **pedir ~** to make an appointment; **dar la ~** to strike the hour; **horas de oficina/trabajo** office/working hours; **horas de visita** visiting times; **horas extras** o **extraordinarias** overtime sg; **horas pico** (LAM) rush o peak hours; **horas punta** (ESP) rush hours

horario, -a [o'rarjo, a] adj hourly, hour cpd ▷ nm timetable; **horario comercial** business hours pl

horca ['orka] nf gallows sg

horcajadas [orka'xaðas]: **a ~** adv astride

horchata [or'tʃata] nf cold drink made from tiger nuts and water, tiger nut milk

horizontal [oriθon'tal] adj

h

horizontal

horizonte [ori'θonte] *nm* horizon

horma ['orma] *nf* mould

hormiga [or'miɣa] *nf* ant; **hormigas** *nfpl* (*Med*) pins and needles

hormigón [ormi'ɣon] *nm* concrete; **hormigón armado/pretensado** reinforced/prestressed concrete; **hormigonera** *nf* cement mixer

hormigueo [ormi'ɣeo] *nm* (*comezón*) itch

hormona [or'mona] *nf* hormone

hornillo [or'niʎo] *nm* (*cocina*) portable stove; **hornillo de gas** gas ring

horno ['orno] *nm* (*Culin*) oven; (*Tec*) furnace; **alto ~** blast furnace

horóscopo [o'roskopo] *nm* horoscope

horquilla [or'kiʎa] *nf* hairpin; (*Agr*) pitchfork

horrendo, -a [o'rrendo, a] *adj* horrendous, frightful

horrible [o'rriβle] *adj* horrible, dreadful

horripilante [orripi'lante] *adj* hair-raising, horrifying

horror [o'rror] *nm* horror, dread; (*atrocidad*) atrocity; **¡qué ~!** (*fam*) how awful!; **horrorizar** *vt* to horrify, frighten; **horrorizarse** *vr* to be horrified; **horroroso, -a** *adj* horrifying, ghastly

hortaliza [orta'liθa] *nf* vegetable

hortelano, -a [orte'lano, a] *nm/f* (market) gardener

hortera [or'tera] (*fam*) *adj* tacky

hospedar [ospe'ðar] *vt* to put up; **hospedarse** *vr* to stay, lodge

hospital [ospi'tal] *nm* hospital

hospitalario, -a [ospita'larjo, a] *adj* (*acogedor*) hospitable; **hospitalidad** *nf* hospitality

hostal [os'tal] *nm* small hotel

hostelería [ostele'ria] *nf* hotel business *o* trade

hostia ['ostja] *nf* (*Rel*) host, consecrated wafer; (*fam!: golpe*) whack, punch ▷ *excl* (*fam!*): **¡~(s)!** damn!

hostil [os'til] *adj* hostile

hotdog [ot'dog] (*LAM*) *nm* hot dog

hotel [o'tel] *nm* hotel; **hotelero, -a** *adj* hotel *cpd* ▷ *nm/f* hotelier

● **HOTEL**
●
● In Spain you can choose from
● the following categories of
● accommodation, in descending
● order of quality and price: **hotel**
● (from 5 stars to 1), **hostal**, **pensión**,
● **casa de huéspedes**, **fonda**. The
● State also runs luxury hotels called
● **paradores**, which are usually sited
● in places of particular historical
● interest and are often historic
● buildings themselves.

hoy [oi] *adv* (*este día*) today; (*la actualidad*) now(adays) ▷ *nm* present time; **~ (en) día** now(adays)

hoyo ['ojo] *nm* hole, pit

hoz [oθ] *nf* sickle

hube *etc vb* V **haber**

hucha ['utʃa] *nf* money box

hueco, -a ['weko, a] *adj* (*vacío*) hollow, empty; (*resonante*) booming ▷ *nm* hollow, cavity

huelga *etc* ['welɣa] *vb* V **holgar** ▷ *nf* strike; **declararse en ~** to go on strike, come out on strike; **huelga de hambre** hunger strike; **huelga general** general strike

huelguista [wel'ɣista] *nmf* striker

huella ['weʎa] *nf* (*pisada*) tread; (*marca del paso*) footprint, footstep; (: *de animal, máquina*) track; **huella dactilar** fingerprint

huelo *etc vb* V **oler**

huérfano, -a ['werfano, a] *adj* orphan(ed) ▷ *nm/f* orphan

huerta ['werta] *nf* market garden; (*en Murcia y Valencia*) irrigated region

huerto ['werto] *nm* kitchen garden; (*de árboles frutales*) orchard

hueso ['weso] *nm* (*Anat*) bone; (*de fruta*) stone

huésped ['wespeð] nmf guest

hueva ['weβa] nf roe

huevera [we'βera] nf eggcup

huevo ['weβo] nm egg; **huevo a la copa** (CS) soft-boiled egg; **huevo duro/escalfado** hard-boiled/poached egg; **huevo estrellado** (LAM) fried egg; **huevo frito** (ESP) fried egg; **huevo pasado por agua** soft-boiled egg; **huevos revueltos** scrambled eggs; **huevo tibio** (MÉX) soft-boiled egg

huida [u'iða] nf escape, flight

huir [u'ir] vi (escapar) to flee, escape; (evitar) to avoid

hule ['ule] nm oilskin; (MÉX: goma) rubber

hulera [u'lera] (MÉX) nf catapult

humanidad [umani'ðað] nf (género humano) man(kind); (cualidad) humanity

humanitario, -a [umani'tarjo, a] adj humanitarian

humano, -a [u'mano, a] adj (gen) human; (humanitario) humane ▷ nm human; **ser ~** human being

humareda [uma'reða] nf cloud of smoke

humedad [ume'ðað] nf (de clima) humidity; (de pared etc) dampness; **a prueba de ~** damp-proof; **humedecer** vt to moisten, wet; **humedecerse** vr to get wet

húmedo, -a ['umeðo, a] adj (mojado) damp, wet; (tiempo etc) humid

humilde [u'milde] adj humble, modest

humillación [umiʎa'θjon] nf humiliation; **humillante** adj humiliating

humillar [umi'ʎar] vt to humiliate

humo ['umo] nm (de fuego) smoke; (gas nocivo) fumes pl; (vapor) steam, vapour; **humos** nmpl (fig) conceit sg

humor [u'mor] nm (disposición) mood, temper; (lo que divierte) humour; **de buen/mal ~** in a good/bad mood; **humorista** nmf comic; **humorístico, -a** adj funny, humorous

hundimiento [undi'mjento] nm (gen) sinking; (colapso) collapse

hundir [un'dir] vt to sink; (edificio, plan) to ruin, destroy; **hundirse** vr to sink, collapse

húngaro, -a ['ungaro, a] adj, nm/f Hungarian

Hungría [un'gria] nf Hungary

huracán [ura'kan] nm hurricane

huraño, -a [u'raɲo, a] adj (antisocial) unsociable

hurgar [ur'xar] vt to poke, jab; (remover) to stir (up); **hurgarse** vr: **~se (las narices)** to pick one's nose

hurón, -ona [u'ron, ona] nm (Zool) ferret

hurtadillas [urta'ðiʎas]: **a ~** adv stealthily, on the sly

hurtar [ur'tar] vt to steal; **hurto** nm theft, stealing

husmear [usme'ar] vt (oler) to sniff out, scent; (fam) to pry into

huyo etc vb V **huir**

iba etc vb V **ir**

ibérico, -a [i'βeriko, a] adj Iberian

iberoamericano, -a [iβeroameri'kano, a] adj, nm/f Latin American

Ibiza [i'βiθa] nf Ibiza

iceberg [iθe'βer] nm iceberg

icono [i'kono] nm ikon, icon

ida ['iða] nf going, departure; **~ y vuelta** round trip, return

idea [i'ðea] nf idea; **no tengo la menor ~** I haven't a clue

ideal [iðe'al] adj, nm ideal; **idealista** nmf idealist; **idealizar** vt to idealize

ídem ['iðem] pron ditto

idéntico, -a [i'ðentiko, a] adj identical

identidad [iðenti'ðað] nf identity

identificación [iðentifika'θjon] nf identification

identificar [iðentifi'kar] vt to identify; **identificarse** vr: **~se con** to identify with

ideología [iðeolo'xia] nf ideology

idilio [i'ðiljo] nm love-affair

idioma [i'ðjoma] nm (gen) language
No confundir **idioma** con la palabra inglesa **idiom**.

idiota [i'ðjota] adj idiotic ▷ nmf idiot

ídolo ['iðolo] nm (tb fig) idol

idóneo, -a [i'ðoneo, a] adj suitable

iglesia [i'ɣlesja] nf church

ignorante [iɣno'rante] adj ignorant, uninformed ▷ nmf ignoramus

ignorar [iɣno'rar] vt not to know, be ignorant of; (no hacer caso a) to ignore

igual [i'ɣwal] adj (gen) equal; (similar) like, similar; (mismo) (the) same; (constante) constant; (temperatura) even ▷ nmf equal; **~ que** like, the same as; **me da o es ~** I don't care; **son ~es** they're the same; **al ~ que** (prep, conj) like, just like

igualar [iɣwa'lar] vt (gen) to equalize, make equal; (allanar, nivelar) to level (off), even (out); **igualarse** vr (platos de balanza) to balance out

igualdad [iɣwal'dað] nf equality; (similaridad) sameness; (uniformidad) uniformity

igualmente [iɣwal'mente] adv equally; (también) also, likewise ▷ excl the same to you!

ilegal [ile'ɣal] adj illegal

ilegítimo, -a [ile'xitimo, a] adj illegitimate

ileso, -a [i'leso, a] adj unhurt

ilimitado, -a [ilimi'taðo, a] adj unlimited

iluminación [ilumina'θjon] nf illumination; (alumbrado) lighting

iluminar [ilumi'nar] vt to illuminate, light (up); (fig) to enlighten

ilusión [ilu'sjon] nf illusion; (quimera) delusion; (esperanza) hope; **hacerse ilusiones** to build up one's hopes; **ilusionado, -a** adj excited; **ilusionar** vi: **le ilusiona ir de vacaciones** he's looking forward to going on holiday; **ilusionarse** vr: **ilusionarse (con)** to get excited (about)

iluso, -a [i'luso, a] adj easily deceived ▷ nm/f dreamer

ilustración [ilustra'θjon] *nf*
illustration; (*saber*) learning, erudition;
la l~ the Enlightenment; **ilustrado, -a**
adj illustrated; learned

ilustrar [ilus'trar] *vt* to illustrate;
(*instruir*) to instruct; (*explicar*) to
explain, make clear

ilustre [i'lustre] *adj* famous,
illustrious

imagen [i'maxen] *nf* (*gen*) image;
(*dibujo*) picture

imaginación [imaxina'θjon] *nf*
imagination

imaginar [imaxi'nar] *vt* (*gen*) to
imagine; (*idear*) to think up; (*suponer*) to
suppose; **imaginarse** *vr* to imagine;
imaginario, -a *adj* imaginary;
imaginativo, -a *adj* imaginative

imán [i'man] *nm* magnet

imbécil [im'beθil] *nmf* imbecile, idiot

imitación [imita'θjon] *nf* imitation,
de ~ imitation *cpd*

imitar [imi'tar] *vt* to imitate;
(*parodiar, remedar*) to mimic, ape

impaciente [impa'θjente] *adj*
impatient; (*nervioso*) anxious

impacto [im'pakto] *nm* impact

impar [im'par] *adj* odd

imparcial [impar'θjal] *adj* impartial,
fair

impecable [impe'kaβle] *adj*
impeccable

impedimento [impeði'mento] *nm*
impediment, obstacle

impedir [impe'ðir] *vt* (*obstruir*) to
impede, obstruct; (*estorbar*) to prevent;
~ a algn hacer *o* **que algn haga algo**
to prevent sb (from) doing sth, stop
sb doing sth

imperativo, -a [impera'tiβo, a] *adj*
(*urgente, Ling*) imperative

imperdible [imper'ðiβle] *nm*
safety pin

imperdonable [imperðo'naβle] *adj*
unforgivable, inexcusable

imperfecto, -a [imper'fekto, a] *adj*
imperfect

imperio [im'perjo] *nm* empire;

(*autoridad*) rule, authority; (*fig*) pride,
haughtiness

impermeable [imperme'aβle] *adj*
waterproof ▷ *nm* raincoat, mac (BRIT)

impersonal [imperso'nal] *adj*
impersonal

impertinente [imperti'nente] *adj*
impertinent

ímpetu ['impetu] *nm* (*impulso*)
impetus, impulse; (*impetuosidad*)
impetuosity; (*violencia*) violence

implantar [implan'tar] *vt* to
introduce

implemento [imple'mento] (LAM)
nm tool, implement

implicar [impli'kar] *vt* to involve;
(*entrañar*) to imply

implícito, -a [im'pliθito, a] *adj*
(*tácito*) implicit; (*sobreentendido*)
implied

imponente [impo'nente] *adj*
(*impresionante*) impressive, imposing;
(*solemne*) grand

imponer [impo'ner] *vt* (*gen*) to
impose; (*exigir*) to exact; **imponerse**
vr to assert o.s.; (*prevalecer*) to prevail;
imponible *adj* (*Com*) taxable

impopular [impopu'lar] *adj*
unpopular

importación [importa'θjon]
nf (*acto*) importing; (*mercancías*)
imports *pl*

importancia [impor'tanθja] *nf*
importance; (*valor*) value, significance;
(*extensión*) size, magnitude; **no
tiene ~** it's nothing; **importante** *adj*
important; valuable, significant

importar [impor'tar] *vt* (*del
extranjero*) to import; (*costar*) to amount
to ▷ *vi* to be important, matter; **me
importa un rábano** I couldn't care
less; **no importa** it doesn't matter;
¿le importa que fume? do you mind
if I smoke?

importe [im'porte] *nm* (*total*)
amount; (*valor*) value

imposible [impo'siβle] *adj* (*gen*)
impossible; (*insoportable*) unbearable,

intolerable

imposición [imposi'θjon] *nf*
imposition; (*Com: impuesto*) tax;
(*: inversión*) deposit

impostor, a [impos'tor, a] *nm/f*
impostor

impotencia [impo'tenθja] *nf*
impotence; **impotente** *adj* impotent

impreciso, -a [impre'θiso, a] *adj*
imprecise, vague

impregnar [imprex'nar] *vt* to
impregnate; **impregnarse** *vr* to
become impregnated

imprenta [im'prenta] *nf* (*acto*)
printing; (*aparato*) press; (*casa*)
printer's; (*letra*) print

imprescindible [impresθin'diβle]
adj essential, vital

impresión [impre'sjon] *nf* (*gen*)
impression; (*Imprenta*) printing;
(*edición*) edition; (*Foto*) print; (*marca*)
imprint; **impresión digital** fingerprint

impresionante [impresjo'nante]
adj impressive; (*tremendo*) tremendous;
(*maravilloso*) great, marvellous

impresionar [impresjo'nar] *vt*
(*conmover*) to move; (*afectar*) to impress,
strike; (*película fotográfica*) to expose;
impresionarse *vr* to be impressed;
(*conmoverse*) to be moved

impreso, -a [im'preso, a] *pp de*
imprimir ▷ *adj* printed; **impresos**
nmpl printed matter; **impresora** *nf*
printer

imprevisto, -a [impre'βisto, a]
adj (*gen*) unforeseen; (*inesperado*)
unexpected

imprimir [impri'mir] *vt* to imprint,
impress, stamp; (*textos*) to print;
(*Inform*) to output, print out

improbable [impro'βaβle] *adj*
improbable; (*inverosímil*) unlikely

impropio, -a [im'propjo, a] *adj*
improper

improvisado, -a [improβi'saðo, a]
adj improvised

improvisar [improβi'sar] *vt* to
improvise

improviso, -a [impro'βiso, a] *adj*: **de**
~ unexpectedly, suddenly

imprudencia [impru'ðenθja] *nf*
imprudence; (*indiscreción*) indiscretion;
(*descuido*) carelessness; **imprudente**
adj unwise, imprudent; (*indiscreto*)
indiscreet

impuesto, -a [im'pwesto, a] *adj*
imposed ▷ *nm* tax; **impuesto al valor**
agregado *o* **añadido** (*LAM*) value added
tax (*BRIT*) ≈ sales tax (*US*); **impuesto**
sobre el valor añadido (*ESP*) value
added tax (*BRIT*) ≈ sales tax (*US*)

impulsar [impul'sar] *vt* to drive;
(*promover*) to promote, stimulate

impulsivo, -a [impul'siβo, a] *adj*
impulsive; **impulso** *nm* impulse;
(*fuerza, empuje*) thrust, drive;
(*fig: sentimiento*) urge, impulse

impureza [impu're θa] *nf* impurity;
impuro, -a *adj* impure

inaccesible [inakθe'siβle] *adj*
inaccessible

inaceptable [inaθep'taβle] *adj*
unacceptable

inactivo, -a [inak'tiβo, a] *adj*
inactive

inadecuado, -a [inaðe'kwaðo, a]
adj (*insuficiente*) inadequate; (*inapto*)
unsuitable

inadvertido, -a [inaðβer'tiðo, a] *adj*
(*no visto*) unnoticed

inaguantable [inaɣwan'taβle] *adj*
unbearable

inanimado, -a [inani'maðo, a] *adj*
inanimate

inaudito, -a [inau'ðito, a] *adj*
unheard-of

inauguración [inauɣura'θjon] *nf*
inauguration; opening

inaugurar [inauɣu'rar] *vt* to
inaugurate; (*exposición*) to open

inca ['inka] *nmf* Inca

incalculable [inkalku'laβle] *adj*
incalculable

incandescente [inkandes'θente]
adj incandescent

incansable [inkan'saβle] *adj*

tireless, untiring

incapacidad [inkapaθi'ðað] *nf* incapacity; (*incompetencia*) incompetence; **incapacidad física/mental** physical/mental disability

incapacitar [inkapaθi'tar] *vt* (*inhabilitar*) to incapacitate, render unfit; (*descalificar*) to disqualify

incapaz [inka'paθ] *adj* incapable

incautarse [inkau'tarse] *vr*: **~ de** to seize, confiscate

incauto, -a [in'kauto, a] *adj* (*imprudente*) incautious, unwary

incendiar [inθen'djar] *vt* to set fire to; (*fig*) to inflame; **incendiarse** *vr* to catch fire; **incendiario, -a** *adj* incendiary

incendio [in'θendjo] *nm* fire

incentivo [inθen'tiβo] *nm* incentive

incertidumbre [inθerti'ðumbre] *nf* (*inseguridad*) uncertainty; (*duda*) doubt

incesante [inθe'sante] *adj* incessant

incesto [in'θesto] *nm* incest

incidencia [inθi'ðenθja] *nf* (*Mat*) incidence

incidente [inθi'ðente] *nm* incident

incidir [inθi'ðir] *vi* (*influir*) to influence; (*afectar*) to affect

incienso [in'θjenso] *nm* incense

incierto, -a [in'θjerto, a] *adj* uncertain

incineración [inθinera'θjon] *nf* incineration; (*de cadáveres*) cremation

incinerar [inθine'rar] *vt* to burn; (*cadáveres*) to cremate

incisión [inθi'sjon] *nf* incision

incisivo, -a [inθi'siβo, a] *adj* sharp, cutting; (*fig*) incisive

incitar [inθi'tar] *vt* to incite, rouse

inclemencia [inkle'menθja] *nf* (*severidad*) harshness, severity; (*del tiempo*) inclemency

inclinación [inklina'θjon] *nf* (*gen*) inclination; (*de tierras*) slope, incline; (*de cabeza*) nod, bow; (*fig*) leaning, bent

inclinar [inkli'nar] *vt* to incline; (*cabeza*) to nod, bow ▷ *vi* to lean, slope; **inclinarse** *vr* to bow; (*encorvarse*) to

stoop; **~se a** (*parecerse a*) to take after, resemble; **~se ante** to bow down to; **me inclino a pensar que ...** I'm inclined to think that ...

incluir [inklu'ir] *vt* to include; (*incorporar*) to incorporate; (*meter*) to enclose

inclusive [inklu'siβe] *adv* inclusive ▷ *prep* including

incluso [in'kluso] *adv* even

incógnita [in'koɣnita] *nf* (*Mat*) unknown quantity

incógnito [in'koɣnito] *nm*: **de ~** incognito

incoherente [inkoe'rente] *adj* incoherent

incoloro, -a [inko'loro, a] *adj* colourless

incomodar [inkomo'ðar] *vt* to inconvenience; (*molestar*) to bother, trouble; (*fastidiar*) to annoy

incomodidad [inkomoði'ðað] *nf* inconvenience; (*fastidio, enojo*) annoyance; (*de vivienda*) discomfort

incómodo, -a [in'komoðo, a] *adj* (*inconfortable*) uncomfortable; (*molesto*) annoying; (*inconveniente*) inconvenient

incomparable [inkompa'raβle] *adj* incomparable

incompatible [inkompa'tiβle] *adj* incompatible

incompetente [inkompe'tente] *adj* incompetent

incompleto, -a [inkom'pleto, a] *adj* incomplete, unfinished

incomprensible [inkompren'siβle] *adj* incomprehensible

incomunicado, -a [inkomuni'kaðo, a] *adj* (*aislado*) cut off, isolated; (*confinado*) in solitary confinement

incondicional [inkondiθjo'nal] *adj* unconditional; (*apoyo*) wholehearted; (*partidario*) staunch

inconfundible [inkonfun'diβle] *adj* unmistakable

incongruente [inkon'grwente] *adj* incongruous

inconsciente [inkons'θjente] *adj*

unconscious; thoughtless

inconsecuente [inkonse'kwente] adj inconsistent

inconstante [inkons'tante] adj inconstant

incontable [inkon'taβle] adj countless, innumerable

inconveniencia [inkombe'njenθja] nf unsuitability, inappropriateness; (descortesía) impoliteness; **inconveniente** adj unsuitable; impolite ▷ nm obstacle; (desventaja) disadvantage; **el inconveniente es que ...** the trouble is that ...

incordiar [inkor'ðjar] (fam) vt to bug, annoy

incorporar [inkorpo'rar] vt to incorporate; **incorporarse** vr to sit up; **~se a** to join

incorrecto, -a [inko'rrekto, a] adj (gen) incorrect, wrong; (comportamiento) bad-mannered

incorregible [inkorre'xiβle] adj incorrigible

incrédulo, -a [in'kreðulo, a] adj incredulous, unbelieving; sceptical

increíble [inkre'iβle] adj incredible

incremento [inkre'mento] nm increment; (aumento) rise, increase

increpar [inkre'par] vt to reprimand

incruento, -a [in'krwento, a] adj bloodless

incrustar [inkrus'tar] vt to incrust; (piedras: en joya) to inlay

incubar [inku'βar] vt to incubate

inculcar [inkul'kar] vt to inculcate

inculto, -a [in'kulto, a] adj (persona) uneducated; (grosero) uncouth ▷ nm/f ignoramus

incumplimiento [inkumpli'mjento] nm non-fulfilment; **incumplimiento de contrato** breach of contract

incurrir [inku'rrir] vi: **~ en** to incur; (crimen) to commit

indagar [inda'ɣar] vt to investigate; to search; (averiguar) to ascertain

indecente [inde'θente] adj indecent,

improper; (lascivo) obscene

indeciso, -a [inde'θiso, a] adj (por decidir) undecided; (vacilante) hesitant

indefenso, -a [inde'fenso, a] adj defenceless

indefinido, -a [indefi'niðo, a] adj indefinite; (vago) vague, undefined

indemne [in'demne] adj (objeto) undamaged; (persona) unharmed, unhurt

indemnizar [indemni'θar] vt to indemnify; (compensar) to compensate

independencia [indepen'denθja] nf independence

independiente [indepen'djente] adj (libre) independent; (autónomo) self-sufficient

indeterminado, -a [indetermi'naðo, a] adj indefinite; (desconocido) indeterminate

India ['indja] nf: **la ~** India

indicación [indika'θjon] nf indication; (señal) sign; (sugerencia) suggestion, hint

indicado, -a [indi'kaðo, a] adj (momento, método) right; (tratamiento) appropriate; (solución) likely

indicador [indika'ðor] nm indicator; (Tec) gauge, meter

indicar [indi'kar] vt (mostrar) to indicate, show; (termómetro etc) to read, register; (señalar) to point to

índice ['indiθe] nm index; (catálogo) catalogue; (Anat) index finger, forefinger; **índice de materias** table of contents

indicio [in'diθjo] nm indication, sign; (en pesquisa etc) clue

indiferencia [indife'renθja] nf indifference; (apatía) apathy; **indiferente** adj indifferent

indígena [in'dixena] adj indigenous, native ▷ nmf native

indigestión [indixes'tjon] nf indigestion

indigesto, -a [indi'xesto, a] adj (alimento) indigestible; (fig) turgid

indignación [indixna'θjon] nf

indignation

indignar [indix'nar] vt to anger, make indignant; **indignarse** vr: **~se por** to get indignant about

indigno, -a [in'dixno, a] adj (despreciable) low, contemptible; (inmerecido) unworthy

indio, -a ['indjo, a] adj, nm/f Indian

indirecta [indi'rekta] nf insinuation, innuendo; (sugerencia) hint

indirecto, -a [indi'rekto, a] adj indirect

indiscreción [indiskre'θjon] nf (imprudencia) indiscretion; (irreflexión) tactlessness; (acto) gaffe, faux pas

indiscreto, -a [indis'kreto, a] adj indiscreet

indiscutible [indisku'tiβle] adj indisputable, unquestionable

indispensable [indispen'saβle] adj indispensable, essential

indispuesto, -a [indis'pwesto, a] adj (enfermo) unwell, indisposed

indistinto, -a [indis'tinto, a] adj indistinct; (vago) vague

individual [indiβi'ðwal] adj individual; (habitación) single ▷ nm (Deporte) singles sg

individuo, -a [indi'βiðwo, a] adj, nm individual

índole ['indole] nf (naturaleza) nature; (clase) sort, kind

inducir [indu'θir] vt to induce; (inferir) to infer; (persuadir) to persuade

indudable [indu'ðaβle] adj undoubted; (incuestionable) unquestionable

indultar [indul'tar] vt (perdonar) to pardon, reprieve; (librar de pago) to exempt; **indulto** nm pardon; exemption

industria [in'dustrja] nf industry; (habilidad) skill; **industrial** adj industrial ▷ nm industrialist

inédito, -a [in'eðito, a] adj (texto) unpublished; (nuevo) new

ineficaz [inefi'kaθ] adj (inútil) ineffective; (ineficiente) inefficient

ineludible [inelu'ðiβle] adj inescapable, unavoidable

ineptitud [inepti'tuð] nf ineptitude, incompetence; **inepto, -a** adj inept, incompetent

inequívoco, -a [ine'kiβoko, a] adj unequivocal; (inconfundible) unmistakable

inercia [in'erθja] nf inertia; (pasividad) passivity

inerte [in'erte] adj inert; (inmóvil) motionless

inesperado, -a [inespe'raðo, a] adj unexpected, unforeseen

inestable [ines'taβle] adj unstable

inevitable [ineβi'taβle] adj inevitable

inexacto, -a [inek'sakto, a] adj inaccurate; (falso) untrue

inexperto, -a [inek'sperto, a] adj (novato) inexperienced

infalible [infa'liβle] adj infallible; (plan) foolproof

infame [in'fame] adj infamous; (horrible) dreadful; **infamia** nf infamy; (deshonra) disgrace

infancia [in'fanθja] nf infancy, childhood

infantería [infante'ria] nf infantry

infantil [infan'til] adj (pueril, aniñado) infantile; (cándido) childlike; (literatura, ropa etc) children's

infarto [in'farto] nm (tb: **~ de miocardio**) heart attack

infatigable [infati'ɣaβle] adj tireless, untiring

infección [infek'θjon] nf infection; **infeccioso, -a** adj infectious

infectar [infek'tar] vt to infect; **infectarse** vr to become infected

infeliz [infe'liθ] adj unhappy, wretched ▷ nmf wretch

inferior [infe'rjor] adj inferior; (situación) lower ▷ nmf inferior, subordinate

inferir [infe'rir] vt (deducir) to infer, deduce; (causar) to cause

infidelidad [infiðeli'ðað] nf (gen)

infidelity, unfaithfulness

infiel [in'fjel] *adj* unfaithful, disloyal; (*erróneo*) inaccurate ▷ *nmf* infidel, unbeliever

infierno [in'fjerno] *nm* hell

infiltrarse [infil'trarse] *vr*: **~ en** to infiltrate in(to); (*persona*) to work one's way in(to)

ínfimo, -a ['infimo, a] *adj* (*más bajo*) lowest; (*despreciable*) vile, mean

infinidad [infini'ðað] *nf* infinity; (*abundancia*) great quantity

infinito, -a [infi'nito, a] *adj, nm* infinite

inflación [infla'θjon] *nf* (*hinchazón*) swelling; (*monetaria*) inflation; (*fig*) conceit

inflamable [infl'maβle] *adj* flammable

inflamar [infla'mar] *vt* (*Med: fig*) to inflame; **inflamarse** *vr* to catch fire; to become inflamed

inflar [in'flar] *vt* (*hinchar*) to inflate, blow up; (*fig*) to exaggerate; **inflarse** *vr* to swell (up); (*fig*) to get conceited

inflexible [inflek'siβle] *adj* inflexible; (*fig*) unbending

influencia [influ'enθja] *nf* influence

influir [influ'ir] *vt* to influence

influjo [in'fluxo] *nm* influence

influya *etc vb* V **influir**

influyente [influ'jente] *adj* influential

información [informa'θjon] *nf* information; (*noticias*) news *sg*; (*Jur*) inquiry; **I~** (*oficina*) Information Office; (*mostrador*) Information Desk; (*Tel*) Directory Enquiries

informal [infor'mal] *adj* (*gen*) informal

informar [infor'mar] *vt* (*gen*) to inform; (*revelar*) to reveal, make known ▷ *vi* (*Jur*) to plead; (*denunciar*) to inform; (*dar cuenta de*) to report on; **informarse** *vr* to find out; **~se de** to inquire into

informática [infor'matika] *nf* computer science, information technology

informe [in'forme] *adj* shapeless ▷ *nm* report

infracción [infrak'θjon] *nf* infraction, infringement

infravalorar [infrabalo'rar] *vt* to undervalue, underestimate

infringir [infrin'xir] *vt* to infringe, contravene

infundado, -a [infun'daðo, a] *adj* groundless, unfounded

infundir [infun'dir] *vt* to infuse, instil

infusión [infu'sjon] *nf* infusion; **infusión de manzanilla** camomile tea

ingeniería [inxenje'ria] *nf* engineering; **ingeniería genética** genetic engineering; **ingeniero, -a** *nm/f* engineer; **ingeniero civil** *o* **de caminos** civil engineer

ingenio [in'xenjo] *nm* (*talento*) talent; (*agudeza*) wit; (*habilidad*) ingenuity, inventiveness; **ingenio azucarero** (*LAM*) sugar refinery; **ingenioso, -a** [inxe'njoso, a] *adj* ingenious, clever; (*divertido*) witty; **ingenuo, -a** *adj* ingenuous

ingerir [inxe'rir] *vt* to ingest; (*tragar*) to swallow; (*consumir*) to consume

Inglaterra [ingla'terra] *nf* England

ingle ['ingle] *nf* groin

inglés, -esa [in'gles, esa] *adj* English ▷ *nm/f* Englishman(-woman) ▷ *nm* (*Ling*) English

ingrato, -a [in'grato, a] *adj* (*gen*) ungrateful

ingrediente [ingre'ðjente] *nm* ingredient

ingresar [ingre'sar] *vt* (*dinero*) to deposit ▷ *vi* to come in; **~ en el hospital** to go into hospital

ingreso [in'greso] *nm* (*entrada*) entry; (*en hospital etc*) admission; **ingresos** *nmpl* (*dinero*) income *sg*; (*Com*) takings *pl*

inhabitable [inaβi'taβle] *adj* uninhabitable

inhalar [ina'lar] *vt* to inhale

inhibir [ini'βir] *vt* to inhibit

inhóspito, -a [i'nospito, a] adj
(región, paisaje) inhospitable

inhumano, -a [inu'mano, a] adj
inhuman

inicial [ini'θjal] adj, nf initial

iniciar [ini'θjar] vt (persona) to
initiate; (empezar) to begin, commence;
(conversación) to start up

iniciativa [iniθja'tiβa] nf initiative;
iniciativa privada private enterprise

ininterrumpido, -a
[ininterrum'piðo, a] adj
uninterrupted

injertar [inxer'tar] vt to graft;
injerto nm graft

injuria [in'xurja] nf (agravio, ofensa)
offence; (insulto) insult

⏐ No confundir **injuria** con la palabra
  inglesa injury.

injusticia [inxus'tiθja] nf injustice

injusto, -a [in'xusto, a] adj unjust,
unfair

inmadurez [inmaðu'reθ] nf
immaturity

inmediaciones [inmeðja'θjones]
nfpl neighbourhood sg, environs

inmediato, -a [inme'ðjato,
a] adj immediate; (contiguo)
adjoining; (rápido) prompt; (próximo)
neighbouring, next; **de ~** immediately

inmejorable [inmexu'raβle] adj
unsurpassable; (precio) unbeatable

inmenso, -a [in'menso, a] adj
immense, huge

inmigración [inmixra'θjon] nf
immigration

inmobiliarla [inmoβi'ljarja] nf
estate agency

inmolar [inmo'lar] vt to immolate,
sacrifice

inmoral [inmo'ral] adj immoral

inmortal [inmor'tal] adj immortal;
inmortalizar vt to immortalize

inmóvil [in'moβil] adj immobile

inmueble [in'mweβle] adj: **bienes
~s** real estate, landed property ▷ nm
property

inmundo, -a [in'mundo, a] adj

filthy

inmune [in'mune] adj: **~ (a)** (Med)
immune (to)

inmunidad [inmuni'ðað] nf
immunity

inmutarse [inmu'tarse] vr to turn
pale; **no se inmutó** he didn't turn a hair

innato, -a [in'nato, a] adj innate

innecesario, -a [inneθe'sarjo, a] adj
unnecessary

innovación [innoβa'θjon] nf
innovation

innovar [inno'βar] vt to introduce

inocencia [ino'θenθja] nf innocence

inocentada [inoθen'taða] nf
practical joke

inocente [ino'θente] adj (ingenuo)
naive, innocent; (inculpable) innocent;
(sin malicia) harmless ▷ nmf simpleton;
el día de los (Santos) l~s ≈ April
Fools' Day

⬤ **DÍA DE LOS (SANTOS)**
⬤ **INOCENTES**
⬤
⬤ The 28th December, el **día de los
⬤ (Santos) Inocentes**, is when
⬤ the Church commemorates the
⬤ story of Herod's slaughter of the
⬤ innocent children of Judaea.
⬤ On this day Spaniards play
⬤ **inocentadas** (practical jokes) on
⬤ each other, much like our April
⬤ Fool's Day pranks.

inodoro [ino'ðoro] nm toilet,
lavatory (BRIT)

inofensivo, -a [inofen'siβo, a] adj
inoffensive, harmless

inolvidable [inolβi'ðaβle] adj
unforgettable

inoportuno, -a [inopor'tuno, a] adj
untimely; (molesto) inconvenient

inoxidable [inoksi'ðaβle] adj: **acero
~** stainless steel

inquietar [inkje'tar] vt to worry,
trouble; **inquietarse** vr to worry,
get upset; **inquieto, -a** adj anxious,

worried; **inquietud** nf anxiety, worry

inquilino, -a [inki'lino, a] nm/f
tenant

insaciable [insa'θjaβle] adj
insatiable

inscribir [inskri'βir] vt to inscribe; ~
a algn en (lista) to put sb on; (censo) to
register sb on

inscripción [inskrip'θjon] nf
inscription; (Escol etc) enrolment; (en
censo) registration

insecticida [insekti'θiða] nm
insecticide

insecto [in'sekto] nm insect

inseguridad [inseɣuri'ðað] nf
insecurity; **inseguridad ciudadana**
lack of safety in the streets

inseguro, -a [inse'ɣuro, a] adj
insecure; (inconstante) unsteady;
(incierto) uncertain

insensato, -a [insen'sato, a] adj
foolish, stupid

insensible [insen'siβle] adj
(gen) insensitive; (movimiento)
imperceptible; (sin sentido) numb

insertar [inser'tar] vt to insert

inservible [inser'βiβle] adj useless

insignia [in'siɣnja] nf (señal
distintiva) badge; (estandarte) flag

insignificante [insiɣnifi'kante] adj
insignificant

insinuar [insi'nwar] vt to insinuate,
imply

insípido, -a [in'sipiðo, a] adj insipid

insistir [insis'tir] vi to insist; ~ **en
algo** to insist on sth; (enfatizar) to
stress sth

insolación [insola'θjon] nf (Med)
sunstroke

insolente [inso'lente] adj insolent

insólito, -a [in'solito, a] adj unusual

insoluble [inso'luβle] adj insoluble

insomnio [in'somnjo] nm insomnia

insonorizado, -a [insonori'θaðo, a]
adj (cuarto etc) soundproof

insoportable [insopor'taβle] adj
unbearable

inspección [inspek'θjon] nf

inspection, check; **inspeccionar**
vt (examinar) to inspect, examine;
(controlar) to check

inspector, a [inspek'tor, a] nm/f
inspector

inspiración [inspira'θjon] nf
inspiration

inspirar [inspi'rar] vt to inspire;
(Med) to inhale; **inspirarse** vr: **~se en**
to be inspired by

instalación [instala'θjon] nf (equipo)
fittings pl, equipment; **instalación
eléctrica** wiring

instalar [insta'lar] vt (establecer)
to instal; (erguir) to set up, erect;
instalarse vr to establish o.s.; (en una
vivienda) to move into

instancia [ins'tanθja] nf (Jur)
petition; (ruego) request; **en última ~**
as a last resort

instantáneo, -a [instan'taneo,
a] adj instantaneous; **café ~** instant
coffee

instante [ins'tante] nm instant,
moment; **al ~** right now

instar [ins'tar] vt to press, urge

instaurar [instau'rar] vt (costumbre)
to establish; (normas, sistema) to bring
in, introduce; (gobierno) to instal

instigar [insti'ɣar] vt to instigate

instinto [ins'tinto] nm instinct; **por
~** instinctively

institución [institu'θjon] nf
institution, establishment

instituir [institu'ir] vt to establish;
(fundar) to found; **instituto** nm (gen)
institute; (ESP Escol) ≈ comprehensive
(BRIT) o high (US) school

institutriz [institu'triθ] nf
governess

instrucción [instruk'θjon] nf
instruction

instructor [instruk'tor] nm
instructor

instruir [instru'ir] vt (gen) to
instruct; (enseñar) to teach, educate

instrumento [instru'mento] nm
(gen) instrument; (herramienta) tool,

implement

insubordinarse [insuβorði'narse] vr to rebel

insuficiente [insufi'θjente] adj (gen) insufficient; (Escol: calificación) unsatisfactory

insular [insu'lar] adj insular

insultar [insul'tar] vt to insult; **insulto** nm insult

insuperable [insupe'raβle] adj (excelente) unsurpassable; (problema etc) insurmountable

insurrección [insurrek'θjon] nf insurrection, rebellion

intachable [inta'tʃaβle] adj irreproachable

intacto, -a [in'takto, a] adj intact

integral [inte'ɣral] adj integral; (completo) complete; **pan ~** wholemeal (BRIT) o wholewheat (US) bread

integrar [inte'ɣrar] vt to make up, compose; (Mat: fig) to integrate

integridad [inteɣri'ðað] nf wholeness; (carácter) integrity; **íntegro, -a** adj whole, entire; (honrado) honest

intelectual [intelek'twal] adj, nmf intellectual

inteligencia [inteli'xenθja] nf intelligence; (ingenio) ability; **inteligente** adj intelligent

intemperie [intem'perje] nf: **a la ~** out in the open, exposed to the elements

intención [inten'θjon] nf (gen) intention, purpose; **con segundas intenciones** maliciously; **con ~** deliberately

intencionado, -a [intenθjo'naðo, a] adj deliberate; **mal ~** ill-disposed, hostile

intensidad [intensi'ðað] nf (gen) intensity; (Elec, Tec) strength; **llover con ~** to rain hard

intenso, -a [in'tenso, a] adj intense; (sentimiento) profound, deep

intentar [inten'tar] vt (tratar) to try, attempt; **intento** nm attempt

interactivo, -a [interak'tiβo, a] adj (Inform) interactive

intercalar [interka'lar] vt to insert

intercambio [inter'kambjo] nm exchange, swap

interceder [interθe'ðer] vi to intercede

interceptar [interθep'tar] vt to intercept

interés [inte'res] nm (gen) interest; (parte) share, part; (pey) self-interest; **intereses creados** vested interests

interesado, -a [intere'saðo, a] adj interested; (prejuiciado) prejudiced; (pey) mercenary, self-seeking

interesante [intere'sante] adj interesting

interesar [intere'sar] vt, vi to interest, be of interest to: **interesarse** vr: **~se en** o **por** to take an interest in

interferir [interfe'rir] vt to interfere with; (Tel) to jam ▷ vi to interfere

interfón [inter'fon] (MÉX) nm entry phone

interino, -a [inte'rino, a] adj temporary ▷ nm/f temporary holder of a post; (Med) locum; (Escol) supply teacher

interior [inte'rjor] adj inner, inside; (Com) domestic, internal ▷ nm interior, inside; (fig) soul, mind; **Ministerio del I~** ≈ Home Office (BRIT) ≈ Department of the Interior (US); **interiorista** (ESP) nmf interior designer

interjección [interxek'θjon] nf interjection

interlocutor, a [interloku'tor, a] nm/f speaker

intermedio, -a [inter'meðjo, a] adj intermediate ▷ nm interval

interminable [intermi'naβle] adj endless

intermitente [intermi'tente] adj intermittent ▷ nm (Auto) indicator

internacional [internaθjo'nal] adj international

internado [inter'naðo] nm boarding

school

internar [inter'nar] vt to intern; (en un manicomio) to commit; **internarse** vr (penetrar) to penetrate

internauta [inter'nauta] nmf web surfer, Internet user

Internet, internet [inter'net] nm o f Internet

interno, -a [in'terno, a] adj internal, interior; (Pol etc) domestic ▷ nm/f (alumno) boarder

interponer [interpo'ner] vt to interpose, put in; **interponerse** vr to intervene

interpretación [interpreta'θjon] nf interpretation

interpretar [interpre'tar] vt to interpret; (Teatro, Mús) to perform, play; **intérprete** nmf (Ling) interpreter, translator; (Mús, Teatro) performer, artist(e)

interrogación [interroxa'θjon] nf interrogation; (Ling: tb: **signo de ~**) question mark

interrogar [interro'xar] vt to interrogate, question

interrumpir [interrum'pir] vt to interrupt

interrupción [interrup'θjon] nf interruption

interruptor [interrup'tor] nm (Elec) switch

intersección [intersek'θjon] nf intersection

interurbano, -a [interur'βano, a] adj: **llamada interurbana** long-distance call

intervalo [inter'βalo] nm interval; (descanso) break

intervenir [interβe'nir] vt (controlar) to control, supervise; (Med) to operate on ▷ vi (participar) to take part, participate; (mediar) to intervene

interventor, a [interβen'tor, a] nm/f inspector; (Com) auditor

intestino [intes'tino] nm (Med) intestine

intimar [inti'mar] vi to become friendly

intimidad [intimi'ðað] nf intimacy; (familiaridad) familiarity; (vida privada) private life; (Jur) privacy

íntimo, -a ['intimo, a] adj intimate

intolerable [intole'raβle] adj intolerable, unbearable

intoxicación [intoksika'θjon] nf poisoning; **intoxicación alimenticia** food poisoning

intranet [intra'net] nf intranet

intranquilo, -a [intran'kilo, a] adj worried

intransitable [intransi'taβle] adj impassable

intrépido, -a [in'trepiðo, a] adj intrepid

intriga [in'trixa] nf intrigue; (plan) plot; **intrigar** vt, vi to intrigue

intrínseco, -a [in'trinseko, a] adj intrinsic

introducción [introðuk'θjon] nf introduction

introducir [introðu'θir] vt (gen) to introduce; (moneda etc) to insert; (Inform) to input, enter

intromisión [intromi'sjon] nf interference, meddling

introvertido, -a [introβer'tiðo, a] adj, nm/f introvert

intruso, -a [in'truso, a] adj intrusive ▷ nm/f intruder

intuición [intwi'θjon] nf intuition

inundación [inunda'θjon] nf flood(ing); **inundar** vt to flood; (fig) to swamp, inundate

inusitado, -a [inusi'taðo, a] adj unusual, rare

inútil [in'util] adj useless; (esfuerzo) vain, fruitless

inutilizar [inutili'θar] vt to make o render useless

invadir [imba'ðir] vt to invade

inválido, -a [im'baliðo, a] adj invalid ▷ nm/f invalid

invasión [imba'sjon] nf invasion

invasor, a [imba'sor, a] adj invading ▷ nm/f invader

invención [imben'θjon] *nf* invention

inventar [imben'tar] *vt* to invent

inventario [imben'tarjo] *nm* inventory

invento [im'bento] *nm* invention

inventor, a [imben'tor, a] *nm/f* inventor

invernadero [imberna'ðero] *nm* greenhouse

inverosímil [imbero'simil] *adj* implausible

inversión [imber'sjon] *nf* (Com) investment

inverso, -a [im'berso, a] *adj* inverse, opposite; **en el orden ~** in reverse order; **a la inversa** inversely, the other way round

inversor, a [imber'sor, a] *nm/f* (Com) investor

invertir [imber'tir] *vt* (Com) to invest; (volcar) to turn upside down; (tiempo etc) to spend

investigación [imbestiɣa'θjon] *nf* investigation; (Escol) research; **investigación y desarrollo** research and development

investigar [imbesti'ɣar] *vt* to investigate; (Escol) to do research into

invierno [im'bjerno] *nm* winter

invisible [imbi'siβle] *adj* invisible

invitación [imbita'θjon] *nf* invitation

invitado, -a [imbi'taðo, a] *nm/f* guest

invitar [imbi'tar] *vt* to invite; (incitar) to entice; (pagar) to buy, pay for

invocar [imbo'kar] *vt* to invoke, call on

involucrar [imbolu'krar] *vt*: **~ en** to involve in; **involucrarse** *vr* (persona): **~se en** to get mixed up in

involuntario, -a [imbolun'tarjo, a] *adj* (movimiento, gesto) involuntary; (error) unintentional

inyección [injek'θjon] *nf* injection

inyectar [injek'tar] *vt* to inject

iPod® ['ipoð] (pl ~s) *nm* iPod®

○ **PALABRA CLAVE**

ir [ir] *vi* **1** to go; (a pie) to walk; (viajar) to travel; **ir caminando** to walk; **fui en tren** I went o travelled by train; **¡(ahora) voy!** (I'm just) coming!

2: **ir (a) por**: **ir (a) por el médico** to fetch the doctor

3 (progresar: persona, cosa) to go; **el trabajo va muy bien** work is going very well; **¿cómo te va?** how are things going?; **me va muy bien** I'm getting on very well; **le fue fatal** it went awfully badly for him

4 (funcionar): **el coche no va muy bien** the car isn't running very well

5: **te va estupendamente ese color** that colour suits you fantastically well

6 (locuciones): **¿vino? – ¡que va!** did he come? – of course not!; **vamos, no llores** come on, don't cry; **¡vaya coche!** what a car!, that's some car!

7: **no vaya a ser: tienes que correr, no vaya a ser que pierdas el tren** you'll have to run so as not to miss the train

8 (+ pp): **iba vestido muy bien** he was very well dressed

9: **ni me** etc **va ni me** etc **viene** I etc don't care

▷ *vb aux* **1** **ir a: voy/iba a hacerlo hoy** I am/was going to do it today

2 (+ gerundio): **iba anocheciendo** it was getting dark; **todo se me iba aclarando** everything was gradually becoming clearer to me

3 (+ pp: = pasivo): **van vendidos 300 ejemplares** 300 copies have been sold so far

irse *vr* **1**: **¿por dónde se va al zoológico?** which is the way to the zoo?

2 (marcharse) to leave; **ya se habrán ido** they must already have left o gone

ira ['ira] *nf* anger, rage

Irak [i'rak] *nm* = **Iraq**

Irán [i'ran] *nm* Iran; **iraní** *adj, nmf* Iranian

Iraq [i'rak] *nm* Iraq; **iraquí** *adj, nmf* Iraqi

iris ['iris] *nm inv* (*tb*: **arco ~**) rainbow; (*Anat*) iris

Irlanda [ir'landa] *nf* Ireland; **Irlanda del Norte** Northern Ireland; **irlandés, -esa** *adj* Irish ▷ *nm/f* Irishman(-woman); **los irlandeses** the Irish

ironía [iro'nia] *nf* irony; **irónico, -a** *adj* ironic(al)

IRPF *nm abr* (= *Impuesto sobre la Renta de las Personas Físicas*) (personal) income tax

irreal [irre'al] *adj* unreal

irregular [irreɣu'lar] *adj* (*gen*) irregular; (*situación*) abnormal

irremediable [irreme'ðjaβle] *adj* irremediable; (*vicio*) incurable

irreparable [irrepa'raβle] *adj* (*daños*) irreparable; (*pérdida*) irrecoverable

irrespetuoso, -a [irrespe'twoso, a] *adj* disrespectful

irresponsable [irrespon'saβle] *adj* irresponsible

irreversible [irreβer'sible] *adj* irreversible

irrigar [irri'ɣar] *vt* to irrigate

irrisorio, -a [irri'sorjo, a] *adj* derisory, ridiculous

irritar [irri'tar] *vt* to irritate, annoy

irrupción [irrup'θjon] *nf* irruption; (*invasión*) invasion

isla ['isla] *nf* island

Islam [is'lam] *nm* Islam; **las enseñanzas del ~** the teachings of Islam; **islámico, -a** *adj* Islamic

islandés, -esa [islan'des, esa] *adj* Icelandic ▷ *nm/f* Icelander

Islandia [is'landja] *nf* Iceland

isleño, -a [is'leɲo, a] *adj* island *cpd* ▷ *nm/f* islander

Israel [isra'el] *nm* Israel; **israelí** *adj, nmf* Israeli

istmo ['istmo] *nm* isthmus

Italia [i'talja] *nf* Italy; **italiano, -a** *adj, nm/f* Italian

itinerario [itine'rarjo] *nm* itinerary, route

ITV (*ESP*) *nf abr* (= *inspección técnica de vehículos*) roadworthiness test, ≈ MOT (*BRIT*)

IVA ['iβa] *nm abr* (= *impuesto sobre el valor añadido*) VAT

izar [i'θar] *vt* to hoist

izdo, -a *abr* (= *izquierdo, a*) l

izquierda [iθ'kjerda] *nf* left; (*Pol*) left (wing); **a la ~** (*estar*) on the left; (*torcer etc*) (to the) left

izquierdo, -a [iθ'kjerðo, a] *adj* left

j

jabalí [xaβa'li] *nm* wild boar
jabalina [xaβa'lina] *nf* javelin
jabón [xa'βon] *nm* soap
jaca ['xaka] *nf* pony
jacal [xa'kal] (*MÉX*) *nm* shack
jacinto [xa'θinto] *nm* hyacinth
jactarse [xak'tarse] *vr* to boast, brag
jadear [xaðe'ar] *vi* to pant, gasp
  for breath
jaguar [xa'ɣwar] *nm* jaguar
jaiba ['xaiβa] (*LAM*) *nf* crab
jalar [xa'lar] (*LAM*) *vt* to pull
jalea [xa'lea] *nf* jelly
jaleo [xa'leo] *nm* racket, uproar;
  armar un ~ to kick up a racket
jalón [xa'lon] (*LAM*) *nm* tug
jamás [xa'mas] *adv* never
jamón [xa'mon] *nm* ham; **jamón
  dulce** *o* **de York** cooked ham; **jamón
  serrano** cured ham
Japón [xa'pon] *nm* Japan; **japonés,
  -esa** *adj, nm/f* Japanese ▷ *nm* (*Ling*)
  Japanese
jaque ['xake] *nm* (*Ajedrez*) check;
  jaque mate checkmate

jaqueca [xa'keka] *nf* (very bad)
  headache, migraine
jarabe [xa'raβe] *nm* syrup
jardín [xar'ðin] *nm* garden; **jardín
  infantil** *o* **de infancia** nursery (school);
  jardinería *nf* gardening; **jardinero, -a**
  nm/f gardener
jardinaje [xarði'naxe] *nm* gardening
jarra ['xarra] *nf* jar; (*jarro*) jug
jarro ['xarro] *nm* jug
jarrón [xa'rron] *nm* vase
jaula ['xaula] *nf* cage
jauría [xau'ria] *nf* pack of hounds
jazmín [xaθ'min] *nm* jasmine
J.C. *abr* (=*Jesucristo*) J.C.
jeans [jins, dʒins] (*LAM*) *nmpl* jeans,
  denims; **unos ~** a pair of jeans
jefatura [xefa'tura] *nf* (*tb*: **~ de
  policía**) police headquarters *sg*
jefe, -a ['xefe, a] *nm/f* (*gen*) chief,
  head; (*patrón*) boss; **jefe de cocina**
  chef; **jefe de estación** stationmaster;
  jefe de Estado head of state; **jefe de
  estudios** (*Escol*) director of studies;
  jefe de gobierno head of government
jengibre [xen'xiβre] *nm* ginger
jeque ['xeke] *nm* sheik
jerárquico, -a [xe'rarkiko, a] *adj*
  hierarchic(al)
jerez [xe'reθ] *nm* sherry
jerga ['xerxa] *nf* jargon
jeringa [xe'ringa] *nf* syringe;
  (*LAM: molestia*) annoyance, bother;
  jeringuilla *nf* syringe
jeroglífico [xero'xlifiko] *nm*
  hieroglyphic
jersey [xer'sei] (*pl* **~s**) *nm* jersey,
  pullover, jumper
Jerusalén [xerusa'len] *n* Jerusalem
Jesucristo [xesu'kristo] *nm* Jesus
  Christ
jesuita [xe'swita] *adj, nm* Jesuit
Jesús [xe'sus] *nm* Jesus; **¡~!** good
  heavens!; (*al estornudar*) bless you!
jinete [xi'nete] *nmf*
  horseman(-woman), rider
jipijapa [xipi'xapa] (*LAM*) *nm* straw
  hat

jirafa [xi'rafa] nf giraffe

jirón [xi'ron] nm rag, shred

jitomate [xito'mate] (MÉX) nm tomato

joder [xo'ðer] (fam!) vt, vi to fuck (!)

jogging ['joɣin] (RPL) nm tracksuit (BRIT), sweat suit (US)

jornada [xor'naða] nf (viaje de un día) day's journey; (camino o viaje entero) journey; (día de trabajo) working day

jornal [xor'nal] nm (day's) wage; **jornalero, -a** [xorna'lero, a] nm (day) labourer

joroba [xo'roβa] nf hump, hunched back; **jorobado, -a** adj hunchbacked ▷ nm/f hunchback

jota ['xota] nf (the letter) J; (danza) Aragonese dance; **no saber ni ~** to have no idea

joven ['xoβen] (pl **jóvenes**) adj young ▷ nm young man, youth ▷ nf young woman, girl

joya ['xoja] nf jewel, gem; (fig: persona) gem; **joyas de fantasía** costume o imitation jewellery; **joyería** nf (joyas) jewellery; (tienda) jeweller's (shop); **joyero** nm (persona) jeweller; (caja) jewel case

juanete [xwa'nete] nm (del pie) bunion

jubilación [xuβila'θjon] nf (retiro) retirement

jubilado, -a [xuβi'laðo, a] adj retired ▷ nm/f pensioner (BRIT), senior citizen

jubilar [xuβi'lar] vt to pension off, retire; (fam) to discard; **jubilarse** vr to retire

júbilo ['xuβilo] nm joy, rejoicing; **jubiloso, -a** adj jubilant

judía [xu'ðia] (ESP) nf (Culin) bean; **judía blanca/verde** haricot/French bean; V tb **judío**

judicial [xuði'θjal] adj judicial

judío, -a [xu'ðio, a] adj Jewish ▷ nm/f Jew(ess)

judo ['juðo] nm judo

juego etc ['xweɣo] vb V **jugar** ▷ nm (gen) play; (pasatiempo, partido) game; (en casino) gambling; (conjunto) set; fuera de ~ (Deporte: persona) offside; (: pelota) out of play; **juego de mesa** board game; **juego de palabras** pun, play on words; **Juegos Olímpicos** Olympic Games

juerga ['xwerɣa] (ESP: fam) nf binge; (fiesta) party; **ir de ~** to go out on a binge

jueves ['xweβes] nm inv Thursday

juez [xweθ] nmf judge; **juez de instrucción** examining magistrate; **juez de línea** linesman; **juez de salida** starter

jugada [xu'ɣaða] nf play; **buena ~** good move o shot o stroke etc

jugador, a [xuɣa'ðor, a] nm/f player; (en casino) gambler

jugar [xu'ɣar] vt, vi to play; (en casino) to gamble; (apostar) to bet; **~ al fútbol** to play football

juglar [xu'ɣlar] nm minstrel

jugo ['xuɣo] nm (Bot) juice; (fig) essence, substance; **jugo de naranja** (LAM) orange juice; **jugoso, -a** adj juicy; (fig) substantial, important

juguete [xu'ɣete] nm toy; **juguetear** vi to play; **juguetería** nf toyshop

juguetón, -ona [xuɣe'ton, ona] adj playful

juicio ['xwiθjo] nm judgement; (razón) sanity, reason; (opinión) opinion

julio ['xuljo] nm July

jumper ['dʒumper] (LAM) nm pinafore dress (BRIT), jumper (US)

junco ['xunko] nm rush, reed

jungla ['xungla] nf jungle

junio ['xunjo] nm June

junta ['xunta] nf (asamblea) meeting, assembly; (comité, consejo) council, committee; (Com, Finanzas) board; (Tec) joint; **junta directiva** board of directors

juntar [xun'tar] vt to join, unite; (maquinaria) to assemble, put together; (dinero) to collect; **juntarse** vr to join, meet; (reunirse: personas) to meet, assemble; (arrimarse) to approach, draw closer; **~se con algn** to join sb

junto, -a ['xunto, a] *adj* joined;
(*unido*) united; (*anexo*) near, close;
(*contiguo, próximo*) next, adjacent
▷ *adv*: **todo ~** all at once; **~s** together;
~ a near (to), next to; **~ con** (together)
with

jurado [xu'raðo] *nm* (*Jur: individuo*)
juror; (: *grupo*) jury; (*de concurso: grupo*)
panel (of judges); (: *individuo*) member
of a panel

juramento [xura'mento] *nm* oath;
(*maldición*) oath, curse; **prestar ~** to
take the oath; **tomar ~ a** to swear in,
administer the oath to

jurar [xu'rar] *vt, vi* to swear; **~ en
falso** to commit perjury; **tenérsela
jurada a algn** to have it in for sb

jurídico, -a [xu'riðiko, a] *adj* legal

jurisdicción [xurisðik'θjon]
nf (*poder, autoridad*) jurisdiction;
(*territorio*) district

justamente [xusta'mente] *adv*
justly, fairly; (*precisamente*) just, exactly

justicia [xus'tiθja] *nf* justice;
(*equidad*) fairness, justice

justificación [xustifika'θjon] *nf*
justification; **justificar** *vt* to justify

justo, -a ['xusto, a] *adj* (*equitativo*)
just, fair, right; (*preciso*) exact, correct;
(*ajustado*) tight ▷ *adv* (*precisamente*)
exactly, precisely; (*LAM: apenas a tiempo*)
just in time

juvenil [xuβe'nil] *adj* youthful

juventud [xuβen'tuð] *nf*
(*adolescencia*) youth; (*jóvenes*) young
people *pl*

juzgado [xuθ'ɣaðo] *nm* tribunal;
(*Jur*) court

juzgar [xuθ'ɣar] *vt* to judge; **a ~ por
...** to judge by ..., judging by ...

kárate ['karate] *nm* karate

kg *abr* (= *kilogramo*) kg

kilo ['kilo] *nm* kilo; **kilogramo**
nm kilogramme; **kilometraje** *nm*
distance in kilometres ≈ mileage;
kilómetro *nm* kilometre; **kilovatio**
nm kilowatt

kiosco ['kjosko] *nm* = **quiosco**

kleenex® [kli'neks] *nm* paper
handkerchief, tissue

Kosovo [ko'soβo] *nm* Kosovo

km *abr* (= *kilómetro*) km

kv *abr* (= *kilovatio*) kw

l *abr* (= *litro*) l

la [la] *art def* the ▷ *pron* her; (*Ud.*) you; (*cosa*) it ▷ *nm* (*Mús*) la; **~ del sombrero rojo** the girl in the red hat; *V tb* **el**

laberinto [laβe'rinto] *nm* labyrinth

labio ['laβjo] *nm* lip

labor [la'βor] *nf* labour; (*Agr*) farm work; (*tarea*) job, task; (*Costura*) needlework; **labores domésticas** *o* **del hogar** household chores; **laborable** *adj* (*Agr*) workable; **día laborable** working day; **laboral** *adj* (*accidente*) at work; (*jornada*) working

laboratorio [laβora'torjo] *nm* laboratory

laborista [laβo'rista] *adj*: **Partido L~** Labour Party

labrador, a [laβra'ðor, a] *adj* farming *cpd* ▷ *nm/f* farmer

labranza [la'βranθa] *nf* (*Agr*) cultivation

labrar [la'βrar] *vt* (*gen*) to work; (*madera etc*) to carve; (*fig*) to cause, bring about

laca ['laka] *nf* lacquer

lacio, -a ['laθjo, a] *adj* (*pelo*) straight

lacón [la'kon] *nm* shoulder of pork

lactancia [lak'tanθja] *nf* lactation

lácteo, -a ['lakteo, a] *adj*: **productos ~s** dairy products

ladear [laðe'ar] *vt* to tip, tilt ▷ *vi* to tilt; **ladearse** *vr* to lean

ladera [la'ðera] *nf* slope

lado ['laðo] *nm* (*gen*) side; (*fig*) protection; (*Mil*) flank; **al ~ de** beside; **poner de ~** to put on its side; **poner a un ~** to put aside; **por todos ~s** on all sides, all round (BRIT)

ladrar [la'ðrar] *vi* to bark; **ladrido** *nm* bark, barking

ladrillo [la'ðriʎo] *nm* (*gen*) brick; (*azulejo*) tile

ladrón, -ona [la'ðron, ona] *nm/f* thief

lagartija [laɣar'tixa] *nf* (*Zool*) (small) lizard

lagarto [la'ɣarto] *nm* (*Zool*) lizard

lago ['laɣo] *nm* lake

lágrima ['laɣrima] *nf* tear

laguna [la'ɣuna] *nf* (*lago*) lagoon; (*hueco*) gap

lamentable [lamen'taβle] *adj* lamentable, regrettable; (*miserable*) pitiful

lamentar [lamen'tar] *vt* (*sentir*) to regret; (*deplorar*) to lament; **lamentarse** *vr* to lament; **lo lamento mucho** I'm very sorry

lamer [la'mer] *vt* to lick

lámina ['lamina] *nf* (*plancha delgada*) sheet; (*para estampar, estampa*) plate

lámpara ['lampara] *nf* lamp; **lámpara de alcohol/gas** spirit/gas lamp; **lámpara de pie** standard lamp

lana ['lana] *nf* wool

lancha ['lantʃa] *nf* launch; **lancha motora** motorboat, speedboat

langosta [lan'gosta] *nf* (*crustáceo*) lobster; (: *de río*) crayfish; **langostino** *nm* Dublin Bay prawn

lanza ['lanθa] *nf* (*arma*) lance, spear

lanzamiento [lanθa'mjento] *nm* (*gen*) throwing; (*Náut, Com*) launch, launching; **lanzamiento de peso** putting the shot

lanzar [lan'θar] vt (gen) to throw; (Deporte: pelota) to bowl; (Náut, Com) to launch; (Jur) to evict; **lanzarse** vr to throw o.s.

lapa ['lapa] nf limpet

lapicero [lapi'θero] (CAM) nm (bolígrafo) ballpoint pen, Biro®

lápida ['lapiða] nf stone; **lápida mortuoria** headstone

lápiz ['lapiθ] nm pencil; **lápiz de color** coloured pencil; **lápiz de labios** lipstick; **lápiz de ojos** eyebrow pencil

largar [lar'ɣar] vt (soltar) to release; (aflojar) to loosen; (lanzar) to launch; (fam) to let fly; (velas) to unfurl; (LAM: lanzar) to throw; **largarse** vr (fam) to beat it; **~se a** (CS: empezar) to start to

largo, -a ['larɣo, a] adj (longitud) long; (tiempo) lengthy; (fig) generous ▷ nm length; (Mus) largo; **dos años ~s** two long years; **tiene 9 metros de ~** it is 9 metres long; **a la larga** in the long run; **a lo ~ de** along; (tiempo) all through, throughout

▎ No confundir **largo** con la palabra inglesa large.

largometraje nm feature film

laringe [la'rinxe] nf larynx; **laringitis** nf laryngitis

las [las] art def the ▷ pron them; **~ que cantan** the ones o women o girls who sing; V tb **el**

lasaña [la'saɲa] nf lasagne, lasagna

láser ['laser] nm laser

lástima ['lastima] nf (pena) pity; **dar ~** to be pitiful; **es una ~ que ...** It's a pity that ...; **¡qué ~!** what a pity!; **está hecha una ~** she looks pitiful

lastimar [lasti'mar] vt (herir) to wound; (ofender) to offend; **lastimarse** vr to hurt o.s.

lata ['lata] nf (metal) tin; (caja) tin (BRIT), can; (fam) nuisance; **en ~** tinned (BRIT), canned; **dar la ~** to be a nuisance

latente [la'tente] adj latent

lateral [late'ral] adj side cpd, lateral ▷ nm (Teatro) wings

latido [la'tiðo] nm (de corazón) beat

latifundio [lati'fundjo] nm large estate

latigazo [lati'xaθo] nm (golpe) lash; (sonido) crack

látigo ['latixo] nm whip

latín [la'tin] nm Latin

latino, -a [la'tino, a] adj Latin; **latinoamericano, -a** adj, nm/f Latin-American

latir [la'tir] vi (corazón, pulso) to beat

latitud [lati'tuð] nf (Geo) latitude

latón [la'ton] nm brass

laurel [lau'rel] nm (Bot) laurel; (Culin) bay

lava ['laβa] nf lava

lavabo [la'βaβo] nm (pila) washbasin; (tb. **~s**) toilet

lavado [la'βaðo] nm washing; (de ropa) laundry; (Arte) wash; **lavado de cerebro** brainwashing; **lavado en seco** dry-cleaning

lavadora [laβa'ðora] nf washing machine

lavanda [la'βanda] nf lavender

lavandería [laβande'ria] nf laundry; (automática) launderette

lavaplatos [laβa'platos] nm inv dishwasher

lavar [la'βar] vt to wash; (borrar) to wipe away; **lavarse** vr to wash o.s.; **~se las manos** to wash one's hands; **~se los dientes** to brush one's teeth; **~ y marcar** (pelo) to shampoo and set; **~ en seco** to dry-clean; **~ los platos** to wash the dishes

lavarropas [laβa'rropas] (RPL) nm inv washing machine

lavavajillas [laβaβa'xiʎas] nm inv dishwasher

laxante [lak'sante] nm laxative

lazarillo [laθa'riʎo] nm (tb: **perro ~**) guide dog

lazo ['laθo] nm knot; (lazada) bow; (para animales) lasso; (trampa) snare;

(*vínculo*) tie

le [le] *pron* (*directo*) him (*o* her); (: *usted*) you; (*indirecto*) to him (*o* her *o* it); (: *usted*) to you

leal [le'al] *adj* loyal; **lealtad** *nf* loyalty

lección [lek'θjon] *nf* lesson

leche ['letʃe] *nf* milk; **tiene mala ~** (*fam!*) he's a swine (!); **leche condensada** condensed milk; **leche desnatada** skimmed milk

lechería [letʃe'ria] *nf* dairy

lecho ['letʃo] *nm* (*cama: de río*) bed; (*Geo*) layer

lechón [le'tʃon] *nm* sucking (*BRIT*) *o* suckling (*US*) pig

lechoso, -a [le'tʃoso, a] *adj* milky

lechuga [le'tʃuɣa] *nf* lettuce

lechuza [le'tʃuθa] *nf* owl

lector, a [lek'tor, a] *nm/f* reader ▷ *nm:* **~ de discos compactos** CD player

lectura [lek'tura] *nf* reading

leer [le'er] *vt* to read

legado [le'ɣaðo] *nm* (*don*) bequest; (*herencia*) legacy; (*enviado*) legate

legajo [le'ɣaxo] *nm* file

legal [le'ɣal] *adj* (*gen*) legal; (*persona*) trustworthy; **legalizar** [leɣali'θar] *vt* to legalize; (*documento*) to authenticate

legaña [le'ɣaɲa] *nf* sleep (*in eyes*)

legión [le'xjon] *nf* legion; **legionario, -a** *adj* legionary ▷ *nm* legionnaire

legislación [lexisla'θjon] *nf* legislation

legislar [lexis'lar] *vi* to legislate

legislatura [lexisla'tura] *nf* (*Pol*) period of office

legítimo, -a [le'xitimo, a] *adj* (*genuino*) authentic; (*legal*) legitimate

legua [le'ɣwa] *nf* league

legumbres [le'ɣumbres] *nfpl* pulses

leído, -a [le'iðo, a] *adj* well-read

lejanía [lexa'nia] *nf* distance; **lejano, -a** *adj* far-off; (*en el tiempo*) distant; (*fig*) remote

lejía [le'xia] *nf* bleach

lejos ['lexos] *adv* far, far away; **a lo ~** in the distance; **de** *o* **desde ~** from afar;

~ de far from

lema ['lema] *nm* motto; (*Pol*) slogan

lencería [lenθe'ria] *nf* linen, drapery

lengua ['lengwa] *nf* tongue; (*Ling*) language; **morderse la ~** to hold one's tongue

lenguado [len'gwaðo] *nm* sole

lenguaje [len'gwaxe] *nm* language; **lenguaje de programación** program(m)ing language

lengüeta [len'gweta] *nf* (*Anat*) epiglottis; (*zapatos*) tongue; (*Mús*) reed

lente ['lente] *nf* lens; (*lupa*) magnifying glass; **lentes** *nfpl* lenses ▷ *nmpl* (*LAM: gafas*) glasses; **lentes bifocales/de sol** (*LAM*) bifocals/ sunglasses; **lentes de contacto** contact lenses

lenteja [len'texa] *nf* lentil; **lentejuela** *nf* sequin

lentilla [len'tiʎa] *nf* contact lens

lentitud [lenti'tuð] *nf* slowness; **con ~** slowly

lento, -a ['lento, a] *adj* slow

leña ['leɲa] *nf* firewood; **leñador, a** *nm/f* woodcutter

leño ['leɲo] *nm* (*trozo de árbol*) log; (*madero*) timber; (*fig*) blockhead

Leo ['leo] *nm* Leo

león [le'on] *nm* lion; **león marino** sea lion

leopardo [leo'parðo] *nm* leopard

leotardos [leo'tarðos] *nmpl* tights

lepra ['lepra] *nf* leprosy; **leproso, -a** *nm/f* leper

les [les] *pron* (*directo*) them; (: *ustedes*) you; (*indirecto*) to them; (: *ustedes*) to you

lesbiana [les'βjana] *adj, nf* lesbian

lesión [le'sjon] *nf* wound, lesion; (*Deporte*) injury; **lesionado, -a** *adj* injured ▷ *nm/f* injured person

letal [le'tal] *adj* lethal

letanía [leta'nia] *nf* litany

letra ['letra] *nf* letter; (*escritura*) handwriting; (*Mús*) lyrics *pl*; **letra de cambio** bill of exchange; **letra de imprenta** print; **letrado, -a** *adj*

learned ▷ nm/f lawyer; **letrero** nm
(cartel) sign; (etiqueta) label

letrina [le'trina] nf latrine

leucemia [leu'θemja] nf leukaemia

levadura [leβa'ðura] nf (para el pan)
yeast; (de cerveza) brewer's yeast

levantar [leβan'tar] vt (gen) to raise;
(del suelo) to pick up; (hacia arriba) to lift
(up); (plan) to make, draw up; (mesa)
to clear; (campamento) to strike; (fig)
to cheer up, hearten; **levantarse** vr
to get up; (enderezarse) to straighten
up; (rebelarse) to rebel; **~ el ánimo** to
cheer up

levante [le'βante] nm east coast; **el
L~** region of Spain extending from Castellón
to Murcia

levar [le'βar] vt to weigh

leve ['leβe] adj light; (fig) trivial

levita [le'βita] nf frock coat

léxico ['leksiko] nm (vocabulario)
vocabulary

ley [lei] nf (gen) law; (metal) standard

leyenda [le'jenda] nf legend

leyó etc vb V **leer**

liar [li'ar] vt to tie (up); (unir) to bind;
(envolver) to wrap (up); (enredar) to
confuse; (cigarrillo) to roll; **liarse** vr
(fam) to get involved; **~se a palos** to get
involved in a fight

Líbano ['liβano] nm: **el ~** the Lebanon

libélula [li'βelula] nf dragonfly

liberación [liβera'θjon] nf
liberation; (de la cárcel) release

liberal [liβe'ral] adj, nmf liberal

liberar [liβe'rar] vt to liberate

libertad [liβer'tað] nf liberty,
freedom; **libertad bajo fianza** bail,
libertad bajo palabra parole; **libertad
condicional** probation; **libertad
de culto/de prensa/de comercio**
freedom of worship/of the press/of
trade

libertar [liβer'tar] vt (preso) to set
free; (de una obligación) to release;
(eximir) to exempt

libertino, -a [liβer'tino, a] adj
permissive ▷ nm/f permissive person

libra ['liβra] nf pound; **L~** (Astrología)
Libra; **libra esterlina** pound sterling

libramiento [liβra'mjento] (MÉX)
nm ring road (BRIT), beltway (US)

librar [li'βrar] vt (de peligro) to save;
(batalla) to wage, fight; (de impuestos)
to exempt; (cheque) to make out; (Jur) to
exempt; **librarse** vr: **~se de** to escape
from, free o.s. from

libre ['liβre] adj free; (lugar)
unoccupied; (asiento) vacant; (de
deudas) free of debts; **~ de impuestos**
free of tax; **tiro ~** free kick; **los 100
metros ~s** the 100 metres free-style
(race); **al aire ~** in the open air

librería [liβre'ria] nf (tienda)
bookshop

▌ No confundir **librería** con la palabra
inglesa library.

librero, -a nm/f bookseller

libreta [li'βreta] nf notebook

libro ['liβro] nm book; **libro de
bolsillo** paperback; **libro de texto**
textbook; **libro electrónico** e-book

Lic. abr = **licenciado, a**

licencia [li'θenθja] nf (gen) licence;
(permiso) permission; **licencia de
caza** game licence; **licencia por
enfermedad** (MÉX, RPL) sick leave;
licenciado, -a adj licensed ▷ nm/f
graduate; **licenciar** vt (empleado) to
dismiss; (permitir) to permit, allow;
(soldado) to discharge; (estudiante) to
confer a degree upon; **licenciarse**
vr: **licenciarse en Derecho** to graduate
in law

licenciatura [liθenθja'tura] nf
(título) degree; (estudios) degree course

lícito, -a ['liθito, a] adj (legal) lawful;
(justo) fair, just; (permisible) permissible

licor [li'kor] nm spirits pl (BRIT), liquor
(US); (de frutas etc) liqueur

licuadora [likwa'ðora] nf blender

líder ['liðer] nmf leader; **liderato** nm
leadership; **liderazgo** nm leadership

lidia ['liðja] nf bullfighting; (una lidia)
bullfight; **toros de ~** fighting bulls;
lidiar vt, vi to fight

liebre ['ljeβre] *nf* hare

lienzo ['ljenθo] *nm* linen; (*Arte*) canvas; (*Arq*) wall

liga ['liɣa] *nf* (*de medias*) garter, suspender; (*LAM: goma*) rubber band; (*confederación*) league

ligadura [liɣa'ðura] *nf* bond, tie; (*Med, Mús*) ligature

ligamento [liɣa'mento] *nm* ligament

ligar [li'ɣar] *vt* (*atar*) to tie; (*unir*) to join; (*Med*) to bind up; (*Mús*) to slur ▷ *vi* to mix, blend; (*fam*): **(él) liga mucho** he pulls a lot of women; **ligarse** *vr* to commit o.s.

ligero, -a [li'xero, a] *adj* (*de peso*) light; (*tela*) thin; (*rápido*) swift, quick; (*ágil*) agile, nimble; (*de importancia*) slight; (*de carácter*) flippant, superficial ▷ *adv*: **a la ligera** superficially

liguero [li'ɣero] *nm* suspender (*BRIT*) *o* garter (*US*) belt

lija ['lixa] *nf* (*Zool*) dogfish; (*tb:* **papel de ~**) sandpaper

lila ['lila] *nf* lilac

lima ['lima] *nf* file; (*Bot*) lime; **lima de uñas** nailfile; **limar** *vt* to file

limitación [limita'θjon] *nf* limitation, limit

limitar [limi'tar] *vt* to limit; (*reducir*) to reduce, cut down ▷ *vi*: **~ con** to border on; **limitarse** *vr*: **~se a** to limit o.s. to

límite ['limite] *nm* (*gen*) limit; (*fin*) end; (*frontera*) border; **límite de velocidad** speed limit

limítrofe [li'mitrofe] *adj* neighbouring

limón [li'mon] *nm* lemon ▷ *adj*: **amarillo ~** lemon-yellow; **limonada** *nf* lemonade

limosna [li'mosna] *nf* alms *pl*; **vivir de ~** to live on charity

limpiador [limpja'ðor] (*MÉX*) *nm* = **limpiaparabrisas**

limpiaparabrisas [limpjapara'βrisas] *nm inv* windscreen (*BRIT*) *o* windshield (*US*) wiper

limpiar [lim'pjar] *vt* to clean; (*con trapo*) to wipe; (*quitar*) to wipe away; (*zapatos*) to shine, polish; (*Inform*) to debug; (*fig*) to clean up

limpieza [lim'pjeθa] *nf* (*estado*) cleanliness; (*acto*) cleaning; (*: de las calles*) cleansing; (*: de zapatos*) polishing; (*habilidad*) skill; (*fig: Policía*) clean-up; (*pureza*) purity; (*Mil*): **operación de ~** mopping-up operation; **limpieza en seco** dry cleaning

limpio, -a ['limpjo, a] *adj* clean; (*moralmente*) pure; (*Com*) clear, net; (*fam*) honest ▷ *adv*: **jugar ~** to play fair; **pasar a** (*ESP*) *o* **en** (*LAM*) **~** to make a clean copy of

lince ['linθe] *nm* lynx

linchar [lin'tʃar] *vt* to lynch

lindar [lin'dar] *vi* to adjoin; **~ con** to border on

lindo, -a ['lindo, a] *adj* pretty, lovely ▷ *adv*: **nos divertimos de lo ~** we had a marvellous time; **canta muy ~** (*LAM*) he sings beautifully

línea ['linea] *nf* (*gen*) line; **en ~** (*Inform*) on line; **línea aérea** airline; **línea de meta** goal line; (*en carrera*) finishing line; **línea discontinua** (*Auto*) broken line; **línea recta** straight line

lingote [lin'gote] *nm* ingot

lingüista [lin'gwista] *nmf* linguist; **lingüística** *nf* linguistics *sg*

lino ['lino] *nm* linen; (*Bot*) flax

linterna [lin'terna] *nf* torch (*BRIT*), flashlight (*US*)

lío ['lio] *nm* bundle; (*fam*) fuss; (*desorden*) muddle, mess; **armar un ~** to make a fuss

liquen ['liken] *nm* lichen

liquidación [likiða'θjon] *nf* liquidation; **venta de ~** clearance sale

liquidar [liki'ðar] *vt* (*mercancías*) to liquidate; (*deudas*) to pay off; (*empresa*) to wind up

líquido, -a ['likiðo, a] *adj* liquid; (*ganancia*) net ▷ *nm* liquid; **líquido imponible** net taxable income

lira ['lira] *nf* (*Mús*) lyre; (*moneda*) lira

lírico, -a ['liriko, a] *adj* lyrical

lirio ['lirjo] *nm* (*Bot*) iris

lirón [li'ron] *nm* (*Zool*) dormouse; (*fig*) sleepyhead

Lisboa [lis'βoa] *n* Lisbon

lisiar [li'sjar] *vt* to maim

liso, -a ['liso, a] *adj* (*terreno*) flat; (*cabello*) straight; (*superficie*) even; (*tela*) plain

lista ['lista] *nf* list; (*de alumnos*) school register; (*de libros*) catalogue; (*de platos*) menu; (*de precios*) price list; **pasar ~** to call the roll; **tela de ~s** striped material; **lista de espera** waiting list; **lista de precios** price list; **listín** *nm* (*tb*: **listín telefónico** *o* **de teléfonos**) telephone directory

listo, -a ['listo, a] *adj* (*perspicaz*) smart, clever; (*preparado*) ready

listón [lis'ton] *nm* (*de madera, metal*) strip

litera [li'tera] *nf* (*en barco, tren*) berth; (*en dormitorio*) bunk, bunk bed

literal [lite'ral] *adj* literal

literario, -a [lite'rarjo, a] *adj* literary

literato, -a [lite'rato, a] *adj* literary ▷ *nm/f* writer

literatura [litera'tura] *nf* literature

litigio [li'tixjo] *nm* (*Jur*) lawsuit; (*fig*): **en ~ con** in dispute with

litografía [litoɣra'fia] *nf* lithography; (*una litografía*) lithograph

litoral [lito'ral] *adj* coastal ▷ *nm* coast, seaboard

litro ['litro] *nm* litre

lívido, -a ['liβiðo, a] *adj* livid

llaga ['ʎaɣa] *nf* wound

llama ['ʎama] *nf* flame; (*Zool*) llama

llamada [ʎa'maða] *nf* call; **llamada a cobro revertido** reverse-charge (*BRIT*) *o* collect (*US*) call; **llamada al orden** call to order; **llamada de atención** warning; **llamada local** (*LAM*) local call; **llamada metropolitana** (*ESP*) local call; **llamada por cobrar** (*MÉX*) reverse-charge (*BRIT*) *o* collect (*US*) call

llamamiento [ʎama'mjento] *nm* call

llamar [ʎa'mar] *vt* to call; (*atención*) to attract ▷ *vi* (*por teléfono*) to telephone; (*a la puerta*) to knock (*o* ring); (*por señas*) to beckon; (*Mil*) to call up; **llamarse** *vr* to be called, be named; **¿cómo se llama (usted)?** what's your name?

llamativo, -a [ʎama'tiβo, a] *adj* showy; (*color*) loud

llano, -a ['ʎano, a] *adj* (*superficie*) flat; (*persona*) straightforward; (*estilo*) clear ▷ *nm* plain, flat ground

llanta ['ʎanta] *nf* (*ESP*) (wheel) rim; **llanta (de goma)** (*LAM*: *neumático*) tyre; (: *cámara*) inner (tube); **llanta de repuesto** (*LAM*) spare tyre

llanto ['ʎanto] *nm* weeping

llanura [ʎa'nura] *nf* plain

llave ['ʎaβe] *nf* key; (*del agua*) tap; (*Mecánica*) spanner; (*de la luz*) switch; (*Mús*) key; **echar la ~ a** to lock up; **llave de contacto** (*ESP Auto*) ignition key; **llave de encendido** (*LAM Auto*) ignition key; **llave de paso** stopcock; **llave inglesa** monkey wrench; **llave maestra** master key; **llavero** *nm* keyring

llegada [ʎe'ɣaða] *nf* arrival

llegar [ʎe'ɣar] *vi* to arrive; (*alcanzar*) to reach; (*bastar*) to be enough; **llegarse** *vr*: **~se a** to approach; **~ a** to manage to, succeed in; **~ a saber** to find out; **~ a ser** to become; **~ a las manos de** to come into the hands of

llenar [ʎe'nar] *vt* to fill; (*espacio*) to cover; (*formulario*) to fill in *o* up; (*fig*) to heap

lleno, -a ['ʎeno, a] *adj* full, filled; (*repleto*) full up ▷ *nm* (*Teatro*) full house; **dar de ~ contra un muro** to hit a wall head-on

llevadero, -a [ʎeβa'ðero, a] *adj* bearable, tolerable

llevar [ʎe'βar] *vt* to take; (*ropa*) to wear; (*cargar*) to carry; (*quitar*) to take away; (*en coche*) to drive; (*transportar*) to transport; (*traer: dinero*) to carry; (*conducir*) to lead; (*Mat*) to carry ▷ *vi* (*suj: camino etc*): **~ a** to lead to; **llevarse**

vr to carry off, take away; **llevamos dos días aquí** we have been here for two days; **él me lleva 2 años** he's 2 years older than me; **~ los libros** (Com) to keep the books; **~se bien** to get on well (together)

llorar [ʎo'rar] *vt, vi* to cry, weep; **~ de risa** to cry with laughter

llorón, -ona [ʎo'ron, ona] *adj* tearful ▷ *nm/f* cry-baby

lloroso, -a [ʎo'roso, a] *adj* (*gen*) weeping, tearful; (*triste*) sad, sorrowful

llover [ʎo'βer] *vi* to rain

llovizna [ʎo'βiθna] *nf* drizzle; **lloviznar** *vi* to drizzle

llueve *etc vb* V **llover**

lluvia [ˈʎuβja] *nf* rain; **lluvia radioactiva** (radioactive) fallout; **lluvioso, -a** *adj* rainy

lo [lo] *art def:* **~ bel-** the beautiful, what is beautiful, that which is beautiful ▷ *pron* (*persona*) him; (*cosa*) it; **~ que sea** whatever; V *tb* **el**

loable [lo'aβle] *adj* praiseworthy

lobo [ˈloβo] *nm* wolf; **lobo de mar** (*fig*) sea dog

lóbulo [ˈloβulo] *nm* lobe

local [lo'kal] *adj* local ▷ *nm* place, site; (*oficinas*) premises *pl*; **localidad** *nf* (*barrio*) locality; (*lugar*) location; (*Teatro*) seat, ticket; **localizar** *vt* (*ubicar*) to locate, find; (*restringir*) to localize; (*situar*) to place

loción [lo'θjon] *nf* lotion

loco, -a [ˈloko, a] *adj* mad ▷ *nm/f* lunatic, mad person; **estar ~ con** *o* **por algo/por algn** to be mad about sth/sb

locomotora [lokomo'tora] *nf* engine, locomotive

locuaz [lo'kwaθ] *adj* loquacious

locución [loku'θjon] *nf* expression

locura [lo'kura] *nf* madness; (*acto*) crazy act

locutor, a [loku'tor, a] *nm/f* (*Radio*) announcer; (*comentarista*) commentator; (*TV*) newsreader

locutorio [loku'torjo] *nm* (*en telefónica*) telephone booth

lodo [ˈloðo] *nm* mud

lógica [ˈloxika] *nf* logic

lógico, -a [ˈloxiko, a] *adj* logical

login [ˈloxin] *nm* login

logística [lo'xistika] *nf* logistics *sg*

logotipo [loðo'tipo] *nm* logo

logrado, -a [lo'ðraðo, a] *adj* (*interpretación, reproducción*) polished, excellent

lograr [lo'ɣrar] *vt* to achieve; (*obtener*) to get, obtain; **~ hacer** to manage to do; **~ que algn venga** to manage to get sb to come

logro [ˈloɣro] *nm* achievement, success

lóker [ˈloker] (LAM) *nm* locker

loma [ˈloma] *nf* hillock (BRIT), small hill

lombriz [lom'briθ] *nf* worm

lomo [ˈlomo] *nm* (*de animal*) back; (*Culin: de cerdo*) pork loin; (: *de vaca*) rib steak; (*de libro*) spine

lona [ˈlona] *nf* canvas

loncha [ˈlontʃa] *nf* = **lonja**

lonchería [lontʃe'ria] (LAM) *nf* snack bar, diner (US)

Londres [ˈlondres] *n* London

longaniza [longa'niθa] *nf* pork sausage

longitud [lonxi'tuð] *nf* length; (*Geo*) longitude; **tener 3 metros de ~** to be 3 metres long; **longitud de onda** wavelength

lonja [ˈlonxa] *nf* slice; (*de tocino*) rasher; **lonja de pescado** fish market

loro [ˈloro] *nm* parrot

los [los] *art def* the ▷ *pron* them; (*ustedes*) you; **mis libros y ~ tuyos** my books and yours; V *tb* **el**

losa [ˈlosa] *nf* stone

lote [ˈlote] *nm* portion; (*Com*) lot

lotería [lote'ria] *nf* lottery; (*juego*) lotto

● **LOTERÍA**
●
● Millions of pounds are spent
● on lotteries each year in Spain,
● two of which are state-run: the

● **Lotería Primitiva** and the **Lotería**
● **Nacional**, with money raised
● going directly to the government.
● One of the most famous lotteries is
● run by the wealthy and influential
● society for the blind, "la ONCE".

loza ['loθa] *nf* crockery
lubina [lu'βina] *nf* sea bass
lubricante [luβri'kante] *nm*
lubricant
lubricar [luβri'kar] *vt* to lubricate
lucha ['lutʃa] *nf* fight, struggle; **lucha**
de clases class struggle; **lucha libre**
wrestling; **luchar** *vi* to fight
lúcido, -a ['luθido, a] *adj* (*persona*)
lucid; (*mente*) logical; (*idea*) crystal-clear
luciérnaga [lu'θjernaɣa] *nf* glow-
worm
lucir [lu'θir] *vt* to illuminate, light
(up); (*ostentar*) to show off ▷ *vi* (*brillar*)
to shine; **lucirse** *vr* (*irónico*) to make
a fool of o.s.
lucro ['lukro] *nm* profit, gain
lúdico, -a ['ludiko, a] *adj* (*aspecto*,
actividad) play *cpd*
luego ['lweɣo] *adv* (*después*) next; (*más*
tarde) later, afterwards
lugar [lu'ɣar] *nm* place; (*sitio*) spot; **en**
primer ~ in the first place, firstly; **en ~**
de instead of; **hacer ~** to make room;
fuera de ~ out of place; **sin ~ a dudas**
without doubt, undoubtedly; **dar ~ a**
to give rise to; **tener ~** to take place;
yo en su ~ if I were him; **lugar común**
commonplace
lúgubre ['luɣuβre] *adj* mournful
lujo ['luxo] *nm* luxury; (*fig*) profusion,
abundance; **de ~** luxury *cpd*, de luxe;
lujoso, -a *adj* luxurious
lujuria [lu'xurja] *nf* lust
lumbre ['lumbre] *nf* fire; (*para*
cigarrillo) light
luminoso, -a [lumi'noso, a] *adj*
luminous, shining
luna ['luna] *nf* moon; (*de un espejo*)
glass; (*de gafas*) lens; (*fig*) crescent;
estar en la ~ to have one's head in the

clouds; **luna de miel** honeymoon; **luna**
llena/nueva full/new moon
lunar [lu'nar] *adj* lunar ▷ *nm* (*Anat*)
mole; **tela de ~es** spotted material
lunes ['lunes] *nm inv* Monday
lupa ['lupa] *nf* magnifying glass
lustre ['lustre] *nm* polish; (*fig*) lustre;
dar ~ a to polish
luto ['luto] *nm* mourning; **llevar el o**
vestirse de ~ to be in mourning
Luxemburgo [luksem'burɣo] *nm*
Luxembourg
luz [luθ] (*pl* **luces**) *nf* light; **dar a ~ un**
niño to give birth to a child; **sacar a**
la ~ to bring to light; **dar o encender**
(*ESP*) *o* **prender** (*LAM*)/**apagar la ~** to
switch the light on/off; **tener pocas**
luces to be dim *o* stupid; **traje de luces**
bullfighter's costume; **luces de tráfico**
traffic lights; **luz de freno** brake light;
luz roja/verde red/green light

l

m *abr* (= *metro*) m; (= *minuto*) m

macana [ma'kana] (*MÉX*) *nf* truncheon (*BRIT*), billy club (*US*)

macarrones [maka'rrones] *nmpl* macaroni *sg*

macedonia [maθe'ðonja] *nf* (*tb:* **~ de frutas**) fruit salad

maceta [ma'θeta] *nf* (*de flores*) pot of flowers; (*para plantas*) flowerpot

machacar [matʃa'kar] *vt* to crush, pound ▷ *vi* (*insistir*) to go on, keep on

machete [ma'tʃete] *nm* machete, (large) knife

machetear [matʃete'ar] (*MÉX*) *vt* to swot (*BRIT*), grind away (*US*)

machismo [ma'tʃismo] *nm* male chauvinism; **machista** *adj, nm* sexist

macho ['matʃo] *adj* male; (*fig*) virile ▷ *nm* male; (*fig*) he-man

macizo, -a [ma'θiθo, a] *adj* (*grande*) massive; (*fuerte, sólido*) solid ▷ *nm* mass, chunk

madeja [ma'ðexa] *nf* (*de lana*) skein, hank; (*de pelo*) mass, mop

madera [ma'ðera] *nf* wood; (*fig*) nature, character; **una ~** a piece of wood

madrastra [ma'ðrastra] *nf* stepmother

madre ['maðre] *adj* mother *cpd* ▷ *nf* mother; (*de vino etc*) dregs *pl*; **madre política/soltera** mother-in-law/ unmarried mother

Madrid [ma'ðrið] *n* Madrid

madriguera [maðri'ɣera] *nf* burrow

madrileño, -a [maðri'leɲo, a] *adj* of o from Madrid ▷ *nm/f* native of Madrid

madrina [ma'ðrina] *nf* godmother; (*Arq*) prop, shore; (*Tec*) brace; (*de boda*) bridesmaid

madrugada [maðru'ɣaða] *nf* early morning; (*alba*) dawn, daybreak

madrugador, a [maðruɣa'ðor, a] *adj* early-rising

madrugar [maðru'ɣar] *vi* to get up early; (*fig*) to get ahead

madurar [maðu'rar] *vt, vi* (*fruta*) to ripen; (*fig*) to mature; **madurez** *nf* ripeness; maturity; **maduro, -a** *adj* ripe; mature

maestra *nf* V **maestro**

maestría [maes'tria] *nf* mastery; (*habilidad*) skill, expertise

maestro, -a [ma'estro, a] *adj* masterly; (*principal*) main ▷ *nm/f* master/mistress; (*profesor*) teacher ▷ *nm* (*autoridad*) authority; (*Mús*) maestro; (*experto*) master; **maestro albañil** master mason

magdalena [maɣða'lena] *nf* fairy cake

magia ['maxja] *nf* magic; **mágico, -a** *adj* magic(al) ▷ *nm/f* magician

magisterio [maxis'terjo] *nm* (*enseñanza*) teaching; (*profesión*) teaching profession; (*maestros*) teachers *pl*

magistrado [maxis'traðo] *nm* magistrate

magistral [maxis'tral] *adj* magisterial; (*fig*) masterly

magnate [maɣ'nate] *nm* magnate, tycoon

magnético, -a [maɣ'netiko, a] *adj*
magnetic

magnetofón [maɣneto'fon] *nm*
tape recorder

magnetófono [maɣne'tofono] *nm* =
magnetofón

magnífico, -a [maɣ'nifiko, a] *adj*
splendid, magnificent

magnitud [maɣni'tuð] *nf*
magnitude

mago, -a ['maɣo, a] *nm/f* magician;
los Reyes M~s the Three Wise Men

magro, -a ['maɣro, a] *adj* (*carne*) lean

mahonesa [mao'nesa] *nf*
mayonnaise

maître ['metre] *nm* head waiter

maíz [ma'iθ] *nm* maize (*BRIT*), corn
(*US*); sweet corn

majestad [maxes'taθ] *nf* majesty

majo, -a ['maxo, a] *adj* nice; (*guapo*)
attractive, good-looking; (*elegante*)
smart

mal [mal] *adv* badly; (*equivocadamente*)
wrongly ▷ *adj* = **malo** ▷ *nm* evil;
(*desgracia*) misfortune; (*daño*) harm,
damage; (*Med*) illness; **~ que bien**
rightly or wrongly; **ir de ~ en peor** to
get worse and worse

malabarista [malaβa'rista] *nmf*
juggler

malaria [ma'larja] *nf* malaria

malcriado, -a [mal'krjaðo, a] *adj*
spoiled

maldad [mal'daθ] *nf* evil,
wickedness

maldecir [malde'θir] *vt* to curse

maldición [maldi'θjon] *nf* curse

maldito, -a [mal'dito, a] *adj*
(*condenado*) damned; (*perverso*) wicked;
¡~ sea! damn it!

malecón [male'kon] (*LAM*) *nm* sea
front, promenade

maleducado, -a [maleðu'kaðo, a]
adj bad-mannered, rude

malentendido [malenten'diðo] *nm*
misunderstanding

malestar [males'tar] *nm* (*gen*)
discomfort; (*fig: inquietud*) uneasiness;

(*Pol*) unrest

maleta [ma'leta] *nf* case, suitcase;
(*Auto*) boot (*BRIT*), trunk (*US*); **hacer las
~s** to pack; **maletero** *nm* (*Auto*) boot
(*BRIT*), trunk (*US*); **maletín** *nm* small
case, bag

maleza [ma'leθa] *nf* (*malas hierbas*)
weeds *pl*; (*arbustos*) thicket

malgastar [malɣas'tar] *vt* (*tiempo,
dinero*) to waste; (*salud*) to ruin

malhechor, a [male'tʃor, a] *nm/f*
delinquent

malhumorado, -a [malumo'raðo,
a] *adj* bad-tempered

malicia [ma'liθja] *nf* (*maldad*)
wickedness; (*astucia*) slyness, guile;
(*mala intención*) malice, spite; (*carácter
travieso*) mischievousness

maligno, -a [ma'liɣno, a] *adj* evil;
(*malévolo*) malicious; (*Med*) malignant

malla ['maʎa] *nf* mesh; (*de baño*)
swimsuit; (*de ballet, gimnasia*) leotard;
mallas *nfpl* tights; **malla de alambre**
wire mesh

Mallorca [ma'ʎorka] *nf* Majorca

malo, -a ['malo, a] *adj* bad, false
▷ *nm/f* villain; **estar ~** to be ill

malograr [malo'ɣrar] *vt* to spoil;
(*plan*) to upset; (*ocasión*) to waste

malparado, -a [malpa'raðo, a]
adj: **salir ~** to come off badly

malpensado, -a [malpen'saðo, a]
adj nasty

malteada [malte'aða] (*LAM*) *nf*
milkshake

maltratar [maltra'tar] *vt* to ill treat,
mistreat

malvado, -a [mal'βaðo, a] *adj* evil,
villainous

Malvinas [mal'βinas] *nfpl* (*tb*: **Islas
~**) Falklands, Falkland Islands

mama ['mama] *nf* (*de animal*) teat; (*de
mujer*) breast

mamá [ma'ma] (*pl* **~s**) (*fam*) *nf* mum,
mummy

mamar [ma'mar] *vt, vi* to suck

mamarracho [mama'rratʃo] *nm*
sight, mess

mameluco [mameluko] (RPL) nm
dungarees pl (BRIT), overalls pl (US)
mamífero [ma'mifero] nm mammal
mampara [mam'para] nf (entre
habitaciones) partition; (biombo) screen
mampostería [mamposte'ria] nf
masonry
manada [ma'naða] nf (Zool) herd;
(: de leones) pride; (: de lobos) pack
manantial [manan'tjal] nm spring
mancha ['mantʃa] nf stain, mark;
(Zool) patch; **manchar** vt (gen) to
stain, mark; (ensuciar) to soil, dirty
manchego, -a [man'tʃexo, a] adj of
o from La Mancha
manco, -a ['manko, a] adj (de un
brazo) one-armed; (de una mano) one-
handed; (fig) defective, faulty
mancuernas [man'kwernas] (MÉX)
nfpl cufflinks
mandado [man'daðo] (LAM) nm
errand
mandamiento [manda'mjento]
nm (orden) order, command; (Rel)
commandment
mandar [man'dar] vt (ordenar) to
order; (dirigir) to lead, command;
(enviar) to send; (pedir) to order, ask for
▷ vi to be in charge; (pey) to be bossy;
¿mande? (MÉX: ¿cómo dice?) pardon?,
excuse me?; **~ hacer un traje** to have
a suit made
mandarina [manda'rina] (ESP) nf
tangerine, mandarin (orange)
mandato [man'dato] nm (orden)
order; (Pol: período) term of office;
(: territorio) mandate
mandíbula [man'diβula] nf jaw
mandil [man'dil] nm apron
mando ['mando] nm (Mil) command;
(de país) rule; (el primer lugar) lead; (Pol)
term of office; (Tec) control; **~ a la
izquierda** left-hand drive; **mando a
distancia** remote control
mandón, -ona [man'don, ona] adj
bossy, domineering
manejar [mane'xar] vt to manage;
(máquina) to work, operate; (caballo

etc) to handle; (casa) to run, manage;
(LAM: coche) to drive; **manejarse**
vr (comportarse) to act, behave;
(arreglárselas) to manage; **manejo**
nm (de bicicleta) handling; (de negocio)
management, running; (LAM Auto)
driving; (facilidad de trato) ease,
confidence; **manejos** nmpl (intrigas)
intrigues
manera [ma'nera] nf way, manner,
fashion; **maneras** nfpl (modales)
manners; **su ~ de ser** the way he
is; (aire) his manner; **de ninguna
~** no way, by no means; **de otra ~**
otherwise; **de todas ~s** at any rate; **no
hay ~ de persuadirle** there's no way of
convincing him
manga ['manga] nf (de camisa) sleeve;
(de riego) hose
mango ['mango] nm handle; (Bot)
mango
manguera [man'gera] nf hose
maní [ma'ni] (LAM) nm peanut
manía [ma'nia] nf (Med) mania;
(fig: moda) rage, craze; (disgusto) dislike;
(malicia) spite; **coger ~ a algn** to take a
dislike to sb; **tener ~ a algn** to dislike
sb; **maníaco, -a** adj maniac(al) ▷ nm/f
maniac
maniático, -a [ma'njatiko, a] adj
maniac(al) ▷ nm/f maniac
manicomio [mani'komjo] nm
mental hospital (BRIT), insane asylum
(US)
manifestación [manifesta'θjon] nf
(declaración) statement, declaration;
(de emoción) show, display; (Pol: desfile)
demonstration; (: concentración) mass
meeting
manifestar [manifes'tar] vt to
show, manifest; (declarar) to state,
declare; **manifiesto, -a** adj clear,
manifest ▷ nm manifesto
manillar [mani'ʎar] nm handlebars pl
maniobra [ma'njoβra] nf
manoeuvre; **maniobras** nfpl (Mil)
manoeuvres; **maniobrar** vt to
manoeuvre

manipulación [manipula'θjon] nf
manipulation

manipular [manipu'lar] vt to
manipulate; (manejar) to handle

maniquí [mani'ki] nm dummy
▷ nmf model

manivela [mani'βela] nf crank

manjar [man'xar] nm (tasty) dish

mano ['mano] nf hand; (Zool) foot,
paw; (de pintura) coat; (serie) lot, series;
a ~ by hand; **a ~ derecha/izquierda**
on the right(-hand side)/left(-hand
side); **de primera ~** (at) first hand; **de
segunda ~** (at) second hand; **robo a ~
armada** armed robbery; **estrechar la
~ a algn** to shake sb's hand; **mano de
obra** labour, manpower; **manos libres**
adj inv (teléfono, dispositivo) hands-free
▷ nm inv hands-free kit

manojo [ma'noxo] nm handful,
bunch; (de llaves) bunch

manopla [ma'nopla] nf mitten

manosear [manose'ar] vt (tocar)
to handle, touch; (desordenar) to mess
up, rumple; (insistir en) to overwork;
(LAM: acariciar) to caress, fondle

manotazo [mano'taθo] nm slap,
smack

mansalva [man'salβa]: **a ~** adv
indiscriminately

mansión [man'sjon] nf mansion

manso, -a ['manso, a] adj gentle,
mild; (animal) tame

manta ['manta] (ESP) nf blanket

manteca [man'teka] nf fat;
(CS: mantequilla) butter, **manteca de
cerdo** lard

mantecado [mante'kaðo] (ESP) nm
Christmas sweet made from flour, almonds
and lard

mantel [man'tel] nm tablecloth

mantendré etc vb V **mantener**

mantener [mante'ner] vt to
support, maintain; (alimentar) to
sustain; (conservar) to keep; (Tec) to
maintain, service; **mantenerse** vr
(seguir de pie) to be still standing;
(no ceder) to hold one's ground;

(subsistir) to sustain o.s., keep going;
mantenimiento nm maintenance;
sustenance; (sustento) support

mantequilla [mante'kiʎa] nf butter

mantilla [man'tiʎa] nf mantilla;
mantillas nfpl (de bebé) baby clothes

manto ['manto] nm (capa) cloak; (de
ceremonia) robe, gown

mantuve etc vb V **mantener**

manual [ma'nwal] adj manual ▷ nm
manual, handbook

manuscrito, -a [manus'krito, a] adj
handwritten ▷ nm manuscript

manutención [manuten'θjon] nf
maintenance; (sustento) support

manzana [man'θana] nf apple; (Arq)
block (of houses)

manzanilla [manθa'niʎa] nf (planta)
camomile; (infusión) camomile tea

manzano [man'θano] nm apple tree

maña ['maɲa] nf (gen) skill, dexterity;
(pey) guile; (destreza) trick, knack

mañana [ma'ɲana] adv tomorrow
▷ nm future ▷ nf morning; **de o por
la ~** in the morning; **¡hasta ~!** see you
tomorrow!; **~ por la ~** tomorrow morning

mapa ['mapa] nm map

maple ['maple] (LAM) nm maple

maqueta [ma'keta] nf (scale) model

maquiladora [makila'ðora] (MÉX) nf
(Com) bonded assembly plant

maquillaje [maki'ʎaxe] nm make-
up; (acto) making up

maquillar [maki'ʎar] vt to make
up; **maquillarse** vr to put on (some)
make-up

máquina ['makina] nf machine;
(de tren) locomotive, engine; (Foto)
camera; (fig) machinery; **escrito a
~** typewritten; **máquina de afeitar**
electric razor; **máquina de coser**
sewing machine; **máquina de escribir**
typewriter; **máquina fotográfica**
camera

maquinaria [maki'narja] nf
(máquinas) machinery; (mecanismo)
mechanism, works pl

maquinilla [maki'niʎa] (ESP) nf

m

(*tb:* **~ de afeitar**) razor

maquinista [maki'nista] *nmf* (*de tren*) engine driver; (*Tec*) operator; (*Náut*) engineer

mar [mar] *nm o f* sea; **~ adentro** out at sea; **en alta ~** on the high seas; **la ~ de** (*fam*) lots of; **el Mar Negro/Báltico** the Black/Baltic Sea

maraña [ma'raɲa] *nf* (*maleza*) thicket; (*confusión*) tangle

maravilla [mara'βiʎa] *nf* marvel, wonder; (*Bot*) marigold; **maravillar** *vt* to astonish, amaze; **maravillarse** *vr* to be astonished, be amazed; **maravilloso, -a** *adj* wonderful, marvellous

marca ['marka] *nf* (*gen*) mark; (*sello*) stamp; (*Com*) make, brand; **de ~** excellent, outstanding; **marca de fábrica** trademark; **marca registrada** registered trademark

marcado, -a [mar'kaðo, a] *adj* marked, strong

marcador [marka'ðor] *nm* (*Deporte*) scoreboard; (*: persona*) scorer

marcapasos [marka'pasos] *nm inv* pacemaker

marcar [mar'kar] *vt* (*gen*) to mark; (*número de teléfono*) to dial; (*gol*) to score; (*números*) to record, keep a tally of; (*pelo*) to set ▷ *vi* (*Deporte*) to score; (*Tel*) to dial

marcha ['martʃa] *nf* march; (*Tec*) running, working; (*Auto*) gear; (*velocidad*) speed; (*fig*) progress; (*dirección*) course; **poner en ~** to put into gear; (*fig*) to set in motion, get going; **dar ~ atrás** to reverse, put into reverse; **estar en ~** to be under way, be in motion

marchar [mar'tʃar] *vi* (*ir*) to go; (*funcionar*) to work, go; **marcharse** *vr* to go (away), leave

marchitar [martʃi'tar] *vt* to wither, dry up; **marchitarse** *vr* (*Bot*) to wither; (*fig*) to fade away; **marchito, -a** *adj* withered, faded; (*fig*) in decline

marciano, -a [mar'θjano, a] *adj,*

nm/f Martian

marco ['marko] *nm* frame; (*moneda*) mark; (*fig*) framework

marea [ma'rea] *nf* tide; **marea negra** oil slick

marear [mare'ar] *vt* (*fig*) to annoy, upset; (*Med*): **~ a algn** to make sb feel sick; **marearse** *vr* (*tener náuseas*) to feel sick; (*desvanecerse*) to feel faint; (*aturdirse*) to feel dizzy; (*fam: emborracharse*) to get tipsy

maremoto [mare'moto] *nm* tidal wave

mareo [ma'reo] *nm* (*náusea*) sick feeling; (*en viaje*) travel sickness; (*aturdimiento*) dizziness; (*fam: lata*) nuisance

marfil [mar'fil] *nm* ivory

margarina [marɣa'rina] *nf* margarine

margarita [marɣa'rita] *nf* (*Bot*) daisy; (*Tip*) daisywheel

margen ['marxen] *nm* (*borde*) edge, border; (*fig*) margin, space ▷ *nf* (*de río etc*) bank; **dar ~ para** to give an opportunity for; **mantenerse al ~** to keep out (of things)

marginar [marxi'nar] *vt* (*socialmente*) to marginalize, ostracize

mariachi [ma'rjatʃi] *nm* (*persona*) mariachi musician; (*grupo*) mariachi band

⬤ MARIACHI

Mariachi music is the musical style most characteristic of Mexico. From the state of Jalisco in the 19th century, this music spread rapidly throughout the country, until each region had its own particular style of the Mariachi "sound". A Mariachi band can be made up of several singers, up to eight violins, two trumpets, guitars, a "vihuela" (an old form of guitar), and a harp. The dance associated with this music is called the "zapateado".

marica [maˈrika] (fam) nm
sissy

maricón [mariˈkon] (fam) nm
queer

marido [maˈriðo] nm husband

marihuana [mariˈwana] nf
marijuana, cannabis

marina [maˈrina] nf navy; **marina
mercante** merchant navy

marinero, -a [mariˈnero, a] adj sea
cpd ▷ nm sailor, seaman

marino, -a [maˈrino, a] adj sea cpd,
marine ▷ nm sailor

marioneta [marjoˈneta] nf
puppet

mariposa [mariˈposa] nf
butterfly

mariquita [mariˈkita] nf ladybird
(BRIT), ladybug (US)

marisco [maˈrisko] (ESP) nm shellfish
inv, seafood; **mariscos** (LAM) nmpl =
marisco

marítimo, -a [maˈritimo, a] adj sea
cpd, maritime

mármol [ˈmarmol] nm marble

marqués, -esa [marˈkes, esa] nm/f
marquis/marchioness

marrón [maˈrron] adj brown

marroquí [marroˈki] adj, nmf
Moroccan ▷ nm Morocco (leather)

Marruecos [maˈrrwekos] nm
Morocco

martes [ˈmartes] nm inv Tuesday; **~ y
trece** ≈ Friday 13th

⚫ **MARTES Y TRECE**

⚫
⚫ According to Spanish superstition
⚫ Tuesday is an unlucky day, even
⚫ more so if it falls on the 13th of
⚫ the month.

martillo [marˈtiʎo] nm hammer

mártir [ˈmartir] nmf martyr;
martirio nm martyrdom; (fig) torture,
torment

marxismo [markˈsismo] nm
Marxism

marzo [ˈmarθo] nm March

○ **PALABRA CLAVE**

más [mas] adj, adv 1: **más (que** o **de)**
(compar) more (than), ...+ er (than); **más
grande/inteligente** bigger/
more intelligent; **trabaja más (que
yo)** he works more (than me); V tb **cada**

2 (superl): **el más** the most, ...+ est; **el
más grande/inteligente (de)** the
biggest/most intelligent (in)

3 (negativo): **no tengo más dinero** I
haven't got any more money; **no viene
más por aquí** he doesn't come round
here any more

4 (adicional): **no le veo más solución
que ...** I see no other solution than to
...; **¿quién más?** anybody else?

5 (+ adj: valor intensivo): **¡qué perro
más sucio!** what a filthy dog!; **¡es más
tonto!** he's so stupid!

6 (locuciones): **más o menos** more or
less; **los más** most people; **es más**
furthermore; **más bien** rather;
¡qué más da! what does it matter!;
V tb **no**

7: **por más: por más que te esfuerces**
no matter how hard you try; **por más
que quisiera ...** much as I should
like to ...

8: **de más: veo que aquí estoy de más**
I can see I'm not needed here; **tenemos
uno de más** we've got one extra

▷ prep: **2 más 2 son 4** 2 and 2 plus 2 are 4

▷ nm inv: **este trabajo tiene sus más
y sus menos** this job's got its good
points and its bad points

mas [mas] conj but

masa [ˈmasa] nf (mezcla) dough;
(volumen) volume, mass; (Física) mass;
en ~ en masse; **las ~s** (Pol) the masses

masacre [maˈsakre] nf massacre

masaje [maˈsaxe] nm massage

máscara [ˈmaskara] nf mask;
máscara antigás/de oxígeno
gas/oxygen mask; **mascarilla** nf (de

m

belleza, Med) mask

masculino, -a [masku'lino, a] *adj*
masculine; *(Bio)* male

masía [ma'sia] *nf* farmhouse

masivo, -a [ma'siβo, a] *adj* mass *cpd*

masoquista [maso'kista] *nmf*
masochist

máster ['master] *(ESP) nm* master

masticar [masti'kar] *vt* to chew

mástil ['mastil] *nm (de navío)* mast;
(de guitarra) neck

mastín [mas'tin] *nm* mastiff

masturbarse [mastur'βarse] *vr* to
masturbate

mata ['mata] *nf (arbusto)* bush, shrub;
(de hierba) tuft

matadero [mata'ðero] *nm*
slaughterhouse, abattoir

matador, a [mata'ðor, a] *adj* killing
▷ *nm/f* killer ▷ *nm (Taur)* matador,
bullfighter

matamoscas [mata'moskas] *nm inv*
(pala) fly swat

matanza [ma'tanθa] *nf* slaughter

matar [ma'tar] *vt, vi* to kill; **matarse**
vr (suicidarse) to kill o.s., commit
suicide; *(morir)* to be o get killed; **~ el
hambre** to stave off hunger

matasellos [mata'seʎos] *nm inv*
postmark

mate ['mate] *adj* matt ▷ *nm (en
ajedrez)* (check)mate; *(LAM: hierba)*
maté; *(: vasija)* gourd

matemáticas [mate'matikas] *nfpl*
mathematics; **matemático, -a** *adj*
mathematical ▷ *nm/f* mathematician

materia [ma'terja] *nf (gen)* matter;
(Tec) material; *(Escol)* subject; **en ~
de** on the subject of; **materia prima**
raw material; **material** *adj* material
▷ *nm* material; *(Tec)* equipment;
materialista *adj* materialist(ic);
materialmente *adv* materially; *(fig)*
absolutely

maternal [mater'nal] *adj* motherly,
maternal

maternidad [materni'ðað] *nf*
motherhood, maternity; **materno, -a**

adj maternal; *(lengua)* mother *cpd*

matinal [mati'nal] *adj* morning *cpd*

matiz [ma'tiθ] *nm* shade; **matizar** *vt*
(variar) to vary; *(Arte)* to blend; **matizar
de** to tinge with

matón [ma'ton] *nm* bully

matorral [mato'rral] *nm* thicket

matrícula [ma'trikula] *nf (registro)*
register; *(Auto)* registration number;
(: placa) number plate; **matrícula de
honor** *(Univ)* top marks in a subject at
university with the right to free registration
the following year; **matricular** *vt* to
register, enrol

matrimonio [matri'monjo] *nm*
(pareja) (married) couple; *(unión)*
marriage

matriz [ma'triθ] *nf (Anat)* womb;
(Tec) mould

matrona [ma'trona] *nf (persona de
edad)* matron; *(comadrona)* midwife

matufia [ma'tufja] *(RPL: fam) nf*
put-up job

maullar [mau'ʎar] *vi* to mew, miaow

maxilar [maksi'lar] *nm* jaw(bone)

máxima ['maksima] *nf* maxim

máximo, -a ['maksimo, a] *adj*
maximum; *(más alto)* highest; *(más
grande)* greatest ▷ *nm* maximum;
como ~ at most

mayo ['majo] *nm* May

mayonesa [majo'nesa] *nf*
mayonnaise

mayor [ma'jor] *adj* main, chief;
(adulto) adult; *(de edad avanzada)*
elderly; *(Mús)* major; *(compar: de
tamaño)* bigger; *(: de edad)* older;
(superl: de tamaño) biggest; *(: de edad)*
oldest ▷ *nm (adulto)* adult; **mayores**
nmpl (antepasados) ancestors; **al por ~**
wholesale; **mayor de edad** adult

mayoral [majo'ral] *nm* foreman

mayordomo [major'ðomo] *nm*
butler

mayoría [majo'ria] *nf* majority,
greater part

mayorista [majo'rista] *nmf*
wholesaler

mayoritario, -a [majori'tarjo, a]
adj majority *cpd*

mayúscula [ma'juskula] *nf* capital
letter

mazapán [maθa'pan] *nm* marzipan

mazo ['maθo] *nm* (*martillo*) mallet; (*de
flores*) bunch; (*Deporte*) bat

me [me] *pron* (*directo*) me; (*indirecto*)
(to) me; (*reflexivo*) (to) myself; **¡dá~lo!**
give it to me!

mear [me'ar] (*fam*) *vi* to pee, piss (!)

mecánica [me'kanika] *nf* (*Escol*)
mechanics *sg*; (*mecanismo*) mechanism;
V tb **mecánico**

mecánico, -a [me'kaniko, a] *adj*
mechanical ⊳ *nm/f* mechanic

mecanismo [meka'nismo] *nm*
mechanism; (*marcha*) gear

mecanografía [mekanoɣra'fia]
nf typewriting; **mecanógrafo, -a**
nm/f typist

mecate [me'kate] (*MÉX, CAM*) *nm* rope

mecedora [meθe'ðora] *nf* rocking
chair

mecer [me'θer] *vt* (*cuna*) to rock;
mecerse *vr* to rock; (*rama*) to sway

mecha ['metʃa] *nf* (*de vela*) wick; (*de
bomba*) fuse

mechero [me'tʃero] *nm* (cigarette)
lighter

mechón [me'tʃon] *nm* (*gen*) tuft; (*de
pelo*) lock

medalla [me'ðaʎa] *nf* medal

media ['meðja] *nf* stocking;
(*LAM: calcetín*) sock; (*promedio*) average;
medias [me'ðjas] *nfpl* (*ropa interior*)
tights

mediado, -a [me'ðjaðo, a] *adj* half-
full; (*trabajo*) half-completed; **a ~s de** in
the middle of, halfway through

mediano, -a [me'ðjano, a] *adj*
(*regular*) medium, average; (*mediocre*)
mediocre

medianoche [meðja'notʃe] *nf*
midnight

mediante [me'ðjante] *adv* by
(means of), through

mediar [me'ðjar] *vi* (*interceder*) to
mediate, intervene

medicamento [meðika'mento] *nm*
medicine, drug

medicina [meði'θina] *nf* medicine

médico, -a ['meðiko, a] *adj* medical
⊳ *nm/f* doctor

medida [me'ðiða] *nf* measure;
(*medición*) measurement; (*prudencia*)
moderation, prudence; **en cierta/
gran ~** up to a point/to a great extent;
un traje a la ~ a made-to-measure
suit; **~ de cuello** collar size; **a ~ de**
in proportion to; (*de acuerdo con*) in
keeping with; **a ~ que** (*conforme*) as;
medidor (*LAM*) *nm* meter

medio, -a ['meðjo, a] *adj* half (a);
(*punto*) mid, middle; (*promedio*) average
⊳ *adv* half ⊳ *nm* (*centro*) middle,
centre; (*promedio*) average; (*método*)
means, way; (*ambiente*) environment;
medios *nmpl* means, resources;
~ litro half a litre; **las tres y media**
half past three; **a ~ terminar** half
finished; **pagar a medias** to share the
cost; **medio ambiente** environment;
medio de transporte means of
transport; **Medio Oriente** Middle East;
medios de comunicación media;
medioambiental *adj* (*política, efectos*)
environmental

mediocre [me'ðjokre] *adj*
mediocre

mediodía [meðjo'ðia] *nm* midday,
noon

medir [me'ðir] *vt, vi* (*gen*) to measure

meditar [meði'tar] *vt* to ponder,
think over, meditate on; (*planear*) to
think out

mediterráneo, -a [meðite'rraneo,
a] *adj* Mediterranean ⊳ *nm*: **el M~** the
Mediterranean

médula ['meðula] *nf* (*Anat*) marrow;
médula espinal spinal cord

medusa [me'ðusa] (*ESP*) *nf* jellyfish

megáfono [me'ɣafono] *nm*
megaphone

megapíxel [meɣa'piksel] (*pl*
megapixels or **~es**) *nm* megapixel

m

mejicano, -a [mexi'kano, a] *adj,
nm/f* Mexican
Méjico ['mexiko] *nm* Mexico
mejilla [me'xiʎa] *nf* cheek
mejillón [mexi'ʎon] *nm* mussel
mejor [me'xor] *adj, adv (compar)*
better; *(superl)* best; **a lo ~** probably;
(quizá) maybe; **~ dicho** rather; **tanto ~**
so much the better
mejora [me'xora] *nf* improvement;
mejorar *vt* to improve, make better
▷ *vi* to improve, get better; **mejorarse**
vr to improve, get better
melancólico, -a [melan'koliko, a]
adj (triste) sad, melancholy; *(soñador)*
dreamy
melena [me'lena] *nf (de persona)* long
hair; *(Zool)* mane
mellizo, -a [me'ʎiθo, a] *adj, nm/f*
twin
melocotón [meloko'ton] *(ESP) nm*
peach
melodía [melo'ðia] *nf* melody, tune
melodrama [melo'ðrama] *nm*
melodrama; **melodramático, -a** *adj*
melodramatic
melón [me'lon] *nm* melon
membrete [mem'brete] *nm*
letterhead
membrillo [mem'briʎo] *nm* quince;
(carne de) ~ quince jelly
memoria [me'morja] *nf (gen)*
memory; **memorias** *nfpl (de autor)*
memoirs; **memorizar** *vt* to memorize
menaje [me'naxe] *nm (tb: **artículos
de ~**)* household items
mencionar [menθjo'nar] *vt* to
mention
mendigo, -a [men'diɣo, a] *nm/f*
beggar
menear [mene'ar] *vt* to move;
menearse *vr* to shake; *(balancearse)*
to sway; *(moverse)* to move; *(fig)* to get
a move on
menestra [me'nestra] *nf (tb: **~ de
verduras**)* vegetable stew
menopausia [meno'pausja] *nf*
menopause

menor [me'nor] *adj (más
pequeño: compar)* smaller; *(: superl)*
smallest; *(más joven: compar)* younger;
(: superl) youngest; *(Mús)* minor ▷ *nmf
(joven)* young person, juvenile; **no
tengo la ~ idea** I haven't the faintest
idea; **al por ~** retail; **menor de edad**
person under age
Menorca [me'norka] *nf* Minorca

○ **PALABRA CLAVE**

menos [menos] *adj* **1**: **menos
(que *o* de)** *(compar: cantidad)* less
(than); *(: número)* fewer (than);
con menos entusiasmo with less
enthusiasm; **menos gente** fewer
people; *V tb* **cada**
2 *(superl)*: **es el que menos culpa tiene**
he is the least to blame
▷ *adv* **1** *(compar)*: **menos (que *o* de)** less
(than); **me gusta menos que el otro** I
like it less than the other one
2 *(superl)*: **es el menos listo (de su
clase)** he's the least bright in his class;
**de todas ellas es la que menos me
agrada** out of all of them she's the one
I like least
3 *(locuciones)*: **no quiero verle y menos
visitarle** I don't want to see him, let
alone visit him; **tenemos siete de
menos** we're seven short; **(por) lo
menos** at (the very) least; **¡menos mal!**
thank goodness!
▷ *prep* except; *(cifras)* minus; **todos
menos él** everyone except (for) him;
5 menos 2 5 minus 2; **las 7 menos 10**
(hora) 10 to 7
▷ *conj*: **a menos que**: **a menos que
venga mañana** unless he comes
tomorrow

menospreciar [menospre'θjar] *vt*
to underrate, undervalue; *(despreciar)*
to scorn, despise
mensaje [men'saxe] *nm* message;
enviar un ~ a algn *(por móvil)* to text
sb, send sb a text message; **mensaje**

de texto text message **mensaje electrónico** email; **mensajero, -a** nm/f messenger

menso, -a ['menso, a] (MÉX: fam) adj stupid

menstruación [menstrua'θjon] nf menstruation

mensual [men'swal] adj monthly; **100 euros ~es** 100 euros a month; **mensualidad** nf (salario) monthly salary; (Com) monthly payment, monthly instalment

menta ['menta] nf mint

mental [men'tal] adj mental; **mentalidad** nf mentality; **mentalizar** vt (sensibilizar) to make aware; (convencer) to convince; (padres) to prepare (mentally); **mentalizarse** vr (concienciarse) to become aware; **mentalizarse (de)** to get used to the idea (of); **mentalizarse de que ...** (convencerse) to get it into one's head that ...

mente ['mente] nf mind

mentir [men'tir] vi to lie

mentira [men'tira] nf (una mentira) lie; (acto) lying; (invención) fiction; **parece mentira que ...** it seems incredible that ..., I can't believe that ...; **mentiroso, -a** [menti'roso, a] adj lying ▷ nm/f liar

menú [me'nu] (pl ~s) nm menu; **menú del día** set menu; **menú turístico** tourist menu

menudencias [menu'ðenθjas] (LAM) nfpl giblets

menudo, -a [me'nuðo, a] adj (pequeño) small, tiny; (sin importancia) petty, insignificant; **¡~ negocio!** (fam) some deal!; **a ~** often, frequently

meñique [me'ɲike] nm little finger

mercadillo [merka'ðiʎo] (ESP) nm flea market

mercado [mer'kaðo] nm market; **mercado de pulgas** (LAM) flea market

mercancía [merkan'θia] nf commodity; **mercancías** nfpl goods, merchandise sg

mercenario, -a [merθe'narjo, a] adj, nm mercenary

mercería [merθe'ria] nf haberdashery (BRIT), notions pl (US); (tienda) haberdasher's (BRIT), notions store (US)

mercurio [mer'kurjo] nm mercury

merecer [mere'θer] vt to deserve, merit ▷ vi to be deserving, be worthy; **merece la pena** it's worthwhile; **merecido, -a** adj (well) deserved; **llevar su merecido** to get one's deserts

merendar [meren'dar] vt to have for tea ▷ vi to have tea; (en el campo) to have a picnic; **merendero** nm open-air cafe

merengue [me'renge] nm meringue

meridiano [meri'ðjano] nm (Geo) meridian

merienda [me'rjenda] nf (light) tea, afternoon snack; (de campo) picnic

mérito ['merito] nm merit; (valor) worth, value

merluza [mer'luθa] nf hake

mermelada [merme'laða] nf jam

mero, -a ['mero, a] adj mere; (MÉX, CAM: fam) very

merodear [meroðe'ar] vi: **~ por** to prowl about

mes [mes] nm month

mesa ['mesa] nf table; (de trabajo) desk; (Geo) plateau; **poner/quitar la ~** to lay/clear the table; **mesa electoral** officials in charge of a polling station; **mesa redonda** (reunión) round table; **mesero, -a** (LAM) nm/f waiter/waitress

meseta [me'seta] nf (Geo) plateau, tableland

mesilla [me'siʎa] nf (tb: **~ de noche**) bedside table

mesón [me'son] nm inn

mestizo, -a [mes'tiθo, a] adj half-caste, of mixed race ▷ nm/f half-caste

meta ['meta] nf goal; (de carrera) finish

metabolismo [metaβo'lismo] nm metabolism

m

metáfora [me'tafora] *nf* metaphor

metal [me'tal] *nm* (*materia*) metal; (*Mús*) brass; **metálico, -a** *adj* metallic; (*de metal*) metal ▷ *nm* (*dinero contante*) cash

meteorología [meteorolo'xia] *nf* meteorology

meter [me'ter] *vt* (*colocar*) to put, place; (*introducir*) to put in, insert; (*involucrar*) to involve; (*causar*) to make, cause; **meterse** *vr*: **~se en** to go into, enter; (*fig*) to interfere in, meddle in; **~se a** to start; **~se a escritor** to become a writer; **~se con uno** to provoke sb, pick a quarrel with sb

meticuloso, -a [metiku'loso, a] *adj* meticulous, thorough

metódico, -a [me'toðiko, a] *adj* methodical

método [me'toðo] *nm* method

metralleta [metra'ʎeta] *nf* sub-machine-gun

métrico, -a ['metriko, a] *adj* metric

metro ['metro] *nm* metre; (*tren*) underground (*BRIT*), subway (*US*)

metrosexual [metrosek'swal] *adj*, *nm* metrosexual

mexicano, -a [mexi'kano, a] *adj*, *nm/f* Mexican

México ['mexiko] *nm* Mexico; **Ciudad de ~** Mexico City

mezcla ['meθkla] *nf* mixture; **mezcladora** (*MÉX*) *nf* (*tb*: **mezcladora de cemento**) cement mixer; **mezclar** *vt* to mix (up); **mezclarse** *vr* to mix, mingle; **mezclarse en** to get mixed up in, get involved in

mezquino, -a [meθ'kino, a] *adj* mean

mezquita [meθ'kita] *nf* mosque

mg. *abr* (= *miligramo*) mg

mi [mi] *adj pos* my ▷ *nm* (*Mús*) E

mí [mi] *pron* me; myself

mía *pron* V **mío**

michelín [mitʃe'lin] (*fam*) *nm* (*de grasa*) spare tyre

microbio [mi'kroβjo] *nm* microbe

micrófono [mi'krofono] *nm* microphone

microondas [mikro'ondas] *nm inv* (*tb*: **horno ~**) microwave (oven)

microscopio [mikro'skopjo] *nm* microscope

miedo ['mjeðo] *nm* fear; (*nerviosismo*) apprehension, nervousness; **tener ~** to be afraid; **de ~** wonderful, marvellous; **hace un frío de ~** (*fam*) it's terribly cold; **miedoso, -a** *adj* fearful, timid

miel [mjel] *nf* honey

miembro ['mjembro] *nm* limb; (*socio*) member; **miembro viril** penis

mientras ['mjentras] *conj* while; (*duración*) as long as ▷ *adv* meanwhile; **~ tanto** meanwhile

miércoles ['mjerkoles] *nm inv* Wednesday

mierda ['mjerða] (*fam!*) *nf* shit (!)

miga ['miɣa] *nf* crumb; (*fig*: *meollo*) essence; **hacer buenas ~s** (*fam*) to get on well

mil [mil] *num* thousand; **dos ~ libras** two thousand pounds

milagro [mi'laɣro] *nm* miracle; **milagroso, -a** *adj* miraculous

milésima [mi'lesima] *nf* (*de segundo*) thousandth

mili ['mili] (*ESP*: *fam*) *nf*: **hacer la ~** to do one's military service

milímetro [mi'limetro] *nm* millimetre

militante [mili'tante] *adj* militant

militar [mili'tar] *adj* military ▷ *nmf* soldier ▷ *vi* (*Mil*) to serve; (*en un partido*) to be a member

milla ['miʎa] *nf* mile

millar [mi'ʎar] *nm* thousand

millón [mi'ʎon] *num* million; **millonario, -a** *nm/f* millionaire

milusos [mi'lusos] (*MÉX*) *nm inv* odd-job man

mimar [mi'mar] *vt* to spoil, pamper

mimbre ['mimbre] *nm* wicker

mímica ['mimika] *nf* (*para comunicarse*) sign language; (*imitación*) mimicry

mimo ['mimo] *nm* (*caricia*) caress; (*de*

niño) spoiling; (*Teatro*) mime; (: *actor*) mime artist

mina ['mina] *nf* mine

mineral [mine'ral] *adj* mineral ▷ *nm* (*Geo*) mineral; (*mena*) ore

minero, -a [mi'nero, a] *adj* mining *cpd* ▷ *nm/f* miner

miniatura [minja'tura] *adj inv, nf* miniature

minidisco [mini'disko] *nm* MiniDisc®

minifalda [mini'falda] *nf* miniskirt

mínimo, -a ['minimo, a] *adj, nm* minimum

minino, -a [mi'nino, a] (*fam*) *nm/f* puss, pussy

ministerio [minis'terjo] *nm* Ministry; **Ministerio de Hacienda/de Asuntos Exteriores** Treasury (*BRIT*), Treasury Department (*US*)/Foreign Office (*BRIT*), State Department (*US*)

ministro, -a [mi'nistro, a] *nm/f* minister

minoría [mino'ria] *nf* minority

minúscula [mi'nuskula] *nf* small letter

minúsculo, -a [mi'nuskulo, a] *adj* tiny, minute

minusválido, -a [minus'βaliðo, a] *adj* (physically) handicapped ▷ *nm/f* (physically) handicapped person

minuta [mi'nuta] *nf* (*de comida*) menu

minutero [minu'tero] *nm* minute hand

minuto [mi'nuto] *nm* minute

mío, -a ['mio, a] *pron*: **el ~/la mía** mine; **un amigo ~** a friend of mine; **lo ~** what is mine

miope [mi'ope] *adj* short-sighted

mira ['mira] *nf* (*de arma*) sight(s) (*pl*); (*fig*) aim, intention

mirada [mi'raða] *nf* look, glance; (*expresión*) look, expression; **clavar la ~ en** to stare at; **echar una ~ a** to glance at

mirado, -a [mi'raðo, a] *adj* (*sensato*) sensible; (*considerado*) considerate;

bien/mal ~ (*estimado*) well/not well thought of; **bien ~ ...** all things considered ...

mirador [mira'ðor] *nm* viewpoint, vantage point

mirar [mi'rar] *vt* to look at; (*observar*) to watch; (*considerar*) to consider, think over; (*vigilar, cuidar*) to watch, look after ▷ *vi* to look; (*Arq*) to face; **mirarse** *vr* (*dos personas*) to look at each other; **~ bien/mal** to think highly of/have a poor opinion of; **~se al espejo** to look at o.s. in the mirror

mirilla [mi'riʎa] *nf* spyhole, peephole

mirlo ['mirlo] *nm* blackbird

misa ['misa] *nf* mass

miserable [mise'raβle] *adj* (*avaro*) mean, stingy; (*nimio*) miserable, paltry; (*lugar*) squalid; (*fam*) vile, despicable ▷ *nmf* (*malvado*) rogue

miseria [mi'serja] *nf* (*pobreza*) poverty; (*tacañería*) meanness, stinginess; (*condiciones*) squalor; **una ~** a pittance

misericordia [miseri'korðja] *nf* (*compasión*) compassion, pity; (*piedad*) mercy

misil [mi'sil] *nm* missile

misión [mi'sjon] *nf* mission; **misionero, -a** *nm/f* missionary

mismo, -a ['mismo, a] *adj* (*semejante*) same; (*después de pron*) -self; (*para énfasis*) very ▷ *adv*: **aquí/hoy ~** right here/this very day, **ahora ~** right now ▷ *conj*: **lo ~ que** just like o as; **el ~ traje** the same suit; **en ese ~ momento** at that very moment; **vino el ~ ministro** the minister himself came; **yo ~ lo vi** I saw it myself; **lo ~** the same (thing); **da lo ~** it's all the same; **quedamos en las mismas** we're no further forward; **por lo ~** for the same reason

misterio [mis'terjo] *nm* mystery; **misterioso, -a** *adj* mysterious

mitad [mi'tað] *nf* (*medio*) half; (*centro*) middle; **a ~ de precio** (at) half-price; **en** *o* **a ~ del camino** halfway along the

m

road; **cortar por la ~** to cut through the middle

mitin ['mitin] (pl **mítines**) nm meeting

mito ['mito] nm myth

mixto, -a ['miksto, a] adj mixed

ml. abr (= mililitro) ml

mm. abr (= milímetro) mm

mobiliario [moβi'ljarjo] nm furniture

mochila [mo'tʃila] nf rucksack (BRIT), back-pack

moco ['moko] nm mucus; **mocos** nmpl (fam) snot; **limpiarse los ~s de la nariz** (fam) to wipe one's nose

moda ['moða] nf fashion; (estilo) style; **a la o de ~** in fashion, fashionable; **pasado de ~** out of fashion

modales [mo'ðales] nmpl manners

modelar [moðe'lar] vt to model

modelo [mo'ðelo] adj inv, nmf model

módem ['moðem] nm (Inform) modem

moderado, -a [moðe'raðo, a] adj moderate

moderar [moðe'rar] vt to moderate; (violencia) to restrain, control; (velocidad) to reduce; **moderarse** vr to restrain o.s., control o.s.

modernizar [moðerni'θar] vt to modernize

moderno, -a [mo'ðerno, a] adj modern; (actual) present-day

modestia [mo'ðestja] nf modesty; **modesto, -a** adj modest

modificar [moðifi'kar] vt to modify

modisto, -a [mo'ðisto, a] nm/f (diseñador) couturier, designer; (que confecciona) dressmaker

modo ['moðo] nm way, manner; (Mús) mode; **modos** nmpl manners; **de ningún ~** in no way; **de todos ~s** at any rate; **modo de empleo** directions pl (for use)

mofarse [mo'farse] vr: **~ de** to mock, scoff at

mofle ['mofle] (MÉX, CAM) nm silencer (BRIT), muffler (US)

mogollón [moɣo'ʎon] (ESP: fam) adv a hell of a lot

moho ['moo] nm mould, mildew; (en metal) rust

mojar [mo'xar] vt to wet; (humedecer) to damp(en), moisten; (calar) to soak; **mojarse** vr to get wet

molcajete [molka'xete] (MÉX) nm mortar

molde ['molde] nm mould; (Costura) pattern; (fig) model; **moldeado** nm soft perm; **moldear** vt to mould

mole ['mole] nf mass, bulk; (edificio) pile

moler [mo'ler] vt to grind, crush

molestar [moles'tar] vt to bother; (fastidiar) to annoy; (incomodar) to inconvenience, put out ▷ vi to be a nuisance; **molestarse** vr to bother; (incomodarse) to go to trouble; (ofenderse) to take offence; **¿(no) te molesta si ...?** do you mind if ...?

▌ No confundir **molestar** con la palabra inglesa **molest**.

molestia [mo'lestja] nf bother, trouble; (incomodidad) inconvenience; (Med) discomfort; **es una ~** it's a nuisance; **molesto, -a** adj (que fastidia) annoying; (incómodo) inconvenient; (inquieto) uncomfortable, ill at ease; (enfadado) annoyed

molido, -a [mo'liðo, a] adj: **estar ~** (fig) to be exhausted o dead beat

molinillo [moli'niʎo] nm hand mill; **molinillo de café** coffee grinder

molino [mo'lino] nm (edificio) mill; (máquina) grinder

momentáneo, -a [momen'taneo, a] adj momentary

momento [mo'mento] nm moment; **de ~** at o for the moment

momia ['momja] nf mummy

monarca [mo'narka] nmf monarch, ruler; **monarquía** nf monarchy

monasterio [monas'terjo] nm monastery

mondar [mon'dar] vt to peel; **mondarse** vr (ESP): **~se de risa** (fam)

to split one's sides laughing
mondongo [mon'dongo] (*LAM*)
nm tripe
moneda [mo'neða] *nf* (*tipo de dinero*)
currency, money; (*pieza*) coin; **una ~
de 2 euros** a 2 euro piece; **monedero**
nm purse
monitor, a [moni'tor, a] *nm/f*
instructor, coach ▷ *nm* (*TV*) set;
(*Inform*) monitor
monja ['monxa] *nf* nun
monje ['monxe] *nm* monk
mono, -a ['mono, a] *adj* (*bonito*)
lovely, pretty; (*gracioso*) nice, charming
▷ *nm/f* monkey, ape ▷ *nm* dungarees
pl; (*overoles*) overalls *pl*
monopatín [monopa'tin] *nm*
skateboard
monopolio [mono'poljo] *nm*
monopoly; **monopolizar** *vt* to
monopolize
monótono, -a [mo'notono, a] *adj*
monotonous
monstruo ['monstrwo] *nm* monster
▷ *adj inv* fantastic; **monstruoso, -a** *adj*
monstrous
montaje [mon'taxe] *nm* assembly;
(*Teatro*) décor; (*Cine*) montage
montaña [mon'taɲa] *nf* (*monte*)
mountain; (*sierra*) mountains *pl*,
mountainous area; **montaña rusa**
roller coaster; **montañero, -a**
nm/f mountaineer; **montañismo** *nm*
mountaineering
montar [mon'tar] *vt* (*subir a*) to
mount, get on; (*Tec*) to assemble, put
together; (*negocio*) to set up; (*arma*) to
cock; (*colocar*) to lift on to; (*Culin*) to
beat ▷ *vi* to mount, get on; (*sobresalir*)
to overlap; **~ en bicicleta** to ride a
bicycle; **~ en cólera** to get angry; **~ a
caballo** to ride, go horseriding
monte ['monte] *nm* (*montaña*)
mountain; (*bosque*) woodland; (*área sin
cultivar*) wild area, wild country; **monte
de piedad** pawnshop
montón [mon'ton] *nm* heap, pile;
(*fig*): **un ~ de** heaps *o* lots of

monumento [monu'mento] *nm*
monument
moño ['moɲo] *nm* bun
moqueta [mo'keta] *nf* fitted carpet
mora ['mora] *nf* blackberry; *V tb*
moro
morado, -a [mo'raðo, a] *adj* purple,
violet ▷ *nm* bruise
moral [mo'ral] *adj* moral ▷ *nf*
(*ética*) ethics *pl*; (*moralidad*) morals *pl*,
morality; (*ánimo*) morale
moraleja [mora'lexa] *nf* moral
morboso, -a [mor'βoso, a] *adj*
morbid
morcilla [mor'θiʎa] *nf* blood sausage
≈ black pudding (*BRIT*)
mordaza [mor'ðaθa] *nf* (*para la boca*)
gag; (*Tec*) clamp
morder [mor'ðer] *vt* to bite;
(*fig: consumir*) to eat away, eat into;
mordisco *nm* bite
moreno, -a [mo'reno, a] *adj* (*color*)
(dark) brown; (*de tez*) dark; (*de pelo
moreno*) dark-haired; (*negro*) black
morfina [mor'fina] *nf* morphine
moribundo, -a [mori'βundo, a]
adj dying
morir [mo'rir] *vi* to die; (*fuego*) to die
down; (*luz*) to go out; **morirse** *vr* to
die; (*fig*) to be dying; **murió en
un accidente** he was killed in an
accident; **~se por algo** to be dying
for sth
moro, -a ['moro, a] *adj* Moorish
▷ *nm/f* Moor
moroso, -a [mo'roso, a] *nm/f* bad
debtor, defaulter
morraña [mo'rraɲa] (*MÉX*) *nf*
(*cambio*) small *o* loose change
morro ['morro] *nm* (*Zool*) snout, nose;
(*Auto, Aviac*) nose
morsa ['morsa] *nf* walrus
mortadela [morta'ðela] *nf*
mortadella
mortal [mor'tal] *adj* mortal;
(*golpe*) deadly; **mortalidad** *nf*
mortality
mortero [mor'tero] *nm* mortar

mosca ['moska] *nf* fly

Moscú [mos'ku] *n* Moscow

mosquearse [moske'arse] *(fam)* *vr* *(enojarse)* to get cross; *(ofenderse)* to take offence

mosquitero [moski'tero] *nm* mosquito net

mosquito [mos'kito] *nm* mosquito

mostaza [mos'taθa] *nf* mustard

mosto ['mosto] *nm* (unfermented) grape juice

mostrador [mostra'ðor] *nm* *(de tienda)* counter; *(de café)* bar

mostrar [mos'trar] *vt* to show; *(exhibir)* to display, exhibit; *(explicar)* to explain; **mostrarse** *vr:* **~se amable** to be kind; to prove to be kind; **no se muestra muy inteligente** he doesn't seem (to be) very intelligent

mota ['mota] *nf* speck, tiny piece; *(en diseño)* dot

mote ['mote] *nm* nickname

motín [mo'tin] *nm* *(del pueblo)* revolt, rising; *(del ejército)* mutiny

motivar [moti'βar] *vt* *(causar)* to cause, motivate; *(explicar)* to explain, justify; **motivo** *nm* motive, reason

moto ['moto] *(fam)* *nf* = **motocicleta**

motocicleta [motoθi'kleta] *nf* motorbike (*BRIT*), motorcycle

motociclista [motoθik'lista] *nmf* motorcyclist, biker

motoneta [moto'neta] *(cs)* *nf* scooter

motor [mo'tor] *nm* motor, engine; **motor a chorro** o **de reacción/de explosión** jet engine/internal combustion engine

motora [mo'tora] *nf* motorboat

movedizo, -a *adj* V **arena**

mover [mo'βer] *vt* to move; *(cabeza)* to shake; *(accionar)* to drive; *(fig)* to cause, provoke; **moverse** *vr* to move; *(fig)* to get a move on

móvil ['moβil] *adj* mobile; *(pieza de máquina)* moving; *(mueble)* movable ▷ *nm* *(motivo)* motive; *(teléfono)* mobile; *(US)* cellphone

movimiento [moβi'mjento] *nm* movement; *(Tec)* motion; *(actividad)* activity

mozo, -a ['moθo, a] *adj* *(joven)* young ▷ *nm/f* youth, young man/girl; *(cs: mesero)* waiter/waitress

MP3 *nm* MP3; **reproductor (de) ~** MP3 player

mucama [mu'kama] *(RPL)* *nf* maid

muchacho, -a [mu'tʃatʃo, a] *nm/f* *(niño)* boy/girl; *(criado)* servant; *(criada)* maid

muchedumbre [mutʃe'ðumbre] *nf* crowd

○ PALABRA CLAVE

---

mucho, -a ['mutʃo, a] *adj* **1** *(cantidad)* a lot of, much; *(número)* lots of, a lot of, many; **mucho dinero** a lot of money; **hace mucho calor** it's very hot; **muchas amigas** lots o a lot of friends

2 *(sg: grande)*: **ésta es mucha casa para él** this house is much too big for him

▷ *pron:* **tengo mucho que hacer** I've got a lot to do; **muchos dicen que ...** a lot of people say that ...; V *tb* **tener**

▷ *adv* **1** **me gusta mucho** I like it a lot; **lo siento mucho** I'm very sorry; **come mucho** he eats a lot; **¿te vas a quedar mucho?** are you going to be staying long?

2 *(respuesta)* very; **¿estás cansado? – ¡mucho!** are you tired? – very!

3 *(locuciones)*: **como mucho** at (the) most; **con mucho: el mejor con mucho** by far the best; **ni mucho menos: no es rico ni mucho menos** he's far from being rich

4: **por mucho que: por mucho que le creas** no matter how o however much you believe her

---

muda ['muða] *nf* change of clothes

mudanza [mu'ðanθa] *nf* *(de casa)* move

mudar [mu'ðar] vt to change; (Zool) to shed ▷ vi to change; **mudarse** vr (ropa) to change; **~se de casa** to move house

mudo, -a ['muðo, a] adj dumb; (callado, Cine) silent

mueble ['mweβle] nm piece of furniture; **muebles** nmpl furniture sg

mueca ['mweka] nf face, grimace; **hacer ~s a** to make faces at

muela ['mwela] nf back tooth; **muela del juicio** wisdom tooth

muelle ['mweʎe] nm spring; (Náut) wharf; (malecón) pier

muero etc vb V **morir**

muerte ['mwerte] nf death; (homicidio) murder; **dar ~ a** to kill

muerto, -a ['mwerto, a] pp de **morir** ▷ adj dead ▷ nm/f dead man/woman; (difunto) deceased; (cadáver) corpse; **estar ~ de cansancio** to be dead tired; **Día de los Muertos** (MÉx) All Souls' Day

- **DÍA DE LOS MUERTOS**
-
- All Souls' Day (or "Day of the Dead")
- in Mexico coincides with All
- Saints' Day, which is celebrated
- in the Catholic countries of Latin
- America on November 1st and
- 2nd. All Souls' Day is actually
- a celebration which begins
- in the evening of October 31st
- and continues until November
- 2nd. It is a combination of the
- Catholic tradition of honouring
- the Christian saints and martyrs,
- and the ancient Mexican or Aztec
- traditions, in which death was not
- something sinister. For this reason
- all the dead are honoured by
- bringing offerings of food, flowers
- and candles to the cemetery.

muestra ['mwestra] nf (señal) indication, sign; (demostración) demonstration; (prueba) proof; (estadística) sample; (modelo) model, pattern; (testimonio) token

muestro etc vb V **mostrar**

muevo etc vb V **mover**

mugir [mu'xir] vi (vaca) to moo

mugre ['muɣre] nf dirt, filth

mujer [mu'xer] nf woman; (esposa) wife; **mujeriego** nm womanizer

mula ['mula] nf mule

muleta [mu'leta] nf (para andar) crutch; (Taur) stick with red cape attached

multa ['multa] nf fine; **poner una ~ a** to fine; **multar** vt to fine

multicines [multi'θines] nmpl multiscreen cinema sg

multinacional [multinaθjo'nal] nf multinational

múltiple ['multiple] adj multiple; (pl) many, numerous

multiplicar [multipli'kar] vt (Mat) to multiply; (fig) to increase; **multiplicarse** vr (Bio) to multiply; (fig) to be everywhere at once

multitud [multi'tuð] nf (muchedumbre) crowd; **~ de** lots of

mundial [mun'djal] adj world-wide, universal; (guerra, récord) world cpd

mundo ['mundo] nm world; **todo el ~** everybody; **tener ~** to be experienced, know one's way around

munición [muni'θjon] nf ammunition

municipal [muniθi'pal] adj municipal, local

municipio [muni'θipjo] nm (ayuntamiento) town council, corporation; (territorio administrativo) town, municipality

muñeca [mu'ɲeka] nf (Anat) wrist; (juguete) doll

muñeco [mu'ɲeko] nm (figura) figure; (marioneta) puppet; (fig) puppet, pawn

mural [mu'ral] adj mural, wall cpd ▷ nm mural

muralla [mu'raʎa] nf (city) wall(s) (pl)

murciélago [mur'θjelaɣo] nm bat

murmullo [mur'muʎo] nm

m

murmur(ing); (*cuchicheo*) whispering
murmurar [murmu'rar] *vi* to
murmur, whisper; (*cotillear*) to gossip
muro ['muro] *nm* wall
muscular [musku'lar] *adj* muscular
músculo ['muskulo] *nm* muscle
museo [mu'seo] *nm* museum; **museo de arte** art gallery
musgo ['musɣo] *nm* moss
música ['musika] *nf* music; V *tb* **músico**
músico, -a ['musiko, a] *adj* musical
▷ *nm/f* musician
muslo ['muslo] *nm* thigh
musulmán, -ana [musul'man, ana] *nm/f* Moslem
mutación [muta'θjon] *nf* (*Bio*) mutation; (*cambio*) (sudden) change
mutilar [muti'lar] *vt* to mutilate; (*a una persona*) to maim
mutuo, -a ['mutwo, a] *adj* mutual
muy [mwi] *adv* very; (*demasiado*) too;
M~ Señor mío Dear Sir; **~ de noche** very late at night; **eso es ~ de él** that's just like him

N *abr* (= *norte*) N
nabo ['naβo] *nm* turnip
nacer [na'θer] *vi* to be born; (*de huevo*) to hatch; (*vegetal*) to sprout; (*río*) to rise; **nací en Barcelona** I was born in Barcelona; **nacido, -a** *adj* born; **recién nacido** newborn; **nacimiento** *nm* birth; (*de Navidad*) Nativity; (*de río*) source
nación [na'θjon] *nf* nation; **nacional** *adj* national; **nacionalismo** *nm* nationalism
nacionalidad [naθjonali'ðað] *nf* nationality
nada ['naða] *pron* nothing ▷ *adv* not at all, in no way; **no decir ~** to say nothing, not to say anything; **~ más** nothing else; **de ~** don't mention it
nadador, a [naða'ðor, a] *nm/f* swimmer
nadar [na'ðar] *vi* to swim
nadie ['naðje] *pron* nobody, no-one; **~ habló** nobody spoke; **no había ~** there was nobody there, there wasn't anybody there

nado ['naðo] **a nado**: *adv*: **pasar a ~** to swim across

nafta ['nafta] (*RPL*) *nf* petrol (*BRIT*), gas (*US*)

naipe ['naipe] *nm* (playing) card; **naipes** *nmpl* cards

nalgas ['nalɣas] *nfpl* buttocks

nalguear [nalɣe'ar] (*MÉX, CAM*) *vt* to spank

nana ['nana] (*ESP*) *nf* lullaby

naranja [na'ranxa] *adj inv, nf* orange; **media ~** (*fam*) better half; **naranjada** *nf* orangeade; **naranjo** *nm* orange tree

narciso [nar'θiso] *nm* narcissus

narcótico, -a [nar'kotiko, a] *adj, nm* narcotic; **narcotizar** *vt* to drug; **narcotráfico** *nm* drug trafficking *o* running

nariz [na'riθ] *nf* nose; **nariz chata/respingona** snub/turned-up nose

narración [narra'θjon] *nf* narration

narrar [na'rrar] *vt* to narrate, recount; **narrativa** *nf* narrative

nata ['nata] *nf* cream; **nata montada** whipped cream

natación [nata'θjon] *nf* swimming

natal [na'tal] *adj*: **ciudad ~** home town; **natalidad** *nf* birth rate

natillas [na'tiʎas] *nfpl* custard *sg*

nativo, -a [na'tiβo, a] *adj, nm/f* native

natural [natu'ral] *adj* natural; (*fruta etc*) fresh ▷ *nmf* native ▷ *nm* (*disposición*) nature

naturaleza [natura'leθa] *nf* nature; (*género*) nature, kind; **naturaleza muerta** still life

naturalmente [natural'mente] *adv* (*de modo natural*) in a natural way; **¡~!** of course!

naufragar [naufra'ɣar] *vi* to sink; **naufragio** *nm* shipwreck

nauseabundo, -a [nausea'βundo, a] *adj* nauseating, sickening

náuseas ['nauseas] *nfpl* nausea *sg*; **me da ~** it makes me feel sick

náutico, -a ['nautiko, a] *adj* nautical

navaja [na'βaxa] *nf* knife; (*de barbero, peluquero*) razor

naval [na'βal] *adj* naval

Navarra [na'βarra] *n* Navarre

nave ['naβe] *nf* (*barco*) ship, vessel; (*Arq*) nave; **nave espacial** spaceship; **nave industrial** factory premises *pl*

navegador [naβexa'ðor] *nm* (*Inform*) browser

navegante [naβe'xante] *nmf* navigator

navegar [naβe'xar] *vi* (*barco*) to sail; (*avión*) to fly; **~ por Internet** to surf the Net

Navidad [naβi'ðað] *nf* Christmas; **Navidades** *nfpl* Christmas time; **¡Feliz ~!** Merry Christmas!; **navideño, -a** *adj* Christmas *cpd*

nazca *etc vb* V **nacer**

nazi ['naθi] *adj, nmf* Nazi

NE *abr* (= *nor(d)este*) NE

neblina [ne'βlina] *nf* mist

necesario, -a [neθe'sarjo, a] *adj* necessary

neceser [neθe'ser] *nm* toilet bag; (*bolsa grande*) holdall

necesidad [neθesi'ðað] *nf* need; (*lo inevitable*) necessity; (*miseria*) poverty; **en caso de ~** in case of need *o* emergency; **hacer sus ~es** to relieve o.s.

necesitado, -a [neθesi'taðo, a] *adj* needy, poor; **~ de** in need of

necesitar [neθesi'tar] *vt* to need, require

necio, -a ['neθjo, a] *adj* foolish

nectarina [nekta'rina] *nf* nectarine

nefasto, -a [ne'fasto, a] *adj* ill-fated, unlucky

negación [neɣa'θjon] *nf* negation; (*rechazo*) refusal, denial

negar [ne'ɣar] *vt* (*renegar, rechazar*) to refuse; (*prohibir*) to refuse, deny; (*desmentir*) to deny; **negarse** *vr*: **~se a** to refuse to

negativa [neɣa'tiβa] *nf* negative; (*rechazo*) refusal, denial

negativo, -a [neɣa'tiβo, a] *adj, nm*

negative

negligente [neɣli'xente] adj
negligent

negociación [neɣoθja'θjon] nf
negotiation

negociante [neɣo'θjante] nmf
businessman/woman

negociar [neɣo'θjar] vt, vi to
negotiate; **~ en** to deal o trade in

negocio [ne'ɣoθjo] nm (Com)
business; (asunto) affair, business;
(operación comercial) deal, transaction;
(lugar) place of business; **los ~s**
business sg; **hacer ~** to do business

negra ['neɣra] nf (Mús) crotchet; V
tb **negro**

negro, -a ['neɣra, a] adj black;
(suerte) awful ▷ nm black ▷ nm/f black
man/woman

nene, -a ['nene, a] nm/f baby,
small child

neón [ne'on] nm: **luces/lámpara de ~**
neon lights/lamp

neoyorquino, -a [neojor'kino, a]
adj (of) New York

nervio ['nerβjo] nm nerve;
nerviosismo nm nervousness, nerves
pl; **nervioso, -a** adj nervous

neto, -a ['neto, a] adj net

neumático, -a [neu'matiko, a] adj
pneumatic ▷ nm (ESP) tyre (BRIT),
tire (US); **neumático de recambio**
spare tyre

neurólogo, -a [neu'roloɣo, a] nm/f
neurologist

neurona [neu'rona] nf nerve cell

neutral [neu'tral] adj neutral;
neutralizar vt to neutralize;
(contrarrestar) to counteract

neutro, -a ['neutro, a] adj (Bio,
Ling) neuter

neutrón [neu'tron] nm neutron

nevada [ne'βaða] nf snowstorm;
(caída de nieve) snowfall

nevar [ne'βar] vi to snow

nevera [ne'βera] (ESP) nf refrigerator
(BRIT), icebox (US)

nevería [neβe'ria] (MÉX) nf ice-cream

parlour

nexo ['nekso] nm link, connection

ni [ni] conj nor, neither; (tb: **~ siquiera**)
not … even; **~ aunque** not even
if; **~ blanco ~ negro** neither white
nor black

Nicaragua [nika'raɣwa] nf
Nicaragua; **nicaragüense** adj, nmf
Nicaraguan

nicho ['nitʃo] nm niche

nicotina [niko'tina] nf nicotine

nido ['niðo] nm nest

niebla ['njeβla] nf fog; (neblina) mist

niego etc vb V **negar**

nieto, -a ['njeto, a] nm/f grandson/
daughter; **nietos** nmpl grandchildren

nieve etc ['njeβe] vb V **nevar** ▷ nf
snow; (MÉX: helado) ice cream

NIF nm abr (= Número de Identificación
Fiscal) personal identification number used
for financial and tax purposes

ninfa ['ninfa] nf nymph

ningún adj V **ninguno**

ninguno, -a [nin'guno, a] (adj
ningún) no pron (nadie) nobody; (ni
uno) none, not one; (ni uno ni otro)
neither; **de ninguna manera** by no
means, not at all

niña ['nina] nf (Anat) pupil; V tb **niño**

niñera [ni'nera] nf nursemaid, nanny

niñez [ni'neθ] nf childhood; (infancia)
infancy

niño, -a ['nino, a] adj (joven) young;
(inmaduro) immature ▷ nm/f child,
boy/girl

nipón, -ona [ni'pon, ona] adj, nm/f
Japanese

níquel ['nikel] nm nickel

níspero ['nispero] nm medlar

nítido, -a ['nitiðo, a] adj clear; sharp

nitrato [ni'trato] nm nitrate

nitrógeno [ni'troxeno] nm nitrogen

nivel [ni'βel] nm (Geo) level; (norma)
level, standard; (altura) height; **nivel
de aceite** oil level; **nivel de aire** spirit
level; **nivel de vida** standard of living;
nivelar vt to level out; (fig) to even up;
(Com) to balance

no [no] *adv* no; not; *(con verbo)* not
▷ *excl* no!; ~ **tengo nada** I don't have
anything, I have nothing; ~ **es el mío**
it's not mine; **ahora** ~ not now; ¿~ **lo
sabes?** don't you know?; ~ **mucho** not
much; ~ **bien termine, lo entregaré** as
soon as I finish, I'll hand it over; ~ **más:
ayer** ~ **más** just yesterday; **¡pase ~
más!** come in!; **¡a que ~ lo sabes!** I bet
you don't know!; **¡cómo ~!** of course!;
la ~ intervención non-intervention

noble ['noβle] *adj, nmf* noble; **nobleza**
nf nobility

noche ['notʃe] *nf* night, night-time;
(la tarde) evening; **de ~, por la ~** at
night; **es de ~** it's dark; **Noche de San
Juan** *see note*

○ **NOCHE DE SAN JUAN**
○
○ The **Noche de San Juan** on the
○ 24th June is a **fiesta** coinciding
○ with the summer solstice and
○ which has taken the place of
○ other ancient pagan festivals.
○ Traditionally fire plays a major
○ part in these festivities with
○ celebrations and dancing taking
○ place around bonfires in towns
○ and villages across the country.

nochebuena [notʃe'βwena] *nf*
Christmas Eve

○ **NOCHEBUENA**
○
○ Traditional Christmas
○ celebrations in Spanish-speaking
○ countries mainly take place
○ on the night of **Nochebuena**,
○ Christmas Eve. Families gather
○ together for a large meal and the
○ more religiously inclined attend
○ Midnight Mass. While presents are
○ traditionally given by **los Reyes
○ Magos** on the 6th January, more
○ and more people are exchanging
○ gifts on Christmas Eve.

nochevieja [notʃe'βjexa] *nf* New
Year's Eve

nocivo, -a [no'θiβo, a] *adj* harmful

noctámbulo, -a [nok'tambulo, a]
nm/f sleepwalker

nocturno, -a [nok'turno, a] *adj (de
la noche)* nocturnal, night *cpd*; *(de la
tarde)* evening *cpd* ▷ *nm* nocturne

nogal [no'ɣal] *nm* walnut tree

nómada ['nomaða] *adj* nomadic
▷ *nmf* nomad

nombrar [nom'brar] *vt (designar)*
to name; *(mencionar)* to mention; *(dar
puesto a)* to appoint

nombre ['nombre] *nm* name;
(sustantivo) noun; ~ **y apellidos** name
in full; **poner** ~ to call, name; **nombre
común/propio** common/proper
noun; **nombre de pila/de soltera**
Christian/maiden name

nómina ['nomina] *nf (lista)* payroll;
(hoja) payslip

nominal [nomi'nal] *adj* nominal

nominar [nomi'nar] *vt* to nominate

nominativo, -a [nomina'tiβo, a]
adj (Com): **cheque ~ a X** cheque made
out to X

nordeste [nor'ðeste] *adj* north-east,
north-eastern, north-easterly ▷ *nm*
north-east

nórdico, -a ['norðiko, a] *adj* Nordic

noreste [no'reste] *adj, nm* = **nordeste**

noria ['norja] *nf (Agr)* waterwheel; *(de
carnaval)* big (BRIT) o Ferris (US) wheel

norma ['norma] *nf* rule (of thumb)

normal [nor'mal] *adj (corriente)*
normal; *(habitual)* usual, natural;
normalizarse *vr* to return to normal;
normalmente *adv* normally

normativa [norma'tiβa] *nf* (set of)
rules *pl*, regulations *pl*

noroeste [noro'este] *adj* north-west,
north-western, north-westerly ▷ *nm*
north-west

norte ['norte] *adj* north, northern,
northerly ▷ *nm* north; *(fig)* guide

norteamericano, -a
[norteameri'kano, a] *adj, nm/f*

n

(North) American

Noruega [no'rweɣa] nf Norway

noruego, -a [no'rweɣo, a] adj, nm/f Norwegian

nos [nos] pron (directo) us; (indirecto) us; to us; for us; from us; (reflexivo) (to) ourselves; (recíproco) (to) each other; ~ **levantamos a las 7** we get up at 7

nosotros, -as [no'sotros, as] pron (sujeto) we; (después de prep) us

nostalgia [nos'talxja] nf nostalgia

nota ['nota] nf note; (Escol) mark

notable [no'taβle] adj notable; (Escol) outstanding

notar [no'tar] vt to notice, note; **notarse** vr to be obvious; **se nota que ...** one observes that ...

notario [no'tarjo] nm notary

noticia [no'tiθja] nf (información) piece of news; **las ~s** the news sg; **tener ~s de algn** to hear from sb

▌ No confundir **noticia** con la palabra inglesa notice.

noticiero [noti'θjero] (LAM) nm news bulletin

notificar [notifi'kar] vt to notify, inform

notorio, -a [no'torjo, a] adj (público) well-known; (evidente) obvious

novato, -a [no'βato, a] adj inexperienced ▷ nm/f beginner, novice

novecientos, -as [noβe'θjentos, as] num nine hundred

novedad [noβe'ðað] nf (calidad de nuevo) newness; (noticia) piece of news; (cambio) change, (new) development

novel [no'βel] adj new; (inexperto) inexperienced ▷ nmf beginner

novela [no'βela] nf novel

noveno, -a [no'βeno, a] adj ninth

noventa [no'βenta] num ninety

novia nf V **novio**

noviazgo [no'βjaθɣo] nm engagement

novicio, -a [no'βiθjo, a] nm/f novice

noviembre [no'βjembre] nm November

novillada [noβi'ʎaða] nf (Taur) bullfight with young bulls; **novillero** nm novice bullfighter; **novillo** nm young bull, bullock; **hacer novillos** (fam) to play truant

novio, -a ['noβjo, a] nm/f boyfriend/ girlfriend; (prometido) fiancé/fiancée; (recién casado) bridegroom/bride; **los ~s** the newly-weds

nube ['nuβe] nf cloud

nublado, -a [nu'βlaðo, a] adj cloudy; **nublarse** vr to grow dark

nubosidad [nuβosi'ðað] nf cloudiness; **había mucha ~** it was very cloudy

nuboso [nu'boso] adj cloudy

nuca ['nuka] nf nape of the neck

nuclear [nukle'ar] adj nuclear

núcleo ['nukleo] nm (centro) core; (Física) nucleus; **núcleo urbano** city centre

nudillo [nu'ðiʎo] nm knuckle

nudista [nu'ðista] adj nudist

nudo ['nuðo] nm knot; (de carreteras) junction

nuera ['nwera] nf daughter-in-law

nuestro, -a ['nwestro, a] adj pos our ▷ pron ours; ~ **padre** our father; **un amigo ~** a friend of ours; **es el ~** it's ours

Nueva York [-jɔrk] n New York

Nueva Zelanda [-θe'landa] nf New Zealand

nueve ['nweβe] num nine

nuevo, -a ['nweβo, a] adj (gen) new; **de ~** again

nuez [nweθ] nf walnut; (Anat) Adam's apple; **nuez moscada** nutmeg

nulo, -a ['nulo, a] adj (inepto, torpe) useless; (inválido) (null and) void; (Deporte) drawn, tied

núm. abr (= número) no.

numerar [nume'rar] vt to number

número ['numero] nm (gen) number; (tamaño: de zapato) size; (ejemplar: de diario) number, issue; **sin ~** numberless, unnumbered; **número atrasado** back number; **número de matrícula/**

teléfono registration/telephone number; **número impar/par** odd/even number; **número romano** Roman numeral

numeroso, -a [nume'roso, a] *adj* numerous

nunca ['nunka] *adv* (*jamás*) never; **~ lo pensé** I never thought it; **no viene ~** he never comes; **~ más** never again; **más que ~** more than ever

nupcias ['nupθjas] *nfpl* wedding *sg*, nuptials

nutria ['nutrja] *nf* otter

nutrición [nutri'θjon] *nf* nutrition

nutrir [nu'trir] *vt* (*alimentar*) to nourish; (*dar de comer*) to feed; (*fig*) to strengthen; **nutritivo, -a** *adj* nourishing, nutritious

nylon [ni'lon] *nm* nylon

ñango, -a ['ɲaŋgo, a] (*MÉX*) *adj* puny

ñapa ['ɲapa] (*LAM*) *nf* extra

ñata ['ɲata] (*LAM: fam*) *nf* nose; V *tb* **ñato**

ñato, -a ['ɲato, a] (*LAM*) *adj* snub-nosed

ñoñería [ɲoɲe'ria] *nf* insipidness

ñoño, -a ['ɲoɲo, a] *adj* (*fam: tonto*) silly, stupid; (*soso*) insipid; (*persona*) spineless; (*ESP: película, novela*) sentimental

O

O abr (= oeste) W

o [o] conj or; **o ... o** either ... or

oasis [o'asis] nm inv oasis

obcecarse [oβθe'karse] vr to get o become stubborn

obedecer [oβeðe'θer] vt to obey; **obediente** adj obedient

obertura [oβer'tura] nf overture

obeso, -a [o'βeso, a] adj obese

obispo [o'βispo] nm bishop

obituario [oβɪ'twarjo] (LAM) nm obituary

objetar [oβxe'tar] vt, vi to object

objetivo, -a [oβxe'tiβo, a] adj, nm objective

objeto [oβ'xeto] nm (cosa) object; (fin) aim

objetor, a [oβxe'tor, a] nm/f objector

obligación [oβlixa'θjon] nf obligation; (Com) bond

obligar [oβli'ɣar] vt to force; **obligarse** vr to bind o.s.; **obligatorio, -a** adj compulsory, obligatory

oboe [o'βoe] nm oboe

obra ['oβra] nf work; (Arq) construction, building; (Teatro) play; **por ~ de** thanks to (the efforts of); **obra maestra** masterpiece; **obras públicas** public works; **obrar** vt to work; (tener efecto) to have an effect on ▷ vi to act, behave; (tener efecto) to have an effect; **la carta obra en su poder** the letter is in his/her possession

obrero, -a [o'βrero, a] adj (clase) working; (movimiento) labour cpd ▷ nm/ f (gen) worker; (sin oficio) labourer

obsceno, -a [oβs'θeno, a] adj obscene

obscu... = **oscu...**

obsequiar [oβse'kjar] vt (ofrecer) to present with; (agasajar) to make a fuss of, lavish attention on; **obsequio** nm (regalo) gift; (cortesía) courtesy, attention

observación [oβserβa'θjon] nf observation; (reflexión) remark

observador, a [oβserβa'ðor, a] nm/f observer

observar [oβser'βar] vt to observe; (anotar) to notice; **observarse** vr to keep to, observe

obsesión [oβse'sjon] nf obsession; **obsesivo, -a** adj obsessive

obstáculo [oβs'takulo] nm obstacle; (impedimento) hindrance, drawback

obstante [oβs'tante]: **no ~** adv nevertheless

obstinado, -a [oβsti'naðo, a] adj obstinate, stubborn

obstinarse [oβsti'narse] vr to be obstinate; **~ en** to persist in

obstruir [oβstru'ir] vt to obstruct

obtener [oβte'ner] vt (gen) to obtain; (premio) to win

obturador [oβtura'ðor] nm (Foto) shutter

obvio, -a ['oββjo, a] adj obvious

oca ['oka] nf (animal) goose; (juego) ≈ snakes and ladders

ocasión [oka'sjon] nf (oportunidad) opportunity, chance; (momento) occasion, time; (causa) cause; **de ~**

secondhand; **ocasionar** vt to cause

ocaso [o'kaso] nm (fig) decline

occidente [okθi'ðente] nm west

OCDE nf abr (= Organización de Cooperación y Desarrollo Económico) OECD

océano [o'θeano] nm ocean; **Océano índico** Indian Ocean

ochenta [o'tʃenta] num eighty

ocho ['otʃo] num eight; **dentro de ~ días** within a week

ocio ['oθjo] nm (tiempo) leisure; (pey) idleness

octavilla [okta'viʎa] nf leaflet, pamphlet

octavo, -a [ok'taβo, a] adj eighth

octubre [ok'tuβre] nm October

oculista [oku'lista] nmf oculist

ocultar [okul'tar] vt (esconder) to hide; (callar) to conceal; **oculto, -a** adj hidden; (fig) secret

ocupación [okupa'θjon] nf occupation

ocupado, -a [oku'paðo, a] adj (persona) busy; (plaza) occupied, taken; (teléfono) engaged; **ocupar** vt (gen) to occupy, **ocuparse** vr: **ocuparse de o en** (gen) to concern o.s. with; (cuidar) to look after

ocurrencia [oku'rrenθja] nf (idea) bright idea

ocurrir [oku'rrir] vi to happen; **ocurrirse** vr: **se me ocurrió que ...** it occurred to me that ...

odiar [o'ðjar] vt to hate; **odio** nm hate, hatred; **odioso, -a** adj (gen) hateful; (malo) nasty

odontólogo, -a [oðon'toloxo, a] nm/f dentist, dental surgeon

oeste [o'este] nm west; **una película del ~** a western

ofender [ofen'der] vt (agraviar) to offend; (insultar) to insult; **ofenderse** vr to take offence; **ofensa** nf offence; **ofensiva** nf offensive; **ofensivo, -a** adj offensive

oferta [o'ferta] nf offer; (propuesta) proposal; **la ~ y la demanda** supply and demand; **artículos en ~** goods on offer

oficial [ofi'θjal] adj official ▷ nm (Mil) officer

oficina [ofi'θina] nf office; **oficina de correos** post office; **oficina de información** information bureau; **oficina de turismo** tourist office; **oficinista** nmf clerk

oficio [o'fiθjo] nm (profesión) profession; (puesto) post; (Rel) service; **ser del ~** to be an old hand; **tener mucho ~** to have a lot of experience; **oficio de difuntos** funeral service

ofimática [ofi'matika] nf office automation

ofrecer [ofre'θer] vt (dar) to offer; (proponer) to propose; **ofrecerse** vr (persona) to offer o.s., volunteer; (situación) to present itself; **¿qué se le ofrece?, ¿se le ofrece algo?** what can I do for you?, can I get you anything?

ofrecimiento [ofreθi'mjento] nm offer

oftalmólogo, -a [oftal'moloxo, a] nm/f ophthalmologist

oída [o'iða] nf: **de ~s** by hearsay

oído [o'iðo] nm (Anat) ear; (sentido) hearing

oigo etc vb V **oír**

oír [o'ir] vt (gen) to hear; (atender a) to listen to; **¡oiga!** listen!; **~ misa** to attend mass

OIT nf abr (= Organización Internacional del Trabajo) ILO

ojal [o'xal] nm buttonhole

ojalá [oxa'la] excl if only (it were so)!, some hope! ▷ conj if only ...!, would that ...!; **~ (que) venga hoy** I hope he comes today

ojeada [oxe'aða] nf glance

ojera [o'xera] nf: **tener ~s** to have bags under one's eyes

ojo ['oxo] nm eye; (de puente) span; (de cerradura) keyhole ▷ excl careful!; **tener ~ para** to have an eye for; **ojo de buey** porthole

okey ['okei] (LAM) excl O.K.

okupa [o'kupa] (*ESP: fam*) *nmf* squatter

ola ['ola] *nf* wave

olé [o'le] *excl* bravo!, olé!

oleada [ole'aða] *nf* big wave, swell; (*fig*) wave

oleaje [ole'axe] *nm* swell

óleo ['oleo] *nm* oil; **oleoducto** *nm* (oil) pipeline

oler [o'ler] *vt* (*gen*) to smell; (*inquirir*) to pry into; (*fig: sospechar*) to sniff out ▷ *vi* to smell; **~ a** to smell of

olfatear [olfate'ar] *vt* to smell; (*inquirir*) to pry into; **olfato** *nm* sense of smell

olimpiada [olim'piaða] *nf*: **las O~s** the Olympics; **olímpico, -a** [o'limpiko, a] *adj* Olympic

oliva [o'liβa] *nf* (*aceituna*) olive; **aceite de ~** olive oil; **olivo** *nm* olive tree

olla ['oʎa] *nf* pan; (*comida*) stew; **olla exprés** *o* **a presión** (*ESP*) pressure cooker; **olla podrida** *type of Spanish stew*

olmo ['olmo] *nm* elm (tree)

olor [o'lor] *nm* smell; **oloroso, -a** *adj* scented

olvidar [olβi'ðar] *vt* to forget; (*omitir*) to omit; **olvidarse** *vr* (*fig*) to forget o.s.; **se me olvidó** I forgot

olvido [ol'βiðo] *nm* oblivion; (*despiste*) forgetfulness

ombligo [om'blixo] *nm* navel

omelette [ome'lete] (*LAM*) *nf* omelet(te)

omisión [omi'sjon] *nf* (*abstención*) omission; (*descuido*) neglect

omiso, -a [o'miso, a] *adj*: **hacer caso ~ de** to ignore, pass over

omitir [omi'tir] *vt* to omit

omnipotente [omnipo'tente] *adj* omnipotent

omóplato [o'moplato] *nm* shoulder blade

OMS *nf abr* (= *Organización Mundial de la Salud*) WHO

once ['onθe] *num* eleven; **onces** (*cs*) *nfpl* tea break *sg*

onda ['onda] *nf* wave; **onda corta/larga/media** short/long/medium wave; **ondear** *vt, vi* to wave; (*tener ondas*) to be wavy; (*agua*) to ripple

ondulación [ondula'θjon] *nf* undulation; **ondulado, -a** *adj* wavy

ONG *nf abr* (= *organización no gubernamental*) NGO

ONU ['onu] *nf abr* (= *Organización de las Naciones Unidas*) UNO

opaco, -a [o'pako, a] *adj* opaque

opción [op'θjon] *nf* (*gen*) option; (*derecho*) right, option

OPEP ['opep] *nf abr* (= *Organización de Países Exportadores de Petróleo*) OPEC

ópera ['opera] *nf* opera; **ópera bufa** *o* **cómica** comic opera

operación [opera'θjon] *nf* (*gen*) operation; (*Com*) transaction, deal

operador, a [opera'ðor, a] *nm/f* operator; (*Cine: de proyección*) projectionist; (: *de rodaje*) cameraman

operar [ope'rar] *vt* (*producir*) to produce, bring about; (*Med*) to operate on ▷ *vi* (*Com*) to operate, deal; **operarse** *vr* to occur; (*Med*) to have an operation

opereta [ope'reta] *nf* operetta

opinar [opi'nar] *vt* to think ▷ *vi* to give one's opinion; **opinión** *nf* (*creencia*) belief; (*criterio*) opinion

opio ['opjo] *nm* opium

oponer [opo'ner] *vt* (*resistencia*) to put up, offer; **oponerse** *vr* (*objetar*) to object; (*estar frente a frente*) to be opposed; (*dos personas*) to oppose each other; **~ A a B** to set A against B; **me opongo a pensar que ...** I refuse to believe o think that ...

oportunidad [oportuni'ðað] *nf* (*ocasión*) opportunity; (*posibilidad*) chance

oportuno, -a [opor'tuno, a] *adj* (*en su tiempo*) opportune, timely; (*respuesta*) suitable; **en el momento ~** at the right moment

oposición [oposi'θjon] *nf* opposition; **oposiciones** *nfpl* (*Escol*) public examinations

opositor, a [oposi'tor, a] *nm/f*
(*adversario*) opponent; (*candidato*): **~ (a)**
candidate (for)

opresión [opre'sjon] *nf* oppression;
opresor, a *nm/f* oppressor

oprimir [opri'mir] *vt* to squeeze; (*fig*)
to oppress

optar [op'tar] *vi* (*elegir*) to choose;
~ por to opt for; **optativo, -a** *adj*
optional

óptico, -a ['optiko, a] *adj* optic(al)
▷ *nm/f* optician; **óptica** *nf* optician's
(shop); **desde esta óptica** from this
point of view

optimismo [opti'mismo] *nm*
optimism; **optimista** *nmf* optimist

opuesto, -a [o'pwesto, a] *adj*
(*contrario*) opposite; (*antagónico*)
opposing

oración [ora'θjon] *nf* (*Rel*) prayer;
(*Ling*) sentence

orador, a [ora'ðor, a] *nm/f*
(*conferenciante*) speaker, orator

oral [o'ral] *adj* oral

orangután [orangu'tan] *nm*
orangutan

orar [o'rar] *vi* to pray

oratoria [ora'torja] *nf* oratory

órbita ['orβita] *nf* orbit

orden ['orðen] *nm* (*gen*) order ▷ *nf*
(*gen*) order; (*Inform*) command; **en ~ de
prioridad** in order of priority; **orden
del día** agenda

ordenado, -a [orðe'naðo, a] *adj*
(*metódico*) methodical, (*arreglado*)
orderly

ordenador [orðena'ðor] *nm*
computer; **ordenador central**
mainframe computer

ordenar [orðe'nar] *vt* (*mandar*) to
order; (*poner orden*) to put in order,
arrange; **ordenarse** *vr* (*Rel*) to be
ordained

ordeñar [orðe'nar] *vt* to milk

ordinario, -a [orði'narjo, a] *adj*
(*común*) ordinary, usual; (*vulgar*) vulgar,
common

orégano [o'reɣano] *nm* oregano

oreja [o'rexa] *nf* ear; (*Mecánica*) lug,
flange

orfanato [orfa'nato] *nm* orphanage

orfebrería [orfeβre'ria] *nf* gold/
silver work

orgánico, -a [or'ɣaniko, a] *adj*
organic

organismo [orɣa'nismo] *nm* (*Bio*)
organism; (*Pol*) organization

organización [orɣaniθa'θjon]
nf organization; **organizar** *vt* to
organize

órgano ['orɣano] *nm* organ

orgasmo [or'ɣasmo] *nm* orgasm

orgía [or'xia] *nf* orgy

orgullo [or'ɣuʎo] *nm* pride;
orgulloso, -a *adj* (*gen*) proud;
(*altanero*) haughty

orientación [orjenta'θjon] *nf*
(*posición*) position; (*dirección*) direction

oriental [orjen'tal] *adj* eastern; (*del
Extremo Oriente*) oriental

orientar [orjen'tar] *vt* (*situar*) to
orientate; (*señalar*) to point; (*dirigir*) to
direct; (*guiar*) to guide; **orientarse** *vr*
to get one's bearings

oriente [o'rjente] *nm* east; **el O-
Medio** the Middle East; **el Próximo/
Extremo O~** the Near/Far East

origen [o'rixen] *nm* origin

original [orixi'nal] *adj* (*nuevo*)
original; (*extraño*) odd, strange;
originalidad *nf* originality

originar [orixi'nar] *vt* to start, cause;
originarse *vr* to originate; **originario,
-a** *adj* original; **originario de** native of

orilla [o'riʎa] *nf* (*borde*) border; (*de
río*) bank; (*de bosque, tela*) edge; (*de
mar*) shore

orina [o'rina] *nf* urine; **orinal** *nm*
(chamber) pot; **orinar** *vi* to urinate;
orinarse *vr* to wet o.s.

oro ['oro] *nm* gold; **oros** *nmpl* (*Naipes*)
hearts

orquesta [or'kesta] *nf* orchestra;
orquesta sinfónica symphony
orchestra

orquídea [orˈkiðea] nf orchid

ortiga [orˈtiɣa] nf nettle

ortodoxo, -a [ortoˈðokso, a] adj orthodox

ortografía [ortoɣraˈfia] nf spelling

ortopedia [ortoˈpeðja] nf orthopaedics sg; **ortopédico, -a** adj orthopaedic

oruga [oˈruɣa] nf caterpillar

orzuelo [orˈθwelo] nm stye

os [os] pron (gen) you; (a vosotros) to you

osa [ˈosa] nf (she-)bear; **Osa Mayor/Menor** Great/Little Bear

osadía [osaˈðia] nf daring

osar [oˈsar] vi to dare

oscilación [osθilaˈθjon] nf (movimiento) oscillation; (fluctuación) fluctuation

oscilar [osθiˈlar] vi to oscillate; to fluctuate

oscurecer [oskureˈθer] vt to darken ▷ vi to grow dark; **oscurecerse** vr to grow o get dark

oscuridad [oskuriˈðað] nf obscurity; (tinieblas) darkness

oscuro, -a [osˈkuro, a] adj dark; (fig) obscure; **a oscuras** in the dark

óseo, -a [ˈoseo, a] adj bone cpd

oso [ˈoso] nm bear; **oso de peluche** teddy bear; **oso hormiguero** anteater

ostentar [ostenˈtar] vt (gen) to show; (pey) to flaunt, show off; (poseer) to have, possess

ostión [osˈtjon] (MÉX) nm = **ostra**

ostra [ˈostra] nf oyster

OTAN [ˈotan] nf abr (= Organización del Tratado del Atlántico Norte) NATO

otitis [oˈtitis] nf earache

otoñal [otoˈɲal] adj autumnal

otoño [oˈtoɲo] nm autumn

otorgar [otorˈɣar] vt (conceder) to concede; (dar) to grant

otorrino, -a [otoˈrrino, a], **otorrinolaringólogo, -a** [otorrinolarinˈɣoloɣo, a] nm/f ear,

nose and throat specialist

○ **PALABRA CLAVE**

otro, -a [ˈotro, a] adj **1** (distinto: sg) another; (: pl) other; **con otros amigos** with other o different friends

2 (adicional): **tráigame otro café (más), por favor** can I have another coffee please; **otros diez días más** another ten days

▷ pron **1** **el otro** the other one; **(los) otros** (the) others; **de otro** somebody else's; **que lo haga otro** let somebody else do it

2 (recíproco): **se odian (la) una a (la) otra** they hate one another o each other

3: **otro tanto: comer otro tanto** to eat the same o as much again; **recibió una decena de telegramas y otras tantas llamadas** he got about ten telegrams and as many calls

ovación [oβaˈθjon] nf ovation

oval [oˈβal] adj oval; **ovalado, -a** adj oval; **óvalo** nm oval

ovario [oˈβario] nm ovary

oveja [oˈβexa] nf sheep

overol [oβeˈrol] (LAM) nm overalls pl

ovillo [oˈβiʎo] nm (de lana) ball of wool

OVNI [ˈoβni] nm abr (= objeto volante no identificado) UFO

ovulación [oβulaˈθjon] nf ovulation; **óvulo** nm ovum

oxidación [oksiðaˈθjon] nf rusting

oxidar [oksiˈðar] vt to rust; **oxidarse** vr to go rusty

óxido [ˈoksiðo] nm oxide

oxigenado, -a [oksixeˈnaðo, a] adj (Quím) oxygenated; (pelo) bleached

oxígeno [okˈsixeno] nm oxygen

oyente [oˈjente] nmf listener

oyes etc vb V **oír**

ozono [oˈθono] nm ozone

P

pabellón [paβe'ʎon] *nm* bell tent; (*Arq*) pavilion; (*de hospital etc*) block, section; (*bandera*) flag

pacer [pa'θer] *vi* to graze

paciencia [pa'θjenθja] *nf* patience

paciente [pa'θjente] *adj, nmf* patient

pacificación [paθifika'θjon] *nf* pacification

pacífico, -a [pa'θifiko, a] *adj* (*persona*) peaceable; (*existencia*) peaceful; **el (Océano) P~** the Pacific (Ocean)

pacifista [paθi'fista] *nmf* pacifist

pacotilla [pako'tiʎa] *nf*: **de ~** (*actor, escritor*) third-rate

pactar [pak'tar] *vt* to agree to o on ▷ *vi* to come to an agreement

pacto [pakto] *nm* (*tratado*) pact; (*acuerdo*) agreement

padecer [paðe'θer] *vt* (*sufrir*) to suffer; (*soportar*) to endure, put up with; **padecimiento** *nm* suffering

padrastro [pa'ðrastro] *nm* stepfather

padre ['paðre] *nm* father ▷ *adj* (*fam*): **un éxito ~** a tremendous success; **padres** *nmpl* parents; **padre político** father-in-law

padrino [pa'ðrino] *nm* (*Rel*) godfather; (*tb*: **~ de boda**) best man; (*fig*) sponsor, patron; **padrinos** *nmpl* godparents

padrón [pa'ðron] *nm* (*censo*) census, roll

padrote [pa'ðrote] (*MÉX: fam*) *nm* pimp

paella [pa'eʎa] *nf* paella, *dish of rice with meat, shellfish etc*

paga ['paɣa] *nf* (*pago*) payment; (*sueldo*) pay, wages *pl*

pagano, -a [pa'ɣano, a] *adj, nm/f* pagan, heathen

pagar [pa'ɣar] *vt* to pay; (*las compras, crimen*) to pay for; (*fig: favor*) to repay ▷ *vi* to pay; **~ al contado/a plazos** to pay (in) cash/in instalments

pagaré [paɣa're] *nm* I.O.U.

página ['paxina] *nf* page; **página de inicio** (*Inform*) home page; **página web** (*Inform*) web page

pago ['paɣo] *nm* (*dinero*) payment; **en ~ de** in return for; **pago anticipado/a cuenta/contra reembolso/en especie** advance payment/payment on account/cash on delivery/payment in kind

pág(s). *abr* (= *página(s)*) p(p).

pague *etc vb V* **pagar**

país [pa'is] *nm* (*gen*) country; (*región*) land; **los P~es Bajos** the Low Countries; **el P~ Vasco** the Basque Country

paisaje [pai'saxe] *nm* landscape, scenery

paisano, -a [pai'sano, a] *adj* of the same country ▷ *nm/f* (*compatriota*) fellow countryman/woman; **vestir de ~** (*soldado*) to be in civvies; (*guardia*) to be in plain clothes

paja ['paxa] *nf* straw; (*fig*) rubbish (*BRIT*), trash (*US*)

pajarita [paxa'rita] *nf* (*corbata*) bow tie

pájaro ['paxaro] nm bird; **pájaro carpintero** woodpecker

pajita [pa'xita] nf (drinking) straw

pala ['pala] nf spade, shovel; (raqueta etc) bat; (: de tenis) racquet; (Culin) slice; **pala mecánica** power shovel

palabra [pa'laβra] nf word; (facultad) (power of) speech; (derecho de hablar) right to speak; **tomar la ~** (en mitin) to take the floor

palabrota [pala'βrota] nf swearword

palacio [pa'laθjo] nm palace; (mansión) mansion, large house; **palacio de justicia** courthouse; **palacio municipal** town o city hall

paladar [pala'ðar] nm palate; **paladear** vt to taste

palanca [pa'lanka] nf lever; (fig) pull, influence

palangana [palan'gana] nf washbasin

palco ['palko] nm box

Palestina [pales'tina] nf Palestine; **palestino, -a** nm/f Palestinian

paleta [pa'leta] nf (de pintor) palette; (de albañil) trowel; (de ping-pong) bat; (MÉX, CAM: helado) ice lolly (BRIT), Popsicle® (US)

palidecer [paliðe'θer] vi to turn pale; **palidez** nf paleness; **pálido, -a** adj pale

palillo [pa'liʎo] nm (mondadientes) toothpick; (para comer) chopstick

palito [pa'lito] (RPL) nm (helado) ice lolly (BRIT), Popsicle® (US)

paliza [pa'liθa] nf beating, thrashing

palma ['palma] nf (Anat) palm; (árbol) palm tree; **batir** o **dar ~s** to clap, applaud; **palmada** nf slap; **palmadas** nfpl clapping sg, applause sg

palmar [pal'mar] (fam) vi (tb: **~la**) to die, kick the bucket

palmear [palme'ar] vi to clap

palmera [pal'mera] nf (Bot) palm tree

palmo ['palmo] nm (medida) span; (fig) small amount; **~ a ~** inch by inch

palo ['palo] nm stick; (poste) post; (de tienda de campaña) pole; (mango) handle, shaft; (golpe) blow, hit; (de golf) club; (de béisbol) bat; (Náut) mast; (Naipes) suit

paloma [pa'loma] nf dove, pigeon

palomitas [palo'mitas] nfpl popcorn sg

palpar [pal'par] vt to touch, feel

palpitar [palpi'tar] vi to palpitate; (latir) to beat

palta ['palta] (CS) nf avocado

paludismo [palu'ðismo] nm malaria

pamela [pa'mela] nf picture hat, sun hat

pampa ['pampa] nf pampas, prairie

pan [pan] nm bread; (una barra) loaf; **pan integral** wholemeal (BRIT) o wholewheat (US) bread; **pan rallado** breadcrumbs pl; **pan tostado** (MÉX: tostada) toast

pana ['pana] nf corduroy

panadería [panaðe'ria] nf baker's (shop); **panadero, -a** nm/f baker

Panamá [pana'ma] nm Panama; **panameño, -a** adj Panamanian

pancarta [pan'karta] nf placard, banner

panceta [pan'θeta] (ESP, RPL) nf bacon

pancho ['pantʃo] (RPL) nm hot dog

pancito [pan'θito] nm (bread) roll

panda ['panda] nm (Zool) panda

pandereta [pande'reta] nf tambourine

pandilla [pan'diʎa] nf set, group; (de criminales) gang; (pey: camarilla) clique

panecillo [pane'θiʎo] (ESP) nm (bread) roll

panel [pa'nel] nm panel; **panel solar** solar panel

panfleto [pan'fleto] nm pamphlet

pánico ['paniko] nm panic

panorama [pano'rama] nm panorama; (vista) view

panqueque [pan'keke] (LAM) nm pancake

pantalla [pan'taʎa] nf (de cine) screen; (de lámpara) lampshade

pantalón [panta'lon] nm trousers;
pantalones nmpl trousers;
pantalones cortes shorts

pantano [pan'tano] nm (ciénaga)
marsh, swamp; (depósito: de agua)
reservoir; (fig) jam, difficulty

panteón [pante'on] nm (monumento)
pantheon

pantera [pan'tera] nf panther

pantimedias [panti'meðjas] (MÉX)
nfpl = **pantis**

pantis ['pantis] nmpl tights (BRIT),
pantyhose (US)

pantomima [panto'mima] nf
pantomime

pantorrilla [panto'rriʎa] nf calf
(of the leg)

pants [pants] (MÉX) nmpl tracksuit
(BRIT), sweat suit (US)

pantufla [pan'tufla] nf slipper

panty(s) ['panti(s)] nm(pl) tights
(BRIT), pantyhose (US)

panza ['panθa] nf belly, paunch

pañal [pa'ɲal] nm nappy (BRIT),
diaper (US); **pañales** nmpl (fig) early
stages, infancy sg

paño ['paɲo] nm (tela) cloth; (pedazo de
tela) (piece of) cloth; (trapo) duster, rag;
paños menores underclothes

pañuelo [pa'ɲwelo] nm
handkerchief, hanky; (fam: para la
cabeza) (head)scarf

papa ['papa] nm: **el P~** the Pope ▷ nf
(LAM: patata) potato; **papas fritas** (LAM)
French fries, chips (BRIT); (de bolsa)
crisps (BRIT), potato chips (US)

papá [pa'pa] (fam) nm dad(dy), pa (US)

papada [pa'paða] nf double chin

papagayo [papa'ɣajo] nm parrot

papalote [papa'lote] (MÉX, CAM)
nm kite

papanatas [papa'natas] (fam) nm
inv simpleton

papaya [pa'paja] nf papaya

papear [pape'ar] (fam) vt, vi to scoff

papel [pa'pel] nm paper; (hoja de
papel) sheet of paper; (Teatro: fig) role;
papel de aluminio aluminium (BRIT)

o aluminum (US) foil; **papel de arroz/
envolver/fumar** rice/wrapping/
cigarette paper; **papel de estaño** o
plata tinfoil; **papel de lija** sandpaper;
papel higiénico toilet paper; **papel
moneda** paper money; **papel pintado**
wallpaper; **papel secante** blotting
paper

papeleo [pape'leo] nm red tape

papelera [pape'lera] nf wastepaper
basket; (en la calle) litter bin; **papelera
(de reciclaje)** (Inform) wastebasket

papelería [papele'ria] nf stationer's
(shop)

papeleta [pape'leta] (ESP) nf (Pol)
ballot paper

paperas [pa'peras] nfpl mumps sg

papilla [pa'piʎa] nf (de bebé) baby
food

paquete [pa'kete] nm (de cigarrillos
etc) packet; (Correos etc) parcel

par [par] adj (igual) like, equal; (Mat)
even ▷ nm equal; (de guantes) pair; (de
veces) couple; (Pol) peer; (Golf, Com) par;
abrir de ~ en ~ to open wide

para ['para] prep for; **no es ~ comer**
it's not for eating; **decir ~ sí** to say to
o.s.; **¿~ qué lo quieres?** what do you
want it for?; **se casaron ~ separarse
otra vez** they married only to separate
again; **lo tendré ~ mañana** I'll have
it (for) tomorrow; **ir ~ casa** to go
home, head for home; **~ profesor es
muy estúpido** he's very stupid for a
teacher; **¿quién es usted ~ gritar así?**
who are you to shout like that?; **tengo
bastante ~ vivir** I have enough to live
on; V tb **con**

parabién [para'βjen] nm
congratulations pl

parábola [pa'raβola] nf parable;
(Mat) parabola; **parabólica** nf
(tb: **antena parabólica**) satellite dish

parabrisas [para'βrisas] nm inv
windscreen (BRIT), windshield (US)

paracaídas [paraka'iðas] nm
inv parachute; **paracaidista** nmf
parachutist; (Mil) paratrooper

p

parachoques [para'tʃokes] nm inv
(Auto) bumper; (Mecánica etc) shock
absorber

parada [pa'raða] nf stop; (acto)
stopping; (de industria) shutdown,
stoppage; (lugar) stopping place;
parada de autobús bus stop; **parada
de taxis** taxi stand o rank (BRIT)

paradero [para'ðero] nm stopping-
place; (situación) whereabouts

parado, -a [pa'raðo, a] adj (persona)
motionless, standing still; (fábrica)
closed, at a standstill; (coche) stopped;
(LAM: de pie) standing (up); (ESP: sin
empleo) unemployed, idle

paradoja [para'ðoxa] nf paradox

parador [para'ðor] nm parador,
state-run hotel

paragolpes [para'golpes] (RPL) nm
inv (Auto) bumper, fender (US)

paraguas [pa'raɣwas] nm inv
umbrella

Paraguay [para'ɣwai] nm Paraguay;
paraguayo, -a adj, nm/f Paraguayan

paraíso [para'iso] nm paradise,
heaven

paraje [pa'raxe] nm place, spot

paralelo, -a [para'lelo, a] adj
parallel

parálisis [pa'ralisis] nf inv paralysis;
paralítico, -a adj, nm/f paralytic

paralizar [parali'θar] vt to paralyse;
paralizarse vr to become paralysed;
(fig) to come to a standstill

páramo ['paramo] nm bleak plateau

paranoico, -a [para'noiko, a] nm/f
paranoiac

parapente [para'pente] nm (deporte)
paragliding; (aparato) paraglider

parapléjico, -a [para'plexiko, a] adj,
nm/f paraplegic

parar [pa'rar] vt to stop; (golpe) to
ward off ▷ vi to stop; **pararse** vr to
stop; (LAM: ponerse de pie) to stand up;
ha parado de llover it has stopped
raining; **van a ir a ~ a comisaría**
they're going to end up in the police
station; **~se en** to pay attention to

pararrayos [para'rrajos] nm inv
lightning conductor

parásito, -a [pa'rasito, a] nm/f
parasite

parasol [para'sol] nm parasol,
sunshade

parcela [par'θela] nf plot, piece of
ground

parche ['partʃe] nm (gen) patch

parchís [par'tʃis] nm ludo

parcial [par'θjal] adj (pago) part-;
(eclipse) partial; (Jur) prejudiced, biased;
(Pol) partisan

parecer [pare'θer] nm (opinión)
opinion, view; (aspecto) looks pl
▷ vi (tener apariencia) to seem, look;
(asemejarse) to look o seem like;
(aparecer, llegar) to appear; **parecerse**
vr to look alike, resemble each
other; **al ~** apparently; **según parece**
evidently, apparently; **~se a** to look
like, resemble; **me parece que** I think
(that), it seems to me that

parecido, -a [pare'θiðo, a] adj
similar ▷ nm similarity, likeness,
resemblance; **bien ~** good-looking,
nice-looking

pared [pa'reð] nf wall

pareja [pa'rexa] nf (par) pair; (dos
personas) couple; (otro: de un par) other
one (of a pair); (persona) partner

parentesco [paren'tesko] nm
relationship

paréntesis [pa'rentesis] nm inv
parenthesis; (en escrito) bracket

parezco etc vb V **parecer**

pariente [pa'rjente] nmf relative,
relation

⏐ No confundir **pariente** con la
palabra inglesa *parent*.

parir [pa'rir] vt to give birth to ▷ vi
(mujer) to give birth, have a baby

París [pa'ris] n Paris

parka ['parka] (LAM) nf anorak

parking ['parkin] nm car park (BRIT),
parking lot (US)

parlamentar [parlamen'tar] vi
to parley

parlamentario, -a [parlamen'tarjo, a] *adj* parliamentary ▷ *nm/f* member of parliament

parlamento [parla'mento] *nm* parliament

parlanchín, -ina [parlan'tʃin, ina] *adj* indiscreet ▷ *nm/f* chatterbox

parlar [par'lar] *vi* to chatter (away)

paro ['paro] *nm* (*huelga*) stoppage (of work), strike; (*ESP: desempleo*) unemployment; (: *subsidio*) unemployment benefit; **estar en ~** (*ESP*) to be unemployed; **paro cardíaco** cardiac arrest

parodia [pa'roðja] *nf* parody; **parodiar** *vt* to parody

parpadear [parpaðe'ar] *vi* (*ojos*) to blink; (*luz*) to flicker

párpado ['parpaðo] *nm* eyelid

parque ['parke] *nm* (*lugar verde*) park; (*MÉX: munición*) ammunition; **parque de atracciones** fairground; **parque de bomberos** (*ESP*) fire station; **parque infantil/temático/zoológico** playground/theme park/zoo

parqué [par'ke] *nm* parquet (flooring)

parquímetro [par'kimetro] *nm* parking meter

parra ['parra] *nf* (grape)vine

párrafo ['parrafo] *nm* paragraph; **echar un ~** (*fam*) to have a chat

parranda [pa'rranda] (*fam*) *nf* spree, binge

parrilla [pa'rriʎa] *nf* (*Culin*) grill; (*de coche*) grille; **(carne a la) ~** barbecue; **parrillada** *nf* barbecue

párroco ['parroko] *nm* parish priest

parroquia [pa'rrokja] *nf* parish; (*iglesia*) parish church; (*Com*) clientele, customers *pl*; **parroquiano, -a** *nm/f* parishioner; (*Com*) client, customer

parte ['parte] *nm* message; (*informe*) report ▷ *nf* part; (*lado, cara*) side; (*de reparto*) share; (*Jur*) party; **en alguna ~ de Europa** somewhere in Europe; **en o por todas ~s** everywhere; **en gran ~** to a large extent; **la mayor ~**

de los españoles most Spaniards; **de un tiempo a esta ~** for some time past; **de ~ de algn** on sb's behalf; **¿de ~ de quién?** (*Tel*) who is speaking?; **por ~ de** on the part of; **yo por mi ~** I for my part; **por otra ~** on the other hand; **dar ~** to inform; **tomar ~** to take part; **parte meteorológico** weather forecast o report

participación [partiθipa'θjon] *nf* (*acto*) participation, taking part; (*parte, Com*) share; (*de lotería*) shared prize; (*aviso*) notice, notification

participante [partiθi'pante] *nmf* participant

participar [partiθi'par] *vt* to notify, inform ▷ *vi* to take part, participate

partícipe [par'tiθipe] *nmf* participant

particular [partiku'lar] *adj* (*especial*) particular, special; (*individual, personal*) private, personal ▷ *nm* (*punto, asunto*) particular, point; (*individuo*) individual; **tiene coche ~** he has a car of his own

partida [par'tiða] *nf* (*salida*) departure; (*Com*) entry, item; (*juego*) game; (*grupo de personas*) band, group; **mala ~** dirty trick; **partida de nacimiento/matrimonio/defunción** (*ESP*) birth/marriage/death certificate

partidario, -a [parti'ðarjo, a] *adj* partisan ▷ *nm/f* supporter, follower

partido [par'tiðo] *nm* (*Pol*) party; (*Deporte*) game, match; **sacar ~ de** to profit o benefit from; **tomar ~** to take sides

partir [par'tir] *vt* (*dividir*) to split, divide; (*compartir, distribuir*) to share (out), distribute; (*romper*) to break open, split open; (*rebanada*) to cut (off) ▷ *vi* (*ponerse en camino*) to set off o out; (*comenzar*) to start (off o out); **partirse** *vr* to crack o split o break (in two *etc*); **a ~ de** (starting) from

partitura [parti'tura] *nf* (*Mús*) score

parto ['parto] *nm* birth; (*fig*) product, creation; **estar de ~** to be in labour

parvulario [parβu'larjo] (*ESP*) *nm*

nursery school, kindergarten

pasa ['pasa] nf raisin; **pasa de Corinto** currant

pasacintas [pasa'θintas] (LAM) nm cassette player

pasada [pa'saða] nf passing, passage; **de ~** in passing, incidentally; **una mala ~** a dirty trick

pasadizo [pasa'ðiθo] nm (pasillo) passage, corridor; (callejuela) alley

pasado, -a [pa'saðo, a] adj past; (malo: comida, fruta) bad; (muy cocido) overdone; (anticuado) out of date ▷ nm past; **~ mañana** the day after tomorrow; **el mes ~** last month

pasador [pasa'ðor] nm (cerrojo) bolt; (de pelo) hair slide; (horquilla) grip

pasaje [pa'saxe] nm passage; (pago de viaje) fare; (los pasajeros) passengers pl; (pasillo) passageway

pasajero, -a [pasa'xero, a] adj passing, (situación, estado) temporary; (amor, enfermedad) brief ▷ nm/f passenger

pasamontañas [pasamon'taɲas] nm inv balaclava helmet

pasaporte [pasa'porte] nm passport

pasar [pa'sar] vt to pass; (tiempo) to spend; (desgracias) to suffer, endure; (noticia) to give, pass on; (río) to cross; (barrera) to pass through; (falta) to overlook, tolerate; (contrincante) to surpass, do better than; (coche) to overtake; (Cine) to show; (enfermedad) to give, infect with; **~ la aspiradora** to do the vacuuming, to hoover o do the hoovering ▷ vi (gen) to pass; (terminarse) to be over; (ocurrir) to happen; **pasarse** vr (flores) to fade; (comida) to go bad o off; (fig) to overdo it, go too far; **~ de** to go beyond, exceed; **~ por** (LAM) to fetch; **~lo bien/ mal** to have a good/bad time; **¡pase!** come in!; **hacer ~** to show in; **lo que pasa es que ...** the thing is ...; **~se al enemigo** to go over to the enemy; **se me pasó** I forgot; **no se le pasa nada** he misses nothing; **pase lo que pase** come what may; **¿qué pasa?** what's going on?, what's up?; **¿qué te pasa?** what's wrong?

pasarela [pasa'rela] nf footbridge; (en barco) gangway

pasatiempo [pasa'tjempo] nm pastime, hobby

Pascua ['paskwa] nf (en Semana Santa) Easter; **Pascuas** nfpl Christmas (time); **¡felices ~s!** Merry Christmas!

pase ['pase] nm pass; (Cine) performance, showing

pasear [pase'ar] vt to take for a walk; (exhibir) to parade, show off ▷ vi to walk, go for a walk; **pasearse** vr to walk, go for a walk; **~ en coche** to go for a drive; **paseo** nm (avenida) avenue; (distancia corta) walk, stroll; **dar un o ir de paseo** to go for a walk; **paseo marítimo** (ESP) promenade

pasillo [pa'siʎo] nm passage, corridor

pasión [pa'sjon] nf passion

pasivo, -a [pa'siβo, a] adj passive; (inactivo) inactive ▷ nm (Com) liabilities pl, debts pl

pasmoso, -a [pas'moso, a] adj amazing, astonishing

paso, -a ['paso, a] adj dried ▷ nm step; (modo de andar) walk; (huella) footprint; (rapidez) speed, pace, rate; (camino accesible) way through, passage; (cruce) crossing; (Geo) pass; (estrecho) strait; **a ese ~** (fig) at that rate; **salir al ~ de o a** to waylay; **estar de ~** to be passing through; **prohibido el ~** no entry; **ceda el ~** give way; **paso a nivel** (Ferro) level-crossing; **paso (de) cebra** (ESP) zebra crossing; **paso de peatones** pedestrian crossing; **paso elevado** flyover

pasota [pa'sota] (ESP: fam) adj, nmf ≈ dropout; **ser un ~** to be a bit of a dropout; (ser indiferente) not to care about anything

pasta ['pasta] nf paste; (Culin: masa) dough; (: de bizcochos etc) pastry; (fam) dough; **pastas** nfpl (bizcochos) pastries, small cakes; (*fideos, espaguetis etc*) pasta; **pasta dentífrica** *o* **de dientes** toothpaste

pastar [pas'tar] *vt, vi* to graze

pastel [pas'tel] *nm* (*dulce*) cake; (*Arte*) pastel; **pastel de carne** meat pie; **pastelería** *nf* cake shop

pastilla [pas'tiʎa] *nf* (*de jabón, chocolate*) bar; (*píldora*) tablet, pill

pasto ['pasto] *nm* (*hierba*) grass; (*lugar*) pasture, field; **pastor, a** [pas'tor, a] *nm/f* shepherd/ess ▷ *nm* (*Rel*) clergyman, pastor; **pastor alemán** Alsatian

pata ['pata] *nf* (*pierna*) leg; (*pie*) foot; (*de muebles*) leg; **~s arriba** upside down; **metedura de ~** (*fam*) gaffe; **meter la ~** (*fam*) to put one's foot in it; **tener buena/mala ~** to be lucky/unlucky; **pata de cabra** (*Tec*) crowbar; **patada** *nf* kick; (*en el suelo*) stamp

patata [pa'tata] *nf* potato; **patatas fritas** chips, French fries; (*de bolsa*) crisps

paté [pa'te] *nm* pâté

patente [pa'tente] *adj* obvious, evident; (*Com*) patent ▷ *nf* patent

paternal [pater'nal] *adj* fatherly, paternal; **paterno, -a** *adj* paternal

patético, -a [pa'tetiko, a] *adj* pathetic, moving

patilla [pa'tiʎa] *nf* (*de gafas*) side(piece); **patillas** *nfpl* sideburns

patín [pa'tin] *nm* skate; (*de trineo*) runner; **patín de ruedas** roller skate; **patinaje** *nm* skating; **patinar** *vi* to skate; (*resbalarse*) to skid, slip; (*fam*) to slip up, blunder

patineta [pati'neta] *nf* (MÉX: **patinete**) scooter; (CS: **monopatín**) skateboard

patinete [pati'nete] *nm* scooter

patio ['patjo] *nm* (*de casa*) patio, courtyard; **patio de recreo** playground

pato ['pato] *nm* duck; **pagar el ~** (*fam*) to take the blame, carry the can

patoso, -a [pa'toso, a] (*fam*) *adj* clumsy

patotero [pato'tero] (CS) *nm* hooligan, lout

patraña [pa'traɲa] *nf* story, fib

patria ['patrja] *nf* native land, mother country

patrimonio [patri'monjo] *nm* inheritance; (*fig*) heritage

patriota [pa'trjota] *nmf* patriot

patrocinar [patroθi'nar] *vt* to sponsor

patrón, -ona [pa'tron, ona] *nm/f* (*jefe*) boss, chief, master(mistress); (*propietario*) landlord/lady; (*Rel*) patron saint ▷ *nm* (*Tec, Costura*) pattern

patronato [patro'nato] *nm* sponsorship; (*acto*) patronage; (*fundación benéfica*) trust, foundation

patrulla [pa'truʎa] *nf* patrol

pausa ['pausa] *nf* pause, break

pauta ['pauta] *nf* line, guide line

pava ['paβa] (RPL) *nf* kettle

pavimento [paβi'mento] *nm* (*de losa*) pavement, paving

pavo ['paβo] *nm* turkey; **pavo real** peacock

payaso, -a [pa'jaso, a] *nm/f* clown

payo, -a ['pajo, a] *nm/f* non-gipsy

paz [paθ] *nf* peace; (*tranquilidad*) peacefulness, tranquillity; **hacer las paces** to make peace; (*fig*) to make up; **¡déjame en ~!** leave me alone!

PC *nm* (= *posdata*) PC, personal computer

P.D. *abr* (= *posdata*) P.S., p.s.

peaje [pe'axe] *nm* toll

peatón [pea'ton] *nm* pedestrian; **peatonal** *adj* pedestrian

peca ['peka] *nf* freckle

pecado [pe'kaðo] *nm* sin; **pecador, a** *adj* sinful ▷ *nm/f* sinner

pecaminoso, -a [pekami'noso, a] *adj* sinful

pecar [pe'kar] *vi* (*Rel*) to sin, **peca de generoso** he is generous to a fault

pecera [pe'θera] *nf* fish tank; (*redonda*) goldfish bowl

pecho ['petʃo] *nm* (*Anat*) chest; (*de mujer*) breast; **dar el ~ a** to breast-feed; **tomar algo a ~** to take sth to heart

pechuga [pe'tʃuxa] *nf* breast

P

peculiar [peku'ljar] *adj* special, peculiar; (*característico*) typical, characteristic

pedal [pe'ðal] *nm* pedal; **pedalear** *vi* to pedal

pédalo ['pedalo] *nm* pedalo, pedal boat

pedante [pe'ðante] *adj* pedantic ▷ *nmf* pedant

pedazo [pe'ðaθo] *nm* piece, bit; **hacerse ~s** to smash, shatter

pediatra [pe'ðjatra] *nmf* paediatrician

pedido [pe'ðiðo] *nm* (*Com*) order; (*petición*) request

pedir [pe'ðir] *vt* to ask for, request; (*comida, Com: mandar*) to order; (*necesitar*) to need, demand, require ▷ *vi* to ask; **me pidió que cerrara la puerta** he asked me to shut the door; **¿cuánto piden por el coche?** how much are they asking for the car?

pedo ['peðo] (*fam!*) *nm* fart

pega ['peɣa] *nf* snag; **poner ~s (a)** to complain (about)

pegadizo, -a [peɣa'ðiθo, a] *adj* (*Mús*) catchy

pegajoso, -a [peɣa'xoso, a] *adj* sticky, adhesive

pegamento [peɣa'mento] *nm* gum, glue

pegar [pe'ɣar] *vt* (*papel, sellos*) to stick (on); (*cartel*) to stick up; (*coser*) to sew (on); (*unir: partes*) to join, fix together; (*Comput*) to paste; (*Med*) to give, infect with; (*dar: golpe*) to give, deal ▷ *vi* (*adherirse*) to stick, adhere; (*ir juntos: colores*) to match, go together; (*golpear*) to hit; (*quemar: el sol*) to strike hot, burn; **pegarse** *vr* (*gen*) to stick; (*dos personas*) to hit each other, fight; (*fam*): **~ un grito** to let out a yell; **~ un salto** to jump (with fright); **~ en** to touch; **~se un tiro** to shoot o.s.: **~ fuego** to catch fire

pegatina [peɣa'tina] *nf* sticker

pegote [pe'ɣote] (*fam*) *nm* eyesore, sight

peinado [pei'naðo] *nm* hairstyle

peinar [pei'nar] *vt* to comb; (*hacer estilo*) to style; **peinarse** *vr* to comb one's hair

peine ['peine] *nm* comb; **peineta** *nf* ornamental comb

p.ej. *abr* (= *por ejemplo*) e.g.

Pekín [pe'kin] *n* Pekin(g)

pelado, -a [pe'laðo, a] *adj* (*fruta, patata etc*) peeled; (*cabeza*) shorn; (*campo, fig*) bare; (*fam: sin dinero*) broke

pelar [pe'lar] *vt* (*fruta, patatas etc*) to peel; (*cortar el pelo a*) to cut the hair of; (*quitar la piel: animal*) to skin; **pelarse** *vr* (*la piel*) to peel off; **voy a ~me** I'm going to get my hair cut

peldaño [pel'daɲo] *nm* step

pelea [pe'lea] *nf* (*lucha*) fight; (*discusión*) quarrel, row; **peleado, -a** [pele'aðo, a] *adj*: **estar peleado (con algn)** to have fallen out (with sb); **pelear** [pele'ar] *vi* to fight; **pelearse** *vr* to fight; (*reñirse*) to fall out, quarrel

pelela [pe'lela] (*cs*) *nf* potty

peletería [pelete'ria] *nf* furrier's, fur shop

pelícano [pe'likano] *nm* pelican

película [pe'likula] *nf* film; (*cobertura ligera*) thin covering; (*Foto: rollo*) roll o reel of film; **película de dibujos (animados)/del oeste** cartoon/western

peligro [pe'liɣro] *nm* danger; (*riesgo*) risk; **correr ~ de** to run the risk of; **peligroso, -a** *adj* dangerous; risky

pelirrojo, -a [peli'rroxo, a] *adj* red-haired, red-headed ▷ *nm/f* redhead

pellejo [pe'ʎexo] *nm* (*de animal*) skin, hide

pellizcar [peʎiθ'kar] *vt* to pinch, nip

pelma ['pelma] (*ESP: fam*) *nmf* pain (in the neck)

pelmazo [pel'maθo] (*fam*) *nm* = **pelma**

pelo ['pelo] *nm* (*cabellos*) hair; (*de barba, bigote*) whisker; (*de animal: pellejo*) hair, fur, coat; **venir al ~** to be exactly what one needs; **un**

hombre de ~ en pecho a brave man;
por los ~s by the skin of one's teeth; **no
tener ~s en la lengua** to be outspoken,
not to mince one's words; **con ~s y
señales** in minute detail; **tomar el ~ a
algn** to pull sb's leg

pelota [pe'lota] *nf* ball; **en ~** stark
naked; **hacer la ~ (a algn)** (ESP: *fam*) to
creep (to sb); **pelota vasca** pelota

pelotón [pelo'ton] *nm* (*Mil*) squad,
detachment

peluca [pe'luka] *nf* wig

peluche [pe'lutʃe] *nm*: **oso/muñeco
de ~** teddy bear/soft toy

peludo, -a [pe'luðo, a] *adj* hairy,
shaggy

peluquería [peluke'ria] *nf*
hairdresser's; **peluquero, -a** *nm/f*
hairdresser

pelusa [pe'lusa] *nf* (*Bot*) down; (*en
tela*) fluff

pena ['pena] *nf* (*congoja*) grief,
sadness; (*remordimiento*) regret;
(*dificultad*) trouble; (*dolor*) pain; (*Jur*)
sentence; **merecer o valer la ~** to be
worthwhile; **a duras ~s** with great
difficulty; **¡qué ~!** what a shame!; **pena
capital** capital punishment; **pena de
muerte** death penalty

penal [pe'nal] *adj* penal ⊳ *nm* (*cárcel*)
prison

penalidad [penali'ðað] *nf* (*problema,
dificultad*) trouble, hardship; (*Jur*)
penalty, punishment; **penalidades**
nfpl trouble *sg*, hardship *sg*

penalti [pe'nalti] *nm* = **penalty**

penalty [pe'nalti] (*pl* **~s** *o* **penalties**)
nm penalty (kick)

pendiente [pen'djente] *adj* pending,
unsettled ⊳ *nm* earring ⊳ *nf* hill, slope

pene ['pene] *nm* penis

penetrante [pene'trante] *adj*
(*herida*) deep; (*persona, arma*) sharp;
(*sonido*) penetrating, piercing; (*mirada*)
searching; (*viento, ironía*) biting

penetrar [pene'trar] *vt* to penetrate,
pierce; (*entender*) to grasp ⊳ *vi* to
penetrate, go in; (*entrar*) to enter, go in;

(*líquido*) to soak in; (*fig*) to pierce

penicilina [peniθi'lina] *nf* penicillin

península [pe'ninsula] *nf* peninsula;
peninsular *adj* peninsular

penique [pe'nike] *nm* penny

penitencia [peni'tenθja] *nf* penance

penoso, -a [pe'noso, a] *adj*
(*lamentable*) distressing; (*difícil*)
arduous, difficult

pensador, a [pensa'ðor, a] *nm/f*
thinker

pensamiento [pensa'mjento] *nm*
thought; (*mente*) mind; (*idea*) idea

pensar [pen'sar] *vt* to think;
(*considerar*) to think over, think out;
(*proponerse*) to intend, plan; (*imaginarse*)
to think up, invent ⊳ *vi* to think; **~ en**
to aim at, aspire to; **pensativo, -a** *adj*
thoughtful, pensive

pensión [pen'sjon] *nf* (*casa*) boarding
o guest house; (*dinero*) pension; (*cama
y comida*) board and lodging; **media
~** half-board; **pensión completa** full
board; **pensionista** *nmf* (*jubilado*) (old-
age) pensioner; (*huésped*) lodger

penúltimo, -a [pe'nultimo, a] *adj*
penultimate, last but one

penumbra [pe'numbra] *nf* half-light

peña ['peɲa] *nf* (*roca*) rock; (*cuesta*)
cliff, crag; (*grupo*) group, circle;
(LAM: *club*) folk club

peñasco [pe'ɲasko] *nm* large rock,
boulder

peñón [pe'ɲon] *nm* wall of rock; **el P~**
the Rock (of Gibraltar)

peón [pe'on] *nm* labourer; (LAM *Agr*)
farm labourer, farmhand; (*Ajedrez*)
pawn

peonza [pe'onθa] *nf* spinning top

peor [pe'or] *adj* (*comparativo*) worse;
(*superlativo*) worst ⊳ *adv* worse; worst;
de mal en ~ from bad to worse

pepinillo [pepi'niʎo] *nm* gherkin

pepino [pe'pino] *nm* cucumber; **(no)
me importa un ~** I don't care one bit

pepita [pe'pita] *nf* (*Bot*) pip; (*Minería*)
nugget

pepito [pe'pito] (ESP) *nm* (*tb*: **~ de**

P

ternera) steak sandwich

pequeño, -a [pe'keɲo, a] adj small, little

pera ['pera] nf pear; **peral** nm pear tree

percance [per'kanθe] nm setback, misfortune

percatarse [perka'tarse] vr: **~ de** to notice, take note of

percebe [per'θeβe] nm barnacle

percepción [perθep'θjon] nf (vista) perception; (idea) notion, idea

percha ['pertʃa] nf (coat)hanger; (ganchos) coat hooks pl; (de ave) perch

percibir [perθi'βir] vt to perceive, notice; (Com) to earn, get

percusión [perku'sjon] nf percussion

perdedor, a [perðe'ðor, a] adj losing ▷ nm/f loser

perder [per'ðer] vt to lose; (tiempo, palabras) to waste; (oportunidad) to lose, miss; (tren) to miss ▷ vi to lose; **perderse** vr (extraviarse) to get lost; (desaparecer) to disappear, be lost to view; (arruinarse) to be ruined; **echar a ~** (comida) to spoil, ruin; (oportunidad) to waste

pérdida ['perðiða] nf loss; (de tiempo) waste; **pérdidas** nfpl (Com) losses

perdido, -a [per'ðiðo, a] adj lost

perdiz [per'ðiθ] nf partridge

perdón [per'ðon] nm (disculpa) pardon, forgiveness; (clemencia) mercy; ¡~! sorry!, I beg your pardon!; **perdonar** vt to pardon, forgive; (la vida) to spare; (excusar) to exempt, excuse; **¡perdone (usted)!** sorry!, I beg your pardon!

perecedero, -a [pereθe'ðero, a] adj perishable

perecer [pere'θer] vi to perish, die

peregrinación [pereɣrina'θjon] nf (Rel) pilgrimage

peregrino, -a [pere'ɣrino, a] adj (idea) strange, absurd ▷ nm/f pilgrim

perejil [pere'xil] nm parsley

perenne [pe'renne] adj everlasting, perennial

pereza [pe'reθa] nf laziness, idleness; **perezoso, -a** adj lazy, idle

perfección [perfek'θjon] nf perfection; **perfeccionar** vt to perfect; (mejorar) to improve; (acabar) to complete, finish

perfecto, -a [per'fekto, a] adj perfect; (total) complete

perfil [per'fil] nm profile; (contorno) silhouette, outline; (Arq) (cross) section; **perfiles** nmpl features

perforación [perfora'θjon] nf perforation; (con taladro) drilling; **perforadora** nf punch

perforar [perfo'rar] vt to perforate; (agujero) to drill, bore; (papel) to punch a hole in ▷ vi to drill, bore

perfume [per'fume] nm perfume, scent

periferia [peri'ferja] nf periphery; (de ciudad) outskirts pl

periférico [peri'feriko] (LAM) nm ring road (BRIT), beltway (US)

perilla [pe'riʎa] nf (de barba) goatee; (LAM: de puerta) doorknob, door handle

perímetro [pe'rimetro] nm perimeter

periódico, -a [pe'rjoðiko, a] adj periodic(al) ▷ nm newspaper

periodismo [perjo'ðismo] nm journalism; **periodista** nmf journalist

periodo [pe'rjoðo] nm period

período [pe'rioðo] nm = **periodo**

periquito [peri'kito] nm budgerigar, budgie

perito, -a [pe'rito, a] adj (experto) expert; (diestro) skilled, skilful ▷ nm/f expert; skilled worker; (técnico) technician

perjudicar [perxuði'kar] vt (gen) to damage, harm; **perjudicial** adj damaging, harmful; (en detrimento) detrimental; **perjuicio** nm damage, harm

perjurar [perxu'rar] vi to commit perjury

perla ['perla] nf pearl; **me viene de ~s** it suits me fine

permanecer [permane'θer] vi
(*quedarse*) to stay, remain; (*seguir*) to
continue to be

permanente [perma'nente] adj
permanent, constant ▷ nf perm

permiso [per'miso] nm permission;
(*licencia*) permit, licence; **con ~** excuse
me; **estar de ~** (*Mil*) to be on leave;
permiso de conducir driving licence
(*BRIT*), driver's license (*US*); **permiso
por enfermedad** (*LAM*) sick leave

permitir [permi'tir] vt to permit,
allow

pernera [per'nera] nf trouser leg

pero ['pero] conj but; (*aún*) yet ▷ nm
(*defecto*) flaw, defect; (*reparo*) objection

perpendicular [perpendiku'lar] adj
perpendicular

perpetuo, -a [per'petwo, a] adj
perpetual

perplejo, -a [per'plexo, a] adj
perplexed, bewildered

perra ['perra] nf (*Zool*) bitch; **estar sin
una ~** (*ESP: fam*) to be flat broke

perrera [pe'rrera] nf kennel

perrito [pe'rrito] nm (*tb: ~ **caliente**)
hot dog

perro ['perro] nm dog

persa ['persa] adj, nmf Persian

persecución [perseku'θjon] nf
pursuit, chase; (*Rel, Pol*) persecution

perseguir [perse'xir] vt to pursue,
hunt; (*cortejar*) to chase after; (*molestar*)
to pester, annoy; (*Rel, Pol*) to persecute

persiana [per'sjana] nf (*Veneti*an)
blind

persistente [persis'tente] adj
persistent

persistir [persis'tir] vi to persist

persona [per'sona] nf person;
persona mayor elderly person

personaje [perso'naxe] nm
important person, celebrity; (*Teatro
etc*) character

personal [perso'nal] adj (*particular*)
personal; (*para una persona*) single, for
one person ▷ nm personnel, staff;
personalidad nf personality

personarse [perso'narse] vr to
appear in person

personificar [personifi'kar] vt to
personify

perspectiva [perspek'tiβa] nf
perspective; (*vista, panorama*) view,
panorama; (*posibilidad futura*) outlook,
prospect

persuadir [perswa'ðir] vt (*gen*) to
persuade; (*convencer*) to convince;
persuadirse vr to become convinced;
persuasión nf persuasion

pertenecer [pertene'θer] vi to
belong; (*fig*) to concern; **perteneciente**
adj: **perteneciente a** belonging
to; **pertenencia** nf ownership;
pertenencias nfpl (*bienes*)
possessions, property sg

pertenezca etc vb V **pertenecer**

pértiga ['pertixa] nf: **salto de ~**
pole vault

pertinente [perti'nente] adj
relevant, pertinent; (*apropiado*)
appropriate; **~ a** concerning, relevant
to

perturbación [perturβa'θjon]
nf (*Pol*) disturbance; (*Med*) upset,
disturbance

Perú [pe'ru] nm Peru; **peruano, -a**
adj, nm/f Peruvian

perversión [perβer'sjon] nf
perversion; **perverso, -a** adj perverse;
(*depravado*) depraved

pervertido, -a [perβer'tiðo, a] adj
perverted ▷ nm/f pervert

pervertir [perβer'tir] vt to pervert,
corrupt

pesa ['pesa] nf weight; (*Deporte*) shot

pesadez [pesa'ðeθ] nf (*peso*)
heaviness; (*lentitud*) slowness;
(*aburrimiento*) tediousness

pesadilla [pesa'ðiʎa] nf nightmare,
bad dream

pesado, -a [pe'saðo, a] adj heavy;
(*lento*) slow; (*difícil, duro*) tough, hard;
(*aburrido*) boring, tedious; (*tiempo*)
sultry

pésame ['pesame] nm expression of

condolence, message of sympathy; **dar el ~** to express one's condolences

pesar [pe'sar] *vt* to weigh ▷ *vi* to weigh; (*ser pesado*) to weigh a lot, be heavy; (*fig: opinión*) to carry weight; **no pesa mucho** it's not very heavy ▷ *nm* (*arrepentimiento*) regret; (*pena*) grief, sorrow; **a ~ de** o **pese a (que)** in spite of, despite

pesca ['peska] *nf* (*acto*) fishing; (*lo pescado*) catch; **ir de ~** to go fishing

pescadería [peskaðe'ria] *nf* fish shop, fishmonger's (BRIT)

pescadilla [peska'ðiʎa] *nf* whiting

pescado [pes'kaðo] *nm* fish

pescador, a [peska'ðor, a] *nm/f* fisherman/woman

pescar [pes'kar] *vt* (*tomar*) to catch; (*intentar tomar*) to fish for; (*conseguir: trabajo*) to manage to get ▷ *vi* to fish, go fishing

pesebre [pe'seβre] *nm* manger

peseta [pe'seta] *nf* (Hist) peseta

pesimista [pesi'mista] *adj* pessimistic ▷ *nmf* pessimist

pésimo, -a ['pesimo, a] *adj* awful, dreadful

peso ['peso] *nm* weight; (*balanza*) scales *pl*; (*moneda*) peso; **vender al ~** to sell by weight; **peso bruto/neto** gross/net weight; **peso pesado/ pluma** heavyweight/featherweight

pesquero, -a [pes'kero, a] *adj* fishing *cpd*

pestaña [pes'taɲa] *nf* (Anat) eyelash; (*borde*) rim

peste ['peste] *nf* plague; (*mal olor*) stink, stench

pesticida [pesti'θiða] *nm* pesticide

pestillo [pes'tiʎo] *nm* (*cerrojo*) bolt; (*picaporte*) door handle

petaca [pe'taka] *nf* (*de cigarros*) cigarette case; (*de pipa*) tobacco pouch; (MÉX: *maleta*) suitcase

pétalo ['petalo] *nm* petal

petardo [pe'tardo] *nm* firework, firecracker

petición [peti'θjon] *nf* (*pedido*) request, plea; (*memorial*) petition; (Jur) plea

peto ['peto] (ESP) *nm* dungarees *pl*, overalls *pl* (US)

petróleo [pe'troleo] *nm* oil, petroleum; **petrolero, -a** *adj* petroleum *cpd* ▷ *nm* (oil) tanker

peyorativo, -a [pejora'tiβo, a] *adj* pejorative

pez [peθ] *nm* fish; **pez dorado/ de colores** goldfish; **pez espada** swordfish

pezón [pe'θon] *nm* teat, nipple

pezuña [pe'θuɲa] *nf* hoof

pianista [pja'nista] *nmf* pianist

piano ['pjano] *nm* piano

piar [pjar] *vi* to cheep

pibe, -a ['piβe, a] (RPL) *nm/f* boy/girl

picadero [pika'ðero] *nm* riding school

picadillo [pika'ðiʎo] *nm* mince, minced meat

picado, -a [pi'kaðo, a] *adj* pricked, punctured; (Culin) minced, chopped; (*mar*) choppy; (*diente*) bad; (*tabaco*) cut; (*enfadado*) cross

picador [pika'ðor] *nm* (Taur) picador; (*minero*) faceworker

picadura [pika'ðura] *nf* (*pinchazo*) puncture; (*de abeja*) sting; (*de mosquito*) bite; (*tabaco picado*) cut tobacco

picante [pi'kante] *adj* hot; (*comentario*) racy, spicy

picaporte [pika'porte] *nm* (*manija*) doorhandle; (*pestillo*) latch

picar [pi'kar] *vt* (*agujerear, perforar*) to prick, puncture; (*abeja*) to sting; (*mosquito, serpiente*) to bite; (Culin) to mince, chop; (*incitar*) to incite, goad; (*dañar, irritar*) to annoy, bother; (*quemar: lengua*) to burn, sting ▷ *vi* (*pez*) to bite, take the bait; (*sol*) to burn, scorch; (*abeja, Med*) to sting; (*mosquito*) to bite; **picarse** *vr* (*agriarse*) to turn sour, go off; (*ofenderse*) to take offence

picardía [pikar'ðia] *nf* villainy; (*astucia*) slyness, craftiness; (*una picardía*) dirty trick; (*palabra*) rude/bad word o expression

pícaro, -a ['pikaro, a] *adj* (*malicioso*) villainous; (*travieso*) mischievous ▷ *nm* (*astuto*) crafty sort; (*sinvergüenza*) rascal, scoundrel

pichi ['pitʃi] (*ESP*) *nm* pinafore dress (*BRIT*), jumper (*US*)

pichón [pi'tʃon] *nm* young pigeon

pico ['piko] *nm* (*de ave*) beak; (*punta*) sharp point; (*Tec*) pick, pickaxe; (*Geo*) peak, summit; **y ~** and a bit; **las seis y ~** six and a bit

picor [pi'kor] *nm* itch

picoso, -a [pi'koso, a] (*MÉX*) *adj* (*comida*) hot

picudo, -a [pi'kuðo, a] *adj* pointed, with a point

pidió *etc vb* V **pedir**

pido *etc vb* V **pedir**

pie [pje] (*pl* **~s**) *nm* foot; (*fig: motivo*) motive, basis; (*: fundamento*) foothold; **ir a ~** to go on foot, walk; **estar de ~** to be standing (up); **ponerse de ~** to stand up; **de ~s a cabeza** from top to bottom; **al ~ de la letra** (*citar*) literally, verbatim; (*copiar*) exactly, word for word; **en ~ de guerra** on a war footing; **dar ~ a** to give cause for; **hacer ~** (*en el agua*) to touch (the) bottom

piedad [pje'ðað] *nf* (*lástima*) pity, compassion; (*clemencia*) mercy; (*devoción*) piety, devotion

piedra ['pjeðra] *nf* stone; (*roca*) rock; (*de mechero*) flint; (*Meteorología*) hailstone; **piedra preciosa** precious stone

piel [pjel] *nf* (*Anat*) skin; (*Zool*) skin, hide, fur; (*cuero*) leather; (*Bot*) skin, peel

pienso *etc vb* V **pensar**

pierdo *etc vb* V **perder**

pierna ['pjerna] *nf* leg

pieza ['pjeθa] *nf* piece; (*habitación*) room; **pieza de recambio** o **repuesto** spare (part)

pigmeo, -a [piɣ'meo, a] *adj, nm/f* pigmy

pijama [pi'xama] *nm* pyjamas *pl* (*BRIT*), pajamas *pl* (*US*)

pila ['pila] *nf* (*Elec*) battery; (*montón*) heap, pile; (*lavabo*) sink

píldora ['pildora] *nf* pill; **la ~ (anticonceptiva)** the (contraceptive) pill

pileta [pi'leta] (*RPL*) *nf* (*fregadero*) (kitchen) sink; (*piscina*) swimming pool

pillar [pi'ʎar] *vt* (*saquear*) to pillage, plunder; (*fam: coger*) to catch; (*: agarrar*) to grasp, seize; (*: entender*) to grasp, catch on to; **pillarse** *vr*: **~se un dedo con la puerta** to catch one's finger in the door

pillo, -a ['piʎo, a] *adj* villainous; (*astuto*) sly, crafty ▷ *nm/f* rascal, rogue, scoundrel

piloto [pi'loto] *nm* pilot; (*de aparato*) (pilot) light; (*Auto: luz*) tail o rear light; (*: conductor*) driver; **piloto automático** automatic pilot

pimentón [pimen'ton] *nm* paprika

pimienta [pi'mjenta] *nf* pepper

pimiento [pi'mjento] *nm* pepper, pimiento

pin [pin] (*pl* **~s**) *nm* badge

pinacoteca [pinako'teka] *nf* art gallery

pinar [pi'nar] *nm* pine forest (*BRIT*), pine grove (*US*)

pincel [pin'θel] *nm* paintbrush

pinchadiscos [pintʃa'ðiskos] (*ESP*) *nmf inv* disc-jockey, DJ

pinchar [pin'tʃar] *vt* (*perforar*) to prick, pierce; (*neumático*) to puncture; (*fig*) to prod; (*Inform*) to click

pinchazo [pin'tʃaθo] *nm* (*perforación*) prick; (*de neumático*) puncture; (*fig*) prod

pincho ['pintʃo] *nm* savoury (snack); **pincho de tortilla** small slice of omelette; **pincho moruno** shish kebab

ping-pong ['pin'pon] *nm* table tennis

pingüino [pin'gwino] *nm* penguin

pino ['pino] *nm* pine (tree)

pinta ['pinta] *nf* spot; (*de líquidos*) spot, drop; (*aspecto*) appearance, look(s) (*pl*); **pintado, -a** *adj* spotted; (*de colores*) colourful; **pintadas** *nfpl* graffiti *sg*

pintalabios [pinta'laβjos] (*ESP*) *nm inv* lipstick

pintar [pin'tar] *vt* to paint ▷ *vi* to paint; (*fam*) to count, be important; **pintarse** *vr* to put on make-up

pintor, a [pin'tor, a] *nm/f* painter

pintoresco, -a [pinto'resko, a] *adj* picturesque

pintura [pin'tura] *nf* painting; **pintura al óleo** oil painting

pinza [pin'θa] *nf* (*Zool*) claw; (*para colgar ropa*) clothes peg; (*Tec*) pincers *pl*; **pinzas** *nfpl* (*para depilar etc*) tweezers *pl*

piña [ˈpiɲa] *nf* (*de pino*) pine cone; (*fruta*) pineapple; (*fig*) group

piñata [piˈɲata] *nf* container hung up at parties to be beaten with sticks until sweets or presents fall out

---

◦ **PIÑATA**
◦
◦ **Piñata** is a very popular party
◦ game in Mexico. The **piñata** itself
◦ is a hollow figure made of papier
◦ maché, or, traditionally, from
◦ adobe, in the shape of an object,
◦ a star, a person or an animal. It is
◦ filled with either sweets and toys,
◦ or fruit and yam beans. The game
◦ consists of hanging the **piñata**
◦ from the ceiling, and beating it
◦ with a stick, blindfolded, until it
◦ breaks and the presents fall out.

---

piñón [piˈɲon] *nm* (*fruto*) pine nut; (*Tec*) pinion

pío, -a [ˈpio, a] *adj* (*devoto*) pious, devout; (*misericordioso*) merciful

piojo [ˈpjoxo] *nm* louse

pipa [ˈpipa] *nf* pipe; **pipas** *nfpl* (*Bot*) (edible) sunflower seeds

pipí [piˈpi] (*fam*) *nm*; **hacer ~** to have a wee(-wee) (*BRIT*), have to go (wee-wee) (*US*)

pique [ˈpike] *nm* (*resentimiento*) pique, resentment; (*rivalidad*)

rivalry, competition; **irse a ~** to sink; (*esperanza, familia*) to be ruined

piqueta [piˈketa] *nf* pick(axe)

piquete [piˈkete] *nm* (*Mil*) squad, party; (*de obreros*) picket; (*MÉX: de insecto*) bite; **piquetear** (*LAM*) *vt* to picket

pirado, -a [piˈraðo, a] (*fam*) *adj* round the bend ▷ *nm/f* nutter

piragua [piˈraxwa] *nf* canoe; **piragüismo** *nm* canoeing

pirámide [piˈramiðe] *nf* pyramid

pirata [piˈrata] *adj, nmf* pirate; **pirata informático** hacker

Pirineo(s) [piriˈneo(s)] *nm(pl)* Pyrenees *pl*

pirómano, -a [piˈromano, a] *nm/f* (*Med, Jur*) arsonist

piropo [piˈropo] *nm* compliment, (piece of) flattery

pirueta [piˈrweta] *nf* pirouette

piruleta [piruˈleta] (*ESP*) *nf* lollipop

pis [pis] (*fam*) *nm* pee, piss; **hacer ~** to have a pee; (*para niños*) to wee-wee

pisada [piˈsaða] *nf* (*paso*) footstep; (*huella*) footprint

pisar [piˈsar] *vt* (*caminar sobre*) to walk on, tread on; (*apretar con el pie*) to press; (*fig*) to trample on, walk all over ▷ *vi* to tread, step, walk

piscina [pisˈθina] *nf* swimming pool

Piscis [ˈpisθis] *nm* Pisces

piso [ˈpiso] *nm* (*suelo, planta*) floor; (*ESP: apartamento*) flat (*BRIT*), apartment; **primer ~** (*ESP*) first floor; (*LAM: planta baja*) ground floor

pisotear [pisoteˈar] *vt* to trample (on *o* underfoot)

pista [ˈpista] *nf* track, trail; (*indicio*) clue; **pista de aterrizaje** runway; **pista de baile** dance floor; **pista de hielo** ice rink; **pista de tenis** (*ESP*) tennis court

pistola [pisˈtola] *nf* pistol; (*Tec*) spray-gun

pistón [pisˈton] *nm* (*Tec*) piston; (*Mús*) key

pitar [piˈtar] *vt* (*silbato*) to blow; (*rechiflar*) to whistle at, boo ▷ *vi* to whistle; (*Auto*) to sound o toot one's horn; (*LAM: fumar*) to smoke

pitillo [pi'tiʎo] *nm* cigarette

pito ['pito] *nm* whistle; (*de coche*) horn

pitón [pi'ton] *nm* (*Zool*) python

pitonisa [pito'nisa] *nf* fortune-teller

pitorreo [pito'rreo] *nm* joke; **estar de ~** to be joking

píxel ['piksel] (*pl* **pixels** or **~es**) *nm* pixel

piyama [pi'jama] (*LAM*) *nm* pyjamas *pl* (*BRIT*), pajamas *pl* (*US*)

pizarra [pi'θarra] *nf* (*piedra*) slate; (*ESP: encerado*) blackboard; **pizarra blanca** whiteboard; **pizarra interactiva** interactive whiteboard

pizarrón [piθa'rron] (*LAM*) *nm* blackboard

pizca ['piθka] *nf* pinch, spot; (*fig*) spot, speck; **ni ~** not a bit

placa ['plaka] *nf* plate; (*distintivo*) badge, insignia; **placa de matrícula** (*LAM*) number plate

placard [pla'kar] (*RPL*) *nm* cupboard

placer [pla'θer] *nm* pleasure ▷ *vt* to please

plaga ['plaxa] *nf* pest; (*Med*) plague; (*abundancia*) abundance

plagio ['plaxjo] *nm* plagiarism

plan [plan] *nm* (*esquema, proyecto*) plan; (*idea, intento*) idea, intention; **tener ~** (*fam*) to have a date; **tener un ~** (*fam*) to have an affair; **en ~ económico** (*fam*) on the cheap; **vamos en ~ de turismo** we're going as tourists; **si te pones en ese ~ ...** if that's your attitude ...

plana ['plana] *nf* sheet (of paper), page; (*Tec*) trowel; **en primera ~** on the front page

plancha ['plantʃa] *nf* (*para planchar*) iron; (*rótulo*) plate, sheet; (*Náut*) gangway; **a la ~** (*Culin*) grilled; **planchar** *vt* to iron ▷ *vi* to do the ironing

planear [plane'ar] *vt* to plan ▷ *vi* to glide

planeta [pla'neta] *nm* planet

plano, -a ['plano, a] *adj* flat, level, even ▷ *nm* (*Mat, Tec*) plane; (*Foto*) shot; (*Arq*) plan; (*Geo*) map; (*de ciudad*) map, street plan; **primer ~** close-up

planta ['planta] *nf* (*Bot, Tec*) plant; (*Anat*) sole of the foot, foot; (*piso*) floor; (*LAM: personal*) staff; **planta baja** ground floor

plantar [plan'tar] *vt* (*Bot*) to plant; (*levantar*) to erect, set up; **plantarse** *vr* to stand firm; **~ a algn en la calle** to throw sb out; **dejar plantado a algn** (*fam*) to stand sb up

plantear [plante'ar] *vt* (*problema*) to pose; (*dificultad*) to raise

plantilla [plan'tiʎa] *nf* (*de zapato*) insole; (*ESP: personal*) personnel; **ser de ~** (*ESP*) to be on the staff

plantón [plan'ton] *nm* (*Mil*) guard, sentry; (*fam*) long wait; **dar (un) ~ a algn** to stand sb up

plasta ['plasta] (*ESP: fam*) *adj inv* boring ▷ *nmf* bore

plástico, -a ['plastiko, a] *adj* plastic ▷ *nm* plastic

Plastilina® [plasti'lina] *nf* Plasticine®

plata ['plata] *nf* (*metal*) silver; (*cosas hechas de plata*) silverware; (*CS: dinero*) cash, dough

plataforma [plata'forma] *nf* platform; **plataforma de lanzamiento/perforación** launch(ing) pad/drilling rig

plátano ['platano] *nm* (*fruta*) banana; (*árbol*) plane tree; banana tree

platea [pla'tea] *nf* (*Teatro*) pit

plática ['platika] *nf* talk, chat; **platicar** *vi* to talk, chat

platillo [pla'tiʎo] *nm* saucer; **platillos** *nmpl* (*Mús*) cymbals; **platillo volante** flying saucer

platino [pla'tino] *nm* platinum; **platinos** *nmpl* (*Auto*) contact points

plato ['plato] *nm* plate, dish; (*parte de comida*) course; (*comida*) dish; **primer ~** first course; **plato combinado** set main course (*served on one plate*); **plato**

fuerte main course

playa ['plaja] nf beach; (costa)
seaside; **playa de estacionamiento**
(cs) car park (BRIT), parking lot (US)

playera [pla'jera] nf (MÉX: camiseta)
T-shirt; **playeras** nfpl (zapatos) canvas
shoes

plaza ['plaθa] nf square; (mercado)
market(place); (sitio) room, space; (de
vehículo) seat, place; (colocación) post,
job; **plaza de toros** bullring

plazo ['plaθo] nm (lapso de tiempo)
time, period; (fecha de vencimiento)
expiry date; (pago parcial) instalment;
a corto/largo ~ short-/long-term;
comprar algo a ~s to buy sth on hire
purchase (BRIT) o on time (US)

plazoleta [plaθo'leta] nf small
square

plebeyo, -a [ple'βejo, a] adj
plebeian; (pey) coarse, common

plegable [ple'ɣaβle] adj collapsible;
(silla) folding

pleito ['pleito] nm (Jur) lawsuit, case;
(fig) dispute, feud

plenitud [pleni'tuð] nf plenitude,
fullness; (abundancia) abundance

pleno, -a ['pleno, a] adj full;
(completo) complete ▷ nm plenum; **en
~ día** in broad daylight; **en ~ verano** at
the height of summer; **en plena cara**
full in the face

pliego etc ['pljeɣo] vb V **plegar**
▷ nm (hoja) sheet (of paper); (carta)
sealed letter/document; **pliego de
condiciones** details pl, specifications
pl

pliegue etc ['pljeɣe] vb V **plegar** ▷ nm
fold, crease; (de vestido) pleat

plomería [plome'ria] (LAM) nf
plumbing; **plomero** (LAM) nm plumber

plomo ['plomo] nm (metal) lead; (Elec)
fuse; **sin ~** unleaded

pluma ['pluma] nf feather; (para
escribir): **~ (estilográfica)** ink pen; **~
fuente** (LAM) fountain pen

plumero [plu'mero] nm (para el polvo)
feather duster

plumón [plu'mon] nm (de ave) down

plural [plu'ral] adj plural

pluriempleo [pluriem'pleo] nm
having more than one job

plus [plus] nm bonus

población [poβla'θjon] nf
population; (pueblo, ciudad) town, city

poblado, -a [po'βlaðo, a] adj
inhabited ▷ nm (aldea) village; (pueblo)
(small) town; **densamente ~** densely
populated

poblador, a [poβla'ðor, a] nm/f
settler, colonist

pobre ['poβre] adj poor ▷ nmf poor
person; **pobreza** nf poverty

pocilga [po'θilɣa] nf pigsty

○ **PALABRA CLAVE**

poco, -a ['poko, a] adj **1** (sg) little,
not much; **poco tiempo** little o not
much time; **de poco interés** of little
interest, not very interesting; **poca
cosa** not much
2 (pl) few, not many; **unos pocos** a
few, some; **pocos niños comen lo que
les conviene** few children eat what
they should
▷ adv **1** little, not much; **cuesta poco** it
doesn't cost much
2 (+ adj: negativo, antónimo): **poco
amable/inteligente** not very nice/
intelligent
3: **por poco me caigo** I almost fell
4: **a poco: a poco de haberse casado**
shortly after getting married
5: **poco a poco** little by little
▷ nm a little, a bit; **un poco triste/de
dinero** a little sad/money

podar [po'ðar] vt to prune

podcast ['poðkast] nm podcast;
podcastear [poðkaste'ar] vi to
podcast

○ **PALABRA CLAVE**

poder [po'ðer] vi **1** (tener capacidad)

can, be able to; **no puedo hacerlo** I can't do it, I'm unable to do it

2 (*tener permiso*) can, may, be allowed to; **¿se puede?** may I (*o* we)?; **puedes irte ahora** you may go now; **no se puede fumar en este hospital** smoking is not allowed in this hospital

3 (*tener posibilidad*) may, might, could; **puede llegar mañana** he may *o* might arrive tomorrow; **pudiste haberte hecho daño** you might *o* could have hurt yourself; **¡podías habérmelo dicho antes!** you might have told me before!

4: **puede ser** perhaps; **puede ser que lo sepa Tomás** Tomás may *o* might know

5: **¡no puedo más!** I've had enough!; **es tonto a más no poder** he's as stupid as they come

6: **poder con: no puedo con este crío** this kid's too much for me
▷ *nm* power; **detentar** *o* **ocupar** *o* **estar en el poder** to be in power; **poder adquisitivo/ejecutivo/legislativo** purchasing/executive/legislative power; **poder judicial** judiciary

poderoso, -a [poðeroso, a] *adj* (*político, país*) powerful

podio [podjo] *nm* (*Deporte*) podium

podium [poðjum] = **podio**

podrido, -a [po'ðriðo, a] *adj* rotten, bad; (*fig*) rotten, corrupt

podrir [po'ðrir] = **pudrir**

poema [po'ema] *nm* poem

poesía [poe'sia] *nf* poetry

poeta [po'eta] *nmf* poet; **poético, -a** *adj* poetic(al)

poetisa [poe'tisa] *nf* (woman) poet

póker [poker] *nm* poker

polaco, -a [po'lako, a] *adj* Polish ▷ *nm/f* Pole

polar [po'lar] *adj* polar

polea [po'lea] *nf* pulley

polémica [po'lemika] *nf* polemics

sg; (*una polémica*) controversy, polemic

polen ['polen] *nm* pollen

policía [poli'θia] *nmf* policeman/woman ▷ *nf* police; **policíaco, -a** *adj* police *cpd*; **novela policíaca** detective story; **policial** *adj* police *cpd*

polideportivo [poliðepor'tiβo] *nm* sports centre *o* complex

polígono [po'liɣono] *nm* (*Mat*) polygon; **polígono industrial** (*ESP*) industrial estate

polilla [po'liʎa] *nf* moth

polio ['poljo] *nf* polio

política [po'litika] *nf* politics *sg*; (*económica, agraria etc*) policy; V *tb* **político**

político, -a [po'litiko, a] *adj* political; (*discreto*) tactful; (*de familia*) ...-in law ▷ *nm/f* politician; **padre ~** father-in-law

póliza [poliθa] *nf* certificate, voucher; (*impuesto*) tax stamp; **póliza de seguro(s)** insurance policy

polizón [poli'θon] *nm* stowaway

pollera [po'ʎera] (*CS*) *nf* skirt

pollo ['poʎo] *nm* chicken

polo ['polo] *nm* (*Geo, Elec*) pole; (*helado*) ice lolly (*BRIT*), Popsicle® (*US*); (*Deporte*) polo; (*suéter*) polo-neck; **polo Norte/Sur** North/South Pole

Polonia [po'lonja] *nf* Poland

poltrona [pol'trona] *nf* easy chair

polución [polu'θjon] *nf* pollution

polvera [pol'βera] *nf* powder compact

polvo ['polβo] *nm* dust; (*Quím, Culin, Med*) powder; **polvos** *nmpl* (*maquillaje*) powder *sg*; **en ~** powdered; **quitar el ~** to dust; **estar hecho ~** (*fam*) to be worn out *o* exhausted; **polvos de talco** talcum powder *sg*

pólvora ['polβora] *nf* gunpowder

polvoriento, -a [polβo'rjento, a] *adj* (*superficie*) dusty; (*sustancia*) powdery

pomada [po'maða] *nf* cream, ointment

pomelo [po'melo] nm grapefruit

pómez ['pomeθ] nf: **piedra ~** pumice stone

pomo ['pomo] nm doorknob

pompa ['pompa] nf (burbuja) bubble; (bomba) pump; (esplendor) pomp, splendour

pómulo ['pomulo] nm cheekbone

pon [pon] vb V **poner**

ponchadura [pontʃa'dura] (MÉX) nf puncture (BRIT), flat (US); **ponchar** (MÉX) vt (llanta) to puncture

ponche ['pontʃe] nm punch

poncho ['pontʃo] nm poncho

pondré etc vb V **poner**

○ **PALABRA CLAVE**

poner [po'ner] vt **1** (colocar) to put; (telegrama) to send; (obra de teatro) to put on; (película) to show; **ponlo más fuerte** turn it up; **¿qué ponen en el Excelsior?** what's on at the Excelsior?

2 (tienda) to open; (instalar: gas etc) to put in; (radio, TV) to switch o turn on

3 (suponer): **pongamos que ...** let's suppose that ...

4 (contribuir): **el gobierno ha puesto otro millón** the government has contributed another million

5 (Tel): **póngame con el Sr. López** can you put me through to Mr. López?

6: **poner de: le han puesto de director general** they've appointed him general manager

7 (+ adj) to make; **me estás poniendo nerviosa** you're making me nervous

8 (dar nombre): **al hijo le pusieron Diego** they called their son Diego

▷ vi (gallina) to lay

ponerse vr **1** (colocarse): **se puso a mi lado** he came and stood beside me; **tú ponte en esa silla** you go and sit on that chair; **ponerse en camino** to set off

2 (vestido, cosméticos) to put on; **¿por qué no te pones el vestido nuevo?** why don't you put on o wear your new dress?

3 (+ adj) to turn; to get, become; **se puso muy serio** he got very serious; **después de lavarla la tela se puso azul** after washing it the material turned blue

4: **ponerse a: se puso a llorar** he started to cry; **tienes que ponerte a estudiar** you must get down to studying

pongo etc vb V **poner**

poniente [po'njente] nm (occidente) west; (viento) west wind

pontífice [pon'tifiθe] nm pope, pontiff

pop [pop] adj inv, nm (Mus) pop

popa ['popa] nf stern

popote [po'pote] (MÉX) nm straw

popular [popu'lar] adj popular; (cultura) of the people, folk cpd; **popularidad** nf popularity

○ **PALABRA CLAVE**

por [por] prep **1** (objetivo) for; **luchar por la patria** to fight for one's country

2 (+ infin): **por no llegar tarde** so as not to arrive late; **por citar unos ejemplos** to give a few examples

3 (causa) out of, because of; **por escasez de fondos** through o for lack of funds

4 (tiempo): **por la mañana/noche** in the morning/at night; **se queda por una semana** she's staying (for) a week

5 (lugar): **pasar por Madrid** to pass through Madrid; **ir a Guayaquil por Quito** to go to Guayaquil via Quito; **caminar por la calle** to walk along the street; **¿Hay un banco por aquí?** Is there a bank near here?; V tb **todo**

6 (cambio, precio): **te doy uno nuevo por el que tienes** I'll give you a new one (in return) for the one you've got

7 (valor distributivo): **6 euros por**

hora/cabeza 6 euros an o per hour/a
o per head
8 (modo, medio) by; **por correo/avión**
by post/air; **entrar por la entrada
principal** to go in through the main
entrance
9: **10 por 10 son 100** 10 times 10 is 100
10 (en lugar de): **vino él por su jefe** he
came instead of his boss
11: **por mí que revienten** as far as I'm
concerned they can drop dead
12: **¿por qué?** why?; **¿por qué no?**
why not?

porcelana [porθe'lana] nf porcelain;
(china) china
porcentaje [porθen'taxe] nm
percentage
porción [por'θjon] nf (parte) portion,
share; (cantidad) quantity, amount
porfiar [por'fjar] vi to persist, insist;
(disputar) to argue stubbornly
pormenor [porme'nor] nm detail,
particular
pornografía [pornoxra'fia] nf
pornography
poro ['poro] nm pore
pororó [poro'ro] (RPL) nm popcorn
poroso, -a [po'roso, a] adj porous
poroto [po'roto] (CS) nm bean
porque ['porke] conj (a causa de)
because; (ya que) since; (con el fin de) so
that, in order that
porqué [por'ke] nm reason, cause
porquería [porke'ria] nf (suciedad)
filth, dirt; (acción) dirty trick; (objeto)
small thing, trifle; (fig) rubbish
porra ['porra] (ESP) nf (arma) stick,
club
porrazo [po'rraθo] nm blow, bump
porro ['porro] (fam) nm (droga) joint
(fam)
porrón [po'rron] nm glass wine jar with
a long spout
portaaviones [porta'(a)βjones] nm
inv aircraft carrier
portada [por'taða] nf (de revista)
cover

portador, a [porta'ðor, a] nm/f
carrier, bearer; (Com) bearer, payee
portaequipajes [portaeki'paxes]
nm inv (Auto: maletero) boot; (: baca)
luggage rack
portafolio [porta'foljo] (LAM) nm
briefcase
portal [por'tal] nm (entrada)
vestibule, hall; (portada) porch,
doorway; (puerta de entrada) main door;
(Internet) portal; **portales** nmpl (LAM)
arcade sg
portamaletas [portama'letas]
nm inv (Auto: maletero) boot; (: baca)
roof rack
portamonedas [portamo'neðas]
nm inv purse
portarse [por'tarse] vr to behave,
conduct o.s.
portátil [por'tatil] adj portable;
(ordenador) **portátil** laptop computer
portavoz [porta'βoθ] nmf
spokesman/woman
portazo [por'taθo] nm: **dar un ~** to
slam the door
porte ['porte] nm (Com) transport;
(precio) transport charges pl
portentoso, -a [porten'toso, a] adj
marvellous, extraordinary
porteño, -a [por'teɲo, a] adj of o
from Buenos Aires
portería [porte'ria] nf (oficina)
porter's office; (Deporte) goal
portero, -a [por'tero, a] nm/f porter;
(conserje) caretaker; (ujier) doorman;
(Deporte) goalkeeper; **portero
automático** (ESP) entry phone
pórtico ['portiko] nm (patio) portico,
porch; (fig) gateway; (arcada) arcade
portorriqueño, -a [portorri'keɲo,
a] adj Puerto Rican
Portugal [portu'ɣal] nm Portugal;
portugués, -esa adj, nm/f Portuguese
▷ nm (Ling) Portuguese
porvenir [porβe'nir] nm future
pos [pos] prep: **en ~ de** after, in
pursuit of
posaderas [posa'ðeras] nfpl

P

backside *sg*, buttocks

posar [po'sar] *vt* (*en el suelo*) to lay down, put down; (*la mano*) to place, put gently ▷ *vi* (*modelo*) to sit, pose; **posarse** *vr* to settle; (*pájaro*) to perch; (*avión*) to land, come down

posavasos [posa'basos] *nm inv* coaster; (*para cerveza*) beermat

posdata [pos'ðata] *nf* postscript

pose ['pose] *nf* pose

poseedor, a [posee'ðor, a] *nm/f* owner, possessor; (*de récord, puesto*) holder

poseer [pose'er] *vt* to possess, own; (*ventaja*) to enjoy; (*récord, puesto*) to hold

posesivo, -a [pose'siβo, a] *adj* possessive

posibilidad [posiβili'ðað] *nf* possibility; (*oportunidad*) chance; **posibilitar** *vt* to make possible; (*hacer realizable*) to make feasible

posible [po'siβle] *adj* possible; (*realizable*) feasible; **de ser ~** if possible; **en lo ~** as far as possible

posición [posi'θjon] *nf* position; (*rango social*) status

positivo, -a [posi'tiβo, a] *adj* positive

poso ['poso] *nm* sediment; (*heces*) dregs *pl*

posponer [pospo'ner] *vt* (*relegar*) to put behind/below; (*aplazar*) to postpone

posta ['posta] *nf*: **a ~** deliberately, on purpose

postal [pos'tal] *adj* postal ▷ *nf* postcard

poste ['poste] *nm* (*de telégrafos etc*) post, pole; (*columna*) pillar

póster ['poster] (*pl* **-es, ~s**) *nm* poster

posterior [poste'rjor] *adj* back, rear; (*siguiente*) following, subsequent; (*más tarde*) later

postgrado [post'graðo] *nm* = **posgrado**

postizo, -a [pos'tiθo, a] *adj* false, artificial ▷ *nm* hairpiece

postre ['postre] *nm* sweet, dessert

póstumo, -a ['postumo, a] *adj* posthumous

postura [pos'tura] *nf* (*del cuerpo*) posture, position; (*fig*) attitude, position

potable [po'taβle] *adj* drinkable; **agua ~** drinking water

potaje [po'taxe] *nm* thick vegetable soup

potencia [po'tenθja] *nf* power; **potencial** [poten'θjal] *adj, nm* potential

potente [po'tente] *adj* powerful

potro, -a ['potro, a] *nm/f* (*Zool*) colt/ filly ▷ *nm* (*de gimnasia*) vaulting horse

pozo ['poθo] *nm* well; (*de río*) deep pool; (*de mina*) shaft

PP (*ESP*) *nm abr* = **Partido Popular**

práctica ['praktika] *nf* practice; (*método*) method; (*arte, capacidad*) skill; **en la ~** in practice

practicable [prakti'kaβle] *adj* practicable; (*camino*) passable

practicante [prakti'kante] *nmf* (*Med: ayudante de doctor*) medical assistant; (: *enfermero*) nurse; (*quien practica algo*) practitioner ▷ *adj* practising

practicar [prakti'kar] *vt* to practise; (*Deporte*) to play; (*realizar*) to carry out, perform

práctico, -a ['praktiko, a] *adj* practical; (*instruído: persona*) skilled, expert

practique *etc vb* V **practicar**

pradera [pra'ðera] *nf* meadow; (*US etc*) prairie

prado ['praðo] *nm* (*campo*) meadow, field; (*pastizal*) pasture

Praga ['praxa] *n* Prague

pragmático, -a [prax'matiko, a] *adj* pragmatic

precario, -a [pre'karjo, a] *adj* precarious

precaución [prekau'θjon] *nf* (*medida preventiva*) preventive measure, precaution; (*prudencia*) caution, wariness

precedente [preθe'ðente] *adj* preceding; (*anterior*) former ▷ *nm* precedent

preceder [preθe'ðer] *vt, vi* to precede, go before, come before

precepto [pre'θepto] *nm* precept

precinto [pre'θinto] *nm* (*tb*: **~ de garantía**) seal

precio ['preθjo] *nm* price; (*costo*) cost; (*valor*) value, worth; (*de viaje*) fare; **precio al contado/de coste/de oportunidad** cash/cost/bargain price; **precio al por menor** retail price; **precio de ocasión** bargain price; **precio de venta al público** retail price; **precio tope** top price

preciosidad [preθjosi'ðað] *nf* (*valor*) (high) value, (great) worth; (*encanto*) charm; (*cosa bonita*) beautiful thing; **es una ~** it's lovely, it's really beautiful

precioso, -a [pre'θjoso, a] *adj* precious; (*de mucho valor*) valuable; (*fam*) lovely, beautiful

precipicio [preθi'piθjo] *nm* cliff, precipice; (*fig*) abyss

precipitación [preθipita'θjon] *nf* haste; (*lluvia*) rainfall

precipitado, -a [preθipi'taðo, a] *adj* (*conducta*) hasty, rash; (*salida*) hasty, sudden

precipitar [preθipi'tar] *vt* (*arrojar*) to hurl down, throw; (*apresurar*) to hasten; (*acelerar*) to speed up, accelerate; **precipitarse** *vr* to throw o.s.; (*apresurarse*) to rush; (*actuar sin pensar*) to act rashly

precisamente [preθisa'mente] *adv* precisely; (*exactamente*) precisely, exactly

precisar [preθi'sar] *vt* (*necesitar*) to need, require; (*fijar*) to determine exactly, fix; (*especificar*) to specify

precisión [preθi'sjon] *nf* (*exactitud*) precision

preciso, -a [pre'θiso, a] *adj* (*exacto*) precise; (*necesario*) necessary, essential

preconcebido, -a [prekonθe'βiðo, a] *adj* preconceived

precoz [pre'koθ] *adj* (*persona*) precocious; (*calvicie etc*) premature

predecir [preðe'θir] *vt* to predict, forecast

predestinado, -a [preðesti'naðo, a] *adj* predestined

predicar [preði'kar] *vt, vi* to preach

predicción [preðik'θjon] *nf* prediction

predilecto, -a [preði'lekto, a] *adj* favourite

predisposición [preðisposi'θjon] *nf* inclination; prejudice, bias

predominar [preðomi'nar] *vt* to dominate ▷ *vi* to predominate; (*prevalecer*) to prevail; **predominio** *nm* predominance; prevalence

preescolar [prc(e)sko'lar] *adj* preschool

prefabricado, -a [prefaβri'kaðo, a] *adj* prefabricated

prefacio [pre'faθjo] *nm* preface

preferencia [prefe'renθja] *nf* preference; **de ~** preferably, for preference

preferible [prefe'riβle] *adj* preferable

preferido, -a [prefe'riðo, a] *adj, nm/f* favourite, favorite (*us*)

preferir [prefe'rir] *vt* to prefer

prefiero *etc vb* V **preferir**

prefijo [pre'fixo] *nm* (*Tel*) (dialling) code

pregunta [pre'ɣunta] *nf* question; **hacer una ~** to ask a question; **preguntas frecuentes** FAQs, frequently asked questions

preguntar [preɣun'tar] *vt* to ask; (*cuestionar*) to question ▷ *vi* to ask; **preguntarse** *vr* to wonder; **preguntar por algn** to ask for sb; **preguntón, -ona** [preɣun'ton, ona] *adj* inquisitive

prehistórico, -a [preis'toriko, a] *adj* prehistoric

prejuicio [pre'xwiθjo] *nm* (*acto*) prejudgement; (*idea preconcebida*) preconception; (*parcialidad*) prejudice,

p

bias

preludio [pre'luðjo] *nm* prelude

prematuro, -a [prema'turo, a] *adj* premature

premeditar [premeði'tar] *vt* to premeditate

premiar [pre'mjar] *vt* to reward; (*en un concurso*) to give a prize to

premio ['premjo] *nm* reward; prize; (*Com*) premium

prenatal [prena'tal] *adj* antenatal, prenatal

prenda ['prenda] *nf* (*ropa*) garment, article of clothing; (*garantía*) pledge; **prendas** *nfpl* (*talentos*) talents, gifts

prender [pren'der] *vt* (*captar*) to catch, capture; (*detener*) to arrest; (*Costura*) to pin, attach; (*sujetar*) to fasten ▷ *vi* to catch; (*arraigar*) to take root; **prenderse** *vr* (*encenderse*) to catch fire

prendido, -a [pren'diðo, a] (*LAM*) *adj* (*luz etc*) on

prensa ['prensa] *nf* press; **la ~** the press

preñado, -a [pre'ɲaðo, a] *adj* pregnant; **~ de** pregnant with, full of

preocupación [preokupa'θjon] *nf* worry, concern; (*ansiedad*) anxiety

preocupado, -a [preoku'paðo, a] *adj* worried, concerned; (*ansioso*) anxious

preocupar [preoku'par] *vt* to worry; **preocuparse** *vr* to worry; **~se de algo** (*hacerse cargo*) to take care of sth

preparación [prepara'θjon] *nf* (*acto*) preparation; (*estado*) readiness; (*entrenamiento*) training

preparado, -a [prepa'raðo, a] *adj* (*dispuesto*) prepared; (*Culin*) ready (to serve) ▷ *nm* preparation

preparar [prepa'rar] *vt* (*disponer*) to prepare, get ready; (*Tec: tratar*) to prepare, process; (*entrenar*) to teach, train; **prepararse** *vr*: **~se a** *o* **para** to prepare to *o* for, get ready to *o* for; **preparativo, -a** *adj* preparatory, preliminary; **preparativos** *nmpl*

preparations; **preparatoria** (*MÉX*) *nf* sixth-form college (*BRIT*), senior high school (*US*)

presa ['presa] *nf* (*cosa apresada*) catch; (*víctima*) victim; (*de animal*) prey; (*de agua*) dam

presagiar [presa'xjar] *vt* to presage, forebode; **presagio** *nm* omen

prescindir [presθin'dir] *vi*: **~ de** (*privarse de*) to do *o* go without; (*descartar*) to dispense with

prescribir [preskri'βir] *vt* to prescribe

presencia [pre'senθja] *nf* presence; **presenciar** *vt* to be present at; (*asistir a*) to attend; (*ver*) to see, witness

presentación [presenta'θjon] *nf* presentation; (*introducción*) introduction

presentador, a [presenta'ðor, a] *nm/f* presenter, compère

presentar [presen'tar] *vt* to present; (*ofrecer*) to offer; (*mostrar*) to show, display; (*a una persona*) to introduce; **presentarse** *vr* (*llegar inesperadamente*) to appear, turn up; (*ofrecerse: como candidato*) to run, stand; (*aparecer*) to show, appear; (*solicitar empleo*) to apply

presente [pre'sente] *adj* present ▷ *nm* present; **hacer ~** to state, declare; **tener ~** to remember, bear in mind

presentimiento [presenti'mjento] *nm* premonition, presentiment

presentir [presen'tir] *vt* to have a premonition of

preservación [preserβa'θjon] *nf* protection, preservation

preservar [preser'βar] *vt* to protect, preserve; **preservativo** *nm* sheath, condom

presidencia [presi'ðenθja] *nf* presidency; (*de comité*) chairmanship

presidente [presi'ðente] *nmf* president; (*de comité*) chairman/woman

presidir [presi'ðir] *vt* (*dirigir*) to preside at, preside over; (*: comité*) to take the chair at; (*dominar*) to dominate, rule ▷ vi to preside; to take the chair

presión [pre'sjon] nf pressure; **presión atmosférica** atmospheric o air pressure; **presionar** vt to press; (fig) to press, put pressure on ▷ vi: **presionar para** to press for

preso, -a ['preso, a] nm/f prisoner; **tomar** o **llevar ~ a algn** to arrest sb, take sb prisoner

prestación [presta'θjon] nf service; (subsidio) benefit; **prestaciones** nfpl (Tec, Auto) performance features

prestado, -a [pres'taðo, a] adj on loan; **pedir ~** to borrow

prestamista [presta'mista] nmf moneylender

préstamo ['prestamo] nm loan; **préstamo hipotecario** mortgage

prestar [pres'tar] vt to lend, loan; (atención) to pay; (ayuda) to give

prestigio [pres'tixjo] nm prestige; **prestigioso, -a** adj (honorable) prestigious; (famoso, renombrado) renowned, famous

presumido, -a [presu'miðo, a] adj (persona) vain

presumir [presu'mir] vt to presume ▷ vi (tener aires) to be conceited; **presunto, -a** adj (supuesto) supposed, presumed; (así llamado) so-called; **presuntuoso, -a** adj conceited, presumptuous

presupuesto [presu'pwesto] pp de **presuponer** ▷ nm (Finanzas) budget; (estimación: de costo) estimate

pretencioso, -a [preten'θjoso, a] adj pretentious

pretender [preten'der] vt (intentar) to try to, seek to; (reivindicar) to claim; (buscar) to seek, try for; (cortejar) to woo, court; **~ que** to expect that

No confundir **pretender** con la palabra inglesa pretend.

pretendiente nmf (amante) suitor; (al trono) pretender; **pretensión** nf (aspiración) aspiration; (reivindicación) claim; (orgullo) pretension

pretexto [pre'teksto] nm pretext; (excusa) excuse

prevención [preβen'θjon] nf prevention; (precaución) precaution

prevenido, -a [preβe'niðo, a] adj prepared, ready; (cauteloso) cautious

prevenir [preβe'nir] vt (impedir) to prevent; (predisponer) to prejudice, bias; (avisar) to warn; (preparar) to prepare, get ready; **prevenirse** vr to get ready, prepare; **~se contra** to take precautions against; **preventivo, -a** adj preventive, precautionary

prever [pre'βer] vt to foresee

previo, -a ['preβjo, a] adj (anterior) previous; (preliminar) preliminary ▷ prep: **~ acuerdo de los otros** subject to the agreement of the others

previsión [preβi'sjon] nf (perspicacia) foresight; (predicción) forecast; **previsto, -a** adj anticipated, forecast

prima ['prima] nf (Com) bonus; (de seguro) premium; V th **primo**

primario, -a [pri'marjo, a] adj primary

primavera [prima'βera] nf spring(-time)

primera [pri'mera] nf (Auto) first gear; (Ferro: tb: **~ clase**) first class; **de ~** (fam) first-class, first-rate

Primer Ministro [pri'mer-] nm Prime Minister

primero, -a [pri'mero, a] (adj **primer**) first; (principal) prime adv first; (más bien) sooner, rather, **primera plana** front page

primitivo, -a [primi'tiβo, a] adj primitive; (original) original

primo, -a ['primo, a] adj prime ▷ nm/f cousin; (fam) fool, idiot; **materias primas** raw materials; **primo hermano** first cousin

primogénito, -a [primo'xenito, a] adj first-born

primoroso, -a [primo'roso, a] adj exquisite, delicate

princesa [prin'θesa] nf princess

principal [prinθi'pal] adj principal,

P

main ▷ *nm* (*jefe*) chief, principal

príncipe ['prinθipe] *nm* prince

principiante [prinθi'pjante] *nmf* beginner

principio [prin'θipjo] *nm* (*comienzo*) beginning, start; (*origen*) origin; (*primera etapa*) rudiment, basic idea; (*moral*) principle; **desde el ~** from the first; **en un ~** at first; **a ~s de** at the beginning of

pringue ['pringe] *nm* (*grasa*) grease, fat, dripping

prioridad [priori'ðað] *nf* priority

prisa ['prisa] *nf* (*apresuramiento*) hurry, haste; (*rapidez*) speed; (*urgencia*) (sense of) urgency; **a o de ~** quickly; **correr ~** to be urgent; **darse ~** to hurry up; **tener ~** to be in a hurry

prisión [pri'sjon] *nf* (*cárcel*) prison; (*período de cárcel*) imprisonment; **prisionero, -a** *nm/f* prisoner

prismáticos [pris'matikos] *nmpl* binoculars

privado, -a [pri'βaðo, a] *adj* private

privar [pri'βar] *vt* to deprive; **privativo, -a** *adj* exclusive

privilegiar [priβile'xjar] *vt* to grant a privilege to; (*favorecer*) to favour

privilegio [priβi'lexjo] *nm* privilege; (*concesión*) concession

pro [pro] *nm o f* profit, advantage ▷ *prep*: **asociación ~ ciegos** association for the blind ▷ *prefijo*: **~ americano** pro-American; **en ~ de** on behalf of, for; **los ~s y los contras** the pros and cons

proa ['proa] *nf* bow, prow; **de ~** bow *cpd*, fore

probabilidad [proβaβili'ðað] *nf* probability, likelihood; (*oportunidad, posibilidad*) chance, prospect; **probable** *adj* probable, likely

probador [proβa'ðor] *nm* (*en tienda*) fitting room

probar [pro'βar] *vt* (*demostrar*) to prove; (*someter a prueba*) to test, try out; (*ropa*) to try on; (*comida*) to taste ▷ *vi* to try; **~se un traje** to try on a suit

probeta [pro'βeta] *nf* test tube

problema [pro'βlema] *nm* problem

procedente [proθe'ðente] *adj* (*razonable*) reasonable; (*conforme a derecho*) proper, fitting; **~ de** coming from, originating in

proceder [proθe'ðer] *vi* (*avanzar*) to proceed; (*actuar*) to act; (*ser correcto*) to be right (and proper), be fitting ▷ *nm* (*comportamiento*) behaviour, conduct; **~ de** to come from, originate in; **procedimiento** *nm* procedure; (*proceso*) process; (*método*) means *pl*, method

procesador [proθesa'ðor] *nm* processor; **procesador de textos** word processor

procesar [proθe'sar] *vt* to try, put on trial

procesión [proθe'sjon] *nf* procession

proceso [pro'θeso] *nm* process; (*Jur*) trial

proclamar [prokla'mar] *vt* to proclaim

procrear [prokre'ar] *vt, vi* to procreate

procurador, a [prokura'ðor, a] *nm/f* attorney

procurar [proku'rar] *vt* (*intentar*) to try, endeavour; (*conseguir*) to get, obtain; (*asegurar*) to secure; (*producir*) to produce

prodigio [pro'ðixjo] *nm* prodigy; (*milagro*) wonder, marvel; **prodigioso, -a** *adj* prodigious, marvellous

pródigo, -a ['proðixo, a] *adj*: **hijo ~** prodigal son

producción [proðuk'θjon] *nf* (*gen*) production; (*producto*) output; **producción en serie** mass production

producir [proðu'θir] *vt* to produce; (*causar*) to cause, bring about; **producirse** *vr* (*cambio*) to come about; (*accidente*) to take place; (*problema etc*) to arise; (*hacerse*) to be produced, be made; (*estallar*) to break out

productividad [proðuktiβi'ðað] *nf* productivity; **productivo, -a** *adj* productive; (*provechoso*) profitable

producto [pro'ðukto] *nm* product

productor, a [produk'tor, a] *adj*
productive, producing ▷ *nm/f* producer

proeza [pro'eθa] *nf* exploit, feat

profano, -a [pro'fano, a] *adj* profane
▷ *nm/f* layman/woman

profecía [profe'θia] *nf* prophecy

profesión [profe'sjon] *nf* profession;
(*en formulario*) occupation; **profesional**
adj professional

profesor, a [profe'sor, a] *nm/f*
teacher; **profesorado** *nm* teaching
profession

profeta [pro'feta] *nmf* prophet

prófugo, -a ['profuɣo, a] *nm/f*
fugitive; (*Mil: desertor*) deserter

profundidad [profundi'ðað] *nf*
depth; **profundizar** *vi*: **profundizar
en** to go deeply into; **profundo, -a** *adj*
deep; (*misterio, pensador*) profound

progenitor [proxeni'tor] *nm*
ancestor; **progenitores** *nmpl* (*padres*)
parents

programa [pro'xrama] *nm*
programme (BRIT), program (US);
programa de estudios curriculum,
syllabus; **programación** *nf*
programming; **programador, a**
nm/f programmer; **programar** *vt* to
program

progresar [proxre'sar] *vi* to
progress, make progress; **progresista**
adj, nmf progressive; **progresivo,
-a** *adj* progressive; (*gradual*) gradual;
(*continuo*) continuous; **progreso** *nm*
progress

prohibición [proiβi'θjon] *nf*
prohibition, ban

prohibir [proi'βir] *vt* to prohibit, ban,
forbid; **prohibido o se prohibe fumar**
no smoking; **"prohibido el paso"**
"no entry"

prójimo, -a ['proximo, a] *nm/f*
fellow man; (*vecino*) neighbour

prólogo ['proloxo] *nm* prologue

prolongar [prolon'xar] *vt* to extend;
(*reunión etc*) to prolong; (*calle, tubo*)
to extend

promedio [pro'meðjo] *nm* average;
(*de distancia*) middle, mid-point

promesa [pro'mesa] *nf* promise

prometer [prome'ter] *vt* to promise
▷ *vi* to show promise; **prometerse** *vr*
(*novios*) to get engaged; **prometido,
-a** *adj* promised; engaged ▷ *nm/f*
fiancé/fiancée

prominente [promi'nente] *adj*
prominent

promoción [promo'θjon] *nf*
promotion

promotor [promo'tor] *nm* promoter;
(*instigador*) instigator

promover [promo'βer] *vt* to
promote; (*causar*) to cause; (*instigar*) to
instigate, stir up

promulgar [promul'xar] *vt* to
promulgate; (*anunciar*) to proclaim

pronombre [pro'nombre] *nm*
pronoun

pronosticar [pronosti'kar] *vt* to
predict, foretell, forecast; **pronóstico**
nm prediction, forecast; **pronóstico
del tiempo** weather forecast

pronto, -a ['pronto, a] *adj* (*rápido*)
prompt, quick; (*preparado*) ready ▷ *adv*
quickly, promptly; (*en seguida*) at once,
right away; (*dentro de poco*) soon;
(*temprano*) early ▷ *nm*: **tiene unos
~s muy malos** he gets ratty all of a
sudden (*inf*); **de ~** suddenly; **por lo ~**
meanwhile, for the present

pronunciación [pronunθja'θjon] *nf*
pronunciation

pronunciar [pronun'θjar] *vt* to
pronounce; (*discurso*) to make, deliver;
pronunciarse *vr* to revolt, rebel;
(*declararse*) to declare o.s.

propagación [propaxa'θjon] *nf*
propagation

propaganda [propa'xanda] *nf* (*Pol*)
propaganda; (*Com*) advertising

propenso, -a [pro'penso, a] *adj*
inclined to; **ser ~ a** to be inclined to,
have a tendency to

propicio, -a [pro'piθjo, a] *adj*

favourable, propitious

propiedad [propje'ðað] nf property; (posesión) possession, ownership; **propiedad particular** private property

propietario, -a [propje'tarjo, a] nm/f owner, proprietor

propina [pro'pina] nf tip

propio, -a ['propjo, a] adj own, of one's own; (característico) characteristic, typical; (debido) proper; (mismo) selfsame, very; **el ~ ministro** the minister himself; **¿tienes casa propia?** have you a house of your own?

proponer [propo'ner] vt to propose, put forward; (problema) to pose; **proponerse** vr to propose, intend

proporción [propor'θjon] nf proportion; (Mat) ratio; **proporciones** nfpl (dimensiones) dimensions; (fig) size sg; **proporcionado, -a** adj proportionate; (regular) medium, middling; (justo) just right; **proporcionar** vt (dar) to give, supply, provide

proposición [proposi'θjon] nf proposition; (propuesta) proposal

propósito [pro'posito] nm purpose; (intento) aim, intention ▷ adv: **a ~** by the way, incidentally; (a posta) on purpose, deliberately; **a ~ de** about, with regard to

propuesta [pro'pwesta] vb V **proponer** ▷ nf proposal

propulsar [propul'sar] vt to drive, propel; (fig) to promote, encourage; **propulsión** nf propulsion; **propulsión a chorro** o **por reacción** jet propulsion

prórroga ['prorroxa] nf extension; (Jur) stay; (Com) deferment; (Deporte) extra time; **prorrogar** vt (período) to extend; (decisión) to defer, postpone

prosa ['prosa] nf prose

proseguir [prose'xir] vt to continue, carry on ▷ vi to continue, go on

prospecto [pros'pekto] nm prospectus

prosperar [prospe'rar] vi to prosper, thrive, flourish; **prosperidad** nf prosperity; (éxito) success; **próspero,**

-a adj prosperous, flourishing; (que tiene éxito) successful

prostíbulo [pros'tiβulo] nm brothel (BRIT), house of prostitution (US)

prostitución [prostitu'θjon] nf prostitution

prostituir [prosti'twir] vt to prostitute; **prostituirse** vr to prostitute o.s., become a prostitute

prostituta [prosti'tuta] nf prostitute

protagonista [protaxo'nista] nmf protagonist

protección [protek'θjon] nf protection

protector, a [protek'tor, a] adj protective, protecting ▷ nm/f protector

proteger [prote'xer] vt to protect; **protegido, -a** nm/f protégé/protégée

proteína [prote'ina] nf protein

protesta [pro'testa] nf protest; (declaración) protestation

protestante [protes'tante] adj Protestant

protestar [protes'tar] vt to protest, declare ▷ vi to protest

protocolo [proto'kolo] nm protocol

prototipo [proto'tipo] nm prototype

provecho [pro'βetʃo] nm advantage, benefit; (Finanzas) profit; **¡buen ~!** bon appétit!; **en ~ de** to the benefit of; **sacar ~ de** to benefit from, profit by

provenir [proβe'nir] vi: **~ de** to come o stem from

proverbio [pro'βerβjo] nm proverb

providencia [proβi'ðenθja] nf providence

provincia [pro'βinθja] nf province

provisión [proβi'sjon] nf provision; (abastecimiento) provision, supply; (medida) measure, step

provisional [proβisjo'nal] adj provisional

provocar [proβo'kar] vt to provoke; (alentar) to tempt, invite; (causar) to bring about, lead to; (promover) to promote; (estimular) to rouse, stimulate; **¿te provoca un café?** (CAM) would you like a coffee?; **provocativo,**

-a adj provocative
proxeneta [prokse'neta] nm pimp
próximamente [proksima'mente] adv shortly, soon
proximidad [proksimi'ðað] nf closeness, proximity; **próximo, -a** adj near, close; (vecino) neighbouring; (siguiente) next
proyectar [projek'tar] vt (objeto) to hurl, throw; (luz) to cast, shed; (Cine) to screen, show; (planear) to plan
proyectil [projek'til] nm projectile, missile
proyecto [pro'jekto] nm plan; (estimación de costo) detailed estimate
proyector [projek'tor] nm (Cine) projector
prudencia [pru'ðenθja] nf (sabiduría) wisdom; (cuidado) care; **prudente** adj sensible, wise; (conductor) careful
prueba etc ['prweβa] vb V **probar** ▷ nf proof; (ensayo) test, trial; (degustación) tasting, sampling; (de ropa) fitting; **a ~** on trial; **a ~ de** proof against; **a ~ de agua/fuego** waterproof/fireproof; **someter a ~** to put to the test
psico... [siko] prefijo psycho...; **psicología** nf psychology; **psicológico, -a** adj psychological; **psicólogo, -a** nm/f psychologist; **psicópata** nmf psychopath; **psicosis** nf inv psychosis
psiquiatra [si'kjatra] nmf psychiatrist; **psiquiátrico, -a** adj psychiatric
PSOE [pe'soe] (ESP) nm abr = **Partido Socialista Obrero Español**
púa ['pua] nf (Bot, Zool) prickle, spine; (para guitarra) plectrum (BRIT), pick (US); **alambre de ~** barbed wire
pubertad [puβer'tað] nf puberty
publicación [puβlika'θjon] nf publication
publicar [puβli'kar] vt (editar) to publish; (hacer público) to publicize; (divulgar) to make public, divulge
publicidad [puβliθi'ðað] nf publicity; (Com: propaganda)

advertising; **publicitario, -a** adj publicity cpd; advertising cpd
público, -a ['puβliko, a] adj public ▷ nm public; (Teatro etc) audience
puchero [pu'tʃero] nm (Culin: guiso) stew; (: olla) cooking pot; **hacer ~s** to pout
pucho ['putʃo] (cs: fam) nm cigarette, fag (BRIT)
pude etc vb V **poder**
pudiente [pu'ðjente] adj (rico) wealthy, well-to-do
pudiera etc vb V **poder**
pudor [pu'ðor] nm modesty
pudrir [pu'ðrir] vt to rot; **pudrirse** vr to rot, decay
pueblo ['pweβlo] nm people, (nación) nation; (aldea) village
puedo etc vb V **poder**
puente ['pwente] nm bridge; **hacer ~** (fam) to take extra days off work between 2 public holidays; to take a long weekend; **puente aéreo** shuttle service, **puente colgante** suspension bridge; **puente levadizo** drawbridge

🔵 **HACER PUENTE**
🔵
🔵 When a public holiday in Spain
🔵 falls on a Tuesday or Thursday it is
🔵 common practice for employers
🔵 to make the Monday or Friday
🔵 a holiday as well and to give
🔵 everyone a four-day weekend. This
🔵 is known as **hacer puente**. When
🔵 a named public holiday such as the
🔵 **Día de la Constitución** falls on a
🔵 Tuesday or Thursday, people refer
🔵 to the whole holiday period as e.g.
🔵 the **puente de la Constitución**.

puerco, -a ['pwerko, a] nm/f pig/ sow ▷ adj (sucio) dirty, filthy; (obsceno) disgusting; **puerco espín** porcupine
pueril [pwe'ril] adj childish
puerro ['pwerro] nm leek
puerta ['pwerta] nf door; (de jardín) gate; (portal) doorway; (fig) gateway;

(*portería*) goal; **a la ~** at the door; **a ~ cerrada** behind closed doors; **puerta giratoria** revolving door

puerto ['pwerto] *nm* port; (*paso*) pass; (*fig*) haven, refuge

Puerto Rico [pwerto'riko] *nm* Puerto Rico; **puertorriqueño, -a** *adj, nm/f* Puerto Rican

pues [pwes] *adv* (*entonces*) then; (*bueno*) well, well then; (*así que*) so ▷ *conj* (*ya que*) since; **i~ sí!** yes!, certainly!

puesta ['pwesta] *nf* (*apuesta*) bet, stake; **puesta al día** updating; **puesta a punto** fine tuning; **puesta de sol** sunset; **puesta en marcha** starting

puesto, -a ['pwesto, a] *pp de* **poner** ▷ *adj*: **tener algo ~** to have sth on, be wearing sth ▷ *nm* (*lugar, posición*) place; (*trabajo*) post, job; (*Com*) stall ▷ *conj*: **~ que** since, as

púgil ['puxil] *nm* boxer

pulga ['pulɣa] *nf* flea

pulgada [pul'ɣaða] *nf* inch

pulgar [pul'ɣar] *nm* thumb

pulir [pu'lir] *vt* to polish; (*alisar*) to smooth; (*fig*) to polish up, touch up

pulmón [pul'mon] *nm* lung; **pulmonía** *nf* pneumonia

pulpa ['pulpa] *nf* pulp; (*de fruta*) flesh, soft part

pulpería [pulpe'ria] (*LAM*) *nf* (*tienda*) small grocery store

púlpito ['pulpito] *nm* pulpit

pulpo ['pulpo] *nm* octopus

pulque ['pulke] *nm* pulque

● **PULQUE**
●
● **Pulque** is a thick, white, alcoholic
● drink which is very popular in
● Mexico. In ancient times it was
● considered sacred by the Aztecs.
● It is produced by fermenting the
● juice of the **maguey**, a Mexican
● cactus similar to the agave. It can
● be drunk by itself or mixed with
● fruit or vegetable juice.

pulsación [pulsa'θjon] *nf* beat; **pulsaciones** pulse rate

pulsar [pul'sar] *vt* (*tecla*) to touch, tap; (*Mús*) to play; (*botón*) to press, push ▷ *vi* to pulsate; (*latir*) to beat, throb

pulsera [pul'sera] *nf* bracelet

pulso ['pulso] *nm* (*Anat*) pulse; (*fuerza*) strength; (*firmeza*) steadiness, steady hand

pulverizador [pulβeriθa'ðor] *nm* spray, spray gun

pulverizar [pulβeri'θar] *vt* to pulverize; (*líquido*) to spray

puna ['puna] (*CAM*) *nf* mountain sickness

punta ['punta] *nf* point, tip; (*extremo*) end; (*fig*) touch, trace; **horas ~** peak *o* rush hours; **sacar ~ a** to sharpen

puntada [pun'taða] *nf* (*Costura*) stitch

puntal [pun'tal] *nm* prop, support

puntapié [punta'pje] *nm* kick

puntería [punte'ria] *nf* (*de arma*) aim, aiming; (*destreza*) marksmanship

puntero, -a [pun'tero, a] *adj* leading ▷ *nm* (*palo*) pointer

puntiagudo, -a [puntja'ɣuðo, a] *adj* sharp, pointed

puntilla [pun'tiʎa] *nf* (*encaje*) lace edging *o* trim; **(andar) de ~s** (to walk) on tiptoe

punto ['punto] *nm* (*gen*) point; (*señal diminuta*) spot, dot; (*Costura, Med*) stitch; (*lugar*) spot, place; (*momento*) point, moment; **a ~** ready; **estar a ~ de** to be on the point of *o* about to; **en ~** on the dot; **hasta cierto ~** to some extent; **hacer ~** (*ESP: tejer*) to knit; **dos ~s** (*Ling*) colon; **punto de interrogación** question mark; **punto de vista** point of view, viewpoint; **punto final** full stop (*BRIT*), period (*US*); **punto muerto** dead center; (*Auto*) neutral (*gear*); **punto y aparte** (*en dictado*) full stop, new paragraph; **punto y coma** semicolon

puntocom [punto'kom] *adj inv, nf inv* dotcom

puntuación [puntwaˈθjon] *nf* punctuation; (*puntos: en examen*) mark(s) (*pl*); (*Deporte*) score

puntual [punˈtwal] *adj* (*a tiempo*) punctual; (*exacto*) exact, accurate; **puntualidad** *nf* punctuality; exactness, accuracy

puntuar [punˈtwar] *vi* (*Deporte*) to score, count

punzante [punˈθante] *adj* (*dolor*) shooting, sharp; (*herramienta*) sharp

puñado [puˈɲaðo] *nm* handful

puñal [puˈɲal] *nm* dagger; **puñalada** *nf* stab

puñetazo [puɲeˈtaθo] *nm* punch

puño [ˈpuɲo] *nm* (*Anat*) fist; (*cantidad*) fistful, handful; (*Costura*) cuff; (*de herramienta*) handle

pupila [puˈpila] *nf* pupil

pupitre [puˈpitre] *nm* desk

puré [puˈre] *nm* purée; (*sopa*) (thick) soup; **puré de papas** (*LAM*) mashed potatoes; **puré de patatas** (*ESP*) mashed potatoes

purga [ˈpurɣa] *nf* purge; **purgante** *adj, nm* purgative

purgatorio [purɣaˈtorjo] *nm* purgatory

purificar [purifiˈkar] *vt* to purify; (*refinar*) to refine

puritano, -a [puriˈtano, a] *adj* (*actitud*) puritanical; (*iglesia, tradición*) puritan ▷ *nm/f* puritan

puro, -a [ˈpuro, a] *adj* pure; (*verdad*) simple, plain ▷ *nm* cigar

púrpura [ˈpurpura] *nf* purple

pus [pus] *nm* pus

puse *etc vb* V **poder**

pusiera *etc vb* V **poder**

puta [ˈputa] (*fam!*) *nf* whore, prostitute

putrefacción [putrefakˈθjon] *nf* rotting, putrefaction

PVP *nm abr* (= *precio de venta al público*) RRP

pyme, PYME [ˈpime] *nf abr* (= *Pequeña y Mediana Empresa*) SME

○ **PALABRA CLAVE**

que [ke] *conj* **1** (*con oración subordinada: muchas veces no se traduce*) that; **dijo que vendría** he said (that) he would come; **espero que lo encuentres** I hope (that) you find it; *V tb* **el**

2 (*en oración independiente*): **¡que entre!** send him in; **¡que aproveche!** enjoy your meal!; **¡que se mejore tu padre!** I hope your father gets better

3 (*enfático*): **¿me quieres? – ¡que sí!** do you love me? – of course!

4 (*consecutivo: muchas veces no se traduce*) that; **es tan grande que no lo puedo levantar** it's so big (that) I can't lift it

5 (*comparaciones*) than; **yo que tú/él** if I were you/him; *V tb* **más, menos, mismo**

6 (*valor disyuntivo*): **que le guste o no** whether he likes it or not; **que venga o que no venga** whether he comes or not

7 (*porque*): **no puedo, que tengo que quedarme en casa** I can't, I've got to stay in
▷ *pron* **1** (*cosa*) that, which; (+ *prep*) which; **el sombrero que te compraste** the hat (that *o* which) you bought; **la cama en que dormí** the bed (that *o* which) I slept in
2 (*persona: suj*) that, who; (: *objeto*) that, whom; **el amigo que me acompañó al museo** the friend that *o* who went to the museum with me; **la chica que invité** the girl (that *o* whom) I invited

qué [ke] *adj* what?, which? ▷ *pron* what?; **¡~ divertido!** how funny!; **¿~ edad tienes?** how old are you?; **¿de ~ me hablas?** what are you saying to me?; **¿~ tal?** how are you?, how are things?; **¿~ hay (de nuevo)?** what's new?

quebrado, -a [ke'βraðo, a] *adj* (*roto*) broken ▷ *nm/f* bankrupt ▷ *nm* (*Mat*) fraction

quebrantar [keβran'tar] *vt* (*infringir*) to violate, transgress

quebrar [ke'βrar] *vt* to break, smash ▷ *vi* to go bankrupt

quedar [ke'ðar] *vi* to stay, remain; (*encontrarse: sitio*) to be; (*haber aún*) to remain, be left; **quedarse** *vr* to remain, stay (behind); **~se (con) algo** to keep sth; **~ en** (*acordar*) to agree on/to; **~ en nada** to come to nothing; **~ por hacer** to be still to be done; **~ ciego/mudo** to be left blind/dumb; **no te queda bien ese vestido** that dress doesn't suit you; **eso queda muy lejos** that's a long way (away); **quedamos a las seis** we agreed to meet at six

quedo, -a ['keðo, a] *adj* still ▷ *adv* softly, gently

quehacer [kea'θer] *nm* task, job; **quehaceres (domésticos)** *nmpl* household chores

queja ['kexa] *nf* complaint; **quejarse** *vr* (*enfermo*) to moan, groan; (*protestar*) to complain; **quejarse de que** to complain (about the fact) that; **quejido** *nm* moan

quemado, -a [ke'maðo, a] *adj* burnt

quemadura [kema'ðura] *nf* burn, scald

quemar [ke'mar] *vt* to burn; (*fig: malgastar*) to burn up, squander ▷ *vi* to be burning hot; **quemarse** *vr* (*consumirse*) to burn (up); (*del sol*) to get sunburnt

quemarropa [kema'rropa]: **a ~** *adv* point-blank

quepo *etc vb* V **caber**

querella [ke'reʎa] *nf* (*Jur*) charge; (*disputa*) dispute

⊙ **PALABRA CLAVE**

querer [ke'rer] *vt* **1** (*desear*) to want; **quiero más dinero** I want more money; **quisiera** *o* **querría un té** I'd like a tea; **sin querer** unintentionally; **quiero ayudar/que vayas** I want to help/you to go
2 (*preguntas: para pedir algo*): **¿quiere abrir la ventana?** could you open the window?; **¿quieres echarme una mano?** can you give me a hand?
3 (*amar*) to love; (*tener cariño a*) to be fond of; **te quiero** I love you; **quiere mucho a sus hijos** he's very fond of his children
4 **le pedí que me dejara ir pero no quiso** I asked him to let me go but he refused

querido, -a [ke'riðo, a] *adj* dear ▷ *nm/f* darling; (*amante*) lover

queso ['keso] *nm* cheese; **queso crema** (*LAM*) cream cheese; **queso de untar** (*ESP*) cream cheese; **queso manchego** sheep's milk cheese made in La Mancha; **queso rallado** grated cheese

quicio ['kiθjo] *nm* hinge; **sacar a algn de ~** to get on sb's nerves

quiebra ['kjeβra] *nf* break, split; (*Com*) bankruptcy; (*Econ*) slump

quiebro ['kjeβro] *nm* (*del cuerpo*)

swerve

quien [kjen] *pron* who; **hay ~ piensa que** there are those who think that; **no hay ~ lo haga** no-one will do it

quién [kjen] *pron* who, whom; **¿~ es?** who's there?

quienquiera [kjen'kjera] (*pl* **quienesquiera**) *pron* whoever

quiero *etc vb* V **querer**

quieto, -a ['kjeto, a] *adj* still; (*carácter*) placid

> No confundir **quieto** con la palabra inglesa *quiet*.

quietud *nf* stillness

quilate [ki'late] *nm* carat

químico, -a ['kimiko, a] *adj* chemical ▷ *nm/f* chemist ▷ *nf* chemistry

quincalla [kin'kaʎa] *nf* hardware, ironmongery (BRIT)

quince ['kinθe] *num* fifteen; **~ días** a fortnight; **quinceañero, -a** *nm/f* teenager; **quincena** *nf* fortnight; (*pago*) fortnightly pay; **quincenal** *adj* fortnightly

quiniela [ki'njela] *nf* football pools *pl*; **quinielas** *nfpl* (*impreso*) pools coupon *sg*

quinientos, -as [ki'njentos, as] *adj*, *num* five hundred

quinto, -a ['kinto, a] *adj* fifth ▷ *nf* country house; (*Mil*) call-up, draft

quiosco ['kjosko] *nm* (*de música*) bandstand; (*de periódicos*) news stand

quirófano [ki'rofano] *nm* operating theatre

quirúrgico, -a [ki'rurxiko, a] *adj* surgical

quise *etc vb* V **querer**

quisiera *etc vb* V **querer**

quisquilloso, -a [kiski'ʎoso, a] *adj* (*susceptible*) touchy; (*meticuloso*) pernickety

quiste ['kiste] *nm* cyst

quitaesmalte [kitaes'malte] *nm* nail-polish remover

quitamanchas [kita'mantʃas] *nm inv* stain remover

quitanieves [kita'njeβes] *nm inv* snowplough (BRIT), snowplow (US)

quitar [ki'tar] *vt* to remove, take away; (*ropa*) to take off; (*dolor*) to relieve; **¡quita de ahí!** get away!; **quitarse** *vr* to withdraw; (*ropa*) to take off; **se quitó el sombrero** he took off his hat

Quito ['kito] *n* Quito

quizá(s) [ki'θa(s)] *adv* perhaps, maybe

q

r

rábano ['raβano] *nm* radish; **me importa un ~** I don't give a damn

rabia ['raβja] *nf* (*Med*) rabies *sg*; (*ira*) fury, rage; **rabiar** *vi* to have rabies; to rage, be furious; **rabiar por algo** to long for sth

rabieta [ra'βjeta] *nf* tantrum, fit of temper

rabino [ra'βino] *nm* rabbi

rabioso, -a [ra'βjoso, a] *adj* rabid; (*fig*) furious

rabo ['raβo] *nm* tail

racha ['ratʃa] *nf* gust of wind; **buena/mala ~** spell of good/bad luck

racial [ra'θjal] *adj* racial, race *cpd*

racimo [ra'θimo] *nm* bunch

ración [ra'θjon] *nf* portion; **raciones** *nfpl* rations

racional [raθjo'nal] *adj* (*razonable*) reasonable; (*lógico*) rational

racionar [raθjo'nar] *vt* to ration (out)

racismo [ra'θismo] *nm* racism; **racista** *adj, nm* racist

radar [ra'ðar] *nm* radar

radiador [raðja'ðor] *nm* radiator

radiante [ra'ðjante] *adj* radiant

radical [raði'kal] *adj, nmf* radical

radicar [raði'kar] *vi*: **~ en** (*dificultad, problema*) to lie in; (*solución*) to consist in

radio ['raðjo] *nf* radio; (*aparato*) radio (set) ▷ *nm* (*Mat*) radius; (*Quím*) radium; **radioactividad** *nf* radioactivity; **radioactivo, -a** *adj* radioactive; **radiografía** *nf* X-ray; **radioterapia** *nf* radiotherapy; **radioyente** *nmf* listener

ráfaga ['rafaxa] *nf* gust; (*de luz*) flash; (*de tiros*) burst

raíz [ra'iθ] *nf* root; **a ~ de** as a result of; **raíz cuadrada** square root

raja ['raxa] *nf* (*de melón etc*) slice; (*grieta*) crack; **rajar** *vt* to split; (*fam*) to slash; **rajarse** *vr* to split, crack; **rajarse de** to back out of

rajatabla [raxa'taβla]: **a ~** *adv* (*estrictamente*) strictly, to the letter

rallador [raʎa'ðor] *nm* grater

rallar [ra'ʎar] *vt* to grate

rama ['rama] *nf* branch; **ramaje** *nm* branches *pl*, foliage; **ramal** *nm* (*de cuerda*) strand; (*Ferro*) branch line (*BRIT*); (*Auto*) branch (road) (*BRIT*)

rambla ['rambla] *nf* (*avenida*) avenue

ramo ['ramo] *nm* branch; (*sección*) department, section

rampa ['rampa] *nf* ramp; **rampa de acceso** entrance ramp

rana ['rana] *nf* frog; **salto de ~** leapfrog

ranchero [ran'tʃero] (*MÉX*) *nm* (*hacendado*) rancher; smallholder

rancho ['rantʃo] *nm* (*grande*) ranch; (*pequeño*) small farm

rancio, -a ['ranθjo, a] *adj* (*comestibles*) rancid; (*vino*) aged, mellow; (*fig*) ancient

rango ['rango] *nm* rank, standing

ranura [ra'nura] *nf* groove; (*de teléfono etc*) slot

rapar [ra'par] *vt* to shave; (*los cabellos*) to crop

rapaz [ra'paθ] (*nf ~a*) *nmf* young

boy/girl ▷ *adj* (*Zool*) predatory
rape ['rape] *nm* (*pez*) monkfish; **al
~** cropped
rapé [ra'pe] *nm* snuff
rapidez [rapi'ðeθ] *nf* speed, rapidity;
rápido, -a *adj* fast, quick ▷ *adv*
quickly ▷ *nm* (*Ferro*) express; **rápidos**
nmpl rapids
rapiña [ra'piɲa] *nm* robbery; **ave de
~** bird of prey
raptar [rap'tar] *vt* to kidnap; **rapto**
nm kidnapping; (*impulso*) sudden
impulse; (*éxtasis*) ecstasy, rapture
raqueta [ra'keta] *nf* racquet
raquítico, -a [ra'kitiko, a] *adj*
stunted; (*fig*) poor, inadequate
rareza [ra'reθa] *nf* rarity; (*fig*)
eccentricity
raro, -a ['raro, a] *adj* (*poco común*)
rare; (*extraño*) odd, strange; (*excepcional*)
remarkable
ras [ras] *nm*: **a ~ de** level with; **a ~ de
tierra** at ground level
rasar [ra'sar] *vt* (*igualar*) to level
rascacielos [raska'θjelos] *nm inv*
skyscraper
rascar [ras'kar] *vt* (*con las uñas etc*) to
scratch; (*raspar*) to scrape; **rascarse** *vr*
to scratch (o.s.)
rasgar [ras'ɣar] *vt* to tear, rip (up)
rasgo ['rasɣo] *nm* (*con pluma*) stroke;
rasgos *nmpl* (*facciones*) features,
characteristics; **a grandes ~s** in
outline, broadly
rasguño [ras'ɣuɲo] *nm* scratch
raso, -a ['raso, a] *adj* (*liso*) flat, level;
(*a baja altura*) very low ▷ *nm* satin;
cielo ~ clear sky
raspadura [raspa'ðura] *nf* (*acto*)
scrape, scraping; (*marca*) scratch;
raspaduras *nfpl* (*de papel etc*)
scrapings
raspar [ras'par] *vt* to scrape; (*arañar*)
to scratch; (*limar*) to file
rastra ['rastra] *nf* (*Agr*) rake; **a ~s** by
dragging; (*fig*) unwillingly
rastrear [rastre'ar] *vt* (*seguir*) to track
rastrero, -a [ras'trero, a] *adj* (*Bot,*

Zool) creeping; (*fig*) despicable, mean
rastrillo [ras'triʎo] *nm* rake
rastro ['rastro] *nm* (*Agr*) rake; (*pista*)
track, trail; (*vestigio*) trace; **el R~** (*ESP*)
the Madrid fleamarket
rasurado [rasu'raðo] (*MÉX*) *nm*
shaving; **rasuradora** [rasura'ðora]
(*MÉX*) *nf* electric shaver; **rasurar**
[rasu'rar] (*MÉX*) *vt* to shave; **rasurarse**
vr to shave
rata ['rata] *nf* rat
ratear [rate'ar] *vt* (*robar*) to steal
ratero, -a [ra'tero, a] *adj*
light-fingered ▷ *nm/f* (*carterista*)
pickpocket; (*ladrón*) petty thief
rato ['rato] *nm* while, short time;
a ~s from time to time; **hay para ~**
there's still a long way to go; **al poco
~** soon afterwards; **pasar el ~** to kill
time; **pasar un buen/mal ~** to have a
good/rough time; **en mis ~s libres** in
my spare time
ratón [ra'ton] *nm* mouse; **ratonera**
nf mousetrap
raudal [rau'ðal] *nm* torrent; **a ~es** in
abundance
raya ['raja] *nf* line; (*marca*) scratch,
(*en tela*) stripe; (*de pelo*) parting; (*límite*)
boundary; (*pez*) ray; (*puntuación*) dash;
a ~s striped; **pasarse de la ~** to go
too far; **tener a ~** to keep in check;
rayar *vt* to line; to scratch; (*subrayar*)
to underline ▷ *vi*: **rayar en** *o* **con** to
border on
rayo ['rajo] *nm* (*del sol*) ray, beam, (*de
luz*) shaft; (*en una tormenta*) (flash of)
lightning; **rayos X** X-rays
raza ['raθa] *nf* race; **raza humana**
human race
razón [ra'θon] *nf* reason; (*justicia*)
right, justice; (*razonamiento*) reasoning;
(*motivo*) reason, motive; (*Mat*) ratio:
a ~ de 10 cada día at the rate of 10
a day; **en ~ de** with regard to; **dar
~ a algn** to agree that sb is right;
tener ~ to be right; **razón de ser**
raison d'être; **razón directa/inversa**
direct/inverse proportion; **razonable**

adj reasonable; (*justo, moderado*) fair; **razonamiento** *nm* (*juicio*) judg(e)ment; (*argumento*) reasoning; **razonar** *vt, vi* to reason, argue

re [re] *nm* (*Mús*) D

reacción [reak'θjon] *nf* reaction; **avión a ~** jet plane; **reacción en cadena** chain reaction; **reaccionar** *vi* to react

reacio, -a [re'aθjo, a] *adj* stubborn

reactivar [reakti'βar] *vt* to revitalize

reactor [reak'tor] *nm* reactor

real [re'al] *adj* real; (*del rey, fig*) royal

realidad [reali'ðað] *nf* reality, fact; (*verdad*) truth

realista [rea'lista] *nmf* realist

realización [realiθa'θjon] *nf* fulfilment

realizador, a [realiθa'ðor, a] *nm/f* film-maker

realizar [reali'θar] *vt* (*objetivo*) to achieve; (*plan*) to carry out; (*viaje*) to make, undertake; **realizarse** *vr* to come about, come true

realmente [real'mente] *adv* really, actually

realzar [real'θar] *vt* to enhance; (*acentuar*) to highlight

reanimar [reani'mar] *vt* to revive; (*alentar*) to encourage; **reanimarse** *vr* to revive

reanudar [reanu'ðar] *vt* (*renovar*) to renew; (*historia, viaje*) to resume

reaparición [reapari'θjon] *nf* reappearance

rearme [re'arme] *nm* rearmament

rebaja [re'βaxa] *nf* (*Com*) reduction; (: *descuento*) discount; **rebajas** *nfpl* (*Com*) sale; **rebajar** *vt* (*bajar*) to lower; (*reducir*) to reduce; (*disminuir*) to lessen; (*humillar*) to humble

rebanada [reβa'naða] *nf* slice

rebañar [reβa'ɲar] *vt* (*comida*) to scrape up; (*plato*) to scrape clean

rebaño [re'βaɲo] *nm* herd; (*de ovejas*) flock

rebatir [reβa'tir] *vt* to refute

rebeca [re'βeka] *nf* cardigan

rebelarse [reβe'larse] *vr* to rebel, revolt

rebelde [re'βelde] *adj* rebellious; (*niño*) unruly ▷ *nmf* rebel; **rebeldía** *nf* rebelliousness; (*desobediencia*) disobedience

rebelión [reβe'ljon] *nf* rebellion

reblandecer [reβlande'θer] *vt* to soften

rebobinar [reβoβi'nar] *vt* (*cinta, película de video*) to rewind

rebosante [reβo'sante] *adj* overflowing

rebosar [reβo'sar] *vi* (*líquido, recipiente*) to overflow; (*abundar*) to abound, be plentiful

rebotar [reβo'tar] *vt* to bounce; (*rechazar*) to repel ▷ *vi* (*pelota*) to bounce; (*bala*) to ricochet; **rebote** *nm* rebound; **de rebote** on the rebound

rebozado, -a [reβo'θaðo, a] *adj* fried in batter *o* breadcrumbs

rebozar [reβo'θar] *vt* to wrap up; (*Culin*) to fry in batter *o* breadcrumbs

rebuscado, -a [reβus'kaðo, a] *adj* (*amanerado*) affected; (*palabra*) recherché; (*idea*) far-fetched

rebuscar [reβus'kar] *vi*: **~ (en/por)** to search carefully (in/for)

recado [re'kaðo] *nm* (*mensaje*) message; (*encargo*) errand; **tomar un ~** (*Tel*) to take a message

recaer [reka'er] *vi* to relapse; **~ en** to fall to *o* on; (*criminal etc*) to fall back into, relapse into; **recaída** *nf* relapse

recalcar [rekal'kar] *vt* (*fig*) to stress, emphasize

recalentar [rekalen'tar] *vt* (*volver a calentar*) to reheat; (*calentar demasiado*) to overheat

recámara [re'kamara] (*MÉX*) *nf* bedroom

recambio [re'kambjo] *nm* spare; (*de pluma*) refill

recapacitar [rekapaθi'tar] *vi* to reflect

recargado, -a [rekar'ɣaðo, a] *adj* overloaded

recargar [rekar'xar] vt to overload; (batería) to recharge; ~ **el saldo de** (Tel) to top up; **recargo** nm surcharge; (aumento) increase

recatado, -a [reka'taðo, a] adj (modesto) modest, demure; (prudente) cautious

recaudación [rekauða'θjon] nf (acción) collection; (cantidad) takings pl; (en deporte) gate; **recaudador, a** nm/f tax collector

recelar [reθe'lar] vt: ~ **que ...** (sospechar) to suspect that ...; (temer) to fear that ... ▷ vi: ~ **de** to distrust; **recelo** nm distrust, suspicion

recepción [reθep'θjon] nf reception; **recepcionista** nmf receptionist

receptor, a [reθep'tor, a] nm/f recipient ▷ nm (Tel) receiver

recesión [reθe'sjon] nf (Com) recession

receta [re'θeta] nf (Culin) recipe; (Med) prescription

No confundir **receta** con la palabra inglesa receipt.

rechazar [retʃa'θar] vt to reject; (oferta) to turn down; (ataque) to repel

rechazo [re'tʃaθo] nm rejection

rechinar [retʃi'nar] vi to creak; (dientes) to grind

rechistar [retʃis'tar] vi: **sin ~** without a murmur

rechoncho, -a [re'tʃontʃo, a] (fam) adj thickset (BRIT), heavy-set (US)

rechupete [retʃu'pete]: **de ~** adj (comida) delicious, scrumptious

recibidor [reθiβi'ðor] nm entrance hall

recibimiento [reθiβi'mjento] nm reception, welcome

recibir [reθi'βir] vt to receive; (dar la bienvenida) to welcome ▷ vi to entertain; **recibo** nm receipt

reciclable [reθi'klaβle] adj recyclable

reciclar [reθi'klar] vt to recycle

recién [re'θjen] adv recently, newly; **los ~ casados** the newly-weds; **el ~ llegado** the newcomer; **el ~ nacido** the newborn child

reciente [re'θjente] adj recent; (fresco) fresh

recinto [re'θinto] nm enclosure; (área) area, place

recio, -a ['reθjo, a] adj strong, tough; (voz) loud ▷ adv hard, loud(ly)

recipiente [reθi'pjente] nm receptacle

recíproco, -a [re'θiproko, a] adj reciprocal

recital [reθi'tal] nm (Mús) recital; (Literatura) reading

recitar [reθi'tar] vt to recite

reclamación [reklama'θjon] nf claim, demand; (queja) complaint; **libro de reclamaciones** complaints book

reclamar [rekla'mar] vt to claim, demand ▷ vi: ~ **contra** to complain about; **reclamo** nm (anuncio) advertisement; (tentación) attraction

reclinar [rekli'nar] vt to recline, lean; **reclinarse** vr to lean back

reclusión [reklu'sjon] nf (prisión) prison; (refugio) seclusion

recluta [re'kluta] nmf recruit ▷ nf recruitment; **reclutar** vt (datos) to collect; (dinero) to collect up; **reclutamiento** nm recruitment

recobrar [reko'βrar] vt (salud) to recover; (rescatar) to get back; **recobrarse** vr to recover

recodo [re'koðo] nm (de río, camino) bend

recogedor [rekoxe'ðor] nm dustpan

recoger [reko'xer] vt to collect; (Agr) to harvest; (levantar) to pick up; (juntar) to gather; (pasar a buscar) to come for, get; (dar asilo) to give shelter to; (faldas) to gather up; (pelo) to put up; **recogerse** vr (retirarse) to retire; **recogido, -a** adj (lugar) quiet, secluded; (pequeño) small ▷ nf (Correos) collection; (Agr) harvest

recolección [rekolek'θjon] nf (Agr) harvesting; (colecta) collection

recomendación [rekomenda'θjon] nf (sugerencia) suggestion, recommendation; (*referencia*) reference

recomendar [rekomen'dar] *vt* to suggest, recommend; (*confiar*) to entrust

recompensa [rekom'pensa] *nf* reward, recompense; **recompensar** *vt* to reward, recompense

reconciliación [rekonθilja'θjon] *nf* reconciliation

reconciliar [rekonθi'ljar] *vt* to reconcile; **reconciliarse** *vr* to become reconciled

recóndito, -a [re'kondito, a] *adj* (*lugar*) hidden, secret

reconocer [rekono'θer] *vt* to recognize; (*registrar*) to search; (*Med*) to examine; **reconocido, -a** *adj* recognized; (*agradecido*) grateful; **reconocimiento** *nm* recognition; search; examination; gratitude; (*confesión*) admission

reconquista [rekon'kista] *nf* reconquest; **la R~** the Reconquest (of Spain)

reconstituyente [rekonstitu'jente] *nm* tonic

reconstruir [rekonstru'ir] *vt* to reconstruct

reconversión [rekonβer'sjon] *nf* (*reestructuración*) restructuring; **reconversión industrial** industrial rationalization

recopilación [rekopila'θjon] *nf* (*resumen*) summary; (*compilación*) compilation; **recopilar** *vt* to compile

récord ['rekorð] (*pl* **~s**) *adj inv, nm* record

recordar [rekor'ðar] *vt* (*acordarse de*) to remember; (*acordar a otro*) to remind ▷ *vi* to remember

▍ No confundir **recordar** con la palabra inglesa *record*.

recorrer [reko'rrer] *vt* (*país*) to cross, travel through; (*distancia*) to cover; (*registrar*) to search; (*repasar*) to look over; **recorrido** *nm* run, journey; **tren de largo recorrido** main-line train

recortar [rekor'tar] *vt* to cut out;

recorte *nm* (*acción, de prensa*) cutting; (*de telas, chapas*) trimming; **recorte presupuestario** budget cut

recostar [rekos'tar] *vt* to lean; **recostarse** *vr* to lie down

recoveco [reko'βeko] *nm* (*de camino, río etc*) bend; (*en casa*) cubby hole

recreación [rekrea'θjon] *nf* recreation

recrear [rekre'ar] *vt* (*entretener*) to entertain; (*volver a crear*) to recreate; **recreativo, -a** *adj* recreational; **recreo** *nm* recreation; (*Escol*) break, playtime

recriminar [rekrimi'nar] *vt* to reproach ▷ *vi* to recriminate; **recriminarse** *vr* to reproach each other

recrudecer [rekruðe'θer] *vt, vi* to worsen; **recrudecerse** *vr* to worsen

recta ['rekta] *nf* straight line

rectángulo, -a [rek'tangulo, a] *adj* rectangular ▷ *nm* rectangle

rectificar [rektifi'kar] *vt* to rectify; (*volverse recto*) to straighten ▷ *vi* to correct o.s.

rectitud [rekti'tuð] *nf* straightness

recto, -a ['rekto, a] *adj* straight; (*persona*) honest, upright; **siga todo ~** go straight on ▷ *nm* rectum

rector, a [rek'tor, a] *adj* governing

recuadro [re'kwaðro] *nm* box; (*Tip*) inset

recubrir [reku'βrir] *vt*: **~ (con)** (*pintura, crema*) to cover (with)

recuento [re'kwento] *nm* inventory; **hacer el ~ de** to count o reckon up

recuerdo [re'kwerðo] *nm* souvenir; **recuerdos** *nmpl* (*memorias*) memories; **¡~s a tu madre!** give my regards to your mother!

recular [reku'lar] *vi* to back down

recuperación [rekupera'θjon] *nf* recovery

recuperar [rekupe'rar] *vt* to recover; (*tiempo*) to make up; **recuperarse** *vr* to recuperate

recurrir [reku'rrir] *vi* (*Jur*) to appeal;

~ a to resort to; (*persona*) to turn to; **recurso** *nm* resort; (*medios*) means *pl*, resources *pl*; (*Jur*) appeal

red [reð] *nf* net, mesh; (*Ferro etc*) network; (*trampa*) trap; **la R~** (*Internet*) the Net

redacción [reðak'θjon] *nf* (*acción*) editing; (*personal*) editorial staff; (*Escol*) essay, composition

redactar [reðak'tar] *vt* to draw up, draft; (*periódico*) to edit

redactor, a [reðak'tor, a] *nm/f* editor

redada [re'ðaða] *nf* (*de policía*) raid, round-up

rededor [reðe'ðor] *nm*: **al** *o* **en ~** around, round about

redoblar [reðo'βlar] *vt* to redouble ▷ *vi* (*tambor*) to roll

redonda [re'ðonda] *nf*: **a la ~** around, round about

redondear [reðonde'ar] *vt* to round, round off

redondel [reðon'del] *nm* (*círculo*) circle; (*Taur*) bullring, arena

redondo, -a [re'ðondo, a] *adj* (*circular*) round; (*completo*) complete

reducción [reðuk'θjon] *nf* reduction

reducido, -a [reðu'θiðo, a] *adj* reduced; (*limitado*) limited; (*pequeño*) small

reducir [reðu'θir] *vt* to reduce; to limit; **reducirse** *vr* to diminish

redundancia [reðun'danθja] *nf* redundancy

reembolsar [re(e)mbol'sar] *vt* (*persona*) to reimburse; (*dinero*) to repay, pay back; (*depósito*) to refund; **reembolso** *nm* reimbursement; refund

reemplazar [re(e)mpla'θar] *vt* to replace; **reemplazo** *nm* replacement; **de reemplazo** (*Mil*) reserve

reencuentro [re(e)n'kwentro] *nm* reunion

reescribible [reeskri'βiβle] *adj* rewritable

refacción [refak'θjon] (*MÉX*) *nf* spare (part)

referencia [refe'renθja] *nf* reference; **con ~ a** with reference to

referéndum [refe'rendum] (*pl* **~s**) *nm* referendum

referente [refe'rente] *adj*: **~ a** concerning, relating to

réferi ['referi] (*LAM*) *nmf* referee

referir [refe'rir] *vt* (*contar*) to tell, recount; (*relacionar*) to refer, relate; **referirse** *vr*: **~se a** to refer to

refilón [refi'lon]: **de ~** *adv* obliquely

refinado, -a [refi'naðo, a] *adj* refined

refinar [refi'nar] *vt* to refine; **refinería** *nf* refinery

reflejar [refle'xar] *vt* to reflect; **reflejo, -a** *adj* reflected; (*movimiento*) reflex ▷ *nm* reflection; (*Anat*) reflex

reflexión [reflek'sjon] *nf* reflection; **reflexionar** *vt* to reflect on ▷ *vi* to reflect; (*detenerse*) to pause (to think)

reflexivo, -a [reflek'siβo, a] *adj* thoughtful; (*Ling*) reflexive

reforma [re'forma] *nf* reform; (*Arq etc*) repair; **reforma agraria** agrarian reform

reformar [refor'mar] *vt* to reform; (*modificar*) to change, alter; (*Arq*) to repair; **reformarse** *vr* to mend one's ways

reformatorio [reforma'torjo] *nm* reformatory

reforzar [refor'θar] *vt* to strengthen; (*Arq*) to reinforce; (*fig*) to encourage

refractario, -a [refrak'tarjo, a] *adj* (*Tec*) heat-resistant

refrán [re'fran] *nm* proverb, saying

refregar [refre'xar] *vt* to scrub

refrescante [refres'kante] *adj* refreshing, cooling

refrescar [refres'kar] *vt* to refresh ▷ *vi* to cool down; **refrescarse** *vr* to get cooler; (*tomar aire fresco*) to go out for a breath of fresh air; (*beber*) to have a drink

refresco [re'fresko] *nm* soft drink, cool drink; **"~s"** "refreshments"

refriega [re'frjeɣa] *nf* scuffle, brawl

refrigeración [refrixera'θjon] *nf*
refrigeration; (*de sala*) air-conditioning

refrigerador [refrixera'ðor] *nm*
refrigerator (BRIT), icebox (US)

refrigerar [refrixe'rar] *vt* to
refrigerate; (*sala*) to air-condition

refuerzo [re'fwerθo] *nm*
reinforcement; (*Tec*) support

refugiado, -a [refu'xjaðo, a] *nm/f*
refugee

refugiarse [refu'xjarse] *vr* to take
refuge, shelter

refugio [re'fuxjo] *nm* refuge;
(*protección*) shelter

refunfuñar [refunfu'ɲar] *vi* to
grunt, growl; (*quejarse*) to grumble

regadera [reɣa'ðera] *nf* watering can

regadío [reɣa'ðio] *nm* irrigated land

regalado, -a [reɣa'laðo, a] *adj*
comfortable, luxurious; (*gratis*) free,
for nothing

regalar [reɣa'lar] *vt* (*dar*) to give (as
a present); (*entregar*) to give away;
(*mimar*) to pamper, make a fuss of

regaliz [reɣa'liθ] *nm* liquorice

regalo [re'ɣalo] *nm* (*obsequio*) gift,
present; (*gusto*) pleasure

regañadientes [reɣaɲa'ðjentes]: **a ~**
adv reluctantly

regañar [reɣa'ɲar] *vt* to scold ▷*vi* to
grumble; **regañón, -ona** *adj* nagging

regar [re'ɣar] *vt* to water, irrigate;
(*fig*) to scatter, sprinkle

regatear [reɣate'ar] *vt* (*Com*) to
bargain over; (*escatimar*) to be mean
with ▷*vi* to bargain, haggle; (*Deporte*)
to dribble; **regateo** *nm* bargaining;
dribbling; (*del cuerpo*) swerve, dodge

regazo [re'ɣaθo] *nm* lap

regenerar [rexene'rar] *vt* to
regenerate

régimen ['reximen] (*pl* **regímenes**)
nm regime; (*Med*) diet

regimiento [rexi'mjento] *nm*
regiment

regio, -a ['rexjo, a] *adj* royal, regal;
(*fig: suntuoso*) splendid; (*cs: fam*) great,
terrific

región [re'xjon] *nf* region

regir [re'xir] *vt* to govern, rule;
(*dirigir*) to manage, run ▷*vi* to apply,
be in force

registrar [rexis'trar] *vt* (*buscar*) to
search; (: *en cajón*) to look through;
(*inspeccionar*) to inspect; (*anotar*)
to register, record; (*Inform*) to log;
registrarse *vr* to register; (*ocurrir*)
to happen

registro [re'xistro] *nm* (*acto*)
registration; (*Mús, libro*) register;
(*inspección*) inspection, search;
registro civil registry office

regla ['reɣla] *nf* (*ley*) rule, regulation;
(*de medir*) ruler, rule; (*Med: período*)
period; **en ~** in order

reglamentación [reɣlamenta'θjon]
nf (*acto*) regulation; (*lista*) rules *pl*

reglamentar [reɣlamen'tar] *vt*
to regulate; **reglamentario, -a** *adj*
statutory; **reglamento** *nm* rules *pl*,
regulations *pl*

regocijarse [reɣoθi'xarse] *vr*
(*alegrarse*) to rejoice; **regocijo** *nm* joy,
happiness

regrabadora [reɣraβa'ðora] *nf*
rewriter; **regrabadora de DVD** DVD
rewriter

regresar [reɣre'sar] *vi* to come back,
go back, return; **regreso** *nm* return

reguero [re'ɣero] *nm* (*de sangre etc*)
trickle; (*de humo*) trail

regulador [reɣula'ðor] *nm* regulator;
(*de radio etc*) knob, control

regular [reɣu'lar] *adj* regular;
(*normal*) normal, usual; (*común*)
ordinary; (*organizado*) regular, orderly;
(*mediano*) average; (*fam*) not bad, so-so
▷*adv* so-so, alright ▷*vt* (*controlar*) to
control, regulate; (*Tec*) to adjust; **por lo
~** as a rule; **regularidad** *nf* regularity;
regularizar *vt* to regularize

rehabilitación [reaβilita'θjon] *nf*
rehabilitation; (*Arq*) restoration

rehabilitar [reaβili'tar] *vt* to
rehabilitate; (*Arq*) to restore; (*reintegrar*)

to reinstate

rehacer [rea'θer] vt (reparar) to mend, repair; (volver a hacer) to redo, repeat; **rehacerse** vr (Med) to recover

rehén [re'en] nm hostage

rehuir [reu'ir] vt to avoid, shun

rehusar [reu'sar] vt, vi to refuse

reina ['reina] nf queen; **reinado** nm reign

reinar [rei'nar] vi to reign

reincidir [reinθi'ðir] vi to relapse

reincorporarse [reinkorpo'rarse] vr: **~ a** to rejoin

reino ['reino] nm kingdom; **reino animal/vegetal** animal/plant kingdom; **el Reino Unido** the United Kingdom

reintegrar [reinte'xrar] vt (reconstituir) to reconstruct; (persona) to reinstate; (dinero) to refund, pay back; **reintegrarse** vr: **~se a** to return to

reír [re'ir] vi to laugh; **reírse** vr to laugh; **~se de** to laugh at

reiterar [reite'rar] vt to reiterate

reivindicación [reiβindika'θjon] nf (demanda) claim, demand; (justificación) vindication

reivindicar [reiβindi'kar] vt to claim

reja ['rexa] nf (de ventana) grille, bars pl; (en la calle) grating

rejilla [re'xiʎa] nf grating, grille; (muebles) wickerwork; (de ventilación) vent; (de coche etc) luggage rack

rejoneador [rexonea'ðor] nm mounted bullfighter

rejuvenecer [rexuβene'θer] vt, vi to rejuvenate

relación [rela'θjon] nf relation, relationship; (Mat) ratio; (narración) report; **con ~ a, en ~ con** in relation to; **relaciones públicas** public relations; **relacionar** vt to relate, connect; **relacionarse** vr to be connected, be linked

relajación [relaxa'θjon] nf relaxation

relajar [rela'xar] vt to relax; **relajarse** vr to relax

relamerse [rela'merse] vr to lick one's lips

relámpago [re'lampaxo] nm flash of lightning; **visita ~** lightning visit

relatar [rela'tar] vt to tell, relate

relativo, -a [rela'tiβo, a] adj relative; **en lo ~ a** concerning

relato [re'lato] nm (narración) story, tale

relegar [rele'xar] vt to relegate

relevante [rele'βante] adj eminent, outstanding

relevar [rele'βar] vt (sustituir) to relieve; **relevarse** vr to relay; **~ a algn de un cargo** to relieve sb of his post

relevo [re'leβo] nm relief; **carrera de ~s** relay race

relieve [re'ljeβe] nm (Arte, Tec) relief; (fig) prominence, importance; **bajo ~** bas-relief

religión [reli'xjon] nf religion; **religioso, -a** adj religious ▷ nm/f monk/nun

relinchar [relin'tʃar] vi to neigh

reliquia [re'likja] nf relic; **reliquia de familia** heirloom

rellano [re'ʎano] nm (Arq) landing

rellenar [reʎe'nar] vt (llenar) to fill up; (Culin) to stuff; (Costura) to pad; **relleno, -a** adj full up; stuffed ▷ nm stuffing; (de tapicería) padding

reloj [re'lo(x)] nm clock; **poner el ~ (en hora)** to set one's watch (o the clock); **reloj (de pulsera)** wristwatch; **reloj despertador** alarm (clock); **reloj digital** digital watch; **relojero, -a** nm/f clockmaker; watchmaker

reluciente [relu'θjente] adj brilliant, shining

relucir [relu'θir] vi to shine; (fig) to excel

remachar [rema'tʃar] vt to rivet; (fig) to hammer home, drive home; **remache** nm rivet

remangar [reman'gar] vt to roll up

remanso [re'manso] nm pool

remar [re'mar] vi to row

rematado, -a [rema'taðo, a] adj

complete, utter

rematar [rema'tar] *vt* to finish off;
(*Com*) to sell off cheap ▷ *vi* to end,
finish off; (*Deporte*) to shoot

remate [re'mate] *nm* end, finish;
(*punta*) tip; (*Deporte*) shot; (*Arq*) top;
de *o* **para ~** to crown it all (*BRIT*), to
top it off

remedar [reme'ðar] *vt* to imitate

remediar [reme'ðjar] *vt* to remedy;
(*subsanar*) to make good, repair; (*evitar*)
to avoid

remedio [re'meðjo] *nm* remedy;
(*alivio*) relief, help; (*Jur*) recourse,
remedy; **poner ~ a** to correct, stop; **no
tener más ~** to have no alternative;
¡qué ~! there's no choice!; **sin ~**
hopeless

remendar [remen'dar] *vt* to repair;
(*con parche*) to patch

remiendo [re'mjendo] *nm* mend;
(*con parche*) patch; (*cosido*) darn

remilgado, -a [remil'ɣaðo, a] *adj*
prim; (*afectado*) affected

remiso, -a [re'miso, a] *adj* slack,
slow

remite [re'mite] *nm* (*en sobre*) name
and address of sender

remitir [remi'tir] *vt* to remit, send
▷ *vi* to slacken; (*en carta*): **remite: X**
sender: X; **remitente** *nmf* sender

remo ['remo] *nm* (*de barco*) oar;
(*Deporte*) rowing

remojar [remo'xar] *vt* to steep, soak;
(*galleta etc*) to dip, dunk

remojo [re'moxo] *nm*: **dejar la ropa
en ~** to leave clothes to soak

remolacha [remo'latʃa] *nf* beet,
beetroot

remolcador [remolka'ðor] *nm*
(*Náut*) tug; (*Auto*) breakdown lorry

remolcar [remol'kar] *vt* to tow

remolino [remo'lino] *nm* eddy; (*de
agua*) whirlpool; (*de viento*) whirlwind;
(*de gente*) crowd

remolque [re'molke] *nm* tow,
towing; (*cuerda*) towrope; **llevar a
~** to tow

remontar [remon'tar] *vt* to mend;
remontarse *vr* to soar; **~se a** (*Com*) to
amount to; **~ el vuelo** to soar

remorder [remor'ðer] *vt* to
distress, disturb; **~le la conciencia
a algn** to have a guilty conscience;
remordimiento *nm* remorse

remoto, -a [re'moto, a] *adj* remote

remover [remo'βer] *vt* to stir; (*tierra*)
to turn over; (*objetos*) to move round

remuneración [remunera'θjon] *nf*
remuneration

remunerar [remune'rar] *vt* to
remunerate; (*premiar*) to reward

renacer [rena'θer] *vi* to be reborn;
(*fig*) to revive; **renacimiento** *nm*
rebirth; **el Renacimiento** the
Renaissance

renacuajo [rena'kwaxo] *nm* (*Zool*)
tadpole

renal [re'nal] *adj* renal, kidney *cpd*

rencilla [ren'θiʎa] *nf* quarrel

rencor [ren'kor] *nm* rancour,
bitterness; **rencoroso, -a** *adj* spiteful

rendición [rendi'θjon] *nf* surrender

rendido, -a [ren'diðo, a] *adj* (*sumiso*)
submissive; (*cansado*) worn-out,
exhausted

rendija [ren'dixa] *nf* (*hendedura*)
crack, cleft

rendimiento [rendi'mjento]
nm (*producción*) output; (*Tec, Com*)
efficiency

rendir [ren'dir] *vt* (*vencer*) to defeat;
(*producir*) to produce; (*dar beneficio*) to
yield; (*agotar*) to exhaust ▷ *vi* to pay;
rendirse *vr* (*someterse*) to surrender;
(*cansarse*) to wear o.s. out; **~ homenaje
o **culto a** to pay homage to

renegar [rene'ɣar] *vi* (*renunciar*) to
renounce; (*blasfemar*) to blaspheme;
(*quejarse*) to complain

RENFE ['renfe] *nf abr* (= *Red Nacional
de los Ferrocarriles Españoles*)

renglón [ren'glon] *nm* (*línea*) line;
(*Com*) item, article; **a ~ seguido**
immediately after

renombre [re'nombre] *nm* renown

renovación [renoβa'θjon] nf (de contrato) renewal; (Arq) renovation

renovar [reno'βar] vt to renew; (Arq) to renovate

renta ['renta] nf (ingresos) income; (beneficio) profit; (alquiler) rent; **renta vitalicia** annuity; **rentable** adj profitable

renuncia [re'nunθja] nf resignation; **renunciar** [renun'θjar] vt to renounce; (tabaco, alcohol etc): **renunciar a** to give up; (oferta, oportunidad) to turn down; (puesto) to resign ▷ vi to resign

reñido, -a [re'niðo, a] adj (batalla) bitter, hard-fought; **estar ~ con algn** to be on bad terms with sb

reñir [re'nir] vt (regañar) to scold ▷ vi (estar peleado) to quarrel, fall out; (combatir) to fight

reo ['reo] nmf culprit, offender; (acusado) accused, defendant

reojo [re'oxo] : **de ~** adv out of the corner of one's eye

reparación [repara'θjon] nf (acto) mending, repairing; (Tec) repair; (fig) amends pl, reparation

reparador, a [repara'ðor] adj refreshing; (comida) fortifying ▷ nm repairer

reparar [repa'rar] vt to repair; (fig) to make amends for; (observar) to observe ▷ vi: **~ en** (darse cuenta de) to notice; (prestar atención a) to pay attention to

reparo [re'paro] nm (advertencia) observation; (duda) doubt; (dificultad) difficulty; **poner ~s (a)** to raise objections

repartidor, a [reparti'ðor, a] nm/f distributor

repartir [repar'tir] vt to distribute, share out; (Correos) to deliver; **reparto** nm distribution; delivery; (Teatro, Cine) cast; (CAM: urbanización) housing estate (BRIT), real estate development (US)

repasar [repa'sar] vt (Escol) to revise; (Mecánica) to check, overhaul; (Costura) to mend; **repaso** nm revision;

overhaul, checkup; mending

repecho [re'petʃo] nm steep incline

repelente [repe'lente] adj repellent, repulsive

repeler [repe'ler] vt to repel

repente [re'pente] nm: **de ~** suddenly

repentino, -a [repen'tino, a] adj sudden

repercusión [reperku'sjon] nf repercussion

repercutir [reperku'tir] vi (objeto) to rebound; (sonido) to echo; **~ en** (fig) to have repercussions on

repertorio [reper'torjo] nm list; (Teatro) repertoire

repetición [repeti'θjon] nf repetition

repetir [repe'tir] vt to repeat; (plato) to have a second helping of ▷ vi to repeat; (sabor) to come back; **repetirse** vr (volver sobre un tema) to repeat o.s.

repetitivo, -a [repeti'tiβo, a] adj repetitive, repetitious

repique [re'pike] nm pealing, ringing; **repiqueteo** nm pealing; (de tambor) drumming

repisa [re'pisa] nf ledge, shelf; (de ventana) windowsill; **la ~ de la chimenea** the mantelpiece

repito etc vb V **repetir**

replantearse [replante'arse] vr: **~ un problema** to reconsider a problem

repleto, -a [re'pleto, a] adj replete, full up

réplica ['replika] nf answer; (Arte) replica

replicar [repli'kar] vi to answer; (objetar) to argue, answer back

repliegue [re'pljexe] nm (Mil) withdrawal

repoblación [repoβla'θjon] nf repopulation; (de río) restocking; **repoblación forestal** reafforestation

repoblar [repo'βlar] vt to repopulate; (con árboles) to reafforest

repollito [repo'ʎito] (cs) nm: **~s de Bruselas** (Brussels) sprouts

repollo [re'poʎo] nm cabbage

reponer [repo'ner] vt to replace, put back; (*Teatro*) to revive; **reponerse** vr to recover; **~ que ...** to reply that ...

reportaje [repor'taxe] nm report, article

reportero, -a [repor'tero, a] nm/f reporter

reposacabezas [reposaka'βeθas] nm inv headrest

reposar [repo'sar] vi to rest, repose

reposera [repo'sera] (RPL) nf deck chair

reposición [reposi'θjon] nf replacement; (*Cine*) remake

reposo [re'poso] nm rest

repostar [repos'tar] vt to replenish; (*Auto*) to fill up (with petrol (BRIT) o gasoline (US))

repostería [reposte'ria] nf confectioner's (shop)

represa [re'presa] nf dam; (*lago artificial*) lake, pool

represalia [repre'salja] nf reprisal

representación [representa'θjon] nf representation; (*Teatro*) performance; **representante** nmf representative; performer

representar [represen'tar] vt to represent; (*Teatro*) to perform; (*edad*) to look; **representarse** vr to imagine; **representativo, -a** adj representative

represión [repre'sjon] nf repression

reprimenda [repri'menda] nf reprimand, rebuke

reprimir [repri'mir] vt to repress

reprobar [repro'βar] vt to censure, reprove

reprochar [repro'tʃar] vt to reproach; **reproche** nm reproach

reproducción [reproðuk'θjon] nf reproduction

reproducir [reproðu'θir] vt to reproduce; **reproducirse** vr to breed; (*situación*) to recur

reproductor, a [reproðuk'tor, a] adj reproductive ▷ nm player; **reproductor de CD** CD player

reptil [rep'til] nm reptile

república [re'puβlika] nf republic; **República Dominicana** Dominican Republic; **republicano, -a** adj, nm republican

repudiar [repu'ðjar] vt to repudiate; (*fe*) to renounce

repuesto [re'pwesto] nm (*pieza de recambio*) spare (part); (*abastecimiento*) supply; **rueda de ~** spare wheel

repugnancia [repuɣ'nanθja] nf repugnance; **repugnante** adj repugnant, repulsive

repugnar [repuɣ'nar] vt to disgust

repulsa [re'pulsa] nf rebuff

repulsión [repul'sjon] nf repulsion, aversion; **repulsivo, -a** adj repulsive

reputación [reputa'θjon] nf reputation

requerir [reke'rir] vt (*pedir*) to ask, request; (*exigir*) to require; (*llamar*) to send for, summon

requesón [reke'son] nm cottage cheese

requete... [re'kete] prefijo extremely

réquiem ['rekjem] (pl **~s**) nm requiem

requisito [reki'sito] nm requirement, requisite

res [res] nf beast, animal

resaca [re'saka] nf (*de mar*) undertow, undercurrent; (*fam*) hangover

resaltar [resal'tar] vi to project, stick out; (*fig*) to stand out

resarcir [resar'θir] vt to compensate; **resarcirse** vr to make up for

resbaladero [resβala'ðero] (MÉX) nm slide

resbaladizo, -a [resβala'ðiθo, a] adj slippery

resbalar [resβa'lar] vi to slip, slide; (*fig*) to slip (up); **resbalarse** vr to slip, slide; to slip (up); **resbalón** nm (*acción*) slip

rescatar [reska'tar] vt (*salvar*) to save, rescue; (*objeto*) to get back, recover; (*cautivos*) to ransom

rescate [res'kate] nm rescue; (*de objeto*) recovery; **pagar un ~** to pay a ransom

rescindir [resθin'dir] *vt* to rescind

rescisión [resθi'sjon] *nf* cancellation

resecar [rese'kar] *vt* to dry thoroughly; (*Med*) to cut out, remove; **resecarse** *vr* to dry up

reseco, -a [re'seko, a] *adj* very dry; (*fig*) skinny

resentido, -a [resen'tiðo, a] *adj* resentful

resentimiento [resenti'mjento] *nm* resentment, bitterness

resentirse [resen'tirse] *vr* (*debilitarse: persona*) to suffer; **~ de** (*consecuencias*) to feel the effects of; **~ de** (*o* **por**) **algo** to resent sth, be bitter about sth

reseña [re'seɲa] *nf* (*cuenta*) account; (*informe*) report; (*Literatura*) review

reseñar [rese'ɲar] *vt* to describe; (*Literatura*) to review

reserva [re'serβa] *nf* reserve; (*reservación*) reservation

reservación [reserβaθ'jon] *nf* reservation

reservado, -a [reser'βaðo, a] *adj* reserved; (*retraído*) cold, distant ▷ *nm* private room

reservar [reser'βar] *vt* (*guardar*) to keep; (*habitación, entrada*) to reserve; **reservarse** *vr* to save o.s.; (*callar*) to keep to o.s.

resfriado [resfri'aðo] *nm* cold; **resfriarse** *vr* to cool; (*Med*) to catch a cold

resguardar [resɣwar'ðar] *vt* to protect, shield; **resguardarse** *vr*: **~se de** to guard against; **resguardo** *nm* defence, (*vale*) voucher; (*recibo*) receipt, slip

residencia [resi'ðenθja] *nf* residence; **residencia de ancianos** residential home, old people's home; **residencia universitaria** hall of residence; **residencial** *nf* (*urbanización*) housing estate

residente [resi'ðente] *adj, nmf* resident

residir [resi'ðir] *vi* to reside, live; **~ en** to reside in, lie in

residuo [re'siðwo] *nm* residue

resignación [resiɣna'θjon] *nf* resignation; **resignarse** *vr*: **resignarse a** *o* **con** to resign o.s. to, be resigned to

resina [re'sina] *nf* resin

resistencia [resis'tenθja] *nf* (*dureza*) endurance, strength; (*oposición, Elec*) resistance; **resistente** *adj* strong, hardy; resistant

resistir [resis'tir] *vt* (*soportar*) to bear; (*oponerse a*) to resist, oppose; (*aguantar*) to put up with ▷ *vi* to resist; (*aguantar*) to last, endure; **resistirse** *vr*: **~se a** to refuse to, resist

resoluto, -a [reso'luto, a] *adj* resolute

resolver [resol'βer] *vt* to resolve; (*solucionar*) to solve, resolve; (*decidir*) to decide, settle; **resolverse** *vr* to make up one's mind

resonar [reso'nar] *vi* to ring, echo

resoplar [reso'plar] *vi* to snort; **resoplido** *nm* heavy breathing

resorte [re'sorte] *nm* spring; (*fig*) lever

resortera [resor'tera] (*MÉX*) *nf* catapult

respaldar [respal'dar] *vt* to back (up), support; **respaldarse** *vr* to lean back; **~se con** *o* **en** (*fig*) to take one's stand on; **respaldo** *nm* (*de sillón*) back; (*fig*) support, backing

respectivo, -a [respek'tiβo, a] *adj* respective; **en lo ~ a** with regard to

respecto [res'pekto] *nm*: **al ~ on** this matter; **con ~ a, ~ de** with regard to, in relation to

respetable [respe'taβle] *adj* respectable

respetar [respe'tar] *vt* to respect; **respeto** *nm* respect; (*acatamiento*) deference; **respetos** *nmpl* respects; **respetuoso, -a** *adj* respectful

respingo [res'pingo] *nm* start, jump

respiración [respira'θjon] *nf* breathing; (*Med*) respiration;

r

(*ventilación*) ventilation; **respiración asistida** artificial respiration (*by machine*)

respirar [respi'rar] *vi* to breathe; **respiratorio, -a** *adj* respiratory; **respiro** *nm* breathing; (*fig: descanso*) respite

resplandecer [resplande'θer] *vi* to shine; **resplandeciente** *adj* resplendent, shining; **resplandor** *nm* brilliance, brightness; (*de luz, fuego*) blaze

responder [respon'der] *vt* to answer ▷ *vi* to answer; (*fig*) to respond; (*pey*) to answer back; **~ de o por** to answer for; **respondón, -ona** *adj* cheeky

responsabilidad [responsaβili'ðað] *nf* responsibility

responsabilizarse [responsaβili'θarse] *vr* to make o.s. responsible, take charge

responsable [respon'saβle] *adj* responsible

respuesta [res'pwesta] *nf* answer, reply

resquebrajar [reskeβra'xar] *vt* to crack, split; **resquebrajarse** *vr* to crack, split

resquicio [res'kiθjo] *nm* chink; (*hendedura*) crack

resta ['resta] *nf* (*Mat*) remainder

restablecer [restaβle'θer] *vt* to re-establish, restore; **restablecerse** *vr* to recover

restante [res'tante] *adj* remaining; **lo ~** the remainder

restar [res'tar] *vt* (*Mat*) to subtract; (*fig*) to take away ▷ *vi* to remain, be left

restauración [restaura'θjon] *nf* restoration

restaurante [restau'rante] *nm* restaurant

restaurar [restau'rar] *vt* to restore

restituir [restitu'ir] *vt* (*devolver*) to return, give back; (*rehabilitar*) to restore

resto ['resto] *nm* (*residuo*) rest, remainder; (*apuesta*) stake; **restos** *nmpl* remains

restorán [resto'ran] *nm* (*Lam*) restaurant

restregar [restre'ɣar] *vt* to scrub, rub

restricción [restrik'θjon] *nf* restriction

restringir [restrin'xir] *vt* to restrict, limit

resucitar [resuθi'tar] *vt, vi* to resuscitate, revive

resuelto, -a [re'swelto, a] *pp de* **resolver** ▷ *adj* resolute, determined

resultado [resul'taðo] *nm* result; (*conclusión*) outcome; **resultante** *adj* resulting, resultant

resultar [resul'tar] *vi* (*ser*) to be; (*llegar a ser*) to turn out to be; (*salir bien*) to turn out well; (*Com*) to amount to; **~ de** to stem from; **me resulta difícil hacerlo** it's difficult for me to do it

resumen [re'sumen] (*pl* **resúmenes**) *nm* summary, résumé; **en ~** in short

resumir [resu'mir] *vt* to sum up; (*cortar*) to abridge, cut down; (*condensar*) to summarize

> No confundir **resumir** con la palabra inglesa *resume*.

resurgir [resur'xir] *vi* (*reaparecer*) to reappear

resurrección [resurre(k)'θjon] *nf* resurrection

retablo [re'taβlo] *nm* altarpiece

retaguardia [reta'ɣwarðja] *nf* rearguard

retahíla [reta'ila] *nf* series, string

retal [re'tal] *nm* remnant

retar [re'tar] *vt* to challenge; (*desafiar*) to defy, dare

retazo [re'taθo] *nm* snippet (*BRIT*), fragment

retención [reten'θjon] *nf* (*tráfico*) hold-up; **retención fiscal** deduction for tax purposes

retener [rete'ner] *vt* (*intereses*) to withhold

reticente [reti'θente] *adj* (*tono*) insinuating; (*postura*) reluctant; **ser ~ a hacer algo** to be reluctant o unwilling to do sth

retina [re'tina] nf retina

retintín [retin'tin] nm jangle, jingle

retirada [reti'raða] nf (Mil, refugio) retreat, (de dinero) withdrawal; (de embajador) recall; **retirado, -a** adj (lugar) remote; (vida) quiet; (jubilado) retired

retirar [reti'rar] vt to withdraw; (quitar) to remove; (jubilar) to retire, pension off; **retirarse** vr to retreat, withdraw; to retire; (acostarse) to retire, go to bed; **retiro** nm retreat; retirement; (pago) pension

reto ['reto] nm dare, challenge

retocar [reto'kar] vt (fotografía) to touch up, retouch

retoño [re'toɲo] nm sprout, shoot; (fig) offspring, child

retoque [re'toke] nm retouching

retorcer [retor'θer] vt to twist; (manos, lavado) to wring; **retorcerse** vr to become twisted; (mover el cuerpo) to writhe

retorcido, -a [retor'θiðo, a] adj (persona) devious

retorcijón [retorθi'xon] (LAM) nm (tb: **~ de tripas**) stomach cramp

retórica [re'torika] nf rhetoric; (pey) affectedness

retorno [re'torno] nm return

retortijón [retorti'xon] (ESP) nm (tb: **~ de tripas**) stomach cramp

retozar [reto'θar] vi (juguetear) to frolic, romp; (saltar) to gambol

retracción [retrak'θjon] nf retraction

retraerse [retra'erse] vr to retreat, withdraw; **retraído, -a** adj shy, retiring; **retraimiento** nm retirement; (timidez) shyness

retransmisión [retransmi'sjon] nf repeat (broadcast)

retransmitir [retransmi'tir] vt (mensaje) to relay; (TV etc) to repeat, retransmit; (: en vivo) to broadcast live

retrasado, -a [retra'saðo, a] adj late; (Med) mentally retarded; (país etc) backward, underdeveloped

retrasar [retra'sar] vt (demorar) to postpone, put off; (retardar) to slow down ▷ vi (atrasarse) to be late; (reloj) to be slow; (producción) to fall (off); (quedarse atrás) to lag behind; **retrasarse** vr to be late; to be slow; to fall (off); to lag behind

retraso [re'traso] nm (demora) delay; (lentitud) slowness; (tardanza) lateness; (atraso) backwardness; **retrasos** nmpl (Finanzas) arrears; **llegar con ~** to arrive late; **retraso mental** mental deficiency

retratar [retra'tar] vt (Arte) to paint the portrait of; (fotografiar) to photograph; (fig) to depict, describe; **retrato** nm portrait; (fig) likeness; **retrato-robot** (ESP) nm Identikit®

retrete [re'trete] nm toilet

retribuir [retri'βwir] vt (recompensar) to reward; (pagar) to pay

retro... ['retro] prefijo retro...

retroceder [retroθe'ðer] vi (echarse atrás) to move back(wards); (fig) to back down

retroceso [retro'θeso] nm backward movement; (Med) relapse; (fig) backing down

retrospectivo, -a [retrospek'tiβo, a] adj retrospective

retrovisor [retroβi'sor] nm (tb: **espejo ~**) rear-view mirror

retumbar [retum'bar] vi to echo, resound

reúma [re'uma], **reuma** ['reuma] nm rheumatism

reunión [reu'njon] nf (asamblea) meeting; (fiesta) party

reunir [reu'nir] vt (juntar) to reunite, join (together); (recoger) to gather (together); (personas) to get together; (cualidades) to combine; **reunirse** vr (personas: en asamblea) to meet, gather

revalidar [reβali'ðar] vt (ratificar) to confirm, ratify

revalorizar [reβalori'θar] vt to revalue, reassess

revancha [re'βantʃa] nf revenge

r

revelación [reβela'θjon] *nf*
revelation

revelado [reβe'laðo] *nm* developing

revelar [reβe'lar] *vt* to reveal; (*Foto*)
to develop

reventa [re'βenta] *nf* (*de
entradas: para concierto*) touting

reventar [reβen'tar] *vt* to burst,
explode

reventón [reβen'ton] *nm* (*Auto*)
blow-out (BRIT), flat (US)

reverencia [reβe'renθja] *nf*
reverence; **reverenciar** *vt* to revere

reverendo, -a [reβe'rendo, a] *adj*
reverend

reverente [reβe'rente] *adj* reverent

reversa [re'βersa] (MÉX, CAM) *nf*
reverse (gear)

reversible [reβer'siβle] *adj* (*prenda*)
reversible

reverso [re'βerso] *nm* back, other
side; (*de moneda*) reverse

revertir [reβer'tir] *vi* to revert

revés [re'βes] *nm* back, wrong
side; (*fig*) reverse, setback; (*Deporte*)
backhand; **al ~** the wrong way round;
(*de arriba abajo*) upside down; (*ropa*)
inside out; **volver algo del ~** to turn
sth round; (*ropa*) to turn sth inside out

revisar [reβi'sar] *vt* (*examinar*) to
check; (*texto etc*) to revise; **revisión**
nf revision; **revisión salarial** wage
review

revisor, a [reβi'sor, a] *nm/f*
inspector; (*Ferro*) ticket collector

revista [re'βista] *nf* magazine,
review; (*Teatro*) revue; (*inspección*)
inspection; **pasar ~ a** to review,
inspect; **revista del corazón** *magazine
featuring celebrity gossip and real-life
romance stories*

revivir [reβi'βir] *vi* to revive

revolcarse [reβol'karse] *vr* to roll
about

revoltijo [reβol'tixo] *nm* mess, jumble

revoltoso, -a [reβol'toso, a] *adj*
(*travieso*) naughty, unruly

revolución [reβolu'θjon] *nf*

revolution; **revolucionario, -a** *adj,
nm/f* revolutionary

revolver [reβol'βer] *vt* (*desordenar*)
to disturb, mess up; (*mover*) to move
about ▷ *vi*: **~ en** to go through,
rummage (about) in; **revolverse** *vr*
(*volver contra*) to turn on *o* against

revólver [re'βolβer] *nm* revolver

revuelo [re'βwelo] *nm* fluttering; (*fig*)
commotion

revuelta [re'βwelta] *nf* (*motín*) revolt;
(*agitación*) commotion

revuelto, -a [re'βwelto, a] *pp de*
revolver ▷ *adj* (*mezclado*) mixed-up,
in disorder

rey [rei] *nm* king; **Día de R~es** Twelfth
Night; **los R~es Magos** the Three Wise
Men, the Magi

● **REYES MAGOS**
●
● On the night before the 6th
● January (the Epiphany), children
● go to bed expecting **los Reyes**
● **Magos** (the Three Wise Men) to
● bring them presents. Twelfth
● Night processions, known as
● **cabalgatas**, take place that
● evening when 3 people dressed
● as **los Reyes Magos** arrive in the
● town by land or sea to the delight
● of the children.

reyerta [re'jerta] *nf* quarrel, brawl

rezagado, -a [reθa'ɣaðo, a] *nm/f*
straggler

rezar [re'θar] *vi* to pray; **~ con** (*fam*)
to concern, have to do with; **rezo**
nm prayer

rezumar [reθu'mar] *vt* to ooze

ría ['ria] *nf* estuary

riada [ri'aða] *nf* flood

ribera [ri'βera] *nf* (*de río*) bank; (: *área*)
riverside

ribete [ri'βete] *nm* (*de vestido*) border;
(*fig*) addition

ricino [ri'θino] *nm*: **aceite de ~**
castor oil

rico, -a ['riko, a] *adj* rich; *(adinerado)* wealthy, rich; *(lujoso)* luxurious; *(comida)* delicious; *(niño)* lovely, cute ▷ *nm/f* rich person

ridiculez [riðiku'leθ] *nf* absurdity

ridiculizar [riðikuli'θar] *vt* to ridicule

ridículo, -a [ri'ðikulo, a] *adj* ridiculous; **hacer el ~** to make a fool of o.s.; **poner a algn en ~** to make a fool of sb

riego ['rjexo] *nm (aspersión)* watering; *(irrigación)* irrigation; **riego sanguíneo** blood flow o circulation

riel [rjel] *nm* rail

rienda ['rjenda] *nf* rein; **dar ~ suelta a** to give free rein to

riesgo ['rjesxo] *nm* risk; **correr el ~ de** to run the risk of

rifa ['rifa] *nf (lotería)* raffle; **rifar** *vt* to raffle

rifle ['rifle] *nm* rifle

rigidez [rixi'ðeθ] *nf* rigidity, stiffness; *(fig)* strictness; **rígido, -a** *adj* rigid, stiff; strict, inflexible

rigor [ri'xor] *nm* strictness, rigour; *(Inclemencia)* harshness; **de ~** de rigueur, essential; **riguroso, -a** *adj* rigorous; harsh; *(severo)* severe

rimar [ri'mar] *vi* to rhyme

rimbombante [rimbom'bante] *adj* pompous

rímel ['rimel] *nm* mascara

rímmel ['rimel] *nm* = **rímel**

rin [rin] *(MÉX) nm (wheel)* rim

rincón [rin'kon] *nm* corner *(inside)*

rinoceronte [rinoθe'ronte] *nm* rhinoceros

riña ['riɲa] *nf (disputa)* argument; *(pelea)* brawl

riñón [ri'ɲon] *nm* kidney

río *etc* ['rio] *vb* V **reír** ▷ *nm* river; *(fig)* torrent, stream; **río abajo/arriba** downstream/upstream; **Río de la Plata** River Plate

rioja [ri'oxa] *nm (vino)* rioja (wine)

rioplatense [riopla'tense] *adj* of o from the River Plate region

riqueza [ri'keθa] *nf* wealth, riches *pl*; *(cualidad)* richness

risa ['risa] *nf* laughter; *(una risa)* laugh; **¡qué ~!** what a laugh!

risco ['risko] *nm* crag, cliff

ristra ['ristra] *nf* string

risueño, -a [ri'sweɲo, a] *adj* *(sonriente)* smiling; *(contento)* cheerful

ritmo ['ritmo] *nm* rhythm; **a ~ lento** slowly; **trabajar a ~ lento** to go slow; **ritmo cardíaco** heart rate

rito ['rito] *nm* rite

ritual [ri'twal] *adj, nm* ritual

rival [ri'βal] *adj, nmf* rival; **rivalidad** *nf* rivalry; **rivalizar** *vi*: **rivalizar con** to rival, vie with

rizado, -a [ri'θaðo, a] *adj* curly ▷ *nm* curls *pl*

rizar [ri'θar] *vt* to curl; **rizarse** *vr* *(pelo)* to curl; *(agua)* to ripple; **rizo** *nm* curl; ripple

RNE *nf abr* = **Radio Nacional de España**

robar [ro'βar] *vt* to rob; *(objeto)* to steal; *(casa etc)* to break into; *(Naipes)* to draw

roble ['roβle] *nm* oak; **robledal** *nm* oakwood

robo ['roβo] *nm* robbery, theft

robot [ro'βot] *nm* robot; **robot (de cocina)** *(ESP)* food processor

robustecer [roβuste'θer] *vt* to strengthen

robusto, -a [ro'βusto, a] *adj* robust, strong

roca ['roka] *nf* rock

roce ['roθe] *nm (caricia)* brush; *(Tec)* friction; *(en la piel)* graze; **tener ~ con** to be in close contact with

rociar [ro'θjar] *vt* to spray

rocín [ro'θin] *nm* nag, hack

rocío [ro'θio] *nm* dew

rocola [ro'kola] *(LAM) nf* jukebox

rocoso, -a [ro'koso, a] *adj* rocky

rodaballo [roða'βaʎo] *nm* turbot

rodaja [ro'ðaxa] *nf* slice

rodaje [ro'ðaxe] *nm (Cine)* shooting, filming; *(Auto)*: **en ~** running in

rodar [ro'ðar] *vt (vehículo)* to wheel (along); *(escalera)* to roll down; *(viajar*

r

por) to travel (over) ▷ *vi* to roll; (*coche*)
to go, run; (*Cine*) to shoot, film
rodear [roðe'ar] *vt* to surround ▷ *vi*
to go round; **rodearse** *vr*: **~se de**
amigos to surround o.s. with friends
rodeo [ro'ðeo] *nm* (*ruta indirecta*)
detour; (*evasión*) evasion; (*Deporte*)
rodeo; **hablar sin ~s** to come to the
point, speak plainly
rodilla [ro'ðiʎa] *nf* knee; **de ~s**
kneeling; **ponerse de ~s** to kneel (down)
rodillo [ro'ðiʎo] *nm* roller; (*Culin*)
rolling-pin
roedor, a [roe'ðor, a] *adj* gnawing
▷ *nm* rodent
roer [ro'er] *vt* (*masticar*) to gnaw;
(*corroer, fig*) to corrode
rogar [ro'xar] *vt, vi* (*pedir*) to ask for;
(*suplicar*) to beg, plead; **se ruega no**
fumar please do not smoke
rojizo, -a [ro'xiθo, a] *adj* reddish
rojo, -a ['roxo, a] *adj, nm* red; **al ~**
vivo red-hot
rol [rol] *nm* list, roll; (*papel*) role
rollito [ro'ʎito] *nm* (*tb*: **~ de**
primavera) spring roll
rollizo, -a [ro'ʎiθo, a] *adj* (*objeto*)
cylindrical; (*persona*) plump
rollo ['roʎo] *nm* roll; (*de cuerda*) coil;
(*madera*) log; (*ESP: fam*) bore; **¡qué ~!**
(*ESP: fam*) what a carry-on!
Roma ['roma] *n* Rome
romance [ro'manθe] *nm* (*amoroso*)
romance; (*Literatura*) ballad
romano, -a [ro'mano, a] *adj, nm/f*
Roman; **a la romana** in batter
romanticismo [romanti'θismo] *nm*
romanticism
romántico, -a [ro'mantiko, a] *adj*
romantic
rombo ['rombo] *nm* (*Geom*) rhombus
romería [rome'ria] *nf* (*Rel*)
pilgrimage; (*excursión*) trip, outing

● **ROMERÍA**
●
● Originally a pilgrimage to a shrine
● or church to express devotion to
● the Virgin Mary or a local Saint,
● the **romería** has also become a
● rural festival which accompanies
● the pilgrimage. People come from
● all over to attend, bringing their
● own food and drink, and spend the
● day in celebration.

romero, -a [ro'mero, a] *nm/f* pilgrim
▷ *nm* rosemary
romo, -a ['romo, a] *adj* blunt;
(*fig*) dull
rompecabezas [rompeka'βeθas]
nm inv riddle, puzzle; (*juego*) jigsaw
(puzzle)
rompehuelgas [rompe'welɣas]
(*LAM*) *nm inv* strikebreaker, scab
rompeolas [rompe'olas] *nm inv*
breakwater
romper [rom'per] *vt* to break; (*hacer*
pedazos) to smash; (*papel, tela etc*)
to tear, rip ▷ *vi* (*olas*) to break; (*sol,*
diente) to break through; **romperse**
vr to break; **~ un contrato** to break
a contract; **~ a** (*empezar a*) to start
(suddenly) to; **~ a llorar** to burst into
tears; **~ con algn** to fall out with sb
ron [ron] *nm* rum
roncar [ron'kar] *vi* to snore
ronco, -a ['ronko, a] *adj* (*afónico*)
hoarse; (*áspero*) raucous
ronda ['ronda] *nf* (*gen*) round;
(*patrulla*) patrol; **rondar** *vt* to patrol
▷ *vi* to patrol; (*fig*) to prowl round
ronquido [ron'kiðo] *nm* snore,
snoring
ronronear [ronrone'ar] *vi* to purr
roña ['roɲa] *nf* (*Veterinaria*) mange;
(*mugre*) dirt, grime; (*óxido*) rust
roñoso, -a [ro'ɲoso, a] *adj*
(*mugriento*) filthy; (*tacaño*) mean
ropa ['ropa] *nf* clothes *pl*, clothing;
ropa blanca linen; **ropa de cama** bed
linen; **ropa de color** coloureds *pl*; **ropa**
interior underwear; **ropa sucia** dirty
washing; **ropaje** *nm* gown, robes *pl*
ropero [ro'pero] *nm* linen cupboard;
(*guardarropa*) wardrobe

rosa ['rosa] *adj* pink ▷ *nf* rose
rosado, -a [ro'saðo, a] *adj* pink
▷ *nm* rosé
rosal [ro'sal] *nm* rosebush
rosario [ro'sarjo] *nm* (*Rel*) rosary;
rezar el ~ to say the rosary
rosca ['roska] *nf* (*de tornillo*) thread;
(*de humo*) coil, spiral; (*pan, postre*) ring-
shaped roll/pastry
rosetón [rose'ton] *nm* rosette; (*Arq*)
rose window
rosquilla [ros'kiʎa] *nf* doughnut-
shaped fritter
rostro ['rostro] *nm* (*cara*) face
rotativo, -a [rota'tiβo, a] *adj* rotary
roto, -a ['roto, a] *pp de* **romper** ▷ *adj*
broken
rotonda [ro'tonda] *nf* roundabout
rótula ['rotula] *nf* kneecap; (*Tec*) ball-
and-socket joint
rotulador [rotula'ðor] *nm* felt-tip
pen
rótulo ['rotulo] *nm* heading, title;
label; (*letrero*) sign
rotundamente [rotunda'mente]
adv (*negar*) flatly; (*responder, afirmar*)
emphatically; **rotundo, -a** *adj* round;
(*enfático*) emphatic
rotura [ro'tura] *nf* (*acto*) breaking;
(*Med*) fracture
rozadura [roθa'ðura] *nf* abrasion,
graze
rozar [ro'θar] *vt* (*frotar*) to rub;
(*arañar*) to scratch; (*tocar ligeramente*)
to shave, touch lightly; **rozarse** *vr* to
rub (together); **~se con** (*fam*) to rub
shoulders with
rte. *abr* (= *remite, remitente*) sender
RTVE *nf abr* = **Radiotelevisión
Española**
rubí [ru'βi] *nm* ruby; (*de reloj*) jewel
rubio, -a ['ruβjo, a] *adj* fair-haired,
blond(e) ▷ *nm/f* blond/blonde;
tabaco ~ Virginia tobacco
rubor [ru'βor] *nm* (*sonrojo*) blush;
(*timidez*) bashfulness; **ruborizarse**
vr to blush
rúbrica ['ruβrika] *nf* (*de la firma*)

flourish; **rubricar** *vt* (*firmar*) to sign
with a flourish; (*concluir*) to sign
and seal
rudimentario, -a [ruðimen'tarjo,
a] *adj* rudimentary
rudo, -a ['ruðo, a] *adj* (*sin pulir*)
unpolished; (*grosero*) coarse; (*violento*)
violent; (*sencillo*) simple
rueda ['rweða] *nf* wheel; (*círculo*)
ring, circle; (*rodaja*) slice, round; **rueda
de auxilio** (*RPL*) spare tyre; **rueda
delantera/trasera/de repuesto**
front/back/spare wheel; **rueda de
prensa** press conference; **rueda
gigante** (*LAM*) big (*BRIT*) o Ferris (*US*)
wheel
ruedo ['rweðo] *nm* (*círculo*) circle;
(*Taur*) arena, bullring
ruego *etc* ['rweɣo] *vb* V **rogar** ▷ *nm*
request
rugby ['ruɣβi] *nm* rugby
rugido [ru'xiðo] *nm* roar
rugir [ru'xir] *vi* to roar
rugoso, -a [ru'ɣoso, a] *adj* (*arrugado*)
wrinkled; (*áspero*) rough; (*desigual*)
ridged
ruido ['rwiðo] *nm* noise; (*sonido*)
sound; (*alboroto*) racket, row;
(*escándalo*) commotion, rumpus;
ruidoso, -a *adj* noisy, loud; (*fig*)
sensational
ruin [rwin] *adj* contemptible, mean
ruina ['rwina] *nf* ruin, (*colapso*)
collapse; (*de persona*) ruin, downfall
ruinoso, -a [rwi'noso, a] *adj*
ruinous; (*destartalado*) dilapidated,
tumbledown; (*Com*) disastrous
ruiseñor [rwise'nor] *nm* nightingale
rulero [ru'lero] (*RPL*) *nm* roller
ruleta [ru'leta] *nf* roulette
rulo ['rulo] *nm* (*para el pelo*) curler
Rumanía [ruma'nia] *nf* Rumania
rumba ['rumba] *nf* rumba
rumbo ['rumbo] *nm* (*ruta*) route,
direction; (*ángulo de dirección*) course,
bearing; (*fig*) course of events; **ir con ~
a** to be heading for
rumiante [ru'mjante] *nm* ruminant

rumiar [ru'mjar] *vt* to chew; (*fig*) to chew over ▷ *vi* to chew the cud
rumor [ru'mor] *nm* (*ruido sordo*) low sound; (*murmuración*) murmur, buzz; **rumorearse** *vr*: **se rumorea que ...** it is rumoured that ...
rupestre [ru'pestre] *adj* rock *cpd*
ruptura [rup'tura] *nf* rupture
rural [ru'ral] *adj* rural
Rusia ['rusja] *nf* Russia; **ruso, -a** *adj*, *nm/f* Russian
rústico, -a ['rustiko, a] *adj* rustic; (*ordinario*) coarse, uncouth ▷ *nm/f* yokel
ruta ['ruta] *nf* route
rutina [ru'tina] *nf* routine

S

S *abr* (= *santo, a*) St; (= *sur*) S
s. *abr* (= *siglo*) C.; (= *siguiente*) foll
S.A. *abr* (= *Sociedad Anónima*) Ltd. (BRIT), Inc. (US)
sábado ['saβaðo] *nm* Saturday
sábana ['saβana] *nf* sheet
sabañón [saβa'ɲon] *nm* chilblain
saber [sa'βer] *vt* to know; (*llegar a conocer*) to find out, learn; (*tener capacidad de*) to know how to ▷ *vi*: **~ a** to taste of, taste like ▷ *nm* knowledge, learning; **a ~** namely; **¿sabes conducir/nadar?** can you drive/swim?; **¿sabes francés?** do you speak French?; **~ de memoria** to know by heart; **hacer ~ algo a algn** to inform sb of sth, let sb know sth
sabiduría [saβiðu'ria] *nf* (*conocimientos*) wisdom; (*instrucción*) learning
sabiendas [sa'βjendas]: **a ~** *adv* knowingly
sabio, -a ['saβjo, a] *adj* (*docto*) learned; (*prudente*) wise, sensible
sabor [sa'βor] *nm* taste, flavour;

saborear vt to taste, savour; (fig) to relish

sabotaje [saβo'taxe] nm sabotage

sabré etc vb V **saber**

sabroso, -a [sa'βroso, a] adj tasty; (fig: fam) racy, salty

sacacorchos [saka'kortʃos] nm inv corkscrew

sacapuntas [saka'puntas] nm inv pencil sharpener

sacar [sa'kar] vt to take out; (fig: extraer) to get (out); (quitar) to remove, get out; (hacer salir) to bring out; (conclusión) to draw; (novela etc) to publish, bring out; (ropa) to take off; (obra) to make; (premio) to receive; (entradas) to get; (Tenis) to serve; **~ adelante** (niño) to bring up; (negocio) to carry on, go on with; **~ a algn a bailar** to get sb up to dance; **~ una foto** to take a photo, **~ la lengua** to stick out one's tongue; **~ buenas/malas notas** to get good/bad marks

sacarina [saka'rina] nf saccharin(e)

sacerdote [saθer'ðote] nm priest

saciar [sa'θjar] vt (hambre, sed) to satisfy; **saciarse** vr (de comida) to get full up

saco ['sako] nm bag; (grande) sack; (su contenido) bagful; (LAM: chaqueta) jacket; **saco de dormir** sleeping bag

sacramento [sakra'mento] nm sacrament

sacrificar [sakrifi'kar] vt to sacrifice; **sacrificio** nm sacrifice

sacristía [sakris'tia] nf sacristy

sacudida [saku'ðiða] nf (agitación) shake, shaking; (sacudimiento) jolt, bump; **sacudida eléctrica** electric shock

sacudir [saku'ðir] vt to shake; (golpear) to hit

Sagitario [saxi'tarjo] nm Sagittarius

sagrado, -a [sa'ɣraðo, a] adj sacred, holy

Sáhara ['saara] nm: **el ~** the Sahara (desert)

sal [sal] vb V **salir** ▷ nf salt; **sales de**

baño bath salts

sala ['sala] nf room; (tb: **~ de estar**) living room; (Teatro) house, auditorium; (de hospital) ward; **sala de espera** waiting room; **sala de estar** living room; **sala de fiestas** dance hall

salado, -a [sa'laðo, a] adj salty; (fig) witty, amusing; **agua salada** salt water

salar [sa'lar] vt to salt, add salt to

salariado [sala'rjaðo] adj (empleado) salaried

salario [sa'larjo] nm wage, pay

salchicha [sal'tʃitʃa] nf (pork) sausage; **salchichón** nm (salami-type) sausage

saldo ['saldo] nm (pago) settlement; (de una cuenta) balance; (lo restante) remnant(s) (pl), remainder; (de móvil) credit; **saldos** nmpl (en tienda) sale

saldré etc vb V **salir**

salero [sa'lero] nm salt cellar

salgo etc vb V **salir**

salida [sa'liða] nf (puerta etc) exit, way out; (acto) leaving, going out; (de tren, Aviac) departure; (Tec) output, production; (fig) way out; (Com) opening; (Geo, válvula) outlet; (de gas) leak; **calle sin ~** cul-de-sac; **salida de baño** (RPL) bathrobe; **salida de emergencia/incendios** emergency exit/fire escape

○ **PALABRA CLAVE**

salir [sa'lir] vi **1** (partir: tb: **salir de**) to leave; **Juan ha salido** Juan is out; **salió de la cocina** he came out of the kitchen

2 (aparecer) to appear; (disco, libro) to come out; **anoche salió en la tele** she appeared o was on TV last night; **salió en todos los periódicos** it was in all the papers

3 (resultar): **la muchacha nos salió muy trabajadora** the girl turned out to be a very hard worker; **la comida te ha salido exquisita** the food was delicious; **sale muy caro** it's very expensive

4: **salirle a uno algo**: **la entrevista que hice me salió bien/mal** the interview I did went o turned out well/badly

5: **salir adelante**: **no sé como haré para salir adelante** I don't know how I'll get by

salirse vr (líquido) to spill; (animal) to escape

saliva [sa'liβa] nf saliva

salmo ['salmo] nm psalm

salmón [sal'mon] nm salmon

salmonete [salmo'nete] nm red mullet

salón [sa'lon] nm (de casa) living room, lounge; (muebles) lounge suite; **salón de actos** assembly hall; **salón de baile** dance hall; **salón de belleza** beauty parlour

salpicadera [salpika'ðera] (MÉX) nf mudguard (BRIT), fender (US)

salpicadero [salpika'ðero] nm (Auto) dashboard

salpicar [salpi'kar] vt (rociar) to sprinkle, spatter; (esparcir) to scatter

salpicón [salpi'kon] nm (tb: ~ de marisco) seafood salad

salsa ['salsa] nf sauce; (con carne asada) gravy; (fig) spice

saltamontes [salta'montes] nm inv grasshopper

saltar [sal'tar] vt to jump (over), leap (over); (dejar de lado) to skip, miss out ▷ vi to jump, leap; (pelota) to bounce; (al aire) to fly up; (quebrarse) to break; (al agua) to dive; (fig) to explode, blow up

salto ['salto] nm jump, leap; (al agua) dive; **salto de agua** waterfall; **salto de altura/longitud** high/long jump

salud [sa'luð] nf health; **¡(a su) ~!** cheers!, good health!; **saludable** adj (de buena salud) healthy; (provechoso) good, beneficial

saludar [salu'ðar] vt to greet; (Mil) to salute; **saludo** nm greeting;

"saludos" (en carta) "best wishes", "regards"

salvación [salβa'θjon] nf salvation; (rescate) rescue

salvado [sal'βaðo] nm bran

salvaje [sal'βaxe] adj wild; (tribu) savage

salvamanteles [salβaman'teles] nm inv table mat

salvamento [salβa'mento] nm rescue

salvapantallas [salβapan'taʎas] nm inv screen saver

salvar [sal'βar] vt (rescatar) to save, rescue; (resolver) to overcome, resolve; (cubrir distancias) to cover, travel; (hacer excepción) to except, exclude; (barco) to salvage

salvavidas [salβa'βiðas] adj inv: **bote/chaleco ~** lifeboat/life jacket

salvo, -a ['salβo, a] adj safe ▷ adv except (for), save; **a ~** out of danger; **~ que** unless

san [san] adj saint; **S~ Juan** St John

sanar [sa'nar] vt (herida) to heal; (persona) to cure ▷ vi (persona) to get well, recover; (herida) to heal

sanatorio [sana'torjo] nm sanatorium

sanción [san'θjon] nf sanction

sancochado, -a [sanko'tʃado, a] (MÉX) adj (Culin) underdone, rare

sandalia [san'dalja] nf sandal

sandía [san'dia] nf watermelon

sandwich ['sandwitʃ] (pl **~s**, **~es**) nm sandwich

sanfermines [sanfer'mines] nmpl festivities in celebration of San Fermín (Pamplona)

● **SANFERMINES**
●
●
● The **Sanfermines** is a week-long
● festival in Pamplona made famous
● by Ernest Hemingway. From the
● 7th July, the feast of "San Fermín",
● crowds of mainly young people
● take to the streets drinking,

singing and dancing. Early in the morning bulls are released along the narrow streets leading to the bullring, and young men risk serious injury to show their bravery by running out in front of them, a custom which is also typical of many Spanish villages.

sangrar [san'grar] vt, vi to bleed; **sangre** nf blood

sangría [san'gria] nf sangria, *sweetened drink of red wine with fruit*

sangriento, -a [san'grjento, a] adj bloody

sanguíneo, -a [san'gineo, a] adj blood cpd

sanidad [sani'ðað] nf (tb: **~ pública**) public health

San Isidro [sani'siðro] nm *patron saint of Madrid*

sanitario, -a [sani'tarjo, a] adj health cpd; **sanitarios** nmpl toilets (BRIT), washroom (US)

sano, -a ['sano, a] adj healthy; (sin daños) sound; (comida) wholesome; (entero) whole, intact; **~ y salvo** safe and sound

No confundir **sano** con la palabra inglesa *sane*.

Santiago [san'tjaɣo] nm: **~ (de Chile)** Santiago

santiamén [santja'men] nm: **en un ~** in no time at all

santidad [santi'ðað] nf holiness, sanctity

santiguarse [santi'ɣwarse] vr to make the sign of the cross

santo, -a ['santo, a] adj holy; (fig) wonderful, miraculous ▷ nm/f saint ▷ nm saint's day; **~ y seña** password

santuario [san'twarjo] nm sanctuary, shrine

sapo ['sapo] nm toad

saque ['sake] nm (Tenis) service, serve; (Fútbol) throw-in; **saque de esquina** corner (kick)

saquear [sake'ar] vt (Mil) to sack; (robar) to loot, plunder; (fig) to ransack

sarampión [saram'pjon] nm measles sg

sarcástico, -a [sar'kastiko, a] adj sarcastic

sardina [sar'ðina] nf sardine

sargento [sar'xento] nm sergeant

sarmiento [sar'mjento] nm (Bot) vine shoot

sarna ['sarna] nf itch; (Med) scabies

sarpullido [sarpu'ʎiðo] nm (Med) rash

sarro ['sarro] nm (en dientes) tartar, plaque

sartén [sar'ten] nf frying pan

sastre ['sastre] nm tailor; **sastrería** nf (arte) tailoring; (tienda) tailor's (shop)

Satanás [sata'nas] nm Satan

satélite [sa'telite] nm satellite

sátira ['satira] nf satire

satisfacción [satisfak'θjon] nf satisfaction

satisfacer [satisfa'θer] vt to satisfy; (gastos) to meet; (pérdida) to make good; **satisfacerse** vr to satisfy o.s., be satisfied; (vengarse) to take revenge; **satisfecho, -a** adj satisfied; (contento) content(ed), happy; (tb: **satisfecho de sí mismo**) self-satisfied, smug

saturar [satu'rar] vt to saturate; **saturarse** vr (mercado, aeropuerto) to reach saturation point

sauce ['sauθe] nm willow; **sauce llorón** weeping willow

sauna ['sauna] nf sauna
savia ['saβja] nf sap
saxofón [sakso'fon] nm saxophone
sazonar [saθo'nar] vt to ripen; (Culin) to flavour, season
scooter [e'skuter] (ESP) nf scooter
Scotch® [skotʃ] (LAM) nm Sellotape® (BRIT), Scotch tape® (US)
SE abr (= sudeste) SE

○ **PALABRA CLAVE**

se [se] pron **1** (reflexivo: sg: m) himself; (: f) herself; (: pl) themselves; (: cosa) itself; (: de Vd) yourself; (: de Vds) yourselves; **se está preparando** she's preparing herself
2 (con complemento indirecto) to him; to her; to them; to it; to you; **a usted se lo dije ayer** I told you yesterday; **se compró un sombrero** he bought himself a hat; **se rompió la pierna** he broke his leg
3 (uso recíproco) each other, one another; **se miraron (el uno al otro)** they looked at each other o one another
4 (en oraciones pasivas): **se han vendido muchos libros** a lot of books have been sold
5 (impers): **se dice que ...** people say that ..., it is said that ...; **allí se come muy bien** the food there is very good, you can eat very well there

sé etc [se] vb V **saber; ser**
sea etc vb V **ser**
sebo ['seβo] nm fat, grease
secador [seka'ðor] nm: **~ de pelo** hair-dryer
secadora [seka'ðora] nf tumble dryer
secar [se'kar] vt to dry; **secarse** vr to dry (off); (río, planta) to dry up
sección [sek'θjon] nf section
seco, -a ['seko, a] adj dry; (carácter) cold; (respuesta) sharp, curt; **parar en ~** to stop dead; **decir algo a secas** to say sth curtly

secretaría [sekreta'ria] nf secretariat
secretario, -a [sekre'tarjo, a] nm/f secretary
secreto, -a [se'kreto, a] adj secret; (persona) secretive ▷ nm secret; (calidad) secrecy
secta ['sekta] nf sect
sector [sek'tor] nm sector
secuela [se'kwela] nf consequence
secuencia [se'kwenθja] nf sequence
secuestrar [sekwes'trar] vt to kidnap; (bienes) to seize, confiscate; **secuestro** nm kidnapping; seizure, confiscation
secundario, -a [sekun'darjo, a] adj secondary
sed [seð] nf thirst; **tener ~** to be thirsty
seda ['seða] nf silk
sedal [se'ðal] nm fishing line
sedán [se'ðan] (LAM) nm saloon (BRIT), sedan (US)
sedante [se'ðante] nm sedative
sede ['seðe] nf (de gobierno) seat; (de compañía) headquarters pl; **Santa S~** Holy See
sedentario, -a [seðen'tario, a] adj sedentary
sediento, -a [se'ðjento, a] adj thirsty
sedimento [seði'mento] nm sediment
seducción [seðuk'θjon] nf seduction
seducir [seðu'θir] vt to seduce; (cautivar) to charm, fascinate; (atraer) to attract; **seductor, a** adj seductive; charming, fascinating; attractive ▷ nm/f seducer
segar [se'ɣar] vt (mies) to reap, cut; (hierba) to mow, cut
seglar [se'ɣlar] adj secular, lay
seguida [se'ɣiða] nf: **en ~** at once, right away
seguido, -a [se'ɣiðo, a] adj (continuo) continuous, unbroken; (recto) straight ▷ adv (directo) straight (on); (después) after; (LAM: a menudo) often; **~s**

consecutive, successive; **5 días ~s** 5 days running, 5 days in a row

seguir [se'ɣir] vt to follow; (*venir después*) to follow on, come after; (*proseguir*) to continue; (*perseguir*) to chase, pursue ▷ vi (*gen*) to follow; (*continuar*) to continue, carry o go on; **seguirse** vr to follow; **sigo sin comprender** I still don't understand; **sigue lloviendo** it's still raining

según [se'ɣun] prep according to ▷ adv: **¿irás? ~ ~** are you going? – it all depends ▷ conj as; **~ caminamos** while we walk

segundo, -a [se'ɣundo, a] adj second ▷ nm second ▷ nf second meaning; **de segunda mano** second-hand; **segunda (clase)** second class; **segunda (marcha)** (*Auto*) second (gear)

seguramente [seɣura'mɛntɛ] adv surely; (*con certeza*) for sure, with certainty

seguridad [seɣuri'ðað] nf safety; (*del estado, de casa etc*) security; (*certidumbre*) certainty; (*confianza*) confidence; (*estabilidad*) stability; **seguridad social** social security

seguro, -a [se'ɣuro, a] adj (*cierto*) sure, certain; (*fiel*) trustworthy; (*libre de peligro*) safe; (*bien defendido, firme*) secure ▷ adv for sure, certainly ▷ nm (*Com*) insurance; **seguro contra terceros/a todo riesgo** third party/comprehensive insurance; **seguros sociales** social security sg

seis [seis] num six

seísmo [se'ismo] nm tremor, earthquake

selección [selek'θjon] nf selection; **seleccionar** vt to pick, choose, select

selectividad [selektiβi'ðað] (ESP) nf university entrance examination

selecto, -a [se'lekto, a] adj select, choice; (*escogido*) selected

sellar [se'ʎar] vt (*documento oficial*) to seal; (*pasaporte, visado*) to stamp

sello ['seʎo] nm stamp; (*precinto*) seal

selva ['selβa] nf (*bosque*) forest, woods pl; (*jungla*) jungle

semáforo [se'maforo] nm (*Auto*) traffic lights pl; (*Ferro*) signal

semana [se'mana] nf week; **entre ~** during the week; **Semana Santa** Holy Week; **semanal** adj weekly; **semanario** nm weekly magazine

● **SEMANA SANTA**
●
●
● In Spain celebrations for **Semana**
● **Santa** (Holy Week) are often
● spectacular. "Viernes Santo",
● "Sábado Santo" and "Domingo de
● Resurrección" (Good Friday, Holy
● Saturday, Easter Sunday) are all
● national public holidays, with
● additional days being given as
● local holidays. There are fabulous
● **procesiones** all over the country,
● with members of "cofradías"
● (brotherhoods) dressing in hooded
● robes and parading their "pasos"
● (religious floats and sculptures)
● through the streets. Seville has
● the most famous Holy Week
● processions.

sembrar [sem'brar] vt to sow; (*objetos*) to sprinkle, scatter about; (*noticias etc*) to spread

semejante [seme'xante] adj (*parecido*) similar ▷ nm fellow man, fellow creature; **~s** alike, similar; **nunca hizo cosa ~** he never did any such thing; **semejanza** nf similarity, resemblance

semejar [seme'xar] vi to seem like, resemble; **semejarse** vr to look alike, be similar

semen ['semen] nm semen

semestral [semes'tral] adj half-yearly, bi-annual

semicírculo [semi'θirkulo] nm semicircle

semidesnatado, -a [semiðesna'taðo, a] adj semi-

skimmed
semifinal [semifi'nal] nf semifinal
semilla [se'miʎa] nf seed
seminario [semi'narjo] nm (Rel) seminary; (Escol) seminar
sémola ['semola] nf semolina
senado [se'naðo] nm senate; **senador, a** nm/f senator
sencillez [senθi'ʎeθ] nf simplicity; (de persona) naturalness; **sencillo, -a** adj simple; natural, unaffected
senda ['senda] nf path, track
senderismo [sende'rismo] nm hiking
sendero [sen'dero] nm path, track
sendos, -as ['sendos, as] adj pl: **les dio ~ golpes** he hit both of them
senil [se'nil] adj senile
seno ['seno] nm (Anat) bosom, bust; (fig) bosom; **~s** breasts
sensación [sensa'θjon] nf sensation; (sentido) sense; (sentimiento) feeling; **sensacional** adj sensational
sensato, -a [sen'sato, a] adj sensible
sensible [sen'sible] adj sensitive; (apreciable) perceptible, appreciable; (pérdida) considerable

▌No confundir **sensible** con la palabra inglesa sensible.

sensiblero, -a adj sentimental
sensitivo, -a [sensi'tiβo, a] adj sense cpd
sensorial [senso'rjal] adj sensory
sensual [sen'swal] adj sensual
sentada [sen'taða] nf sitting; (protesta) sit-in
sentado, -a [sen'taðo, a] adj: **estar ~** to sit, be sitting (down); **dar por ~** to take for granted, assume
sentar [sen'tar] vt to sit, seat; (fig) to establish ▷ vi (vestido) to suit; (alimento): **~ bien/mal a** to agree/disagree with; **sentarse** vr (persona) to sit, sit down; (los depósitos) to settle
sentencia [sen'tenθja] nf (máxima) maxim, saying; (Jur) sentence; **sentenciar** vt to sentence
sentido, -a [sen'tiðo, a] adj (pérdida)

regrettable; (carácter) sensitive ▷ nm sense; (sentimiento) feeling; (significado) sense, meaning; (dirección) direction; **mi más ~ pésame** my deepest sympathy; **tener ~** to make sense; **sentido común** common sense; **sentido del humor** sense of humour; **sentido único** one-way (street)
sentimental [sentimen'tal] adj sentimental; **vida ~** love life
sentimiento [senti'mjento] nm feeling
sentir [sen'tir] vt to feel; (percibir) to perceive, sense; (lamentar) to regret, be sorry for ▷ vi (tener la sensación) to feel; (lamentarse) to feel sorry ▷ nm opinion, judgement; **~se bien/mal** to feel well/ill; **lo siento** I'm sorry
seña ['seɲa] nf sign; (Mil) password; **señas** nfpl (dirección) address sg; **señas personales** personal description sg
señal [se'ɲal] nf sign; (síntoma) symptom; (Ferro, Tel) signal; (marca) mark; (Com) deposit; **en ~ de** as a token o sign of; **señalar** vt to mark; (indicar) to point out, indicate
señor [se'ɲor] nm (hombre) man; (caballero) gentleman; (dueño) owner, master; (trato: antes de nombre propio) Mr; (: hablando directamente) sir; **muy ~ mío** Dear Sir; **el ~ alcalde/presidente** the mayor/president
señora [se'ɲora] nf (dama) lady; (trato: antes de nombre propio) Mrs; (: hablando directamente) madam; (esposa) wife; **Nuestra S~** Our Lady
señorita [seɲo'rita] nf (con nombre y/o apellido) Miss; (mujer joven) young lady
señorito [seɲo'rito] nm young gentleman; (pey) rich kid
sepa etc vb V **saber**
separación [separa'θjon] nf separation; (división) division; (hueco) gap
separar [sepa'rar] vt to separate; (dividir) to divide; **separarse** vr (parte) to come away; (partes) to come apart;

(persona) to leave, go away; (matrimonio) to separate; **separatismo** nm separatism

sepia ['sepja] nf cuttlefish

septentrional [septentrjo'nal] adj northern

se(p)tiembre [sep'tjembre] nm September

séptimo, -a ['septimo, a] adj, nm seventh

sepulcral [sepul'kral] adj (fig: silencio, atmósfera) deadly; **sepulcro** nm tomb, grave

sepultar [sepul'tar] vt to bury; **sepultura** nf (acto) burial; (tumba) grave, tomb

sequía [se'kia] nf drought

séquito ['sekito] nm (de rey etc) retinue; (seguidores) followers pl

○ **PALABRA CLAVE**

ser [ser] vi **1** (descripción) to be; **es médica/muy alta** she's a doctor/very tall; **la familia es de Cuzco** his (o her etc) family is from Cuzco; **soy Ana** (Tel) Ana speaking o here

2 (propiedad): **es de Joaquín** it's Joaquín's, it belongs to Joaquín

3 (horas, fechas, números): **es la una** it's one o'clock; **son las seis y media** it's half-past six; **es el 1 de junio** it's the first of June; **somos/son seis** there are six of us/them

4 (en oraciones pasivas): **ha sido descubierto ya** it's already been discovered

5: **es de esperar que ...** it is to be hoped o I etc hope that ...

6 (locuciones con sub): **o sea** that is to say; **sea él sea su hermana** either him or his sister

7: **a no ser por él ...** but for him ...

8: **a no ser que: a no ser que tenga uno ya** unless he's got one already ▷ nm being; **ser humano** human being

sereno, -a [se'reno, a] adj (persona) calm, unruffled; (el tiempo) fine, settled; (ambiente) calm, peaceful ▷ nm night watchman

serial [ser'jal] nm serial

serie ['serje] nf series; (cadena) sequence, succession; **fuera de ~** out of order; (fig) special, out of the ordinary; **fabricación en ~** mass production

seriedad [serje'ðað] nf seriousness; (formalidad) reliability; **serio, -a** adj serious; reliable, dependable; grave, serious; **en serio** adv seriously

serigrafía [seriɣra'fia] nf silk-screen printing

sermón [ser'mon] nm (Rel) sermon

seropositivo, -a [seroposi'tiβo] adj HIV positive

serpentear [serpente'ar] vi to wriggle; (camino, río) to wind, snake

serpentina [serpen'tina] nf streamer

serpiente [ser'pjente] nf snake; **serpiente de cascabel** rattlesnake

serranía [serra'nia] nf mountainous area

serrar [se'rrar] vt = **aserrar**

serrín [se'rrin] nm sawdust

serrucho [se'rrutʃo] nm saw

service ['serβis] (RPL) nm (Auto) service

servicio [ser'βiθjo] nm service; (LAM Auto) service; **servicios** nmpl (ESP) toilet(s); **servicio incluido** service charge included; **servicio militar** military service

servidumbre [serβi'ðumbre] nf (sujeción) servitude; (criados) servants pl, staff

servil [ser'βil] adj servile

servilleta [serβi'ʎeta] nf serviette, napkin

servir [ser'βir] vt to serve ▷ vi to serve; (tener utilidad) to be of use, be useful; **servirse** vr to serve o help o.s.; **~se de algo** to make use of sth, use sth; **sírvase pasar** please come in

sesenta [se'senta] *num* sixty
sesión [se'sjon] *nf* (*Pol*) session, sitting; (*Cine*) showing
seso ['seso] *nm* brain; **sesudo, -a** *adj* sensible, wise
seta ['seta] *nf* mushroom; **seta venenosa** toadstool
setecientos, -as [sete'θjentos, as] *adj, num* seven hundred
setenta [se'tenta] *num* seventy
seto ['seto] *nm* hedge
severo, -a [se'βero, a] *adj* severe
Sevilla [se'βiʎa] *n* Seville; **sevillano, -a** *adj* of o from Seville ▷ *nm/f* native o inhabitant of Seville
sexo ['sekso] *nm* sex
sexto, -a ['seksto, a] *adj, nm* sixth
sexual [sek'swal] *adj* sexual; **vida ~** sex life
si [si] *conj* if ▷ *nm* (*Mús*) B; **me pregunto ~ ...** I wonder if o whether ...
sí [si] *adv* yes ▷ *nm* consent ▷ *pron* (*uso impersonal*) oneself; (*sg: m*) himself; (: *f*) herself; (: *de cosa*) itself; (*de usted*) yourself; (*pl*) themselves; (*de ustedes*) yourselves; (*recíproco*) each other; **él no quiere pero yo ~** he doesn't want to but I do; **ella ~ vendrá** she will certainly come, she is sure to come; **claro que ~** of course; **creo que ~** I think so
siamés, -esa [sja'mes, esa] *adj, nm/f* Siamese
SIDA ['siða] *nm abr* (= *Síndrome de Inmunodeficiencia Adquirida*) AIDS
siderúrgico, -a [siðe'rurxico, a] *adj* iron and steel *cpd*
sidra ['siðra] *nf* cider
siembra ['sjembra] *nf* sowing
siempre ['sjempre] *adv* always; (*todo el tiempo*) all the time; **~ que** (*cada vez*) whenever; (*dado que*) provided that; **como ~** as usual; **para ~** for ever
sien [sjen] *nf* temple
siento *etc* ['sjento] *vb* V **sentar; sentir**
sierra ['sjerra] *nf* (*Tec*) saw; (*cadena de montañas*) mountain range

siervo, -a ['sjerβo, a] *nm/f* slave
siesta ['sjesta] *nf* siesta, nap; **echar la ~** to have an afternoon nap o a siesta
siete ['sjete] *num* seven
sifón [si'fon] *nm* syphon
sigla ['siɣla] *nf* abbreviation; acronym
siglo ['siɣlo] *nm* century; (*fig*) age
significado [siɣnifi'kaðo] *nm* (*de palabra etc*) meaning
significar [siɣnifi'kar] *vt* to mean, signify; (*notificar*) to make known, express
significativo, -a [siɣnifika'tiβo, a] *adj* significant
signo ['siɣno] *nm* sign; **signo de admiración** o **exclamación** exclamation mark; **signo de interrogación** question mark
sigo *etc vb* V **seguir**
siguiente [si'ɣjente] *adj* next, following
siguió *etc vb* V **seguir**
sílaba ['silaβa] *nf* syllable
silbar [sil'βar] *vt, vi* to whistle; **silbato** *nm* whistle; **silbido** *nm* whistle, whistling
silenciador [silenθja'ðor] *nm* silencer
silenciar [silen'θjar] *vt* (*persona*) to silence; (*escándalo*) to hush up; **silencio** *nm* silence, quiet; **silencioso, -a** *adj* silent, quiet
silla ['siʎa] *nf* (*asiento*) chair; (*tb*: **~ de montar**) saddle; **silla de ruedas** wheelchair
sillón [si'ʎon] *nm* armchair, easy chair
silueta [si'lweta] *nf* silhouette; (*de edificio*) outline; (*figura*) figure
silvestre [sil'βestre] *adj* wild
simbólico, -a [sim'boliko, a] *adj* symbolic(al)
simbolizar [simboli'θar] *vt* to symbolize
símbolo ['simbolo] *nm* symbol
similar [simi'lar] *adj* similar
simio ['simjo] *nm* ape
simpatía [simpa'tia] *nf* liking; (*afecto*) affection; (*amabilidad*) kindness;

simpático, -a adj nice, pleasant; kind ▪ No confundir **simpático** con la palabra inglesa *sympathetic*.

simpatizante [simpati'θante] nmf sympathizer

simpatizar [simpati'θar] vi: **~ con** to get on well with

simple ['simple] adj simple; (*elemental*) simple, easy; (*mero*) mere; (*puro*) pure, sheer ▷ nmf simpleton; **simpleza** nf simpleness; (*necedad*) silly thing; **simplificar** vt to simplify

simposio [sim'posjo] nm symposium

simular [simu'lar] vt to simulate

simultáneo, -a [simul'taneo, a] adj simultaneous

sin [sin] prep without; **la ropa está ~ lavar** the clothes are unwashed; **~ que** without; **~ embargo** however, still

sinagoga [sina'ɣoɣa] nf synagogue

sinceridad [sinθeri'ðað] nf sincerity; **sincero, -a** adj sincere

sincronizar [sinkroni'θar] vt to synchronize

sindical [sindi'kal] adj union cpd, trade union cpd; **sindicalista** adj, nmf trade unionist

sindicato [sindi'kato] nm (*de trabajadores*) trade(s) union; (*de negociantes*) syndicate

síndrome ['sindrome] nm (Med) syndrome; **síndrome de abstinencia** (Med) withdrawal symptoms; **síndrome de de la clase turista** (Med) economy-class syndrome

sinfín [sin'fin] nm: **un ~ de** a great many, no end of

sinfonía [sinfo'nia] nf symphony

singular [singu'lar] adj singular; (*fig*) outstanding, exceptional; (*raro*) peculiar, odd

siniestro, -a [si'njestro, a] adj sinister ▷ nm (*accidente*) accident

sinnúmero [sin'numero] nm = **sinfín**

sino ['sino] nm fate, destiny ▷ conj (*pero*) but; (*salvo*) except, save

sinónimo, -a [si'nonimo, a] adj

synonymous ▷ nm synonym

síntesis ['sintesis] nf synthesis; **sintético, -a** adj synthetic

sintió vb V **sentir**

síntoma ['sintoma] nm symptom

sintonía [sinto'nia] nf (Radio, Mús: *de programa*) tuning; **sintonizar** vt (Radio: *emisora*) to tune (in)

sinvergüenza [simber'ɣwenθa] nmf rogue, scoundrel; **¡es un ~!** he's got a nerve!

siquiera [si'kjera] conj even if, even though ▷ adv at least; **ni ~** not even

Siria ['sirja] nf Syria

sirviente, -a [sir'βjente, a] nm/f servant

sirvo etc vb V **servir**

sistema [sis'tema] nm system, (*método*) method, **sistema educativo** education system; **sistemático, -a** adj systematic

SISTEMA EDUCATIVO

The reform of the Spanish **sistema educativo** (education system) begun in the early 90s has replaced the courses **EGB**, **BUP** and **COU** with the following: "Primaria" a compulsory 6 years; "Secundaria" a compulsory 4 years and "Bachillerato" an optional 2-year secondary school course, essential for those wishing to go on to higher education.

sitiar [si'tjar] vt to besiege, lay siege to

sitio ['sitjo] nm (*lugar*) place; (*espacio*) room, space; (*Mil*) siege; **sitio de taxis** (MÉX: *parada*) taxi stand o rank (BRIT); **sitio web** (*Inform*) website

situación [sitwa'θjon] nf situation, position; (*estatus*) position, standing

situado, -a [situ'aðo] adj situated, placed

situar [si'twar] vt to place, put; (*edificio*) to locate, situate

slip [slip] *nm* pants *pl*, briefs *pl*

smoking ['smokin, es'mokin] (*pl* **~s**) *nm* dinner jacket (*BRIT*), tuxedo (*US*)

▌ No confunda **smoking** con la palabra inglesa *smoking*.

SMS *nm* (*mensaje*) text message, SMS message

snob [es'nob] = **esnob**

SO *abr* (= *suroeste*) SW

sobaco [so'βako] *nm* armpit

sobar [so'βar] *vt* (*ropa*) to rumple; (*comida*) to play around with

soberanía [soβera'nia] *nf* sovereignty; **soberano, -a** *adj* sovereign; (*fig*) supreme ▷ *nm/f* sovereign

soberbia [so'βerβja] *nf* pride; haughtiness, arrogance; magnificence

soberbio, -a [so'βerβjo, a] *adj* (*orgulloso*) proud; (*altivo*) arrogant; (*estupendo*) magnificent, superb

sobornar [soβor'nar] *vt* to bribe; **soborno** *nm* bribe

sobra ['soβra] *nf* excess, surplus; **sobras** *nfpl* left-overs, scraps; **de ~** surplus, extra; **tengo de ~** I've more than enough; **sobrado, -a** *adj* (*más que suficiente*) more than enough; (*superfluo*) excessive; **sobrante** *adj* remaining, extra ▷ *nm* surplus, remainder

sobrar [so'βrar] *vt* to exceed, surpass ▷ *vi* (*tener de más*) to be more than enough; (*quedar*) to remain, be left (over)

sobrasada [soβra'saða] *nf* pork sausage spread

sobre ['soβre] *prep* (*gen*) on; (*encima*) on (top of); (*por encima de, arriba de*) over, above; (*más que*) more than; (*además*) in addition to, besides; (*alrededor de*) about ▷ *nm* envelope; **~ todo** above all

sobrecama [soβre'kama] *nf* bedspread

sobrecargar [soβrekar'ɣar] *vt* (*camión*) to overload; (*Com*) to surcharge

sobredosis [soβre'ðosis] *nf inv* overdose

sobreentender [soβre(e)nten'der] *vt* to deduce, infer; **sobreentenderse** *vr*: **se sobreentiende que ...** it is implied that ...

sobrehumano, -a [soβreu'mano, a] *adj* superhuman

sobrellevar [soβreʎe'βar] *vt* to bear, endure

sobremesa [soβre'mesa] *nf*: **durante la ~** after dinner

sobrenatural [soβrenatu'ral] *adj* supernatural

sobrenombre [soβre'nombre] *nm* nickname

sobrepasar [soβrepa'sar] *vt* to exceed, surpass

sobreponerse [soβrepo'nerse] *vr*: **~ a** to overcome

sobresaliente [soβresa'ljente] *adj* outstanding, excellent

sobresalir [soβresa'lir] *vi* to project, jut out; (*fig*) to stand out, excel

sobresaltar [soβresal'tar] *vt* (*asustar*) to scare, frighten; (*sobrecoger*) to startle; **sobresalto** *nm* (*movimiento*) start; (*susto*) scare; (*turbación*) sudden shock

sobretodo [soβre'toðo] *nm* overcoat

sobrevenir [soβreβe'nir] *vi* (*ocurrir*) to happen (unexpectedly); (*resultar*) to follow, ensue

sobrevivir [soβreβi'βir] *vi* to survive

sobrevolar [soβreβo'lar] *vt* to fly over

sobriedad [soβrje'ðað] *nf* sobriety, soberness; (*moderación*) moderation, restraint

sobrino, -a [so'βrino, a] *nm/f* nephew/niece

sobrio, -a ['soβrjo, a] *adj* sober; (*moderado*) moderate, restrained

socarrón, -ona [soka'rron, ona] *adj* (*sarcástico*) sarcastic, ironic(al)

socavón [soka'βon] *nm* (*hoyo*) hole

sociable [so'θjaβle] *adj* (*persona*) sociable, friendly; (*animal*) social

social [so'θjal] *adj* social; (*Com*) company *cpd*

socialdemócrata [soθjalde'mokrata] *nmf* social democrat

socialista [soθja'lista] *adj, nm* socialist

socializar [soθjali'θar] *vt* to socialize

sociedad [soθje'ðað] *nf* society; (*Com*) company; **sociedad anónima** limited company; **sociedad de consumo** consumer society

socio, -a ['soθjo, a] *nm/f* (*miembro*) member; (*Com*) partner

sociología [soθjolo'xia] *nf* sociology; **sociólogo, -a** *nm/f* sociologist

socorrer [soko'rrer] *vt* to help; **socorrista** *nmf* first aider; (*en piscina, playa*) lifeguard; **socorro** *nm* (*ayuda*) help, aid; (*Mil*) relief; **¡socorro!** help!

soda ['soða] *nf* (*sosa*) soda; (*bebida*) soda (water)

sofá [so'fa] (*pl* **~s**) *nm* sofa, settee; **sofá-cama** *nm* studio couch; sofa bed

sofocar [sofo'kar] *vt* to suffocate; (*apagar*) to smother, put out; **sofocarse** *vr* to suffocate; (*fig*) to blush, feel embarrassed; **sofoco** *nm* suffocation; embarrassment

sofreír [sofre'ir] *vt* (*Culin*) to fry lightly

software ['sofwer] *nm* (*Inform*) software

soga ['soγa] *nf* rope

sois *etc vb* V **ser**

soja ['soxa] *nf* soya

sol [sol] *nm* sun; (*luz*) sunshine, sunlight; (*Mús*) G; **hace ~** it's sunny

solamente [sola'mente] *adv* only, just

solapa [so'lapa] *nf* (*de chaqueta*) lapel; (*de libro*) jacket

solapado, -a [sola'paðo, a] *adj* (*intenciónes*) underhand; (*gestos, movimiento*) sly

solar [so'lar] *adj* solar, sun *cpd*; (*terreno*) plot (of ground)

soldado [sol'daðo] *nm* soldier; **soldado raso** private

soldador [solda'ðor] *nm* soldering iron; (*persona*) welder

soldar [sol'dar] *vt* to solder, weld

soleado, -a [sole'aðo, a] *adj* sunny

soledad [sole'ðað] *nf* solitude; (*estado infeliz*) loneliness

solemne [so'lemne] *adj* solemn

soler [so'ler] *vi* to be in the habit of, be accustomed to; **suele salir a las ocho** she usually goes out at eight o'clock

solfeo [sol'feo] *nm* solfa

solicitar [soliθi'tar] *vt* (*permiso*) to ask for, seek; (*puesto*) to apply for; (*votos*) to canvass for; (*atención*) to attract

solícito, -a [so'liθito, a] *adj* (*diligente*) diligent; (*cuidadoso*) careful; **solicitud** *nf* (*calidad*) great care; (*petición*) request; (*a un puesto*) application

solidaridad [soliðari'ðað] *nf* solidarity; **solidario, -a** *adj* (*participación*) joint, common; (*compromiso*) mutually binding

sólido, -a [so'liðo, a] *adj* solid

soliloquio [soli'lokjo] *nm* soliloquy

solista [so'lista] *nmf* soloist

solitario, -a [soli'tarjo, a] *adj* (*persona*) lonely, solitary; (*lugar*) lonely, desolate ▷ *nm/f* (*recluso*) recluse; (*en la sociedad*) loner ▷ *nm* solitaire

sollozar [soʎo'θar] *vi* to sob; **sollozo** *nm* sob

solo, -a ['solo, a] *adj* (*único*) single, sole; (*sin compañía*) alone; (*solitario*) lonely; **hay una sola dificultad** there is just one difficulty; **a solas** alone, by oneself

sólo ['solo] *adv* only, just

solomillo [solo'miʎo] *nm* sirloin

soltar [sol'tar] *vt* (*dejar ir*) to let go of; (*desprender*) to unfasten, loosen; (*librar*) to release, set free; (*risa etc*) to let out

soltero, -a [sol'tero, a] *adj* single, unmarried ▷ *nm/f* bachelor/single woman; **solterón, -ona** *nm/f* old bachelor/spinster

soltura [sol'tura] *nf* looseness,

slackness; (*de los miembros*) agility, ease of movement; (*en el hablar*) fluency, ease

soluble [so'luβle] *adj* (*Quím*) soluble; (*problema*) solvable; **~ en agua** soluble in water

solución [solu'θjon] *nf* solution; **solucionar** *vt* (*problema*) to solve; (*asunto*) to settle, resolve

solventar [solβen'tar] *vt* (*pagar*) to settle, pay; (*resolver*) to resolve; **solvente** *adj* (*Econ: empresa, persona*) solvent

sombra ['sombra] *nf* shadow; (*como protección*) shade; **sombras** *nfpl* (*oscuridad*) darkness *sg*, shadows; **tener buena/mala ~** to be lucky/unlucky

sombrero [som'brero] *nm* hat

sombrilla [som'briʎa] *nf* parasol, sunshade

sombrío, -a [som'brio, a] *adj* (*oscuro*) dark; (*triste*) sombre, sad; (*persona*) gloomy

someter [some'ter] *vt* (*país*) to conquer; (*persona*) to subject to one's will; (*informe*) to present, submit; **someterse** *vr* to give in, yield, submit; **~ a** to subject to

somier [so'mjer] (*pl* **~s**) *n* spring mattress

somnífero [som'nifero] *nm* sleeping pill

somos *vb* V **ser**

son [son] *vb* V **ser** ▷ *nm* sound

sonaja [so'naxa] (*MÉX*) *nf* = **sonajero**

sonajero [sona'xero] *nm* (baby's) rattle

sonambulismo [sonambu'lismo] *nm* sleepwalking; **sonámbulo, -a** *nm/f* sleepwalker

sonar [so'nar] *vt* to ring ▷ *vi* to sound; (*hacer ruido*) to make a noise; (*pronunciarse*) to be sounded, be pronounced; (*ser conocido*) to sound familiar; (*campana*) to ring; (*reloj*) to strike, chime; **sonarse** *vr*: **~se (las narices)** to blow one's nose; **me suena ese nombre** that name rings a bell

sonda ['sonda] *nf* (*Náut*) sounding; (*Tec*) bore, drill; (*Med*) probe

sondear [sonde'ar] *vt* to sound; to bore (into), drill; to probe, sound; (*fig*) to sound out; **sondeo** *nm* sounding; boring, drilling; (*fig*) poll, enquiry

sonido [so'niðo] *nm* sound

sonoro, -a [so'noro, a] *adj* sonorous; (*resonante*) loud, resonant

sonreír [sonre'ir] *vi* to smile; **sonreírse** *vr* to smile; **sonriente** *adj* smiling; **sonrisa** *nf* smile

sonrojarse [sonro'xarse] *vr* to blush, go red; **sonrojo** *nm* blush

soñador, a [soɲa'ðor, a] *nm/f* dreamer

soñar [so'ɲar] *vt, vi* to dream; **~ con** to dream about *o* of

soñoliento, -a [soɲo'ljento, a] *adj* sleepy, drowsy

sopa ['sopa] *nf* soup

soplar [so'plar] *vt* (*polvo*) to blow away, blow off; (*inflar*) to blow up; (*vela*) to blow out ▷ *vi* to blow; **soplo** *nm* blow, puff; (*de viento*) puff, gust

soplón, -ona [so'plon, ona] (*fam*) *nm/f* (*niño*) telltale; (*de policía*) grass (*fam*)

soporífero [sopo'rifero] *nm* sleeping pill

soportable [sopor'taβle] *adj* bearable

soportar [sopor'tar] *vt* to bear, carry; (*fig*) to bear, put up with

▌ No confundir **soportar** con la palabra inglesa *support*.

soporte *nm* support; (*fig*) pillar, support

soprano [so'prano] *nf* soprano

sorber [sor'βer] *vt* (*chupar*) to sip; (*absorber*) to soak up, absorb

sorbete [sor'βete] *nm* iced fruit drink

sorbo ['sorβo] *nm* (*trago: grande*) gulp, swallow; (: *pequeño*) sip

sordera [sor'ðera] *nf* deafness

sórdido, -a ['sorðiðo, a] *adj* dirty, squalid

sordo, -a ['sorðo, a] *adj* (*persona*) deaf

▷ nm/f deaf person; **sordomudo, -a** adj deaf and dumb

sorna ['sorna] nf sarcastic tone

soroche [so'rotʃe] (CAM) nm mountain sickness

sorprendente [sorpren'dente] adj surprising

sorprender [sorpren'der] vt to surprise; **sorpresa** nf surprise

sortear [sorte'ar] vt to draw lots for; (rifar) to raffle; (dificultad) to avoid; **sorteo** nm (en lotería) draw; (rifa) raffle

sortija [sor'tixa] nf ring; (rizo) ringlet, curl

sosegado, -a [sose'xaðo, a] adj quiet, calm

sosiego [so'sjexo] nm quiet(ness), calm(ness)

soso, -a ['soso, a] adj (Culin) tasteless; (aburrido) dull, uninteresting

sospecha [sos'petʃa] nf suspicion; **sospechar** vt to suspect; **sospechoso, -a** adj suspicious; (testimonio, opinión) suspect ▷ nm/f suspect

sostén [sos'ten] nm (apoyo) support; (sujetador) bra; (alimentación) sustenance, food

sostener [soste'ner] vt to support; (mantener) to keep up, maintain; (alimentar) to sustain, keep going; **sostenerse** vr to support o.s.; (seguir) to continue, remain; **sostenido, -a** adj continuous, sustained; (prolongado) prolonged

sotana [so'tana] nf (Rel) cassock

sótano ['sotano] nm basement

soy [soi] vb V **ser**

soya ['soja] (LAM) nf soya (BRIT), soy (US)

Sr. abr (= Señor) Mr

Sra. abr (= Señora) Mrs

Sras. abr (= Señoras) Mrs

Sres. abr (= Señores) Messrs

Srta. abr (= Señorita) Miss

Sta. abr (= Santa) St

Sto. abr (= Santo) St

su [su] pron (de él) his; (de ella) her; (de una cosa) its; (de ellos, ellas) their; (de usted, ustedes) your

suave ['swaβe] adj gentle; (superficie) smooth; (trabajo) easy; (música, voz) soft, sweet; **suavidad** nf gentleness; smoothness; softness, sweetness; **suavizante** nm (de ropa) softener; (del pelo) conditioner; **suavizar** vt to soften; (quitar la aspereza) to smooth (out)

subasta [su'βasta] nf auction; **subastar** vt to auction (off)

subcampeón, -ona [suβkampe'on, ona] nm/f runner-up

subconsciente [suβkon'sθjente] adj, nm subconscious

subdesarrollado, -a [suβðesarro'ʎaðo, a] adj underdeveloped

subdesarrollo [suβðesa'rroʎo] nm underdevelopment

subdirector, a [suβðirek'tor, a] nm/f assistant director

súbdito, -a [su'βðito, a] nm/f subject

subestimar [suβesti'mar] vt to underestimate, underrate

subida [su'βiða] nf (de montaña etc) ascent, climb; (de precio) rise, increase; (pendiente) slope, hill

subir [su'βir] vt (objeto) to raise, lift up; (cuesta, calle) to go up, (colina, montaña) to climb; (precio) to raise, put up ▷ vi to go up, come up; (a un coche) to get in; (a un autobús, tren o avión) to get on, board; (precio) to rise, go up; (río, marea) to rise; **subirse** vr to get up, climb

súbito, -a ['suβito, a] adj (repentino) sudden; (imprevisto) unexpected

subjetivo, -a [suβxe'tiβo, a] adj subjective

sublevar [suβle'βar] vt to rouse to revolt; **sublevarse** vr to revolt, rise

sublime [su'βlime] adj sublime

submarinismo [suβmari'nismo] nm scuba diving

submarino, -a [suβma'rino, a] adj

underwater ▷ *nm* submarine
subnormal [suβnor'mal] *adj*
subnormal ▷ *nmf* subnormal person
subordinado, -a [suβorði'naðo, a]
adj, nm/f subordinate
subrayar [suβra'jar] *vt* to underline
subsanar [suβsa'nar] *vt* to rectify
subsidio [suβ'siðjo] *nm* (*ayuda*) aid,
financial help; (*subvención*) subsidy,
grant; (*de enfermedad, paro etc*) benefit,
allowance
subsistencia [suβsis'tenθja] *nf*
subsistence
subsistir [suβsis'tir] *vi* to subsist;
(*sobrevivir*) to survive, endure
subte ['suβte] (*RPL*) *nm* underground
(*BRIT*), subway (*US*)
subterráneo, -a [suβte'rraneo, a]
adj underground, subterranean ▷ *nm*
underpass, underground passage
subtitulado, -a [suβtitu'laðo] *adj*
subtitled
subtítulo [suβ'titulo] *nm* (*Cine*)
subtitle
suburbio [su'βurβjo] *nm* (*barrio*)
slum quarter
subvención [suββen'θjon] *nf* (*Econ*)
subsidy, grant; **subvencionar** *vt* to
subsidize
sucedáneo, -a [suθe'ðaneo, a] *adj*
substitute ▷ *nm* substitute (food)
suceder [suθe'ðer] *vt, vi* to happen;
(*seguir*) to succeed, follow; **lo que
sucede es que ...** the fact is that
...; **sucesión** *nf* succession; (*serie*)
sequence, series
sucesivamente [suθesiβa'mente]
adv: **y así ~** and so on
sucesivo, -a [suθe'siβo, a] *adj*
successive, following; **en lo ~** in future,
from now on
suceso [su'θeso] *nm* (*hecho*) event,
happening; (*incidente*) incident

▌ No confundir **suceso** con la palabra
inglesa *success*.

suciedad [suθje'ðað] *nf* (*estado*)
dirtiness; (*mugre*) dirt, filth
sucio, -a ['suθjo, a] *adj* dirty

suculento, -a [suku'lento, a] *adj*
succulent
sucumbir [sukum'bir] *vi* to succumb
sucursal [sukur'sal] *nf* branch
(office)
sudadera [suða'ðera] *nf* sweatshirt
Sudáfrica [suð'afrika] *nf* South
Africa
Sudamérica [suða'merika] *nf* South
America; **sudamericano, -a** *adj, nm/f*
South American
sudar [su'ðar] *vt, vi* to sweat
sudeste [su'ðeste] *nm* south-east
sudoeste [suðo'este] *nm* south-west
sudoku [su'doku] *nm* sudoku
sudor [su'ðor] *nm* sweat; **sudoroso,
-a** *adj* sweaty, sweating
Suecia ['sweθja] *nf* Sweden; **sueco,
-a** *adj* Swedish ▷ *nm/f* Swede
suegro, -a ['sweɣro, a] *nm/f* father-/
mother-in-law
suela ['swela] *nf* sole
sueldo ['sweldo] *nm* pay, wage(s) (*pl*)
suele *etc* *vb* V **soler**
suelo ['swelo] *nm* (*tierra*) ground; (*de
casa*) floor
suelto, -a ['swelto, a] *adj* loose;
(*libre*) free; (*separado*) detached; (*ágil*)
quick, agile ▷ *nm* (loose) change,
small change
sueñito [swe'ɲito] (*LAM*) *nm* nap
sueño *etc* *vb* V **soñar**
▷ *nm* sleep; (*somnolencia*) sleepiness,
drowsiness; (*lo soñado, fig*) dream;
tener ~ to be sleepy
suero ['swero] *nm* (*Med*) serum; (*de
leche*) whey
suerte ['swerte] *nf* (*fortuna*) luck;
(*azar*) chance; (*destino*) fate, destiny;
(*especie*) sort, kind; **tener ~** to be lucky
suéter ['sweter] *nm* sweater
suficiente [sufi'θjente] *adj* enough,
sufficient ▷ *nm* (*Escol*) pass
sufragio [su'fraxjo] *nm* (*voto*) vote;
(*derecho de voto*) suffrage
sufrido, -a [su'friðo, a] *adj* (*persona*)
tough; (*paciente*) long-suffering,
patient

sufrimiento [sufri'mjento] nm
(dolor) suffering
sufrir [su'frir] vt (padecer) to suffer;
(soportar) to bear, put up with; (apoyar)
to hold up, support ▷ vi to suffer
sugerencia [suxe'renθja] nf
suggestion
sugerir [suxe'rir] vt to suggest;
(sutilmente) to hint
sugestión [suxes'tjon] nf
suggestion; (sutil) hint; **sugestionar**
vt to influence
sugestivo, -a [suxes'tiβo, a] adj
stimulating; (fascinante) fascinating
suicida [sui'θiða] adj suicidal ▷ nmf
suicidal person; (muerto) suicide,
person who has committed suicide;
suicidarse vr to commit suicide, kill
o.s.; **suicidio** nm suicide
Suiza ['swiθa] nf Switzerland; **suizo,
-a** adj, nm/f Swiss
sujeción [suxe'θjon] nf subjection
sujetador [suxeta'ðor] nm (sostén)
bra
sujetar [suxe'tar] vt (fijar) to fasten;
(detener) to hold down; **sujetarse** vr to
subject o.s.; **sujeto, -a** adj fastened,
secure ▷ nm subject; (individuo)
individual; **sujeto a** subject to
suma ['suma] nf (cantidad) total,
sum; (de dinero) sum; (acto) adding (up),
addition; **en ~** in short
sumamente [suma'mente] adv
extremely, exceedingly
sumar [su'mar] vt to add (up) ▷ vi
to add up
sumergir [sumer'xir] vt to
submerge; (hundir) to sink
suministrar [sumini'strar] vt to
supply, provide; **suministro** nm
supply; (acto) supplying, providing
sumir [su'mir] vt to sink, submerge;
(fig) to plunge
sumiso, -a [su'miso, a] adj
submissive, docile
sumo, -a ['sumo, a] adj great,
extreme; (autoridad) highest, supreme
suntuoso, -a [sun'twoso, a] adj

sumptuous, magnificent
supe etc vb V **saber**
super... [super] prefijo super..., over...
superbueno, -a [super'bweno, a]
adj great, fantastic
súper ['super] nf (gasolina) four-star
(petrol)
superar [supe'rar] vt (sobreponerse
a) to overcome; (rebasar) to surpass,
do better than; (pasar) to go beyond;
superarse vr to excel o.s.
superficial [superfi'θjal] adj
superficial; (medida) surface cpd, of
the surface
superficie [super'fiθje] nf surface;
(área) area
superfluo, -a [su'perflwo, a] adj
superfluous
superior [supe'rjor] adj (piso, clase)
upper; (temperatura, número, nivel)
higher; (mejor: calidad, producto)
superior, better ▷ nmf superior;
superioridad nf superiority
supermercado [supermer'kaðo] nm
supermarket
superponer [superpo'ner] vt to
superimpose
superstición [supersti'θjon] nf
superstition; **supersticioso, -a** adj
superstitious
supervisar [superβi'sar] vt to
supervise
supervivencia [superβi'βenθja]
nf survival
superviviente [superβi'βjente] adj
surviving
supiera etc vb V **saber**
suplantar [suplan'tar] vt to
supplant
suplementario, -a
[suplemen'tarjo, a] adj
supplementary
suplemento [suple'mento] nm
supplement
suplente [su'plente] adj, nm
substitute
supletorio, -a [suple'torjo, a] adj
supplementary ▷ nm supplement;

teléfono ~ extension

súplica ['suplika] nf request; (Jur) petition

suplicar [supli'kar] vt (cosa) to beg (for), plead for; (persona) to beg, plead with

suplicio [su'pliθjo] nm torture

suplir [su'plir] vt (compensar) to make good, make up for; (reemplazar) to replace, substitute ▷ vi: **~ a** to take the place of, substitute for

supo etc vb V **saber**

suponer [supo'ner] vt to suppose; **suposición** nf supposition

suprimir [supri'mir] vt to suppress; (derecho, costumbre) to abolish; (palabra etc) to delete; (restricción) to cancel, lift

supuesto, -a [su'pwesto, a] pp de **suponer** ▷ adj (hipotético) supposed ▷ nm assumption, hypothesis; **~ que** since; **por ~** of course

sur [sur] nm south

suramericano, -a [surameri'kano, a] adj South American ▷ nm/f South American

surcar [sur'kar] vt to plough; **surco** nm (en metal, disco) groove; (Agr) furrow

surfear [surfe'ar] vt: **~ el Internet** to surf the internet

surgir [sur'xir] vi to arise, emerge; (dificultad) to come up, crop up

suroeste [suro'este] nm south-west

surtido, -a [sur'tiðo, a] adj mixed, assorted ▷ nm (selección) selection, assortment; (abastecimiento) supply, stock; **surtidor** nm (tb: **surtidor de gasolina**) petrol pump (BRIT), gas pump (US)

surtir [sur'tir] vt to supply, provide ▷ vi to spout, spurt

susceptible [susθep'tiβle] adj susceptible; (sensible) sensitive; **~ de** capable of

suscitar [susθi'tar] vt to cause, provoke; (interés, sospechas) to arouse

suscribir [suskri'βir] vt (firmar) to sign; (respaldar) to subscribe to, endorse; **suscribirse** vr to subscribe;

suscripción nf subscription

susodicho, -a [suso'ðitʃo, a] adj above-mentioned

suspender [suspen'der] vt (objeto) to hang (up), suspend; (trabajo) to stop, suspend; (Escol) to fail; (interrumpir) to adjourn; (atrasar) to postpone

suspense [sus'pense] (ESP) nm suspense; **película/novela de ~** thriller

suspensión [suspen'sjon] nf suspension; (fig) stoppage, suspension

suspenso, -a [sus'penso, a] adj hanging, suspended; (ESP Escol) failed ▷ nm (ESP Escol) fail; **película o novela de ~** (LAM) thriller; **quedar o estar en ~** to be pending

suspicaz [suspi'kaθ] adj suspicious, distrustful

suspirar [suspi'rar] vi to sigh; **suspiro** nm sigh

sustancia [sus'tanθja] nf substance

sustento [sus'tento] nm support; (alimento) sustenance, food

sustituir [sustitu'ir] vt to substitute, replace; **sustituto, -a** nm/f substitute, replacement

susto ['susto] nm fright, scare

sustraer [sustra'er] vt to remove, take away; (Mat) to subtract

susurrar [susu'rrar] vi to whisper; **susurro** nm whisper

sutil [su'til] adj (aroma, diferencia) subtle; (tenue) thin; (inteligencia, persona) sharp

suyo, -a ['sujo, a] (con artículo o después del verbo **ser**) adj (de él) his; (de ella) hers; (de ellos, ellas) theirs; (de Ud, Uds) yours; **un amigo ~** a friend of his (o hers o theirs o yours)

t

Tabacalera [taβaka'lera] *nf Spanish state tobacco monopoly*

tabaco [ta'βako] *nm* tobacco; (*ESP: fam*) cigarettes *pl*

tabaquería [tabake'ria] (*LAM*) *nf* tobacconist's (shop) (*BRIT*), smoke shop (*US*); **tabaquero, -a** (*LAM*) *nm/f* tobacconist

taberna [ta'βerna] *nf* bar, pub (*BRIT*)

tabique [ta'βike] *nm* partition (wall)

tabla ['taβla] *nf* (*de madera*) plank; (*estante*) shelf; (*de vestido*) pleat; (*Arte*) panel; **tablas** *nfpl*: **estar** *o* **quedar en ~s** to draw; **tablado** *nm* (*plataforma*) platform; (*Teatro*) stage

tablao [ta'βlao] *nm* (*tb: ~ flamenco*) flamenco show

tablero [ta'βlero] *nm* (*de madera*) plank, board; (*de ajedrez, damas*) board; **tablero de mandos** (*LAM Auto*) dashboard

tableta [ta'βleta] *nf* (*Med*) tablet; (*de chocolate*) bar

tablón [ta'βlon] *nm* (*de suelo*) plank; (*de techo*) beam; **tablón de anuncios** notice (*BRIT*) *o* bulletin (*US*) board

tabú [ta'βu] *nm* taboo

taburete [taβu'rete] *nm* stool

tacaño, -a [ta'kaɲo, a] *adj* mean

tacha ['tatʃa] *nf* flaw; (*Tec*) stud; **tachar** *vt* (*borrar*) to cross out; **tachar de** to accuse of

tacho ['tatʃo] (*CS*) *nm* (*balde*) bucket; **tacho de la basura** rubbish bin (*BRIT*), trash can (*US*)

taco ['tako] *nm* (*Billar*) cue; (*de billetes*) book; (*CS: de zapato*) heel; (*tarugo*) peg; (*palabrota*) swear word

tacón [ta'kon] *nm* heel; **de ~ alto** high-heeled

táctica ['taktika] *nf* tactics *pl*

táctico, -a ['taktiko, a] *adj* tactical

tacto ['takto] *nm* touch; (*fig*) tact ▷

tajada [ta'xaða] *nf* slice

tajante [ta'xante] *adj* sharp

tajo ['taxo] *nm* (*corte*) cut; (*Geo*) cleft

tal [tal] *adj* such ▷ *pron* (*persona*) someone, such a one; (*cosa*) something, such a thing ▷ *adv*: **~ como** (*igual*) just as ▷ *conj*: **con ~ de que** provided that; **~ cual** (*como es*) just as it is; **~ vez** perhaps; **~ como** such as; **~ para cual** (*dos iguales*) two of a kind; **¿qué ~?** how are things?; **¿qué ~ te gusta?** how do you like it?

taladrar [tala'ðrar] *vt* to drill; **taladro** *nm* drill

talante [ta'lante] *nm* (*humor*) mood; (*voluntad*) will, willingness

talar [ta'lar] *vt* to fell, cut down; (*devastar*) to devastate

talco ['talko] *nm* (*polvos*) talcum powder

talento [ta'lento] *nm* talent; (*capacidad*) ability

TALGO ['talxo] (*ESP*) *nm abr* (= *tren articulado ligero Goicoechea-Oriol*) ≈ HST (*BRIT*)

talismán [talis'man] *nm* talisman

talla ['taʎa] *nf* (*estatura, fig, Med*) height, stature; (*palo*) measuring rod; (*Arte*) carving; (*medida*) size

tallar [ta'ʎar] *vt* (*madera*) to carve;

(*metal etc*) to engrave; (*medir*) to measure
tallarines [taʎaˈrines] *nmpl* noodles
talle [ˈtaʎe] *nm* (*Anat*) waist; (*fig*) appearance
taller [taˈʎer] *nm* (*Tec*) workshop; (*de artista*) studio
tallo [ˈtaʎo] *nm* (*de planta*) stem; (*de hierba*) blade; (*brote*) shoot
talón [taˈlon] *nm* (*Anat*) heel; (*Com*) counterfoil; (*cheque*) cheque (BRIT), check (US)
talonario [taloˈnarjo] *nm* (*de cheques*) chequebook (BRIT), checkbook (US); (*de recibos*) receipt book
tamaño, -a [taˈmaɲo, a] *adj* (*tan grande*) such a big; (*tan pequeño*) such a small ▷ *nm* size; **de ~ natural** full-size
tamarindo [tamaˈrindo] *nm* tamarind
tambalearse [tambaleˈarse] *vr* (*persona*) to stagger; (*vehículo*) to sway
también [tamˈbjen] *adv* (*igualmente*) also, too, as well; (*además*) besides
tambor [tamˈbor] *nm* drum; (*Anat*) eardrum; **tambor del freno** brake drum
Támesis [ˈtamesis] *nm* Thames
tamizar [tamiˈθar] *vt* to sieve
tampoco [tamˈpoko] *adv* nor, neither; **yo ~ lo compré** I didn't buy it either
tampón [tamˈpon] *nm* tampon
tan [tan] *adv* so; **~ es así que ...** so much so that ...
tanda [ˈtanda] *nf* (*gen*) series; (*turno*) shift
tangente [tanˈxente] *nf* tangent
tangerina [tanxeˈrina] (LAM) *nf* tangerine
tangible [tanˈxiβle] *adj* tangible
tanque [ˈtanke] *nm* (*cisterna, Mil*) tank; (*Auto*) tanker
tantear [tanteˈar] *vt* (*calcular*) to reckon (up); (*medir*) to take the measure of; (*probar*) to test, try out; (*tomar la medida: persona*) to take the measurements of; (*situación*) to weigh up; (*persona: opinión*) to sound out ▷ *vi* (*Deporte*) to score; **tanteo** *nm* (*cálculo*)

(rough) calculation; (*prueba*) test, trial; (*Deporte*) scoring
tanto, -a [ˈtanto, a] *adj* (*cantidad*) so much, as much ▷ *adv* (*cantidad*) so much, as much; (*tiempo*) so long, as long ▷ *conj*: **en ~ que** while ▷ *nm* (*suma*) certain amount; (*proporción*) so much; (*punto*) point; (*gol*) goal; **un ~ perezoso** somewhat lazy ▷ *pron*: **cado uno paga ~** each one pays so much; **~s** so many, as many; **20 y ~s** 20-odd; **hasta ~ (que)** until such time as; **~ tú como yo** both you and I; **~ como eso** as much as that; **~ más ... cuanto que** all the more ... because; **~ mejor/peor** so much the better/the worse; **~ si viene como si va** whether he comes or whether he goes; **~ es así que** so much so that; **por (lo) ~** therefore; **entre ~** meanwhile; **estar al ~** to be up to date; **me he vuelto ronco de *o* con ~ hablar** I have become hoarse with so much talking; **a ~s de agosto** on such and such a day in August
tapa [ˈtapa] *nf* (*de caja, olla*) lid; (*de botella*) top; (*de libro*) cover; (*comida*) snack
tapadera [tapaˈðera] *nf* lid, cover
tapar [taˈpar] *vt* (*cubrir*) to cover; (*envolver*) to wrap *o* cover up; (*la vista*) to obstruct; (*persona, falta*) to conceal; (MÉX, CAM: *diente*) to fill; **taparse** *vr* to wrap o.s. up
taparrabo [tapaˈrraβo] *nm* loincloth
tapete [taˈpete] *nm* table cover
tapia [ˈtapja] *nf* (*garden*) wall
tapicería [tapiθeˈria] *nf* tapestry; (*para muebles*) upholstery; (*tienda*) upholsterer's (shop)
tapiz [taˈpiθ] *nm* (*alfombra*) carpet; (*tela tejida*) tapestry; **tapizar** *vt* (*muebles*) to upholster
tapón [taˈpon] *nm* (*de botella*) top; (*de lavabo*) plug; **tapón de rosca** screw-top
taquigrafía [takiɣraˈfia] *nf* shorthand; **taquígrafo, -a** *nm/f* shorthand writer, stenographer
taquilla [taˈkiʎa] *nf* (*donde se*

compra) booking office; (*suma recogida*) takings *pl*

tarántula [ta'rantula] *nf* tarantula

tararear [tarare'ar] *vi* to hum

tardar [tar'ðar] *vi* (*tomar tiempo*) to take a long time; (*llegar tarde*) to be late; (*demorar*) to delay; **¿tarda mucho el tren?** does the train take (very) long?; **a más ~** at the latest; **no tardes en venir** come soon

tarde ['tarðe] *adv* late ▷ *nf* (*de día*) afternoon; (*al anochecer*) evening; **de ~ en ~** from time to time; **¡buenas ~s!** good afternoon!; **a o por la ~** in the afternoon; in the evening

tardío, -a [tar'ðio, a] *adj* (*retrasado*) late; (*lento*) slow (to arrive)

tarea [ta'rea] *nf* task; (*faena*) chore; (*Escol*) homework

tarifa [ta'rifa] *nf* (*lista de precios*) price list; (*precio*) tariff

tarima [ta'rima] *nf* (*plataforma*) platform

tarjeta [tar'xeta] *nf* card; **tarjeta de crédito/de Navidad/postal/ telefónica** credit card/Christmas card/postcard/phonecard; **tarjeta de embarque** boarding pass; **tarjeta de memoria** memory card; **tarjeta prepago** top-up card; **tarjeta SIM** SIM card

tarro ['tarro] *nm* jar, pot

tarta ['tarta] *nf* (*pastel*) cake; (*de base dura*) tart

tartamudear [tartamuðe'ar] *vi* to stammer; **tartamudo, -a** *adj* stammering ▷ *nm/f* stammerer

tártaro, -a ['tartaro, a] *adj*: **salsa tártara** tartar(e) sauce

tasa ['tasa] *nf* (*precio*) (fixed) price, rate; (*valoración*) valuation; (*medida, norma*) measure, standard; **tasa de cambio/interés** exchange/interest rate; **tasas de aeropuerto** airport tax; **tasas universitarias** university fees

tasar [ta'sar] *vt* (*arreglar el precio*) to fix a price for; (*valorar*) to value, assess

tasca ['taska] (*fam*) *nf* pub

tatarabuelo, -a [tatara'βwelo, a] *nm/f* great-great-grandfather/mother

tatuaje [ta'twaxe] *nm* (*dibujo*) tattoo; (*acto*) tattooing

tatuar [ta'twar] *vt* to tattoo

taurino, -a [tau'rino, a] *adj* bullfighting *cpd*

Tauro ['tauro] *nm* Taurus

tauromaquia [tauro'makja] *nf* tauromachy, (art of) bullfighting

taxi ['taksi] *nm* taxi; **taxista** [tak'sista] *nmf* taxi driver

taza ['taθa] *nf* cup; (*de retrete*) bowl; **~ para café** coffee cup; **taza de café** cup of coffee; **tazón** *nm* (*taza grande*) mug, large cup; (*de fuente*) basin

te [te] *pron* (*complemento de objeto*) you; (*complemento indirecto*) (to) you; (*reflexivo*) (to) yourself; **¿~ duele mucho el brazo?** does your arm hurt a lot?; **~ equivocas** you're wrong; **¡cálma~!** calm down!

té [te] *nm* tea

teatral [tea'tral] *adj* theatre *cpd*; (*fig*) theatrical

teatro [te'atro] *nm* theatre; (*Literatura*) plays *pl*, drama

tebeo [te'βeo] *nm* comic

techo ['tetʃo] *nm* (*externo*) roof; (*interno*) ceiling; **techo corredizo** sunroof

tecla ['tekla] *nf* key; **teclado** *nm* keyboard; **teclear** *vi* (*Mús*) to strum; (*con los dedos*) to tap ▷ *vt* (*Inform*) to key in

técnica ['teknika] *nf* technique; (*tecnología*) technology; *V tb* **técnico**

técnico, -a ['tekniko, a] *adj* technical ▷ *nm/f* technician; (*experto*) expert

tecnología [teknolo'xia] *nf* technology; **tecnológico, -a** *adj* technological

tecolote [teko'lote] (*MÉX*) *nm* owl

tedioso, -a [te'ðjoso, a] *adj* boring, tedious

teja ['texa] *nf* tile; (*Bot*) lime (tree); **tejado** *nm* (tiled) roof

tejanos [te'xanos] *nmpl* (*vaqueros*) jeans

tejemaneje [texema'nexe] nm (lío) fuss; (intriga) intrigue

tejer [te'xer] vt to weave; (hacer punto) to knit; (fig) to fabricate; **tejido** nm (tela) material, fabric; (telaraña) web; (Anat) tissue

tel [tel] abr (= teléfono) tel

tela ['tela] nf (tejido) material; (telaraña) web; (en líquido) skin; **telar** nm (máquina) loom

telaraña [tela'raɲa] nf cobweb

tele ['tele] (fam) nf telly (BRIT), tube (US)

tele... ['tele] prefijo tele...; **telebasura** nf trashTV; **telecomunicación** nf telecommunication; **telediario** nm television news; **teledirigido, -a** adj remote-controlled

teleférico [tele'feriko] nm (de esquí) ski-lift

telefonear [telefone'ar] vi to telephone

telefónico, -a [tele'foniko, a] adj telephone cpd

telefonillo [telefo'niʎo] nm (de puerta) intercom

telefonista [telefo'nista] nmf telephonist

teléfono [te'lefono] nm (tele)phone; **estar hablando al ~** to be on the phone; **llamar a algn por ~** to ring sb (up) o phone sb (up); **teléfono celular** (LAM) mobile phone; **teléfono con cámara** camera phone; **teléfono inalámbrico** cordless phone; **teléfono móvil** (ESP) mobile phone

telégrafo [te'leɣrafo] nm telegraph

telegrama [tele'ɣrama] nm telegram

tele: **telenovela** nf soap (opera); **teleobjetivo** nm telephoto lens; **telepatía** nf telepathy; **telepático, -a** adj telepathic; **telerrealidad** nf realityTV; **telescopio** nm telescope; **telesilla** nm chairlift; **telespectador, a** nm/f viewer; **telesquí** nm ski-lift; **teletarjeta** nf phonecard; **teletexto** nm teletext; **teletipo** nm teletype; **teletrabajador, a** nm/f teleworker;

teletrabajo nm teleworking; **televentas** nfpl telesales

televidente [teleβi'ðente] nmf viewer

televisar [teleβi'sar] vt to televise

televisión [teleβi'sjon] nf television; **televisión digital** digital television

televisor [teleβi'sor] nm television set

télex ['teleks] nm inv telex

telón [te'lon] nm curtain; **telón de acero** (Pol) iron curtain; **telón de fondo** backcloth, background

tema ['tema] nm (asunto) subject, topic; (Mús) theme; **temático, -a** adj thematic

temblar [tem'blar] vi to shake, tremble; (por frío) to shiver; **temblor** nm trembling; (de tierra) earthquake; **tembloroso, -a** adj trembling

temer [te'mer] vt to fear ⊳ vi to be afraid; **temo que llegue tarde** I am afraid he may be late

temible [te'miβle] adj fearsome

temor [te'mor] nm (miedo) fear; (duda) suspicion

témpano ['tempano] nm (tb: ~ de hielo) ice-floe

temperamento [tempera'mento] nm temperament

temperatura [tempera'tura] nf temperature

tempestad [tempes'tað] nf storm

templado, -a [tem'plaðo, a] adj (moderado) moderate; (frugal) frugal; (agua) lukewarm; (clima) mild; (Mús) well-tuned; **templanza** nf moderation; mildness

templar [tem'plar] vt (moderar) to moderate; (furia) to restrain; (calor) to reduce; (afinar) to tune (up); (acero) to temper; (tuerca) to tighten up; **temple** nm (ajuste) tempering; (afinación) tuning; (pintura) tempera

templo ['templo] nm (iglesia) church; (pagano etc) temple

temporada [tempo'raða] nf time, period; (estación) season

temporal [tempo'ral] adj (no permanente) temporary ▷ nm storm

temprano, -a [tem'prano, a] adj early; (demasiado pronto) too soon, too early

ten vb V **tener**

tenaces [te'naθes] adj pl V **tenaz**

tenaz [te'naθ] adj (material) tough; (persona) tenacious; (creencia, resistencia) stubborn

tenaza(s) [te'naθa(s)] nf(pl) (Med) forceps; (Tec) pliers; (Zool) pincers

tendedero [tende'ðero] nm (para ropa) drying place; (cuerda) clothes line

tendencia [ten'denθja] nf tendency; **tener ~ a** to tend to, have a tendency to

tender [ten'der] vt (extender) to spread out; (colgar) to hang out; (vía férrea, cable) to lay; (estirar) to stretch ▷ vi: **~ a** to tend to, have a tendency towards; **tenderse** vr to lie down; **~ la cama/mesa** (LAM) to make the bed/lay (BRIT) o set (US) the table

tenderete [tende'rete] nm (puesto) stall; (exposición) display of goods

tendero, -a [ten'dero, a] nm/f shopkeeper

tendón [ten'don] nm tendon

tendré etc vb V **tener**

tenebroso, -a [tene'βroso, a] adj (oscuro) dark; (fig) gloomy

tenedor [tene'ðor] nm (Culin) fork

tenencia [te'nenθja] nf (de casa) tenancy; (de oficio) tenure; (de propiedad) possession

○ **PALABRA CLAVE**

tener [te'ner] vt **1** (poseer, gen) to have; (en la mano) to hold; **¿tienes un boli?** have you got a pen?; **va a tener un niño** she's going to have a baby; **¡ten (o tenga)!, ¡aquí tienes (o tiene)!** here you are!

2 (edad, medidas) to be; **tiene 7 años** she's 7 (years old); **tiene 15 cm de largo** it's 15 cm long; V **calor; hambre** etc

3 (considerar): **lo tengo por brillante** I

consider him to be brilliant; **tener en mucho a algn** to think very highly of sb

4 (+ pp: = pretérito): **tengo terminada ya la mitad del trabajo** I've done half the work already

5: **tener que hacer algo** to have to do sth; **tengo que acabar este trabajo hoy** I have to finish this job today

6: **¿qué tienes, estás enfermo?** what's the matter with you, are you ill?

tenerse vr **1 tenerse en pie** to stand up

2 tenerse por to think o.s.

tengo etc vb V **tener**

tenia ['tenja] nf tapeworm

teniente [te'njente] nm (rango) lieutenant, (ayudante) deputy

tenis ['tenis] nm tennis; **tenis de mesa** table tennis; **tenista** nmf tennis player

tenor [te'nor] nm (sentido) meaning; (Mús) tenor; **a ~ de** on the lines of

tensar [ten'sar] vt to tighten; (arco) to draw

tensión [ten'sjon] nf tension; (Tec) stress; **tener la ~ alta** to have high blood pressure; **tensión arterial** blood pressure

tenso, -a ['tenso, a] adj tense

tentación [tenta'θjon] nf temptation

tentáculo [ten'takulo] nm tentacle

tentador, a [tenta'ðor, a] adj tempting

tentar [ten'tar] vt (seducir) to tempt; (atraer) to attract

tentempié [tentem'pje] nm snack

tenue ['tenwe] adj (delgado) thin, slender; (neblina) light; (lazo, vínculo) slight

teñir [te'nir] vt to dye; (fig) to tinge; **teñirse** vr to dye; **~se el pelo** to dye one's hair

teología [teolo'xia] nf theology

teoría [teo'ria] nf theory; **en ~** in theory; **teórico, -a** adj theoretic(al) ▷ nm/f theoretician, theorist; **teorizar**

vi to theorize

terapéutico, -a [tera'peutiko, a] adj therapeutic

terapia [te'rapja] nf therapy

tercer adj V **tercero**

tercermundista [terθermun'dista] adj Third World cpd

tercero, -a [ter'θero, a] (delante de nmsg: **tercer**) adj third ▷ nm (Jur) third party

terceto [ter'θeto] nm trio

terciar [ter'θjar] vi (participar) to take part; (hacer de árbitro) to mediate; **terciario, -a** adj tertiary

tercio ['terθjo] nm third

terciopelo [terθjo'pelo] nm velvet

terco, -a ['terko, a] adj obstinate

tergal® [ter'ɣal] nm type of polyester

tergiversar [terxiβer'sar] vt to distort

termal [ter'mal] adj thermal

termas ['termas] nfpl hot springs

térmico, -a ['termiko, a] adj thermal

terminal [termi'nal] adj, nm, nf terminal

terminante [termi'nante] adj (final) final, definitive; (tajante) categorical; **terminantemente** adv: **terminantemente prohibido** strictly forbidden

terminar [termi'nar] vt (completar) to complete, finish; (concluir) to end ▷ vi (llegar a su fin) to end; (parar) to stop; (acabar) to finish; **terminarse** vr to come to an end; **~ por hacer algo** to end up (by) doing sth

término ['termino] nm end, conclusion; (parada) terminus; (límite) boundary; **en último ~** (a fin de cuentas) in the last analysis; (como último recurso) as a last resort; **término medio** average; (fig) middle way

termómetro [ter'mometro] nm thermometer

termo(s)® ['termo(s)] nm Thermos®

termostato [termo'stato] nm thermostat

ternero, -a [ter'nero, a] nm/f (animal) calf ▷ nf (carne) veal, beef

ternura [ter'nura] nf (trato) tenderness; (palabra) endearment; (cariño) fondness

terrado [te'rraðo] nm terrace

terraplén [terra'plen] nm embankment

terrateniente [terrate'njente] nmf landowner

terraza [te'rraθa] nf (balcón) balcony; (tejado) (flat) roof; (Agr) terrace

terremoto [terre'moto] nm earthquake

terrenal [terre'nal] adj earthly

terreno [te'rreno] nm (tierra) land; (parcela) plot; (suelo) soil; (fig) field; **un ~** a piece of land

terrestre [te'rrestre] adj terrestrial; (ruta) land cpd

terrible [te'rriβle] adj terrible, awful

territorio [terri'torjo] nm territory

terrón [te'rron] nm (de azúcar) lump; (de tierra) clod, lump

terror [te'rror] nm terror; **terrorífico, -a** adj terrifying; **terrorista** adj, nmf terrorist; **terrorista suicida** suicide bomber

terso, -a ['terso, a] adj (liso) smooth; (pulido) polished

tertulia [ter'tulja] nf (reunión informal) social gathering; (grupo) group, circle

tesis ['tesis] nf inv thesis

tesón [te'son] nm (firmeza) firmness; (tenacidad) tenacity

tesorero, -a [teso'rero, a] nm/f treasurer

tesoro [te'soro] nm treasure; (Com, Pol) treasury

testamento [testa'mento] nm will

testarudo, -a [testa'ruðo, a] adj stubborn

testículo [tes'tikulo] nm testicle

testificar [testifi'kar] vt to testify; (fig) to attest ▷ vi to give evidence

testigo [tes'tiɣo] nmf witness; **testigo de cargo/descargo** witness for the prosecution/defence; **testigo ocular** eye witness

testimonio [testi'monjo] nm testimony

teta ['teta] nf (de biberón) teat; (Anat: fam) breast

tétanos ['tetanos] nm tetanus

tetera [te'tera] nf teapot

tétrico, -a ['tetriko, a] adj gloomy, dismal

textear [tekste'ar] vt to text

textil [teks'til] adj textile

texto ['teksto] nm text; **textual** adj textual

textura [teks'tura] nf (de tejido) texture

tez [teθ] nf (cutis) complexion

ti [ti] pron you; (reflexivo) yourself

tía ['tia] nf (pariente) aunt; (fam) chick, bird

tibio, -a ['tiβjo, a] adj lukewarm

tiburón [tiβu'ron] nm shark

tic [tik] nm (ruido) click; (de reloj) tick; (Med): **~ nervioso** nervous tic

tictac [tik'tak] nm (de reloj) tick tock

tiempo ['tjempo] nm time; (época, período) age, period; (Meteorología) weather; (Ling) tense; (Deporte) half; **a ~** in time; **a un o al mismo ~** at the same time; **al poco ~** very soon (after); **se quedó poco ~** he didn't stay very long; **hace poco ~** not long ago; **mucho ~** a long time; **de ~ en ~** from time to time, **hace buen/mal ~** the weather is fine/bad; **estar a ~** to be in time; **hace ~** some time ago; **hacer ~** to while away the time; **motor de 2 ~s** two-stroke engine; **primer ~** first half

tienda ['tjenda] nf shop, store; **tienda de abarrotes** (MÉX, CAM) grocer's (BRIT), grocery store (US); **tienda de alimentación o comestibles** grocer's (BRIT), grocery store (US); **tienda de campaña** tent

tienes etc vb V **tener**

tienta etc ['tjenta] vb V **tentar**
▷ nf: **andar a ~s** to grope one's way along

tiento etc ['tjento] vb V **tentar** ▷ nm

(tacto) touch; (precaución) wariness

tierno, -a ['tjerno, a] adj (blando) tender; (fresco) fresh; (amable) sweet

tierra ['tjerra] nf earth; (suelo) soil; (mundo) earth, world; (país) country, land; **~ adentro** inland

tieso, -a ['tjeso, a] adj (rígido) rigid; (duro) stiff; (fam: orgulloso) conceited

tiesto ['tjesto] nm flowerpot

tifón [ti'fon] nm typhoon

tifus ['tifus] nm typhus

tigre ['tixre] nm tiger

tijera [ti'xera] nf scissors pl; (Zool) claw; **tijeras** nfpl scissors; (para plantas) shears

tila ['tila] nf lime blossom tea

tildar [til'dar] vt: **~ de** to brand as

tilde ['tilde] nf (Tip) tilde

tilín [ti'lin] nm tinkle

timar [ti'mar] vt (estafar) to swindle

timbal [tim'bal] nm small drum

timbre ['timbre] nm (sello) stamp; (campanilla) bell, (tono) timbre; (Com) stamp duty

timidez [timi'ðeθ] nf shyness; **tímido, -a** adj shy

timo ['timo] nm swindle

timón [ti'mon] nm helm, rudder; **timonel** nm helmsman

tímpano ['timpano] nm (Anat) eardrum; (Mús) small drum

tina ['tina] nf tub; (baño) bath(tub); **tinaja** nf large jar

tinieblas [ti'njeβlas] nfpl darkness sg; (sombras) shadows

tino ['tino] nm (habilidad) skill; (juicio) insight

tinta ['tinta] nf ink; (Tec) dye; (Arte) colour

tinte ['tinte] nm dye

tintero [tin'tero] nm inkwell

tinto ['tinto] nm red wine

tintorería [tintore'ria] nf dry cleaner's

tío ['tio] nm (pariente) uncle; (fam: individuo) bloke (BRIT), guy

tiovivo [tio'βiβo] nm merry-go-round

típico, -a ['tipiko, a] *adj* typical
tipo ['tipo] *nm* (*clase*) type, kind; (*hombre*) fellow; (*Anat: de hombre*) build; (*: de mujer*) figure; (*Imprenta*) type; **tipo bancario/de descuento/de interés/de cambio** bank/discount/interest/exchange rate
tipografía [tipoɣra'fia] *nf* printing *cpd*
tíquet ['tiket] (*pl ~s*) *nm* ticket; (*en tienda*) cash slip
tiquismiquis [tikis'mikis] *nm inv* fussy person ▷ *nmpl* (*querellas*) squabbling *sg*; (*escrúpulos*) silly scruples
tira ['tira] *nf* strip; (*fig*) abundance; **tira y afloja** give and take
tirabuzón [tiraβu'θon] *nm* (*rizo*) curl
tirachinas [tira'tʃinas] *nm inv* catapult
tirada [ti'raða] *nf* (*acto*) cast, throw; (*serie*) series; (*Tip*) printing, edition; **de una ~** at one go
tirado, -a [ti'raðo, a] *adj* (*barato*) dirt-cheap; (*fam: fácil*) very easy
tirador [tira'ðor] *nm* (*mango*) handle
tirano, -a [ti'rano, a] *adj* tyrannical ▷ *nm/f* tyrant
tirante [ti'rante] *adj* (*cuerda etc*) tight, taut; (*relaciónes*) strained ▷ *nm* (*Arq*) brace; (*Tec*) stay; **tirantes** *nmpl* (*de pantalón*) braces (BRIT), suspenders (US); **tirantez** *nf* tightness; (*fig*) tension
tirar [ti'rar] *vt* to throw; (*dejar caer*) to drop; (*volcar*) to upset; (*derribar*) to knock down o over; (*desechar*) to throw out o away; (*dinero*) to squander; (*imprimir*) to print ▷ *vi* (*disparar*) to shoot; (*de la puerta etc*) to pull; (*fam: andar*) to go; (*tender a, buscar realizar*) to tend to; (*Deporte*) to shoot; **tirarse** *vr* to throw o.s.; **~ abajo** to bring down, destroy; **tira más a su padre** he takes more after his father; **ir tirando** to manage
tirita [ti'rita] *nf* (sticking) plaster (BRIT), Bandaid® (US)
tiritar [tiri'tar] *vi* to shiver

tiro ['tiro] *nm* (*lanzamiento*) throw; (*disparo*) shot; (*Deporte*) shot; (*Golf, Tenis*) drive; (*alcance*) range; **caballo de ~** cart-horse; **tiro al blanco** target practice
tirón [ti'ron] *nm* (*sacudida*) pull, tug; **de un ~** in one go, all at once
tiroteo [tiro'teo] *nm* exchange of shots, shooting
tisis ['tisis] *nf inv* consumption, tuberculosis
títere ['titere] *nm* puppet
titubear [tituβe'ar] *vi* to stagger; to stammer; (*fig*) to hesitate; **titubeo** *nm* staggering; stammering; hesitation
titulado, -a [titu'laðo, a] *adj* (*libro*) entitled; (*persona*) titled
titular [titu'lar] *adj* titular ▷ *nmf* holder ▷ *nm* headline ▷ *vt* to title; **titularse** *vr* to be entitled; **título** *nm* title; (*de diario*) headline; (*certificado*) professional qualification; (*universitario*) (university) degree; **a título de** in the capacity of
tiza ['tiθa] *nf* chalk
toalla [to'aʎa] *nf* towel
tobillo [to'βiʎo] *nm* ankle
tobogán [toβo'ɣan] *nm* (*montaña rusa*) roller-coaster; (*de niños*) chute, slide
tocadiscos [toka'ðiskos] *nm inv* record player
tocado, -a [to'kaðo, a] *adj* (*fam*) touched ▷ *nm* headdress
tocador [toka'ðor] *nm* (*mueble*) dressing table; (*cuarto*) boudoir; (*fam*) ladies' toilet (BRIT) o room (US)
tocar [to'kar] *vt* to touch; (*Mús*) to play; (*referirse a*) to allude to; (*timbre*) to ring ▷ *vi* (*a la puerta*) to knock (on o at the door); (*ser de turno*) to fall to, be the turn of; (*ser hora*) to be due; **tocarse** *vr* (*cubrirse la cabeza*) to cover one's head; (*tener contacto*) to touch (each other); **por lo que a mí me toca** as far as I am concerned; **te toca a ti** it's your turn
tocayo, -a [to'kajo, a] *nm/f* namesake

tocino [to'θino] nm bacon

todavía [toða'βia] adv (aun) even; (aún) still, yet; **~ más** yet more; **~ no** not yet

O **PALABRA CLAVE**

todo, -a ['toðo, a] adj **1** (con artículo sg) all; **toda la carne** all the meat; **toda la noche** all night, the whole night; **todo el libro** the whole book; **toda una botella** a whole bottle; **todo lo contrario** quite the opposite; **está toda sucia** she's all dirty; **por todo el país** throughout the whole country
2 (con artículo pl) all; every; **todos los libros** all the books; **todas las noches** every night; **todos los que quieran salir** all those who want to leave
▷ pron **1** everything, all; **todos** everyone, everybody; **lo sabemos todo** we know everything; **todos querían más tiempo** everybody o everyone wanted more time; **nos marchamos todos** all of us left
2: con todo: **con todo él me sigue gustando** even so I still like him
▷ adv all; **vaya todo seguido** keep straight on o ahead
▷ nm: **como un todo** as a whole; **del todo: no me agrada del todo** I don't entirely like it

todopoderoso, -a [toðopoðe'roso, a] adj all powerful; (Rel) almighty
todoterreno [toðote'rreno] sm inv four-wheel drive, SUV (ESP US)
toga ['toɣa] nf toga; (Escol) gown
Tokio ['tokjo] n Tokyo
toldo ['toldo] nm (para el sol) sunshade (BRIT), parasol; (tienda) marquee
tolerancia [tole'ranθja] nf tolerance; **tolerante** adj (sociedad) liberal; (persona) open-minded
tolerar [tole'rar] vt to tolerate; (resistir) to endure

toma ['toma] nf (acto) taking; (Med) dose; **toma de corriente** socket; **toma de tierra** earth (wire); **tomacorriente** (LAM) nm socket
tomar [to'mar] vt to take; (aspecto) to take on; (beber) to drink ▷ vi to take; (LAM: beber) to drink; **tomarse** vr to take; **~se por** to consider o.s. to be; **~ a bien/mal** to take well/badly; **~ en serio** to take seriously; **~ el pelo a algn** to pull sb's leg; **~la con algn** to pick a quarrel with sb; **¡toma!** here you are!; **~ el sol** to sunbathe
tomate [to'mate] nm tomato
tomillo [to'miʎo] nm thyme
tomo ['tomo] nm (libro) volume
ton [ton] abr =**tonelada** ▷ nm: **sin ~ ni son** without rhyme or reason
tonalidad [tonali'ðað] nf tone
tonel [to'nel] nm barrel
tonelada [tone'laða] nf ton; **tonelaje** nm tonnage
tónica ['tonika] nf (Mús) tonic; (fig) keynote
tónico, -a ['toniko, a] adj tonic ▷ nm (Med) tonic
tono ['tono] nm tone; **fuera de ~** inappropriate; **tono de llamada** ringtone
tontería [tonte'ria] nf (estupidez) foolishness; (cosa) stupid thing; (acto) foolish act; **tonterías** nfpl (disparates) rubbish sg, nonsense sg
tonto, -a ['tonto, a] adj stupid, silly ▷ nm/f fool
topar [to'par] vi: **~ contra** o **en** to run into; **~ con** to run up against
tope ['tope] adj maximum ▷ nm (fin) end; (límite) limit; (Ferro) buffer; (Auto) bumper; **al ~** end to end
tópico, -a ['topiko, a] adj topical ▷ nm platitude
topo ['topo] nm (Zool) mole; (fig) blunderer
toque etc ['toke] vb V **tocar** ▷ nm touch; (Mús) beat; (de campana) peal; **dar un ~ a** to warn; **toque de queda** curfew

toqué etc vb V **tocar**

toquetear [tokete'ar] vt to finger

toquilla [to'kiʎa] nf (pañuelo) headscarf; (chal) shawl

tórax ['toraks] nm thorax

torbellino [torbe'ʎino] nm whirlwind; (fig) whirl

torcedura [torθe'ðura] nf twist; (Med) sprain

torcer [tor'θer] vt to twist; (la esquina) to turn; (Med) to sprain ▷ vi (desviar) to turn off; **torcerse** vr (ladearse) to bend; (desviarse) to go astray; (fracasar) to go wrong; **torcido, -a** adj twisted; (fig) crooked ▷ nm curl

tordo, -a ['torðo, a] adj dappled ▷ nm thrush

torear [tore'ar] vt (fig: evadir) to avoid; (jugar con) to tease ▷ vi to fight bulls; **toreo** nm bullfighting; **torero, -a** nm/f bullfighter

tormenta [tor'menta] nf storm; (fig: confusión) turmoil

tormento [tor'mento] nm torture; (fig) anguish

tornar [tor'nar] vt (devolver) to return, give back; (transformar) to transform ▷ vi to go back

tornasolado, -a [tornaso'laðo, a] adj (brillante) iridescent; (reluciente) shimmering

torneo [tor'neo] nm tournament

tornillo [tor'niʎo] nm screw

torniquete [torni'kete] nm (Med) tourniquet

torno ['torno] nm (Tec) winch; (tambor) drum; **en ~ (a)** round, about

toro ['toro] nm bull; (fam) he-man; **los ~s** bullfighting

toronja [to'ronxa] nf grapefruit

torpe ['torpe] adj (poco hábil) clumsy, awkward; (necio) dim; (lento) slow

torpedo [tor'peðo] nm torpedo

torpeza [tor'peθa] nf (falta de agilidad) clumsiness; (lentitud) slowness; (error) mistake

torre ['torre] nf tower; (de petróleo) derrick

torrefacto, -a [torre'fakto, a] adj roasted

torrente [to'rrente] nm torrent

torrija [to'rrixa] nf French toast

torsión [tor'sjon] nf twisting

torso ['torso] nm torso

torta ['torta] nf cake; (fam) slap

tortícolis [tor'tikolis] nm inv stiff neck

tortilla [tor'tiʎa] nf omelette; (LAM: de maíz) maize pancake; **tortilla de papas** (LAM) potato omelette; **tortilla de patatas** (ESP) potato omelette; **tortilla francesa** (ESP) plain omelette

tórtola ['tortola] nf turtledove

tortuga [tor'tuɣa] nf tortoise

tortuoso, -a [tor'twoso, a] adj winding

tortura [tor'tura] nf torture; **torturar** vt to torture

tos [tos] nf cough; **tos ferina** whooping cough

toser [to'ser] vi to cough

tostada [tos'taða] nf piece of toast; **tostado, -a** adj toasted; (por el sol) dark brown; (piel) tanned

tostador [tosta'ðor] (ESP) nm toaster; **tostadora** (LAM) nf = **tostador**

tostar [tos'tar] vt to toast; (café) to roast; (persona) to tan; **tostarse** vr to get brown

total [to'tal] adj total ▷ adv in short; (al fin y al cabo) when all is said and done ▷ nm total; **en ~** in all; **~ que ...** to cut (BRIT) o make (US) a long story short ...

totalidad [totali'ðað] nf whole

totalitario, -a [totali'tarjo, a] adj totalitarian

tóxico, -a ['toksiko, a] adj toxic ▷ nm poison; **toxicómano, -a** nm/f drug addict

toxina [to'ksina] nf toxin

tozudo, -a [to'θuðo, a] adj obstinate

trabajador, a [traβaxa'ðor, a] adj hard-working ▷ nm/f worker; **trabajador autónomo o por cuenta propia** self-employed person

trabajar [traβa'xar] *vt* to work; (*Agr*) to till; (*empeñarse en*) to work at; (*convencer*) to persuade ▷ *vi* to work; (*esforzarse*) to strive; **trabajo** *nm* work; (*tarea*) task; (*Pol*) labour; (*fig*) effort; **tomarse el trabajo de** to take the trouble to; **trabajo a destajo** piecework; **trabajo en equipo** teamwork; **trabajo por turnos** shift work; **trabajos forzados** hard labour *sg*

trabalenguas [traβa'lengwas] *nm inv* tongue twister

tracción [trak'θjon] *nf* traction; **tracción delantera/trasera** front-wheel/rear-wheel drive

tractor [trak'tor] *nm* tractor

tradición [traði'θjon] *nf* tradition; **tradicional** *adj* traditional

traducción [traðuk'θjon] *nf* translation

traducir [traðu'θir] *vt* to translate; **traductor, a** *nm/f* translator

traer [tra'er] *vt* to bring; (*llevar*) to carry; (*llevar puesto*) to wear; (*incluir*) to carry; (*causar*) to cause; **traerse** *vr*: **~se algo** to be up to sth

traficar [trafi'kar] *vi* to trade

tráfico ['trafiko] *nm* (*Com*) trade; (*Auto*) traffic

tragaluz [traγa'luθ] *nm* skylight

tragamonedas [traγamo'neðas] (*LAM*) *nf inv* slot machine

tragaperras [traγa'perras] (*ESP*) *nf inv* slot machine

tragar [tra'γar] *vt* to swallow; (*devorar*) to devour, bolt down; **tragarse** *vr* to swallow

tragedia [tra'xeðja] *nf* tragedy; **trágico, -a** *adj* tragic

trago ['traγo] *nm* (*líquido*) drink; (*bocado*) gulp; (*fam: de bebida*) swig; (*desgracia*) blow; **echar un ~** to have a drink

traición [trai'θjon] *nf* treachery; (*Jur*) treason; (*una traición*) act of treachery; **traicionar** *vt* to betray

traidor, a [trai'ðor, a] *adj*

treacherous ▷ *nm/f* traitor

traigo *etc vb* V **traer**

traje ['traxe] *vb* V **traer** ▷ *nm* (*de hombre*) suit; (*de mujer*) dress; (*vestido típico*) costume; **traje de baño/chaqueta** swimsuit/suit; **traje de etiqueta** dress suit; **traje de luces** bullfighter's costume

trajera *etc vb* V **traer**

trajín [tra'xin] *nm* (*fam: movimiento*) bustle; **trajinar** *vi* (*moverse*) to bustle about

trama ['trama] *nf* (*intriga*) plot; (*de tejido*) weft (BRIT), woof (US); **tramar** *vt* to plot; (*Tec*) to weave

tramitar [trami'tar] *vt* (*asunto*) to transact; (*negociar*) to negotiate

trámite ['tramite] *nm* (*paso*) step; (*Jur*) transaction; **trámites** *nmpl* (*burocracia*) procedure *sg*; (*Jur*) proceedings

tramo ['tramo] *nm* (*de tierra*) plot; (*de escalera*) flight; (*de vía*) section

trampa ['trampa] *nf* trap; (*en el suelo*) trapdoor; (*truco*) trick; (*engaño*) fiddle; **trampear** *vt*, *vi* to cheat

trampolín [trampo'lin] *nm* (*de piscina etc*) diving board

tramposo, -a [tram'poso, a] *adj* crooked, cheating ▷ *nm/f* crook, cheat

tranca ['tranka] *nf* (*palo*) stick; (*de puerta, ventana*) bar; **trancar** *vt* to bar

trance ['tranθe] *nm* (*momento difícil*) difficult moment *o* juncture; (*estado hipnotizado*) trance

tranquilidad [trankili'ðað] *nf* (*calma*) calmness, stillness; (*paz*) peacefulness

tranquilizar [trankili'θar] *vt* (*calmar*) to calm (down); (*asegurar*) to reassure; **tranquilizarse** *vr* to calm down; **tranquilo, -a** *adj* (*calmado*) calm; (*apacible*) peaceful; (*mar*) calm; (*mente*) untroubled

transacción [transak'θjon] *nf* transaction

transbordador [transβorða'ðor] *nm* ferry

t

transbordo [trans'βorðo] *nm*
transfer; **hacer ~** to change (trains *etc*)
transcurrir [transku'rrir] *vi* (*tiempo*)
to pass; (*hecho*) to take place
transcurso [trans'kurso] *nm*: **~ del**
tiempo lapse (of time)
transeúnte [transe'unte] *nmf*
passer-by
transferencia [transfe'renθja] *nf*
transference; (*Com*) transfer
transferir [transfe'rir] *vt* to transfer
transformación [transforma'θjon]
nf transformation
transformador [transforma'ðor]
nm (*Elec*) transformer
transformar [transfor'mar] *vt* to
transform; (*convertir*) to convert
transfusión [transfu'sjon] *nf*
transfusion
transgénico, -a [trans'xeniko, a]
adj genetically modified, GM
transición [transi'θjon] *nf* transition
transigir [transi'xir] *vi* to
compromise, make concessions
transitar [transi'tar] *vi* to go (from
place to place); **tránsito** *nm* transit;
(*Auto*) traffic; **transitorio, -a** *adj*
transitory
transmisión [transmi'sjon] *nf* (*Tec*)
transmission; (*transferencia*) transfer;
transmisión exterior/en directo
outside/live broadcast
transmitir [transmi'tir] *vt* to
transmit; (*Radio, TV*) to broadcast
transparencia [transpa'renθja]
nf transparency; (*claridad*) clearness,
clarity; (*foto*) slide
transparentar [transparen'tar]
vt to reveal ▷ *vi* to be transparent;
transparente *adj* transparent;
(*claro*) clear
transpirar [transpi'rar] *vi* to perspire
transportar [transpor'tar] *vt* to
transport; (*llevar*) to carry; **transporte**
nm transport; (*Com*) haulage
transversal [transβer'sal] *adj*
transverse, cross
tranvía [tram'bia] *nm* tram

trapeador [trapea'ðor] (*LAM*) *nm*
mop; **trapear** (*LAM*) *vt* to mop
trapecio [tra'peθjo] *nm* trapeze;
trapecista *nmf* trapeze artist
trapero, -a [tra'pero, a] *nm/f*
ragman
trapicheo [trapi'tʃeo] (*fam*) *nm*
scheme, fiddle
trapo ['trapo] *nm* (*tela*) rag; (*de*
cocina) cloth
tráquea ['trakea] *nf* windpipe
traqueteo [trake'teo] *nm* rattling
tras [tras] *prep* (*detrás*) behind;
(*después*) after
trasatlántico [trasat'lantiko] *nm*
(*barco*) (cabin) cruiser
trascendencia [trasθen'denθja] *nf*
(*importancia*) importance; (*Filosofía*)
transcendence
trascendental [trasθenden'tal] *adj*
important; (*Filosofía*) transcendental
trasero, -a [tra'sero, a] *adj* back,
rear ▷ *nm* (*Anat*) bottom
trasfondo [tras'fondo] *nm*
background
trasgredir [trasɣre'ðir] *vt* to
contravene
trashumante [trasu'mante] *adj*
(*animales*) migrating
trasladar [trasla'ðar] *vt* to move;
(*persona*) to transfer; (*postergar*) to
postpone; (*copiar*) to copy; **trasladarse**
vr (*mudarse*) to move; **traslado** *nm*
move; (*mudanza*) move, removal
traslucir [traslu'θir] *vt* to show
trasluz [tras'luθ] *nm* reflected light;
al ~ against *o* up to the light
trasnochador, a [trasnotʃa'ðor, a]
nm/f night owl
trasnochar [trasno'tʃar] *vi* (*acostarse*
tarde) to stay up late
traspapelar [traspape'lar] *vt*
(*documento, carta*) to mislay, misplace
traspasar [traspa'sar] *vt* (*suj: bala*
etc) to pierce, go through; (*propiedad*)
to sell, transfer; (*calle*) to cross over;
(*límites*) to go beyond; (*ley*) to break;
traspaso *nm* (*venta*) transfer, sale

traspatio [tras'patʃo] (*LAM*) *nm* backyard

traspié [tras'pje] *nm* (*tropezón*) trip; (*error*) blunder

trasplantar [trasplan'tar] *vt* to transplant

traste ['traste] *nm* (*Mús*) fret; **dar al ~ con algo** to ruin sth

trastero [tras'tero] *nm* storage room

trastienda [tras'tjenda] *nf* back of shop

trasto ['trasto] (*pey*) *nm* (*cosa*) piece of junk; (*persona*) dead loss

trastornado, -a [trastor'naðo, a] *adj* (*loco*) mad, crazy

trastornar [trastor'nar] *vt* (*fig: planes*) to disrupt; (: *nervios*) to shatter; (: *persona*) to drive crazy; **trastornarse** *vr* (*volverse loco*) to go mad o crazy; **trastorno** *nm* (*acto*) overturning; (*confusión*) confusion

tratable [tra'taβle] *adj* friendly

tratado [tra'taðo] *nm* (*Pol*) treaty; (*Com*) agreement

tratamiento [trata'mjento] *nm* treatment; **tratamiento de textos** (*Inform*) word processing *cpd*

tratar [tra'tar] *vt* (*ocuparse de*) to treat; (*manejar, Tec*) to handle; (*Med*) to treat; (*dirigirse a: persona*) to address ▷ *vi*: **~ de** (*hablar sobre*) to deal with, be about; (*intentar*) to try to; **tratarse** *vr* to treat each other; **~ con** (*Com*) to trade in; (*negociar*) to negotiate with; (*tener contactos*) to have dealings with; **¿de qué se trata?** what's it about?; **trato** *nm* dealings *pl*; (*relaciónes*) relationship; (*comportamiento*) manner; (*Com*) agreement

trauma ['trauma] *nm* trauma

través [tra'βes] *nm* (*fig*) reverse; **al ~** across, crossways; **a ~ de** across; (*sobre*) over; (*por*) through

travesaño [traβe'saɲo] *nm* (*Arq*) crossbeam; (*Deporte*) crossbar

travesía [traβe'sia] *nf* (*calle*) cross-street; (*Náut*) crossing

travesura [traβe'sura] *nf* (*broma*)

prank; (*ingenio*) wit

travieso, -a [tra'βjeso, a] *adj* (*niño*) naughty

trayecto [tra'jekto] *nm* (*ruta*) road, way; (*viaje*) journey; (*tramo*) stretch; **trayectoria** *nf* trajectory; (*fig*) path

traza ['traθa] *nf* (*aspecto*) looks *pl*; (*señal*) sign; **trazado, -a** *adj*: **bien trazado** shapely, well-formed ▷ *nm* (*Arq*) plan, design; (*fig*) outline

trazar [tra'θar] *vt* (*Arq*) to plan; (*Arte*) to sketch; (*fig*) to trace; (*plan*) to draw up; **trazo** *nm* (*línea*) line; (*bosquejo*) sketch

trébol ['treβol] *nm* (*Bot*) clover

trece ['treθe] *num* thirteen

trecho ['tretʃo] *nm* (*distancia*) distance; (*tiempo*) while

tregua ['treɣwa] *nf* (*Mil*) truce; (*fig*) respite

treinta ['treinta] *num* thirty

tremendo, -a [tre'mendo, a] *adj* (*terrible*) terrible; (*imponente: cosa*) imposing; (*fam: fabuloso*) tremendous

tren [tren] *nm* train; **tren de aterrizaje** undercarriage; **tren de cercanías** suburban train

trenca ['trenka] *nf* duffel coat

trenza ['trenθa] *nf* (*de pelo*) plait (*BRIT*), braid (*US*)

trepadora [trepa'ðora] *nf* (*Bot*) climber

trepar [tre'par] *vt, vi* to climb

tres [tres] *num* three

tresillo [tre'siʎo] *nm* three-piece suite; (*Mús*) triplet

treta ['treta] *nf* trick

triángulo ['trjangulo] *nm* triangle

tribu ['triβu] *nf* tribe

tribuna [tri'βuna] *nf* (*plataforma*) platform; (*Deporte*) (grand)stand

tribunal [triβu'nal] *nm* (*Jur*) court; (*comisión, fig*) tribunal; **~ popular** jury

tributo [tri'βuto] *nm* (*Com*) tax

trigal [tri'ɣal] *nm* wheat field

trigo ['triɣo] *nm* wheat

trigueño, -a [tri'ɣeɲo, a] *adj* (*pelo*) corn-coloured

trillar [tri'ʎar] vt (Agr) to thresh
trimestral [trimes'tral] adj quarterly; (Escol) termly
trimestre [tri'mestre] nm (Escol) term
trinar [tri'nar] vi (pájaros) to sing; (rabiar) to fume, be angry
trinchar [trin'tʃar] vt to carve
trinchera [trin'tʃera] nf (fosa) trench
trineo [tri'neo] nm sledge
trinidad [trini'ðað] nf trio; (Rel): **la T~** the Trinity
tripa ['tripa] nf (Anat) intestine; (fam: tb: **~s**) insides pl
triple ['triple] adj triple
triplicado, -a [tripli'kaðo, a] adj: **por ~** in triplicate
tripulación [tripula'θjon] nf crew
tripulante [tripu'lante] nmf crewman/woman
tripular [tripu'lar] vt (barco) to man; (Auto) to drive
triquiñuela [triki'ɲwela] nf trick
tris [tris] nm inv crack
triste ['triste] adj sad; (lamentable) sorry, miserable; **tristeza** nf (aflicción) sadness; (melancolía) melancholy
triturar [tritu'rar] vt (moler) to grind; (mascar) to chew
triunfar [trjun'far] vi (tener éxito) to triumph; (ganar) to win; **triunfo** nm triumph
trivial [tri'βjal] adj trivial
triza ['triθa] nf: **hacer ~s** to smash to bits; (papel) to tear to shreds
trocear [troθe'ar] vt (carne, manzana) to cut up, cut into pieces
trocha ['trotʃa] nf short cut
trofeo [tro'feo] nm (premio) trophy; (éxito) success
tromba ['tromba] nf downpour
trombón [trom'bon] nm trombone
trombosis [trom'bosis] nf inv thrombosis
trompa ['trompa] nf horn; (trompo) humming top; (hocico) snout; (fam): **cogerse una ~** to get tight
trompazo [trom'paθo] nm bump, bang

trompeta [trom'peta] nf trumpet; (clarín) bugle
trompicón [trompi'kon]: **a trompicones** adv in fits and starts
trompo ['trompo] nm spinning top
trompón [trom'pon] nm bump
tronar [tro'nar] vt (MÉX, CAM: fusilar) to shoot; (MÉX: examen) to flunk ▷ vi to thunder; (fig) to rage
tronchar [tron'tʃar] vt (árbol) to chop down; (fig: vida) to cut short; (: esperanza) to shatter; (persona) to tire out; **troncharse** vr to fall down
tronco ['tronko] nm (de árbol, Anat) trunk
trono ['trono] nm throne
tropa ['tropa] nf (Mil) troop; (soldados) soldiers pl
tropezar [trope'θar] vi to trip, stumble; (errar) to slip up; **~ con** to run into; (topar con) to bump into; **tropezón** nm trip; (fig) blunder
tropical [tropi'kal] adj tropical
trópico ['tropiko] nm tropic
tropiezo [tro'pjeθo] vb V **tropezar** ▷ nm (error) slip, blunder; (desgracia) misfortune; (obstáculo) snag
trotamundos [trota'mundos] nm inv globetrotter
trotar [tro'tar] vi to trot; **trote** nm trot; (fam) travelling; **de mucho trote** hard-wearing
trozar [tro'θar] (LAM) vt to cut up, cut into pieces
trozo ['troθo] nm bit, piece
trucha ['trutʃa] nf trout
truco ['truko] nm (habilidad) knack; (engaño) trick
trueno ['trweno] nm thunder; (estampido) bang
trueque etc ['trweke] vb V **trocar** ▷ nm exchange; (Com) barter
trufa ['trufa] nf (Bot) truffle
truhán, -ana [tru'an, ana] nm/f rogue
truncar [trun'kar] vt (cortar) to truncate; (fig: la vida etc) to cut short; (: el desarrollo) to stunt

tu [tu] *adj* your

tú [tu] *pron* you

tubérculo [tu'βerkulo] *nm* (*Bot*) tuber

tuberculosis [tuβerku'losis] *nf inv* tuberculosis

tubería [tuβe'ria] *nf* pipes *pl*; (*conducto*) pipeline

tubo ['tuβo] *nm* tube, pipe; **tubo de ensayo** test tube; **tubo de escape** exhaust (pipe)

tuerca ['twerka] *nf* nut

tuerto, -a ['twerto, a] *adj* blind in one eye ▷ *nm/f* one-eyed person

tuerza *etc vb* V **torcer**

tuétano ['twetano] *nm* marrow; (*Bot*) pith

tufo ['tufo] *nm* (*hedor*) stench

tul [tul] *nm* tulle

tulipán [tuli'pan] *nm* tulip

tullido, -a [tu'ʎiðo, a] *adj* crippled

tumba ['tumba] *nf* (*sepultura*) tomb

tumbar [tum'bar] *vt* to knock down; **tumbarse** *vr* (*echarse*) to lie down; (*extenderse*) to stretch out

tumbo ['tumbo] *nm*: **dar -s** to stagger

tumbona [tum'bona] *nf* (*butaca*) easy chair; (*de playa*) deckchair (BRIT), beach chair (US)

tumor [tu'mor] *nm* tumour

tumulto [tu'multo] *nm* turmoil

tuna ['tuna] *nf* (*Mús*) student music group; V tb **tuno**

⬤ **TUNA**
⬤
⬤ A **tuna** is a musical group made
⬤ up of university students or
⬤ former students who dress up
⬤ in costumes from the "Edad de
⬤ Oro", the Spanish Golden Age.
⬤ These groups go through the
⬤ town playing their guitars, lutes
⬤ and tambourines and serenade
⬤ the young ladies in the halls of
⬤ residence or make impromptu
⬤ appearances at weddings or
⬤ parties singing traditional
⬤ Spanish songs for a few coins.

tunante [tu'nante] *nmf* rascal

tunear [tune'ar] *vt* (*Auto*) to style, mod (*inf*)

túnel ['tunel] *nm* tunnel

tuning ['tunin] *nm* (*Auto*) car styling, modding (*inf*)

tuno, -a ['tuno, a] *nm/f* (*fam*) rogue ▷ *nm* member of student music group

tupido, -a [tu'piðo, a] *adj* (*denso*) dense; (*tela*) close-woven

turbante [tur'βante] *nm* turban

turbar [tur'βar] *vt* (*molestar*) to disturb; (*incomodar*) to upset

turbina [tur'βina] *nf* turbine

turbio, -a ['turβjo, a] *adj* cloudy; (*tema etc*) confused

turbulencia [turβu'lenθja] *nf* turbulence; (*fig*) restlessness; **turbulento, -a** *adj* turbulent; (*fig: intranquilo*) restless; (: *ruidoso*) noisy

turco, -a ['turko, a] *adj* Turkish ▷ *nm/f* Turk

turismo [tu'rismo] *nm* tourism; (*coche*) car; **turista** *nmf* tourist; **turístico, -a** *adj* tourist *cpd*

turnar [tur'nar] *vi* to take (it in) turns; **turnarse** *vr* to take (it in) turns; **turno** *nm* (*de trabajo*) shift; (*en juegos etc*) turn

turquesa [tur'kesa] *nf* turquoise

Turquía [tur'kia] *nf* Turkey

turrón [tu'rron] *nm* (*dulce*) nougat

tutear [tute'ar] *vt* to address as familiar "tú"; **tutearse** *vr* to be on familiar terms

tutela [tu'tela] *nf* (*legal*) guardianship; **tutelar** *adj* tutelary ▷ *vt* to protect

tutor, a [tu'tor, a] *nm/f* (*legal*) guardian; (*Escol*) tutor

tuve *etc vb* V **tener**

tuviera *etc vb* V **tener**

tuyo, -a ['tujo, a] *adj* yours, of yours ▷ *pron* yours; **un amigo ~** a friend of yours; **los ~s** (*fam*) your relations o family

TV *nf abr* (= *televisión*) TV

TVE *nf abr* = **Televisión Española**

u [u] *conj* or

reciente) latest, most recent; (*más bajo*) bottom; (*más alto*) top; **en las últimas** on one's last legs; **por ~** finally

ultra ['ultra] *adj* ultra ▷ *nmf* extreme right-winger

ultraje [ul'traxe] *nm* outrage; insult

ultramar [ultra'mar] *nm*: **de** *o* **en ~** abroad, overseas

ultramarinos [ultrama'rinos] *nmpl* groceries; **tienda de ~** grocer's (shop)

ultranza [ul'tranθa]: **a ~** *adv* (*a todo trance*) at all costs; (*completo*) outright

umbral [um'bral] *nm* (*gen*) threshold

○ **PALABRA CLAVE**

un, una [un, 'una] *art indef* a; (*antes de vocal*) an; **una mujer/naranja** a woman/an orange
▷ *adj*: **unos** (*o* **unas**): **hay unos regalos para ti** there are some presents for you; **hay unas cervezas en la nevera** there are some beers in the fridge

ubicar [uβi'kar] *vt* to place, situate; (*LAM: encontrar*) to find; **ubicarse** *vr* (*LAM: encontrarse*) to lie, be located

ubre ['uβre] *nf* udder

UCI *nf abr* (= *Unidad de Cuidados Intensivos*) ICU

Ud(s) *abr* = **usted(es)**

UE *nf abr* (= *Unión Europea*) EU

ufanarse [ufa'narse] *vr* to boast; **ufano, -a** *adj* (*arrogante*) arrogant; (*presumido*) conceited

UGT (*ESP*) *nf abr* = **Unión General de Trabajadores**

úlcera ['ulθera] *nf* ulcer

ulterior [ulte'rjor] *adj* (*más allá*) farther, further; (*subsecuente, siguiente*) subsequent

últimamente ['ultimamente] *adv* (*recientemente*) lately, recently

ultimar [ulti'mar] *vt* to finish; (*finalizar*) to finalize; (*LAM: matar*) to kill

ultimátum [ulti'matum] (*pl* **~s**) *nm* ultimatum

último, -a ['ultimo, a] *adj* last; (*más

unánime [u'nanime] *adj* unanimous; **unanimidad** *nf* unanimity

undécimo, -a [un'deθimo, a] *adj* eleventh

ungir [un'xir] *vt* to anoint

ungüento [un'gwento] *nm* ointment

único, -a ['uniko, a] *adj* only, sole; (*sin par*) unique

unidad [uni'ðað] *nf* unity; (*Com, Tec etc*) unit

unido, -a [u'niðo, a] *adj* joined, linked; (*fig*) united

unificar [unifi'kar] *vt* to unite, unify

uniformar [unifor'mar] *vt* to make uniform, level up; (*persona*) to put into uniform

uniforme [uni'forme] *adj* uniform, equal; (*superficie*) even ▷ *nm* uniform

unilateral [unilate'ral] *adj* unilateral

unión [u'njon] *nf* union; (*acto*) uniting, joining; (*unidad*) unity; (*Tec*) joint; **Unión Europea** European Union

unir [u'nir] *vt* (*juntar*) to join, unite;

(atar) to tie, fasten; (combinar) to combine; **unirse** vr to join together, unite; (empresas) to merge

unísono [u'nisono] nm: **al ~** in unison

universal [uniβer'sal] adj universal; (mundial) world cpd

universidad [uniβersi'ðað] nf university

universitario, -a [uniβersi'tarjo, a] adj university cpd ⊳ nm/f (profesor) lecturer; (estudiante) (university) student; (graduado) graduate

universo [uni'βerso] nm universe

○ **PALABRA CLAVE**

uno, -a ['uno, a] adj one; **unos pocos** a few; **unos cien** about a hundred ⊳ pron **1** one; **quiero sólo uno** I only want one; **uno de ellos** one of them **2** (alguien) somebody, someone; **conozco a uno que se te parece** I know somebody o someone who looks like you; **uno mismo** oneself; **unos querían quedarse** some (people) wanted to stay

3 (los) unos ... (los) otros ... some ... others
⊳ nf one; **es la una** it's one o'clock
⊳ nm (number) one

untar [un'tar] vt (mantequilla) to spread; (engrasar) to grease, oil

uña ['uɲa] nf (Anat) nail; (garra) claw; (casco) hoof; (arrancaclavos) claw

uranlo [u'ranjo] nm uranium

urbanización [urβaniθa'θjon] nf (barrio, colonia) housing estate

urbanizar [urβani'θar] vt (zona) to develop, urbanize

urbano, -a [ur'βano, a] adj (de ciudad) urban; (cortés) courteous, polite

urbe ['urβe] nf large city

urdir [ur'ðir] vt to warp; (complot) to plot, contrive

urgencia [ur'xenθja] nf urgency; (prisa) haste, rush; (emergencia) emergency; **servicios de ~** emergency services; **"U~s"** "Casualty"; **urgente** adj urgent

urgir [ur'xir] vi to be urgent; **me urge** I'm in a hurry for it

urinario, -a [uri'narjo, a] adj urinary ⊳ nm urinal

urna ['urna] nf urn; (Pol) ballot box

urraca [u'rraka] nf magpie

URSS [urs] nf (Hist): **la URSS** the USSR

Uruguay [uru'xwai] nm (tb: **el ~**) Uruguay; **uruguayo, -a** adj, nm/f Uruguayan

usado, -a [u'saðo, a] adj used; (de segunda mano) secondhand

usar [u'sar] vt to use; (ropa) to wear; (tener costumbre) to be in the habit of; **usarse** vr to be used; **uso** nm use; wear; (costumbre) usage, custom; (moda) fashion; **al uso** in keeping with custom; **al uso de** in the style of; **de uso externo** (Med) for external use

usted [us'teð] pron (sg) you sg; (pl): **~es** you pl

usual [u'swal] adj usual

usuario, -a [usu'arjo, a] nm/f user

usura [u'sura] nf usury; **usurero, -a** nm/f usurer

usurpar [usur'par] vt to usurp

utensilio [uten'siljo] nm tool; (Culin) utensil

útero ['utero] nm uterus, womb

útil ['util] adj useful ⊳ nm tool; **utilidad** nf usefulness; (Com) profit; **utilizar** vt to use, utilize

utopía [uto'pia] nf Utopia; **utópico, -a** adj Utopian

uva ['uβa] nf grape

u

● **LAS UVAS**
●
●
● In Spain **Las uvas** play a big part on
● New Year's Eve (**Nochevieja**), when
● on the stroke of midnight people
● gather at home, in restaurants or
● in the **plaza mayor** and eat a grape
● for each stroke of the clock of the
● **Puerta del Sol** in Madrid. It is said
● to bring luck for the following year.

v *abr* (= *voltio*) v

va *vb* V **ir**

vaca ['baka] *nf* (*animal*) cow; **carne de ~** beef

vacaciones [baka'θjones] *nfpl* holidays

vacante [ba'kante] *adj* vacant, empty ▷ *nf* vacancy

vaciar [ba'θjar] *vt* to empty out; (*ahuecar*) to hollow out; (*moldear*) to cast; **vaciarse** *vr* to empty

vacilar [baθi'lar] *vi* to be unsteady; (*al hablar*) to falter; (*dudar*) to hesitate, waver; (*memoria*) to fail

vacío, -a [ba'θio, a] *adj* empty; (*puesto*) vacant; (*desocupado*) idle; (*vano*) vain ▷ *nm* emptiness; (*Física*) vacuum; (*un vacío*) (empty) space

vacuna [ba'kuna] *nf* vaccine; **vacunar** *vt* to vaccinate

vacuno, -a [ba'kuno, a] *adj* cow *cpd*; **ganado ~** cattle

vadear [baðe'ar] *vt* (*río*) to ford; **vado** *nm* ford; **'vado permanente'** 'keep clear'

vagabundo, -a [baɣa'βundo, a] *adj* wandering ▷ *nm* tramp

vagancia [ba'ɣanθja] *nf* (*pereza*) idleness, laziness

vagar [ba'ɣar] *vi* to wander; (*no hacer nada*) to idle

vagina [ba'xina] *nf* vagina

vago, -a ['baɣo, a] *adj* vague; (*perezoso*) lazy ▷ *nm/f* (*vagabundo*) tramp; (*flojo*) lazybones *sg*, idler

vagón [ba'ɣon] *nm* (*Ferro: de pasajeros*) carriage; (*: de mercancías*) wagon

vaho ['bao] *nm* (*vapor*) vapour, steam; (*respiración*) breath

vaina ['baina] *nf* sheath

vainilla [bai'niʎa] *nf* vanilla

vais *vb* V **ir**

vaivén [bai'βen] *nm* to-and-fro movement; (*de tránsito*) coming and going; **vaivenes** *nmpl* (*fig*) ups and downs

vajilla [ba'xiʎa] *nf* crockery, dishes *pl*; (*juego*) service, set

valdré *etc vb* V **valer**

vale ['bale] *nm* voucher; (*recibo*) receipt; (*pagaré*) IOU

valedero, -a [bale'ðero, a] *adj* valid

valenciano, -a [balen'θjano, a] *adj* Valencian

valentía [balen'tia] *nf* courage, bravery

valer [ba'ler] *vt* to be worth; (*Mat*) to equal; (*costar*) to cost ▷ *vi* (*ser útil*) to be useful; (*ser válido*) to be valid; **valerse** *vr* to take care of oneself; **~se de** to make use of, take advantage of; **~ la pena** to be worthwhile; **¿vale?** (*ESP*) OK?; **más vale que nos vayamos** we'd better go; **¡eso a mí no me vale!** (*MÉX: fam: no importar*) I couldn't care less about that

valeroso, -a [bale'roso, a] *adj* brave, valiant

valgo *etc vb* V **valer**

valía [ba'lia] *nf* worth, value

validar [bali'ðar] *vt* to validate; **validez** *nf* validity; **válido, -a** *adj* valid

valiente [ba'ljente] *adj* brave, valiant
▷ *nm* hero

valija [ba'lixa] (cs) *nf* (suit)case

valioso, -a [ba'ljoso, a] *adj* valuable

valla ['baʎa] *nf* fence; (*Deporte*) hurdle;
valla publicitaria hoarding; **vallar** *vt*
to fence in

valle ['baʎe] *nm* valley

valor [ba'lor] *nm* value, worth;
(*precio*) price; (*valentía*) valour, courage;
(*importancia*) importance; **valores**
nmpl (*Com*) securities; **valorar** *vt*
to value

vals [bals] *nm inv* waltz

válvula ['balβula] *nf* valve

vamos *vb* V **ir**

vampiro, -resa [bam'piro, 'resa]
nm/f vampire

van *vb* V **ir**

vanguardia [ban'ɣwarðja] *nf*
vanguard; (*Arte etc*) avant-garde

vanidad [bani'ðað] *nf* vanity;
vanidoso, -a *adj* vain, conceited

vano, -a ['bano, a] *adj* vain

vapor [ba'por] *nm* vapour; (*vaho*)
steam; **al ~** (*Culin*) steamed; **vapor de
agua** water vapour; **vaporizador** *nm*
atomizer; **vaporizar** *vt* to vaporize;
vaporoso, -a *adj* vaporous

vaquero, -a [ba'kero, a] *adj* cattle
cpd ▷ *nm* cowboy; **vaqueros** *nmpl*
(*pantalones*) jeans

vaquilla [ba'kiʎa] *nf* (*Zool*) heifer

vara ['bara] *nf* stick; (*Tec*) rod

variable [ba'rjaβle] *adj, nf* variable

variación [barja'θjon] *nf* variation

variar [bar'jar] *vt* to vary; (*modificar*)
to modify; (*cambiar de posición*) to
switch around ▷ *vi* to vary

varicela [bari'θela] *nf* chickenpox

varices [ba'riθes] *nfpl* varicose veins

variedad [barje'ðað] *nf* variety

varilla [ba'riʎa] *nf* stick; (*Bot*) twig;
(*Tec*) rod; (*de rueda*) spoke

vario, -a ['barjo, a] *adj* varied; **~s**
various, several

varita [ba'rita] *nf* (*tb:* **~ mágica**)
magic wand

varón [ba'ron] *nm* male, man; **varonil**
adj manly, virile

Varsovia [bar'soβja] *n* Warsaw

vas *vb* V **ir**

vasco, -a ['basko, a] *adj,
nm/f* Basque; **vascongado, -a**
[baskoŋ'gaðo, a] *adj* Basque; **las
Vascongadas** the Basque Country

vaselina [base'lina] *nf* Vaseline®

vasija [ba'sixa] *nf* container, vessel

vaso ['baso] *nm* glass, tumbler;
(*Anat*) vessel

⎸ No confundir **vaso** con la palabra
⎸ inglesa *vase*.

vástago ['bastaɣo] *nm* (*Bot*) shoot;
(*Tec*) rod; (*fig*) offspring

vasto, -a ['basto, a] *adj* vast, huge

Vaticano [bati'kano] *nm*: **el ~** the
Vatican

vatio ['batjo] *nm* (*Elec*) watt

vaya *etc vb* V **ir**

Vd(s) *abr* = **usted(es)**

ve [be] *vb* V **ir**; **ver**

vecindad [beθin'dað] *nf*
neighbourhood; (*habitantes*) residents
pl

vecindario [beθin'darjo] *nm*
neighbourhood; residents *pl*

vecino, -a [be'θino, a] *adj*
neighbouring ▷ *nm/f* neighbour;
(*residente*) resident

veda ['beða] *nf* prohibition; **vedar**
[be'ðar] *vt* (*prohibir*) to ban, prohibit;
(*impedir*) to stop, prevent

vegetación [bexeta'θjon] *nf*
vegetation

vegetal [bexe'tal] *adj, nm* vegetable

vegetariano, -a [bexeta'rjano, a]
adj, nm/f vegetarian

vehículo [be'ikulo] *nm* vehicle;
(*Med*) carrier

veía *etc vb* V **ver**

veinte ['beinte] *num* twenty

vejar [be'xar] *vt* (*irritar*) to annoy, vex;
(*humillar*) to humiliate

vejez [be'xeθ] *nf* old age

vejiga [be'xiɣa] *nf* (*Anat*) bladder

vela ['bela] *nf* (*de cera*) candle; (*Náut*)

sail; (*insomnio*) sleeplessness; (*vigilia*) vigil; (*Mil*) sentry duty; **estar a dos ~s** (*fam: sin dinero*) to be skint

velado, -a [be'laðo, a] *adj* veiled; (*sonido*) muffled; (*Foto*) blurred ▷ *nf* soirée

velar [be'lar] *vt* (*vigilar*) to keep watch over ▷ *vi* to stay awake; **~ por** to watch over, look after

velatorio [bela'torjo] *nm* (funeral) wake

velero [be'lero] *nm* (*Náut*) sailing ship; (*Aviac*) glider

veleta [be'leta] *nf* weather vane

veliz [be'lis] (*MÉX*) *nm* (suit)case

vello ['beʎo] *nm* down, fuzz

velo ['belo] *nm* veil

velocidad [beloθi'ðað] *nf* speed; (*Tec, Auto*) gear

velocímetro [belo'θimetro] *nm* speedometer

velorio [be'lorjo] (*LAM*) *nm* (funeral) wake

veloz [be'loθ] *adj* fast

ven *vb* V **venir**

vena ['bena] *nf* vein

venado [be'naðo] *nm* deer

vencedor, a [benθe'ðor, a] *adj* victorious ▷ *nm/f* victor, winner

vencer [ben'θer] *vt* (*dominar*) to defeat, beat; (*derrotar*) to vanquish; (*superar, controlar*) to overcome, master ▷ *vi* (*triunfar*) to win (through), triumph; (*plazo*) to expire; **vencido, -a** *adj* (*derrotado*) defeated, beaten; (*Com*) due ▷ *adv*: **pagar vencido** to pay in arrears

venda ['benda] *nf* bandage; **vendaje** *nm* bandage, dressing; **vendar** *vt* to bandage; **vendar los ojos** to blindfold

vendaval [benda'βal] *nm* (*viento*) gale

vendedor, a [bende'ðor, a] *nm/f* seller

vender [ben'der] *vt* to sell; **venderse** *vr* (*estar a la venta*) to be on sale; **~ al contado/al por mayor/al por menor** to sell for cash/wholesale/retail; **"se vende"** "for sale"

vendimia [ben'dimja] *nf* grape harvest

vendré *etc vb* V **venir**

veneno [be'neno] *nm* poison; (*de serpiente*) venom; **venenoso, -a** *adj* poisonous; venomous

venerable [bene'raβle] *adj* venerable; **venerar** *vt* (*respetar*) to revere; (*adorar*) to worship

venéreo, -a [be'nereo, a] *adj*: **enfermedad venérea** venereal disease

venezolano, -a [beneθo'lano, a] *adj* Venezuelan

Venezuela [bene'θwela] *nf* Venezuela

venganza [ben'ganθa] *nf* vengeance, revenge; **vengar** *vt* to avenge; **vengarse** *vr* to take revenge; **vengativo, -a** *adj* (*persona*) vindictive

vengo *etc vb* V **venir**

venia ['benja] *nf* (*perdón*) pardon; (*permiso*) consent

venial [be'njal] *adj* venial

venida [be'niða] *nf* (*llegada*) arrival; (*regreso*) return

venidero, -a [beni'ðero, a] *adj* coming, future

venir [be'nir] *vi* to come; (*llegar*) to arrive; (*ocurrir*) to happen; (*fig*): **~ de** to stem from; **~ bien/mal** to be suitable/unsuitable; **el año que viene** next year; **~se abajo** to collapse

venta ['benta] *nf* (*Com*) sale; **"en ~"** "for sale"; **estar a la** *o* **en ~** to be (up) for sale *o* on the market; **venta a domicilio** door-to-door selling; **venta a plazos** hire purchase; **venta al contado/al por mayor/al por menor** cash sale/wholesale/retail

ventaja [ben'taxa] *nf* advantage; **ventajoso, -a** *adj* advantageous

ventana [ben'tana] *nf* window; **ventanilla** *nf* (*de taquilla*) window (of booking office etc)

ventilación [bentila'θjon] *nf* ventilation; (*corriente*) draught

ventilador [bentila'ðor] nm fan

ventilar [benti'lar] vt to ventilate; (para secar) to put out to dry; (asunto) to air, discuss

ventisca [ben'tiska] nf blizzard

ventrílocuo, -a [ben'trilokwo, a] nm/f ventriloquist

ventura [ben'tura] nf (felicidad) happiness; (buena suerte) luck; (destino) fortune; **a la (buena) ~** at random; **venturoso, -a** adj happy; (afortunado) lucky, fortunate

veo etc vb V **ver**

ver [ber] vt to see; (mirar) to look at, watch; (entender) to understand; (investigar) to look into ▷ vi to see; to understand; **verse** vr (encontrarse) to meet; (dejarse ver) to be seen; (hallarse: en un apuro) to find o.s., be; **(vamos) a** ~ let's see; **no tener nada que** ~ **con** to have nothing to do with; **a mi modo de** ~ as I see it; **ya ~emos** we'll see

vera ['bera] nf edge, verge; (de río) bank

veraneante [berane'ante] nm/f holidaymaker, (summer) vacationer (us)

veranear [berane'ar] vi to spend the summer; **veraneo** nm summer holiday; **veraniego, -a** adj summer cpd

verano [be'rano] nm summer

veras ['beras] nfpl truth sg; **de** ~ really, truly

verbal [ber'ßal] adj verbal

verbena [ber'ßena] nf (baile) open-air dance

verbo ['berßo] nm verb

verdad [ber'ðað] nf truth; (fiabilidad) reliability; **de** ~ real, proper, **a decir** ~ to tell the truth; **verdadero, -a** adj (veraz) true, truthful; (fiable) reliable; (fig) real

verde ['berðe] adj green; (chiste) blue, dirty ▷ nm green; **viejo** ~ dirty old man; **verdear** vi to turn green; **verdor** nm greenness

verdugo [ber'ðuxo] nm executioner

verdulero, -a [berðu'lero, a] nm/f greengrocer

verduras [ber'ðuras] nfpl (Culin) greens

vereda [be'reða] nf path; (cs: acera) pavement (BRIT), sidewalk (us)

veredicto [bere'ðikto] nm verdict

vergonzoso, -a [berxon'θoso, a] adj shameful; (tímido) timid, bashful

vergüenza [ber'xwenθa] nf shame, sense of shame; (timidez) bashfulness; (pudor) modesty; **me da** ~ I'm ashamed

verídico, -a [be'riðiko, a] adj true, truthful

verificar [berifi'kar] vt to check; (corroborar) to verify; (llevar a cabo) to carry out; **verificarse** vr (predicción) to prove to be true

verja ['berxa] nf (cancela) iron gate; (valla) iron railings pl; (de ventana) grille

vermut [ber'mut] (pl ~s) nm vermouth

verosímil [bero'simil] adj likely, probable; (relato) credible

verruga [be'rruxa] nf wart

versátil [ber'satil] adj versatile

versión [ber'sjon] nf version

verso ['berso] nm verse; **un** ~ a line of poetry

vértebra ['berteßra] nf vertebra

verter [ber'ter] vt (líquido. adrede) to empty, pour (out); (: sin querer) to spill; (basura) to dump ▷ vi to flow

vertical [berti'kal] adj vertical

vértice ['bertiθe] nm vertex, apex

vertidos [ber'tiðos] nmpl waste sg

vertiente [ber'tjente] nf slope; (fig) aspect

vértigo ['bertixo] nm vertigo; (mareo) dizziness

vesícula [be'sikula] nf blister

vespino® [bes'pino] nm o nf moped

vestíbulo [bes'tißulo] nm hall; (de teatro) foyer

vestido [bes'tiðo] nm (ropa) clothes pl, clothing; (de mujer) dress, frock ▷ pp de **vestir**; **~ de azul/marinero** dressed in blue/as a sailor

vestidor [besti'ðor] (MÉX) nm
(Deporte) changing (BRIT) o locker
(US) room

vestimenta [besti'menta] nf
clothing

vestir [bes'tir] vt (poner: ropa) to put
on; (llevar: ropa) to wear; (proveer de ropa
a) to clothe; (sastre) to make clothes for
▷ vi to dress; (verse bien) to look good;
vestirse vr to get dressed, dress o.s.

vestuario [bes'twarjo] nm clothes
pl, wardrobe; (Teatro: cuarto) dressing
room; (Deporte) changing (BRIT) o locker
(US) room

vetar [be'tar] vt to veto

veterano, -a [bete'rano, a] adj,
nm veteran

veterinaria [beteri'narja] nf
veterinary science; V tb **veterinario**

veterinario, -a [beteri'narjo, a]
nm/f vet(erinary surgeon)

veto ['beto] nm veto

vez [beθ] nf time; (turno) turn; **a la ~
que** at the same time as; **a su ~** in its
turn; **otra ~** again; **una ~** once; **de una
~** in one go; **de una ~ para siempre**
once and for all; **en ~ de** instead of;
a o algunas veces sometimes; **una
y otra ~** repeatedly; **de ~ en cuando**
from time to time; **7 veces 9** 7 times
9; **hacer las veces de** to stand in for;
tal ~ perhaps

vía ['bia] nf track, route; (Ferro) line;
(fig) way; (Anat) passage, tube ▷ prep
via, by way of; **por ~ judicial** by legal
means; **en ~s de** in the process of; **vía
aérea** airway; **Vía Láctea** Milky Way;
vía pública public road o thoroughfare

viable ['bjaβle] adj (solución, plan,
alternativa) feasible

viaducto [bja'ðukto] nm viaduct

viajante [bja'xante] nm commercial
traveller

viajar [bja'xar] vi to travel; **viaje** nm
journey; (gira) tour; (Náut) voyage;
estar de viaje to be on a trip; **viaje
de ida y vuelta** round trip; **viaje**

de novios honeymoon; **viajero,
-a** adj travelling; (Zool) migratory
▷ nm/f (quien viaja) traveller; (pasajero)
passenger

víbora ['biβora] nf (Zool) viper;
(: (MÉX: venenoso) poisonous snake

vibración [biβra'θjon] nf vibration

vibrar [bi'βrar] vt, vi to vibrate

vicepresidente [biθepresi'ðente]
nmf vice-president

viceversa [biθe'βersa] adv vice versa

vicio ['biθjo] nm vice; (mala costumbre)
bad habit; **vicioso, -a** adj (muy malo)
vicious; (corrompido) depraved ▷ nm/f
depraved person

víctima ['biktima] nf victim

victoria [bik'torja] nf victory;
victorioso, -a adj victorious

vid [bið] nf vine

vida ['biða] nf (gen) life; (duración)
lifetime; **de por ~** for life; **en la o mi
~** never; **estar con ~** to be still alive;
ganarse la ~ to earn one's living

vídeo ['biðeo] nm video ▷ adj
inv: **película de ~** video film;
videocámara nf camcorder;
videocasete nm video cassette,
videotape; **videoclub** nm video
club; **videojuego** nm video game;
videollamada nf video call;
videoteléfono nf videophone

vidrio ['biðrjo] nm glass

vieira ['bjeira] nf scallop

viejo, -a ['bjexo, a] adj old ▷ nm/f
old man/woman; **hacerse ~** to get old

Viena ['bjena] n Vienna

vienes etc vb V **venir**

vienés, -esa [bje'nes, esa] adj
Viennese

viento ['bjento] nm wind; **hacer ~**
to be windy

vientre ['bjentre] nm belly; (matriz)
womb

viernes ['bjernes] nm inv Friday;
Viernes Santo Good Friday

Vietnam [bjet'nam] nm Vietnam;
vietnamita adj Vietnamese

viga ['bixa] nf beam, rafter; (de metal)

girder

vigencia [biˈxenθja] nf validity; **estar en ~** to be in force; **vigente** adj valid, in force; (*imperante*) prevailing

vigésimo, -a [biˈxesimo, a] adj twentieth

vigía [biˈxia] nm look-out

vigilancia [bixiˈlanθja] nf: **tener a algn bajo ~** to keep watch on sb

vigilar [bixiˈlar] vt to watch over ▷ vi (*gen*) to be vigilant; (*hacer guardia*) to keep watch; **~ por** to take care of

vigilia [viˈxilja] nf wakefulness, being awake; (*Rel*) fast

vigor [biˈɣor] nm vigour, vitality; **en ~** in force; **entrar/poner en ~** to come/put into effect; **vigoroso, -a** adj vigorous

VIH nm abr (= *virus de la inmunodeficiencia humana*) HIV; **VIH negativo/positivo** HIV-negative/-positive

vil [bil] adj vile, low

villa [ˈbiʎa] nf (*casa*) villa; (*pueblo*) small town; (*municipalidad*) municipality

villancico [biʎanˈθiko] nm (Christmas) carol

vilo [ˈbilo]: **en ~** adv in the air, suspended; (*fig*) on tenterhooks, in suspense

vinagre [biˈnaɣre] nm vinegar

vinagreta [binaˈɣreta] nf vinaigrette, French dressing

vinculación [binkulaˈθjon] nf (*lazo*) link, bond; (*acción*) linking

vincular [binkuˈlar] vt to link, bind; **vínculo** nm link, bond

vine etc vb V **venir**

vinicultor, a [binikulˈtor] nm/f wine grower

vinicultura [binikulˈtura] nf wine growing

viniera etc vb V **venir**

vino [ˈbino] vb V **venir** ▷ nm wine; **vino blanco/tinto** white/red wine

viña [ˈbiɲa] nf vineyard; **viñedo** nm vineyard

viola [ˈbjola] nf viola

violación [bjolaˈθjon] nf violation; (*sexual*) rape

violar [bjoˈlar] vt to violate; (*sexualmente*) to rape

violencia [bjoˈlenθja] nf violence, force; (*incomodidad*) embarrassment; (*acto injusto*) unjust act; **violentar** vt to force; (*casa*) to break into; (*agredir*) to assault; (*violar*) to violate; **violento, -a** adj violent; (*furioso*) furious; (*situación*) embarrassing; (*acto*) forced, unnatural

violeta [bjoˈleta] nf violet

violín [bjoˈlin] nm violin

violón [bjoˈlon] nm double bass

virar [biˈrar] vi to change direction

virgen [ˈbirxen] adj, nf virgin

Virgo [ˈbirɣo] nm Virgo

viril [biˈril] adj virile; **virilidad** nf virility

virtud [birˈtuð] nf virtue; **en ~ de** by virtue of; **virtuoso, -a** adj virtuous ▷ nm/f virtuoso

viruela [biˈrwela] nf smallpox

virulento, -a [biruˈlento, a] adj virulent

virus [ˈbirus] nm inv virus

visa [ˈbisa] (*LAM*) nf = **visado**

visado [biˈsaðo] (*ESP*) nm visa

víscera [ˈbisθera] nf (*Anat, Zool*) gut, bowel; **vísceras** nfpl entrails

visceral [bisθeˈral] adj (*odio*) intense; **reacción ~** gut reaction

vísera [biˈsera] nf visor

visibilidad [bisiβiliˈðað] nf visibility; **visible** adj visible; (*fig*) obvious

visillos [biˈsiʎos] nmpl lace curtains

visión [biˈsjon] nf (*Anat*) vision, (eye)sight; (*fantasía*) vision, fantasy

visita [biˈsita] nf call, visit; (*persona*) visitor; **hacer una ~** to pay a visit; **visitar** [bisiˈtar] vt to visit, call on

visitante [bisiˈtante] adj visiting ▷ nmf visitor

visón [biˈson] nm mink

visor [biˈsor] nm (*Foto*) viewfinder

víspera [ˈbispera] nf: **la ~ de …** the day before …

vista ['bista] nf sight, vision; (capacidad de ver) (eye)sight; (mirada) look(s) (pl); **a primera ~** at first glance; **hacer la ~ gorda** to turn a blind eye; **volver la ~** to look back; **está a la ~ que** it's obvious that; **en ~ de** in view of; **en ~ de que** in view of the fact that; **¡hasta la ~!** so long!, see you!; **con ~ a** with a view to; **vistazo** nm glance; **dar o echar un vistazo a** to glance at

visto, -a ['bisto, a] pp de **ver** ▷ vb V tb **vestir** ▷ adj seen; (considerado) considered ▷ nm: **~ bueno** approval; **por lo ~** apparently; **está ~ que** it's clear that; **está bien/mal ~** it's acceptable/unacceptable; **~ que** since, considering that

vistoso, -a [bis'toso, a] adj colourful

visual [bi'swal] adj visual

vital [bi'tal] adj life cpd, living cpd; (fig) vital; (persona) lively, vivacious; **vitalicio, -a** adj for life; **vitalidad** nf (de persona, negocio) energy; (de ciudad) liveliness

vitamina [bita'mina] nf vitamin

vitorear [bitore'ar] vt to cheer, acclaim

vitrina [bi'trina] nf show case; (LAM: escaparate) shop window

viudo, -a ['bjuðo, a] nm/f widower/widow

viva ['biβa] excl hurrah!; **¡~ el rey!** long live the king!

vivaracho, -a [biβa'ratʃo, a] adj jaunty, lively; (ojos) bright, twinkling

vivaz [bi'βaθ] adj lively

víveres ['biβeres] nmpl provisions

vivero [bi'βero] nm (para plantas) nursery; (para peces) fish farm; (fig) hotbed

viveza [bi'βeθa] nf liveliness; (agudeza: mental) sharpness

vivienda [bi'βjenda] nf housing; (una vivienda) house; (piso) flat (BRIT), apartment (US)

viviente [bi'βjente] adj living

vivir [bi'βir] vt, vi to live ▷ nm life, living

vivo, -a ['biβo, a] adj living, alive; (fig: descripción) vivid; (persona: astuto) smart, clever; **en ~** (transmisión etc) live

vocablo [bo'kaβlo] nm (palabra) word; (término) term

vocabulario [bokaβu'larjo] nm vocabulary

vocación [boka'θjon] nf vocation; **vocacional** (LAM) nf ≈ technical college

vocal [bo'kal] adj vocal ▷ nf vowel; **vocalizar** vt to vocalize

vocero [bo'θero] (LAM) nmf spokesman/woman

voces ['boθes] pl de **voz**

vodka ['boðka] nm o f vodka

vol abr = **volumen**

volado [bo'laðo] (MÉX) adv in a rush, hastily

volador, a [bola'ðor, a] adj flying

volandas [bo'landas]: **en ~** adv in the air

volante [bo'lante] adj flying ▷ nm (de coche) steering wheel; (de reloj) balance

volar [bo'lar] vt (edificio) to blow up ▷ vi to fly

volátil [bo'latil] adj volatile

volcán [bol'kan] nm volcano; **volcánico, -a** adj volcanic

volcar [bol'kar] vt to upset, overturn; (tumbar, derribar) to knock over; (vaciar) to empty out ▷ vi to overturn; **volcarse** vr to tip over

voleibol [bolei'βol] nm volleyball

volqué etc vb V **volcar**

voltaje [bol'taxe] nm voltage

voltear [bolte'ar] vt to turn over; (volcar) to turn upside down

voltereta [bolte'reta] nf somersault

voltio ['boltjo] nm volt

voluble [bo'luβle] adj fickle

volumen [bo'lumen] (pl **volúmenes**) nm volume; **voluminoso, -a** adj voluminous; (enorme) massive

voluntad [bolun'tað] nf will; (resolución) willpower; (deseo) desire, wish

voluntario, -a [bolun'tarjo, a] adj voluntary ▷ nm/f volunteer

volver [bol'βer] vt (gen) to turn; (dar vuelta a) to turn (over); (voltear) to turn round, turn upside down; (poner al revés) to turn inside out; (devolver) to return ▷ vi to return, go back, come back; **volverse** vr to turn round; ~ **la espalda** to turn one's back; ~ **triste** etc **a algn** to make sb sad etc; ~ **a hacer** to do again; ~ **en sí** to come to; ~**se insoportable/muy caro** to get o become unbearable/very expensive; ~**se loco** to go mad

vomitar [bomi'tar] vt, vi to vomit; **vómito** nm vomit

voraz [bo'raθ] adj voracious

vos [bos] (LAM) pron you

vosotros, -as [bo'sotros, as] (ESP) pron you; (reflexivo): **entre/para** ~ among/for yourselves

votación [bota'θjon] nf (acto) voting; (voto) vote

votar [bo'tar] vi to vote; **voto** nm vote; (promesa) vow; **votos** nmpl (good) wishes

voy vb V **ir**

voz [boθ] nf voice; (grito) shout; (rumor) rumour; (Ling) word; **dar voces** to shout, yell; **de viva** ~ verbally; **en** ~ **alta** aloud; **en** ~ **baja** in a low voice, in a whisper; **voz de mando** command

vuelco ['bwelko] vb V **volcar** ▷ nm spill, overturning

vuelo ['bwelo] vb V **volar** ▷ nm flight; (encaje) lace, frill; **coger al** ~ to catch in flight; **vuelo chárter/regular** charter/scheduled flight; **vuelo libre** (Deporte) hang-gliding

vuelque etc vb V **volcar**

vuelta ['bwelta] nf (gen) turn; (curva) bend, curve; (regreso) return; (revolución) revolution; (de circuito) lap; (de papel, tela) reverse; (cambio) change; **a la** ~ on one's return; **a la** ~ **(de la esquina)** round the corner; **a** ~ **de correo** by return of post; **dar** ~**s** (cabeza) to spin; **dar(se) la** ~ (volverse) to turn round;

dar ~**s a una idea** to turn over an idea (in one's head); **estar de** ~ to be back; **dar una** ~ to go for a walk; (en coche) to go for a drive; **vuelta ciclista** (Deporte) (cycle) tour

vuelto ['bwelto] pp de **volver**

vuelvo etc vb V **volver**

vuestro, -a ['bwestro, a] adj pos your; **un amigo** ~ a friend of yours ▷ pron: **el** ~**/la vuestra, los** ~**s/las vuestras** yours

vulgar [bul'xar] adj (ordinario) vulgar; (común) common; **vulgaridad** nf commonness; (acto) vulgarity; (expresión) coarse expression

vulnerable [bulne'raβle] adj vulnerable

vulnerar [bulne'rar] vt (ley, acuerdo) to violate, breach; (derechos, intimidad) to violate; (reputación) to damage

V

walkie-talkie [walki-'talki] (*pl* **~s**)
nm walkie-talkie

Walkman® ['walkman] *nm*
Walkman®

wáter ['bater] *nm* (*taza*) toilet;
(*LAM*: *lugar*) toilet (*BRIT*), rest room (*US*)

web [web] *nm o f* (*página*) website;
(*red*) (World Wide) Web; **webcam**
nf webcam; **webmaster** *nmf*
webmaster; **website** *nm* website

western ['western] (*pl* **~s**) *nm*
western

whisky ['wiski] *nm* whisky, whiskey

wifi [waɪfaɪ] *nm* Wi-Fi

windsurf ['winsurf] *nm*
windsurfing; **hacer ~** to go
windsurfing

xenofobia [kseno'foβja] *nf*
xenophobia

xilófono [ksi'lofono] *nm* xylophone

xocoyote, -a [ksoko'yote, a] (*MÉX*)
nm/f baby of the family, youngest child

yogur(t) [joˈɣur(t)] *nm* yoghurt
yuca [ˈjuka] *nf* (*alimento*) cassava,
manioc root
Yugoslavia [juɣosˈlaβja] *nf* (*Hist*)
Yugoslavia
yugular [juɣuˈlar] *adj* jugular
yunque [ˈjunke] *nm* anvil
yuyo [ˈjujo] (RPL) *nm* (*mala hierba*)
weed

y [i] *conj* and; (*tiempo*) **la una y cinco**
five past one
ya [ja] *adv* (*gen*) already; (*ahora*) now;
(*en seguida*) at once; (*pronto*) soon ▷ *excl*
all right! ▷ *conj* (*ahora que*) now that;
~ lo sé I know; **~ que ...** since; **¡~ está
bien!** that's (quite) enough!; **¡~ voy!**
coming!
yacaré [jakaˈre] (CS) *nm* cayman
yacer [jaˈθer] *vi* to lie
yacimiento [jaθiˈmjento] *nm* (*de
mineral*) deposit; (*arqueológico*) site
yanqui [ˈjanki] *adj, nmf* Yankee
yate [ˈjate] *nm* yacht
yazco *etc vb* V **yacer**
yedra [ˈjeðra] *nf* ivy
yegua [ˈjeɣwa] *nf* mare
yema [ˈjema] *nf* (*del huevo*) yolk; (*Bot*)
leaf bud; (*fig*) best part; **yema del dedo**
fingertip
yerno [ˈjerno] *nm* son-in-law
yeso [ˈjeso] *nm* plaster
yo [jo] *pron* I; **soy ~** it's me
yodo [ˈjoðo] *nm* iodine
yoga [ˈjoɣa] *nm* yoga

Z

zafar [θa'far] *vt* (*soltar*) to untie; (*superficie*) to clear; **zafarse** *vr* (*escaparse*) to escape; (*Tec*) to slip off

zafiro [θa'firo] *nm* sapphire

zaga ['θaɣa] *nf*: **a la ~** behind

zaguán [θa'ɣwan] *nm* hallway

zalamero, -a [θala'mero, a] *adj* flattering; (*cobista*) suave

zamarra [θa'marra] *nf* (*chaqueta*) sheepskin jacket

zambullirse [θambu'ʎirse] *vr* to dive

zampar [θam'par] *vt* to gobble down

zanahoria [θana'orja] *nf* carrot

zancadilla [θanka'ðiʎa] *nf* trip

zanco ['θanko] *nm* stilt

zanja ['θanxa] *nf* ditch; **zanjar** *vt* (*resolver*) to resolve

zapata [θa'pata] *nf* (*Mecánica*) shoe

zapatería [θapate'ria] *nf* (*oficio*) shoemaking; (*tienda*) shoe shop; (*fábrica*) shoe factory; **zapatero, -a** *nm/f* shoemaker

zapatilla [θapa'tiʎa] *nf* slipper; **zapatilla de deporte** training shoe

zapato [θa'pato] *nm* shoe

zapping ['θapin] *nm* channel-hopping; **hacer ~** to channel-hop

zar [θar] *nm* tsar, czar

zarandear [θarande'ar] (*fam*) *vt* to shake vigorously

zarpa ['θarpa] *nf* (*garra*) claw

zarpar [θar'par] *vi* to weigh anchor

zarza ['θarθa] *nf* (*Bot*) bramble; **zarzamora** *nf* blackberry

zarzuela [θar'θwela] *nf* Spanish light opera

zigzag [θiɣ'θaɣ] *nm* zigzag

zinc [θink] *nm* zinc

zíper ['θiper] (*MÉX, CAM*) *nm* zip (fastener) (*BRIT*), zipper (*US*)

zócalo ['θokalo] *nm* (*Arq*) plinth, base; (*de pared*) skirting board (*BRIT*), baseboard (*US*); (*MÉX: plaza*) main o public square

zoclo ['θoklo] *nm* skirting board (*BRIT*), baseboard (*US*)

zodíaco [θo'ðiako] *nm* zodiac

zona ['θona] *nf* zone; **zona fronteriza** border area; **zona roja** (*LAM*) red-light district

zonzo, -a (*LAM: fam*) ['θonθo, a] *adj* silly ▷ *nm/f* fool

zoo ['θoo] *nm* zoo

zoología [θoolo'xia] *nf* zoology; **zoológico, -a** *adj* zoological ▷ *nm* (*tb*: **parque zoológico**) zoo; **zoólogo, -a** *nm/f* zoologist

zoom [θum] *nm* zoom lens

zopilote [θopi'lote] (*MÉX, CAM*) *nm* buzzard

zoquete [θo'kete] *nm* (*fam*) blockhead

zorro, -a ['θorro, a] *adj* crafty ▷ *nm/f* fox/vixen

zozobrar [θoθo'βrar] *vi* (*hundirse*) to capsize; (*fig*) to fail

zueco ['θweko] *nm* clog

zumbar [θum'bar] *vt* (*golpear*) to hit ▷ *vi* to buzz; **zumbido** *nm* buzzing

zumo ['θumo] *nm* juice

zurcir [θur'θir] *vt* (*coser*) to darn

zurdo, -a ['θurðo, a] *adj* left-handed

zurrar [θu'rrar] (*fam*) *vt* to wallop

Spanish in focus

Introduction

Spanish in focus gives you a fascinating introduction to the Spanish-speaking world. The following pages look at where Spanish is spoken throughout the world, helping you to get to know the language and the people that speak it. Practical language tips and notes on common translation difficulties will allow you to become more confident in Spanish and a useful correspondence section gives you all the information you need to be able to communicate effectively.

We've also included a number of links to useful websites, which will give you the opportunity to read and learn more about Spanish-speaking countries and the Spanish language.

We hope that you will enjoy using your *Spanish in focus* supplement. We are sure that it will help you to find out more about Spanish-speaking countries and become more confident in writing and speaking Spanish.

¡Vamos!

Spain and its regions

Spellings

The English spellings of Seville, Majorca and Andalusia are not used in Spanish; *Sevilla*, *Mallorca* and *Andalucía* are the Spanish forms. Remember the accent on *Málaga*, *Córdoba* and *Cádiz* in Spanish.

Spain and its regions

The six biggest Spanish cities

City	Name of inhabitants	Population
Madrid	los madrileños	2,938,700
Barcelona	los barceloneses	1,504,900
Valencia	los valencianos	738,500
Sevilla	los sevillanos	683,600
Zaragoza	los zaragozanos	614,900
Málaga	los malagueños	524,400

Spain shares the Iberian Peninsula with Portugal, its neighbour to the west. The Spanish state consists of the mainland; the Balearic Islands in the Mediterranean; and the Canary Islands in the Atlantic, north-west of Africa. The towns of Ceuta and Melilla, on the coast of Morocco, are also Spanish.

The head of state is the King, Juan Carlos I. The Prime Minister, leader of the party that has the majority in parliament, heads the government and is elected every four years.

Spain is organized into seventeen administrative regions called *comunidades autónomas*. Each region, made up of several smaller *provincias*, has its own parliament and can legislate in areas such as housing, infrastructure, health and education. Central government retains jurisdiction for matters such as defence, foreign affairs and the legal system, which affect the country as a whole.

Regional identity is strong in many parts of Spain, and though the majority of people speak Castilian Spanish (*castellano*) as their first language, other languages and dialects are also important, and for significant numbers of people are their mother tongue. Three of these languages are called *lenguas cooficiales*: Basque (*euskera*), Catalan (*catalán*) and Galician (*gallego*). They have official status under the Constitution and are therefore used in official documents, education and so on.

A snapshot of Spain

- Spain is the second biggest country by area in Western Europe, covering 504 800 km² (well over twice the size of the UK).

- Spain's highest mountain is in the Canary Islands: Teide (3718 m), in Tenerife.

- The river Ebro is around 910km long, rising in the Cantabrian Mountains and flowing into the Mediterranean.

- 40.8 million people live in Spain. The population is one of the slowest-growing in the world.

- The main religion in Spain is Roman Catholicism.

- Spain is the world's tenth largest economy (the US is first and the UK fourth).

- Only France is more popular with foreign tourists; almost 52 million visit Spain every year. The British and Germans head the list, and Andalusia is the most popular destination.

Useful links:

www.ine.es
  The Spanish statistical office.

www.cervantes.es
  Information about Spanish language and culture.

The Spanish-speaking world

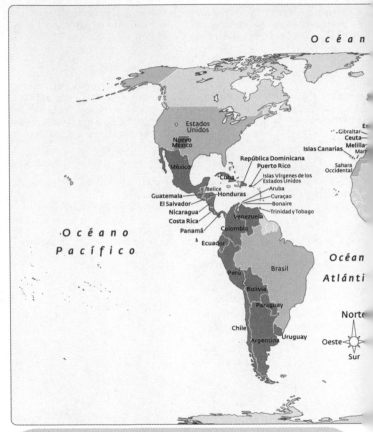

Spellings

Don't forget the accent on *Perú*, *Panamá* and *México* in Spanish. *República Dominicana* is the Spanish-speaking Dominican Republic (not to be confused with English-speaking Dominica). Cuba's capital, Havana, is *la Habana* in Spanish.

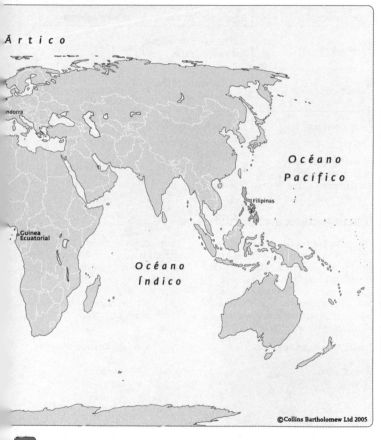

Ártico

Andorra

Guinea
Ecuatorial

Océano
Pacífico

Filipinas

Océano
Índico

©Collins Bartholomew Ltd 2005

Countries or regions where Spanish is the main language or an official language

Countries or regions where many of the population speak Spanish

Other languages of Spain

Language	Brief description	Where spoken
Basque (*euskera*)	Not related to any other known language	In the Basque Country (on the border with France)
Catalan (*catalán*)	Closely related to both French and Spanish	In Catalonia (north-eastern Spain), Valencia and the Balearics
Galician (*gallego*)	Close to Portuguese	In Galicia (north-west Spain)

A useful link:
www.la-moncloa.es
Information on the Prime Minister and government.

Latin American Spanish

There are 417 million speakers of Spanish worldwide; only Chinese has more. Latin American Spanish differs from the Spanish spoken in Europe (peninsular Spanish). There is also a huge variation in the type of Spanish spoken throughout the Americas. For example, a 'light bulb' is *un foco* in Mexico, but *una bujía* in Central America. Accents and pronunciation can also vary dramatically throughout the region.

Some words are common to most Latin American countries. For example:

Latin American Spanish	English	Peninsular Spanish
carro	car	*coche*
computadora	computer	*ordenador*
papa	potato	*patata*

> **Two Amerindian languages**
> *Náhuatl* was the language of the Aztecs and is still spoken by a million Mexicans. It gave us words such as 'tomato', 'avocado', 'chocolate' and 'chilli'.
> *Quechua* is still used by 13 million descendants of the Incas in the Andean region. 'Llama', 'condor' and 'puma' all come from Quechua.

A snapshot of Spanish-speaking America

• Argentina is the biggest Spanish-speaking country by area in South and Central America, covering 2 780 000 km². Next come Mexico (1 958 000 km²) and Peru (1 285 000 km²).

• Mexico has by far the biggest population (101 million), but is outstripped by tiny El Salvador in terms of population density (310 people per km², compared with 246 in the UK and just 31 in the US).

• The highest mountain in the world outside the Himalayas, Cerro Aconcagua (6959 m) lies in Argentina, on the border with Chile. The lowest point in South America, Península Valdés (40 m below sea level), is also in Argentina

• At an altitude of 3630 m, the Bolivian city of La Paz is the highest capital in the Americas.

• The Atacama Desert (lying mainly in northern Chile) is the driest place on earth.

• The second longest river in the world, the Amazon, rises in the Peruvian Andes and flows east through Brazil to the Atlantic. Angel Falls in Venezuela is the world's highest waterfall.

• Latin America has only two landlocked countries: Bolivia and Paraguay.

• Chile is over 4000 km long but only 177 km wide on average.

• Mexico is the world's ninth largest economy (the US is first and the UK fourth).

• The USA has the fifth largest Spanish-speaking population in the world (28 million, or 10% of the population).

A useful link:

http://lanic.utexas.edu/index.html ·
Aspects of life in Spanish-speaking America.

Improving your pronunciation

There are a number of different methods you can use to improve your accent and increase your confidence in speaking Spanish:

- read out loud to yourself to improve your confidence

- listen to Spanish-language radio

- watch Spanish-language films

- chat with Spanish-speakers

A useful link:
www.geocities.com/spanishradio/
A selection of Spanish and Latin American stations.

Some special Spanish sounds

- **Z and c**. Most Spaniards say *z* and the *c* in *ce* and *ci* like 'th' in English '**th**in' (e.g. *cena* = 'thena'; *diez* = 'dieth'). Latin Americans tend to use an 's' sound, as in English '**s**ame'.

- **Ll**. The pronunciation of this (e.g. *llamar, ella*) is rather variable – all over the Spanish-speaking world you'll hear speakers who pronounce it like English '**y**et', while others pronounce it like 'mi**lli**on'.

- **J and g**. *J* in any position and *g* before *e* or *i*, sound similar to English 'lo**ch**' (e.g. *jefe, ajo, gente*) in Spain, but in Latin America they are softer, more like English *h*.

- **B and v**. These sound exactly the same: at the start of a word and after *m* and *n* (e.g. *vaso, ambulancia*) they are similar to English **b**oy. Otherwise to say them try saying a 'b', but don't let your lips touch (e.g. *obra, uva*).

- **D**. Between vowels and after consonants other than *l* or *n* (e.g. *modo, ardiente*), *d* is very like 'th' in English '**th**ough'.

- **H**. In Spanish, *h* is always silent (e.g. *hablar* is pronounced 'ablah').

- **R and rr**. *Rr* is strongly trilled, like Scots *r* (e.g. *perro*). *R* is said with a single trill (e.g. *pero*), but sounds like *rr* at the start of a word and after *l, n* or *s* (e.g. *rápido*).

- **Ñ**. A *tilde* changes the sound of *n* to one similar to English 'o**ni**on' (e.g. *baño*).

Improving your fluency

Conversational words and phrases

In English we insert lots of words and phrases, such as *so, then, by the way* into our conversation, to give our thoughts a structure and often to show our attitude. The Spanish words shown below do the same thing. If you use them they will make you sound more fluent and natural.

- *además*
  Además, *no tienes nada que perder.* (= besides)

- *está bien*
  *¡**Está bien**! Lo haré.* (= all right!)

- *bueno*
  *¡**Bueno**! Haremos lo que tú quieras.* (= all right!)

- *por cierto*
  Por cierto, *¿has sacado las entradas?* (= by the way)

- *claro*
  *¿Te gusta el fútbol? – ¡**Claro que sí/no**!* (= of course!/of course not!)

- *desde luego*
  Desde luego *que me gusta!* (= of course)

- *entonces*
  *Si no es tu padre, ¿**entonces** quién es?* (= then)
  *¿**Entonces**, vienes o te quedas?* (= so)

- *pues*
  Pues, *como te iba contando ...* (= well)

- *por supuesto*
  Por supuesto *que iré.* (= of course)

- *de todas formas/maneras*
  De todas formas/maneras *iremos.* (= anyway, in any case)

- *vale*
  *¿Vamos a tomar algo? – ¡**Vale**!* (= OK)

- *venga*
  *¡**Venga**, vámonos!* (= come on; used in Spain)

Improving your fluency

Varying the words you use to get your message across will make you sound more fluent in Spanish. For example, you already know *Me gusta el mar*, but for a change you could say *Me encanta el mar* to mean the same thing. Here are some other suggestions:

Saying what you like or dislike

Me ha gustado mucho tu regalo.	I was delighted with ...
Estaba encantado/encantada con el regalo.	I (really) liked ...
No me gusta comer fuera de casa.	I don't like ...
Mi vecina *me cae muy mal*.	I don't like ... (at all).
Detesto cualquier tipo de violencia.	I hate ...

Expressing your opinion

Creo que es demasiado caro.	I think ...
Pienso que es normal.	I think ...
Me parece que le va a encantar tu visita.	I think ...
Estoy seguro/segura de que no es culpa tuya.	I'm sure ...
En mi opinión, fue un error.	In my opinion ...

Agreeing or disagreeing

Tienes razón.	You're right.
Estoy (No estoy) de acuerdo contigo.	I (don't) agree with you.
¡Claro que sí!	Of course!
¡Naturalmente!	Of course!
En eso te equivocas.	You're wrong there.

Correspondence

The following section on correspondence has been designed to help you communicate confidently in written as well as spoken Spanish. Sample letters, emails and sections on text messaging and making telephone calls will ensure that you have all the vocabulary you need to correspond successfully in Spanish.

Text messaging

Abbreviation	Spanish	English
+trd	*más tarde*	later
2	*tú*	you
a2	*adiós*	goodbye
bboo	*besos*	love (from)
find	*fin de semana*	weekend
gnl	*genial*	wonderful
h lgo HL	*hasta luego*	see you later
LAP	*lo antes posible*	asap (as soon as possible)
msj	*mensaje*	message
NLS	*no lo sé*	I don't know
q acc? q hcs?	*¿qué haces?*	what are you doing?
QT1BD	*¡que tengas un buen día!*	have a good day!
q tl?	*¿qué tal?*	how are you?
salu2	*saludos*	best wishes
tq	*te quiero*	I love you
x	*por*	for, by etc
xdon	*perdón*	sorry
xq	*porque*	because
xq?	*¿por qué?*	why?

Writing an email

| Archivo | Edición | Ver | Herramientas | **Correo** | Ayuda | Enviar |

A: belen.huertas@glnet.es

Nuevo mensaje
Responder al autor
Responder a todos
Reenviar
Archivo adjunto

Cc:

Copia oculta:

Asunto: Concierto

Hola, ¿qué tal el fin de semana?

Me sobran dos entradas para el concierto de mañana, de unos amigos que no pueden venir. Si te interesa, o conoces a alguien que quiera ir, avísame en cuanto puedas.

Un beso,

E.

Saying your email address
In Spanish, when you tell someone your email address, you say:
belen punto huertas arroba glnet punto es

archivo	file	*responder a todos*	reply to all
edición (f)	edit	*reenviar*	forward
ver	view	*archivo adjunto*	attachment
herramientas (fpl)	tools	*A*	to
correo	mail	*CC*	cc (carbon copy)
ayuda	help	*copia oculta*	bcc (blind carbon copy)
enviar	send	*asunto*	subject
nuevo mensaje (m)	new	*de*	from
responder al autor	reply to sender	*fecha*	sent

Here is some additional useful Internet vocabulary:

adelante	forward	*e-mail* or *email (m)*	e-mail or email; e-mail or email address
atrás	back	*enlaces (mpl)*	links
banda ancha	broadband	*historial (m)*	history
bajarse algo de Internet	to download something from the Internet	*icono*	icon
borrar	to delete	*Internet (m or f)*	the Internet
buscador (m)	search engine	*mandar un e-mail* or *un email a alguien*	to e-mail or email someone
buscar	to search	*navegar por Internet*	to surf the Net
clicar en or *hacer clic en*	to click on		
copia de seguridad	backup	*página de inicio*	home page
copiar	to copy	*página web*	web page
correo basura	spam	*preguntas frecuentes*	FAQs
cortar y pegar	to cut and paste	*sitio web*	website
descargarse algo de Internet	to download something from the Internet	*el* or *la web*	the (World-Wide) Web

Writing a personal letter

Town/city you are writing from, and the date; your full address is not given → *Barcelona,*
5 de junio de 2010

Queridos amigos: ← Use a colon here

Muchas gracias por la preciosa pulsera que me mandasteis por mi cumpleaños, que me ha gustado muchísimo. Voy a disfrutar de verdad poniéndomela para mi fiesta del sábado, y estoy segura de que a Cristina le va a dar una envidia tremenda.

En realidad no hay demasiadas cosas nuevas que contaros, ya que últimamente parece que no hago otra cosa que estudiar para los exámenes, que ya están a la vuelta de la esquina. No sabéis las ganas que tengo de terminarlos todos y poder empezar a pensar en las vacaciones.

Paloma me encarga que os dé recuerdos de su parte.

Muchos besos de

Ana

Writing a personal letter

Other ways of starting a personal letter	Other ways of ending a personal letter
Querido Juan *Mi querida Marta* *Queridísimo Antonio*	*Con mucho cariño* *Un fuerte abrazo de ...* *Un beso muy fuerte* *Afectuosamente*

Some useful phrases

Muchas gracias por la carta.	Thank you for your letter.
Me alegró mucho recibir noticias tuyas.	It was great to hear from you.
Perdona que no te haya escrito antes.	Sorry for not writing sooner.
Dale un beso a Eduardo de mi parte.	Give my love to Eduardo.
Mamá te manda recuerdos.	Mum sends her best wishes.
Escríbeme pronto.	Write soon

Writing a formal letter

José Arteaga Pérez ← Your own name and address
Plaza San Agustín 45, 3º A
34012 Zaragoza

19 de marzo de 2010 ← Date

Hotel Sol y Mar ← Name and address of the person/company you are writing to
Paseo Marítimo 12
08005 Barcelona

Estimados señores: ← Use a colon here

Como continuación a nuestra conversación telefónica de esta mañana, les escribo para confirmarles la reserva de una habitación doble con baño para las noches del miércoles 1 y el jueves 2 de julio de 2010.

Como hemos acordado, le adjunto un cheque de 30 € como garantía para la reserva.

Sin otro particular, les envío un atento saludo.

José Arteaga Pérez

In much of the Spanish-speaking world, and especially in Spain, most people use two *apellidos*, or surnames. The first is their father's first surname, and the second their mother's first surname. For example, the children of Juan Arteaga López, married to Carmen Pérez Rodríguez would be called Arteaga Pérez. A married woman normally retains her own surname instead of taking her husband's.

Writing a formal letter

Other ways of starting a formal letter	Other ways of ending a formal letter
Estimado señor (García) *Estimados señores* *Muy señor mío/Muy señores míos* (used especially in Spain) *De nuestra consideración* (used especially in Latin America)	*Reciba un atento saludo de ...* *Un cordial saludo* *Le/les saluda atentamente*

Some useful phrases

Agradecemos su carta de ...	Thank you for your letter of ...
En relación con ...	With reference to ...
Les ruego que me envíen ...	Please send me ...
Sin otro particular, quedo a la espera de su respuesta.	I look forward to hearing from you.
Muchas gracias de antemano por ...	Thank you in advance for ...

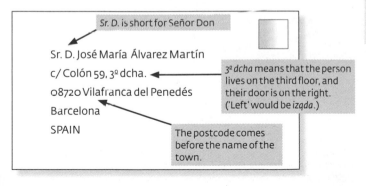

Sr. D. is short for Señor Don

Sr. D. José María Álvarez Martín

c/ Colón 59, 3º dcha.

3º dcha means that the person lives on the third floor, and their door is on the right. ('Left' would be *izqda*.)

08720 Vilafranca del Penedés

Barcelona

SPAIN

The postcode comes before the name of the town.

Making a call

Asking for information

¿Cuál es el prefijo de Léon?	What's the code for Léon?
¿Qué hay que hacer para obtener línea externa?	How do I get an outside line?
¿Podría decirme cuál es la extensión del Sr. Ruiz?	Please could you tell me what Sr. Ruiz's extension number is?

When your number answers

Hola, ¿está Susana?	Hello! Is Susana there?
Por favor, ¿podría hablar con Carlos García?	Could I speak to Carlos García, please?
¿Es usted la Sra. Reyes?	Is that Sra. Reyes?
¿Puede decirle que me llame?	Could you ask him/her to call me back?
Le vuelvo a llamar dentro de media hora.	I'll call back in half an hour.
¿Podría dejar un recado?	Could I leave a message, please?

When you answer the telephone

¿Diga?/ ¿Dígame?/¿Sí?	Hello? (used in Spain)
¿Aló?	(used in Latin America)
¿Hola?	(used in the Southern Cone)
¿Bueno?	(used in Mexico)
¿Con quién hablo?	Who's speaking?
Soy Marcos.	It's Marcos speaking.
Sí, soy yo.	Speaking.
¿Quiere dejar un mensaje?	Would you like to leave a message?

Making a call

What you may hear

¿De parte de quién?	Who's calling?
Le paso.	I'm putting you through now.
No cuelgue.	Please hold.
No contesta.	There's no reply.
Comunica.	The line is engaged (Brit)/busy (US).
¿Quiere dejar un mensaje?	Would you like to leave a message?

If you have a problem

Perdone, me he equivocado de número.	Sorry, I dialled the wrong number.
No se oye bien.	This is a bad line.
Se corta.	You're breaking up.
Me estoy quedando sin batería.	My battery's low.
Se oye muy mal.	I can't hear you.

Saying your phone number

To tell someone your phone number in Spanish, you divide the number up into pairs instead of saying each digit separately. For example:

88 73 14

ochenta y ocho / setenta y tres / catorce

If there's an extra number, you make a group of three and say those numbers separately. For example:

959 48 32 94

nueve-cinco-nueve / cuarenta y ocho / treinta y dos / noventa y cuatro

Spanish phrases and sayings

In Spanish, as in many languages, people use vivid expressions based on images from their experience of real life. We've grouped the common expressions below according to the type of image they use. For fun, we have given you the word-for-word translation as well as the true English equivalent.

Food and drink

en todas partes cuecen habas
→ it's the same the whole world over
    word for word: *broad beans are cooked everywhere*

llamar al pan pan y al vino vino
→ to call a spade a spade
    word for word: *to call bread bread and wine wine*

eso es pedir peras al olmo
→ that's asking the impossible
    word for word: *that's asking the elm tree for pears*

llegar para los postres
→ to come very late
    word for word: *to arrive in time for pudding*

ahogarse en un vaso de agua
→ to make a mountain out of a molehill
    word for word: *to drown in a glass of water*

Animals and insects

aburrirse como una ostra
→ to be bored stiff
    word for word: *to get as bored as an oyster*

si los burros volaran
→ pigs might fly
    word for word: *if donkeys could fly*

estar más loco que una cabra
→ to be as mad as a hatter
    word for word: *to be madder than a goat*

a paso de tortuga
→ at a snail's pace
    word for word: *at a tortoise's pace*

Spanish phrases and sayings

Objects

consultar algo con la almohada   →   to sleep on something

     word for word: *to discuss something with one's pillow*

empezar la casa por el tejado   →   to put the cart before the horse

     word for word: *to start the house with the roof*

estar en la luna   →   to have one's head in the clouds

     word for word: *to be on the moon*

Weather

ha llovido mucho desde entonces   →   a lot of water has flowed under the bridge since then

     word for word: *it's rained a lot since then*

nunca llueve a gusto de todos   →   you can't please everyone

     word for word: *it never rains to everyone's liking*

una tormenta en un vaso de agua   →   a storm in a teacup

     word for word: *a storm in a glass of water*

Parts of the body

romperse la cabeza   →   to rack one's brains

     word for word: *to break one's head*

tener la cabeza sobre los hombros   →   to have one's head screwed on (the right way)

     word for word: *to have one's head on one's shoulders*

costar un ojo de la cara   →   to cost an arm and a leg

     word for word: *to cost an eye from one's face*

me costó un riñón   →   it cost me a fortune

     word for word: *it cost me a kidney*

23

Spanish phrases and sayings

Clothes

cambiar de chaqueta
→ to change sides
    word for word: *to change one's jacket*

estar hasta el gorro
→ to be fed up
    word for word: *to be up to one's hat*

querer nadar y guardar la ropa
→ to want to have it both ways
    word for word: *to want to swim and keep one's clothes on*

estar todavía en pañales
→ to be still wet behind the ears
    word for word: *to be still in nappies*

Colours

no distinguir lo blanco de lo negro
→ to be unable to tell right from wrong
    word for word: *not to be able to tell what's white from what's black*

ponerse de mil colores
→ to go bright red
    word for word: *to turn a thousand colours*

verlo todo de color de rosa
→ to see everything through rose-tinted spectacles
    word for word: *to see everything in pink*

estar más rojo que un cangrejo
→ to be lobster-pink or lobster-red
    word for word: *to be redder than a crab*

Some common translation difficulties

On the following pages we have shown some of the translation difficulties that you are most likely to come across. We hope that the tips we have given will help you to avoid these common pitfalls when writing and speaking Spanish.

'I, you, he, she, they...?'

Yo, tú, él, and so on are not normally used before a verb if the ending or context make it clear who is performing the action:

I speak Spanish.	→	*Hablo español.*
We have two cars.	→	*Tenemos dos coches.*

But use *yo, tú, él* and the other subject pronouns for emphasis, contrast or where it helps make it clear who is being talked about:

You don't need to come.	→	*Tú no tienes por qué venir.*
He drives but she doesn't.	→	*Él conduce pero ella no.*

Usted and *ustedes*, the polite words for 'you', are used more than the other pronouns.

Personal *a*

When the direct object of a verb is a specific person or pet, put *a* in front of it (except after *tener*):

I look after **my little sister**.	→	*Cuido **a mi hermana pequeña**.*
They love **their dog**.	→	*Quieren mucho **a su perro**.*

Some common translation difficulties

In Spanish the word for 'you' and the form of the verb depend on who you are talking to:

• With one person you know well, use the **tú** form of the verb:

Will you lend me this CD?	➜	¿Me **prestas** este CD?

• With one person you do not know so well, use **usted** and the **usted** form of the verb:

Have you met my wife?	➜	¿**Usted conoce** a mi mujer?

• With more than one person you know well, in Spain use the **vosotros/as** form of the verb:

Do you understand, children?	➜	¿**Entendéis**, niños?

Elsewhere, use **ustedes** and the **ustedes** form:

Are you coming too?	➜	¿Vienen también **ustedes**?

• With more than one person you do not know so well, use **ustedes** and the **ustedes** form:

Please come this way.	➜	Pasen **ustedes** por aquí.

> **Vos and tú**
>
> In Argentina and parts of Central America, vos is preferred to tú.

Some common translation difficulties

Showing possession

In English, you can use 's and s' to show who or what something belongs to; in Spanish, you have to use a different construction:

my brother**'s** car	➜	*el coche **de** mi hermano*
the girl**s'** bedroom	➜	*el cuarto **de** las niñas*

Translating 'to'

To is generally translated by **a** but remember:

• When you are talking about the time, use **menos:**

five **to** ten	➜	*las diez **menos** cinco*
at a quarter **to** seven	➜	*a las siete **menos** cuarto*

• In front of verbs, it is often just shown by the Spanish verb ending:

to sing	➜	*cantar*
to eat	➜	*comer*
I want **to go out**.	➜	*Quiero **salir**.*

• When you mean 'in order to', use **para:**

I did it **(in order) to** help you.	➜	*Lo hice **para** ayudaros.*

Some common translation difficulties

'There is' and 'there are'

In Spanish these are both translated by **hay**:

There is a gentleman at the door. → **Hay** un señor en la puerta.
There are five books on the table. → **Hay** cinco libros en la mesa.

Translating 'and'

The normal word for 'and' is y. But to avoid two 'i' sounds coming together, you use e instead before words beginning with i or hi (but not hie):

Spain **and** Italy → España **e** Italia
grapes **and** figs → uvas **e** higos

Translating 'or'

The normal word for 'or' is o, but to avoid two 'o' sounds coming together, you use u instead before words beginning with o or ho:

for one reason **or** another → por un motivo **u** otro

Translating -ing

In Spanish you use the infinitive (the Spanish verb ending in -ar, -er and -ir) after verbs like gustar, encantar, preferir, ver and oír as well as after prepositions, even though in English we use the -ing form of the verb:

I like **going** to the cinema. → Me gusta **ir** al cine.
We love **dancing**. → Nos encanta **bailar**.
We prefer **travelling** by train. → Preferimos **viajar** en tren.
I've heard her **singing**. → La he oído **cantar**.
Before **leaving**... → Antes de **salir**...

Some common translation difficulties

There are two main verbs which mean 'be' in Spanish, *ser* and *estar*.

Ser is used:

• to link nouns and pronouns (words like 'he' and 'him'):

Pablo **is** a teacher.	➔	*Pablo **es** profesor.*
It's me.	➔	***Soy** yo.*
It's five o'clock.	➔	***Son** las cinco.*
Three and two **are** five.	➔	*Tres y dos **son** cinco.*

• with adjectives that give the idea of inherent and fundamental characteristics:

He's tall.	➔	***Es** alto.*
Marta**'s** very attractive.	➔	*Marta **es** muy guapa.*
They're fair.	➔	***Son** rubios.*
He's a bachelor.	➔	***Es** soltero.*
They're Italian.	➔	***Son** italianos.*

Estar is used:

• when describing more temporary qualities:

The coffee**'s** cold.	➔	*El café **está** frío.*
She's in a bad mood.	➔	***Está** de mal humor.*
You're looking very pretty today.	➔	***Estás** muy guapa hoy.*

• to talk about location and with past participles (the *–ado/-ido* form of regular verbs) used as adjectives:

I'm in Madrid.	➔	***Estoy** en Madrid.*
Madrid **is** in Spain.	➔	*Madrid **está** en España.*
She's married.	➔	***Está** casada.*
The window**'s** broken.	➔	*La ventana **está** rota.*

Some common translation difficulties

Translating 'to be' by other verbs

Other verbs can be used in certain contexts instead of *ser* and *estar* to translate 'to be':

- Use **tener** in phrases describing how you feel:

I'm hot/cold.	➜	**Tengo** *calor/frío*.
We're hungry/thirsty.	➜	**Tenemos** *hambre/sed*.
Don't be afraid.	➜	**No tengas** *miedo*.
You're right.	➜	**Tienes** *razón*.

- Use **tener** when talking about your age:

How old **are you**?	➜	*¿Cuántos años* **tienes**?
I'm fifteen.	➜	**Tengo** *quince (años)*.

- Use **hacer** when talking about the weather:

What**'s** the weather like?	➜	*¿Qué tiempo* **hace**?
It's lovely.	➜	**Hace** *bueno*.
It's hot.	➜	**Hace** *calor*.
It's windy.	➜	**Hace** *viento*.

Translating verbs

Many English verbs can be followed by a preposition or adverb such as 'on' or 'back' – 'to go on', 'to give back'. These additions often give the verb a new meaning. There is no similar way of doing this in Spanish – you just use a different word, for example:

to go	➜	*ir*
to go on	➜	*seguir, continuar*
to give	➜	*dar*
to give back	➜	*devolver*

Some common translation difficulties

Sentences that contain a verb and preposition in English might not contain a preposition in Spanish, and vice versa. The dictionary can help you with these.

For example:

- Verb + preposition: Verb without preposition:

  to look **for** something   →   *buscar algo*

- Verb without preposition: Verb + preposition:

  to attend something   →   *asistir **a** algo*

'Can', 'be able'

There are different ways of saying what someone can do in Spanish:

- Use **poder** to talk about someone's physical ability to do something:

  I **can't** go out with you.   →   **No puedo** *salir contigo*.

- Use **saber** to talk about things you *know how to* do:

  Can you swim?   →   *¿**Sabes** nadar?*

- Don't translate *can* when it's used with verbs of sensing, seeing and hearing:

  I **can't see** anything.   →   **No veo** *nada*.
  Can't you **hear** me?   →   *¿Es que **no** me **oyes**?*

A useful link:
www.spanish.about.com/od/learnspanishgrammar

A [eɪ] *n* (*Mus*) la *m*

○ **KEYWORD**

a [ə] (*before vowel or silent h: an*) *indef art*
1 un(a); **a book** un libro; **an apple** una manzana; **she's a doctor** (ella) es médica
2 (*instead of the number "one"*) un(a); **a year ago** hace un año; **a hundred/ thousand** *etc* **pounds** cien/mil *etc* libras
3 (*in expressing ratios, prices etc*): **3 a day/week** 3 al día/a la semana; **10 km an hour** 10 km por hora; **£5 a person** £5 por persona; **30p a kilo** 30p el kilo

A2 (*BRIT: Scol*) *n* segunda parte de los "A levels"
A.A. *n abbr* (*BRIT:* = *Automobile Association*) ≈ RACE *m* (*SP*); (= *Alcoholics Anonymous*) Alcohólicos Anónimos
A.A.A. (*US*) *n abbr* (= *American Automobile Association*) ≈ RACE *m* (*SP*)
aback [ə'bæk] *adv*: **to be taken ~**
quedar desconcertado
abandon [ə'bændən] *vt* abandonar; (*give up*) renunciar a
abattoir ['æbətwɑ:*] (*BRIT*) *n* matadero
abbey ['æbɪ] *n* abadía
abbreviation [ə'bri:vɪ'eɪʃən] *n* (*short form*) abreviatura
abdomen ['æbdəmən] *n* abdomen *m*
abduct [æb'dʌkt] *vt* raptar, secuestrar
abide [ə'baɪd] *vt*: **I can't ~ it/him** no lo/le puedo ver; **abide by** *vt fus* atenerse a
ability [ə'bɪlɪtɪ] *n* habilidad *f*, capacidad *f*; (*talent*) talento
able ['eɪbl] *adj* capaz; (*skilled*) hábil; **to be ~ to do sth** poder hacer algo
abnormal [æb'nɔ:məl] *adj* anormal
aboard [ə'bɔ:d] *adv* a bordo ▷ *prep* a bordo de
abolish [ə'bɔlɪʃ] *vt* suprimir, abolir
abolition [æbəu'lɪʃən] *n* supresión *f*, abolición *f*
abort [ə'bɔ:t] *vt, vi* abortar; **abortion** [ə'bɔ:ʃən] *n* aborto; **to have an abortion** abortar, hacerse abortar

○ **KEYWORD**

about [ə'baut] *adv* **1** (*approximately*) más o menos, aproximadamente; **about a hundred/thousand** *etc* unos(unas) cien/mil *etc*; **it takes about 10 hours** se tarda unas *or* más o menos 10 horas; **at about 2 o'clock** sobre las dos; **I've just about finished** casi he terminado
2 (*referring to place*) por todas partes; **to leave things lying about** dejar las cosas (tiradas) por ahí; **to run about** correr por todas partes; **to walk about** pasearse, ir y venir
3: **to be about to do sth** estar a punto de hacer algo
▷ *prep* **1** (*relating to*) de, sobre, acerca de; **a book about London** un libro sobre *or* acerca de Londres; **what is it**

about? ¿de qué se trata?; **we talked about it** hablamos de eso or ello; **what** or **how about doing this?** ¿qué tal si hacemos esto?
2 (referring to place) por; **to walk about the town** caminar por la ciudad

above [ə'bʌv] adv encima, por encima, arriba ▷ prep encima de; (greater than: in number) más de; (: in rank) superior a; **mentioned ~** susodicho; **~ all** sobre todo
abroad [ə'brɔːd] adv (to be) en el extranjero; (to go) al extranjero
abrupt [ə'brʌpt] adj (sudden) brusco; (curt) áspero
abscess ['æbsɪs] n absceso
absence ['æbsəns] n ausencia
absent ['æbsənt] adj ausente; **absent-minded** adj distraído
absolute ['æbsəluːt] adj absoluto; **absolutely** [-'luːtlɪ] adv (totally) totalmente; (certainly!) ¡por supuesto (que sí)!
absorb [əb'zɔːb] vt absorber; **to be ~ed in a book** estar absorto en un libro; **absorbent cotton** (US) n algodón m hidrófilo; **absorbing** adj absorbente
abstain [əb'steɪn] vi: **to ~ (from)** abstenerse (de)
abstract ['æbstrækt] adj abstracto
absurd [əb'səːd] adj absurdo
abundance [ə'bʌndəns] n abundancia
abundant [ə'bʌndənt] adj abundante
abuse [n ə'bjuːs, vb ə'bjuːz] n (insults) insultos mpl, injurias fpl; (ill-treatment) malos tratos mpl; (misuse) abuso ▷ vt insultar; maltratar; abusar de; **abusive** adj ofensivo
abysmal [ə'bɪzməl] adj pésimo; (failure) garrafal; (ignorance) supino
academic [ækə'dɛmɪk] adj académico, universitario; (pej: issue) puramente teórico ▷ n estudioso/a, profesor(a) m/f universitario/a; **academic year** n (Univ) año m

académico; (Scol) año m escolar
academy [ə'kædəmɪ] n (learned body) academia; (school) instituto, colegio; **~ of music** conservatorio
accelerate [æk'sɛləreɪt] vt, vi acelerar; **acceleration** [æksɛlə'reɪʃən] n aceleración f; **accelerator** (BRIT) n acelerador m
accent ['æksɛnt] n acento; (fig) énfasis m
accept [ək'sɛpt] vt aceptar; (responsibility, blame) admitir; **acceptable** adj aceptable; **acceptance** n aceptación f
access ['æksɛs] n acceso; **to have ~ to** tener libre acceso a; **accessible** [-'sɛsəbl] adj (place, person) accesible; (knowledge etc) asequible
accessory [æk'sɛsərɪ] n accesorio; (Law): **~ to** cómplice de
accident ['æksɪdənt] n accidente m; (chance event) casualidad f; **by ~** (unintentionally) sin querer; (by chance) por casualidad; **accidental** [-'dɛntl] adj accidental, fortuito; **accidentally** [-'dɛntəlɪ] adv sin querer; por casualidad; **Accident and Emergency Department** n (BRIT) Urgencias fpl; **accident insurance** n seguro contra accidentes
acclaim [ə'kleɪm] vt aclamar, aplaudir ▷ n aclamación f, aplausos mpl
accommodate [ə'kɔmədeɪt] vt (person) alojar, hospedar; (: car, hotel etc) tener cabida para; (oblige, help) complacer
accommodation [əkɔmə'deɪʃən] (US **accommodations**) n alojamiento
accompaniment [ə'kʌmpənɪmənt] n acompañamiento
accompany [ə'kʌmpənɪ] vt acompañar
accomplice [ə'kʌmplɪs] n cómplice mf
accomplish [ə'kʌmplɪʃ] vt (finish) concluir; (achieve) lograr; **accomplishment** n (skill: gen pl)

talento; (*completion*) realización *f*
accord [ə'kɔːd] *n* acuerdo
▷ *vt* conceder; **of his own ~**
espontáneamente; **accordance**
n: **in accordance with** de acuerdo
con; **according** ▷ **according to** *prep*
según; (*in accordance with*) conforme
a; **accordingly** *adv* (*appropriately*)
de acuerdo con esto; (*as a result*) en
consecuencia
account [ə'kaunt] *n* (*Comm*)
cuenta; (*report*) informe *m*; **accounts**
npl (*Comm*) cuentas *fpl*; **of no ~** de
ninguna importancia; **on ~** a cuenta;
on no ~ bajo ningún concepto; **on ~
of** a causa de, por motivo de; **to take
into ~, take ~ of** tener en cuenta;
account for *vt fus* (*explain*) explicar;
(*represent*) representar; **accountable**
adj: **accountable (to)** responsable
(ante); **accountant** *n* contable *mf*,
contador(a) *m/f*; **account number** *n*
(*at bank etc*) número de cuenta
accumulate [ə'kjuːmjuleɪt] *vt*
acumular ▷ *vi* acumularse
accuracy ['ækjurəsɪ] *n* (*of total*)
exactitud *f*; (*of description etc*)
precisión *f*
accurate ['ækjurɪt] *adj* (*total*) exacto;
(*description*) preciso; (*person*) cuidadoso;
(*device*) de precisión; **accurately** *adv*
con precisión
accusation [ækju'zeɪʃən] *n*
acusación *f*
accuse [ə'kjuːz] *vt*: **to ~ sb (of sth)**
acusar a algn (de algo), **accused** *n*
(*Law*) acusado/a
accustomed [ə'kʌstəmd] *adj*: **~ to**
acostumbrado a
ace [eɪs] *n* as *m*
ache [eɪk] *n* dolor *m* ▷ *vi* doler; **my
head ~s** me duele la cabeza
achieve [ə'tʃiːv] *vt* (*aim, result*)
alcanzar; (*success*) lograr, conseguir;
achievement *n* (*completion*)
realización *f*; (*success*) éxito
acid ['æsɪd] *adj* ácido; (*taste*) agrio ▷ *n*
(*Chem, inf: LSD*) ácido

acknowledge [ək'nɔlɪdʒ] *vt*
(*letter: also*: **~ receipt of**) acusar recibo
de; (*fact, situation, person*) reconocer;
acknowledgement *n* acuse *m* de
recibo
acne ['æknɪ] *n* acné *m*
acorn ['eɪkɔːn] *n* bellota
acoustic [ə'kuːstɪk] *adj* acústico
acquaintance [ə'kweɪntəns] *n*
(*person*) conocido/a; (*with person,
subject*) conocimiento
acquire [ə'kwaɪə*] *vt* adquirir;
acquisition [ækwɪ'zɪʃən] *n*
adquisición *f*
acquit [ə'kwɪt] *vt* absolver, exculpar;
to ~ o.s. well salir con éxito
acre ['eɪkə*] *n* acre *m*
acronym ['ækrənɪm] *n* siglas *fpl*
across [ə'krɔs] *prep* (*on the other side
of*) al otro lado de, del otro lado de;
(*crosswise*) a través de ▷ *adv* de un lado
a otro, de una parte a otra; a través, al
través; (*measurement*). **the road is 10m
~** la carretera tiene 10m de ancho; **to
run/swim ~** atravesar corriendo/
nadando; **~ from** enfrente de
acrylic [ə'krɪlɪk] *adj* acrílico ▷ *n*
acrílica
act [ækt] *n* acto, acción *f*; (*of play*)
acto; (*in music hall etc*) número;
(*Law*) decreto, ley *f* ▷ *vi* (*behave*)
comportarse; (*have effect: drug,
chemical*) hacer efecto; (*Theatre*) actuar;
(*pretend*) fingir; (*take action*) obrar ▷ *vt*
(*part*) hacer el papel de; **in the ~ of: to
catch sb in the ~ of ...** pillar a algn en
el momento en que ...; **to ~ as** actuar
or hacer de; **act up** (*inf*) *vi* (*person*)
portarse mal; **acting** *adj* suplente
▷ *n* (*activity*) actuación *f*; (*profession*)
profesión *f* de actor
action ['ækʃən] *n* acción *f*, acto;
(*Mil*) acción *f*, batalla; (*Law*) proceso,
demanda; **out of ~** (*person*) fuera de
combate; (*thing*) estropeado; **to take ~**
tomar medidas; **action replay** *n* (*TV*)
repetición *f*
activate ['æktɪveɪt] *vt* activar

active ['æktɪv] adj activo, enérgico;
(volcano) en actividad; **actively** adv
(participate) activamente; (discourage,
dislike) enérgicamente

activist ['æktɪvɪst] n activista m/f

activity [-'tɪvɪtɪ] n actividad f;
activity holiday n vacaciones con
actividades organizadas

actor ['æktə*] n actor m, actriz f

actress ['æktrɪs] n actriz f

actual ['æktjuəl] adj verdadero, real;
(emphatic use) propiamente dicho
▌ Be careful not to translate **actual** by
the Spanish word actual.

actually ['æktjuəlɪ] adv realmente,
en realidad; (even) incluso
▌ Be careful not to translate **actually**
by the Spanish word actualmente.

acupuncture ['ækjupʌŋktʃə*] n
acupuntura

acute [ə'kju:t] adj agudo

ad [æd] n abbr = **advertisement**

A.D. adv abbr (= anno Domini) DC

adamant ['ædəmənt] adj firme,
inflexible

adapt [ə'dæpt] vt adaptar ▷ vi: **to
~ (to)** adaptarse (a), ajustarse (a);
adapter (US **adaptor**) n (Elec)
adaptador m; (for several plugs) ladrón m

add [æd] vt añadir, agregar; **add up** vt
(figures) sumar ▷ vi (fig): **it doesn't add
up** no tiene sentido; **add up to** vt fus
(Math) sumar, ascender a; (fig: mean)
querer decir, venir a ser

addict ['ædɪkt] n adicto/a;
(enthusiast) entusiasta mf; **addicted**
[ə'dɪktɪd] adj: **to be addicted to** ser
adicto a, ser fanático de; **addiction**
[ə'dɪkʃən] n (to drugs etc) adicción f;
addictive [ə'dɪktɪv] adj que causa
adicción

addition [ə'dɪʃən] n (adding up)
adición f; (thing added) añadidura,
añadido; **in ~** además, por añadidura;
in ~ to además de; **additional** adj
adicional

additive ['ædɪtɪv] n aditivo

address [ə'drɛs] n dirección f, señas

fpl; (speech) discurso ▷ vt (letter) dirigir;
(speak to) dirigirse a, dirigir la palabra
a; (problem) tratar; **address book** n
agenda (de direcciones)

adequate ['ædɪkwɪt] adj
(satisfactory) adecuado; (enough)
suficiente

adhere [əd'hɪə*] vi: **to ~ to** (stick
to) pegarse a; (fig: abide by) observar;
(: belief etc) ser partidario de

adhesive [əd'hi:zɪv] n adhesivo;
adhesive tape n (BRIT) cinta
adhesiva; (US Med) esparadrapo

adjacent [ə'dʒeɪsənt] adj: **~ to**
contiguo a, inmediato a

adjective ['ædʒɛktɪv] n adjetivo

adjoining [ə'dʒɔɪnɪŋ] adj contiguo,
vecino

adjourn [ə'dʒə:n] vt aplazar ▷ vi
suspenderse

adjust [ə'dʒʌst] vt (change) modificar;
(clothing) arreglar; (machine) ajustar
▷ vi: **to ~ (to)** adaptarse (a); **adjustable**
adj ajustable; **adjustment** n
adaptación f; (to machine, prices)
ajuste m

administer [əd'mɪnɪstə*] vt
administrar; **administration**
[-'treɪʃən] n (management)
administración f; (government)
gobierno; **administrative** [-trətɪv] adj
administrativo

administrator [əd'mɪnɪstreɪtə*] n
administrador(a) m/f

admiral ['ædmərəl] n almirante m

admiration [ædmə'reɪʃən] n
admiración f

admire [əd'maɪə*] vt admirar;
admirer n (fan) admirador(a) m/f

admission [əd'mɪʃən] n (to university,
club) ingreso; (entry fee) entrada;
(confession) confesión f

admit [əd'mɪt] vt (confess) confesar;
(permit to enter) dejar entrar, dar
entrada a; (to club, organization)
admitir; (accept: defeat) reconocer;
to be ~ted to hospital ingresar en el
hospital; **admit to** vt fus confesarse

culpable de; **admittance** n entrada;
admittedly adv es cierto que
adolescent [ædəu'lɛsnt] adj, n
adolescente mf
adopt [ə'dɔpt] vt adoptar; **adopted**
adj adoptivo; **adoption** [ə'dɔpʃən] n
adopción f
adore [ə'dɔ:*] vt adorar
adorn [ə'dɔ:n] vt adornar
Adriatic [eɪdrɪ'ætɪk] n: **the ~ (Sea)** el
(Mar) Adriático
adrift [ə'drɪft] adv a la deriva
ADSL abbr (= asymmetrical digital
subscriber line) ADSL m
adult ['ædʌlt] n adulto/a ▷ adj
(grown-up) adulto; (for adults)
para adultos; **adult education** n
educación f para adultos
adultery [ə'dʌltərɪ] n adulterio
advance [əd'vɑ:ns] n (progress)
adelanto, progreso; (money) anticipo,
préstamo; (Mil) avance m ▷ adj: ~
booking venta anticipada; ~ **notice,**
~ **warning** previo aviso ▷ vt (money)
anticipar; (theory, idea) proponer
(para la discusión) ▷ vi avanzar,
adelantarse; **to make ~s (to sb)**
hacer proposiciones (a algn); **in ~** por
adelantado; **advanced** adj avanzado;
(Scol: studies) adelantado
advantage [əd'vɑ:ntɪdʒ] n (also
Tennis) ventaja; **to take ~ of** (person)
aprovecharse de; (opportunity)
aprovechar
advent ['ædvənt] n advenimiento;
A~ Adviento
adventure [əd'vɛntʃə*] n aventura;
adventurous [-tʃərəs] adj atrevido;
aventurero
adverb ['ædvə:b] n adverbio
adversary ['ædvəsərɪ] n adversario,
contrario
adverse ['ædvə:s] adj adverso,
contrario
advert ['ædvə:t] (BRIT) n abbr =
advertisement
advertise ['ædvətaɪz] vi anunciar,
hacer publicidad; **to ~ for** buscar por

medio de anuncios ▷ vt anunciar;
advertisement [əd'və:tɪsmənt]
n (Comm) anuncio; **advertiser**
n anunciante mf; **advertising** n
publicidad f, anuncios mpl; (industry)
industria publicitaria
advice [əd'vaɪs] n consejo, consejos
mpl; (notification) aviso; **a piece of ~** un
consejo; **to take legal ~** consultar con
un abogado
advisable [əd'vaɪzəbl] adj
aconsejable, conveniente
advise [əd'vaɪz] vt aconsejar;
(inform): **to ~ sb of sth** informar a algn
de algo; **to ~ sb against sth/doing sth**
desaconsejar algo a algn/aconsejar
a algn que no haga algo; **adviser,**
advisor n consejero/a; (consultant)
asesor(a) m/f; **advisory** adj consultivo
advocate [vb 'ædvəkeɪt, n -kɪt] vt
abogar por ▷ n (lawyer) abogado/a;
(supporter): ~ **of** defensor(a) m/f de
Aegean [i:'dʒi:ən] n: **the ~ (Sea)** el
(Mar) Egeo
aerial ['ɛərɪəl] n antena ▷ adj aéreo
aerobics [ɛə'rəubɪks] n aerobic m
aeroplane ['ɛərəpleɪn] (BRIT) n
avión m
aerosol ['ɛərəsɔl] n aerosol m
affair [ə'fɛə*] n asunto; (also: **love ~**)
aventura (amorosa)
affect [ə'fɛkt] vt (influence) afectar,
influir en; (afflict, concern) afectar;
(move) conmover; **affected** adj
afectado; **affection** n afecto, cariño;
affectionate adj afectuoso, cariñoso
afflict [ə'flɪkt] vt afligir
affluent ['æfluənt] adj (wealthy)
acomodado; **the ~ society** la sociedad
opulenta
afford [ə'fɔ:d] vt (provide)
proporcionar; **can we ~ (to buy)**
it? ¿tenemos bastante dinero para
comprarlo?; **affordable** adj asequible
Afghanistan [æf'gænɪstæn] n
Afganistán m
afraid [ə'freɪd] adj: **to be ~ of** (person)
tener miedo a; (thing) tener miedo de;

to be ~ to tener miedo de, temer; **I am ~ that** me temo que; **I am ~ not/so** lo siento, pero no/es así

Africa ['æfrɪkə] n África; **African** adj, n africano/a m/f; **African-American** adj, n afroamericano/a

after ['ɑːftə*] prep (time) después de; (place, order) detrás de, tras ▷ adv después ▷ conj después (de) que; **what/who are you ~?** ¿qué/a quién busca usted?; **~ having done/he left** después de haber hecho/después de que se marchó; **to name sb ~ sb** llamar a algn por algn; **it's twenty ~ eight** (us) son las ocho y veinte; **to ask ~ sb** preguntar por algn; **~ all** después de todo, al fin y al cabo; **~ you!** ¡pase usted!; **after-effects** npl consecuencias fpl, efectos mpl; **aftermath** n consecuencias fpl, resultados mpl; **afternoon** n tarde f; **after-shave (lotion)** n aftershave m; **aftersun (lotion/cream)** n loción f/crema para después del sol, aftersun m; **afterwards** (us **afterward**) adv después, más tarde

again [ə'gɛn] adv otra vez, de nuevo; **to do sth ~** volver a hacer algo; **~ and ~** una y otra vez

against [ə'gɛnst] prep (in opposition to) en contra de; (leaning on, touching) contra, junto a

age [eɪdʒ] n edad f; (period) época ▷ vi envejecer(se) ▷ vt envejecer; **she is 20 years of ~** tiene 20 años; **to come of ~** llegar a la mayoría de edad; **it's been ~s since I saw you** hace siglos que no te veo; **~d 10** de 10 años de edad; **age group** n: **to be in the same age group** tener la misma edad; **age limit** n edad f mínima (or máxima)

agency ['eɪdʒənsɪ] n agencia

agenda [ə'dʒɛndə] n orden m del día
▌Be careful not to translate **agenda** by the Spanish word agenda.

agent ['eɪdʒənt] n agente mf; (Comm: holding concession) representante mf, delegado/a; (Chem,

fig) agente m

aggravate ['ægrəveɪt] vt (situation) agravar; (person) irritar

aggression [ə'grɛʃən] n agresión f

aggressive [ə'grɛsɪv] adj (belligerent) agresivo; (assertive) enérgico

agile ['ædʒaɪl] adj ágil

agitated ['ædʒɪteɪtɪd] adj agitado

AGM n abbr (= annual general meeting) asamblea anual

ago [ə'gəu] adv: **2 days ~** hace 2 días; **not long ~** hace poco; **how long ~?** ¿hace cuánto tiempo?

agony ['ægənɪ] n (pain) dolor m agudo; (distress) angustia; **to be in ~** retorcerse de dolor

agree [ə'griː] vt (price, date) acordar, quedar en ▷ vi (have same opinion): **to ~ (with/that)** estar de acuerdo (con/que); (correspond) coincidir, concordar; (consent) acceder; **to ~ with** (person) estar de acuerdo con, ponerse de acuerdo con; (: food) sentar bien a; (Ling) concordar con; **to ~ to sth/to do sth** consentir en algo/aceptar hacer algo; **to ~ that** (admit) estar de acuerdo en que; **agreeable** adj (sensation) agradable; (person) simpático; (willing) de acuerdo, conforme; **agreed** adj (time, place) convenido; **agreement** n acuerdo; (contract) contrato; **in agreement** de acuerdo, conforme

agricultural [ægrɪ'kʌltʃərəl] adj agrícola

agriculture ['ægrɪkʌltʃə*] n agricultura

ahead [ə'hɛd] adv (in front) delante; (into the future): **she had no time to think ~** no tenía tiempo de hacer planes para el futuro; **~ of** delante de; (in advance of) antes de; **~ of time** antes de la hora; **go right** or **straight ~** (direction) siga adelante; (permission) hazlo (or hágalo)

aid [eɪd] n ayuda, auxilio; (device) aparato ▷ vt ayudar, auxiliar; **in ~ of** a beneficio de

aide [eɪd] n (person, also Mil) ayudante

a

mf

AIDS [eɪdz] n abbr (= acquired immune deficiency syndrome) SIDA m

ailing ['eɪlɪŋ] adj (person, economy) enfermizo

ailment ['eɪlmənt] n enfermedad f, achaque m

aim [eɪm] vt (gun, camera) apuntar; (missile, remark) dirigir; (blow) asestar ▷ vi (also: **take ~**) apuntar ▷ n (in shooting: skill) puntería; (objective) propósito, meta; **to ~ at** (with weapon) apuntar a; (objective) aspirar a, pretender; **to ~ to do** tener la intención de hacer

ain't [eɪnt] (inf) = **am not; aren't; isn't**

air [ɛə*] n aire m; (appearance) aspecto ▷ vt (room) ventilar; (clothes, ideas) airear ▷ cpd aéreo; **to throw sth into the ~** (ball etc) lanzar algo al aire; **by ~** (travel) en avión; **to be on the ~** (Radio, TV) estar en antena; **airbag** n airbag m inv; **airbed** (BRIT) n colchón m neumático; **airborne** adj (in the air) en el aire; **as soon as the plane was airborne** tan pronto como el avión estuvo en el aire; **air-conditioned** adj climatizado; **air conditioning** n aire acondicionado; **aircraft** n inv avión m; **airfield** n campo de aviación; **Air Force** n fuerzas fpl aéreas, aviación f; **air hostess** (BRIT) n azafata; **airing cupboard** n (BRIT) armario m para oreo; **airlift** n puente m aéreo; **airline** n línea aérea; **airliner** n avión m de pasajeros; **airmail** n: **by airmail** por avión; **airplane** (US) n avión m; **airport** n aeropuerto; **air raid** n ataque m aéreo; **airsick** adj: **to be airsick** marearse (en avión); **airspace** n espacio aéreo; **airstrip** n pista de aterrizaje; **air terminal** n terminal f; **airtight** adj hermético; **air-traffic controller** n controlador(a) m/f aéreo/a; **airy** adj (room) bien ventilado; (fig: manner) desenfadado

aisle [aɪl] n (of church) nave f; (of theatre, supermarket) pasillo; **aisle seat**

n (on plane) asiento de pasillo

ajar [ə'dʒɑ:*] adj entreabierto

à la carte [ælæ'kɑ:t] adv a la carta

alarm [ə'lɑ:m] n (in shop, bank) alarma; (anxiety) inquietud f ▷ vt asustar, inquietar; **alarm call** n (in hotel etc) alarma; **alarm clock** n despertador m; **alarmed** adj (person) alarmado, asustado; (house, car etc) con alarma; **alarming** adj alarmante

Albania [æl'beɪnɪə] n Albania

albeit [ɔ:l'bi:ɪt] conj aunque

album ['ælbəm] n álbum m; (L.P.) elepé m

alcohol ['ælkəhɔl] n alcohol m; **alcohol-free** adj sin alcohol; **alcoholic** [-'hɔlɪk] adj, n alcohólico/a m/f

alcove ['ælkəuv] n nicho, hueco

ale [eɪl] n cerveza

alert [ə'lə:t] adj (attentive) atento; (to danger, opportunity) alerta ▷ n alerta m, alarma ▷ vt poner sobre aviso; **to be on the ~** (also Mil) estar alerta or sobre aviso

algebra ['ældʒɪbrə] n álgebra

Algeria [æl'dʒɪərɪə] n Argelia

alias ['eɪlɪəs] adv alias, conocido por ▷ n (of criminal) apodo; (of writer) seudónimo

alibi ['ælɪbaɪ] n coartada

alien ['eɪlɪən] n (foreigner) extranjero/a; (extraterrestrial) extraterrestre mf ▷ adj: **~ to** ajeno a; **alienate** vt enajenar, alejar

alight [ə'laɪt] adj ardiendo; (eyes) brillante ▷ vi (person) apearse, bajar; (bird) posarse

align [ə'laɪn] vt alinear

alike [ə'laɪk] adj semejantes, iguales ▷ adv igualmente, del mismo modo; **to look ~** parecerse

alive [ə'laɪv] adj vivo; (lively) alegre

○ **KEYWORD**

all [ɔ:l] adj (sg) todo/a; (pl) todos/as; **all day** todo el día; **all night** toda la noche; **all men** todos los hombres;

all five came vinieron los cinco; **all the books** todos los libros; **all his life** toda su vida
▷ *pron* **1** todo; **I ate it all, I ate all of it** me lo comí todo; **all of us went** fuimos todos; **all the boys went** fueron todos los chicos; **is that all?** ¿eso es todo?, ¿algo más?; (*in shop*) ¿algo más?, ¿alguna cosa más?
2 (*in phrases*): **above all** sobre todo; por encima de todo; **after all** después de todo; **at all: not at all** (*in answer to question*) en absoluto; (*in answer to thanks*) ¡de nada!, ¡no hay de qué!; **I'm not at all tired** no estoy nada cansado/a; **anything at all will do** cualquier cosa viene bien; **all in all** a fin de cuentas
▷ *adv*: **all alone** completamente solo/a; **it's not as hard as all that** no es tan difícil como lo pintas; **all the more/the better** tanto más/mejor; **all but** casi; **the score is 2 all** están empatados a 2

Allah ['ælə] *n* Alá *m*
allegation [ælɪ'geɪʃən] *n* alegato
alleged [ə'ledʒd] *adj* supuesto, presunto; **allegedly** *adv* supuestamente, según se afirma
allegiance [ə'li:dʒəns] *n* lealtad *f*
allergic [ə'lə:dʒɪk] *adj*: **~ to** alérgico a
allergy ['ælədʒɪ] *n* alergia
alleviate [ə'li:vɪeɪt] *vt* aliviar
alley ['ælɪ] *n* callejuela
alliance [ə'laɪəns] *n* alianza
allied ['ælaɪd] *adj* aliado
alligator ['ælɪgeɪtə*] *n* (*Zool*) caimán *m*
all-in (BRIT) ['ɔ:lɪn] *adj, adv* (*charge*) todo incluido
allocate ['æləkeɪt] *vt* (*money etc*) asignar
allot [ə'lɒt] *vt* asignar
all-out ['ɔ:laʊt] *adj* (*effort etc*) supremo
allow [ə'laʊ] *vt* permitir, dejar; (*a claim*) admitir; (*sum, time etc*)

dar, conceder; (*concede*): **to ~ that** reconocer que; **to ~ sb to do** permitir a algn hacer; **he is ~ed to ...** se le permite ...; **allow for** *vt fus* tener en cuenta;
allowance *n* subvención *f*; (*welfare payment*) subsidio, pensión *f*; (*pocket money*) dinero de bolsillo; (*tax allowance*) desgravación *f*; **to make allowances for** (*person*) disculpar a; (*thing*) tener en cuenta
all right *adv* bien; (*as answer*) ¡conforme!, ¡está bien!
ally ['ælaɪ] *n* aliado/a ▷ *vt*: **to ~ o.s. with** aliarse con
almighty [ɔ:l'maɪtɪ] *adj* todopoderoso; (*row etc*) imponente
almond ['ɑ:mənd] *n* almendra
almost ['ɔ:lməʊst] *adv* casi
alone [ə'ləʊn] *adj, adv* solo; **to leave sb ~** dejar a algn en paz; **to leave sth ~** no tocar algo, dejar algo sin tocar; **let ~ ...** y mucho menos ...
along [ə'lɒŋ] *prep* a lo largo de, por ▷ *adv*: **is he coming ~ with us?** ¿viene con nosotros?; **he was limping ~** iba cojeando; **~ with** junto con; **all ~** (*all the time*) desde el principio; **alongside** *prep* al lado de ▷ *adv* al lado
aloof [ə'lu:f] *adj* reservado ▷ *adv*: **to stand ~** mantenerse apartado
aloud [ə'laʊd] *adv* en voz alta
alphabet ['ælfəbet] *n* alfabeto
Alps [ælps] *npl*: **the ~** los Alpes
already [ɔ:l'redɪ] *adv* ya
alright ['ɔ:l'raɪt] (BRIT) *adv* = **all right**
also ['ɔ:lsəʊ] *adv* también, además
altar ['ɒltə*] *n* altar *m*
alter ['ɒltə*] *vt* cambiar, modificar ▷ *vi* cambiar; **alteration** [ɒltə'reɪʃən] *n* cambio; (*to clothes*) arreglo; (*to building*) arreglos *mpl*
alternate [*adj* ɒl'tə:nɪt, *vb* 'ɒltə:neɪt] *adj* (*actions etc*) alternativo; (*events*) alterno; (*US*) = **alternative** ▷ *vi*: **to ~ (with)** alternar (con); **on ~ days** un día sí y otro no
alternative [ɒl'tə:nətɪv] *adj* alternativo ▷ *n* alternativa; **~**

medicine medicina alternativa;
alternatively adv: **alternatively one
could ...** por otra parte se podría ...
although [ɔːl'ðəu] conj aunque
altitude [ˈæltɪtjuːd] n altura
altogether [ɔːltəˈgɛðə*] adv
completamente, del todo; (on the
whole) en total, en conjunto
aluminium [æljuˈmɪnɪəm] (BRIT),
aluminum [əˈluːmɪnəm] (US) n
aluminio
always [ˈɔːlweɪz] adv siempre
Alzheimer's (disease)
[ˈæltshaɪməz-] n enfermedad f de
Alzheimer
am [æm] vb see **be**
amalgamate [əˈmælgəmeɪt] vi
amalgamarse ▷ vt amalgamar, unir
amass [əˈmæs] vt amontonar,
acumular
amateur [ˈæmətə*] n aficionado/a,
amateur mf
amaze [əˈmeɪz] vt asombrar, pasmar;
to be ~d (at) quedar pasmado (de);
amazed adj asombrado; **amazement**
n asombro, sorpresa; **amazing** adj
extraordinario; (fantastic) increíble
Amazon [ˈæməzən] n (Geo)
Amazonas m
ambassador [æmˈbæsədə*] n
embajador(a) m/f
amber [ˈæmbə*] n ámbar m; **at ~**
(BRIT Aut) en el amarillo
ambiguous [æmˈbɪgjuəs] adj
ambiguo
ambition [æmˈbɪʃən] n ambición f;
ambitious [-ʃəs] adj ambicioso
ambulance [ˈæmbjuləns] n
ambulancia
ambush [ˈæmbuʃ] n emboscada ▷ vt
tender una emboscada a
amen [ɑːˈmɛn] excl amén
amend [əˈmɛnd] vt enmendar; **to
make ~s** dar cumplida satisfacción;
amendment n enmienda
amenities [əˈmiːnɪtɪz] npl
comodidades fpl
America [əˈmɛrɪkə] n (USA)

Estados mpl Unidos; **American** adj, n
norteamericano/a; estadounidense
mf; **American football** n (BRIT) fútbol
m americano
amicable [ˈæmɪkəbl] adj amistoso,
amigable
amid(st) [əˈmɪd(st)] prep entre, en
medio de
ammunition [æmjuˈnɪʃən] n
municiones fpl
amnesty [ˈæmnɪstɪ] n amnistía
among(st) [əˈmʌŋ(st)] prep entre,
en medio de
amount [əˈmaunt] n (gen) cantidad
f; (of bill etc) suma, importe m ▷ vi: **to
~ to** sumar; (be same as) equivaler a,
significar
amp(ère) [ˈæmp(ɛə*)] n amperio
ample [ˈæmpl] adj (large) grande;
(abundant) abundante; (enough)
bastante, suficiente
amplifier [ˈæmplɪfaɪə*] n
amplificador m
amputate [ˈæmpjuteɪt] vt amputar
Amtrak [ˈæmtræk] (US) n empresa
nacional de ferrocarriles de los EEUU
amuse [əˈmjuːz] vt divertir; (distract)
distraer, entretener; **amusement**
n diversión f; (pastime) pasatiempo;
(laughter) risa; **amusement arcade** n
salón m de juegos; **amusement park** n
parque m de atracciones
amusing [əˈmjuːzɪŋ] adj divertido
an [æn] indef art see **a**
anaemia [əˈniːmɪə] (US **anemia**)
n anemia
anaemic [əˈniːmɪk] (US **anemic**) adj
anémico; (fig) soso, insípido
anaesthetic [ænɪsˈθɛtɪk] (US
anesthetic) n anestesia
analog(ue) [ˈænəlɔg] adj (computer,
watch) analógico
analogy [əˈnælədʒɪ] n analogía
analyse [ˈænəlaɪz] (US **analyze**)
vt analizar; **analysis** [əˈnæləsɪs] (pl
analyses) n análisis m inv; **analyst**
[-lɪst] n (political analyst, psychoanalyst)
analista mf

analyze ['ænəlaɪz] (US) vt = **analyse**

anarchy ['ænəkɪ] n anarquía, desorden m

anatomy [ə'nætəmɪ] n anatomía

ancestor ['ænsɪstə*] n antepasado

anchor ['æŋkə*] n ancla, áncora ▷ vi (also: **to drop ~**) anclar ▷ vt anclar; **to weigh ~** levar anclas

anchovy ['æntʃəvɪ] n anchoa

ancient ['eɪnʃənt] adj antiguo

and [ænd] conj y; (before i-, hi- + consonant) e; **men ~ women** hombres y mujeres; **father ~ son** padre e hijo; **trees ~ grass** árboles y hierba; **~ so on** etcétera, y así sucesivamente; **try ~ come** procura venir; **he talked ~ talked** habló sin parar; **better ~ better** cada vez mejor

Andes ['ændiːz] npl: **the ~** los Andes

Andorra [æn'dɔːrə] n Andorra

anemia etc [ə'niːmɪə] (US) = **anaemia** etc

anesthetic [ænɪs'θetɪk] (US) = **anaesthetic**

angel ['eɪndʒəl] n ángel m

anger ['æŋgə*] n cólera

angina [æn'dʒaɪnə] n angina (del pecho)

angle ['æŋgl] n ángulo; **from their ~** desde su punto de vista

angler ['æŋglə*] n pescador(a) m/f (de caña)

Anglican ['æŋglɪkən] adj, n anglicano/a m/f

angling ['æŋglɪŋ] n pesca con caña

angrily ['æŋgrɪlɪ] adv coléricamente, airadamente

angry ['æŋgrɪ] adj enfadado, airado; (wound) inflamado; **to be ~ with sb/at sth** estar enfadado con algn/por algo; **to get ~** enfadarse, enojarse

anguish ['æŋgwɪʃ] n (physical) tormentos mpl; (mental) angustia

animal ['ænɪməl] n animal m; (pej: person) bestia ▷ adj animal

animated [-meɪtɪd] adj animado

animation [ænɪ'meɪʃən] n animación f

aniseed ['ænɪsiːd] n anís m

ankle ['æŋkl] n tobillo

annex [n 'æneks, vb æ'neks] n (BRIT: also: **~e**: building) edificio anexo ▷ vt (territory) anexionar

anniversary [ænɪ'vɜːsərɪ] n aniversario

announce [ə'nauns] vt anunciar; **announcement** n anuncio; (official) declaración f; **announcer** n (Radio) locutor(a) m/f; (TV) presentador(a) m/f

annoy [ə'nɔɪ] vt molestar, fastidiar; **don't get ~ed!** ¡no se enfade!; **annoying** adj molesto, fastidioso; (person) pesado

annual ['ænjuəl] adj anual ▷ n (Bot) anual m; (book) anuario; **annually** adv anualmente, cada año

annum ['ænəm] n see **per**

anonymous [ə'nɒnɪməs] adj anónimo

anorak ['ænəræk] n anorak m

anorexia [ænə'reksɪə] n (Med: also: **~ nervosa**) anorexia

anorexic [ænə'reksɪk] adj, n anoréxico/a m/f

another [ə'nʌðə*] adj (one more, a different one) otro ▷ pron otro; see **one**

answer ['ɑːnsə*] n contestación f, respuesta; (to problem) solución f ▷ vi contestar, responder ▷ vt (reply to) contestar a, responder a; (problem) resolver; (prayer) escuchar; **in ~ to your letter** contestando or en contestación a su carta; **to ~ the phone** contestar or coger el teléfono; **to ~ the bell** or **the door** acudir a la puerta; **answer back** vi replicar, ser respondón/ona; **answerphone** n (esp BRIT) contestador m (automático)

ant [ænt] n hormiga

Antarctic [ænt'ɑːktɪk] n: **the ~** el Antártico

antelope ['æntɪləup] n antílope m

antenatal ['æntɪ'neɪtl] adj antenatal, prenatal

antenna [æn'tenə, pl -niː] (pl **antennae**) n antena

anthem [ˈænθəm] n: **national ~**
himno nacional
anthology [ænˈθɒlədʒɪ] n
antología
anthrax [ˈænθræks] n ántrax m
anthropology [ænθrəˈpɒlədʒɪ] n
antropología
anti [ˈæntɪ] prefix anti; **antibiotic**
[-baɪˈɒtɪk] n antibiótico; **antibody**
[ˈæntɪbɒdɪ] n anticuerpo
anticipate [ænˈtɪsɪpeɪt] vt prever;
(expect) esperar, contar con; (look
forward to) esperar con ilusión; (do
first) anticiparse a, adelantarse a;
anticipation [-ˈpeɪʃən] n (expectation)
previsión f; (eagerness) ilusión f,
expectación f
anticlimax [æntɪˈklaɪmæks] n
decepción f
anticlockwise [æntɪˈklɒkwaɪz]
(BRIT) adv en dirección
contraria a la de las agujas
del reloj
antics [ˈæntɪks] npl gracias
fpl
anti: **antidote** [ˈæntɪdəʊt] n
antídoto; **antifreeze** [ˈæntɪfriːz] n
anticongelante m; **antihistamine**
[-ˈhɪstəmiːn] n antihistamínico;
antiperspirant [ˈæntɪpəːspɪrənt] n
antitranspirante m
antique [ænˈtiːk] n antigüedad f
▷ adj antiguo; **antique shop** n tienda
de antigüedades
antiseptic [æntɪˈsɛptɪk] adj, n
antiséptico
antisocial [æntɪˈsəʊʃəl] adj
antisocial
antivirus [æntɪˈvaɪərəs] adj (program,
software) antivirus inv
antlers [ˈæntləz] npl cuernas fpl,
cornamenta sg
anxiety [æŋˈzaɪətɪ] n inquietud
f; (Med) ansiedad f; **~ to do** deseo
de hacer
anxious [ˈæŋkʃəs] adj inquieto,
preocupado; (worrying) preocupante;
(keen): **to be ~ to do** tener muchas

ganas de hacer

○ **KEYWORD**

any [ˈɛnɪ] adj **1** (in questions etc)
algún/alguna; **have you any butter/**
children? ¿tienes mantequilla/
hijos?; **if there are any tickets left** si
quedan billetes, si queda algún
billete
2 (with negative): **I haven't any money/**
books no tengo dinero/libros
3 (no matter which) cualquier; **any**
excuse will do valdrá or servirá
cualquier excusa; **choose any book**
you like escoge el libro que quieras
4 (in phrases): **in any case** de todas
formas, en cualquier caso; **any day**
now cualquier día (de estos); **at any**
moment en cualquier momento, de
un momento a otro; **at any rate** en
todo caso; **any time: come (at) any**
time ven cuando quieras; **he might**
come (at) any time podría llegar de un
momento a otro
▷ pron **1** (in questions etc): **have you got**
any? ¿tienes alguno(s)/a(s)?; **can any**
of you sing? ¿sabe cantar alguno de
vosotros/ustedes?
2 (with negative): **I haven't any (of**
them) no tengo ninguno
3 (no matter which one(s)): **take any of**
those books (you like) toma el libro
que quieras de ésos
▷ adv **1** (in questions etc): **do you**
want any more soup/sandwiches?
¿quieres más sopa/bocadillos?; **are**
you feeling any better? ¿te sientes
algo mejor?
2 (with negative): **I can't hear him any**
more ya no le oigo; **don't wait any**
longer no esperes más

any: **anybody** pron cualquiera;
(in interrogative sentences) alguien;
(in negative sentences): **I don't see**
anybody no veo a nadie; **if anybody**
should phone ... si llama alguien

...; **anyhow** adv (at any rate) de todos modos, de todas formas; (haphazard): **do it anyhow you like** hazlo como quieras; **she leaves things just anyhow** deja las cosas como quiera or de cualquier modo; **I shall go anyhow** de todos modos iré; **anyone** pron = **anybody**; **anything** pron (in questions etc) algo, alguna cosa; (with negative) nada; **can you see anything?** ¿ves algo?; **if anything happens to me** ... si algo me ocurre ...; (no matter what): **you can say anything you like** puedes decir lo que quieras; **anything will do** vale todo or cualquier cosa; **he'll eat anything** come de todo or lo que sea; **anytime** adv (at any moment) en cualquier momento, de un momento a otro; (whenever) no importa cuándo, cuando quiera; **anyway** adv (at any rate) de todos modos, de todas formas; **I shall go anyway** iré de todos modos; (besides): **anyway, I couldn't come even if I wanted to** además, no podría venir aunque quisiera; **why are you phoning, anyway?** ¿entonces, por qué llamas?, ¿por qué llamas, pues?; **anywhere** adv (in questions etc): **can you see him anywhere?** ¿le ves por algún lado?; **are you going anywhere?** ¿vas a algún sitio?; (with negative): **I can't see him anywhere** no le veo por ninguna parte; **anywhere in the world** (no matter where) en cualquier parte (del mundo); **put the books down anywhere** deja los libros donde quieras

apart [ə'pɑːt] adv (aside) aparte; (situation): **~ (from)** separado (de); (movement): **to pull ~** separar; **10 miles ~** separados por 10 millas; **to take ~** desmontar; **~ from** prep aparte de

apartment [ə'pɑːtmənt] n (US) piso (SP), departamento (LAM), apartamento; (room) cuarto; **apartment building** (US) n edificio de apartamentos

apathy ['æpəθɪ] n apatía, indiferencia

ape [eɪp] n mono ▷ vt imitar, remedar

aperitif [ə'perɪtɪf] n aperitivo

aperture ['æpətʃuə*] n rendija, resquicio; (Phot) abertura

APEX ['eɪpeks] n abbr (= Advanced Purchase Excursion Fare) tarifa f APEX

apologize [ə'pɒlədʒaɪz] vi: **to ~ (for sth to sb)** disculparse (con algn de algo)

apology [ə'pɒlədʒɪ] n disculpa, excusa

> Be careful not to translate **apology** by the Spanish word apología.

apostrophe [ə'pɒstrəfɪ] n apóstrofo

appal [ə'pɔːl] (US **appall**) vt horrorizar, espantar; **appalling** adj espantoso; (awful) pésimo

apparatus [æpə'reɪtəs] n (equipment) equipo; (organization) aparato; (in gymnasium) aparatos mpl

apparent [ə'pærənt] adj aparente; (obvious) evidente; **apparently** adv por lo visto, al parecer

appeal [ə'piːl] vi (Law) apelar ▷ n (Law) apelación f; (request) llamamiento; (plea) petición f; (charm) atractivo; **to ~ for** reclamar; **to ~ to** (be attractive to) atraer; **it doesn't ~ to me** no me atrae, no me llama la atención; **appealing** adj (attractive) atractivo

appear [ə'pɪə*] vi aparecer, presentarse; (Law) comparecer; (publication) salir (a luz), publicarse; (seem) parecer; **to ~ on TV/in "Hamlet"** salir por la tele/hacer un papel en "Hamlet"; **it would ~ that** parecería que; **appearance** n aparición f; (look) apariencia, aspecto

appendices [ə'pendɪsiːz] npl of **appendix**

appendicitis [əpendɪ'saɪtɪs] n apendicitis f

appendix [ə'pendɪks] (pl **appendices**) n apéndice m

appetite ['æpɪtaɪt] n apetito; (fig) deseo, anhelo

appetizer ['æpıtaızə*] n (drink)
aperitivo; (food) tapas fpl (SP)
applaud [ə'plɔːd] vt, vi aplaudir
applause [ə'plɔːz] n aplausos mpl
apple ['æpl] n manzana; **apple pie**
n pastel m de manzana, pay m de
manzana (LAM)
appliance [ə'plaıəns] n aparato
applicable [ə'plıkəbl] adj
(relevant): **to be ~ (to)** referirse (a)
applicant ['æplıkənt] n candidato/
a; solicitante mf
application [æplı'keıʃən] n
aplicación f; (for a job etc) solicitud
f, petición f; **application form** n
solicitud f
apply [ə'plaı] vt (paint etc) poner;
(law etc: put into practice) poner en
vigor ▷ vi: **to ~ to** (ask) dirigirse a;
(be applicable) ser aplicable a; **to ~ for**
(permit, grant, job) solicitar; **to ~ o.s. to**
aplicarse a, dedicarse a
appoint [ə'pɔınt] vt (to post)
nombrar a

Be careful not to translate **appoint**
by the Spanish word apuntar.

appointment n (with client) cita;
(act) nombramiento; (post) puesto;
(at hairdresser etc): **to have an
appointment** tener hora; **to make
an appointment (with sb)** citarse
(con algn)
appraisal [ə'preızl] n valoración f
appreciate [ə'priːʃıeıt] vt apreciar,
tener en mucho; (be grateful for)
agradecer; (be aware) comprender
▷ vi (Comm) aumentar(se) en valor;
appreciation [-'eıʃən] n apreciación
f; (gratitude) reconocimiento,
agradecimiento; (Comm) aumento
en valor
apprehension [æprı'henʃən] n
(fear) aprensión f
apprehensive [æprı'hensıv] adj
aprensivo
apprentice [ə'prentıs] n aprendiz(a)
m/f
approach [ə'prəutʃ] vi acercarse

▷ vt acercarse a; (ask, apply to) dirigirse
a; (situation, problem) abordar ▷ n
acercamiento; (access) acceso; (to
problem, situation): **~ (to)** actitud f
(ante)
appropriate [adj ə'prəupriıt, vb
ə'prəuprieıt] adj apropiado,
conveniente ▷ vt (take) apropiarse de
approval [ə'pruːvəl] n aprobación
f, visto bueno; (permission)
consentimiento; **on ~** (Comm) a prueba
approve [ə'pruːv] vt aprobar;
approve of vt fus (thing) aprobar;
(person): **they don't approve of her**
(ella) no les parece bien
approximate [ə'prɒksımıt] adj
aproximado; **approximately** adv
aproximadamente, más o menos
Apr. abbr (= April) abr
apricot ['eıprıkɒt] n albaricoque m,
chabacano (MEX), damasco (RPL)
April ['eıprəl] n abril m; **April Fools'
Day** n el primero de abril, ≈ día m de
los Inocentes (28 December)
apron ['eıprən] n delantal m
apt [æpt] adj acertado, apropiado;
(likely): **~ to do** propenso a hacer
aquarium [ə'kwεərıəm] n acuario
Aquarius [ə'kwεərıəs] n Acuario
Arab ['ærəb] adj, n árabe mf
Arabia [ə'reıbıə] n Arabia; **Arabian**
adj árabe; **Arabic** ['ærəbık] adj árabe;
(numerals) arábigo ▷ n árabe m
arbitrary ['ɑːbıtrərı] adj arbitrario
arbitration [ɑːbı'treıʃən] n
arbitraje m
arc [ɑːk] n arco
arcade [ɑː'keıd] n (round a square)
soportales mpl; (shopping mall) galería
comercial
arch [ɑːtʃ] n arco; (of foot) arco del pie
▷ vt arquear
archaeology [ɑːkı'ɒlədʒı] (US
archeology) n arqueología
archbishop [ɑːtʃ'bıʃəp] n arzobispo
archeology [ɑːkı'ɒlədʒı] (US) =
archaeology
architect ['ɑːkıtɛkt] n arquitecto/a;

architectural [ɑːkɪ'tɛktʃərəl] *adj*
arquitectónico; **architecture** *n*
arquitectura
archive ['ɑːkaɪv] *n* (*often pl: also*
Comput) archivo
Arctic ['ɑːktɪk] *adj* ártico ▷ *n*: **the**
~ el Ártico
are [ɑː*] *vb see* **be**
area ['ɛərɪə] *n* área, región *f*; (*part of*
place) zona; (*Math etc*) área, superficie
f; (*in room: e.g. dining area*) parte *f*; (*of*
knowledge, experience) campo; **area**
code (*us*) *n* (*Tel*) prefijo
arena [ə'riːnə] *n* estadio; (*of circus*)
pista
aren't [ɑːnt] = **are not**
Argentina [ɑːdʒən'tiːnə] *n*
Argentina; **Argentinian** [-'tɪnɪən] *adj*,
n argentino/a *m/f*
arguably ['ɑːgjuəblɪ] *adv*
posiblemente
argue ['ɑːgjuː] *vi* (*quarrel*) discutir,
pelearse; (*reason*) razonar, argumentar;
to ~ that sostener que
argument ['ɑːgjumənt] *n* discusión
f, pelea; (*reasons*) argumento
Aries ['ɛərɪz] *n* Aries *m*
arise [ə'raɪz] (*pt* **arose**, *pp* **arisen**) *vi*
surgir, presentarse
arithmetic [ə'rɪθmətɪk] *n*
aritmética
arm [ɑːm] *n* brazo ▷ *vt* armar;
arms *npl* armas *fpl*; **~ in ~** cogidos del
brazo; **armchair** ['ɑːmtʃɛə*] *n* sillón
m, butaca
armed [ɑːmd] *adj* armado; **armed**
robbery *n* robo a mano armada
armour ['ɑːmə*] (*us* **armor**) *n*
armadura; (*Mil: tanks*) blindaje *m*
armpit ['ɑːmpɪt] *n* sobaco, axila
armrest ['ɑːmrɛst] *n* apoyabrazos
m inv
army ['ɑːmɪ] *n* ejército; (*fig*)
multitud *f*
A road *n* (*BRIT*) ≈ carretera *f* nacional
aroma [ə'rəumə] *n* aroma *m*,
fragancia; **aromatherapy** *n*
aromaterapia

arose [ə'rəuz] *pt of* **arise**
around [ə'raund] *adv* alrededor;
(*in the area*): **there is no one else ~**
no hay nadie más por aquí ▷ *prep*
alrededor de
arouse [ə'rauz] *vt* despertar; (*anger*)
provocar
arrange [ə'reɪndʒ] *vt* arreglar,
ordenar; (*organize*) organizar; **to**
~ to do sth quedar en hacer algo;
arrangement *n* arreglo; (*agreement*)
acuerdo; **arrangements** *npl*
(*preparations*) preparativos *mpl*
array [ə'reɪ] *n*: **~ of** (*things*) serie *f* de;
(*people*) conjunto de
arrears [ə'rɪəz] *npl* atrasos *mpl*; **to be**
in ~ with one's rent estar retrasado en
el pago del alquiler
arrest [ə'rɛst] *vt* detener; (*sb's*
attention) llamar ▷ *n* detención *f*;
under ~ detenido
arrival [ə'raɪvəl] *n* llegada; **new ~**
recién llegado/a; (*baby*) recién nacido
arrive [ə'raɪv] *vi* llegar; (*baby*) nacer;
arrive at *vt fus* (*decision, solution*)
llegar a
arrogance ['ærəgəns] *n* arrogancia,
prepotencia *LAM*
arrogant ['ærəgənt] *adj* arrogante
arrow ['ærəu] *n* flecha
arse [ɑːs] (*BRIT*: *inf!*) *n* culo, trasero
arson ['ɑːsn] *n* incendio premeditado
art [ɑːt] *n* arte *m*; (*skill*) destreza; **art**
college *n* escuela *f* de Bellas Artes
artery ['ɑːtərɪ] *n* arteria
art gallery *n* pinacoteca; (*saleroom*)
galería de arte
arthritis [ɑː'θraɪtɪs] *n* artritis *f*
artichoke ['ɑːtɪtʃəuk] *n* alcachofa;
Jerusalem ~ aguaturma
article ['ɑːtɪkl] *n* artículo
articulate [*adj* ɑː'tɪkjulɪt, *vb*
ɑː'tɪkjuleɪt] *adj* claro, bien expresado
▷ *vt* expresar
artificial [ɑːtɪ'fɪʃəl] *adj* artificial;
(*affected*) afectado
artist ['ɑːtɪst] *n* artista *mf*; (*Mus*)
intérprete *mf*; **artistic** [ɑː'tɪstɪk] *adj*

artístico
art school n escuela de bellas artes

○ KEYWORD

as [æz] conj **1** (referring to time)
cuando, mientras; a medida que; **as
the years went by** con el paso de los
años; **he came in as I was leaving**
entró cuando me marchaba; **as
from tomorrow** desde or a partir de
mañana
2 (in comparisons): **as big as** tan grande
como; **twice as big as** el doble de
grande que; **as much money/many
books as** tanto dinero/tantos libros
como; **as soon as** en cuanto
3 (since, because) como, ya que; **he left
early as he had to be home by 10** se
fue temprano ya que tenía que estar en
casa a las 10
4 (referring to manner, way): **do as you
wish** haz lo que quieras; **as she said**
como dijo; **he gave it to me as a
present** me lo dio de regalo
5 (in the capacity of): **he works as
a barman** trabaja de barman; **as
chairman of the company, he ...**
como presidente de la compañía ...
6 (concerning): **as for** or **to that** por or en
lo que respecta a eso
7: **as if** or **though** como si; **he looked
as if he was ill** parecía como si
estuviera enfermo, tenía aspecto de
enfermo; see also **long; such; well**

a.s.a.p. abbr (= as soon as possible)
cuanto antes
asbestos [æz'bɛstəs] n asbesto,
amianto
ascent [ə'sɛnt] n subida; (slope)
cuesta, pendiente f
ash [æʃ] n ceniza; (tree) fresno
ashamed [ə'ʃeɪmd] adj avergonzado,
apenado (LAM); **to be ~ of** avergonzarse
de
ashore [ə'ʃɔː*] adv en tierra; (swim
etc) a tierra

ashtray ['æʃtreɪ] n cenicero
Ash Wednesday n miércoles m
de Ceniza
Asia ['eɪʃə] n Asia; **Asian** adj, n
asiático/a m/f
aside [ə'saɪd] adv a un lado ▷ n
aparte m
ask [ɑːsk] vt (question) preguntar;
(invite) invitar; **to ~ sb sth/to do sth**
preguntar algo a algn/pedir a algn que
haga algo; **to ~ sb about sth** preguntar
algo a algn; **to ~ (sb) a question** hacer
una pregunta (a algn); **to ~ sb out to
dinner** invitar a cenar a algn; **ask for** vt
fus pedir; (trouble) buscar
asleep [ə'sliːp] adj dormido; **to fall ~**
dormirse, quedarse dormido
asparagus [əs'pærəgəs] n (plant)
espárrago; (food) espárragos mpl
aspect ['æspɛkt] n aspecto,
apariencia; (direction in which a building
etc faces) orientación f
aspirations [æspə'reɪʃənz] npl
aspiraciones fpl; (ambition) ambición f
aspire [əs'paɪə*] vi: **to ~ to** aspirar a,
ambicionar
aspirin ['æsprɪn] n aspirina
ass [æs] n asno, burro; (inf: idiot)
imbécil mf; (us: inf!) culo, trasero
assassin [ə'sæsɪn] n asesino/a;
assassinate vt asesinar
assault [ə'sɔːlt] n asalto; (Law)
agresión f ▷ vt asaltar, atacar;
(sexually) violar
assemble [ə'sɛmbl] vt reunir, juntar;
(Tech) montar ▷ vi reunirse, juntarse
assembly [ə'sɛmblɪ] n reunión f,
asamblea; (parliament) parlamento;
(construction) montaje m
assert [ə'sɜːt] vt afirmar; (authority)
hacer valer; **assertion** [-ʃən] n
afirmación f
assess [ə'sɛs] vt valorar, calcular;
(tax, damages) fijar; (for tax) gravar;
assessment n valoración f; (for tax)
gravamen m
asset ['æsɛt] n ventaja; **assets**
npl (Comm) activo; (property, funds)

fondos *mpl*
assign [ə'saɪn] *vt*: **to ~ (to)** (*date*) fijar (para); (*task*) asignar (a); (*resources*) destinar (a); **assignment** *n* tarea
assist [ə'sɪst] *vt* ayudar; **assistance** *n* ayuda, auxilio; **assistant** *n* ayudante *mf*; (BRIT: *also*: **shop assistant**) dependiente/a *m/f*
associate [*adj, n* ə'səʊʃɪɪt, *vb* ə'səʊʃɪeɪt] *adj* asociado ▷ *n* (*at work*) colega *mf* ▷ *vt* asociar; (*ideas*) relacionar ▷ *vi*: **to ~ with sb** tratar con algn
association [əsəʊsɪ'eɪʃən] *n* asociación *f*
assorted [ə'sɔ:tɪd] *adj* surtido, variado
assortment [ə'sɔ:tmənt] *n* (*of shapes, colours*) surtido; (*of books*) colección *f*; (*of people*) mezcla
assume [ə'sju:m] *vt* suponer; (*responsibilities*) asumir; (*attitude*) adoptar, tomar
assumption [ə'sʌmpʃən] *n* suposición *f*, presunción *f*; (*of power etc*) toma
assurance [ə'ʃʊərəns] *n* garantía, promesa; (*confidence*) confianza, aplomo; (*insurance*) seguro
assure [ə'ʃʊə*] *vt* asegurar
asterisk ['æstərɪsk] *n* asterisco
asthma ['æsmə] *n* asma
astonish [ə'stɒnɪʃ] *vt* asombrar, pasmar; **astonished** *adj* estupefacto, pasmado; **to be astonished (at)** asombrarse (de); **astonishing** *adj* asombroso, pasmoso; **I find it astonishing that ...** me asombra *or* pasma que ...; **astonishment** *n* asombro, sorpresa
astound [ə'staund] *vt* asombrar, pasmar
astray [ə'streɪ] *adv*: **to go ~** extraviarse; **to lead ~** (*morally*) llevar por mal camino
astrology [æs'trɒlədʒɪ] *n* astrología
astronaut ['æstrənɔ:t] *n* astronauta *mf*

astronomer [əs'trɒnəmə*] *n* astrónomo/a
astronomical [æstrə'nɒmɪkəl] *adj* astronómico
astronomy [əs'trɒnəmɪ] *n* astronomía
astute [əs'tju:t] *adj* astuto
asylum [ə'saɪləm] *n* (*refuge*) asilo; (*mental hospital*) manicomio

○ **KEYWORD**

at [æt] *prep* **1** (*referring to position*) en; (*direction*) a; **at the top** en lo alto; **at home/school** en casa/la escuela; **to look at sth/sb** mirar algo/a algn
2 (*referring to time*): **at 4 o'clock** a las 4; **at night** por la noche; **at Christmas** en Navidad; **at times** a veces
3 (*referring to rates, speed etc*): **at £1 a kilo** a una libra el kilo; **two at a time** de dos en dos; **at 50 km/h** a 50 km/h
4 (*referring to manner*): **at a stroke** de un golpe; **at peace** en paz
5 (*referring to activity*): **to be at work** estar trabajando; (*in the office etc*) estar en el trabajo; **to play at cowboys** jugar a los vaqueros; **to be good at sth** ser bueno en algo
6 (*referring to cause*): **shocked/surprised/annoyed at sth** asombrado/sorprendido/fastidiado por algo; **I went at his suggestion** fui a instancias suyas
7 (*symbol*) arroba

ate [eɪt] *pt of* **eat**
atheist ['eɪθɪɪst] *n* ateo/a
Athens ['æθɪnz] *n* Atenas
athlete ['æθli:t] *n* atleta *mf*
athletic [æθ'letɪk] *adj* atlético; **athletics** *n* atletismo
Atlantic [ət'læntɪk] *adj* atlántico ▷ *n*: **the ~ (Ocean)** el (Océano) Atlántico
atlas ['ætləs] *n* atlas *m inv*
A.T.M. *n abbr* (= *automated telling*

machine) cajero automático

atmosphere ['ætməsfɪə*] *n* atmósfera; (*of place*) ambiente *m*

atom ['ætəm] *n* átomo; **atomic** [ə'tɔmɪk] *adj* atómico; **atom(ic) bomb** *n* bomba atómica

A to Z® *n* (*map*) callejero

atrocity [ə'trɔsɪtɪ] *n* atrocidad *f*

attach [ə'tætʃ] *vt* (*fasten*) atar; (*join*) unir, sujetar; (*document, email, letter*) adjuntar; (*importance etc*) dar, conceder; **to be ~ed to sb/sth** (*to like*) tener cariño a algn/algo; **attachment** (*tool*) accesorio; (*Comput*) archivo, documento adjunto; (*love*): **attachment (to)** apego (a)

attack [ə'tæk] *vt* atacar; (*criminal*) agredir, asaltar; (*criticize*) criticar; (*task*) emprender ▷ *n* ataque *m*, asalto; (*on sb's life*) atentado; (*fig: criticism*) crítica; (*of illness*) ataque *m*; **heart ~** infarto (de miocardio); **attacker** *n* agresor(a) *m/f*, asaltante *mf*

attain [ə'teɪn] *vt* (*also: ~ to*) alcanzar; (*achieve*) lograr, conseguir

attempt [ə'tɛmpt] *n* tentativa, intento; (*attack*) atentado ▷ *vt* intentar

attend [ə'tɛnd] *vt* asistir a; (*patient*) atender; **attend to** *vt fus* ocuparse de; (*customer, patient*) atender a; **attendance** *n* asistencia, presencia; (*people present*) concurrencia; **attendant** *n* ayudante *mf*; (*in garage etc*) encargado/a ▷ *adj* (*dangers*) concomitante

attention [ə'tɛnʃən] *n* atención *f*; (*care*) atenciones *fpl* ▷ *excl* (*Mil*) ¡firme(s)!; **for the ~ of ...** (*Admin*) atención ...

attic ['ætɪk] *n* desván *m*

attitude ['ætɪtjuːd] *n* actitud *f*; (*disposition*) disposición *f*

attorney [ə'təːnɪ] *n* (*lawyer*) abogado/a; **Attorney General** *n* (*BRIT*) ≈ Presidente *m* del Consejo del Poder Judicial (*SP*); (*US*) ≈ ministro

de Justicia

attract [ə'trækt] *vt* atraer; (*sb's attention*) llamar; **attraction** [ə'trækʃən] *n* encanto; (*gen pl: amusements*) diversiones *fpl*; (*Physics*) atracción *f*; (*fig: towards sb, sth*) atractivo; **attractive** *adj* guapo; (*interesting*) atrayente

attribute [*n* 'ætrɪbjuːt, *vb* ə'trɪbjuːt] *n* atributo ▷ *vt*: **to ~ sth to** atribuir algo a

aubergine ['əubəʒiːn] (*BRIT*) *n* berenjena; (*colour*) morado

auburn ['ɔːbən] *adj* color castaño rojizo

auction ['ɔːkʃən] *n* (*also: sale by ~*) subasta ▷ *vt* subastar

audible ['ɔːdɪbl] *adj* audible, que se puede oír

audience ['ɔːdɪəns] *n* público; (*Radio*) radioescuchas *mpl*; (*TV*) telespectadores *mpl*; (*interview*) audiencia

audit ['ɔːdɪt] *vt* revisar, intervenir

audition [ɔː'dɪʃən] *n* audición *f*

auditor ['ɔːdɪtə*] *n* interventor(a) *m/f*, censor(a) *m/f* de cuentas

auditorium [ɔːdɪ'tɔːrɪəm] *n* auditorio

Aug. *abbr* (= *August*) ag

August ['ɔːgəst] *n* agosto

aunt [ɑːnt] *n* tía; **auntie** *n diminutive of* **aunt**, **aunty** *n diminutive of* **aunt**

au pair ['əu'pɛə*] *n* (*also: ~ girl*) (chica) au pair *f*

aura ['ɔːrə] *n* aura; (*atmosphere*) ambiente *m*

austerity [ɔ'stɛrɪtɪ] *n* austeridad *f*

Australia [ɔs'treɪlɪə] *n* Australia; **Australian** *adj*, *n* australiano/a *m/f*

Austria ['ɔstrɪə] *n* Austria; **Austrian** *adj*, *n* austríaco/a *m/f*

authentic [ɔː'θɛntɪk] *adj* auténtico

author ['ɔːθə*] *n* autor(a) *m/f*

authority [ɔː'θɔrɪtɪ] *n* autoridad *f*; (*official permission*) autorización *f*; **the authorities** *npl* las autoridades

authorize ['ɔːθəraɪz] *vt* autorizar

auto ['ɔːtəu] (US) n coche m (SP), carro
(LAM), automóvil m
auto: autobiography [ɔːtəbaɪ'ɒgrəfɪ]
n autobiografía; **autograph**
['ɔːtəgrɑːf] n autógrafo ▷ vt
(photo etc) dedicar; (programme)
firmar; **automatic** [ɔːtə'mætɪk]
adj automático ▷ n (gun)
pistola automática; (car) coche m
automático; **automatically** adv
automáticamente; **automobile**
['ɔːtəməbiːl] (US) n coche m (SP), carro
(LAM), automóvil m; **autonomous**
[ɔː'tɒnəməs] adj autónomo;
autonomy [ɔː'tɒnəmɪ] n autonomía
autumn ['ɔːtəm] n otoño
auxiliary [ɔːg'zɪlɪərɪ] adj, n auxiliar
mf
avail [ə'veɪl] vt: **to ~ o.s. of**
aprovechar(se) de ▷ n: **to no ~** en vano,
sin resultado
availability [əveɪlə'bɪlɪtɪ] n
disponibilidad f
available [ə'veɪləbl] adj disponible;
(unoccupied) libre; (person: unattached)
soltero y sin compromiso
avalanche ['ævəlɑːnʃ] n alud m,
avalancha
Ave. abbr = avenue
avenue ['ævənjuː] n avenida; (fig)
camino
average ['ævərɪdʒ] n promedio,
término medio ▷ adj medio, de
término medio; (ordinary) regular,
corriente ▷ vt sacar un promedio de;
on ~ por regla general
avert [ə'vəːt] vt prevenir; (blow)
desviar; (one's eyes) apartar
avid ['ævɪd] adj ávido
avocado [ævə'kɑːdəu] n (also BRIT: ~
pear) aguacate m, palta (SC)
avoid [ə'vɔɪd] vt evitar, eludir
await [ə'weɪt] vt esperar, aguardar
awake [ə'weɪk] (pt **awoke**, pp **awoken**
or **awaked**) adj despierto ▷ vt
despertar ▷ vi despertarse; **to be ~**
estar despierto
award [ə'wɔːd] n premio;

(Law: damages) indemnización f ▷ vt
otorgar, conceder; (Law: damages)
adjudicar
aware [ə'wɛə*] adj: **~ (of)** consciente
(de); **to become ~ of/that** (realize)
darse cuenta de/de que; (learn)
enterarse de/de que; **awareness** n
conciencia; (knowledge) conocimiento
away [ə'weɪ] adv fuera;
(movement): **she went ~** se marchó;
far ~ lejos; **two kilometres ~** a dos
kilómetros de distancia; **two hours
~ by car** a dos horas en coche; **the
holiday was two weeks ~** faltaban dos
semanas para las vacaciones; **he's ~ for
a week** estará ausente una semana;
to take ~ (from) quitar (a); (subtract)
substraer (de); **to work/pedal ~** seguir
trabajando/pedaleando; **to fade ~**
(colour) desvanecerse; (sound) apagarse
awe [ɔː] n admiración f respetuosa;
awesome ['ɔːsəm] (US) adj (excellent)
formidable
awful ['ɔːfəl] adj horroroso;
(quantity): **an ~ lot (of)** cantidad (de);
awfully adv (very) terriblemente
awkward ['ɔːkwəd] adj desmañado,
torpe; (shape) incómodo; (embarrassing)
delicado, difícil
awoke [ə'wəuk] pt of awake
awoken [ə'wəukən] pp of awake
axe [æks] (US **ax**) n hacha ▷ vt
(project) cortar; (jobs) reducir
axle ['æksl] n eje m, árbol m
ay(e) [aɪ] excl sí
azalea [ə'zeɪlɪə] n azalea

b

B [biː] n (Mus) si m

B.A. abbr = **Bachelor of Arts**

baby ['beɪbɪ] n bebé mf;
(US: inf: darling) mi amor; **baby
carriage** (US) n cochecito; **baby-sit**
vi hacer de canguro; **baby-sitter** n
canguro/a; **baby wipe** n toallita
húmeda (para bebés)

bachelor ['bætʃələ*] n soltero; **B~ of
Arts/Science** licenciado/a en Filosofía
y Letras/Ciencias

back [bæk] n (of person) espalda;
(of animal) lomo; (of hand) dorso; (as
opposed to front) parte f de atrás; (of
chair) respaldo; (of page) reverso; (of
book) final m; (Football) defensa m; (of
crowd): **the ones at the ~** los del fondo
▷ vt (candidate: also: **~ up**) respaldar,
apoyar; (horse: at races) apostar a; (car)
dar marcha atrás a or con ▷ vi (car etc)
ir (or salir or entrar) marcha atrás ▷ adj
(payment, rent) atrasado; (seats, wheels)
de atrás ▷ adv (not forward) (hacia)
atrás; (returned): **he's ~** está de vuelta,
ha vuelto; **he ran ~** volvió corriendo;

(restitution): **throw the ball ~** devuelve
la pelota; **can I have it ~?** ¿me lo
devuelve?; (again): **he called ~** llamó de
nuevo; **back down** vi echarse atrás;
back out vi (of promise) volverse atrás;
back up vt (person) apoyar, respaldar;
(theory) defender; (Comput) hacer
una copia preventiva or de reserva;
backache n dolor m de espalda;
backbencher (BRIT) n miembro
del parlamento sin cargo relevante;
backbone n columna vertebral; **back
door** n puerta f trasera; **backfire**
vi (Aut) petardear; (plans) fallar, salir
mal; **backgammon** n backgammon
m; **background** n fondo; (of events)
antecedentes mpl; (basic knowledge)
bases fpl; (experience) conocimientos
mpl, educación f; **family background**
origen m, antecedentes mpl; **backing**
n (fig) apoyo, respaldo; **backlog**
n: **backlog of work** trabajo atrasado;
backpack n mochila; **backpacker**
n mochilero/a; **backslash** n pleca,
barra inversa; **backstage** adv entre
bastidores; **backstroke** n espalda;
backup adj suplementario; (Comput)
de reserva ▷ n (support) apoyo; (also:
backup file) copia preventiva or de
reserva; **backward** adj (person, country)
atrasado; **backwards** adv hacia atrás;
(read a list) al revés; (fall) de espaldas;
backyard n traspatio

bacon ['beɪkən] n tocino, beicon m

bacteria [bæk'tɪərɪə] npl bacterias fpl

bad [bæd] adj malo; (mistake, accident)
grave; (food) podrido, pasado; **his ~ leg**
su pierna lisiada; **to go ~** (food) pasarse

badge [bædʒ] n insignia; (policeman's)
chapa, placa

badger ['bædʒə*] n tejón m

badly ['bædlɪ] adv mal; **to reflect
~ on sb** influir negativamente en
la reputación de algn; **~ wounded**
gravemente herido; **he needs it ~**
le hace gran falta; **to be ~ off (for
money)** andar mal de dinero

bad-mannered ['bæd'mænəd] adj

mal educado
badminton ['bædmɪntən] n
bádminton m
bad-tempered ['bæd'tɛmpəd] adj
de mal genio or carácter; (temporarily)
de mal humor
bag [bæg] n bolsa; (handbag) bolso;
(satchel) mochila; (case) maleta; **~s**
of (inf) un montón de; **baggage** n
equipaje m; **baggage allowance** n
límite m de equipaje; **baggage**
reclaim n recogida de equipajes;
baggy adj amplio; **bagpipes** npl
gaita
bail [beɪl] n fianza ▷ vt
(prisoner: gen: grant bail to) poner en
libertad bajo fianza; (boat: also: **~ out**)
achicar; **on ~** (prisoner) bajo fianza; **to**
~ sb out obtener la libertad de algn
bajo fianza
bait [beɪt] n cebo ▷ vt poner cebo en;
(tease) tomar el pelo a
bake [beɪk] vt cocer (al horno) ▷ vi
cocerse; **baked beans** npl judías fpl
en salsa de tomate; **baked potato** n
patata al horno; **baker** n panadero;
bakery n panadería; (for cakes)
pastelería; **baking** n (act) amasar m;
(batch) hornada; **baking powder** n
levadura (en polvo)
balance ['bæləns] n equilibrio;
(Comm: sum) balance m; (remainder)
resto; (scales) balanza ▷ vt equilibrar;
(budget) nivelar; (account) saldar;
(make equal) equilibrar; **~ of trade/**
payments balanza de comercio/
pagos; **balanced** adj (personality, diet)
equilibrado; (report) objetivo; **balance**
sheet n balance m
balcony ['bælkənɪ] n (open) balcón m;
(closed) galería; (in theatre) anfiteatro
bald [bɔːld] adj calvo; (tyre) liso
Balearics [bælɪ'ærɪks] npl: **the ~** las
Baleares
ball [bɔːl] n pelota; (football) balón m;
(of wool, string) ovillo; (dance) baile m; **to**
play ~ (fig) cooperar
ballerina [bælə'riːnə] n bailarina

ballet ['bæleɪ] n ballet m; **ballet**
dancer n bailarín/ina m/f
balloon [bə'luːn] n globo
ballot ['bælət] n votación f
ballpoint (pen) ['bɔːlpɔɪnt-] n
bolígrafo
ballroom ['bɔːlrum] n salón m
de baile
Baltic ['bɔːltɪk] n: **the ~ (Sea)** el (Mar)
Báltico
bamboo [bæm'buː] n bambú m
ban [bæn] n prohibición f,
proscripción f ▷ vt prohibir, proscribir
banana [bə'nɑːnə] n plátano, banana
(LAM), banano (CAM)
band [bænd] n grupo; (strip) faja, tira;
(stripe) lista; (Mus: jazz) orquesta; (: rock)
grupo; (Mil) banda
bandage ['bændɪdʒ] n venda,
vendaje m ▷ vt vendar
Band-Aid® ['bændeɪd] (US) n tirita
bandit ['bændɪt] n bandido
bang [bæŋ] n (of gun, exhaust)
estallido, detonación f; (of door)
portazo; (blow) golpe m ▷ vt (door)
cerrar de golpe; (one's head) golpear ▷ vi
estallar; (door) cerrar de golpe
Bangladesh [bɑːŋglə'dɛʃ] n
Bangladesh m
bangle ['bæŋgl] n brazalete m,
ajorca
bangs [bæŋz] (US) npl flequillo
banish ['bænɪʃ] vt desterrar
banister(s) ['bænɪstə(z)] n(pl)
barandilla, pasamanos m inv
banjo ['bændʒəu] (pl **~es** or **~s**) n
banjo
bank [bæŋk] n (Comm) banco; (of river,
lake) ribera, orilla; (of earth) terraplén
m ▷ vi (Aviat) ladearse; **bank on** vt fus
contar con; **bank account** n cuenta
de banco; **bank balance** n saldo;
bank card n tarjeta bancaria; **bank**
charges npl comisión fsg; **banker** n
banquero; **bank holiday** n (BRIT) día m
festivo or de fiesta; **banking** n banca;
bank manager n director(a) m/f
(de sucursal) de banco; **banknote** n

billete m de banco

● **BANK HOLIDAY**

El término **bank holiday** se aplica
en el Reino Unido a todo día festivo
oficial en el que cierran bancos y
comercios. Los más importantes
son en Navidad, Semana Santa,
finales de mayo y finales de
agosto y, al contrario que en los
países de tradición católica, no
coinciden necesariamente con una
celebración religiosa.

bankrupt ['bæŋkrʌpt] *adj* quebrado,
insolvente; **to go ~** hacer bancarrota;
to be ~ estar en quiebra; **bankruptcy**
n quiebra

bank statement *n* balance m or
detalle m de cuenta

banner ['bænə*] *n* pancarta

bannister(s) ['bænɪstə(z)] *n(pl)* =
banister(s)

banquet ['bæŋkwɪt] *n* banquete m

baptism ['bæptɪzəm] *n* bautismo;
(*act*) bautizo

baptize [bæp'taɪz] *vt* bautizar

bar [bɑː*] *n* (*pub*) bar m; (*counter*)
mostrador m; (*rod*) barra; (*of window,
cage*) reja; (*of soap*) pastilla; (*of
chocolate*) tableta; (*fig: hindrance*)
obstáculo; (*prohibition*) proscripción
f; (*Mus*) barra ▷ *vt* (*road*) obstruir;
(*person*) excluir; (*activity*) prohibir; **the
B~** (*Law*) la abogacía; **behind ~s** entre
rejas; **~ none** sin excepción

barbaric [bɑː'bærɪk] *adj* bárbaro

barbecue ['bɑːbɪkjuː] *n* barbacoa

barbed wire ['bɑːbd-] *n* alambre
m de púas

barber ['bɑːbə*] *n* peluquero,
barbero; **barber's (shop)** (*us* **barber
(shop)**) *n* peluquería

bar code *n* código de barras

bare [bɛə*] *adj* desnudo; (*trees*) sin
hojas; (*necessities etc*) básico ▷ *vt*
desnudar; (*teeth*) enseñar; **barefoot**

adj, adv descalzo; **barely** *adv* apenas

bargain ['bɑːgɪn] *n* pacto, negocio;
(*good buy*) ganga ▷ *vi* negociar; (*haggle*)
regatear; **into the ~** además, por
añadidura; **bargain for** *vt fus*: **he got
more than he bargained for** le resultó
peor de lo que esperaba

barge [bɑːdʒ] *n* barcaza; **barge in**
vi irrumpir; (*interrupt: conversation*)
interrumpir

bark [bɑːk] *n* (*of tree*) corteza; (*of dog*)
ladrido ▷ *vi* ladrar

barley ['bɑːlɪ] *n* cebada

barmaid ['bɑːmeɪd] *n* camarera

barman ['bɑːmən] (*irreg*) *n* camarero,
barman m

barn [bɑːn] *n* granero

barometer [bə'rɒmɪtə*] *n*
barómetro

baron ['bærən] *n* barón m; (*press baron
etc*) magnate m; **baroness** *n* baronesa

barracks ['bærəks] *npl* cuartel m

barrage [bærɑːʒ] *n* (*Mil*) descarga,
bombardeo; (*dam*) presa; (*of criticism*)
lluvia, aluvión m

barrel ['bærəl] *n* barril m; (*of gun*)
cañón m

barren ['bærən] *adj* estéril

barrette [bə'ret] (*us*) *n* pasador m
(*LAM, SP*), broche m (*MEX*)

barricade [bærɪ'keɪd] *n* barricada

barrier ['bærɪə*] *n* barrera

barring ['bɑːrɪŋ] *prep* excepto, salvo

barrister ['bærɪstə*] (*BRIT*) *n*
abogado/a

barrow ['bærəu] *n* (*cart*) carretilla
(de mano)

bartender ['bɑːtendə*] (*us*) *n*
camarero, barman m

base [beɪs] *n* base f ▷ *vt*: **to ~ sth on**
basar or fundar algo en ▷ *adj* bajo,
infame

baseball ['beɪsbɔːl] *n* béisbol m;
baseball cap *n* gorra f de béisbol

basement ['beɪsmənt] *n* sótano

bases[1] ['beɪsiːz] *npl of* **basis**

bases[2] ['beɪsiz] *npl of* **base**

bash [bæʃ] (*inf*) *vt* golpear

basic ['beɪsɪk] *adj* básico; **basically** *adv* fundamentalmente, en el fondo; (*simply*) sencillamente; **basics** *npl*: **the basics** los fundamentos

basil ['bæzl] *n* albahaca

basin ['beɪsn] *n* cuenco, tazón *m*; (*Geo*) cuenca; (*also*: **wash~**) lavabo

basis ['beɪsɪs] (*pl* **bases**) *n* base *f*; **on a part-time/trial ~** a tiempo parcial/a prueba

basket ['bɑːskɪt] *n* cesta, cesto; canasta; **basketball** *n* baloncesto

bass [beɪs] *n* (*Mus: instrument*) bajo; (*double bass*) contrabajo; (*singer*) bajo

bastard ['bɑːstəd] *n* bastardo; (*inf!*) hijo de puta (!)

bat [bæt] *n* (*Zool*) murciélago; (*for ball games*) palo; (*BRIT: for table tennis*) pala ▷ *vt*: **he didn't ~ an eyelid** ni pestañeó

batch [bætʃ] *n* (*of bread*) hornada; (*of letters etc*) lote *m*

bath [bɑːθ, *pl* bɑːðz] *n* (*action*) baño; (*bathtub*) bañera (*SP*), tina (*LAM*), bañadera (*RPL*) ▷ *vt* bañar; **to have a ~** bañarse, tomar un baño; *see also* **baths**

bathe [beɪð] *vi* bañarse ▷ *vt* (*wound*) lavar

bathing ['beɪðɪŋ] *n* el bañarse; **bathing costume** (*US* **bathing suit**) *n* traje *m* de baño

bath: bathrobe *n* (*man's*) batín *m*; (*woman's*) bata; **bathroom** *n* (cuarto de) baño; **baths** [bɑːðz] *npl* (*also*: **swimming baths**) piscina; **bath towel** *n* toalla de baño; **bathtub** *n* bañera

baton ['bætən] *n* (*Mus*) batuta; (*Athletics*) testigo; (*weapon*) porra

batter ['bætə*] *vt* maltratar; (*rain etc*) azotar ▷ *n* masa (para rebozar); **battered** *adj* (*hat, pan*) estropeado

battery ['bætərɪ] *n* (*Aut*) batería; (*of torch*) pila; **battery farming** *n* cría intensiva

battle ['bætl] *n* batalla; (*fig*) lucha ▷ *vi* luchar; **battlefield** *n* campo *m* de batalla

bay [beɪ] *n* (*Geo*) bahía; **B~ of Biscay** ≈ mar Cantábrico; **to hold sb at ~** mantener a algn a raya

bazaar [bə'zɑː*] *n* bazar *m*; (*fete*) venta con fines benéficos

B. & B. *n abbr* = **bed and breakfast**; (*place*) pensión *f*; (*terms*) cama y desayuno

BBC *n abbr* (= British Broadcasting Corporation) cadena de radio y televisión estatal británica

B.C. *adv abbr* (= before Christ) a. de C.

○ **KEYWORD**

be [biː] (*pt* **was, were**, *pp* **been**) *aux vb* **1** (*with present participle: forming continuous tenses*): **what are you doing?** ¿qué estás haciendo?, ¿qué haces?; **they're coming tomorrow** vienen mañana; **I've been waiting for you for hours** llevo horas esperándote **2** (*with pp: forming passives*) ser (*but often replaced by active or reflexive constructions*); **to be murdered** ser asesinado; **the box had been opened** habían abierto la caja; **the thief was nowhere to be seen** no se veía al ladrón por ninguna parte **3** (*in tag questions*): **it was fun, wasn't it?** fue divertido, ¿no? or ¿verdad?; **he's good-looking, isn't he?** es guapo, ¿no te parece?; **she's back again, is she?** entonces, ¿ha vuelto? **4** (*+to +infin*): **the house is to be sold** (*necessity*) hay que vender la casa; (*future*) van a vender la casa; **he's not to open it** no tiene que abrirlo ▷ *vb +complement* **1** (*with n or num complement, but see also 3, 4, 5 and impers vb below*) ser; **he's a doctor** es médico; **2 and 2 are 4** 2 y 2 son 4 **2** (*with adj complement: expressing permanent or inherent quality*) ser; (: *expressing state seen as temporary or reversible*) estar; **I'm English** soy inglés/esa; **she's tall/pretty** es alta/bonita; **he's young** es joven; **be careful/good/quiet** ten cuidado/

pórtate bien/cállate; **I'm tired** estoy cansado/a; **it's dirty** está sucio/a
3 (*of health*) estar; **how are you?** ¿cómo estás?; **he's very ill** está muy enfermo; **I'm better now** ya estoy mejor
4 (*of age*) tener; **how old are you?** ¿cuántos años tienes?; **I'm sixteen (years old)** tengo dieciséis años
5 (*cost*) costar; ser; **how much was the meal?** ¿cuánto fue *or* costó la comida?; **that'll be £5.75, please** son £5.75, por favor; **this shirt is £17** esta camisa cuesta £17
▷ vi **1** (*exist, occur etc*) existir, haber; **the best singer that ever was** el mejor cantante que existió jamás; **is there a God?** ¿hay un Dios?, ¿existe Dios?; **be that as it may** sea como sea; **so be it** así sea
2 (*referring to place*) estar; **I won't be here tomorrow** no estaré aquí mañana
3 (*referring to movement*): **where have you been?** ¿dónde has estado?
▷ impers vb **1** (*referring to time*): **it's 5 o'clock** son las 5; **it's the 28th of April** estamos a 28 de abril
2 (*referring to distance*): **it's 10 km to the village** el pueblo está a 10 km
3 (*referring to the weather*): **it's too hot/cold** hace demasiado calor/frío; **it's windy today** hace viento hoy
4 (*emphatic*): **it's me** soy yo; **it was Maria who paid the bill** fue María la que pagó la cuenta

beach [biːtʃ] *n* playa ▷ vt varar
beacon ['biːkən] *n* (*lighthouse*) faro; (*marker*) guía
bead [biːd] *n* cuenta; (*of sweat etc*) gota; **beads** npl (*necklace*) collar m
beak [biːk] *n* pico
beam [biːm] *n* (*Arch*) viga, travesaño; (*of light*) rayo, haz m de luz ▷ vi brillar; (*smile*) sonreír
bean [biːn] *n* judía; **runner/broad ~** habichuela/haba; **coffee ~** grano de café; **beansprouts** npl brotes

mpl de soja
bear [bɛə*] (*pt* bore, *pp* borne) *n* oso ▷ vt (*weight etc*) llevar; (*cost*) pagar; (*responsibility*) tener; (*endure*) soportar, aguantar; (*children*) parir, tener; (*fruit*) dar ▷ vi: **to ~ right/left** torcer a la derecha/izquierda
beard [biəd] *n* barba
bearer ['bɛərə*] *n* portador(a) m/f
bearing ['bɛəriŋ] *n* porte m, comportamiento; (*connection*) relación f
beast [biːst] *n* bestia; (*inf*) bruto, salvaje m
beat [biːt] (*pt* ~, *pp* beaten) *n* (*of heart*) latido; (*Mus*) ritmo, compás m; (*of policeman*) ronda ▷ vt pegar, golpear; (*eggs*) batir; (*defeat: opponent*) vencer, derrotar; (: *record*) sobrepasar ▷ vi (*heart*) latir; (*drum*) redoblar; (*rain, wind*) azotar; **off the ~en track** aislado; **to ~ it** (*inf*) largarse; **beat up** vt (*attack*) dar una paliza a; **beating** *n* paliza
beautiful ['bjuːtɪful] *adj* precioso, hermoso, bello; **beautifully** *adv* maravillosamente
beauty ['bjuːtɪ] *n* belleza; **beauty parlour** (*US* **beauty parlor**) *n* salón m de belleza; **beauty salon** *n* salón m de belleza; **beauty spot** *n* (*Tourism*) lugar m pintoresco
beaver ['biːvə*] *n* castor m
became [bɪ'keɪm] *pt of* **become**
because [bɪ'kɔz] *conj* porque; **~ of** debido a, a causa de
beckon ['bɛkən] *vt* (*also*: **~ to**) llamar con señas
become [bɪ'kʌm] (*pt* became, *pp* ~) vt (*suit*) favorecer, sentar bien a ▷ vi (+ *n*) hacerse, llegar a ser; (+ *adj*) ponerse, volverse; **to ~ fat** engordar
bed [bɛd] *n* cama; (*of flowers*) macizo; (*of coal, clay*) capa; (*of river*) lecho; (*of sea*) fondo; **to go to ~** acostarse; **bed and breakfast** (*place*) pensión f; (*terms*) cama y desayuno; **bedclothes** npl ropa de cama; **bedding** *n* ropa de cama; **bed linen** *n* (*BRIT*) ropa f

de cama

bed: bedroom n dormitorio; **bedside**
n: **at the bedside of** a la cabecera de;
  bedside lamp n lámpara de noche;
  bedside table n mesilla de noche;
  bedsit(ter) (BRIT) n cuarto de alquiler;
  bedspread n cubrecama m, colcha;
  bedtime n hora de acostarse
bee [biː] n abeja
beech [biːtʃ] n haya
beef [biːf] n carne f de vaca; **roast ~**
rosbif m; **beefburger** n hamburguesa;
  Beefeater n alabardero de la Torre
de Londres
been [biːn] pp of **be**
beer [bɪə*] n cerveza; **beer garden**
n (BRIT) terraza f de verano, jardín m
(de un bar)
beet [biːt] (US) n (also: **red ~**)
remolacha
beetle ['biːtl] n escarabajo
beetroot ['biːtruːt] (BRIT) n
remolacha
before [bɪ'fɔː*] prep (of time) antes
de; (of space) delante de ▷ conj antes
(de) que ▷ adv antes, anteriormente;
delante, adelante; **~ going** antes de
marcharse; **~ she goes** antes de que se
vaya; **the week ~** la semana anterior;
I've never seen it ~ no lo he visto
nunca; **beforehand** adv de antemano,
con anticipación
beg [beg] vi pedir limosna ▷ vt pedir,
rogar; (entreat) suplicar; **to ~ sb to do
sth** rogar a algn que haga algo; see
also **pardon**

began [bɪ'gæn] pt of **begin**
beggar ['begə*] n mendigo/a
begin [bɪ'gɪn] (pt **began**, pp **begun**) vt,
vi empezar, comenzar; **to ~ doing** or **to
do sth** empezar a hacer algo; **beginner**
n principiante mf; **beginning** n
principio, comienzo
begun [bɪ'gʌn] pp of **begin**
behalf [bɪ'hɑːf] n: **on ~ of** en nombre
de, por; (for benefit of) en beneficio de;
on my/his ~ por mí/él
behave [bɪ'heɪv] vi (person)
portarse, comportarse; (well: also:
~ o.s.) portarse bien; **behaviour**
(US **behavior**) n comportamiento,
conducta
behind [bɪ'haɪnd] prep detrás de;
(supporting): **to be ~ sb** apoyar a
algn ▷ adv detrás, por detrás, atrás
▷ n trasero; **to be ~ (schedule)** ir
retrasado; **~ the scenes** (fig) entre
bastidores
beige [beɪʒ] adj color beige
Beijing ['beɪ'dʒɪŋ] n Pekín m
being ['biːɪŋ] n ser m; (existence): **in ~**
existente; **to come into ~** aparecer
belated [bɪ'leɪtɪd] adj atrasado,
tardío
belch [beltʃ] vi eructar ▷ vt (gen: belch
out: smoke etc) arrojar
Belgian ['beldʒən] adj, n belga mf
Belgium ['beldʒəm] n Bélgica
belief [bɪ'liːf] n opinión f; (faith) fe f
believe [bɪ'liːv] vt, vi creer; **to ~ in**
creer en; **believer** n partidario/a; (Rel)
creyente mf, fiel mf
bell [bel] n campana; (small)
campanilla; (on door) timbre m
bellboy ['belbɔɪ] (BRIT) n botones
m inv
bellhop ['belhɒp] (US) n = **bellboy**
bellow ['beləʊ] vi bramar; (person)
rugir
bell pepper n (esp US) pimiento,
pimentón m (LAM)
belly ['belɪ] n barriga, panza; **belly
button** (inf) n ombligo
belong [bɪ'lɒŋ] vi: **to ~ to** pertenecer

a; (*club etc*) ser socio de; **this book ~s here** este libro va aquí; **belongings** *npl* pertenencias *fpl*

beloved [bɪ'lʌvɪd] *adj* querido/a

below [bɪ'ləu] *prep* bajo, debajo de; (*less than*) inferior a ▷ *adv* abajo, (por) debajo; **see ~** véase más abajo

belt [bɛlt] *n* cinturón *m*; (*Tech*) correa, cinta ▷ *vt* (*thrash*) pegar con correa; **beltway** (*US*) *n* (*Aut*) carretera de circunvalación

bemused [bɪ'mju:zd] *adj* perplejo

bench [bɛntʃ] *n* banco; (*BRIT Pol*): **the Government/Opposition ~es** (los asientos de) los miembros del Gobierno/de la Oposición; **the B~** (*Law: judges*) magistratura

bend [bɛnd] (*pt, pp* **bent**) *vt* doblar ▷ *vi* inclinarse ▷ *n* (*BRIT: in road, river*) curva; (*in pipe*) codo; **bend down** *vi* inclinarse, doblarse; **bend over** *vi* inclinarse

beneath [bɪ'ni:θ] *prep* bajo, debajo de; (*unworthy*) indigno de ▷ *adv* abajo, (por) debajo

beneficial [bɛnɪ'fɪʃəl] *adj* beneficioso

benefit ['bɛnɪfɪt] *n* beneficio; (*allowance of money*) subsidio ▷ *vt* beneficiar ▷ *vi*: **he'll ~ from it** le sacará provecho

benign [bɪ'naɪn] *adj* benigno; (*smile*) afable

bent [bɛnt] *pt, pp of* **bend** ▷ *n* inclinación *f* ▷ *adj*: **to be ~ on** estar empeñado en

bereaved [bɪ'ri:vd] *npl*: **the ~** los íntimos de una persona afligidos por su muerte

beret ['bɛreɪ] *n* boina

Berlin [bə:'lɪn] *n* Berlín

Bermuda [bə:'mju:də] *n* las Bermudas

berry ['bɛrɪ] *n* baya

berth [bə:θ] *n* (*bed*) litera; (*cabin*) camarote *m*; (*for ship*) amarradero ▷ *vi* atracar, amarrar

beside [bɪ'saɪd] *prep* junto a, al lado de; **to be ~ o.s. with anger** estar fuera de sí; **that's ~ the point** eso no tiene nada que ver; **besides** *adv* además ▷ *prep* además de

best [bɛst] *adj* (el/la) mejor ▷ *adv* (lo) mejor; **the ~ part of** (*quantity*) la mayor parte de; **at ~** en el mejor de los casos; **to make the ~ of sth** sacar el mejor partido de algo; **to do one's ~** hacer todo lo posible; **to the ~ of my knowledge** que yo sepa; **to the ~ of my ability** como mejor puedo; **best-before date** *n* fecha de consumo preferente; **best man** (*irreg*) *n* padrino de boda; **bestseller** *n* éxito de librería, bestseller *m*

bet [bɛt] (*pt, pp ~ or ~ted*) *n* apuesta ▷ *vt*: **to ~ money on** apostar dinero por ▷ *vi* apostar; **to ~ sb sth** apostar algo a algn

betray [bɪ'treɪ] *vt* traicionar; (*trust*) faltar a

better ['bɛtə*] *adj, adv* mejor ▷ *vt* superar ▷ *n*: **to get the ~ of sb** quedar por encima de algn; **you had ~ do it** más vale que lo hagas; **he thought ~ of it** cambió de parecer; **to get ~** (*Med*) mejorar(se)

betting ['bɛtɪŋ] *n* juego, el apostar; **betting shop** (*BRIT*) *n* agencia de apuestas

between [bɪ'twi:n] *prep* entre ▷ *adv* (*time*) mientras tanto; (*place*) en medio

beverage ['bɛvərɪdʒ] *n* bebida

beware [bɪ'wɛə*] *vi*: **to ~ (of)** tener cuidado (con); **"~ of the dog"** "perro peligroso"

bewildered [bɪ'wɪldəd] *adj* aturdido, perplejo

beyond [bɪ'jɔnd] *prep* más allá de; (*past: understanding*) fuera de; (*after: date*) después de, más allá de; (*above*) superior a ▷ *adv* (*in space*) más allá; (*in time*) posteriormente; **~ doubt** fuera de toda duda; **~ repair** irreparable

bias ['baɪəs] *n* (*prejudice*) prejuicio, pasión *f*; (*preference*) predisposición *f*; **bias(s)ed** *adj* parcial

bib [bɪb] *n* babero
Bible ['baɪbl] *n* Biblia
bicarbonate of soda [baɪ'kɑːbənɪt-] *n* bicarbonato sódico
biceps ['baɪsɛps] *n* bíceps *m*
bicycle ['baɪsɪkl] *n* bicicleta; **bicycle pump** *n* bomba de bicicleta
bid [bɪd] (*pt* **bade** *or* ~, *pp* **bidden** *or* ~) *n* oferta, postura; (*in tender*) licitación *f*; (*attempt*) tentativa, conato ▷ *vi* hacer una oferta ▷ *vt* (*offer*) ofrecer; **to ~ sb good day** dar a algn los buenos días; **bidder** *n*: **the highest bidder** el mejor postor
bidet ['biːdeɪ] *n* bidet *m*
big [bɪg] *adj* grande; (*brother, sister*) mayor; **bigheaded** *adj* engreído; **big toe** *n* dedo gordo (del pie)
bike [baɪk] *n* bici *f*; **bike lane** *n* carril-bici *m*
bikini [bɪ'kiːnɪ] *n* bikini *m*
bilateral [baɪ'lætərl] *adj* (*agreement*) bilateral
bilingual [baɪ'lɪŋgwəl] *adj* bilingüe
bill [bɪl] *n* cuenta; (*invoice*) factura; (*Pol*) proyecto de ley; (*us: banknote*) billete *m*; (*of bird*) pico; (*of show*) programa *m*; **"post no ~s"** "prohibido fijar carteles"; **to fit** *or* **fill the ~** (*fig*) cumplir con los requisitos; **billboard** (*us*) *n* cartelera; **billfold** ['bɪlfəuld] (*us*) *n* cartera
billiards ['bɪljədz] *n* billar *m*
billion ['bɪljən] *n* (*BRIT*) billón *m* (*millón de millones*); (*us*) mil millones *mpl*
bin [bɪn] *n* (*for rubbish*) cubo *or* bote *m* (*MEX*) *or* tacho (*sc*) de la basura; (*container*) recipiente *m*
bind [baɪnd] (*pt, pp* **bound**) *vt* atar; (*book*) encuadernar; (*oblige*) obligar ▷ *n* (*inf: nuisance*) lata
binge [bɪndʒ] (*inf*) *n*: **to go on a ~** ir de juerga
bingo ['bɪŋgəu] *n* bingo *m*
binoculars [bɪ'nɔkjuləz] *npl* prismáticos *mpl*
bio... ['baɪə'] *prefix*: **biochemistry** *n*

bioquímica; **biodegradable** [baɪəudɪ'greɪdəbl] *adj* biodegradable;
biography [baɪ'ɔgrəfɪ] *n* biografía;
biological *adj* biológico; **biology** [baɪ'ɔlədʒɪ] *n* biología; **biometric** [baɪə'mɛtrɪk] *adj* biométrico
birch [bəːtʃ] *n* (*tree*) abedul *m*
bird [bəːd] *n* ave *f*, pájaro; (*BRIT: inf: girl*) chica; **bird flu** *n* gripe *f* aviar; **bird of prey** *n* ave *f* de presa; **birdwatching** *n*: **he likes to go birdwatching on Sundays** los domingos le gusta ir a ver pájaros
Biro® ['baɪrəu] *n* boli
birth [bəːθ] *n* nacimiento; **to give ~ to** parir, dar a luz; **birth certificate** *n* partida de nacimiento; **birth control** *n* (*policy*) control *m* de natalidad; (*methods*) métodos *mpl* anticonceptivos; **birthday** *n* cumpleaños *m inv* ▷ *cpd* (*cake, card etc*) de cumpleaños; **birthmark** *n* antojo, marca de nacimiento; **birthplace** *n* lugar *m* de nacimiento
biscuit ['bɪskɪt] (*BRIT*) *n* galleta
bishop ['bɪʃəp] *n* obispo; (*Chess*) alfil *m*
bistro ['biːstrəu] *n* café-bar *m*
bit [bɪt] *pt of* **bite** ▷ *n* trozo, pedazo, pedacito; (*Comput*) bit *m*, bitio; (*for horse*) freno, bocado; **a ~ of** un poco de; **a ~ mad** un poco loco; **~ by ~** poco a poco
bitch [bɪtʃ] *n* perra; (*inf!: woman*) zorra (!)
bite [baɪt] (*pt* **bit**, *pp* **bitten**) *vt, vi* morder; (*insect etc*) picar ▷ *n* (*insect bite*) picadura; (*mouthful*) bocado; **to ~ one's nails** comerse las uñas; **let's have a ~ (to eat)** (*inf*) vamos a comer algo
bitten ['bɪtn] *pp of* **bite**
bitter ['bɪtə*] *adj* amargo; (*wind*) cortante, penetrante; (*battle*) encarnizado ▷ *n* (*BRIT: beer*) cerveza típica británica a base de lúpulos
bizarre [bɪ'zɑː*] *adj* raro, extraño
black [blæk] *adj* negro; (*tea, coffee*) solo ▷ *n* color *m* negro; (*person*): **B~**

negro/a ▷ vt (BRIT Industry) boicotear;
to give sb a ~ eye ponerle a algn
el ojo morado; **~ and blue** (bruised)
amoratado; **to be in the ~** (bank
account) estar en números negros;
black out vi (faint) desmayarse;
blackberry n zarzamora; **blackbird**
n mirlo; **blackboard** n pizarra; **black
coffee** n café m solo; **blackcurrant**
n grosella negra; **black ice** n hielo
invisible en la carretera; **blackmail**
n chantaje m ▷ vt chantajear; **black
market** n mercado negro; **blackout**
n (Mil) oscurecimiento; (power cut)
apagón m; (TV, Radio) interrupción f de
programas; (fainting) desvanecimiento;
black pepper n pimienta f negra;
black pudding n morcilla f; **Black Sea**
n: **the Black Sea** el Mar Negro
bladder ['blædə*] n vejiga
blade [bleɪd] n hoja; (of propeller)
paleta; **a ~ of grass** una brizna de
hierba
blame [bleɪm] n culpa ▷ vt: **to ~ sb
for sth** echar a algn la culpa de algo; **to
be to ~ (for)** tener la culpa (de)
bland [blænd] adj (music, taste) soso
blank [blæŋk] adj en blanco; (look) sin
expresión ▷ n (of memory): **my mind is
a ~** no puedo recordar nada; (on form)
blanco, espacio en blanco; (cartridge)
cartucho sin bala or de fogueo
blanket ['blæŋkɪt] n manta (SP),
cobija (LAM); (of snow) capa; (of fog)
manto
blast [blɑːst] n (of wind) ráfaga, soplo;
(of explosive) explosión f ▷ vt (blow
up) volar
blatant ['bleɪtənt] adj descarado
blaze [bleɪz] n (fire) fuego; (fig: of
colour) despliegue m; (: of glory)
esplendor m ▷ vi arder en llamas; (fig)
brillar ▷ vt: **to ~ a trail** (fig) abrir (un)
camino; **in a ~ of publicity** con gran
publicidad
blazer ['bleɪzə*] n chaqueta de uniforme
de colegial o de socio de club
bleach [bliːtʃ] n (also: **household ~**)

lejía ▷ vt blanquear; **bleachers** (US)
npl (Sport) gradas fpl al sol
bleak [bliːk] adj (countryside) desierto;
(prospect) poco prometedor(a);
(weather) crudo; (smile) triste
bled [bled] pt, pp of **bleed**
bleed [bliːd] (pt, pp **bled**) vt, vi
sangrar; **my nose is ~ing** me está
sangrando la nariz
blemish ['blemɪʃ] n marca, mancha;
(on reputation) tacha
blend [blend] n mezcla ▷ vt mezclar;
(colours etc) combinar, mezclar ▷ vi
(colours etc: also: **~ in**) combinarse,
mezclarse; **blender** n (Culin) batidora
bless [bles] (pt, pp **~ed** or **blest**) vt
bendecir; **~ you!** (after sneeze) ¡Jesús!;
blessing n (approval) aprobación f;
(godsend) don m del cielo, bendición f;
(advantage) beneficio, ventaja
blew [bluː] pt of **blow**
blight [blaɪt] vt (hopes etc) frustrar,
arruinar
blind [blaɪnd] adj ciego; (fig): **~ (to)**
ciego (a) ▷ n (for window) persiana ▷ vt
cegar; (dazzle) deslumbrar; (deceive): **to
~ sb to ...** cegar a algn a ... ; **the blind**
npl los ciegos; **blind alley** n callejón
m sin salida; **blindfold** n venda ▷ adv
con los ojos vendados ▷ vt vendar
los ojos a
blink [blɪŋk] vi parpadear, pestañear;
(light) oscilar
bliss [blɪs] n felicidad f
blister ['blɪstə*] n ampolla ▷ vi
(paint) ampollarse
blizzard ['blɪzəd] n ventisca
bloated ['bləʊtɪd] adj hinchado;
(person: full) ahíto
blob [blɒb] n (drop) gota; (indistinct
object) bulto
block [blɒk] n bloque m; (in pipes)
obstáculo; (of buildings) manzana
(SP), cuadra (LAM) ▷ vt obstruir,
cerrar; (progress) estorbar; **~ of flats**
(BRIT) bloque m de pisos; **mental ~**
bloqueo mental; **block up** vt tapar,
obstruir; (pipe) atascar; **blockade**

[-'keɪd] n bloqueo ▷ vt bloquear;
blockage n estorbo, obstrucción f;
blockbuster n (book) bestseller m;
(film) éxito de público; **block capitals**
npl mayúsculas fpl; **block letters** npl
mayúsculas fpl

blog [blɔg] n blog m

bloke [bləuk] (BRIT: inf) n tipo, tío

blond(e) [blɔnd] adj, n rubio/a m/f

blood [blʌd] n sangre f; **blood donor**
n donante mf de sangre; **blood group**
n grupo sanguíneo; **blood poisoning**
n envenenamiento de la sangre; **blood
pressure** n presión f sanguínea;
bloodshed n derramamiento de
sangre; **bloodshot** adj inyectado en
sangre; **bloodstream** n corriente
f sanguínea; **blood test** n análisis
m inv de sangre; **blood transfusion**
n transfusión f de sangre; **blood
type** n grupo sanguíneo; **blood
vessel** n vaso sanguíneo; **bloody**
adj sangriento; (nose etc) lleno de
sangre; (BRIT: inf!): **this bloody ...**
este condenado o puñetero ... (!)
▷ adv: **bloody strong/good** (BRIT: inf!)
terriblemente fuerte/bueno

bloom [blu:m] n flor f ▷ vi florecer

blossom ['blɔsəm] n flor f ▷ vi
florecer

blot [blɔt] n borrón m; (fig) mancha
▷ vt (stain) manchar

blouse [blauz] n blusa

blow [bləu] (pt **blew**, pp **blown**) n
golpe m; (with sword) espadazo ▷ vi
soplar; (dust, sand etc) volar; (fuse)
fundirse ▷ vt (wind) llevarse; (fuse)
quemar; (instrument) tocar; **to ~ one's
nose** sonarse; **blow away** vt llevarse,
arrancar; **blow out** vi apagarse; **blow
up** vi estallar ▷ vt volar; (tyre) inflar;
(Phot) ampliar; **blow-dry** n moldeado
(con secador)

blown [bləun] pp of **blow**

blue [blu:] adj azul; (depressed)
deprimido; **~ film/joke** película/chiste
m verde; **out of the ~** (fig) de repente;
bluebell n campanilla, campánula

azul; **blueberry** n arándano; **blue
cheese** n queso azul; **blues** npl: **the
blues** (Mus) el blues; **to have the blues**
estar triste; **bluetit** n herrerillo m
(común)

bluff [blʌf] vi tirarse un farol, farolear
▷ n farol m; **to call sb's ~** coger a algn
la palabra

blunder ['blʌndə*] n patinazo,
metedura de pata ▷ vi cometer un
error, meter la pata

blunt [blʌnt] adj (pencil) despuntado;
(knife) desafilado, romo; (person) franco,
directo

blur [blə:*] n (shape): **to become
a ~** hacerse borroso ▷ vt (vision)
enturbiar; (distinction) borrar; **blurred**
adj borroso

blush [blʌʃ] vi ruborizarse, ponerse
colorado ▷ n rubor m; **blusher** n
colorete m

board [bɔ:d] n (cardboard) cartón m;
(wooden) tabla, tablero; (on wall) tablón
m; (for chess etc) tablero; (committee)
junta, consejo; (in firm) mesa or junta
directiva; (Naut, Aviat): **on ~** a bordo
▷ vt (ship) embarcarse en; (train) subir
a; **full ~** (BRIT) pensión completa; **half
~** (BRIT) media pensión; **to go by the ~**
(fig) ser abandonado or olvidado; **board
game** n juego de tablero; **boarding
card** (BRIT) n tarjeta de embarque;
boarding pass (US) n = **boarding
card**; **boarding school** n internado;
board room n sala de juntas

boast [bəust] vi: **to ~ (about or of)**
alardear (de)

boat [bəut] n barco, buque m; (small)
barca, bote m

bob [bɔb] vi (also: **~ up and down**)
menearse, balancearse

bobby pin ['bɔbɪ-] (US) n horquilla

body ['bɔdɪ] n cuerpo; (corpse) cadáver
m; (of car) caja, carrocería; (fig: group)
grupo; (: organization) organismo;
body-building n culturismo;
bodyguard n guardaespaldas m inv;
bodywork n carrocería

bog [bɒg] n pantano, ciénaga ▷ vt: **to get ~ged down** (fig) empantanarse, atascarse

bogus ['bəʊgəs] adj falso, fraudulento

boil [bɔɪl] vt (water) hervir; (eggs) pasar por agua, cocer ▷ vi hervir; (fig: with anger) estar furioso; (: with heat) asfixiarse ▷ n (Med) furúnculo, divieso; **to come to the ~, to come to a ~** (us) comenzar a hervir; **to ~ down to** (fig) reducirse a; **boil over** vi salirse, rebosar; (anger etc) llegar al colmo; **boiled egg** n (soft) huevo tibio (MEX) or pasado por agua or a la copa (SC); (hard) huevo duro; **boiled potatoes** npl patatas fpl (SP) or papas fpl (LAM) cocidas; **boiler** n caldera; **boiling** ['bɔɪlɪŋ] adj: **I'm boiling (hot)** (inf) estoy asado; **boiling point** n punto de ebullición

bold [bəʊld] adj valiente, audaz; (pej) descarado; (colour) llamativo

Bolivia [bə'lɪvɪə] n Bolivia; **Bolivian** adj, n boliviano/a m/f

bollard ['bɒləd] n (Aut) poste m

bolt [bəʊlt] n (lock) cerrojo; (with nut) perno, tornillo ▷ adv: **~ upright** rígido, erguido ▷ vt (door) echar el cerrojo a; (also: **~ together**) sujetar con tornillos; (food) engullir ▷ vi fugarse; (horse) desbocarse

bomb [bɒm] n bomba ▷ vt bombardear; **bombard** [bɒm'bɑːd] vt bombardear; (fig) asediar; **bomber** n (Aviat) bombardero; **bomb scare** n amenaza de bomba

bond [bɒnd] n (promise) fianza; (Finance) bono; (link) vínculo, lazo; (Comm): **in ~** en depósito bajo fianza; **bonds** npl (chains) cadenas fpl

bone [bəʊn] n hueso; (of fish) espina ▷ vt deshuesar; quitar las espinas a

bonfire ['bɒnfaɪə*] n hoguera, fogata

bonnet ['bɒnɪt] n gorra; (BRIT: of car) capó m

bonus ['bəʊnəs] n (payment) paga extraordinaria, plus m; (fig) bendición f

boo [buː] excl ¡uh! ▷ vt abuchear,

rechiflar

book [buk] n libro; (of tickets) taco; (of stamps etc) librito ▷ vt (ticket) sacar; (seat, room) reservar; **books** npl (Comm) cuentas fpl, contabilidad f; **book in** vi (at hotel) registrarse; **book up** vt: **to be booked up** (hotel) estar completo; **bookcase** n librería, estante m para libros; **booking** n reserva; **booking office** n (BRIT Rail) despacho de billetes (SP) or boletos (LAM); (Theatre) taquilla (SP), boletería (LAM); **book-keeping** n contabilidad f; **booklet** n folleto; **bookmaker** n corredor m de apuestas; **bookmark** n (also Comput) marcador; **bookseller** n librero; **bookshelf** n estante m (para libros); **bookshop, book store** n librería

boom [buːm] n (noise) trueno, estampido; (in prices etc) alza rápida; (Econ, in population) boom m ▷ vi (cannon) hacer gran estruendo, retumbar; (Econ) estar en alza

boost [buːst] n estímulo, empuje m ▷ vt estimular, empujar

boot [buːt] n bota; (BRIT: of car) maleta, maletero ▷ vt (Comput) arrancar; **to ~** (in addition) además, por añadidura

booth [buːð] n (telephone booth, voting booth) cabina

booze [buːz] n (inf) n bebida

border ['bɔːdə*] n borde m, margen m; (of a country) frontera; (for flowers) arriate m ▷ vt (road) bordear; (another country: also: **~ on**) lindar con; **borderline** n: **on the borderline** en el límite

bore [bɔː*] pt of **bear** ▷ vt (hole) hacer un agujero en; (well) perforar; (person) aburrir ▷ n (person) pelmazo, pesado; (of gun) calibre m; **bored** adj aburrido; **he's bored to tears** or **to death** or **stiff** está aburrido como una ostra, está muerto de aburrimiento; **boredom** n aburrimiento

boring ['bɔːrɪŋ] adj aburrido

born [bɔːn] adj: **to be ~** nacer; **I was ~**

in 1960 nací en 1960
borne [bɔːn] *pp of* **bear**
borough ['bʌrə] *n* municipio
borrow ['bɔrəu] *vt*: **to ~ sth (from sb)** tomar algo prestado (a algn)
Bosnia(-Herzegovina) ['bɔːsnɪə(hɛrzə'gəuviːnə)] *n* Bosnia(-Herzegovina); **Bosnian** ['bɔznɪən] *adj*, *n* bosnio/a
bosom ['buzəm] *n* pecho
boss [bɔs] *n* jefe *m* ▷ *vt* (*also*: **~ about or around**) mangonear; **bossy** *adj* mandón/ona
both [bəuθ] *adj*, *pron* ambos/as, los dos(las dos); **~ of us went, we ~ went** fuimos los dos, ambos fuimos ▷ *adv*: **~ A and B** tanto A como B
bother ['bɔðə*] *vt* (*worry*) preocupar; (*disturb*) molestar, fastidiar ▷ *vi* (*also*: **~ o.s.**) molestarse ▷ *n* (*trouble*) dificultad *f*; (*nuisance*) molestia, lata; **to ~ doing** tomarse la molestia de hacer
bottle ['bɔtl] *n* botella; (*small*) frasco; (*baby's*) biberón *m* ▷ *vt* embotellar; **bottle bank** *n* contenedor *m* de vidrio; **bottle-opener** *n* abrebotellas *m inv*
bottom ['bɔtəm] *n* (*of box, sea*) fondo *m*; (*buttocks*) trasero, culo; (*of page*) pie *m*; (*of list*) final *m*; (*of class*) último/a ▷ *adj* (*lowest*) más bajo; (*last*) último
bought [bɔːt] *pt, pp of* **buy**
boulder ['bəuldə*] *n* canto rodado
bounce [bauns] *vi* (*ball*) (re)botar; (*cheque*) ser rechazado ▷ *vt* hacer (re)botar ▷ *n* (*rebound*) (re)bote *m*; **bouncer** (*inf*) *n* gorila *m* (*que echa a los alborotadores de un bar, club etc*)
bound [baund] *pt, pp of* **bind** ▷ *n* (*leap*) salto; (*gen pl*: *limit*) límite *m* ▷ *vi* (*leap*) saltar ▷ *vt* (*border*) rodear ▷ *adj*: **~ by** rodeado de; **to be ~ to do sth** (*obliged*) tener el deber de hacer algo; **he's ~ to come** es seguro que vendrá; **out of ~s** prohibido el paso; **~ for** con destino a
boundary ['baundrɪ] *n* límite *m*
bouquet ['bukeɪ] *n* (*of flowers*) ramo
bourbon ['buəbən] (US) *n* (*also*: **~**

whiskey) whisky *m* americano, bourbon *m*
bout [baut] *n* (*of malaria etc*) ataque *m*; (*of activity*) período; (*Boxing etc*) combate *m*, encuentro
boutique [buː'tiːk] *n* boutique *f*, tienda de ropa
bow¹ [bəu] *n* (*knot*) lazo; (*weapon, Mus*) arco
bow² [bau] *n* (*of the head*) reverencia; (*Naut*: *also*: **~s**) proa ▷ *vi* inclinarse, hacer una reverencia
bowels [bauəlz] *npl* intestinos *mpl*, vientre *m*; (*fig*) entrañas *fpl*
bowl [bəul] *n* tazón *m*, cuenco; (*ball*) bola ▷ *vi* (*Cricket*) arrojar la pelota; *see also* **bowls**; **bowler** *n* (*Cricket*) lanzador *m* (de la pelota); (*BRIT*: *also*: **bowler hat**) hongo, bombín *m*; **bowling** *n* (*game*) bochas *fpl*, bolos *mpl*; **bowling alley** *n* bolera; **bowling green** *n* pista para bochas; **bowls** *n* juego de las bochas, bolos *mpl*
bow tie ['bəu-] *n* corbata de lazo, pajarita
box [bɔks] *n* (*also*: **cardboard ~**) caja, cajón *m*; (*Theatre*) palco ▷ *vt* encajonar ▷ *vi* (*Sport*) boxear; **boxer** ['bɔksə*] *n* (*person*) boxeador *m*; **boxer shorts** ['bɔksəfɔːts] *pl n* bóxers; **a pair of boxer shorts** unos bóxers; **boxing** ['bɔksɪŋ] *n* (*Sport*) boxeo; **Boxing Day** (*BRIT*) *n* día en que se dan los aguinaldos, 26 de diciembre; **boxing gloves** *npl* guantes *mpl* de boxeo; **boxing ring** *n* ring *m*, cuadrilátero; **box office** *n* taquilla (*SP*), boletería (*LAM*)
boy [bɔɪ] *n* (*young*) niño; (*older*) muchacho, chico; (*son*) hijo; **boy band** *n* boy band *m* (*grupo musical de chicos*)
boycott ['bɔɪkɔt] *n* boicot *m* ▷ *vt* boicotear
boyfriend ['bɔɪfrɛnd] *n* novio
bra [brɑː] *n* sostén *m*, sujetador *m*
brace [breɪs] *n* (*BRIT*: *also*: **~s**: *on teeth*) corrector *m*, aparato; (*tool*) berbiquí *m* ▷ *vt* (*knees, shoulders*) tensionar; **braces** *npl* (*BRIT*) tirantes *mpl*; **to ~ o.s.** (*fig*)

prepararse

bracelet ['breɪslɪt] n pulsera, brazalete m

bracket ['brækɪt] n (Tech) soporte m, puntal m; (group) clase f, categoría; (also: **brace ~**) soporte m, abrazadera; (also: **round ~**) paréntesis m inv; (also: **square ~**) corchete m ▷ vt (word etc) poner entre paréntesis

brag [bræg] vi jactarse

braid [breɪd] n (trimming) galón m; (of hair) trenza

brain [breɪn] n cerebro; **brains** npl sesos mpl; **she's got ~s** es muy lista

braise [breɪz] vt cocer a fuego lento

brake [breɪk] n (on vehicle) freno ▷ vi frenar; **brake light** n luz f de frenado

bran [bræn] n salvado

branch [brɑːntʃ] n rama; (Comm) sucursal f; **branch off** vi: **a small road branches off to the right** hay una carretera pequeña que sale hacia la derecha; **branch out** vi (fig) extenderse

brand [brænd] n marca; (fig: type) tipo ▷ vt (cattle) marcar con hierro candente; **brand name** n marca; **brand-new** adj flamante, completamente nuevo

brandy ['brændɪ] n coñac m

brash [bræʃ] adj (forward) descarado

brass [brɑːs] n latón m; **the ~** (Mus) los cobres; **brass band** n banda de metal

brat [bræt] n (pej) n mocoso/a

brave [breɪv] adj valiente, valeroso ▷ vt (face up to) desafiar; **bravery** n valor m, valentía

brawl [brɔːl] n pelea, reyerta

Brazil [brə'zɪl] n (el) Brasil; **Brazilian** adj, n brasileño/a m/f

breach [briːtʃ] vt abrir brecha en ▷ n (gap) brecha; (breaking): **~ of contract** infracción f de contrato; **~ of the peace** perturbación f del órden público

bread [brɛd] n pan m; **breadbin** n panera; **breadbox** (US) n panera; **breadcrumbs** npl migajas fpl; (Culin) pan rallado

breadth [brɛtθ] n anchura; (fig) amplitud f

break [breɪk] (pt **broke**, pp **broken**) vt romper; (promise) faltar a; (law) violar, infringir; (record) batir ▷ vi romperse, quebrarse; (storm) estallar; (weather) cambiar; (dawn) despuntar; (news etc) darse a conocer ▷ n (gap) abertura; (fracture) fractura; (time) intervalo; (: at school) (período de) recreo; (chance) oportunidad f; **to ~ the news to sb** comunicar la noticia a algn; **break down** vt (figures, data) analizar, descomponer ▷ vi (machine) estropearse; (Aut) averiarse; (person) romper a llorar; (talks) fracasar; **break in** vt (horse etc) domar ▷ vi (burglar) forzar una entrada; (interrupt) interrumpir; **break into** vt fus (house) forzar; **break off** vi (speaker) pararse, detenerse; (branch) partir; **break out** vi estallar; (prisoner) escaparse; **to break out in spots** salirle a algn granos; **break up** vi (ship) hacerse pedazos; (crowd, meeting) disolverse; (marriage) deshacerse; (Scol) terminar (el curso); (line) cortarse ▷ vt (rocks etc) partir; (journey) partir; (fight etc) acabar con; **the line's** or **you're breaking up** se corta; **breakdown** n (Aut) avería; (in communications) interrupción f; (Med: also: **nervous breakdown**) colapso, crisis f nerviosa; (of marriage, talks) fracaso; (of statistics) análisis m inv; **breakdown truck, breakdown van** n (camión m) grúa

breakfast ['brɛkfəst] n desayuno

break: break-in n robo con allanamiento de morada; **breakthrough** n (also fig) avance m

breast [brɛst] n (of woman) pecho, seno; (chest) pecho; (of bird) pechuga; **breast-feed** (pt, pp **breast-fed**) vt, vi amamantar, criar a los pechos; **breast-stroke** n braza (de pecho)

breath [brɛθ] n aliento, respiración f; **to take a deep ~** respirar hondo; **out of ~** sin aliento, sofocado

Breathalyser® ['brɛθəlaɪzə*] (BRIT)
n alcoholímetro
breathe [bri:ð] vt, vi respirar;
breathe in vt, vi aspirar; **breathe
out** vt, vi espirar; **breathing** n
respiración f
breath: breathless adj sin aliento,
jadeante; **breathtaking** adj
imponente, pasmoso; **breath test** n
prueba de la alcoholemia
bred [bred] pt, pp of **breed**
breed [bri:d] (pt, pp **bred**) vt criar ▷ vi
reproducirse, procrear ▷ n (Zool) raza,
casta; (type) tipo
breeze [bri:z] n brisa
breezy ['bri:zɪ] adj de mucho viento,
ventoso; (person) despreocupado
brew [bru:] vt (tea) hacer; (beer)
elaborar ▷ vi (fig: trouble) prepararse;
(storm) amenazar; **brewery** n fábrica
de cerveza, cervecería
bribe [braɪb] n soborno ▷ vt
sobornar, cohechar; **bribery** n
soborno, cohecho
bric-a-brac ['brɪkabræk] n inv
baratijas fpl
brick [brɪk] n ladrillo; **bricklayer** n
albañil m
bride [braɪd] n novia; **bridegroom** n
novio; **bridesmaid** n dama de honor
bridge [brɪdʒ] n puente m; (Naut)
puente m de mando; (of nose) caballete
m; (Cards) bridge m ▷ vt (fig): **to ~ a gap**
llenar un vacío
bridle ['braɪdl] n brida, freno
brief [bri:f] adj breve, corto ▷ n (Law)
escrito; (task) cometido, encargo
▷ vt informar; **briefs** npl (for men)
calzoncillos mpl; (for women) bragas fpl;
briefcase n cartera (SP), portafolio
(LAM); **briefing** n (Press) informe m;
briefly adv (glance) fugazmente; (say)
en pocas palabras
brigadier [brɪgə'dɪə*] n general m
de brigada
bright [braɪt] adj brillante; (room)
luminoso; (day) de sol; (person: clever)
listo, inteligente; (: lively) alegre;

(colour) vivo; (future) prometedor(a)
brilliant ['brɪljənt] adj brillante; (inf)
fenomenal
brim [brɪm] n borde m; (of hat) ala
brine [braɪn] n (Culin) salmuera
bring [brɪŋ] (pt, pp **brought**) vt (thing,
person: with you) traer; (: to sb) llevar,
conducir; (trouble, satisfaction) causar;
bring about vt ocasionar, producir;
bring back vt volver a traer; (return)
devolver; **bring down** vt (government,
plane) derribar; (price) rebajar; **bring
in** vt (harvest) recoger; (person) hacer
entrar o pasar; (object) traer; (Pol: bill,
law) presentar; (produce: income)
producir, rendir; **bring on** vt (illness,
attack) producir, causar; (player,
substitute) sacar (de la reserva), hacer
salir; **bring out** vt sacar; (book etc)
publicar; (meaning) subrayar; **bring
up** vt subir; (person) educar, criar;
(question) sacar a colación; (food: vomit)
devolver, vomitar
brink [brɪŋk] n borde m
brisk [brɪsk] adj (abrupt: tone) brusco;
(person) enérgico, vigoroso; (pace)
rápido; (trade) activo
bristle ['brɪsl] n cerda ▷ vi: **to ~ in
anger** temblar de rabia
Brit [brɪt] n abbr (inf: = British person)
británico/a
Britain ['brɪtən] n (also: **Great ~**)
Gran Bretaña
British ['brɪtɪʃ] adj británico
▷ npl: **the ~** los británicos; **British Isles**
npl: **the British Isles** las Islas Británicas
Briton ['brɪtən] n británico/a
brittle ['brɪtl] adj quebradizo, frágil
broad [brɔ:d] adj ancho; (range)
amplio; (smile) abierto; (general. outlines
etc) general; (accent) cerrado; **in ~
daylight** en pleno día; **broadband** n
banda ancha; **broad bean** n haba;
broadcast (pt, pp **~**) n emisión f
▷ vt (Radio) emitir; (TV) transmitir
▷ vi emitir; transmitir; **broaden** vt
ampliar ▷ vi ensancharse; **to broaden
one's mind** hacer más tolerante a

algn; **broadly** adv en general; **broad-minded** adj tolerante, liberal

broccoli ['brɔkəlɪ] n brécol m

brochure ['brəuʃjuə*] n folleto

broil [brɔɪl] vt (Culin) asar a la parrilla

broiler ['brɔɪlə*] n (grill) parrilla

broke [brəuk] pt of **break** ▷ adj (inf) pelado, sin blanca

broken ['brəukən] pp of **break** ▷ adj roto; (machine: also: **~ down**) averiado; **~ leg** pierna rota; **in ~ English** en un inglés imperfecto

broker ['brəukə*] n agente mf, bolsista mf; (insurance broker) agente de seguros

bronchitis [brɔŋ'kaɪtɪs] n bronquitis f

bronze [brɔnz] n bronce m

brooch [brəutʃ] n prendedor m, broche m

brood [bru:d] n camada, cría ▷ vi (person) dejarse obsesionar

broom [brum] n escoba; (Bot) retama

Bros. abbr (= Brothers) Hnos

broth [brɔθ] n caldo

brothel ['brɔθl] n burdel m

brother ['brʌðə*] n hermano; **brother-in-law** n cuñado

brought [brɔ:t] pt, pp of **bring**

brow [brau] n (forehead) frente m; (eyebrow) ceja; (of hill) cumbre f

brown [braun] adj (colour) marrón; (hair) castaño; (tanned) bronceado, moreno ▷ n (colour) color m marrón or pardo ▷ vt (Culin) dorar; **brown bread** n pan integral

Brownie ['braunɪ] n niña exploradora

brown rice n arroz m integral

brown sugar n azúcar m terciado

browse [brauz] vi (through book) hojear; (in shop) mirar; **browser** n (Comput) navegador m

bruise [bru:z] n cardenal m (SP), moretón m ▷ vt magullar

brunette [bru:'nɛt] n morena

brush [brʌʃ] n cepillo; (for painting, shaving etc) brocha; (artist's) pincel m;

(with police etc) roce m ▷ vt (sweep) barrer; (groom) cepillar; (also: **~ against**) rozar al pasar

Brussels ['brʌslz] n Bruselas

Brussels sprout n col f de Bruselas

brutal ['bru:tl] adj brutal

B.Sc. abbr (= Bachelor of Science) licenciado en Ciencias

BSE n abbr (= bovine spongiform encephalopathy) encefalopatía espongiforme bovina

bubble ['bʌbl] n burbuja ▷ vi burbujear, borbotar; **bubble bath** n espuma para el baño; **bubble gum** n chicle m de globo; **bubblejet printer** ['bʌbldʒɛt-] n impresora de injección por burbujas

buck [bʌk] n (rabbit) conejo macho, (deer) gamo; (us: inf) dólar m ▷ vi corcovear; **to pass the ~ (to sb)** echar (a algn) el muerto

bucket ['bʌkɪt] n cubo, balde m

buckle ['bʌkl] n hebilla ▷ vt abrochar con hebilla ▷ vi combarse

bud [bʌd] n (of plant) brote m, yema; (of flower) capullo ▷ vi brotar, echar brotes

Buddhism ['budɪzm] n Budismo

Buddhist ['budɪst] adj, n budista m/f

buddy ['bʌdɪ] (us) n compañero, compinche m

budge [bʌdʒ] vt mover; (fig) hacer ceder ▷ vi moverse, ceder

budgerigar ['bʌdʒərɪgɑ:*] n periquito

budget ['bʌdʒɪt] n presupuesto ▷ vi: **to ~ for sth** presupuestar algo

budgie ['bʌdʒɪ] n = **budgerigar**

buff [bʌf] adj (colour) color de ante ▷ n (inf: enthusiast) entusiasta mf

buffalo ['bʌfələu] (pl ~ or ~es) n (BRIT) búfalo; (us: bison) bisonte m

buffer ['bʌfə*] n (Comput) memoria intermedia; (Rail) tope m

buffet¹ ['bʌfɪt] vt golpear

buffet² ['bufeɪ] n (BRIT: in station) bar m, cafetería; (food) buffet m; **buffet car** (BRIT) n (Rail) coche-comedor m

bug [bʌg] n (esp us: insect) bicho, sabandija; (Comput) error m; (germ) microbio, bacilo; (spy device) micrófono oculto ▷ vt (inf: annoy) fastidiar; (room) poner micrófono oculto en

buggy ['bʌgɪ] n cochecito de niño

build [bɪld] (pt, pp built) n (of person) tipo ▷ vt construir, edificar; **build up** vt (morale, forces, production) acrecentar; (stocks) acumular; **builder** n (contractor) contratista mf; **building** n construcción f; (structure) edificio; **building site** n obra; **building society** (BRIT) n sociedad f inmobiliaria

built [bɪlt] pt, pp of **build**; **built-in** adj (cupboard) empotrado; (device) interior, incorporado; **built-up** adj (area) urbanizado

bulb [bʌlb] n (Bot) bulbo; (Elec) bombilla, foco (MEX), bujía (CAM), bombita (RPL)

Bulgaria [bʌlˈgɛərɪə] n Bulgaria; **Bulgarian** adj, n búlgaro/a m/f

bulge [bʌldʒ] n bulto, protuberancia ▷ vi bombearse, pandearse; (pocket etc): **to ~ (with)** rebosar (de)

bulimia [bəˈlɪmɪə] n bulimia

bulimic [bjuːˈlɪmɪk] adj, n bulímico/a m/f

bulk [bʌlk] n masa, mole f; **in ~** (Comm) a granel; **the ~ of** la mayor parte de; **bulky** adj voluminoso, abultado

bull [bul] n toro; (male elephant, whale) macho

bulldozer ['buldəuzə*] n bulldozer m

bullet ['bulɪt] n bala

bulletin ['bulɪtɪn] n anuncio, parte m; (journal) boletín m; **bulletin board** n (us) tablón m de anuncios; (Comput) tablero de noticias

bullfight ['bulfaɪt] n corrida de toros; **bullfighter** n torero; **bullfighting** n los toros, el toreo

bully ['bulɪ] n valentón m, matón m ▷ vt intimidar, tiranizar

bum [bʌm] n (inf: backside) culo; (esp us: tramp) vagabundo

bumblebee ['bʌmblbiː] n abejorro

bump [bʌmp] n (blow) tope m, choque m; (jolt) sacudida; (on road etc) bache m; (on head etc) chichón m ▷ vt (strike) chocar contra; **bump into** vt fus chocar contra, tropezar con; (person) topar con; **bumper** n (Aut) parachoques m inv ▷ adj: **bumper crop** or **harvest** cosecha abundante; **bumpy** adj (road) lleno de baches

bun [bʌn] n (BRIT: cake) pastel m; (us: bread) bollo; (of hair) moño

bunch [bʌntʃ] n (of flowers) ramo; (of keys) manojo; (of bananas) piña; (of people) grupo; (pej) pandilla; **bunches** npl (in hair) coletas fpl

bundle ['bʌndl] n bulto, fardo; (of sticks) haz m; (of papers) legajo ▷ vt (also: **~ up**) atar, envolver; **to ~ sth/sb into** meter algo/a algn precipitadamente en

bungalow ['bʌŋgələu] n bungalow m, chalé m

bungee jumping ['bʌndʒiː'dʒʌmpɪŋ] n puenting m, banyi m

bunion ['bʌnjən] n juanete m

bunk [bʌŋk] n litera; **bunk beds** npl literas fpl

bunker ['bʌŋkə*] n (coal store) carbonera; (Mil) refugio; (Golf) bunker m

bunny ['bʌnɪ] n (inf: also: **~ rabbit**) conejito

buoy [bɔɪ] n boya; **buoyant** adj (ship) capaz de flotar; (economy) boyante; (person) optimista

burden ['bəːdn] n carga ▷ vt cargar

bureau [bjuəˈrəu] (pl **~x**) n (BRIT: writing desk) escritorio, buró m; (us: chest of drawers) cómoda; (office) oficina, agencia

bureaucracy [bjuəˈrɔkrəsɪ] n burocracia

bureaucrat ['bjuərəkræt] n burócrata m/f

bureau de change [-dəˈʃɑːʒ] (pl **bureaux de change**) n caja f de cambio

bureaux ['bjuərəuz] npl of **bureau**

b

burger ['bə:gə*] n hamburguesa
burglar ['bə:glə*] n ladrón/ona m/f;
burglar alarm n alarma f antirrobo;
burglary n robo con allanamiento,
robo de una casa
burial ['bɛrɪəl] n entierro
burn [bə:n] (pt, pp **~ed** or **~t**) vt
quemar; (house) incendiar ▷ vi
quemarse, arder; incendiarse; (sting)
escocer ▷ n quemadura; **burn down**
vt incendiar; **burn out** vt (writer
etc): **to burn o.s. out** agotarse;
burning adj (building etc) en llamas;
(hot: sand etc) abrasador(a); (ambition)
ardiente
Burns' Night [bə:nz-] n ver recuadro

burnt [bə:nt] pt, pp of **burn**
burp [bə:p] (inf) n eructo ▷ vi eructar
burrow ['bʌrəʊ] n madriguera ▷ vi
hacer una madriguera; (rummage)
hurgar
burst [bə:st] (pt, pp **~**) vt reventar;
(river: banks etc) romper ▷ vi
reventarse; (tyre) pincharse ▷ n (of
gunfire) ráfaga; (also: **~ pipe**) reventón
m; **a ~ of energy/speed/enthusiasm**
una explosión de energía/un
ímpetu de velocidad/un arranque
de entusiasmo; **to ~ into flames**

estallar en llamas; **to ~ into tears**
deshacerse en lágrimas; **to ~ out
laughing** soltar la carcajada; **to ~
open** abrirse de golpe; **to be ~ing with**
(container) estar lleno a rebosar de;
(: person) reventar por or de; **burst into**
vt fus (room etc) irrumpir en
bury ['bɛrɪ] vt enterrar; (body)
enterrar, sepultar
bus [bʌs] (pl **~es**) n autobús m; **bus
conductor** n cobrador(a) m/f
bush [bʊʃ] n arbusto; (scrub land)
monte m; **to beat about the ~**
andar(se) con rodeos
business ['bɪznɪs] n (matter) asunto;
(trading) comercio, negocios mpl; (firm)
empresa, casa; (occupation) oficio;
to be away on ~ estar en viaje de
negocios; **it's my ~ to ...** me toca or
corresponde ...; **it's none of my ~** yo no
tengo nada que ver; **he means ~** habla
en serio; **business class** n (Aer) clase f
preferente; **businesslike** adj eficiente;
businessman (irreg) n hombre m de
negocios; **business trip** n viaje m de
negocios; **businesswoman** (irreg) n
mujer f de negocios
busker ['bʌskə*] (BRIT) n músico/a
ambulante
bus: bus pass n bonobús; **bus shelter**
n parada cubierta; **bus station** n
estación f de autobuses; **bus-stop** n
parada de autobús
bust [bʌst] n (Anat) pecho; (sculpture)
busto ▷ adj (inf: broken) roto,
estropeado; **to go ~** quebrar
bustling ['bʌslɪŋ] adj (town)
animado, bullicioso
busy ['bɪzɪ] adj ocupado, atareado;
(shop, street) concurrido, animado;
(Tel: line) comunicando ▷ vt: **to ~ o.s.
with** ocuparse en; **busy signal** (US) n
(Tel) señal f de comunicando

○ **KEYWORD**

but [bʌt] conj **1** pero; **he's not very
bright, but he's hard-working** no es

muy inteligente, pero es trabajador
2 (*in direct contradiction*) sino; **he's not English but French** no es inglés sino francés; **he didn't sing but he shouted** no cantó sino que gritó
3 (*showing disagreement, surprise etc*): **but that's far too expensive!** ¡pero eso es carísimo!; **but it does work!** ¡(pero) sí que funciona!
▷ *prep* (*apart from, except*) menos, salvo; **we've had nothing but trouble** no hemos tenido más que problemas; **no-one but him can do it** nadie más que él puede hacerlo; **who but a lunatic would do such a thing?** ¡sólo un loco haría una cosa así!; **but for you/your help** si no fuera por ti/tu ayuda; **anything but that** cualquier cosa menos eso
▷ *adv* (*just, only*): **she's but a child** no es más que una niña; **had I but known** si lo hubiera sabido; **I can but try** al menos lo puedo intentar; **it's all but finished** está casi acabado

butcher ['butʃə*] *n* carnicero ▷ *vt* hacer una carnicería con; (*cattle etc*) matar; **butcher's (shop)** *n* carnicería
butler ['bʌtlə*] *n* mayordomo
butt [bʌt] *n* (*barrel*) tonel *m*; (*of gun*) culata; (*of cigarette*) colilla; (BRIT: *fig: target*) blanco ▷ *vt* dar cabezadas contra, top(et)ar
butter ['bʌtə*] *n* mantequilla ▷ *vt* untar con mantequilla; **buttercup** *n* botón *m* de oro
butterfly ['bʌtəflaɪ] *n* mariposa; (*Swimming: also:* **~ stroke**) braza de mariposa
buttocks ['bʌtəks] *npl* nalgas *fpl*
button ['bʌtn] *n* botón *m*; (us) placa, chapa ▷ *vt* (*also:* **~ up**) abotonar, abrochar ▷ *vi* abrocharse
buy [baɪ] (*pt, pp* **bought**) *vt* comprar ▷ *n* compra; **to ~ sb sth/sth from sb** comprarle algo a algn; **to ~ sb a drink** invitar a algn a tomar algo; **buy out** *vt*

(*partner*) comprar la parte de; **buy up** *vt* (*property*) acaparar; (*stock*) comprar todas las existencias de; **buyer** *n* comprador(a) *m/f*
buzz [bʌz] *n* zumbido; (inf: *phone call*) llamada (por teléfono) ▷ *vi* zumbar; **buzzer** *n* timbre *m*

○ **KEYWORD**

by [baɪ] *prep* **1** (*referring to cause, agent*) por; de; **killed by lightning** muerto por un relámpago; **a painting by Picasso** un cuadro de Picasso
2 (*referring to method, manner, means*): **by bus/car/train** en autobús/coche/tren; **to pay by cheque** pagar con un cheque; **by moonlight/candlelight** a la luz de la luna/una vela; **by saving hard he ...** ahorrando ...
3 (*via, through*) por; **we came by Dover** vinimos por Dover
4 (*close to, past*): **the house by the river** la casa junto al río; **she rushed by me** pasó a mi lado como una exhalación; **I go by the post office every day** paso por delante de Correos todos los días
5 (*time: not later than*) para; (: *during*): **by daylight** de día; **by 4 o'clock** para las cuatro; **by this time tomorrow** mañana a estas horas; **by the time I got here it was too late** cuando llegué ya era demasiado tarde
6 (*amount*): **by the metre/kilo** por metro/kilo; **paid by the hour** pagado por hora
7 (*Math, measure*): **to divide/multiply by 3** dividir/multiplicar por 3; **a room 3 metres by 4** una habitación de 3 metros por 4; **it's broader by a metre** es un metro más ancho
8 (*according to*) según, de acuerdo con; **it's 3 o'clock by my watch** según mi reloj, son las tres; **it's all right by me** por mí, está bien
9: **(all) by oneself** *etc* todo solo; **he did it (all) by himself** lo hizo él solo;

he was standing (all) by himself in a corner estaba de pie solo en un rincón
10: **by the way** a propósito, por cierto; **this wasn't my idea, by the way** pues, no fue idea mía
▷ adv **1** see **go**; **pass** etc
2: **by and by** finalmente; **they'll come back by and by** acabarán volviendo; **by and large** en líneas generales, en general

bye(-bye) ['baɪ('baɪ)] excl adiós, hasta luego
by-election (BRIT) n elección f parcial
bypass ['baɪpɑːs] n carretera de circunvalación; (Med) (operación f de) by-pass f ▷ vt evitar
byte [baɪt] n (Comput) byte m, octeto

C [siː] n (Mus) do m
cab [kæb] n taxi m; (of truck) cabina
cabaret ['kæbəreɪ] n cabaret m
cabbage ['kæbɪdʒ] n col f, berza
cabin ['kæbɪn] n cabaña; (on ship) camarote m; (on plane) cabina; **cabin crew** n tripulación f de cabina
cabinet ['kæbɪnɪt] n (Pol) consejo de ministros; (furniture) armario; (also: **display ~**) vitrina; **cabinet minister** n ministro/a (del gabinete)
cable ['keɪbl] n cable m ▷ vt cablegrafiar; **cable car** n teleférico; **cable television** n televisión f por cable
cactus ['kæktəs] (pl **cacti**) n cacto
café ['kæfeɪ] n café m
cafeteria [kæfɪ'tɪərɪə] n cafetería
caffein(e) ['kæfiːn] n cafeína
cage [keɪdʒ] n jaula
cagoule [kə'guːl] n chubasquero
cake [keɪk] n (Culin: large) tarta; (: small) pastel m; (of soap) pastilla
calcium ['kælsɪəm] n calcio
calculate ['kælkjuleɪt] vt calcular;

calculation [-'leɪʃən] n cálculo, cómputo; **calculator** n calculadora
calendar ['kæləndə*] n calendario
calf [kɑ:f] (pl **calves**) n (of cow) ternero, becerro; (of other animals) cría; (also: ~**skin**) piel f de becerro; (Anat) pantorrilla
calibre ['kælɪbə*] (US **caliber**) n calibre m
call [kɔ:l] vt llamar; (meeting) convocar ▷ vi (shout) llamar; (Tel) llamar (por teléfono); (visit: also: ~ **in**, ~ **round**) hacer una visita ▷ n llamada; (of bird) canto; **to be ~ed** llamarse; **on ~** (on duty) de guardia; **call back** vi (return) volver; (Tel) volver a llamar; **call for** vt fus (demand) pedir, exigir; (fetch) pasar a recoger; **call in** vt (doctor, expert, police) llamar; **call off** vt (cancel: meeting, race) cancelar; (: deal) anular; (: strike) desconvocar; **call on** vt fus (visit) visitar; (turn to) acudir a; **call out** vi gritar; **call up** vt (Mil) llamar al servicio militar; (Tel) llamar; **callbox** (BRIT) n cabina telefónica; **call centre** (US **call center**) n centro de atención al cliente; **caller** n visita; (Tel) usuario/a
callous ['kæləs] adj insensible, cruel
calm [kɑ:m] adj tranquilo; (sea) liso, en calma ▷ n calma, tranquilidad f ▷ vt calm, tranquilizar; **calm down** vi calmarse, tranquilizarse ▷ vt calmar, tranquilizar; **calmly** ['kɑ:mlɪ] adv tranquilamente, con calma
Calor gas® ['kælə*-] n butano
calorie ['kælərɪ] n caloría
calves [kɑ:vz] npl of **calf**
camcorder ['kæmkɔ:də*] n videocámara
came [keɪm] pt of **come**
camel ['kæməl] n camello
camera ['kæmərə] n máquina fotográfica; (Cinema, TV) cámara; **in ~** (Law) a puerta cerrada; **cameraman** (irreg) n cámara m; **camera phone** n teléfono con cámara
camouflage ['kæməflɑ:ʒ] n

camuflaje m ▷ vt camuflar
camp [kæmp] n campamento, camping m; (Mil) campamento; (for prisoners) campo; (fig: faction) bando ▷ vi acampar ▷ adj afectado, afeminado
campaign [kæm'peɪn] n (Mil, Pol etc) campaña ▷ vi hacer campaña; **campaigner** n: **campaigner for** defensor(a) m/f de
camp: campbed (BRIT) n cama de campaña; **camper** n campista mf; (vehicle) caravana; **campground** (US) n camping m, campamento; **camping** n camping m; **to go camping** hacer camping; **campsite** n camping m
campus ['kæmpəs] n ciudad f universitaria
can¹ [kæn] n (of oil, water) bidón m; (tin) lata, bote m ▷ vt enlatar

○ **KEYWORD**

can² [kæn] (negative **cannot**, **can't**, conditional and pt **could**) aux vb **1** (be able to) poder; **you can do it if you try** puedes hacerlo si lo intentas; **I can't see you** no te veo
2 (know how to) saber; **I can swim/play tennis/drive** sé nadar/jugar al tenis/ conducir; **can you speak French?** ¿hablas or sabes hablar francés?
3 (may) poder; **can I use your phone?** ¿me dejas or puedo usar tu teléfono?
4 (expressing disbelief, puzzlement etc): **it can't be true!** ¡no puede ser (verdad)!; **what can he want?** ¿qué querrá?
5 (expressing possibility, suggestion etc): **he could be in the library** podría estar en la biblioteca; **she could have been delayed** pudo haberse retrasado

Canada ['kænədə] n (el) Canadá; **Canadian** [kə'neɪdɪən] adj, n canadiense mf
canal [kə'næl] n canal m
canary [kə'nɛərɪ] n canario
Canary Islands [kə'nɛərɪ'aɪləndz]

npl: **the ~** las (Islas) Canarias
cancel ['kænsəl] *vt* cancelar; (*train*)
suprimir; (*cross out*) tachar, borrar;
cancellation [-'leɪʃən] *n* cancelación
f; supresión *f*
Cancer ['kænsə*] *n* (*Astrology*)
Cáncer *m*
cancer ['kænsə*] *n* cáncer *m*
candidate ['kændɪdeɪt] *n*
candidato/a
candle ['kændl] *n* vela; (*in church*)
cirio; **candlestick** *n* (*single*) candelero;
(*low*) palmatoria; (*bigger, ornate*)
candelabro
candy ['kændɪ] *n* azúcar *m* cande;
(*US*) caramelo; **candy bar** (*US*) *n*
barrita (*dulce*); **candyfloss** (*BRIT*) *n*
algodón *m* (azucarado)
cane [keɪn] *n* (*Bot*) caña; (*stick*) vara,
palmeta; (*for furniture*) mimbre *f* ▷ *vt*
(*BRIT: Scol*) castigar (con vara)
canister ['kænɪstə*] *n* bote *m*, lata;
(*of gas*) bombona
cannabis ['kænəbɪs] *n* marijuana
canned [kænd] *adj* en lata, de lata
cannon ['kænən] (*pl ~ or ~s*) *n*
cañón *m*
cannot ['kænɔt] = **can not**
canoe [kə'nu:] *n* canoa; (*Sport*)
piragua; **canoeing** *n* piragüismo
canon ['kænən] *n* (*clergyman*)
canónigo; (*standard*) canon *m*
can-opener ['kænəupnə*] *n*
abrelatas *m inv*
can't [kænt] = **can not**
canteen [kæn'ti:n] *n* (*eating place*)
cantina; (*BRIT: of cutlery*) juego
canter ['kæntə*] *vi* ir a medio galope
canvas ['kænvəs] *n* (*material*) lona;
(*painting*) lienzo; (*Naut*) velas *fpl*
canvass ['kænvəs] *vi* (*Pol*): **to ~
for** solicitar votos por ▷ *vt* (*Comm*)
sondear
canyon ['kænjən] *n* cañón *m*
cap [kæp] *n* (*hat*) gorra; (*of pen*)
capuchón *m;* (*of bottle*) tapa, tapón *m;*
(*contraceptive*) diafragma *m;* (*for toy gun*)
cápsula ▷ *vt* (*outdo*) superar; (*limit*)

recortar
capability [keɪpə'bɪlɪtɪ] *n* capacidad
f
capable ['keɪpəbl] *adj* capaz
capacity [kə'pæsɪtɪ] *n* capacidad *f;*
(*position*) calidad *f*
cape [keɪp] *n* capa; (*Geo*) cabo
caper ['keɪpə*] *n* (*Culin: gen pl*)
alcaparra; (*prank*) broma
capital ['kæpɪtl] *n* (*also:* **~ city**)
capital *f;* (*money*) capital *m;* (*also:*
~ letter) mayúscula; **capitalism**
n capitalismo; **capitalist** *adj, n*
capitalista *mf;* **capital punishment** *n*
pena de muerte
Capitol ['kæpɪtl] *n ver recuadro*

○ **CAPITOL**
○
○
○ El Capitolio **(Capitol)** es el edificio
○ del Congreso **(Congress)** de
○ los Estados Unidos, situado en
○ la ciudad de Washington. Por
○ extensión, también se suele llamar
○ así al edificio en el que tienen lugar
○ las sesiones parlamentarias de
○ la cámara de representantes de
○ muchos de los estados.

Capricorn ['kæprɪkɔ:n] *n*
Capricornio
capsize [kæp'saɪz] *vt* volcar, hacer
zozobrar ▷ *vi* volcarse, zozobrar
capsule ['kæpsju:l] *n* cápsula
captain ['kæptɪn] *n* capitán *m*
caption ['kæpʃən] *n* (*heading*) título;
(*to picture*) leyenda
captivity [kæp'tɪvɪtɪ] *n* cautiverio
capture ['kæptʃə*] *vt* prender,
apresar; (*animal, Comput*) capturar;
(*place*) tomar; (*attention*) captar, llamar
▷ *n* apresamiento; captura; toma;
(*data capture*) formulación *f* de datos
car [kɑ:*] *n* coche *m*, carro (*LAM*),
automóvil *m;* (*US Rail*) vagón *m*
carafe [kə'ræf] *n* jarra
caramel ['kærəməl] *n* caramelo
carat ['kærət] *n* quilate *m*

caravan ['kærəvæn] n (BRIT) caravana, rulɔ́ f; (in desert) caravana; **caravan site** (BRIT) n camping m para caravanas

carbohydrate [kɑːbəu'haɪdreɪt] n hidrato de carbono; (food) fécula

carbon ['kɑːbən] n carbono; **carbon dioxide** n dióxido de carbono, anhídrido carbónico; **carbon footprint** n huella de carbono; **carbon monoxide** n monóxido de carbono

car boot sale n mercadillo organizado en un aparcamiento, en el que se exponen las mercancías en el maletero del coche

carburettor [kɑːbju'rɛtə*] (US **carburetor**) n carburador m

card [kɑːd] n (material) cartulina; (index card etc) ficha; (playing card) carta, naipe m; (visiting card, greetings card etc) tarjeta; **cardboard** n cartón m; **card game** n juego de naipes or cartas

cardigan ['kɑːdɪgən] n rebeca

cardinal ['kɑːdɪnl] adj cardinal; (importance, principal) esencial ⊳ n cardenal m

cardphone ['kɑːdfəun] n cabina que funciona con tarjetas telefónicas

care [kɛə*] n cuidado; (worry) inquietud f; (charge) cargo, custodia ⊳ vi: **to ~ about** (person, animal) tener cariño a; (thing, idea) preocuparse por; **~ of** en casa de, al cuidado de; **in sb's ~** a cargo de algn; **to take ~ to** cuidarse de, tener cuidado de; **to take ~ of** cuidar; (problem etc) ocuparse de; **I don't ~** no me importa; **I couldn't ~ less** eso me trae sin cuidado; **care for** vt fus cuidar a; (like) querer

career [kə'rɪə*] n profesión f; (in work, school) carrera ⊳ vi (also: **~ along**) correr a toda velocidad

care: carefree adj despreocupado; **careful** adj cuidadoso; (cautious) cauteloso; **(be) careful!** ¡tenga cuidado!; **carefully** adv con cuidado; **caregiver** (US) n (professional) enfermero/a m/f; (unpaid) persona que cuida a un pariente o vecino; **careless** adj descuidado; (heedless) poco atento; **carelessness** n descuido, falta de atención; **carer** ['kɛərə*] n (professional) enfermero/a m/f; (unpaid) persona que cuida a un pariente o vecino; **caretaker** n portero/a, conserje mf

car-ferry ['kɑːfɛrɪ] n transbordador m para coches

cargo ['kɑːgəu] (pl **~es**) n cargamento, carga

car hire n alquiler m de automóviles

Caribbean [kærɪ'biːən] n: **the ~ (Sea)** el (Mar) Caribe

caring ['kɛərɪŋ] adj humanitario; (behaviour) afectuoso

carnation [kɑː'neɪʃən] n clavel m

carnival ['kɑːnɪvəl] n carnaval m; (US: funfair) parque m de atracciones

carol ['kærəl] n: **(Christmas) ~** villancico

carousel [kærə'sɛl] (US) n tiovivo, caballitos mpl

car park (BRIT) n aparcamiento, parking m

carpenter ['kɑːpɪntə*] n carpintero/a

carpet ['kɑːpɪt] n alfombra; (fitted) moqueta ⊳ vt alfombrar

car rental (US) n alquiler m de coches

carriage ['kærɪdʒ] n (BRIT Rail) vagón m; (horse-drawn) coche m; (of goods) transporte m; (: cost) porte m, flete m; **carriageway** (BRIT) n (part of road) calzada

carrier ['kærɪə*] n (transport company) transportista, empresa de transportes; (Med) portador(a) m/f; **carrier bag** (BRIT) n bolsa de papel or plástico

carrot ['kærət] n zanahoria

carry ['kærɪ] vt (person) llevar; (transport) transportar; (involve: responsibilities etc) entrañar, implicar; (Med) ser portador de ⊳ vi (sound) oírse; **to get carried away** (fig) entusiasmarse; **carry on** vi (continue) seguir (adelante), continuar ⊳ vt proseguir, continuar; **carry out** vt (*orders*) cumplir; (*investigation*) llevar a cabo, realizar

cart [kɑːt] *n* carro, carreta ▷ *vt* (*inf: transport*) acarrear

carton ['kɑːtən] *n* (*box*) caja (de cartón); (*of milk etc*) bote *m*; (*of yogurt*) tarrina

cartoon [kɑː'tuːn] *n* (*Press*) caricatura; (*comic strip*) tira cómica; (*film*) dibujos *mpl* animados

cartridge ['kɑːtrɪdʒ] *n* cartucho; (*of pen*) recambio

carve [kɑːv] *vt* (*meat*) trinchar; (*wood, stone*) cincelar, esculpir; (*initials etc*) grabar; **carving** *n* (*object*) escultura; (*design*) talla; (*art*) tallado

car wash *n* lavado de coches

case [keɪs] *n* (*container*) caja; (*Med*) caso; (*for jewels etc*) estuche *m*; (*Law*) causa, proceso; (*BRIT: also*: **suit~**) maleta; **in ~ of** en caso de; **in any ~** en todo caso; **just in ~** por si acaso

cash [kæʃ] *n* dinero en efectivo, dinero contante ▷ *vt* cobrar, hacer efectivo; **to pay (in) ~** pagar al contado; **~ on delivery** cóbrese al entregar; **cashback** *n* (*discount*) devolución *f*; (*at supermarket etc*) retirada de dinero en efectivo de un establecimiento donde se ha pagado con tarjeta; también dinero retirado; **cash card** *n* tarjeta *f* dinero; **cash desk** (*BRIT*) *n* caja; **cash dispenser** *n* cajero automático

cashew [kæ'ʃuː] *n* (*also*: **~ nut**) anacardo

cashier [kæ'ʃɪə*] *n* cajero/a

cashmere ['kæʃmɪə*] *n* cachemira

cash point *n* cajero automático

cash register *n* caja

casino [kə'siːnəu] *n* casino

casket ['kɑːskɪt] *n* cofre *m*, estuche *m*; (*US: coffin*) ataúd *m*

casserole ['kæsərəul] *n* (*food, pot*) cazuela

cassette [kæ'sɛt] *n* casete *f*; **cassette player, cassette recorder** *n* casete *m*

cast [kɑːst] (*pt, pp* **~**) *vt* (*throw*) echar, arrojar, lanzar; (*glance, eyes*) dirigir;

(*Theatre*): **to ~ sb as Othello** dar a algn el papel de Otelo ▷ *vi* (*Fishing*) lanzar ▷ *n* (*Theatre*) reparto; (*also*: **plaster ~**) vaciado; **to ~ one's vote** votar; **to ~ doubt on** suscitar dudas acerca de; **cast off** *vi* (*Naut*) desamarrar; (*Knitting*) cerrar (los puntos)

castanets [kæstə'nɛts] *npl* castañuelas *fpl*

caster sugar ['kɑːstə*-] (*BRIT*) *n* azúcar *m* extrafino

Castile [kæs'tiːl] *n* Castilla; **Castilian** *adj, n* castellano/a *m/f*

cast-iron ['kɑːstaɪən] *adj* (*lit*) (hecho) de hierro fundido; (*fig: case*) irrebatible

castle ['kɑːsl] *n* castillo; (*Chess*) torre *f*

casual ['kæʒjul] *adj* fortuito; (*irregular: work etc*) eventual, temporero; (*unconcerned*) despreocupado; (*clothes*) informal

▌ Be careful not to translate **casual** by the Spanish word *casual*.

casualty ['kæʒjultɪ] *n* víctima, herido/a; (*dead*) muerto/a; (*Med: department*) urgencias *fpl*

cat [kæt] *n* gato; (*big cat*) felino

Catalan ['kætəlæn] *adj, n* catalán/ ana *m/f*

catalogue ['kætəlɔg] (*US* **catalog**) *n* catálogo ▷ *vt* catalogar

Catalonia [kætə'ləunɪə] *n* Cataluña

catalytic converter [kætə'lɪtɪkkən'vəːtə*] *n* catalizador *m*

cataract ['kætərækt] *n* (*Med*) cataratas *fpl*

catarrh [kə'tɑː*] *n* catarro

catastrophe [kə'tæstrəfɪ] *n* catástrofe *f*

catch [kætʃ] (*pt, pp* **caught**) *vt* coger (*SP*), agarrar (*LAM*); (*arrest*) detener; (*grasp*) asir; (*breath*) contener; (*surprise: person*) sorprender; (*attract: attention*) captar; (*hear*) oír; (*Med*) contagiarse de, coger; (*also*: **~ up**) alcanzar ▷ *vi* (*fire*) encenderse; (*in branches etc*) enredarse ▷ *n* (*fish etc*) pesca; (*act of catching*) cogida; (*hidden problem*) dificultad *f*; (*game*) pilla-pilla; (of lock) pestillo, cerradura; **to ~ fire** encenderse; **to ~ sight of** divisar; **catch up** vi (fig) ponerse al día; **catching** ['kætʃɪŋ] adj (Med) contagioso

category ['kætɪgərɪ] n categoría, clase f

cater ['keɪtə*] vi: **to ~ for** (BRIT) abastecer a; (needs) atender a; (Comm: parties etc) proveer comida a

caterpillar ['kætəpɪlə*] n oruga, gusano

cathedral [kə'θiːdrəl] n catedral f

Catholic ['kæθəlɪk] adj, n (Rel) católico/a m/f

Catseye® ['kætsˈaɪ] (BRIT) n (Aut) catafoto

cattle ['kætl] npl ganado

catwalk ['kætwɔːk] n pasarela

caught [kɔːt] pt, pp of **catch**

cauliflower ['kɔlɪflauə*] n coliflor f

cause [kɔːz] n causa, motivo, razón f; (principle: also Pol) causa ▷ vt causar

caution ['kɔːʃən] n cautela, prudencia; (warning) advertencia, amonestación f ▷ vt amonestar; **cautious** adj cauteloso, prudente, precavido

cave [keɪv] n cueva, caverna; **cave in** vi (roof etc) derrumbarse, hundirse

caviar(e) ['kævɪɑː*] n caviar m

cavity ['kævɪtɪ] n hueco, cavidad f

cc abbr (= cubic centimetres) c.c.; (= carbon copy) copia hecha con papel del carbón

CCTV n abbr (= closed-circuit television) circuito cerrado de televisión

CD n abbr (= compact disc) CD m; (player) (reproductor m de) CD; **CD player** n reproductor m de CD; **CD-ROM** [siːdiːˈrɔm] n abbr CD-ROM m; **CD writer** n grabadora de CD

cease [siːs] vt, vi cesar; **ceasefire** n alto m el fuego

cedar ['siːdə*] n cedro

ceilidh ['keɪlɪ] n baile con música y danzas tradicionales escocesas o irlandesas

ceiling ['siːlɪŋ] n techo; (fig) límite m

celebrate ['selɪbreɪt] vt celebrar ▷ vi

divertirse; **celebration** [-'breɪʃən] n fiesta, celebración f

celebrity [sɪ'lɛbrɪtɪ] n celebridad f

celery ['sɛlərɪ] n apio

cell [sɛl] n celda; (Biol) célula; (Elec) elemento

cellar ['sɛlə*] n sótano; (for wine) bodega

cello ['tʃɛləu] n violoncelo

Cellophane® ['sɛləfeɪn] n celofán m

cellphone ['sɛlfəʊn] n móvil

Celsius ['sɛlsɪəs] adj centígrado

Celtic ['kɛltɪk] adj celta

cement [sə'mɛnt] n cemento

cemetery ['sɛmɪtrɪ] n cementerio

censor ['sɛnsə*] n censor m ▷ vt (cut) censurar; **censorship** n censura

census ['sɛnsəs] n censo

cent [sɛnt] n (unit of dollar) centavo, céntimo; (unit of euro) céntimo; see also **per**

centenary [sɛn'tiːnərɪ] n centenario

centennial [sɛn'tɛnɪəl] (US) n centenario

center ['sɛntə*] (US) = **centre**

centi... [sɛntɪ] prefix: **centigrade** adj centígrado; **centimetre** (US **centimeter**) n centímetro; **centipede** ['sɛntɪpiːd] n ciempiés m inv

central ['sɛntrəl] adj central; (of house etc) céntrico; **Central America** n Centroamérica; **central heating** n calefacción f central; **central reservation** n (BRIT Aut) mediana

centre ['sɛntə*] (US **center**) n centro; (fig) núcleo ▷ vt centrar; **centre-forward** n (Sport) delantero centro; **centre-half** n (Sport) medio centro

century ['sɛntjurɪ] n siglo; **20th ~** siglo veinte

CEO n abbr = **chief executive officer**

ceramic [sɪ'ræmɪk] adj cerámico

cereal ['siːrɪəl] n cereal m

ceremony ['sɛrɪmənɪ] n ceremonia; **to stand on ~** hacer ceremonias, estar de cumplido

certain ['səːtən] adj seguro;

(*person*): **a ~ Mr Smith** un tal Sr. Smith; (*particular, some*) cierto; **for ~** a ciencia cierta; **certainly** *adv* (*undoubtedly*) ciertamente; (*of course*) desde luego, por supuesto; **certainty** *n* certeza, certidumbre *f*; seguridad *f*; (*inevitability*) certeza

certificate [sə'tɪfɪkɪt] *n* certificado

certify ['sɜːtɪfaɪ] *vt* certificar; (*award diploma to*) conceder un diploma a; (*declare insane*) declarar loco

cf. *abbr* (= *compare*) cfr

CFC *n abbr* (= *chlorofluorocarbon*) CFC *m*

chain [tʃeɪn] *n* cadena; (*of mountains*) cordillera; (*of events*) sucesión *f* ▷ *vt* (*also: ~ up*) encadenar; **chain-smoke** *vi* fumar un cigarrillo tras otro

chair [tʃɛə*] *n* silla; (*armchair*) sillón *m*, butaca; (*of university*) cátedra; (*of meeting etc*) presidencia ▷ *vt* (*meeting*) presidir; **chairlift** *n* telesilla; **chairman** (*irreg*) *n* presidente *m*; **chairperson** *n* presidente/a *m/f*; **chairwoman** (*irreg*) *n* presidenta

chalet ['ʃæleɪ] *n* chalet *m* (de madera)

chalk [tʃɔːk] *n* (*Geo*) creta; (*for writing*) tiza, gis *m* (*MEX*); **chalkboard** (*US*) *n* pizarrón (*LAM*), pizarra (*SP*)

challenge ['tʃælɪndʒ] *n* desafío, reto ▷ *vt* desafiar, retar; (*statement, right*) poner en duda; **to ~ sb to do sth** retar a algn a que haga algo; **challenging** *adj* exigente; (*tone*) de desafío

chamber ['tʃeɪmbə*] *n* cámara, sala; (*Pol*) cámara; (*BRIT Law: gen pl*) despacho; **~ of commerce** cámara de comercio; **chambermaid** *n* camarera

champagne [ʃæm'peɪn] *n* champaña *m*, champán *m*

champion ['tʃæmpɪən] *n* campeón/ona *m/f*; (*of cause*) defensor(a) *m/f*; **championship** *n* campeonato

chance [tʃɑːns] *n* (*opportunity*) ocasión *f*, oportunidad *f*; (*likelihood*) posibilidad *f*; (*risk*) riesgo ▷ *vt* arriesgar, probar ▷ *adj* fortuito, casual; **to ~ it** arriesgarse, intentarlo; **to take a ~** arriesgarse; **by ~** por casualidad

chancellor ['tʃɑːnsələ*] *n* canciller *m*; **Chancellor of the Exchequer** (*BRIT*) *n* Ministro de Hacienda

chandelier [ʃændə'lɪə*] *n* araña (de luces)

change [tʃeɪndʒ] *vt* cambiar; (*replace*) cambiar, reemplazar; (*gear, clothes, job*) cambiar de; (*transform*) transformar ▷ *vi* cambiar(se); (*change trains*) hacer transbordo; (*traffic lights*) cambiar de color; (*be transformed*): **to ~ into** transformarse en ▷ *n* cambio; (*alteration*) modificación *f*; (*transformation*) transformación *f*; (*of clothes*) muda; (*coins*) suelto, sencillo; (*money returned*) vuelta; **to ~ gear** (*Aut*) cambiar de marcha; **to ~ one's mind** cambiar de opinión *or* idea; **for a ~** para variar; **change over** *vi* (*from sth to sth*) cambiar; (*players etc*) cambiar(se) ▷ *vt* cambiar; **changeable** *adj* (*weather*) cambiable; **change machine** *n* máquina de cambio; **changing room** (*BRIT*) *n* vestuario

channel ['tʃænl] *n* (*TV*) canal *m*; (*of river*) cauce *m*; (*groove*) conducto; (*fig: medium*) medio ▷ *vt* (*river etc*) encauzar; **the (English) C~** el Canal (de la Mancha); **the C~ Islands** las Islas Normandas; **Channel Tunnel** *n*: **the Channel Tunnel** el túnel del Canal de la Mancha, el Eurotúnel

chant [tʃɑːnt] *n* (*of crowd*) gritos *mpl*; (*Rel*) canto ▷ *vt* (*slogan, word*) repetir a gritos

chaos ['keɪɔs] *n* caos *m*

chaotic [keɪ'ɔtɪk] *adj* caótico

chap [tʃæp] (*BRIT: inf*) *n* (*man*) tío, tipo

chapel ['tʃæpəl] *n* capilla

chapped [tʃæpt] *adj* agrietado

chapter ['tʃæptə*] *n* capítulo

character ['kærɪktə*] *n* carácter *m*, naturaleza, índole *f*; (*moral strength, personality*) carácter; (*in novel, film*) personaje *m*; **characteristic** [-'rɪstɪk] *adj* característico ▷ *n* característica; **characterize** ['kærɪktəraɪz] *vt* caracterizar

charcoal ['tʃɑːkəʊl] n carbón m vegetal; (Art) carboncillo

charge [tʃɑːdʒ] n (Law) cargo, acusación f; (cost) precio, coste m; (responsibility) cargo ▷ vt (Law): **to ~ (with)** acusar (de); (battery) cargar; (price) pedir; (customer) cobrar ▷ vi precipitarse; (Mil) cargar, atacar; **charge card** n tarjeta de cuenta; **charger** n (also: **battery charger**) cargador m (de baterías)

charismatic [kærɪz'mætɪk] adj carismático

charity ['tʃærɪtɪ] n caridad f; (organization) sociedad f benéfica; (money, gifts) limosnas fpl; **charity shop** n (BRIT) tienda de artículos de segunda mano que dedica su recaudación a causas benéficas

charm [tʃɑːm] n encanto, atractivo; (talisman) hechizo; (on bracelet) dije m ▷ vt encantar; **charming** adj encantador(a)

chart [tʃɑːt] n (diagram) cuadro; (graph) gráfica; (map) carta de navegación ▷ vt (course) trazar; (progress) seguir; **charts** npl (Top 40): **the ~s** ≈ los 40 principales (SP)

charter ['tʃɑːtə*] vt (plane) alquilar; (ship) fletar ▷ n (document) carta; (of university, company) estatutos mpl; **chartered accountant** (BRIT) n contable m/f diplomado/a; **charter flight** n vuelo chárter

chase [tʃeɪs] vt (pursue) perseguir; (also: **~ away**) ahuyentar ▷ n persecución f

chat [tʃæt] vi (also: **have a ~**) charlar; (on Internet) chatear ▷ n charla; **chat up** vt (inf: girl) ligar con, enrollarse con; **chat room** n (Internet) chat m, canal m de charla; **chat show** (BRIT) n programa m de entrevistas

chatter ['tʃætə*] vi (person) charlar; (teeth) castañetear ▷ n (of birds) parloteo; (of people) charla, cháchara

chauffeur ['ʃəʊfə*] n chófer m

chauvinist ['ʃəʊvɪnɪst] n (male chauvinist) machista m; (nationalist) chovinista mf

cheap [tʃiːp] adj barato; (joke) de mal gusto; (poor quality) de mala calidad ▷ adv barato; **cheap day return** n billete de ida y vuelta el mismo día; **cheaply** adv barato, a bajo precio

cheat [tʃiːt] vi hacer trampa ▷ vt: **to ~ sb (out of sth)** estafar (algo) a algn ▷ n (person) tramposo/a; **cheat on** vt fus engañar

Chechnya [tʃɪtʃ'njɑː] n Chechenia

check [tʃek] vt (examine) controlar; (facts) comprobar; (halt) parar, detener; (restrain) refrenar, restringir ▷ n (inspection) control m, inspección f; (curb) freno; (us: bill) nota, cuenta; (us) = **cheque**; (pattern: gen pl) cuadro; **check in** vi (at hotel) firmar el registro; (at airport) facturar el equipaje ▷ vt (luggage) facturar; **check off** vt (esp us: check) comprobar; (cross off) tachar; **check out** vi (of hotel) marcharse; **check up** vi: **to check up on sth** comprobar algo; **to check up on sb** investigar a algn; **checkbook** (US) = **chequebook**; **checked** adj a cuadros; **checkers** (US) n juego de damas; **check-in** n (also: **check-in desk**: at airport) mostrador m de facturación; **checking account** (US) n cuenta corriente; **checklist** n lista (de control); **checkmate** n jaque m mate; **checkout** n caja; **checkpoint** n (punto de) control m; **checkroom** (US) n consigna; **checkup** n (Med) reconocimiento general

cheddar ['tʃedə*] n (also: **~ cheese**) queso m cheddar

cheek [tʃiːk] n mejilla; (impudence) descaro; **what a ~!** ¡qué cara!; **cheekbone** n pómulo; **cheeky** adj fresco, descarado

cheer [tʃɪə*] vt vitorear, aplaudir; (gladden) alegrar, animar ▷ vi dar vivas ▷ n viva m; **cheer up** vi animarse ▷ vt alegrar, animar; **cheerful** adj alegre

cheerio [tʃɪərɪ'əʊ] (BRIT) excl ¡hasta luego!
cheerleader ['tʃɪəliːdə*] n animador(a) m/f
cheese [tʃiːz] n queso; **cheeseburger** n hamburguesa con queso; **cheesecake** n pastel m de queso
chef [ʃɛf] n jefe/a m/f de cocina
chemical ['kɛmɪkəl] adj químico ▷ n producto químico
chemist ['kɛmɪst] n (BRIT: pharmacist) farmacéutico/a; (scientist) químico/a; **chemistry** n química; **chemist's (shop)** (BRIT) n farmacia
cheque [tʃɛk] (US **check**) n cheque m; **chequebook** n talonario de cheques (SP), chequera (LAM); **cheque card** n tarjeta de cheque
cherry ['tʃɛrɪ] n cereza; (also: **~ tree**) cerezo
chess [tʃɛs] n ajedrez m
chest [tʃɛst] n (Anat) pecho; (box) cofre m, cajón m
chestnut ['tʃɛsnʌt] n castaña; (also: **~ tree**) castaño
chest of drawers n cómoda
chew [tʃuː] vt mascar, masticar; **chewing gum** n chicle m
chic [ʃiːk] adj elegante
chick [tʃɪk] n pollito, polluelo; (inf: girl) chica
chicken ['tʃɪkɪn] n gallina, pollo; (food) pollo; (inf: coward) gallina mf; **chicken out** (inf) vi rajarse; **chickenpox** n varicela
chickpea ['tʃɪkpiː] n garbanzo
chief [tʃiːf] n jefe/a m/f ▷ adj principal; **chief executive (officer)** n director(a) m/f general; **chiefly** adv principalmente
child [tʃaɪld] (pl **~ren**) n niño/a; (offspring) hijo/a; **child abuse** n (with violence) malos tratos mpl a niños; (sexual) abuso m sexual de niños; **child benefit** n (BRIT) subsidio por cada hijo pequeño; **childbirth** n parto; **child-care** n cuidado de los niños; **childhood** n niñez f, infancia; **childish**

adj pueril, aniñado; **child minder** (BRIT) n madre f de día; **children** ['tʃɪldrən] npl of **child**
Chile ['tʃɪlɪ] n Chile m; **Chilean** adj, n chileno/a m/f
chill [tʃɪl] n frío; (Med) resfriado ▷ vt enfriar; (Culin) congelar; **chill out** vi (esp US: inf) tranquilizarse
chil(l)i ['tʃɪlɪ] (BRIT) n chile m, ají m (SC)
chilly ['tʃɪlɪ] adj frío
chimney ['tʃɪmnɪ] n chimenea
chimpanzee [tʃɪmpæn'ziː] n chimpancé m
chin [tʃɪn] n mentón m, barbilla
China ['tʃaɪnə] n China
china ['tʃaɪnə] n porcelana; (crockery) loza
Chinese [tʃaɪ'niːz] adj chino ▷ n inv chino/a m/f; (Ling) chino
chip [tʃɪp] n (gen pl: Culin: BRIT) patata (SP) or papa (LAM) frita; (: US: also: **potato ~**) patata or papa frita; (of wood) astilla; (of glass, stone) lasca; (at poker) ficha; (Comput) chip m ▷ vt (cup, plate) desconchar; **chip shop** n pescadería (donde se vende principalmente pescado rebozado y patatas fritas)
chiropodist [kɪ'rɔpədɪst] (BRIT) n pedicuro/a, callista m/f
chisel ['tʃɪzl] n (for wood) escoplo; (for stone) cincel m
chives [tʃaɪvz] npl cebollinos mpl
chlorine ['klɔːriːn] n cloro
choc-ice ['tʃɒkaɪs] n (BRIT) helado m cubierto de chocolate
chocolate ['tʃɒklɪt] n chocolate m; (sweet) bombón m
choice [tʃɔɪs] n elección f, selección f; (option) opción f; (preference) preferencia ▷ adj escogido
choir ['kwaɪə*] n coro
choke [tʃəʊk] vi ahogarse; (on food) atragantarse ▷ vt estrangular, ahogar; (block): **to be ~d with** estar atascado de ▷ n (Aut) estárter m
cholesterol [kə'lɛstərɒl] n colesterol m
choose [tʃuːz] (pt **chose**, pp **chosen**)

vt escoger, elegir; (*team*) seleccionar; **to ~ to do sth** optar por hacer algo

chop [tʃɔp] *vt* (*wood*) cortar, tajar; (*Culin: also:* **~ up**) picar ▷ *n* (*Culin*) chuleta; **chop down** *vt* (*tree*) talar; **chop off** *vt* cortar (de un tajo); **chopsticks** ['tʃɔpstɪks] *npl* palillos *mpl*

chord [kɔ:d] *n* (*Mus*) acorde *m*

chore [tʃɔ:*] *n* faena, tarea; (*routine task*) trabajo rutinario

chorus ['kɔ:rəs] *n* coro; (*repeated part of song*) estribillo

chose [tʃəuz] *pt of* **choose**

chosen ['tʃəuzn] *pp of* **choose**

Christ [kraɪst] *n* Cristo

christen ['krɪsn] *vt* bautizar; **christening** *n* bautizo

Christian ['krɪstɪən] *adj*, *n* cristiano/a *m/f*; **Christianity** [-'ænɪtɪ] *n* cristianismo; **Christian name** *n* nombre *m* de pila

Christmas ['krɪsməs] *n* Navidad *f*; **Merry ~!** ¡Felices Pascuas!; **Christmas card** *n* crismas *m inv*, tarjeta de Navidad; **Christmas carol** *n* villancico *m*; **Christmas Day** *n* día *m* de Navidad; **Christmas Eve** *n* Nochebuena; **Christmas pudding** *n* (*esp BRIT*) pudin *m* de Navidad; **Christmas tree** *n* árbol *m* de Navidad

chrome [krəum] *n* cromo

chronic ['krɔnɪk] *adj* crónico

chrysanthemum [krɪ'sænθəməm] *n* crisantemo

chubby ['tʃʌbɪ] *adj* regordete

chuck [tʃʌk] (*inf*) *vt* lanzar, arrojar; (*BRIT: also:* **~ up**) abandonar; **chuck out** *vt* (*person*) echar (fuera); (*rubbish etc*) tirar

chuckle ['tʃʌkl] *vi* reírse entre dientes

chum [tʃʌm] *n* compañero/a

chunk [tʃʌŋk] *n* pedazo, trozo

church [tʃə:tʃ] *n* iglesia; **churchyard** *n* cementerio

churn [tʃə:n] *n* (*for butter*) mantequera; (*for milk*) lechera

chute [ʃu:t] *n* (*also:* **rubbish ~**) vertedero; (*for coal etc*) rampa de caída

chutney ['tʃʌtnɪ] *n* condimento a base de frutas de la India

CIA (*us*) *n abbr* (= *Central Intelligence Agency*) CIA *f*

CID (*BRIT*) *n abbr* (= *Criminal Investigation Department*) ≈ B.I.C. *f* (*SP*)

cider ['saɪdə*] *n* sidra

cigar [sɪ'gɑ:*] *n* puro

cigarette [sɪgə'rɛt] *n* cigarrillo; **cigarette lighter** *n* mechero

cinema ['sɪnəmə] *n* cine *m*

cinnamon ['sɪnəmən] *n* canela

circle ['sə:kl] *n* círculo; (*in theatre*) anfiteatro ▷ *vi* dar vueltas ▷ *vt* (*surround*) rodear, cercar; (*move round*) dar la vuelta a

circuit ['sə:kɪt] *n* circuito; (*tour*) gira; (*track*) pista; (*lap*) vuelta

circular ['sə:kjulə*] *adj* circular ▷ *n* circular *f*

circulate ['sə:kjuleɪt] *vi* circular; (*person: at party etc*) hablar con los invitados ▷ *vt* poner en circulación; **circulation** [-'leɪʃən] *n* circulación *f*; (*of newspaper*) tirada

circumstances ['sə:kəmstənsɪz] *npl* circunstancias *fpl*; (*financial condition*) situación *f* económica

circus ['sə:kəs] *n* circo

cite [saɪt] *vt* citar

citizen ['sɪtɪzn] *n* (*Pol*) ciudadano/a; (*of city*) vecino/a, habitante *mf*; **citizenship** *n* ciudadanía; (*BRIT: Scol*) civismo

citrus fruits ['sɪtrəs-] *npl* agrios *mpl*

city ['sɪtɪ] *n* ciudad *f*; **the C~** *centro financiero de Londres*; **city centre** (*BRIT*) *n* centro de la ciudad; **city technology college** *n* centro de formación profesional (*centro de enseñanza secundaria que da especial importancia a la ciencia y tecnología*.)

civic ['sɪvɪk] *adj* cívico; (*authorities*) municipal

civil ['sɪvɪl] *adj* civil; (*polite*) atento, cortés; **civilian** [sɪ'vɪlɪən] *adj* civil (*no militar*) ▷ *n* civil *mf*, paisano/a

civilization [sɪvɪlaɪˈzeɪʃən] n civilización f

civilized [ˈsɪvɪlaɪzd] adj civilizado

civil: civil law n derecho civil; **civil rights** npl derechos mpl civiles; **civil servant** n funcionario/a del Estado; **Civil Service** n administración f pública; **civil war** n guerra civil

CJD n abbr (= Creutzfeldt-Jakob disease) enfermedad de Creutzfeldt-Jakob

claim [kleɪm] vt exigir, reclamar; (rights etc) reivindicar; (assert) pretender ▷ vi (for insurance) reclamar ▷ n reclamación f; pretensión f; **claim form** n solicitud f

clam [klæm] n almeja

clamp [klæmp] n abrazadera, grapa ▷ vt (two things together) cerrar fuertemente; (one thing on another) afianzar (con abrazadera); (Aut: wheel) poner el cepo a

clan [klæn] n clan m

clap [klæp] vi aplaudir

claret [ˈklærət] n burdeos m inv

clarify [ˈklærɪfaɪ] vt aclarar

clarinet [klærɪˈnɛt] n clarinete m

clarity [ˈklærɪtɪ] n claridad f

clash [klæʃ] n enfrentamiento; choque m; desacuerdo; estruendo ▷ vi (fight) enfrentarse; (beliefs) chocar; (disagree) estar en desacuerdo; (colours) desentonar; (two events) coincidir

clasp [klɑːsp] n (hold) apretón m; (of necklace, bag) cierre m ▷ vt apretar; abrazar

class [klɑːs] n clase f ▷ vt clasificar

classic [ˈklæsɪk] adj, n clásico; **classical** adj clásico

classification [klæsɪfɪˈkeɪʃən] n clasificación f

classify [ˈklæsɪfaɪ] vt clasificar

classmate [ˈklɑːsmeɪt] n compañero/a de clase

classroom [ˈklɑːsrum] n aula; **classroom assistant** n profesor(a) m/f de apoyo

classy [ˈklɑːsɪ] adj (inf) elegante, con estilo

clatter [ˈklætə*] n estrépito ▷ vi hacer ruido or estrépito

clause [klɔːz] n cláusula; (Ling) oración f

claustrophobic [klɔːstrəˈfəubɪk] adj claustrofóbico; **I feel ~** me entra claustrofobia

claw [klɔː] n (of cat) uña; (of bird of prey) garra; (of lobster) pinza

clay [kleɪ] n arcilla

clean [kliːn] adj limpio; (record, reputation) bueno, intachable; (joke) decente ▷ vt limpiar; (hands etc) lavar; **clean up** vt limpiar, asear; **cleaner** n (person) asistenta; (substance) producto para la limpieza; **cleaner's** n tintorería; **cleaning** n limpieza

cleanser [ˈklɛnzə*] n (for face) crema limpiadora

clear [klɪə*] adj claro; (road, way) libre; (conscience) limpio, tranquilo; (skin) terso; (sky) despejado ▷ vt (space) despejar, limpiar; (Law: suspect) absolver; (obstacle) salvar, saltar por encima de; (cheque) aceptar ▷ vi (fog etc) despejarse ▷ adv: **~ of** a distancia de; **to ~ the table** recoger or levantar la mesa; **clear away** vt (things, clothes etc) quitar (de en medio); (dishes) retirar; **clear up** vt limpiar; (mystery) aclarar, resolver; **clearance** n (removal) despeje m; (permission) acreditación f; **clear-cut** adj bien definido, nítido; **clearing** n (in wood) claro; **clearly** adv claramente; (evidently) sin duda; **clearway** (BRIT) n carretera donde no se puede parar

clench [klɛntʃ] vt apretar, cerrar

clergy [ˈklɜːdʒɪ] n clero

clerk [klɑːk, (US) klɜːrk] n (BRIT) oficinista mf; (US) dependiente/a m/f

clever [ˈklɛvə*] adj (intelligent) inteligente, listo; (skilful) hábil; (device, arrangement) ingenioso

cliché [ˈkliːʃeɪ] n cliché m, frase f hecha

click [klɪk] vt (tongue) chasquear; (heels) taconear ▷ vi (Comput) hacer clic; **to ~ on an icon** hacer clic en un icono

client ['klaɪənt] *n* cliente *m/f*

cliff [klɪf] *n* acantilado

climate ['klaɪmɪt] *n* clima *m*; **climate change** *n* cambio climático

climax ['klaɪmæks] *n* (*of battle, career*) apogeo; (*of film, book*) punto culminante; (*sexual*) orgasmo

climb [klaɪm] *vt* subir; (*plant*) trepar; (*move with effort*): **to ~ over a wall/into a car** trepar a una tapia/subir a un coche ▷ *vt* (*stairs*) subir; (*tree*) trepar a; (*mountain*) escalar ▷ *n* subida; **climb down** *vi* (*fig*) volverse atrás; **climber** *n* alpinista *mf* (*SP, MEX*), andinista *mf* (*LAM*); **climbing** *n* alpinismo (*SP, MEX*), andinismo (*LAM*)

clinch [klɪntʃ] *vt* (*deal*) cerrar; (*argument*) remachar

cling [klɪŋ] (*pt, pp* **clung**) *vi*: **to ~ to** agarrarse a; (*clothes*) pegarse a

Clingfilm® ['klɪŋfɪlm] *n* plástico adherente

clinic ['klɪnɪk] *n* clínica

clip [klɪp] *n* (*for hair*) horquilla; (*also:* **paper ~**) sujetapapeles *m inv*, clip *m*; (*TV, Cinema*) fragmento ▷ *vt* (*cut*) cortar; (*also:* **~ together**) unir; **clipping** *n* (*newspaper*) recorte *m*

cloak [kləuk] *n* capa, manto ▷ *vt* (*fig*) encubrir, disimular; **cloakroom** *n* guardarropa; (*BRIT: WC*) lavabo (*SP*), aseos *mpl* (*SP*), baño (*LAM*)

clock [klɔk] *n* reloj *m*; **clock in** *or* **on** *vi* (*with card*) fichar, picar; (*start work*) entrar a trabajar; **clock off** *or* **out** *vi* (*with card*) fichar *or* picar la salida; (*leave work*) salir del trabajar; **clockwise** *adv* en el sentido de las agujas del reloj; **clockwork** *n* aparato de relojería ▷ *adj* (*toy*) de cuerda

clog [klɔg] *n* zueco, chanclo ▷ *vt* atascar ▷ *vi* (*also:* **~ up**) atascarse

clone [kləun] *n* clon *m* ▷ *vt* clonar

close¹ [kləus] *adj* (*near*): **~ (to)** cerca (de); (*friend*) íntimo; (*connection*) estrecho; (*examination*) detallado, minucioso; (*weather*) bochornoso ▷ *adv* cerca; **~ by**, **~ at hand** muy cerca; **to have a ~ shave** (*fig*) escaparse por un pelo

close² [kləuz] *vt* (*shut*) cerrar; (*end*) concluir, terminar ▷ *vi* (*shop etc*) cerrarse; (*end*) concluirse, terminarse ▷ *n* (*end*) fin *m*, final *m*, conclusión *f*; **close down** *vi* cerrarse definitivamente; **closed** *adj* (*shop etc*) cerrado

closely ['kləuslɪ] *adv* (*study*) con detalle; (*watch*) de cerca; (*resemble*) estrechamente

closet ['klɔzɪt] *n* armario

close-up ['kləusʌp] *n* primer plano

closing time *n* hora de cierre

closure ['kləuʒə*] *n* cierre *m*

clot [klɔt] *n* (*gen*) coágulo; (*inf: idiot*) imbécil *m/f* ▷ *vi* (*blood*) coagularse

cloth [klɔθ] *n* (*material*) tela, paño; (*rag*) trapo

clothes [kləuðz] *npl* ropa; **clothes line** *n* cuerda (para tender la ropa); **clothes peg** (*US* **clothes pin**) *n* pinza

clothing ['kləuðɪŋ] *n* = **clothes**

cloud [klaud] *n* nube *f*; **cloud over** *vi* (*also fig*) nublarse; **cloudy** *adj* nublado, nubloso; (*liquid*) turbio

clove [kləuv] *n* clavo; **~ of garlic** diente *m* de ajo

clown [klaun] *n* payaso ▷ *vi* (*also:* **~ about**, **~ around**) hacer el payaso

club [klʌb] *n* (*society*) club *m*; (*weapon*) porra, cachiporra; (*also:* **golf ~**) palo ▷ *vt* aporrear ▷ *vi*: **to ~ together** (*for gift*) comprar entre todos; **clubs** *npl* (*Cards*) tréboles *mpl*; **club class** *n* (*Aviat*) clase *f* preferente

clue [klu:] *n* pista; (*in crosswords*) indicación *f*; **I haven't a ~** no tengo ni idea

clump [klʌmp] *n* (*of trees*) grupo

clumsy ['klʌmzɪ] *adj* (*person*) torpe, desmañado; (*tool*) difícil de manejar; (*movement*) desgarbado

clung [klʌŋ] *pt, pp of* **cling**

cluster ['klʌstə*] *n* grupo ▷ *vi*

agruparse, apiñarse

clutch [klʌtʃ] n (Aut) embrague m; (grasp): **~es** garras fpl ▷ vt asir; agarrar

cm abbr (= centimetre) cm

Co. abbr (= county; company)

c/o abbr (= care of) c/a, a/c

coach [kəutʃ] n autocar m (SP), coche m de línea; (horse-drawn) coche m; (of train) vagón m, coche m; (Sport) entrenador(a) m/f, instructor(a) m/f; (tutor) profesor(a) m/f particular ▷ vt (Sport) entrenar; (student) preparar, enseñar; **coach station** n (BRIT) estación f de autobuses etc; **coach trip** n excursión f en autocar

coal [kəul] n carbón m

coalition [kəuə'lɪʃən] n coalición f

coarse [kɔːs] adj basto, burdo; (vulgar) grosero, ordinario

coast [kəust] n costa, litoral m ▷ vi (Aut) ir en punto muerto; **coastal** adj costero, costanero; **coastguard** n guardacostas m inv; **coastline** n litoral m

coat [kəut] n abrigo; (of animal) pelaje m, lana; (of paint) mano f, capa ▷ vt cubrir, revestir; **coat hanger** n percha (SP), gancho (LAM); **coating** n capa, baño

coax [kəuks] vt engatusar

cob [kɔb] n see **corn**

cobbled ['kɔbld] adj: **~ street** calle f empedrada, calle f adoquinada

cobweb ['kɔbwɛb] n telaraña

cocaine [kə'keɪn] n cocaína

cock [kɔk] n (rooster) gallo; (male bird) macho ▷ vt (gun) amartillar; **cockerel** n gallito

cockney ['kɔknɪ] n habitante de ciertos barrios de Londres

cockpit ['kɔkpɪt] n cabina

cockroach ['kɔkrəutʃ] n cucaracha

cocktail ['kɔkteɪl] n coctel m, cóctel m

cocoa ['kəukəu] n cacao; (drink) chocolate m

coconut ['kəukənʌt] n coco

cod [kɔd] n bacalao

C.O.D. abbr (= cash on delivery) C.A.E.

code [kəud] n código; (cipher) clave f; (dialling code) prefijo; (post code) código postal

coeducational [kəuɛdju'keɪʃənl] adj mixto

coffee ['kɔfɪ] n café m; **coffee bar** (BRIT) n cafetería; **coffee bean** n grano de café; **coffee break** n descanso (para tomar café); **coffee maker** n máquina de hacer café, cafetera; **coffeepot** n cafetera; **coffee shop** n café m; **coffee table** n mesita (para servir el café)

coffin ['kɔfɪn] n ataúd m

cog [kɔg] n (wheel) rueda dentada; (tooth) diente m

cognac ['kɔnjæk] n coñac m

coherent [kəu'hɪərənt] adj coherente

coil [kɔɪl] n rollo; (Elec) bobina, carrete m; (contraceptive) espiral f ▷ vt enrollar

coin [kɔɪn] n moneda ▷ vt (word) inventar, idear

coincide [kəuɪn'saɪd] vi coincidir; (agree) estar de acuerdo; **coincidence** [kəu'ɪnsɪdəns] n casualidad f

Coke® [kəuk] n Coca-Cola®

coke [kəuk] n (coal) coque m

colander ['kɔləndə*] n colador m, escurridor m

cold [kəuld] adj frío ▷ n frío; (Med) resfriado; **it's ~** hace frío; **to be ~** (person) tener frío; **to catch (a) ~** resfriarse; **in ~ blood** a sangre fría; **cold sore** n herpes mpl or fpl

coleslaw ['kəulslɔː] n especie de ensalada de col

colic ['kɔlɪk] n cólico

collaborate [kə'læbəreɪt] vi colaborar

collapse [kə'læps] vi hundirse, derrumbarse; (Med) sufrir un colapso ▷ n hundimiento, derrumbamiento; (Med) colapso

collar ['kɔlə*] n (of coat, shirt) cuello; (of dog etc) collar; **collarbone** n clavícula

colleague [ˈkɔliːg] n colega mf; (at work) compañero/a
collect [kəˈlɛkt] vt (litter, mail etc) recoger; (as a hobby) coleccionar; (BRIT: call and pick up) recoger; (debts, subscriptions etc) recaudar ▷ vi reunirse; (dust) acumularse; **to call ~** (US Tel) llamar a cobro revertido; **collection** [kəˈlɛkʃən] n colección f; (of mail, for charity) recogida; **collective** [kəˈlɛktɪv] adj colectivo; **collector** n coleccionista mf
college [ˈkɔlɪdʒ] n colegio mayor; (of agriculture, technology) escuela universitaria
collide [kəˈlaɪd] vi chocar
collision [kəˈlɪʒən] n choque m
cologne [kəˈləʊn] n (also: **eau de ~**) (agua de) colonia
Colombia [kəˈlɔmbɪə] n Colombia; **Colombian** adj, n colombiano/a
colon [ˈkəʊlən] n (sign) dos puntos; (Med) colon m
colonel [ˈkɜːnl] n coronel m
colonial [kəˈləʊnɪəl] adj colonial
colony [ˈkɔlənɪ] n colonia
colour etc [ˈkʌlə*] (US **color** etc) n color m ▷ vt color(e)ar; (dye) teñir; (fig: account) adornar; (: judgement) distorsionar ▷ vi (blush) sonrojarse; **colour in** vt colorear; **colour-blind** adj daltónico; **coloured** adj de color; (photo) en color; **colour film** n película en color; **colourful** adj lleno de color; (story) fantástico; (person) excéntrico; **colouring** n (complexion) tez f; (in food) colorante m; **colour television** n televisión f en color
column [ˈkɔləm] n columna
coma [ˈkəʊmə] n coma m
comb [kəʊm] n peine m; (ornamental) peineta ▷ vt (hair) peinar; (area) registrar a fondo
combat [ˈkɔmbæt] n combate m ▷ vt combatir
combination [kɔmbɪˈneɪʃən] n combinación f
combine [vb kəmˈbaɪn, n ˈkɔmbaɪn]

vt combinar; (qualities) reunir ▷ vi combinarse ▷ n (Econ) cartel m

come [kʌm] (pt **came**, pp **come**) vi
1 (movement towards) venir; **to come running** venir corriendo
2 (arrive) llegar; **he's come here to work** ha venido aquí para trabajar; **to come home** volver a casa
3 (reach): **to come to** llegar a; **the bill came to £40** la cuenta ascendía a cuarenta libras
4 (occur): **an idea came to me** se me ocurrió una idea
5 (be, become): **to come loose/undone** etc aflojarse/desabrocharse/desatarse etc; **I've come to like him** por fin ha llegado a gustarme
come across vt fus (person) topar con; (thing) dar con
come along vi (BRIT: progress) ir
come back vi (return) volver
come down vi (price) bajar; (tree, building) ser derribado
come from vt fus (place, source) ser de
come in vi (visitor) entrar; (train, report) llegar; (fashion) ponerse de moda; (on deal etc) entrar
come off vi (button) soltarse, desprenderse; (attempt) salir bien
come on vi (pupil) progresar; (work, project) desarrollarse; (lights) encenderse; (electricity) volver; **come on!** ¡vamos!
come out vi (fact) salir a la luz; (book, sun) salir; (stain) quitarse
come round vi (after faint, operation) volver en sí
come to vi (wake) volver en sí
come up vi (sun) salir; (problem) surgir; (event) aproximarse; (in conversation) mencionarse
come up with vt fus (idea) sugerir; (money) conseguir

comeback [ˈkʌmbæk] n: **to make a ~**

(*Theatre*) volver a las tablas
comedian [kə'miːdɪən] *n* humorista *mf*
comedy ['kɒmɪdɪ] *n* comedia; (*humour*) comicidad *f*
comet ['kɒmɪt] *n* cometa *m*
comfort ['kʌmfət] *n* bienestar *m*; (*relief*) alivio ▷ *vt* consolar; **comfortable** *adj* cómodo; (*financially*) acomodado; (*easy*) fácil; **comfort station** (*US*) *n* servicios *mpl*
comic ['kɒmɪk] *adj* (*also*: **~al**) cómico ▷ *n* (*comedian*) cómico; (*BRIT: for children*) tebeo; (*BRIT: for adults*) comic *m*; **comic book** (*US*) *n* libro *m* de cómics; **comic strip** *n* tira cómica
comma ['kɒmə] *n* coma
command [kə'mɑːnd] *n* orden *f*, mandato; (*Mil: authority*) mando; (*mastery*) dominio ▷ *vt* (*troops*) mandar; (*give orders to*): **to ~ sb to do** mandar or ordenar a algn hacer; **commander** *n* (*Mil*) comandante *mf*, jefe/a *m/f*
commemorate [kə'mɛmərɛit] *vt* conmemorar
commence [kə'mɛns] *vt, vi* comenzar, empezar; **commencement** (*US*) *n* (*Univ*) (ceremonia de) graduación *f*
commend [kə'mɛnd] *vt* elogiar, alabar; (*recommend*) recomendar
comment ['kɒmɛnt] *n* comentario ▷ *vi*: **to ~ on** hacer comentarios sobre; **"no ~"** (*written*) "sin comentarios"; (*spoken*) "no tengo nada que decir"; **commentary** ['kɒməntərɪ] *n* comentario; **commentator** ['kɒmənteɪtə*] *n* comentarista *mf*
commerce ['kɒməːs] *n* comercio
commercial [kə'məːʃəl] *adj* comercial ▷ *n* (*TV, Radio*) anuncio; **commercial break** *n* intermedio para publicidad
commission [kə'mɪʃən] *n* (*committee, fee*) comisión *f* ▷ *vt* (*work of art*) encargar; **out of ~** fuera de servicio; **commissioner** *n* (*Police*)

comisario de policía
commit [kə'mɪt] *vt* (*act*) cometer; (*resources*) dedicar; (*to sb's care*) entregar; **to ~ o.s. (to do)** comprometerse (a hacer); **to ~ suicide** suicidarse; **commitment** *n* compromiso; (*to ideology etc*) entrega
committee [kə'mɪtɪ] *n* comité *m*
commodity [kə'mɒdɪtɪ] *n* mercancía
common ['kɒmən] *adj* común; (*pej*) ordinario ▷ *n* campo común; **commonly** *adv* comúnmente; **commonplace** *adj* de lo más común; **Commons** (*BRIT*) *npl* (*Pol*): **the Commons** (la Cámara de) los Comunes; **common sense** *n* sentido común; **Commonwealth** *n*: **the Commonwealth** la Commonwealth
communal ['kɒmjuːnl] *adj* (*property*) comunal; (*kitchen*) común
commune [*n* 'kɒmjuːn, *vb* kə'mjuːn] *n* (*group*) comuna ▷ *vi*: **to ~ with** comulgar or conversar con
communicate [kə'mjuːnɪkeɪt] *vt* comunicar ▷ *vi*: **to ~ (with)** comunicarse (con); (*in writing*) estar en contacto (con)
communication [kəmjuːnɪ'keɪʃən] *n* comunicación *f*
communion [kə'mjuːnɪən] *n* (*also*: **Holy ~**) comunión *f*
communism ['kɒmjunɪzəm] *n* comunismo; **communist** *adj, n* comunista *mf*
community [kə'mjuːnɪtɪ] *n* comunidad *f*; (*large group*) colectividad *f*; **community centre** (*US* **community center**) *n* centro social; **community service** *n* trabajo *m* comunitario (*prestado en lugar de cumplir una pena de prisión*)
commute [kə'mjuːt] *vi* viajar a diario de la casa al trabajo ▷ *vt* conmutar; **commuter** *n* persona que viaja a diario de la casa al trabajo
compact [*adj* kəm'pækt, *n* 'kɒmpækt] *adj* compacto ▷ *n* (*also*: **powder ~**)

polvera; **compact disc** n compact disc m; **compact disc player** n reproductor m de disco compacto, compact disc m

companion [kəm'pænɪən] n compañero/a

company ['kʌmpənɪ] n compañía; (Comm) sociedad f, compañía; **to keep sb ~** acompañar a algn; **company car** n coche m de la empresa; **company director** n director(a) m/f de empresa

comparable ['kɔmpərəbl] adj comparable

comparative [kəm'pærətɪv] adj relativo; (study) comparativo; **comparatively** adv (relatively) relativamente

compare [kəm'pɛə*] vt: **to ~ sth/sb with** or **to** comparar algo/a algn con ▷ vi: **to ~ (with)** compararse (con); **comparison** [-'pærɪsn] n comparación f

compartment [kəm'pɑːtmənt] n (also: Rail) compartim(i)ento

compass ['kʌmpəs] n brújula; **compasses** npl (Math) compás m

compassion [kəm'pæʃən] n compasión f

compatible [kəm'pætɪbl] adj compatible

compel [kəm'pɛl] vt obligar; **compelling** adj (fig: argument) convincente

compensate ['kɔmpənseɪt] vt compensar ▷ vi: **to ~ for** compensar; **compensation** [-'seɪʃən] n (for loss) indemnización f

compete [kəm'piːt] vi (take part) tomar parte, concurrir; (vie with): **to ~ with** competir con, hacer competencia a

competent ['kɔmpɪtənt] adj competente, capaz

competition [kɔmpɪ'tɪʃən] n (contest) concurso; (rivalry) competencia

competitive [kəm'pɛtɪtɪv] adj (Econ, Sport) competitivo

competitor [kəm'pɛtɪtə*] n (rival) competidor(a) m/f; (participant) concursante mf

complacent [kəm'pleɪsənt] adj autocomplaciente

complain [kəm'pleɪn] vi quejarse; (Comm) reclamar; **complaint** n queja; reclamación f; (Med) enfermedad f

complement [n 'kɔmplɪmənt, vb 'kɔmplɪment] n complemento; (esp of ship's crew) dotación f ▷ vt (enhance) complementar; **complementary** [kɔmplɪ'mentərɪ] adj complementario

complete [kəm'pliːt] adj (full) completo; (finished) acabado ▷ vt (fulfil) completar; (finish) acabar; (a form) llenar; **completely** adv completamente; **completion** [-'pliːʃən] n terminación f; (of contract) realización f

complex ['kɔmplɛks] adj, n complejo

complexion [kəm'plɛkʃən] n (of face) tez f, cutis m

compliance [kəm'plaɪəns] n (submission) sumisión f; (agreement) conformidad f; **in ~ with** de acuerdo con

complicate ['kɔmplɪkeɪt] vt complicar; **complicated** adj complicado; **complication** [-'keɪʃən] n complicación f

compliment [n 'kɔmplɪmənt] n (formal) cumplido ▷ vt felicitar; **complimentary** [-'mentərɪ] adj lisonjero; (free) de favor

comply [kəm'plaɪ] vi: **to ~ with** cumplir con

component [kəm'pəunənt] adj componente ▷ n (Tech) pieza

compose [kəm'pəuz] vt: **to be ~d of** componerse de; (music etc) componer; **to ~ o.s.** tranquilizarse; **composer** n (Mus) compositor(a) m/f; **composition** [kɔmpə'zɪʃən] n composición f

composure [kəm'pəuʒə*] n serenidad f, calma

compound ['kɔmpaund] n (Chem)

compuesto; (*Ling*) palabra compuesta; (*enclosure*) recinto ▷ *adj* compuesto; (*fracture*) complicado

comprehension [-'hɛnʃən] *n* comprensión *f*

comprehensive [kɔmprɪ'hɛnsɪv] *adj* exhaustivo; (*Insurance*) contra todo riesgo; **comprehensive (school)** *n* centro estatal de enseñanza secundaria ≈ Instituto Nacional de Bachillerato (SP)

compress [*vb* kəm'prɛs, *n* 'kɔmprɛs] *vt* comprimir; (*information*) condensar ▷ *n* (*Med*) compresa

comprise [kəm'praɪz] *vt* (*also*: **be ~ of**) comprender, constar de; (*constitute*) constituir

compromise ['kɔmprəmaɪz] *n* (*agreement*) arreglo ▷ *vt* comprometer ▷ *vi* transigir

compulsive [kəm'pʌlsɪv] *adj* compulsivo; (*viewing, reading*) obligado

compulsory [kəm'pʌlsərɪ] *adj* obligatorio

computer [kəm'pjuːtə*] *n* ordenador *m*, computador *m*, computadora *f*; **computer game** *n* juego para ordenador; **computer-generated** *adj* realizado por ordenador, creado por ordenador; **computerize** *vt* (*data*) computerizar; (*system*) informatizar; **we're computerized now** ya nos hemos informatizado; **computer programmer** *n* programador(a) *m/f*; **computer programming** *n* programación *f*; **computer science** *n* informática; **computer studies** *npl* informática *fsg*, computación *fsg* (LAM); **computing** [kəm'pjuːtɪŋ] *n* (*activity, science*) informática

con [kɔn] *vt* (*deceive*) engañar; (*cheat*) estafar ▷ *n* estafa

conceal [kən'siːl] *vt* ocultar

concede [kən'siːd] *vt* (*point, argument*) reconocer; (*territory*) ceder; **to ~ (defeat)** darse por vencido; **to ~ that** admitir que

conceited [kən'siːtɪd] *adj* presumido

conceive [kən'siːv] *vt, vi* concebir

concentrate ['kɔnsəntreɪt] *vi* concentrarse ▷ *vt* concentrar

concentration [kɔnsən'treɪʃən] *n* concentración *f*

concept ['kɔnsɛpt] *n* concepto

concern [kən'səːn] *n* (*matter*) asunto; (*Comm*) empresa; (*anxiety*) preocupación *f* ▷ *vt* (*worry*) preocupar; (*involve*) afectar; (*relate to*) tener que ver con; **to be ~ed (about)** interesarse (por), preocuparse (por); **concerning** *prep* sobre, acerca de

concert ['kɔnsət] *n* concierto; **concert hall** *n* sala de conciertos

concerto [kən'tʃəːtəu] *n* concierto

concession [kən'sɛʃən] *n* concesión *f*; **tax ~** privilegio fiscal

concise [kən'saɪs] *adj* conciso

conclude [kən'kluːd] *vt* concluir; (*treaty etc*) firmar; (*agreement*) llegar a; (*decide*) llegar a la conclusión de; **conclusion** [-'kluːʒən] *n* conclusión *f*, firma

concrete ['kɔnkriːt] *n* hormigón *m* ▷ *adj* de hormigón; (*fig*) concreto

concussion [kən'kʌʃən] *n* conmoción *f* cerebral

condemn [kən'dɛm] *vt* condenar; (*building*) declarar en ruina

condensation [kɔndɛn'seɪʃən] *n* condensación *f*

condense [kən'dɛns] *vi* condensarse ▷ *vt* condensar, abreviar

condition [kən'dɪʃən] *n* condición *f*, estado; (*requirement*) condición *f* ▷ *vt* condicionar; **on ~ that** a condición (de) que; **conditional** [kən'dɪʃənl] *adj* condicional; **conditioner** *n* suavizante

condo ['kɔndəu] (US) *n* (*inf*) = **condominium**

condom ['kɔndəm] *n* condón *m*

condominium [kɔndə'mɪnɪəm] (US) *n* (*building*) bloque *m* de pisos or apartamentos (*propiedad de quienes lo habitan*), condominio (LAM); (*apartment*) piso or apartamento (en propiedad),

condominio (*LAM*)
condone [kən'dəun] *vt* condonar
conduct [*n* 'kɒndʌkt, *vb* kən'dʌkt]
n conducta, comportamiento ▷ *vt*
(*lead*) conducir; (*manage*) llevar a
cabo, dirigir; (*Mus*) dirigir; **to ~ o.s.**
comportarse; **conducted tour** (*BRIT*)
n visita acompañada; **conductor** *n*
(*of orchestra*) director *m*; (*US: on train*)
revisor(a) *m/f*; (*on bus*) cobrador *m*;
(*Elec*) conductor *m*
cone [kəun] *n* cono; (*pine cone*)
piña; (*on road*) pivote *m*; (*for ice-cream*)
cucurucho
confectionery [kən'fɛkʃənrɪ] *n*
dulces *mpl*
confer [kən'fə:*] *vt*: **to ~ sth on**
otorgar algo a ▷ *vi* conferenciar
conference ['kɒnfərns] *n* (*meeting*)
reunión *f*; (*convention*) congreso
confess [kən'fɛs] *vt* confesar ▷ *vi*
admitir; **confession** [-'fɛʃən] *n*
confesión *f*
confide [kən'faɪd] *vi*: **to ~ in** confiar
en
confidence ['kɒnfɪdns] *n* (*also*: **self-
~**) confianza; (*secret*) confidencia; **in ~**
(*speak, write*) en confianza; **confident**
adj seguro de sí mismo; (*certain*)
seguro; **confidential** [kɒnfɪ'dɛnʃəl]
adj confidencial
confine [kən'faɪn] *vt* (*limit*) limitar;
(*shut up*) encerrar; **confined** *adj* (*space*)
reducido
confirm [kən'fə:m] *vt* confirmar;
confirmation [kɒnfə'meɪʃən] *n*
confirmación *f*
confiscate ['kɒnfɪskeɪt] *vt* confiscar
conflict [*n* 'kɒnflɪkt, *vb* kən'flɪkt] *n*
conflicto ▷ *vi* (*opinions*) chocar
conform [kən'fɔ:m] *vi* conformarse;
to ~ to ajustarse a
confront [kən'frʌnt] *vt* (*problems*)
hacer frente a; (*enemy, danger*)
enfrentarse con; **confrontation**
[kɒnfrən'teɪʃən] *n* enfrentamiento
confuse [kən'fju:z] *vt* (*perplex*)
aturdir, desconcertar; (*mix up*)

confundir; (*complicate*) complicar;
confused *adj* confuso; (*person*)
perplejo; **confusing** *adj* confuso;
confusion [-'fju:ʒən] *n* confusión *f*
congestion [kən'dʒɛstʃən] *n*
congestión *f*
congratulate [kən'grætjuleɪt]
vt: **to ~ sb (on)** felicitar a algn (por);
congratulations [-'leɪʃənz] *npl*
felicitaciones *fpl*; **congratulations!**
¡enhorabuena!
congregation [-'geɪʃən] *n* (*of a
church*) feligreses *mpl*
congress ['kɒngrɛs] *n* congreso;
(*US*): **C~** Congreso; **congressman**
(*irreg*: *US*) *n* miembro del Congreso;
congresswoman (*irreg*: *US*) *n*
diputada, miembro *f* del Congreso
conifer ['kɒnɪfə*] *n* conífera
conjugate ['kɒndʒugeɪt] *vt* conjugar
conjugation [kɒndʒə'geɪʃən] *n*
conjugación *f*
conjunction [kən'dʒʌŋkʃən] *n*
conjunción *f*; **in ~ with** junto con
conjure ['kʌndʒə*] *vi* hacer juegos
de manos
connect [kə'nɛkt] *vt* juntar, unir;
(*Elec*) conectar; (*Tel: subscriber*) poner;
(: *caller*) poner al habla; (*fig*) relacionar,
asociar ▷ *vi*: **to ~ with** (*train*) enlazar
con; **to be ~ed with** (*associated*) estar
relacionado con; **connecting flight** *n*
vuelo *m* de enlace; **connection**
[-ʃən] *n* juntura, unión *f*; (*Elec*)
conexión *f*; (*Rail*) enlace *m*; (*Tel*)
comunicación *f*; (*fig*) relación *f*
conquer ['kɒŋkə*] *vt* (*territory*)
conquistar; (*enemy, feelings*) vencer
conquest ['kɒŋkwɛst] *n* conquista
cons [kɒnz] *npl see* **convenience;
pro; mod**
conscience ['kɒnʃəns] *n* conciencia
conscientious [kɒnʃɪ'ɛnʃəs] *adj*
concienzudo; (*objection*) de conciencia
conscious ['kɒnʃəs] *adj* (*deliberate*)
deliberado; (*awake, aware*) consciente;
consciousness *n* conciencia; (*Med*)
conocimiento

consecutive [kən'sɛkjutɪv] *adj*
consecutivo; **on 3 ~ occasions** en 3
ocasiones consecutivas

consensus [kən'sɛnsəs] *n* consenso

consent [kən'sɛnt] *n*
consentimiento ▷ *vi*: **to ~ (to)**
consentir (en)

consequence ['kɔnsɪkwəns]
n consecuencia; (*significance*)
importancia

consequently ['kɔnsɪkwəntlɪ] *adv*
por consiguiente

conservation [kɔnsə'veɪʃən] *n*
conservación *f*

conservative [kən'sə:vətɪv]
adj conservador(a); (*estimate etc*)
cauteloso; **Conservative** (BRIT) *adj, n*
(*Pol*) conservador(a) *m/f*

conservatory [kən'sə:vətrɪ] *n*
invernadero; (*Mus*) conservatorio

consider [kən'sɪdə*] *vt* considerar;
(*take into account*) tener en cuenta;
(*study*) estudiar, examinar; **to ~
doing sth** pensar en (la posibilidad
de) hacer algo; **considerable** *adj*
considerable; **considerably** *adv*
notablemente; **considerate** *adj*
considerado; **consideration** [-'reɪʃə
n] *n* consideración *f*; (*factor*) factor
m; **to give sth further consideration**
estudiar algo más a fondo;
considering *prep* teniendo en cuenta

consignment [kən'saɪnmənt]
n envío

consist [kən'sɪst] *vi*: **to ~ of** consistir
en

consistency [kən'sɪstənsɪ]
n (*of argument etc*) coherencia;
consecuencia; (*thickness*) consistencia

consistent [kən'sɪstənt] *adj* (*person*)
consecuente; (*argument etc*) coherente

consolation [kɔnsə'leɪʃən] *n*
consuelo

console¹ [kən'səul] *vt* consolar

console² ['kɔnsəul] *n* consola

consonant ['kɔnsənənt] *n*
consonante *f*

conspicuous [kən'spɪkjuəs] *adj*

(*visible*) visible

conspiracy [kən'spɪrəsɪ] *n* conjura,
complot *m*

constable ['kʌnstəbl] (BRIT) *n* policía
mf; **chief ~** ≈ jefe *m* de policía

constant ['kɔnstənt] *adj* constante;
constantly *adv* constantemente

constipated ['kɔnstɪpeɪtəd] *adj*
estreñido

Be careful not to translate
constipated by the Spanish word
constipado.

constipation [kɔnstɪ'peɪʃən] *n*
estreñimiento

constituency [kən'stɪtjuənsɪ] *n*
(*Pol: area*) distrito electoral; (: *electors*)
electorado

constitute ['kɔnstɪtju:t] *vt*
constituir

constitution [kɔnstɪ'tju:ʃən] *n*
constitución *f*

constraint [kən'streɪnt] *n*
obligación *f*; (*limit*) restricción *f*

construct [kən'strʌkt] *vt* construir;
construction [-ʃən] *n* construcción *f*;
constructive *adj* constructivo

consul ['kɔnsl] *n* cónsul *mf*;
consulate ['kɔnsjulɪt] *n* consulado

consult [kən'sʌlt] *vt* consultar;
consultant *n* (BRIT Med) especialista
mf; (*other specialist*) asesor(a)
m/f; **consultation** [kɔnsəl'teɪʃən] *n*
consulta; **consulting room** (BRIT) *n*
consultorio

consume [kən'sju:m] *vt* (*eat*)
comerse; (*drink*) beberse; (*fire etc,
Comm*) consumir; **consumer** *n*
consumidor(a) *m/f*

consumption [kən'sʌmpʃən] *n*
consumo

cont. *abbr* (= *continued*) sigue

contact ['kɔntækt] *n* contacto;
(*person*) contacto; (: *pej*) enchufe *m* ▷ *vt*
ponerse en contacto con; **contact
lenses** *npl* lentes *fpl* de contacto

contagious [kən'teɪdʒəs] *adj*
contagioso

contain [kən'teɪn] *vt* contener;

to ~ o.s. contenerse; **container**
n recipiente m; (for shipping etc)
contenedor m
contaminate [kən'tæmɪneɪt] vt
contaminar
cont'd abbr (= continued) sigue
contemplate ['kɔntəmpleɪt] vt
contemplar; (reflect upon) considerar
contemporary [kən'tɛmpərərɪ] adj,
n contemporáneo/a m/f
contempt [kən'tɛmpt] n desprecio;
~ of court (Law) desacato (a los
tribunales)
contend [kən'tɛnd] vt (argue) afirmar
▷ vi: **to ~ with/for** luchar contra/por
content [adj, vb kən'tɛnt, n
'kɔntɛnt] adj (happy) contento;
(satisfied) satisfecho ▷ vt contentar;
satisfacer ▷ n contenido; **contents**
npl contenido; **(table of) ~s** índice m
de materias; **contented** adj contento;
satisfecho
contest [n 'kɔntɛst, vb kən'tɛst] n
lucha; (competition) concurso ▷ vt
(dispute) impugnar; (Pol) presentarse
como candidato/a en

　┃ Be careful not to translate **contest**
　┃ by the Spanish word contestar.

contestant [kən'tɛstənt] n
concursante mf; (in fight) contendiente
mf
context ['kɔntɛkst] n contexto
continent ['kɔntɪnənt] n continente
m; **the C~** (BRIT) el continente
europeo; **continental** [-'nɛntl] adj
continental; **continental breakfast** n
desayuno estilo europeo; **continental
quilt** (BRIT) n edredón m
continual [kən'tɪnjuəl] adj
continuo; **continually** adv
constantemente
continue [kən'tɪnjuː] vi, vt seguir,
continuar
continuity [kɔntɪ'njuɪtɪ] n (also
Cine) continuidad f
continuous [kən'tɪnjuəs] adj
continuo; **continuous assessment**
n (BRIT) evaluación f continua;

continuously adv continuamente
contour ['kɔntuə*] n contorno; (also:
~ line) curva de nivel
contraception [kɔntrə'sɛpʃən] n
contracepción f
contraceptive [kɔntrə'sɛptɪv] adj, n
anticonceptivo
contract [n 'kɔntrækt, vb kən'trækt]
n contrato ▷ vi (Comm): **to ~ to do
sth** comprometerse por contrato a
hacer algo; (become smaller) contraerse,
encogerse ▷ vt contraer; **contractor**
n contratista m
contradict [kɔntrə'dɪkt] vt
contradecir; **contradiction** [-ʃən] n
contradicción f
contrary¹ ['kɔntrərɪ] adj contrario
▷ n lo contrario; **on the ~** al contrario;
unless you hear to the ~ a no ser que
le digan lo contrario
contrary² [kən'trɛərɪ] adj (perverse)
terco
contrast [n 'kɔntrɑːst, vt kən'trɑːst]
n contraste m ▷ vt comparar; **in ~ to**
en contraste con
contribute [kən'trɪbjuːt] vi
contribuir ▷ vt: **to ~ £10/an article to**
contribuir con 10 libras/un artículo
a; **to ~ to** (charity) donar a; (newspaper)
escribir para; (discussion) intervenir en;
contribution [kɔntrɪ'bjuːʃən]
n (donation) donativo; (BRIT: for social
security) cotización f; (to debate)
intervención f; (to journal) colaboración
f; **contributor** n contribuyente mf; (to
newspaper) colaborador(a) m/f
control [kən'trəul] vt controlar;
(process etc) dirigir; (machinery)
manejar; (temper) dominar; (disease)
contener ▷ n control m; **controls** npl
(of vehicle) instrumentos mpl de mando;
(of radio) controles mpl; (governmental)
medidas fpl de control; **under ~** bajo
control; **to be in ~ of** tener el mando
de; **the car went out of ~** se perdió
el control del coche; **control tower** n
(Aviat) torre f de control
controversial [kɔntrə'və:ʃl] adj

polémico

controversy [ˈkɒntrəvəːsɪ] n
polémica

convenience [kənˈviːnɪəns] n
(easiness) comodidad f; (suitability)
idoneidad f; (advantage) ventaja; **at
your ~** cuando le sea conveniente;
all modern ~s, all mod cons (BRIT)
todo confort

convenient [kənˈviːnɪənt] adj
(useful) útil; (place, time) conveniente

convent [ˈkɒnvənt] n convento

convention [kənˈvɛnʃən] n
convención f; (meeting) asamblea;
(agreement) convenio; **conventional**
adj convencional

conversation [kɒnvəˈseɪʃən] n
conversación f

conversely [-ˈvəːslɪ] adv a la inversa

conversion [kənˈvɔːʃən] n
conversión f

convert [vb kənˈvəːt, n ˈkɒnvəːt] vt
(Rel, Comm) convertir; (alter): **to ~ sth
into/to** transformar algo en/convertir
algo a ⊳ n converso/a; **convertible**
adj convertible ⊳ n descapotable m

convey [kənˈveɪ] vt llevar; (thanks)
comunicar; (idea) expresar; **conveyor
belt** n cinta transportadora

convict [vb kənˈvɪkt, n ˈkɒnvɪkt] vt
(find guilty) declarar culpable a ⊳ n
presidiario/a; **conviction** [-ʃən] n
condena; (belief, certainty) convicción f

convince [kənˈvɪns] vt convencer;
convinced adj: **convinced of/that**
convencido de/de que; **convincing** adj
convincente

convoy [ˈkɒnvɔɪ] n convoy m

cook [kʊk] vt (stew etc) guisar; (meal)
preparar ⊳ vi cocer; (person) cocinar
⊳ n cocinero/a; **cook book** n libro de
cocina; **cooker** n cocina; **cookery** n
cocina; **cookery book** (BRIT) n =**cook
book**; **cookie** (US) n galleta; **cooking**
n cocina

cool [kuːl] adj fresco; (not afraid)
tranquilo; (unfriendly) frío ⊳ vt enfriar
⊳ vi enfriarse; **cool down** vi enfriarse;

(fig: person, situation) calmarse; **cool
off** vi (become calmer) calmarse,
apaciguarse; (lose enthusiasm) perder
(el) interés, enfriarse

cop [kɒp] (inf) n poli mf (SP), tira
mf (MEX)

cope [kəup] vi: **to ~ with** (problem)
hacer frente a

copper [ˈkɒpə*] n (metal) cobre m;
(BRIT: inf) poli mf, tira mf (MEX)

copy [ˈkɒpɪ] n copia; (of book etc)
ejemplar m ⊳ vt copiar; **copyright** n
derechos mpl de autor

coral [ˈkɒrəl] n coral m

cord [kɔːd] n cuerda; (Elec) cable
m; (fabric) pana; **cords** npl (trousers)
pantalones mpl de pana; **cordless** adj
sin hilos

corduroy [ˈkɔːdərɔɪ] n pana

core [kɔː*] n centro, núcleo; (of fruit)
corazón m; (of problem) meollo ⊳ vt
quitar el corazón de

coriander [kɒrɪˈændə*] n culantro

cork [kɔːk] n corcho; (tree) alcornoque
m; **corkscrew** n sacacorchos m inv

corn [kɔːn] n (BRIT: cereal crop) trigo;
(US: maize) maíz m; (on foot) callo; **~ on
the cob** (Culin) mazorca, elote m (MEX),
choclo (SC)

corned beef [ˈkɔːnd-] n carne f
acecinada (en lata)

corner [ˈkɔːnə*] n (outside) esquina;
(inside) rincón m; (in road) curva;
(Football) córner m; (Boxing) esquina
⊳ vt (trap) arrinconar; (Comm) acaparar
⊳ vi (in car) tomar las curvas; **corner
shop** (BRIT) tienda de la esquina

cornflakes [ˈkɔːnfleɪks] npl copos
mpl de maíz, cornflakes mpl

cornflour [ˈkɔːnflauə*] (BRIT) n
harina de maíz

cornstarch [ˈkɔːnstaːtʃ] (US) n =
cornflour

Cornwall [ˈkɔːnwəl] n Cornualles m

coronary [ˈkɒrənərɪ] n (also: ~
thrombosis) infarto

coronation [kɒrəˈneɪʃən] n
coronación f

coroner ['kɒrənə*] n juez mf de
instrucción

corporal ['kɔ:pərl] n cabo ▷ adj: ~
punishment castigo corporal

corporate ['kɔ:pərɪt] adj (action,
ownership) colectivo; (finance, image)
corporativo

corporation [kɔ:pə'reɪʃən] n
(of town) ayuntamiento; (Comm)
corporación f

corps [kɔ:*, pl kɔ:z] n inv cuerpo;
diplomatic ~ cuerpo diplomático;
press ~ gabinete m de prensa

corpse [kɔ:ps] n cadáver m

correct [kə'rekt] adj justo, exacto;
(proper) correcto ▷ vt corregir; (exam)
corregir, calificar; **correction**
[-ʃən] n (act) corrección f; (instance)
rectificación f

correspond [kɒrɪs'pɒnd] vi
(write): **to ~ (with)** escribirse (con); (be
equivalent to): **to ~ (to)** corresponder
(a); (be in accordance): **to ~ (with)**
corresponder (con); **correspondence**
n correspondencia; **correspondent** n
corresponsal mf; **corresponding** adj
correspondiente

corridor ['kɒrɪdɔ:*] n pasillo

corrode [kə'rəud] vt corroer ▷ vi
corroerse

corrupt [kə'rʌpt] adj (person)
corrupto; (Comput) corrompido
▷ vt corromper; (Comput) degradar;
corruption n corrupción f; (of data)
alteración f

Corsica ['kɔ:sɪkə] n Córcega

cosmetic [kɒz'metɪk] adj, n
cosmético; **cosmetic surgery** n
cirugía f estética

cosmopolitan [kɒzmə'pɒlɪtn] adj
cosmopolita

cost [kɒst] (pt, pp ~) n (price) precio
▷ vi costar, valer ▷ vt preparar el
presupuesto de; **how much does it ~?**
¿cuánto cuesta?; **to ~ sb time/effort**
costarle a algn tiempo/esfuerzo; **it ~
him his life** le costó la vida; **at all ~s**
cueste lo que cueste; **costs** npl (Comm)

costes mpl; (Law) costas fpl

co-star ['kəustɑ:*] n coprotagonista
mf

Costa Rica [kɒstə'ri:kə] n
Costa Rica; **Costa Rican** adj, n
costarriqueño/a

costly ['kɒstlɪ] adj costoso

cost of living n costo or coste m (Sp)
de la vida

costume ['kɒstju:m] n traje m;
(BRIT: also: **swimming ~**) traje de baño

cosy ['kəuzɪ] (US **cozy**) adj (person)
cómodo; (room) acogedor(a)

cot [kɒt] n (BRIT: child's) cuna;
(US: campbed) cama de campaña

cottage ['kɒtɪdʒ] n casita de campo;
(rustic) barraca; **cottage cheese** n
requesón m

cotton ['kɒtn] n algodón m; (thread)
hilo; **cotton on** vi (inf): **to cotton on
(to sth)** caer en la cuenta (de algo);
cotton bud n (BRIT) bastoncillo m
de algodón; **cotton candy** (US) n
algodón m (azucarado); **cotton wool**
(BRIT) n algodón m (hidrófilo)

couch [kautʃ] n sofá m; (doctor's etc)
diván m

cough [kɒf] vi toser ▷ n tos f; **cough
mixture** n jarabe m para la tos

could [kud] pt of **can²**; **couldn't** =
could not

council ['kaunsl] n consejo; **city or
town ~** consejo municipal; **council
estate** (BRIT) n urbanización de
viviendas municipales de alquiler; **council
house** (BRIT) n vivienda municipal de
alquiler; **councillor** (US **councilor**) n
concejal(a) m/f; **council tax** n (BRIT)
contribución f municipal (dependiente
del valor de la vivienda)

counsel ['kaunsl] n (advice) consejo;
(lawyer) abogado/a ▷ vt aconsejar;
counselling (US **counseling**) n (Psych)
asistencia f psicológica; **counsellor** (US
counselor) n consejero/a, abogado/a

count [kaunt] vt contar; (include)
incluir ▷ vi contar ▷ n cuenta;
(of votes) escrutinio; (level) nivel m;

(*nobleman*) conde *m*; **count in** (*inf*) *vt*: **to count sb in on sth** contar con algn para algo; **count on** *vt fus* contar con; **countdown** *n* cuenta atrás

counter ['kauntə*] *n* (*in shop*) mostrador *m*; (*in games*) ficha ▷ *vt* contrarrestar ▷ *adv*: **to run ~ to** ser contrario a, ir en contra de; **counter clockwise** (*us*) *adv* en sentido contrario al de las agujas del reloj

counterfeit ['kauntəfɪt] *n* falsificación *f*, simulación *f* ▷ *vt* falsificar ▷ *adj* falso, falsificado

counterpart ['kauntəpɑ:t] *n* homólogo/a

countess ['kauntɪs] *n* condesa

countless ['kauntlɪs] *adj* innumerable

country ['kʌntrɪ] *n* país *m*; (*native land*) patria; (*as opposed to town*) campo; (*region*) región *f*, tierra; **country and western (music)** *n* música country; **country house** *n* casa de campo; **countryside** *n* campo

county ['kauntɪ] *n* condado

coup [ku:] (*pl* **~s**) *n* (*also*: **~ d'état**) golpe *m* (de estado); (*achievement*) éxito

couple ['kʌpl] *n* (*of things*) par *m*; (*of people*) pareja; (*married couple*) matrimonio; **a ~ of** un par de

coupon ['ku:pɔn] *n* cupón *m*; (*voucher*) valé *m*

courage ['kʌrɪdʒ] *n* valor *m*, valentía; **courageous** [kə'reɪdʒəs] *adj* valiente

courgette [kuə'ʒet] (*BRIT*) *n* calabacín *m*, calabacita (*MEX*)

courier ['kurɪə*] *n* mensajero/a; (*for tourists*) guía *mf* (de turismo)

course [kɔ:s] *n* (*direction*) dirección *f*; (*of river, Scol*) curso; (*process*) transcurso; (*Med*): **~ of treatment** tratamiento; (*of ship*) rumbo; (*part of meal*) plato; (*Golf*) campo; **of ~** desde luego, naturalmente; **of ~!** ¡claro!

court [kɔ:t] *n* (*royal*) corte *f*; (*Law*) tribunal *m*, juzgado; (*Tennis etc*) pista, cancha ▷ *vt* (*woman*) cortejar a; **to take to ~** demandar

courtesy ['kə:təsɪ] *n* cortesía; **(by) ~ of** por cortesía de; **courtesy bus, courtesy coach** *n* autobús *m* gratuito

court: **court-house** ['kɔ:thaus] (*us*) *n* palacio de justicia; **courtroom** ['kɔ:trum] *n* sala de justicia; **courtyard** ['kɔ:tjɑ:d] *n* patio

cousin ['kʌzn] *n* primo/a; **first ~** primo/a carnal, primo/a hermano/a

cover ['kʌvə*] *vt* cubrir; (*feelings, mistake*) ocultar; (*with lid*) tapar; (*book etc*) forrar; (*distance*) recorrer; (*include*) abarcar; (*protect: also: Insurance*) cubrir; (*Press*) investigar; (*discuss*) tratar ▷ *n* cubierta; (*lid*) tapa; (*for chair etc*) funda; (*envelope*) sobre *m*; (*for book*) forro; (*of magazine*) portada; (*shelter*) abrigo; (*Insurance*) cobertura; (*of spy*) cobertura; **covers** *npl* (*on bed*) sábanas; mantas; **to take ~** (*shelter*) protegerse, resguardarse; **under ~** (*indoors*) bajo techo; **under ~ of darkness** al amparo de la oscuridad; **under separate ~** (*Comm*) por separado; **cover up** *vi*: **to cover up for sb** encubrir a algn; **coverage** *n* (*TV, Press*) cobertura; **cover charge** *n* precio del cubierto; **cover-up** *n* encubrimiento

cow [kau] *n* vaca; (*inf!: woman*) bruja ▷ *vt* intimidar

coward ['kauəd] *n* cobarde *mf*; **cowardly** *adj* cobarde

cowboy ['kaubɔɪ] *n* vaquero

cozy ['kəuzɪ] (*us*) *adj* = **cosy**

crab [kræb] *n* cangrejo

crack [kræk] *n* grieta; (*noise*) crujido; (*drug*) crack *m* ▷ *vt* agrietar, romper; (*nut*) cascar; (*solve: problem*) resolver; (: *code*) descifrar; (*whip etc*) chasquear; (*knuckles*) crujir; (*joke*) contar ▷ *adj* (*expert*) de primera; **crack down on** *vt fus* adoptar fuertes medidas contra; **cracked** *adj* (*cup, window*) rajado; (*wall*) resquebrajado; **cracker** *n* (*biscuit*) cráquer *m*; (*Christmas cracker*) petardo sorpresa

crackle ['krækl] *vi* crepitar

cradle ['kreɪdl] *n* cuna

craft [krɑːft] n (skill) arte m; (trade) oficio; (cunning) astucia; (boat: pl inv) barco; (plane: pl inv) avión m; **craftsman** (irreg) n artesano; **craftsmanship** n (quality) destreza

cram [kræm] vt (fill): **to ~ sth with** llenar algo (a reventar) de; (put): **to ~ sth into** meter algo a la fuerza en ▷ vi (for exams) empollar

cramp [kræmp] n (Med) calambre m; **cramped** adj apretado, estrecho

cranberry ['krænbəri] n arándano agrio

crane [kreɪn] n (Tech) grúa; (bird) grulla

crap [kræp] n (inf!) mierda (!)

crash [kræʃ] n (noise) estrépito; (of cars etc) choque m; (of plane) accidente m de aviación; (Comm) quiebra ▷ vt (car, plane) estrellar ▷ vi (car, plane) estrellarse; (two cars) chocar; (Comm) quebrar; **crash course** n curso acelerado; **crash helmet** n casco (protector)

crate [kreɪt] n cajón m de embalaje; (for bottles) caja

crave [kreɪv] vt, vi: **to ~ (for)** ansiar, anhelar

crawl [krɔːl] vi (drag o.s.) arrastrarse; (child) andar a gatas, gatear; (vehicle) avanzar (lentamente) ▷ n (Swimming) crol m

crayfish ['kreɪfɪʃ] n inv (freshwater) cangrejo de río; (saltwater) cigala

crayon ['kreɪən] n lápiz m de color

craze [kreɪz] n (fashion) moda

crazy ['kreɪzi] adj (person) loco; (idea) disparatado; (inf: keen): **~ about sb/sth** loco por algn/algo

creak [kriːk] vi (floorboard) crujir; (hinge etc) chirriar, rechinar

cream [kriːm] n (of milk) nata, crema; (lotion) crema; (fig) flor f y nata ▷ adj (colour) color crema; **cream cheese** n queso blanco; **creamy** adj cremoso

crease [kriːs] n (fold) pliegue m; (in trousers) raya; (wrinkle) arruga ▷ vt (wrinkle) arrugar ▷ vi (wrinkle up) arrugarse

create [kriː'eɪt] vt crear; **creation** [-ʃən] n creación f; **creative** adj creativo; **creator** n creador(a) m/f

creature ['kriːtʃə*] n (animal) animal m, bicho; (person) criatura

crèche [kreʃ] n guardería (infantil)

credentials [krɪ'denʃlz] npl (references) referencias fpl; (identity papers) documentos mpl de identidad

credibility [kredɪ'bɪlɪtɪ] n credibilidad f

credible ['kredɪbl] adj creíble; (trustworthy) digno de confianza

credit ['kredɪt] n crédito; (merit) honor m, mérito ▷ vt (Comm) abonar; (believe: also: **give ~ to**) creer, prestar fe a ▷ adj crediticio; **credits** npl (Cinema) fichas fpl técnicas; **to be in ~** (person) tener saldo a favor; **to ~ sb with** (fig) reconocer a algn el mérito de; **credit card** n tarjeta de crédito; **credit crunch** n crisis f crediticia

creek [kriːk] n cala, ensenada; (US) riachuelo

creep [kriːp] (pt, pp **crept**) vi arrastrarse

cremate [krɪ'meɪt] vt incinerar

crematorium [kremə'tɔːrɪəm] (pl **crematoria**) n crematorio

crept [krept] pt, pp of **creep**

crescent ['kresnt] n media luna; (street) calle f (en forma de semicírculo)

cress [kres] n berro

crest [krest] n (of bird) cresta; (of hill) cima, cumbre f; (of coat of arms) blasón m

crew [kruː] n (of ship etc) tripulación f; (TV, Cinema) equipo; **crew-neck** n cuello a la caja

crib [krɪb] n cuna ▷ vt (inf) plagiar

cricket ['krɪkɪt] n (insect) grillo; (game) críquet m; **cricketer** n jugador(a) m/f de críquet

crime [kraɪm] n (no pl: illegal activities) crimen m; (illegal action) delito; **criminal** ['krɪmɪnl] n criminal mf, delincuente mf ▷ adj criminal; (illegal) delictivo; (*law*) penal

crimson ['krɪmzn] *adj* carmesí

cringe [krɪndʒ] *vi* agacharse, encogerse

cripple ['krɪpl] *n* lisiado/a, cojo/a ▷ *vt* lisiar, mutilar

crisis ['kraɪsɪs] (*pl* **crises**) *n* crisis *f inv*

crisp [krɪsp] *adj* fresco; (*vegetables etc*) crujiente; (*manner*) seco; **crispy** *adj* crujiente

criterion [kraɪ'tɪərɪən] (*pl* **criteria**) *n* criterio

critic ['krɪtɪk] *n* crítico/a; **critical** *adj* crítico; (*illness*) grave; **criticism** ['krɪtɪsɪzm] *n* crítica; **criticize** ['krɪtɪsaɪz] *vt* criticar

Croat ['krəuæt] *adj, n* = **Croatian**

Croatia [krəu'eɪʃə] *n* Croacia; **Croatian** *adj, n* croata *m/f* ▷ *n* (*Ling*) croata *m*

crockery ['krɒkərɪ] *n* loza, vajilla

crocodile ['krɒkədaɪl] *n* cocodrilo

crocus ['krəukəs] *n* croco, crocus *m*

croissant ['krwʌsɴ] *n* croissant *m*, medialuna (*esp LAM*)

crook [kruk] *n* ladrón/ona *m/f*; (*of shepherd*) cayado; **crooked** ['krukɪd] *adj* torcido; (*dishonest*) nada honrado

crop [krɒp] *n* (*produce*) cultivo; (*amount produced*) cosecha; (*riding crop*) látigo de montar ▷ *vt* cortar, recortar; **crop up** *vi* surgir, presentarse

cross [krɒs] *n* cruz *f*; (*hybrid*) cruce *m* ▷ *vt* (*street etc*) cruzar, atravesar ▷ *adj* de mal humor, enojado; **cross off** *vt* tachar; **cross out** *vt* tachar; **cross over** *vi* cruzar; **cross-Channel ferry** ['krɒs'tʃænl-] *n* transbordador *m* que cruza el Canal de la Mancha; **crosscountry (race)** *n* carrera a campo traviesa, cross *m*; **crossing** *n* (*sea passage*) travesía; (*also:* **pedestrian crossing**) paso para peatones; **crossing guard** (*us*) *n* persona encargada de ayudar a los niños a cruzar la calle; **crossroads** *n* cruce *m*, encrucijada; **crosswalk** (*us*) *n* paso de peatones; **crossword** *n* crucigrama *m*

crotch [krɒtʃ] *n* (*Anat, of garment*) entrepierna

crouch [krautʃ] *vi* agacharse, acurrucarse

crouton ['kru:tɒn] *n* cubito de pan frito

crow [krəu] *n* (*bird*) cuervo; (*of cock*) canto, cacareo ▷ *vi* (*cock*) cantar

crowd [kraud] *n* muchedumbre *f*, multitud *f* ▷ *vt* (*fill*) llenar ▷ *vi* (*gather*): **to ~ round** reunirse en torno a; (*cram*): **to ~ in** entrar en tropel; **crowded** *adj* (*full*) atestado; (*densely populated*) superpoblado

crown [kraun] *n* corona; (*of head*) coronilla; (*for tooth*) funda; (*of hill*) cumbre *f* ▷ *vt* coronar; (*fig*) completar, rematar; **crown jewels** *npl* joyas *fpl* reales

crucial ['kru:ʃl] *adj* decisivo

crucifix ['kru:sɪfɪks] *n* crucifijo

crude [kru:d] *adj* (*materials*) bruto; (*fig: basic*) tosco; (*: vulgar*) ordinario; **crude (oil)** *n* (*petróleo*) crudo

cruel ['kruəl] *adj* cruel; **cruelty** *n* crueldad *f*

cruise [kru:z] *n* crucero ▷ *vi* (*ship*) hacer un crucero; (*car*) ir a velocidad de crucero

crumb [krʌm] *n* miga, migaja

crumble ['krʌmbl] *vt* desmenuzar ▷ *vi* (*building, also fig*) desmoronarse

crumpet ['krʌmpɪt] *n* ≈ bollo para tostar

crumple ['krʌmpl] *vt* (*paper*) estrujar; (*material*) arrugar

crunch [krʌntʃ] *vt* (*with teeth*) mascar; (*underfoot*) hacer crujir ▷ *n* (*fig*) hora or momento de la verdad; **crunchy** *adj* crujiente

crush [krʌʃ] *n* (*crowd*) aglomeración *f*; (*infatuation*): **to have a ~ on sb** estar loco por algn; (*drink*): **lemon ~** limonada ▷ *vt* aplastar; (*paper*) estrujar; (*cloth*) arrugar; (*fruit*) exprimir; (*opposition*) aplastar; (*hopes*) destruir

crust [krʌst] *n* corteza; (*of snow, ice*) costra; **crusty** *adj* (*bread*) crujiente;

(*person*) de mal carácter

crutch [krʌtʃ] n muleta

cry [krai] vi llorar ▷ n (*shriek*) chillido; (*shout*) grito; **cry out** vi (*call out, shout*) lanzar un grito, echar un grito ▷ vt gritar

crystal ['krɪstl] n cristal m

cub [kʌb] n cachorro; (*also:* ~ **scout**) niño explorador

Cuba ['kju:bə] n Cuba; **Cuban** adj, n cubano/a m/f

cube [kju:b] n cubo ▷ vt (*Math*) cubicar

cubicle ['kju:bɪkl] n (*at pool*) caseta; (*for bed*) cubículo

cuckoo ['kuku:] n cuco

cucumber ['kju:kʌmbə*] n pepino

cuddle ['kʌdl] vt abrazar ▷ vi abrazarse

cue [kju:] n (*snooker cue*) taco; (*Theatre etc*) señal f

cuff [kaf] n (*of sleeve*) puño; (*US: of trousers*) vuelta; (*blow*) bofetada ▷ **off the** ~ adv de improviso; **cufflinks** npl gemelos mpl

cuisine [kwɪ'zi:n] n cocina

cul-de-sac ['kʌldəsæk] n callejón m sin salida

cull [kʌl] vt (*idea*) sacar ▷ n (*of animals*) matanza selectiva

culminate ['kʌlmɪneɪt] vi: **to** ~ **in** terminar en

culprit ['kʌlprɪt] n culpable mf

cult [kʌlt] n culto

cultivate ['kʌltɪveɪt] vt cultivar

cultural ['kʌltʃərəl] adj cultural

culture ['kʌltʃə*] n (*also fig*) cultura; (*Biol*) cultivo

cumin ['kʌmɪn] n (*spice*) comino

cunning ['kʌnɪŋ] n astucia ▷ adj astuto

cup [kʌp] n taza; (*as prize*) copa

cupboard ['kʌbəd] n armario; (*in kitchen*) alacena

cup final n (*Football*) final f de copa

curator [kjuə'reɪtə*] n director(a) m/f

curb [kə:b] vt refrenar; (*person*)

reprimir ▷ n freno; (*US*) bordillo

curdle ['kə:dl] vi cuajarse

cure [kjuə*] vt curar ▷ n cura, curación f; (*fig: solution*) remedio

curfew ['kə:fju:] n toque m de queda

curiosity [kjuərɪ'ɔsɪtɪ] n curiosidad f

curious ['kjuərɪəs] adj curioso; (*person: interested*): **to be** ~ sentir curiosidad

curl [kə:l] n rizo ▷ vt (*hair*) rizar ▷ vi rizarse; **curl up** vi (*person*) hacerse un ovillo; **curler** n rulo; **curly** adj rizado

currant ['kʌrnt] n pasa (de Corinto); (*blackcurrant, redcurrant*) grosella

currency ['kʌrnsɪ] n moneda; **to gain** ~ (*fig*) difundirse

current ['kʌrnt] n corriente f ▷ adj (*accepted*) corriente; (*present*) actual; **current account** (BRIT) n cuenta corriente; **current affairs** npl noticias fpl de actualidad; **currently** adv actualmente

curriculum [kə'rɪkjuləm] (pl ~**s** or **curricula**) n plan m de estudios; **curriculum vitae** n currículum m

curry ['kʌrɪ] n curry m ▷ vt: **to** ~ **favour with** buscar favores con; **curry powder** n curry m en polvo

curse [kə:s] vi soltar tacos ▷ vt maldecir ▷ n maldición f; (*swearword*) palabrota, taco

cursor ['kə:sə*] n (*Comput*) cursor m

curt [kə:t] adj corto, seco

curtain ['kə:tn] n cortina; (*Theatre*) telón m

curve [kə:v] n curva ▷ vi (*road*) hacer una curva; (*line etc*) curvarse; **curved** adj curvo

cushion ['kuʃən] n cojín m; (*of air*) colchón m ▷ vt (*shock*) amortiguar

custard ['kʌstəd] n natillas fpl

custody ['kʌstədɪ] n custodia; **to take into** ~ detener

custom ['kʌstəm] n costumbre f; (*Comm*) clientela

customer ['kʌstəmə*] n cliente m/f

customized ['kʌstəmaɪzd] adj (*car etc*) hecho a encargo

customs ['kʌstəmz] *npl* aduana;
  customs officer *n* aduanero/a
cut [kʌt] (*pt, pp* ~) *vt* cortar; (*price*)
  rebajar; (*text, programme*) acortar;
  (*reduce*) reducir ▷ *vi* cortar ▷ *n* (*of
  garment*) corte *m*; (*in skin*) cortadura;
  (*in salary etc*) rebaja; (*in spending*)
  reducción *f*, recorte *m*; (*slice of meat*)
  tajada; **to ~ a tooth** echar un diente;
  to ~ and paste (*Comput*) cortar y pegar;
  cut back *vt* (*plants*) podar; (*production,
  expenditure*) reducir; **cut down** *vt*
  (*tree*) derribar; (*reduce*) reducir; **cut
  off** *vt* cortar; (*person, place*) aislar;
  (*Tel*) desconectar; **cut out** *vt* (*shape*)
  recortar; (*stop: activity etc*) dejar;
  (*remove*) quitar; **cut up** *vt* cortar (en
  pedazos); **cutback** *n* reducción *f*
cute [kjuːt] *adj* mono
cutlery ['kʌtlərɪ] *n* cubiertos *mpl*
cutlet ['kʌtlɪt] *n* chuleta; (*nut etc
  cutlet*) plato vegetariano hecho con nueces
  y verdura en forma de chuleta
cut-price ['kʌt'praɪs] (*BRIT*) *adj* a
  precio reducido
cut-rate ['kʌt'reɪt] (*US*) *adj* =
  cut-price
cutting ['kʌtɪŋ] *adj* (*remark*) mordaz
  ▷ *n* (*BRIT: from newspaper*) recorte *m*;
  (*from plant*) esqueje *m*
CV *n abbr* = **curriculum vitae**
cwt *abbr* = **hundredweight(s)**
cybercafé ['saɪbəkæfeɪ] *n* cibercafé
  m
cyberspace ['saɪbəspeɪs] *n*
  ciberespacio
cycle ['saɪkl] *n* ciclo; (*bicycle*) bicicleta
  ▷ *vi* ir en bicicleta; **cycle hire** *n*
  alquiler *m* de bicicletas; **cycle lane** *n*
  carril-bici *m*; **cycle path** *n* carril-bici
  m; **cycling** *n* ciclismo; **cyclist** *n*
  ciclista *mf*
cyclone ['saɪkləun] *n* ciclón *m*
cylinder ['sɪlɪndə*] *n* cilindro; (*of gas*)
  bombona
cymbal ['sɪmbl] *n* címbalo, platillo
cynical ['sɪnɪkl] *adj* cínico
Cypriot ['sɪprɪət] *adj, n* chipriota *m/f*

Cyprus ['saɪprəs] *n* Chipre *f*
cyst [sɪst] *n* quiste *m*; **cystitis**
  [-'taɪtɪs] *n* cistitis *f*
czar [zɑː*] *n* zar *m*
Czech [tʃɛk] *adj, n* checo/a *m/f*; **Czech
  Republic** *n*: **the Czech Republic** la
  República Checa

D [di:] n (Mus) re m

dab [dæb] vt (eyes, wound) tocar (ligeramente); (paint, cream) poner un poco de

dad [dæd] n = **daddy**

daddy ['dædɪ] n papá m

daffodil ['dæfədɪl] n narciso

daft [dɑ:ft] adj tonto

dagger ['dægə*] n puñal m, daga

daily ['deɪlɪ] adj diario, cotidiano ▷ adv todos los días, cada día

dairy ['dɛərɪ] n (shop) lechería; (on farm) vaquería; **dairy produce** n productos mpl lácteos

daisy ['deɪzɪ] n margarita

dam [dæm] n presa ▷ vt construir una presa sobre, represar

damage ['dæmɪdʒ] n lesión f; daño; (dents etc) desperfectos mpl; (fig) perjuicio ▷ vt dañar, perjudicar; (spoil, break) estropear; **damages** npl (Law) daños mpl y perjuicios

damn [dæm] vt condenar; (curse) maldecir ▷ n (inf): **I don't give a ~** me importa un pito ▷ adj (inf: also: **~ed**) maldito; **~ (it)!** ¡maldito sea!

damp [dæmp] adj húmedo, mojado ▷ n humedad f ▷ vt (also: **~en**: cloth, rag) mojar; (: enthusiasm) enfriar

dance [dɑ:ns] n baile m ▷ vi bailar; **dance floor** n pista f de baile; **dancer** n bailador(a) m/f; (professional) bailarín/ina m/f; **dancing** n baile m

dandelion ['dændɪlaɪən] n diente m de león

dandruff ['dændrəf] n caspa

Dane [deɪn] n danés/esa m/f

danger ['deɪndʒə*] n peligro; (risk) riesgo; **~!** (on sign) ¡peligro de muerte!; **to be in ~ of** correr riesgo de; **dangerous** adj peligroso

dangle ['dæŋgl] vt colgar ▷ vi pender, colgar

Danish ['deɪnɪʃ] adj danés/esa ▷ n (Ling) danés m

dare [dɛə*] vt: **to ~ sb to do** desafiar a algn a hacer ▷ vi: **to ~ (to) do sth** atreverse a hacer algo; **I ~ say** (I suppose) puede ser (que); **daring** adj atrevido, osado ▷ n atrevimiento, osadía

dark [dɑ:k] adj oscuro; (hair, complexion) moreno ▷ n: **in the ~** a oscuras; **to be in the ~ about** (fig) no saber nada de; **after ~** después del anochecer; **darken** vt (colour) hacer más oscuro ▷ vi oscurecerse; **darkness** n oscuridad f; **darkroom** n cuarto oscuro

darling ['dɑ:lɪŋ] adj, n querido/a m/f

dart [dɑ:t] n dardo; (in sewing) sisa ▷ vi precipitarse; **dartboard** n diana; **darts** n (game) dardos mpl

dash [dæʃ] n (small quantity: of liquid) gota, chorrito; (sign) raya ▷ vt (throw) tirar; (hopes) defraudar ▷ vi precipitarse, ir de prisa

dashboard ['dæʃbɔ:d] n (Aut) salpicadero

data ['deɪtə] npl datos mpl; **database** n base f de datos; **data processing** n proceso de datos

date [deɪt] n (day) fecha; (with

friend) cita; (fruit) dátil m ▷ vt fechar;
(person) salir con; **~ of birth** fecha de
nacimiento; **to ~** adv hasta la fecha;
dated adj anticuado

daughter ['dɔːtə*] n hija; **daughter-
in-law** n nuera, hija política

daunting ['dɔːntɪŋ] adj
desalentador(a)

dawn [dɔːn] n alba, amanecer m;
(fig) nacimiento ▷ vi (day) amanecer;
(fig): **it ~ed on him that ...** cayó en la
cuenta de que ...

day [deɪ] n día m; (working day)
jornada; (heyday) tiempos mpl, días
mpl; **the ~ before/after** el día anterior/
siguiente; **the ~ after tomorrow**
pasado mañana; **the ~ before
yesterday** anteayer; **the following ~**
el día siguiente; **by ~** de día; **day-care
centre** ['deɪkɛə-] n centro de día; (for
children) guardería infantil; **daydream**
vi soñar despierto; **daylight** n luz f
(del día); **day return** (BRIT) n billete m
de ida y vuelta (en un día); **daytime** n
día m; **day-to-day** adj cotidiano; **day
trip** n excursión f (de un día)

dazed [deɪzd] adj aturdido

dazzle ['dæzl] vt deslumbrar;
dazzling adj (light, smile)
deslumbrante; (colour) fuerte

DC abbr (= direct current) C.C.

dead [dɛd] adj muerto; (limb)
dormido; (telephone) cortado;
(battery) agotado ▷ adv (completely)
totalmente; (exactly) exactamente;
to shoot sb ~ matar a algn a tiros; **~
tired** muerto (de cansancio); **to stop ~**
parar en seco; **dead end** n callejón m
sin salida; **deadline** n fecha (or hora)
tope; **deadly** adj mortal, fatal; **Dead
Sea** n: **the Dead Sea** el Mar Muerto

deaf [dɛf] adj sordo; **deafen**
vt ensordecer; **deafening** adj
ensordecedor/a

deal [diːl] (pt, pp **~t**) n (agreement)
pacto, convenio; (business deal) trato
▷ vt dar; (card) repartir; **a great ~
(of)** bastante, mucho; **deal with**

vt fus (people) tratar con; (problem)
ocuparse de; (subject) tratar de; **dealer**
n comerciante m/f; (Cards) mano f;
dealings npl (Comm) transacciones
fpl; (relations) relaciones fpl

dealt [dɛlt] pt, pp of **deal**

dean [diːn] n (Rel) deán m; (Scol: BRIT)
decano; (: US) decano; rector m

dear [dɪə*] adj querido; (expensive)
caro ▷ n: **my ~** mi querido/a ▷ excl: **~
me!** ¡Dios mío!; **D~ Sir/Madam** (in
letter) Muy Señor Mío, Estimado
Señor/Estimada Señora; **D~ Mr/Mrs
X** Estimado/a Señor(a) X; **dearly** adv
(love) mucho; (pay) caro

death [dɛθ] n muerte f; **death
penalty** n pena de muerte; **death
sentence** n condena a muerte

debate [dɪ'beɪt] n debate m ▷ vt discutir

debit ['dɛbɪt] n debe m ▷ vt: **to ~ a
sum to sb** or **to sb's account** cargar
una suma en cuenta a algn; **debit card**
n tarjeta f de débito

debris ['dɛbriː] n escombros mpl

debt [dɛt] n deuda; **to be in ~** tener
deudas

debug [diː'bʌg] vt (Comput) limpiar

debut [deɪ'bjuː] n presentación f

Dec. abbr (= December) dic

decade ['dɛkeɪd] n decenio, década

decaffeinated [dɪ'kæfɪneɪtɪd] adj
descafeinado

decay [dɪ'keɪ] n (of building)
desmoronamiento; (of tooth) caries f
inv ▷ vi (rot) pudrirse

deceased [dɪ'siːst] n: **the ~** el(la)
difunto/a

deceit [dɪ'siːt] n engaño; **deceive**
[dɪ'siːv] vt engañar

December [dɪ'sɛmbə*] n diciembre m

decency ['diːsənsɪ] n decencia

decent ['diːsənt] adj (proper) decente;
(person: kind) amable, bueno

deception [dɪ'sɛpʃən] n engaño

> Be careful not to translate
> **deception** by the Spanish word
> decepción.

deceptive [dɪ'sɛptɪv] adj engañoso

decide [dɪ'saɪd] vt (person) decidir; (question, argument) resolver ▷ vi decidir; **to ~ to do/that** decidir hacer/que; **to ~ on sth** decidirse por algo

decimal ['dɛsɪməl] adj decimal ▷ n decimal m

decision [dɪ'sɪʒən] n decisión f

decisive [dɪ'saɪsɪv] adj decisivo; (person) decidido

deck [dɛk] n (Naut) cubierta; (of bus) piso; (record deck) platina; (of cards) baraja; **deckchair** n tumbona

declaration [dɛklə'reɪʃən] n declaración f

declare [dɪ'klɛə*] vt declarar

decline [dɪ'klaɪn] n disminución f, descenso ▷ vt rehusar ▷ vi (person, business) decaer; (strength) disminuir

decorate ['dɛkəreɪt] vt (adorn): **to ~ (with)** adornar (de), decorar (de); (paint) pintar; (paper) empapelar; **decoration** [-'reɪʃən] n adorno; (act) decoración f; (medal) condecoración f; **decorator** n (workman) pintor m (decorador)

decrease [n 'diːkriːs, vb dɪ'kriːs] n: **~ (in)** disminución f (de) ▷ vt disminuir, reducir ▷ vi reducirse

decree [dɪ'kriː] n decreto

dedicate ['dɛdɪkeɪt] vt dedicar; **dedicated** adj dedicado; (Comput) especializado; **dedicated word processor** procesador m de textos especializado or dedicado; **dedication** [-'keɪʃən] n (devotion) dedicación f; (in book) dedicatoria

deduce [dɪ'djuːs] vt deducir

deduct [dɪ'dʌkt] vt restar; descontar; **deduction** [dɪ'dʌkʃən] n (amount deducted) descuento; (conclusion) deducción f, conclusión f

deed [diːd] n hecho, acto; (feat) hazaña; (Law) escritura

deem [diːm] vt (formal) juzgar, considerar

deep [diːp] adj profundo; (expressing measurements) de profundidad; (voice) bajo; (breath) profundo; (colour) intenso ▷ adv: **the spectators stood 20 ~** los espectadores se formaron de 20 en fondo; **to be 4 metres ~** tener 4 metros de profundidad; **deep-fry** vt freír en aceite abundante; **deeply** adv (breathe) a pleno pulmón; (interested, moved, grateful) profundamente, hondamente

deer [dɪə*] n inv ciervo

default [dɪ'fɔːlt] n: **by ~** (win) por incomparecencia ▷ adj (Comput) por defecto

defeat [dɪ'fiːt] n derrota ▷ vt derrotar, vencer

defect [n 'diːfɛkt, vb dɪ'fɛkt] n defecto ▷ vi: **to ~ to the enemy** pasarse al enemigo; **defective** [dɪ'fɛktɪv] adj defectuoso

defence [dɪ'fɛns] (us **defense**) n defensa

defend [dɪ'fɛnd] vt defender; **defendant** n acusado/a; (in civil case) demandado/a; **defender** n defensor(a) m/f; (Sport) defensa mf

defense [dɪ'fɛns] (us) = **defence**

defensive [dɪ'fɛnsɪv] adj defensivo ▷ n: **on the ~** a la defensiva

defer [dɪ'fəː*] vt aplazar

defiance [dɪ'faɪəns] n desafío; **in ~ of** en contra de; **defiant** [dɪ'faɪənt] adj (challenging) desafiante, retador(a)

deficiency [dɪ'fɪʃənsɪ] n (lack) falta; (defect) defecto; **deficient** [dɪ'fɪʃənt] adj deficiente

deficit ['dɛfɪsɪt] n déficit m

define [dɪ'faɪn] vt (word etc) definir; (limits etc) determinar

definite ['dɛfɪnɪt] adj (fixed) determinado; (obvious) claro; (certain) indudable; **he was ~ about it** no dejó lugar a dudas (sobre ello); **definitely** adv desde luego, por supuesto

definition [dɛfɪ'nɪʃən] n definición f; (clearness) nitidez f

deflate [diː'fleɪt] vt desinflar

deflect [dɪ'flɛkt] vt desviar

defraud [dɪ'frɔːd] vt: **to ~ sb of sth** estafar algo a algn

defrost [diːˈfrɒst] vt descongelar
defuse [diːˈfjuːz] vt desactivar; (*situation*) calmar
defy [dɪˈfaɪ] vt (*resist*) oponerse a; (*challenge*) desafiar; (*fig*): **it defies description** resulta imposible describirlo
degree [dɪˈgriː] n grado; (*Scol*) título; **to have a ~ in maths** tener una licenciatura en matemáticas; **by ~s** (*gradually*) poco a poco, por etapas; **to some ~** hasta cierto punto
dehydrated [diːhaɪˈdreɪtɪd] adj deshidratado; (*milk*) en polvo
de-icer [diːˈaɪsə*] n descongelador m
delay [dɪˈleɪ] vt demorar, aplazar; (*person*) entretener; (*train*) retrasar ▷ vi tardar ▷ n demora, retraso; **to be ~ed** retrasarse; **without ~** en seguida, sin tardar
delegate [n ˈdɛlɪgɪt, vb ˈdɛlɪgeɪt] n delegado/a ▷ vt (*person*) delegar en; (*task*) delegar
delete [dɪˈliːt] vt suprimir, tachar
deli [ˈdɛlɪ] n = **delicatessen**
deliberate [adj dɪˈlɪbərɪt, vb dɪˈlɪbəreɪt] adj (*intentional*) intencionado; (*slow*) pausado, lento ▷ vi deliberar; **deliberately** adv (*on purpose*) a propósito
delicacy [ˈdɛlɪkəsɪ] n delicadeza; (*choice food*) manjar m
delicate [ˈdɛlɪkɪt] adj delicado; (*fragile*) frágil
delicatessen [dɛlɪkəˈtɛsn] n ultramarinos mpl finos
delicious [dɪˈlɪʃəs] adj delicioso
delight [dɪˈlaɪt] n (*feeling*) placer m, deleite m; (*person, experience etc*) encanto, delicia ▷ vt encantar, deleitar; **to take ~ in** deleitarse en; **delighted** adj: **delighted (at** or **with/to do)** encantado (con/de hacer); **delightful** adj encantador(a), delicioso
delinquent [dɪˈlɪŋkwənt] adj, n delincuente mf
deliver [dɪˈlɪvə*] vt (*distribute*)

repartir; (*hand over*) entregar; (*message*) comunicar; (*speech*) pronunciar; (*Med*) asistir al parto de; **delivery** n reparto; entrega; (*of speaker*) modo de expresarse; (*Med*) parto, alumbramiento; **to take delivery of** recibir
delusion [dɪˈluːʒən] n ilusión f, engaño
de luxe [dəˈlʌks] adj de lujo
delve [dɛlv] vi: **to ~ into** hurgar en
demand [dɪˈmɑːnd] vt (*gen*) exigir; (*rights*) reclamar ▷ n exigencia; (*claim*) reclamación f; (*Econ*) demanda; **to be in ~** ser muy solicitado; **on ~** a solicitud; **demanding** adj (*boss*) exigente; (*work*) absorbente
demise [dɪˈmaɪz] n (*death*) fallecimiento
demo [ˈdɛməu] (*inf*) n abbr (= *demonstration*) manifestación f
democracy [dɪˈmɒkrəsɪ] n democracia; **democrat** [ˈdɛməkræt] n demócrata mf; **democratic** [dɛməˈkrætɪk] adj democrático; (*us*) demócrata
demolish [dɪˈmɒlɪʃ] vt derribar, demoler; (*fig: argument*) destruir
demolition [dɛməˈlɪʃən] n derribo, demolición f
demon [ˈdiːmən] n (*evil spirit*) demonio
demonstrate [ˈdɛmənstreɪt] vt demostrar; (*skill, appliance*) mostrar ▷ vi manifestarse; **demonstration** [-ˈstreɪʃən] n (*Pol*) manifestación f; (*proof, exhibition*) demostración f; **demonstrator** n (*Pol*) manifestante mf; (*Comm*) demostrador(a) m/f; vendedor(a) m/f
demote [dɪˈməut] vt degradar
den [dɛn] n (*of animal*) guarida; (*room*) habitación f
denial [dɪˈnaɪəl] n (*refusal*) negativa; (*of report etc*) negación f
denim [ˈdɛnɪm] n tela vaquera; **denims** npl vaqueros mpl
Denmark [ˈdɛnmɑːk] n Dinamarca

denomination [dɪnɒmɪˈneɪʃən] n
valor m; (Rel) confesión f
denounce [dɪˈnauns] vt denunciar
dense [dɛns] adj (crowd) denso; (thick)
espeso; (: foliage etc) tupido; (inf: stupid)
torpe
density [ˈdɛnsɪtɪ] n densidad f
▷ **single/double-~ disk** n (Comput)
disco de densidad sencilla/de doble
densidad
dent [dɛnt] n abolladura ▷vt
(also: **make a ~ in**) abollar
dental [ˈdɛntl] adj dental; **dental
floss** [-flɒs] n seda dental; **dental
surgery** n clínica f dental, consultorio
m dental
dentist [ˈdɛntɪst] n dentista mf
dentures [ˈdɛntʃəz] npl dentadura
(postiza)
deny [dɪˈnaɪ] vt negar; (charge)
rechazar
deodorant [diːˈəudərənt] n
desodorante m
depart [dɪˈpɑːt] vi irse, marcharse;
(train) salir; **to ~ from** (fig: differ from)
apartarse de
department [dɪˈpɑːtmənt] n
(Comm) sección f; (Scol) departamento;
(Pol) ministerio; **department store** n
gran almacén m
departure [dɪˈpɑːtʃə*] n partida, ida;
(of train) salida; (of employee) marcha;
a new ~ un nuevo rumbo; **departure
lounge** n (at airport) sala de embarque
depend [dɪˈpɛnd] vi: **to ~ on** depender
de; (rely on) contar con; **it ~s** depende,
según; **~ing on the result** según el
resultado; **dependant** n dependiente
mf; **dependent** adj: **to be dependent
on** depender de ▷ n = **dependant**
depict [dɪˈpɪkt] vt (in picture) pintar;
(describe) representar
deport [dɪˈpɔːt] vt deportar
deposit [dɪˈpɒzɪt] n depósito; (Chem)
sedimento; (of ore, oil) yacimiento ▷vt
(gen) depositar; **deposit account** (BRIT)
n cuenta de ahorros
depot [ˈdɛpəu] n (storehouse)

depósito; (for vehicles) parque m; (US)
estación f
depreciate [dɪˈpriːʃɪeɪt] vi
depreciarse, perder valor
depress [dɪˈprɛs] vt deprimir; (wages
etc) hacer bajar; (press down) apretar;
depressed adj deprimido; **depressing**
adj deprimente; **depression**
[dɪˈprɛʃən] n depresión f
deprive [dɪˈpraɪv] vt: **to ~ sb of** privar
a algn de; **deprived** adj necesitado
dept. abbr (=department) dto
depth [dɛpθ] n profundidad f; (of
cupboard) fondo; **to be in the ~s of
despair** sentir la mayor desesperación;
to be out of one's ~ (in water) no hacer
pie; (fig) sentirse totalmente perdido
deputy [ˈdɛpjutɪ] adj: **~ head**
subdirector(a) m/f ▷ n sustituto/a,
suplente mf; (US Pol) diputado/a;
(US: also: **~ sheriff**) agente m del sheriff
derail [dɪˈreɪl] vt: **to be ~ed**
descarrilarse
derelict [ˈdɛrɪlɪkt] adj abandonado
derive [dɪˈraɪv] vt (benefit etc) obtener
▷ vi: **to ~ from** derivarse de
descend [dɪˈsɛnd] vt, vi descender,
bajar; **to ~ from** descender de; **to
~ to** rebajarse a; **descendant** n
descendiente mf
descent [dɪˈsɛnt] n descenso; (origin)
descendencia
describe [dɪsˈkraɪb] vt describir;
description [-ˈkrɪpʃən] n descripción
f; (sort) clase f, género
desert [n ˈdɛzət, vb dɪˈzəːt] n desierto
▷vt abandonar ▷vi (Mil) desertar;
deserted [dɪˈzəːtɪd] adj desierto
deserve [dɪˈzəːv] vt merecer, ser
digno de
design [dɪˈzaɪn] n (sketch) bosquejo;
(layout, shape) diseño; (pattern) dibujo;
(intention) intención f ▷vt diseñar;
design and technology (BRIT: Scol) n
≈ dibujo y tecnología
designate [vb ˈdɛzɪgneɪt, adj
ˈdɛzɪgnɪt] vt (appoint) nombrar;
(destine) designar ▷ adj designado

designer [dɪ'zaɪnə*] n diseñador(a) m/f; (fashion designer) modisto/a, diseñador(a) m/f de moda

desirable [dɪ'zaɪərəbl] adj (proper) deseable; (attractive) atractivo

desire [dɪ'zaɪə*] n deseo ▷ vt desear

desk [dɛsk] n (in office) escritorio; (for pupil) pupitre m; (in hotel, at airport) recepción f; (in shop, restaurant) caja; **desk-top publishing** ['dɛsktɔp-] n autoedición f

despair [dɪs'pɛə*] n desesperación f ▷ vi: **to ~ of** perder la esperanza de

despatch [dɪs'pætʃ] n, vt = **dispatch**

desperate ['dɛspərɪt] adj desesperado; (fugitive) peligroso; **to be ~ for sth/to do** necesitar urgentemente algo/hacer; **desperately** adv desesperadamente; (very) terriblemente, gravemente

desperation [dɛspə'reɪʃən] n desesperación f; **in (sheer) ~** (absolutamente) desesperado

despise [dɪs'paɪz] vt despreciar

despite [dɪs'paɪt] prep a pesar de, pese a

dessert [dɪ'zə:t] n postre m; **dessertspoon** n cuchara (de postre)

destination [dɛstɪ'neɪʃən] n destino

destined ['dɛstɪnd] adj: **~ for London** con destino a Londres

destiny ['dɛstɪnɪ] n destino

destroy [dɪs'trɔɪ] vt destruir; (animal) sacrificar

destruction [dɪs'trʌkʃən] n destrucción f

destructive [dɪs'trʌktɪv] adj destructivo, destructor(a)

detach [dɪ'tætʃ] vt separar; (unstick) despegar; **detached** adj (attitude) objetivo, imparcial; **detached house** n ≈ chalé m, ≈ chalet m

detail ['di:teɪl] n detalle m; (no pl: in picture etc) detalles mpl; (trifle) pequeñez f ▷ vt detallar; (Mil) destacar; **in ~** detalladamente; **detailed** adj detallado

detain [dɪ'teɪn] vt retener; (in captivity) detener

detect [dɪ'tɛkt] vt descubrir; (Med, Police) identificar; (Mil, Radar, Tech) detectar; **detection** [dɪ'tɛkʃən] n descubrimiento; identificación f; **detective** n detective mf; **detective story** n novela policíaca

detention [dɪ'tɛnʃən] n detención f, arresto; (Scol) castigo

deter [dɪ'tə:*] vt (dissuade) disuadir

detergent [dɪ'tə:dʒənt] n detergente m

deteriorate [dɪ'tɪərɪəreɪt] vi deteriorarse

determination [dɪtə:mɪ'neɪʃən] n resolución f

determine [dɪ'tə:mɪn] vt determinar; **determined** adj (person) resuelto, decidido; **determined to do** resuelto a hacer

deterrent [dɪ'tɛrənt] n (Mil) fuerza de disuasión

detest [dɪ'tɛst] vt aborrecer

detour ['di:tuə*] n (gen, us Aut) desviación f

detract [dɪ'trækt] vt: **to ~ from** quitar mérito a, desvirtuar

detrimental [dɛtrɪ'mɛntl] adj: **~ (to)** perjudicial(a)

devastating ['dɛvəsteɪtɪŋ] adj devastador(a); (fig) arrollador(a)

develop [dɪ'vɛləp] vt desarrollar; (Phot) revelar; (disease) coger; (habit) adquirir; (fault) empezar a tener ▷ vi desarrollarse; (advance) progresar; (facts, symptoms) aparecer; **developing country** n país m en (vías de) desarrollo; **development** n desarrollo; (advance) progreso; (of affair, case) desenvolvimiento; (of land) urbanización f

device [dɪ'vaɪs] n (apparatus) aparato, mecanismo

devil ['dɛvl] n diablo, demonio

devious ['di:vɪəs] adj taimado

devise [dɪ'vaɪz] vt idear, inventar

devote [dɪ'vəut] vt: **to ~ sth to** dedicar algo a; **devoted** adj (loyal) leal, fiel; **to be devoted to sb** querer con devoción a algn; **the book is devoted to politics** el libro trata de la política; **devotion** n dedicación f; (Rel) devoción f

devour [dɪ'vauə*] vt devorar

devout [dɪ'vaut] adj devoto

dew [djuː] n rocío

diabetes [daɪə'biːtiːz] n diabetes f

diabetic [daɪə'bɛtɪk] adj, n diabético/a m/f

diagnose ['daɪəgnəuz] vt diagnosticar

diagnosis [daɪəg'nəusɪs] (pl **-ses**) n diagnóstico

diagonal [daɪ'ægənl] adj, n diagonal f

diagram ['daɪəgræm] n diagrama m, esquema m

dial ['daɪəl] n esfera (SP), cara (LAM); (on radio etc) dial m; (of phone) disco ⊳ vt (number) marcar

dialect ['daɪəlɛkt] n dialecto

dialling code ['daɪəlɪŋ-] n prefijo

dialling tone (US **dial tone**) n (BRIT) señal f or tono de marcar

dialogue ['daɪəlɔg] (US **dialog**) n diálogo

diameter [daɪ'æmɪtə*] n diámetro

diamond ['daɪəmənd] n diamante m; (shape) rombo; **diamonds** npl (Cards) diamantes mpl

diaper ['daɪəpə*] (US) n pañal m

diarrhoea [daɪə'riːə] (US **diarrhea**) n diarrea

diary ['daɪərɪ] n (daily account) diario; (book) agenda

dice [daɪs] n inv dados mpl ⊳ vt (Culin) cortar en cuadritos

dictate [dɪk'teɪt] vt dictar; (conditions) imponer; **dictation** [-'teɪʃən] n dictado; (giving of orders) órdenes fpl

dictator [dɪk'teɪtə*] n dictador m

dictionary ['dɪkʃənrɪ] n diccionario

did [dɪd] pt of **do**

didn't ['dɪdənt] = **did not**

die [daɪ] vi morir; (fig: fade)

desvanecerse, desaparecer; **to be dying for sth/to do sth** morirse por algo/de ganas de hacer algo; **die down** vi apagarse; (wind) amainar; **die out** vi desaparecer

diesel ['diːzəl] n vehículo con motor Diesel

diet ['daɪət] n dieta; (restricted food) régimen m ⊳ vi (also: **be on a ~**) estar a dieta, hacer régimen

differ ['dɪfə*] vi: **to ~ (from)** (be different) ser distinto (a), diferenciarse (de); (disagree) discrepar (de); **difference** n diferencia; (disagreement) desacuerdo; **different** adj diferente, distinto; **differentiate** [-'rɛnʃɪeɪt] vi: **to differentiate (between)** distinguir (entre); **differently** adv de otro modo, en forma distinta

difficult ['dɪfɪkəlt] adj difícil; **difficulty** n dificultad f

dig [dɪg] (pt, pp **dug**) vt (hole, ground) cavar ⊳ n (prod) empujón m; (archaeological) excavación f; (remark) indirecta; **to ~ one's nails into** clavar las uñas en; **dig up** vt (information) desenterrar; (plant) desarraigar

digest [vb daɪ'dʒɛst, n 'daɪdʒɛst] vt (food) digerir; (facts) asimilar ⊳ n resumen m; **digestion** [dɪ'dʒɛstʃən] n digestión f

digit ['dɪdʒɪt] n (number) dígito; (finger) dedo; **digital** adj digital; **digital camera** n cámara digital; **digital TV** n televisión f digital

dignified ['dɪgnɪfaɪd] adj grave, solemne

dignity ['dɪgnɪtɪ] n dignidad f

digs [dɪgz] (BRIT: inf) npl pensión f, alojamiento

dilemma [daɪ'lɛmə] n dilema m

dill [dɪl] n eneldo

dilute [daɪ'luːt] vt diluir

dim [dɪm] adj (light) débil; (outline) indistinto; (room) oscuro; (inf: stupid) lerdo ⊳ vt (light) bajar

dime [daɪm] (US) n moneda de diez centavos

dimension [dɪ'mɛnʃən] n dimensión f

diminish [dɪ'mɪnɪʃ] vt, vi disminuir

din [dɪn] n estruendo, estrépito

dine [daɪn] vi cenar; **diner** n (person) comensal mf

dinghy ['dɪŋgɪ] n bote m; (also: **rubber ~**) lancha (neumática)

dingy ['dɪndʒɪ] adj (room) sombrío; (colour) sucio

dining car ['daɪnɪŋ-] (BRIT) n (Rail) coche-comedor m

dining room ['daɪnɪŋ-] n comedor m

dining table n mesa f de comedor

dinner ['dɪnə*] n (evening meal) cena; (lunch) comida; (public) cena, banquete m; **dinner jacket** n smoking m; **dinner party** n cena; **dinner time** n (evening) hora de cenar; (midday) hora de comer

dinosaur ['daɪnəsɔ:*] n dinosaurio

dip [dɪp] n (slope) pendiente m; (in sea) baño; (Culin) salsa ▷ vt (in water) mojar; (ladle etc) meter; (BRIT Aut): **to ~ one's lights** poner luces de cruce ▷ vi (road etc) descender, bajar

diploma [dɪ'pləumə] n diploma m

diplomacy [dɪ'pləuməsɪ] n diplomacia

diplomat ['dɪpləmæt] n diplomático/a; **diplomatic** [dɪplə'mætɪk] adj diplomático

dipstick ['dɪpstɪk] (BRIT) n (Aut) varilla de nivel (del aceite)

dire [daɪə*] adj calamitoso

direct [daɪ'rɛkt] adj directo; (challenge) claro; (person) franco ▷ vt dirigir; (order): **to ~ sb to do sth** mandar a algn hacer algo ▷ adv derecho; **can you ~ me to ...?** ¿puede indicarme dónde está ...?; **direct debit** (BRIT) n domiciliación f bancaria de recibos

direction [dɪ'rɛkʃən] n dirección f; **sense of ~** sentido de la dirección; **directions** npl (instructions) instrucciones fpl; **~s for use** modo de empleo

directly [dɪ'rɛktlɪ] adv (in straight line)

directamente; (at once) en seguida

director [dɪ'rɛktə*] n director(a) m/f

directory [dɪ'rɛktərɪ] n (Tel) guía (telefónica); (Comput) directorio; **directory enquiries** (US **directory assistance**) n (servicio de) información f

dirt [də:t] n suciedad f; (earth) tierra; **dirty** adj sucio; (joke) verde, colorado (MEX) ▷ vt ensuciar; (stain) manchar

disability [dɪsə'bɪlɪtɪ] n incapacidad f

disabled [dɪs'eɪbld] adj: **to be physically ~** ser minusválido/a; **to be mentally ~** ser deficiente mental

disadvantage [dɪsəd'vɑ:ntɪdʒ] n desventaja, inconveniente m

disagree [dɪsə'gri:] vi (differ) discrepar; **to ~ (with)** no estar de acuerdo (con); **disagreeable** adj desagradable; (person) antipático; **disagreement** n desacuerdo

disappear [dɪsə'pɪə*] vi desaparecer; **disappearance** n desaparición f

disappoint [dɪsə'pɔɪnt] vt decepcionar, defraudar; **disappointed** adj decepcionado; **disappointing** adj decepcionante; **disappointment** n decepción f

disapproval [dɪsə'pru:vəl] n desaprobación f

disapprove [dɪsə'pru:v] vi: **to ~ of** ver mal

disarm [dɪs'ɑ:m] vt desarmar; **disarmament** [dɪs'ɑ:məmənt] n desarme m

disaster [dɪ'zɑ:stə*] n desastre m

disastrous [dɪ'zɑ:strəs] adj desastroso

disbelief [dɪsbə'li:f] n incredulidad f

disc [dɪsk] n disco; (Comput) = **disk**

discard [dɪs'kɑ:d] vt (old things) tirar; (fig) descartar

discharge [vb dɪs'tʃɑ:dʒ, n 'dɪstʃɑ:dʒ] vt (task, duty) cumplir; (waste) verter; (patient) dar de alta; (employee) despedir; (soldier) licenciar; (defendant) poner en libertad ▷ n (Elec) descarga; (*Med*) supuración *f*; (*dismissal*) despedida; (*of duty*) desempeño; (*of debt*) pago, descargo

discipline ['dɪsɪplɪn] *n* disciplina ▷ *vt* disciplinar; (*punish*) castigar

disc jockey *n* pinchadiscos *mf inv*

disclose [dɪs'kləʊz] *vt* revelar

disco ['dɪskəʊ] *n abbr* discoteca

discoloured [dɪs'kʌləd] (*US* **discolored**) *adj* descolorido

discomfort [dɪs'kʌmfət] *n* incomodidad *f*; (*unease*) inquietud *f*; (*physical*) malestar *m*

disconnect [dɪskə'nɛkt] *vt* separar; (*Elec etc*) desconectar

discontent [dɪskən'tɛnt] *n* descontento

discontinue [dɪskən'tɪnjuː] *vt* interrumpir; (*payments*) suspender; "**~d**" (*Comm*) "ya no se fabrica"

discount [*n* 'dɪskaʊnt, *vb* dɪs'kaʊnt] *n* descuento ▷ *vt* descontar

discourage [dɪs'kʌrɪdʒ] *vt* desalentar; (*advise against*): **to ~ sb from doing** disuadir a algn de hacer

discover [dɪs'kʌvə*] *vt* descubrir; (*error*) darse cuenta de; **discovery** *n* descubrimiento

discredit [dɪs'krɛdɪt] *vt* desacreditar

discreet [dɪ'skriːt] *adj* (*tactful*) discreto; (*careful*) prudente

discrepancy [dɪ'skrɛpənsɪ] *n* diferencia

discretion [dɪ'skrɛʃən] *n* (*tact*) discreción *f*; **at the ~ of** a criterio de

discriminate [dɪ'skrɪmɪneɪt] *vi*: **to ~ between** distinguir entre; **to ~ against** discriminar contra; **discrimination** [-'neɪʃən] *n* (*discernment*) perspicacia; (*bias*) discriminación *f*

discuss [dɪ'skʌs] *vt* discutir; (*a theme*) tratar; **discussion** [dɪ'skʌʃən] *n* discusión *f*

disease [dɪ'ziːz] *n* enfermedad *f*

disembark [dɪsɪm'bɑːk] *vt, vi* desembarcar

disgrace [dɪs'greɪs] *n* ignominia; (*shame*) vergüenza, escándalo ▷ *vt* deshonrar; **disgraceful** *adj* vergonzoso

disgruntled [dɪs'grʌntld] *adj* disgustado, descontento

disguise [dɪs'gaɪz] *n* disfraz *m* ▷ *vt* disfrazar; **in ~** disfrazado

disgust [dɪs'gʌst] *n* repugnancia ▷ *vt* repugnar, dar asco a

■ Be careful not to translate **disgust** by the Spanish word *disgustar*.

disgusted [dɪs'gʌstɪd] *adj* indignado

■ Be careful not to translate **disgusted** by the Spanish word *disgustado*.

disgusting [dɪs'gʌstɪŋ] *adj* repugnante, asqueroso; (*behaviour etc*) vergonzoso

dish [dɪʃ] *n* (*gen*) plato; **to do** *or* **wash the ~es** fregar los platos; **dishcloth** *n* estropajo

dishonest [dɪs'ɔnɪst] *adj* (*person*) poco honrado, tramposo; (*means*) fraudulento

dishtowel ['dɪʃtaʊəl] (*US*) *n* estropajo

dishwasher ['dɪʃwɔʃə*] *n* lavaplatos *m inv*

disillusion [dɪsɪ'luːʒən] *vt* desilusionar

disinfectant [dɪsɪn'fɛktənt] *n* desinfectante *m*

disintegrate [dɪs'ɪntɪgreɪt] *vi* disgregarse, desintegrarse

disk [dɪsk] *n* (*esp US*) = **disc**; (*Comput*) disco, disquete *m*; **single-/double-sided ~** disco de una cara/dos caras; **disk drive** *n* disc drive *m*; **diskette** *n* = **disk**

dislike [dɪs'laɪk] *n* antipatía, aversión *f* ▷ *vt* tener antipatía a

dislocate ['dɪsləkeɪt] *vt* dislocar

disloyal [dɪs'lɔɪəl] *adj* desleal

dismal ['dɪzml] *adj* (*gloomy*) deprimente, triste; (*very bad*) malísimo, fatal

dismantle [dɪs'mæntl] *vt* desmontar, desarmar

dismay [dɪs'meɪ] n consternación f
▷ vt consternar
dismiss [dɪs'mɪs] vt (worker)
despedir; (pupils) dejar marchar;
(soldiers) dar permiso para irse; (idea,
Law) rechazar; (possibility) descartar;
dismissal n despido
disobedient [dɪsə'biːdɪənt] adj
desobediente
disobey [dɪsə'beɪ] vt desobedecer
disorder [dɪs'ɔːdə*] n desorden m;
(rioting) disturbios mpl; (Med) trastorno
disorganized [dɪs'ɔːgənaɪzd] adj
desorganizado
disown [dɪs'əʊn] vt (action) renegar
de; (person) negar cualquier tipo de
relación con
dispatch [dɪs'pætʃ] vt enviar ▷ n
(sending) envío; (Press) informe m; (Mil)
parte m
dispel [dɪs'pɛl] vt disipar
dispense [dɪs'pɛns] vt (medicines)
preparar; **dispense with** vt fus
prescindir de; **dispenser** n (container)
distribuidor m automático
disperse [dɪs'pɜːs] vt dispersar ▷ vi
dispersarse
display [dɪs'pleɪ] n (in shop window)
escaparate m; (exhibition) exposición
f; (Comput) visualización f; (of feeling)
manifestación f ▷ vt exponer;
manifestar; (ostentatiously) lucir
displease [dɪs'pliːz] vt (offend)
ofender; (annoy) fastidiar
disposable [dɪs'pəʊzəbl] adj
desechable; (income) disponible
disposal [dɪs'pəʊzl] n (of rubbish)
destrucción f; **at one's ~** a su
disposición
dispose [dɪs'pəʊz] vi: **to ~ of**
(unwanted goods) deshacerse de;
(problem etc) resolver; **disposition**
[dɪspə'zɪʃən] n (nature)
temperamento; (inclination)
propensión f
disproportionate [dɪsprə'pɔːʃənət]
adj desproporcionado
dispute [dɪs'pjuːt] n disputa; (also:

industrial ~) conflicto (laboral) ▷ vt
(argue) disputar, discutir; (question)
cuestionar
disqualify [dɪs'kwɔlɪfaɪ] vt (Sport)
desclasificar; **to ~ sb for sth/from
doing sth** incapacitar a algn para
algo/hacer algo
disregard [dɪsrɪ'gɑːd] vt (ignore) no
hacer caso de
disrupt [dɪs'rʌpt] vt (plans)
desbaratar, trastornar; (conversation)
interrumpir; **disruption**
[dɪs'rʌpʃən] n trastorno,
desbaratamiento; interrupción f
dissatisfaction [dɪssætɪs'fækʃən] n
disgusto, descontento
dissatisfied [dɪs'sætɪsfaɪd] adj
insatisfecho
dissect [dɪ'sɛkt] vt disecar
dissent [dɪ'sɛnt] n disensión f
dissertation [dɪsə'teɪʃən] n tesina
dissolve [dɪ'zɔlv] vt disolver
▷ vi disolverse; **to ~ in(to) tears**
deshacerse en lágrimas
distance ['dɪstəns] n distancia; **in
the ~** a lo lejos
distant ['dɪstənt] adj lejano; (manner)
reservado, frío
distil [dɪs'tɪl] (us **distill**) vt destilar;
distillery n destilería
distinct [dɪs'tɪŋkt] adj (different)
distinto; (clear) claro; (unmistakeable)
inequívoco; **as ~ from** a diferencia
de; **distinction** [dɪs'tɪŋkʃən] n
distinción f; (honour) honor m; (in
exam) sobresaliente m; **distinctive** adj
distintivo
distinguish [dɪs'tɪŋgwɪʃ] vt
distinguir; **to ~ o.s.** destacarse;
distinguished adj (eminent)
distinguido
distort [dɪs'tɔːt] vt distorsionar;
(shape, image) deformar
distract [dɪs'trækt] vt distraer;
distracted adj distraído; **distraction**
[dɪs'trækʃən] n distracción f;
(confusion) aturdimiento
distraught [dɪs'trɔːt] adj loco de

inquietud

distress [dɪs'trɛs] n (*anguish*)
angustia, aflicción f ▷ vt afligir;
distressing adj angustioso; doloroso

distribute [dɪs'trɪbjuːt] vt distribuir;
(*share out*) repartir; **distribution**
[-'bjuːʃən] n distribución f, reparto;
distributor n (*Aut*) distribuidor m;
(*Comm*) distribuidora

district [dɪstrɪkt] n (*of country*)
zona, región f; (*of town*) barrio; (*Admin*)
distrito; **district attorney** (*US*) n
fiscal mf

distrust [dɪs'trʌst] n desconfianza
▷ vt desconfiar de

disturb [dɪs'təːb] vt (*person: bother,
interrupt*) molestar; (: *upset*)
perturbar, inquietar; (*disorganize*)
alterar; **disturbance** n (*upheaval*)
perturbación f; (*political etc: gen
pl*) disturbio; (*of mind*) trastorno;
disturbed adj (*worried, upset*)
preocupado, angustiado; **emotionally
disturbed** trastornado; (*childhood*)
inseguro; **disturbing** adj inquietante,
perturbador(a)

ditch [dɪtʃ] n zanja; (*irrigation ditch*)
acequia ▷ vt (*inf: partner*) deshacerse
de; (: *plan, car etc*) abandonar

ditto ['dɪtəu] adv ídem, lo mismo

dive [daɪv] n (*from board*) salto;
(*underwater*) buceo; (*of submarine*)
sumersión f ▷ vi (*swimmer: into water*)
saltar; (: *under water*) zambullirse,
bucear; (*fish, submarine*) sumergirse;
(*bird*) lanzarse en picado; **to ~ into** (*bag
etc*) meter la mano en; (*place*) meterse
de prisa en; **diver** n (*underwater*) buzo

diverse [daɪ'vəːs] adj diversos/as,
varios/as

diversion [daɪ'vəːʃən] n (*BRIT Aut*)
desviación f; (*distraction, Mil*) diversión
f; (*of funds*) distracción f

diversity [daɪ'vəːsɪtɪ] n diversidad f

divert [daɪ'vəːt] vt (*turn aside*) desviar

divide [dɪ'vaɪd] vt dividir; (*separate*)
separar ▷ vi dividirse; (*road*)
bifurcarse; **divided highway** (*US*) n

carretera de doble calzada

divine [dɪ'vaɪn] adj (*also fig*) divino

diving ['daɪvɪŋ] n (*Sport*) salto;
(*underwater*) buceo; **diving board** n
trampolín m

division [dɪ'vɪʒən] n división f;
(*sharing out*) reparto; (*disagreement*)
diferencias fpl; (*Comm*) sección f

divorce [dɪ'vɔːs] n divorcio
▷ vt divorciarse de; **divorced** adj
divorciado; **divorcee** [-'siː] n
divorciado/a

D.I.Y. (*BRIT*) adj, n abbr = **do-it-
yourself**

dizzy ['dɪzɪ] adj (*spell*) de mareo; **to
feel ~** marearse

DJ n abbr = **disc jockey**

DNA n abbr (= *deoxyribonucleic acid*)
ADN m

○ **KEYWORD**

do [duː] (pt **did**, pp **done**) n (*inf: party
etc*): **we're having a little do on
Saturday** damos una fiestecita el
sábado; **it was rather a grand do** fue
un acontecimiento a lo grande
▷ aux vb **1** (*in negative constructions: not
translated*): **I don't understand** no
entiendo
2 (*to form questions: not translated*):
didn't you know? ¿no lo sabías?; **what
do you think?** ¿qué opinas?
3 (*for emphasis, in polite expressions*):
**people do make mistakes
sometimes** sí que se cometen errores
a veces; **she does seem rather late**
a mí también me parece que se ha
retrasado; **do sit down/help yourself**
siéntate/sírvete por favor; **do take
care!** ¡ten cuidado(, te pido)!
4 (*used to avoid repeating vb*): **she sings
better than I do** canta mejor que yo;
do you agree? – yes, I do/no, I don't
¿estás de acuerdo? – sí (lo estoy)/no
(lo estoy); **she lives in Glasgow – so
do I** vive en Glasgow – yo también; **he
didn't like it and neither did we** no

le gustó y a nosotros tampoco; **who made this mess? – I did** ¿quién hizo esta chapuza? – yo; **he asked me to help him and I did** me pidió que le ayudara y lo hice

5 (*in question tags*): **you like him, don't you?** te gusta, ¿verdad? *or* ¿no?; **I don't know him, do I?** creo que no le conozco

▷ vt **1** (*gen, carry out, perform etc*): **what are you doing tonight?** ¿qué haces esta noche?; **what can I do for you?** ¿en qué puedo servirle?; **to do the washing-up/cooking** fregar los platos/cocinar; **to do one's teeth/hair/nails** lavarse los dientes/arreglarse el pelo/arreglarse las uñas

2 (*Aut etc*): **the car was doing 100** el coche iba a 100; **we've done 200 km already** ya hemos hecho 200 km; **he can do 100 in that car** puede ir a 100 en ese coche

▷ vi **1** (*act, behave*) hacer; **do as I do** haz como yo

2 (*get on, fare*): **he's doing well/badly at school** va bien/mal en la escuela; **the firm is doing well** la empresa anda *or* va bien; **how do you do?** mucho gusto; (*less formal*) ¿qué tal?

3 (*suit*): **will it do?** ¿sirve?, ¿está *or* va bien?

4 (*be sufficient*) bastar; **will £10 do?** ¿será bastante con £10?; **that'll do** así está bien; **that'll do!** (*in annoyance*) ¡ya está bien!, ¡basta ya!; **to make do (with)** arreglárselas (con)

do up vt (*laces*) atar; (*zip, dress, shirt*) abrochar; (*renovate: room, house*) renovar

do with vt fus (*need*): **I could do with a drink/some help** no me vendría mal un trago/un poco de ayuda; (*be connected*) tener que ver con; **what has it got to do with you?** ¿qué tiene que ver contigo?

do without vi pasar sin; **if you're late for tea then you'll do without** si llegas tarde tendrás que quedarte sin cenar

▷ vt fus pasar sin; **I can do without a car** puedo pasar sin coche

dock [dɔk] n (*Naut*) muelle m; (*Law*) banquillo (de los acusados) ▷ vi (*enter dock*) atracar (la) muelle; (*Space*) acoplarse; **docks** npl (*Naut*) muelles mpl, puerto sg

doctor ['dɔktə*] n médico/a; (*Ph. D. etc*) doctor(a) m/f ▷ vt (*drink etc*) adulterar; **Doctor of Philosophy** n Doctor en Filosofía y Letras

document ['dɔkjumənt] n documento; **documentary** [-'mɛntəri] adj documental ▷ n documental m; **documentation** [-mɛn'teɪʃən] n documentación f

dodge [dɔdʒ] n (*fig*) truco ▷ vt evadir; (*blow*) esquivar

dodgy ['dɔdʒɪ] adj (*inf: uncertain*) dudoso; (*suspicious*) sospechoso; (*risky*) arriesgado

does [dʌz] vb see **do**

doesn't ['dʌznt] = **does not**

dog [dɔg] n perro ▷ vt seguir los pasos de; (*bad luck*) perseguir; **doggy bag** ['dɔgɪ-] n bolsa para llevarse las sobras de la comida

do-it-yourself ['duːɪtjɔː'sɛlf] n bricolaje m

dole [dəʊl] (*BRIT*) n (*payment*) subsidio de paro, **on the ~** parado

doll [dɔl] n muñeca; (*US: inf: woman*) muñeca, gachí f

dollar ['dɔlə*] n dólar m

dolphin ['dɔlfɪn] n delfín m

dome [dəʊm] n (*Arch*) cúpula

domestic [də'mɛstɪk] adj (*animal, duty*) doméstico; (*flight, policy*) nacional; **domestic appliance** n aparato m doméstico, aparato m de uso doméstico

dominant ['dɔmɪnənt] adj dominante

dominate ['dɔmɪneɪt] vt dominar

domino ['dɔmɪnəʊ] (*pl* ~es) n ficha de dominó; **dominoes** n (*game*) dominó

donate [də'neɪt] vt donar; **donation** [də'neɪʃən] n donativo

done [dʌn] pp of **do**

donkey ['dɒŋkɪ] n burro

donor ['dəunə*] n donante mf; **donor card** n carnet m de donante

don't [dəunt] = **do not**

doodle ['du:dl] vi hacer dibujitos or garabatos

doom [du:m] n (fate) suerte f ▷ vt: **to be ~ed to failure** estar condenado al fracaso

door [dɔ:*] n puerta; **doorbell** n timbre m; **door handle** n tirador m; (of car) manija; **doorknob** n pomo m de la puerta, manilla f (LAM); **doorstep** n peldaño; **doorway** n entrada, puerta

dope [dəup] n (inf: illegal drug) droga; (: person) imbécil mf ▷ vt (horse etc) drogar

dormitory ['dɔ:mɪtrɪ] n (BRIT) dormitorio; (US) colegio mayor

DOS n abbr (= disk operating system) DOS m

dosage ['dəusɪdʒ] n dosis f inv

dose [dəus] n dosis f inv

dot [dɒt] n punto ▷ vi: **~ted with** salpicado de; **on the ~** en punto; **dotcom** [dɒt'kɒm] n puntocom f inv; **dotted line** ['dɒtɪd-] n: **to sign on the dotted line** firmar

double ['dʌbl] adj doble ▷ adv (twice): **to cost ~** costar el doble ▷ n doble m ▷ vt doblar ▷ vi doblarse; **on the ~, at the ~** = (BRIT) corriendo; **double back** vi (person) volver sobre sus pasos; **double bass** n contrabajo; **double bed** n cama de matrimonio; **double-check** vt volver a revisar ▷ vi: **I'll double-check** voy a revisarlo otra vez; **double-click** vi (Comput) hacer doble clic; **double-cross** vt (trick) engañar; (betray) traicionar; **doubledecker** n autobús m de dos pisos; **double glazing** (BRIT) n doble acristalamiento; **double room** n habitación f doble; **doubles** n (Tennis) juego de dobles; **double yellow lines** npl (BRIT: Aut) línea doble amarilla de prohibido aparcar, ≈ línea fsg amarilla continua

doubt [daut] n duda ▷ vt dudar; (suspect) dudar de; **to ~ that** dudar que; **doubtful** adj dudoso; (person): **to be doubtful about sth** tener dudas sobre algo; **doubtless** adv sin duda

dough [dəu] n masa, pasta; **doughnut** (US **donut**) n ≈ rosquilla

dove [dʌv] n paloma

down [daun] n (feathers) plumón m, flojel m ▷ adv (downwards) abajo, hacia abajo; (on the ground) por or en tierra ▷ prep abajo ▷ vt (inf: drink) beberse; **~ with X!** ¡abajo X!; **down-and-out** n vagabundo/a; **downfall** n caída, ruina; **downhill** adv: **to go downhill** (also fig) ir cuesta abajo

Downing Street ['daunɪŋ-] n (BRIT) Downing Street f

down: download vt (Comput) bajar; **downloadable** adj (Comput) descargable; **downright** adj (nonsense, lie) manifiesto; (refusal) terminante

Down's syndrome ['daunz-] n síndrome m de Down

down: downstairs adv (below) (en el piso de) abajo; (downwards) escaleras abajo; **down-to-earth** adj práctico; **downtown** adv en el centro de la ciudad; **down under** adv en Australia (or Nueva Zelanda); **downward** [-wəd] adj, adv hacia abajo; **downwards** [-wədz] adv hacia abajo

doz. abbr = **dozen**

doze [dəuz] vi dormitar

dozen ['dʌzn] n docena; **a ~ books** una docena de libros; **~s of** cantidad de

Dr. abbr = **doctor; drive**

drab [dræb] adj gris, monótono

draft [drɑ:ft] n (first copy) borrador m; (Pol: of bill) anteproyecto; (US: call-up) quinta ▷ vt (plan) preparar; (write roughly) hacer un borrador de; see also **draught**

drag [dræg] vt arrastrar; (river) dragar,

rastrear ▷ vi (time) pasar despacio; (play, film etc) hacerse pesado ▷ n (inf) lata; (women's clothing): **in ~** vestido de travesti; **to ~ and drop** (Comput) arrastrar y soltar

dragon ['drægən] n dragón m

dragonfly ['drægənflaɪ] n libélula

drain [dreɪn] n desaguadero; (in street) sumidero; (source of loss): **to be a ~ on** consumir, agotar ▷ vt (land, marshes) desaguar; (reservoir) desecar; (vegetables) escurrir ▷ vi escurrirse; **drainage** n (act) desagüe m; (Med, Agr) drenaje m; (sewage) alcantarillado; **drainpipe** n tubo de desagüe

drama ['drɑːmə] n (art) teatro; (play) drama m; (excitement) emoción f; **dramatic** [drə'mætɪk] adj dramático; (sudden, marked) espectacular

drank [dræŋk] pt of **drink**

drape [dreɪp] vt (cloth) colocar; (flag) colgar; **drapes** npl (US) cortinas fpl

drastic ['dræstɪk] adj (measure) severo; (change) radical, drástico

draught [drɑːft] (US **draft**) n (of air) corriente f de aire; (Naut) calado; **on ~** (beer) de barril; **draught beer** n cerveza de barril; **draughts** (BRIT) n (game) juego de damas

draw [drɔː] (pt **drew**, pp **drawn**) vt (picture) dibujar; (cart) tirar de; (curtain) correr; (take out) sacar; (attract) atraer; (money) retirar, (wages) cobrar ▷ vi (Sport) empatar ▷ n (Sport) empate m; (lottery) sorteo; **draw out** vi (lengthen) alargarse ▷ vt sacar; **draw up** vi (stop) pararse ▷ vt (chair) acercar; (document) redactar; **drawback** n inconveniente m, desventaja

drawer [drɔː*] n cajón m

drawing ['drɔːɪŋ] n dibujo; **drawing pin** (BRIT) n chincheta; **drawing room** n salón m

drawn [drɔːn] pp of **draw**

dread [drɛd] n pavor m, terror m ▷ vt temer, tener miedo or pavor a; **dreadful** adj horroroso

dream [driːm] (pt, pp **~ed** or **~t**) n

sueño ▷ vt, vi soñar; **dreamer** n soñador(a) m/f

dreamt [drɛmt] pt, pp of **dream**

dreary ['drɪərɪ] adj monótono

drench [drɛntʃ] vt empapar

dress [drɛs] n vestido; (clothing) ropa ▷ vt vestir; (wound) vendar ▷ vi vestirse; **to get ~ed** vestirse; **dress up** vi vestirse de etiqueta; (in fancy dress) disfrazarse; **dress circle** (BRIT) n principal m; **dresser** n (furniture) aparador m; (: US) cómoda (con espejo); **dressing** n (Med) vendaje m; (Culin) aliño; **dressing gown** (BRIT) n bata; **dressing room** n (Theatre) camarín m; (Sport) vestuario; **dressing table** n tocador m; **dressmaker** n modista, costurera

drew [druː] pt of **draw**

dribble ['drɪbl] vi (baby) babear ▷ vt (ball) regatear

dried [draɪd] adj (fruit) seco; (milk) en polvo

drier ['draɪə*] n = **dryer**

drift [drɪft] n (of current etc) flujo; (of snow) ventisquero; (meaning) significado ▷ vi (boat) ir a la deriva; (sand, snow) amontonarse

drill [drɪl] n (drill bit) broca; (tool for DIY etc) taladro; (of dentist) fresa; (for mining etc) perforadora, barrena; (Mil) instrucción f ▷ vt perforar, taladrar; (troops) enseñar la instrucción a ▷ vi (for oil) perforar

drink [drɪŋk] (pt **drank**, pp **drunk**) n bebida; (sip) trago ▷ vt, vi beber; **to have a ~** tomar algo; tomar una copa or un trago; **a ~ of water** un trago de agua; **drink-driving** n: **to be charged with drink-driving** ser acusado de conducir borracho or en estado de embriaguez; **drinker** n bebedor(a) m/f; **drinking water** n agua potable

drip [drɪp] n (act) goteo; (one drip) gota; (Med) gota a gota m ▷ vi gotear

drive [draɪv] (pt **drove**, pp **driven**) n (journey) viaje m (en coche); (also: **~way**) entrada; (energy) energía, vigor *m*; (*Comput: also*: **disk ~**) drive *m* ▷ *vt* (*car*) conducir (*SP*), manejar (*LAM*); (*nail*) clavar; (*push*) empujar; (*Tech: motor*) impulsar ▷ *vi* (*Aut: at controls*) conducir; (: *travel*) pasearse en coche; **left-/right-hand ~** conducción *f* a la izquierda/derecha; **to ~ sb mad** volverle loco a algn; **drive out** *vt* (*force out*) expulsar, echar; **drive-in** *adj* (*esp US*): **drive-in cinema** autocine *m*

driven ['drɪvn] *pp of* **drive**

driver ['draɪvə*] *n* conductor(a) *m/f* (*SP*), chofer *mf* (*LAM*); (*of taxi, bus*) chófer *mf* (*SP*), chofer *mf* (*LAM*); **driver's license** (*US*) *n* carnet *m* de conducir

driveway ['draɪvweɪ] *n* entrada

driving ['draɪvɪŋ] *n* el conducir (*SP*), el manejar (*LAM*); **driving instructor** *n* profesor(a) *m/f* de autoescuela (*SP*), instructor(a) *m/f* de manejo (*LAM*); **driving lesson** *n* clase *f* de conducir (*SP*) or manejar (*LAM*); **driving licence** (*BRIT*) *n* licencia de manejo (*LAM*), carnet *m* de conducir (*SP*); **driving test** *n* examen *m* de conducir (*SP*) or manejar (*LAM*)

drizzle ['drɪzl] *n* llovizna

droop [dru:p] *vi* (*flower*) marchitarse; (*shoulders*) encorvarse; (*head*) inclinarse

drop [drɔp] *n* (*of water*) gota; (*lessening*) baja; (*fall*) caída ▷ *vt* dejar caer; (*voice, eyes, price*) bajar; (*passenger*) dejar; (*omit*) omitir ▷ *vi* (*object*) caer; (*wind*) amainar; **drop in** *vi* (*inf: visit*): **to drop in (on)** pasar por casa (de); **drop off** *vi* (*sleep*) dormirse ▷ *vt* (*passenger*) dejar; **drop out** *vi* (*withdraw*) retirarse

drought [draut] *n* sequía

drove [drəuv] *pt of* **drive**

drown [draun] *vt* ahogar ▷ *vi* ahogarse

drowsy ['drauzɪ] *adj* soñoliento; **to be ~** tener sueño

drug [drʌg] *n* medicamento; (*narcotic*) droga ▷ *vt* drogar; **to be on ~s** drogarse; **drug addict** *n* drogadicto/a; **drug dealer** *n* traficante *mf* de drogas; **druggist** (*US*) *n* farmacéutico;

drugstore (*US*) *n* farmacia

drum [drʌm] *n* tambor *m*; (*for oil, petrol*) bidón *m*; **drums** *npl* batería; **drummer** *n* tambor *m*

drunk [drʌŋk] *pp of* **drink** ▷ *adj* borracho ▷ *n* (*also*: **~ard**) borracho/a; **drunken** *adj* borracho; (*laughter, party*) de borrachos

dry [draɪ] *adj* seco; (*day*) sin lluvia; (*climate*) árido, seco ▷ *vt* secar; (*tears*) enjugarse ▷ *vi* secarse; **dry off** *vi* secarse ▷ *vt* secar; **dry up** *vi* (*river*) secarse; **dry-cleaner's** *n* tintorería; **dry-cleaning** *n* lavado en seco; **dryer** *n* (*for hair*) secador *m*; (*US: for clothes*) secadora

DSS *n abbr* = **Department of Social Security**

D & T (*BRIT: Scol*) *n abbr* (= *design and technology*) ≈ dibujo y tecnología

DTP *n abbr* (= *desk-top publishing*) autoedición *f*

dual ['djuəl] *adj* doble; **dual carriageway** (*BRIT*) *n* carretera de doble calzada

dubious ['dju:bɪəs] *adj* indeciso; (*reputation, company*) sospechoso

duck [dʌk] *n* pato ▷ *vi* agacharse

due [dju:] *adj* (*owed*): **he is ~ £10** se le deben 10 libras; (*expected: event*): **the meeting is ~ on Wednesday** la reunión tendrá lugar el miércoles; (: *arrival*): **the train is ~ at 8am** el tren tiene su llegada para las 8; (*proper*) debido ▷ *n*: **to give sb his** (*or* **her**) **~** ser justo con algn ▷ *adv*: **~ north** derecho al norte

duel ['djuəl] *n* duelo

duet [dju:'ɛt] *n* dúo

dug [dʌg] *pt, pp of* **dig**

duke [dju:k] *n* duque *m*

dull [dʌl] *adj* (*light*) débil; (*stupid*) torpe; (*boring*) pesado; (*sound, pain*) sordo; (*weather, day*) gris ▷ *vt* (*pain, grief*) aliviar; (*mind, senses*) entorpecer

dumb [dʌm] *adj* mudo; (*pej: stupid*) estúpido

dummy ['dʌmɪ] *n* (*tailor's dummy*)

maniquí m; (*mock-up*) maqueta;
(BRIT: *for baby*) chupete m ▷ *adj* falso,
postizo
dump [dʌmp] n (*also*: **rubbish ~**)
basurero, vertedero; (*inf*: *place*)
cuchitril m ▷ *vt* (*put down*) dejar; (*get
rid of*) deshacerse de; (*Comput*: *data*)
transferir
dumpling ['dʌmplɪŋ] n *bola de masa
hervida*
dune [djuːn] n duna
dungarees [dʌŋɡə'riːz] *npl* mono
dungeon ['dʌndʒən] n calabozo
duplex ['djuːplɛks] n dúplex m
duplicate [n 'djuːplɪkət, vb
'djuːplɪkeɪt] n duplicado ▷ *vt*
duplicar; (*photocopy*) fotocopiar;
(*repeat*) repetir; **in ~** por duplicado
durable ['djuərəbl] *adj* duradero
duration [djuə'reɪʃən] n duración f
during ['djuərɪŋ] *prep* durante
dusk [dʌsk] n crepúsculo, anochecer
m
dust [dʌst] n polvo ▷ *vt* quitar el
polvo a, desempolvar; (*cake etc*): **to ~
with** espolvorear de; **dustbin** (BRIT)
n cubo or bote m (MEX) or tacho (SC)
de la basura; **duster** n paño, trapo;
dustman (BRIT: *irreg*) n basurero;
dustpan n cogedor m; **dusty** *adj*
polvoriento
Dutch [dʌtʃ] *adj* holandés/esa ▷ n
(*Ling*) holandés m; **the Dutch** *npl* los
holandeses; **to go ~** (*inf*) pagar cada
uno lo suyo; **Dutchman** (*irreg*) n
holandés m; **Dutchwoman** (*irreg*) n
holandésa
duty ['djuːtɪ] n deber m; (*tax*) derechos
mpl de aduana; **on ~** de servicio; (*at
night etc*) de guardia; **off ~** libre (de
servicio); **duty-free** *adj* libre de
impuestos
duvet ['duːveɪ] (BRIT) n edredón m
DVD n *abbr* (= *digital versatile or video
disc*) DVD m; **DVD player** n lector m de
DVD; **DVD writer** n grabadora de DVD
dwarf [dwɔːf] (*pl* **dwarves**) n enano/
a ▷ *vt* empequeñecer

dwell [dwɛl] (*pt*, *pp* **dwelt**) vi morar;
dwell on *vt fus* explayarse en
dwelt [dwɛlt] *pt*, *pp of* **dwell**
dwindle ['dwɪndl] vi disminuir
dye [daɪ] n tinte m ▷ *vt* teñir
dying ['daɪɪŋ] *adj* moribundo
dynamic [daɪ'næmɪk] *adj* dinámico
dynamite ['daɪnəmaɪt] n dinamita
dyslexia [dɪs'lɛksɪə] n dislexia
dyslexic [dɪs'lɛksɪk] *adj*, n disléxico/
a m/f

e

E [iː] *n* (*Mus*) mi *m*

E111 *n abbr* (= *form E111*) impreso E111

each [iːtʃ] *adj* cada *inv* ▷ *pron* cada uno; **~ other** el uno a otro; **they hate ~ other** se odian (entre ellos *or* mutuamente); **they have 2 books ~** tienen 2 libros por persona

eager ['iːgə*] *adj* (*keen*) entusiasmado; **to be ~ to do sth** tener muchas ganas de hacer algo, impacientarse por hacer algo; **to be ~ for** tener muchas ganas de

eagle ['iːgl] *n* águila

ear [ɪə*] *n* oreja; oído; (*of corn*) espiga; **earache** *n* dolor *m* de oídos; **eardrum** *n* tímpano

earl [əːl] *n* conde *m*

earlier ['əːlɪə*] *adj* anterior ▷ *adv* antes

early ['əːlɪ] *adv* temprano; (*before time*) con tiempo, con anticipación ▷ *adj* temprano; (*settlers etc*) primitivo; (*death, departure*) prematuro; (*reply*) pronto; **to have an ~ night** acostarse temprano; **in the ~** *or* **~ in the**

spring/19th century a principios de primavera/del siglo diecinueve; **early retirement** *n* jubilación *f* anticipada

earmark ['ɪəmɑːk] *vt*: **to ~ (for)** reservar (para), destinar (a)

earn [əːn] *vt* (*salary*) percibir; (*interest*) devengar; (*praise*) merecerse

earnest ['əːnɪst] *adj* (*wish*) fervoroso; (*person*) serio, formal; **in ~** en serio

earnings ['əːnɪŋz] *npl* (*personal*) sueldo, ingresos *mpl*; (*company*) ganancias *fpl*

ear: **earphones** *npl* auriculares *mpl*; **earplugs** *npl* tapones *mpl* para los oídos; **earring** *n* pendiente *m*, arete *m*

earth [əːθ] *n* tierra; (*BRIT Elec*) cable *m* de toma de tierra ▷ *vt* (*BRIT Elec*) conectar a tierra; **earthquake** *n* terremoto

ease [iːz] *n* facilidad *f*; (*comfort*) comodidad *f* ▷ *vt* (*lessen: problem*) mitigar; (: *pain*) aliviar; (: *tension*) reducir; **to ~ sth in/out** meter/sacar algo con cuidado; **at ~!** (*Mil*) ¡descansen!

easily ['iːzɪlɪ] *adv* fácilmente

east [iːst] *n* este *m* ▷ *adj* del este, oriental; (*wind*) este ▷ *adv* al este, hacia el este; **the E~** el Oriente; (*Pol*) los países del Este; **eastbound** *adj* en dirección este

Easter ['iːstə*] *n* Pascua (de Resurrección); **Easter egg** *n* huevo de Pascua

eastern ['iːstən] *adj* del este, oriental; (*oriental*) oriental

Easter Sunday *n* Domingo de Resurrección

easy ['iːzɪ] *adj* fácil; (*simple*) sencillo; (*comfortable*) holgado, cómodo; (*relaxed*) tranquilo ▷ *adv*: **to take it** *or* **things ~** (*not worry*) tomarlo con calma; (*rest*) descansar; **easy-going** *adj* acomodadizo

eat [iːt] (*pt* **ate**, *pp* **eaten**) *vt* comer; **eat out** *vi* comer fuera

eavesdrop ['iːvzdrɔp] *vi*: **to ~ (on)** escuchar a escondidas

e-book ['i:buk] *n* libro electrónico

e-business ['i:bɪznɪs] *n* (*company*) negocio electrónico; (*commerce*) comercio electrónico

EC *n abbr* (= *European Community*) CE *f*

eccentric [ɪk'sɛntrɪk] *adj, n* excéntrico/a *m/f*

echo ['ɛkəʊ] (*pl* ~**es**) *n* eco ▷ *vt* (*sound*) repetir ▷ *vi* resonar, hacer eco

eclipse [ɪ'klɪps] *n* eclipse *m*

eco-friendly ['i:kəʊfrɛndlɪ] *adj* ecológico

ecological [i:kə'lɒdʒɪkl] *adj* ecológico

ecology [ɪ'kɒlədʒɪ] *n* ecología

e-commerce *n abbr* comercio electrónico

economic [i:kə'nɒmɪk] *adj* económico; (*business etc*) rentable; **economical** *adj* económico; **economics** *n* (*Scol*) economía ▷ *npl* (*of project etc*) rentabilidad *f*

economist [ɪ'kɒnəmɪst] *n* economista *m/f*

economize [ɪ'kɒnəmaɪz] *vi* economizar, ahorrar

economy [ɪ'kɒnəmɪ] *n* economía; **economy class** *n* (*Aviat*) clase *f* económica; **economy class syndrome** *n* síndrome *m* de la clase turista

ecstasy ['ɛkstəsɪ] *n* éxtasis *m inv*; (*drug*) éxtasis *m inv*; **ecstatic** [ɛks'tætɪk] *adj* extático

eczema ['ɛksɪmə] *n* eczema *m*

edge [ɛdʒ] *n* (*of knife*) filo *m*; (*of object*) borde *m*; (*of lake*) orilla ▷ *vt* (*Sewing*) ribetear; **on** ~ (*fig*) = **edgy**; **to** ~ **away from** alejarse poco a poco de

edgy ['ɛdʒɪ] *adj* nervioso, inquieto

edible ['ɛdɪbl] *adj* comestible

Edinburgh ['ɛdɪnbərə] *n* Edimburgo

edit ['ɛdɪt] *vt* (*be editor of*) dirigir; (*text, report*) corregir, preparar; **edition** [ɪ'dɪʃən] *n* edición *f*; **editor** *n* (*of newspaper*) director(a) *m/f*; (*of column*): **foreign/political editor** encargado de la sección de extranjero/ política; (*of book*) redactor(a) *m/f*;

editorial [-'tɔːrɪəl] *adj* editorial ▷ *n* editorial *m*

educate ['ɛdjʊkeɪt] *vt* (*gen*) educar; (*instruct*) instruir; **educated** ['ɛdjʊkeɪtɪd] *adj* culto

education [ɛdjʊ'keɪʃən] *n* educación *f*; (*schooling*) enseñanza; (*Scol*) pedagogía; **educational** *adj* (*policy etc*) educacional; (*experience*) docente; (*toy*) educativo

eel [i:l] *n* anguila

eerie ['ɪərɪ] *adj* misterioso

effect [ɪ'fɛkt] *n* efecto ▷ *vt* efectuar, llevar a cabo; **to take** ~ (*law*) entrar en vigor *or* vigencia; (*drug*) surtir efecto; **in** ~ en realidad; **effects** *npl* (*property*) efectos *mpl*; **effective** *adj* eficaz; (*actual*) verdadero; **effectively** *adv* eficazmente; (*in reality*) efectivamente

efficiency [ɪ'fɪʃənsɪ] *n* eficiencia; rendimiento

efficient [ɪ'fɪʃənt] *adj* eficiente; (*machine*) de buen rendimiento; **efficiently** *adv* eficientemente, de manera eficiente

effort ['ɛfət] *n* esfuerzo; **effortless** *adj* sin ningún esfuerzo; (*style*) natural

e.g. *adv abbr* (= *exempli gratia*) p. ej.

egg [ɛg] *n* huevo; **hard-boiled/soft-boiled** ~ huevo duro/pasado por agua; **eggcup** *n* huevera; **eggplant** (*esp us*) *n* berenjena; **eggshell** *n* cáscara de huevo; **egg white** *n* clara de huevo; **egg yolk** *n* yema de huevo

ego ['i:gəʊ] *n* ego

Egypt ['i:dʒɪpt] *n* Egipto; **Egyptian** [ɪ'dʒɪpʃən] *adj, n* egipcio/a *m/f*

eight [eɪt] *num* ocho; **eighteen** *num* diez y ocho, dieciocho; **eighteenth** *adj* decimoctavo; **the eighteenth floor** la planta dieciocho; **the eighteenth of August** el dieciocho de agosto; **eighth** *num* octavo; **eightieth** ['eɪtɪɪθ] *adj* octogésimo

eighty ['eɪtɪ] *num* ochenta

Eire ['ɛərə] *n* Eire *m*

either ['aɪðə*] *adj* cualquiera de los dos; (*both, each*) cada ▷ *pron*: ~ **(of**

them) cualquiera (de los dos) ▷ *adv*
tampoco ▷ *conj*: **~ yes or no** o sí o no;
on ~ side en ambos lados; **I don't like ~**
no me gusta ninguno/a de los(las) dos;
no, I don't ~ no, yo tampoco

eject [ɪ'dʒɛkt] *vt* echar, expulsar;
(tenant) desahuciar

elaborate [*adj* ɪ'læbərɪt, *vb* ɪ'læbəreɪt]
adj (complex) complejo ▷ *vt (expand)*
ampliar; *(refine)* refinar ▷ *vi* explicar
con más detalles

elastic [ɪ'læstɪk] *n* elástico ▷ *adj*
elástico; *(fig)* flexible; **elastic band**
(BRIT) *n* gomita

elbow ['ɛlbəʊ] *n* codo

elder ['ɛldə*] *adj* mayor ▷ *n (tree)*
saúco; *(person)* mayor; **elderly** *adj* de
edad, mayor ▷ *npl*: **the elderly** los
mayores

eldest ['ɛldɪst] *adj, n* el/la mayor

elect [ɪ'lɛkt] *vt* elegir ▷ *adj*: **the
president ~** el presidente electo; **to
~ to do** optar por hacer; **election** *n*
elección *f*; **electoral** *adj* electoral;
electorate *n* electorado

electric [ɪ'lɛktrɪk] *adj* eléctrico;
electrical *n* eléctrico; **electric
blanket** *n* manta eléctrica; **electric
fire** *n* estufa eléctrica; **electrician**
[ɪlɛk'trɪʃən] *n* electricista *mf*;
electricity [ɪlɛk'trɪsɪtɪ] *n* electricidad
f; **electric shock** *n* electrochoque
m; **electrify** [ɪ'lɛktrɪfaɪ] *vt (Rail)*
electrificar; *(fig: audience)* electrizar

electronic [ɪlɛk'trɔnɪk] *adj*
electrónico; **electronic mail** *n* correo
electrónico; **electronics** *n* electrónica

elegance ['ɛlɪgəns] *n* elegancia

elegant ['ɛlɪgənt] *adj* elegante

element ['ɛlɪmənt] *n* elemento; *(of
kettle etc)* resistencia

elementary [ɛlɪ'mɛntərɪ] *adj*
elemental; *(primitive)* rudimentario;
elementary school (US) *n* escuela de
enseñanza primaria

elephant ['ɛlɪfənt] *n* elefante *m*

elevate ['ɛlɪveɪt] *vt (gen)* elevar; *(in
rank)* ascender

elevator ['ɛlɪveɪtə*] (US) *n* ascensor
m; *(in warehouse etc)* montacargas *m inv*

eleven [ɪ'lɛvn] *num* once; **eleventh**
num undécimo

eligible ['ɛlɪdʒəbl] *adj*: **an ~ young
man/woman** un buen partido; **to be ~
for sth** llenar los requisitos para algo

eliminate [ɪ'lɪmɪneɪt] *vt (suspect,
possibility)* descartar

elm [ɛlm] *n* olmo

eloquent ['ɛləkwənt] *adj* elocuente

else [ɛls] *adv*: **something ~** otra
cosa; **somewhere ~** en otra parte;
everywhere ~ en todas partes menos
aquí; **where ~?** ¿dónde más?, ¿en qué
otra parte?; **there was little ~ to do**
apenas quedaba otra cosa que hacer;
nobody ~ spoke no habló nadie más;
elsewhere *adv (be)* en otra parte; *(go)*
a otra parte

elusive [ɪ'lu:sɪv] *adj* esquivo; *(quality)*
difícil de encontrar

email ['i:meɪl] *n abbr (= electronic mail)*
correo electrónico, e-mail *m*; **email
address** *n* dirección *f* electrónica,
email *m*

embankment [ɪm'bæŋkmənt] *n*
terraplén *m*

embargo [ɪm'bɑːgəʊ] *(pl* **~es***)* *n*
(Comm, Naut) embargo; *(prohibition)*
prohibición *f*; **to put an ~ on sth** poner
un embargo en algo

embark [ɪm'bɑːk] *vi* embarcarse ▷ *vt*
embarcar; **to ~ on** *(journey)* emprender;
(course of action) lanzarse a

embarrass [ɪm'bærəs] *vt*
avergonzar; *(government etc)* dejar en
mal lugar; **embarrassed** *adj (laugh,
silence)* embarazoso

> Be careful not to translate
> **embarrassed** by the Spanish word
> *embarazada*.

embarrassing *adj (situation)*
violento; *(question)* embarazoso;
embarrassment *n (shame)*
vergüenza; *(problem)*: **to be an
embarrassment for sb** poner en un
aprieto a algn

embassy ['ɛmbəsɪ] *n* embajada
embrace [ɪm'breɪs] *vt* abrazar, dar un abrazo a; (*include*) abarcar ▷ *vi* abrazarse ▷ *n* abrazo
embroider [ɪm'brɔɪdə*] *vt* bordar; **embroidery** *n* bordado
embryo ['ɛmbrɪəu] *n* embrión *m*
emerald ['ɛmərəld] *n* esmeralda
emerge [ɪ'mə:dʒ] *vi* salir; (*arise*) surgir
emergency [ɪ'mə:dʒənsɪ] *n* crisis *f inv*; **in an ~** en caso de urgencia; **state of ~** estado de emergencia; **emergency brake** (*us*) *n* freno de mano; **emergency exit** *n* salida de emergencia; **emergency landing** *n* aterrizaje *m* forzoso; **emergency room** (*us*: *Med*) *n* sala *f* de urgencias; **emergency services** *npl* (*fire, police, ambulance*) servicios *mpl* de urgencia
emigrate ['ɛmɪgreɪt] *vi* emigrar; **emigration** [ɛmɪ'greɪʃən] *n* emigración *f*
eminent ['ɛmɪnənt] *adj* eminente
emissions [ɪ'mɪʃənz] *npl* emisión *f*
emit [ɪ'mɪt] *vt* emitir; (*smoke*) arrojar; (*smell*) despedir; (*sound*) producir
emoticon [ɪ'məutɪkən] *n* emoticon *m*
emotion [ɪ'məuʃən] *n* emoción *f*; **emotional** *adj* (*needs*) emocional; (*person*) sentimental; (*scene*) conmovedor(a), emocionante; (*speech*) emocionado
emperor ['ɛmpərə*] *n* emperador *m*
emphasis ['ɛmfəsɪs] (*pl* -**ses**) *n* énfasis *m inv*
emphasize ['ɛmfəsaɪz] *vt* (*word, point*) subrayar, recalcar; (*feature*) hacer resaltar
empire ['ɛmpaɪə*] *n* imperio
employ [ɪm'plɔɪ] *vt* emplear; **employee** [-'i:] *n* empleado/a; **employer** *n* patrón/ona *m/f*; empresario; **employment** *n* (*work*) trabajo; **employment agency** *n* agencia de colocaciones
empower [ɪm'pauə*] *vt*: **to ~ sb to do sth** autorizar a algn para hacer algo
empress ['ɛmprɪs] *n* emperatriz *f*

emptiness ['ɛmptɪnɪs] *n* vacío; (*of life etc*) vaciedad *f*
empty ['ɛmptɪ] *adj* vacío; (*place*) desierto; (*house*) desocupado; (*threat*) vano ▷ *vt* vaciar; (*place*) dejar vacío ▷ *vi* vaciarse; (*house etc*) quedar desocupado; **empty-handed** *adj* con las manos vacías
EMU *n abbr* (= *European Monetary Union*) UME *f*
emulsion [ɪ'mʌlʃən] *n* emulsión *f*; (*also:* **~ paint**) pintura emulsión
enable [ɪ'neɪbl] *vt*: **to ~ sb to do sth** permitir a algn hacer algo
enamel [ɪ'næməl] *n* esmalte *m*; (*also:* **~ paint**) pintura esmaltada
enchanting [ɪn'tʃɑ:ntɪŋ] *adj* encantador(a)
encl. *abbr* (= *enclosed*) *adj*
enclose [ɪn'kləuz] *vt* (*land*) cercar; (*letter etc*) adjuntar; **please find ~d** le mandamos adjunto
enclosure [ɪn'kləuʒə*] *n* cercado, recinto
encore [ɔŋ'kɔ:*] *excl* ¡otra!, ¡bis! ▷ *n* bis *m*
encounter [ɪn'kauntə*] *n* encuentro ▷ *vt* encontrar, encontrarse con; (*difficulty*) tropezar con
encourage [ɪn'kʌrɪdʒ] *vt* alentar, animar; (*activity*) fomentar; (*growth*) estimular; **encouragement** *n* estímulo; (*of industry*) fomento
encouraging [ɪn'kʌrɪdʒɪŋ] *adj* alentador(a)
encyclop(a)edia [ɛnsaɪkləu'pi:dɪə] *n* enciclopedia
end [ɛnd] *n* fin *m*; (*of table*) extremo; (*of street*) final *m*; (*Sport*) lado ▷ *vt* terminar, acabar; (*also:* **bring to an ~, put an ~ to**) acabar con ▷ *vi* terminar, acabar; **in the ~** al fin; **on ~** (*object*) de punta, de cabeza; **to stand on ~** (*hair*) erizarse; **for hours on ~** hora tras hora; **end up** *vi*: **to end up in** terminar en; (*place*) ir a parar en
endanger [ɪn'deɪndʒə*] *vt* poner en peligro; **an ~ed species** una especie en

peligro de extinción

endearing [ɪn'dɪərɪŋ] *adj* simpático, atractivo

endeavour [ɪn'dɛvə*] (*US* **endeavor**) *n* esfuerzo; (*attempt*) tentativa ▷ *vi*: **to ~ to do** esforzarse por hacer; (*try*) procurar hacer

ending ['ɛndɪŋ] *n* (*of book*) desenlace *m*; (*Ling*) terminación *f*

endless ['ɛndlɪs] *adj* interminable, inacabable

endorse [ɪn'dɔːs] *vt* (*cheque*) endosar; (*approve*) aprobar; **endorsement** *n* (*on driving licence*) nota de inhabilitación

endurance [ɪn'djuərəns] *n* resistencia

endure [ɪn'djuə*] *vt* (*bear*) aguantar, soportar ▷ *vi* (*last*) durar

enemy ['ɛnəmɪ] *adj*, *n* enemigo/a *m/f*

energetic [ɛnə'dʒɛtɪk] *adj* enérgico

energy ['ɛnədʒɪ] *n* energía

enforce [ɪn'fɔːs] *vt* (*Law*) hacer cumplir

engaged [ɪn'geɪdʒd] *adj* (*BRIT*: *busy, in use*) ocupado; (*betrothed*) prometido; **to get ~** prometerse; **engaged tone** (*BRIT*) *n* (*Tel*) señal *f* de comunicando

engagement [ɪn'geɪdʒmənt] *n* (*appointment*) compromiso, cita; (*booking*) contratación *f*; (*to marry*) compromiso; (*period*) noviazgo; **engagement ring** *n* anillo de prometida

engaging [ɪn'geɪdʒɪŋ] *adj* atractivo

engine ['ɛndʒɪn] *n* (*Aut*) motor *m*; (*Rail*) locomotora

engineer [ɛndʒɪ'nɪə*] *n* ingeniero; (*BRIT*: *for repairs*) mecánico; (*on ship, US Rail*) maquinista *m*; **engineering** *n* ingeniería

England ['ɪŋglənd] *n* Inglaterra

English ['ɪŋglɪʃ] *adj* inglés/esa ▷ *n* (*Ling*) inglés *m*; **the English** *npl* los ingleses *mpl*; **English Channel** *n*: **the English Channel** (el Canal de) la Mancha; **Englishman** (*irreg*) *n* inglés *m*; **Englishwoman** (*irreg*) *n* inglésa

engrave [ɪn'greɪv] *vt* grabar

engraving [ɪn'greɪvɪŋ] *n* grabado

enhance [ɪn'hɑːns] *vt* (*gen*) aumentar; (*beauty*) realzar

enjoy [ɪn'dʒɔɪ] *vt* (*health, fortune*) disfrutar de, gozar de; (*like*) gustarle a algn; **to ~ o.s.** divertirse; **enjoyable** *adj* agradable; (*amusing*) divertido; **enjoyment** *n* (*joy*) placer *m*; (*activity*) diversión *f*

enlarge [ɪn'lɑːdʒ] *vt* aumentar; (*broaden*) extender; (*Phot*) ampliar ▷ *vi*: **to ~ on** (*subject*) tratar con más detalles; **enlargement** *n* (*Phot*) ampliación *f*

enlist [ɪn'lɪst] *vt* alistar; (*support*) conseguir ▷ *vi* alistarse

enormous [ɪ'nɔːməs] *adj* enorme

enough [ɪ'nʌf] *adj*: **~ time/books** bastante tiempo/bastantes libros ▷ *pron* bastante(s) ▷ *adv*: **big ~** bastante grande; **he has not worked ~** no ha trabajado bastante; **have you got ~?** ¿tiene usted bastante(s)?; **~ to eat** (lo) suficiente *or* (lo) bastante para comer; **~!** ¡basta ya!; **that's ~, thanks** con eso basta, gracias; **I've had ~ of him** estoy harto de él; **... which, funnily** *or* **oddly ~ ...** ... lo que, por extraño que parezca ...

enquire [ɪn'kwaɪə*] *vt*, *vi* = **inquire**

enquiry [ɪn'kwaɪərɪ] *n* (*official investigation*) investigación

enrage [ɪn'reɪdʒ] *vt* enfurecer

enrich [ɪn'rɪtʃ] *vt* enriquecer

enrol [ɪn'rəul] (*US* **enroll**) *vt* (*members*) inscribir; (*Scol*) matricular ▷ *vi* inscribirse; matricularse; **enrolment** (*US* **enrollment**) *n* inscripción *f*; matriculación *f*

en route [ɔn'ruːt] *adv* durante el viaje

en suite [ɔn'swiːt] *adj*: **with ~ bathroom** con baño

ensure [ɪn'ʃuə*] *vt* asegurar

entail [ɪn'teɪl] *vt* suponer

enter ['ɛntə*] *vt* (*room*) entrar en; (*club*) hacerse socio de; (*army*) alistarse en; (*sb for a competition*) inscribir; (*write* *down)* anotar, apuntar; (*Comput*) meter ▷ *vi* entrar

enterprise ['ɛntəpraɪz] *n* empresa; (*spirit*) iniciativa; **free ~** la libre empresa; **private ~** la iniciativa privada; **enterprising** *adj* emprendedor(a)

entertain [ɛntə'teɪn] *vt* (*amuse*) divertir; (*invite: guest*) invitar (a casa); (*idea*) abrigar; **entertainer** *n* artista *mf*; **entertaining** *adj* divertido, entretenido; **entertainment** *n* (*amusement*) diversión *f*; (*show*) espectáculo

enthusiasm [ɪn'θuːzɪæzəm] *n* entusiasmo

enthusiast [ɪn'θuːzɪæst] *n* entusiasta *mf*; **enthusiastic** [-'æstɪk] *adj* entusiasta; **to be enthusiastic about** entusiasmarse por

entire [ɪn'taɪə*] *adj* entero; **entirely** *adv* totalmente

entitle [ɪn'taɪtl] *vt*: **to ~ sb to sth** dar a algn derecho a algo; **entitled** *adj* (*book*) titulado; **to be entitled to do** tener derecho a hacer

entrance [*n* 'ɛntrəns, *vb* ɪn'trɑːns] *n* entrada ▷ *vt* encantar, hechizar; **to gain ~ to** ingresar en; **entrance examination** *n* examen *m* de ingreso; **entrance fee** *n* cuota; **entrance ramp** (*US*) *n* (*Aut*) rampa de acceso

entrant ['ɛntrənt] *n* (*in race, competition*) participante *mf*; (*in examination*) candidato/a

entrepreneur [ɔntrəprə'nəː] *n* empresario

entrust [ɪn'trʌst] *vt*: **to ~ sth to sb** confiar algo a algn

entry ['ɛntrɪ] *n* entrada; (*in competition*) participación *f*; (*in register*) apunte *m*; (*in account*) partida; (*in reference book*) artículo; **"no ~"** "prohibido el paso"; (*Aut*) "dirección prohibida"; **entry phone** *n* portero automático

envelope ['ɛnvələup] *n* sobre *m*

envious ['ɛnvɪəs] *adj* envidioso; (*look*) de envidia

environment [ɪn'vaɪrnmənt] *n* (*surroundings*) entorno; (*natural world*): **the ~** el medio ambiente; **environmental** [-'mɛntl] *adj* ambiental; medioambiental; **environmentally** [-'mɛntəlɪ] *adv*: **environmentally sound/friendly** ecológico

envisage [ɪn'vɪzɪdʒ] *vt* prever

envoy ['ɛnvɔɪ] *n* enviado

envy ['ɛnvɪ] *n* envidia a; **to ~ sb sth** envidiar algo a algn

epic ['ɛpɪk] *n* épica ▷ *adj* épico

epidemic [ɛpɪ'dɛmɪk] *n* epidemia

epilepsy ['ɛpɪlɛpsɪ] *n* epilepsia

epileptic [ɛpɪ'lɛptɪk] *adj, n* epiléptico/a *m/f*; **epileptic fit** [ɛpɪ'lɛptɪk-] *n* ataque *m* de epilepsia, acceso *m* epiléptico

episode ['ɛpɪsəud] *n* episodio

equal ['iːkwl] *adj* igual; (*treatment*) equitativo ▷ *n* igual *mf* ▷ *vt* ser igual a; (*fig*) igualar; **to be ~ to** (*task*) estar a la altura de; **equality** [iː'kwɔlɪtɪ] *n* igualdad *f*; **equalize** *vi* (*Sport*) empatar; **equally** *adv* igualmente; (*share etc*) a partes iguales

equation [ɪ'kweɪʒən] *n* (*Math*) ecuación *f*

equator [ɪ'kweɪtə*] *n* ecuador *m*

equip [ɪ'kwɪp] *vt* equipar; (*person*) proveer; **to be well ~ped** estar bien equipado; **equipment** *n* equipo; (*tools*) avíos *mpl*

equivalent [ɪ'kwɪvələnt] *adj*: **~ (to)** equivalente (a) ▷ *n* equivalente *m*

ER *abbr* (BRIT: = Elizabeth Regina) la reina Isabel; (*US: Med*) = **emergency room**

era ['ɪərə] *n* era, época

erase [ɪ'reɪz] *vt* borrar; **eraser** *n* goma de borrar

erect [ɪ'rɛkt] *adj* erguido ▷ *vt* erigir, levantar; (*assemble*) montar; **erection** [-ʃən] *n* construcción *f*; (*assembly*) montaje *m*; (*Physiol*) erección *f*

ERM n abbr (= Exchange Rate
Mechanism) tipo de cambio europeo
erode [ɪ'rəud] vt (Geo) erosionar;
(metal) corroer, desgastar; (fig)
desgastar
erosion [ɪ'rəuʒən] n erosión f;
desgaste m
erotic [ɪ'rɒtɪk] adj erótico
errand ['ɛrnd] n recado (SP),
mandado (LAM)
erratic [ɪ'rætɪk] adj desigual, poco
uniforme
error ['ɛrə*] n error m, equivocación f
erupt [ɪ'rʌpt] vi entrar en erupción;
(fig) estallar; **eruption** [ɪ'rʌpʃən] n
erupción f; (of war) estallido
escalate ['ɛskəleɪt] vi extenderse,
intensificarse
escalator ['ɛskəleɪtə*] n escalera
móvil
escape [ɪ'skeɪp] n fuga ▷ vi
escaparse; (flee) huir, evadirse; (leak)
fugarse ▷ vt (responsibility etc) evitar,
eludir; (consequences) escapar a;
(elude) **his name ~s me** no me sale su
nombre; **to ~ from** (place) escaparse de;
(person) escaparse a
escort [n 'ɛskɔːt, vb ɪ'skɔːt] n
acompañante mf; (Mil) escolta mf ▷ vt
acompañar
especially [ɪ'spɛʃlɪ] adv (above all)
sobre todo; (particularly) en particular,
especialmente
espionage ['ɛspɪənɑːʒ] n espionaje
m
essay ['ɛseɪ] n (Literature) ensayo;
(Scol: short) redacción f; (: long)
trabajo
essence ['ɛsns] n esencia
essential [ɪ'sɛnʃl] adj (necessary)
imprescindible; (basic) esencial;
essentially adv esencialmente;
essentials npl lo imprescindible, lo
esencial
establish [ɪ'stæblɪʃ] vt establecer;
(prove) demostrar; (relations) entablar;
(reputation) ganarse; **establishment** n
establecimiento; **the Establishment**

la clase dirigente
estate [ɪ'steɪt] n (land) finca,
hacienda; (inheritance) herencia;
(BRIT: also: **housing ~**) urbanización
f; **estate agent** (BRIT) n agente mf
inmobiliario/a; **estate car** (BRIT) n
furgoneta
estimate [n 'ɛstɪmət, vb 'ɛstɪmeɪt] n
estimación f, apreciación f; (assessment)
tasa, cálculo; (Comm) presupuesto ▷ vt
estimar, tasar; calcular
etc abbr (= et cetera) etc
eternal [ɪ'təːnl] adj eterno
eternity [ɪ'təːnɪtɪ] n eternidad f
ethical ['ɛθɪkl] adj ético; **ethics**
['ɛθɪks] n ética ▷ npl moralidad f
Ethiopia [iːθɪ'əupɪə] n Etiopía
ethnic ['ɛθnɪk] adj étnico; **ethnic
minority** n minoría étnica
e-ticket ['iːtɪkɪt] n billete m
electrónico (SP), boleto electrónico
(LAM)
etiquette ['ɛtɪkɛt] n etiqueta
EU n abbr (= European Union) UE f
euro n euro
Europe ['juərəp] n Europa; **European**
[-'piːən] adj, n europeo/a m/f;
European Community n Comunidad
f Europea; **European Union** n Unión
f Europea
Eurostar® ['juərəustɑː*] n
Eurostar® m
evacuate [ɪ'vækjueɪt] vt (people)
evacuar; (place) desocupar
evade [ɪ'veɪd] vt evadir, eludir
evaluate [ɪ'væljueɪt] vt evaluar;
(value) tasar; (evidence) interpretar
evaporate [ɪ'væpəreɪt] vi
evaporarse; (fig) desvanecerse
eve [iːv] n: **on the ~ of** en vísperas de
even ['iːvn] adj (level) llano; (smooth)
liso; (speed, temperature) uniforme;
(number) par ▷ adv hasta, incluso;
(introducing a comparison) aún, todavía;
~ if, ~ though aunque +subjun; **~
more** aun más; **~ so** aun así; **not ~**
ni siquiera; **~ he was there** hasta él
estuvo allí; **~ on Sundays** incluso los

domingos; **to get ~ with sb** ajustar cuentas con algn

evening ['iːvnɪŋ] *n* tarde *f*; (*late*) noche *f*; **in the ~** por la tarde; **evening class** *n* clase *f* nocturna; **evening dress** *n* (*no pl: formal clothes*) traje *m* de etiqueta; (*woman's*) traje *m* de noche

event [ɪ'vɛnt] *n* suceso, acontecimiento; (*Sport*) prueba; **in the ~ of** en caso de; **eventful** *adj* (*life*) activo; (*day*) ajetreado

eventual [ɪ'vɛntʃuəl] *adj* final

⬛ Be careful not to translate **eventual** by the Spanish word *eventual*.

eventually *adv* (*finally*) finalmente; (*in time*) con el tiempo

ever ['ɛvə*] *adv* (*at any time*) nunca, jamás; (*at all times*) siempre; (*in question*): **why ~ not?** ¿y por qué no?; **the best ~** lo nunca visto; **have you ~ seen it?** ¿lo ha visto usted alguna vez?; **better than ~** mejor que nunca; **~ since** *adv* desde entonces ⊳ *conj* después de que; **evergreen** *n* árbol *m* de hoja perenne

Ⓞ **KEYWORD**

every ['ɛvrɪ] *adj* **1** (*each*) cada; **every one of them** (*persons*) todos ellos/as; (*objects*) cada uno de ellos/as; **every shop in the town was closed** todas las tiendas de la ciudad estaban cerradas

2 (*all possible*) todo/a; **I gave you every assistance** te di toda la ayuda posible; **I have every confidence in him** tiene toda mi confianza; **we wish you every success** te deseamos toda suerte de éxitos

3 (*showing recurrence*) todo/a; **every day/week** todos los días/todas las semanas; **every other car had been broken into** habían forzado uno de cada dos coches; **she visits me every other/third day** me visita cada dos/tres días; **every now and then** de vez en cuando

every: **everybody** *pron* = **everyone**; **everyday** *adj* (*daily*) cotidiano, de todos los días; (*usual*) acostumbrado; **everyone** *pron* todos/as, todo el mundo; **everything** *pron* todo; **this shop sells everything** esta tienda vende de todo; **everywhere** *adv*: **I've been looking for you everywhere** te he estado buscando por todas partes; **everywhere you go you meet ...** en todas partes encuentras ...

evict [ɪ'vɪkt] *vt* desahuciar

evidence ['ɛvɪdəns] *n* (*proof*) prueba; (*of witness*) testimonio; (*sign*) indicios *mpl*; **to give ~** prestar declaración, dar testimonio

evident ['ɛvɪdənt] *adj* evidente, manifiesto; **evidently** *adv* por lo visto

evil ['iːvl] *adj* malo; (*influence*) funesto ⊳ *n* mal *m*

evoke [ɪ'vəuk] *vt* evocar

evolution [iːvə'luːʃən] *n* evolución *f*

evolve [ɪ'vɔlv] *vt* desarrollar ⊳ *vi* evolucionar, desarrollarse

ewe [juː] *n* oveja

ex [ɛks] (*inf*) *n*: **my ~** mi ex

ex- [ɛks] *prefix* ex

exact [ɪg'zækt] *adj* exacto; (*person*) meticuloso ⊳ *vt*: **to ~ sth (from)** exigir algo (de); **exactly** *adv* exactamente; (*indicating agreement*) exacto

exaggerate [ɪg'zædʒəreɪt] *vt*, *vi* exagerar; **exaggeration** [-'reɪʃən] *n* exageración *f*

exam [ɪg'zæm] *n abbr* (*Scol*) = **examination**

examination [ɪgzæmɪ'neɪʃən] *n* examen *m*; (*Med*) reconocimiento

examine [ɪg'zæmɪn] *vt* examinar; (*inspect*) inspeccionar, escudriñar; (*Med*) reconocer; **examiner** *n* examinador(a) *m/f*

example [ɪg'zɑːmpl] *n* ejemplo; **for ~** por ejemplo

exasperated [ɪg'zɑːspəreɪtɪd] *adj* exasperado

excavate ['ɛkskəveɪt] *vt* excavar

exceed [ɪk'siːd] *vt* (*amount*) exceder;

(*number*) pasar de; (*speed limit*)
sobrepasar; (*powers*) excederse en;
(*hopes*) superar; **exceedingly** *adv*
sumamente, sobremanera
excel [ɪk'sɛl] *vi* sobresalir; **to ~ o.s**
lucirse
excellence ['ɛksələns] *n* excelencia
excellent ['ɛksələnt] *adj* excelente
except [ɪk'sɛpt] *prep* (*also*: **~ for, ~ing**)
excepto, salvo ▷ *vt* exceptuar, excluir;
~ if/when excepto si/cuando; **~ that**
salvo que; **exception** [ɪk'sɛpʃən] *n*
excepción *f*; **to take exception to**
ofenderse por; **exceptional**
[ɪk'sɛpʃənl] *adj* excepcional;
exceptionally [ɪk'sɛpʃənəlɪ] *adv*
excepcionalmente, extraordinariamente
excerpt ['ɛksəːpt] *n* extracto
excess [ɪk'sɛs] *n* exceso; **excess
baggage** *n* exceso de equipaje;
excessive *adj* excesivo
exchange [ɪks'tʃeɪndʒ] *n*
intercambio; (*conversation*) diálogo;
(*also*: **telephone ~**) central *f*
(telefónica) ▷ *vt*: **to ~ (for)** cambiar
(por); **exchange rate** *n* tipo de
cambio
excite [ɪk'saɪt] *vt* (*stimulate*)
estimular; (*arouse*) excitar; **excited**
adj: **to get excited** emocionarse;
excitement *n* (*agitation*) excitación
f; (*exhilaration*) emoción *f*; **exciting** *adj*
emocionante
exclaim [ɪk'skleɪm] *vi* exclamar;
exclamation [ɛksklə'meɪʃən] *n*
exclamación *f*; **exclamation mark** *n*
punto de admiración; **exclamation
point** (*US*) = **exclamation mark**
exclude [ɪk'skluːd] *vt* excluir;
exceptuar
excluding [ɪks'kluːdɪŋ] *prep*: **~ VAT**
IVA no incluido
exclusion [ɪk'skluːʒən] *n* exclusión *f*;
to the ~ of con exclusión de
exclusive [ɪk'skluːsɪv] *adj* exclusivo;
(*club, district*) selecto; **~ of tax**
excluyendo impuestos; **exclusively**
adv únicamente

excruciating [ɪk'skruːʃɪeɪtɪŋ]
adj (*pain*) agudísimo, atroz; (*noise,
embarrassment*) horrible
excursion [ɪk'skəːʃən] *n* (*tourist
excursion*) excursión *f*
excuse [*n* ɪk'skjuːs, *vb* ɪk'skjuːz] *n*
disculpa, excusa; (*pretext*) pretexto ▷ *vt*
(*justify*) justificar; (*forgive*) disculpar,
perdonar; **to ~ sb from doing sth**
dispensar a algn de hacer algo; **~
me!** (*attracting attention*) ¡por favor!;
(*apologizing*) ¡perdón!; **if you will ~ me**
con su permiso
ex-directory ['ɛksdɪ'rɛktərɪ] (*BRIT*)
adj que no consta en la guía
execute ['ɛksɪkjuːt] *vt* (*plan*) realizar;
(*order*) cumplir; (*person*) ajusticiar,
ejecutar; **execution** [-'kjuːʃən]
n realización *f*; cumplimiento;
ejecución *f*
executive [ɪg'zɛkjutɪv] *n* (*person,
committee*) ejecutivo; (*Pol*: *committee*)
poder *m* ejecutivo ▷ *adj* ejecutivo
exempt [ɪg'zɛmpt] *adj*: **~ from** exento
de ▷ *vt*: **to ~ sb from** eximir a algn de
exercise ['ɛksəsaɪz] *n* ejercicio ▷ *vt*
(*patience*) usar de; (*right*) valerse de;
(*dog*) llevar de paseo; (*mind*) preocupar
▷ *vi* (*also*: **to take ~**) hacer ejercicio(s);
exercise book *n* cuaderno
exert [ɪg'zəːt] *vt* ejercer; **to ~ o.s.**
esforzarse; **exertion** [-ʃən] *n* esfuerzo
exhale [ɛks'heɪl] *vt* despedir ▷ *vi*
exhalar
exhaust [ɪg'zɔːst] *n* (*Aut*: *also*: **~
pipe**) escape *m*; (: *fumes*) gases *mpl* de
escape ▷ *vt* agotar; **exhausted** *adj*
agotado; **exhaustion** [ɪg'zɔːstʃən] *n*
agotamiento; **nervous exhaustion**
postración *f* nerviosa
exhibit [ɪg'zɪbɪt] *n* (*Art*) obra
expuesta; (*Law*) objeto expuesto ▷ *vt*
(*show*: *emotions*) manifestar; (: *courage,
skill*) demostrar; (*paintings*) exponer;
exhibition [ɛksɪ'bɪʃən] *n* exposición
f; (*of talent etc*) demostración *f*
exhilarating [ɪg'zɪləreɪtɪŋ] *adj*
estimulante, tónico

exile ['ɛksaɪl] n exilio; (person) exiliado/a ▷ vt desterrar, exiliar
exist [ɪg'zɪst] vi existir; (live) vivir; **existence** n existencia; **existing** adj existente, actual
exit ['ɛksɪt] n salida ▷ vi (Theatre) hacer mutis; (Comput) salir (del sistema)

| Be careful not to translate **exit** by the Spanish word éxito.

exit ramp (us) n (Aut) vía de acceso
exotic [ɪg'zɔtɪk] adj exótico
expand [ɪk'spænd] vt ampliar; (number) aumentar ▷ vi (population) aumentar; (trade etc) expandirse; (gas, metal) dilatarse
expansion [ɪk'spænʃən] n (of population) aumento; (of trade) expansión f
expect [ɪk'spɛkt] vt esperar; (require) contar con; (suppose) suponer ▷ vi: **to be ~ing** (pregnant woman) estar embarazada; **expectation** [ɛkspɛk'teɪʃən] n (hope) esperanza; (belief) expectativa
expedition [ɛkspə'dɪʃən] n expedición f
expel [ɪk'spɛl] vt arrojar; (from place) expulsar
expenditure [ɪks'pɛndɪtʃə*] n gastos mpl, desembolso; consumo
expense [ɪk'spɛns] n gasto, gastos mpl; (high cost) costa; **expenses** npl (Comm) gastos mpl, **at the ~ of** a costa de; **expense account** n cuenta de gastos
expensive [ɪk'spɛnsɪv] adj caro, costoso
experience [ɪk'spɪərɪəns] n experiencia ▷ vt experimentar; (suffer) sufrir; **experienced** adj experimentado
experiment [ɪk'spɛrɪmənt] n experimento ▷ vi hacer experimentos; **experimental** [-'mɛntl] adj experimental; **the process is still at the experimental stage** el proceso está todavía en prueba

expert ['ɛkspə:t] adj experto, perito ▷ n experto/a, perito/a; (specialist) especialista mf; **expertise** [-'ti:z] n pericia
expire [ɪk'spaɪə*] vi caducar, vencer; **expiry** n vencimiento; **expiry date** n (of medicine, food item) fecha de caducidad
explain [ɪk'spleɪn] vt explicar; **explanation** [ɛksplə'neɪʃən] n explicación f
explicit [ɪk'splɪsɪt] adj explícito
explode [ɪk'spləud] vi estallar, explotar; (population) crecer rápidamente; (with anger) reventar
exploit [n 'ɛksplɔɪt, vb ɪk'splɔɪt] n hazaña ▷ vt explotar; **exploitation** [-'teɪʃən] n explotación f
explore [ɪk'splɔ:*] vt explorar; (fig) examinar; investigar; **explorer** n explorador(a) m/f
explosion [ɪk'spləuʒən] n explosión f; **explosive** [ɪks'pləusɪv] adj, n explosivo
export [vb ɛk'spɔ:t, n, cpd 'ɛkspɔ:t] vt exportar ▷ n (process) exportación f; (product) producto de exportación ▷ cpd de exportación; **exporter** n exportador m
expose [ɪk'spəuz] vt exponer; (unmask) desenmascarar; **exposed** adj expuesto
exposure [ɪk'spəuʒə*] n exposición f; (publicity) publicidad f; (Phot: speed) velocidad f de obturación; (: shot) fotografía; **to die from ~** (Med) morir de frío
express [ɪk'sprɛs] adj (definite) expreso, explícito; (BRIT: letter etc) urgente ▷ n (train) rápido ▷ vt expresar; **expression** [ɪk'sprɛʃən] n expresión f; (of actor etc) sentimiento; **expressway** (us) n (urban motorway) autopista
exquisite [ɛk'skwɪzɪt] adj exquisito
extend [ɪk'stɛnd] vt (visit, street) prolongar; (building) ampliar; (invitation) ofrecer ▷ vi (land)

extenderse; (*period of time*) prolongarse
extension [ɪk'stɛnʃən] *n* extensión
f; (*building*) ampliación f; (*of time*)
prolongación f; (*Tel: in private house*)
línea derivada; (: *in office*) extensión
f; **extension lead** *n* alargador *m*,
alargadera
extensive [ɪk'stɛnsɪv] *adj* extenso;
(*damage*) importante; (*knowledge*)
amplio
extent [ɪk'stɛnt] *n* (*breadth*)
extensión f; (*scope*) alcance *m*; **to some**
~ hasta cierto punto; **to the ~ of ...**
hasta el punto de ...; **to such an ~ that**
... hasta tal punto que ...; **to what ~?**
¿hasta qué punto?
exterior [ɛk'stɪərɪə*] *adj* exterior,
externo ▷ *n* exterior *m*
external [ɛk'stə:nl] *adj* externo
extinct [ɪk'stɪŋkt] *adj* (*volcano*)
extinguido; (*race*) extinto; **extinction**
n extinción f
extinguish [ɪk'stɪŋgwɪʃ] *vt*
extinguir, apagar
extra ['ɛkstrə] *adj* adicional ▷ *adv* (*in*
addition) de más ▷ *n* (*luxury, addition*)
extra *m*; (*Cinema, Theatre*) extra *mf*,
comparsa *mf*
extract [*vb* ɪk'strækt, *n* 'ɛkstrækt] *vt*
sacar; (*tooth*) extraer; (*money, promise*)
obtener ▷ *n* extracto
extradite ['ɛkstrədaɪt] *vt* extraditar
extraordinary [ɪk'strɔ:dnrɪ] *adj*
extraordinario; (*odd*) raro
extravagance [ɪk'strævəgəns] *n*
derroche *m*, despilfarro; (*thing bought*)
extravagancia
extravagant [ɪk'strævəgənt]
adj (*lavish: person*) pródigo; (: *gift*)
(demasiado) caro; (*wasteful*)
despilfarrador(a)
extreme [ɪk'stri:m] *adj* extremo,
extremado ▷ *n* extremo; **extremely**
adv sumamente, extremadamente
extremist [ɪk'stri:mɪst] *adj, n*
extremista *m/f*
extrovert ['ɛkstrəvə:t] *n*
extrovertido/a

eye [aɪ] *n* ojo ▷ *vt* mirar de soslayo,
ojear; **to keep an ~ on** vigilar; **eyeball**
n globo ocular; **eyebrow** *n* ceja;
eyedrops *npl* gotas *fpl* para los ojos,
colino; **eyelash** *n* pestaña; **eyelid** *n*
párpado; **eyeliner** *n* delineador *m* (de
ojos); **eyeshadow** *n* sombreador *m* de
ojos; **eyesight** *n* vista; **eye witness** *n*
testigo *mf* presencial

f

F [ɛf] *n* (*Mus*) fa *m*

fabric ['fæbrɪk] *n* tejido, tela

> Be careful not to translate **fabric** by the Spanish word *fábrica*.

fabulous ['fæbjuləs] *adj* fabuloso

face [feɪs] *n* (*Anat*) cara, rostro; (*of clock*) esfera (*SP*), cara (*LAM*); (*of mountain*) cara, ladera; (*of building*) fachada ▷ *vt* (*direction*) estar de cara a; (*situation*) hacer frente a; (*facts*) aceptar; **~ down** (*person, card*) boca abajo; **to lose ~** desprestigiarse; **to make** *or* **pull a ~** hacer muecas; **in the ~ of** (*difficulties etc*) ante; **on the ~ of it** a primera vista; **~ to ~** cara a cara; **face up to** *vt fus* hacer frente a, arrostrar; **face cloth** (*BRIT*) *n* manopla; **face pack** *n* (*BRIT*) mascarilla

facial ['feɪʃəl] *adj* de la cara ▷ *n* (*also*: **beauty ~**) tratamiento facial, limpieza

facilitate [fə'sɪlɪteɪt] *vt* facilitar

facilities [fə'sɪlɪtɪz] *npl* (*buildings*) instalaciones *fpl*; (*equipment*) servicios *mpl*; **credit ~** facilidades *fpl* de crédito

fact [fækt] *n* hecho; **in ~** en realidad

faction ['fækʃən] *n* facción *f*

factor ['fæktə*] *n* factor *m*

factory ['fæktərɪ] *n* fábrica

factual ['fæktjuəl] *adj* basado en los hechos

faculty ['fækəltɪ] *n* facultad *f*; (*US: teaching staff*) personal *m* docente

fad [fæd] *n* novedad *f*, moda

fade [feɪd] *vi* desteñirse; (*sound, smile*) desvanecerse; (*light*) apagarse; (*flower*) marchitarse; (*hope, memory*) perderse; **fade away** *vi* (*sound*) apagarse

fag [fæg] (*BRIT: inf*) *n* (*cigarette*) pitillo (*SP*), cigarro

Fahrenheit ['fɑːrənhaɪt] *n* Fahrenheit *m*

fail [feɪl] *vt* (*candidate, test*) suspender (*SP*), reprobar (*LAM*); (*memory etc*) fallar a ▷ *vi* suspender (*SP*), reprobar (*LAM*); (*be unsuccessful*) fracasar; (*strength, brakes*) fallar; (*light*) acabarse; **to ~ to do sth** (*neglect*) dejar de hacer algo; (*be unable*) no poder hacer algo; **without ~** sin falta; **failing** *n* falta, defecto ▷ *prep* a falta de; **failure** ['feɪljə*] *n* fracaso; (*person*) fracasado/a; (*mechanical etc*) fallo

faint [feɪnt] *adj* débil; (*recollection*) vago; (*mark*) apenas visible ▷ *n* desmayo ▷ *vi* desmayarse; **to feel ~** estar mareado, marearse; **faintest** *adj*: **I haven't the faintest idea** no tengo la más remota idea; **faintly** *adv* débilmente; (*vaguely*) vagamente

fair [fɛə*] *adj* justo; (*hair, person*) rubio; (*weather*) bueno; (*good enough*) regular; (*considerable*) considerable ▷ *adv* (*play*) limpio ▷ *n* feria; (*BRIT: funfair*) parque *m* de atracciones; **fairground** *n* recinto ferial; **fair-haired** *adj* (*person*) rubio; **fairly** *adv* (*justly*) con justicia; (*quite*) bastante; **fair trade** *n* comercio justo; **fairway** *n* (*Golf*) calle *f*

fairy ['fɛərɪ] *n* hada; **fairy tale** *n* cuento de hadas

faith [feɪθ] *n* fe *f*; (*trust*) confianza; (*sect*) religión *f*; **faithful** *adj*

(loyal: troops etc) leal; (spouse) fiel;
(account) exacto; **faithfully** adv
fielmente; **yours faithfully** (BRIT: in
letters) le saluda atentamente
fake [feɪk] n (painting etc) falsificación
f; (person) impostor(a) m/f ▷ adj falso
▷ vt fingir; (painting etc) falsificar
falcon ['fɔːlkən] n halcón m
fall [fɔːl] (pt **fell**, pp **fallen**) n caída;
(in price etc) descenso; (US) otoño ▷ vi
caer(se); (price) bajar, descender; **falls**
npl (waterfall) cascada, salto de agua;
to ~ flat (on one's face) caerse (boca
abajo); (plan) fracasar; (joke, story) no
hacer gracia; **fall apart** vi deshacerse;
fall down vi (person) caerse; (building,
hopes) derrumbarse; **fall for** vt fus
(trick) dejarse engañar por; (person)
enamorarse de; **fall off** vi caerse;
(diminish) disminuir; **fall out** vi (friends
etc) reñir; (hair, teeth) caerse; **fall over**
vi caer(se); **fall through** vi (plan,
project) fracasar
fallen ['fɔːlən] pp of **fall**
fallout ['fɔːlaut] n lluvia radioactiva
false [fɔːls] adj falso; **under ~
pretences** con engaños; **false alarm**
n falsa alarma; **false teeth** (BRIT) npl
dentadura postiza
fame [feɪm] n fama
familiar [fəˈmɪlɪə*] adj conocido,
familiar; (tone) de confianza; **to
be ~ with** (subject) conocer (bien);
familiarize [fəˈmɪlɪəraɪz] vt: **to
familiarize o.s. with** familiarizarse
con
family ['fæmɪlɪ] n familia; **family
doctor** n médico/a de cabecera;
family planning n planificación f
familiar
famine ['fæmɪn] n hambre f,
hambruna
famous ['feɪməs] adj famoso, célebre
fan [fæn] n abanico; (Elec) ventilador
m; (of pop star) fan m/f; (Sport) hincha m/f
▷ vt abanicar; (fire, quarrel) atizar
fanatic [fəˈnætɪk] n fanático/a
fan belt n correa del ventilador

fan club n club m de fans
fancy ['fænsɪ] n (whim) capricho,
antojo; (imagination) imaginación f
▷ adj (luxury) lujoso, de lujo ▷ vt (feel
like, want) tener ganas de; (imagine)
imaginarse; (think) creer; **to take a ~ to
sb** tomar cariño a algn; **he fancies her**
(inf) le gusta (ella) mucho; **fancy dress**
n disfraz m
fan heater n calefactor m de aire
fantasize ['fæntəsaɪz] vi fantasear,
hacerse ilusiones
fantastic [fænˈtæstɪk] adj (enormous)
enorme; (strange, wonderful) fantástico
fantasy ['fæntəzɪ] n (dream) sueño;
(unreality) fantasía
fanzine ['fænziːn] n fanzine m
FAQs abbr (= frequently asked questions)
preguntas frecuentes
far [fɑː*] adj (distant) lejano ▷ adv
lejos; (much, greatly) mucho; **~ away, ~
off** (a lo) lejos; **~ better** mucho mejor; **~
from** lejos de; **by ~** con mucho; **go as
~ as the farm** vaya hasta la granja; **as
~ as I know** que yo sepa; **how ~?** ¿hasta
dónde?; (fig) ¿hasta qué punto?
farce [fɑːs] n farsa
fare [fɛə*] n (on trains, buses) precio
(del billete); (in taxi: cost) tarifa; (food)
comida; **half ~** medio pasaje m; **full ~**
pasaje completo
Far East n: **the ~** el Extremo Oriente
farewell [fɛəˈwɛl] excl, n adiós m
farm [fɑːm] n cortijo (SP), hacienda
(LAM), rancho (MEX), estancia (RPL)
▷ vt cultivar; **farmer** n granjero,
hacendado (LAM), ranchero (MEX),
estanciero (RPL); **farmhouse** n granja,
casa del hacendado (LAM), rancho
(MEX), casco de la estancia (RPL);
farming n agricultura; (of crops)
cultivo; (of animals) cría; **farmyard**
n corral m
far-reaching [fɑːˈriːtʃɪŋ] adj (reform,
effect) de gran alcance
fart [fɑːt] (inf!) vi tirarse un pedo (!)
farther ['fɑːðə*] adv más lejos, más
allá ▷ adj más lejano

farthest ['fɑːðɪst] *superlative of* **far**

fascinate ['fæsɪneɪt] *vt* fascinar; **fascinated** *adj* fascinado

fascinating ['fæsɪneɪtɪŋ] *adj* fascinante

fascination [-'neɪʃən] *n* fascinación *f*

fascist ['fæʃɪst] *adj, n* fascista *m/f*

fashion ['fæʃən] *n* moda; (*fashion industry*) industria de la moda; (*manner*) manera ▷ *vt* formar; **in ~** a la moda; **out of ~** pasado de moda; **fashionable** *adj* de moda; **fashion show** *n* desfile *m* de modelos

fast [fɑːst] *adj* rápido; (*dye, colour*) resistente; (*clock*): **to be ~** estar adelantado ▷ *adv* rápidamente, de prisa; (*stuck, held*) firmemente ▷ *n* ayuno ▷ *vi* ayunar; **~ asleep** profundamente dormido

fasten ['fɑːsn] *vt* atar, sujetar; (*coat, belt*) abrochar ▷ *vi* atarse; abrocharse

fast food *n* comida rápida, platos *mpl* preparados

fat [fæt] *adj* gordo; (*book*) grueso; (*profit*) grande, pingüe ▷ *n* grasa; (*on person*) carnes *fpl*; (*lard*) manteca

fatal ['feɪtl] *adj* (*mistake*) fatal; (*injury*) mortal; **fatality** [fə'tælɪtɪ] *n* (*road death etc*) víctima; **fatally** *adv* fatalmente; mortalmente

fate [feɪt] *n* destino; (*of person*) suerte *f*

father ['fɑːðə*] *n* padre *m*; **Father Christmas** *n* Papá *m* Noel; **father-in-law** *n* suegro

fatigue [fə'tiːg] *n* fatiga, cansancio

fattening ['fætnɪŋ] *adj* (*food*) que hace engordar

fatty ['fætɪ] *adj* (*food*) graso ▷ *n* (*inf*) gordito/a, gordinflón/ona *m/f*

faucet ['fɔːsɪt] (*US*) *n* grifo (*SP*), llave *f*, canilla (*RPL*)

fault [fɔːlt] *n* (*blame*) culpa; (*defect: in person, machine*) defecto; (*Geo*) falla ▷ *vt* criticar; **it's my ~** es culpa mía; **to find ~ with** criticar, poner peros a; **at ~** culpable; **faulty** *adj* defectuoso

fauna ['fɔːnə] *n* fauna

favour *etc* ['feɪvə*] (*US* **favor** *etc*) *n* favor *m*; (*approval*) aprobación *f* ▷ *vt* (*proposition*) estar a favor de, aprobar; (*assist*) ser propicio a; **to do sb a ~** hacer un favor a algn; **to find ~ with sb** caer en gracia a algn; **in ~ of** a favor de; **favourable** *adj* favorable; **favourite** ['feɪvrɪt] *adj, n* favorito, preferido

fawn [fɔːn] *n* cervato ▷ *adj* (*also*: **~-coloured**) color de cervato, leonado ▷ *vi*: **to ~ (up)on** adular

fax [fæks] *n* (*document*) fax *m*; (*machine*) telefax *m* ▷ *vt* mandar por telefax

FBI (*US*) *n abbr* (= *Federal Bureau of Investigation*) ≈ BIC *f* (*SP*)

fear [fɪə*] *n* miedo, temor *m*; **for ~ of** por si; tener miedo de, temer; **to find ~ with** criticar, poner peros a; **fearful** *adj* temeroso, miedoso; (*awful*) terrible; **fearless** *adj* audaz

feasible ['fiːzəbl] *adj* factible

feast [fiːst] *n* banquete *m*; (*Rel: also*: **~ day**) fiesta ▷ *vi* festejar

feat [fiːt] *n* hazaña

feather ['feðə*] *n* pluma

feature ['fiːtʃə*] *n* característica; (*article*) artículo de fondo ▷ *vt* (*film*) presentar ▷ *vi*: **to ~ in** tener un papel destacado en; **features** *npl* (*of face*) facciones *fpl*; **feature film** *n* largometraje *m*

Feb. *abbr* (= *February*) feb

February ['februərɪ] *n* febrero

fed [fɛd] *pt, pp of* **feed**

federal ['fɛdərəl] *adj* federal

federation [fɛdə'reɪʃən] *n* federación *f*

fed up [fɛd'ʌp] *adj*: **to be ~ (with)** estar harto (de)

fee [fiː] *n* pago; (*professional*) derechos *mpl*, honorarios *mpl*; (*of club*) cuota; **school ~s** matrícula

feeble ['fiːbl] *adj* débil; (*joke*) flojo

feed [fiːd] (*pt, pp* **fed**) *n* comida; (*of animal*) pienso; (*on printer*) dispositivo de alimentación ▷ *vt* alimentar; (*BRIT: baby: breastfeed*) dar el pecho a; (*animal*) dar de comer a; (*data,*

information): **to ~ into** meter en;
feedback n reacción f, feedback m
feel [fi:l] (*pt, pp* **felt**) n (*sensation*)
sensación f; (*sense of touch*) tacto;
(*impression*): **to have the ~ of** parecerse
a ▷ vt tocar; (*pain etc*) sentir; (*think,
believe*) creer; **to ~ hungry/cold** tener
hambre/frío; **to ~ lonely/better**
sentirse solo/mejor; **I don't ~ well**
no me siento bien; **it ~s soft** es suave
al tacto; **to ~ like** (*want*) tener ganas
de; **feeling** n (*physical*) sensación f;
(*foreboding*) presentimiento; (*emotion*)
sentimiento
feet [fi:t] *npl of* **foot**
fell [fɛl] *pt of* **fall** ▷ vt (*tree*) talar
fellow ['fɛləu] n (*man*) tipo, tío (*SP*);
(*comrade*) compañero; (*of learned
society*) socio/a; **fellow citizen** n
conciudadano/a; **fellow countryman**
(*irreg*) n compatriota m; **fellow men**
npl semejantes *mpl*; **fellowship** n
compañerismo; (*grant*) beca
felony ['fɛlənɪ] n crimen m
felt [fɛlt] *pt, pp of* **feel** ▷ n fieltro;
felt-tip n (*also*: **felt-tip pen**)
rotulador m
female ['fi:meɪl] n (*pej: woman*) mujer
f, tía; (*Zool*) hembra ▷ adj femenino;
hembra
feminine ['fɛmɪnɪn] adj femenino
feminist ['fɛmɪnɪst] n feminista
fence [fɛns] n valla, cerca ▷ vt (*also*: ~
in) cercar ▷ vi (*Sport*) hacer esgrima;
fencing n esgrima
fend [fɛnd] vi: **to ~ for o.s.** valerse por
sí mismo; **fend off** vt (*attack*) rechazar;
(*questions*) evadir
fender ['fɛndə*] (*US*) n guardafuego;
(*Aut*) parachoques m inv
fennel ['fɛnl] n hinojo
ferment [*vb* fə'mɛnt, *n* 'fə:mɛnt] vi
fermentar ▷ n (*fig*) agitación f
fern [fə:n] n helecho
ferocious [fə'rəʊʃəs] adj feroz
ferret ['fɛrɪt] n hurón m
ferry ['fɛrɪ] n (*small*) barca (de pasaje),
balsa; (*large: also*: **~boat**) transbordador

m, ferry m ▷ vt transportar
fertile ['fə:taɪl] adj fértil; (*Biol*)
fecundo; **fertilize** ['fə:tɪlaɪz] vt (*Biol*)
fecundar; (*Agr*) abonar; **fertilizer** n
abono
festival ['fɛstɪvəl] n (*Rel*) fiesta; (*Art,
Mus*) festival m
festive ['fɛstɪv] adj festivo; **the ~
season** (*BRIT: Christmas*) las Navidades
fetch [fɛtʃ] vt ir a buscar; (*sell for*)
venderse por
fête [feɪt] n fiesta
fetus ['fi:təs] (*US*) n = **foetus**
feud [fju:d] n (*hostility*) enemistad f;
(*quarrel*) disputa
fever ['fi:və*] n fiebre f; **feverish**
adj febril
few [fju:] adj (*not many*) pocos ▷ pron
pocos; algunos; **a ~** adj unos pocos,
algunos; **fewer** adj menos; **fewest** adj
los(las) menos
fiancé [fɪ'ɑ̃:ŋseɪ] n novio, prometido;
fiancée n novia, prometida
fiasco [fɪ'æskəu] n fiasco
fib [fɪb] n mentirilla
fibre ['faɪbə*] (*US* **fiber**) n fibra;
fibreglass (*US* **Fiberglass**®) n fibra
de vidrio
fickle ['fɪkl] adj inconstante
fiction ['fɪkʃən] n ficción f; **fictional**
adj novelesco
fiddle ['fɪdl] n (*Mus*) violín m;
(*cheating*) trampa ▷ vt (*BRIT: accounts*)
falsificar; **fiddle with** vt fus juguetear
con
fidelity [fɪ'dɛlɪtɪ] n fidelidad f
field [fi:ld] n campo; (*fig*) campo,
esfera; (*Sport*) campo (*SP*), cancha (*LAM*);
field marshal n mariscal m
fierce [fɪəs] adj feroz; (*wind, heat*)
fuerte; (*fighting, enemy*) encarnizado
fifteen [fɪf'ti:n] num quince;
fifteenth adj decimoquinto; **the
fifteenth floor** la planta quince;
the fifteenth of August el quince
de agosto
fifth [fɪfθ] num quinto
fiftieth ['fɪftɪɪθ] adj quincuagésimo

fifty ['fɪftɪ] *num* cincuenta; **fifty-fifty** *adj* (*deal, split*) a medias ▷ *adv* a medias, mitad por mitad

fig [fɪg] *n* higo

fight [faɪt] (*pt, pp* **fought**) *n* (*gen*) pelea; (*Mil*) combate *m*; (*struggle*) lucha ▷ *vt* luchar contra; (*cancer, alcoholism*) combatir; (*election*) intentar ganar; (*emotion*) resistir ▷ *vi* pelear, luchar; **fight back** *vi* defenderse; (*after illness*) recuperarse ▷ *vt* (*tears*) contener; **fight off** *vt* (*attack, attacker*) rechazar; (*disease, sleep, urge*) luchar contra; **fighting** *n* combate *m*, pelea

figure ['fɪgə*] *n* (*Drawing, Geom*) figura, dibujo; (*number, cipher*) cifra; (*body, outline*) tipo; (*personality*) figura ▷ *vt* (*esp US*) imaginar ▷ *vi* (*appear*) figurar; **figure out** *vt* (*work out*) resolver

file [faɪl] *n* (*tool*) lima; (*dossier*) expediente *m*; (*folder*) carpeta; (*Comput*) fichero; (*row*) fila ▷ *vt* limar; (*Law: claim*) presentar; (*store*) archivar; **filing cabinet** *n* fichero, archivador *m*

Filipino [fɪlɪ'piːnəu] *adj* filipino ▷ *n* (*person*) filipino/a *m/f*; (*Ling*) tagalo

fill [fɪl] *vt* (*space*): **to ~ (with)** llenar (de); (*vacancy, need*) cubrir ▷ *n*: **to eat one's ~** llenarse; **fill in** *vt* rellenar; **fill out** *vt* (*form, receipt*) rellenar; **fill up** *vt* llenar (hasta el borde) ▷ *vi* (*Aut*) poner gasolina

fillet ['fɪlɪt] *n* filete *m*; **fillet steak** *n* filete *m* de ternera

filling ['fɪlɪŋ] *n* (*Culin*) relleno; (*for tooth*) empaste *m*; **filling station** *n* estación *f* de servicio

film [fɪlm] *n* película ▷ *vt* (*scene*) filmar ▷ *vi* rodar (una película); **film star** *n* astro, estrella de cine

filter ['fɪltə*] *n* filtro ▷ *vt* filtrar; **filter lane** (*BRIT*) *n* carril *m* de selección

filth [fɪlθ] *n* suciedad *f*; **filthy** *adj* sucio; (*language*) obsceno

fin [fɪn] *n* (*gen*) aleta

final ['faɪnl] *adj* (*last*) final, último; (*definitive*) definitivo, terminante ▷ *n* (*BRIT Sport*) final *f*; **finals** *npl* (*Scol*) examen *m* final; (*US Sport*) final *f*

finale [fɪ'nɑːlɪ] *n* final *m*

final: finalist *n* (*Sport*) finalista *mf*; **finalize** *vt* concluir, completar; **finally** *adv* (*lastly*) por último, finalmente; (*eventually*) por fin

finance [faɪ'næns] *n* (*money*) fondos *mpl* ▷ *vt* financiar; **finances** *npl* finanzas *fpl*; (*personal finances*) situación *f* económica; **financial** [-'nænʃəl] *adj* financiero; **financial year** *n* ejercicio (financiero)

find [faɪnd] (*pt, pp* **found**) *vt* encontrar, hallar; (*come upon*) descubrir ▷ *n* hallazgo; descubrimiento; **to ~ sb guilty** (*Law*) declarar culpable a algn; **find out** *vt* averiguar; (*truth, secret*) descubrir; **to find out about** (*subject*) informarse sobre; (*by chance*) enterarse de; **findings** *npl* (*Law*) veredicto, fallo; (*of report*) recomendaciones *fpl*

fine [faɪn] *adj* excelente; (*thin*) fino ▷ *adv* (*well*) bien ▷ *n* (*Law*) multa ▷ *vt* (*Law*) multar; **to be ~** (*person*) estar bien; (*weather*) hacer buen tiempo; **fine arts** *npl* bellas artes *fpl*

finger ['fɪŋgə*] *n* dedo ▷ *vt* (*touch*) manosear; **little/index ~** (*dedo*) meñique *m*/índice *m*; **fingernail** *n* uña; **fingerprint** *n* huella dactilar; **fingertip** *n* yema del dedo

finish ['fɪnɪʃ] *n* (*end*) fin *m*; (*Sport*) meta; (*polish etc*) acabado ▷ *vt, vi* terminar; **to ~ doing sth** acabar de hacer algo; **to ~ third** llegar el tercero; **finish off** *vt* acabar, terminar; (*kill*) acabar con; **finish up** *vt* acabar, terminar ▷ *vi* ir a parar, terminar

Finland ['fɪnlənd] *n* Finlandia

Finn [fɪn] *n* finlandés/esa *m/f*; **Finnish** *adj* finlandés/esa ▷ *n* (*Ling*) finlandés *m*

fir [fəː*] *n* abeto

fire ['faɪə*] *n* fuego; (*in hearth*) lumbre *f*; (*accidental*) incendio; (*heater*) estufa ▷ *vt* (*gun*) disparar; (*interest*) despertar; (*inf: dismiss*) despedir ▷ *vi* (*shoot*)

disparar; **on ~** ardiendo, en llamas;
fire alarm n alarma de incendios;
firearm n arma de fuego; **fire brigade**
(us **fire department**) n (cuerpo de)
bomberos mpl; **fire engine** (BRIT) n
coche m de bomberos; **fire escape**
n escalera de incendios; **fire exit** n
salida de incendios; **fire extinguisher**
n extintor m (de incendios); **fireman**
(irreg) n bombero; **fireplace** n
chimenea; **fire station** n parque m
de bomberos; **firetruck** (us) n = **fire
engine**; **firewall** (Internet) firewall
m; **firewood** n leña; **fireworks** npl
fuegos mpl artificiales

firm [fə:m] adj firme; (look, voice)
resuelto ▷ n firma, empresa; **firmly**
adv firmemente; ʀesueltamente

first [fə:st] adj primero ▷ adv (before
others) primero; (when listing reasons
etc) en primer lugar, primeramente
▷ n (person: in race) primero/a; (Aut)
primera; (BRIT Scol) título de licenciado
con calificación de sobresaliente; **at ~** al
principio; **~ of all** ante todo; **first aid** n
primera ayuda, primeros auxilios mpl;
first-aid kit n botiquín m; **first-class**
adj (excellent) de primera (categoría);
(ticket etc) de primera clase; **first-hand**
adj de primera mano; **first lady** n
(esp us) primera dama; **firstly** adv en
primer lugar; **first name** n nombre m
(de pila); **first-rate** adj estupendo

fiscal ['fɪskəl] adj fiscal; **fiscal year** n
año fiscal, ejercicio

fish [fɪʃ] n inv pez m; (food) pescado
▷ vt, vi pescar; **to go ~ing** ir de pesca;
~ and chips pescado frito con patatas
fritas; **fisherman** (irreg) n pescador
m; **fish fingers** (BRIT) npl croquetas
fpl de pescado; **fishing** n pesca;
fishing boat n barca de pesca; **fishing
line** n sedal m; **fishmonger** n (BRIT)
pescadero/a; **fishmonger's (shop)**
(BRIT) n pescadería; **fish sticks** (us)
npl = **fish fingers**; **fishy** (inf) adj
sospechoso

fist [fɪst] n puño

fit [fɪt] adj (healthy) en (buena)
forma; (proper) adecuado, apropiado
▷ vt (clothes) estar or sentar bien a;
(instal) poner; (equip) proveer, dotar;
(facts) cuadrar or corresponder con
▷ vi (clothes) sentar bien; (in space,
gap) caber; (facts) coincidir ▷ n (Med)
ataque m; **~ to** (ready) a punto de; **~ for**
apropiado para; **a ~ of anger/pride**
un arranque de cólera/orgullo; **this
dress is a good ~** este vestido me
sienta bien; **by ~s and starts** a rachas;
fit in vi (fig: person) llevarse bien
(con todos); **fitness** n (Med) salud
f; **fitted** adj (jacket, shirt) entallado;
(sheet) de cuatro picos; **fitted carpet**
n moqueta; **fitted kitchen** n cocina
amueblada; **fitting** adj apropiado ▷ n
(of dress) prueba; (of piece of equipment)
instalación f; **fitting room** n probador
m; **fittings** npl instalaciones fpl

five [faɪv] num cinco; **fiver** (inf) n
(BRIT) billete m de cinco libras; (us)
billete m de cinco dólares

fix [fɪks] vt (secure) fijar, asegurar;
(mend) arreglar; (prepare) preparar
▷ n: **to be in a ~** estar en un aprieto; **fix
up** vt (meeting) arreglar; **to fix sb up
with sth** proveer a algn de algo; **fixed**
adj (prices etc) fijo; **fixture** n (Sport)
encuentro

fizzy ['fɪzɪ] adj (drink) gaseoso

flag [flæg] n bandera; (stone) losa ▷ vi
decaer ▷ vt: **to ~ sb down** hacer señas
a algn para que se pare; **flagpole** n
asta de bandera

flair [flɛə*] n aptitud f especial

flak [flæk] n (Mil) fuego antiaéreo;
(inf: criticism) lluvia de críticas

flake [fleɪk] n (of rust, paint) escama;
(of snow, soap powder) copo ▷ vi (also: ~
off) desconcharse

flamboyant [flæm'bɔɪənt] adj
(dress) vistoso; (person)
extravagante

flame [fleɪm] n llama

flamingo [flə'mɪŋɡəu] n flamenco

flammable ['flæməbl] adj

inflamable

flan [flæn] (BRIT) n tarta

⬛ Be careful not to translate **flan** by
the Spanish word *flan*.

flank [flæŋk] n (of animal) ijar m; (of
army) flanco ▷ vt flanquear

flannel ['flænl] n (BRIT: also: **face ~**)
manopla; (fabric) franela

flap [flæp] n (of pocket, envelope)
solapa ▷ vt (wings, arms) agitar ▷ vi
(sail, flag) ondear

flare [flɛə*] n llamarada; (Mil)
bengala; (in skirt etc) vuelo; **flares** npl
(trousers) pantalones mpl de campana;
flare up vi encenderse; (fig: person)
encolerizarse; (: revolt) estallar

flash [flæʃ] n relámpago; (also:
news ~) noticias fpl de última hora;
(Phot) flash m ▷ vt (light, headlights)
lanzar un destello con; (news, message)
transmitir; (smile) lanzar ▷ vi brillar;
(hazard light etc) lanzar destellos; **in a ~**
en un instante; **he ~ed by** or **past** pasó
como un rayo; **flashback** n (Cinema)
flashback m; **flashbulb** n bombilla
fusible; **flashlight** n linterna

flask [flɑːsk] n frasco; (also: **vacuum
~**) termo

flat [flæt] adj llano; (smooth)
liso; (tyre) desinflado; (battery)
descargado; (beer) muerto; (refusal
etc) rotundo; (Mus) desafinado; (rate)
fijo ▷ n (BRIT: apartment) piso (SP),
departamento (LAM), apartamento
(Aut) pinchazo; (Mus) bemol m; **to work
~ out** trabajar a toda mecha; **flatten** vt
(also: **flatten out**) allanar; (smooth out)
alisar; (building, plants) arrasar

flatter ['flætə*] vt adular, halagar;
flattering adj halagüeño; (dress) que
favorece

flaunt [flɔːnt] vt ostentar, lucir

flavour etc ['fleɪvə*] (US **flavor**
etc) n sabor m, gusto ▷ vt sazonar,
condimentar; **strawberry-flavoured**
con sabor a fresa; **flavouring** n (in
product) aromatizante m

flaw [flɔː] n defecto; **flawless** adj

impecable

flea [fliː] n pulga; **flea market** n
rastro, mercadillo

flee [fliː] (pt, pp **fled**) vt huir de ▷ vi
huir, fugarse

fleece [fliːs] n vellón m; (wool) lana;
(top) forro polar ▷ vt (inf) desplumar

fleet [fliːt] n flota; (of lorries etc)
escuadra

fleeting ['fliːtɪŋ] adj fugaz

Flemish ['flɛmɪʃ] adj flamenco

flesh [flɛʃ] n carne f; (skin) piel f; (of
fruit) pulpa

flew [fluː] pt of **fly**

flex [flɛks] n cordón m ▷ vt (muscles)
tensar; **flexibility** n flexibilidad f;
flexible adj flexible; **flexitime** (US
flextime) n horario flexible

flick [flɪk] n capirotazo; chasquido
▷ vt (with hand) dar un capirotazo a;
(whip etc) chasquear; (switch) accionar;
flick through vt fus hojear

flicker ['flɪkə*] vi (light) parpadear,
(flame) vacilar

flies [flaɪz] npl of **fly**

flight [flaɪt] n vuelo; (escape)
huida, fuga; (also: **~ of steps**) tramo
(de escaleras); **flight attendant** n
auxiliar mf de vuelo

flimsy ['flɪmzɪ] adj (thin) muy ligero;
(building) endeble; (excuse) flojo

flinch [flɪntʃ] vi encogerse; **to ~ from**
retroceder ante

fling [flɪŋ] (pt, pp **flung**) vt arrojar

flint [flɪnt] n pedernal m; (in lighter)
piedra

flip [flɪp] vt dar la vuelta a; (switch: turn
on) encender; (turn) apagar; (coin) echar
a cara o cruz

flip-flops ['flɪpflɒps] npl (esp BRIT)
chancletas fpl

flipper ['flɪpə*] n aleta

flirt [flɜːt] vi coquetear, flirtear ▷ n
coqueta

float [fləʊt] n flotador m; (in
procession) carroza; (money) reserva ▷ vi
flotar; (swimmer) hacer la plancha

flock [flɒk] n (of sheep) rebaño; (of

birds) bandada ▷*vi:* **to ~ to** acudir en tropel a

flood [flʌd] *n* inundación *f*; *(of letters, imports etc)* avalancha ▷*vt* inundar ▷*vi (place)* inundarse; *(people):* **to ~ into** inundar; **flooding** *n* inundaciones *fpl*; **floodlight** *n* foco

floor [flɔː*] *n* suelo; *(storey)* piso; *(of sea)* fondo ▷*vt (question)* dejar sin respuesta; *(: blow)* derribar; **ground ~, first ~** *(us)* planta baja; **first ~, second ~** *(us)* primer piso; **floorboard** *n* tabla; **flooring** *n* suelo; *(material)* solería; **floor show** *n* cabaret *m*

flop [flɔp] *n* fracaso ▷*vi (fail)* fracasar; *(fall)* derrumbarse; **floppy** *adj* flojo ▷*n (Comput: also:* **floppy disk***)* floppy *m*

flora ['flɔːrə] *n* flora

floral ['flɔːrl] *adj (pattern)* floreado

florist ['flɔrɪst] *n* florista *mf*; **florist's (shop)** *n* floristería

flotation [fləu'teɪʃən] *n (of shares)* emisión *f*; *(of company)* lanzamiento

flour ['flauə*] *n* harina

flourish ['flʌrɪʃ] *vi* florecer ▷*n* ademán *m*, movimiento *(ostentoso)*

flow [fləu] *n (movement)* flujo; *(of traffic)* circulación *f*; *(tide)* corriente *f* ▷*vi (river, blood)* fluir; *(traffic)* circular

flower ['flauə*] *n* flor *f* ▷*vi* florecer; **flower bed** *n* macizo; **flowerpot** *n* tiesto

flown [fləun] *pp of* **fly**

fl. oz. *abbr (= fluid ounce)*

flu [fluː] *n:* **to have ~** tener la gripe

fluctuate ['flʌktjueɪt] *vi* fluctuar

fluent ['fluːənt] *adj (linguist)* que habla perfectamente; *(speech)* elocuente; **he speaks ~ French, he's ~ in French** domina el francés

fluff [flʌf] *n* pelusa; **fluffy** *adj* de pelo suave

fluid ['fluːɪd] *adj (movement)* fluido, líquido; *(situation)* inestable ▷*n* fluido, líquido; **fluid ounce** *n* onza *f* líquida

fluke [fluːk] *(inf)* *n* chiripa

flung [flʌŋ] *pt, pp of* **fling**

fluorescent [fluə'rɛsnt] *adj* fluorescente

fluoride ['fluəraɪd] *n* fluoruro

flurry ['flʌrɪ] *n (of snow)* temporal *m*; **~ of activity** frenesí *m* de actividad

flush [flʌʃ] *n* rubor *m*; *(fig: of youth etc)* resplandor *m* ▷*vt* limpiar con agua ▷*vi* ruborizarse ▷*adj:* **~ with** a ras de; **to ~ the toilet** hacer funcionar la cisterna

flute [fluːt] *n* flauta

flutter ['flʌtə*] *n (of wings)* revoloteo, aleteo; *(fig):* **a ~ of panic/excitement** una oleada de pánico/excitación ▷*vi* revolotear

fly [flaɪ] *(pt* **flew***, pp* **flown***) n* mosca; *(on trousers: also:* **flies***)* bragueta ▷*vt (plane)* pilot(e)ar; *(cargo)* transportar (en avión); *(distances)* recorrer (en avión) ▷*vi* volar; *(passengers)* ir en avión; *(escape)* evadirse; *(flag)* ondear; **fly away, fly off** *vi* emprender el vuelo; **fly-drive** *n:* **fly-drive holiday** vacaciones que incluyen vuelo y alquiler de coche; **flying** *n (activity)* (el) volar; *(action)* vuelo ▷*adj:* **flying visit** visita relámpago; **with flying colours** con lucimiento; **flying saucer** *n* platillo volante; **flyover** *(BRIT) n* paso a desnivel *or* superior

FM *abbr (Radio)* (*= frequency modulation)* FM

foal [fəul] *n* potro

foam [fəum] *n* espuma ▷*vi* hacer espuma

focus ['fəukəs] *(pl* **~es***) n* foco; *(centre)* centro ▷*vt (field glasses etc)* enfocar ▷*vi:* **to ~ (on)** enfocar (a); *(issue etc)* centrarse en; **in/out of ~** enfocado/ desenfocado

foetus ['fiːtəs] *(us* **fetus***) n* feto

fog [fɔg] *n* niebla; **foggy** *adj:* **it's foggy** hay niebla, está brumoso; **fog lamp** *(us* **fog light***) n (Aut)* faro de niebla

foil [fɔɪl] *vt* frustrar ▷*n* hoja; *(kitchen foil)* papel *m* (de) aluminio; *(complement)* complemento; *(Fencing)* florete *m*

fold [fəuld] n (bend, crease) pliegue m; (Agr) redil m ▷ vt doblar; (arms) cruzar; **fold up** vi plegarse, doblarse; (business) quebrar ▷ vt (map etc) plegar; **folder** n (for papers) carpeta; (Comput) directorio; **folding** adj (chair, bed) plegable

foliage ['fəulɪɪdʒ] n follaje m

folk [fəuk] npl gente f ▷ adj popular, folklórico; **folks** npl (family) familia sg, parientes mpl; **folklore** ['fəuklɔː*] n folklore m; **folk music** n música folk; **folk song** n canción f popular

follow ['fɔləu] vt seguir ▷ vi seguir; (result) resultar; **to ~ suit** hacer lo mismo; **follow up** vt (letter, offer) responder a; (case) investigar; **follower** n (of person, belief) partidario/a, **following** adj siguiente ▷ n afición f, partidarios mpl; **follow-up** n continuación f

fond [fɔnd] adj (memory, smile etc) cariñoso; (hopes) ilusorio; **to be ~ of** tener cariño a; (pastime, food) ser aficionado a

food [fuːd] n comida; **food mixer** n batidora; **food poisoning** n intoxicación f alimenticia; **food processor** n robot m de cocina; **food stamp** (US) n vale m para comida

fool [fuːl] n tonto/a; (Culin) puré m de frutas con nata ▷ vt engañar ▷ vi (gen) bromear; **fool about, fool around** vi hacer el tonto; **foolish** adj tonto; (careless) imprudente; **foolproof** adj (plan etc) infalible

foot [fut] (pl **feet**) n pie m; (measure) pie m (= 304 mm); (of animal) pata ▷ vt (bill) pagar; **on ~** a pie; **footage** n (Cinema) imágenes fpl; **foot-and-mouth (disease)** [futənd'mauθ-] n fiebre f aftosa; **football** n balón m; (game: BRIT) fútbol m; (: US) fútbol m americano; **footballer** n (BRIT) = **football player**; **football match** n partido de fútbol; **football player** n (BRIT) futbolista mf; (US) jugador m de fútbol americano; **footbridge** n

puente m para peatones; **foothills** npl estribaciones fpl; **foothold** n pie m firme; **footing** n (fig) posición f; **to lose one's footing** perder el pie; **footnote** n nota (al pie de la página); **footpath** n sendero; **footprint** n huella, pisada; **footstep** n paso; **footwear** n calzado

○ **KEYWORD**   **f**

for [fɔː] prep **1** (indicating destination, intention) para; **the train for London** el tren con destino a or de Londres; **he left for Rome** marchó para Roma; **he went for the paper** fue por el periódico; **is this for me?** ¿es esto para mí?; **it's time for lunch** es la hora de comer

2 (indicating purpose) para; **what('s it) for?** ¿para qué (es)?; **to pray for peace** rezar por la paz

3 (on behalf of, representing): **the MP for Hove** el diputado por Hove; **he works for the government/a local firm** trabaja para el gobierno/en una empresa local; **I'll ask him for you** se lo pediré por ti; **G for George** G de Gerona

4 (because of) por esta razón; **for fear of being criticized** por temor a ser criticado

5 (with regard to) para; **it's cold for July** hace frío para Julio; **he has a gift for languages** tiene don de lenguas

6 (in exchange for) por; **I sold it for £5** lo vendí por £5; **to pay 50 pence for a ticket** pagar 50 peniques por un billete

7 (in favour of): **are you for or against us?** ¿estás con nosotros o contra nosotros?; **I'm all for it** estoy totalmente a favor; **vote for X** vote (a) X

8 (referring to distance): **there are roadworks for 5 km** hay obras en 5 km; **we walked for miles** caminamos kilómetros y kilómetros

9 (referring to time): **he was away for two years** estuvo fuera (durante) dos

años; **it hasn't rained for 3 weeks** no ha llovido durante or en 3 semanas; **I have known her for years** la conozco desde hace años; **can you do it for tomorrow?** ¿lo podrás hacer para mañana?
10 (*with infinitive clauses*): **it is not for me to decide** la decisión no es cosa mía; **it would be best for you to leave** sería mejor que te fueras; **there is still time for you to do it** todavía te queda tiempo para hacerlo; **for this to be possible** ... para que esto sea posible ...
11 (*in spite of*) a pesar de; **for all his complaints** a pesar de sus quejas ▷ *conj* (*since, as: rather formal*) puesto que

forbid [fə'bɪd] (*pt* **forbad(e)**, *pp* **forbidden**) *vt* prohibir; **to ~ sb to do sth** prohibir a algn hacer algo; **forbidden** *pt of* **forbid** ▷ *adj* (*food, area*) prohibido; (*word, subject*) tabú
force [fɔ:s] *n* fuerza ▷ *vt* forzar; (*push*) meter a la fuerza; **to ~ o.s. to do** hacer un esfuerzo por hacer; **forced** *adj* forzado; **forceful** *adj* enérgico
ford [fɔ:d] *n* vado
fore [fɔ:*] *n*: **to come to the ~** empezar a destacar; **forearm** *n* antebrazo; **forecast** (*pt, pp* **forecast**) *n* pronóstico ▷ *vt* pronosticar; **forecourt** *n* patio; **forefinger** *n* (dedo) índice *m*; **forefront** *n*: **in the forefront of** en la vanguardia de; **foreground** *n* primer plano; **forehead** ['fɔrɪd] *n* frente *f*
foreign ['fɔrɪn] *adj* extranjero; (*trade*) exterior; (*object*) extraño; **foreign currency** *n* divisas *fpl*; **foreigner** *n* extranjero/a; **foreign exchange** *n* divisas *fpl*; **Foreign Office** (BRIT) *n* Ministerio de Asuntos Exteriores; **Foreign Secretary** (BRIT) *n* Ministro de Asuntos Exteriores
fore: foreman (*irreg*) *n* capataz *m*; (*in construction*) maestro de obras; **foremost** *adj* principal ▷ *adv*: **first**

and foremost ante todo; **forename** *n* nombre *m* (de pila)
forensic [fə'rɛnsɪk] *adj* forense
foresee [fɔ:'si:] (*pt* **foresaw**, *pp* **foreseen**) *vt* prever; **foreseeable** *adj* previsible
forest ['fɔrɪst] *n* bosque *m*; **forestry** *n* silvicultura
forever [fə'rɛvə*] *adv* para siempre; (*endlessly*) constantemente
foreword ['fɔ:wə:d] *n* prefacio
forfeit ['fɔ:fɪt] *vt* perder
forgave [fə'geɪv] *pt of* **forgive**
forge [fɔ:dʒ] *n* herrería ▷ *vt* (*signature, money*) falsificar; (*metal*) forjar; **forger** *n* falsificador(a) *m/f*; **forgery** *n* falsificación *f*
forget [fə'gɛt] (*pt* **forgot**, *pp* **forgotten**) *vt* olvidar ▷ *vi* olvidarse; **forgetful** *adj* despistado
forgive [fə'gɪv] (*pt* **forgave**, *pp* **forgiven**) *vt* perdonar; **to ~ sb for sth** perdonar algo a algn
forgot [fə'gɔt] *pt of* **forget**
forgotten [fə'gɔtn] *pp of* **forget**
fork [fɔ:k] *n* (*for eating*) tenedor *m*; (*for gardening*) horca; (*of roads*) bifurcación *f* ▷ *vi* (*road*) bifurcarse
forlorn [fə'lɔ:n] *adj* (*person*) triste, melancólico; (*place*) abandonado; (*attempt, hope*) desesperado
form [fɔ:m] *n* forma; (BRIT Scol) clase *f*; (*document*) formulario ▷ *vt* formar; (*idea*) concebir; (*habit*) adquirir; **in top ~** en plena forma; **to ~ a queue** hacer cola
formal ['fɔ:məl] *adj* (*offer, receipt*) por escrito; (*person etc*) correcto; (*occasion, dinner*) de etiqueta; (*dress*) correcto; (*garden*) (de estilo) clásico; **formality** [-'mælɪtɪ] *n* (*procedure*) trámite *m*; corrección *f*; etiqueta
format ['fɔ:mæt] *n* formato ▷ *vt* (*Comput*) formatear
formation [fɔ:'meɪʃən] *n* formación *f*
former ['fɔ:mə*] *adj* anterior; (*earlier*) antiguo; (*ex*) ex; **the ~ ... the latter ...** aquél ... éste ...; **formerly** *adv* antes

formidable ['fɔ:mɪdəbl] *adj*
formidable

formula ['fɔ:mjulə] *n* fórmula

fort [fɔ:t] *n* fuerte *m*

forthcoming [fɔ:θ'kʌmɪŋ] *adj*
próximo, venidero; (*help, information*)
disponible; (*character*) comunicativo

fortieth ['fɔ:tɪɪθ] *adj* cuadragésimo

fortify ['fɔ:tɪfaɪ] *vt* (*city*) fortificar;
(*person*) fortalecer

fortnight ['fɔ:tnaɪt] (*BRIT*) *n* quince
días *mpl*; quincena; **fortnightly** *adj*
de cada quince días, quincenal ▷ *adv*
cada quince días, quincenalmente

fortress ['fɔ:trɪs] *n* fortaleza

fortunate ['fɔ:tʃənɪt] *adj*
afortunado; **it is ~ that ...** (es una)
suerte que ...; **fortunately** *adv*
afortunadamente

fortune ['fɔ:tʃən] *n* suerte *f*; (*wealth*)
fortuna; **fortune-teller** *n* adivino/a

forty ['fɔ:tɪ] *num* cuarenta

forum ['fɔ:rəm] *n* foro

forward ['fɔ:wəd] *adj* (*movement,
position*) avanzado; (*front*) delantero;
(*in time*) adelantado; (*not shy*) atrevido
▷ *n* (*Sport*) delantero ▷ *vt* (*letter*)
remitir; (*career*) promocionar; **to move
~** avanzar; **forwarding address** *n*
destinatario; **forward(s)** *adv* (hacia)
adelante; **forward slash** *n* barra
diagonal

fossil ['fɔsl] *n* fósil *m*

foster ['fɔstə*] *vt* (*child*) acoger en
una familia; fomentar; **foster child** *n*
hijo/a adoptivo/a; **foster mother** *n*
madre *f* adoptiva

fought [fɔ:t] *pt, pp of* **fight**

foul [faul] *adj* sucio, puerco; (*weather,
smell etc*) asqueroso; (*language*) grosero;
(*temper*) malísimo ▷ *n* (*Sport*) falta
▷ *vt* (*dirty*) ensuciar; **foul play** *n* (*Law*)
muerte *f* violenta

found [faund] *pt, pp of* **find** ▷ *vt*
fundar; **foundation** [-'deɪʃən]
n (*act*) fundación *f*; (*basis*) base *f*;
(*also*: **foundation cream**) crema
base; **foundations** *npl* (*of building*)
cimientos *mpl*

founder ['faundə*] *n* fundador(a) *m/f*
▷ *vi* hundirse

fountain ['fauntɪn] *n* fuente *f*;
fountain pen *n* (pluma) estilográfica
(*SP*), pluma-fuente *f* (*LAM*)

four [fɔ:*] *num* cuatro; **on all ~s** a
gatas; **four-letter word** *n* taco; **four-
poster** *n* (*also*: **four-poster bed**) cama
de columnas; **fourteen** *num* catorce;
fourteenth *adj* decimocuarto; **fourth**
num cuarto; **four-wheel drive** *n*
tracción *f* a las cuatro ruedas

fowl [faul] *n* ave *f* (de corral)

fox [fɔks] *n* zorro ▷ *vt* confundir

foyer ['fɔɪeɪ] *n* vestíbulo

fraction ['frækʃən] *n* fracción *f*

fracture ['fræktʃə*] *n* fractura

fragile ['frædʒaɪl] *adj* frágil

fragment ['frægmənt] *n* fragmento

fragrance ['freɪɡrəns] *n* fragancia

frail [freɪl] *adj* frágil; (*person*) débil

frame [freɪm] *n* (*Tech*) armazón *m*;
(*of person*) cuerpo; (*of picture, door etc*)
marco; (*of spectacles: also*: **~s**) montura
▷ *vt* enmarcar; **framework** *n* marco

France [frɑ:ns] *n* Francia

franchise ['fræntʃaɪz] *n* (*Pol*) derecho
de votar, sufragio; (*Comm*) licencia,
concesión *f*

frank [fræŋk] *adj* franco ▷ *vt* (*letter*)
franquear; **frankly** *adv* francamente

frantic ['fræntɪk] *adj* (*distraught*)
desesperado; (*hectic*) frenético

fraud [frɔ:d] *n* fraude *m*; (*person*)
impostor/a *m/f*

fraught [frɔ:t] *adj*: **~ with** lleno de

fray [freɪ] *vi* deshilacharse

freak [fri:k] *n* (*person*) fenómeno;
(*event*) suceso anormal

freckle ['frɛkl] *n* peca

free [fri:] *adj* libre; (*gratis*) gratuito
▷ *vt* (*prisoner etc*) poner en libertad;
(*jammed object*) soltar; **~ (of charge),
for ~** gratis; **freedom** *n* libertad
f; **Freefone®** *n* número gratuito;
free gift *n* prima; **free kick** *n* tiro
libre; **freelance** *adj* independiente

▷ adv por cuenta propia; **freely** adv libremente; (liberally) generosamente; **Freepost**® n porte m pagado; **free-range** adj (hen, eggs) de granja; **freeway** (US) n autopista; **free will** n libre albedrío; **of one's own free will** por su propia voluntad

freeze [friːz] (pt **froze**, pp **frozen**) vi (weather) helar; (liquid, pipe, person) helarse, congelarse ▷ vt helar; (food, prices, salaries) congelar ▷ n helada; (on arms, wages) congelación f; **freezer** n congelador m, freezer m (SC)

freezing ['friːzɪŋ] adj helado; **three degrees below ~** tres grados bajo cero; **freezing point** n punto de congelación

freight [freɪt] n (goods) carga; (money charged) flete m; **freight train** (US) n tren m de mercancías

French [frɛntʃ] adj francés/esa ▷ n (Ling) francés m; **the French** npl los franceses; **French bean** n judía verde; **French bread** n pan m francés; **French dressing** n (Culin) vinagreta; **French fried potatoes, French fries** (US) npl patatas fpl (SP) or papas fpl (LAM) fritas; **Frenchman** (irreg) n francés m; **Frenchwoman** (irreg) n francésa; **French stick** n barra de pan; **French window** n puerta de cristal

frenzy ['frɛnzɪ] n frenesí m

frequency ['friːkwənsɪ] n frecuencia

frequent [adj 'friːkwənt, vb frɪ'kwɛnt] adj frecuente ▷ vt frecuentar; **frequently** [-əntlɪ] adv frecuentemente, a menudo

fresh [frɛʃ] adj fresco; (bread) tierno; (new) nuevo; **freshen** vi (wind, air) soplar más recio; **freshen up** vi (person) arreglarse, lavarse; **fresher** (BRIT: inf) n (Univ) estudiante mf de primer año; **freshly** adv (made, painted etc) recién; **freshman** (US: irreg) n = **fresher**; **freshwater** adj (fish) de agua dulce

fret [frɛt] vi inquietarse

Fri abbr (= Friday) vier

friction ['frɪkʃən] n fricción f

Friday ['fraɪdɪ] n viernes m inv

fridge [frɪdʒ] (BRIT) n frigorífico (SP), nevera (SP), refrigerador m (LAM), heladera (RPL)

fried [fraɪd] adj frito

friend [frɛnd] n amigo/a; **friendly** adj simpático; (government) amigo; (place) acogedor(a); (match) amistoso; **friendship** n amistad f

fries [fraɪz] (esp US) npl = **French fried potatoes**

frigate ['frɪgɪt] n fragata

fright [fraɪt] n (terror) terror m; (scare) susto; **to take ~** asustarse; **frighten** vt asustar; **frightened** adj asustado; **frightening** adj espantoso; **frightful** adj espantoso, horrible

frill [frɪl] n volante m

fringe [frɪndʒ] n (BRIT: of hair) flequillo; (on lampshade etc) flecos mpl; (of forest etc) borde m, margen m

Frisbee® ['frɪzbɪ] n frisbee® m

fritter ['frɪtə*] n buñuelo

frivolous ['frɪvələs] adj frívolo

fro [frəu] see **to**

frock [frɔk] n vestido

frog [frɔg] n rana; **frogman** (irreg) n hombre-rana m

○ KEYWORD

from [frɔm] prep **1** (indicating starting place) de, desde; **where do you come from?** ¿de dónde eres?; **from London to Glasgow** de Londres a Glasgow; **to escape from sth/sb** escaparse de algo/algn

2 (indicating origin etc) de; **a letter/ telephone call from my sister** una carta/llamada de mi hermana; **tell him from me that ...** dígale de mi parte que ...

3 (indicating time): **from one o'clock to** or **until** or **till two** de(sde) la una a or hasta las dos; **from January (on)** a partir de enero

4 (indicating distance) de; **the hotel is**

1 km from the beach el hotel está a 1 km de la playa

5 (*indicating price, number etc*) de; **prices range from £10 to £50** los precios van desde £10 a o hasta £50; **the interest rate was increased from 9% to 10%** el tipo de interés fue incrementado de un 9% a un 10%

6 (*indicating difference*) de; **he can't tell red from green** no sabe distinguir el rojo del verde; **to be different from sb/sth** ser diferente a algn/algo

7 (*because of, on the basis of*): **from what he says** por lo que dice; **weak from hunger** debilitado por el hambre

front [frʌnt] *n* (*foremost part*) parte *f* delantera; (*of house*) fachada; (*of dress*) delantero; (*promenade: also:* **sea ~**) paseo marítimo; (*Mil, Pol, Meteorology*) frente *m*; (*fig: appearances*) apariencias *fpl* ▷ *adj* (*wheel, leg*) delantero; (*row, line*) primero; **in ~ (of)** delante (de); **front door** *n* puerta principal; **frontier** ['frʌntɪə*] *n* frontera; **front page** *n* primera plana; **front-wheel drive** *n* tracción *f* delantera

frost [frɔst] *n* helada; (*also:* **hoar~**) escarcha; **frostbite** *n* congelación *f*; **frosting** *n* (*esp us: icing*) glaseado; **frosty** *adj* (*weather*) de helada; (*welcome etc*) glacial

froth [frɔθ] *n* espuma

frown [fraun] *vi* fruncir el ceño

froze [frəuz] *pt of* **freeze**

frozen ['frəuzn] *pp of* **freeze**

fruit [fruːt] *n inv* fruta; fruto; (*fig*) fruto; resultados *mpl*; **fruit juice** *n* zumo (SP) or jugo (LAM) de fruta; **fruit machine** (BRIT) *n* máquina *f* tragaperras; **fruit salad** *n* macedonia (SP) or ensalada (LAM) de frutas

frustrate [frʌs'treɪt] *vt* frustrar; **frustrated** *adj* frustrado

fry [fraɪ] (*pt, pp* **fried**) *vt* freír; **small ~** gente *f* menuda; **frying pan** *n* sartén *f*

ft. *abbr* = **foot; feet**

fudge [fʌdʒ] *n* (*Culin*) caramelo blando

fuel [fjuəl] *n* (*for heating*) combustible *m*; (*coal*) carbón *m*; (*wood*) leña; (*for engine*) carburante *m*; **fuel tank** *n* depósito (de combustible)

fulfil [ful'fɪl] *vt* (*function*) cumplir con; (*condition*) satisfacer; (*wish, desire*) realizar

full [ful] *adj* lleno; (*fig*) pleno; (*complete*) completo; (*maximum*) máximo; (*information*) detallado; (*price*) íntegro; (*skirt*) amplio ▷ *adv*: **to know ~ well that** saber perfectamente que; **I'm ~ (up)** no puedo más; **~ employment** pleno empleo; **a ~ two hours** dos horas completas; **at ~ speed** a máxima velocidad; **in ~** (*reproduce, quote*) íntegramente; **full-length** *adj* (*novel etc*) entero; (*coat*) largo; (*portrait*) de cuerpo entero; **full moon** *n* luna llena; **full-scale** *adj* (*attack, war*) en gran escala; (*model*) de tamaño natural; **full stop** *n* punto; **full-time** *adj* (*work*) de tiempo completo ▷ *adv*: **to work full-time** trabajar a tiempo completo; **fully** *adv* completamente; (*at least*) por lo menos

fumble ['fʌmbl] *vi*: **to ~ with** manejar torpemente

fume [fjuːm] *vi* (*rage*) estar furioso; **fumes** *npl* humo, gases *mpl*

fun [fʌn] *n* (*amusement*) diversión *f*; **to have ~** divertirse; **for ~** en broma; **to make ~ of** burlarse de

function ['fʌŋkʃən] *n* función *f* ▷ *vi* funcionar

fund [fʌnd] *n* fondo; (*reserve*) reserva; **funds** *npl* (*money*) fondos *mpl*

fundamental [fʌndə'mɛntl] *adj* fundamental

funeral ['fjuːnərəl] *n* (*burial*) entierro; (*ceremony*) funerales *mpl*; **funeral director** *n* director(a) *m/f* de pompas fúnebres; **funeral parlour** (BRIT) *n* funeraria

funfair ['fʌnfɛə*] (BRIT) *n* parque *m* de atracciones

fungus ['fʌŋgəs] (*pl* **fungi**) *n* hongo; (*mould*) moho

funnel ['fʌnl] n embudo; (of ship) chimenea

funny ['fʌnɪ] adj gracioso, divertido; (strange) curioso, raro

fur [fə:*] n piel f; (BRIT: in kettle etc) sarro; **fur coat** n abrigo de pieles

furious ['fjuərɪəs] adj furioso; (effort) violento

furnish ['fə:nɪʃ] vt amueblar; (supply) suministrar; (information) facilitar; **furnishings** npl muebles mpl

furniture ['fə:nɪtʃə*] n muebles mpl; **piece of ~** mueble m

furry ['fə:rɪ] adj peludo

further ['fə:ðə*] adj (new) nuevo, adicional ▷ adv más lejos; (more) más; (moreover) además ▷ vt promover, adelantar; **further education** n educación f superior; **furthermore** adv además

furthest ['fə:ðɪst] superlative of **far**

fury ['fjuərɪ] n furia

fuse [fju:z] (US **fuze**) n fusible m; (for bomb etc) mecha ▷ vt (metal) fundir; (fig) fusionar ▷ vi fundirse; fusionarse; (BRIT Elec): **to ~ the lights** fundir los plomos; **fuse box** n caja de fusibles

fusion ['fju:ʒən] n fusión f

fuss [fʌs] n (excitement) conmoción f; (trouble) alboroto; **to make a ~** armar un lío or jaleo; **to make a ~ of sb** mimar a algn; **fussy** adj (person) exigente; (too ornate) recargado

future ['fju:tʃə*] adj futuro; (coming) venidero ▷ n futuro; (prospects) porvenir m; **in ~** de ahora en adelante; **futures** npl (Comm) operaciones fpl a término, futuros mpl

fuze [fju:z] (US) = **fuse**

fuzzy ['fʌzɪ] adj (Phot) borroso; (hair) muy rizado

G [dʒi:] n (Mus) sol m

g. abbr (= gram(s)) gr.

gadget ['gædʒɪt] n aparato

Gaelic ['geɪlɪk] adj, n (Ling) gaélico

gag [gæg] n (on mouth) mordaza; (joke) chiste m ▷ vt amordazar

gain [geɪn] n: **~ (in)** aumento (de); (profit) ganancia ▷ vt ganar ▷ vi (watch) adelantarse; **to ~ from/by sth** sacar provecho de algo; **to ~ on sb** ganar terreno a algn; **to ~ 3 lbs (in weight)** engordar 3 libras

gal. abbr = **gallon**

gala ['gɑ:lə] n fiesta

galaxy ['gæləksɪ] n galaxia

gale [geɪl] n (wind) vendaval m

gall bladder ['gɔ:l-] n vesícula biliar

gallery ['gælərɪ] n (also: **art ~**: public) pinacoteca; (: private) galería de arte; (for spectators) tribuna

gallon ['gæln] n galón m (BRIT = 4,546 litros, US = 3,785 litros)

gallop ['gæləp] n galope m ▷ vi galopar

gallstone ['gɔ:lstəun] n cálculo

biliario

gamble ['gæmbl] n (risk) riesgo ▷ vt jugar, apostar ▷ vi (take a risk) jugárselas; (bet) apostar; **to ~ on** apostar a; (success etc) contar con; **gambler** n jugador(a) m/f; **gambling** n juego

game [geɪm] n juego; (match) partido; (of cards) partida; (Hunting) caza ▷ adj (willing): **to be ~ for anything** atreverse a todo; **big ~** caza mayor (contest) juegos; (BRIT: Scol) deportes mpl; **games console** [geɪmz-] n consola de juegos; **game show** n programa m concurso m, concurso

gammon ['gæmən] n (bacon) tocino ahumado; (ham) jamón m ahumado

gang [gæŋ] n (of criminals) pandilla; (of friends etc) grupo; (of workmen) brigada

gangster ['gæŋstə*] n gángster m

gap [gæp] n vacío (SP), hueco (LAM); (in trees, traffic) claro; (in time) intervalo; (difference): **~ (between)** diferencia (entre)

gape [geɪp] vi mirar boquiabierto; (shirt etc) abrirse (completamente)

gap year n año sabático (antes de empezar a estudiar en la universidad)

garage ['gærɑ:ʒ] n garaje m; (for repairs) taller m; **garage sale** n venta de objetos usados (en el jardín de una casa particular)

garbage ['gɑ:bɪdʒ] (US) n basura; (inf: nonsense) tonterías fpl; **garbage can** n cubo or bote m (MEX) or tacho (SC) de la basura; **garbage collector** (US) n basurero/a

garden ['gɑ:dn] n jardín m; **gardens** npl (park) parque m; **garden centre** (BRIT) n centro de jardinería; **gardener** n jardinero/a; **gardening** n jardinería

garlic ['gɑ:lɪk] n ajo

garment ['gɑ:mənt] n prenda (de vestir)

garnish ['gɑ:nɪʃ] vt (Culin) aderezar

garrison ['gærɪsn] n guarnición f

gas [gæs] n gas m; (fuel) combustible m; (US: gasoline) gasolina ▷ vt asfixiar con gas; **gas cooker** (BRIT) n cocina de gas; **gas cylinder** n bombona de gas; **gas fire** n estufa de gas

gasket ['gæskɪt] n (Aut) junta de culata

gasoline ['gæsəli:n] (US) n gasolina

gasp [gɑ:sp] n boqueada; (of shock etc) grito sofocado ▷ vi (pant) jadear

gas: gas pedal n (esp US) acelerador m; **gas station** (US) n gasolinera; **gas tank** (US) n (Aut) depósito (de gasolina)

gate [geɪt] n puerta; (iron gate) verja

gateau ['gætəʊ] (pl **~x**) n tarta

gatecrash ['geɪtkræʃ] (BRIT) vt colarse en

gateway ['geɪtweɪ] n puerta

gather ['gæðə*] vt (flowers, fruit) coger (SP), recoger; (assemble) reunir; (pick up) recoger; (Sewing) fruncir; (understand) entender ▷ vi (assemble) reunirse; **to ~ speed** ganar velocidad; **gathering** n reunión f, asamblea

gauge [geɪdʒ] n (instrument) indicador m ▷ vt medir; (fig) juzgar

gave [geɪv] pt of **give**

gay [geɪ] adj (homosexual) gay; (joyful) alegre; (colour) vivo

gaze [geɪz] n mirada fija ▷ vi: **to ~ at sth** mirar algo fijamente

GB abbr = **Great Britain**

GCSE (BRIT) n abbr (= General Certificate of Secondary Education) examen de reválida que se hace a los 16 años

gear [gɪə*] n equipo, herramientas fpl; (Tech) engranaje m; (Aut) velocidad f, marcha ▷ vt (fig: adapt): **to ~ sth to** adaptar or ajustar algo a; **top** or **high** (US)**/low ~** cuarta/primera velocidad; **in ~** en marcha; **gear up** vi prepararse; **gear box** n caja de cambios; **gear lever** n palanca de cambios; **gear shift** (US) n = **gear lever**; **gear stick** n (BRIT) palanca de cambios

geese [gi:s] npl of **goose**

gel [dʒɛl] *n* gel *m*

gem [dʒɛm] *n* piedra preciosa

Gemini ['dʒɛmɪnaɪ] *n* Géminis *m*, Gemelos *mpl*

gender ['dʒɛndə*] *n* género

gene [dʒiːn] *n* gen(e) *m*

general ['dʒɛnərl] *n* general *m* ▷ *adj* general; **in ~** en general; **general anaesthetic** (US **general anesthetic**) *n* anestesia general; **general election** *n* elecciones *fpl* generales; **generalize** *vi* generalizar; **generally** *adv* generalmente, en general; **general practitioner** *n* médico general; **general store** *n* tienda (*que vende de todo*) (LAM, SP), almacén *m* (SC, SP)

generate ['dʒɛnəreɪt] *vt* (*Elec*) generar; (*jobs, profits*) producir

generation [dʒɛnə'reɪʃən] *n* generación *f*

generator ['dʒɛnəreɪtə*] *n* generador *m*

generosity [dʒɛnə'rɔsɪtɪ] *n* generosidad *f*

generous ['dʒɛnərəs] *adj* generoso

genetic [dʒɪ'nɛtɪk] *adj*: **~ engineering** ingeniería genética; **~ fingerprinting** identificación *f* genética; **genetically modified** *adj* transgénico; **genetics** *n* genética

genitals ['dʒɛnɪtlz] *npl* (órganos *mpl*) genitales *mpl*

genius ['dʒiːnɪəs] *n* genio

genome ['giːnəum] *n* genoma *m*

gent [dʒɛnt] *n abbr* (BRIT *inf*) = **gentleman**

gentle ['dʒɛntl] *adj* apacible, dulce; (*animal*) manso; (*breeze, curve etc*) suave

▍ Be careful not to translate **gentle** by the Spanish word *gentil*.

gentleman ['dʒɛntlmən] (*irreg*) *n* señor *m*; (*well-bred man*) caballero

gently ['dʒɛntlɪ] *adv* dulcemente; suavemente

gents [dʒɛnts] *n* aseos *mpl* (de caballeros)

genuine ['dʒɛnjuɪn] *adj* auténtico; (*person*) sincero; **genuinely** *adv*

sinceramente

geographic(al) [dʒɪə'græfɪk(l)] *adj* geográfico

geography [dʒɪ'ɔgrəfɪ] *n* geografía

geology [dʒɪ'ɔlədʒɪ] *n* geología

geometry [dʒɪ'ɔmətrɪ] *n* geometría

geranium [dʒɪ'reɪnjəm] *n* geranio

gerbil ['dʒəːbɪl] *n* gerbo

geriatric [dʒɛrɪ'ætrɪk] *adj, n* geriátrico/a *m/f*

germ [dʒəːm] *n* (*microbe*) microbio, bacteria; (*seed, fig*) germen *m*

German ['dʒəːmən] *adj* alemán/ana ▷ *n* alemán/ana *m/f*; (*Ling*) alemán *m*; **German measles** *n* rubéola

Germany ['dʒəːmənɪ] *n* Alemania

gesture ['dʒɛstjə*] *n* gesto; (*symbol*) muestra

⭕ **KEYWORD**

get [gɛt] (*pt, pp* **got**, *pp* **gotten** (US)) *vi*
1 (*become, be*) ponerse, volverse; **to get old/tired** envejecer/cansarse; **to get drunk** emborracharse; **to get dirty** ensuciarse; **when do I get paid?** ¿cuándo me pagan *or* se me paga?; **it's getting late** se está haciendo tarde
2 (*go*): **to get to/from** llegar a/de; **to get home** llegar a casa
3 (*begin*) empezar a; **to get to know sb** (llegar a) conocer a algn; **I'm getting to like him** me está empezando a gustar; **let's get going** *or* **started** ¡vamos (a empezar)!
4 (*modal aux vb*): **you've got to do it** tienes que hacerlo
▷ *vt* **1**: **to get sth done** (*finish*) terminar algo; (*have done*) mandar hacer algo; **to get one's hair cut** cortarse el pelo; **to get the car going** *or* **to go** arrancar el coche; **to get sb to do sth** conseguir *or* hacer que algn haga algo; **to get sth/sb ready** preparar algo/a algn
2 (*obtain: money, permission, results*) conseguir; (*find: job, flat*) encontrar; (*fetch: person, doctor*) buscar; (*object*) ir a buscar, traer; **to get sth for sb**

conseguir algo para algn; **get me Mr Jones, please** (*Tel*) póngame (*SP*) or comuníqueme (*LAM*) con el Sr. Jones, por favor; **can I get you a drink?** ¿quieres algo de beber?
3 (*receive: present, letter*) recibir; (*acquire: reputation*) alcanzar; (*: prize*) ganar; **what did you get for your birthday?** ¿qué te regalaron por tu cumpleaños?; **how much did you get for the painting?** ¿cuánto sacaste por el cuadro?
4 (*catch*) coger (*SP*), agarrar (*LAM*); (*hit: target etc*) dar en; **to get sb by the arm/throat** coger or agarrar a algn por el brazo/cuello; **get him!** ¡cógelo! (*SP*), ¡atrápalo! (*LAM*); **the bullet got him in the leg** la bala le dio en la pierna
5 (*take, move*) llevar; **to get sth to sb** hacer llegar algo a algn; **do you think we'll get it through the door?** ¿crees que lo podremos meter por la puerta?
6 (*catch, take: plane, bus etc*) coger (*SP*), tomar (*LAM*); **where do I get the train for Birmingham?** ¿dónde se coge or se toma el tren para Birmingham?
7 (*understand*) entender; (*hear*) oír; **I've got it!** ¡ya lo tengo!, ¡eureka!; **I don't get your meaning** no te entiendo; **I'm sorry, I didn't get your name** lo siento, no cogí tu nombre
8 (*have, possess*): **to have got** tener
get away *vi* marcharse; (*escape*) escaparse
get away with *vt fus* hacer impunemente
get back *vi* (*return*) volver ▷ *vt* recobrar
get in *vi* entrar; (*train*) llegar; (*arrive home*) volver a casa, regresar
get into *vt fus* entrar en; (*vehicle*) subir a; **to get into a rage** enfadarse
get off *vi* (*from train etc*) bajar; (*depart: person, car*) marcharse ▷ *vt* (*remove*) quitar ▷ *vt fus* (*train, bus*) bajar de
get on *vi* (*at exam etc*): **how are you getting on?** ¿cómo te va?; (*agree*): **to**

get on (with) llevarse bien (con) ▷ *vt fus* subir a
get out *vi* salir; (*of vehicle*) bajar ▷ *vt* sacar
get out of *vt fus* salir de; (*duty etc*) escaparse de
get over *vt fus* (*illness*) recobrarse de
get through *vi* (*Tel*) (lograr) comunicarse
get up *vi* (*rise*) levantarse ▷ *vt fus* subir

getaway ['gɛtəweɪ] *n* fuga
Ghana ['gɑːnə] *n* Ghana
ghastly ['gɑːstlɪ] *adj* horrible
ghetto ['gɛtəʊ] *n* gueto
ghost [gəʊst] *n* fantasma *m*
giant ['dʒaɪənt] *n* gigante *mf* ▷ *adj* gigantesco, gigante
gift [gɪft] *n* regalo; (*ability*) talento; **gifted** *adj* dotado; **gift shop** (*US* **gift store**) *n* tienda de regalos; **gift token, gift voucher** *n* vale *m* canjeable por un regalo
gig [gɪg] *n* (*inf: concert*) actuación *f*
gigabyte ['dʒɪgəbaɪt] *n* gigabyte *m*
gigantic [dʒaɪ'gæntɪk] *adj* gigantesco
giggle ['gɪgl] *vi* reírse tontamente
gills [gɪlz] *npl* (*of fish*) branquias *fpl*, agallas *fpl*
gilt [gɪlt] *adj, n* dorado
gimmick ['gɪmɪk] *n* truco
gin [dʒɪn] *n* ginebra
ginger ['dʒɪndʒə*] *n* jengibre *m*
gipsy ['dʒɪpsɪ] *n* = **gypsy**
giraffe [dʒɪ'rɑːf] *n* jirafa
girl [gəːl] *n* (*small*) niña; (*young woman*) chica, joven *f*, muchacha; (*daughter*) hija; **an English ~** una (chica) inglesa; **girl band** *n* girl band *m* (*grupo musical de chicas*); **girlfriend** *n* (*of girl*) amiga; (*of boy*) novia; **Girl Scout** (*US*) *n* = **Girl Guide**
gist [dʒɪst] *n* lo esencial
give [gɪv] (*pt* **gave**, *pp* **given**) *vt* dar; (*deliver*) entregar; (*as gift*) regalar ▷ *vi* (*break*) romperse; (*stretch: fabric*) dar

de sí; **to ~ sb sth, ~ sth to sb** dar algo a algn; **give away** vt (*give free*) regalar; (*betray*) traicionar; (*disclose*) revelar; **give back** vt devolver; **give in** vi ceder ⊳ vt entregar; **give out** vt distribuir; **give up** vi rendirse, darse por vencido ⊳ vt renunciar a; **to give up smoking** dejar de fumar; **to give o.s. up** entregarse

given ['gɪvn] pp of **give** ⊳ adj (*fixed: time, amount*) determinado ⊳ conj: **~ (that) ...** dado (que) ...; **~ the circumstances ...** dadas las circunstancias ...

glacier ['glæsɪə*] n glaciar m

glad [glæd] adj contento; **gladly** ['-lɪ] adv con mucho gusto

glamour ['glæmər] (US **glamor**) n encanto, atractivo; **glamorous** adj encantador(a), atractivo

glance [glɑ:ns] n ojeada, mirada ⊳ vi: **to ~ at** echar una ojeada a

gland [glænd] n glándula

glare [glɛə*] n (*of anger*) mirada feroz; (*of light*) deslumbramiento, brillo; **to be in the ~ of publicity** ser el foco de la atención pública ⊳ vi deslumbrar; **to ~ at** mirar con odio a; **glaring** adj (*mistake*) manifiesto

glass [glɑ:s] n vidrio, cristal m; (*for drinking*) vaso; (: *with stem*) copa; **glasses** npl (*spectacles*) gafas fpl

glaze [gleɪz] vt (*window*) poner cristales a; (*pottery*) vidriar ⊳ n vidriado

gleam [gli:m] vi brillar

glen [glɛn] n cañada

glide [glaɪd] vi deslizarse; (*Aviat: birds*) planear; **glider** n (*Aviat*) planeador m

glimmer ['glɪmə*] n luz f tenue; (*of interest*) muestra; (*of hope*) rayo

glimpse [glɪmps] n vislumbre m ⊳ vt vislumbrar, entrever

glint [glɪnt] vi centellear

glisten ['glɪsn] vi relucir, brillar

glitter ['glɪtə*] vi relucir, brillar

global ['gləʊbl] adj mundial; **globalization** n globalización f;

global warming n (re)calentamiento global or de la tierra

globe [gləʊb] n globo; (*model*) globo terráqueo

gloom [glu:m] n oscuridad f; (*sadness*) tristeza; **gloomy** adj (*dark*) oscuro; (*sad*) triste; (*pessimistic*) pesimista

glorious ['glɔ:rɪəs] adj glorioso; (*weather etc*) magnífico

glory ['glɔ:rɪ] n gloria

gloss [glɔs] n (*shine*) brillo; (*paint*) pintura de aceite

glossary ['glɔsərɪ] n glosario

glossy ['glɔsɪ] adj lustroso; (*magazine*) de lujo

glove [glʌv] n guante m; **glove compartment** n (*Aut*) guantera

glow [gləʊ] vi brillar

glucose ['glu:kəʊs] n glucosa

glue [glu:] n goma (de pegar), cemento ⊳ vt pegar

GM adj abbr (= *genetically modified*) transgénico

gm abbr (= *gram*) g

GMO n abbr (= *genetically modified organism*) organismo transgénico

GMT abbr (= *Greenwich Mean Time*) GMT

gnaw [nɔ:] vt roer

go [gəʊ] (pt **went**, pp **gone**, pl **~es**) vi ir; (*travel*) viajar; (*depart*) irse, marcharse; (*work*) funcionar, marchar; (*be sold*) venderse; (*time*) pasar; (*fit, suit*): **to ~ with** hacer juego con; (*become*) ponerse; (*break etc*) estropearse, romperse ⊳ n: **to have a ~ (at)** probar suerte (con); **to be on the ~** no parar; **whose ~ is it?** ¿a quién le toca?; **he's ~ing to do it** va a hacerlo; **to ~ for a walk** ir de paseo; **to ~ dancing** ir a bailar; **how did it ~?** ¿qué tal salió or resultó?, ¿cómo ha ido?; **to ~ round the back** pasar por detrás; **go ahead** vi seguir adelante; **go away** vi irse, marcharse; **go back** vi volver; **go by** vi (*time*) pasar ⊳ vt fus guiarse por; **go down** vi bajar; (*ship*) hundirse; (*sun*) ponerse ⊳ vt fus bajar; **go for** vt fus (*fetch*) ir por; (*like*) gustar; (*attack*) atacar; **go in** vi entrar; **go into** vt fus entrar en; (investigate) investigar; (embark on) dedicarse a; **go off** vi irse, marcharse; (food) pasarse; (explode) estallar; (event) realizarse ▷ vt fus dejar de gustar; **I'm going off him/the idea** ya no me gusta tanto él/la idea; **go on** vi (continue) seguir, continuar; (happen) pasar, ocurrir; **to go on doing sth** seguir haciendo algo; **go out** vi salir; (fire, light) apagarse; **go over** vi (ship) zozobrar ▷ vt fus (check) revisar; **go past** vi, vt fus pasar; **go round** vi (circulate: news, rumour) correr; (suffice) alcanzar, bastar; (revolve) girar, dar vueltas; (visit): **to go round (to sb's)** pasar a ver (a algn); **to go round (by)** (make a detour) dar la vuelta (por); **go through** vt fus (town etc) atravesar; **go up** vi, vt fus subir; **go with** vt fus (accompany) ir con, acompañar a; **go without** vt fus pasarse sin

go-ahead ['gəuəhɛd] adj (person) dinámico; (firm) innovador(a) ▷ n luz f verde

goal [gəul] n meta; (score) gol m; **goalkeeper** n portero; **goal-post** n poste m (de la portería)

goat [gəut] n cabra

gobble ['gɔbl] vt (also: **~ down, ~ up**) tragarse, engullir

God [gɔd] n Dios m; **godchild** n ahijado/a; **goddaughter** n ahijada; **goddess** n diosa; **godfather** n padrino; **godmother** n madrina; **godson** n ahijado

goggles ['gɔglz] npl gafas fpl

going ['gəuɪŋ] n (conditions) estado del terreno ▷ adj: **the ~ rate** la tarifa corriente or en vigor

gold [gəuld] n oro ▷ adj de oro; **golden** adj (made of gold) de oro; (gold in colour) dorado; **goldfish** n pez m de colores; **goldmine** n (also fig) mina de oro; **gold-plated** adj chapado en oro

golf [gɔlf] n golf m; **golf ball** n (for game) pelota de golf; (on typewriter) esfera; **golf club** n club m de golf;

(stick) palo (de golf); **golf course** n campo de golf; **golfer** n golfista mf

gone [gɔn] pp of **go**

gong [gɔŋ] n gong m

good [gud] adj bueno; (pleasant) agradable; (kind) bueno, amable; (well-behaved) educado ▷ n bien m, provecho; **goods** npl (Comm) mercancías fpl; **~!** ¡qué bien!; **to be ~ at** tener aptitud para; **to be ~ for** servir para; **it's ~ for you** te hace bien; **would you be ~ enough to ...?** ¿podría hacerme el favor de ...?, ¿sería tan amable de ...?; **a ~ deal (of)** mucho; **a ~ many** muchos; **to make ~** reparar; **it's no ~ complaining** no vale la pena quejarse; **for ~** para siempre, definitivamente; **~ morning/afternoon!** ¡buenos días/buenas tardes!; **~ evening!** ¡buenas noches!; **~ night!** ¡buenas noches!

goodbye [gud'baɪ] excl ¡adiós!; **to say ~ (to)** (person) despedirse (de)

good: Good Friday n Viernes m Santo; **good-looking** adj guapo; **good-natured** adj amable, simpático; **goodness** n (of person) bondad f; **for goodness sake!** ¡por Dios!; **goodness gracious!** ¡Dios mío!; **goods train** (BRIT) n tren m de mercancías; **goodwill** n buena voluntad f

Google® ['guːgəl] n Google® m ▷ vi hacer búsquedas en Internet ▷ vt buscar información en Internet sobre

goose [guːs] n (pl **geese**) ganso, oca

gooseberry ['guzbərɪ] n grosella espinosa; **to play ~** hacer de carabina

goose bumps, goose pimples npl carne f de gallina

gorge [gɔːdʒ] n barranco ▷ vr: **to ~ o.s. (on)** atracarse (de)

gorgeous ['gɔːdʒəs] adj (thing) precioso; (weather) espléndido; (person) guapísimo

gorilla [gə'rɪlə] n gorila m

gosh [gɔʃ] (inf) excl ¡cielos!

gospel ['gɔspl] n evangelio

gossip ['gɔsɪp] n (scandal)

g

cotilleo, chismes *mpl*; (*chat*) charla; (*scandalmonger*) cotilla *m/f*, chismoso/a ▷ *vi* cotillear; **gossip column** *n* ecos *mpl* de sociedad

got [gɔt] *pt, pp of* **get**

gotten (US) ['gɔtn] *pp of* **get**

gourmet ['guəmeɪ] *n* gastrónomo/a *m/f*

govern ['gʌvən] *vt* gobernar; (*influence*) dominar; **government** *n* gobierno; **governor** *n* gobernador(a) *m/f*; (*of school etc*) miembro del consejo; (*of jail*) director(a) *m/f*

gown [gaun] *n* traje *m*; (*of teacher, BRIT: of judge*) toga

G.P. *n abbr* = **general practitioner**

grab [græb] *vt* coger (SP), agarrar (LAM), arrebatar ▷ *vi*: **to ~ at** intentar agarrar

grace [greɪs] *n* gracia ▷ *vt* honrar; (*adorn*) adornar; **5 days' ~** un plazo de 5 días; **graceful** *adj* grácil, ágil; (*style, shape*) elegante, gracioso; **gracious** ['greɪʃəs] *adj* amable

grade [greɪd] *n* (*quality*) clase *f*, calidad *f*; (*in hierarchy*) grado; (*Scol: mark*) nota; (*US: school class*) curso ▷ *vt* clasificar; **grade crossing** (US) *n* paso a nivel; **grade school** (US) *n* escuela primaria

gradient ['greɪdɪənt] *n* pendiente *f*

gradual ['grædjuəl] *adj* paulatino; **gradually** *adv* paulatinamente

graduate [*n* 'grædjuɪt, *vb* 'grædjueɪt] *n* (US: *of high school*) graduado/a; (*of university*) licenciado/a ▷ *vi* graduarse; licenciarse; **graduation** [-'eɪʃən] *n* (*ceremony*) entrega del título

graffiti [grə'fiːtɪ] *n* pintadas *fpl*

graft [grɑːft] *n* (Agr, Med) injerto; (BRIT: inf) trabajo duro; (*bribery*) corrupción *f* ▷ *vt* injertar

grain [greɪn] *n* (*single particle*) grano; (*corn*) granos *mpl*, cereales *mpl*; (*of wood*) fibra

gram [græm] *n* gramo

grammar ['græmə*] *n* gramática; **grammar school** (BRIT) *n* ≈ instituto

de segunda enseñanza, liceo (SP)

gramme [græm] *n* = **gram**

gran [græn] (*inf*) *n* (BRIT) abuelita

grand [grænd] *adj* magnífico, imponente; (*gesture etc*) grandioso; **grandad** (*inf*) *n* = **granddad**; **grandchild** (*pl* **grandchildren**) *n* nieto/a *m/f*; **granddad** (*inf*) *n* yayo, abuelito; **granddaughter** *n* nieta; **grandfather** *n* abuelo; **grandma** (*inf*) *n* yaya, abuelita; **grandmother** *n* abuela; **grandpa** (*inf*) *n* = **granddad**; **grandparents** *npl* abuelos *mpl*; **grand piano** *n* piano de cola; **Grand Prix** ['grɑ̃ː'priː] *n* (Aut) gran premio, Grand Prix *m*; **grandson** *n* nieto

granite ['grænɪt] *n* granito

granny ['grænɪ] (*inf*) *n* abuelita, yaya

grant [grɑːnt] *vt* (*concede*) conceder; (*admit*) reconocer ▷ *n* (Scol) beca; (Admin) subvención *f*; **to take sth/sb for ~ed** dar algo por sentado/no hacer ningún caso a algn

grape [greɪp] *n* uva

grapefruit ['greɪpfruːt] *n* pomelo (SP, SC), toronja (LAM)

graph [grɑːf] *n* gráfica; **graphic** ['græfɪk] *adj* gráfico; **graphics** *n* artes *fpl* gráficas ▷ *npl* (*drawings*) dibujos *mpl*

grasp [grɑːsp] *vt* agarrar, asir; (*understand*) comprender ▷ *n* (*grip*) asimiento; (*understanding*) comprensión *f*

grass [grɑːs] *n* hierba; (*lawn*) césped *m*; **grasshopper** *n* saltamontes *m inv*

grate [greɪt] *n* parrilla de chimenea ▷ *vi*: **to ~ (on)** chirriar (sobre) ▷ *vt* (Culin) rallar

grateful ['greɪtful] *adj* agradecido

grater ['greɪtə*] *n* rallador *m*

gratitude ['grætɪtjuːd] *n* agradecimiento

grave [greɪv] *n* tumba ▷ *adj* serio, grave

gravel ['grævl] *n* grava

gravestone ['greɪvstəun] *n* lápida

graveyard ['greɪvjɑːd] n cementerio
gravity ['grævɪtɪ] n gravedad f
gravy ['greɪvɪ] n salsa de carne
gray [greɪ] adj = **grey**
graze [greɪz] vi pacer ▷ vt (touch lightly) rozar; (scrape) raspar ▷ n (Med) abrasión f
grease [griːs] n (fat) grasa; (lubricant) lubricante m ▷ vt engrasar; lubrificar; **greasy** adj grasiento
great [greɪt] adj grande; (inf) magnífico, estupendo; **Great Britain** n Gran Bretaña; **great-grandfather** n bisabuelo; **great-grandmother** n bisabuela; **greatly** adv muy; (with verb) mucho
Greece [griːs] n Grecia
greed [griːd] n (also: **~iness**) codicia, avaricia; (for food) gula; (for power etc) avidez f; **greedy** adj avaro; (for food) glotón/ona
Greek [griːk] adj griego/a; ▷ n griego/a; (Ling) griego
green [griːn] adj (also Pol) verde; (inexperienced) novato ▷ n verde m; (stretch of grass) césped m; (Golf) green; m **greens** npl (vegetables) verduras fpl; **green card** n (Aut) carta verde; (US: work permit) permiso de trabajo para los extranjeros en EE. UU.; **greengage** n (ciruela) claudia; **greengrocer** (BRIT) n verdulero/a; **greenhouse** n invernadero; **greenhouse effect** n efecto invernadero
Greenland ['griːnlənd] n Groenlandia
green salad n ensalada f (de lechuga, pepino, pimiento verde, etc)
greet [griːt] vt (welcome) dar la bienvenida a; (receive: news) recibir; **greeting** n (welcome) bienvenida; **greeting(s) card** n tarjeta de felicitación
grew [gruː] pt of **grow**
grey [greɪ] (US **gray**) adj gris; (weather) sombrío; **grey-haired** adj canoso; **greyhound** n galgo
grid [grɪd] n reja; (Elec) red f; **gridlock**

n (traffic jam) retención f
grief [griːf] n dolor m, pena
grievance ['griːvəns] n motivo de queja, agravio
grieve [griːv] vi afligirse, acongojarse ▷ vt dar pena a; **to ~ for** llorar por
grill [grɪl] n (on cooker) parrilla; (also: **mixed ~**) parillada ▷ vt (BRIT) asar a la parrilla; (inf: question) interrogar
grille [grɪl] n reja; (Aut) rejilla
grim [grɪm] adj (place) sombrío; (situation) triste; (person) ceñudo
grime [graɪm] n mugre f, suciedad f
grin [grɪn] n sonrisa abierta ▷ vi sonreír abiertamente
grind [graɪnd] (pt, pp **ground**) vt (coffee, pepper etc) moler; (US: meat) picar; (make sharp) afilar ▷ n (work) rutina
grip [grɪp] n (hold) asimiento; (control) control m, dominio; (of tyre etc): **to have a good/bad ~** agarrarse bien/mal; (handle) asidero; (holdall) maletín m ▷ vt agarrar; (viewer, reader) fascinar; **to get to ~s with** enfrentarse con; **gripping** adj absorbente
grit [grɪt] n gravilla; (courage) valor m ▷ vt (road) poner gravilla en; **to ~ one's teeth** apretar los dientes
grits [grɪts] (US) npl maíz msg a medio moler
groan [grəun] n gemido; quejido ▷ vi gemir; quejarse
grocer ['grəusə*] n tendero (de ultramarinos (SP)); **groceries** npl comestibles mpl; **grocer's (shop)** n tienda de comestibles or (MEX, CAM) abarrotes, almacén (SC); **grocery** n (shop) tienda de ultramarinos
groin [grɔɪn] n ingle f
groom [gruːm] n mozo/a de cuadra; (also: **bride~**) novio ▷ vt (horse) almohazar; (fig): **to ~ sb for** preparar a algn para; **well-~ed** de buena presencia
groove [gruːv] n ranura, surco
grope [grəup] vi: **to ~ for** buscar a tientas
gross [grəus] adj (neglect, injustice) grave; (vulgar: behaviour) grosero;

(: *appearance*) de mal gusto; (*Comm*) bruto; **grossly** adv (*greatly*) enormemente

grotesque [grə'tɛsk] adj grotesco

ground [graund] pt, pp of **grind** ▷ n suelo, tierra; (*Sport*) campo, terreno; (*reason: gen pl*) causa, razón f; (*us: also*: **~ wire**) tierra ▷ vt (*plane*) mantener en tierra; (*us Elec*) conectar con tierra; **grounds** npl (*of coffee etc*) poso; (*gardens etc*) jardines mpl, parque m; **on the ~** en el suelo; **to the ~** al suelo; **to gain/lose ~** ganar/perder terreno; **ground floor** n (*BRIT*) planta baja; **groundsheet** (*BRIT*) n tela impermeable; suelo; **groundwork** n preparación f

group [gru:p] n grupo; (*musical*) conjunto ▷ vt (*also*: **~ together**) agrupar ▷ vi (*also*: **~ together**) agruparse

grouse [graus] n inv (*bird*) urogallo ▷ vi (*complain*) quejarse

grovel ['grɔvl] vi (*fig*): **to ~ before** humillarse ante

grow [grəu] (pt **grew**, pp **grown**) vi crecer; (*increase*) aumentar; (*expand*) desarrollarse; (*become*) volverse; **to ~ rich/weak** enriquecerse/debilitarse ▷ vt cultivar; (*hair, beard*) dejar crecer; **grow on** vt fus: **that painting is growing on me** ese cuadro me gusta cada vez más; **grow up** vi crecer, hacerse hombre/mujer

growl [graul] vi gruñir

grown [grəun] pp of **grow**; **grown-up** n adulto/a, mayor mf

growth [grəuθ] n crecimiento, desarrollo; (*what has grown*) brote m; (*Med*) tumor m

grub [grʌb] n larva, gusano; (*inf: food*) comida

grubby ['grʌbɪ] adj sucio, mugriento

grudge [grʌdʒ] n (*motivo de*) rencor m ▷ vt: **to ~ sb sth** dar algo a algn de mala gana; **to bear sb a ~** guardar rencor a algn

gruelling ['gruəlɪŋ] (*us* **grueling**) adj penoso, duro

gruesome ['gru:səm] adj horrible

grumble ['grʌmbl] vi refunfuñar, quejarse

grumpy ['grʌmpɪ] adj gruñón/ona

grunt [grʌnt] vi gruñir

guarantee [gærən'ti:] n garantía ▷ vt garantizar

guard [gɑːd] n (*squad*) guardia; (*one man*) guardia mf; (*BRIT Rail*) jefe m de tren; (*on machine*) dispositivo de seguridad; (*also*: **fire~**) rejilla de protección ▷ vt guardar; (*prisoner*) vigilar; **to be on one's ~** estar alerta; **guardian** n guardián/ana m/f; (*of minor*) tutor(a) m/f

guerrilla [gə'rɪlə] n guerrillero/a

guess [gɛs] vi adivinar; (*us*) suponer ▷ vt adivinar; suponer ▷ n suposición f, conjetura; **to take or have a ~** tratar de adivinar

guest [gɛst] n invitado/a; (*in hotel*) huésped mf; **guest house** n casa de huéspedes, pensión f; **guest room** n cuarto de huéspedes

guidance ['gaɪdəns] n (*advice*) consejos mpl

guide [gaɪd] n (*person*) guía mf; (*book, fig*) guía; (*also*: **Girl ~**) guía ▷ vt (*round museum etc*) guiar; (*lead*) conducir; (*direct*) orientar; **guidebook** n guía; **guide dog** n perro m guía; **guided tour** n visita f con guía; **guidelines** npl (*advice*) directrices fpl

guild [gɪld] n gremio

guilt [gɪlt] n culpabilidad f; **guilty** adj culpable

guinea pig ['gɪnɪ-] n cobaya; (*fig*) conejillo de Indias

guitar [gɪ'tɑ:*] n guitarra; **guitarist** n guitarrista m/f

gulf [gʌlf] n golfo; (*abyss*) abismo

gull [gʌl] n gaviota

gulp [gʌlp] vi tragar saliva ▷ vt (*also*: **~ down**) tragarse

gum [gʌm] n (*Anat*) encía; (*glue*) goma, cemento; (*sweet*) caramelo de goma; (*also*: **chewing-~**) chicle m ▷ vt pegar con goma

gun [gʌn] n (small) pistola, revólver m; (shotgun) escopeta; (rifle) fusil m; (cannon) cañón m; **gunfire** n disparos mpl; **gunman** (irreg) n pistolero; **gunpoint** n: **at gunpoint** a mano armada; **gunpowder** n pólvora; **gunshot** n escopetazo

gush [gʌʃ] vi salir a raudales; (person) deshacerse en efusiones

gust [gʌst] n (of wind) ráfaga

gut [gʌt] n intestino; **guts** npl (Anat) tripas fpl; (courage) valor m

gutter ['gʌtə*] n (of roof) canalón m; (in street) cuneta

guy [gaɪ] n (also: ~rope) cuerda; (inf: man) tío (SP), tipo; (figure) monigote m

Guy Fawkes' Night [gaɪ'fɔːks-] n ver recuadro

gym [dʒɪm] n gimnasio; **gymnasium** n gimnasio mf; **gymnast** n gimnasta mf; **gymnastics** n gimnasia; **gym shoes** npl zapatillas fpl (de deporte)

gynaecologist [gaɪnɪ'kɒlədʒɪst] (US **gynecologist**) n ginecólogo/a

gypsy ['dʒɪpsɪ] n gitano/a

haberdashery [hæbə'dæʃərɪ] (BRIT) n mercería

habit ['hæbɪt] n hábito, costumbre f; (drug habit) adicción f; (costume) hábito

habitat ['hæbɪtæt] n hábitat m

hack [hæk] vt (cut) cortar; (slice) tajar ▷ n (pej: writer) escritor(a) m/f a sueldo; **hacker** n (Comput) pirata mf informático/a

had [hæd] pt, pp of **have**

haddock ['hædək] (pl ~ or ~s) n especie de merluza

hadn't ['hædnt] = **had not**

haemorrhage ['hɛmərɪdʒ] (US **hemorrhage**) n hemorragia

haemorrhoids ['hɛmərɔɪdz] (US **hemorrhoids**) npl hemorroides fpl

haggle ['hægl] vi regatear

Hague [heɪg] n: **The ~** La Haya

hail [heɪl] n granizo; (fig) lluvia ▷ vt saludar; (taxi) llamar a; (acclaim) aclamar ▷ vi granizar; **hailstone** n (piedra de) granizo

hair [hɛə*] n pelo, cabellos mpl; (one hair) pelo, cabello; (on legs etc) vello;

to do one's ~ arreglarse el pelo; **to have grey ~** tener canas *fpl*; **hairband** *n* cinta; **hairbrush** *n* cepillo (para el pelo); **haircut** *n* corte *m* (de pelo); **hairdo** *n* peinado; **hairdresser** *n* peluquero/a; **hairdresser's** *n* peluquería; **hair dryer** *n* secador *m* de pelo; **hair gel** *n* fijador; **hair spray** *n* laca; **hairstyle** *n* peinado; **hairy** *adj* peludo; velludo; (*inf: frightening*) espeluznante

hake [heɪk] (*pl* **~** or **~s**) *n* merluza

half [hɑːf] (*pl* **halves**) *n* mitad *f*; (*of beer*) ≈ caña (*SP*), media pinta; (*Rail, Bus*) billete *m* de niño ▷ *adj* medio ▷ *adv* medio, a medias; **two and a ~** dos y media; **~ a dozen** media docena; **~ a pound** media libra; **to cut sth in ~** cortar algo por la mitad; **half board** *n* (*BRIT: in hotel*) media pensión; **half-brother** *n* hermanastro; **half day** *n* medio día *m*, media jornada; **half fare** *n* medio pasaje *m*; **half-hearted** *adj* indiferente, poco entusiasta; **half-hour** *n* media hora; **half-price** *adj*, *adv* a mitad de precio; **half term** (*BRIT*) *n* (*Scol*) vacaciones de mediados del trimestre; **half-time** *n* descanso; **halfway** *adv* a medio camino; **halfway through** a mitad de

hall [hɔːl] *n* (*for concerts*) sala; (*entrance way*) hall *m*; vestíbulo

hallmark ['hɔːlmɑːk] *n* sello

hallo [hə'ləu] *excl* = **hello**

hall of residence (*BRIT*) *n* residencia

Hallowe'en [hæləu'iːn] *n* víspera de Todos los Santos

hallucination [həluːsɪ'neɪʃən] *n* alucinación *f*

hallway ['hɔːlweɪ] *n* vestíbulo

halo ['heɪləu] *n* (*of saint*) halo, aureola

halt [hɔːlt] *n* (*stop*) alto, parada ▷ *vt* parar; interrumpir ▷ *vi* pararse

halve [hɑːv] *vt* partir por la mitad

halves [hɑːvz] *npl of* **half**

ham [hæm] *n* jamón *m* (cocido)

hamburger ['hæmbəːgə*] *n* hamburguesa

hamlet ['hæmlɪt] *n* aldea

hammer ['hæmə*] *n* martillo ▷ *vt* (*nail*) clavar; (*force*): **to ~ an idea into sb/a message home** meter una idea en la cabeza a algn/machacar una idea ▷ *vi* dar golpes

hammock ['hæmək] *n* hamaca

hamper ['hæmpə*] *vt* estorbar ▷ *n* cesto

hamster ['hæmstə*] *n* hámster *m*

hamstring ['hæmstrɪŋ] *n* (*Anat*) tendón *m* de la corva

hand [hænd] *n* mano *f*; (*of clock*) aguja; (*writing*) letra; (*worker*) obrero ▷ *vt* dar, pasar; **to give** or **lend sb a ~** echar una mano a algn, ayudar a algn; **at ~** a mano; **in ~** (*time*) libre; (*job etc*) entre manos; **on ~** (*person, services*) a mano, al alcance; **to ~** (*information etc*) a mano; **on the one ~ ..., on the other ~ ...** por una parte ... por otra (parte) ...; **hand down** *vt* pasar, bajar; (*tradition*) transmitir; (*heirloom*) dejar en herencia; (*US: sentence, verdict*) imponer; **hand in** *vt* entregar; **hand out** *vt* distribuir; **hand over** *vt* (*deliver*) entregar; **handbag** *n* bolso (*SP*), cartera (*LAM*), bolsa (*MEX*); **hand baggage** *n* = **hand luggage**; **handbook** *n* manual *m*; **handbrake** *n* freno de mano; **handcuffs** *npl* esposas *fpl*; **handful**

n puñado

handicap ['hændɪkæp] *n*
minusvalía; (*disadvantage*) desventaja;
(*Sport*) handicap *m* ▷ *vt* estorbar; **to be
mentally ~ped** ser mentalmente *m/f*
discapacitado; **to be physically ~ped**
ser minusválido/a

handkerchief ['hæŋkətʃɪf] *n*
pañuelo

handle ['hændl] *n* (*of door etc*)
tirador *m*; (*of cup etc*) asa; (*of knife etc*)
mango; (*for winding*) manivela ▷ *vt*
(*touch*) tocar; (*deal with*) encargarse de;
(*treat: people*) manejar; **"~ with care"**
"(manéjese) con cuidado"; **to fly off
the ~** perder los estribos; **handlebar(s)**
n(pl) manillar *m*

hand: hand luggage *n* equipaje *m*
de mano; **handmade** *adj* hecho a
mano; **handout** *n* (*money etc*) limosna;
(*leaflet*) folleto; **hands-free** *adj* (*phone*)
manos libres *inv*; **hands-free kit** *n*
manos libres *m inv*

handsome ['hænsəm] *adj* guapo;
(*building*) bello; (*fig: profit*) considerable

handwriting ['hændraɪtɪŋ] *n* letra

handy ['hændɪ] *adj* (*close at hand*)
a la mano; (*tool etc*) práctico; (*skilful*)
hábil, diestro

hang [hæŋ] (*pt, pp* **hung**) *vt* colgar;
(*criminal: pt, pp* hanged) ahorcar ▷ *vi*
(*painting, coat etc*) colgar; (*hair, drapery*)
caer; **to get the ~ of sth** (*inf*) lograr
dominar algo; **hang about** *or* **around**
vi haraganear; **hang down** *vi* colgar,
pender; **hang on** *vi* (*wait*) esperar;
hang out *vt* (*washing*) tender, colgar
▷ *vi* (*inf: live*) vivir; (*spend time*) pasar
el rato; **to hang out of sth** colgar
fuera de algo; **hang round** *vi* = **hang
around, hang up** *vi* (*Tel*) colgar ▷ *vt*
colgar

hanger ['hæŋə*] *n* percha

hang-gliding ['-glaɪdɪŋ] *n* vuelo
libre

hangover ['hæŋəuvə*] *n* (*after
drinking*) resaca

hankie, hanky ['hæŋkɪ] *n abbr* =

handkerchief

happen ['hæpən] *vi* suceder, ocurrir;
(*chance*): **he ~ed to hear/see** dió la
casualidad de que oyó/vió; **as it ~s** da
la casualidad de que

happily ['hæpɪlɪ] *adv* (*luckily*)
afortunadamente; (*cheerfully*)
alegremente

happiness ['hæpɪnɪs] *n* felicidad *f*;
(*cheerfulness*) alegría

happy ['hæpɪ] *adj* feliz; (*cheerful*)
alegre; **to be ~ (with)** estar contento
(con); **to be ~ to do** estar encantado de
hacer; **~ birthday!** ¡feliz cumpleaños!

harass ['hærəs] *vt* acosar, hostigar;
harassment *n* persecución *f*

harbour ['hɑːbə*] (*us* **harbor**) *n*
puerto ▷ *vt* (*fugitive*) dar abrigo a; (*hope
etc*) abrigar

hard [hɑːd] *adj* duro; (*difficult*) difícil;
(*work*) arduo; (*person*) severo; (*fact*)
innegable ▷ *adv* (*work*) mucho, duro;
(*think*) profundamente; **to look ~ at**
clavar los ojos en; **to try ~** esforzarse;
no ~ feelings! ¡sin rencor(es)!; **to be
~ of hearing** ser duro de oído; **to be
~ done by** ser tratado injustamente;
hardback *n* libro en cartoné;
hardboard *n* aglomerado *m* (*de
madera*); **hard disk** *n* (*Comput*) disco
duro *or* rígido; **harden** *vt* endurecer;
(*fig*) curtir ▷ *vi* endurecerse; curtirse

hardly ['hɑːdlɪ] *adv* apenas; **~ ever**
casi nunca

hard: hardship *n* privación *f*; **hard
shoulder** (*BRIT*) *n* (*Aut*) arcén *m*; **hard-
up** (*inf*) *adj* sin un duro (*SP*), pelado, sin
un centavo (*MEX*), pato (*SC*); **hardware**
n ferretería; (*Comput*) hardware *m*;
(*Mil*) armamento; **hardware shop**
(*us* **hardware store**) ferretería; **hard-
working** *adj* trabajador(a)

hardy ['hɑːdɪ] *adj* fuerte; (*plant*)
resistente

hare [hɛə*] *n* liebre *f*

harm [hɑːm] *n* daño, mal *m* ▷ *vt*
(*person*) hacer daño a; (*health, interests*)
perjudicar; (*thing*) dañar; **out of ~'s**

way a salvo; **harmful** adj dañino;
harmless adj (person) inofensivo; (joke
etc) inocente

harmony ['hɑːmənɪ] n armonía

harness ['hɑːnɪs] n arreos mpl; (for
child) arnés m; (safety harness) arneses
mpl ▷ vt (horse) enjaezar; (resources)
aprovechar

harp [hɑːp] n arpa ▷ vi: **to ~ on
(about)** machacar (con)

harsh [hɑːʃ] adj (cruel) duro, cruel;
(severe) severo; (sound) áspero; (light)
deslumbrador(a)

harvest ['hɑːvɪst] n (harvest time)
siega; (of cereals etc) cosecha; (of grapes)
vendimia ▷ vt cosechar

has [hæz] vb see **have**

hasn't ['hæznt] = **has not**

hassle ['hæsl] (inf) n lata

haste [heɪst] n prisa; **hasten** ['heɪsn]
vt acelerar ▷ vi darse prisa; **hastily**
adv de prisa; precipitadamente; **hasty**
adj apresurado; (rash) precipitado

hat [hæt] n sombrero

hatch [hætʃ] n (Naut: also: **~way**)
escotilla; (also: **service ~**) ventanilla
▷ vi (bird) salir del cascarón ▷ vt
incubar; (plot) tramar; **5 eggs have ~ed**
han salido 5 pollos

hatchback ['hætʃbæk] n (Aut) tres or
cinco puertas m

hate [heɪt] vt odiar, aborrecer ▷ n
odio; **hatred** ['heɪtrɪd] n odio

haul [hɔːl] vt tirar ▷ n (of fish) redada;
(of stolen goods etc) botín m

haunt [hɔːnt] vt (ghost) aparecerse
en; (obsess) obsesionar ▷ n guarida;
haunted adj (castle etc) embrujado;
(look) de angustia

○ **KEYWORD**

have [hæv] (pt, pp **had**) aux vb **1** (gen)
haber; **to have arrived/eaten** haber
llegado/comido; **having finished** or
when he had finished, he left cuando
hubo acabado, se fue

2 (in tag questions): **you've done it,**

haven't you? lo has hecho, ¿verdad?
or ¿no?

3 (in short answers and questions): **I
haven't** no; **so I have** pues, es verdad;
we haven't paid – yes we have!
no hemos pagado – ¡sí que hemos
pagado!; **I've been there before, have
you?** he estado allí antes, ¿y tú?
▷ modal aux vb (be obliged): **to have
(got) to do sth** tener que hacer algo;
you haven't to tell her no hay que or
no debes decírselo
▷ vt **1** (possess): **he has (got) blue
eyes/dark hair** tiene los ojos azules/el
pelo negro

2 (referring to meals etc): **to have
breakfast/lunch/dinner** desayunar/
comer/cenar; **to have a drink/a
cigarette** tomar algo/fumar un
cigarrillo

3 (receive) recibir; (obtain) obtener; **may
I have your address?** ¿puedes darme
tu dirección?; **you can have it for
£5** te lo puedes quedar por £5; **I must
have it by tomorrow** lo necesito para
mañana; **to have a baby** tener un
niño or bebé

4 (maintain, allow): **I won't have it/this
nonsense!** ¡no lo permitiré!/¡no
permitiré estas tonterías!; **we can't
have that** no podemos permitir eso

5 to have sth done hacer or mandar
hacer algo; **to have one's hair cut**
cortarse el pelo; **to have sb do sth**
hacer que algn haga algo

6 (experience, suffer): **to have a cold/flu**
tener un resfriado/la gripe; **she had
her bag stolen/her arm broken** le
robaron el bolso/se rompió un brazo;
to have an operation operarse

7 (+ noun): **to have a swim/walk/
bath/rest** nadar/dar un paseo/darse
un baño/descansar; **let's have a look**
vamos a ver; **to have a meeting/
party** celebrar una reunión/una fiesta;
let me have a try déjame intentarlo

haven ['heɪvn] n puerto; (fig) refugio

haven't ['hævnt] = **have not**

havoc ['hævək] n estragos mpl

Hawaii [hə'waiːɪ] n (Islas fpl)
Hawai fpl

hawk [hɔːk] n halcón m

hawthorn ['hɔːθɔːn] n espino

hay [heɪ] n heno; **hay fever** n fiebre f
del heno; **haystack** n almiar m

hazard ['hæzəd] n peligro ▷ vt
aventurar; **hazardous** adj peligroso;
hazard warning lights npl (Aut)
señales fpl de emergencia

haze [heɪz] n neblina

hazel ['heɪzl] n (tree) avellano ▷ adj
(eyes) color m de avellano; **hazelnut**
n avellana

hazy ['heɪzɪ] adj brumoso; (idea) vago

he [hiː] pron él; **~ who ...** él que ...,
quien ...

head [hɛd] n cabeza; (leader) jefe/a
m/f; (of school) director(a) m/f ▷ vt
(list) encabezar; (group) capitanear;
(company) dirigir; **~s (or tails)** cara (o
cruz); **~ first** de cabeza; **~ over heels**
(in love) perdidamente; **to ~ the ball**
cabecear (la pelota); **head for** vt fus
dirigirse a; (disaster) ir camino de; **head
off** vt (threat, danger) evitar; **headache**
n dolor m de cabeza; **heading** n título;
headlamp (BRIT) n = **headlight**;
headlight n faro; **headline** n titular
m; **head office** n oficina central,
central f; **headphones** npl auriculares
mpl; **headquarters** npl sede f central;
(Mil) cuartel m general; **headroom** n
(in car) altura interior; (under bridge)
(límite m de) altura; **headscarf** n
pañuelo; **headset** n cascos mpl;
headteacher n director(directora);
head waiter n maître m

heal [hiːl] vt curar ▷ vi cicatrizarse

health [hɛlθ] n salud f; **health
care** n asistencia sanitaria; **health
centre** (BRIT) n ambulatorio, centro
médico; **health food** n alimentos mpl
orgánicos; **Health Service** (BRIT) n el
servicio de salud pública, ≈ el Insalud
(SP); **healthy** adj sano, saludable

heap [hiːp] n montón m ▷ vt: **to
~ (up)** amontonar; **to ~ sth with**
llenar algo hasta arriba de; **~s of** un
montón de

hear [hɪə*] (pt, pp **~d**) vt (also Law) oír;
(news) saber ▷ vi oír; **to ~ about** oír
hablar de; **to ~ from sb** tener noticias
de algn

heard [hɜːd] pt, pp of **hear**

hearing ['hɪərɪŋ] n (sense) oído; (Law)
vista; **hearing aid** n audífono

hearse [hɜːs] n coche m fúnebre

heart [hɑːt] n corazón m; (fig) valor
m; (of lettuce) cogollo; **hearts** npl
(Cards) corazones mpl; **to lose/take
~** descorazonarse/cobrar ánimo; **at
~** en el fondo; **by ~** (learn, know) de
memoria; **heart attack** n infarto (de
miocardio); **heartbeat** n latido (del
corazón); **heartbroken** adj: **she was
heartbroken about it** esto le partió el
corazón; **heartburn** n acedía; **heart
disease** n enfermedad f cardíaca

hearth [hɑːθ] n (fireplace) chimenea

heartless ['hɑːtlɪs] adj despiadado

hearty ['hɑːtɪ] adj (person)
campechano; (laugh) sano; (dislike,
support) absoluto

heat [hiːt] n calor m; (Sport: also:
qualifying ~) prueba eliminatoria ▷ vt
calentar; **heat up** vi calentarse ▷ vt
calentar; **heated** adj caliente; (fig)
acalorado, **heater** n estufa; (in car)
calefacción f

heather ['hɛðə*] n brezo

heating ['hiːtɪŋ] n calefacción f

heatwave ['hiːtweɪv] n ola de calor

heaven ['hɛvn] n cielo; (fig) una
maravilla; **heavenly** adj celestial; (fig)
maravilloso

heavily ['hɛvɪlɪ] adv pesadamente;
(drink, smoke) con exceso; (sleep, sigh)
profundamente; (depend) mucho

heavy ['hɛvɪ] adj pesado; (work,
blow) duro; (sea, rain, meal) fuerte;
(drinker, smoker) grande; (responsibility)
grave; (schedule) ocupado; (weather)
bochornoso

Hebrew ['hi:bru:] *adj, n* (*Ling*) hebreo
hectare ['hɛktɑ:*] *n* (BRIT) hectárea
hectic ['hɛktɪk] *adj* agitado
he'd [hi:d] = **he would; he had**
hedge [hɛdʒ] *n* seto ▷ *vi* contestar
con evasivas; **to ~ one's bets** (*fig*)
cubrirse
hedgehog ['hɛdʒhɔg] *n* erizo
heed [hi:d] *vt* (*also*: **take ~**: *pay
attention to*) hacer caso de
heel [hi:l] *n* talón *m*; (*of shoe*) tacón *m*
▷ *vt* (*shoe*) poner tacón a
hefty ['hɛftɪ] *adj* (*person*) fornido;
(*parcel, profit*) gordo
height [haɪt] *n* (*of person*) estatura;
(*of building*) altura; (*high ground*) cerro;
(*altitude*) altitud *f*; (*fig*: *of season*): **at the
~ of summer** en los días más calurosos
del verano; (: *of power etc*) cúspide *f*;
(: *of stupidity etc*) colmo; **heighten** *vt*
elevar; (*fig*) aumentar
heir [ɛə*] *n* heredero; **heiress** *n*
heredera
held [hɛld] *pt, pp of* **hold**
helicopter ['hɛlɪkɔptə*] *n*
helicóptero
hell [hɛl] *n* infierno; **~!** (*inf*)
¡demonios!
he'll [hi:l] = **he will; he shall**
hello [hə'ləu] *excl* ¡hola!; (*to attract
attention*) ¡oiga!; (*surprise*) ¡caramba!
helmet ['hɛlmɪt] *n* casco
help [hɛlp] *n* ayuda; (*cleaner etc*)
criada, asistenta ▷ *vt* ayudar; **~!**
¡socorro!; **~ yourself** sírvete; **he can't
~ it** no es culpa suya; **help out** *vi*
ayudar, echar una mano ▷ *vt*: **to help
sb out** ayudar a algn, echar una mano
a algn; **helper** *n* ayudante *mf*; **helpful**
adj útil; (*person*) servicial; (*advice*)
útil; **helping** *n* ración *f*; **helpless**
adj (*incapable*) incapaz; (*defenceless*)
indefenso; **helpline** *n* teléfono de
asistencia al público
hem [hɛm] *n* dobladillo ▷ *vt* poner or
coser el dobladillo de
hemisphere ['hɛmɪsfɪə*] *n*
hemisferio

hemorrhage ['hɛmərɪdʒ] (US) *n* =
haemorrhage
hemorrhoids ['hɛmərɔɪdz] (US) *npl* =
haemorrhoids
hen [hɛn] *n* gallina; (*female bird*)
hembra
hence [hɛns] *adv* (*therefore*) por lo
tanto; **2 years ~** de aquí a 2 años
hen night, hen party *n* (*inf*)
despedida de soltera
hepatitis [hɛpə'taɪtɪs] *n* hepatitis *f*
her [hə:*] *pron* (*direct*) la; (*indirect*) le;
(*stressed, after prep*) ella ▷ *adj* su; *see
also* **me; my**
herb [hə:b] *n* hierba; **herbal** *adj* de
hierbas; **herbal tea** *n* infusión *f* de
hierbas
herd [hə:d] *n* rebaño
here [hɪə*] *adv* aquí; (*at this point*)
en este punto; **~!** (*present*) ¡presente!;
~ is/are aquí está/están; **~ she is**
aquí está
hereditary [hɪ'rɛdɪtrɪ] *adj*
hereditario
heritage ['hɛrɪtɪdʒ] *n* patrimonio
hernia ['hə:nɪə] *n* hernia
hero ['hɪərəu] (*pl* **~es**) *n* héroe *m*;
(*in book, film*) protagonista *m*; **heroic**
[hɪ'rəuɪk] *adj* heroico
heroin ['hɛrəuɪn] *n* heroína
heroine ['hɛrəuɪn] *n* heroína; (*in
book, film*) protagonista
heron ['hɛrən] *n* garza
herring ['hɛrɪŋ] *n* arenque *m*
hers [hə:z] *pron* (el) suyo/(la) suya *etc*;
see also **mine¹**
herself [hə:'sɛlf] *pron* (*reflexive*) se;
(*emphatic*) ella misma; (*after prep*) sí
(misma); *see also* **oneself**
he's [hi:z] = **he is; he has**
hesitant ['hɛzɪtənt] *adj* vacilante
hesitate ['hɛzɪteɪt] *vi* vacilar; (*in
speech*) titubear; (*be unwilling*) resistirse
a; **hesitation** ['-teɪʃən] *n* indecisión *f*;
titubeo; dudas *fpl*
heterosexual [hɛtərəu'sɛksjuəl] *adj*
heterosexual
hexagon ['hɛksəgən] *n* hexágono

hey [heɪ] *excl* ¡oye!, ¡oiga!
heyday ['heɪdeɪ] *n*: **the ~ of** el
apogeo de
HGV *n abbr* (= *heavy goods vehicle*)
vehículo pesado
hi [haɪ] *excl* ¡hola!; (*to attract attention*)
¡oiga!
hibernate ['haɪbəneɪt] *vi* invernar
hiccough ['hɪkʌp] = **hiccup**
hiccup ['hɪkʌp] *vi* hipar
hid [hɪd] *pt of* **hide**
hidden ['hɪdn] *pp of* **hide** ▷ *adj*: **~
agenda** plan *m* encubierto
hide [haɪd] (*pt* **hid**, *pp* **hidden**) *n* (*skin*)
piel *f* ▷ *vt* esconder, ocultar ▷ *vi*: **to
~ (from sb)** esconderse *or* ocultarse
(de algn)
hideous ['hɪdɪəs] *adj* horrible
hiding ['haɪdɪŋ] *n* (*beating*) paliza; **to
be in ~** (*concealed*) estar escondido
hi-fi ['haɪfaɪ] *n* estéreo, hifi *m* ▷ *adj*
de alta fidelidad
high [haɪ] *adj* alto; (*speed, number*)
grande; (*price*) elevado; (*wind*) fuerte;
(*voice*) agudo ▷ *adv* alto, a gran altura;
it is 20 m ~ tiene 20 m de altura; **~
in the air** en las alturas; **highchair**
n silla alta; **high-class** *adj* (*hotel*)
de lujo; (*person*) distinguido, de
categoría; (*food*) de alta categoría;
higher education *n* educación *f*
or enseñanza superior; **high heels**
npl (*heels*) tacones *mpl* altos; (*shoes*)
zapatos *mpl* de tacón; **high jump** *n*
(*Sport*) salto de altura; **highlands**
['haɪləndz] *npl* tierras *fpl* altas; **the
Highlands** (*in Scotland*) las Tierras Altas
de Escocia; **highlight** *n* (*fig*: *of event*)
punto culminante ▷ *vt* subrayar;
highlights *npl* (*in hair*) reflejos *mpl*;
highlighter *n* rotulador; **highly** *adv*
(*paid*) muy bien; (*critical, confidential*)
sumamente; (*a lot*): **to speak/think
highly of** hablar muy bien de/tener
en mucho a; **highness** *n* altura;
Her/His Highness Su Alteza; **high-rise**
n (*also*: **high-rise block, high-rise
building**) torre *f* de pisos; **high school**

n ≈ Instituto Nacional de Bachillerato
(*sp*); **high season** (*BRIT*) *n* temporada
alta; **high street** (*BRIT*) *n* calle *f* mayor;
high-tech (*inf*) *adj* al-tec (*inf*), de alta
tecnología; **highway** *n* carretera;
(*us*) carretera nacional; autopista;
Highway Code (*BRIT*) *n* código de la
circulación
hijack ['haɪdʒæk] *vt* secuestrar;
hijacker *n* secuestrador(a) *m/f*
hike [haɪk] *vi* (*go walking*) ir de
excursión (a pie) ▷ *n* caminata;
hiker *n* excursionista *mf*; **hiking** *n*
senderismo
hilarious [hɪ'lɛərɪəs] *adj*
divertidísimo
hill [hɪl] *n* colina; (*high*) montaña;
(*slope*) cuesta; **hillside** *n* ladera; **hill
walking** *n* senderismo (de montaña);
hilly *adj* montañoso
him [hɪm] *pron* (*direct*) le, lo; (*indirect*)
le; (*stressed, after prep*) él; *see also* **me**;
himself *pron* (*reflexive*) se; (*emphatic*)
él mismo; (*after prep*) sí (mismo); *see
also* **oneself**
hind [haɪnd] *adj* posterior
hinder ['hɪndə*] *vt* estorbar, impedir
hindsight ['haɪndsaɪt] *n*: **with ~** en
retrospectiva
Hindu ['hɪndu:] *n* hindú *mf*;
Hinduism *n* (*Rel*) hinduismo
hinge [hɪndʒ] *n* bisagra, gozne *m* ▷ *vi*
(*fig*): **to ~ on** depender de
hint [hɪnt] *n* indirecta; (*advice*)
consejo; (*sign*) dejo ▷ *vt*: **to ~ that**
insinuar que ▷ *vi*: **to ~ at** hacer
alusión a
hip [hɪp] *n* cadera
hippie ['hɪpɪ] *n* hippie *m/f*, jipi *m/f*
hippo ['hɪpəu] (*pl* **~s**) *n* hipopótamo
hippopotamus [hɪpə'pɒtəməs] (*pl*
~es *or* **hippopotami**) *n* hipopótamo
hippy ['hɪpɪ] *n* = **hippie**
hire ['haɪə*] *vt* (*BRIT*: *car, equipment*)
alquilar; (*worker*) contratar ▷ *n* alquiler
m; **for ~** se alquila; (*taxi*) libre; **hire(d)
car** (*BRIT*) *n* coche *m* de alquiler; **hire
purchase** (*BRIT*) *n* compra a plazos

his [hɪz] *pron* (el) suyo((la) suya) *etc*
▷ *adj* su; *see also* **mine¹; my**
Hispanic [hɪsˈpænɪk] *adj* hispánico
hiss [hɪs] *vi* silbar
historian [hɪˈstɔːrɪən] *n*
historiador(a) *m/f*
historic(al) [hɪˈstɔrɪk(l)] *adj*
histórico
history [ˈhɪstərɪ] *n* historia
hit [hɪt] (*pt, pp* **~**) *vt* (*strike*) golpear,
pegar; (*reach: target*) alcanzar; (*collide
with: car*) chocar contra; (*fig: affect*)
afectar ▷ *n* golpe *m*; (*success*) éxito;
(*on website*) visita; (*in web search*)
correspondencia; **to ~ it off with
sb** llevarse bien con algn; **hit back**
vi defenderse; (*fig*) devolver golpe
por golpe
hitch [hɪtʃ] *vt* (*fasten*) atar, amarrar;
(*also:* **~ up**) remangar ▷ *n* (*difficulty*)
dificultad *f*; **to ~ a lift** hacer
autostop
hitch-hike [ˈhɪtʃhaɪk] *vi* hacer
autostop; **hitch-hiker** *n* autostopista
m/f; **hitch-hiking** *n* autostop *m*
hi-tech [haɪˈtɛk] *adj* de alta
tecnología
hitman [ˈhɪtmæn] (*irreg*) *n* asesino
a sueldo
HIV *n abbr* (= *human immunodeficiency
virus*) VIH *m*; **~-negative/positive**
VIH negativo/positivo
hive [haɪv] *n* colmena
hoard [hɔːd] *n* (*treasure*) tesoro;
(*stockpile*) provisión *f* ▷ *vt* acumular;
(*goods in short supply*) acaparar
hoarse [hɔːs] *adj* ronco
hoax [həuks] *n* trampa
hob [hɔb] *n* quemador *m*
hobble [ˈhɔbl] *vi* cojear
hobby [ˈhɔbɪ] *n* pasatiempo, afición
f
hobo [ˈhəubəu] (*US*) *n* vagabundo
hockey [ˈhɔkɪ] *n* hockey *m*; **hockey
stick** *n* palo *m* de hockey
hog [hɔg] *n* cerdo, puerco ▷ *vt* (*fig*)
acaparar; **to go the whole ~** poner
toda la carne en el asador

Hogmanay [hɔgməˈneɪ] *n* ver
recuadro

● **HOGMANAY**
●
● La Nochevieja o "New Year's Eve"
● se conoce como "Hogmanay"
● en Escocia, donde se festeje de
● forma especial. La familia y los
● amigos se suelen juntar para oír
● las campanadas del reloj y luego se
● hace el "first-footing", costumbre
● que consiste en visitar a los amigos
● y vecinos llevando algo de beber
● (generalmente whisky) y un trozo
● de carbón que se supone que traerá
● buena suerte para el año entrante.

hoist [hɔɪst] *n* (*crane*) grúa ▷ *vt*
levantar, alzar; (*flag, sail*) izar
hold [həuld] (*pt, pp* **held**) *vt* sostener;
(*contain*) contener; (*have: power,
qualification*) tener; (*keep back*) retener;
(*believe*) sostener; (*consider*) considerar;
(*keep in position*) **to ~ one's head up**
mantener la cabeza alta; (*meeting*)
celebrar ▷ *vi* (*withstand pressure*)
resistir; (*be valid*) valer ▷ *n* (*grasp*)
asimiento; (*fig*) dominio; **~ the line!**
(*Tel*) ¡no cuelgue!; **to ~ one's own** (*fig*)
defenderse; **to catch** *or* **get (a) ~ of**
agarrarse *or* asirse de; **hold back** *vt*
retener; (*secret*) ocultar; **hold on** *vi*
agarrarse bien; (*wait*) esperar; **hold
on!** (*Tel*) ¡(espere) un momento!; **hold
out** *vt* ofrecer ▷ *vi* (*resist*) resistir;
hold up *vt* (*raise*) levantar; (*support*)
apoyar; (*delay*) retrasar; (*rob*) asaltar;
holdall (*BRIT*) *n* bolsa; **holder** *n*
(*container*) receptáculo; (*of ticket, record*)
poseedor(a) *m/f*; (*of office, title etc*)
titular *mf*
hole [həul] *n* agujero
holiday [ˈhɔlədɪ] *n* vacaciones
fpl; (*public holiday*) (día *m* de) fiesta,
día *m* feriado; **on ~** de vacaciones;
holiday camp *n* (*BRIT: also*: **holiday
centre**) centro de vacaciones; **holiday**

job n (BRIT) trabajillo extra para las vacaciones; **holiday-maker** (BRIT) n turista mf; **holiday resort** n centro turístico

Holland ['hɔlənd] n Holanda

hollow ['hɔləu] adj hueco; (claim) vacío; (eyes) hundido; (sound) sordo ▷ n hueco; (in ground) hoyo ▷ vt: **to ~ out** excavar

holly ['hɔlɪ] n acebo

Hollywood ['hɔlɪwud] n Hollywood m

holocaust ['hɔləkɔːst] n holocausto

holy ['həulɪ] adj santo, sagrado; (water) bendito

home [həum] n casa; (country) patria; (institution) asilo ▷ cpd (domestic) casero, de casa; (Econ, Pol) nacional ▷ adv (direction) a casa; (right in: nail etc) a fondo; **at ~** en casa; (in country) en el país; (fig) como pez en el agua; **to go/come ~** ir/volver a casa; **make yourself at ~** ¡estás en tu casa!; **home address** n domicilio; **homeland** n tierra natal; **homeless** adj sin hogar, sin casa; **homely** adj (simple) sencillo; **home-made** adj casero; **home match** n partido en casa; **Home Office** (BRIT) n Ministerio del Interior; **home owner** n propietario/a m/f de una casa; **home page** n página de inicio; **Home Secretary** (BRIT) n Ministro del Interior; **homesick** adj: **to be homesick** tener morriña, sentir nostalgia; **home town** n ciudad f natal; **homework** n deberes mpl

homicide ['hɔmɪsaɪd] (US) n homicidio

homoeopathic [həumɪə'pæθɪk] (US **homeopathic**) adj homeopático

homoeopathy [həumɪ'ɔpəθɪ] (US **homeopathy**) n homeopatía

homosexual [hɔməu'sɛksjuəl] adj, n homosexual mf

honest ['ɔnɪst] adj honrado; (sincere) franco, sincero; **honestly** adv honradamente; francamente; **honesty** n honradez f

honey ['hʌnɪ] n miel f; **honeymoon** n luna de miel; **honeysuckle** n madreselva

Hong Kong ['hɔŋ'kɔŋ] n Hong-Kong m

honorary ['ɔnərərɪ] adj (member, president) de honor; (title) honorífico; **~ degree** doctorado honoris causa

honour ['ɔnə*] (US **honor**) vt honrar; (commitment, promise) cumplir con ▷ n honor m, honra; **to graduate with ~s** ≈ licenciarse con matrícula (de honor); **honourable** (US **honorable**) adj honorable; **honours degree** n (Scol) título de licenciado con calificación alta

hood [hud] n capucha; (BRIT Aut) capota; (US Aut) capó m; (of cooker) campana de humos; **hoodie** n (top) jersey m con capucha

hoof [huːf] (pl **hooves**) n pezuña

hook [huk] n gancho; (on dress) corchete m, broche m; (for fishing) anzuelo ▷ vt enganchar; (fish) pescar

hooligan ['huːlɪgən] n gamberro

hoop [huːp] n aro

hooray [huː'reɪ] excl = **hurray**

hoot [huːt] (BRIT) vi (Aut) tocar el pito, pitar; (siren) (hacer) sonar; (owl) ulular

Hoover® ['huːvə*] (BRIT) n aspiradora ▷ vt: **to hoover** pasar la aspiradora por

hooves [huːvz] npl of **hoof**

hop [hɔp] vi saltar, brincar; (on one foot) saltar con un pie

hope [həup] vt, vi esperar ▷ n esperanza; **I ~ so/not** espero que sí/no; **hopeful** adj (person) optimista; (situation) prometedor(a); **hopefully** adv con esperanza; (one hopes): **hopefully he will recover** esperamos que se recupere; **hopeless** adj desesperado; (person): **to be hopeless** ser un desastre

hops [hɔps] npl lúpulo

horizon [hə'raɪzn] n horizonte m; **horizontal** [hɔrɪ'zɔntl] adj horizontal

hormone ['hɔːməun] n hormona

horn [hɔːn] n cuerno; (Mus: also:

French ~) trompa; (*Aut*) pito, claxon *m*

horoscope ['hɔrəskəup] *n* horóscopo

horrendous [hɔ'rɛndəs] *adj* horrendo

horrible ['hɔrɪbl] *adj* horrible

horrid ['hɔrɪd] *adj* horrible, horroroso

horrific [hɔ'rɪfɪk] *adj* (*accident*) horroroso; (*film*) horripilante

horrifying ['hɔrɪfaɪɪŋ] *adj* horroroso

horror ['hɔrə*] *n* horror *m*; **horror film** *n* película de horror

hors d'œuvre [ɔː'dəːvrə] *n* entremeses *mpl*

horse [hɔːs] *n* caballo; **on horseback** a caballo; **horse chestnut** *n* (*tree*) castaño de Indias; (*nut*) castaña de Indias; **horsepower** *n* caballo (de fuerza); **horse-racing** *n* carreras *fpl* de caballos; **horseradish** *n* rábano picante; **horse riding** *n* (*BRIT*) equitación *f*

hose [həuz] *n* manguera; **hosepipe** *n* manguera

hospital ['hɔspɪtl] *n* hospital *m*

hospitality [hɔspɪ'tælɪtɪ] *n* hospitalidad *f*

host [həust] *n* anfitrión *m*; (*TV, Radio*) presentador *m*; (*Rel*) hostia; (*large number*): **a ~ of** multitud de

hostage ['hɔstɪdʒ] *n* rehén *m*

hostel ['hɔstl] *n* hostal *m*; **(youth) ~** albergue *m* juvenil

hostess ['həustɪs] *n* anfitriona; (*BRIT: air hostess*) azafata; (*TV, Radio*) presentadora

hostile ['hɔstaɪl] *adj* hostil

hostility [hɔ'stɪlɪtɪ] *n* hostilidad *f*

hot [hɔt] *adj* caliente; (*weather*) caluroso, de calor; (*as opposed to warm*) muy caliente; (*spicy*) picante: **to be ~** (*person*) tener calor; (*object*) estar caliente; (*weather*) hacer calor; **hot dog** *n* perro caliente

hotel [həu'tɛl] *n* hotel *m*

hotspot ['hɔtspɔt] *n* (*Comput*): **wireless hotspot** punto *m* de acceso inalámbrico

hot-water bottle [hɔt'wɔːtə*-] *n* bolsa de agua caliente

hound [haund] *vt* acosar ▷ *n* perro (de caza)

hour ['auə*] *n* hora; **hourly** *adj* (de) cada hora

house [*n* haus, *pl* 'hauzɪz, *vb* hauz] *n* (*gen, firm*) casa; (*Pol*) cámara; (*Theatre*) sala ▷ *vt* (*person*) alojar; (*collection*) albergar; **on the ~** (*fig*) la casa invita; **household** *n* familia; (*home*) casa; **householder** *n* propietario/a; (*head of house*) cabeza de familia; **housekeeper** *n* ama de llaves; **housekeeping** *n* (*work*) trabajos *mpl* domésticos; **housewife** (*irreg*) *n* ama de casa; **house wine** *n* vino *m* de la casa; **housework** *n* faenas *fpl* (de la casa)

housing ['hauzɪŋ] *n* (*act*) alojamiento; (*houses*) viviendas *fpl*; **housing development, housing estate** (*BRIT*) *n* urbanización *f*

hover ['hɔvə*] *vi* flotar (en el aire); **hovercraft** *n* aerodeslizador *m*

how [hau] *adv* (*in what way*) cómo; **~ are you?** ¿cómo estás?; **~ much milk/ many people?** ¿cuánta leche/gente?; **~ much does it cost?** ¿cuánto cuesta?; **~ long have you been here?** ¿cuánto hace que estás aquí?; **~ old are you?** ¿cuántos años tienes?; **~ tall is he?** ¿cómo es de alto?; **~ is school?** ¿cómo (te) va (en) la escuela?; **~ was the film?** ¿qué tal la película?; **~ lovely/awful!** ¡qué bonito/horror!

however [hau'ɛvə*] *adv*: **~ I do it** lo haga como lo haga; **~ cold it is** por mucho frío que haga; **~ did you do it?** ¿cómo lo hiciste? ▷ *conj* sin embargo, no obstante

howl [haul] *n* aullido ▷ *vi* aullar; (*person*) dar alaridos; (*wind*) ulular

H.P. *n abbr* = **hire purchase**

h.p. *abbr* = **horsepower**

HQ *n abbr* = **headquarters**

hr(s) *abbr* (= *hour(s)*) h

HTML *n abbr* (= *hypertext markup language*) lenguaje *m* de hipertexto

hubcap ['hʌbkæp] *n* tapacubos *m inv*

huddle ['hʌdl] *vi*: **to ~ together**

acurrucarse

huff [hʌf] n: **in a ~** enojado

hug [hʌg] vt abrazar; (thing) apretar con los brazos

huge [hju:dʒ] adj enorme

hull [hʌl] n (of ship) casco

hum [hʌm] vt tararear, canturrear ▷ vi tararear, canturrear; (insect) zumbar

human ['hju:mən] adj, n humano

humane [hju:'meɪn] adj humano, humanitario

humanitarian [hju:mænɪ'teərɪən] adj humanitario

humanity [hju:'mænɪtɪ] n humanidad f

human rights npl derechos mpl humanos

humble ['hʌmbl] adj humilde

humid ['hju:mɪd] adj húmedo; **humidity** [-'mɪdɪtɪ] n humedad f

humiliate [hju:'mɪlɪeɪt] vt humillar

humiliating [hju:'mɪlɪeɪtɪŋ] adj humillante, vergonzoso

humiliation [hju:mɪlɪ'eɪʃən] n humillación f

hummus ['huməs] n paté de garbanzos

humorous ['hju:mərəs] adj gracioso, divertido

humour ['hju:mə*] (US **humor**) n humorismo, sentido del humor; (mood) humor m ▷ vt (person) complacer

hump [hʌmp] n (in ground) montículo; (camel's) giba

hunch [hʌntʃ] n (premonition) presentimiento

hundred ['hʌndrəd] num ciento; (before n) cien; **~s of** centenares de; **hundredth** [-ɪdθ] adj centésimo

hung [hʌŋ] pt, pp of **hang**

Hungarian [hʌŋ'geərɪən] adj, n húngaro/a m/f

Hungary ['hʌŋgərɪ] n Hungría

hunger ['hʌŋgə*] n hambre f ▷ vi: **to ~ for** (fig) tener hambre de, anhelar

hungry ['hʌŋgrɪ] adj: **~ (for)** hambriento (de); **to be ~** tener hambre

hunt [hʌnt] vt (seek) buscar; (Sport) cazar ▷ vi (search): **to ~ (for)** buscar; (Sport) cazar ▷ n búsqueda; caza, cacería; **hunter** n cazador(a) m/f; **hunting** n caza

hurdle ['hə:dl] n (Sport) valla; (fig) obstáculo

hurl [hə:l] vt lanzar, arrojar

hurrah [hu:'rɑ:] excl = **hurray**

hurray [hu'reɪ] excl ¡viva!

hurricane ['hʌrɪkən] n huracán m

hurry ['hʌrɪ] n prisa ▷ vt (also: ~ up: person) dar prisa a; (: work) apresurar, hacer de prisa; **to be in a ~** tener prisa; **hurry up** vi darse prisa, apurarse (LAM)

hurt [hə:t] (pt, pp ~) vt hacer daño a ▷ vi doler ▷ adj lastimado

husband ['hʌzbənd] n marido

hush [hʌʃ] n silencio ▷ vt hacer callar; **~!** ¡chitón!, ¡cállate!

husky ['hʌskɪ] adj ronco ▷ n perro esquimal

hut [hʌt] n cabaña; (shed) cobertizo

hyacinth ['haɪəsɪnθ] n jacinto

hydrangea [haɪ'dreɪnʒə] n hortensia

hydrofoil ['haɪdrəfoɪl] n aerodeslizador m

hydrogen ['haɪdrədʒən] n hidrógeno

hygiene ['haɪdʒi:n] n higiene f; **hygienic** [-'dʒi:nɪk] adj higiénico

hymn [hɪm] n himno

hype [haɪp] (inf) n bombardeo publicitario

hyperlink ['haɪpəlɪŋk] n hiperlink m

hyphen ['haɪfn] n guión m

hypnotize ['hɪpnətaɪz] vt hipnotizar

hypocrite ['hɪpəkrɪt] n hipócrita mf

hypocritical [hɪpə'krɪtɪkl] adj hipócrita

hypothesis [haɪ'pɔθɪsɪs] (pl **hypotheses**) n hipótesis f inv

hysterical [hɪ'sterɪkl] adj histérico; (funny) para morirse de risa

hysterics [hɪ'sterɪks] npl histeria; **to be in ~** (fig) morirse de risa

I [aɪ] *pron* yo

ice [aɪs] *n* hielo; (*ice cream*) helado ▷ *vt* (*cake*) alcorzar ▷ *vi* (*also:* **~ over, ~ up**) helarse; **iceberg** *n* iceberg *m*; **ice cream** *n* helado; **ice cube** *n* cubito de hielo; **ice hockey** *n* hockey *m* sobre hielo

Iceland ['aɪslənd] *n* Islandia; **Icelander** *n* islandés/esa *m/f*; **Icelandic** [aɪs'lændɪk] *adj* islandés/esa ▷ *n* (*Ling*) islandés *m*

ice: ice lolly (BRIT) *n* polo; **ice rink** *n* pista de hielo; **ice skating** *n* patinaje *m* sobre hielo

icing ['aɪsɪŋ] *n* (*Culin*) alcorza; **icing sugar** (BRIT) *n* azúcar *m* glas(eado)

icon ['aɪkɒn] *n* icono

ICT (BRIT: *Scol*) *n abbr* (= *information and communications technology*) informática

icy ['aɪsɪ] *adj* helado

I'd [aɪd] = **I would**; **I had**

ID card *n* (*identity card*) DNI *m*

idea [aɪ'dɪə] *n* idea

ideal [aɪ'dɪəl] *n* ideal *m* ▷ *adj* ideal; **ideally** [-dɪəlɪ] *adv* idealmente;

---

they're ideally suited hacen una pareja ideal

identical [aɪ'dɛntɪkl] *adj* idéntico

identification [aɪdɛntɪfɪ'keɪʃən] *n* identificación *f*; **(means of) ~** documentos *mpl* personales

identify [aɪ'dɛntɪfaɪ] *vt* identificar

identity [aɪ'dɛntɪtɪ] *n* identidad *f*; **identity card** *n* carnet *m* de identidad; **identity theft** *n* robo de identidad

ideology [aɪdɪ'ɔlədʒɪ] *n* ideología

idiom ['ɪdɪəm] *n* modismo; (*style of speaking*) lenguaje *m*

> Be careful not to translate **idiom** by the Spanish word *idioma*.

idiot ['ɪdɪət] *n* idiota *mf*

idle ['aɪdl] *adj* (*inactive*) ocioso; (*lazy*) holgazán/ana; (*unemployed*) parado, desocupado; (*machinery etc*) parado; (*talk etc*) frívolo ▷ *vi* (*machine*) marchar en vacío

idol ['aɪdl] *n* ídolo

idyllic [ɪ'dɪlɪk] *adj* idílico

i.e. *abbr* (= *that is*) esto es

if [ɪf] *conj* si; **~ necessary** si fuera necesario, si hiciese falta; **~ I were you** yo en tu lugar; **~ so/not** de ser así/si no; **~ only I could!** ¡ojalá pudiera!; *see also* **as**; **even**

ignite [ɪg'naɪt] *vt* (*set fire to*) encender ▷ *vi* encenderse

ignition [ɪg'nɪʃən] *n* (*Aut: process*) ignición *f*; (: *mechanism*) encendido; **to switch on/off the ~** arrancar/apagar el motor

ignorance ['ɪgnərəns] *n* ignorancia

ignorant ['ɪgnərənt] *adj* ignorante; **to be ~ of** ignorar

ignore [ɪg'nɔ:*] *vt* (*person, advice*) no hacer caso de; (*fact*) pasar por alto

I'll [aɪl] = **I will**; **I shall**

ill [ɪl] *adj* enfermo, malo ▷ *n* mal *m* ▷ *adv* mal; **to be taken ~** ponerse enfermo

illegal [ɪ'li:gl] *adj* ilegal

illegible [ɪ'lɛdʒɪbl] *adj* ilegible

illegitimate [ɪlɪ'dʒɪtɪmət] *adj*

ilegítimo

ill health n mala salud f; **to be in ~** estar mal de salud

illiterate [ɪ'lɪtərət] adj analfabeto

illness ['ɪlnɪs] n enfermedad f

illuminate [ɪ'lu:mɪneɪt] vt (room, street) iluminar, alumbrar

illusion [ɪ'lu:ʒən] n ilusión f; (trick) truco

illustrate ['ɪləstreɪt] vt ilustrar

illustration [ɪlə'streɪʃən] n (act of illustrating) ilustración f; (example) ejemplo, ilustración f; (in book) lámina

I'm [aɪm] = **I am**

image ['ɪmɪdʒ] n imagen f

imaginary [ɪ'mædʒɪnərɪ] adj imaginario

imagination [ɪmædʒɪ'neɪʃən] n imaginación f; (inventiveness) inventiva

imaginative [ɪ'mædʒɪnətɪv] adj imaginativo

imagine [ɪ'mædʒɪn] vt imaginarse

imbalance [ɪm'bæləns] n desequilibrio

imitate ['ɪmɪteɪt] vt imitar; **imitation** [ɪmɪ'teɪʃən] n imitación f; (copy) copia

immaculate [ɪ'mækjulət] adj inmaculado

immature [ɪmə'tjuə*] adj (person) inmaduro

immediate [ɪ'mi:dɪət] adj inmediato; (pressing) urgente, apremiante; (nearest: family) próximo, (: neighbourhood) inmediato; **immediately** adv (at once) en seguida; (directly) inmediatamente; **immediately next to** muy junto a

immense [ɪ'mɛns] adj inmenso, enorme; (importance) enorme; **immensely** adv enormemente

immerse [ɪ'mə:s] vt (submerge) sumergir; **to be ~d in** (fig) estar absorto en

immigrant ['ɪmɪgrənt] n inmigrante mf; **immigration** [ɪmɪ'greɪʃən] n inmigración f

imminent ['ɪmɪnənt] adj inminente

immoral [ɪ'mɔrəl] adj inmoral

immortal [ɪ'mɔ:tl] adj inmortal

immune [ɪ'mju:n] adj: **~ (to)** inmune (a); **immune system** n sistema m inmunitario

immunize ['ɪmjunaɪz] vt inmunizar

impact ['ɪmpækt] n impacto

impair [ɪm'pɛə*] vt perjudicar

impartial [ɪm'pɑ:ʃl] adj imparcial

impatience [ɪm'peɪʃəns] n impaciencia

impatient [ɪm'peɪʃənt] adj impaciente; **to get** or **grow ~** impacientarse

impeccable [ɪm'pɛkəbl] adj impecable

impending [ɪm'pɛndɪŋ] adj inminente

imperative [ɪm'pɛrətɪv] adj (tone) imperioso; (need) imprescindible

imperfect [ɪm'pə:fɪkt] adj (goods etc) defectuoso ▷ n (Ling: also: **~ tense**) imperfecto

imperial [ɪm'pɪərɪəl] adj imperial

impersonal [ɪm'pə:sənl] adj impersonal

impersonate [ɪm'pə:səneɪt] vt hacerse pasar por; (Theatre) imitar

impetus ['ɪmpətəs] n ímpetu m; (fig) impulso

implant [ɪm'plɑ:nt] vt (Med) injertar, implantar; (fig: idea, principle) inculcar

implement [n 'ɪmplɪmənt, vb 'ɪmplɪment] n herramienta; (for cooking) utensilio ▷ vt (regulation) hacer efectivo; (plan) realizar

implicate ['ɪmplɪkeɪt] vt (compromise) comprometer; **to ~ sb in sth** comprometer a algn en algo

implication [ɪmplɪ'keɪʃən] n consecuencia; **by ~** indirectamente

implicit [ɪm'plɪsɪt] adj implícito; (belief, trust) absoluto

imply [ɪm'plaɪ] vt (involve) suponer; (hint) dar a entender que

impolite [ɪmpə'laɪt] adj mal educado

import [vb ɪmˈpɔːt, n ˈɪmpɔːt] vt
importar ▷ n (Comm) importación
f; (: article) producto importado;
(meaning) significado, sentido
importance [ɪmˈpɔːtəns] n
importancia
important [ɪmˈpɔːtənt] adj
importante; **it's not ~** no importa, no
tiene importancia
importer [ɪmˈpɔːtə*] n
importador(a) m/f
impose [ɪmˈpəuz] vt imponer
▷ vi: **to ~ on sb** abusar de algn;
imposing adj imponente,
impresionante
impossible [ɪmˈpɔsɪbl] adj
imposible; (person) insoportable
impotent [ˈɪmpətənt] adj impotente
impoverished [ɪmˈpɔvərɪʃt] adj
necesitado
impractical [ɪmˈpræktɪkl] adj
(person, plan) poco práctico
impress [ɪmˈpres] vt impresionar;
(mark) estampar; **to ~ sth on sb** hacer
entender algo a algn
impression [ɪmˈpreʃən] n
impresión f; (imitation) imitación f; **to
be under the ~ that** tener la impresión
de que
impressive [ɪmˈpresɪv] adj
impresionante
imprison [ɪmˈprɪzn] vt encarcelar;
imprisonment n encarcelamiento;
(term of imprisonment) cárcel f
improbable [ɪmˈprɔbəbl] adj
improbable, inverosímil
improper [ɪmˈprɔpə*] adj
(unsuitable: conduct etc) incorrecto;
(: activities) deshonesto
improve [ɪmˈpruːv] vt mejorar;
(foreign language) perfeccionar
▷ vi mejorarse; **improvement** n
mejoramiento; perfección f;
progreso
improvise [ˈɪmprəvaɪz] vt, vi
improvisar
impulse [ˈɪmpʌls] n impulso; **to act
on ~** obrar sin reflexión; **impulsive**

[ɪmˈpʌlsɪv] adj irreflexivo

○ **KEYWORD**

in [ɪn] prep **1** (indicating place,
position, with place names) en; **in the
house/garden** en (la) casa/el jardín;
in here/there aquí/ahí or allí dentro;
in London/England en Londres/
Inglaterra
2 (indicating time) en; **in spring** en (la)
primavera; **in the afternoon** por la
tarde; **at 4 o'clock in the afternoon**
a las 4 de la tarde; **I did it in 3 hours/
days** lo hice en 3 horas/días; **I'll see
you in 2 weeks** or **in 2 weeks' time** te
veré dentro de 2 semanas
3 (indicating manner etc) en; **in a loud/
soft voice** en voz alta/baja; **in pencil/
ink** a lápiz/bolígrafo; **the boy in the
blue shirt** el chico de la camisa azul
4 (indicating circumstances): **in the sun/
shade/rain** al sol/a la sombra/bajo la
lluvia; **a change in policy** un cambio
de política
5 (indicating mood, state): **in tears** en
lágrimas, llorando; **in anger/despair**
enfadado/desesperado; **to live in
luxury** vivir lujosamente
6 (with ratios, numbers): **1 in 10
households, 1 household in 10** una
de cada 10 familias; **20 pence in the
pound** 20 peniques por libra; **they
lined up in twos** se alinearon de dos
en dos
7 (referring to people, works) en; entre;
the disease is common in children la
enfermedad es común entre los niños;
in (the works of) Dickens en (las
obras de) Dickens
8 (indicating profession etc): **to be in
teaching** estar en la enseñanza
9 (after superlative) de; **the best pupil
in the class** el(la) mejor alumno/a
de la clase
10 (with present participle): **in saying
this** al decir esto
▷ adv: **to be in** (person: at home) estar en

casa; (*at work*) estar; (*train, ship, plane*) haber llegado; (*in fashion*) estar de moda; **she'll be in later today** llegará más tarde hoy; **to ask sb in** hacer pasar a algn; **to run/limp** *etc* **in** entrar corriendo/cojeando *etc*
▷ *n*: **the ins and outs** (*of proposal, situation etc*) los detalles

inability [ɪnə'bɪlɪtɪ] *n*: **~ (to do)** incapacidad *f* (de hacer)

inaccurate [ɪn'ækjurət] *adj* inexacto, incorrecto

inadequate [ɪn'ædɪkwət] *adj* (*income, reply etc*) insuficiente; (*person*) incapaz

inadvertently [ɪnəd'vəːtntlɪ] *adv* por descuido

inappropriate [ɪnə'prəupriət] *adj* inadecuado; (*improper*) poco oportuno

inaugurate [ɪ'nɔːgjureɪt] *vt* inaugurar; (*president, official*) investir

Inc. (*us*) *abbr* (= *incorporated*) S.A.

incapable [ɪn'keɪpəbl] *adj* incapaz

incense [*n* 'ɪnsɛns, *vb* ɪn'sɛns] *n* incienso ▷ *vt* (*anger*) indignar, encolerizar

incentive [ɪn'sɛntɪv] *n* incentivo, estímulo

inch [ɪntʃ] *n* pulgada; **to be within an ~ of** estar a dos dedos de; **he didn't give an ~** no dio concesión alguna

incidence ['ɪnsɪdns] *n* (*of crime, disease*) incidencia

incident ['ɪnsɪdnt] *n* incidente *m*

incidentally [ɪnsɪ'dɛntəlɪ] *adv* (*by the way*) a propósito

inclination [ɪnklɪ'neɪʃən] *n* (*tendency*) tendencia, inclinación *f*; (*desire*) deseo; (*disposition*) propensión *f*

incline [*n* 'ɪnklaɪn, *vb* ɪn'klaɪn] *n* pendiente *m*, cuesta ▷ *vt* (*head*) poner de lado ▷ *vi* inclinarse; **to be ~d to** (*tend*) tener tendencia a hacer algo

include [ɪn'kluːd] *vt* (*incorporate*) incluir; (*in letter*) adjuntar; **including** *prep* incluso, inclusive

inclusion [ɪn'kluːʒən] *n* inclusión *f*

inclusive [ɪn'kluːsɪv] *adj* inclusivo; **~ of tax** incluidos los impuestos

income ['ɪŋkʌm] *n* (*earned*) ingresos *mpl*; (*from property etc*) renta; (*from investment etc*) rédito; **income support** *n* (BRIT) ≈ ayuda familiar; **income tax** *n* impuesto sobre la renta

incoming ['ɪnkʌmɪŋ] *adj* (*flight, government etc*) entrante

incompatible [ɪnkəm'pætɪbl] *adj* incompatible

incompetence [ɪn'kɔmpɪtəns] *n* incompetencia

incompetent [ɪn'kɔmpɪtənt] *adj* incompetente

incomplete [ɪnkəm'pliːt] *adj* (*partial: achievement etc*) incompleto; (*unfinished: painting etc*) inacabado

inconsistent [ɪnkən'sɪstənt] *adj* inconsecuente; (*contradictory*) incongruente; **~ with** (que) no concuerda con

inconvenience [ɪnkən'viːnjəns] *n* inconvenientes *mpl*; (*trouble*) molestia, incomodidad *f* ▷ *vt* incomodar

inconvenient [ɪnkən'viːnjənt] *adj* incómodo, poco práctico; (*time, place, visitor*) inoportuno

incorporate [ɪn'kɔːpəreɪt] *vt* incorporar; (*contain*) comprender; (*add*) agregar

incorrect [ɪnkə'rɛkt] *adj* incorrecto

increase [*n* 'ɪnkriːs, *vb* ɪn'kriːs] *n* aumento ▷ *vi* aumentar; (*grow*) crecer; (*price*) subir ▷ *vt* aumentar; (*price*) subir; **increasingly** *adv* cada vez más, más y más

incredible [ɪn'krɛdɪbl] *adj* increíble; **incredibly** *adv* increíblemente

incur [ɪn'kəː*] *vt* (*expenditure*) incurrir; (*loss*) sufrir; (*anger, disapproval*) provocar

indecent [ɪn'diːsnt] *adj* indecente

indeed [ɪn'diːd] *adv* efectivamente, en realidad; (*in fact*) en efecto; (*furthermore*) es más; **yes ~!** ¡claro!

que sí!

indefinitely [ɪnˈdɛfɪnɪtlɪ] *adv* (*wait*)
indefinidamente

independence [ɪndɪˈpɛndns] *n*
independencia; **Independence Day**
(*US*) *n* Día *m* de la Independencia

● **INDEPENDENCE DAY**
●
● El cuatro de julio es **Independence**
● **Day**, la fiesta nacional de Estados
● Unidos, que se celebra en
● conmemoración de la Declaración
● de Independencia, escrita por
● Thomas Jefferson y aprobada
● en 1776. En ella se proclamaba
● la independencia total de Gran
● Bretaña de las trece colonias
● americanas que serían el origen de
● los Estados Unidos de América.

independent [ɪndɪˈpɛndənt] *adj*
independiente; **independent school**
n (*BRIT*) escuela *f* privada, colegio *m*
privado

index [ˈɪndɛks] (*pl* **-es**) *n* (*in book*)
índice *m*; (: *in library etc*) catálogo; (*pl*
indices: *ratio, sign*) exponente *m*

India [ˈɪndɪə] *n* la India; **Indian** *adj, n*
indio/a; **Red Indian** piel roja *mf*

indicate [ˈɪndɪkeɪt] *vt* indicar;
indication [-ˈkeɪʃən] *n* indicio, señal
f; **indicative** [ɪnˈdɪkətɪv] *adj*: **to be**
indicative of indicar; **indicator** *n*
indicador *m*; (*Aut*) intermitente *m*

indices [ˈɪndɪsiːz] *npl of* **index**

indict [ɪnˈdaɪt] *vt* acusar; **indictment**
n acusación *f*

indifference [ɪnˈdɪfrəns] *n*
indiferencia

indifferent [ɪnˈdɪfrənt] *adj*
indiferente; (*mediocre*) regular

indigenous [ɪnˈdɪdʒɪnəs] *adj*
indígena

indigestion [ɪndɪˈdʒɛstʃən] *n*
indigestión *f*

indignant [ɪnˈdɪgnənt] *adj*: **to be**
~ at sth/with sb indignarse por

algo/con algn

indirect [ɪndɪˈrɛkt] *adj* indirecto

indispensable [ɪndɪˈspɛnsəbl] *adj*
indispensable, imprescindible

individual [ɪndɪˈvɪdjuəl] *n* individuo
▷ *adj* individual; (*personal*) personal;
(*particular*) particular; **individually** *adv*
(*singly*) individualmente

Indonesia [ɪndəˈniːzɪə] *n* Indonesia

indoor [ˈɪndɔː*] *adj* (*swimming pool*)
cubierto; (*plant*) de interior; (*sport*) bajo
cubierta; **indoors** [ɪnˈdɔːz] *adv* dentro

induce [ɪnˈdjuːs] *vt* inducir,
persuadir; (*bring about*) producir;
(*labour*) provocar

indulge [ɪnˈdʌldʒ] *vt* (*whim*)
satisfacer; (*person*) complacer; (*child*)
mimar ▷ *vi*: **to ~ in** darse el gusto de;
indulgent *adj* indulgente

industrial [ɪnˈdʌstrɪəl] *adj*
industrial; **industrial estate** (*BRIT*) *n*
polígono (*SP*) *or* zona (*LAM*) industrial;
industrialist *n* industrial *mf*;
industrial park (*US*) *n* = **industrial**
estate

industry [ˈɪndəstrɪ] *n* industria;
(*diligence*) aplicación *f*

inefficient [ɪnɪˈfɪʃənt] *adj* ineficaz,
ineficiente

inequality [ɪnɪˈkwɔlɪtɪ] *n*
desigualdad *f*

inevitable [ɪnˈɛvɪtəbl] *adj* inevitable;
inevitably *adv* inevitablemente

inexpensive [ɪnɪkˈspɛnsɪv] *adj*
económico

inexperienced [ɪnɪkˈspɪərɪənst] *adj*
inexperto

inexplicable [ɪnɪkˈsplɪkəbl] *adj*
inexplicable

infamous [ˈɪnfəməs] *adj* infame

infant [ˈɪnfənt] *n* niño/a; (*baby*) niño/
a pequeño/a, bebé *mf*; (*pej*) aniñado

infantry [ˈɪnfəntrɪ] *n* infantería

infant school (*BRIT*) *n* parvulario

infect [ɪnˈfɛkt] *vt* (*wound*) infectar;
(*food*) contaminar; (*person, animal*)
contagiar; **infection** [ɪnˈfɛkʃən] *n*
infección *f*; (*fig*) contagio; **infectious**

[ɪnˈfɛkʃəs] adj (also fig) contagioso

infer [ɪnˈfəː*] vt deducir, inferir

inferior [ɪnˈfɪərɪə*] adj, n inferior mf

infertile [ɪnˈfəːtaɪl] adj estéril; (person) infecundo

infertility [ɪnfəˈtɪlɪtɪ] n esterilidad f; infecundidad f

infested [ɪnˈfɛstɪd] adj: **~ with** plagado de

infinite [ˈɪnfɪnɪt] adj infinito; **infinitely** adv infinitamente

infirmary [ɪnˈfəːmərɪ] n hospital m

inflamed [ɪnˈfleɪmd] adj: **to become ~** inflamarse

inflammation [ɪnfləˈmeɪʃən] n inflamación f

inflatable [ɪnˈfleɪtəbl] adj (ball, boat) inflable

inflate [ɪnˈfleɪt] vt (tyre, price etc) inflar; (fig) hinchar; **inflation** [ɪnˈfleɪʃən] n (Econ) inflación f

inflexible [ɪnˈflɛksəbl] adj (rule) rígido; (person) inflexible

inflict [ɪnˈflɪkt] vt: **to ~ sth on sb** infligir algo en algn

influence [ˈɪnfluəns] n influencia ▷ vt influir en, influenciar; **under the ~ of alcohol** en estado de embriaguez; **influential** [-ˈɛnʃl] adj influyente

influx [ˈɪnflʌks] n afluencia

info (inf) [ˈɪnfəu] n = **information**

inform [ɪnˈfɔːm] vt: **to ~ sb of sth** informar a algn sobre or de algo ▷ vi: **to ~ on sb** delatar a algn

informal [ɪnˈfɔːməl] adj (manner, tone) familiar; (dress, interview, occasion) informal; (visit, meeting) extraoficial

information [ɪnfəˈmeɪʃən] n información f; (knowledge) conocimientos mpl; **a piece of ~** un dato; **Information office** n información f; **information technology** n informática

informative [ɪnˈfɔːmətɪv] adj informativo

infra-red [ɪnfrəˈrɛd] adj infrarrojo

infrastructure [ˈɪnfrəstrʌktʃə*] n (of system etc) infraestructura

infrequent [ɪnˈfriːkwənt] adj infrecuente

infuriate [ɪnˈfjuərɪeɪt] vt: **to become ~d** ponerse furioso

infuriating [ɪnˈfjuərɪeɪtɪŋ] adj (habit, noise) enloquecedor(a)

ingenious [ɪnˈdʒiːnjəs] adj ingenioso

ingredient [ɪnˈgriːdɪənt] n ingrediente m

inhabit [ɪnˈhæbɪt] vt vivir en; **inhabitant** n habitante mf

inhale [ɪnˈheɪl] vt inhalar ▷ vi (breathe in) aspirar; (in smoking) tragar; **inhaler** n inhalador m

inherent [ɪnˈhɪərənt] adj: **~ in or to** inherente a

inherit [ɪnˈhɛrɪt] vt heredar; **inheritance** n herencia; (fig) patrimonio

inhibit [ɪnˈhɪbɪt] vt inhibir, impedir; **inhibition** [-ˈbɪʃən] n cohibición f

initial [ɪˈnɪʃl] adj primero ▷ n inicial f ▷ vt firmar con las iniciales; **initials** npl (as signature) iniciales fpl; (abbreviation) siglas fpl; **initially** adv al principio

initiate [ɪˈnɪʃɪeɪt] vt iniciar; **to ~ proceedings against sb** (Law) entablar proceso contra algn

initiative [ɪˈnɪʃətɪv] n iniciativa

inject [ɪnˈdʒɛkt] vt inyectar; **to ~ sb with sth** inyectar algo a algn; **injection** [ɪnˈdʒɛkʃən] n inyección f

injure [ˈɪndʒə*] vt (hurt) herir, lastimar; (fig: reputation etc) perjudicar; **injured** adj (person, arm) herido, lastimado; **injury** n herida, lesión f; (wrong) perjuicio, daño

⎸ Be careful not to translate **injury** by the Spanish word injuria.

injustice [ɪnˈdʒʌstɪs] n injusticia

ink [ɪŋk] n tinta; **ink-jet printer** [ˈɪŋkdʒɛt-] n impresora de chorro de tinta

inland [adj ˈɪnlənd, adv ɪnˈlænd] adj (waterway, port etc) interior ▷ adv tierra adentro; **Inland Revenue** (BRIT) n departamento de impuestos ≈

Hacienda (sp)

in-laws ['ɪnlɔːz] npl suegros mpl

inmate ['ɪnmeɪt] n (in prison) preso/a, presidiario/a; (in asylum) internado/a

inn [ɪn] n posada, mesón m

inner ['ɪnə*] adj (courtyard, calm) interior; (feelings) íntimo; **inner-city** adj (schools, problems) de las zonas céntricas pobres, de los barrios céntricos pobres

inning ['ɪnɪŋ] n (US: Baseball) inning m, entrada; **~s** (Cricket) entrada, turno

innocence ['ɪnəsns] n inocencia

innocent ['ɪnəsnt] adj inocente

innovation [ɪnəu'veɪʃən] n novedad f

innovative ['ɪnəu'veɪtɪv] adj innovador

in-patient ['ɪnpeɪʃənt] n paciente m/f interno/a

input ['ɪnput] n entrada; (of resources) inversión f; (Comput) entrada de datos

inquest ['ɪnkwɛst] n (coroner's) encuesta judicial

inquire [ɪn'kwaɪə*] vi preguntar ▷ vt: **to ~ whether** preguntar si; **to ~ about** (person) preguntar por; (fact) informarse de; **inquiry** n pregunta; (investigation) investigación f, pesquisa; **"Inquiries"** "Información"

ins. abbr = **inches**

insane [ɪn'seɪn] adj loco; (Med) demente

insanity [ɪn'sænɪtɪ] n demencia, locura

insect ['ɪnsɛkt] n insecto; **insect repellent** n loción f contra insectos

insecure [ɪnsɪ'kjuə*] adj inseguro

insecurity [ɪnsɪ'kjuərɪtɪ] n inseguridad f

insensitive [ɪn'sɛnsɪtɪv] adj insensible

insert [vb ɪn'sə:t, n 'ɪnsə:t] vt (into sth) introducir ▷ n encarte m

inside ['ɪn'saɪd] n interior m ▷ adj interior, interno ▷ adv (be) (por) dentro; (go) hacia dentro ▷ prep dentro de; (of time): **~ 10 minutes** en menos

de 10 minutos; **inside lane** n (Aut: in Britain) carril m izquierdo; (: in US, Europe etc) carril m derecho; **inside out** adv (turn) al revés; (know) a fondo

insight ['ɪnsaɪt] n perspicacia

insignificant [ɪnsɪg'nɪfɪknt] adj insignificante

insincere [ɪnsɪn'sɪə*] adj poco sincero

insist [ɪn'sɪst] vi insistir; **to ~ on** insistir en; **to ~ that** insistir en que; (claim) exigir que; **insistent** adj insistente; (noise, action) persistente

insomnia [ɪn'sɔmnɪə] n insomnio

inspect [ɪn'spɛkt] vt inspeccionar, examinar; (troops) pasar revista a; **inspection** [ɪn'spɛkʃən] n inspección f, examen m; (of troops) revista; **inspector** n inspector(a) m/f; (BRIT: on buses, trains) revisor(a) m/f

inspiration [ɪnspə'reɪʃən] n inspiración f; **inspire** [ɪn'spaɪə*] vt inspirar; **inspiring** adj inspirador(a)

instability [ɪnstə'bɪlɪtɪ] n inestabilidad f

install [ɪn'stɔ:l] (US **instal**) vt instalar; (official) nombrar; **installation** [ɪnstə'leɪʃən] n instalación f

installment [ɪn'stɔ:lmənt] (US **installment**) n plazo; (of story) entrega; (of TV serial etc) capítulo; **in ~s** (pay, receive) a plazos

instance ['ɪnstəns] n ejemplo, caso; **for ~** por ejemplo; **in the first ~** en primer lugar

instant ['ɪnstənt] n instante m, momento ▷ adj inmediato; (coffee etc) instantáneo; **instantly** adv en seguida; **instant messaging** n mensajería instantánea

instead [ɪn'stɛd] adv en cambio; **~ of** en lugar de, en vez de

instinct ['ɪnstɪŋkt] n instinto; **instinctive** adj instintivo

institute ['ɪnstɪtjuːt] n instituto; (professional body) colegio ▷ vt (begin) iniciar, empezar; (proceedings) entablar; (system, rule) establecer

institution [ɪnstɪˈtjuːʃən] n
institución f; (Med: home) asilo;
(: asylum) manicomio; (of system etc)
establecimiento; (of custom)
iniciación f

instruct [ɪnˈstrʌkt] vt: **to ~ sb in sth**
instruir a algn en or sobre algo; **to ~ sb**
to do sth dar instrucciones a algn de
hacer algo; **instruction** [ɪnˈstrʌkʃən]
n (teaching) instrucción f; **instructions**
npl (orders) órdenes fpl; **instructions**
(for use) modo de empleo; **instructor**
n instructor(a) m/f

instrument [ˈɪnstrəmənt] n
instrumento; **instrumental** [-ˈmɛntl]
adj (Mus) instrumental; **to be**
instrumental in ser (el) artífice de

insufficient [ɪnsəˈfɪʃənt] adj
insuficiente

insulate [ˈɪnsjuleɪt] vt aislar;
insulation [-ˈleɪʃən] n aislamiento

insulin [ˈɪnsjulɪn] n insulina

insult [n ˈɪnsʌlt, vb ɪnˈsʌlt] n insulto
▷ vt insultar; **insulting** adj insultante

insurance [ɪnˈʃuərəns] n seguro;
fire/life ~ seguro contra incendios/
sobre la vida; **insurance company**
n compañía f de seguros; **insurance**
policy n póliza (de seguros)

insure [ɪnˈʃuə*] vt asegurar

intact [ɪnˈtækt] adj íntegro;
(unharmed) intacto

intake [ˈɪnteɪk] n (of food) ingestión f;
(of air) consumo; (BRIT Scol): **an ~ of 200**
a year 200 matriculados al año

integral [ˈɪntɪɡrəl] adj (whole)
íntegro; (part) integrante

integrate [ˈɪntɪɡreɪt] vt integrar ▷ vi
integrarse

integrity [ɪnˈtɛɡrɪtɪ] n honradez f,
rectitud f

intellect [ˈɪntəlɛkt] n intelecto;
intellectual [-ˈlɛktjuəl] adj, n
intelectual mf

intelligence [ɪnˈtɛlɪdʒəns] n
inteligencia

intelligent [ɪnˈtɛlɪdʒənt] adj
inteligente

intend [ɪnˈtɛnd] vt (gift etc): **to ~ sth**
for destinar algo a; **to ~ to do sth** tener
intención de or pensar hacer algo

intense [ɪnˈtɛns] adj intenso

intensify [ɪnˈtɛnsɪfaɪ] vt intensificar;
(increase) aumentar

intensity [ɪnˈtɛnsɪtɪ] n (gen)
intensidad f

intensive [ɪnˈtɛnsɪv] adj intensivo;
intensive care n: **to be in intensive**
care estar bajo cuidados intensivos;
intensive care unit n unidad f de
vigilancia intensiva

intent [ɪnˈtɛnt] n propósito; (Law)
premeditación f ▷ adj (absorbed)
absorto; (attentive) atento; **to all ~s**
and purposes prácticamente; **to**
be ~ on doing sth estar resuelto a
hacer algo

intention [ɪnˈtɛnʃən] n intención f,
propósito; **intentional** adj deliberado

interact [ɪntərˈækt] vi influirse
mutuamente; **interaction**
[ɪntərˈækʃən] n interacción f, acción
f recíproca; **interactive** adj (Comput)
interactivo

intercept [ɪntəˈsɛpt] vt interceptar;
(stop) detener

interchange [ˈɪntətʃeɪndʒ] n
intercambio; (on motorway)
intersección f

intercourse [ˈɪntəkɔːs] n (sexual)
relaciones fpl sexuales

interest [ˈɪntrɪst] n (also Comm)
interés m ▷ vt interesar; **interested**
adj interesado; **to be interested**
in interesarse por; **interesting** adj
interesante; **interest rate** n tipo or
tasa de interés

interface [ˈɪntəfeɪs] n (Comput)
junción f

interfere [ɪntəˈfɪə*] vi: **to ~ in**
entrometerse en; **to ~ with** (hinder)
estorbar; (damage) estropear

interference [ɪntəˈfɪərəns] n
intromisión f; (Radio, TV) interferencia

interim [ˈɪntərɪm] n: **in the ~** en el
ínterin ▷ adj provisional

interior [ɪnˈtɪərɪə*] n interior m ▷ adj interior; **interior design** n interiorismo, decoración f de interiores

intermediate [ɪntəˈmiːdɪət] adj intermedio

intermission [ɪntəˈmɪʃən] n intermisión f; (Theatre) descanso

intern [vb ɪnˈtəːn, n ˈɪntəːn] (US) vt internar ▷ n interno/a

internal [ɪnˈtəːnl] adj (layout, pipes, security) interior; (injury, structure, memo) internal; **Internal Revenue Service** (US) n departamento de impuestos, ≈ Hacienda (SP)

international [ɪntəˈnæʃənl] adj internacional ▷ n (BRIT: match) partido internacional

Internet [ˈɪntənɛt] n: **the ~** Internet m or f; **Internet café** n cibercafé m; **Internet Service Provider** n proveedor m de (acceso a) Internet; **Internet user** n internauta mf

interpret [ɪnˈtəːprɪt] vt interpretar; (translate) traducir; (understand) entender ▷ vi hacer de intérprete; **interpretation** [ɪntəːprɪˈteɪʃən] n interpretación f; traducción f; **interpreter** n intérprete mf

interrogate [ɪnˈtɛrəʊɡeɪt] vt interrogar; **interrogation** [-ˈɡeɪʃən] n interrogatorio

interrogative [ɪntəˈrɔɡətɪv] adj interrogativo

interrupt [ɪntəˈrʌpt] vt, vi interrumpir; **interruption** [-ˈrʌpʃən] n interrupción f

intersection [ɪntəˈsɛkʃən] n (of roads) cruce m

interstate [ˈɪntəsteɪt] (US) n carretera interestatal

interval [ˈɪntəvl] n intervalo; (BRIT Theatre, Sport) descanso; (Scol) recreo; **at ~s** a ratos, de vez en cuando

intervene [ɪntəˈviːn] vi intervenir; (event) interponerse; (time) transcurrir

interview [ˈɪntəvjuː] n entrevista ▷ vt entrevistarse con; **interviewer** n

entrevistador(a) m/f

intimate [adj ˈɪntɪmət, vb ˈɪntɪmeɪt] adj íntimo; (friendship) estrecho; (knowledge) profundo ▷ vt dar a entender

intimidate [ɪnˈtɪmɪdeɪt] vt intimidar, amedrentar

intimidating [ɪnˈtɪmɪdeɪtɪŋ] adj amedrentador, intimidante

into [ˈɪntuː] prep en; (towards) a; (inside) hacia el interior de; **~ 3 pieces/ French** en 3 pedazos/al francés

intolerant [ɪnˈtɔlərənt] adj: **~ (of)** intolerante (con or para)

intranet [ˈɪntrənɛt] n intranet f

intransitive [ɪnˈtrænsɪtɪv] adj intransitivo

intricate [ˈɪntrɪkət] adj (design, pattern) intrincado

intrigue [ɪnˈtriːɡ] n intriga ▷ vt fascinar; **intriguing** adj fascinante

introduce [ɪntrəˈdjuːs] vt introducir, meter; (speaker, TV show etc) presentar; **to ~ sb (to sb)** presentar a algn (a algn); **to ~ sb to** (pastime, technique) introducir a algn a; **introduction** [-ˈdʌkʃən] n introducción f; (of person) presentación f; **introductory** [-ˈdʌktərɪ] adj introductorio; (lesson, offer) de introducción

intrude [ɪnˈtruːd] vi (person) entrometerse; **to ~ on** estorbar; **intruder** n intruso/a

intuition [ɪntjuːˈɪʃən] n intuición f

inundate [ˈɪnʌndeɪt] vt: **to ~ with** inundar de

invade [ɪnˈveɪd] vt invadir

invalid [n ˈɪnvəlɪd, adj ɪnˈvælɪd] n (Med) minusválido/a ▷ adj (not valid) inválido, nulo

invaluable [ɪnˈvæljuəbl] adj inestimable

invariably [ɪnˈvɛərɪəblɪ] adv sin excepción, siempre; **she is ~ late** siempre llega tarde

invasion [ɪnˈveɪʒən] n invasión f

invent [ɪnˈvɛnt] vt inventar; **invention** [ɪnˈvɛnʃən] n invento;

(lie) ficción f, mentira; **inventor** n inventor(a) m/f

inventory ['ɪnvəntrɪ] n inventario

inverted commas [ɪn'və:tɪd-] (BRIT) npl comillas fpl

invest [ɪn'vɛst] vt invertir ▷ vi: **to ~ in** *(company etc)* invertir dinero en; *(fig: sth useful)* comprar

investigate [ɪn'vɛstɪgeɪt] vt investigar; **investigation** [-'geɪʃən] n investigación f, pesquisa

investigator [ɪn'vɛstɪgeɪtə*] n investigador(a) m/f; **private ~** investigador(a) m/f privado/a

investment [ɪn'vɛstmənt] n inversión f

investor [ɪn'vɛstə*] n inversionista mf

invisible [ɪn'vɪzɪbl] adj invisible

invitation [ɪnvɪ'teɪʃən] n invitación f

invite [ɪn'vaɪt] vt invitar; *(opinions etc)* solicitar, pedir; **inviting** adj atractivo; *(food)* apetitoso

invoice ['ɪnvɔɪs] n factura ▷ vt facturar

involve [ɪn'vɔlv] vt suponer, implicar; tener que ver con; *(concern, affect)* corresponder; **to ~ sb (in sth)** comprometer a algn (con algo); **involved** adj complicado; **to be involved in** *(take part)* tomar parte en; *(be engrossed)* estar muy metido en; **involvement** n participación f; dedicación f

inward ['ɪnwəd] adj *(movement)* interior, interno; *(thought, feeling)* íntimo; **inward(s)** adv hacia dentro

iPod ® ['aɪpɔd] n iPod ® m

IQ n abbr (= intelligence quotient) cociente m intelectual

IRA n abbr (= Irish Republican Army) IRA m

Iran [ɪ'rɑːn] n Irán m; **Iranian** [ɪ'reɪnɪən] adj, n iraní mf

Iraq [ɪ'rɑːk] n Iraq; **Iraqi** adj, n iraquí mf

Ireland ['aɪələnd] n Irlanda

iris ['aɪrɪs] (pl **~es**) n *(Anat)* iris m; *(Bot)* lirio

Irish ['aɪrɪʃ] adj irlandés/esa ▷ npl: **the ~** los irlandeses; **Irishman** *(irreg)* n irlandés m; **Irishwoman** *(irreg)* n irlandésa

iron ['aɪən] n hierro; *(for clothes)* plancha ▷ cpd de hierro ▷ vt *(clothes)* planchar

ironic(al) [aɪ'rɔnɪk(l)] adj irónico; **ironically** adv irónicamente

ironing ['aɪənɪŋ] n *(activity)* planchado; *(clothes: ironed)* ropa planchada; *(: to be ironed)* ropa por planchar; **ironing board** n tabla de planchar

irony ['aɪrənɪ] n ironía

irrational [ɪ'ræʃənl] adj irracional

irregular [ɪ'rɛgjulə*] adj irregular; *(surface)* desigual, *(action, event)* anómalo; *(behaviour)* poco ortodoxo

irrelevant [ɪ'rɛləvənt] adj fuera de lugar, inoportuno

irresistible [ɪrɪ'zɪstɪbl] adj irresistible

irresponsible [ɪrɪ'spɔnsɪbl] adj *(act)* irresponsable; *(person)* poco serio

irrigation [ɪrɪ'geɪʃən] n riego

irritable ['ɪrɪtəbl] adj *(person)* de mal humor

irritate ['ɪrɪteɪt] vt fastidiar; *(Med)* picar; **irritating** adj fastidioso; **irritation** [-'teɪʃən] n fastidio; enfado; picazón f

IRS (US) n abbr = **Internal Revenue Service**

is [ɪz] vb see **be**

ISDN n abbr (= Integrated Services Digital Network) RDSI f

Islam ['ɪzlɑːm] n Islam m; **Islamic** [ɪz'læmɪk] adj islámico

island ['aɪlənd] n isla; **islander** n isleño/a

isle [aɪl] n isla

isn't ['ɪznt] = **is not**

isolated ['aɪsəleɪtɪd] adj aislado

isolation [aɪsə'leɪʃən] n aislamiento

ISP n abbr = **Internet Service Provider**

Israel ['ɪzreɪl] n Israel m; **Israeli**

[ɪz'reɪlɪ] *adj, n* israelí *mf*

issue ['ɪsjuː] *n* (*problem, subject*) cuestión *f*; (*outcome*) resultado; (*of banknotes etc*) emisión *f*; (*of newspaper etc*) edición *f* ▷ *vt* (*rations, equipment*) distribuir, repartir; (*orders*) dar; (*certificate, passport*) expedir; (*decree*) promulgar; (*magazine*) publicar; (*cheques*) extender; (*banknotes, stamps*) emitir; **at ~** en cuestión; **to take ~ with sb (over)** estar en desacuerdo con algn (sobre); **to make an ~ of sth** hacer una cuestión de algo

IT *n abbr* = **information technology**

○ **KEYWORD**

it [ɪt] *pron* **1** (*specific subject: not generally translated*) él (ella); (*: direct object*) lo, la; (*: indirect object*) le; (*after prep*) él (ella); (*abstract concept*) ello; **it's on the table** está en la mesa; **I can't find it** no lo (*or* la) encuentro; **give it to me** dámelo (*or* dámela); **I spoke to him about it** le hablé del asunto; **what did you learn from it?** ¿qué aprendiste de él (*or* ella)?; **did you go to it?** (*party, concert etc*) ¿fuiste?

2 (*impersonal*): **it's raining** llueve, está lloviendo; **it's 6 o'clock/the 10th of August** son las 6/es el 10 de agosto; **how far is it? – it's 10 miles/2 hours on the train** ¿a qué distancia está? – a 10 millas/2 horas en tren; **who is it? – it's me** ¿quién es? – soy yo

Italian [ɪ'tæljən] *adj* italiano ▷ *n* italiano/a; (*Ling*) italiano

italics [ɪ'tælɪks] *npl* cursiva

Italy ['ɪtəlɪ] *n* Italia

itch [ɪtʃ] *n* picazón *f* ▷ *vi* (*part of body*) picar; **to ~ to do sth** rabiar por hacer algo; **itchy** *adj*: **my hand is itchy** me pica la mano

it'd ['ɪtd] = **it would; it had**

item ['aɪtəm] *n* artículo; (*on agenda*) asunto (a tratar); (*also*: **news ~**) noticia

itinerary [aɪ'tɪnərərɪ] *n* itinerario

it'll ['ɪtl] = **it will; it shall**

its [ɪts] *adj* su; sus *pl*

it's [ɪts] = **it is; it has**

itself [ɪt'sɛlf] *pron* (*reflexive*) sí mismo/a; (*emphatic*) él mismo(ella misma)

ITV *n abbr* (BRIT: = *Independent Television*) cadena de televisión comercial independiente del Estado

I've [aɪv] = **I have**

ivory ['aɪvərɪ] *n* marfil *m*

ivy ['aɪvɪ] *n* (*Bot*) hiedra

j

jab [dʒæb] *vt*: **to ~ sth into sth** clavar algo en algo ▷ *n* (*inf: Med*) pinchazo
jack [dʒæk] *n* (*Aut*) gato; (*Cards*) sota
jacket ['dʒækɪt] *n* chaqueta, americana (*SP*), saco (*LAM*); (*of book*) sobrecubierta; **jacket potato** *n* patata asada (con piel)
jackpot ['dʒækpɔt] *n* premio gordo
Jacuzzi® [dʒə'ku:zɪ] *n* jacuzzi® *m*
jagged ['dʒægɪd] *adj* dentado
jail [dʒeɪl] *n* cárcel *f* ▷ *vt* encarcelar; **jail sentence** *n* pena *f* de cárcel
jam [dʒæm] *n* mermelada; (*also*: **traffic ~**) embotellamiento; (*inf: difficulty*) apuro ▷ *vt* (*passage etc*) obstruir; (*mechanism, drawer etc*) atascar; (*Radio*) interferir ▷ *vi* atascarse, trabarse; **to ~ sth into sth** meter algo a la fuerza en algo
Jamaica [dʒə'meɪkə] *n* Jamaica
jammed [dʒæmd] *adj* atascado
Jan *abbr* (= *January*) ene
janitor ['dʒænɪtə*] *n* (*caretaker*) portero, conserje *m*
January ['dʒænjuərɪ] *n* enero

Japan [dʒə'pæn] *n* (el) Japón; **Japanese** [dʒæpə'ni:z] *adj* japonés/esa ▷ *n inv* japonés/esa *m/f*; (*Ling*) japonés *m*
jar [dʒɑ:*] *n* tarro, bote *m* ▷ *vi* (*sound*) chirriar; (*colours*) desentonar
jargon ['dʒɑ:gən] *n* jerga
javelin ['dʒævlɪn] *n* jabalina
jaw [dʒɔ:] *n* mandíbula
jazz [dʒæz] *n* jazz *m*
jealous ['dʒɛləs] *adj* celoso; (*envious*) envidioso; **jealousy** *n* celos *mpl*; envidia
jeans [dʒi:nz] *npl* vaqueros *mpl*, tejanos *mpl*
Jello® ['dʒɛləʊ] (*US*) *n* gelatina
jelly ['dʒɛlɪ] *n* (*jam*) jalea; (*dessert etc*) gelatina; **jellyfish** *n inv* medusa, aguaviva (*RPL*)
jeopardize ['dʒɛpədaɪz] *vt* arriesgar, poner en peligro
jerk [dʒə:k] *n* (*jolt*) sacudida; (*wrench*) tirón *m*; (*inf*) imbécil *mf* ▷ *vt* tirar bruscamente de ▷ *vi* (*vehicle*) traquetear
Jersey ['dʒə:zɪ] *n* Jersey *m*
jersey ['dʒə:zɪ] *n* jersey *m*; (*fabric*) (tejido de) punto
Jesus ['dʒi:zəs] *n* Jesús *m*
jet [dʒɛt] *n* (*of gas, liquid*) chorro; (*Aviat*) avión *m* a reacción; **jet lag** *n* desorientación *f* después de un largo vuelo; **jet-ski** *vi* practicar el motociclismo acuático
jetty ['dʒɛtɪ] *n* muelle *m*, embarcadero
Jew [dʒu:] *n* judío/a
jewel ['dʒu:əl] *n* joya; (*in watch*) rubí *m*; **jeweller** (*US* **jeweler**) *n* joyero/a; **jeweller's (shop)** (*US* **jewelry store**) *n* joyería; **jewellery** (*US* **jewelry**) *n* joyas *fpl*, alhajas *fpl*
Jewish ['dʒu:ɪʃ] *adj* judío
jigsaw ['dʒɪgsɔ:] *n* (*also*: **~ puzzle**) rompecabezas *m inv*, puzle *m*
job [dʒɔb] *n* (*task*) tarea; (*post*) empleo; **it's not my ~** no me incumbe a mí; **it's a good ~ that ...** menos mal que

...; **just the ~!** ¡estupendo!; **job centre**
(BRIT) n oficina estatal de colocaciones;
jobless adj sin trabajo
jockey ['dʒɔkɪ] n jockey mf ▷ vi: **to ~**
for position maniobrar para conseguir
una posición
jog [dʒɔg] vt empujar (ligeramente)
▷ vi (run) hacer footing; **to ~ sb's**
memory refrescar la memoria a algn;
jogging n footing m
join [dʒɔɪn] vt (things) juntar, unir;
(club) hacerse socio de; (Pol: party)
afiliarse a; (queue) ponerse en;
(meet: people) reunirse con ▷ vi (roads)
juntarse; (rivers) confluir ▷ n juntura;
join in vi tomar parte, participar ▷ vt
fus tomar parte or participar en; **join**
up vi reunirse; (Mil) alistarse
joiner ['dʒɔɪnə*] (BRIT) n carpintero/a
joint [dʒɔɪnt] n (Tech) junta, unión f;
(Anat) articulación f; (BRIT Culin) pieza
de carne (para asar); (inf: place) tugurio;
(: of cannabis) porro ▷ adj (common)
común; (combined) combinado; **joint**
account n (with bank etc) cuenta
común; **jointly** adv (gen) en común;
(together) conjuntamente
joke [dʒəuk] n chiste m; (also:
practical ~) broma ▷ vi bromear; **to**
play a ~ on gastar una broma a; **joker**
n (Cards) comodín m
jolly ['dʒɔlɪ] adj (merry) alegre;
(enjoyable) divertido ▷ adv (BRIT: inf)
muy, terriblemente
jolt [dʒəult] n (jerk) sacudida;
(shock) susto ▷ vt (physically) sacudir;
(emotionally) asustar
Jordan ['dʒɔːdən] n (country) Jordania;
(river) Jordán m
journal ['dʒəːnl] n (magazine) revista;
(diary) periódico, diario; **journalism** n
periodismo; **journalist** n periodista
mf, reportero/a
journey ['dʒəːnɪ] n viaje m; (distance
covered) trayecto
joy [dʒɔɪ] n alegría; **joyrider** n
gamberro que roba un coche para dar una
vuelta y luego abandonarlo; **joy stick** n

(Aviat) palanca de mando; (Comput)
palanca de control
Jr abbr = **junior**
judge [dʒʌdʒ] n juez mf; (fig: expert)
perito ▷ vt juzgar; (consider)
considerar
judo ['dʒuːdəu] n judo
jug [dʒʌg] n jarra
juggle ['dʒʌgl] vi hacer juegos
malabares; **juggler** n malabarista mf
juice [dʒuːs] n zumo (SP), jugo (LAM);
juicy adj jugoso
Jul abbr (= July) jul
July [dʒuːˈlaɪ] n julio
jumble ['dʒʌmbl] n revoltijo ▷ vt
(also: **~ up**) revolver; **jumble sale**
(BRIT) n venta de objetos usados con
fines benéficos

jumbo ['dʒʌmbəu] n (also: **~ jet**)
jumbo
jump [dʒʌmp] vi saltar, dar saltos;
(with fear etc) pegar un bote; (increase)
aumentar ▷ vt saltar ▷ n salto;
aumento; **to ~ the queue** (BRIT) colarse
jumper ['dʒʌmpə*] n (BRIT: pullover)
suéter m, jersey m; (US: dress) mandil m
jumper cables (US) npl = **jump leads**
jump leads (BRIT) npl cables mpl
puente de batería
Jun. abbr = **junior**
junction ['dʒʌŋkʃən] n (BRIT: of roads)
cruce m; (Rail) empalme m
June [dʒuːn] n junio
jungle ['dʒʌŋgl] n selva, jungla
junior ['dʒuːnɪə*] adj (in age) menor,
más joven; (brother/sister etc): **seven**

years her **~** siete años menor que ella; (*position*) subalterno ▷ *n* menor *mf*, joven *mf*; **junior high school** (*US*) *n* centro de educación secundaria; *see also* **high school**; **junior school** (*BRIT*) *n* escuela primaria

junk [dʒʌŋk] *n* (*cheap goods*) baratijas *fpl*; (*rubbish*) basura; **junk food** *n* alimentos preparados y envasados de escaso valor nutritivo

junkie ['dʒʌŋkɪ] (*inf*) *n* drogadicto/a, yonqui *mf*

junk mail *n* propaganda de buzón

Jupiter ['dʒuːpɪtə*] *n* (*Mythology, Astrology*) Júpiter *m*

jurisdiction [dʒuərɪs'dɪkʃən] *n* jurisdicción *f*; **it falls** *or* **comes within/ outside our ~** es/no es de nuestra competencia

jury ['dʒuərɪ] *n* jurado

just [dʒʌst] *adj* justo ▷ *adv* (*exactly*) exactamente; (*only*) sólo, solamente; **he's ~ done it/left** acaba de hacerlo/ irse; **~ right** perfecto; **~ two o'clock** las dos en punto; **she's ~ as clever as you** (*ella*) es tan lista como tú; **~ as well that ...** menos mal que ...; **~ as he was leaving** en el momento en que se marchaba; **~ before/enough** justo antes/lo suficiente; **~ here** aquí mismo; **he ~ missed** ha fallado por poco; **~ listen to this** escucha esto un momento

justice ['dʒʌstɪs] *n* justicia; (*US: judge*) juez *mf*; **to do ~ to** (*fig*) hacer justicia a

justification [dʒʌstɪfɪ'keɪʃən] *n* justificación *f*

justify ['dʒʌstɪfaɪ] *vt* justificar; (*text*) alinear

jut [dʒʌt] *vi* (*also*: **~ out**) sobresalir

juvenile ['dʒuːvənaɪl] *adj* (*court*) de menores; (*humour, mentality*) infantil ▷ *n* menor *m* de edad

K *abbr* (= *one thousand*) mil; (= *kilobyte*) kilobyte *m*, kiloocteto

kangaroo [kæŋgə'ruː] *n* canguro

karaoke [kɑːrə'əʊkɪ] *n* karaoke

karate [kə'rɑːtɪ] *n* karate *m*

kebab [kə'bæb] *n* pincho moruno

keel [kiːl] *n* quilla; **on an even ~** (*fig*) en equilibrio

keen [kiːn] *adj* (*interest, desire*) grande, vivo; (*eye, intelligence*) agudo; (*competition*) reñido; (*edge*) afilado; (*eager*) entusiasta; **to be ~ to do** *or* **on doing sth** tener muchas ganas de hacer algo; **to be ~ on sth/sb** interesarse por algo/algn

keep [kiːp] (*pt, pp* **kept**) *vt* (*preserve, store*) guardar; (*hold back*) quedarse con; (*maintain*) mantener; (*detain*) detener; (*shop*) ser propietario de; (*feed: family etc*) mantener; (*promise*) cumplir; (*chickens, bees etc*) criar; (*accounts*) llevar; (*diary*) escribir; (*prevent*): **to ~ sb from doing sth** impedir a algn hacer algo ▷ *vi* (*food*) conservarse; (*remain*) seguir, continuar ▷ *n* (*of* *castle*) torreón m; (*food etc*) comida, subsistencia; (*inf*): **for ~s** para siempre; **to ~ doing sth** seguir haciendo algo; **to ~ sb happy** tener a algn contento; **to ~ a place tidy** mantener un lugar limpio; **to ~ sth to o.s.** guardar algo para sí mismo; **to ~ sth (back) from sb** ocultar algo a algn; **to ~ time** (*clock*) mantener la hora exacta; **keep away** vt: **to keep sth/sb away from sb** mantener algo/a algn apartado de algn ▷ vi: **to keep away (from)** mantenerse apartado (de); **keep back** vt (*crowd, tears*) contener; (*money*) quedarse con; (*conceal: information*): **to keep sth back from sb** ocultar algo a algn ▷ vi hacerse a un lado; **keep off** vt (*dog, person*) mantener a distancia ▷ vi: **if the rain keeps off** so no lleuve; **keep your hands off!** ¡no toques!; **"keep off the grass"** "prohibido pisar el césped"; **keep on** vi: **to keep on doing** seguir or continuar haciendo; **to keep on (about sth)** no parar de hablar (de algo); **keep out** vi (*stay out*) permanecer fuera; **"keep out"** "prohibida la entrada"; **keep up** vt mantener, conservar ▷ vi no retrasarse; **to keep up with** (*pace*) ir al paso de; (*level*) mantenerse a la altura de; **keeper** n guardián/ana m/f; **keeping** n (*care*) cuidado; **in keeping with** de acuerdo con

kennel ['kɛnl] n perrera; **kennels** npl residencia canina

Kenya ['kɛnjə] n Kenia

kept [kɛpt] pt, pp of **keep**

kerb [kə:b] (BRIT) n bordillo

kerosene ['kɛrəsi:n] n keroseno

ketchup ['kɛtʃəp] n salsa de tomate, catsup m

kettle ['kɛtl] n hervidor m de agua

key [ki:] n llave f; (*Mus*) tono; (*of piano, typewriter*) tecla ▷ adj (*issue etc*) clave inv ▷ vt (*also:* **~ in**) teclear; **keyboard** n teclado; **keyhole** n ojo (de la cerradura); **keyring** n llavero

kg abbr (= kilogram) kg

khaki ['kɑ:kɪ] n caqui

kick [kɪk] vt dar una patada or un puntapié a; (*inf: habit*) quitarse de ▷ vi (*horse*) dar coces ▷ n patada; puntapié m; (*of animal*) coz f; (*thrill*): **he does it for ~s** lo hace por pura diversión; **kick off** vi (*Sport*) hacer el saque inicial; **kick-off** n saque inicial; **the kick-off is at 10 o'clock** el partido empieza a las diez

kid [kɪd] n (*inf: child*) chiquillo/a; (*animal*) cabrito; (*leather*) cabritilla ▷ vi (*inf*) bromear

kidnap ['kɪdnæp] vt secuestrar; **kidnapping** n secuestro

kidney ['kɪdnɪ] n riñón m; **kidney bean** n judía, alubia

kill [kɪl] vt matar; (*murder*) asesinar ▷ n matanza; **to ~ time** matar el tiempo; **killer** n asesino/a; **killing** n (*one*) asesinato; (*several*) matanza; **to make a killing** (*fig*) hacer su agosto

kiln [kɪln] n horno

kilo ['ki:ləu] n kilo; **kilobyte** n (*Comput*) kilobyte m, kiloocteto; **kilogram(me)** n kilo, kilogramo; **kilometre** ['kɪləmi:tə*] (US **kilometer**) n kilómetro; **kilowatt** n kilovatio

kilt [kɪlt] n falda escocesa

kin [kɪn] n see **next-of-kin**

kind [kaɪnd] adj amable, atento ▷ n clase f, especie f; (*species*) género; **in ~** (*Comm*) en especie; **a ~ of** una especie de; **to be two of a ~** ser tal para cual

kindergarten ['kɪndəgɑ:tn] n jardín m de la infancia

kindly ['kaɪndlɪ] adj bondadoso; cariñoso ▷ adv bondadosamente, amablemente; **will you ~ ...** sea usted tan amable de ...

kindness ['kaɪndnɪs] n (*quality*) bondad f, amabilidad f; (*act*) favor m

king [kɪŋ] n rey m; **kingdom** n reino; **kingfisher** n martín m pescador; **king-size(d) bed** n cama de matrimonio extragrande

kiosk ['ki:ɔsk] n quiosco; (BRIT Tel) cabina

kipper ['kɪpə*] n arenque m ahumado

kiss [kɪs] n beso ▷ vt besar; **to ~ (each other)** besarse; **kiss of life** n respiración f boca a boca

kit [kɪt] n (equipment) equipo; (tools etc) (caja de) herramientas fpl; (assembly kit) juego de armar

kitchen ['kɪtʃɪn] n cocina

kite [kaɪt] n (toy) cometa

kitten ['kɪtn] n gatito/a

kiwi ['kiːwiː-] n (also: **~ fruit**) kiwi m

km abbr (= kilometre) km

km/h abbr (= kilometres per hour) km/h

knack [næk] n: **to have the ~ of doing sth** tener el don de hacer algo

knee [niː] n rodilla; **kneecap** n rótula

kneel [niːl] (pt, pp **knelt**) vi (also: **~ down**) arrodillarse

knelt [nɛlt] pt, pp of **kneel**

knew [njuː] pt of **know**

knickers ['nɪkəz] (BRIT) npl bragas fpl

knife [naɪf] (pl **knives**) n cuchillo ▷ vt acuchillar

knight [naɪt] n caballero; (Chess) caballo

knit [nɪt] vt tejer, tricotar ▷ vi hacer punto, tricotar; (bones) soldarse; **to ~ one's brows** fruncir el ceño; **knitting** n labor f de punto; **knitting needle** n aguja de hacer punto; **knitwear** n prendas fpl de punto

knives [naɪvz] npl of **knife**

knob [nɔb] n (of door) tirador m; (of stick) puño, (on radio, TV) botón m

knock [nɔk] vt (strike) golpear; (bump into) chocar contra; (inf) criticar ▷ vi (at door etc): **to ~ at/on** llamar a ▷ n golpe m; (on door) llamada; **knock down** vt atropellar; **knock off** (inf) vi (finish) salir del trabajo ▷ vt (from price) descontar; (inf: steal) birlar; **knock out** vt dejar sin sentido; (Boxing) poner fuera de combate, dejar K.O.; (in competition) eliminar; **knock over** vt (object) tirar; (person) atropellar; **knockout** n (Boxing) K.O. m, knockout m ▷ cpd (competition etc) eliminatorio

knot [nɔt] n nudo ▷ vt anudar

know [nəu] (pt **knew**, pp **known**) vt (facts) saber; (be acquainted with) conocer; (recognize) reconocer, conocer; **to ~ how to swim** saber nadar; **to ~ about** or **of sb/sth** saber de algn/algo; **know-all** n sabelotodo mf; **know-how** n conocimientos mpl; **knowing** adj (look) de complicidad; **knowingly** adv (purposely) adrede; (smile, look) con complicidad; **know-it-all** (US) n = **know-all**

knowledge ['nɔlɪdʒ] n conocimiento; (learning) saber m, conocimientos mpl; **knowledgeable** adj entendido

known [nəun] pp of **know** ▷ adj (thief, facts) conocido; (expert) reconocido

knuckle ['nʌkl] n nudillo

koala [kəu'uːlə] n (also: **~ bear**) koala m

Koran [kɔ'raːn] n Corán m

Korea [kə'rɪə] n Corea; **Korean** adj, n coreano/a m/f

kosher ['kəuʃə*] adj autorizado por la ley judía

Kosovar ['kɔsəvɑ*], **Kosovan** ['kɔːsəvən] adj kosovar

Kosovo ['kɔsəvəu] n Kosovo

Kremlin ['kremlɪn] n: **the ~** el Kremlin

Kuwait [ku'weɪt] n Kuwait m

k

L

L (BRIT) abbr = **learner driver**

l. abbr (= litre) l

lab [læb] n abbr = **laboratory**

label ['leɪbl] n etiqueta ▷ vt poner etiqueta a

labor etc ['leɪbə*] (US) = **labour** etc

laboratory [lə'bɔrətərɪ] n laboratorio

Labor Day (US) n día m de los trabajadores (primer lunes de septiembre)

labor union (US) n sindicato

labour ['leɪbə*] (US **labor**) n (hard work) trabajo; (labour force) mano f de obra; (Med): **to be in ~** estar de parto ▷ vi: **to ~ (at sth)** trabajar (en algo) ▷ vt: **to ~ a point** insistir en un punto; **L~, the L~ party** (BRIT) el partido laborista, los laboristas mpl; **labourer** n peón m; **farm labourer** peón m; (day labourer) jornalero

lace [leɪs] n encaje m; (of shoe etc) cordón m ▷ vt (shoes: also: **~ up**) atarse (los zapatos)

lack [læk] n (absence) falta ▷ vt faltarle a algn, carecer de; **through** or **for ~ of** por falta de; **to be ~ing** faltar, no haber; **to be ~ing in sth** faltarle a algn algo

lacquer ['lækə*] n laca

lacy ['leɪsɪ] adj (of lace) de encaje; (like lace) como de encaje

lad [læd] n muchacho, chico

ladder ['lædə*] n escalera (de mano); (BRIT: in tights) carrera

ladle ['leɪdl] n cucharón m

lady ['leɪdɪ] n señora; (dignified, graceful) dama; **"ladies and gentlemen ..."** "señoras y caballeros ..."; **young ~** señorita; **the ladies' (room)** los servicios de señoras; **ladybird** (US **ladybug**) n mariquita

lag [læg] n retraso ▷ vi (also: **~ behind**) retrasarse, quedarse atrás ▷ vt (pipes) revestir

lager ['lɑːgə*] n cerveza (rubia)

lagoon [lə'guːn] n laguna

laid [leɪd] pt, pp of **lay**; **laid back** (inf) adj relajado

lain [leɪn] pp of **lie**

lake [leɪk] n lago

lamb [læm] n cordero; (meat) (carne f de) cordero

lame [leɪm] adj cojo; (excuse) poco convincente

lament [lə'mɛnt] n quejo ▷ vt lamentarse de

lamp [læmp] n lámpara; **lamppost** (BRIT) n (poste m de) farol m; **lampshade** n pantalla

land [lænd] n tierra; (country) país m; (piece of land) terreno; (estate) tierras fpl, finca ▷ vi (from ship) desembarcar; (Aviat) aterrizar; (fig: fall) caer, terminar ▷ vt (passengers, goods) desembarcar; **to ~ sb with sth** (inf) hacer cargar a algn con algo; **landing** n aterrizaje m; (of staircase) rellano; **landing card** n tarjeta de desembarque; **landlady** n (of rented house, pub etc) dueña; **landlord** n propietario; (of pub etc) patrón m; **landmark** n lugar m conocido; **to be a landmark** (fig) marcar un hito histórico; **landowner** n terrateniente *mf*; **landscape** *n* paisaje *m*; **landslide** *n* (Geo) corrimiento de tierras; (fig: Pol) victoria arrolladora

lane [leɪn] *n* (in country) camino; (Aut) carril *m*; (in race) calle *f*

language ['læŋgwɪdʒ] *n* lenguaje *m*; (national tongue) idioma *m*, lengua; **bad ~** palabrotas *fpl*; **language laboratory** *n* laboratorio de idiomas; **language school** *n* academia de idiomas

lantern ['læntn] *n* linterna, farol *m*

lap [læp] *n* (of track) vuelta; (of body) regazo ▷ vi (also: **~ up**) beber a lengüetadas ▷ vi (waves) chapotear; **to sit on sb's ~** sentarse en las rodillas de algn

lapel [lə'pɛl] *n* solapa

lapse [læps] *n* fallo; (moral) desliz *m*; (of time) intervalo ▷ vi (expire) caducar; (time) pasar, transcurrir; **to ~ into bad habits** caer en malos hábitos

laptop (computer) ['læptɔp-] *n* (ordenador *m*) portátil *m*

lard [lɑːd] *n* manteca (de cerdo)

larder ['lɑːdə*] *n* despensa

large [lɑːdʒ] *adj* grande; **at ~** (free) en libertad; (generally) en general

　Be careful not to translate **large** by the Spanish word *largo*.

largely *adv* (mostly) en su mayor parte; (introducing reason) en gran parte; **large-scale** *adj* (map) en gran escala; (fig) importante

lark [lɑːk] *n* (bird) alondra; (joke) broma

laryngitis [lærɪn'dʒaɪtɪs] *n* laringitis *f*

lasagne [lə'zænjə] *n* lasaña

laser ['leɪzə*] *n* láser *m*; **laser printer** *n* impresora (por) láser

lash [læʃ] *n* latigazo; (also: **eye~**) pestaña ▷ vt azotar; (tie): **to ~ to/ together** atar a/atar; **lash out** *vi*: **to lash out (at sb)** (hit) arremeter (contra algn); **to lash out against sb** lanzar invectivas contra algn

lass [læs] (BRIT) *n* chica

last [lɑːst] *adj* último; (end: of series etc) final ▷ adv (most recently) la última vez; (finally) por último ▷ vi durar; (continue) continuar, seguir; **~ night** anoche; **~ week** la semana pasada; **at ~** por fin; **~ but one** penúltimo; **lastly** adv por último, finalmente; **last-minute** *adj* de última hora

latch [lætʃ] *n* pestillo; **latch onto** *vt fus* (person, group) pegarse a; (idea) agarrarse a

late [leɪt] *adj* (far on: in time, process etc) al final de; (not on time) tarde, atrasado; (dead) fallecido ▷ adv tarde; (behind time, schedule) con retraso; **of ~** últimamente; **~ at night** a última hora de la noche; **in ~ May** hacia fines de mayo; **the ~ Mr X** el difunto Sr X; **latecomer** *n* recién llegado/a; **lately** adv últimamente; **later** *adj* (date etc) posterior; (version etc) más reciente ▷ adv más tarde, después; **latest** ['leɪtɪst] *adj* último; **at the latest** a más tardar

lather ['lɑːðə*] *n* espuma (de jabón) ▷ vt enjabonar

Latin ['lætɪn] *n* latín *m* ▷ adj latino; **Latin America** *n* América Latina; **Latin American** *adj, n* latinoamericano/a *m/f*

latitude ['lætɪtjuːd] *n* latitud *f*; (fig) libertad *f*

latter ['lætə*] *adj* último; (of two) segundo ▷ *n*: **the ~** el último, éste

laugh [lɑːf] *n* risa ▷ vi reír(se); **(to do sth) for a ~** (hacer algo) en broma; **laugh at** *vt fus* reírse de; **laughter** *n* risa

launch [lɔːntʃ] *n* lanzamiento; (boat) lancha ▷ vt (ship) botar; (rocket etc) lanzar; (fig) comenzar; **launch into** *vt fus* lanzarse a

launder ['lɔːndə*] *vt* lavar

Launderette® [lɔːn'drɛt] (BRIT) *n* lavandería (automática)

Laundromat® ['lɔːndrəmæt] (US) *n* = **Launderette**

laundry ['lɔːndrɪ] *n* (dirty) ropa sucia; (clean) colada; (room) lavadero

lava ['lɑːvə] n lava

lavatory ['lævətərɪ] n wáter m

lavender ['lævəndə*] n lavanda

lavish ['lævɪʃ] adj (amount) abundante; (person): ~ **with** pródigo en ▷ vt: **to ~ sth on sb** colmar a algn de algo

law [lɔː] n ley f; (Scol) derecho; (a rule) regla; (professions connected with law) jurisprudencia; **lawful** adj legítimo, lícito; **lawless** adj (action) criminal

lawn [lɔːn] n césped m; **lawnmower** n cortacésped m

lawsuit ['lɔːsuːt] n pleito

lawyer ['lɔːjə*] n abogado/a; (for sales, wills etc) notario/a

lax [læks] adj laxo

laxative ['læksətɪv] n laxante m

lay [leɪ] (pt, pp **laid**) pt of **lie** ▷ adj laico; (not expert) lego ▷ vt (place) colocar; (eggs, table) poner; (cable) tender; (carpet) extender; **lay down** vt (pen etc) dejar; (rules etc) establecer; **to lay down the law** (pej) imponer las normas; **lay off** vt (workers) despedir; **lay on** vt (meal, facilities) proveer; **lay out** vt (spread out) disponer, exponer; **lay-by** n (BRIT Aut) área de aparcamiento

layer ['leɪə*] n capa

layman ['leɪmən] (irreg) n lego

layout ['leɪaut] n (design) plan m, trazado m; (Press) composición f

lazy ['leɪzɪ] adj perezoso, vago; (movement) lento

lb. abbr = **pound** (weight)

lead¹ [liːd] (pt, pp **led**) n (front position) delantera; (clue) pista; (Elec) cable m; (for dog) correa; (Theatre) papel m principal ▷ vt (walk etc in front) ir a la cabeza de; (guide): **to ~ sb somewhere** conducir a algn a algún sitio; (be leader) dirigir; (start, guide: activity) protagonizar ▷ vi (road, pipe etc) conducir a; (Sport) ir primero; **to be in the ~** (Sport) llevar la delantera; (fig) ir a la cabeza; **to ~ the way** llevar la delantera; **lead up to** vt fus (events)

conducir a; (in conversation) preparar el terreno para

lead² [lɛd] n (metal) plomo; (in pencil) mina

leader ['liːdə*] n jefe/a m/f, líder m/f; (Sport) líder m/f; **leadership** n dirección f; (position) mando; (quality) iniciativa

lead-free ['lɛdfriː] adj sin plomo

leading ['liːdɪŋ] adj (main) principal; (first) primero; (front) delantero

lead singer [liːd-] n cantante m/f

leaf [liːf] (pl **leaves**) n hoja ▷ vi: **to ~ through** hojear; **to turn over a new ~** reformarse

leaflet ['liːflɪt] n folleto

league [liːg] n sociedad f; (Football) liga; **to be in ~ with** haberse confabulado con

leak [liːk] n (of liquid, gas) escape m, fuga; (in pipe) agujero; (in roof) gotera; (in security) filtración f ▷ vi (shoes, ship) hacer agua; (pipe) tener (un) escape; (roof) gotear; (liquid, gas) escaparse, fugarse; (fig) divulgarse ▷ vt (fig) filtrar

lean [liːn] (pt, pp **~ed** or **~t**) adj (thin) flaco; (meat) magro ▷ vt: **to ~ sth on sth** apoyar algo en algo ▷ vi (slope) inclinarse; **to ~ against** apoyarse contra; **to ~ on** apoyarse en; **lean forward** vi inclinarse hacia adelante; **lean over** vi inclinarse; **leaning** n: **leaning (towards)** inclinación f (hacia)

leant [lɛnt] pt, pp of **lean**

leap [liːp] (pt, pp **~ed** or **~t**) n salto ▷ vi saltar

leapt [lɛpt] pt, pp of **leap**

leap year n año bisiesto

learn [lɜːn] (pt, pp **~ed** or **~t**) vt aprender ▷ vi aprender; **to ~ about sth** enterarse de algo; **to ~ to do sth** aprender a hacer algo; **learner** n (BRIT: also: **learner driver**) principiante m/f; **learning** n el saber m, conocimientos mpl

learnt [lɜːnt] pp of **learn**

lease [liːs] n arriendo ▷ vt arrendar

leash [liːʃ] n correa

least [liːst] *adj*: **the ~** (*slightest*) el menor, el más pequeño; (*smallest amount of*) mínimo ▷ *adv* (*+ vb*) menos; (*+ adj*): **the ~ expensive** el (la) menos costoso/a; **the ~ possible effort** el menor esfuerzo posible; **at ~** por lo menos, al menos; **you could at ~ have written** por lo menos podías haber escrito; **not in the ~** en absoluto

leather ['lɛðə*] *n* cuero

leave [liːv] (*pt, pp* **left**) *vt* dejar; (*go away from*) abandonar; (*place etc: permanently*) salir de ▷ *vi* irse; (*train etc*) salir ▷ *n* permiso; **to ~ sth to sb** (*money etc*) legar algo a algn; (*responsibility etc*) encargar a algn de algo; **to be left** quedar, sobrar; **there's some milk left over** sobra *or* queda algo de leche; **on ~** de permiso; **leave behind** *vt* (*on purpose*) dejar; (*accidentally*) dejarse; **leave out** *vt* omitir

leaves [liːvz] *npl of* **leaf**

Lebanon ['lɛbənən] *n*: **the ~** el Líbano

lecture ['lɛktʃə*] *n* conferencia; (*Scol*) clase *f* ▷ *vi* dar una clase ▷ *vt* (*scold*): **to ~ sb on** *or* **about sth** echar una reprimenda a algn por algo; **to give a ~ on** dar una conferencia sobre; **lecture hall** *n* sala de conferencias; (*Univ*) aula; **lecturer** *n* conferenciante *mf*; (*BRIT: at university*) profesor(a) *m/f*; **lecture theatre** *n* = **lecture hall**

led [lɛd] *pt, pp of* **lead**¹

ledge [lɛdʒ] *n* repisa; (*of window*) alféizar *m*; (*of mountain*) saliente *m*

leek [liːk] *n* puerro

left [lɛft] *pt, pp of* **leave** ▷ *adj* izquierdo; (*remaining*): **there are two ~** quedan dos ▷ *n* izquierda ▷ *adv* a la izquierda; **on** *or* **to the ~** a la izquierda; **the L~** (*Pol*) la izquierda; **left-hand** *adj*: **the left-hand side** la izquierda; **left-hand drive** *adj*: **a left-hand drive car** un coche con el volante a la izquierda; **left-handed** *adj* zurdo; **left-luggage locker** *n* (*BRIT*) consigna *f* automática; **left-luggage**

(office) (*BRIT*) *n* consigna; **left-overs** *npl* sobras *fpl*; **left-wing** *adj* (*Pol*) de izquierdas, izquierdista

leg [lɛg] *n* pierna; (*of animal, chair*) pata; (*trouser leg*) pernera; (*Culin: of lamb*) pierna; (: *of chicken*) pata; (*of journey*) etapa

legacy ['lɛgəsɪ] *n* herencia

legal ['liːgl] *adj* (*permitted by law*) lícito; (*of law*) legal; **legal holiday** (*US*) *n* fiesta oficial; **legalize** *vt* legalizar; **legally** *adv* legalmente

legend ['lɛdʒənd] *n* (*also fig: person*) leyenda; **legendary** [-ərɪ] *adj* legendario

leggings ['lɛgɪŋz] *npl* mallas *fpl*, leggins *mpl*

legible ['lɛdʒəbl] *adj* legible

legislation [lɛdʒɪsˈleɪʃən] *n* legislación *f*

legislative ['lɛdʒɪslətɪv] *adj* legislativo

legitimate [lɪˈdʒɪtɪmət] *adj* legítimo

leisure ['lɛʒə*] *n* ocio, tiempo libre; **at ~** con tranquilidad; **leisure centre** (*BRIT*) *n* centro de recreo; **leisurely** *adj* sin prisa; lento

lemon ['lɛmən] *n* limón *m*; **lemonade** *n* (*fizzy*) gaseosa; **lemon tea** *n* té *m* con limón

lend [lɛnd] (*pt, pp* **lent**) *vt*: **to ~ sth to sb** prestar algo a algn

length [lɛŋθ] *n* (*size*) largo, longitud *f*; (*distance*): **the ~ of** todo lo largo de; (*of swimming pool, cloth*) largo; (*of wood, string*) trozo; (*amount of time*) duración *f*; **at ~** (*at last*) por fin, finalmente; (*lengthily*) largamente; **lengthen** *vt* alargar ▷ *vi* alargarse; **lengthways** *adv* a lo largo; **lengthy** *adj* largo, extenso

lens [lɛnz] *n* (*of spectacles*) lente *f*; (*of camera*) objetivo

Lent [lɛnt] *n* Cuaresma

lent [lɛnt] *pt, pp of* **lend**

lentil ['lɛntl] *n* lenteja

Leo ['liːəʊ] *n* Leo

leopard ['lɛpəd] *n* leopardo

leotard ['li:ǝtɑ:d] *n* mallas *fpl*
leprosy ['lɛprǝsɪ] *n* lepra
lesbian ['lɛzbɪǝn] *n* lesbiana
less [lɛs] *adj* (*in size, degree etc*)
menor; (*in quality*) menos ▷ *pron, adv*
menos ▷ *prep*: **~ tax/10% discount**
menos impuestos/el 10 por ciento
de descuento; **~ than half** menos
de la mitad; **~ than ever** menos que
nunca; **~ and ~** cada vez menos; **the
~ he works ...** cuanto menos trabaja
...; **lessen** *vi* disminuir, reducirse ▷ *vt*
disminuir, reducir; **lesser** ['lɛsǝ*] *adj*
menor; **to a lesser extent** en menor
grado
lesson ['lɛsn] *n* clase *f*; (*warning*)
lección *f*
let [lɛt] (*pt, pp* **~**) *vt* (*allow*) dejar,
permitir; (*BRIT: lease*) alquilar; **to ~ sb
do sth** dejar que algn haga algo; **to ~
sb know sth** comunicar algo a algn;
~'s go ¡vamos!; **~ him come** que venga;
"to ~" "se alquila"; **let down** *vt* (*tyre*)
desinflar; (*disappoint*) defraudar; **let in**
vt dejar entrar; (*visitor etc*) hacer pasar;
let off *vt* (*culprit*) dejar escapar; (*gun*)
disparar; (*bomb*) accionar; (*firework*)
hacer estallar; **let out** *vt* dejar salir;
(*sound*) soltar
lethal ['li:θl] *adj* (*weapon*) mortífero;
(*poison, wound*) mortal
letter ['lɛtǝ*] *n* (*of alphabet*) letra;
(*correspondence*) carta; **letterbox** (*BRIT*)
n buzón *m*
lettuce ['lɛtɪs] *n* lechuga
leukaemia [lu:'ki:mɪǝ] (*US* **leukemia**)
n leucemia
level ['lɛvl] *adj* (*flat*) llano ▷ *adv*: **to
draw ~ with** llegar a la altura de ▷ *n*
nivel *m*; (*height*) altura ▷ *vt* nivelar;
allanar; (*destroy: building*) derribar;
(: *forest*) arrasar; **to be ~ with** estar
a nivel de; **A ~s** (*BRIT*) ≈ exámenes
mpl de bachillerato superior, B.U.P.;
AS ~ (*BRIT*) asignatura aprobada entre
los "GCSEs" y los "A levels"; **on the ~**
(*fig: honest*) serio; **level crossing** (*BRIT*)
n paso a nivel

lever ['li:vǝ*] *n* (*also fig*) palanca
▷ *vt*: **to ~ up** levantar con palanca;
leverage *n* (*using bar etc*)
apalancamiento; (*fig: influence*)
influencia
levy ['lɛvɪ] *n* impuesto ▷ *vt* exigir,
recaudar
liability [laɪǝ'bɪlǝtɪ] *n* (*pej: person,
thing*) estorbo, lastre *m*; (*Jur:
responsibility*) responsabilidad *f*
liable ['laɪǝbl] *adj* (*subject*): **~ to** sujeto
a; (*responsible*): **~ for** responsable de;
(*likely*): **~ to do** propenso a hacer
liaise [lɪ'eɪz] *vi*: **to ~ with** enlazar con
liar ['laɪǝ*] *n* mentiroso/a
liberal ['lɪbǝrǝl] *adj* liberal; (*offer,
amount etc*) generoso; **Liberal
Democrat** *n* (*BRIT*) demócrata *m/f*
liberal
liberate ['lɪbǝreɪt] *vt* (*people: from
poverty etc*) librar; (*prisoner*) libertar;
(*country*) liberar
liberation [lɪbǝ'reɪʃǝn] *n* liberación *f*
liberty ['lɪbǝtɪ] *n* libertad *f*; **to be at
~** (*criminal*) estar en libertad; **to be at
~ to do** estar libre para hacer; **to take
the ~ of doing sth** tomarse la libertad
de hacer algo
Libra ['li:brǝ] *n* Libra
librarian [laɪ'brɛǝrɪǝn] *n*
bibliotecario/a
library ['laɪbrǝrɪ] *n* biblioteca
▌ Be careful not to translate **library**
by the Spanish word *librería*.
Libya ['lɪbɪǝ] *n* Libia
lice [laɪs] *npl of* **louse**
licence ['laɪsǝns] (*US* **license**) *n*
licencia; (*permit*) permiso; (*also*: **driving
~**) carnet *m* de conducir (*SP*), licencia de
manejo (*LAM*)
license ['laɪsǝns] *n* (*US*) = **licence** ▷ *vt*
autorizar, dar permiso a; **licensed** *adj*
(*for alcohol*) autorizado para vender
bebidas alcohólicas; (*car*) matriculado;
license plate (*US*) *n* placa (de
matrícula); **licensing hours** (*BRIT*) *npl*
*horas durante las cuales se permite la venta
y consumo de alcohol* (*en un bar etc*)

lick [lɪk] vt lamer; (inf: defeat) dar una paliza a; **to ~ one's lips** relamerse

lid [lɪd] n (of box, case) tapa; (of pan) tapadera

lie [laɪ] (pt **lay**, pp **lain**) vi (rest) estar echado, estar acostado; (of object: be situated) estar, encontrarse; (tell lies: pt, pp **lied**) mentir ▷ n mentira; **to ~ low** (fig) mantenerse a escondidas; **lie about** or **around** vi (things) estar tirado; (BRIT: people) estar tumbado; **lie down** vi echarse, tumbarse

Liechtenstein ['lɪktənstaɪn] n Liechtenstein m

lie-in ['laɪɪn] (BRIT) n: **to have a ~** quedarse en la cama

lieutenant [leftenənt, US luː'tɛnənt] n (Mil) teniente mf

life [laɪf] (pl **lives**) n vida; **to come to ~** animarse; **life assurance** (BRIT) n seguro de vida; **lifeboat** n lancha de socorro; **lifeguard** n vigilante mf, socorrista mf; **life insurance** n ~ **life assurance**; **life jacket** n chaleco salvavidas; **lifelike** adj (model etc) que parece vivo; (realistic) realista; **life preserver** (US) n cinturón m/chaleco salvavidas; **life sentence** n cadena perpetua; **lifestyle** n estilo de vida; **lifetime** n (of person) vida; (of thing) período de vida

lift [lɪft] vt levantar; (end: ban, rule) levantar, suprimir ▷ vi (fog) disiparse ▷ n (BRIT: machine) ascensor m; **to give sb a ~** (BRIT) llevar a algn en el coche; **lift up** vt levantar; **lift-off** n despegue m

light [laɪt] (pt, pp **~ed** or **lit**) n luz f; (lamp) luz f, lámpara; (Aut) faro; (for cigarette etc): **have you got a ~?** ¿tienes fuego? ▷ vt (candle, cigarette, fire) encender (SP), prender (LAM); (room) alumbrar ▷ adj (colour) claro; (not heavy, also fig) ligero; (room) con mucha luz; (gentle, graceful) ágil; **lights** npl (traffic lights) semáforos mpl; **to come to ~** salir a luz; **in the ~ of** (new evidence etc) a la luz de; **light up** vi (smoke) encender un cigarrillo; (face) iluminarse ▷ vt (illuminate) iluminar, alumbrar; (set fire to) encender; **light bulb** n bombilla (SP), foco (MEX), bujía (CAM), bombita (RPL) etc) **lighten** vt (make less heavy) aligerar; **lighter** n (also: **cigarette lighter**) encendedor m, mechero; **light-hearted** adj (person) alegre; (remark etc) divertido; **lighthouse** n faro; **lighting** n (system) alumbrado; **lightly** adv ligeramente; (not seriously) con poca seriedad; **to get off lightly** ser castigado con poca severidad

lightning ['laɪtnɪŋ] n relámpago, rayo

lightweight ['laɪtweɪt] adj (suit) ligero ▷ n (Boxing) peso ligero

like [laɪk] vt gustarle a algn ▷ prep como ▷ adj parecido, semejante ▷ n: **and the ~** y otros por el estilo; **his ~s and dislikes** sus gustos y aversiones; **I would ~, I'd ~** me gustaría; (for purchase) quisiera; **would you ~ a coffee?** ¿te apetece un café? **I ~ swimming** me gusta nadar; **she ~s apples** le gustan las manzanas; **to be or look ~ sb/sth** parecerse a algn/algo; **what does it taste/sound ~?** ¿cómo es/a qué sabe/cómo suena ~? **that's just ~ him** es muy de él, es característico de él; **do it ~ this** hazlo así; **it is nothing ~ ...** no tiene parecido alguno con ...; **likeable** adj simpático, agradable

likelihood ['laɪklɪhud] n probabilidad f

likely ['laɪklɪ] adj probable; **he's ~ to leave** es probable que se vaya; **not ~!** ¡ni hablar!

likewise ['laɪkwaɪz] adv igualmente; **to do ~** hacer lo mismo

liking ['laɪkɪŋ] n: **~ (for)** (person) cariño (a); (thing) afición (a); **to be to sb's ~** ser del gusto de algn

lilac ['laɪlək] n (tree) lilo; (flower) lila

Lilo® ['laɪləu] n colchoneta inflable

lily ['lɪlɪ] n lirio, azucena; **~ of the**

valley lirio de los valles

limb [lɪm] n miembro

limbo ['lɪmbəu] n: **to be in ~** (fig) quedar a la expectativa

lime [laɪm] n (tree) limero; (fruit) lima; (Geo) cal f

limelight ['laɪmlaɪt] n: **to be in the ~** (fig) ser el centro de atención

limestone ['laɪmstəun] n piedra caliza

limit ['lɪmɪt] n límite m ▷ vt limitar; **limited** adj limitado; **to be limited to** limitarse a

limousine ['lɪməziːn] n limusina

limp [lɪmp] n: **to have a ~** tener cojera ▷ vi cojear ▷ adj flojo; (material) fláccido

line [laɪn] n línea; (rope) cuerda; (for fishing) sedal m; (wire) hilo; (row, series) fila, hilera; (of writing) renglón m, línea; (of song) verso; (on face) arruga; (Rail) vía ▷ vt (road etc) llenar; (Sewing) forrar; **to ~ the streets** llenar las aceras; **in ~ with** alineado con; (according to) de acuerdo con; **line up** vi hacer cola ▷ vt alinear; (prepare) preparar; organizar

linear ['lɪnɪə*] adj lineal

linen ['lɪnɪn] n ropa blanca; (cloth) lino

liner ['laɪnə*] n vapor m de línea, transatlántico; (for bin) bolsa (de basura)

line-up ['laɪnʌp] n (US: queue) cola; (Sport) alineación f

linger ['lɪŋgə*] vi retrasarse, tardar en marcharse; (smell, tradition) persistir

lingerie ['lænʒəriː] n lencería

linguist ['lɪŋgwɪst] n lingüista mf; **linguistic** adj lingüístico

lining ['laɪnɪŋ] n forro; (Anat) (membrana) mucosa

link [lɪŋk] n (of a chain) eslabón m; (relationship) relación f, vínculo; (Internet) link m, enlace m ▷ vt vincular, unir; (associate): **to ~ with** or **to** relacionar con; **links** npl (Golf) campo de golf; **link up** vt acoplar ▷ vi unirse

lion ['laɪən] n león m; **lioness** n leona

lip [lɪp] n labio; **lipread** vi leer los labios; **lip salve** n crema protectora para labios; **lipstick** n lápiz m de labios, carmín m

liqueur [lɪ'kjuə*] n licor m

liquid ['lɪkwɪd] adj, n líquido; **liquidizer** [-aɪzə*] n licuadora

liquor ['lɪkə*] n licor m, bebidas fpl alcohólicas; **liquor store** (US) n bodega, tienda de vinos y bebidas alcohólicas

Lisbon ['lɪzbən] n Lisboa

lisp [lɪsp] n ceceo ▷ vi cecear

list [lɪst] n lista ▷ vt (mention) enumerar; (put on a list) poner en una lista

listen ['lɪsn] vi escuchar, oír; **to ~ to sb/sth** escuchar a algn/algo; **listener** n oyente mf; (Radio) radioyente mf

lit [lɪt] pt, pp of **light**

liter ['liːtə*] (US) n = **litre**

literacy ['lɪtərəsɪ] n capacidad f de leer y escribir

literal ['lɪtərl] adj literal; **literally** adv literalmente

literary ['lɪtərərɪ] adj literario

literate ['lɪtərət] adj que sabe leer y escribir; (educated) culto

literature ['lɪtərɪtʃə*] n literatura; (brochures etc) folletos mpl

litre ['liːtə*] (US **liter**) n litro

litter ['lɪtə*] n (rubbish) basura; (young animals) camada, cría; **litter bin** (BRIT) n papelera; **littered** adj: **littered with** (scattered) lleno de

little ['lɪtl] adj (small) pequeño; (not much) poco ▷ adv poco; **a ~** un poco (de); **~ house/bird** casita/pajarito; **a ~ bit** un poquito; **~ by ~** poco a poco; **little finger** n dedo meñique

live¹ [laɪv] adj (animal) vivo; (wire) conectado; (broadcast) en directo; (shell) cargado

live² [lɪv] vi vivir; **live together** vi vivir juntos; **live up to** vt fus (fulfil) cumplir con

livelihood ['laɪvlɪhud] n sustento

lively ['laɪvlɪ] adj vivo;

(interesting: place, book etc) animado

liven up ['laɪvn-] vt animar ▷ vi animarse

liver ['lɪvə*] n hígado

lives [laɪvz] npl of **life**

livestock ['laɪvstɔk] n ganado

living ['lɪvɪŋ] adj *(alive)* vivo ▷ n: **to earn** or **make a ~** ganarse la vida; **living room** n sala (de estar)

lizard ['lɪzəd] n lagarto; *(small)* lagartija

load [ləud] n carga; *(weight)* peso ▷ vt *(Comput)* cargar; *(also:* **~ up**): **to ~ (with)** cargar (con or de); **a ~ of rubbish** *(inf)* tonterías fpl; **a ~ of, ~s of** *(fig)* (gran) cantidad de, montones de; **loaded** adj *(vehicle)*: **to be loaded with** estar cargado de

loaf [ləuf] *(pl* **loaves)** n (barra de) pan m

loan [ləun] n préstamo ▷ vt prestar; **on ~** prestado

loathe [ləuð] vt aborrecer; *(person)* odiar

loaves [ləuvz] npl of **loaf**

lobby ['lɔbɪ] n vestíbulo, sala de espera; *(Pol: pressure group)* grupo de presión ▷ vt presionar

lobster ['lɔbstə*] n langosta

local ['ləukl] adj local ▷ n *(pub)* bar m; **the locals** npl los vecinos, los del lugar; **local anaesthetic** n *(Med)* anestesia local; **local authority** n municipio, ayuntamiento (sp); **local government** n gobierno municipal; **locally** [-kəlɪ] adv en la vecindad; por aquí

locate [ləu'keɪt] vt *(find)* localizar; *(situate)*: **to be ~d in** estar situado en

location [ləu'keɪʃən] n situación f; **on ~** *(Cinema)* en exteriores

loch [lɔx] n lago

lock [lɔk] n *(of door, box)* cerradura; *(of canal)* esclusa; *(of hair)* mechón m ▷ vt *(with key)* cerrar (con llave) ▷ vi *(door etc)* cerrarse (con llave); *(wheels)* trabarse; **lock in** vt encerrar; **lock out** vt *(person)* cerrar la puerta a; **lock up** vt *(criminal)* meter en la cárcel; *(mental*

patient) encerrar; *(house)* cerrar (con llave) ▷ vi echar la llave

locker ['lɔkə*] n casillero; **locker-room** *(us)* n *(Sport)* vestuario

locksmith ['lɔksmɪθ] n cerrajero/a

locomotive [ləukə'məutɪv] n locomotora

lodge [lɔdʒ] n casita (del guarda) ▷ vi *(person)*: **to ~ (with)** alojarse (en casa de); *(bullet, bone)* incrustarse ▷ vt presentar; **lodger** n huésped mf

lodging ['lɔdʒɪŋ] n alojamiento, hospedaje m

loft [lɔft] n desván m

log [lɔg] n *(of wood)* leño, tronco; *(written account)* diario ▷ vt anotar; **log in, log on** vi *(Comput)* entrar en el sistema, hacer un login; **log off, log out** vi *(Comput)* salir del sistema

logic ['lɔdʒɪk] n lógica; **logical** adj lógico

login ['lɔgɪn] n *(Comput)* login m

lollipop ['lɔlɪpɔp] n piruli m; **lollipop man/lady** *(BRIT: irreg)* n persona encargada de ayudar a los niños a cruzar la calle

lolly ['lɔlɪ] n *(inf: ice cream)* polo; *(: lollipop)* piruleta; *(: money)* guita

London ['lʌndən] n Londres; **Londoner** n londinense mf

lone [ləun] adj solitario

loneliness ['ləunlɪnɪs] n soledad f; aislamiento

lonely ['ləunlɪ] adj *(situation)* solitario; *(person)* solo; *(place)* aislado

long [lɔŋ] adj largo ▷ adv mucho tiempo, largamente ▷ vi: **to ~ for sth** anhelar algo; **so** or **as ~ as** mientras, con tal que; **don't be ~!** ¡no tardes!, ¡vuelve pronto!; **how ~ is the street?** ¿cuánto tiene la calle de largo?; **how ~ is the lesson?** ¿cuánto dura la clase?; **6 metres ~** que mide 6 metros, de 6 metros de largo; **6 months ~** que dura 6 meses, de 6 meses de duración; **all night ~** toda la noche; **he no ~er comes** ya no viene; **I can't stand it any ~er** ya no lo aguanto más; **~ before**

mucho antes; **before ~** (+ *future*) dentro de poco; (+ *past*) poco tiempo después; **at ~ last** al fin, por fin; **long-distance** *adj* (*race*) de larga distancia; (*call*) interurbano; **long-haul** *adj* (*flight*) de larga distancia; **longing** *n* anhelo, ansia; (*nostalgia*) nostalgia ▷ *adj* anhelante

longitude ['lɒŋgɪtjuːd] *n* longitud *f*

long: long jump *n* salto de longitud; **long-life** *adj* (*batteries*) de larga duración; (*milk*) uperizado; **long-sighted** (BRIT) *adj* présbita; **long-standing** *adj* de mucho tiempo; **long-term** *adj* a largo plazo

loo [luː] (BRIT: *inf*) *n* wáter *m*

look [luk] *vi* mirar; (*seem*) parecer; (*building etc*): **to ~ south/on to the sea** dar al sur/al mar ▷ *n* (*gen*): **to have a ~** (*glance*) mirada; (*appearance*) aire *m*, aspecto; **looks** *npl* (*good looks*) belleza; **~ (here)!** (*expressing annoyance etc*) ¡oye!; **~!** (*expressing surprise*) ¡mira!; **look after** *vt fus* (*care for*) cuidar a; (*deal with*) encargarse de; **look around** *vi* echar una mirada alrededor; **look at** *vt fus* mirar; (*read quickly*) echar un vistazo a; **look back** *vi* mirar hacia atrás; **look down on** *vt fus* (*fig*) despreciar, mirar con desprecio; **look for** *vt fus* buscar; **look forward to** *vt fus* esperar con ilusión; (*in letters*): **we look forward to hearing from you** quedamos a la espera de sus gratas noticias; **look into** *vt* investigar; **look out** *vi* (*beware*): **to look out (for)** tener cuidado (de); **look out for** *vt fus* (*seek*) buscar; (*await*) esperar; **look round** *vi* volver la cabeza; **look through** *vt fus* (*examine*) examinar; **look up** *vi* mirar hacia arriba; (*improve*) mejorar ▷ *vt* (*word*) buscar; **look up to** *vt fus* admirar; **lookout** *n* (*tower etc*) puesto de observación; (*person*) vigía *mf*; **to be on the lookout for sth** estar al acecho de algo

loom [luːm] *vi*: **~ (up)** (*threaten*) surgir, amenazar; (*event: approach*) aproximarse

loony ['luːnɪ] (*inf*) *n, adj* loco/a *m/f*

loop [luːp] *n* lazo ▷ *vt*: **to ~ sth round sth** pasar algo alrededor de algo; **loophole** *n* escapatoria

loose [luːs] *adj* suelto; (*clothes*) ancho; (*morals, discipline*) relajado; **to be on the ~** estar en libertad; **to be at a ~ end** *or* **at ~ ends** (US) no saber qué hacer; **loosely** *adv* libremente, aproximadamente; **loosen** *vt* aflojar

loot [luːt] *n* botín *m* ▷ *vt* saquear

lop-sided ['lɒp'saɪdɪd] *adj* torcido

lord [lɔːd] *n* señor *m*; **L~ Smith** Lord Smith; **the L~** el Señor; **my ~** (*to bishop*) Ilustrísima; (*to noble etc*) Señor; **good L~!** ¡Dios mío!; **Lords** *npl* (BRIT: *Pol*): **the (House of) Lords** la Cámara de los Lores

lorry ['lɒrɪ] (BRIT) *n* camión *m*; **lorry driver** (BRIT) *n* camionero/a

lose [luːz] (*pt, pp* **lost**) *vt* perder ▷ *vi* perder, ser vencido; **to ~ (time)** (*clock*) atrasarse; **lose out** *vi* salir perdiendo; **loser** *n* perdedor(a) *m/f*

loss [lɒs] *n* pérdida; **heavy ~es** (*Mil*) grandes pérdidas; **to be at a ~** no saber qué hacer; **to make a ~** sufrir pérdidas

lost [lɒst] *pt, pp* of **lose** ▷ *adj* perdido; **lost property** (US **lost and found**) *n* objetos *mpl* perdidos

lot [lɒt] *n* (*group: of things*) grupo; (*at auctions*) lote *m*; **the ~** el todo, todos; **a ~** (*large number: of books etc*) muchos; (*a great deal*) mucho, bastante; **a ~ of, ~s of** mucho(s) (*pl*); **I read a ~** leo bastante; **to draw ~s (for sth)** echar suertes (para decidir algo)

lotion ['ləʊʃən] *n* loción *f*

lottery ['lɒtərɪ] *n* lotería

loud [laʊd] *adj* (*voice, sound*) fuerte; (*laugh, shout*) estrepitoso; (*condemnation etc*) enérgico; (*gaudy*) chillón/ona ▷ *adv* (*speak etc*) fuerte; **out ~** en voz alta; **loudly** *adv* (*noisily*) fuerte; (*aloud*) en voz alta; **loudspeaker** *n* altavoz *m*

lounge [laʊndʒ] *n* salón *m*, sala (de

estar); (*at airport etc*) sala; (BRIT: *also:* **~-bar**) salón-bar *m* ▷ *vi* (*also:* **~ about** *or* **around**) reposar, holgazanear
louse [laus] (*pl* **lice**) *n* piojo
lousy ['lauzı] (*inf*) *adj* (*bad quality*) malísimo, asqueroso; (*ill*) fatal
love [lʌv] *n* (*romantic, sexual*) amor *m*; (*kind, caring*) cariño ▷ *vt* amar, querer; (*thing, activity*) encantarle a algn; **"~ from Anne"** (*on letter*) "un abrazo (de) Anne"; **to ~ to do** encantarle a algn hacer; **to be/fall in ~ with** estar enamorado/enamorarse de; **to make ~** hacer el amor; **for the ~ of** por amor de; **"15 ~"** (*Tennis*) "15 a cero"; **I ~ you** te quiero; **I ~ paella** me encanta la paella; **love affair** *n* aventura sentimental; **love life** *n* vida sentimental
lovely ['lʌvlı] *adj* (*delightful*) encantador(a); (*beautiful*) precioso
lover ['lʌvə*] *n* amante *mf*; (*person in love*) enamorado; (*amateur*): **a ~ of** un(a) aficionado/a *or* un(a) amante de
loving ['lʌvıŋ] *adj* amoroso, cariñoso; (*action*) tierno
low [ləu] *adj, adv* bajo ▷ *n* (*Meteorology*) área de baja presión; **to be ~ on** (*supplies etc*) andar mal de, **to feel ~** sentirse deprimido; **to turn (down) ~** bajar; **low-alcohol** *adj* de bajo contenido en alcohol; **low-calorie** *adj* bajo en calorías
lower ['ləuə*] *adj* más bajo; (*less important*) menos importante ▷ *vt* bajar; (*reduce*) reducir ▷ *vr*: **to ~ o.s. to** (*fig*) rebajarse a
low-fat *adj* (*milk, yoghurt*) desnatado; (*diet*) bajo en calorías
loyal ['lɔıəl] *adj* leal; **loyalty** *n* lealtad *f*; **loyalty card** *n* tarjeta cliente
L.P. *n abbr* (= *long-playing record*) elepé *m*
L-plates ['εl-] (BRIT) *npl* placas *fpl* de aprendiz de conductor

- **L-PLATES**

- En el Reino Unido las personas que están aprendiendo a conducir deben llevar en la parte delantera y trasera de su vehículo unas placas blancas con una L en rojo conocidas como **L-Plates** (de **learner**). No es necesario que asistan a clases teóricas sino que, desde el principio, se le sentrega un carnet de conducir provisional ("provisional driving licence") para que realicen sus prácticas, aunque no pueden circular por las autopistas y deben ir siempre acompañadas por un conductor con carnet definitivo ("full driving licence").

Lt *abbr* (= *lieutenant*) Tte.
Ltd *abbr* (= *limited company*) S.A.
luck [lʌk] *n* suerte *f*; **bad ~** mala suerte; **good ~!** ¡que tengas suerte!, ¡suerte!; **bad** *or* **hard** *or* **tough ~!** ¡qué pena!; **luckily** *adv* afortunadamente; **lucky** *adj* afortunado; (*at cards etc*) con suerte; (*object*) que trae suerte
lucrative ['lu:krətıv] *adj* lucrativo
ludicrous ['lu:dıkrəs] *adj* absurdo
luggage ['lʌgıdʒ] *n* equipaje *m*; **luggage rack** *n* (*on car*) baca, portaequipajes *m inv*
lukewarm ['lu:kwɔ:m] *adj* tibio
lull [lʌl] *n* tregua ▷ *vt*: **to ~ sb to sleep** arrullar a algn; **to ~ sb into a false sense of security** dar a algn una falsa sensación de seguridad
lullaby ['lʌləbaı] *n* nana
lumber ['lʌmbə*] *n* (*junk*) trastos *mpl* viejos; (*wood*) maderos *mpl*
luminous ['lu:mınəs] *adj* luminoso
lump [lʌmp] *n* terrón *m*; (*fragment*) trozo; (*swelling*) bulto ▷ *vt* (*also:* **~ together**) juntar; **lump sum** *n* suma global; **lumpy** *adj* (*sauce*) lleno de grumos; (*mattress*) lleno de bultos
lunatic ['lu:nətık] *adj* loco
lunch [lʌntʃ] *n* almuerzo, comida ▷ *vi* almorzar; **lunch break, lunch hour** *n* hora del almuerzo; **lunch time** *n* hora de comer

lung [lʌŋ] n pulmón m
lure [luə*] n (attraction) atracción f
▷ vt tentar
lurk [lə:k] vi (person, animal) estar al
acecho; (fig) acechar
lush [lʌʃ] adj exuberante
lust [lʌst] n lujuria; (greed) codicia
Luxembourg ['lʌksəmbə:g] n
Luxemburgo
luxurious [lʌg'zjuəriəs] adj lujoso
luxury ['lʌkʃəri] n lujo ▷ cpd de lujo
Lycra® ['laikrə] n licra®
lying ['laiiŋ] n mentiras fpl ▷ adj
mentiroso
lyrics ['liriks] npl (of song) letra

m. abbr = **metre; mile; million**
M.A. abbr = **Master of Arts**
ma (inf) [mɑ:] n mamá
mac [mæk] (BRIT) n impermeable m
macaroni [mækə'rəuni] n
macarrones mpl
Macedonia [mæsɪ'dəuniə] n
Macedonia; **Macedonian** [-'dəuniən]
adj macedonio ▷ n macedonio/a;
(Ling) macedonio
machine [mə'ʃi:n] n máquina
▷ vt (dress etc) coser a máquina;
(Tech) hacer a máquina; **machine
gun** n ametralladora; **machinery**
n maquinaria; (fig) mecanismo;
machine washable adj lavable a
máquina
macho ['mætʃəu] adj machista
mackerel ['mækrl] n inv caballa
mackintosh ['mækintɔʃ] (BRIT) n
impermeable m
mad [mæd] adj loco; (idea)
disparatado; (angry) furioso; (keen): **to
be ~ about sth** volverle loco a algn algo
Madagascar [mædə'gæskə*] n

Madagascar m

madam ['mædəm] n señora

mad cow disease n encefalopatía espongiforme bovina

made [meɪd] pt, pp of **make**; **made-to-measure** (BRIT) adj hecho a la medida; **made-up** ['meɪdʌp] adj (story) ficticio

madly ['mædlɪ] adv locamente

madman ['mædmən] (irreg) n loco

madness ['mædnɪs] n locura

Madrid [mə'drɪd] n Madrid

Mafia ['mæfɪə] n Mafia

mag [mæg] n abbr (BRIT inf) = **magazine**

magazine [mægə'ziːn] n revista; (Radio, TV) programa m magazina

maggot ['mægət] n gusano

magic ['mædʒɪk] n magia ▷ adj mágico; **magical** adj mágico; **magician** [mə'dʒɪʃən] n mago/a; (conjurer) prestidigitador(a) m/f

magistrate ['mædʒɪstreɪt] n juez mf (municipal)

magnet ['mægnɪt] n imán m; **magnetic** [-'nɛtɪk] adj magnético; (personality) atrayente

magnificent [mæg'nɪfɪsənt] adj magnífico

magnify ['mægnɪfaɪ] vt (object) ampliar; (sound) aumentar; **magnifying glass** n lupa

magpie ['mægpaɪ] n urraca

mahogany [mə'hɔgənɪ] n caoba

maid [meɪd] n criada; **old ~** (pej) solterona

maiden name n nombre m de soltera

mail [meɪl] n correo; (letters) cartas fpl ▷ vt echar al correo; **mailbox** (US) n buzón m; **mailing list** n lista de direcciones; **mailman** (US: irreg) n cartero; **mail-order** n pedido postal

main [meɪn] adj principal, mayor ▷ n (pipe) cañería maestra; (US) red f eléctrica ▷ **the ~s** (BRIT Elec) la red eléctrica; **in the ~** en general; **main course** n (Culin) plato principal; **mainland** n tierra firme; **mainly**

adv principalmente; **main road** n carretera; **mainstream** n corriente f principal; **main street** n calle f mayor

maintain [meɪn'teɪn] vt mantener; **maintenance** ['meɪntənəns] n mantenimiento; (Law) manutención f

maisonette [meɪzə'nɛt] n dúplex m

maize [meɪz] (BRIT) n maíz m, choclo (SC)

majesty ['mædʒɪstɪ] n majestad f; (title): **Your M~** Su Majestad

major ['meɪdʒə*] n (Mil) comandante mf ▷ adj principal; (Mus) mayor

Majorca [mə'jɔːkə] n Mallorca

majority [mə'dʒɔrɪtɪ] n mayoría

make [meɪk] (pt, pp **made**) vt hacer; (manufacture) fabricar; (mistake) cometer; (speech) pronunciar; (cause to be): **to ~ sb sad** poner triste a algn; (force): **to ~ sb do sth** obligar a algn a hacer algo; (earn) ganar; (equal): **2 and 2 ~ 4** 2 y 2 son 4 ▷ n marca; **to ~ the bed** hacer la cama; **to ~ a fool of sb** poner a algn en ridículo; **to ~ a profit/loss** obtener ganancias/sufrir pérdidas; **to ~ it** (arrive) llegar; (achieve sth) tener éxito; **what time do you ~ it?** ¿qué hora tienes?; **to ~ do with** contentarse con; **make off** vi largarse; **make out** vt (decipher) descifrar; (understand) entender; (see) distinguir; (cheque) extender; **make up** vt (invent) inventar; (prepare) hacer; (constitute) constituir ▷ vi reconciliarse; (with cosmetics) maquillarse; **make up for** vt fus compensar; **makeover** ['meɪkəuvə*] n (by beautician) sesión f de maquillaje y peluquería; (change of image) lavado de cara; **maker** n fabricante mf; (of film, programme) autor(a) m/f; **makeshift** adj improvisado; **make-up** n maquillaje m

making ['meɪkɪŋ] n (fig): **in the ~** en vías de formación; **to have the ~s of** (person) tener madera de

malaria [mə'lɛərɪə] n malaria

Malaysia [mə'leɪzɪə] n Malasia,

m

Malaysia

male [meɪl] n (Biol) macho ▷ adj (sex, attitude) masculino; (child etc) varón

malicious [mə'lɪʃəs] adj malicioso; rencoroso

malignant [mə'lɪgnənt] adj (Med) maligno

mall [mɔːl] (US) n (also: **shopping ~**) centro comercial

mallet ['mælɪt] n mazo

malnutrition [mælnjuː'trɪʃən] n desnutrición f

malpractice [mæl'præktɪs] n negligencia profesional

malt [mɔːlt] n malta; (whisky) whisky m de malta

Malta ['mɔːltə] n Malta; **Maltese** [-'tiːz] adj, n inv maltés/esa m/f

mammal ['mæml] n mamífero

mammoth ['mæməθ] n mamut m ▷ adj gigantesco

man [mæn] (pl men) n hombre m; (mankind) el hombre ▷ vt (Naut) tripular; (Mil) guarnecer; (operate: machine) manejar; **an old ~** un viejo; **~ and wife** marido y mujer

manage ['mænɪdʒ] vi arreglárselas, ir tirando ▷ vt (be in charge of) dirigir; (control: person) manejar; (: ship) gobernar; **manageable** adj manejable; **management** n dirección f; **manager** n director(a) m/f; (of pop star) mánager mf; (Sport) entrenador(a) m/f; **manageress** n directora; entrenadora; **managerial** [-ə'dʒɪərɪəl] adj directivo; **managing director** n director(a) m/f general

mandarin ['mændərɪn] n (also: **~ orange**) mandarina; (person) mandarín m

mandate ['mændeɪt] n mandato

mandatory ['mændətərɪ] adj obligatorio

mane [meɪn] n (of horse) crin f; (of lion) melena

maneuver [mə'nuːvə*] (US) = **manoeuvre**

mangetout [mɔnʒ'tuː] n tirabeque

mango ['mæŋgəu] (pl ~es) n mango

man: manhole n agujero de acceso; **manhood** n edad f viril; (state) virilidad f

mania ['meɪnɪə] n manía; **maniac** ['meɪnɪæk] n maníaco/a; (fig) maniático

manic ['mænɪk] adj frenético

manicure ['mænɪkjuə*] n manicura

manifest ['mænɪfest] vt manifestar, mostrar ▷ adj manifiesto

manifesto [mænɪ'festəu] n manifiesto

manipulate [mə'nɪpjuleɪt] vt manipular

man: mankind [mæn'kaɪnd] n humanidad f, género humano; **manly** adj varonil; **man-made** adj artificial

manner ['mænə*] n manera, modo; (behaviour) conducta, manera de ser; (type): **all ~ of things** toda clase de cosas; **manners** npl (behaviour) modales mpl; **bad ~s** mala educación

manoeuvre [mə'nuːvə*] (US **maneuver**) vt, vi maniobrar ▷ n maniobra

manpower ['mænpauə*] n mano f de obra

mansion ['mænʃən] n palacio, casa grande

manslaughter ['mænslɔːtə*] n homicidio no premeditado

mantelpiece ['mæntlpiːs] n repisa, chimenea

manual ['mænjuəl] adj manual ▷ n manual m

manufacture [mænju'fæktʃə*] vt fabricar ▷ n fabricación f; **manufacturer** n fabricante mf

manure [mə'njuə*] n estiércol m

manuscript ['mænjuskrɪpt] n manuscrito

many ['menɪ] adj, pron muchos/as; **a great ~** muchísimos, un buen número de; **~ a time** muchas veces

map [mæp] n mapa m ▷ **to ~ out** vt proyectar

maple ['meɪpl] n arce m, maple m (LAM)

Mar abbr (= March) mar

mar [mɑ:*] vt estropear

marathon ['mærəθən] ↟ maratón m

marble ['mɑ:bl] n mármol m; (toy) canica

March [mɑ:tʃ] n marzo

march [mɑ:tʃ] vi (Mil) marchar; (demonstrators) manifestarse ▷ n marcha; (demonstration) manifestación f

mare [mɛə*] n yegua

margarine [mɑ:dʒə'ri:n] n margarina

margin ['mɑ:dʒɪn] n margen m; (Comm: profit margin) margen m de beneficios; **marginal** adj marginal; **marginally** adv ligeramente

marigold ['mærɪgəuld] n caléndula

marijuana [mærɪ'wɑ:nə] n marijuana

marina [mə'ri:nə] n puerto deportivo

marinade [mɑ:k] n adobo

marinate ['mærɪneɪt] vt marinar

marine [mə'ri:n] adj marino ▷ n soldado de marina

marital ['mærɪtl] adj matrimonial; **marital status** n estado m civil

maritime ['mærɪtaɪm] adj marítimo

marjoram ['mɑ:dʒərəm] n mejorana

mark [mɑ:k] n marca, señal f; (in snow, mud etc) huella; (stain) mancha; (BRIT Scol) nota ▷ vt marcar; manchar; (damage: furniture) rayar; (indicate: place etc) señalar; (BRIT Scol) calificar, corregir; **to ~ time** marcar el paso; (fig) marcar(se) un ritmo; **marked** adj (obvious) marcado, acusado; **marker** n (sign) marcador m; (bookmark) señal f (de libro)

market ['mɑ:kɪt] n mercado ▷ vt (Comm) comercializar; **marketing** n márketing m; **marketplace** n mercado; **market research** n análisis m inv de mercados

marmalade ['mɑ:məleɪd] n mermelada de naranja

maroon [mə'ru:n] vt: **to be ~ed** quedar aislado; (fig) quedar abandonado ▷ n (colour) granate m

marquee [mɑ:'ki:] n entoldado

marriage ['mærɪdʒ] n (relationship, institution) matrimonio; (wedding) boda; (act) casamiento; **marriage certificate** n partida de casamiento

married ['mærɪd] adj casado; (life, love) conyugal

marrow ['mærəu] n médula; (vegetable) calabacín m

marry ['mærɪ] vt casarse con; (father, priest etc) casar ▷ vi (also: **get married**) casarse

Mars [mɑ:z] n Marte m

marsh [mɑ:ʃ] n pantano; (salt marsh) marisma

marshal ['mɑ:ʃl] n (Mil) mariscal m; (at sports meeting etc) oficial m; (US: of police, fire department) jefe/a m/f ▷ vt (thoughts etc) ordenar; (soldiers) formar

martyr ['mɑ:tə*] n mártir mf

marvel ['mɑ:vl] n maravilla, prodigio ▷ vi: **to ~ (at)** maravillarse (de); **marvellous** (US **marvelous**) adj maravilloso

Marxism ['mɑ:ksɪzəm] n marxismo

Marxist ['mɑ:ksɪst] adj, n marxista mf

marzipan ['mɑ:zɪpæn] n mazapán m

mascara [mæs'kɑ:rə] n rímel m

mascot ['mæskət] n mascota

masculine ['mæskjulɪn] adj masculino

mash [mæʃ] vt machacar; **mashed potato(es)** n(pl) puré m de patatas (SP) or papas (LAM)

mask [mɑ:sk] n máscara ▷ vt (cover); **to ~ one's face** ocultarse la cara; (hide: feelings) esconder

mason ['meɪsn] n (also: **stone~**) albañil m; (also: **free~**) masón m; **masonry** n (in building) mampostería

mass [mæs] n (people) muchedumbre f; (of air, liquid etc) masa; (of detail, hair etc) gran cantidad f; (Rel) misa ▷ cpd

masivo ▷ vi reunirse; concentrarse;
the masses npl las masas; **~es of** (inf)
montones de
massacre ['mæsəkə*] n masacre f
massage ['mæsɑ:ʒ] n masaje m ▷ vt
dar masaje en
massive ['mæsɪv] adj enorme;
(support, changes) masivo
mass media npl medios mpl de
comunicación
mass-produce ['mæsprə'dju:s] vt
fabricar en serie
mast [mɑ:st] n (Naut) mástil m; (Radio
etc) torre f
master ['mɑ:stə*] n (of servant)
amo; (of situation) dueño, maestro;
(in primary school) maestro; (in
secondary school) profesor m; (title for
boys): **M~ X** Señorito X ▷ vt dominar;
mastermind n inteligencia superior
▷ vt dirigir, planear; **Master of
Arts/Science** n licenciatura superior
en Letras/Ciencias; **masterpiece** n
obra maestra
masturbate ['mæstəbeɪt] vi
masturbarse
mat [mæt] n estera; (also: **door~**)
felpudo; (also: **table ~**) salvamanteles m
inv, posavasos m inv ▷ adj = **matt**
match [mætʃ] n cerilla, fósforo;
(game) partido; (equal) igual m/f ▷ vt
(go well with) hacer juego con; (equal)
igualar; (correspond to) corresponderse
con; (pair: also: **~ up**) casar con ▷ vi
hacer juego; **to be a good ~** hacer
juego; **matchbox** n caja de cerillas;
matching adj que hace juego
mate [meɪt] n (workmate) colega mf;
(inf: friend) amigo/a; (animal) macho/
hembra; (in merchant navy) segundo
de a bordo ▷ vi acoplarse, aparearse
▷ vt aparear
material [mə'tɪərɪəl] n (substance)
materia; (information) material m;
(cloth) tela, tejido ▷ adj material;
(important) esencial; **materials** npl
materiales mpl
materialize [mə'tɪərɪəlaɪz] vi

materializarse
maternal [mə'tə:nl] adj maternal
maternity [mə'tə:nɪtɪ] n
maternidad f; **maternity hospital** n
hospital m de maternidad; **maternity
leave** n baja por maternidad
math [mæθ] (US) n = **mathematics**
mathematical [mæθə'mætɪkl] adj
matemático
mathematician [mæθəmə'tɪʃən] n
matemático/a
mathematics [mæθə'mætɪks] n
matemáticas fpl
maths [mæθs] (BRIT) n =
mathematics
matinée ['mætɪneɪ] n sesión f de
tarde
matron ['meɪtrən] n enfermera f jefe;
(in school) ama de llaves
matt [mæt] adj mate
matter ['mætə*] n cuestión f, asunto;
(Physics) sustancia, materia; (reading
matter) material m; (Med: pus) pus m
▷ vi importar; **matters** npl (affairs)
asuntos mpl; (complaint) males mpl; **it doesn't ~**
no importa; **what's the ~?** ¿qué pasa?;
no ~ what pase lo que pase; **as a ~
of course** por rutina; **as a ~ of fact**
de hecho
mattress ['mætrɪs] n colchón m
mature [mə'tjuə*] adj maduro
▷ vi madurar; **mature student** n
estudiante de más de 21 años; **maturity**
n madurez f
maul [mɔ:l] vt magullar
mauve [məuv] adj de color malva (SP)
or guinda (LAM)
max abbr = **maximum**
maximize ['mæksɪmaɪz] vt (profits
etc) llevar al máximo; (chances)
maximizar
maximum ['mæksɪməm] (pl
maxima) adj máximo ▷ n máximo
May [meɪ] n mayo
may [meɪ] (conditional **might**) vi
(indicating possibility): **he ~ come** puede
que venga; (be allowed to): **~ I smoke?**
¿puedo fumar?; (wishes): **~ God bless**

you! ¡que Dios le bendiga!; **you ~ as well go** bien puedes irte

maybe ['meɪbi:] adv quizá(s)

May Day n el primero de Mayo

mayhem ['meɪhem] n caos m total

mayonnaise [meɪə'neɪz] n mayonesa

mayor [mɛə*] n alcalde m; **mayoress** n alcaldesa

maze [meɪz] n laberinto

MD n abbr = **managing director**

me [mi:] pron (direct) me; (stressed, after pron) mí; **can you hear ~?** ¿me oyes?; **he heard ME** ¡me oyó a mí!; **it's ~** soy yo; **give them to ~** dámelos/las; **with/without ~** conmigo/sin mí

meadow ['mɛdəʊ] n prado, pradera

meagre ['mi:gə*] (US **meager**) adj escaso, pobre

meal [mi:l] n comida; (flour) harina; **mealtime** n hora de comer

mean [mi:n] (pt, pp **~t**) adj (with money) tacaño; (unkind) mezquino, malo; (shabby) humilde; (average) medio ▷ vt (signify) querer decir, significar; (refer to) referirse a; (intend): **to ~ to do sth** pensar or pretender hacer algo ▷ n medio, término medio; **means** npl (way) medio, manera; (money) recursos mpl, medios mpl; **by ~s of** mediante, por medio de; **by all ~s!** ¡naturalmente!, ¡claro que sí!; **do you ~ it?** ¿lo dices en serio?; **what do you ~?** ¿qué quiere decir?; **to be ~t for sb/sth** ser para algn/algo

meaning ['mi:nɪŋ] n significado, sentido; (purpose) sentido, propósito; **meaningful** adj significativo; **meaningless** adj sin sentido

meant [mɛnt] pt, pp of **mean**

meantime ['mi:ntaɪm] adv (also: **in the ~**) mientras tanto

meanwhile ['mi:nwaɪl] adv = **meantime**

measles ['mi:zlz] n sarampión m

measure ['mɛʒə*] vt, vi medir ▷ n medida; (ruler) regla; **measurement** ['mɛʒəmənt] n (measure) medida;

(act) medición f; **to take sb's measurements** tomar las medidas a algn

meat [mi:t] n carne f; **cold ~** fiambre m; **meatball** n albóndiga

Mecca ['mɛkə] n La Meca

mechanic [mɪ'kænɪk] n mecánico/a; **mechanical** adj mecánico

mechanism ['mɛkənɪzəm] n mecanismo

medal ['mɛdl] n medalla; **medallist** (US **medalist**) n (Sport) medallista mf

meddle ['mɛdl] vi: **to ~ in** entrometerse en; **to ~ with sth** manosear algo

media ['mi:dɪə] npl medios mpl de comunicación ▷ npl of **medium**

mediaeval [mɛdɪ'i:vl] adj = **medieval**

mediate ['mi:dɪeɪt] vi mediar

medical ['mɛdɪkl] adj médico ▷ n reconocimiento médico; **medical certificate** n certificado m médico

medicated ['mɛdɪkeɪtɪd] adj medicinal

medication [mɛdɪ'keɪʃən] n medicación f

medicine ['mɛdsɪn] n medicina; (drug) medicamento

medieval [mɛdɪ'i:vl] adj medieval

mediocre [mi:dɪ'əʊkə*] adj mediocre

meditate ['mɛdɪteɪt] vi meditar

meditation [mɛdɪ'teɪʃən] n meditación f

Mediterranean [mɛdɪtə'reɪnɪən] adj mediterráneo; **the ~ (Sea)** el (Mar) Mediterráneo

medium ['mi:dɪəm] (pl **media**) adj mediano, regular ▷ n (means) medio; (pl **mediums**: person) médium mf; **medium-sized** adj de tamaño mediano; (clothes) de (la) talla mediana; **medium wave** n onda media

meek [mi:k] adj manso, sumiso

meet [mi:t] (pt, pp **met**) vt encontrar; (accidentally) encontrarse con, tropezar con; (by arrangement) reunirse con; (for the first time) conocer; (go and fetch) ir a buscar; (opponent) enfrentarse con; (obligations) cumplir; (encounter: problem) hacer frente a; (need) satisfacer ▷ vi encontrarse; (in session) reunirse; (join: objects) unirse; (for the first time) conocerse; **meet up** vi: **to meet up with sb** reunirse con algn; **meet with** vt fus (difficulty) tropezar con; **to meet with success** tener éxito; **meeting** n encuentro; (arranged) cita, compromiso; (business meeting) reunión f; (Pol) mítin m; **meeting place** n lugar m de reunión or encuentro

megabyte ['mɛgəbaɪt] n (Comput) megabyte m, megaocteto

megaphone ['mɛgəfəʊn] n megáfono

megapixel ['mɛgəpɪksl] n megapíxel m

melancholy ['mɛlənkəlɪ] n melancolía ▷ adj melancólico

melody ['mɛlədɪ] n melodía

melon ['mɛlən] n melón m

melt [mɛlt] vi (metal) fundirse; (snow) derretirse ▷ vt fundir

member ['mɛmbə*] n (gen, Anat) miembro; (of club) socio/a; **Member of Congress** (US) n miembro mf del Congreso; **Member of Parliament** n (BRIT) diputado/a m/f, parlamentario/a m/f; **Member of the European Parliament** n diputado/a m/f del Parlamento Europeo, eurodiputado/a m/f; **Member of the Scottish Parliament** (BRIT) diputado/a del Parlamento escocés; **membership** n (members) número de miembros; (state) filiación f; **membership card** n carnet m de socio

memento [mə'mɛntəʊ] n recuerdo

memo ['mɛməʊ] n apunte m, nota

memorable ['mɛmərəbl] adj memorable

memorandum [mɛmə'rændəm] (pl **memoranda**) n apunte m, nota; (official note) acta

memorial [mɪ'mɔːrɪəl] n monumento conmemorativo ▷ adj conmemorativo

memorize ['mɛmər-aɪz] vt aprender de memoria

memory ['mɛmərɪ] n (also: Comput) memoria; (instance) recuerdo; (of dead person): **in ~ of** a la memoria de; **memory card** n tarjeta de memoria; **memory stick** n barra de memoria

men [mɛn] npl of **man**

menace ['mɛnəs] n amenaza ▷ vt amenazar

mend [mɛnd] vt reparar, arreglar; (darn) zurcir ▷ vi reponerse ▷ n arreglo, reparación f zurcido ▷ n: **to be on the ~** ir mejorando; **to ~ one's ways** enmendar

meningitis [mɛnɪn'dʒaɪtɪs] n meningitis f

menopause ['mɛnəupɔːz] n menopausia

men's room (US) n: **the ~** el servicio de caballeros

menstruation [mɛnstru'eɪʃən] n menstruación f

menswear ['mɛnzwɛə*] n confección f de caballero

mental ['mɛntl] adj mental; **mental hospital** n (hospital m) psiquiátrico; **mentality** [mɛn'tælɪtɪ] n mentalidad f; **mentally** adv: **to be mentally ill** tener una enfermedad mental

menthol ['mɛnθɔl] n mentol m

mention ['mɛnʃən] n mención f ▷ vt mencionar; (speak) hablar de; **don't ~ it!** ¡de nada!

menu ['mɛnjuː] n (set menu) menú m; (printed) carta; (Comput) menú m

MEP n abbr = **Member of the European Parliament**

mercenary ['məːsɪnərɪ] adj, n mercenario/a

merchandise ['məːtʃəndaɪz] n mercancías fpl

merchant ['məːtʃənt] n comerciante mf; **merchant navy** (US), **merchant marine** n marina mercante

merciless ['mɜːsɪlɪs] adj despiadado

mercury ['mɜːkjʊrɪ] n mercurio

mercy ['mɜːsɪ] n compasión f; (Rel) misericordia; **at the ~ of** a la merced de

mere [mɪə*] adj simple, mero; **merely** adv simplemente, sólo

merge [mɜːdʒ] vt (join) unir ▷ vi unirse; (Comm) fusionarse; (colours etc) fundirse; **merger** n (Comm) fusión f

meringue [mə'ræŋ] n merengue m

merit ['mɛrɪt] n mérito ▷ vt merecer

mermaid ['mɜːmeɪd] n sirena

merry ['mɛrɪ] adj alegre; **M~ Christmas!** ¡Felices Pascuas!; **merry-go-round** n tiovivo

mesh [mɛʃ] n malla

mess [mɛs] n (muddle: of situation) confusión f; (: of room) revoltijo; (dirt) porquería; (Mil) comedor m; **mess about** or **around** (inf) vi perder el tiempo; (pass the time) entretenerse; **mess up** vt (spoil) estropear; (dirty) ensuciar; **mess with** (inf) vt fus (challenge, confront) meterse con (inf); (interfere with) interferir con

message ['mɛsɪdʒ] n recado, mensaje m

messenger ['mɛsɪndʒə*] n mensajero/a

Messrs abbr (on letters) (= Messieurs) Sres

messy ['mɛsɪ] adj (dirty) sucio; (untidy) desordenado

met [mɛt] pt, pp of **meet**

metabolism [mɛ'tæbəlɪzəm] n metabolismo

metal ['mɛtl] n metal m; **metallic** [-'tælɪk] adj metálico

metaphor ['mɛtəfə*] n metáfora

meteor ['miːtɪə*] n meteoro; **meteorite** [-aɪt] n meteorito

meteorology [miːtɪə'rɔlədʒɪ] n meteorología

meter ['miːtə*] n (instrument) contador m; (US: unit) = **metre** ▷ vt (US Post) franquear

method ['mɛθəd] n método; **methodical** [mɪ'θɔdɪkl] adj metódico

meths [mɛθs] n (BRIT) alcohol m metilado or desnaturalizado

meticulous [mɛ'tɪkjʊləs] adj meticuloso

metre ['miːtə*] (US **meter**) n metro

metric ['mɛtrɪk] adj métrico

metro ['mɛtrəʊ] n metro

metropolitan [mɛtrə'pɔlɪtən] adj metropolitano; **the M~ Police** (BRIT) la policía londinense

Mexican ['mɛksɪkən] adj, n mexicano/a, mejicano/a

Mexico ['mɛksɪkəʊ] n México, Méjico (SP)

mg abbr (= milligram) mg

mice [maɪs] npl of **mouse**

micro... [maɪkrəʊ] prefix micro...; **microchip** n microplaqueta; **microphone** n micrófono; **microscope** n microscopio; **microwave** n (also: **microwave oven**) horno microondas

mid [mɪd] adj: **in ~ May** a mediados de mayo; **in ~ afternoon** a media tarde; **in ~ air** en el aire; **midday** n mediodía m

middle ['mɪdl] n centro; (half-way point) medio; (waist) cintura ▷ adj de en medio; (course, way) intermedio; **in the ~ of the night** en plena noche; **middle-aged** adj de mediana edad; **Middle Ages** npl: **the Middle Ages** la Edad Media; **middle-class** adj de clase media; **the middle class(es)** la clase media; **Middle East** n Oriente m Medio; **middle name** n segundo nombre; **middle school** n (US) colegio para niños de doce a catorce años; (BRIT) colegio para niños de ocho o nueve a doce o trece años

midge [mɪdʒ] n mosquito

midget ['mɪdʒɪt] n enano/a

midnight ['mɪdnaɪt] n medianoche f

midst [mɪdst] n: **in the ~ of** (crowd) en medio de; (situation, action) en mitad de

midsummer [mɪd'sʌmə*] n: **in ~** en pleno verano

midway ['mɪdweɪ] adj, adv: **~ (between)** a medio camino (entre); **~**

m

through a la mitad (de)
midweek [mɪd'wi:k] *adv* entre semana
midwife ['mɪdwaɪf] (*irreg*) *n* comadrona, partera
midwinter [mɪd'wɪntə*] *n*: **in ~** en pleno invierno
might [maɪt] *vb see* **may** ▷ *n* fuerza, poder *m*; **mighty** *adj* fuerte, poderoso
migraine ['mi:greɪn] *n* jaqueca
migrant ['maɪgrənt] *n, adj* (*bird*) migratorio; (*worker*) emigrante
migrate [maɪ'greɪt] *vi* emigrar
migration [maɪ'greɪʃən] *n* emigración *f*
mike [maɪk] *n abbr* (= *microphone*) micro
mild [maɪld] *adj* (*person*) apacible; (*climate*) templado; (*slight*) ligero; (*taste*) leve; (*illness*) leve; **mildly** ['-lɪ] *adv* ligeramente; suavemente; **to put it mildly** para no decir más
mile [maɪl] *n* milla; **mileage** *n* número de millas ≈ kilometraje *m*; **mileometer** [maɪ'lɒmɪtə] *n* ≈ cuentakilómetros *m inv*; **milestone** *n* mojón *m*
military ['mɪlɪtərɪ] *adj* militar
militia [mɪ'lɪʃə] *n* milicia
milk [mɪlk] *n* leche *f* ▷ *vt* (*cow*) ordeñar; (*fig*) chupar; **milk chocolate** *n* chocolate *m* con leche; **milkman** (*irreg*) *n* lechero; **milky** *adj* lechoso
mill [mɪl] *n* (*windmill etc*) molino; (*coffee mill*) molinillo; (*factory*) fábrica ▷ *vt* moler ▷ *vi* (*also*: **~ about**) arremolinarse
millennium [mɪ'lɛnɪəm] (*pl* **~s** or **millennia**) *n* milenio, milenario
milli... ['mɪlɪ] *prefix*: **milligram(me)** *n* miligramo; **millilitre** (*us* **milliliter**) ['mɪlɪliːtə*] *n* mililitro; **millimetre** (*us* **millimeter**) *n* milímetro
million ['mɪljən] *n* millón *m*; **a ~ times** un millón de veces; **millionaire** [-jə'nɛə*] *n* millonario/a; **millionth** [-θ] *adj* millonésimo
milometer [maɪ'lɒmɪtə*] (*BRIT*) *n* =

mileometer
mime [maɪm] *n* mímica; (*actor*) mimo/a ▷ *vt* remedar ▷ *vi* actuar de mimo
mimic ['mɪmɪk] *n* imitador(a) *m/f* ▷ *adj* mímico ▷ *vt* remedar, imitar
min. *abbr* = **minimum; minute(s)**
mince [mɪns] *vt* picar ▷ *n* (*BRIT Culin*) carne *f* picada; **mincemeat** *n* conserva de fruta picada; (*us*: *meat*) carne *f* picada; **mince pie** *n* empanadilla rellena de fruta picada
mind [maɪnd] *n* mente *f*; (*intellect*) intelecto; (*contrasted with matter*) espíritu *m* ▷ *vt* (*attend to, look after*) ocuparse de, cuidar; (*be careful*) tener cuidado con; (*object to*): **I don't ~ the noise** no me molesta el ruido; **it is on my ~** me preocupa; **to bear sth in ~** tomar or tener algo en cuenta; **to make up one's ~** decidirse; **I don't ~** me es igual; **~ you ...** te advierto que ...; **never ~!** ¡es igual!, ¡no importa!; (*don't worry*) ¡no te preocupes!; **"~ the step"** "cuidado con el escalón"; **mindless** *adj* (*crime*) sin motivo; (*work*) de autómata
mine¹ [maɪn] *pron* el mío/la mía etc; **a friend of ~** un(a) amigo/a mío/mía ▷ *adj*: **this book is ~** este libro es mío
mine² [maɪn] *n* mina ▷ *vt* (*coal*) extraer; (*bomb*: *beach etc*) minar; **minefield** *n* campo de minas; **miner** *n* minero/a
mineral ['mɪnərəl] *adj* mineral ▷ *n* mineral *m*; **mineral water** *n* agua mineral
mingle ['mɪŋgl] *vi*: **to ~ with** mezclarse con
miniature ['mɪnətʃə*] *adj* (en) miniatura ▷ *n* miniatura
minibar ['mɪnɪbɑ:*] *n* minibar *m*
minibus ['mɪnɪbʌs] *n* microbús *m*
minicab ['mɪnɪkæb] *n* taxi *m* (*que sólo puede pedirse por teléfono*)
minimal ['mɪnɪml] *adj* mínimo
minimize ['mɪnɪmaɪz] *vt* minimizar; (*play down*) empequeñecer
minimum ['mɪnɪməm] (*pl* **minima**)

n, adj mínimo

mining ['maɪnɪŋ] *n* explotación *f* minera

miniskirt ['mɪnɪskəːt] *n* minifalda

minister ['mɪnɪstə*] *n* (*BRIT Pol*) ministro/a (*SP*), secretario/a (*LAM*); (*Rel*) pastor *m* ▷ *vi*: **to ~ to** atender a

ministry ['mɪnɪstrɪ] *n* (*BRIT Pol*) ministerio, secretaría (*MEX*); (*Rel*) sacerdocio

minor ['maɪnə*] *adj* (*repairs, injuries*) leve; (*poet, planet*) menor; (*Mus*) menor ▷ *n* (*Law*) menor *m* de edad

Minorca [mɪ'nɔːkə] *n* Menorca

minority [maɪ'nɔrɪtɪ] *n* minoría

mint [mɪnt] *n* (*plant*) menta, hierbabuena; (*sweet*) caramelo de menta ▷ *vt* (*coins*) acuñar; **the (Royal) M~, the (US) M~** la Casa de la Moneda; **in ~ condition** en perfecto estado

minus ['maɪnəs] *n* (*also:* **~ sign**) signo de menos ▷ *prep* menos; **12 ~ 6 equals 6** 12 menos 6 son 6; **~ 24°C** menos 24 grados

minute¹ ['mɪnɪt] *n* minuto; (*fig*) momento; **minutes** *npl* (*of meeting*) actas *fpl*; **at the last ~** a última hora

minute² [maɪ'njuːt] *adj* diminuto; (*search*) minucioso

miracle ['mɪrəkl] *n* milagro

miraculous [mɪ'rækjʊləs] *adj* milagroso

mirage ['mɪrɑːʒ] *n* espejismo

mirror ['mɪrə*] *n* espejo; (*in car*) retrovisor *m*

misbehave [mɪsbɪ'heɪv] *vi* portarse mal

misc. *abbr* = **miscellaneous**

miscarriage ['mɪskærɪdʒ] *n* (*Med*) aborto; **~ of justice** error *m* judicial

miscellaneous [mɪsɪ'leɪnɪəs] *adj* varios/as, diversos/as

mischief ['mɪstʃɪf] *n* travesuras *fpl*, diabluras *fpl*; (*maliciousness*) malicia; **mischievous** [-ʃɪvəs] *adj* travieso

misconception [mɪskən'sɛpʃən] *n* idea equivocada; equivocación *f*

misconduct [mɪs'kɔndʌkt] *n* mala conducta; **professional ~** falta profesional

miser ['maɪzə*] *n* avaro/a

miserable ['mɪzərəbl] *adj* (*unhappy*) triste, desgraciado; (*unpleasant, contemptible*) miserable

misery ['mɪzərɪ] *n* tristeza; (*wretchedness*) miseria, desdicha

misfortune [mɪs'fɔːtʃən] *n* desgracia

misgiving [mɪs'gɪvɪŋ] *n* (*apprehension*) presentimiento; **to have ~s about sth** tener dudas acerca de algo

misguided [mɪs'gaɪdɪd] *adj* equivocado

mishap ['mɪshæp] *n* desgracia, contratiempo

misinterpret [mɪsɪn'təːprɪt] *vt* interpretar mal

misjudge [mɪs'dʒʌdʒ] *vt* juzgar mal

mislay [mɪs'leɪ] *vt* extraviar, perder

mislead [mɪs'liːd] *vt* llevar a conclusiones erróneas; **misleading** *adj* engañoso

misplace [mɪs'pleɪs] *vt* extraviar

misprint ['mɪsprɪnt] *n* errata, error *m* de imprenta

misrepresent [mɪsrɛprɪ'zɛnt] *vt* falsificar

Miss [mɪs] *n* Señorita

miss [mɪs] *vt* (*train etc*) perder, (*fail to hit: target*) errar; (*regret the absence of*): **I ~ him** (yo) le echo de menos *or* a faltar; (*fail to see*): **you can't ~ it** no tiene pérdida ▷ *vi* fallar ▷ *n* (*shot*) tiro fallido *or* perdido; **miss out** (*BRIT*) *vt* omitir; **miss out on** *vt fus* (*fun, party, opportunity*) perderse

missile ['mɪsaɪl] *n* (*Aviat*) mísil *m*; (*object thrown*) proyectil *m*

missing ['mɪsɪŋ] *adj* (*pupil*) ausente; (*thing*) perdido; (*Mil*): **~ in action** desaparecido en combate

mission ['mɪʃən] *n* misión *f*; (*official representation*) delegación *f*; **missionary** *n* misionero/a

misspell [mɪs'spɛl] (*pt, pp* **misspelt**
(BRIT) or **~ed**) *vt* escribir mal

mist [mɪst] *n* (*light*) neblina; (*heavy*)
niebla; (*at sea*) bruma ▷ *vi* (*eyes: also:*
~ over, **~ up**) llenarse de lágrimas;
(BRIT: *windows: also:* **~ over**, **~ up**)
empañarse

mistake [mɪs'teɪk] (*vt: irreg*) *n*
error *m* ▷ *vt* entender mal; **by ~**
por equivocación; **to make a ~**
equivocarse; **to ~ A for B** confundir
A con B; **mistaken** *pp of* **mistake**
▷ *adj* equivocado; **to be mistaken**
equivocarse, engañarse

mister ['mɪstə*] (*inf*) *n* señor *m*;
see **Mr**

mistletoe ['mɪsltəu] *n* muérdago

mistook [mɪs'tuk] *pt of* **mistake**

mistress ['mɪstrɪs] *n* (*lover*) amante
f; (*of house*) señora (de la casa); (BRIT: *in
primary school*) maestra; (*in secondary
school*) profesora; (*of situation*) dueña

mistrust [mɪs'trʌst] *vt* desconfiar de

misty ['mɪstɪ] *adj* (*day*) de niebla;
(*glasses etc*) empañado

misunderstand [mɪsʌndə'stænd]
(*irreg*) *vt, vi* entender mal;
misunderstanding *n* malentendido

misunderstood [mɪsʌndə'stud] *pt,
pp of* **misunderstand** ▷ *adj* (*person*)
incomprendido

misuse [*n* mɪs'juːs, *vb* mɪs'juːz] *n*
mal uso; (*of power*) abuso; (*of funds*)
malversación *f* ▷ *vt* abusar de;
malversar

mitt(en) ['mɪt(n)] *n* manopla

mix [mɪks] *vt* mezclar; (*combine*)
unir ▷ *vi* mezclarse; (*people*) llevarse
bien ▷ *n* mezcla; **mix up** *vt* mezclar;
(*confuse*) confundir; **mixed** *adj* mixto;
(*feelings etc*) encontrado; **mixed grill**
n (BRIT) parrillada mixta; **mixed
salad** *n* ensalada mixta; **mixed-up**
adj (*confused*) confuso, revuelto;
mixer *n* (*for food*) licuadora; (*for
drinks*) coctelera; (*person*): **he's a good
mixer** tiene don de gentes; **mixture** *n*
mezcla; (*also:* **cough mixture**) jarabe

m; **mix-up** *n* confusión *f*

ml *abbr* (= *millilitre(s)*) ml

mm *abbr* (= *millimetre*) mm

moan [məun] *n* gemido ▷ *vi* gemir;
(*inf: complain*): **to ~ (about)** quejarse
(de)

moat [məut] *n* foso

mob [mɔb] *n* multitud *f* ▷ *vt* acosar

mobile ['məubaɪl] *adj* móvil ▷ *n*
móvil *m*; **mobile home** *n* caravana;
mobile phone *n* teléfono móvil

mobility [məu'bɪlɪtɪ] *n* movilidad *f*

mobilize ['məubɪlaɪz] *vt* movilizar

mock [mɔk] *vt* (*ridicule*) ridiculizar;
(*laugh at*) burlarse de ▷ *adj* fingido;
~ exam *examen* examen preparatorio antes de
los exámenes oficiales* (BRIT: Scol: *inf*)
exámenes *mpl* de prueba; **mockery**
n burla

mod cons ['mɔd'kɔnz] *npl*
abbr (= *modern conveniences*) *see*
convenience

mode [məud] *n* modo

model ['mɔdl] *n* modelo; (*fashion
model, artist's model*) modelo *mf* ▷ *adj*
modelo ▷ *vt* (*with clay etc*) modelar;
(*copy*): **to ~ o.s. on** tomar como modelo
a ▷ *vi* ser modelo; **to ~ clothes** pasar
modelos, ser modelo

modem ['məudəm] *n* modem *m*

moderate [*adj* 'mɔdərət, *vb* 'mɔdə
reɪt] *adj* moderado/a ▷ *vi* moderarse,
calmarse ▷ *vt* moderar

moderation [mɔdə'reɪʃən] *n*
moderación *f*; **in ~** con moderación

modern ['mɔdən] *adj* moderno;
modernize *vt* modernizar; **modern
languages** *npl* lenguas *fpl* modernas

modest ['mɔdɪst] *adj* modesto;
(*small*) módico; **modesty** *n* modestia

modification [mɔdɪfɪ'keɪʃən] *n*
modificación *f*

modify ['mɔdɪfaɪ] *vt* modificar

module ['mɔdjuːl] *n* (*unit, component,
Space*) módulo

mohair ['məuhɛə*] *n* mohair *m*

Mohammed [mə'hæmɛd] *n*
Mahoma *m*

moist [mɔɪst] *adj* húmedo; **moisture** ['mɔɪstʃə*] *n* humedad *f*; **moisturizer** ['mɔɪstʃəraɪzə*] *n* crema hidratante

mold *etc* [məuld] (*US*) = **mould** *etc*

mole [məul] *n* (*animal, spy*) topo; (*spot*) lunar *m*

molecule ['mɔlɪkjuːl] *n* molécula

molest [məu'lɛst] *vt* importunar; (*assault sexually*) abusar sexualmente de

> Be careful not to translate **molest** by the Spanish word *molestar*.

molten ['məultən] *adj* fundido; (*lava*) líquido

mom [mɔm] (*US*) *n* = **mum**

moment ['məumənt] *n* momento; **at the ~** de momento, por ahora; **momentarily** ['məuməntrɪlɪ] *adv* momentáneamente; (*US: very soon*) de un momento a otro; **momentary** *adj* momentáneo; **momentous** [-'mɛntə s] *adj* trascendental, importante

momentum [məu'mɛntəm] *n* momento; (*fig*) ímpetu *m*; **to gather ~** cobrar velocidad; (*fig*) ganar fuerza

mommy ['mɔmɪ] (*US*) *n* = **mummy**

Mon *abbr* (= *Monday*) lun

Monaco ['mɔnəkəu] *n* Mónaco

monarch ['mɔnək] *n* monarca *mf*; **monarchy** *n* monarquía

monastery ['mɔnəstərɪ] *n* monasterio

Monday ['mʌndɪ] *n* lunes *m inv*

monetary ['mʌnɪtərɪ] *adj* monetario

money ['mʌnɪ] *n* dinero; (*currency*) moneda; **to make ~** ganar dinero; **money belt** *n* riñonera; **money order** *n* giro

mongrel ['mʌŋgrəl] *n* (*dog*) perro mestizo

monitor ['mɔnɪtə*] *n* (*Scol*) monitor *m*; (*also*: **television ~**) receptor *m* de control; (*of computer*) monitor *m* ▷ *vt* controlar

monk [mʌŋk] *n* monje *m*

monkey ['mʌŋkɪ] *n* mono

monologue ['mɔnəlɔg] *n* monólogo

monopoly [mə'nɔpəlɪ] *n* monopolio

monosodium glutamate [mɔnə'səudɪəm'gluː təmeɪt] *n* glutamato monosódico

monotonous [mə'nɔtənəs] *adj* monótono

monsoon [mɔn'suːn] *n* monzón *m*

monster ['mɔnstə*] *n* monstruo

month [mʌnθ] *n* mes *m*; **monthly** *adj* mensual ▷ *adv* mensualmente

monument ['mɔnjumənt] *n* monumento

mood [muːd] *n* humor *m*; (*of crowd, group*) clima *m*; **to be in a good/bad ~** estar de buen/mal humor; **moody** *adj* (*changeable*) de humor variable; (*sullen*) malhumorado

moon [muːn] *n* luna; **moonlight** *n* luz *f* de la luna

moor [muə*] *n* páramo ▷ *vt* (*ship*) amarrar ▷ *vi* echar las amarras

moose [muːs] *n inv* alce *m*

mop [mɔp] *n* fregona; (*of hair*) greña, melena ▷ *vt* fregar; **mop up** *vt* limpiar

mope [məup] *vi* estar *or* andar deprimido

moped ['məupɛd] *n* ciclomotor *m*

moral ['mɔrl] *adj* moral ▷ *n* moraleja; **morals** *npl* moralidad *f*, moral *f*

morale [mɔ'rɑːl] *n* moral *f*

morality [mə'rælɪtɪ] *n* moralidad *f*

morbid ['mɔːbɪd] *adj* (*interest*) morboso; (*Med*) mórbido

○ KEYWORD

more [mɔː*] *adj* **1** (*greater in number etc*) más; **more people/work than before** más gente/trabajo que antes

2 (*additional*) más; **do you want (some) more tea?** ¿quieres más té?; **is there any more wine?** ¿queda vino?; **it'll take a few more weeks** tardará unas semanas más; **it's 2 kms more to the house** faltan 2 kms para la casa; **more time/letters than we expected**

m

más tiempo del que/más cartas de las que esperábamos
▷ *pron (greater amount, additional amount)* más; **more than 10** más de 10; **it cost more than the other one/than we expected** costó más que el otro/más de lo que esperábamos; **is there any more?** ¿hay más?; **many/much more** muchos(as)/mucho(a) más
▷ *adv* más; **more dangerous/easily (than)** más peligroso/fácilmente (que); **more and more expensive** cada vez más caro; **more or less** más o menos; **more than ever** más que nunca

moreover [mɔː'rəuvə*] *adv* además, por otra parte

morgue [mɔːg] *n* depósito de cadáveres

morning ['mɔːnɪŋ] *n* mañana; *(early morning)* madrugada ▷ *cpd* matutino, de la mañana; **in the ~** por la mañana; **7 o'clock in the ~** las 7 de la mañana; **morning sickness** *n* náuseas *fpl* matutinas

Moroccan [mə'rɔkən] *adj, n* marroquí *m/f*

Morocco [mə'rɔkəu] *n* Marruecos *m*

moron ['mɔːrɔn] *(inf) n* imbécil *mf*

morphine ['mɔːfiːn] *n* morfina

Morse [mɔːs] *n (also: ~ code)* (código) Morse

mortal ['mɔːtl] *adj, n* mortal *m*

mortar ['mɔːtə*] *n* argamasa

mortgage ['mɔːgɪdʒ] *n* hipoteca ▷ *vt* hipotecar

mortician [mɔː'tɪʃən] *(US) n* director/a *m/f* de pompas fúnebres

mortified ['mɔːtɪfaɪd] *adj:* **I was ~** me dio muchísima vergüenza

mortuary ['mɔːtjuərɪ] *n* depósito de cadáveres

mosaic [məu'zeɪɪk] *n* mosaico

Moslem ['mɔzləm] *adj, n* = **Muslim**

mosque [mɔsk] *n* mezquita

mosquito [mɔs'kiːtəu] *(pl ~es) n*

mosquito *(SP)*, zancudo *(LAM)*

moss [mɔs] *n* musgo

most [məust] *adj* la mayor parte de, la mayoría de ▷ *pron* la mayor parte, la mayoría ▷ *adv* el más; *(very)* muy; **the ~** *(also: + adj)* el más; **~ of them** la mayor parte de ellos; **I saw the ~** yo vi el que más; **at the (very) ~** a lo sumo, todo lo más; **to make the ~ of** aprovechar (al máximo); **a ~ interesting book** un libro interesantísimo; **mostly** *adv* en su mayor parte, principalmente

MOT *(BRIT) n abbr* = **Ministry of Transport**; **the ~ (test)** inspección *(anual)* obligatoria de coches y camiones

motel [məu'tɛl] *n* motel *m*

moth [mɔθ] *n* mariposa nocturna; *(clothes moth)* polilla

mother ['mʌðə*] *n* madre *f* ▷ *adj* materno ▷ *vt (care for)* cuidar (como una madre); **motherhood** *n* maternidad *f*; **mother-in-law** *n* suegra; **mother-of-pearl** *n* nácar *m*; **Mother's Day** *n* Día *m* de la Madre; **mother-to-be** *n* futura madre *f*; **mother tongue** *n* lengua materna

motif [məu'tiːf] *n* motivo

motion ['məuʃən] *n* movimiento; *(gesture)* ademán *m*, señal *f*; *(at meeting)* moción *f* ▷ *vt, vi:* **to ~ (to) sb to do sth** hacer señas a algn para que haga algo; **motionless** *adj* inmóvil; **motion picture** *n* película

motivate ['məutɪveɪt] *vt* motivar

motivation [məutɪ'veɪʃən] *n* motivación *f*

motive ['məutɪv] *n* motivo

motor ['məutə*] *n* motor *m*; *(BRIT: inf: vehicle)* coche *m (SP)*, carro *(LAM)*, automóvil *m* ▷ *adj* motor *(f: motora or motriz)*; **motorbike** *n* moto *f*; **motorboat** *n* lancha motora; **motorcar** *(BRIT) n* coche *m*, carro, automóvil *m*; **motorcycle** *n* motocicleta; **motorcyclist** *n* motociclista *mf*; **motoring** *(BRIT) n* automovilismo; **motorist** *n* conductor(a) *m/f*, automovilista *mf*;

motor racing (BRIT) n carreras fpl de coches, automovilismo; **motorway** (BRIT) n autopista

motto ['mɔtəu] (pl **~es**) n lema m; (watchword) consigna

mould [məuld] (US **mold**) n molde m; (mildew) moho ▷ vt moldear; (fig) formar; **mouldy** adj enmohecido

mound [maund] n montón m, montículo

mount [maunt] n monte m ▷ vt montar, subir a; (jewel) engarzar; (picture) enmarcar; (exhibition etc) organizar ▷ vi (increase) aumentar; **mount up** vi aumentar

mountain ['mauntɪn] n montaña ▷ cpd de montaña; **mountain bike** n bicicleta de montaña; **mountaineer** n alpinista mf (SP, MEX), andinista mf (LAM); **mountaineering** n alpinismo (SP, MEX), andinismo (LAM); **mountainous** adj montañoso; **mountain range** n sierra

mourn [mɔ:n] vt llorar, lamentar ▷ vi: **to ~ for** llorar la muerte de; **mourner** n doliente mf; dolorido/a; **mourning** n luto; **in mourning** de luto

mouse [maus] (pl **mice**) n (Zool, Comput) ratón m; **mouse mat** n (Comput) alfombrilla

moussaka [mu'sɑ:kə] n musaca

mousse [mu:s] n (Culin) crema batida; (for hair) espuma (moldeadora)

moustache [məs'tɑ:ʃ] (US **mustache**) n bigote m

mouth [mauθ, pl mauðz] n boca; (of river) desembocadura; **mouthful** n bocado; **mouth organ** n armónica; **mouthpiece** n (of musical instrument) boquilla; (spokesman) portavoz mf; **mouthwash** n enjuague m

move [mu:v] n (movement) movimiento; (in game) jugada; (: turn to play) turno; (change: of house) mudanza; (: of job) cambio de trabajo ▷ vt mover; (emotionally) conmover; (Pol: resolution etc) proponer ▷ vi moverse; (traffic) circular; (also: **~ house**) trasladarse, mudarse; **to ~ sb to do sth** mover a algn a hacer algo; **to get a ~ on** darse prisa; **move back** vi retroceder; **move in** vi (to a house) instalarse; (police, soldiers) intervenir; **move off** vi ponerse en camino; **move on** vi ponerse en camino; **move out** vi (of house) mudarse; **move over** vi apartarse, hacer sitio; **move up** vi (employee) ser ascendido; **movement** n movimiento

movie ['mu:vɪ] n película; **to go to the ~s** ir al cine; **movie theater** (US) n cine m

moving ['mu:vɪŋ] adj (emotional) conmovedor(a); (that moves) móvil

mow [məu] (pt **~ed**, pp **mowed** or **mown**) vt (grass, corn) cortar, segar; **mower** n (also: **lawnmower**) cortacéspedes m inv

Mozambique [məuzæm'bi:k] n Mozambique m

MP n abbr = **Member of Parliament**

MP3 n MP3; **MP3 player** n reproductor m (de) MP3

mpg n abbr = **miles per gallon**

m.p.h. abbr = **miles per hour** (60 m.p.h. = 96 k.p.h.)

Mr ['mɪstə*] (US **Mr.**) n: **~ Smith** (el) Sr. Smith

Mrs ['mɪsɪz] (US **Mrs.**) n: **~ Smith** (la) Sra. Smith

Ms [mɪz] (US **Ms.**) n = **Miss** or **Mrs**; **~ Smith** (la) Sr(t)a. Smith

MSP n abbr = **Member of the Scottish Parliament**

Mt abbr (Geo) (= mount) m

much [mʌtʃ] adj mucho ▷ adv mucho; (before pp) muy ▷ n or pron mucho; **how ~ is it?** ¿cuánto es?, ¿cuánto cuesta?; **too ~** demasiado; **it's not ~** no es mucho; **as ~ as** tanto como; **however ~ he tries** por mucho que se esfuerce

muck [mʌk] n suciedad f; **muck up** (inf) vt arruinar, estropear; **mucky** adj (dirty) sucio

mucus ['mju:kəs] n mucosidad f, moco

mud [mʌd] n barro, lodo

muddle ['mʌdl] n desorden m, confusión f; (mix-up) embrollo, lío ▷ vt (also: ~ up) embrollar, confundir

muddy ['mʌdɪ] adj fangoso, cubierto de lodo

mudguard ['mʌdgɑ:d] n guardabarros m inv

muesli ['mju:zlɪ] n muesli m

muffin ['mʌfɪn] n panecillo dulce

muffled ['mʌfld] adj (noise etc) amortiguado, apagado

muffler (us) ['mʌflə*] n (Aut) silenciador m

mug [mʌg] n taza grande (sin platillo); (for beer) jarra; (inf: face) jeta ▷ vt (assault) asaltar; **mugger** ['mʌgə*] n atracador(a) m/f; **mugging** n asalto

muggy ['mʌgɪ] adj bochornoso

mule [mju:l] n mula

multicoloured ['mʌltɪkʌləd] (us), **multicolored** adj multicolor

multimedia ['mʌltɪ'mi:dɪə] adj multimedia

multinational [mʌltɪ'næʃnl] n multinacional f ▷ adj multinacional

multiple ['mʌltɪpl] adj múltiple ▷ n múltiplo; **multiple choice (test)** n examen m de tipo test; **multiple sclerosis** n esclerosis f múltiple

multiplex cinema ['mʌltɪpleks-] n multicines mpl

multiplication [mʌltɪplɪ'keɪʃən] n multiplicación f

multiply ['mʌltɪplaɪ] vt multiplicar ▷ vi multiplicarse

multistorey [mʌltɪ'stɔ:rɪ] (BRIT) adj de muchos pisos

mum [mʌm] (BRIT: inf) n mamá ▷ adj: **to keep ~** mantener la boca cerrada

mumble ['mʌmbl] vt, vi hablar entre dientes, refunfuñar

mummy ['mʌmɪ] n (BRIT: mother) mamá; (embalmed) momia

mumps [mʌmps] n paperas fpl

munch [mʌntʃ] vt, vi mascar

municipal [mju:'nɪsɪpl] adj municipal

mural ['mjuərl] n (pintura) mural m

murder ['mə:də*] n asesinato; (in law) homicidio ▷ vt asesinar, matar; **murderer** n asesino

murky ['mə:kɪ] adj (water) turbio; (street, night) lóbrego

murmur ['mə:mə*] n murmullo ▷ vt, vi murmurar

muscle ['mʌsl] n músculo; (fig: strength) garra, fuerza; **muscular** ['mʌskjulə*] adj muscular; (person) musculoso

museum [mju:'zɪəm] n museo

mushroom ['mʌʃrum] n seta, hongo; (Culin) champiñón m ▷ vi crecer de la noche a la mañana

music ['mju:zɪk] n música; **musical** adj musical; (sound) melodioso; (person) con talento musical ▷ n (show) comedia musical; **musical instrument** n instrumento musical; **musician** [-'zɪʃən] n músico/a

Muslim ['mʌzlɪm] adj, n musulmán/ana m/f

muslin ['mʌzlɪn] n muselina

mussel ['mʌsl] n mejillón m

must [mʌst] aux vb (obligation): **I ~ do it** debo hacerlo, tengo que hacerlo; (probability): **he ~ be there by now** ya debe (de) estar allí ▷ n: **it's a ~** es imprescindible

mustache ['mʌstæʃ] (us) n = **moustache**

mustard ['mʌstəd] n mostaza

mustn't ['mʌsnt] = **must not**

mute [mju:t] adj, n mudo/a m/f

mutilate ['mju:tɪleɪt] vt mutilar

mutiny ['mju:tɪnɪ] n motín m ▷ vi amotinarse

mutter ['mʌtə*] vt, vi murmurar

mutton ['mʌtn] n carne f de cordero

mutual ['mju:tʃuəl] adj mutuo; (interest) común

muzzle ['mʌzl] n hocico; (for dog) bozal m; (of gun) boca ▷ vt (dog) poner

un bozal a

my [maɪ] *adj* mi(s); **~ house/brother/
sisters** mi casa/mi hermano/mis
hermanas; **I've washed ~ hair/cut ~
finger** me he lavado el pelo/cortado un
dedo; **is this ~ pen or yours?** ¿es este
bolígrafo mío o tuyo?

myself [maɪˈsɛlf] *pron (reflexive)* me;
(emphatic) yo mismo; *(after prep)* mí
(mismo); *see also* **oneself**

mysterious [mɪsˈtɪərɪəs] *adj*
misterioso

mystery [ˈmɪstərɪ] *n* misterio

mystical [ˈmɪstɪkl] *adj* místico

mystify [ˈmɪstɪfaɪ] *vt (perplex)* dejar
perplejo

myth [mɪθ] *n* mito; **mythology**
[mɪˈθɒlədʒɪ] *n* mitología

n/a *abbr (= not applicable)* no interesa

nag [næg] *vt (scold)* regañar

nail [neɪl] *n (human)* uña; *(metal)*
clavo ▷ *vt* clavar; **to ~ sth to sth**
clavar algo en algo; **to ~ sb down
to doing sth** comprometer a algn a
que haga algo; **nailbrush** *n* cepillo
para las uñas; **nailfile** *n* lima para las
uñas; **nail polish** *n* esmalte *m* or laca
para las uñas; **nail polish remover**
n quitaesmalte *m*; **nail scissors** *npl*
tijeras *fpl* para las uñas; **nail varnish**
(*BRIT*) *n* = **nail polish**

naïve [naɪˈiːv] *adj* ingenuo

naked [ˈneɪkɪd] *adj (nude)* desnudo;
(flame) expuesto al aire

name [neɪm] *n* nombre *m*; *(surname)*
apellido; *(reputation)* fama, renombre *m*
▷ *vt (child)* poner nombre a; *(criminal)*
identificar; *(price, date etc)* fijar; **what's
your ~?** ¿cómo se llama?; **by ~** de
nombre; **in the ~ of** en nombre de;
to give one's ~ and address dar sus
señas; **namely** *adv* a saber

nanny [ˈnænɪ] *n* niñera

nap [næp] n (*sleep*) sueñecito, siesta
napkin ['næpkɪn] n (*also:* **table ~**) servilleta
nappy ['næpɪ] (*BRIT*) n pañal m
narcotics npl (*illegal drugs*) estupefacientes mpl, narcóticos mpl
narrative ['nærətɪv] n narrativa ▷ adj narrativo
narrator [nə'reɪtə*] n narrador(a) m/f
narrow ['nærəu] adj estrecho, angosto; (*fig: majority etc*) corto; (: *ideas etc*) estrecho ▷ vi (*road*) estrecharse; (*diminish*) reducirse; **to have a ~ escape** escaparse por los pelos; **narrow down** vt (*search, investigation, possibilities*) restringir, limitar; (*list*) reducir; **narrowly** adv (*miss*) por poco; **narrow-minded** adj de miras estrechas
nasal ['neɪzl] adj nasal
nasty ['nɑːstɪ] adj (*remark*) feo; (*person*) antipático; (*revolting: taste, smell*) asqueroso; (*wound, disease etc*) peligroso, grave
nation ['neɪʃən] n nación f
national ['næʃənl] adj, n nacional m/f; **national anthem** n himno nacional; **national dress** n vestido nacional; **National Health Service** (*BRIT*) n servicio nacional de salud pública ≈ Insalud m (*SP*); **National Insurance** (*BRIT*) n seguro social nacional; **nationalist** adj, n nacionalista mf; **nationality** [-'nælɪtɪ] n nacionalidad f; **nationalize** vt nacionalizar; **national park** (*BRIT*) n parque m nacional; **National Trust** n (*BRIT*) *organización encargada de preservar el patrimonio histórico británico*
nationwide ['neɪʃənwaɪd] adj en escala or a nivel nacional
native ['neɪtɪv] n (*local inhabitant*) natural mf, nacional mf ▷ adj (*indigenous*) indígena; (*country*) natal; (*innate*) natural, innato; **a ~ of Russia** un(a) natural mf de Rusia; **Native American** adj, n americano/a

indígena, amerindio/a; **native speaker** n hablante mf nativo/a
NATO ['neɪtəu] n abbr (= *North Atlantic Treaty Organization*) OTAN f
natural ['nætʃrəl] adj natural; **natural gas** n gas m natural; **natural history** n historia natural; **naturally** adv (*speak etc*) naturalmente; (*of course*) desde luego, por supuesto; **natural resources** npl recursos mpl naturales
nature ['neɪtʃə*] n (*also:* **N~**) naturaleza; (*group, sort*) género, clase f; (*character*) carácter m, genio; **by ~** por or de naturaleza; **nature reserve** n reserva natural
naughty ['nɔːtɪ] adj (*child*) travieso
nausea ['nɔːsɪə] n náuseas fpl
naval ['neɪvl] adj naval, de marina
navel ['neɪvl] n ombligo
navigate ['nævɪgeɪt] vt gobernar ▷ vi navegar; (*Aut*) ir de copiloto; **navigation** [-'geɪʃən] n (*action*) navegación f; (*science*) náutica
navy ['neɪvɪ] n marina de guerra; (*ships*) armada, flota
Nazi ['nɑːtsɪ] n nazi mf
NB abbr (= *nota bene*) nótese
near [nɪə*] adj (*place, relation*) cercano; (*time*) próximo ▷ adv cerca ▷ prep (*also:* **~ to**: *space*) cerca de, junto a; (: *time*) cerca de ▷ vt acercarse a, aproximarse a; **nearby** [nɪə'baɪ] adj cercano, próximo ▷ adv cerca; **nearly** adv casi, por poco; **I nearly fell** por poco me caigo; **near-sighted** adj miope, corto de vista
neat [niːt] adj (*place*) ordenado, bien cuidado; (*person*) pulcro; (*plan*) ingenioso; (*spirits*) solo; **neatly** adv (*tidily*) con esmero; (*skilfully*) ingeniosamente
necessarily ['nɛsɪsrɪlɪ] adv necesariamente
necessary ['nɛsɪsrɪ] adj necesario, preciso
necessity [nɪ'sɛsɪtɪ] n necesidad f
neck [nɛk] n (*of person, garment, bottle*) cuello; (*of animal*) pescuezo ▷ vi

(*inf*) bes>uquearse; **~ and ~** parejos;
necklace ['nɛklɪs] n collar m; **necktie**
['nɛktaɪ] n corbata

nectarine ['nɛktərɪn] n nectarina

need [ni:d] n (*lack*) escasez f, falta;
(*necessity*) necesidad f ▷ vt (*require*)
necesitar; **I ~ to do it** tengo que or debo
hacerlo; **you don't ~ to go** no hace
falta que (te) vayas

needle ['ni:dl] n aguja ▷ vt (*fig: inf*)
picar, fastidiar

needless ['ni:dlɪs] adj innecesario; **~
to say** huelga decir que

needlework ['ni:dlwə:k] n (*activity*)
costura, labor f de aguja

needn't ['ni:dnt] = **need not**

needy ['ni:dɪ] adj necesitado

negative ['nɛgətɪv] n (*Phot*)
negativo; (*Ling*) negación f ▷ adj
negativo

neglect [nɪ'glɛkt] vt (*one's duty*) faltar
a, no cumplir con; (*child*) descuidar,
desatender ▷ n (*of house, garden etc*)
abandono; (*of child*) desatención f; (*of
duty*) incumplimiento

negotiate [nɪ'gəuʃɪeɪt] vt (*treaty,
loan*) negociar; (*obstacle*) franquear;
(*bend in road*) tomar ▷ vi: **to ~ (with)**
negociar (con)

negotiations [nɪgəuʃɪ'eɪʃənz] pl n
negociaciones

negotiator [nɪ'gəuʃɪeɪtə*] n
negociador(a) m/f

neighbour ['neɪbə*] (*US* **neighbor** *etc*)
n vecino/a; **neighbourhood** n (*place*)
vecindad f, barrio; (*people*) vecindario;
neighbouring adj vecino

neither ['naɪðə*] adj ni ▷ conj: **I
didn't move and ~ did John** no me
he movido, ni Juan tampoco ▷ pron
ninguno ▷ adv: **~ good nor bad** ni
bueno ni malo; **~ is true** ninguno/a de
los(las) dos es cierto/a

neon ['ni:ɔn] n neón m

Nepal [nɪ'pɔ:l] n Nepal m

nephew ['nɛvju:] n sobrino

nerve [nə:v] n (*Anat*) nervio; (*courage*)
valor m; (*impudence*) descaro, frescura

(*nervousness*) nerviosismo msg, nervios
mpl; **a fit of ~s** un ataque de nervios

nervous ['nə:vəs] adj (*anxious, Anat*)
nervioso; (*timid*) tímido, miedoso;
nervous breakdown n crisis f
nerviosa

nest [nɛst] n (*of bird*) nido; (*wasps'
nest*) avispero ▷ vi anidar

net [nɛt] n (*gen*) red f; (*fabric*) tul m
▷ adj (*Comm*) neto, líquido ▷ vt coger
(*SP*) or agarrar (*LAM*) con red; (*Sport*)
marcar; **netball** n balonred m

Netherlands ['nɛðələndz] npl: **the ~**
los Países Bajos

nett [nɛt] adj = **net**

nettle ['nɛtl] n ortiga

network ['nɛtwə:k] n red f

neurotic [njuə'rɔtɪk] adj neurótico/a

neuter ['nju:tə*] adj (*Ling*) neutro
▷ vt castrar, capar

neutral ['nju:trəl] adj (*person*)
neutral; (*colour etc, Elec*) neutro ▷ n
(*Aut*) punto muerto

never ['nɛvə*] adv nunca, jamás;
I ~ went no fui nunca; **~ in my life**
jamás en la vida; *see also* **mind**; **never-
ending** adj interminable, sin fin;
nevertheless [nɛvəðə'lɛs] adv sin
embargo, no obstante

new [nju:] adj nuevo; (*brand new*) a
estrenar; (*recent*) reciente; **New Age**
n Nueva Era; **newborn** adj recién
nacido; **newcomer** ['nju:kʌmə*] n
recién venido/a or llegado/a; **newly**
adv nuevamente, recién

news [nju:z] n noticias fpl; **a piece
of ~** una noticia; **the ~** (*Radio, TV*) las
noticias fpl; **news agency** n agencia
de noticias; **newsagent** (*BRIT*) n
vendedor(a) m/f de periódicos;
newscaster n presentador(a) m/f,
locutor(a) m/f; **news dealer** (*US*) n
= **newsagent**; **newsletter** n hoja
informativa, boletín m; **newspaper**
n periódico, diario; **newsreader** n =
newscaster

newt [nju:t] n tritón m

New Year n Año Nuevo; **New Year's**

Day n Día m de Año Nuevo; **New Year's Eve** n Nochevieja

New Zealand [njuː'ziːlənd] n Nueva Zelanda; **New Zealander** n neozelandés/esa m/f

next [nɛkst] adj (house, room) vecino; (bus stop, meeting) próximo; (following: page etc) siguiente ▷ adv después; **the ~ day** el día siguiente; **~ time** la próxima vez; **~ year** el año próximo or que viene; **~ to** junto a, al lado de; **~ to nothing** casi nada; **~ please!** ¡el siguiente!; **next door** adv en la casa de al lado ▷ adj vecino, de al lado; **next-of-kin** n pariente m más cercano

NHS n abbr = **National Health Service**

nibble ['nɪbl] vt mordisquear, mordiscar

nice [naɪs] adj (likeable) simpático; (kind) amable; (pleasant) agradable; (attractive) bonito, lindo (LAM); **nicely** adv amablemente; bien

niche [niːʃ] n (Arch) nicho, hornacina

nick [nɪk] n (wound) rasguño; (cut, indentation) mella, muesca ▷ vt (inf) birlar, robar; **in the ~ of time** justo a tiempo

nickel ['nɪkl] n níquel m; (US) moneda de 5 centavos

nickname ['nɪkneɪm] n apodo, mote m ▷ vt apodar

nicotine ['nɪkətiːn] n nicotina

niece [niːs] n sobrina

Nigeria [naɪ'dʒɪərɪə] n Nigeria

night [naɪt] n noche f; (evening) tarde f; **the ~ before last** anteanoche; **at ~, by ~** de noche, por la noche; **night club** n cabaret m; **nightdress** (BRIT) n camisón m; **nightie** ['naɪtɪ] n = **nightdress**; **nightlife** n vida nocturna; **nightly** adj de todas las noches ▷ adv todas las noches, cada noche; **nightmare** n pesadilla; **night school** n clase(s) f(pl) nocturna(s); **night shift** n turno nocturno or de noche; **night-time** n noche f

nil [nɪl] (BRIT) n (Sport) cero, nada

nine [naɪn] num nueve; **nineteen** num diecinueve, diez y nueve; **nineteenth** [naɪn'tiːnθ] adj decimonoveno, decimonono; **ninetieth** ['naɪntɪɪθ] adj nonagésimo; **ninety** num noventa

ninth [naɪnθ] adj noveno

nip [nɪp] vt (pinch) pellizcar; (bite) morder

nipple ['nɪpl] n (Anat) pezón m

nitrogen ['naɪtrədʒən] n nitrógeno

○ **KEYWORD**

no [nəu] (pl **noes**) adv (opposite of "yes") no; **are you coming? – no (I'm not)** ¿vienes? – no; **would you like some more? – no thank you** ¿quieres más? – no gracias ▷ adj (not any): **I have no money/time/books** no tengo dinero/tiempo/libros; **no other man would have done it** ningún otro lo hubiera hecho; **"no entry"** "prohibido el paso"; **"no smoking"** "prohibido fumar" ▷ n no m

nobility [nəu'bɪlɪtɪ] n nobleza

noble ['nəubl] adj noble

nobody ['nəubədɪ] pron nadie

nod [nɔd] vi saludar con la cabeza; (in agreement) decir que sí con la cabeza; (doze) dar cabezadas ▷ vt: **to ~ one's head** inclinar la cabeza ▷ n inclinación f de cabeza; **nod off** vi dar cabezadas

noise [nɔɪz] n ruido; (din) escándalo, estrépito; **noisy** adj ruidoso; (child) escandaloso

nominal ['nɔmɪnl] adj nominal

nominate ['nɔmɪneɪt] vt (propose) proponer; (appoint) nombrar; **nomination** [nɔmɪ'neɪʃən] n propuesta; nombramiento; **nominee** [-'niː] n candidato/a

none [nʌn] pron ninguno/a ▷ adv de ninguna manera; **~ of you** ninguno de vosotros; **I've ~ left** no me queda ninguno/a; **he's ~ the worse for it** no le ha hecho ningún mal

nonetheless [nʌnðə'les] *adv* sin embargo, no obstante

non-fiction [nɔn'fɪkʃən] *n* literatura no novelesca

nonsense ['nɔnsəns] *n* tonterías *fpl*, disparates *fpl*; **~!** ¡qué tonterías!

non: **non-smoker** *n* no fumador(a) *m/f*; **non-smoking** *adj* (de) no fumador; **non-stick** *adj* (*pan, surface*) antiadherente

noodles ['nu:dlz] *npl* tallarines *mpl*

noon [nu:n] *n* mediodía *m*

no-one ['nəuwʌn] *pron* =**nobody**

nor [nɔ:*] *conj* =**neither** ▷ *adv see* **neither**

norm [nɔ:m] *n* norma

normal ['nɔ:ml] *adj* normal; **normally** *adv* normalmente

north [nɔ:θ] *n* norte *m* ▷ *adj* del norte, norteño ▷ *adv* al or hacia el norte; **North America** *n* América del Norte; **North American** *adj, n* norteamericano/a *m/f*; **northbound** ['nɔ:θbaund] *adj* (*traffic*) que se dirige al norte; (*carriageway*) de dirección norte; **north-east** *n* nor(d)este *m*; **northeastern** *adj* nor(d)este, del nor(d)este; **northern** ['nɔ:ðən] *adj* norteño, del norte; **Northern Ireland** *n* Irlanda del Norte; **North Korea** *n* Corea del Norte; **North Pole** *n* Polo Norte; **North Sea** *n* Mar *m* del Norte; **north-west** *n* nor(d)oeste *m*; **northwestern** ['nɔ:θ'westən] *adj* noroeste, del noroeste

Norway ['nɔ:wei] *n* Noruega; **Norwegian** [-'wi:dʒən] *adj* noruego/a ▷ *n* noruego/a; (*Ling*) noruego

nose [nəuz] *n* (*Anat*) nariz *f*; (*Zool*) hocico; (*sense of smell*) olfato ▷ *vi*: **to ~ about** curiosear; **nosebleed** *n* hemorragia nasal; **nosey** (*inf*) *adj* curioso, fisgón/ona

nostalgia [nɔs'tældʒiə] *n* nostalgia

nostalgic [nɔs'tældʒik] *adj* nostálgico

nostril ['nɔstril] *n* ventana de la nariz

nosy ['nəuzi] (*inf*) *adj* =**nosey**

not [nɔt] *adv* no; **~ that ...** no es que ...; **it's too late, isn't it?** es demasiado tarde, ¿verdad *or* no?; **~ yet/now** todavía/ahora no; **why ~?** ¿por qué no?; *see also* **all**; **only**

notable ['nəutəbl] *adj* notable; **notably** *adv* especialmente

notch [nɔtʃ] *n* muesca, corte *m*

note [nəut] *n* (*Mus, record, letter*) nota; (*banknote*) billete *m*; (*tone*) tono ▷ *vt* (*observe*) notar, observar; (*write down*) apuntar, anotar; **notebook** *n* libreta, cuaderno; **noted** ['nəutid] *adj* célebre, conocido; **notepad** *n* bloc *m*; **notepaper** *n* papel *m* para cartas

nothing ['nʌθiŋ] *n* nada; (*zero*) cero; **he does ~** no hace nada; **~ new** nada nuevo; **~ much** no mucho; **for ~** (*free*) gratis, sin pago; (*in vain*) en balde

notice ['nəutis] *n* (*announcement*) anuncio; (*warning*) aviso; (*dismissal*) despido; (*resignation*) dimisión *f*; (*period of time*) plazo ▷ *vt* (*observe*) notar, observar; **to bring sth to sb's ~** (*attention*) llamar la atención de algn sobre algo; **to take ~ of** tomar nota de, prestar atención a; **at short ~** con poca anticipación; **until further ~** hasta nuevo aviso; **to hand in one's ~** dimitir

⚠ Be careful not to translate **notice** by the Spanish word *noticia*.

noticeable *adj* evidente, obvio

notify ['nəutifai] *vt*: **to ~ sb (of sth)** comunicar (algo) a algn

notion ['nəuʃən] *n* idea; (*opinion*) opinión *f*; **notions** *npl* (*US*) mercería

notorious [nəu'tɔ:riəs] *adj* notorio

notwithstanding [nɔtwiθ'stændiŋ] *adv* no obstante, sin embargo; **~ this** a pesar de esto

nought [nɔ:t] *n* cero

noun [naun] *n* nombre *m*, sustantivo

nourish ['nʌriʃ] *vt* nutrir; (*fig*) alimentar; **nourishment** *n* alimento, sustento

Nov. *abbr* (= *November*) nov

novel ['nɔvl] *n* novela ▷ *adj* (*new*)

nuevo, original; (*unexpected*) insólito;
novelist *n* novelista *mf*; **novelty** *n*
novedad *f*
November [nəu'vɛmbə*] *n*
noviembre *m*
novice ['nɔvɪs] *n* (*Rel*) novicio/a
now [nau] *adv* (*at the present time*)
ahora; (*these days*) actualmente, hoy
día ▷ *conj*: **~ (that)** ya que, ahora que;
right ~ ahora mismo; **by ~** ya; **just
~** ahora mismo; **~ and then, ~ and
again** de vez en cuando; **from ~ on** de
ahora en adelante; **nowadays** ['nauə
deɪz] *adv* hoy (en) día, actualmente
nowhere ['nəuwɛə*] *adv* (*direction*)
a ninguna parte; (*location*) en ninguna
parte
nozzle ['nɔzl] *n* boquilla
nr *abbr* (*BRIT*) = **near**
nuclear ['nju:klɪə*] *adj* nuclear
nucleus ['nju:klɪəs] (*pl* **nuclei**) *n*
núcleo
nude [nju:d] *adj, n* desnudo/a *m/f*; **in
the ~** desnudo
nudge [nʌdʒ] *vt* dar un codazo a
nudist ['nju:dɪst] *n* nudista *mf*
nudity ['nju:dɪtɪ] *n* desnudez *f*
nuisance ['nju:sns] *n* molestia,
fastidio; (*person*) pesado, latoso; **what
a ~!** ¡qué lata!
numb [nʌm] *adj*: **~ with cold/fear**
entumecido por el frío/paralizado
de miedo
number ['nʌmbə*] *n* número;
(*quantity*) cantidad *f* ▷ *vt* (*pages etc*)
numerar, poner número a; (*amount to*)
sumar, ascender a; **to be ~ed among**
figurar entre; **a ~ of** varios, algunos;
they were ten in ~ eran diez; **number
plate** (*BRIT*) *n* matrícula, placa;
Number Ten *n* (*BRIT*: 10 *Downing
Street*) residencia del primer ministro
numerical [nju:'mɛrɪkl] *adj*
numérico
numerous ['nju:mərəs] *adj*
numeroso
nun [nʌn] *n* monja, religiosa
nurse [nə:s] *n* enfermero/a; (*also*:

~maid) niñera ▷ *vt* (*patient*) cuidar,
atender
nursery ['nə:sərɪ] *n* (*institution*)
guardería infantil; (*room*) cuarto de los
niños; (*for plants*) criadero, semillero;
nursery rhyme *n* canción *f* infantil;
nursery school *n* parvulario, escuela
de párvulos; **nursery slope** (*BRIT*) *n*
(*Ski*) cuesta para principiantes
nursing ['nə:sɪŋ] *n* (*profession*)
profesión *f* de enfermera; (*care*)
asistencia, cuidado; **nursing home** *n*
clínica de reposo
nurture ['nə:tʃə*] *vt* (*child, plant*)
alimentar, nutrir
nut [nʌt] *n* (*Tech*) tuerca; (*Bot*) nuez *f*
nutmeg ['nʌtmɛg] *n* nuez *f* moscada
nutrient ['nju:trɪənt] *adj* nutritivo
▷ *n* elemento nutritivo
nutrition [nju:'trɪʃən] *n* nutrición *f*,
alimentación *f*
nutritious [nju:'trɪʃəs] *adj* nutritivo,
alimenticio
nuts [nʌts] (*inf*) *adj* loco
NVQ *n abbr* (*BRIT*) = **National
Vocational Qualification**
nylon ['naɪlɔn] *n* nilón *m* ▷ *adj* de
nilón

O

oath [əuθ] *n* juramento; (*swear word*) palabrota; **on** (BRIT) *or* **under ~** bajo juramento

oak [əuk] *n* roble *m* ▷ *adj* de roble

O.A.P. (BRIT) *n, abbr* = **old-age pensioner**

oar [ɔː*] *n* remo

oasis [əu'eɪsɪs] (*pl* **oases**) *n* oasis *m inv*

oath [əuθ] *n* juramento; (*swear word*) palabrota; **on** (BRIT) *or* **under ~** bajo juramento

oatmeal ['əutmiːl] *n* harina de avena

oats [əuts] *npl* avena

obedience [ə'biːdɪəns] *n* obediencia

obedient [ə'biːdɪənt] *adj* obediente

obese [əu'biːs] *adj* obeso

obesity [əu'biːsɪtɪ] *n* obesidad *f*

obey [ə'beɪ] *vt* obedecer; (*instructions, regulations*) cumplir

obituary [ə'bɪtjuərɪ] *n* necrología

object [*n* 'ɔbdʒɪkt, *vb* əb'dʒɛkt] *n* objeto, cosa; (*purpose*) objeto, propósito; (*Ling*) complemento ▷ *vi*: **to ~ to** estar en contra de; (*proposal*) oponerse a; **to ~ that** objetar que; **expense is no**

~ no importa cuánto cuesta; **I ~!** ¡yo protesto!; **objection** [əb'dʒɛkʃən] *n* protesta; **I have no objection to ...** no tengo inconveniente en que ...; **objective** *adj, n* objetivo

obligation [ɔblɪ'geɪʃən] *n* obligación *f*; (*debt*) deber *m*; **without ~** sin compromiso

obligatory [ə'blɪgətərɪ] *adj* obligatorio

oblige [ə'blaɪdʒ] *vt* (*do a favour for*) complacer, hacer un favor a; **to ~ sb to do sth** forzar *or* obligar a algn a hacer algo; **to be ~d to sb for sth** estarle agradecido a algn por algo

oblique [ə'bliːk] *adj* oblicuo; (*allusion*) indirecto

obliterate [ə'blɪtəreɪt] *vt* borrar

oblivious [ə'blɪvɪəs] *adj*: **~ of** inconsciente de

oblong ['ɔblɔŋ] *adj* rectangular ▷ *n* rectángulo

obnoxious [əb'nɔkʃəs] *adj* odioso, detestable; (*smell*) nauseabundo

oboe ['əubəu] *n* oboe *m*

obscene [əb'siːn] *adj* obsceno

obscure [əb'skjuə*] *adj* oscuro ▷ *vt* oscurecer; (*hide: sun*) esconder

observant [əb'zəːvnt] *adj* observador(a)

observation [ɔbzə'veɪʃən] *n* observación *f*; (*Med*) examen *m*

observatory [əb'zəːvətrɪ] *n* observatorio

observe [əb'zəːv] *vt* observar; (*rule*) cumplir; **observer** *n* observador(a) *m/f*

obsess [əb'sɛs] *vt* obsesionar; **obsession** [əb'sɛʃən] *n* obsesión *f*; **obsessive** *adj* obsesivo; obsesionante

obsolete ['ɔbsəliːt] *adj*: **to be ~** estar en desuso

obstacle ['ɔbstəkl] *n* obstáculo; (*nuisance*) estorbo

obstinate ['ɔbstɪnɪt] *adj* terco, porfiado; (*determined*) obstinado

obstruct [əb'strʌkt] *vt* obstruir; (*hinder*) estorbar, obstaculizar; **obstruction** [əb'strʌkʃən] *n* (*action*)

obstrucción f; (object) estorbo, obstáculo
obtain [əb'teɪn] vt obtener; (achieve)
conseguir
obvious ['ɔbvɪəs] adj obvio, evidente;
obviously adv evidentemente,
naturalmente; **obviously not** por
supuesto que no
occasion [ə'keɪʒən] n oportunidad
f, ocasión f; (event) acontecimiento;
occasional adj poco frecuente,
ocasional; **occasionally** adv de vez
en cuando
occult [ɔ'kʌlt] adj (gen) oculto
occupant ['ɔkjupənt] n (of house)
inquilino/a; (of car) ocupante mf
occupation [ɔkju'peɪʃən] n
ocupación f; (job) trabajo; (pastime)
ocupaciones fpl
occupy ['ɔkjupaɪ] vt (seat, post, time)
ocupar; (house) habitar; **to o.s. in
doing** pasar el tiempo haciendo
occur [ə'kə:*] vi pasar, suceder; **to ~
to sb** ocurrírsele a algn; **occurrence**
[ə'kʌrəns] n acontecimiento;
(existence) existencia
ocean ['əuʃən] n océano
o'clock [ə'klɔk] adv: **it is 5 ~** son las 5
Oct. abbr (= October) oct
October [ɔk'təubə*] n octubre m
octopus ['ɔktəpəs] n pulpo
odd [ɔd] adj extraño, raro; (number)
impar; (sock, shoe etc) suelto; **60-~** 60 y
pico; **at ~ times** de vez en cuando; **to
be the ~ one out** estar de más; **oddly**
adv curiosamente, extrañamente;
see also **enough**; **odds** npl (in betting)
puntos mpl de ventaja; **it makes no
odds** da lo mismo; **at odds** reñidos/as;
odds and ends minucias fpl
odometer [ɔ'dɔmɪtə*] (us) n
cuentakilómetros m inv
odour ['əudə*] (us **odor**) n olor m;
(unpleasant) hedor m

○ **KEYWORD**

of [ɔv, əv] prep **1** (gen) de; **a friend of
ours** un amigo nuestro; **a boy of 10** un

chico de 10 años; **that was kind of you**
eso fue muy amable por or de tu parte
2 (expressing quantity, amount, dates
etc) de; **a kilo of flour** un kilo de
harina; **there were three of them**
había tres; **three of us went** tres de
nosotros fuimos; **the 5th of July** el
5 de julio
3 (from, out of) de; **made of wood**
(hecho) de madera

off [ɔf] adj, adv (engine) desconectado;
(light) apagado; (tap) cerrado;
(BRIT: food: bad) pasado, malo; (: milk)
cortado; (cancelled) cancelado ▷ prep
de; **to be ~** (to leave) irse, marcharse;
to be ~ sick estar enfermo or de baja;
a day ~ un día libre or sin trabajar; **to
have an ~ day** tener un día malo; **he
had his coat ~** se había quitado el
abrigo; **10% ~** (Comm) (con el) 10% de
descuento; **5 km ~ (the road)** a 5 km
(de la carretera); **~ the coast** frente a la
costa; **I'm ~ meat** (no longer eat/like it)
paso de la carne; **on the ~ chance** por
si acaso; **~ and on** de vez en cuando
offence [ə'fɛns] (us **offense**) n (crime)
delito; **to take ~ at** ofenderse por
offend [ə'fɛnd] vt (person) ofender;
offender n delincuente mf
offense [ə'fɛns] (us) n = **offence**
offensive [ə'fɛnsɪv] adj ofensivo;
(smell etc) repugnante ▷ n (Mil)
ofensiva
offer ['ɔfə*] n oferta, ofrecimiento;
(proposal) propuesta ▷ vt ofrecer;
(opportunity) facilitar; **"on ~"** (Comm)
"en oferta"
offhand [ɔf'hænd] adj informal ▷ adv
de improviso
office ['ɔfɪs] n (place) oficina; (room)
despacho; (position) carga, oficio;
doctor's ~ (us) consultorio; **to take
~** entrar en funciones; **office block**
(us), **office building** n bloque m de
oficinas; **office hours** npl horas fpl de
oficina; (us Med) horas fpl de consulta
officer ['ɔfɪsə*] n (Mil etc) oficial mf;

(also: **police ~**) agente mf de policía; (of organization) director(a) m/f

office worker n oficinista mf

official [ə'fɪʃl] adj oficial, autorizado ▷ n funcionario/a, oficial mf

off: off-licence (BRIT) n (shop) bodega tienda de vinos y bebidas alcohólicas; **off-line** adj, adv (Comput) fuera de línea; **off-peak** adj (electricity) de banda económica; (ticket) billete de precio reducido por viajar fuera de las horas punta; **off-putting** (BRIT) adj (person) asqueroso; (remark) desalentador(a); **off-season** adj, adv fuera de temporada

● **OFF-LICENCE**
●
● En el Reino Unido la venta
● de bebidas alcohólicas está
● estrictamente regulada
● y se necesita una licencia
● especial, con la que cuentan
● los bares, restaurantes y los
● establecimientos de **off-licence**,
● los únicos lugares en donde
● se pueden adquirir bebidas
● alcohólicas para su consumo
● fuera del local, de donde viene
● su nombre. También venden
● bebidas no alcohólicas, tabaco,
● chocolatinas, patatas fritas, etc.
● y a menudo forman parte de una
● cadena nacional.

offset ['ɔfsɛt] vt contrarrestar, compensar

offshore [ɔf'ʃɔː*] adj (breeze, island) costera; (fishing) de bajura

offside ['ɔf'saɪd] adj (Sport) fuera de juego; (Aut: in UK) del lado derecho; (: in US, Europe etc) del lado izquierdo

offspring ['ɔfsprɪŋ] n inv descendencia

often ['ɔfn] adv a menudo, con frecuencia; **how ~ do you go?** ¿cada cuánto vas?

oh [əu] excl ¡ah!

oil [ɔɪl] n aceite m; (petroleum) petróleo; (for heating) aceite m combustible ▷ vt engrasar; **oil filter** n (Aut) filtro de aceite; **oil painting** n pintura al óleo; **oil refinery** n refinería de petróleo; **oil rig** n torre f de perforación; **oil slick** n marea negra; **oil tanker** n petrolero; (truck) camión m cisterna; **oil well** n pozo (de petróleo); **oily** adj aceitoso; (food) grasiento

ointment ['ɔɪntmənt] n ungüento

O.K., okay ['əu'keɪ] excl ¡O.K.!, ¡está bien!, ¡vale! (SP) ▷ adj bien ▷ vt dar el visto bueno a

old [əuld] adj viejo; (former) antiguo; **how ~ are you?** ¿cuántos años tienes?, ¿qué edad tienes?; **he's 10 years ~** tiene 10 años; **~er brother** hermano mayor; **old age** n vejez f; **old-age pension** n (BRIT) jubilación f, pensión f; **old-age pensioner** (BRIT) n jubilado/a; **old-fashioned** adj anticuado, pasado de moda; **old people's home** n (esp BRIT) residencia f de ancianos

olive ['ɔlɪv] n (fruit) aceituna; (tree) olivo ▷ adj (also: **~-green**) verde oliva; **olive oil** n aceite m de oliva

Olympic [əu'lɪmpɪk] adj olímpico; **the ~ Games, the ~s** las Olimpiadas

omelet(te) ['ɔmlɪt] n tortilla francesa (SP), omelette f (LAM)

omen ['əumən] n presagio

ominous ['ɔmɪnəs] adj de mal agüero, amenazador(a)

omit [əu'mɪt] vt omitir

○ **KEYWORD**

on [ɔn] prep **1** (indicating position) en; sobre; **on the wall** en la pared; **it's on the table** está sobre or en la mesa; **on the left** a la izquierda
2 (indicating means, method, condition etc): **on foot** a pie; **on the train/**

plane (go) en tren/avión; (be) en el tren/el avión; **on the radio/television/telephone** por or en la radio/televisión/al teléfono; **to be on drugs** drogarse; (Med) estar a tratamiento; **to be on holiday/business** estar de vacaciones/en viaje de negocios
3 (referring to time): **on Friday** el viernes; **on Fridays** los viernes; **on June 20th** el 20 de junio; **a week on Friday** del viernes en una semana; **on arrival** al llegar; **on seeing this** al ver esto
4 (about, concerning) sobre, acerca de; **a book on physics** un libro de or sobre física
▷ adv **1** (referring to dress): **to have one's coat on** tener or llevar el abrigo puesto; **she put her gloves on** se puso los guantes
2 (referring to covering): **"screw the lid on tightly"** "cerrar bien la tapa"
3 (further, continuously): **to walk** etc **on** seguir caminando etc
▷ adj **1** (functioning, in operation: machine, radio, TV, light) encendido/a (SP), prendido/a (LAM); (: tap) abierto/a; (: brakes) echado/a, puesto/a; **is the meeting still on?** (in progress) ¿todavía continúa la reunión?; (not cancelled) ¿va a haber reunión al fin?; **there's a good film on at the cinema** ponen una buena película en el cine
2 **that's not on!** (inf: not possible) ¡eso ni hablar!; (: not acceptable) ¡eso no se hace!

once [wʌns] adv una vez; (formerly) antiguamente ▷ conj una vez que; **~ he had left/it was done** una vez que se había marchado/se hizo; **at ~** en seguida, inmediatamente; (simultaneously) a la vez; **~ a week** una vez por semana; **~ more** otra vez; **~ and for all** de una vez por todas; **~ upon a time** érase una vez
oncoming [ˈɒnkʌmɪŋ] adj (traffic)

que viene de frente

⊙ **KEYWORD**

one [wʌn] num uɾi(ʊ)/una; **one hundred and fifty** ciento cincuenta; **one by one** uno a uno
▷ adj **1** (sole) único; **the one book which** el único libro que; **the one man who** el único que
2 (same) mismo/a; **they came in the one car** vinieron en un solo coche
▷ pron **1** **this one** éste(ésta); **that one** ése(ésa); (more remote) aquél(aquella); **I've already got (a red) one** ya tengo uno/a rojo/a; **one by one** uno/a por uno/a
2 **one another** os (SP), se (+ el uno al otro, unos a otros etc); **do you two ever see one another?** ¿vosotros dos os veis alguna vez? (SP), ¿se ven ustedes dos alguna vez?; **the boys didn't dare look at one another** los chicos no se atrevieron a mirarse (el uno al otro); **they all kissed one another** se besaron unos a otros
3 (impers): **one never knows** nunca se sabe; **to cut one's finger** cortarse el dedo; **one needs to eat** hay que comer
one-off (BRIT: inf) n (event) acontecimiento único

oneself [wʌnˈsɛlf] pron (reflexive) se; (after prep) sí; (emphatic) uno/a mismo/a; **to hurt ~** hacerse daño; **to keep sth for ~** guardarse algo; **to talk to ~** hablar solo
one: one-shot [wʌnˈʃɒt] (US) n =**one-off**; **one-sided** adj (argument) parcial; **one-to-one** adj (relationship) de dos; **one-way** adj (street) de sentido único
ongoing [ˈɒngəʊɪŋ] adj continuo
onion [ˈʌnjən] n cebolla
on-line [ˈɒnlaɪn] adj, adv (Comput) en línea
onlooker [ˈɒnlʊkə*] n espectador(a) m/f

only ['əʊnlɪ] *adv* solamente, sólo ▷ *adj* único, solo ▷ *conj* solamente que, pero; **an ~ child** un hijo único; **not ~ ... but also ...** no sólo ... sino también ...

on-screen [ɒn'skriːn] *adj* (*Comput etc*) en pantalla; (*romance, kiss*) cinematográfico

onset ['ɒnsɛt] *n* comienzo

onto ['ɒntʊ] *prep* = **on to**

onward(s) ['ɒnwəd(z)] *adv* (*move*) (hacia) adelante; **from that time ~** desde entonces en adelante

oops [ʊps] *excl* (*also*: **~-a-daisy!**) ¡huy!

ooze [uːz] *vi* rezumar

opaque [əʊ'peɪk] *adj* opaco

open ['əʊpn] *adj* abierto; (*car*) descubierto; (*road, view*) despejado; (*meeting*) público; (*admiration*) manifiesto ▷ *vt* abrir ▷ *vi* abrirse; (*book etc: commence*) comenzar; **in the ~ (air)** al aire libre; **open up** *vt* abrir; (*blocked road*) despejar ▷ *vi* abrirse, empezar; **open-air** *adj* al aire libre; **opening** *n* abertura; (*start*) comienzo; (*opportunity*) oportunidad *f*; **opening hours** *npl* horario de apertura; **open learning** *n* enseñanza flexible a tiempo parcial; **openly** *adv* abiertamente; **open-minded** *adj* imparcial; **open-necked** *adj* (*shirt*) desabrochado; sin corbata; **open-plan** *adj*: **open-plan office** gran oficina sin particiones; **Open University** *n* (BRIT) ≈ Universidad *f* Nacional de Enseñanza a Distancia, UNED *f*

opera ['ɒpərə] *n* ópera; **opera house** *n* teatro de la ópera; **opera singer** *n* cantante *m/f* de ópera

operate ['ɒpəreɪt] *vt* (*machine*) hacer funcionar; (*company*) dirigir ▷ *vi* funcionar; **to ~ on sb** (*Med*) operar a algn

operating room ['ɒpəreɪtɪŋ-] (US) *n* quirófano, sala de operaciones

operating theatre (BRIT) *n* sala de operaciones

operation [ɒpə'reɪʃən] *n* operación *f*; (*of machine*) funcionamiento; **to be in ~** estar funcionando *or* en funcionamiento; **to have an ~** (*Med*) ser operado; **operational** *adj* operacional, en buen estado

operative ['ɒpərətɪv] *adj* en vigor

operator ['ɒpəreɪtə*] *n* (*of machine*) maquinista *mf*, operario/a; (*Tel*) operador(a) *m/f*, telefonista *mf*

opinion [ə'pɪnɪən] *n* opinión *f*; **in my ~** en mi opinión, a mi juicio; **opinion poll** *n* encuesta, sondeo

opponent [ə'pəʊnənt] *n* adversario/a, contrincante *mf*

opportunity [ɒpə'tjuːnɪtɪ] *n* oportunidad *f*; **to take the ~ of doing** aprovechar la ocasión para hacer

oppose [ə'pəʊz] *vt* oponerse a; **to be ~d to sth** oponerse a algo; **as ~d to** a diferencia de

opposite ['ɒpəzɪt] *adj* opuesto, contrario a; (*house etc*) de enfrente ▷ *adv* en frente ▷ *prep* en frente de, frente a ▷ *n* lo contrario

opposition [ɒpə'zɪʃən] *n* oposición *f*

oppress [ə'prɛs] *vt* oprimir

opt [ɒpt] *vi*: **to ~ for** optar por; **to ~ to do** optar por hacer; **opt out** *vi*: **to opt out of** optar por no hacer

optician [ɒp'tɪʃən] *n* óptico *m/f*

optimism ['ɒptɪmɪzəm] *n* optimismo

optimist ['ɒptɪmɪst] *n* optimista *mf*;

optimistic [-'mɪstɪk] *adj* optimista
optimum ['ɔptɪməm] *adj* óptimo
option ['ɔpʃən] *n* opción *f*; **optional**
adj facultativo, discrecional
or [ɔː*] *conj* o; (*before o, ho*) u; (*with
negative*): **he hasn't seen ~ heard
anything** no ha visto ni oído nada; **~
else** si no
oral ['ɔːrəl] *adj* oral ▷ *n* examen *m* oral
orange ['ɔrɪndʒ] *n* (*fruit*) naranja
▷ *adj* color naranja; **orange juice** *n*
jugo *m* de naranja, zumo *m* de naranja
(*SP*); **orange squash** *n* naranjada
orbit ['ɔːbɪt] *n* órbita ▷ *vt*, *vi* orbitar
orchard ['ɔːtʃəd] *n* huerto
orchestra ['ɔːkɪstrə] *n* orquesta;
(*US: seating*) platea
orchid ['ɔːkɪd] *n* orquídea
ordeal [ɔː'diːl] *n* experiencia
horrorosa
order ['ɔːdə*] *n* orden *m*; (*command*)
orden *f*; (*good order*) buen estado;
(*Comm*) pedido ▷ *vt* (*also*: **put in ~**)
arreglar, poner en orden; (*Comm*)
pedir; (*command*) mandar, ordenar;
in ~ en orden; (*of document*) en regla;
in (working) ~ en funcionamiento;
in ~ to do/that para hacer/que;
on ~ (*Comm*) pedido; **to be out of ~**
estar desordenado; (*not working*) no
funcionar; **to ~ sb to do sth** mandar
a algn hacer algo; **order form** *n* hoja
de pedido; **orderly** *n* (*Mil*) ordenanza
m; (*Med*) enfermero/a (auxiliar) ▷ *adj*
ordenado
ordinary ['ɔːdnrɪ] *adj* corriente,
normal; (*pej*) común y corriente; **out of
the ~** fuera de lo común
ore [ɔː*] *n* mineral *m*
oregano [ɔrɪ'gɑːnəʊ] *n* orégano
organ ['ɔːgən] *n* órgano; **organic**
[ɔː'gænɪk] *adj* orgánico; **organism** *n*
organismo
organization [ɔːgənaɪ'zeɪʃən] *n*
organización *f*
organize ['ɔːgənaɪz] *vt* organizar;
organized ['ɔːgənaɪzd] *adj*
organizado; **organizer** *n*

organizador(a) *m/f*
orgasm ['ɔːgæzəm] *n* orgasmo
orgy ['ɔːdʒɪ] *n* orgía
oriental [ɔːrɪ'ɛntl] *adj* oriental
orientation [ɔːrɪen'teɪʃən] *n*
orientación *f*
origin ['ɔrɪdʒɪn] *n* origen *m*
original [ə'rɪdʒɪnl] *adj* original; (*first*)
primero; (*earlier*) primitivo ▷ *n* original
m; **originally** *adv* al principio
originate [ə'rɪdʒɪneɪt] *vi*: **to ~ from,
to ~ in** surgir de, tener su origen en
Orkneys ['ɔːknɪz] *npl*: **the ~** (*also*: **the
Orkney Islands**) las Orcadas
ornament ['ɔːnəmənt] *n* adorno;
(*trinket*) chuchería; **ornamental**
[-'mɛntl] *adj* decorativo, de adorno
ornate [ɔː'neɪt] *adj* muy ornado,
vistoso
orphan ['ɔːfn] *n* huérfano/a
orthodox ['ɔːθədɔks] *adj* ortodoxo
orthopaedic [ɔːθə'piːdɪk] (*US*
orthopedic) *adj* ortopédico
osteopath ['ɔstɪəpæθ] *n* osteópata
mf
ostrich ['ɔstrɪtʃ] *n* avestruz *m*
other ['ʌðə*] *adj* otro ▷ *pron*: **the ~
(one)** el(la) otro/a ▷ *adv*: **~ than** aparte
de; **otherwise** *adv* de otra manera
▷ *conj* (*if not*) si no
otter ['ɔtə*] *n* nutria
ouch [autʃ] *excl* ¡ay!
ought [ɔːt] (*pt* **~**) *aux vb*: **I ~ to do
it** debería hacerlo; **this ~ to have
been corrected** esto debiera haberse
corregido; **he ~ to win** (*probability*)
debe *or* debiera ganar
ounce [auns] *n* onza (*28.35g*)
our ['auə*] *adj* nuestro; *see also* **my**;
ours *pron* (el) nuestro/(la) nuestra
etc; *see also* **mine**[1]; **ourselves** *pron pl*
(*reflexive, after prep*) nosotros; (*emphatic*)
nosotros mismos; *see also* **oneself**
oust [aust] *vt* desalojar
out [aut] *adv* fuera, afuera; (*not
at home*) fuera (de casa); (*light, fire*)
apagado; **~ there** allí (fuera); **he's ~**
(*absent*) no está, ha salido; **to be ~ in**

one's calculations equivocarse (en sus cálculos); **to run ~** salir corriendo; **~ loud** en alta voz; **~ of** (*outside*) fuera de; (*because of: anger etc*) por; **~ of petrol** sin gasolina; **"~ of order"** "no funciona"; **outback** n interior m; **outbound** adj (*flight*) de salida; (*flight: not return*) de ida; **outbreak** n (*of war*) comienzo; (*of disease*) epidemia; (*of violence etc*) ola; **outburst** n explosión f, arranque m; **outcast** n paria mf; **outcome** n resultado; **outcry** n protestas fpl; **outdated** adj anticuado, fuera de moda; **outdoor** adj exterior, de aire libre; (*clothes*) de calle; **outdoors** adv al aire libre

outer ['autə*] adj exterior, externo; **outer space** n espacio exterior

outfit ['autfit] n (*clothes*) conjunto

out: outgoing adj (*character*) extrovertido; (*retiring: president etc*) saliente; **outgoings** (BRIT) npl gastos mpl; **outhouse** n dependencia

outing ['autɪŋ] n excursión f, paseo

out: outlaw n proscrito ▷ vt proscribir; **outlay** n inversión f; **outlet** n salida; (*of pipe*) desagüe m; (*US Elec*) toma de corriente; (*also:* **retail outlet**) punto de venta; **outline** n (*shape*) contorno, perfil m; (*sketch, plan*) esbozo ▷ vt (*plan etc*) esbozar; **in outline** (*fig*) a grandes rasgos; **outlook** n (*fig: prospects*) perspectivas fpl; (*: for weather*) pronóstico; **outnumber** vt superar en número; **out-of-date** adj (*passport*) caducado; (*clothes*) pasado de moda; **out-of-doors** adv al aire libre; **out-of-the-way** adj apartado; **out-of-town** adj (*shopping centre etc*) en las afueras; **outpatient** n paciente mf externo/a; **outpost** n puesto avanzado; **output** n (*volumen* m de) producción m, rendimiento; (*Comput*) salida

outrage ['autreidʒ] n escándalo; (*atrocity*) atrocidad f ▷ vt ultrajar; **outrageous** [-'reidʒəs] adj monstruoso

outright [adv aut'rait, adj 'autrait] adv (*ask, deny*) francamente; (*refuse*) rotundamente; (*win*) de manera absoluta; (*be killed*) en el acto ▷ adj franco; rotundo

outset ['autset] n principio

outside [aut'said] n exterior m ▷ adj exterior, externo ▷ adv fuera ▷ prep fuera de; (*beyond*) más allá de; **at the ~** (*fig*) a lo sumo; **outside lane** n (*Aut: in Britain*) carril m de la derecha; (*: in US, Europe etc*) carril m de la izquierda; **outside line** n (*Tel*) línea (exterior); **outsider** n (*stranger*) extraño, forastero

out: outsize adj (*clothes*) de talla grande; **outskirts** npl alrededores mpl, afueras fpl; **outspoken** adj muy franco; **outstanding** adj excepcional, destacado; (*remaining*) pendiente

outward ['autwəd] adj externo; (*journey*) de ida; **outwards** adv (*esp* BRIT) = **outward**

outweigh [aut'wei] vt pesar más que

oval ['əuvl] adj ovalado ▷ n óvalo

ovary ['əuvəri] n ovario

oven ['ʌvn] n horno; **oven glove** n guante m para el horno, manopla para el horno; **ovenproof** adj resistente al horno; **oven-ready** adj listo para el horno

over ['əuvə*] adv encima, por encima ▷ adj or adv (*finished*) terminado; (*surplus*) de sobra ▷ prep (por) encima de; (*above*) sobre; (*on the other side of*) al otro lado de; (*more than*) más de; (*during*) durante; **~ here** (por) aquí; **~ there** (por) allí or allá; **all ~** (*everywhere*) por todas partes; **~ and ~ (again)** una y otra vez; **~ and above** además de; **to ask sb ~** invitar a algn a casa; **to bend ~** inclinarse

overall [adj, n 'əuvərɔːl, adv əuvər'ɔːl] adj (*length etc*) total; (*study*) de conjunto ▷ adv en conjunto ▷ n (BRIT) guardapolvo; **overalls** npl (*boiler suit*) mono (SP) or overol m (LAM) (de trabajo)

overboard adv (*Naut*) por la borda

o

overcame [əuvə'keɪm] *pt of*
overcome

overcast ['əuvəkɑ:st] *adj*
encapotado

overcharge [əuvə'tʃɑ:dʒ] *vt*: **to ~ sb**
cobrar un precio excesivo a algn

overcoat ['əuvəkəut] *n* abrigo,
sobretodo

overcome [əuvə'kʌm] *vt* vencer;
(*difficulty*) superar

over: **overcrowded** *adj* atestado de
gente; (*city, country*) superpoblado;
overdo (*irreg*) *vt* exagerar; (*overcook*)
cocer demasiado; **to overdo it** (*work
etc*) pasarse; **overdone** [əuvə'dʌn] *adj*
(*vegetables*) recocido; (*steak*) demasiado
hecho; **overdose** *n* sobredosis *f inv*;
overdraft *n* saldo deudor; **overdrawn**
adj (*account*) en descubierto; **overdue**
adj retrasado; **overestimate** *vt*
sobreestimar

overflow [*vb* əuvə'fləu, *n* 'əuvəfləu]
vi desbordarse ▷ *n* (*also*: **~ pipe**)
(cañería) desagüe *m*

overgrown [əuvə'grəun] *adj* (*garden*)
invadido por la vegetación

overhaul [*vb* əuvə'hɔ:l, *n* 'əuvəhɔ:l]
vt revisar, repasar ▷ *n* revisión *f*

overhead [*adv* əuvə'hɛd, *adj, n* 'əuvə
hɛd] *adv* por arriba *or* encima ▷ *adj*
(*cable*) aéreo ▷ *n* (*US*) = **overheads**;
overhead projector *n* retroproyector;
overheads *npl* (*expenses*) gastos *mpl*
generales

over: **overhear** (*irreg*) *vt* oír por
casualidad; **overheat** *vi* (*engine*)
recalentarse; **overland** *adj, adv*
por tierra; **overlap** [əuvə'læp] *vi*
traslaparse; **overleaf** *adv* al dorso;
overload *vt* sobrecargar; **overlook**
vt (*have view of*) dar a, tener vistas a;
(*miss: by mistake*) pasar por alto; (*excuse*)
perdonar

overnight [əuvə'naɪt] *adv* durante
la noche; (*fig*) de la noche a la mañana
▷ *adj* de noche; **to stay ~** pasar la
noche; **overnight bag** *n* fin *m* de
semana, neceser *m* de viaje

overpass (*US*) ['əuvəpɑ:s] *n* paso
superior

overpower [əuvə'pauə*]
vt dominar; (*fig*) embargar;
overpowering *adj* (*heat*) agobiante;
(*smell*) penetrante

over: **overreact** [əuvərɪ'ækt] *vi*
reaccionar de manera exagerada;
overrule *vt* (*decision*) anular; (*claim*)
denegar; **overrun** (*irreg*) *vt* (*country*)
invadir; (*time limit*) rebasar, exceder

overseas [əuvə'si:z] *adv* (*abroad: live*)
en el extranjero; (*travel*) al extranjero
▷ *adj* (*trade*) exterior; (*visitor*) extranjero

oversee [əuvə'si:] (*irreg*) *vt* supervisar

overshadow [əuvə'ʃædəu] *vt*: **to be
~ed by** estar a la sombra de

oversight ['əuvəsaɪt] *n* descuido

oversleep [əuvə'sli:p] (*irreg*) *vi*
quedarse dormido

overspend [əuvə'spɛnd] (*irreg*) *vi*
gastar más de la cuenta; **we have
overspent by 5 pounds** hemos
excedido el presupuesto en 5 libras

overt [əu'və:t] *adj* abierto

overtake [əuvə'teɪk] (*irreg*) *vt*
sobrepasar; (*BRIT Aut*) adelantar

over: **overthrow** (*irreg*) *vt* (*government*)
derrocar; **overtime** *n* horas *fpl*
extraordinarias

overtook [əuvə'tuk] *pt of* **overtake**

over: **overturn** *vt* tener, volcar; (*fig: plan*)
desbaratar; (: *government*) derrocar ▷ *vi*
volcar; **overweight** *adj* demasiado
gordo *or* pesado; **overwhelm** *vt*
aplastar; (*emotion*) sobrecoger;
overwhelming *adj* (*victory, defeat*)
arrollador(a); (*feeling*) irresistible

ow [au] *excl* ¡ay!

owe [əu] *vt*: **to ~ sb sth, to ~ sth to
sb** deber algo a algn; **owing to** *prep*
debido a, por causa de

owl [aul] *n* búho, lechuza

own [əun] *vt* tener, poseer ▷ *adj*
propio; **a room of my ~** una habitación
propia; **to get one's ~ back** tomar
revancha; **on one's ~** solo, a solas; **own
up** *vi* confesar; **owner** *n* dueño/a;

ownership *n* posesión *f*

ox [ɔks] (*pl* **~en**) *n* buey *m*

Oxbridge ['ɔksbrɪdʒ] *n* universidades de Oxford y Cambridge

oxen ['ɔksən] *npl of* **ox**

oxygen ['ɔksɪdʒən] *n* oxígeno

oyster ['ɔɪstə*] *n* ostra

oz. *abbr* = **ounce(s)**

ozone ['əuzəun] *n* ozono; **ozone friendly** *adj* que no daña la capa de ozono; **ozone layer** *n* capa *f* de ozono

p [piː] *abbr* = **penny; pence**

P.A. *n abbr* = **personal assistant; public address system**

p.a. *abbr* = **per annum**

pace [peɪs] *n* paso ▷ *vi*: **to ~ up and down** pasearse de un lado a otro; **to keep ~ with** llevar el mismo paso que; **pacemaker** *n* (*Med*) regulador *m* cardíaco, marcapasos *m inv*; (*Sport*: *also*: **pacesetter**) liebre *f*

Pacific [pə'sɪfɪk] *n*: **the ~ (Ocean)** el (Océano) Pacífico

pacifier ['pæsɪfaɪə*] (US) *n* (*dummy*) chupete *m*

pack [pæk] *n* (*packet*) paquete *m*; (*of hounds*) jauría; (*of people*) manada, bando; (*of cards*) baraja; (*bundle*) fardo; (US: *of cigarettes*) paquete *m*; (*back pack*) mochila ▷ *vt* (*fill*) llenar; (*in suitcase etc*) meter, poner; (*cram*) llenar, atestar; **to ~ (one's bags)** hacerse la maleta; **to ~ sb off** despachar a algn; **pack in** *vi* (*watch, car*) estropearse ▷ *vt* (*inf*) dejar; **pack it in!** ¡para!, ¡basta ya!; **pack up** *vi* (*inf*: *machine*) estropearse; (*person*) irse

▷ *vt* (*belongings, clothes*) recoger; (*goods, presents*) empaquetar, envolver

package ['pækɪdʒ] *n* paquete *m*; (*bulky*) bulto; (*also:* **~ deal**) acuerdo global; **package holiday** *n* vacaciones *fpl* organizadas; **package tour** *n* viaje *m* organizado

packaging ['pækɪdʒɪŋ] *n* envase *m*

packed [pækt] *adj* abarrotado; **packed lunch** *n* almuerzo frío

packet ['pækɪt] *n* paquete *m*

packing ['pækɪŋ] *n* embalaje *m*

pact [pækt] *n* pacto

pad [pæd] *n* (*of paper*) bloc *m*; (*cushion*) cojinete *m*; (*inf: home*) casa ▷ *vt* rellenar; **padded** *adj* (*jacket*) acolchado; (*bra*) reforzado

paddle ['pædl] *n* (*oar*) canalete *m*; (*us: for table tennis*) paleta ▷ *vt* impulsar con canalete ▷ *vi* (*with feet*) chapotear; **paddling pool** (*BRIT*) *n* estanque *m* de juegos

paddock ['pædək] *n* corral *m*

padlock ['pædlɔk] *n* candado

paedophile ['piːdəfaɪl] (*us* **pedophile**) *adj* de pedófilos ▷ *n* pedófilo/a

page [peɪdʒ] *n* (*of book*) página; (*of newspaper*) plana; (*also:* **~ boy**) paje *m* ▷ *vt* (*in hotel etc*) llamar por altavoz a

pager ['peɪdʒə*] *n* (*Tel*) busca *m*

paid [peɪd] *pt, pp of* **pay** ▷ *adj* (*work*) remunerado; (*holiday*) pagado; (*official etc*) a sueldo; **to put ~ to** (*BRIT*) acabar con

pain [peɪn] *n* dolor *m*; **to be in ~** sufrir; **to take ~s to do sth** tomarse grandes molestias en hacer algo; **painful** *adj* doloroso; (*difficult*) penoso; (*disagreeable*) desagradable; **painkiller** *n* analgésico; **painstaking** ['peɪnzteɪkɪŋ] *adj* (*person*) concienzudo, esmerado

paint [peɪnt] *n* pintura ▷ *vt* pintar; **to ~ the door blue** pintar la puerta de azul; **paintbrush** *n* (*of artist*) pincel *m*; (*of decorator*) brocha; **painter** *n* pintor(a) *m/f*; **painting** *n* pintura

pair [pɛə*] *n* (*of shoes, gloves etc*) par *m*; (*of people*) pareja; **a ~ of scissors** unas tijeras; **a ~ of trousers** unos pantalones, un pantalón

pajamas [pə'dʒɑːməz] (*us*) *npl* pijama *m*

Pakistan [pɑːkɪ'stɑːn] *n* Paquistán *m*; **Pakistani** *adj, n* paquistaní *mf*

pal [pæl] (*inf*) *n* compinche *mf*, compañero/a

palace ['pæləs] *n* palacio

pale [peɪl] *adj* (*gen*) pálido; (*colour*) claro ▷ *n*: **to be beyond the ~** pasarse de la raya

Palestine ['pælɪstaɪn] *n* Palestina; **Palestinian** [-'tɪnɪən] *adj, n* palestino/a *m/f*

palm [pɑːm] *n* (*Anat*) palma; (*also:* **~ tree**) palmera, palma ▷ *vt*: **to ~ sth off on sb** (*inf*) encajar algo a algn

pamper ['pæmpə*] *vt* mimar

pamphlet ['pæmflət] *n* folleto

pan [pæn] *n* (*also:* **sauce~**) cacerola, cazuela, olla; (*also:* **frying ~**) sartén *f*

pancake ['pænkeɪk] *n* crepe *f*

panda ['pændə] *n* panda *m*

pane [peɪn] *n* cristal *m*

panel ['pænl] *n* (*of wood etc*) panel *m*; (*Radio, TV*) panel *m* de invitados

panhandler ['pænhændlə*] (*us*) *n* (*inf*) mendigo/a

panic ['pænɪk] *n* terror *m* pánico ▷ *vi* dejarse llevar por el pánico

panorama [pænə'rɑːmə] *n* panorama *m*

pansy ['pænzɪ] *n* (*Bot*) pensamiento; (*inf, pej*) maricón *m*

pant [pænt] *vi* jadear

panther ['pænθə*] *n* pantera

panties ['pæntɪz] *npl* bragas *fpl*, pantis *mpl*

pantomime ['pæntəmaɪm] (*BRIT*) *n* revista musical representada en Navidad, basada en cuentos de hadas

> **PANTOMIME**
>
> En época navideña se ponen en

escena en los teatros británicos las llamadas **pantomimes**, que son versiones libres de cuentos tradicionales como Aladino o El gato con botas. En ella nunca faltan personajes como la dama ("dame"), papel que siempre interpreta un actor, el protagonista joven ("principal boy"), normalmente interpretado por una actriz, y el malvado ("villain"). Es un espectáculo familiar en el que se anima al público a participar y aunque va dirigido principalmente a los niños, cuenta con grandes dosis de humor para adultos.

pants [pænts] n (BRIT: underwear: woman's) bragas fpl; (: man's) calzoncillos mpl; (US: trousers) pantalones mpl
paper ['peɪpə*] n papel m; (also: **news~**) periódico, diario; (academic essay) ensayo; (exam) examen m ▷ adj de papel ▷ vt empapelar, tapizar (MEX); **papers** npl (also: **identity ~s**) papeles mpl, documentos mpl; **paperback** n libro en rústica; **paper bag** n bolsa de papel; **paper clip** n clip m; **paper shop** (BRIT) n tienda de periódicos; **paperwork** n trabajo administrativo
paprika ['pæprɪkə] n pimentón m
par [pɑː*] n par f; (Golf) par m; **to be on a ~ with** estar a la par con
paracetamol [pærə'siːtəmɔl] (BRIT) n paracetamol m
parachute ['pærəʃuːt] n paracaídas m inv
parade [pə'reɪd] n desfile m ▷ vt (show) hacer alarde de ▷ vi desfilar; (Mil) pasar revista
paradise ['pærədaɪs] n paraíso
paradox ['pærədɔks] n paradoja
paraffin ['pærəfɪn] (BRIT) n (also: ~ oil) parafina
paragraph ['pærəgrɑːf] n párrafo
parallel ['pærəlɛl] adj en paralelo;

(fig) semejante ▷ n (line) paralela; (fig, Geo) paralelo
paralysed ['pærəlaɪzd] adj paralizado
paralysis [pə'rælɪsɪs] n parálisis f inv
paramedic [pærə'mɛdɪk] n auxiliar m/f sanitario/a
paranoid ['pærənɔɪd] adj (person, feeling) paranoico
parasite ['pærəsaɪt] n parásito/a
parcel ['pɑːsl] n paquete m ▷ vt (also: ~ up) empaquetar, embalar
pardon ['pɑːdn] n (Law) indulto ▷ vt perdonar; **~ me!, I beg your ~!** (I'm sorry!) ¡perdone usted!; **(I beg your) ~?, ~ me?** (US: what did you say?) ¿cómo?
parent ['pɛərənt] n (mother) madre f; (father) padre m; **parents** npl padres mpl

Be careful not to translate **parent** by the Spanish word pariente.

parental [pə'rɛntl] adj paternal/ maternal
Paris ['pærɪs] n París
parish ['pærɪʃ] n parroquia
Parisian [pə'rɪzɪən] adj, n parisiense mf
park [pɑːk] n parque m ▷ vt aparcar, estacionar ▷ vi aparcar, estacionarse
parking ['pɑːkɪŋ] n aparcamiento, estacionamiento; **"no ~"** "prohibido estacionarse"; **parking lot** (US) n parking m; **parking meter** n parquímetro; **parking ticket** n multa de aparcamiento
parkway ['pɑːkweɪ] (US) n alameda
parliament ['pɑːləmənt] n parlamento; (Spanish) Cortes fpl; **parliamentary** [-'mɛntərɪ] adj parlamentario

PARLIAMENT

El Parlamento británico (**Parliament**) tiene como sede el palacio de Westminster, también llamado "Houses of Parliament" y consta de dos

cámaras. La Cámara de los
Comunes ("House of Commons"),
compuesta por 650 diputados
(**Members of Parliament**)
elegidos por sufragio universal
en su respectiva circunscripción
electoral (constituency), se reúne
175 días al año y sus sesiones son
moderadas por el Presidente de
la Cámara (**Speaker**). La cámara
alta es la Cámara de los Lores
("House of Lords") y está formada
por miembros que han sido
nombrados por el monarca o que
han heredado su escaño. Su poder
es limitado, aunque actúa como
tribunal supremo de apelación,
excepto en Escocia.

Parmesan [pɑ:mɪ'zæn] n (also: ~
cheese) queso parmesano
parole [pə'rəul] n: **on ~** libre bajo
palabra
parrot ['pærət] n loro, papagayo
parsley ['pɑ:slɪ] n perejil m
parsnip ['pɑ:snɪp] n chirivía
parson ['pɑ:sn] n cura m
part [pɑ:t] n (gen, Mus) parte f; (bit)
trozo; (of machine) pieza; (Theatre etc)
papel m; (of serial) entrega; (us: in hair)
raya ▷ adv = **partly** ▷ vt separar ▷ vi
(people) separarse; (crowd) apartarse; **to
take ~ in** tomar parte or participar en;
to take sth in good ~ tomar algo en
buena parte; **to take sb's ~** defender
a algn; **for my ~** por mi parte; **for the
most ~** en su mayor parte; **to ~ one's
hair** hacerse la raya; **part with** vt fus
ceder, entregar; (money) pagar; **part
of speech** n parte f de la oración,
categoría f gramatical
partial ['pɑ:ʃl] adj parcial; **to be ~ to**
ser aficionado a
participant [pɑ:'tɪsɪpənt] n (in
competition) concursante mf; (in
campaign etc) participante mf
participate [pɑ:'tɪsɪpeɪt] vi: **to ~ in**
participar en

particle ['pɑ:tɪkl] n partícula; (of
dust) grano
particular [pə'tɪkjulə*] adj (special)
particular; (concrete) concreto; (given)
determinado; (fussy) quisquilloso;
(demanding) exigente; **in ~** en
particular; **particularly** adv (in
particular) sobre todo; (difficult, good
etc) especialmente; **particulars**
npl (information) datos mpl; (details)
pormenores mpl
parting ['pɑ:tɪŋ] n (act) separación f;
(farewell) despedida; (BRIT: in hair) raya
▷ adj de despedida
partition [pɑ:'tɪʃən] n (Pol) división f;
(wall) tabique m
partly ['pɑ:tlɪ] adv en parte
partner ['pɑ:tnə*] n (Comm)
socio/a; (Sport, at dance) pareja; (spouse)
cónyuge mf; (lover) compañero/a;
partnership n asociación f; (Comm)
sociedad f
partridge ['pɑ:trɪdʒ] n perdiz f
part-time ['pɑ:t'taɪm] adj, adv a
tiempo parcial
party ['pɑ:tɪ] n (Pol) partido;
(celebration) fiesta; (group) grupo;
(Law) parte f interesada ▷ cpd (Pol)
de partido
pass [pɑ:s] vt (time, object) pasar;
(place) pasar por; (overtake) rebasar;
(exam) aprobar; (approve) aprobar ▷ vi
pasar; (Scol) aprobar, ser aprobado
▷ n (permit) permiso; (membership
card) carnet m; (in mountains) puerto,
desfiladero; (Sport) pase m; (Scol: also:
~ **mark**) to **get a ~ in** aprobar en;
to ~ sth through sth pasar algo por
algo; **to make a ~ at sb** (inf) hacer
proposiciones a algn; **pass away** vi
fallecer; **pass by** vi pasar ▷ vt (ignore)
pasar por alto; **pass on** vt transmitir;
pass out vi desmayarse; **pass over**
vi, vt omitir, pasar por alto; **pass up** vt
(opportunity) renunciar a; **passable** adj
(road) transitable; (tolerable) pasable
passage ['pæsɪdʒ] n (also: **~way**)
pasillo; (act of passing) tránsito; (fare,

in book) pasaje *m*; (*by boat*) travesía; (*Anat*) tubo

passenger ['pæsɪndʒə*] *n* pasajero/a, viajero/a

passer-by [pɑːsə'baɪ] *n* transeúnte *mf*

passing place *n* (*Aut*) apartadero

passion ['pæʃən] *n* pasión *f*; **passionate** *adj* apasionado; **passion fruit** *n* fruta de la pasión, granadilla

passive ['pæsɪv] *adj* (*gen, also Ling*) pasivo

passport ['pɑːspɔːt] *n* pasaporte *m*; **passport control** *n* control *m* de pasaporte; **passport office** *n* oficina de pasaportes

password ['pɑːswɜːd] *n* contraseña

past [pɑːst] *prep* (*in front of*) por delante de; (*further than*) más allá de; (*later than*) después de ▷ *adj* pasado; (*president etc*) antiguo ▷ *n* (*time*) pasado; (*of person*) antecedentes *mpl*; **he's ~ forty** tiene más de cuarenta años; **ten/quarter ~ eight** las ocho y diez/cuarto; **for the ~ few/3 days** durante los últimos días/últimos 3 días; **to run ~ sb** pasar a algn corriendo

pasta ['pæstə] *n* pasta

paste [peɪst] *n* pasta; (*glue*) engrudo ▷ *vt* pegar

pastel ['pæstl] *adj* pastel; (*painting*) al pastel

pasteurized ['pæstəraɪzd] *adj* pasteurizado

pastime ['pɑːstaɪm] *n* pasatiempo

pastor ['pɑːstə*] *n* pastor *m*

past participle [-'pɑːtɪsɪpl] *n* (*Ling*) participio *m* (de) pasado *or* (de) pretérito *or* pasivo

pastry ['peɪstrɪ] *n* (*dough*) pasta; (*cake*) pastel *m*

pasture ['pɑːstʃə*] *n* pasto

pasty¹ ['pæstɪ] *n* empanada

pasty² ['peɪstɪ] *adj* (*complexion*) pálido

pat [pæt] *vt* dar una palmadita a; (*dog etc*) acariciar

patch [pætʃ] *n* (*of material,: eye patch*) parche *m*; (*mended part*) remiendo; (*of*

land) terreno ▷ *vt* remendar; **(to go through) a bad ~** (pasar por) una mala racha; **patchy** *adj* desigual

pâté ['pæteɪ] *n* paté *m*

patent ['peɪtnt] *n* patente *f* ▷ *vt* patentar ▷ *adj* patente, evidente

paternal [pə'tɜːnl] *adj* paternal; (*relation*) paterno

paternity leave [pə'tɜːnɪtɪ-] *n* permiso *m* por paternidad, licencia por paternidad

path [pɑːθ] *n* camino, sendero; (*trail, track*) pista; (*of missile*) trayectoria

pathetic [pə'θetɪk] *adj* patético, lastimoso; (*very bad*) malísimo

pathway ['pɑːθweɪ] *n* sendero, vereda

patience ['peɪʃns] *n* paciencia; (*BRIT Cards*) solitario

patient ['peɪʃnt] *n* paciente *mf* ▷ *adj* paciente, sufrido

patio ['pætɪəu] *n* patio

patriotic [pætrɪ'ɔtɪk] *adj* patriótico

patrol [pə'trəul] *n* patrulla ▷ *vt* patrullar por; **patrol car** *n* coche *m* patrulla

patron ['peɪtrən] *n* (*in shop*) cliente *mf*, (*of charity*) patrocinador(a) *m/f*; **~ of the arts** mecenas *m*

patronizing ['pætrənaɪzɪŋ] *adj* condescendiente

pattern ['pætən] *n* (*Sewing*) patrón *m*; (*design*) dibujo; **patterned** *adj* (*material*) estampado

pause [pɔːz] *n* pausa ▷ *vi* hacer una pausa

pave [peɪv] *vt* pavimentar; **to ~ the way for** preparar el terreno para

pavement ['peɪvmənt] (*BRIT*) *n* acera, banqueta (*MEX*), andén *m* (*CAM*), vereda (*SC*)

pavilion [pə'vɪlɪən] *n* (*Sport*) caseta

paving ['peɪvɪŋ] *n* pavimento, enlosado

paw [pɔː] *n* pata

pawn [pɔːn] *n* (*Chess*) peón *m*; (*fig*) instrumento ▷ *vt* empeñar; **pawn broker** *n* prestamista *mf*

pay [peɪ] (*pt, pp* **paid**) *n* (*wage etc*)
sueldo, salario ▷ *vt* pagar ▷ *vi* (*be
profitable*) rendir; **to ~ attention
(to)** prestar atención (a); **to ~ sb a
visit** hacer una visita a algn; **to ~
one's respects to sb** presentar sus
respetos a algn; **pay back** *vt* (*money*)
reembolsar; (*person*) pagar; **pay for** *vt
fus* pagar; **pay in** *vt* ingresar; **pay off**
vt saldar ▷ *vi* (*scheme, decision*) dar
resultado; **pay out** *vt* (*money*) gastar,
desembolsar; **pay up** *vt* pagar (de
mala gana); **payable** *adj*: **payable to**
pagadero a; **pay day** *n* día *m* de paga;
pay envelope (*us*) *n* = **pay packet**;
payment *n* pago; **monthly payment**
mensualidad *f*; **payout** *n* pago; (*in
competition*) premio en metálico; **pay
packet** (*brit*) *n* sobre *m* (de paga); **pay
phone** *n* teléfono público; **payroll** *n*
nómina; **pay slip** *n* recibo de sueldo;
pay television *n* televisión *f* de pago
PC *n abbr* = **personal computer**; (*brit*)
(= *police constable*) policía *mf* ▷ *adv abbr*
= **politically correct**
p.c. *abbr* = **per cent**
PDA *n abbr* (= *personal digital assistant*)
agenda electrónica
PE *n abbr* (= *physical education*) ed. física
pea [piː] *n* guisante *m* (*sp*), arveja
(*lam*), chícharo (*mex, cam*)
peace [piːs] *n* paz *f*; (*calm*) paz *f*,
tranquilidad *f*; **peaceful** *adj* (*gentle*)
pacífico; (*calm*) tranquilo, sosegado
peach [piːtʃ] *n* melocotón *m* (*sp*),
durazno (*lam*)
peacock ['piːkɔk] *n* pavo real
peak [piːk] *n* (*of mountain*) cumbre
f, cima; (*of cap*) visera; (*fig*) cumbre *f*;
peak hours *npl* horas *fpl* punta
peanut ['piːnʌt] *n* cacahuete *m*
(*sp*), maní *m* (*lam*), cacahuate *m*
(*mex*); **peanut butter** *n* manteca de
cacahuete *or* maní
pear [pɛə*] *n* pera
pearl [pəːl] *n* perla
peasant ['pɛznt] *n* campesino/a
peat [piːt] *n* turba

pebble ['pɛbl] *n* guijarro
peck [pɛk] *vt* (*also*: **~ at**) picotear
▷ *n* picotazo; (*kiss*) besito; **peckish**
(*brit: inf*) *adj*: **I feel peckish** tengo
ganas de picar algo
peculiar [pɪˈkjuːliə*] *adj* (*odd*)
extraño, raro; (*typical*) propio,
característico; **~ to** propio de
pedal ['pɛdl] *n* pedal *m* ▷ *vi* pedalear
pedalo ['pɛdələu] *n* patín *m* a pedal
pedestal ['pɛdəstl] *n* pedestal *m*
pedestrian [pɪˈdɛstriən] *n* peatón/
ona *m/f* ▷ *adj* pedestre; **pedestrian
crossing** (*brit*) *n* paso de peatones;
pedestrianized *adj*: **a pedestrianized
street** una calle peatonal; **pedestrian
precinct** (*us* **pedestrian zone**) *n* zona
peatonal
pedigree ['pɛdɪgriː] *n* genealogía; (*of
animal*) raza, pedigrí *m* ▷ *cpd* (*animal*)
de raza, de casta
pedophile ['piːdəufaɪl] (*us*) *n* =
paedophile
pee [piː] (*inf*) *vi* mear
peek [piːk] *vi* mirar a hurtadillas
peel [piːl] *n* piel *f*; (*of orange, lemon*)
cáscara; (: *removed*) peladuras *fpl* ▷ *vt*
pelar ▷ *vi* (*paint etc*) desconcharse;
(*wallpaper*) despegarse, desprenderse;
(*skin*) pelar
peep [piːp] *n* (*brit: look*) mirada
furtiva; (*sound*) pío ▷ *vi* (*brit: look*)
mirar furtivamente
peer [pɪə*] *vi*: **to ~ at** esudriñar
▷ *n* (*noble*) par *m*; (*equal*) igual *m*;
(*contemporary*) contemporáneo/a
peg [pɛg] *n* (*for coat etc*) gancho,
colgadero; (*brit: also*: **clothes ~**) pinza
pelican ['pɛlɪkən] *n* pelícano;
pelican crossing (*brit*) *n* (*Aut*) paso de
peatones señalizado
pelt [pɛlt] *vt*: **to ~ sb with sth** arrojarle
algo a algn ▷ *vi* (*rain*) llover a cántaros;
(*inf: run*) correr ▷ *n* pellejo
pelvis ['pɛlvɪs] *n* pelvis *f*
pen [pɛn] *n* (*fountain pen*) pluma;
(*ballpoint pen*) bolígrafo; (*for sheep*)
redil *m*

penalty ['pɛnltɪ] n (gen) pena; (fine) multa

pence [pɛns] npl of **penny**

pencil ['pɛnsl] n lápiz m; **pencil in** vt (appointment) apuntar con carácter provisional; **pencil case** n estuche m; **pencil sharpener** n sacapuntas m inv

pendant ['pɛndnt] n pendiente m

pending ['pɛndɪŋ] prep antes de ▷ adj pendiente

penetrate ['pɛnɪtreɪt] vt penetrar

penfriend ['pɛnfrɛnd] (BRIT) n amigo/a por carta

penguin ['pɛŋgwɪn] n pingüino

penicillin [pɛnɪ'sɪlɪn] n penicilina

peninsula [pə'nɪnsjulə] n península

penis ['piːnɪs] n pene m

penitentiary [pɛnɪ'tɛnʃərɪ] (US) n cárcel f, presidio

penknife ['pɛnnaɪf] n navaja

penniless ['pɛnɪlɪs] adj sin dinero

penny ['pɛnɪ] (pl **pennies** or **pence**) (BRIT) n penique m; (US) centavo

penpal ['pɛnpæl] n amigo/a por carta

pension ['pɛnʃən] n (state benefit) jubilación f; **pensioner** (BRIT) n jubilado/a

pentagon ['pɛntəgən] (US) n: **the P~** (Pol) el Pentágono

penthouse ['pɛnthaus] n ático de lujo

penultimate [pɛ'nʌltɪmət] adj penúltimo

people ['piːpl] npl gente f; (citizens) pueblo, ciudadanos mpl; (Pol): **the ~** el pueblo ▷ n (nation, race) pueblo, nación f; **several ~ came** vinieron varias personas; **~ say that ...** dice la gente que ...

pepper ['pɛpə*] n (spice) pimienta; (vegetable) pimiento ▷ vt: **to ~ with** (fig) salpicar de; **peppermint** n (sweet) pastilla de menta

per [pəː*] prep por; **~ day/~son** por día/persona; **~ annum** al año

perceive [pə'siːv] vt percibir; (realize) darse cuenta de

per cent n por ciento

percentage [pə'sɛntɪdʒ] n porcentaje m

perception [pə'sɛpʃən] n percepción f; (insight) perspicacia; (opinion etc) opinión f

perch [pəːtʃ] n (fish) perca; (for bird) percha ▷ vi: **to ~ (on)** (bird) posarse (en); (person) encaramarse (en)

percussion [pə'kʌʃən] n percusión f

perfect [adj, n 'pəːfɪkt, vb pə'fɛkt] adj perfecto ▷ n (also: **~ tense**) perfecto ▷ vt perfeccionar; **perfection** [pə'fɛkʃən] n perfección f; **perfectly** ['pəːfɪktlɪ] adv perfectamente

perform [pə'fɔːm] vt (carry out) realizar, llevar a cabo; (Theatre) representar; (piece of music) interpretar ▷ vi (well, badly) funcionar; **performance** n (of a play) representación f; (of actor, athlete etc) actuación f; (of car, engine, company) rendimiento; (of economy) resultados mpl; **performer** n (actor) actor m, actriz f

perfume ['pəːfjuːm] n perfume m

perhaps [pə'hæps] adv quizá(s), tal vez

perimeter [pə'rɪmɪtə*] n perímetro

period ['pɪərɪəd] n período; (Scol) clase f; (full stop) punto; (Med) regla ▷ adj (costume, furniture) de época; **periodical** [pɪərɪ'ɔdɪkl] n periódico; **periodically** adv de vez en cuando, cada cierto tiempo

P

perish ['pɛrɪʃ] vi perecer; (decay) echarse a perder

perjury ['pəːdʒərɪ] n (Law) perjurio

perk [pəːk] n extra m

perm [pəːm] n permanente f

permanent ['pəːmənənt] adj permanente; **permanently** adv (lastingly) para siempre, de modo definitivo; (all the time) permanentemente

permission [pəˈmɪʃən] n permiso

permit [n 'pəːmɪt, vt pəˈmɪt] n permiso, licencia ▷ vt permitir

perplex [pəˈplɛks] vt dejar perplejo

persecute ['pəːsɪkjuːt] vt perseguir

persecution [pəːsɪˈkjuːʃən] n persecución f

persevere [pəːsɪˈvɪə*] vi persistir

Persian ['pəːʃən] adj, n persa mf; **the ~ Gulf** el Golfo Pérsico

persist [pəˈsɪst] vi: **to ~ (in doing sth)** persistir (en hacer algo); **persistent** adj persistente; (determined) porfiado

person ['pəːsn] n persona; **in ~** en persona; **personal** adj personal; individual; (visit) en persona; **personal assistant** n ayudante mf personal; **personal computer** n ordenador m personal; **personality** [-ˈnælɪtɪ] n personalidad f; **personally** adv personalmente; (in person) en persona; **to take sth personally** tomarse algo a mal; **personal organizer** n agenda; **personal stereo** n Walkman® m

personnel [pəːsəˈnɛl] n personal m

perspective [pəˈspɛktɪv] n perspectiva

perspiration [pəːspɪˈreɪʃən] n transpiración f

persuade [pəˈsweɪd] vt: **to ~ sb to do sth** persuadir a algn para que haga algo

persuasion [pəˈsweɪʒən] n persuasión f; (persuasiveness) persuasiva

persuasive [pəˈsweɪsɪv] adj persuasivo

perverse [pəˈvəːs] adj perverso; (wayward) travieso

pervert [n 'pəːvəːt, vb pəˈvəːt] n pervertido/a ▷ vt pervertir; (truth, sb's words) tergiversar

pessimism ['pɛsɪmɪzəm] n pesimismo

pessimist ['pɛsɪmɪst] n pesimista mf; **pessimistic** [-ˈmɪstɪk] adj pesimista

pest [pɛst] n (insect) insecto nocivo; (fig) lata, molestia

pester ['pɛstə*] vt molestar, acosar

pesticide ['pɛstɪsaɪd] n pesticida m

pet [pɛt] n animal m doméstico ▷ cpd favorito ▷ vt acariciar; **teacher's ~** favorito/a (del profesor); **~ hate** manía

petal ['pɛtl] n pétalo

petite [pəˈtiːt] adj chiquita

petition [pəˈtɪʃən] n petición f

petrified ['pɛtrɪfaɪd] adj horrorizado

petrol ['pɛtrəl] (BRIT) n gasolina

petroleum [pəˈtrəʊlɪəm] n petróleo

petrol: petrol pump (BRIT) n (in garage) surtidor m de gasolina; **petrol station** (BRIT) n gasolinera; **petrol tank** (BRIT) n depósito (de gasolina)

petticoat ['pɛtɪkəʊt] n enaguas fpl

petty ['pɛtɪ] adj (mean) mezquino; (unimportant) insignificante

pew [pjuː] n banco

pewter ['pjuːtə*] n peltre m

phantom ['fæntəm] n fantasma m

pharmacist ['fɑːməsɪst] n farmacéutico/a

pharmacy ['fɑːməsɪ] n farmacia

phase [feɪz] n fase f; **phase in** vt introducir progresivamente; **phase out** vt (machinery, product) retirar progresivamente; (job, subsidy) eliminar por etapas

Ph.D. abbr = **Doctor of Philosophy**

pheasant ['fɛznt] n faisán m

phenomena [fəˈnɔmɪnə] npl of **phenomenon**

phenomenal [fɪˈnɔmɪnl] adj fenomenal, extraordinario

phenomenon [fəˈnɔmɪnən] (pl **phenomena**) n fenómeno

Philippines ['fɪlɪpiːnz] npl: **the ~** las

Filipinas

philosopher [fɪ'lɒsəfə*] n filósofo/a

philosophical [fɪlə'sɒfɪkl] adj filosófico

philosophy [fɪ'lɒsəfɪ] n filosofía

phlegm [flɛm] n flema

phobia ['fəubjə] n fobia

phone [fəun] n teléfono ▷ vt telefonear, llamar por teléfono; **to be on the ~** tener teléfono; (be calling) estar hablando por teléfono; **phone back** vt, vi volver a llamar; **phone up** vt, vi llamar por teléfono; **phone book** n guía telefónica; **phone booth** n cabina telefónica; **phone box** (BRIT) n = **phone booth**; **phone call** n llamada (telefónica); **phonecard** n teletarjeta; **phone number** n número de teléfono

phonetics [fə'nɛtɪks] n fonética

phoney ['fəunɪ] adj falso

photo ['fəutəu] n foto f; **photo album** n álbum m de fotos; **photocopier** n fotocopiadora; **photocopy** n fotocopia ▷ vt fotocopiar

photograph ['fəutəgrɑ:f] n fotografía ▷ vt fotografiar; **photographer** [fə'tɒgrəfə*] n fotógrafo; **photography** [fə'tɒgrəfɪ] n fotografía

phrase [freɪz] n frase f ▷ vt expresar; **phrase book** n libro de frases

physical ['fɪzɪkl] adj físico; **physical education** n educación f física; **physically** adv físicamente

physician [fɪ'zɪʃən] n médico/a

physicist ['fɪzɪsɪst] n físico/a

physics ['fɪzɪks] n física

physiotherapist [fɪzɪəu'θɛrəpɪst] n fisioterapeuta

physiotherapy [fɪzɪəu'θɛrəpɪ] n fisioterapia

physique [fɪ'zi:k] n físico

pianist ['pi:ənɪst] n pianista mf

piano [pɪ'ænəu] n piano

pick [pɪk] n (tool: also: **~-axe**) pico, piqueta ▷ vt (select) elegir, escoger; (gather) coger (SP), recoger; (remove, take out) sacar, quitar; (lock) abrir con ganzúa; **take your ~** escoja lo que quiera; **the ~ of** lo mejor de; **to ~ one's nose/teeth** hurgarse las narices/ limpiarse los dientes; **to ~ a quarrel with sb** meterse con algn; **pick on** vt fus (person) meterse con; **pick out** vt escoger; (distinguish) identificar; **pick up** vi (improve: sales) ir mejor; (: patient) reponerse; (Finance) recobrarse ▷ vt recoger; (learn) aprender; (Police: arrest) detener; (person: for sex) ligar; (Radio) captar; **to pick up speed** acelerarse; **to pick o.s. up** levantarse

pickle ['pɪkl] n (also: **~s**: as condiment) escabeche m; (fig: mess) apuro ▷ vt encurtir

pickpocket ['pɪkpɒkɪt] n carterista mf

pick-up ['pɪkʌp] n (also: **~ truck**) furgoneta, camioneta

picnic ['pɪknɪk] n merienda ▷ vi ir de merienda; **picnic area** n zona de picnic; (Aut) área de descanso

picture ['pɪktʃə*] n cuadro; (painting) pintura; (photograph) fotografía; (TV) imagen f; (film) película; (fig: description) descripción f; (: situation) situación f ▷ vt (imagine) imaginar; **pictures** npl: **the ~s** (BRIT) el cine; **picture frame** n marco; **picture messaging** n (envío de) mensajes con imágenes

picturesque [pɪktʃə'rɛsk] adj pintoresco

pie [paɪ] n pastel m; (open) tarta; (small: of meat) empanada

piece [pi:s] n pedazo, trozo; (of cake) trozo; (item): **a ~ of clothing/ furniture/advice** una prenda (de vestir)/un mueble/un consejo ▷ vt: **to ~ together** juntar; (Tech) armar; **to take to ~s** desmontar

pie chart n gráfico de sectores or tarta

pier [pɪə*] n muelle m, embarcadero

pierce [pɪəs] vt perforar; **pierced** adj: **I've got pierced ears** tengo los agujeros hechos en las orejas

pig [pɪg] n cerdo, chancho (LAM);

P

(*pej: unkind person*) asqueroso; (: *greedy person*) glotón/ona *m/f*

pigeon ['pɪdʒən] *n* paloma; (*as food*) pichón *m*

piggy bank ['pɪgɪ-] *n* hucha (*en forma de cerdito*)

pigsty ['pɪgstaɪ] *n* pocilga

pigtail *n* (*girl's*) trenza

pike [paɪk] *n* (*fish*) lucio

pilchard ['pɪltʃəd] *n* sardina

pile [paɪl] *n* montón *m*; (*of carpet, cloth*) pelo; **pile up** *vi +adv* (*accumulate: work*) amontonarse, acumularse ▷ *vt +adv* (*put in a heap: books, clothes*) apilar, amontonar; (*accumulate*) acumular; **piles** *npl* (*Med*) almorranas *fpl*, hemorroides *mpl*; **pile-up** *n* (*Aut*) accidente *m* múltiple

pilgrimage ['pɪlgrɪmɪdʒ] *n* peregrinación *f*, romería

pill [pɪl] *n* píldora; **the ~** la píldora

pillar ['pɪlə*] *n* pilar *m*

pillow ['pɪləu] *n* almohada; **pillowcase** *n* funda

pilot ['paɪlət] *n* piloto ▷ *cpd* (*scheme etc*) piloto ▷ *vt* pilotar; **pilot light** *n* piloto

pimple ['pɪmpl] *n* grano

PIN *n abbr* (= *personal identification number*) número personal

pin [pɪn] *n* alfiler *m* ▷ *vt* prender (con alfiler); **~s and needles** hormigueo; **to ~ sb down** (*fig*) hacer que algn concrete; **to ~ sth on sb** (*fig*) colgarle a algn el sambenito de algo

pinafore ['pɪnəfɔ:*] *n* delantal *m*

pinch [pɪntʃ] *n* (*of salt etc*) pizca ▷ *vt* pellizcar; (*inf: steal*) birlar; **at a ~** en caso de apuro

pine [paɪn] *n* (*also: ~ tree*) pino ▷ *vi*: **to ~ for** suspirar por

pineapple ['paɪnæpl] *n* piña, ananás *m*

ping [pɪŋ] *n* (*noise*) sonido agudo; **ping-pong**® *n* pingpong® *m*

pink [pɪŋk] *adj* rosado, (color de) rosa ▷ *n* (*colour*) rosa; (*Bot*) clavel *m*, clavellina

pinpoint ['pɪnpɔɪnt] *vt* precisar

pint [paɪnt] *n* pinta (BRIT = 568cc, US = 473cc); (BRIT: *inf: of beer*) pinta de cerveza ≈ jarra (SP)

pioneer [paɪə'nɪə*] *n* pionero/a

pious ['paɪəs] *adj* piadoso, devoto

pip [pɪp] *n* (*seed*) pepita; **the ~s** (BRIT) la señal

pipe [paɪp] *n* tubo, caño; (*for smoking*) pipa ▷ *vt* conducir en cañerías; **pipeline** *n* (*for oil*) oleoducto; (*for gas*) gasoducto; **piper** *n* gaitero/a

pirate ['paɪərət] *n* pirata *mf* ▷ *vt* (*cassette, book*) piratear

Pisces ['paɪsi:z] *n* Piscis *m*

piss [pɪs] (*inf!*) *vi* mear; **pissed** (*inf!*) *adj* (*drunk*) borracho

pistol ['pɪstl] *n* pistola

piston ['pɪstən] *n* pistón *m*, émbolo

pit [pɪt] *n* hoyo; (*also:* **coal ~**) mina; (*in garage*) foso de inspección; (*also:* **orchestra ~**) platea ▷ *vt*: **to ~ one's wits against sb** medir fuerzas con algn

pitch [pɪtʃ] *n* (*Mus*) tono; (BRIT *Sport*) campo, terreno; (*fig*) punto; (*tar*) brea ▷ *vt* (*throw*) arrojar, lanzar ▷ *vi* (*fall*) caer(se); **to ~ a tent** montar una tienda (de campaña); **pitch-black** *adj* negro como boca de lobo

pitfall ['pɪtfɔ:l] *n* riesgo

pith [pɪθ] *n* (*of orange*) médula

pitiful ['pɪtɪful] *adj* (*touching*) lastimoso, conmovedor(a)

pity ['pɪtɪ] *n* compasión *f*, piedad *f* ▷ *vt* compadecer(se de); **what a ~!** ¡qué pena!

pizza ['pi:tsə] *n* pizza

placard ['plækɑ:d] *n* letrero; (*in march etc*) pancarta

place [pleɪs] *n* lugar *m*, sitio; (*seat*) plaza, asiento; (*post*) puesto; (*home*): **at/to his ~** en/a su casa; (*role: in society etc*) papel *m* ▷ *vt* (*object*) poner, colocar; (*identify*) reconocer; **to take ~** tener lugar; **to be ~d** (*in race, exam*) colocarse; **out of ~** (*not suitable*) fuera de lugar; **in the first ~** en primer lugar; **to change ~s with sb** cambiarse de sitio con algn; **~ of birth** lugar m de nacimiento; **place mat** n (wooden etc) salvamanteles m inv; (linen etc) mantel m individual; **placement** n (positioning) colocación f; (at work) emplazamiento

placid ['plæsɪd] adj apacible

plague [pleɪg] n plaga; (Med) peste f ▷ vt (fig) acosar, atormentar

plaice [pleɪs] n inv platija

plain [pleɪn] adj (unpatterned) liso; (clear) claro, evidente; (simple) sencillo; (not handsome) poco atractivo ▷ adv claramente ▷ n llano, llanura; **plain chocolate** n chocolate m amargo; **plainly** adv claramente

plaintiff ['pleɪntɪf] n demandante mf

plait [plæt] n trenza

plan [plæn] n (drawing) plano; (scheme) plan m, proyecto ▷ vt proyectar, planificar ▷ vi hacer proyectos; **to ~ to do** pensar hacer

plane [pleɪn] n (Aviat) avión m; (Math, fig) plano; (also: **~ tree**) plátano; (tool) cepillo

planet ['plænɪt] n planeta m

plank [plæŋk] n tabla

planning ['plænɪŋ] n planificación f; **family ~** planificación familiar

plant [plɑːnt] n planta; (machinery) maquinaria; (factory) fábrica ▷ vt plantar; (field) sembrar; (bomb) colocar

plantation [plæn'teɪʃən] n plantación f; (estate) hacienda

plaque [plæk] n placa

plaster ['plɑːstə*] n (for walls) yeso; (also: **~ of Paris**) yeso mate, escayola (SP); (BRIT: also: **sticking ~**) tirita (SP), curita (LAM) ▷ vt enyesar; (cover): **to ~ with** llenar or cubrir de; **plaster cast** n (Med) escayola; (model, statue) vaciado de yeso

plastic ['plæstɪk] n plástico ▷ adj de plástico; **plastic bag** n bolsa de plástico; **plastic surgery** n cirujía plástica

plate [pleɪt] n (dish) plato; (metal, in book) lámina; (dental plate) placa de

dentadura postiza

plateau ['plætəʊ] (pl **~s** or **~x**) n meseta, altiplanicie f

platform ['plætfɔːm] n (Rail) andén m; (stage, BRIT: on bus) plataforma; (at meeting) tribuna; (Pol) programa m (electoral)

platinum ['plætɪnəm] adj, n platino

platoon [plə'tuːn] n pelotón m

platter ['plætə*] n fuente f

plausible ['plɔːzɪbl] adj verosímil; (person) convincente

play [pleɪ] n (Theatre) obra, comedia ▷ vt (game) jugar; (compete against) jugar contra; (instrument) tocar; (part: in play etc) hacer el papel de; (tape, record) poner ▷ vi jugar; (band) tocar; (tape, record) sonar; **to ~ safe** ir a lo seguro; **play back** vt (tape) poner; **play up** vi (cause trouble to) dar guerra; **player** n jugador(a) m/f; (Theatre) actor(actriz) m/f; (Mus) músico/a; **playful** adj juguetón/ona, **playground** n (in school) patio de recreo; (in park) parque m infantil; **playgroup** n jardín m de niños; **playing card** n naipe m, carta; **playing field** n campo de deportes, **playschool** n =**playgroup**; **playtime** n (Scol) recreo; **playwright** n dramaturgo/a

plc abbr (= public limited company) ≈ S.A.

plea [pliː] n súplica, petición f; (Law) alegato, defensa

plead [pliːd] vt (Law): **to ~ sb's case** defender a algn; (give as excuse) poner como pretexto ▷ vi (Law) declararse; (beg): **to ~ with sb** suplicar or rogar a algn

pleasant ['plɛznt] adj agradable

please [pliːz] excl ¡por favor! ▷ vt (give pleasure to) dar gusto a, agradar ▷ vi (think fit): **do as you ~** haz lo que quieras; **~ yourself!** (inf) ¡haz lo que quieras!, ¡como quieras!; **pleased** adj (happy) alegre, contento; **pleased (with)** satisfecho (de); **pleased to meet you** ¡encantado!, ¡tanto gusto!

pleasure ['plɛʒə*] n placer m, gusto;

"it's a ~" "el gusto es mío"

pleat [pli:t] n pliegue m

pledge [plɛdʒ] n (promise) promesa, voto ▷ vt prometer

plentiful ['plɛntɪful] adj copioso, abundante

plenty ['plɛntɪ] n: **~ of** mucho(s)/a(s)

pliers ['plaɪəz] npl alicates mpl, tenazas fpl

plight [plaɪt] n situación f difícil

plod [plɒd] vi caminar con paso pesado; (fig) trabajar laboriosamente

plonk [plɒŋk] (inf) n (BRIT: wine) vino peleón ▷ vt: **to ~ sth down** dejar caer algo

plot [plɒt] n (scheme) complot m, conjura; (of story, play) argumento; (of land) terreno ▷ vt (mark out) trazar; (conspire) tramar, urdir ▷ vi conspirar

plough [plaʊ] (US **plow**) n arado ▷ vt (earth) arar; **to ~ money into** invertir dinero en

plow [plaʊ] (US) = **plough**

ploy [plɔɪ] n truco, estratagema

pluck [plʌk] vt (fruit) coger (SP), recoger (LAM); (musical instrument) puntear; (bird) desplumar; (eyebrows) depilar; **to ~ up courage** hacer de tripas corazón

plug [plʌg] n tapón m; (Elec) enchufe m, clavija; (Aut: also: **spark(ing) ~**) bujía ▷ vt (hole) tapar; (inf: advertise) dar publicidad a; **plug in** vt (Elec) enchufar; **plughole** n desagüe m

plum [plʌm] n (fruit) ciruela

plumber ['plʌmə*] n fontanero/a (SP, CAM), plomero/a (LAM)

plumbing ['plʌmɪŋ] n (trade) fontanería, plomería; (piping) cañería

plummet ['plʌmɪt] vi: **to ~ (down)** caer a plomo

plump [plʌmp] adj rechoncho, rollizo ▷ vi: **to ~ for** (inf: choose) optar por

plunge [plʌndʒ] n zambullida ▷ vt sumergir, hundir ▷ vi (fall) caer; (dive) saltar; (person) arrojarse; **to take the ~** lanzarse

plural ['pluərl] adj plural ▷ n plural m

plus [plʌs] n (also: **~ sign**) signo más ▷ prep más, y, además de; **ten/twenty ~** más de diez/veinte

ply [plaɪ] vt (a trade) ejercer ▷ vi (ship) ir y venir ▷ n (of wool, rope) cabo; **to ~ sb with drink** insistir en ofrecer a algn muchas copas; **plywood** n madera contrachapada

P.M. n abbr = **Prime Minister**

p.m. adv abbr (= post meridiem) de la tarde or noche

PMS n abbr (= premenstrual syndrome) SPM m

PMT n abbr (= premenstrual tension) SPM m

pneumatic drill [nju:'mætɪk-] n martillo neumático

pneumonia [nju:'məunɪə] n pulmonía

poach [pəutʃ] vt (cook) escalfar; (steal) cazar (or pescar) en vedado ▷ vi cazar (or pescar) en vedado; **poached** adj escalfado

P.O. Box n abbr (= Post Office Box) apdo., aptdo.

pocket ['pɒkɪt] n bolsillo; (fig: small area) bolsa ▷ vt meter en el bolsillo; (steal) embolsar; **to be out of ~** (BRIT) salir perdiendo; **pocketbook** (US) n cartera; **pocket money** n asignación f

pod [pɒd] n vaina

podcast ['pɒdkɑ:st] n podcast m ▷ vi podcastear

podiatrist [pɔ'di:ətrɪst] (US) n pedicuro/a

podium ['pəudɪəm] n podio

poem ['pəuɪm] n poema m

poet ['pəuɪt] n poeta m/f; **poetic** [-'ɛtɪk] adj poético; **poetry** n poesía

poignant ['pɔɪnjənt] adj conmovedor/a

point [pɔɪnt] n punto; (tip) punta; (purpose) fin m, propósito; (use) utilidad f; (significant part) lo significativo; (moment) momento; (Elec) toma (de corriente); (also: **decimal ~**): **2 ~ 3 (2.3)** dos coma tres (2,3) ▷ vt señalar; (gun etc): **to ~ sth at sb** apuntar algo a algn ▷ vi: **to ~ at** señalar; **points** npl (Aut) contactos mpl; (Rail) agujas fpl; **to be on the ~ of doing sth** estar a punto de hacer algo; **to make a ~ of** poner empeño en; **to get/miss the ~** comprender/no comprender; **to come to the ~** ir al meollo; **there's no ~ (in doing)** no tiene sentido (hacer); **point out** vt señalar; **point-blank** adv (say, refuse) sin más hablar; (also: **at point-blank range**) a quemarropa; **pointed** adj (shape) puntiagudo, afilado; (remark) intencionado; **pointer** n (needle) aguja, indicador m; **pointless** adj sin sentido; **point of view** n punto de vista

poison ['pɔɪzn] n veneno ▷ vt envenenar; **poisonous** adj venenoso; (fumes etc) tóxico

poke [pəuk] vt (jab with finger, stick etc) empujar; (put): **to ~ sth in(to)** introducir algo en; **poke about** or **around** vi tisgonear; **poke out** vi (stick out) salir

poker ['pəukə*] n atizador m; (Cards) póker m

Poland ['pəulənd] n Polonia

polar ['pəulə*] adj polar; **polar bear** n oso polar

Pole [pəul] n polaco/a

pole [pəul] n palo; (fixed) poste m; (Geo) polo; **pole bean** (US) n = judía verde; **pole vault** n salto con pértiga

police [pə'li:s] n policía ▷ vt vigilar; **police car** n coche-patrulla m; **police constable** (BRIT) n guardia m, policía m; **police force** n cuerpo de policía; **policeman** (irreg) n policía m, guardia m; **police officer** n guardia m, policía m; **police station** n comisaría; **policewoman** (irreg) n mujer f policía

policy ['pɔlɪsɪ] n política; (also: **insurance ~**) póliza

polio ['pəulɪəu] n polio f

Polish ['pəulɪʃ] adj polaco ▷ n (Ling) polaco

polish ['pɔlɪʃ] n (for shoes) betún m; (for floor) cera (de lustrar); (shine) brillo,

lustre m; (fig: refinement) educación f ▷ vt (shoes) limpiar; (make shiny) pulir, sacar brillo a; **polish off** vt (food) despachar; **polished** adj (fig: person) elegante

polite [pə'laɪt] adj cortés, atento; **politeness** n cortesía

political [pə'lɪtɪkl] adj político; **politically** adv políticamente; **politically correct** políticamente correcto

politician [pɔlɪ'tɪʃən] n político/a

politics ['pɔlɪtɪks] n política

poll [pəul] n (election) votación f; (also: **opinion ~**) sondeo, encuesta ▷ vt encuestar; (votes) obtener

pollen ['pɔlən] n polen m

polling station ['pəulɪŋ-] n centro electoral

pollute [pə'lu:t] vt contaminar

pollution [pə'lu:ʃən] n polución f, contaminación f del medio ambiente

polo ['pəuləu] n (sport) polo; **polo-neck** adj de cuello vuelto ▷ n (sweater) suéter m de cuello vuelto; **polo shirt** n polo, niqui m

polyester [pɔlɪ'estə*] n poliéster m

polystyrene [pɔlɪ'staɪrl:n] n poliestireno

polythene ['pɔlɪθi:n] (BRIT) n politeno; **polythene bag** n bolsa de plástico

pomegranate ['pɔmɪgrænɪt] n granada

pompous ['pɔmpəs] adj pomposo

pond [pɔnd] n (natural) charca; (artificial) estanque m

ponder ['pɔndə*] vt meditar

pony ['pəunɪ] n poni m; **ponytail** n coleta; **pony trekking** (BRIT) n excursión f a caballo

poodle ['pu:dl] n caniche m

pool [pu:l] n (natural) charca; (also: **swimming ~**) piscina, alberca (MEX), pileta (RPL); (fig: of liquid etc) charco; (Sport) chapolín m ▷ vt juntar; **pools** npl quinielas fpl

poor [puə*] adj pobre; (bad) de mala

calidad ▷ *npl*: **the ~** los pobres; **poorly**
adj mal, enfermo ▷ *adv* mal

pop [pɔp] *n* (*sound*) ruido seco; (*Mus*)
(música) pop *m*; (*inf: father*) papá *m*;
(*drink*) gaseosa ▷ *vt* (*put quickly*) meter
(de prisa) ▷ *vi* reventar; (*cork*) saltar;
pop in *vi* entrar un momento; **pop
out** *vi* salir un momento; **popcorn** *n*
palomitas *fpl*

poplar ['pɔplə*] *n* álamo

popper ['pɔpə*] (*BRIT*) *n* automático

poppy ['pɔpɪ] *n* amapola

Popsicle® ['pɔpsɪkl] (*US*) *n* polo

pop star *n* estrella del pop

popular ['pɔpjulə*] *adj* popular;
popularity [pɔpju'lærɪtɪ] *n*
popularidad *f*

population [pɔpju'leɪʃən] *n*
población *f*

pop-up ['pɔpʌp] (*Comput*) *adj* (*menu,
window*) emergente ▷ *n* ventana
emergente, (ventana *f*) pop-up *f*

porcelain ['pɔːslɪn] *n* porcelana

porch [pɔːtʃ] *n* pórtico, entrada; (*US*)
veranda

pore [pɔː*] *n* poro ▷ *vi*: **to ~ over**
engolfarse en

pork [pɔːk] *n* carne *f* de cerdo *or*
(*LAM*) chancho; **pork chop** *n* chuleta
de cerdo; **pork pie** *n* (*BRIT: Culin*)
empanada de carne de cerdo

porn [pɔːn] *adj* (*inf*) porno *inv* ▷ *n*
porno; **pornographic** [pɔːnə'græfɪk]
adj pornográfico; **pornography**
[pɔː'nɔgrəfɪ] *n* pornografía

porridge ['pɔrɪdʒ] *n* gachas *fpl* de
avena

port [pɔːt] *n* puerto; (*Naut: left side*)
babor *m*; (*wine*) vino de Oporto; **~ of
call** puerto de escala

portable ['pɔːtəbl] *adj* portátil

porter ['pɔːtə*] *n* (*for luggage*)
maletero; (*doorkeeper*) portero/a,
conserje *m/f*

portfolio [pɔːt'fəuliəu] *n* cartera

portion ['pɔːʃən] *n* porción *f*; (*of food*)
ración *f*

portrait ['pɔːtreɪt] *n* retrato

portray [pɔː'treɪ] *vt* retratar; (*actor*)
representar

Portugal ['pɔːtjugl] *n* Portugal *m*

Portuguese [pɔːtju'giːz] *adj*
portugués/esa ▷ *n inv* portugués/esa
m/f; (*Ling*) portugués *m*

pose [pəuz] *n* postura, actitud *f* ▷ *vi*
(*pretend*): **to ~ as** hacerse pasar por ▷ *vt*
(*question*) plantear; **to ~ for** posar para

posh [pɔʃ] (*inf*) *adj* elegante, de lujo

position [pə'zɪʃən] *n* posición *f*;
(*job*) puesto; (*situation*) situación *f*
▷ *vt* colocar

positive ['pɔzɪtɪv] *adj* positivo;
(*certain*) seguro; (*definite*) definitivo;
positively *adv* (*affirmatively,
enthusiastically*) de forma positiva;
(*inf: really*) absolutamente

possess [pə'zɛs] *vt* poseer;
possession [pə'zɛʃən] *n* posesión
f; **possessions** *npl* (*belongings*)
pertenencias *fpl*; **possessive** *adj*
posesivo

possibility [pɔsɪ'bɪlɪtɪ] *n* posibilidad
f

possible ['pɔsɪbl] *adj* posible; **as big
as ~** lo más grande posible; **possibly**
adv posiblemente; **I cannot possibly
come** me es imposible venir

post [pəust] *n* (*BRIT: system*) correos
mpl; (*BRIT: letters, delivery*) correo;
(*job, situation*) puesto; (*pole*) poste
m ▷ *vt* (*BRIT: send by post*) echar al
correo; (*BRIT: appoint*): **to ~ to** enviar a;
postage *n* porte *m*, franqueo; **postal**
adj postal, de correos; **postal order** *n*
giro postal; **postbox** (*BRIT*) *n* buzón *m*;
postcard *n* tarjeta postal; **postcode**
(*BRIT*) *n* código postal

poster ['pəustə*] *n* cartel *m*

postgraduate ['pəust'grædjuət] *n*
posgraduado/a

postman ['pəustmən] (*BRIT: irreg*)
n cartero

postmark ['pəustmɑːk] *n*
matasellos *m inv*

post-mortem [-'mɔːtəm] *n*
autopsia

post office n (building) (oficina de) correos m; (organization): **the Post Office** Correos m inv (SP), Dirección f General de Correos (LAM)

postpone [pəs'pəun] vt aplazar

posture ['pɒstʃə*] n postura, actitud f

postwoman ['pəustwumən] (BRIT: irreg) n cartera

pot [pɒt] n (for cooking) olla; (teapot) tetera; (coffeepot) cafetera; (for flowers) maceta; (for jam) tarro, pote m; (inf: marijuana) chocolate m ▷ vt (plant) poner en tiesto; **to go to ~** (inf) irse al traste

potato [pə'teɪtəu] (pl **~es**) n patata (SP), papa (LAM); **potato peeler** n pelapatatas m inv

potent ['pəutnt] adj potente, poderoso, (drink) fuerte

potential [pə'tɛnʃl] adj potencial, posible ▷ n potencial m

pothole ['pɒthəul] n (in road) bache m; (BRIT: underground) gruta

pot plant ['pɒtplɑ:nt] n planta de interior

potter ['pɒtə*] n alfarero/a ▷ vi: **to ~ around** or **about** (BRIT) hacer trabajitos; **pottery** n cerámica; (factory) alfarería

potty ['pɒtɪ] n orinal m de niño

pouch [pautʃ] n (Zool) bolsa; (for tobacco) petaca

poultry ['pəultrɪ] n aves fpl de corral; (meat) pollo

pounce [pauns] vi: **to ~ on** precipitarse sobre

pound [paund] n libra (weight = 453g or 16oz; money = 100 pence) ▷ vt (beat) golpear; (crush) machacar ▷ vi (heart) latir; **pound sterling** n libra esterlina

pour [pɔ:*] vt echar; (tea etc) servir ▷ vi correr, fluir; **to ~ sb a drink** servirle a algn una copa; **pour in** vi (people) entrar en tropel; **pour out** vi salir en tropel ▷ vt (drink) echar, servir; (fig): **to pour out one's feelings** desahogarse; **pouring** adj: **pouring rain** lluvia torrencial

pout [paut] vi hacer pucheros

poverty ['pɒvətɪ] n pobreza, miseria

powder ['paudə*] n polvo; (also: **face ~**) polvos mpl ▷ vt polvorear; **to ~ one's face** empolvarse la cara; **powdered milk** n leche f en polvo

power ['pauə*] n poder m; (strength) fuerza; (nation, Tech) potencia; (drive) empuje m; (Elec) fuerza, energía ▷ vt impulsar; **to be in ~** (Pol) estar en el poder; **power cut** (BRIT) n apagón m; **power failure** n = **power cut**; **powerful** adj poderoso; (engine) potente; (speech etc) convincente; **powerless** adj: **powerless (to do)** incapaz (de hacer); **power point** (BRIT) n enchufe m; **power station** n central f eléctrica

p.p. abbr (= per procurationem); **p.p. J. Smith** p.p. (por poder de) J. Smith; (= pages) págs

PR n abbr = **public relations**

practical ['præktɪkl] adj práctico: **practical joke** n broma pesada; **practically** adv (almost) casi

practice ['præktɪs] n (habit) costumbre f; (exercise) práctica, ejercicio; (training) adiestramiento; (Med: of profession) práctica, ejercicio; (Med, Law: business) consulta ▷ vt, vi (US) = **practise**; **in ~** (in reality) en la práctica; **out of ~** desentrenado

practise ['præktɪs] (US **practice**) vt (carry out) practicar; (profession) ejercer; (train at) practicar ▷ vi ejercer; (train) practicar; **practising** adj (Christian etc) practicante; (lawyer) en ejercicio

practitioner [præk'tɪʃənə*] n (Med) médico/a

pragmatic [præg'mætɪk] adj pragmático

prairie ['prɛərɪ] n pampa

praise [preɪz] n alabanza(s) f(pl), elogio(s) m(pl) ▷ vt alabar, elogiar

pram [præm] (BRIT) n cochecito de niño

prank [præŋk] n travesura

prawn [prɔ:n] n gamba; **prawn**

p

cocktail n cóctel m de gambas

pray [preɪ] vi rezar; **prayer** [preə*] n
oración f, rezo; (entreaty) ruego, súplica

preach [pri:tʃ] vi predicar; **preacher**
n predicador(a) m/f

precarious [prɪ'kɛərɪəs] adj precario

precaution [prɪ'kɔ:ʃən] n
precaución f

precede [prɪ'si:d] vt, vi preceder;
precedent ['prɛsɪdənt] n precedente
m; **preceding** [prɪ'si:dɪŋ] adj anterior

precinct ['pri:sɪŋkt] n recinto

precious ['prɛʃəs] adj precioso

precise [prɪ'saɪs] adj preciso,
exacto; **precisely** adv precisamente,
exactamente

precision [prɪ'sɪʒən] n precisión f

predator ['prɛdətə*] n depredador m

predecessor ['pri:dɪsɛsə*] n
antecesor(a) m/f

predicament [prɪ'dɪkəmənt] n
apuro

predict [prɪ'dɪkt] vt pronosticar;
predictable adj previsible; **prediction**
[-'dɪkʃən] n predicción f

predominantly [prɪ'dɔmɪnəntlɪ]
adv en su mayoría

preface ['prɛfəs] n prefacio

prefect ['pri:fɛkt] (BRIT) n (in school)
monitor(a) m/f

prefer [prɪ'fə:*] vt preferir; **to ~ doing**
or **to do** preferir hacer; **preferable**
['prɛfrəbl] adj preferible; **preferably**
['prɛfrəblɪ] adv de preferencia;
preference ['prɛfrəns] n preferencia;
(priority) prioridad f

prefix ['pri:fɪks] n prefijo

pregnancy ['prɛgnənsɪ] n (of woman)
embarazo; (of animal) preñez f

pregnant ['prɛgnənt] adj (woman)
embarazada; (animal) preñada

prehistoric ['pri:hɪs'tɔrɪk] adj
prehistórico

prejudice ['prɛdʒudɪs] n prejuicio;
prejudiced adj (person) predispuesto

preliminary [prɪ'lɪmɪnərɪ] adj
preliminar

prelude ['prɛlju:d] n preludio

premature ['prɛmətʃuə*] adj
prematuro

premier ['prɛmɪə*] adj primero,
principal ▷ n (Pol) primer(a)
ministro/a

première ['prɛmɪɛə*] n estreno

Premier League [prɛmɪə'li:g] n
primera división

premises ['prɛmɪsɪz] npl (of business
etc) local m; **on the ~** en el lugar mismo

premium ['pri:mɪəm] n premio;
(insurance) prima; **to be at a ~** ser muy
solicitado

premonition [prɛmə'nɪʃən] n
presentimiento

preoccupied [prɪ'ɔkjupaɪd] adj
ensimismado

prepaid [pri:'peɪd] adj porte pagado

preparation [prɛpə'reɪʃən] n
preparación f; **preparations** npl
preparativos mpl

preparatory school [prɪ'pærətərɪ-]
n escuela preparatoria

prepare [prɪ'pɛə*] vt preparar,
disponer; (Culin) preparar ▷ vi: **to ~ for**
(action) prepararse or disponerse para;
(event) hacer preparativos para; **~d to**
dispuesto a; **~d for** listo para

preposition [prɛpə'zɪʃən] n
preposición f

prep school [prɛp-] n = **preparatory
school**

prerequisite [pri:'rɛkwɪzɪt] n
requisito

preschool ['pri:'sku:l] adj preescolar

prescribe [prɪ'skraɪb] vt (Med)
recetar

prescription [prɪ'skrɪpʃən] n (Med)
receta

presence ['prɛzns] n presencia; **in
sb's ~** en presencia de algn; **~ of mind**
aplomo

present [adj, n 'prɛznt, vb prɪ'zɛnt] adj
(in attendance) presente; (current) actual
▷ n (gift) regalo; (actuality): **the ~** la
actualidad, el presente ▷ vt (introduce,
describe) presentar; (expound) exponer;
(give) presentar, dar, ofrecer; (Theatre)

representar; **to give sb a ~** regalar algo a algn; **at ~** actualmente; **presentable** [prɪˈzɛntəbl] adj: **to make o.s. presentable** arreglarse; **presentation** [-ˈteɪʃən] n presentación f; (of report etc) exposición f; (formal ceremony) entrega de un regalo; **present-day** adj actual; **presenter** [prɪˈzɛntə*] n (Radio, TV) locutor(a) m/f; **presently** adv (soon) dentro de poco; (now) ahora; **present participle** n participio (de) presente

preservation [prɛzəˈveɪʃən] n conservación f

preservative [prɪˈzəːvətɪv] n conservante m

preserve [prɪˈzəːv] vt (keep safe) preservar, proteger; (maintain) mantener; (food) conservar ▷ n (for game) coto, vedado; (often pl: jam) conserva, confitura

preside [prɪˈzaɪd] vi presidir

president [ˈprɛzɪdənt] n presidente m/f; **presidential** [-ˈdɛnʃl] adj presidencial

press [prɛs] n (newspapers): **the P~** la prensa; (printer's) imprenta; (of button) pulsación f ▷ vt empujar; (button etc) apretar; (clothes: iron) planchar; (put pressure on: person) presionar; (insist): **to ~ sth on sb** insistir en que algn acepte algo ▷ vi (squeeze) apretar; (pressurize): **to ~ for** presionar por; **we are ~ed for time/money** estamos apurados de tiempo/dinero; **press conference** n rueda de prensa; **pressing** adj apremiante; **press stud** (BRIT) n botón m de presión; **press-up** (BRIT) n plancha

pressure [ˈprɛʃə*] n presión f; **to put ~ on sb** presionar a algn; **pressure cooker** n olla a presión; **pressure group** n grupo de presión

prestige [prɛsˈtiːʒ] n prestigio

prestigious [prɛsˈtɪdʒəs] adj prestigioso

presumably [prɪˈzjuːməblɪ] adv es de suponer que, cabe presumir que

presume [prɪˈzjuːm] vt: **to ~ (that)** presumir (que), suponer (que)

pretence [prɪˈtɛns] (US **pretense**) n fingimiento; **under false ~s** con engaños

pretend [prɪˈtɛnd] vt, vi (feign) fingir

▋ Be careful not to translate **pretend** by the Spanish word pretender.

pretense [prɪˈtɛns] (US) n = **pretence**

pretentious [prɪˈtɛnʃəs] adj presumido; (ostentatious) ostentoso, aparatoso

pretext [ˈpriːtɛkst] n pretexto

pretty [ˈprɪtɪ] adj bonito, lindo (LAM) ▷ adv bastante

prevail [prɪˈveɪl] vi (gain mastery) prevalecer; (be current) predominar; **prevailing** adj (dominant) predominante

prevalent [ˈprɛvələnt] adj (widespread) extendido

prevent [prɪˈvɛnt] vt: **to ~ sb from doing sth** impedir a algn hacer algo; **to ~ sth from happening** evitar que ocurra algo; **prevention** [prɪˈvɛnʃən] n prevención f; **preventive** adj preventivo

preview [ˈpriːvjuː] n (of film) preestreno

previous [ˈpriːvɪəs] adj previo, anterior; **previously** adv antes

prey [preɪ] n presa ▷ vi: **to ~ on** (feed on) alimentarse de; **it was ~ing on his mind** le preocupaba, le obsesionaba

price [praɪs] n precio ▷ vt (goods) fijar el precio de; **priceless** adj que no tiene precio; **price list** n tarifa

prick [prɪk] n (sting) picadura ▷ vt pinchar; (hurt) picar; **to ~ up one's ears** aguzar el oído

prickly [ˈprɪklɪ] adj espinoso; (fig: person) enojadizo

pride [praɪd] n orgullo; (pej) soberbia ▷ vt: **to ~ o.s. on** enorgullecerse de

priest [priːst] n sacerdote m

primarily [ˈpraɪmərɪlɪ] adv ante todo

primary [ˈpraɪmərɪ] adj (first in importance) principal ▷ n (US Pol)

p

elección f primaria; **primary school**
(BRIT) n escuela primaria

prime [praɪm] adj primero, principal;
(excellent) selecto, de primera clase
▷ n: **in the ~ of life** en la flor de la vida
▷ vt (wood: fig) preparar; **~ example**
ejemplo típico; **Prime Minister** n
primer(a) ministro/a

primitive ['prɪmɪtɪv] adj primitivo;
(crude) rudimentario

primrose ['prɪmrəʊz] n primavera,
prímula

prince [prɪns] n príncipe m

princess [prɪn'sɛs] n princesa

principal ['prɪnsɪpl] adj principal,
mayor ▷ n director(a) m/f; **principally**
adv principalmente

principle ['prɪnsɪpl] n principio; **in ~**
en principio; **on ~** por principio

print [prɪnt] n (footprint) huella;
(fingerprint) huella dactilar; (letters)
letra de molde; (fabric) estampado;
(Art) grabado; (Phot) impresión
f ▷ vt imprimir; (cloth) estampar;
(write in capitals) escribir en letras de
molde; **out of ~** agotado; **print out** vt
(Comput) imprimir; **printer** n (person)
impresor(a) m/f; (machine) impresora;
printout n (Comput) impresión f

prior ['praɪə*] adj anterior, previo;
(more important) más importante; **~
to** antes de

priority [praɪ'ɔrɪtɪ] n prioridad f; **to
have ~ (over)** tener prioridad (sobre)

prison ['prɪzn] n cárcel f, prisión f
▷ cpd carcelario; **prisoner** n (in prison)
preso/a; (captured person) prisionero;
prisoner-of-war n prisionero de
guerra

pristine ['prɪstiːn] adj pristino

privacy ['prɪvəsɪ] n intimidad f

private ['praɪvɪt] adj (personal)
particular; (property, industry, discussion
etc) privado; (person) reservado; (place)
tranquilo ▷ n soldado raso; **"~"** (on
envelope) "confidencial"; (on door)
"prohibido el paso"; **in ~** en privado;
privately adv en privado; (in o.s.)

en secreto; **private property** n
propiedad f privada; **private school** n
colegio particular

privatize ['praɪvɪtaɪz] vt privatizar

privilege ['prɪvɪlɪdʒ] n privilegio;
(prerogative) prerrogativa

prize [praɪz] n premio ▷ adj de
primera clase ▷ vt apreciar, estimar;
prize-giving n distribución f de
premios; **prizewinner** n premiado/a

pro [prəʊ] n (Sport) profesional mf
▷ prep a favor de; **the ~s and cons** los
pros y los contras

probability [prɔbə'bɪlɪtɪ] n
probabilidad f; **in all ~** con toda
probabilidad

probable ['prɔbəbl] adj probable

probably ['prɔbəblɪ] adv
probablemente

probation [prə'beɪʃən] n: **on ~**
(employee) a prueba; (Law) en libertad
condicional

probe [prəʊb] n (Med, Space) sonda;
(enquiry) encuesta, investigación f ▷ vt
sondar; (investigate) investigar

problem ['prɔbləm] n problema m

procedure [prə'siːdʒə*] n
procedimiento; (bureaucratic) trámites
mpl

proceed [prə'siːd] vi (do
afterwards): **to ~ to do sth** proceder
a hacer algo; (continue): **to ~ (with)**
continuar o seguir (con); **proceedings**
npl acto(s) (pl); (Law) proceso;
proceeds ['prəʊsiːdz] npl (money)
ganancias fpl, ingresos mpl

process ['prəʊsɛs] n proceso ▷ vt
tratar, elaborar

procession [prə'sɛʃən] n desfile m;
funeral ~ cortejo fúnebre

proclaim [prə'kleɪm] vt (announce)
anunciar

prod [prɔd] vt empujar ▷ n empujón
m

produce [n 'prɔdjuːs, vt prə'djuːs]
n (Agr) productos mpl agrícolas ▷ vt
producir; (play, film, programme)
presentar; **producer** n productor(a)

m/f; (*of film, programme*) director(a) *m/f*; (*of record*) productor(a) *m/f*

product ['prɒdʌkt] *n* producto; **production** [prə'dʌkʃən] *n* producción *f*; (*Theatre*) presentación *f*; **productive** [prə'dʌktɪv] *adj* productivo; **productivity** [prɒdʌk'tɪvɪtɪ] *n* productividad *f*

Prof. [prɒf] *abbr* (= *professor*) Prof

profession [prə'fɛʃən] *n* profesión *f*; **professional** *adj* profesional ▷ *n* profesional *mf*; (*skilled person*) perito

professor [prə'fɛsə*] *n* (BRIT) catedrático/a; (US, CANADA) profesor(a) *m/f*

profile ['prəufaɪl] *n* perfil *m*

profit ['prɒfɪt] *n* (Comm) ganancia ▷ *vi*: **to ~ by** *or* **from** aprovechar *or* sacar provecho de; **profitable** *adj* (Econ) rentable

profound [prə'faund] *adj* profundo

programme ['prəugræm] (US **program**) *n* programa *m* ▷ *vt* programar; **programmer** (US **programer**) *n* programador(a) *m/f*; **programming** (US **programing**) *n* programación *f*

progress [*n* 'prəugrɛs, *vi* prə'grɛs] *n* progreso; (*development*) desarrollo ▷ *vi* progresar, avanzar; **in ~** en curso; **progressive** [-'grɛsɪv] *adj* progresivo; (*person*) progresista

prohibit [prə'hɪbɪt] *vt* prohibir; **to ~ sb from doing sth** prohibir a algn hacer algo

project [*n* 'prɒdʒɛkt, *vb* prə'dʒɛkt] *n* proyecto ▷ *vt* proyectar ▷ *vi* (*stick out*) salir, sobresalir; **projection** [prə'dʒɛkʃən] *n* proyección *f*; (*overhang*) saliente *m*; **projector** [prə'dʒɛktə*] *n* proyector *m*

prolific [prə'lɪfɪk] *adj* prolífico

prolong [prə'lɒŋ] *vt* prolongar, extender

prom [prɒm] *n abbr* = **promenade** (US: *ball*) baile *m* de gala; **the P~s** *ver*

recuadro

promenade [prɒmə'nɑːd] *n* (*by sea*) paseo marítimo

prominent ['prɒmɪnənt] *adj* (*standing out*) saliente; (*important*) eminente, importante

promiscuous [prə'mɪskjuəs] *adj* (*sexually*) promiscuo

promise ['prɒmɪs] *n* promesa ▷ *vt*, *vi* prometer; **promising** *adj* prometedor(a)

promote [prə'məut] *vt* (*employee*) ascender; (*product, pop star*) hacer propaganda por; (*ideas*) fomentar; **promotion** [-'məuʃən] *n* (*advertising campaign*) campaña *f* de promoción; (*in rank*) ascenso

prompt [prɒmpt] *adj* rápido ▷ *adv*: **at 6 o'clock ~** a las seis en punto ▷ *n* (Comput) aviso ▷ *vt* (*urge*) mover, incitar; (*Theatre*) apuntar; **to ~ sb to do sth** instar a algn a hacer algo; **promptly** *adv* rápidamente; (*exactly*) puntualmente

prone [prəun] *adj* (*lying*) postrado; **~ to** propenso a

prong [prɒŋ] *n* diente *m*, punta

pronoun ['prəunaun] *n* pronombre

P

m

pronounce [prə'naʊns] *vt* pronunciar

pronunciation [prənʌnsɪ'eɪʃən] *n* pronunciación *f*

proof [pru:f] *n* prueba ▷ *adj*: ~ **against** a prueba de

prop [prɔp] *n* apoyo *m*; (*fig*) sostén *m* accesorios *mpl*, at(t)rezzo *msg*; **prop up** *vt* (*roof, structure*) apuntalar; (*economy*) respaldar

propaganda [prɔpə'gændə] *n* propaganda

propeller [prə'pɛlə*] *n* hélice *f*

proper ['prɔpə*] *adj* (*suited, right*) propio; (*exact*) justo; (*seemly*) correcto, decente; (*authentic*) verdadero; (*referring to place*): **the village ~** el pueblo mismo; **properly** *adv* (*adequately*) correctamente; (*decently*) decentemente; **proper noun** *n* nombre *m* propio

property ['prɔpətɪ] *n* propiedad *f*; (*personal*) bienes *mpl* muebles

prophecy ['prɔfɪsɪ] *n* profecía

prophet ['prɔfɪt] *n* profeta *m*

proportion [prə'pɔ:ʃən] *n* proporción *f*; (*share*) parte *f*; **proportions** *npl* (*size*) dimensiones *fpl*; **proportional** *adj*: **proportional (to)** en proporción (con)

proposal [prə'pəʊzl] *n* (*offer of marriage*) oferta de matrimonio; (*plan*) proyecto

propose [prə'pəʊz] *vt* proponer ▷ *vi* declararse; **to ~ to do** tener intención de hacer

proposition [prɔpə'zɪʃən] *n* propuesta

proprietor [prə'praɪətə*] *n* propietario/a, dueño/a

prose [prəʊz] *n* prosa

prosecute ['prɔsɪkju:t] *vt* (*Law*) procesar; **prosecution** [-'kju:ʃən] *n* proceso, causa; (*accusing side*) acusación *f*; **prosecutor** *n* acusador(a) *m/f*; (*also:* **public prosecutor**) fiscal *mf*

prospect [*n* 'prɔspɛkt, *vb* prə'spɛkt] *n* (*possibility*) posibilidad *f*; (*outlook*) perspectiva ▷ *vi*: **to ~ for** buscar; **prospects** *npl* (*for work etc*) perspectivas *fpl*; **prospective** [prə'spɛktɪv] *adj* futuro

prospectus [prə'spɛktəs] *n* prospecto

prosper ['prɔspə*] *vi* prosperar; **prosperity** [-'spɛrɪtɪ] *n* prosperidad *f*; **prosperous** *adj* próspero

prostitute ['prɔstɪtju:t] *n* prostituta; (*male*) hombre que se dedica a la prostitución

protect [prə'tɛkt] *vt* proteger; **protection** [-'tɛkʃən] *n* protección *f*; **protective** *adj* protector(a)

protein ['prəʊti:n] *n* proteína

protest [*n* 'prəʊtɛst, *vb* prə'tɛst] *n* protesta ▷ *vi*: **to ~ about** *or* **at/against** protestar de/contra ▷ *vt* (*insist*): **to ~ (that)** insistir en (que)

Protestant ['prɔtɪstənt] *adj, n* protestante *mf*

protester [prə'tɛstə*] *n* manifestante *mf*

protractor [prə'træktə*] *n* (*Geom*) transportador *m*

proud [praʊd] *adj* orgulloso; (*pej*) soberbio, altanero

prove [pru:v] *vt* probar; (*show*) demostrar ▷ *vi*: **to ~ (to be) correct** resultar correcto; **to ~ o.s.** probar su valía

proverb ['prɔvə:b] *n* refrán *m*

provide [prə'vaɪd] *vt* proporcionar, dar; **to ~ sb with sth** proveer a algn de algo; **provide for** *vt fus* (*person*) mantener a; (*problem etc*) tener en cuenta; **provided** *conj*: **provided (that)** con tal de que, a condición de que; **providing** [prə'vaɪdɪŋ] *conj*: **providing (that)** a condición de que, con tal de que

province ['prɔvɪns] *n* provincia; (*fig*) esfera; **provincial** [prə'vɪnʃəl] *adj* provincial; (*pej*) provinciano

provision [prə'vɪʒən] *n* (*supplying*)

suministro, abastecimiento; (*of contract etc*) disposición *f*; **provisions** *npl* (*food*) comestibles *mpl*; **provisional** *adj* provisional

provocative [prə'vɒkətɪv] *adj* provocativo

provoke [prə'vəuk] *vt* (*cause*) provocar, incitar; (*anger*) enojar

prowl [praul] *vi* (*also*: **~ about, ~ around**) merodear ▷ *n*: **on the ~** de merodeo

proximity [prɒk'sɪmɪtɪ] *n* proximidad *f*

proxy ['prɒksɪ] *n*: **by ~** por poderes

prudent ['pru:dənt] *adj* prudente

prune [pru:n] *n* ciruela pasa ▷ *vt* podar

pry [praɪ] *vi*: **to ~ (into)** entrometerse (en)

PS *n abbr* (= *postscript*) P.D.

pseudonym ['sju:dənɪm] *n* seudónimo

PSHE (BRIT: Scol) *n abbr* (= *personal, social and health education*) formación social y sanitaria

psychiatric [saɪkɪ'ætrɪk] *adj* psiquiátrico

psychiatrist [saɪ'kaɪətrɪst] *n* psiquiatra *mf*

psychic ['saɪkɪk] *adj* (*also*: **~al**) psíquico

psychoanalysis [saɪkəuə'nælɪsɪs] *n* psicoanálisis *m inv*

psychological [saɪkə'lɒdʒɪkl] *adj* psicológico

psychologist [saɪ'kɒlədʒɪst] *n* psicólogo/a

psychology [saɪ'kɒlədʒɪ] *n* psicología

psychotherapy [saɪkəu'θɛrəpɪ] *n* psicoterapia

pt *abbr* = **pint(s)**; **point(s)**

PTO *abbr* (= *please turn over*) sigue

pub [pʌb] *n abbr* (= *public house*) pub *m*, bar *m*

puberty ['pju:bətɪ] *n* pubertad *f*

public ['pʌblɪk] *adj* público ▷ *n*: **the ~** el público; **in ~** en público; **to make ~**

hacer público

publication [pʌblɪ'keɪʃən] *n* publicación *f*

public: public company *n* sociedad *f* anónima; **public convenience** (BRIT) *n* aseos *mpl* públicos (SP), sanitarios *mpl* (LAM); **public holiday** *n* (día *m* de) fiesta (SP), (día *m*) feriado (LAM); **public house** (BRIT) *n* bar *m*, pub *m*

publicity [pʌb'lɪsɪtɪ] *n* publicidad *f*

publicize ['pʌblɪsaɪz] *vt* publicitar

public: public limited company *n* sociedad *f* anónima (S.A.); **publicly** *adv* públicamente, en público; **public opinion** *n* opinión *f* pública; **public relations** *n* relaciones *fpl* públicas; **public school** *n* (BRIT) escuela privada; (US) instituto; **public transport** *n* transporte *m* público

publish ['pʌblɪʃ] *vt* publicar; **publisher** *n* (*person*) editor(a) *m/f*; (*firm*) editorial *f*; **publishing** *n* (*industry*) industria del libro

pub lunch *n* almuerzo que se sirve en un pub; **to go for a ~** almorzar o comer en un pub

pudding ['pudɪŋ] *n* pudín *m*; (BRIT: dessert) postre *m*; **black ~** morcilla

puddle ['pʌdl] *n* charco

Puerto Rico [pwɛ:təu'ri:kəu] *n* Puerto Rico

puff [pʌf] *n* soplo; (*of smoke, air*) bocanada; (*of breathing*) resoplido ▷ *vt*: **to ~ one's pipe** chupar la pipa ▷ *vi* (*pant*) jadear; **puff pastry** *n* hojaldre *m*

pull [pul] *n* (*tug*): **to give sth a ~** dar un tirón a algo ▷ *vt* tirar de; (*press: trigger*) apretar; (*haul*) tirar, arrastrar; (*close: curtain*) echar ▷ *vi* tirar; **to ~ to pieces** hacer pedazos; **not to ~ one's punches** no andarse con bromas; **to ~ one's weight** hacer su parte; **to ~ o.s. together** sobreponerse; **to ~ sb's leg** tomar el pelo a algn; **pull apart** *vt* (*break*) romper; **pull away** *vi* (*vehicle: move off*) salir, arrancar; (*draw back*) apartarse bruscamente; **pull back** *vt* (*lever etc*)

P

tirar hacia sí; (*curtains*) descorrer ▷ *vi*
(*refrain*) contenerse; (*Mil: withdraw*)
retirarse; **pull down** *vt* (*building*)
derribar; **pull in** *vi* (*car etc*) parar
(junto a la acera); (*train*) llegar a la
estación; **pull off** *vt* (*deal etc*) cerrar;
pull out *vi* (*car, train etc*) salir ▷ *vt*
sacar, arrancar; **pull over** *vi* (*Aut*)
hacerse a un lado; **pull up** *vi* (*stop*)
parar ▷ *vt* (*raise*) levantar; (*uproot*)
arrancar, desarraigar
pulley ['pulɪ] *n* polea
pullover ['puləuvə*] *n* jersey *m*,
suéter *m*
pulp [pʌlp] *n* (*of fruit*) pulpa
pulpit ['pulpɪt] *n* púlpito
pulse [pʌls] *n* (*Anat*) pulso; (*rhythm*)
pulsación *f*; (*Bot*) legumbre *f*; **pulses** *pl*
n legumbres
puma ['pjuːmə] *n* puma *m*
pump [pʌmp] *n* bomba; (*shoe*)
zapatilla ▷ *vt* sacar con una bomba;
pump up *vt* inflar
pumpkin ['pʌmpkɪn] *n* calabaza
pun [pʌn] *n* juego de palabras
punch [pʌntʃ] *n* (*blow*) golpe *m*,
puñetazo; (*tool*) punzón *m*; (*drink*)
ponche *m* ▷ *vt* (*hit*): **to ~ sb/sth** dar
un puñetazo *or* golpear a algn/algo;
punch-up (*BRIT: inf*) *n* riña
punctual ['pʌŋktjuəl] *adj* puntual
punctuation [pʌŋktju'eɪʃən] *n*
puntuación *f*
puncture ['pʌŋktʃə*] (*BRIT*) *n*
pinchazo ▷ *vt* pinchar
punish ['pʌnɪʃ] *vt* castigar;
punishment *n* castigo
punk [pʌŋk] *n* (*also: ~ rocker*)
punki *mf*; (*also: ~ rock*) música punk;
(*US: inf: hoodlum*) rufián *m*
pup [pʌp] *n* cachorro
pupil ['pjuːpl] *n* alumno/a; (*of eye*)
pupila
puppet ['pʌpɪt] *n* títere *m*
puppy ['pʌpɪ] *n* cachorro, perrito
purchase ['pəːtʃɪs] *n* compra ▷ *vt*
comprar
pure [pjuə*] *adj* puro; **purely** *adv*

puramente
purify ['pjuərɪfaɪ] *vt* purificar,
depurar
purity ['pjuərɪtɪ] *n* pureza
purple ['pəːpl] *adj* purpúreo; morado
purpose ['pəːpəs] *n* propósito; **on ~** a
propósito, adrede
purr [pəː*] *vi* ronronear
purse [pəːs] *n* monedero;
(*US: handbag*) bolso (*SP*), cartera (*LAM*),
bolsa (*MEX*) ▷ *vt* fruncir
pursue [pə'sjuː] *vt* seguir
pursuit [pə'sjuːt] *n* (*chase*) caza;
(*occupation*) actividad *f*
pus [pʌs] *n* pus *m*
push [puʃ] *n* empuje *m*, empujón
m; (*of button*) presión *f*; (*drive*) empuje
m ▷ *vt* empujar; (*button*) apretar;
(*promote*) promover ▷ *vi* empujar;
(*demand*): **to ~ for** luchar por; **push in**
vi colarse; **push off** (*inf*) *vi* largarse;
push on *vi* seguir adelante; **push over**
vt (*cause to fall*) hacer caer, derribar;
(*knock over*) volcar; **push through** *vi*
(*crowd*) abrirse paso a empujones ▷ *vt*
(*measure*) despachar; **pushchair** (*BRIT*)
n sillita de ruedas; **pusher** *n* (*drug
pusher*) traficante *mf* de drogas; **push-
up** (*US*) *n* plancha
pussy(-cat) ['pusɪ-] (*inf*) *n* minino
(*inf*)
put [put] (*pt, pp ~*) *vt* (*place*) poner,
colocar; (*put into*) meter; (*say*) expresar;
(*a question*) hacer; (*estimate*) estimar;
put aside *vt* (*lay down: book etc*) dejar
or poner a un lado; (*save*) ahorrar; (*in
shop*) guardar; **put away** *vt* (*store*)
guardar; **put back** *vt* (*replace*) devolver
a su lugar; (*postpone*) aplazar; **put by**
vt (*money*) guardar; **put down** *vt* (*on
ground*) poner en el suelo; (*animal*)
sacrificar; (*in writing*) apuntar; (*revolt
etc*) sofocar; (*attribute*): **to put sth
down to** atribuir algo a; **put forward**
vt (*ideas*) presentar, proponer; **put
in** *vt* (*complaint*) presentar; (*time*)
dedicar; **put off** *vt* (*postpone*) aplazar;
(*discourage*) desanimar; **put on** *vt*

ponerse; (*light etc*) encender; (*play etc*)
presentar; (*gain*): **to put on weight**
engordar; (*brake*) echar; (*record, kettle
etc*) poner; (*assume*) adoptar; **put out**
vt (*fire, light*) apagar; (*rubbish etc*) sacar;
(*cat etc*) echar; (*one's hand*) alargar;
(*inf: person*): **to be put out** alterarse;
put through *vt* (*Tel*) poner; (*plan etc*)
hacer aprobar; **put together** *vt* unir,
reunir; (*assemble: furniture*) armar,
montar; (*meal*) preparar; **put up** *vt*
(*raise*) levantar, alzar; (*hang*) colgar;
(*build*) construir; (*increase*) aumentar;
(*accommodate*) alojar; **put up with** *vt
fus* aguantar

putt [pʌt] *n* putt *m*, golpe *m* corto;
putting green *n* green *m*; minigolf *m*

puzzle ['pʌzl] *n* rompecabezas *m
inv*; (*also:* **crossword ~**) crucigrama
m; (*mystery*) misterio ▷ *vt* dejar
perplejo, confundir ▷ *vi*: **to ~ over sth**
devanarse los sesos con algo; **puzzled**
adj perplejo; **puzzling** *adj* misterioso,
extraño

pyjamas [pɪ'dʒɑːməz] (BRIT) *npl*
pijama *m*

pylon ['paɪlən] *n* torre *f* de
conducción eléctrica

pyramid ['pɪrəmɪd] *n* pirámide *f*

q

quack [kwæk] *n* graznido; (*pej: doctor*)
curandero/a

quadruple [kwɔ'drupl] *vt, vi*
cuadruplicar

quail [kweɪl] *n* codorniz *f* ▷ *vi*: **to ~ at**
or **before** amedrentarse ante

quaint [kweɪnt] *adj* extraño;
(*picturesque*) pintoresco

quake [kweɪk] *vi* temblar ▷ *n abbr =*
earthquake

qualification [kwɔlɪfɪ'keɪʃən] *n*
(*ability*) capacidad *f*; (*often pl: diploma
etc*) título; (*reservation*) salvedad *f*

qualified ['kwɔlɪfaɪd] *adj*
capacitado; (*professionally*) titulado;
(*limited*) limitado

qualify ['kwɔlɪfaɪ] *vt* (*make competent*)
capacitar; (*modify*) modificar ▷ *vi* (*in
competition*): **to ~ (for)** calificarse
(para); (*pass examination(s)*: **to ~ (as)**
calificarse (de), graduarse (en); (*be
eligible*): **to ~ (for)** reunir los requisitos
(para)

quality ['kwɔlɪtɪ] *n* calidad *f*; (*of
person*) cualidad *f*

qualm [kwɑːm] n escrúpulo
quantify ['kwɒntɪfaɪ] vt cuantificar
quantity ['kwɒntɪtɪ] n cantidad f; **in ~** en grandes cantidades
quarantine ['kwɒrntiːn] n cuarentena
quarrel ['kwɒrl] n riña, pelea ▷ vi reñir, pelearse
quarry ['kwɒrɪ] n cantera
quart [kwɔːt] n ≈ litro
quarter ['kwɔːtə*] n cuarto, cuarta parte f; (US: coin) moneda de 25 centavos; (of year) trimestre m; (district) barrio ▷ vt dividir en cuartos; (Mil: lodge) alojar; **quarters** npl (barracks) cuartel m; (living quarters) alojamiento; **a ~ of an hour** un cuarto de hora; **quarter final** n cuarto de final; **quarterly** adj trimestral ▷ adv cada 3 meses, trimestralmente
quartet(te) [kwɔːˈtɛt] n cuarteto
quartz [kwɔːts] n cuarzo
quay [kiː] n (also: **~side**) muelle m
queasy ['kwiːzɪ] adj: **to feel ~** tener náuseas
queen [kwiːn] n reina; (Cards etc) dama
queer [kwɪə*] adj raro, extraño ▷ n (inf: highly offensive) maricón m
quench [kwɛntʃ] vt: **to ~ one's thirst** apagar la sed
query ['kwɪərɪ] n (question) pregunta ▷ vt dudar de
quest [kwɛst] n busca, búsqueda
question ['kwɛstʃən] n pregunta; (doubt) duda; (matter) asunto, cuestión f ▷ vt (doubt) dudar de; (interrogate) interrogar, hacer preguntas a; **beyond ~** fuera de toda duda; **out of the ~** imposible; ni hablar; **questionable** adj dudoso; **question mark** n punto de interrogación; **questionnaire** [-'nɛə*] n cuestionario
queue [kjuː] (BRIT) n cola ▷ vi (also: **~ up**) hacer cola
quiche [kiːʃ] n quiche m
quick [kwɪk] adj rápido; (agile) ágil; (mind) listo ▷ n: **cut to the ~** (fig) herido en lo vivo; **be ~!** ¡date prisa!; **quickly** adv rápidamente, de prisa
quid [kwɪd] (BRIT: inf) n inv libra
quiet ['kwaɪət] adj (voice, music etc) bajo; (person, place) tranquilo; (ceremony) íntimo ▷ n silencio; (calm) tranquilidad f ▷ vt, vi (US) = **quieten**

⬛ Be careful not to translate **quiet** by the Spanish word quieto.

quietly adv tranquilamente; (silently) silenciosamente
quilt [kwɪlt] n edredón m
quirky ['kwɜːkɪ] adj raro, estrafalario
quit [kwɪt] (pt, pp **~** or **~ted**) vt dejar, abandonar; (premises) desocupar ▷ vi (give up) renunciar; (resign) dimitir
quite [kwaɪt] adv (rather) bastante; (entirely) completamente; **that's not ~ big enough** no acaba de ser lo bastante grande; **~ a few of them** un buen número de ellos; **~ (so)!** ¡así es!, ¡exactamente!
quits [kwɪts] adj: **~ (with)** en paz (con); **let's call it ~** dejémoslo en tablas
quiver ['kwɪvə*] vi estremecerse
quiz [kwɪz] n concurso ▷ vt interrogar
quota ['kwəutə] n cuota
quotation [kwəuˈteɪʃən] n cita; (estimate) presupuesto; **quotation marks** npl comillas fpl
quote [kwəut] n cita; (estimate) presupuesto ▷ vt citar; (price) cotizar ▷ vi: **to ~ from** citar de; **quotes** npl (inverted commas) comillas fpl

r

rabbi ['ræbaɪ] n rabino
rabbit ['ræbɪt] n conejo
rabies ['reɪbiːz] n rabia
RAC (BRIT) n abbr (= Royal Automobile Club) ~ RACE m
rac(c)oon [rə'kuːn] n mapache m
race [reɪs] n carrera; (species) raza ▷ vt (horse) hacer correr; (engine) acelerar ▷ vi (compete) competir; (run) correr; (pulse) latir a ritmo acelerado; **race car** (US) n = **racing car**; **racecourse** n hipódromo; **racehorse** n caballo de carreras; **racetrack** n pista; (for cars) autódromo
racial ['reɪʃl] adj racial
racing ['reɪsɪŋ] n carreras fpl; **racing car** (BRIT) n coche m de carreras; **racing driver** (BRIT) n piloto mf de carreras
racism ['reɪsɪzəm] n racismo; **racist** [-sɪst] adj, n racista mf
rack [ræk] n (also: luggage ~) rejilla; (shelf) estante m; (also: roof ~) baca, portaequipajes m inv; (dish rack) escurreplatos m inv; (clothes rack)

percha ▷ vt atormentar; **to ~ one's brains** devanarse los sesos
racket ['rækɪt] n (for tennis) raqueta; (noise) ruido, estrépito; (swindle) estafa, timo
racquet ['rækɪt] n raqueta
radar ['reɪdɑː*] n radar m
radiation [reɪdɪ'eɪʃən] n radiación f
radiator ['reɪdɪeɪtə*] n radiador m
radical ['rædɪkl] adj radical
radio ['reɪdɪəu] n radio f; **on the ~** por radio; **radioactive** adj radioactivo; **radio station** n emisora
radish ['rædɪʃ] n rábano
RAF n abbr (= Royal Air Force) las Fuerzas Aéreas Británicas
raffle ['ræfl] n rifa, sorteo
raft [rɑːft] n balsa; (also: life ~) balsa salvavidas
rag [ræg] n (piece of cloth) trapo; (torn cloth) harapo; (pej: newspaper) periodicucho; (for charity) actividades estudiantiles benéficas; **rags** npl (torn clothes) harapos mpl
rage [reɪdʒ] n rabia, furor m ▷ vi (person) rabiar, estar furioso; (storm) bramar; **it's all the ~** (very fashionable) está muy de moda
ragged ['rægɪd] adj (edge) desigual, mellado; (appearance) andrajoso, harapiento
raid [reɪd] n (Mil) incursión f; (criminal) asalto; (by police) redada ▷ vt invadir, atacar; asaltar
rail [reɪl] n (on stair) barandilla, pasamanos m inv; (on bridge, balcony) pretil m; (of ship) barandilla; (also: towel ~) toallero; **railcard** n (BRIT) tarjeta para obtener descuentos en el tren; **railing(s)** n(pl) vallado; **railroad** (US) n = **railway**; **railway** (BRIT) n ferrocarril m, vía férrea; **railway line** (BRIT) n línea (de ferrocarril); **railway station** (BRIT) n estación f de ferrocarril
rain [reɪn] n lluvia ▷ vi llover; **in the ~** bajo la lluvia; **it's ~ing** llueve, está lloviendo; **rainbow** n arco iris;

raincoat n impermeable m; **raindrop** n gota de lluvia; **rainfall** n lluvia; **rainforest** n selvas fpl tropicales; **rainy** adj lluvioso

raise [reɪz] n aumento ▷ vt levantar; (increase) aumentar; (improve: morale) subir; (: standards) mejorar; (doubts) suscitar; (a question) plantear; (cattle, family) criar; (crop) cultivar; (army) reclutar; (loan) obtener; **to ~ one's voice** alzar la voz

raisin ['reɪzn] n pasa de Corinto

rake [reɪk] n (tool) rastrillo; (person) libertino ▷ vt (garden) rastrillar

rally ['rælɪ] n (Pol etc) reunión f, mitin m; (Aut) rallye m; (Tennis) peloteo ▷ vt reunir ▷ vi recuperarse

RAM [ræm] n abbr (= random access memory) RAM f

ram [ræm] n carnero; (also: **battering ~**) ariete m ▷ vt (crash into) dar contra, chocar con; (push: fist etc) empujar con fuerza

Ramadan [ræmə'dæn] n ramadán m

ramble ['ræmbl] n caminata, excursión f en el campo ▷ vi (pej: also: ~ **on**) divagar; **rambler** n excursionista mf; (Bot) trepadora; **rambling** adj (speech) inconexo; (house) laberíntico; (Bot) trepador(a)

ramp [ræmp] n rampa; **on/off ~** (us Aut) vía de acceso/salida

rampage [ræm'peɪdʒ] n: **to be on the ~** desmandarse ▷ vi: **they went rampaging through the town** recorrieron la ciudad armando alboroto

ran [ræn] pt of **run**

ranch [rɑːntʃ] n hacienda, estancia

random ['rændəm] adj fortuito, sin orden; (Comput, Math) aleatorio ▷ n: **at ~** al azar

rang [ræŋ] pt of **ring**

range [reɪndʒ] n (of mountains) cadena de montañas, cordillera; (of missile) alcance m; (of voice) registro; (series) serie f; (of products) surtido; (Mil: also: **shooting ~**) campo de tiro;

(also: **kitchen ~**) fogón m ▷ vt (place) colocar; (arrange) arreglar ▷ vi: **to ~ over** (extend) extenderse por; **to ~ from ... to ...** oscilar entre ... y ...

ranger ['reɪndʒə*] n guardabosques mf inv

rank [ræŋk] n (row) fila; (Mil) rango; (status) categoría; (BRIT: also: **taxi ~**) parada de taxis ▷ vi: **to ~ among** figurar entre ▷ adj fétido, rancio; **the ~ and file** (fig) la base

ransom ['rænsəm] n rescate m; **to hold to ~** (fig) hacer chantaje a

rant [rænt] vi divagar, desvariar

rap [ræp] vt golpear, dar un golpecito en ▷ n (music) rap m

rape [reɪp] n violación f; (Bot) colza ▷ vt violar

rapid ['ræpɪd] adj rápido; **rapidly** adv rápidamente; **rapids** npl (Geo) rápidos mpl

rapist ['reɪpɪst] n violador m

rapport [ræ'pɔː*] n simpatía

rare [reə*] adj raro, poco común; (Culin: steak) poco hecho; **rarely** adv pocas veces

rash [ræʃ] adj imprudente, precipitado ▷ n (Med) sarpullido, erupción f (cutánea); (of events) serie f

rasher ['ræʃə*] n lonja

raspberry ['rɑːzbərɪ] n frambuesa

rat [ræt] n rata

rate [reɪt] n (ratio) razón f; (price) precio; (: of hotel etc) tarifa; (of interest) tipo; (speed) velocidad f ▷ vt (value) tasar; (estimate) estimar; **rates** npl (BRIT: property tax) impuesto municipal; (fees) tarifa; **to ~ sth/sb as** considerar algo/a algn como

rather ['rɑːðə*] adv: **it's ~ expensive** es algo caro; (too much) es demasiado caro; (to some extent) más bien; **there's ~ a lot** hay bastante; **I would** or **I'd ~ go** preferiría ir; **or ~** mejor dicho

rating ['reɪtɪŋ] n tasación f; (score) índice m; (of ship) clase f; **ratings** npl (Radio, TV) niveles mpl de audiencia

ratio ['reɪʃɪəu] n razón f; **in the ~ of**

100 to 1 a razón de 100 a 1

ration ['ræʃən] n ración f ▷ vt racionar; **rations** npl víveres mpl

rational ['ræʃənl] adj (solution, reasoning) lógico, razonable; (person) cuerdo, sensato

rattle ['rætl] n golpeteo; (of train etc) traqueteo; (for baby) sonaja, sonajero ▷ vi castañetear; (car, bus): **to ~ along** traquetear ▷ vt hacer sonar agitando

rave [reɪv] vi (in anger) encolerizarse; (with enthusiasm) entusiasmarse; (Med) delirar, desvariar ▷ n (inf: party) rave m

raven ['reɪvən] n cuervo

ravine [rə'viːn] n barranco

raw [rɔː] adj crudo; (not processed) bruto; (sore) vivo; (inexperienced) novato, inexperto; **~ materials** materias primas

ray [reɪ] n rayo; **~ of hope** (rayo de) esperanza

razor ['reɪzə*] n (open) navaja; (safety razor) máquina de afeitar; (electric razor) máquina (eléctrica) de afeitar; **razor blade** n hoja de afeitar

Rd abbr = **road**

RE n abbr (BRIT) = **religious education**

re [riː] prep con referencia a

reach [riːtʃ] n alcance m; (of river etc) extensión f entre dos recodos ▷ vt alcanzar, llegar a; (achieve) lograr ▷ vi extenderse; **within ~** al alcance (de la mano); **out of ~** fuera del alcance; **reach out** vt (hand) tender ▷ vi: **to reach out for sth** alargar or tender la mano para tomar algo

react [riː'ækt] vi reaccionar; **reaction** [-'ækʃən] n reacción f; **reactor** [riː'æktə*] n (also: **nuclear reactor**) reactor m (nuclear)

read [riːd, pt, pp red] (pt, pp **~**) vi leer ▷ vt leer; (understand) entender; (study) estudiar; **read out** vt leer en alta voz; **reader** n lector(a) m/f; (BRIT: at university) profesor(a) m/f adjunto/a

readily ['redɪlɪ] adv (willingly) de buena gana; (easily) fácilmente; (quickly) en seguida

reading ['riːdɪŋ] n lectura; (on instrument) indicación f

ready ['redɪ] adj listo, preparado; (willing) dispuesto; (available) disponible ▷ adv: **~-cooked** listo para comer ▷ n: **at the ~** (Mil) listo para tirar ▷ **to get ~** vi prepararse ▷ **to get ~** vt preparar; **ready-made** adj confeccionado

real [rɪəl] adj verdadero, auténtico; **in ~ terms** en términos reales; **real ale** n cerveza elaborada tradicionalmente; **real estate** n bienes mpl raíces; **realistic** [-'lɪstɪk] adj realista; **reality** [riː'ælɪtɪ] n realidad f; **reality TV** n telerrealidad f

realization [rɪəlaɪ'zeɪʃən] n comprensión f; (fulfilment, Comm) realización f

realize ['rɪəlaɪz] vt (understand) darse cuenta de

really ['rɪəlɪ] adv realmente; (for emphasis) verdaderamente; (actually): **what ~ happened** lo que pasó en realidad; **~?** ¿de veras?; **~!** (annoyance) ¡vamos!, ¡por favor!

realm [relm] n reino; (fig) esfera

realtor ['rɪəltɔ:*] n (US) agente mf inmobiliario/a

reappear [riːə'pɪə*] vi reaparecer

rear [rɪə*] adj trasero ▷ n parte f trasera ▷ vt (cattle, family) criar ▷ vi (also: **~ up**: animal) encabritarse

rearrange [riːə'reɪndʒ] vt ordenar or arreglar de nuevo

rear: rear-view mirror n (Aut) (espejo) retrovisor m; **rear-wheel drive** n tracción f trasera

reason ['riːzn] n razón f ▷ vi: **to ~ with sb** tratar de que algn entre en razón; **it stands to ~ that …** es lógico que …; **reasonable** adj razonable; (sensible) sensato; **reasonably** adv razonablemente; **reasoning** n razonamiento, argumentos mpl

reassurance [riːə'ʃuərəns] n consuelo

reassure [riːə'ʃuə*] vt tranquilizar,

alentar; **to ~ sb that ...** tranquilizar a algn asegurando que ...

rebate ['riːbeɪt] n (on tax etc) desgravación f

rebel [n 'rɛbl, vi rɪ'bɛl] n rebelde mf ▷ vi rebelarse, sublevarse; **rebellion** [rɪ'bɛljən] n rebelión f, sublevación f; **rebellious** [rɪ'bɛljəs] adj rebelde; (child) revoltoso

rebuild [riː'bɪld] vt reconstruir

recall [vb rɪ'kɔːl, n 'riːkɔl] vt (remember) recordar; (ambassador etc) retirar ▷ n recuerdo; retirada

rec'd abbr (= received) rbdo

receipt [rɪ'siːt] n (document) recibo; (for parcel etc) acuse m de recibo; (act of receiving) recepción f; **receipts** npl (Comm) ingresos mpl

> Be careful not to translate **receipt** by the Spanish word receta.

receive [rɪ'siːv] vt recibir; (guest) acoger; (wound) sufrir; **receiver** n (Tel) auricular m; (Radio) receptor m; (of stolen goods) perista mf; (Comm) administrador m jurídico

recent ['riːsnt] adj reciente; **recently** adv recientemente; **recently arrived** recién llegado

reception [rɪ'sɛpʃən] n recepción f; (welcome) acogida; **reception desk** n recepción f; **receptionist** n recepcionista mf

recession [rɪ'sɛʃən] n recesión f

recharge [riː'tʃɑːdʒ] vt (battery) recargar

recipe ['rɛsɪpɪ] n receta; (for disaster, success) fórmula

recipient [rɪ'sɪpɪənt] n recibidor(a) m/f; (of letter) destinatario/a

recital [rɪ'saɪtl] n recital m

recite [rɪ'saɪt] vt (poem) recitar

reckless ['rɛkləs] adj temerario, imprudente; (driving, driver) peligroso

reckon ['rɛkən] vt calcular; (consider) considerar; (think): **I ~ that ...** me parece que ...

reclaim [rɪ'kleɪm] vt (land, waste) recuperar; (land: from sea) rescatar;

(demand back) reclamar

recline [rɪ'klaɪn] vi reclinarse

recognition [rɛkəg'nɪʃən] n reconocimiento; **transformed beyond ~** irreconocible

recognize ['rɛkəgnaɪz] vt: **to ~ (by/as)** reconocer (por/como)

recollection [rɛkə'lɛkʃən] n recuerdo

recommend [rɛkə'mɛnd] vt recomendar; **recommendation** [rɛkəmɛn'deɪʃən] n recomendación f

reconcile ['rɛkənsaɪl] vt (two people) reconciliar; (two facts) compaginar; **to ~ o.s. to sth** conformarse a algo

reconsider [riːkən'sɪdə*] vt repensar

reconstruct [riːkən'strʌkt] vt reconstruir

record [n, adj 'rɛkɔːd, vt rɪ'kɔːd] n (Mus) disco; (of meeting etc) acta; (register) registro, partida; (file) archivo; (also: **criminal ~**) antecedentes mpl; (written) expediente m; (Sport, Comput) récord m ▷ adj récord, sin precedentes ▷ vt registrar; (Mus: song etc) grabar; **in ~ time** en un tiempo récord; **off the ~** adj no oficial ▷ adv confidencialmente; **recorded delivery** (BRIT) n (Post) entrega con acuse de recibo; **recorder** n (Mus) flauta de pico; **recording** n (Mus) grabación f; **record player** n tocadiscos m inv

recount [rɪ'kaunt] vt contar

recover [rɪ'kʌvə*] vt recuperar ▷ vi (from illness, shock) recuperarse; **recovery** n recuperación f

recreate [riːkrɪ'eɪt] vt recrear

recreation [rɛkrɪ'eɪʃən] n recreo; **recreational vehicle** (US) n caravan or rulota pequeña; **recreational drug** droga recreativa

recruit [rɪ'kruːt] n recluta mf ▷ vt reclutar; (staff) contratar; **recruitment** n reclutamiento

rectangle ['rɛktæŋgl] n rectángulo; **rectangular** [-'tæŋgjulə*] adj rectangular

rectify ['rɛktɪfaɪ] vt rectificar

rector ['rɛktə*] n (Rel) párroco
recur [rɪ'kə:*] vi repetirse; (pain, illness) producirse de nuevo; **recurring** adj (problem) repetido, constante
recyclable [ri:'saɪkləbl] adj reciclable
recycle [ri:'saɪkl] vt reciclar
recycling [ri:'saɪklɪŋ] n reciclaje
red [rɛd] n rojo ▷ adj rojo; (hair) pelirrojo; (wine) tinto; **to be in the ~** (account) estar en números rojos; (business) tener un saldo negativo; **to give sb the ~ carpet treatment** recibir a algn con todos los honores; **Red Cross** n Cruz f Roja; **redcurrant** n grosella roja
redeem [rɪ'di:m] vt redimir; (promises) cumplir; (sth in pawn) desempeñar; (fig, also Rel) rescatar
red: red-haired adj pelirrojo; **redhead** n pelirrojo/a; **red-hot** adj candente; **red light** n **to go through a red light** (Aut) pasar la luz roja; **red-light district** n barrio chino
red meat n carne f roja
reduce [rɪ'dju:s] vt reducir; **to ~ sb to tears** hacer llorar a algn; **"~ speed now"** (Aut) "reduzca la velocidad", **reduced** adj (decreased) reducido, rebajado; **at a reduced price** con rebaja or descuento; **"greatly reduced prices"** "grandes rebajas"; **reduction** [rɪ'dʌkʃən] n reducción f; (of price) rebaja; (discount) descuento; (smaller-scale copy) copia reducida
redundancy [rɪ'dʌndənsɪ] n (dismissal) despido; (unemployment) desempleo
redundant [rɪ'dʌndnt] adj (BRIT: worker) parado, sin trabajo; (detail, object) superfluo; **to be made ~** quedar(se) sin trabajo
reed [ri:d] n (Bot) junco, caña; (Mus) lengüeta
reef [ri:f] n (at sea) arrecife m
reel [ri:l] n carrete m, bobina; (of film) rollo; (dance) baile escocés ▷ vt (also: ~ up) devanar; (also: ~ in) sacar ▷ vi

(sway) tambalear(se)
ref [rɛf] (inf) n abbr = **referee**
refectory [rɪ'fɛktərɪ] n comedor m
refer [rɪ'fə:*] vt (send: patient) referir; (: matter) remitir ▷ vi: **to ~ to** (allude to) referirse a, aludir a; (apply to) relacionarse con; (consult) consultar
referee [rɛfə'ri:] n árbitro; (BRIT: for job application): **to be a ~ for sb** proporcionar referencias a algn ▷ vt (match) arbitrar en
reference ['rɛfrəns] n referencia; (for job application: letter) carta de recomendación; **with ~ to** (Comm: in letter) me remito a; **reference number** n número de referencia
refill [vt ri:'fɪl, n 'ri:fɪl] vt rellenar ▷ n repuesto, recambio
refine [rɪ'faɪn] vt refinar; **refined** adj (person) fino; **refinery** n refinería
reflect [rɪ'flɛkt] vt reflejar ▷ vi (think) reflexionar, pensar; **it ~s badly/well on him** le perjudica/le hace honor; **reflection** [-'flɛkʃən] n (act) reflexión f; (image) reflejo; (criticism) crítica; **on reflection** pensándolo bien
reflex ['ri:flɛks] adj, n reflejo
reform [rɪ'fɔ:m] n reforma ▷ vt reformar
refrain [rɪ'freɪn] vi: **to ~ from doing** abstenerse de hacer ▷ n estribillo
refresh [rɪ'frɛʃ] vt refrescar; **refreshing** adj refrescante, **refreshments** npl refrescos mpl
refrigerator [rɪ'frɪdʒəreɪtə*] n frigorífico (SP), nevera (SP), refrigerador m (LAM), heladera (RPL)
refuel [ri:'fjuəl] vi repostar (combustible)
refuge ['rɛfju:dʒ] n refugio, asilo; **to take ~ in** refugiarse en; **refugee** [rɛfju'dʒi:] n refugiado/a
refund [n 'ri:fʌnd, vb rɪ'fʌnd] n reembolso ▷ vt devolver, reembolsar
refurbish [ri:'fə:bɪʃ] vt restaurar, renovar
refusal [rɪ'fju:zəl] n negativa; **to have first ~ on** tener la primera

opción a
refuse¹ [ˈrɛfjuːs] n basura
refuse² [rɪˈfjuːz] vt rechazar;
(invitation) declinar; (permission)
denegar ▷ vi: **to ~ to do sth** negarse a
hacer algo; (horse) rehusar
regain [rɪˈɡeɪn] vt recobrar, recuperar
regard [rɪˈɡɑːd] n mirada; (esteem)
respeto; (attention) consideración f ▷ vt
(consider) considerar; **to give one's ~s
to** saludar de su parte a; **"with kindest
~s"** "con muchos recuerdos"; **as ~s,
with ~ to** con respecto a, en cuanto
a; **regarding** prep con respecto a, en
cuanto a; **regardless** adv a pesar de
todo; **regardless of** sin reparar en
regenerate [rɪˈdʒɛnəreɪt] vt
regenerar
reggae [ˈrɛɡeɪ] n reggae m
regiment [ˈrɛdʒɪmənt] n regimiento
region [ˈriːdʒən] n región f; **in the
~ of** (fig) alrededor de; **regional** adj
regional
register [ˈrɛdʒɪstə*] n registro
▷ vt registrar; (birth) declarar;
(car) matricular; (letter) certificar;
(instrument) marcar, indicar ▷ vi
(at hotel) registrarse; (as student)
matricularse; (make impression)
producir impresión; **registered** adj
(letter, parcel) certificado
registrar [ˈrɛdʒɪstrɑː*] n secretario/a
(del registro civil)
registration [rɛdʒɪsˈtreɪʃən] n (act)
declaración f; (Aut: also: **~ number**)
matrícula
registry office [ˈrɛdʒɪstrɪ-] (BRIT) n
registro civil; **to get married in a ~**
casarse por lo civil
regret [rɪˈɡrɛt] n sentimiento, pesar
m ▷ vt sentir, lamentar; **regrettable**
adj lamentable
regular [ˈrɛɡjulə*] adj regular;
(soldier) profesional; (usual) habitual;
(: doctor) de cabecera ▷ n (client etc)
cliente/a m/f habitual; **regularly** adv
con regularidad; (often) repetidas veces
regulate [ˈrɛɡjuleɪt] vt controlar;

regulation [-ˈleɪʃən] n (rule) regla,
reglamento
rehabilitation [ˈriːəbɪlɪˈteɪʃən] n
rehabilitación f
rehearsal [rɪˈhəːsəl] n ensayo
rehearse [rɪˈhəːs] vt ensayar
reign [reɪn] n reinado; (fig)
predominio ▷ vi reinar; (fig) imperar
reimburse [riːɪmˈbəːs] vt reembolsar
rein [reɪn] n (for horse) rienda
reincarnation [riːɪnkɑːˈneɪʃən] n
reencarnación f
reindeer [ˈreɪndɪə*] n inv reno
reinforce [riːɪnˈfɔːs] vt reforzar;
reinforcements npl (Mil) refuerzos
mpl
reinstate [riːɪnˈsteɪt] vt reintegrar;
(tax, law) reinstaurar
reject [n ˈriːdʒɛkt, vb rɪˈdʒɛkt] n
(thing) desecho ▷ vt rechazar;
(suggestion) descartar; (coin) expulsar;
rejection [rɪˈdʒɛkʃən] n rechazo
rejoice [rɪˈdʒɔɪs] vi: **to ~ at or over**
regocijarse or alegrarse de
relate [rɪˈleɪt] vt (tell) contar,
relatar; (connect) relacionar ▷ vi
relacionarse; **related** adj afín; (person)
emparentado; **related to** (subject)
relacionado con; **relating to** prep
referente a
relation [rɪˈleɪʃən] n (person) familiar
mf, pariente mf; (link) relación f;
relations npl (relatives) familiares
mpl; **relationship** n relación f;
(personal) relaciones fpl; (also: **family
relationship**) parentesco
relative [ˈrɛlətɪv] n pariente mf,
familiar mf ▷ adj relativo; **relatively**
adv (comparatively) relativamente
relax [rɪˈlæks] vi descansar; (unwind)
relajarse ▷ vt (one's grip) soltar,
aflojar; (control) relajar; (mind, person)
descansar; **relaxation** [riːlækˈseɪʃə
n] n descanso; (of rule, control)
relajamiento; (entertainment) diversión
f; **relaxed** adj relajado; (tranquil)
tranquilo; **relaxing** adj relajante
relay [ˈriːleɪ] n (race) carrera de relevos

▷ *vt* (*Radio, TV*) retransmitir
release [rɪ'liːs] *n* (*liberation*)
liberación *f*; (*from prison*) puesta en
libertad; (*of gas etc*) escape *m*; (*of film
etc*) estreno; (*of record*) lanzamiento
▷ *vt* (*prisoner*) poner en libertad; (*gas*)
despedir, arrojar; (*from wreckage*)
soltar; (*catch, spring etc*) desenganchar;
(*film*) estrenar; (*book*) publicar; (*news*)
difundir
relegate ['rɛləgeɪt] *vt* relegar; (*BRIT
Sport*): **to be ~d to** bajar a
relent [rɪ'lɛnt] *vi* ablandarse;
relentless *adj* implacable
relevant ['rɛləvənt] *adj* (*fact*)
pertinente; **~ to** relacionado con
reliable [rɪ'laɪəbl] *adj* (*person, firm*)
de confianza, de fiar; (*method, machine*)
seguro; (*source*) fidedigno
relic ['rɛlɪk] *n* (*Rel*) reliquia; (*of the
past*) vestigio
relief [rɪ'liːf] *n* (*from pain, anxiety*)
alivio; (*help, supplies*) socorro, ayuda;
(*Art, Geo*) relieve *m*
relieve [rɪ'liːv] *vt* (*pain*) aliviar; (*bring
help to*) ayudar, socorrer; (*take over from*)
sustituir; (: *guard*) relevar; **to ~ sb of
sth** quitar algo a algn; **to ~ o.s.** hacer
sus necesidades; **relieved** *adj*: **to be
relieved** sentir un gran alivio
religion [rɪ'lɪdʒən] *n* religión *f*
religious [rɪ'lɪdʒəs] *adj* religioso;
religious education *n* educación *f*
religiosa
relish ['rɛlɪʃ] *n* (*Culin*) salsa;
(*enjoyment*) entusiasmo ▷ *vt* (*food
etc*) saborear; (*enjoy*): **to ~ sth** hacerle
mucha ilusión a algn algo
relocate [riːləʊ'keɪt] *vt* cambiar de
lugar, mudar ▷ *vi* mudarse
reluctance [rɪ'lʌktəns] *n* renuencia
reluctant [rɪ'lʌktənt] *adj* renuente;
reluctantly *adv* de mala gana
rely on [rɪ'laɪ-] *vt fus* depender de;
(*trust*) contar con
remain [rɪ'meɪn] *vi* (*survive*) quedar;
(*be left*) sobrar; (*continue*) quedar(se),
permanecer; **remainder** *n* resto;

remaining *adj* que queda(n);
(*surviving*) restante(s); **remains** *npl*
restos *mpl*
remand [rɪ'mɑːnd] *n*: **on ~** detenido
(bajo custodia) ▷ *vt*: **to be ~ed in
custody** quedar detenido bajo
custodia
remark [rɪ'mɑːk] *n* comentario
▷ *vt* comentar; **remarkable** *adj*
(*outstanding*) extraordinario
remarry [riː'mærɪ] *vi* volver a casarse
remedy ['rɛmədɪ] *n* remedio ▷ *vt*
remediar, curar
remember [rɪ'mɛmbə*] *vt* recordar,
acordarse de; (*bear in mind*) tener
presente; (*send greetings to*): **~ me
to him** dale recuerdos de mi parte;
Remembrance Day *n* ≈ día en el
que se recuerda a los caídos en las dos
guerras mundiales

● **REMEMBRANCE DAY**
●
● En el Reino Unido el domingo
● más próximo al 11 de noviembre
● se conoce como **Remembrance
● Sunday** o **Remembrance
● Day**, aniversario de la firma del
● armisticio de 1918 que puso fin a
● la Primera Guerra Mundial. Ese
● día, a las once de la mañana (hora
● en que se firmó el armisticio), se
● recuerda a los que murieron en
● las dos guerras mundiales con
● dos minutos de silencio ante los
● monumentos a los caídos. Allí se
● colocan coronas de amapolas,
● flor que también se suele llevar
● prendida en el pecho tras pagar un
● donativo destinado a los inválidos
● de guerra.

remind [rɪ'maɪnd] *vt*: **to ~ sb to do
sth** recordar a algn que haga algo; **to ~
sb of sth** (*of fact*) recordar algo a algn;
she ~s me of her mother me recuerda
a su madre; **reminder** *n* notificación *f*;
(*memento*) recuerdo

reminiscent [rɛmɪ'nɪsnt] *adj*: **to be ~ of sth** recordar algo

remnant ['rɛmnənt] *n* resto; (*of cloth*) retal *m*

remorse [rɪ'mɔːs] *n* remordimientos *mpl*

remote [rɪ'məut] *adj* (*distant*) lejano; (*person*) distante; **remote control** *n* telecontrol *m*; **remotely** *adv* remotamente; (*slightly*) levemente

removal [rɪ'muːvəl] *n* (*taking away*) el quitar; (BRIT: *from house*) mudanza; (*from office: dismissal*) destitución *f*; (*Med*) extirpación *f*; **removal man** (*irreg*) *n* (BRIT) mozo de mudanzas; **removal van** (BRIT) *n* camión *m* de mudanzas

remove [rɪ'muːv] *vt* quitar; (*employee*) destituir; (*name: from list*) tachar, borrar; (*doubt*) disipar; (*abuse*) suprimir, acabar con; (*Med*) extirpar

Renaissance [rɪ'neɪsãns] *n*: **the ~** el Renacimiento

rename [riː'neɪm] *vt* poner nuevo nombre a

render ['rɛndə*] *vt* (*thanks*) dar; (*aid*) proporcionar, prestar; (*make*): **to ~ sth useless** hacer algo inútil

rendezvous ['rɔndɪvuː] *n* cita

renew [rɪ'njuː] *vt* renovar; (*resume*) reanudar; (*loan etc*) prorrogar; **renewable** *adj* (*energy*) renovable

renovate ['rɛnəveɪt] *vt* renovar

renowned [rɪ'naund] *adj* renombrado

rent [rɛnt] *n* (*for house*) arriendo, renta ▷ *vt* alquilar; **rental** *n* (*for television, car*) alquiler *m*

reorganize [riː'ɔːgənaɪz] *vt* reorganizar

rep [rɛp] *n abbr* = **representative**

repair [rɪ'pɛə*] *n* reparación *f*, compostura ▷ *vt* reparar, componer; (*shoes*) remendar; **in good/bad ~** en buen/mal estado; **repair kit** *n* caja de herramientas

repay [riː'peɪ] *vt* (*money*) devolver, reembolsar; (*person*) pagar; (*debt*) liquidar; (*sb's efforts*) devolver, corresponder a; **repayment** *n* reembolso, devolución *f*; (*sum of money*) recompensa

repeat [rɪ'piːt] *n* (*Radio, TV*) reposición *f* ▷ *vt* repetir ▷ *vi* repetirse; **repeatedly** *adv* repetidas veces; **repeat prescription** *n* (BRIT) receta renovada

repellent [rɪ'pɛlənt] *adj* repugnante ▷ *n*: **insect ~** crema *or* loción *f* anti-insectos

repercussions [riːpə'kʌʃənz] *npl* consecuencias *fpl*

repetition [rɛpɪ'tɪʃən] *n* repetición *f*

repetitive [rɪ'pɛtɪtɪv] *adj* repetitivo

replace [rɪ'pleɪs] *vt* (*put back*) devolver a su sitio; (*take the place*) reemplazar, sustituir; **replacement** *n* (*act*) reposición *f*; (*thing*) recambio; (*person*) suplente *mf*

replay ['riːpleɪ] *n* (*Sport*) desempate *m*; (*of tape, film*) repetición *f*

replica ['rɛplɪkə] *n* copia, reproducción *f* (exacta)

reply [rɪ'plaɪ] *n* respuesta, contestación *f* ▷ *vi* contestar, responder

report [rɪ'pɔːt] *n* informe *m*; (*Press etc*) reportaje *m*; (BRIT: *also*: **school ~**) boletín *m* escolar; (*of gun*) estallido ▷ *vt* informar de; (*Press etc*) hacer un reportaje sobre; (*notify: accident, culprit*) denunciar ▷ *vi* (*make a report*) presentar un informe; (*present o.s.*): **to ~ (to sb)** presentarse (ante algn); **report card** *n* (US, SCOTTISH) cartilla escolar; **reportedly** *adv* según se dice; **reporter** *n* periodista *mf*

represent [rɛprɪ'zɛnt] *vt* representar; (*Comm*) ser agente de; (*describe*): **to ~ sth as** describir algo como; **representation** [-'teɪʃən] *n* representación *f*; **representative** *n* representante *mf*; (US *Pol*) diputado/a *m/f* ▷ *adj* representativo

repress [rɪ'prɛs] *vt* reprimir; **repression** [-'prɛʃən] *n* represión *f*

reprimand ['rɛprɪmɑːnd] *n*

reprimenda ▷ vt reprender
reproduce [riːprə'djuːs] vt
reproducir ▷ vi reproducirse;
reproduction [-'dʌkʃən] n
reproducción f
reptile ['reptail] n reptil m
republic [rɪ'pʌblɪk] n república;
republican adj, n republicano/a m/f
reputable ['repjutəbl] adj (make etc)
de renombre
reputation [repju'teɪʃən] n
reputación f
request [rɪ'kwest] n petición f;
(formal) solicitud f ▷ vt: **to ~ sth of or
from sb** solicitar algo a algn; **request
stop** (BRIT) n parada discrecional
require [rɪ'kwaɪə*] vt (need: person)
necesitar, tener necesidad de; (: thing,
situation) exigir; (want) pedir; **to ~ sb
to do sth** pedir a algn que haga algo;
requirement n requisito; (need)
necesidad f
resat [riː'sæt] pt, pp of **resit**
rescue ['reskjuː] n rescate m ▷ vt
rescatar
research [rɪ'səːtʃ] n investigaciones
fpl ▷ vt investigar
resemblance [rɪ'zembləns] n
parecido
resemble [rɪ'zembl] vt parecerse a
resent [rɪ'zent] vt tomar a mal;
resentful adj resentido; **resentment**
n resentimiento
reservation [rezə'veɪʃən] n reserva;
reservation desk (US) n (in hotel)
recepción f
reserve [rɪ'zəːv] n reserva; (Sport)
suplente mf ▷ vt (seats etc) reservar;
reserved adj reservado
reservoir ['rezəvwɑː*] n (artificial
lake) embalse m, tank; (small) depósito
residence ['rezɪdəns] n (formal: home)
domicilio; (length of stay) permanencia;
residence permit (BRIT) n permiso de
permanencia
resident ['rezɪdənt] n (of area)
vecino/a; (in hotel) huésped mf ▷ adj
(population) permanente; (doctor)

residente; **residential** [-'denʃəl] adj
residencial
residue ['rezɪdjuː] n resto
resign [rɪ'zaɪn] vt renunciar a
▷ vi dimitir; **to ~ o.s. to** (situation)
resignarse a; **resignation** [rezɪg'neɪʃə
n] n dimisión f; (state of mind)
resignación f
resin ['rezɪn] n resina
resist [rɪ'zɪst] vt resistir, oponerse a;
resistance n resistencia
resit ['riːsɪt] (BRIT) (pt, pp **resat**) vt
(exam) volver a presentarse a; (subject)
recuperar, volver a examinarse de (SP)
resolution [rezə'luːʃən] n resolución
f
resolve [rɪ'zɔlv] n resolución f ▷ vt
resolver ▷ vi: **to ~ to do** resolver hacer
resort [rɪ'zɔːt] n (town) centro
turístico; (recourse) recurso ▷ vi: **to ~
to** recurrir a; **in the last ~** como último
recurso
resource [rɪ'sɔːs] n recurso;
resourceful adj despabilado,
ingenioso
respect [rɪs'pekt] n respeto ▷ vt
respetar; **respectable** adj respetable;
(large: amount) apreciable; (passable)
tolerable; **respectful** adj respetuoso;
respective adj respectivo;
respectively adv respectivamente
respite ['respait] n respiro
respond [rɪs'pɔnd] vi responder;
(react) reaccionar; **response** [-'pɔns] n
respuesta; reacción f
responsibility [rɪspɔnsɪ'bɪlɪti] n
responsabilidad f
responsible [rɪs'pɔnsɪbl] adj
(character) serio, formal; (job) de
confianza; (liable): **~ (for)** responsable
(de); **responsibly** adv con seriedad
responsive [rɪs'pɔnsɪv] adj sensible
rest [rest] n descanso, reposo;
(Mus, pause) pausa, silencio;
(support) apoyo; (remainder) resto
▷ vi descansar; (be supported): **to
~ on** descansar sobre ▷ vt: **to ~
sth on/against** apoyar algo en or

sobre/contra; **the ~ of them** (*people, objects*) los demás; **it ~s with him to ...** depende de él el que ...

restaurant ['rɛstərɔŋ] *n* restaurante *m*; **restaurant car** (BRIT) *n* (*Rail*) coche-comedor *m*

restless ['rɛstlɪs] *adj* inquieto

restoration [rɛstə'reɪʃən] *n* restauración *f*; devolución *f*

restore [rɪ'stɔː*] *vt* (*building*) restaurar; (*sth stolen*) devolver; (*health*) restablecer; (*to power*) volver a poner a

restrain [rɪs'treɪn] *vt* (*feeling*) contener, refrenar; (*person*): **to ~ (from doing)** disuadir (de hacer); **restraint** *n* (*restriction*) restricción *f*; (*moderation*) moderación *f*; (*of manner*) reserva

restrict [rɪs'trɪkt] *vt* restringir, limitar; **restriction** [-kʃən] *n* restricción *f*, limitación *f*

rest room (US) *n* aseos *mpl*

restructure [riː'strʌktʃə*] *vt* reestructurar

result [rɪ'zʌlt] *n* resultado ▷ *vi*: **to ~ in** terminar en, tener por resultado; **as a ~ of** a consecuencia de

resume [rɪ'zjuːm] *vt* reanudar ▷ *vi* comenzar de nuevo

▌ Be careful not to translate **resume** by the Spanish word *resumir*.

résumé ['reɪzjuːmeɪ] *n* resumen *m*; (US) currículum *m*

resuscitate [rɪ'sʌsɪteɪt] *vt* (*Med*) resucitar

retail ['riːteɪl] *adj, adv* al por menor; **retailer** *n* detallista *mf*

retain [rɪ'teɪn] *vt* (*keep*) retener, conservar

retaliation [rɪtælɪ'eɪʃən] *n* represalias *fpl*

retarded [rɪ'tɑːdɪd] *adj* retrasado

retire [rɪ'taɪə*] *vi* (*give up work*) jubilarse; (*withdraw*) retirarse; (*go to bed*) acostarse; **retired** *adj* (*person*) jubilado; **retirement** *n* (*giving up work: state*) retiro; (: *act*) jubilación *f*

retort [rɪ'tɔːt] *vi* contestar

retreat [rɪ'triːt] *n* (*place*) retiro; (*Mil*) retirada ▷ *vi* retirarse

retrieve [rɪ'triːv] *vt* recobrar; (*situation, honour*) salvar; (*Comput*) recuperar; (*error*) reparar

retrospect ['rɛtrəspɛkt] *n*: **in ~** retrospectivamente; **retrospective** [-'spɛktɪv] *adj* retrospectivo; (*law*) retroactivo

return [rɪ'təːn] *n* (*going or coming back*) vuelta, regreso; (*of sth stolen etc*) devolución *f*; (*Finance: from land, shares*) ganancia, ingresos *mpl* ▷ *cpd* (*journey*) de regreso; (BRIT: *ticket*) de ida y vuelta; (*match*) de vuelta ▷ *vi* (*person etc: come or go back*) volver, regresar; (*symptoms etc*) reaparecer; (*regain*): **to ~ to** recuperar ▷ *vt* devolver; (*favour, love etc*) corresponder a; (*verdict*) pronunciar; (*Pol: candidate*) elegir; **returns** *npl* (*Comm*) ingresos *mpl*; **in ~ (for)** a cambio (de); **by ~ of post** a vuelta de correo; **many happy ~s (of the day)!** ¡feliz cumpleaños!; **return ticket** (*esp BRIT*) billete *m* (SP) or boleto *m* (LAM) de ida y vuelta, billete *m* redondo (MEX)

reunion [riː'juːnɪən] *n* (*of family*) reunión *f*; (*of two people, school*) reencuentro

reunite [riːjuː'naɪt] *vt* reunir; (*reconcile*) reconciliar

revamp [riː'væmp] *vt* renovar

reveal [rɪ'viːl] *vt* revelar; **revealing** *adj* revelador(a)

revel ['rɛvl] *vi*: **to ~ in sth/in doing sth** gozar de algo/con hacer algo

revelation [rɛvə'leɪʃən] *n* revelación *f*

revenge [rɪ'vɛndʒ] *n* venganza; **to take ~ on** vengarse de

revenue ['rɛvənjuː] *n* ingresos *mpl*, rentas *fpl*

Reverend ['rɛvərənd] *adj* (*in titles*): **the ~ John Smith** (*Anglican*) el Reverendo John Smith; (*Catholic*) el Padre John Smith; (*Protestant*) el Pastor John Smith

reversal [rɪ'vəːsl] *n* (*of order*)

inversión f; (of direction, policy) cambio; (of decision) revocación f
reverse [rɪ'və:s] n (opposite) contrario; (back: of cloth) revés m; (: of coin) reverso; (: of paper) dorso; (Aut: also: ~ **gear**) marcha atrás, revés m ▷ adj (order) inverso; (direction) contrario; (process) opuesto ▷ vt (decision, Aut) dar marcha atrás a; (position, function) invertir ▷ vi (BRIT Aut) dar marcha atrás; **reverse-charge call** (BRIT) n llamada a cobro revertido; **reversing lights** (BRIT) npl (Aut) luces fpl de retroceso
revert [rɪ'və:t] vi: **to ~ to** volver a
review [rɪ'vju:] n (magazine, Mil) revista; (of book, film) reseña; (US: examination) repaso, examen m ▷ vt repasar, examinar; (Mil) pasar revista a; (book, film) reseñar
revise [rɪ'vaɪz] vt (manuscript) corregir; (opinion) modificar; (price, procedure) revisar ▷ vi (study) repasar; **revision** [rɪ'vɪʒən] n corrección f; modificación f; (for exam) repaso
revival [rɪ'vaɪvəl] n (recovery) reanimación f; (of interest) renacimiento, (Theatre) reestreno; (of faith) despertar m
revive [rɪ'vaɪv] vt resucitar; (custom) restablecer; (hope) despertar; (play) reestrenar ▷ vi (person) volver en sí; (business) reactivarse
revolt [rɪ'vəult] n rebelión f ▷ vi rebelarse, sublevarse ▷ vt dar asco a, repugnar; **revolting** adj asqueroso, repugnante
revolution [rɛvə'lu:ʃən] n revolución f; **revolutionary** adj, n revolucionario/a m/f
revolve [rɪ'vɔlv] vi dar vueltas, girar; (life, discussion): **to ~ (a)round** girar en torno a
revolver [rɪ'vɔlvə*] n revólver m
reward [rɪ'wɔ:d] n premio, recompensa ▷ vt: **to ~ (for)** recompensar or premiar (por); **rewarding** adj (fig) valioso

rewind [ri:'waɪnd] vt rebobinar
rewritable [ri:'raɪtəbl] adj (CD, DVD) reescribible
rewrite [ri:'raɪt] (pt **rewrote**, pp **rewritten**) vt reescribir
rheumatism ['ru:mətɪzəm] n reumatismo, reúma m
rhinoceros [raɪ'nɔsərəs] n rinoceronte m
rhubarb ['ru:bɑ:b] n ruibarbo
rhyme [raɪm] n rima; (verse) poesía
rhythm ['rɪðm] n ritmo
rib [rɪb] n (Anat) costilla ▷ vt (mock) tomar el pelo a
ribbon ['rɪbən] n cinta; **in ~s** (torn) hecho trizas
rice [raɪs] n arroz m; **rice pudding** n arroz m con leche
rich [rɪtʃ] adj rico; (soil) fértil; (food) pesado; (: sweet) empalagoso; (abundant): **~ in** (minerals etc) rico en
rid [rɪd] (pt, pp ~) vt: **to ~ sb of sth** librar a algn de algo; **to get ~ of** deshacerse or desembarazarse de
riddle ['rɪdl] n (puzzle) acertijo; (mystery) enigma m, misterio ▷ vt: **to be ~d with** ser lleno or plagado de
ride [raɪd] (pt **rode**, pp **ridden**) n paseo; (distance covered) viaje m, recorrido ▷ vi (as sport) montar; (go somewhere: on horse, bicycle) dar un paseo, pasearse; (travel: on bicycle, motorcycle, bus) viajar ▷ vt (a horse) montar a; (a bicycle, motorcycle) andar en; (distance) recorrer; **to take sb for a ~** (fig) engañar a algn; **rider** n (on horse) jinete mf; (on bicycle) ciclista mf; (on motorcycle) motociclista mf
ridge [rɪdʒ] n (of hill) cresta; (of roof) caballete m; (wrinkle) arruga
ridicule ['rɪdɪkju:l] n irrisión f, burla ▷ vt poner en ridículo, burlarse de; **ridiculous** [-'dɪkjuləs] adj ridículo
riding ['raɪdɪŋ] n equitación f; **I like ~** me gusta montar a caballo; **riding school** n escuela de equitación
rife [raɪf] adj: **to be ~** ser muy común; **to be ~ with** abundar en

rifle ['raɪfl] n rifle m, fusil m ▷ vt saquear

rift [rɪft] n (in clouds) claro; (fig: disagreement) desavenencia

rig [rɪg] n (also: **oil ~**: at sea) plataforma petrolera ▷ vt (election etc) amañar

right [raɪt] adj (correct) correcto, exacto; (suitable) indicado, debido; (proper) apropiado; (just) justo; (morally good) bueno; (not left) derecho ▷ n bueno; (title, claim) derecho; (not left) derecha ▷ adv bien, correctamente; (not left) a la derecha; (exactly) ~ **now** ahora mismo ▷ vt enderezar; (correct) corregir ▷ excl ¡bueno!, ¡está bien!; **to be ~** (person) tener razón; (answer) ser correcto; **is that the ~ time?** (of clock) ¿es esa la hora buena?; **by ~s** en justicia; **on the ~** a la derecha; **to be in the ~** tener razón; ~ **away** en seguida; ~ **in the middle** exactamente en el centro; **right angle** n ángulo recto; **rightful** adj legítimo; **right-hand** adj: **right-hand drive** conducción f por la derecha; **the right-hand side** derecha; **right-handed** adj diestro; **rightly** adv correctamente, debidamente; (with reason) con razón; **right of way** n (on path etc) derecho de paso; (Aut) prioridad f; **right-wing** adj (Pol) derechista

rigid ['rɪdʒɪd] adj rígido; (person, ideas) inflexible

rigorous ['rɪgərəs] adj riguroso

rim [rɪm] n borde m; (of spectacles) aro; (of wheel) llanta

rind [raɪnd] n (of bacon) corteza; (of lemon etc) cáscara; (of cheese) costra

ring [rɪŋ] (pt **rang**, pp **rung**) n (of metal) aro; (on finger) anillo; (of people) corro; (of objects) círculo; (gang) banda; (for boxing) cuadrilátero; (of circus) pista; (bull ring) ruedo, plaza; (sound of bell) toque m ▷ vi (on telephone) llamar por teléfono; (bell) repicar; (doorbell, phone) sonar; (also: ~ **out**) sonar; (ears) zumbar ▷ vt (BRIT Tel) llamar, telefonear; (bell etc) hacer sonar; (doorbell) tocar; **to give sb a ~** (BRIT Tel) llamar or telefonear a algn; **ring back** (BRIT) vt, vi (Tel) devolver la llamada; **ring off** (BRIT) vi (Tel) colgar, cortar la comunicación; **ring up** (BRIT) vt (Tel) llamar, telefonear; **ringing tone** n (Tel) tono de llamada; **ringleader** n (of gang) cabecilla m; **ring road** (BRIT) n carretera periférica or de circunvalación; **ringtone** n (on mobile) tono de llamada

rink [rɪŋk] n (also: **ice ~**) pista de hielo

rinse [rɪns] n aclarado; (dye) tinte m ▷ vt aclarar; (mouth) enjuagar

riot ['raɪət] n motín m, disturbio ▷ vi amotinarse; **to run ~** desmandarse

rip [rɪp] n rasgón m, rasgadura ▷ vt rasgar, desgarrar ▷ vi rasgarse, desgarrarse; **rip off** vt (inf: cheat) estafar; **rip up** vt hacer pedazos

ripe [raɪp] adj maduro

rip-off ['rɪpɔf] n (inf): **it's a ~!** ¡es una estafa!, ¡es un timo!

ripple ['rɪpl] n onda, rizo; (sound) murmullo ▷ vi rizarse

rise [raɪz] (pt **rose**, pp **risen**) n (slope) cuesta, pendiente f; (hill) altura; (BRIT: in wages) aumento; (in prices, temperature) subida; (fig: to power etc) ascenso ▷ vi subir; (waters) crecer; (sun, moon) salir; (person: from bed etc) levantarse; (also: ~ **up**: rebel) sublevarse; (in rank) ascender; **to give ~ to** dar lugar or origen a; **to ~ to the occasion** ponerse a la altura de las circunstancias; **risen** ['rɪzn] pp of **rise**; **rising** adj (increasing: number) creciente; (: prices) en aumento or alza; (tide) creciente; (sun, moon) naciente

risk [rɪsk] n riesgo, peligro ▷ vt arriesgar; (run the risk of) exponerse a; **to take** or **run the ~ of doing** correr el riesgo de hacer; **at ~** en peligro; **at one's own ~** bajo su propia responsabilidad; **risky** adj arriesgado, peligroso

rite [raɪt] n rito; **last ~s** exequias fpl

ritual ['rɪtjuəl] adj ritual ▷ n ritual

m, rito

rival ['raɪvl] *n* rival *mf*; (*in business*) competidor(a) *m/f* ▷ *adj* rival, opuesto ▷ *vt* competir con; **rivalry** *n* competencia

river ['rɪvə*] *n* río ▷ *cpd* (*port*) de río; (*traffic*) fluvial; **up/down ~** río arriba/ abajo; **riverbank** *n* orilla (del río)

rivet ['rɪvɪt] *n* roblón *m*, remache *m* ▷ *vt* (*fig*) captar

road [rəud] *n* camino; (*motorway etc*) carretera; (*in town*) calle *f* ▷ *cpd* (*accident*) de tráfico; **major/minor ~** carretera principal/secundaria; **roadblock** *n* barricada; **road map** *n* mapa *m* de carreteras; **road rage** *n* agresividad en la carretera; **road safety** *n* seguridad *f* vial; **roadside** *n* borde *m* (del camino); **roadsign** *n* señal *f* de tráfico; **road tax** *n* (*BRIT*) impuesto de rodaje; **roadworks** *npl* obras *fpl*

roam [rəum] *vi* vagar

roar [rɔ:*] *n* rugido; (*of vehicle, storm*) estruendo; (*of laughter*) carcajada ▷ *vi* rugir; hacer estruendo; **to ~ with laughter** reírse a carcajadas; **to do a ~ing trade** hacer buen negocio

roast [rəust] *n* carne *f* asada, asado ▷ *vt* asar; (*coffee*) tostar; **roast beef** *n* rosbif *m*

rob [rɔb] *vt* robar; **to ~ sb of sth** robar algo a algn; (*fig: deprive*) quitar algo a algn; **robber** *n* ladrón/ona *m/f*; **robbery** *n* robo

robe [rəub] *n* (*for ceremony etc*) toga; (*also: bath~*) albornoz *m*

robin ['rɔbɪn] *n* petirrojo

robot ['rəubɔt] *n* robot *m*

robust [rəu'bʌst] *adj* robusto, fuerte

rock [rɔk] *n* roca; (*boulder*) peña, peñasco; (*US: small stone*) piedrecita; (*BRIT: sweet*) ≈ pirulí ▷ *vt* (*swing gently: cradle*) balancear, mecer; (*: child*) arrullar; (*shake*) sacudir ▷ *vi* mecerse, balancearse; sacudirse; **on the ~s** (*drink*) con hielo; (*marriage etc*) en ruinas; **rock and roll** *n* rocanrol *m*; **rock climbing** *n* (*Sport*) escalada

rocket ['rɔkɪt] *n* cohete *m*; **rocking chair** ['rɔkɪŋ-] *n* mecedora

rocky ['rɔkɪ] *adj* rocoso

rod [rɔd] *n* vara, varilla; (*also: fishing ~*) caña

rode [rəud] *pt of* **ride**

rodent ['rəudnt] *n* roedor *m*

rogue [rəug] *n* pícaro, pillo

role [rəul] *n* papel *m*; **role-model** *n* modelo a imitar

roll [rəul] *n* rollo; (*of bank notes*) fajo; (*also: bread ~*) panecillo; (*register, list*) lista, nómina; (*sound of drums etc*) redoble *m* ▷ *vt* hacer rodar; (*also: ~ up: string*) enrollar; (*cigarette*) liar; (*also: ~ out: pastry*) aplanar; (*flatten: road, lawn*) apisonar ▷ *vi* rodar; (*drum*) redoblar; (*ship*) balancearse; **roll over** *vi* dar una vuelta; **roll up** *vi* (*inf: arrive*) aparecer ▷ *vt* (*carpet*) arrollar; (*: sleeves*) arremangar; **roller** *n* rodillo; (*wheel*) rueda; (*for road*) apisonadora; (*for hair*) rulo; **Rollerblades**® *npl* patines *mpl* en línea; **roller coaster** *n* montaña rusa; **roller skates** *npl* patines *mpl* de rueda; **roller-skating** *n* patinaje sobre ruedas; **to go roller-skating** ir a patinar (*sobre ruedas*), **rolling pin** *n* rodillo (de cocina)

ROM [rɔm] *n abbr* (*Comput: = read only memory*) ROM *f*

Roman ['rəumən] (*irreg*) *adj* romano/a; **Roman Catholic** (*irreg*) *adj*, *n* católico/a *m/f* (romano/a)

romance [rə'mæns] *n* (*love affair*) amor *m*; (*charm*) lo romántico; (*novel*) novela de amor

Romania *etc* [ru:'meɪnɪə] *n* = **Rumania** *etc*

Roman numeral *n* número romano

romantic [rə'mæntɪk] *adj* romántico

Rome [rəum] *n* Roma

roof [ru:f] (*pl* **~s**) *n* techo; (*of house*) techo, tejado ▷ *vt* techar, poner techo a; **the ~ of the mouth** el paladar; **roof rack** *n* (*Aut*) baca, portaequipajes *m inv*

rook [ruk] *n* (*bird*) graja; (*Chess*) torre *f*

room [ru:m] n cuarto, habitación f; (also: **bed~**) dormitorio, recámara (MEX), pieza (SC); (in school etc) sala; (space, scope) sitio, cabida; **roommate** n compañero/a de cuarto; **room service** n servicio de habitaciones; **roomy** adj espacioso; (garment) amplio

rooster ['ru:stə*] n gallo

root [ru:t] n raíz f ▷ vi arraigarse

rope [rəup] n cuerda; (Naut) cable m ▷ vt (tie) atar or amarrar con (una) cuerda; (climbers: also: **~ together**) encordarse; (an area: also: **~ off**) acordonar; **to know the ~s** (fig) conocer los trucos (del oficio)

rose [rəuz] pt of **rise** ▷ n rosa; (shrub) rosal m; (on watering can) roseta

rosé ['rəuzei] n vino rosado

rosemary ['rəuzməri] n romero

rosy ['rəuzi] adj rosado, sonrosado; **a ~ future** un futuro prometedor

rot [rɔt] n podredumbre f; (fig: pej) tonterías fpl ▷ vt pudrir ▷ vi pudrirse

rota ['rəutə] n (sistema m de) turnos m

rotate [rəu'teit] vt (revolve) hacer girar, dar vueltas a; (jobs) alternar ▷ vi girar, dar vueltas

rotten ['rɔtn] adj podrido; (dishonest) corrompido; (inf: bad) pocho; **to feel ~** (ill) sentirse fatal

rough [rʌf] adj (skin, surface) áspero; (terrain) quebrado; (road) desigual; (voice) bronco; (person, manner) tosco, grosero; (weather) borrascoso; (treatment) brutal; (sea) picado; (town, area) peligroso; (cloth) basto; (plan) preliminar; (guess) aproximado ▷ n (Golf): **in the ~** en las hierbas altas; **to ~ it** vivir sin comodidades; **to sleep ~** (BRIT) pasar la noche al raso; **roughly** adv (handle) torpemente; (make) toscamente; (speak) groseramente; (approximately) aproximadamente

roulette [ru:'let] n ruleta

round [raund] adj redondo ▷ n círculo; (BRIT: of toast) rebanada; (of policeman) ronda; (of milkman) recorrido; (of doctor) visitas fpl; (game: of cards, in competition) partida; (of ammunition) cartucho; (Boxing) asalto; (of talks) ronda ▷ vt (corner) doblar ▷ prep alrededor de; (surrounding): **~ his neck/the table** en su cuello/alrededor de la mesa; (in a circular movement): **to move ~ the room/sail ~ the world** dar una vuelta a la habitación/circunnavigar el mundo; (in various directions): **to move ~ a room/house** moverse por toda la habitación/casa; (approximately) alrededor de ▷ adv: **all ~** por todos lados; **the long way ~** por el camino menos directo; **all (the) year ~** durante todo el año; **it's just ~ the corner** (fig) está a la vuelta de la esquina; **~ the clock** adv las 24 horas; **to go ~ to sb's (house)** ir a casa de algn; **to go ~ the back** pasar por atrás; **enough to go ~** bastante (para todos); **a ~ of applause** una salva de aplausos; **a ~ of drinks/sandwiches** una ronda de bebidas/bocadillos; **round off** vt (speech etc) acabar, poner término a; **round up** vt (cattle) acorralar; (people) reunir; (price) redondear; **roundabout** (BRIT) n (Aut) isleta; (at fair) tiovivo ▷ adj (route, means) indirecto; **round trip** n viaje m de ida y vuelta; **roundup** n rodeo; (of criminals) redada; (of news) resumen m

rouse [rauz] vt (wake up) despertar; (stir up) suscitar

route [ru:t] n ruta, camino; (of bus) recorrido; (of shipping) derrota

routine [ru:'ti:n] adj rutinario ▷ n rutina; (Theatre) número

row¹ [rəu] n (line) fila, hilera; (Knitting) pasada ▷ vi (in boat) remar ▷ vt conducir remando; **4 days in a ~** 4 días seguidos

row² [rau] n (racket) escándalo; (dispute) bronca, pelea; (scolding) regaño ▷ vi pelear(se)

rowboat ['rəubəut] (US) = **rowing boat**

rowing ['rəʊɪŋ] n remo; **rowing boat** (BRIT) n bote m de remos

royal ['rɔɪəl] adj real; **royalty** n (royal persons) familia real; (payment to author) derechos mpl de autor

rpm abbr (= revs per minute) r.p.m.

R.S.V.P. abbr (= répondez s'il vous plaĉt) SRC

Rt. Hon. abbr (BRIT) (= Right Honourable) título honorífico de diputado

rub [rʌb] vt frotar; (scrub) restregar ▷ n: **to give sth a ~** frotar algo; **to ~ sb up** or **~ sb** (US) **the wrong way** entrarle algn por mal ojo; **rub in** vt (ointment) aplicar frotando; **rub off** vi borrarse; **rub out** vt borrar

rubber ['rʌbə*] n caucho, goma; (BRIT: eraser) goma de borrar; **rubber band** n goma, gomita; **rubber gloves** npl guantes mpl de goma

rubbish ['rʌbɪʃ] (BRIT) n basura; (waste) desperdicios mpl; (fig: pej) tonterías fpl; (junk) pacotilla; **rubbish bin** (BRIT) n cubo or bote m (MEX) or tacho (SC) de la basura; **rubbish dump** (BRIT) n vertedero, basurero

rubble ['rʌbl] n escombros mpl

ruby ['ru:bɪ] n rubí m

rucksack ['rʌksæk] n mochila

rudder ['rʌdə*] n timón m

rude [ru:d] adj (impolite: person) mal educado; (: word, manners) grosero; (crude) crudo; (indecent) indecente

ruffle ['rʌfl] vt (hair) despeinar; (clothes) arrugar; **to get ~d** (fig: person) alterarse

rug [rʌg] n alfombra; (BRIT: blanket) manta

rugby ['rʌgbɪ] n rugby m

rugged ['rʌgɪd] adj (landscape) accidentado; (features) robusto

ruin ['ru:ɪn] n ruina ▷ vt arruinar; (spoil) estropear; **ruins** npl ruinas fpl, restos mpl

rule [ru:l] n (norm) norma, costumbre f; (regulation, ruler) regla; (government) dominio ▷ vt (country, person) gobernar ▷ vi gobernar; (Law) fallar; **as a ~** por regla general; **rule out** vt excluir; **ruler** n (sovereign) soberano; (for measuring) regla; **ruling** adj (party) gobernante; (class) dirigente ▷ n (Law) fallo, decisión f

rum [rʌm] n ron m

Rumania [ru:'meɪnɪə] n Rumanía; **Rumanian** adj rumano/a ▷ n rumano a m/f; (Ling) rumano

rumble ['rʌmbl] n (noise) ruido sordo ▷ vi retumbar, hacer un ruido sordo; (stomach, pipe) sonar

rumour ['ru:mə*] (US **rumor**) n rumor m ▷ vt: **it is ~ed that ...** se rumorea que ...

rump steak n filete m de lomo

run [rʌn] (pt **ran**, pp **run**) n (fast pace): **at a ~** corriendo; (Sport, in tights) carrera; (outing) paseo, excursión f; (distance travelled) trayecto; (series) serie f; (Theatre) temporada; (Ski) pista ▷ vt correr; (operate: business) dirigir; (: competition, course) organizar; (: hotel, house) administrar, llevar; (Comput) ejecutar; (pass: hand) pasar; (Press: feature) publicar ▷ vi correr; (work: machine) funcionar, marchar; (bus, train: operate) circular, ir; (: travel) ir; (continue: play) seguir; (contract) ser válido; (flow: river) fluir; (colours, washing) desteñirse; (in election) ser candidato; **there was a ~ on** (meat, tickets) hubo mucha demanda de; **in the long ~** a la larga; **on the ~** en fuga; **I'll ~ you to the station** te llevaré a la estación (en coche); **to ~ a risk** correr un riesgo; **to ~ a bath** llenar la bañera; **run after** vt fus (to catch up) correr tras; (chase) perseguir; **run away** vi huir; **run down** vt (production) ir reduciendo; (factory) ir restringiendo la producción en; (car) atropellar; (criticize) criticar; **to be run down** (person: tired) estar debilitado; **run into** vt fus (meet: person, trouble) tropezar con; (collide with) chocar con; **run off** vt (water) dejar correr; (copies) sacar ▷ vi huir corriendo; **run out** vi (person) salir

r

corriendo; (*liquid*) irse; (*lease*) caducar, vencer; (*money etc*) acabarse; **run out of** *vt fus* quedar sin; **run over** *vt* (*Aut*) atropellar ▷ *vt fus* (*revise*) repasar; **run through** *vt fus* (*instructions*) repasar; **run up** *vt* (*debt*) contraer; **to run up against** (*difficulties*) tropezar con; **runaway** *adj* (*horse*) desbocado; (*truck*) sin frenos; (*child*) escapado de casa

rung [rʌŋ] *pp of* **ring** ▷ *n* (*of ladder*) escalón *m*, peldaño

runner ['rʌnə*] *n* (*in race: person*) corredor(a) *m/f*; (: *horse*) caballo (*on sledge*) patín *m*; **runner bean** (BRIT) ≈ judía verde; **runner-up** *n* subcampeón/ona *m/f*

running ['rʌnɪŋ] *n* (*sport*) atletismo; (*of business*) administración *f* ▷ *adj* (*water, costs*) corriente; (*commentary*) continuo; **to be in/out of the ~ for sth** tener/no tener posibilidades de ganar algo; **6 days ~** 6 días seguidos

runny ['rʌnɪ] *adj* fluido; (*nose, eyes*) gastante

run-up ['rʌnʌp] *n*: **~ to** (*election etc*) período previo a

runway ['rʌnweɪ] *n* (*Aviat*) pista de aterrizaje

rupture ['rʌptʃə*] *n* (*Med*) hernia ▷ *vt*: **to ~ o.s** causarse una hernia

rural ['ruərl] *adj* rural

rush [rʌʃ] *n* ímpetu *m*; (*hurry*) prisa; (*Comm*) demanda repentina; (*current*) corriente *f* fuerte; (*of feeling*) torrente *m*; (*Bot*) junco ▷ *vt* apresurar; (*work*) hacer de prisa ▷ *vi* correr, precipitarse; **rush hour** *n* horas *fpl* punta

Russia ['rʌʃə] *n* Rusia; **Russian** *adj* ruso/a ▷ *n* ruso/a *m/f*; (*Ling*) ruso

rust [rʌst] *n* herrumbre *f*, moho ▷ *vi* oxidarse

rusty ['rʌstɪ] *adj* oxidado

ruthless ['ru:θlɪs] *adj* despiadado

RV (*us*) *n abbr* = **recreational vehicle**

rye [raɪ] *n* centeno

S

Sabbath ['sæbəθ] *n* domingo; (*Jewish*) sábado

sabotage ['sæbətɑ:ʒ] *n* sabotaje *m* ▷ *vt* sabotear

saccharin(e) ['sækərɪn] *n* sacarina

sachet ['sæʃeɪ] *n* sobrecito

sack [sæk] *n* (*bag*) saco, costal *m* ▷ *vt* (*dismiss*) despedir; (*plunder*) saquear; **to get the ~** ser despedido

sacred ['seɪkrɪd] *adj* sagrado, santo

sacrifice ['sækrɪfaɪs] *n* sacrificio ▷ *vt* sacrificar

sad [sæd] *adj* (*unhappy*) triste; (*deplorable*) lamentable

saddle ['sædl] *n* silla (de montar); (*of cycle*) sillín *m* ▷ *vt* (*horse*) ensillar; **to be ~d with sth** (*inf*) quedar cargado con algo

sadistic [sə'dɪstɪk] *adj* sádico

sadly ['sædlɪ] *adv* lamentablemente; **to be ~ lacking in** estar por desgracia carente de

sadness ['sædnɪs] *n* tristeza

s.a.e. *abbr* (= *stamped addressed envelope*) sobre con las propias señas de *uno y con sello*

safari [sə'fɑːrɪ] n safari m

safe [seɪf] adj (out of danger) fuera de peligro; (not dangerous, sure) seguro; (unharmed) ileso ▷ n caja de caudales, caja fuerte; **~ and sound** sano y salvo; **(just) to be on the ~ side** para mayor seguridad; **safely** adv seguramente, con seguridad; **to arrive safely** llegar bien; **safe sex** n sexo seguro or sin riesgo

safety ['seɪftɪ] n seguridad f; **safety belt** n cinturón m (de seguridad); **safety pin** n imperdible m, seguro (MEX), alfiler m de gancho (sc)

saffron ['sæfrən] n azafrán m

sag [sæg] vi aflojarse

sage [seɪdʒ] n (herb) salvia; (man) sabio

Sagittarius [sædʒɪ'tɛərɪəs] n Sagitario

Sahara [sə'hɑːrə] n: **the ~ (Desert)** el (desierto del) Sáhara

said [sɛd] pt, pp of **say**

sail [seɪl] n (on boat) vela; (trip): **to go for a ~** dar un paseo en barco ▷ vt (boat) gobernar ▷ vi (travel: ship) navegar, (Sport) hacer vela, (begin voyage) salir; **they ~ed into Copenhagen** arribaron a Copenhague; **sailboat** (US) n = **sailing boat**; **sailing** n (Sport) vela; **to go sailing** hacer vela; **sailing boat** n barco de vela; **sailor** n marinero, marino

saint [seɪnt] n santo

sake [seɪk] n: **for the ~ of** por

salad ['sæləd] n ensalada f; **salad cream** (BRIT) n (especie f de) mayonesa; **salad dressing** n aliño

salami [sə'lɑːmɪ] n salami m, salchichón m

salary ['sælərɪ] n sueldo

sale [seɪl] n venta; (at reduced prices) liquidación f, saldo; (auction) subasta; **sales** npl (total amount sold) ventas fpl, facturación f; **"for ~"** "se vende"; **on ~** en venta; **on ~ or return** (goods) venta por reposición; **sales assistant** (US),

sales clerk n dependiente/a m/f; **salesman/woman** (Irreg) n (In shop) dependiente/a m/f; **salesperson** (irreg) n vendedor(a) m/f, dependiente/a m/f; **sales rep** n representante mf, agente mf comercial

saline ['seɪlaɪn] adj salino

saliva [sə'laɪvə] n saliva

salmon ['sæmən] n inv salmón m

salon ['sælɔn] n (hairdressing salon) peluquería; (beauty salon) salón m de belleza

saloon [sə'luːn] n (US) bar m, taberna; (BRIT Aut) coche m (de) turismo; (ship's lounge) cámara, salón m

salt [sɔlt] n sal f ▷ vt salar; (put salt on) poner sal en; **saltwater** adj de agua salada; **salty** adj salado

salute [sə'luːt] n saludo; (of guns) salva ▷ vt saludar

salvage ['sælvɪdʒ] n (saving) salvamento, recuperación f; (things saved) objetos mpl salvados ▷ vt salvar

Salvation Army [sæl'veɪʃən-] n Ejército de Salvación

same [seɪm] adj mismo ▷ pron: **the ~** el(la) mismo/a, los(las) mismos/as; **the ~ book as** el mismo libro que; **at the ~ time** (at the same moment) al mismo tiempo; (yet) sin embargo; **all** or **just the ~** sin embargo, aun así; **to do the ~ (as sb)** hacer lo mismo (que algn); **the ~ to you!** ¡igualmente!

sample ['sɑːmpl] n muestra ▷ vt (food) probar; (wine) catar

sanction ['sæŋkʃən] n aprobación f ▷ vt sancionar; aprobar; **sanctions** npl (Pol) sanciones fpl

sanctuary ['sæŋktjuərɪ] n santuario; (refuge) asilo, refugio; (for wildlife) reserva

sand [sænd] n arena; (beach) playa ▷ vt (also: **~ down**) lijar

sandal ['sændl] n sandalia

sand: **sandbox** (US) n = **sandpit**; **sandcastle** n castillo de arena; **sand dune** n duna; **sandpaper** n papel m de lija; **sandpit** n (for children) cajón m

de arena; **sands** npl playa sg de arena;
sandstone ['sændstəun] n piedra
arenisca
sandwich ['sændwɪtʃ] n sandwich
m ▷ vt intercalar; **~ed between**
apretujado entre; **cheese/ham ~**
sandwich de queso/jamón
sandy ['sændɪ] adj arenoso; (colour)
rojizo
sane [seɪn] adj cuerdo; (sensible)
sensato

▮ Be careful not to translate **sane** by
the Spanish word sano.

sang [sæŋ] pt of **sing**
sanitary towel (US **sanitary napkin**)
n paño higiénico, compresa
sanity ['sænɪtɪ] n cordura; (of
judgment) sensatez f
sank [sæŋk] pt of **sink**
Santa Claus [sæntə'klɔ:z] n San
Nicolás, Papá Noel
sap [sæp] n (of plants) savia ▷ vt
(strength) minar, agotar
sapphire ['sæfaɪə*] n zafiro
sarcasm ['sɑ:kæzm] n sarcasmo
sarcastic [sɑ:'kæstɪk] adj sarcástico
sardine [sɑ:'di:n] n sardina
SASE (US) n abbr (= self-addressed
stamped envelope) sobre con las propias
señas de uno y con sello
Sat. abbr (= Saturday) sáb
sat [sæt] pt, pp of **sit**
satchel ['sætʃl] n (child's) mochila,
cartera (SP)
satellite ['sætəlaɪt] n satélite m;
satellite dish n antena de televisión
por satélite; **satellite television** n
televisión f vía satélite
satin ['sætɪn] n raso ▷ adj de raso
satire ['sætaɪə*] n sátira
satisfaction [sætɪs'fækʃən] n
satisfacción f
satisfactory [sætɪs'fæktərɪ] adj
satisfactorio
satisfied ['sætɪsfaɪd] adj satisfecho;
to be ~ (with sth) estar satisfecho
(de algo)
satisfy ['sætɪsfaɪ] vt satisfacer;

(convince) convencer
Saturday ['sætədɪ] n sábado
sauce [sɔ:s] n salsa; (sweet) crema;
jarabe m; **saucepan** n cacerola, olla
saucer ['sɔ:sə*] n platillo; **Saudi
Arabia** n Arabia Saudí or Saudita
sauna ['sɔ:nə] n sauna
sausage ['sɔsɪdʒ] n salchicha;
sausage roll n empanadita de
salchicha
sautéed ['səuteɪd] adj salteado
savage ['sævɪdʒ] adj (cruel, fierce)
feroz, furioso; (primitive) salvaje ▷ n
salvaje mf ▷ vt (attack) embestir
save [seɪv] vt (rescue) salvar, rescatar;
(money, time) ahorrar; (put by, keep: seat)
guardar; (Comput) salvar (y guardar),
(avoid: trouble) evitar; (Sport) parar ▷ vi
(also: ~ up) ahorrar ▷ n (Sport) parada
▷ prep salvo, excepto
savings ['seɪvɪŋz] npl ahorros mpl;
savings account n cuenta de ahorros;
savings and loan association (US) n
sociedad f de ahorro y préstamo
savoury ['seɪvərɪ] (US **savory**) adj
sabroso; (dish: not sweet) salado
saw [sɔ:] (pt **~ed**, pp **~ed** or **~n**) pt
of **see** ▷ n (tool) sierra ▷ vt serrar;
sawdust n (a)serrín m
sawn [sɔ:n] pp of **saw**
saxophone ['sæksəfəun] n saxófono
say [seɪ] (pt, pp **said**) n: **to have one's
~** expresar su opinión ▷ vt decir; **to
have a** or **some ~ in sth** tener voz or
tener que ver en algo; **to ~ yes/no** decir
que sí/no; **could you ~ that again?**
¿podría repetir eso?; **that is to ~** es
decir; **that goes without ~ing** ni que
decir tiene; **saying** n dicho, refrán m
scab [skæb] n costra; (pej) esquirol m
scaffolding ['skæfəldɪŋ] n andamio,
andamiaje m
scald [skɔ:ld] n escaldadura ▷ vt
escaldar
scale [skeɪl] n (gen, Mus) escala;
(of fish) escama; (of salaries, fees
etc) escalafón m ▷ vt (mountain)
escalar; (tree) trepar; **scales** npl (for

weighing: small) balanza; (: *large*) báscula; **on a large ~** en gran escala; **~ of charges** tarifa, lista de precios
scallion ['skæljən] (*us*) *n* cebolleta
scallop ['skɔləp] *n* (*Zool*) venera; (*Sewing*) festón *m*
scalp [skælp] *n* cabellera ▷ *vt* escalpar
scalpel ['skælpl] *n* bisturí *m*
scam [skæm] *n* (*inf*) estafa, timo
scampi ['skæmpɪ] *npl* gambas *fpl*
scan [skæn] *vt* (*examine*) escudriñar; (*glance at quickly*) dar un vistazo a; (*TV, Radar*) explorar, registrar ▷ *n* (*Med*): **to have a ~** pasar por el escáner
scandal ['skændl] *n* escándalo; (*gossip*) chismes *mpl*
Scandinavia [skændɪ'neɪvɪə] *n* Escandinavia; **Scandinavian** *adj, n* escandinavo/a *m/f*
scanner ['skænə*] *n* (*Radar, Med*) escáner *m*
scapegoat ['skeɪpgəʊt] *n* cabeza de turco, chivo expiatorio
scar [skɑː] *n* cicatriz *f*; (*fig*) señal *f* ▷ *vt* dejar señales en
scarce [skɛəs] *adj* escaso; **to make o.s. ~** (*inf*) esfumarse, **scarcely** *adv* apenas
scare [skɛə*] *n* susto, sobresalto; (*panic*) pánico ▷ *vt* asustar, espantar; **to ~ sb stiff** dar a algn un susto de muerte; **bomb ~** amenaza de bomba; **scarecrow** *n* espantapájaros *m inv*; **scared** *adj*: **to be scared** estar asustado
scarf [skɑːf] (*pl* **~s** *or* **scarves**) *n* (*long*) bufanda; (*square*) pañuelo
scarlet ['skɑːlɪt] *adj* escarlata
scarves [skɑːvz] *npl of* **scarf**
scary ['skɛərɪ] (*inf*) *adj* espeluznante
scatter ['skætə*] *vt* (*spread*) esparcir, desparramar; (*put to flight*) dispersar ▷ *vi* desparramarse; dispersarse
scenario [sɪ'nɑːrɪəʊ] *n* (*Theatre*) argumento; (*Cinema*) guión *m*; (*fig*) escenario
scene [siːn] *n* (*Theatre, fig etc*)

escena; (*of crime etc*) escenario; (*view*) panorama *m*; (*fuss*) escándalo; **scenery** *n* (*Theatre*) decorado; (*landscape*) paisaje *m*

Be careful not to translate **scenery** by the Spanish word *escenario*.

scenic *adj* pintoresco
scent [sɛnt] *n* perfume *m*, olor *m*; (*fig: track*) rastro, pista
sceptical ['skɛptɪkl] *adj* escéptico
schedule ['ʃɛdjuːl] (*us*) ['skɛdjuːl] *n* (*timetable*) horario; (*of events*) programa *m*; (*list*) lista ▷ *vt* (*visit*) fijar la hora de; **to arrive on ~** llegar a la hora debida; **to be ahead of/behind ~** estar adelantado/en retraso; **scheduled flight** *n* vuelo regular
scheme [skiːm] *n* (*plan*) plan *m*, proyecto; (*plot*) intriga; (*arrangement*) disposición *f*; (*pension scheme etc*) sistema *m* ▷ *vi* (*intrigue*) intrigar
schizophrenic [skɪtsə'frɛnɪk] *adj* esquizofrénico
scholar ['skɔlə*] *n* (*pupil*) alumno/a; (*learned person*) sabio/a, erudito/a; **scholarship** *n* erudición *f*; (*grant*) beca
school [skuːl] *n* escuela, colegio; (*in university*) facultad *f* ▷ *cpd* escolar; **schoolbook** *n* libro de texto; **schoolboy** *n* alumno; **school children** *npl* alumnos *mpl*; **schoolgirl** *n* alumna; **schooling** *n* enseñanza; **schoolteacher** *n* (*primary*) maestro/a; (*secondary*) profesor/a *m/f*
science ['saɪəns] *n* ciencia; **science fiction** *n* ciencia-ficción *f*; **scientific** [-'tɪfɪk] *adj* científico; **scientist** *n* científico/a
sci-fi ['saɪfaɪ] *n abbr* (*inf*) = **science fiction**
scissors ['sɪzəz] *npl* tijeras *fpl*; **a pair of ~** unas tijeras
scold [skəʊld] *vt* regañar
scone [skɔn] *n* pastel de pan
scoop [skuːp] *n* (*for flour etc*) pala; (*Press*) exclusiva
scooter ['skuːtə*] *n* moto *f*; (*toy*) patinete *m*

scope [skəup] n (of plan) ámbito; (of person) competencia; (opportunity) libertad f (de acción)

scorching ['skɔːtʃɪŋ] adj (heat, sun) abrasador(a)

score [skɔː*] n (points etc) puntuación f; (Mus) partitura; (twenty) veintena ▷ vt (goal, point) ganar; (mark) rayar; (achieve: success) conseguir ▷ vi marcar un tanto; (Football) marcar (un) gol; (keep score) llevar el tanteo; **~s of** (lots of) decenas de; **on that ~** en lo que se refiere a eso; **to ~ 6 out of 10** obtener una puntuación de 6 sobre 10; **score out** vt tachar; **scoreboard** n marcador m; **scorer** n marcador m; (keeping score) encargado/a del marcador

scorn [skɔːn] n desprecio

Scorpio ['skɔːpɪəu] n Escorpión m

scorpion ['skɔːpɪən] n alacrán m

Scot [skɔt] n escocés/esa m/f

Scotch tape® (US) n cinta adhesiva, celo, scotch® m

Scotland ['skɔtlənd] n Escocia

Scots [skɔts] adj escocés/esa; **Scotsman** (irreg) n escocés; **Scotswoman** (irreg) n escocésa; **Scottish** ['skɔtɪʃ] adj escocés/esa; **Scottish Parliament** n Parlamento escocés

scout [skaut] n (Mil: also: **boy ~**) explorador m; **girl ~** (US) niña exploradora

scowl [skaul] vi fruncir el ceño; **to ~ at sb** mirar con ceño a algn

scramble ['skræmbl] n (climb) subida (difícil); (struggle) pelea ▷ vi: **to ~ through/out** abrirse paso/salir con dificultad; **to ~ for** pelear por; **scrambled eggs** npl huevos mpl revueltos

scrap [skræp] n (bit) pedacito; (fig) pizca; (fight) riña, bronca; (also: **~ iron**) chatarra, hierro viejo ▷ vt (discard) desechar, descartar ▷ vi reñir, armar una bronca; **scraps** npl (waste) sobras fpl, desperdicios mpl; **scrapbook** n álbum m de recortes

scrape [skreip] n: **to get into a ~** meterse en un lío ▷ vt raspar; (skin etc) rasguñar; (scrape against) rozar ▷ vi: **to ~ through** (exam) aprobar por los pelos; **scrap paper** n pedazos mpl de papel

scratch [skrætʃ] n rasguño; (from claw) arañazo ▷ vt (paint, car) rayar; (with claw, nail) rasguñar, arañar; (rub: nose etc) rascarse ▷ vi rascarse; **to start from ~** partir de cero; **to be up to ~** cumplir con los requisitos; **scratch card** n (BRIT) tarjeta f de "rasque y gane"

scream [skriːm] n chillido ▷ vi chillar

screen [skriːn] n (Cinema, TV) pantalla; (movable barrier) biombo ▷ vt (conceal) tapar; (from the wind etc) proteger; (film) proyectar; (candidates etc) investigar a; **screening** n (Med) investigación f médica; **screenplay** n guión m; **screen saver** n (Comput) protector m de pantalla

screw [skruː] n tornillo ▷ vt (also: **~ in**) atornillar; **screw up** vt (paper etc) arrugar; **to screw up one's eyes** arrugar el entrecejo; **screwdriver** n destornillador m

scribble ['skrɪbl] n garabatos mpl ▷ vt, vi garabatear

script [skrɪpt] n (Cinema etc) guión m; (writing) escritura, letra

scroll [skrəul] n rollo

scrub [skrʌb] n (land) maleza ▷ vt fregar, restregar; (inf: reject) cancelar, anular

scruffy ['skrʌfɪ] adj desaliñado, piojoso

scrum(mage) ['skrʌm(mɪdʒ)] n (Rugby) melée f

scrutiny ['skruːtɪnɪ] n escrutinio, examen m

scuba diving ['skuːbə'daɪvɪŋ] n submarinismo

sculptor ['skʌlptə*] n escultor(a) m/f

sculpture ['skʌlptʃə*] n escultura

scum [skʌm] n (on liquid) espuma;

(pej: people) escoria

scurry ['skʌrɪ] vi correr; **to ~ off** escabullirse

sea [si:] n mar m ▷cpd de mar, marítimo; **by ~** (travel) en barco; **on the ~** (boat) en el mar; (town) junto al mar; **to be all at ~** (fig) estar despistado; **out to ~**, **at ~** en alta mar; **seafood** n mariscos mpl; **sea front** n paseo marítimo; **seagull** n gaviota

seal [si:l] n (animal) foca; (stamp) sello ▷vt (close) cerrar; **seal off** vt (area) acordonar

sea level n nivel m del mar

seam [si:m] n costura; (of metal) juntura; (of coal) veta, filón m

search [sə:tʃ] n (for person, thing) busca, búsqueda; (Comput) búsqueda; (inspection: of sb's home) registro ▷vt (look in) buscar en; (examine) examinar; (person, place) registrar ▷vi: **to ~ for** buscar; **in ~ of** en busca de; **search engine** n (Comput) buscador m; **search party** n pelotón m de salvamento

sea: seashore n playa, orilla del mar; **seasick** adj mareado; **seaside** n playa, orilla del mar; **seaside resort** n centro turístico costero

season ['si:zn] n (of year) estación f; (sporting etc) temporada; (of films etc) ciclo ▷vt (food) sazonar; **in/out of ~** en sazón/fuera de temporada; **seasonal** adj estacional; **seasoning** n condimento, aderezo; **season ticket** n abono

seat [si:t] n (in bus, train) asiento; (chair) silla; (Parliament) escaño; (buttocks) culo, trasero; (of trousers) culera ▷vt sentar; (have room for) tener cabida para; **to be ~ed** sentarse; **seat belt** n cinturón m de seguridad; **seating** n asientos mpl

sea: sea water n agua del mar; **seaweed** n alga marina

sec. abbr = **second(s)**

secluded [si'klu:dɪd] adj retirado

second ['sɛkənd] adj segundo ▷adv en segundo lugar ▷n segundo; (Aut: also: **~ gear**) segunda; (Comm) artículo con algún desperfecto; (BRIT Scol: degree) título de licenciado con calificación de notable ▷vt (motion) apoyar; **secondary** adj secundario; **secondary school** n escuela secundaria; **second-class** adj de segunda clase ▷adv (Rail) en segunda; **secondhand** adj de segunda mano, usado; **secondly** adv en segundo lugar; **second-rate** adj de segunda categoría; **second thoughts**: **to have second thoughts** cambiar de opinión; **on second thoughts** or **thought** (US) pensándolo bien

secrecy ['si:krəsɪ] n secreto

secret ['si:krɪt] adj, n secreto; **in ~** en secreto

secretary ['sɛkrətərɪ] n secretario/a; **S~ of State (for)** (BRIT Pol) Ministro (de)

secretive ['si:krətɪv] adj reservado, sigiloso

secret service n servicio secreto

sect [sɛkt] n secta

section ['sɛkʃən] n sección f; (part) parte f; (of document) artículo; (of opinion) sector m; (cross-section) corte m transversal

sector ['sɛktə*] n sector m

secular ['sɛkjulə*] adj secular, seglar

secure [sɪ'kjuə*] adj seguro; (firmly fixed) firme, fijo ▷vt (fix) asegurar, afianzar; (get) conseguir

security [sɪ'kjuərɪtɪ] n seguridad f; (for loan) fianza; (: object) prenda; **securities** npl (Comm) valores mpl, títulos mpl; **security guard** n guardia m/f de seguridad

sedan [sɪ'dæn] (US) n (Aut) sedán m

sedate [sɪ'deɪt] adj tranquilo ▷vt tratar con sedantes

sedative ['sɛdɪtɪv] n sedante m, sedativo

seduce [sɪ'dju:s] vt seducir; **seductive** [-'dʌktɪv] adj seductor(a)

see [si:] (pt saw, pp seen) vt ver; (accompany): **to ~ sb to the door**

s

acompañar a algn a la puerta;
(*understand*) ver, comprender ▷ *vi* ver
▷ *n* (arz)obispado; **to ~ that** (*ensure*)
asegurar que; **~ you soon!** ¡hasta
pronto!; **see off** *vt* despedir; **see out**
vt (*take to the door*) acompañar hasta la
puerta; **see through** *vt fus* (*fig*) calar
▷ *vt* (*plan*) llevar a cabo; **see to** *vt fus*
atender a, encargarse de

seed [siːd] *n* semilla; (*in fruit*) pepita;
(*fig: gen pl*) germen *m*; (*Tennis etc*)
preseleccionado/a; **to go to ~** (*plant*)
granar; (*fig*) descuidarse

seeing ['siːɪŋ] *conj*: **~ (that)** visto que,
en vista de que

seek [siːk] (*pt, pp* **sought**) *vt* buscar;
(*post*) solicitar

seem [siːm] *vi* parecer; **there ~s to
be ...** parece que hay ...; **seemingly** *adv*
aparentemente, según parece

seen [siːn] *pp of* **see**

seesaw ['siːsɔː] *n* subibaja

segment ['sɛgmənt] *n* (*part*) sección
f; (*of orange*) gajo

segregate ['sɛgrɪgeɪt] *vt* segregar

seize [siːz] *vt* (*grasp*) agarrar,
asir; (*take possession of*) secuestrar;
(: *territory*) apoderarse de; (*opportunity*)
aprovecharse de

seizure ['siːʒə*] *n* (*Med*) ataque *m*;
(*Law, of power*) incautación *f*

seldom ['sɛldəm] *adv* rara vez

select [sɪ'lɛkt] *adj* selecto, escogido
▷ *vt* escoger, elegir; (*Sport*) seleccionar;
selection *n* selección *f*, elección
f; (*Comm*) surtido; **selective** *adj*
selectivo

self [sɛlf] (*pl* **selves**) *n* uno mismo;
the ~ el yo ▷ *prefix* auto...; **self-
assured** *adj* seguro de sí mismo;
self-catering (*BRIT*) *adj* (*flat etc*)
con cocina; **self-centred** (*US*
self-centered) *adj* egocéntrico;
self-confidence *n* confianza en sí
mismo; **self-confident** *adj* seguro
de sí (mismo), lleno de confianza en sí
mismo; **self-conscious** *adj* cohibido;
self-contained (*BRIT*) *adj* (*flat*) con

entrada particular; **self-control** *n*
autodominio; **self-defence** (*US* **self-
defense**) *n* defensa propia; **self-drive**
adj (*BRIT*) sin chofer or (*SP*) chófer; **self-
employed** *adj* que trabaja por cuenta
propia; **self-esteem** *n* amor *m* propio;
self-indulgent *adj* autocomplaciente;
self-interest *n* egoísmo; **selfish**
adj egoísta; **self-pity** *n* lástima de
sí mismo; **self-raising** [sɛlf'reɪzɪŋ]
(*US* **self-rising**) *adj*: **self-raising flour**
harina con levadura; **self-respect** *n*
amor *m* propio; **self-service** *adj* de
autoservicio

sell [sɛl] (*pt, pp* **sold**) *vt* vender ▷ *vi*
venderse; **to ~ at** or **for £10** venderse a
10 libras; **sell off** *vt* liquidar; **sell out**
vi: **to sell out of tickets/milk** vender
todas las entradas/toda la leche; **sell-
by date** *n* fecha de caducidad; **seller**
n vendedor(a) *m/f*

Sellotape® ['sɛləʊteɪp] (*BRIT*) *n* celo
(*SP*), cinta Scotch® (*LAM*) or Dúrex®
(*MEX, ARG*)

selves [sɛlvz] *npl of* **self**

semester [sɪ'mɛstə*] (*US*) *n*
semestre *m*

semi... [sɛmɪ] *prefix* semi...,
medio...; **semicircle** *n* semicírculo;
semidetached (house) *n* (*casa*)
semiseparada; **semi-final** *n* semi-
final *m*

seminar ['sɛmɪnɑː*] *n* seminario

semi-skimmed [sɛmɪ'skɪmd] *adj*
semidesnatado; **semi-skimmed
(milk)** *n* leche semidesnatada

senate ['sɛnɪt] *n* senado; **the S~** (*US*)
el Senado; **senator** *n* senador(a) *m/f*

send [sɛnd] (*pt, pp* **sent**) *vt* mandar,
enviar; (*signal*) transmitir; **send back**
vt devolver; **send for** *vt fus* mandar
traer; **send in** *vt* (*report, application,
resignation*) mandar; **send off** *vt*
(*goods*) despachar; (*BRIT Sport: player*)
expulsar; **send on** *vt* (*letter, luggage*)
remitir; (*person*) mandar; **send out**
vt (*invitation*) mandar; (*signal*) emitir;
send up *vt* (*person, price*) hacer subir;

(BRIT: *parody*) parodiar; **sender** *n* remitente *mf*; **send-off** *n*: **a good send-off** una buena despedida

senile ['si:naɪl] *adj* senil

senior ['si:nɪə*] *adj* (*older*) mayor, más viejo; (: *on staff*) de más antigüedad; (*of higher rank*) superior; **senior citizen** *n* persona de la tercera edad; **senior high school** (US) *n* ≈ instituto de enseñanza media; *see also* **high school**

sensation [sɛn'seɪʃən] *n* sensación *f*; **sensational** *adj* sensacional

sense [sɛns] *n* (*faculty, meaning*) sentido; (*feeling*) sensación *f*; (*good sense*) sentido común, juicio ▷ *vt* sentir, percibir; **it makes ~** tiene sentido; **senseless** *adj* estúpido, insensato; (*unconscious*) sin conocimiento; **sense of humour** (BRIT) *n* sentido del humor

sensible ['sɛnsɪbl] *adj* sensato; (*reasonable*) razonable, lógico

Be careful not to translate **sensible** by the Spanish word *sensible*.

sensitive ['sɛnsɪtɪv] *adj* sensible; (*touchy*) susceptible

sensual ['sɛnsjʊəl] *adj* sensual

sensuous ['sɛnsjʊəs] *adj* sensual

sent [sɛnt] *pt, pp of* **send**

sentence ['sɛntns] *n* (*Ling*) oración *f*; (*Law*) sentencia, fallo ▷ *vt*: **to ~ sb to death/to 5 years (in prison)** condenar a algn a muerte/a 5 años de cárcel

sentiment ['sɛntɪmənt] *n* sentimiento; (*opinion*) opinión *f*; **sentimental** [-'mɛntl] *adj* sentimental

Sep. *abbr* (= *September*) sep., set.

separate [*adj* 'sɛprɪt, *vb* 'sɛpəreɪt] *adj* separado; (*distinct*) distinto ▷ *vt* separar; (*part*) dividir ▷ *vi* separarse; **separately** *adv* por separado; **separates** *npl* (*clothes*) coordinados *mpl*; **separation** [-'reɪʃən] *n* separación *f*

September [sɛp'tɛmbə*] *n* se(p)tiembre *m*

septic ['sɛptɪk] *adj* séptico; **septic tank** *n* fosa séptica

sequel ['si:kwl] *n* consecuencia, resultado; (*of story*) continuación *f*

sequence ['si:kwəns] *n* sucesión *f*, serie *f*; (*Cinema*) secuencia

sequin ['si:kwɪn] *n* lentejuela

Serb [sə:b] *adj, n* = **Serbian**

Serbian ['sə:bɪən] *adj* serbio ▷ *n* serbio/a; (*Ling*) serbio

serial ['sɪərɪəl] *n* (*TV*) telenovela, serie *f* televisiva; (*Book*) serie *f*; **serial killer** *n* asesino/a múltiple; **serial number** *n* número de serie

series ['sɪəri:s] *n inv* serie *f*

serious ['sɪərɪəs] *adj* serio; (*grave*) grave; **seriously** *adv* en serio; (*ill, wounded etc*) gravemente

sermon ['sə:mən] *n* sermón *m*

servant ['sə:vənt] *n* servidor(a) *m/f*; (*house servant*) criado/a

serve [sə:v] *vt* servir; (*customer*) atender; (*train*) pasar por; (*apprenticeship*) hacer; (*prison term*) cumplir ▷ *vi* (*at table*) servir; (*Tennis*) sacar; **to ~ as/for/to do** servir de/para/para hacer ▷ *n* (*Tennis*) saque *m*; **it ~s him right** se lo tiene merecido; **server** *n* (*Comput*) servidor *m*

service ['sə:vɪs] *n* servicio; (*Rel*) misa; (*Aut*) mantenimiento; (*dishes etc*) juego ▷ *vt* (*car etc*) revisar; (: *repair*) reparar; **to be of ~ to sb** ser útil a algn; **~ included/not included** servicio incluido/no incluido (*Econ: tertiary sector*) sector *m* terciario or (de) servicios; (BRIT: *on motorway*) área de servicio; (*Mil*): **the S~s** las fuerzas armadas; **service area** *n* (*on motorway*) área de servicio; **service charge** (BRIT) *n* servicio; **serviceman** (*irreg*) *n* militar *m*; **service station** *n* estación *f* de servicio

serviette [sə:vɪ'ɛt] (BRIT) *n* servilleta

session ['sɛʃən] *n* sesión *f*; **to be in ~** estar en sesión

set [sɛt] (*pt, pp ~*) *n* juego; (*Radio*) aparato; (*TV*) televisor *m*; (*of utensils*)

batería; (of cutlery) cubierto; (of books) colección f; (Tennis) set m; (group of people) grupo; (Cinema) plató m; (Theatre) decorado; (Hairdressing) marcado ▷ adj (fixed) fijo; (ready) listo ▷ vt (place) poner, colocar; (fix) fijar; (adjust) ajustar, arreglar; (decide: rules etc) establecer, decidir ▷ vi (sun) ponerse; (jam, jelly) cuajarse; (concrete) fraguar; (bone) componerse; **to be ~ on doing sth** estar empeñado en hacer algo; **to ~ to music** poner música a; **to ~ on fire** incendiar, poner fuego a; **to ~ free** poner en libertad; **to ~ sth going** poner algo en marcha; **to ~ sail** zarpar, hacerse a la vela; **set aside** vt poner aparte, dejar de lado; (money, time) reservar; **set down** vt (bus, train) dejar; **set in** vi (infection) declararse; (complications) comenzar; **the rain has set in for the day** parece que va a llover todo el día; **set off** vi partir ▷ vt (bomb) hacer estallar; (events) poner en marcha; (show up well) hacer resaltar; **set out** vi partir ▷ vt (arrange) disponer; (state) exponer; **to set out to do sth** proponerse hacer algo; **set up** vt establecer; **setback** n revés m, contratiempo; **set menu** n menú m
settee [sɛ'tiː] n sofá m
setting ['sɛtɪŋ] n (scenery) marco; (position) disposición f; (of sun) puesta; (of jewel) engaste m, montadura
settle ['sɛtl] vt (argument) resolver; (accounts) ajustar, liquidar; (Med: calm) calmar, sosegar ▷ vi (dust etc) depositarse; (weather) serenarse; **to ~ for sth** convenir en aceptar algo; **to ~ on sth** decidirse por algo; **settle down** vi (get comfortable) ponerse cómodo, acomodarse; (calm down) calmarse, tranquilizarse; (live quietly) echar raíces; **settle in** vi instalarse; **settle up** vi: **to settle up with sb** ajustar cuentas con algn; **settlement** n (payment) liquidación f; (agreement) acuerdo, convenio; (village etc) pueblo
setup ['sɛtʌp] n sistema m; (situation)

situación f
seven ['sɛvn] num siete; **seventeen** num diez y siete, diecisiete; **seventeenth** [sɛvn'tiːnθ] adj decimoséptimo; **seventh** num séptimo; **seventieth** ['sɛvntɪɪθ] adj septuagésimo; **seventy** num setenta
sever ['sɛvə*] vt cortar; (relations) romper
several ['sɛvərl] adj, pron varios/as m/fpl, algunos/as m/fpl; **~ of us** varios de nosotros
severe [sɪ'vɪə*] adj severo; (serious) grave; (hard) duro; (pain) intenso
sew [səʊ] (pt **~ed**, pp **~n**) vt, vi coser
sewage ['suːɪdʒ] n aguas fpl residuales
sewer ['suːə*] n alcantarilla, cloaca
sewing ['səʊɪŋ] n costura; **sewing machine** n máquina de coser
sewn [səʊn] pp of **sew**
sex [sɛks] n sexo; (lovemaking): **to have ~** hacer el amor; **sexism** ['sɛksɪzəm] n sexismo; **sexist** adj, n sexista mf; **sexual** ['sɛksjʊəl] adj sexual; **sexual intercourse** n relaciones fpl sexuales; **sexuality** [sɛksju'ælɪtɪ] n sexualidad f; **sexy** adj sexy
shabby ['ʃæbɪ] adj (person) desharrapado; (clothes) raído, gastado; (behaviour) ruin inv
shack [ʃæk] n choza, chabola
shade [ʃeɪd] n sombra; (for lamp) pantalla; (for eyes) visera; (of colour) matiz m, tonalidad f; (small quantity): **a ~ (too big/more)** un poquitín (grande/más) ▷ vt dar sombra a; (eyes) proteger del sol; **in the ~** en la sombra; **shades** npl (sunglasses) gafas fpl de sol
shadow ['ʃædəʊ] n sombra ▷ vt (follow) seguir y vigilar; **shadow cabinet** (BRIT) n (Pol) gabinete paralelo formado por el partido de oposición
shady ['ʃeɪdɪ] adj sombreado; (fig: dishonest) sospechoso; (: deal) turbio
shaft [ʃɑːft] n (of arrow, spear) astil m; (Aut, Tech) eje m, árbol m; (of mine) pozo;

(of lift) hueco, caja; (of light) rayo
shake [ʃeɪk] (pt **shook**, pp **shaken**)
vt sacudir; (building) hacer temblar;
(bottle, cocktail) agitar ▷ vi (tremble)
temblar; **to ~ one's head** (in refusal)
negar con la cabeza; (in dismay) mover
or menear la cabeza, incrédulo; **to
~ hands with sb** estrechar la mano
a algn; **shake off** vt sacudirse; (fig)
deshacerse de; **shake up** vt agitar;
(fig) reorganizar; **shaky** adj (hand,
voice) trémulo; (building) inestable
shall [ʃæl] aux vb: **~ I help you?**
¿quieres que te ayude?; **I'll buy three, ~
I?** compro tres, ¿no te parece?
shallow [ˈʃæləu] adj poco profundo;
(fig) superficial
sham [ʃæm] n fraude m, engaño
shambles [ˈʃæmblz] n confusión f
shame [ʃeɪm] n vergüenza ▷ vt
avergonzar; **it is a ~ that/to do** es una
lástima que/hacer; **what a ~!** ¡qué
lástima!; **shameful** adj vergonzoso;
shameless adj desvergonzado
shampoo [ʃæmˈpuː] n champú m
▷ vt lavar con champú
shandy [ˈʃændɪ] n mezcla de cerveza
con gaseosa
shan't [ʃɑːnt] = **shall not**
shape [ʃeɪp] n forma ▷ vt formar, dar
forma a; (sb's ideas) formar; (sb's life)
determinar; **to take ~** tomar forma
share [ʃɛə*] n (part) parte f,
porción f; (contribution) cuota;
(Comm) acción f ▷ vt dividir; (have
in common) compartir; **to ~ out
(among or between)** repartir (entre);
shareholder (BRIT) n accionista m/f
shark [ʃɑːk] n tiburón m
sharp [ʃɑːp] adj (blade, nose) afilado;
(point) puntiagudo; (outline) definido;
(pain) intenso; (Mus) desafinado;
(contrast) marcado; (voice) agudo;
(person: quick-witted) astuto;
(: dishonest) poco escrupuloso ▷ n
(Mus) sostenido ▷ adv: **at 2 o'clock ~**
a las 2 en punto; **sharpen** vt afilar;
(pencil) sacar punta a; (fig) agudizar;

sharpener n (also: **pencil sharpener**)
sacapuntas m inv; **sharply** adv
(turn, stop) bruscamente; (stand out,
contrast) claramente; (criticize, retort)
severamente
shatter [ˈʃætə*] vt hacer añicos or
pedazos; (fig: ruin) destruir, acabar con
▷ vi hacerse añicos; **shattered** adj
(grief-stricken) destrozado, deshecho;
(exhausted) agotado, hecho polvo
shave [ʃeɪv] vt afeitar, rasurar ▷ vi
afeitarse, rasurarse ▷ n: **to have a
~** afeitarse; **shaver** n (also: **electric
shaver**) máquina de afeitar (eléctrica)
shavings [ˈʃeɪvɪŋz] npl (of wood etc)
virutas fpl
shaving cream [ˈʃeɪvɪŋ-] n crema
de afeitar
shaving foam n espuma de afeitar
shawl [ʃɔːl] n chal m
she [ʃiː] pron ella
sheath [ʃiːθ] n vaina; (contraceptive)
preservativo
shed [ʃɛd] (pt, pp **~**) n cobertizo ▷ vt
(skin) mudar; (tears, blood) derramar;
(load) derramar; (workers) despedir
she'd [ʃiːd] = **she had**; **she would**
sheep [ʃiːp] n inv oveja; **sheepdog**
n perro pastor; **sheepskin** n piel f
de carnero
sheer [ʃɪə*] adj (utter) puro, completo;
(steep) escarpado; (material) diáfano
▷ adv verticalmente
sheet [ʃiːt] n (on bed) sábana; (of
paper) hoja; (of glass, metal) lámina; (of
ice) capa
sheik(h) [ʃeɪk] n jeque m
shelf [ʃɛlf] (pl **shelves**) n estante m
shell [ʃɛl] n (on beach) concha; (of egg,
nut etc) cáscara; (explosive) proyectil
m, obús m; (of building) armazón f ▷ vt
(peas) desenvainar; (Mil) bombardear
she'll [ʃiːl] = **she will**; **she shall**
shellfish [ˈʃɛlfɪʃ] n inv crustáceo; (as
food) mariscos mpl
shelter [ˈʃɛltə*] n abrigo, refugio ▷ vt
(aid) amparar, proteger; (give lodging
to) abrigar ▷ vi abrigarse, refugiarse;

sheltered *adj* (*life*) protegido; (*spot*) abrigado

shelves [ʃɛlvz] *npl of* **shelf**

shelving [ˈʃɛlvɪŋ] *n* estantería

shepherd [ˈʃɛpəd] *n* pastor *m* ▷ *vt* (*guide*) guiar, conducir; **shepherd's pie** (BRIT) *n* pastel de carne y patatas

sheriff [ˈʃɛrɪf] (US) *n* sheriff *m*

sherry [ˈʃɛrɪ] *n* jerez *m*

she's [ʃiːz] = **she is; she has**

Shetland [ˈʃɛtlənd] *n* (*also*: **the ~s, the ~ Isles**) las Islas de Zetlandia

shield [ʃiːld] *n* escudo; (*protection*) blindaje *m* ▷ *vt*: **to ~ (from)** proteger (de)

shift [ʃɪft] *n* (*change*) cambio; (*at work*) turno ▷ *vt* trasladar; (*remove*) quitar ▷ *vi* moverse

shin [ʃɪn] *n* espinilla

shine [ʃaɪn] (*pt, pp* **shone**) *n* brillo, lustre *m* ▷ *vi* brillar, relucir ▷ *vt* (*shoes*) lustrar, sacar brillo a; **to ~ a torch on sth** dirigir una linterna hacia algo

shingles [ˈʃɪŋglz] *n* (*Med*) herpes *mpl or fpl*

shiny [ˈʃaɪnɪ] *adj* brillante, lustroso

ship [ʃɪp] *n* buque *m*, barco ▷ *vt* (*goods*) embarcar; (*send*) transportar *or* enviar por vía marítima; **shipment** *n* (*goods*) envío; **shipping** *n* (*act*) embarque *m*; (*traffic*) buques *mpl*; **shipwreck** *n* naufragio ▷ *vt*: **to be shipwrecked** naufragar; **shipyard** *n* astillero

shirt [ʃəːt] *n* camisa; **in (one's) ~ sleeves** en mangas de camisa

shit [ʃɪt] (*inf!*) *excl* ¡mierda! (*!*)

shiver [ˈʃɪvə*] *n* escalofrío ▷ *vi* temblar, estremecerse; (*with cold*) tiritar

shock [ʃɔk] *n* (*impact*) choque *m*; (*Elec*) descarga (eléctrica); (*emotional*) conmoción *f*; (*start*) sobresalto, susto; (*Med*) postración *f* ▷ *vt* dar un susto a; (*offend*) escandalizar; **shocking** *adj* (*awful*) espantoso; (*outrageous*) escandaloso

shoe [ʃuː] *n* (*pt, pp* **shod**) *n* zapato; (*for horse*) herradura ▷ *vt* (*horse*) herrar; **shoelace** *n* cordón *m*; **shoe polish** *n* betún *m*; **shoeshop** *n* zapatería

shone [ʃɔn] *pt, pp of* **shine**

shook [ʃuk] *pt of* **shake**

shoot [ʃuːt] (*pt, pp* **shot**) *n* (*on branch, seedling*) retoño, vástago ▷ *vt* disparar; (*kill*) matar a tiros; (*wound*) pegar un tiro; (*execute*) fusilar; (*film*) rodar, filmar ▷ *vi* (*Football*) chutar; **shoot down** *vt* (*plane*) derribar; **shoot up** *vi* (*prices*) dispararse; **shooting** *n* (*shots*) tiros *mpl*; (*Hunting*) caza con escopeta

shop [ʃɔp] *n* tienda; (*workshop*) taller *m* ▷ *vi* (*also*: **go ~ping**) ir de compras; **shop assistant** (BRIT) *n* dependiente/a *m/f*; **shopkeeper** *n* tendero/a; **shoplifting** *n* mechería; **shopping** *n* (*goods*) compras *fpl*; **shopping bag** *n* bolsa (de compras); **shopping centre** (US **shopping center**) *n* centro comercial; **shopping mall** *n* centro comercial; **shopping trolley** *n* (BRIT) carrito de la compra; **shop window** *n* escaparate *m* (SP), vidriera (LAM)

shore [ʃɔː*] *n* orilla ▷ *vt*: **to ~ (up)** reforzar; **on ~** en tierra

short [ʃɔːt] *adj* corto; (*in time*) breve, de corta duración; (*person*) bajo; (*curt*) brusco, seco; (*insufficient*) insuficiente; **(a pair of) ~s** (unos) pantalones *mpl* cortos; **to be ~ of sth** estar falto de algo; **in ~** en pocas palabras; **~ of doing ...** fuera de hacer ...; **it is ~ for** es la forma abreviada de; **to cut ~** (*speech, visit*) interrumpir, terminar inesperadamente; **everything ~ of ...** todo menos ...; **to fall ~ of** no alcanzar; **to run ~ of** quedarle a algn poco; **to stop ~** parar en seco; **to stop ~ of** detenerse antes de; **shortage** *n*: **a shortage of** una falta de; **shortbread** *n* especie de mantecada; **shortcoming** *n* defecto, deficiencia; **short(crust) pastry** (BRIT) *n* pasta quebradiza; **shortcut** *n* atajo; **shorten** *vt* acortar; (*visit*) interrumpir; **shortfall** *n* déficit *m*; **shorthand** (BRIT) *n*

taquigrafía; **short-lived** adj efímero;
shortly adv en breve, dentro de poco;
shorts npl pantalones mpl cortos; (US)
calzoncillos mpl; **short-sighted** (BRIT)
adj miope; (fig) imprudente; **short-
sleeved** adj de manga corta; **short
story** n cuento; **short-tempered** adj
enojadizo; **short-term** adj (effect) a
corto plazo

shot [ʃɒt] pt, pp of **shoot** ▷ n (sound)
tiro, disparo; (try) tentativa; (injection)
inyección f; (Phot) toma, fotografía;
to be a good/poor ~ (person) tener
buena/mala puntería; **like a ~** (without
any delay) como un rayo; **shotgun** n
escopeta

should [ʃʊd] aux vb: **I ~ go now** debo
irme ahora; **he ~ be there now** debe
de haber llegado (ya); **I ~ go if I were
you** yo en tu lugar me iría; **I ~ like to**
me gustaría

shoulder ['ʃəʊldə*] n hombro ▷ vt
(fig) cargar con; **shoulder blade** n
omóplato

shouldn't ['ʃʊdnt] = **should not**

shout [ʃaʊt] n grito ▷ vt gritar ▷ vi
gritar, dar voces

shove [ʃʌv] n empujón m ▷ vt
empujar; (inf: put): **to ~ sth in** meter
algo a empellones

shovel ['ʃʌvl] n pala; (mechanical)
excavadora ▷ vt mover con pala

show [ʃəʊ] (pt **~ed**, pp **~n**) n (of
emotion) demostración f; (semblance)
apariencia; (exhibition) exposición
f; (Theatre) función f, espectáculo;
(TV) show m ▷ vt mostrar, enseñar;
(courage etc) mostrar, manifestar;
(exhibit) exponer; (film) proyectar ▷ vi
mostrarse; (appear) aparecer; **for ~**
para impresionar; **on ~** (exhibits etc)
expuesto; **show in** vt (person) hacer
pasar; **show off** (pej) vi presumir ▷ vt
(display) lucir; **show out** vt: **to show
sb out** acompañar a algn a la puerta;
show up vi (stand out) destacar;
(inf: turn up) aparecer ▷ vt (unmask)
desenmascarar; **show business** n

mundo del espectáculo

shower ['ʃaʊə*] n (rain) chaparrón
m, chubasco; (of stones etc) lluvia;
(for bathing) ducha, regadera (MEX)
▷ vi llover ▷ vt (fig): **to ~ sb with sth**
colmar a algn de algo; **to have a ~**
ducharse; **shower cap** n gorro de
baño; **shower gel** n gel m de ducha

showing ['ʃəʊɪŋ] n (of film)
proyección f

show jumping n hípica

shown [ʃəʊn] pp of **show**

show: show-off (inf) n (person)
presumido/a; **showroom** n sala de
muestras

shrank [ʃræŋk] pt of **shrink**

shred [ʃrɛd] n (gen pl) triza, jirón m
▷ vt hacer trizas; (Culin) desmenuzar

shrewd [ʃruːd] adj astuto

shriek [ʃriːk] n chillido ▷ vi chillar

shrimp [ʃrɪmp] n camarón m

shrine [ʃraɪn] n santuario, sepulcro

shrink [ʃrɪŋk] (pt **shrank**, pp **shrunk**)
vi encogerse; (be reduced) reducirse;
(also: **~ away**) retroceder ▷ vt encoger
▷ n (inf, pej) loquero/a; **to ~ from
(doing) sth** no atreverse a hacer algo

shrivel ['ʃrɪvl] (also: **~ up**) vt (dry) secar
▷ vi secarse

shroud [ʃraʊd] n sudario ▷ vt: **~ed in
mystery** envuelto en el misterio

Shrove Tuesday ['ʃrəʊv-] n martes
m de carnaval

shrub [ʃrʌb] n arbusto

shrug [ʃrʌg] n encogimiento
de hombros ▷ vt, vi: **to ~ (one's
shoulders)** encogerse de hombros;
shrug off vt negar importancia a

shrunk [ʃrʌŋk] pp of **shrink**

shudder ['ʃʌdə*] n estremecimiento,
escalofrío ▷ vi estremecerse

shuffle ['ʃʌfl] vt (cards) barajar ▷ vi: **to
~ (one's feet)** arrastrar los pies

shun [ʃʌn] vt rehuir, esquivar

shut [ʃʌt] (pt, pp **~**) vt cerrar ▷ vi
cerrarse; **shut down** vt, vi cerrar;
shut up vi (inf: keep quiet) callarse
▷ vt (close) cerrar; (silence) hacer callar;

s

shutter n contraventana; (Phot) obturador m

shuttle ['ʃʌtl] n lanzadera; (also: ~ **service**) servicio rápido y continuo entre dos puntos; (Aviat) puente m aéreo; **shuttlecock** n volante m

shy [ʃaɪ] adj tímido

sibling ['sɪblɪŋ] n (formal) hermano/a

sick [sɪk] adj (ill) enfermo; (nauseated) mareado; (humour) negro; (vomiting): **to be ~** (BRIT) vomitar; **to feel ~** tener náuseas; **to be ~ of** (fig) estar harto de; **sickening** adj (fig) asqueroso; **sick leave** n baja por enfermedad; **sickly** adj enfermizo; (smell) nauseabundo; **sickness** n enfermedad f, mal m; (vomiting) náuseas fpl

side [saɪd] n (gen) lado; (of body) costado; (of lake) orilla; (of hill) ladera; (team) equipo ▷ adj (door, entrance) lateral ▷ vi: **to ~ with sb** tomar el partido de algn; **by the ~ of** al lado de; **~ by ~** juntos/as; **from ~ to ~** de un lado para otro; **to take ~s (with)** tomar partido (con); **sideboard** n aparador m; **sideboards** (BRIT) npl = **sideburns**; **sideburns** npl patillas fpl; **sidelight** n (Aut) luz f lateral; **sideline** n (Sport) línea de banda; (fig) empleo suplementario; **side order** n plato de acompañamiento; **side road** n (BRIT) calle f lateral; **side street** n calle f lateral; **sidetrack** vt (fig) desviar (de su propósito); **sidewalk** (US) n acera; **sideways** adv de lado

siege [siːdʒ] n cerco, sitio

sieve [sɪv] n colador m ▷ vt cribar

sift [sɪft] vt cribar; (fig: information) escudriñar

sigh [saɪ] n suspiro ▷ vi suspirar

sight [saɪt] n (faculty) vista; (spectacle) espectáculo; (on gun) mira, alza ▷ vt divisar; **in ~** a la vista; **out of ~** fuera de (la) vista; **on ~** (shoot) sin previo aviso; **sightseeing** n excursionismo, turismo; **to go sightseeing** hacer turismo

sign [saɪn] n (with hand) señal f, seña; (trace) huella, rastro; (notice) letrero; (written) signo ▷ vt firmar; (Sport) fichar; **to ~ sth over to sb** firmar el traspaso de algo a algn; **sign for** vt fus (item) firmar el recibo de; **sign in** vi firmar el registro (al entrar); **sign on** vi (BRIT: as unemployed) registrarse como desempleado; (for course) inscribirse ▷ vt (Mil) alistar; (employee) contratar; **sign up** vi (Mil) alistarse; (for course) inscribirse ▷ vt (player) fichar

signal ['sɪgnl] n señal f ▷ vi señalizar ▷ vt (person) hacer señas a; (message) comunicar por señales

signature ['sɪgnətʃə*] n firma

significance [sɪg'nɪfɪkəns] n (importance) trascendencia

significant [sɪg'nɪfɪkənt] adj significativo; (important) trascendente

signify ['sɪgnɪfaɪ] vt significar

sign language n lenguaje m para sordomudos

signpost ['saɪnpəust] n indicador m

Sikh [siːk] adj, n sij mf

silence ['saɪlns] n silencio ▷ vt acallar; (guns) reducir al silencio

silent ['saɪlnt] adj silencioso; (not speaking) callado; (film) mudo; **to remain ~** guardar silencio

silhouette [sɪluː'et] n silueta

silicon chip ['sɪlɪkən-] n plaqueta de silicio

silk [sɪlk] n seda ▷ adj de seda

silly ['sɪlɪ] adj (person) tonto; (idea) absurdo

silver ['sɪlvə*] n plata; (money) moneda suelta ▷ adj de plata; (colour) plateado; **silver-plated** adj plateado

SIM card ['sɪm-] n (Tel) SIM card mf; tarjeta f SIM

similar ['sɪmɪlə*] adj: **~ (to)** parecido or semejante (a); **similarity** [-'lærɪtɪ] n semejanza; **similarly** adv del mismo modo

simmer ['sɪmə*] vi hervir a fuego lento

simple ['sɪmpl] adj (easy) sencillo; (foolish, Comm: interest) simple;

simplicity [-'plɪsɪtɪ] n sencillez f;
simplify ['sɪmplɪfaɪ] vt simplificar;
simply adv (live, talk) sencillamente;
(just, merely) sólo
simulate ['sɪmju:leɪt] vt fingir,
simular
simultaneous [sɪməl'teɪnɪəs] adj
simultáneo; **simultaneously** adv
simultáneamente
sin [sɪn] n pecado ▷ vi pecar
since [sɪns] adv desde entonces,
después ▷ prep desde ▷ conj (time)
desde que; (because) ya que, puesto
que; **~ then, ever ~** desde entonces
sincere [sɪn'sɪə*] adj sincero;
sincerely adv: **yours sincerely** (in
letters) le saluda atentamente
sing [sɪŋ] (pt **sang**, pp **sung**) vt, vi
cantar
Singapore [sɪŋə'pɔː*] n Singapur m
singer ['sɪŋə*] n cantante mf
singing ['sɪŋɪŋ] n canto
single ['sɪŋgl] adj único, solo,
(unmarried) soltero; (not double) simple,
sencillo ▷ n (BRIT: also: **~ ticket**) billete
m sencillo; (record) sencillo, single
m; **singles** npl (Tennis) individual
m; **single out** vt (choose) escoger;
single bed n cama individual; **single
file** n: **in single file** en fila de uno;
single-handed adv sin ayuda; **single-
minded** adj resuelto, firme; **single
parent** n padre m soltero, madre f
soltera (o divorciado etc); **single parent
family** familia monoparental; **single
room** n cuarto individual
singular ['sɪŋgjulə*] adj (odd) raro,
extraño; (outstanding) excepcional ▷ n
(Ling) singular m
sinister ['sɪnɪstə*] adj siniestro
sink [sɪŋk] (pt **sank**, pp **sunk**) n
fregadero ▷ vt (ship) hundir, echar
a pique; (foundations) excavar ▷ vi
hundirse; **to ~ sth into** hundir algo en;
sink in vi (fig) penetrar, calar
sinus ['saɪnəs] n (Anat) seno
sip [sɪp] n sorbo ▷ vt sorber, beber
a sorbitos

sir [sə*] n señor m; **S~ John Smith** Sir
John Smith; **yes ~** sí, señor
siren ['saɪərn] n sirena
sirloin ['sə:lɔɪn] n (also: **~ steak**)
solomillo
sister ['sɪstə*] n hermana;
(BRIT: nurse) enfermera jefe; **sister-in-
law** n cuñada
sit [sɪt] (pt, pp **sat**) vi sentarse; (be
sitting) estar sentado; (assembly)
reunirse; (for painter) posar ▷ vt (exam)
presentarse a; **sit back** vi (in seat)
recostarse; **sit down** vi sentarse;
sit on vt fus (jury, committee) ser
miembro de, formar parte de; **sit up** vi
incorporarse; (not go to bed) velar
sitcom ['sɪtkɔm] n abbr (= situation
comedy) comedia de situación
site [saɪt] n sitio; (also: **building ~**)
solar m ▷ vt situar
sitting ['sɪtɪŋ] n (of assembly etc)
sesión f; (in canteen) turno; **sitting
room** n sala de estar
situated ['sɪtjueɪtɪd] adj situado
situation [sɪtju'eɪʃən] n situación f;
"~s vacant" (BRIT) "ofrecen trabajo"
six [sɪks] num seis; **sixteen** num diez
y seis, dieciséis; **sixteenth** [sɪks'ti:nθ]
adj decimosexto; **sixth** [sɪksθ] num
sexto; **sixth form** n (BRIT) clase f de
alumnos del sexto año (de 16 a 18 años de
edad); **sixth-form college** n instituto
m para alumnos de 16 a 18 años;
sixtieth ['sɪkstɪɪθ] adj sexagésimo;
sixty num sesenta
size [saɪz] n tamaño; (extent)
extensión f; (of clothing) talla; (of shoes)
número; **sizeable** adj importante,
considerable
sizzle ['sɪzl] vi crepitar
skate [skeɪt] n patín m; (fish: pl
inv) raya ▷ vi patinar; **skateboard**
n monopatín m; **skateboarding** n
monopatín m; **skater** n patinador(a)
m/f; **skating** n patinaje m; **skating
rink** n pista de patinaje
skeleton ['skelɪtn] n esqueleto;
(Tech) armazón f; (outline) esquema m

skeptical ['skɛptɪkl] (US) = **sceptical**

sketch [skɛtʃ] n (drawing) dibujo; (outline) esbozo, bosquejo; (Theatre) sketch m ▷ vt dibujar; (plan etc: also: ~ out) esbozar

skewer ['skjuːə*] n broqueta

ski: [skiː] n esquí m ▷ vi esquiar; **ski boot** n bota de esquí

skid [skɪd] n patinazo ▷ vi patinar

ski: skier n esquiador(a) m/f; **skiing** n esquí m

skilful ['skɪlful] (US **skillful**) adj diestro, experto

ski lift n telesilla m, telesquí m

skill [skɪl] n destreza, pericia, técnica; **skilled** adj hábil, diestro; (worker) cualificado

skim [skɪm] vt (milk) desnatar; (glide over) rozar, rasar ▷ vi: **to ~ through** (book) hojear; **skimmed milk** (US **skim milk**) n leche f desnatada

skin [skɪn] n piel f; (complexion) cutis m ▷ vt (fruit etc) pelar; (animal) despellejar; **skinhead** n cabeza m/f rapada, skin(head) m/f; **skinny** adj flaco

skip [skɪp] n brinco, salto; (BRIT: container) contenedor m ▷ vi brincar; (with rope) saltar a la comba ▷ vt saltarse

ski: ski pass n forfait m (de esquí); **ski pole** n bastón m de esquiar

skipper ['skɪpə*] n (Naut, Sport) capitán m

skipping rope ['skɪpɪŋ-] (US **skip rope**) n comba

skirt [skəːt] n falda, pollera (SC) ▷ vt (go round) ladear

skirting board ['skəːtɪŋ-] (BRIT) n rodapié m

ski slope n pista de esquí

ski suit n traje m de esquiar

skull [skʌl] n calavera; (Anat) cráneo

skunk [skʌŋk] n mofeta

sky [skaɪ] n cielo; **skyscraper** n rascacielos m inv

slab [slæb] n (stone) bloque m; (flat) losa; (of cake) trozo

slack [slæk] adj (loose) flojo; (slow) de poca actividad; (careless) descuidado; **slacks** npl pantalones mpl

slain [sleɪn] pp of **slay**

slam [slæm] vt (throw) arrojar (violentamente); (criticize) criticar duramente ▷ vi (door) cerrarse de golpe; **to ~ the door** dar un portazo

slander ['slɑːndə*] n calumnia, difamación f

slang [slæŋ] n argot m; (jargon) jerga

slant [slɑːnt] n sesgo, inclinación f; (fig) interpretación f

slap [slæp] n palmada; (in face) bofetada ▷ vt dar una palmada or bofetada a; (paint etc): **to ~ sth on sth** embadurnar algo con algo ▷ adv (directly) exactamente, directamente

slash [slæʃ] vt acuchillar; (fig: prices) fulminar

slate [sleɪt] n pizarra ▷ vt (fig: criticize) criticar duramente

slaughter ['slɔːtə*] n (of animals) matanza; (of people) carnicería ▷ vt matar; **slaughterhouse** n matadero

Slav [slɑːv] adj eslavo

slave [sleɪv] n esclavo/a ▷ vi (also: ~ away) sudar tinta; **slavery** n esclavitud f

slay [sleɪ] (pt **slew**, pp **slain**) vt matar

sleazy ['sliːzɪ] adj de mala fama

sled [slɛd] (US) = **sledge**

sledge [slɛdʒ] n trineo

sleek [sliːk] adj (shiny) lustroso; (car etc) elegante

sleep [sliːp] (pt, pp **slept**) n sueño ▷ vi dormir; **to go to ~** quedarse dormido; **sleep in** vi (oversleep) quedarse dormido; **sleep together** vi (have sex) acostarse juntos; **sleeper** n (person) durmiente mf; (BRIT Rail: on track) traviesa; (: train) coche-cama m; **sleeping bag** n saco de dormir; **sleeping car** n coche-cama m; **sleeping pill** n somnífero; **sleepover** n: **we're having a sleepover at Jo's** nos vamos a quedar a dormir en casa de Jo; **sleepwalk** vi caminar dormido;

(*habitually*) ser sonámbulo; **sleepy** *adj* soñoliento; (*place*) soporífero

sleet [sli:t] *n* aguanieve *f*

sleeve [sli:v] *n* manga; (*Tech*) manguito; (*of record*) portada; **sleeveless** *adj* sin mangas

sleigh [sleɪ] *n* trineo

slender ['slɛndə*] *adj* delgado; (*means*) escaso

slept [slɛpt] *pt, pp of* **sleep**

slew [slu:] *pt of* **slay** ▷ *vi* (BRIT: *veer*) torcerse

slice [slaɪs] *n* (*of meat*) tajada; (*of bread*) rebanada; (*of lemon*) rodaja; (*utensil*) pala ▷ *vt* cortar (en tajos), rebanar

slick [slɪk] *adj* (*skilful*) hábil, diestro; (*clever*) astuto ▷ *n* (*also*: **oil ~**) marea negra

slide [slaɪd] (*pt, pp* **slid**) *n* (*movement*) descenso, desprendimiento; (*in playground*) tobogán *m*; (*Phot*) diapositiva; (BRIT: *also*: **hair ~**) pasador *m* ▷ *vt* correr, deslizar ▷ *vi* (*slip*) resbalarse; (*glide*) deslizarse; **sliding** *adj* (*door*) corredizo

slight [slaɪt] *adj* (*slim*) delgado; (*frail*) delicado; (*pain etc*) leve; (*trivial*) insignificante; (*small*) pequeño ▷ *n* desaire *m* ▷ *vt* (*insult*) ofender, desairar; **not in the ~est** en absoluto; **slightly** *adv* ligeramente, un poco

slim [slɪm] *adj* delgado, esbelto; (*fig: chance*) remoto ▷ *vi* adelgazar; **slimming** *n* adelgazamiento

slimy ['slaɪmɪ] *adj* cenagoso

sling [slɪŋ] (*pt, pp* **slung**) *n* (*Med*) cabestrillo; (*weapon*) honda ▷ *vt* tirar, arrojar

slip [slɪp] *n* (*slide*) resbalón *m*; (*mistake*) descuido; (*underskirt*) combinación *f*; (*of paper*) papelito ▷ *vt* (*slide*) deslizar ▷ *vi* deslizarse; (*stumble*) resbalar(se); (*decline*) decaer; (*move smoothly*): **to ~ into/out of** introducirse en/salirse de; **to give sb the ~** eludir a algn; **a ~ of the tongue** un lapsus; **to ~ sth on/off** ponerse/quitarse algo;

slip up *vi* (*make mistake*) equivocarse; meter la pata

slipper ['slɪpə*] *n* zapatilla, pantufla

slippery ['slɪpərɪ] *adj* resbaladizo; **slip road** (BRIT) *n* carretera de acceso

slit [slɪt] (*pt, pp ~*) *n* raja; (*cut*) corte *m* ▷ *vt* rajar; cortar

slog [slɔg] (BRIT) *vi* sudar tinta; **it was a ~** costó trabajo (hacerlo)

slogan ['sləugən] *n* eslogan *m*, lema *m*

slope [sləup] *n* (*up*) cuesta, pendiente *f*; (*down*) declive *m*; (*side of mountain*) falda, vertiente *m* ▷ *vi*: **to ~ down** estar en declive; **to ~ up** inclinarse; **sloping** *adj* en pendiente; en declive; (*writing*) inclinado

sloppy ['slɔpɪ] *adj* (*work*) descuidado; (*appearance*) desaliñado

slot [slɔt] *n* ranura ▷ *vt*: **to ~ into** encajar en; **slot machine** *n* (BRIT: *vending machine*) distribuidor *m* automático, (*for gambling*) tragaperras *m inv*

Slovakia [sləu'vækɪə] *n* Eslovaquia

Slovene [sləu'vi:n] *adj* esloveno ▷ *n* esloveno/a; (*Ling*) esloveno; **Slovenia** [sləu'vi:nɪə] *n* Eslovenia, **Slovenian** *adj, n* = **Slovene**

slow [sləu] *adj* lento; (*not clever*) lerdo; (*watch*): **to be ~** atrasar ▷ *adv* lentamente, despacio ▷ *vt, vi* retardar; **"~"** (*road sign*) "disminuir velocidad"; **slow down** *vi* reducir la marcha; **slowly** *adv* lentamente, despacio; **slow motion** *n*: **in slow motion** a cámara lenta

slug [slʌg] *n* babosa; (*bullet*) posta; **sluggish** *adj* lento; (*person*) perezoso

slum [slʌm] *n* casucha

slump [slʌmp] *n* (*economic*) depresión *f* ▷ *vi* hundirse; (*prices*) caer en picado

slung [slʌŋ] *pt, pp of* **sling**

slur [slə:*] *n*: **to cast a ~ on** insultar ▷ *vt* (*speech*) pronunciar mal

sly [slaɪ] *adj* astuto; (*smile*) taimado

smack [smæk] *n* bofetada ▷ *vt* dar con la mano a; (*child, on face*) abofetear

s

▷ *vi*: **to ~ of** saber a, oler a

small [smɔːl] *adj* pequeño; **small ads** (*BRIT*) *npl* anuncios *mpl* por palabras; **small change** *n* suelto, cambio

smart [smɑːt] *adj* elegante; (*clever*) listo, inteligente; (*quick*) rápido, vivo ▷ *vi* escocer, picar; **smartcard** *n* tarjeta inteligente; **smart phone** *n* smartphone *m*

smash [smæʃ] *n* (*also*: **~-up**) choque *m*; (*Mus*) exitazo ▷ *vt* (*break*) hacer pedazos; (*car etc*) estrellar; (*Sport: record*) batir ▷ *vi* hacerse pedazos; (*against wall etc*) estrellarse; **smashing** (*inf*) *adj* estupendo

smear [smɪə*] *n* mancha; (*Med*) frotis *m inv* ▷ *vt* untar; **smear test** *n* (*Med*) citología, frotis *m inv* (cervical)

smell [smɛl] (*pt, pp* **smelt** *or* **~ed**) *n* olor *m*; (*sense*) olfato ▷ *vt, vi* oler; **smelly** *adj* maloliente

smelt [smɛlt] *pt, pp of* **smell**

smile [smaɪl] *n* sonrisa ▷ *vi* sonreír

smirk [smə:k] *n* sonrisa falsa *or* afectada

smog [smɔg] *n* esmog *m*

smoke [sməuk] *n* humo ▷ *vi* fumar; (*chimney*) echar humo ▷ *vt* (*cigarettes*) fumar; **smoke alarm** *n* detector *m* de humo, alarma contra incendios; **smoked** *adj* (*bacon, glass*) ahumado; **smoker** *n* fumador(a) *m/f*; (*Rail*) coche *m* fumador; **smoking** *n*: **"no smoking"** "prohibido fumar"

▌ Be careful not to translate **smoking** by the Spanish word *smoking*.

smoky *adj* (*room*) lleno de humo; (*taste*) ahumado

smooth [smuːð] *adj* liso; (*sea*) tranquilo; (*flavour, movement*) suave; (*sauce*) fino; (*person: pej*) meloso ▷ *vt* (*also*: **~ out**) alisar; (*creases, difficulties*) allanar

smother ['smʌðə*] *vt* sofocar; (*repress*) contener

SMS *n abbr* (= *short message service*) (servicio) SMS; **SMS message** *n* (mensaje *m*) SMS

smudge [smʌdʒ] *n* mancha ▷ *vt* manchar

smug [smʌg] *adj* presumido; oronda

smuggle ['smʌgl] *vt* pasar de contrabando; **smuggling** *n* contrabando

snack [snæk] *n* bocado; **snack bar** *n* cafetería

snag [snæg] *n* problema *m*

snail [sneɪl] *n* caracol *m*

snake [sneɪk] *n* serpiente *f*

snap [snæp] *n* (*sound*) chasquido; (*photograph*) foto *f* ▷ *adj* (*decision*) instantáneo ▷ *vt* (*break*) quebrar; (*fingers*) castañetear ▷ *vi* quebrarse; (*fig: speak sharply*) contestar bruscamente; **to ~ shut** cerrarse de golpe; **snap at** *vt fus* (*dog*) intentar morder; **snap up** *vt* agarrar; **snapshot** *n* foto *f* (instantánea)

snarl [snɑːl] *vi* gruñir

snatch [snætʃ] *n* (*small piece*) fragmento ▷ *vt* (*snatch away*) arrebatar; (*fig*) agarrar; **to ~ some sleep** encontrar tiempo para dormir

sneak [sniːk] (*pt* (*US*) **snuck**) *vi*: **to ~ in/out** entrar/salir a hurtadillas ▷ *n* (*inf*) soplón/ona *m/f*; **to ~ up on sb** aparecérsele de improviso a algn; **sneakers** *npl* zapatos *mpl* de lona

sneer [snɪə*] *vi* reír con sarcasmo; (*mock*): **to ~ at** burlarse de

sneeze [sniːz] *vi* estornudar

sniff [snɪf] *vi* sollozar ▷ *vt* husmear, oler; (*drugs*) esnifar

snigger ['snɪgə*] *vi* reírse con disimulo

snip [snɪp] *n* tijeretazo; (*BRIT: inf: bargain*) ganga ▷ *vt* tijeretear

sniper ['snaɪpə*] *n* francotirador(a) *m/f*

snob [snɔb] *n* (e)snob *mf*

snooker ['snuːkə*] *n* especie de billar

snoop [snuːp] *vi*: **to ~ about** fisgonear

snooze [snuːz] *n* siesta ▷ *vi* echar una siesta

snore [snɔː*] *n* ronquido ▷ *vi* roncar

snorkel ['snɔːkl] *n* (tubo) respirador *m*

snort [snɔːt] n bufido ▷ vi bufar
snow [snəu] n nieve f ▷ vi nevar;
snowball n bola de nieve ▷ vi (fig)
agrandirse, ampliarse; **snowstorm** n
nevada, nevasca
snub [snʌb] vt (person) desairar ▷ n
desaire m, repulsa
snug [snʌg] adj (cosy) cómodo; (fitted)
ajustado

○ **KEYWORD**

so [səu] adv **1** (thus, likewise) así, de este
modo; **if so** de ser así; **I like swimming
– so do I** a mí me gusta nadar – a mí
también; **I've got work to do – so has
Paul** tengo trabajo que hacer – Paul
también; **it's 5 o'clock – so it is!** son las
cinco – ¡pues es verdad!; **I hope/think
so** espero/creo que sí; **so far** hasta
ahora; (in past) hasta este momento
2 (in comparisons etc: to such a degree)
tan; **so quickly (that)** tan rápido (que),
she's not so clever as her brother
no es tan lista como su hermano;
we were so worried estábamos
preocupadísimos
3. so much adj, adv tanto; **so many**
tantos/as
4 (phrases): **10 or so** unos 10, 10 o así; **so
long!** (inf: goodbye) ¡hasta luego!
▷ conj **1** (expressing purpose): **so as to do**
para hacer; **so (that)** para que +subjun
2 (expressing result) así que; **so you see,
I could have gone** así que ya ves, (yo)
podría haber ido

soak [səuk] vt (drench) empapar;
(steep in water) remojar ▷ vi remojarse,
estar a remojo; **soak up** vt absorber;
soaking adj (also: **soaking wet**)
calado or empapado (hasta los huesos
or el tuétano)
so-and-so ['səuənsəu] n (somebody)
fulano/a de tal
soap [səup] n jabón m; **soap opera**
n telenovela; **soap powder** n jabón
m en polvo

soar [sɔː*] vi (on wings) remontarse;
(rocket: prices) dispararse; (building etc)
elevarse
sob [sɔb] n sollozo ▷ vi sollozar
sober ['səubə*] adj (serious) serio; (not
drunk) sobrio; (colour, style) discreto;
sober up vt quitar la borrachera
so-called ['səu'kɔːld] adj así llamado
soccer ['sɔkə*] n fútbol m
sociable ['səuʃəbl] adj sociable
social ['səuʃl] adj social ▷ n velada,
fiesta; **socialism** n socialismo;
socialist adj, n socialista mf; **socialize**
vi: **to socialize** alternar; **social life** n
vida social; **socially** adv socialmente;
social networking n interacción
social a través de la red; **social security**
n seguridad f social; **social services**
npl servicios mpl sociales; **social work**
n asistencia social; **social worker** n
asistente/a m/f social
society [sə'saɪətɪ] n sociedad f;
(club) asociación f, (also: **high ~**) alta
sociedad
sociology [səusɪ'ɔlədʒɪ] n sociología
sock [sɔk] n calcetín m
socket ['sɔkɪt] n cavidad f; (BRIT Elec)
enchufe m
soda ['səudə] n (Chem) sosa; (also: **~
water**) soda; (us: also: **~ pop**) gaseosa
sodium ['səudɪəm] n sodio
sofa ['səufə] n sofá m; **sofa bed** n
sofá-cama m
soft [sɔft] adj (lenient, not hard) blando;
(gentle, not bright) suave; **soft drink** n
bebida no alcohólica; **soft drugs** npl
drogas fpl blandas; **soften** ['sɔfn] vt
ablandar; suavizar; (effect) amortiguar
▷ vi ablandarse; suavizarse; **softly** adv
suavemente; (gently) delicadamente,
con delicadeza; **software** n (Comput)
software m
soggy ['sɔgɪ] adj empapado
soil [sɔɪl] n (earth) tierra, suelo ▷ vt
ensuciar
solar ['səulə*] adj solar; **solar power**
n energía solar; **solar system** n
sistema m solar

s

sold [səʊld] *pt, pp of* **sell**
soldier ['səʊldʒə*] *n* soldado; (*army man*) militar *m*
sold out *adj* (*Comm*) agotado
sole [səʊl] *n* (*of foot*) planta; (*of shoe*) suela; (*fish: pl inv*) lenguado ▷ *adj* único; **solely** *adv* únicamente, sólo, solamente; **I will hold you solely responsible** le consideraré el único responsable
solemn ['sɒləm] *adj* solemne
solicitor [sə'lɪsɪtə*] (*BRIT*) *n* (*for wills etc*) ≈ notario/a; (*in court*) ≈ abogado/a
solid ['sɒlɪd] *adj* sólido; (*gold etc*) macizo ▷ *n* sólido
solitary ['sɒlɪtərɪ] *adj* solitario, solo
solitude ['sɒlɪtjuːd] *n* soledad *f*
solo ['səʊləʊ] *n* solo ▷ *adv* (*fly*) en solitario; **soloist** *n* solista *m/f*
soluble ['sɒljuːbl] *adj* soluble
solution [sə'luːʃən] *n* solución *f*
solve [sɒlv] *vt* resolver, solucionar
solvent ['sɒlvənt] *adj* (*Comm*) solvente ▷ *n* (*Chem*) solvente *m*
sombre ['sɒmbə*] (*US* **somber**) *adj* sombrío

○ **KEYWORD**

some [sʌm] *adj* **1** (*a certain amount or number*): **some tea/water/biscuits** té/agua/(unas) galletas; **there's some milk in the fridge** hay leche en el frigo; **there were some people outside** había algunas personas fuera; **I've got some money, but not much** tengo algo de dinero, pero no mucho
2 (*certain: in contrasts*) algunos/as; **some people say that ...** hay quien dice que ...; **some films were excellent, but most were mediocre** hubo películas excelentes, pero la mayoría fueron mediocres
3 (*unspecified*): **some woman was asking for you** una mujer estuvo preguntando por ti; **he was asking for some book (or other)** pedía un libro;

some day algún día; **some day next week** un día de la semana que viene ▷ *pron* **1** (*a certain number*): **I've got some** (*books etc*) tengo algunos/as
2 (*a certain amount*) algo; **I've got some** (*money, milk*) tengo algo; **could I have some of that cheese?** ¿me puede dar un poco de ese queso?; **I've read some of the book** he leído parte del libro ▷ *adv*: **some 10 people** unas 10 personas, una decena de personas

some: somebody ['sʌmbədɪ] *pron* = **someone**; **somehow** *adv* de alguna manera; (*for some reason*) por una u otra razón; **someone** *pron* alguien; **someplace** (*US*) *adv* = **somewhere**; **something** *pron* algo; **would you like something to eat/drink?** ¿te gustaría cenar/tomar algo?; **sometime** *adv* (*in future*) algún día, en algún momento; (*in past*): **sometime last month** durante el mes pasado; **sometimes** *adv* a veces; **somewhat** *adv* algo; **somewhere** *adv* (*be*) en alguna parte; (*go*) a alguna parte; **somewhere else** (*be*) en otra parte; (*go*) a otra parte
son [sʌn] *n* hijo
song [sɒŋ] *n* canción *f*
son-in-law ['sʌnɪnlɔː] *n* yerno
soon [suːn] *adv* pronto, dentro de poco; **~ afterwards** poco después; *see also* **as**; **sooner** *adv* (*time*) antes, más temprano; (*preference: rather*): **I would sooner do that** preferiría hacer eso; **sooner or later** tarde o temprano
soothe [suːð] *vt* tranquilizar; (*pain*) aliviar
sophisticated [sə'fɪstɪkeɪtɪd] *adj* sofisticado
sophomore ['sɒfəmɔː*] (*US*) *n* estudiante *mf* de segundo año
soprano [sə'prɑːnəʊ] *n* soprano *f*
sorbet ['sɔːbeɪ] *n* sorbete *m*
sordid ['sɔːdɪd] *adj* (*place etc*) sórdido; (*motive etc*) mezquino
sore [sɔː*] *adj* (*painful*) doloroso, que duele ▷ *n* llaga

sorrow ['sɒrəʊ] n pena, dolor m
sorry ['sɒrɪ] adj (regretful) arrepentido; (condition, excuse) lastimoso; **~!** ¡perdón!, ¡perdone!; **~?** ¿cómo?; **to feel ~ for sb** tener lástima a algn; **I feel ~ for him** me da lástima
sort [sɔːt] n clase f, género, tipo; **sort out** vt (papers) clasificar; (organize) ordenar, organizar; (resolve: problem, situation etc) arreglar, solucionar
SOS n SOS m
so-so ['səʊsəʊ] adv regular, así así
sought [sɔːt] pt, pp of **seek**
soul [səʊl] n alma
sound [saʊnd] n (noise) sonido, ruido; (volume: on TV etc) volumen m; (Geo) estrecho ▷ adj (safe, not damaged) en buen estado; (reliable: person) digno de confianza; (sensible) sensato, razonable; (secure: investment) seguro ▷ adv: **~ asleep** profundamente dormido ▷ vt (alarm) sonar ▷ vi sonar, resonar; (fig: seem) parecer; **to ~ like** sonar a; **soundtrack** n (of film) banda sonora
soup [suːp] n (thick) sopa; (thin) caldo
sour ['saʊə*] adj agrio; (milk) cortado; **it's ~ grapes** (fig) están verdes
source [sɔːs] n fuente f
south [saʊθ] n sur m ▷ adj del sur, sureño ▷ adv al sur, hacia el sur; **South Africa** n África del Sur; **South African** adj, n sudafricano/a m/f; **South America** n América del Sur, Sudamérica; **South American** adj, n sudamericano/a m/f; **southbound** adj (con) rumbo al sur; **southeastern** [saʊθ'iːstən] adj sureste, del sureste; **southern** ['sʌðən] adj del sur, meridional; **South Korea** n Corea del Sur; **South Pole** n Polo Sur; **southward(s)** adv hacia el sur; **southwest** n suroeste m; **southwestern** [saʊθ'westən] adj suroeste
souvenir [suːvə'nɪə*] n recuerdo
sovereign ['sɒvrɪn] adj, n soberano/a m/f
sow[1] [səʊ] (pt **~ed**, pp **sown**) vt sembrar
sow[2] [saʊ] n cerda, puerca
soya ['sɔɪə] (BRIT) n soja
spa [spɑː] n balneario
space [speɪs] n espacio; (room) sitio ▷ cpd espacial ▷ vt (also: **~ out**) espaciar; **spacecraft** n nave f espacial; **spaceship** n = **spacecraft**
spacious ['speɪʃəs] adj amplio
spade [speɪd] n (tool) pala, laya; **spades** npl (Cards: British) picas fpl; (: Spanish) espadas fpl
spaghetti [spə'getɪ] n espaguetis mpl, fideos mpl
Spain [speɪn] n España
spam [spæm] n (junk email) spam m
span [spæn] n (of bird, plane) envergadura; (of arch) luz f; (in time) lapso ▷ vt extenderse sobre, cruzar; (fig) abarcar
Spaniard ['spænjəd] n español(a) m/f
Spanish ['spænɪʃ] adj español(a) ▷ n (Ling) español m, castellano; **the Spanish** npl los españoles
spank [spæŋk] vt zurrar
spanner ['spænə*] (BRIT) n llave f (inglesa)
spare [speə*] adj de reserva; (surplus) sobrante, de más ▷ n = **spare part** ▷ vt (do without) pasarse sin; (refrain from hurting) perdonar; **to ~** (surplus) sobrante, de sobra; **spare part** n pieza de repuesto; **spare room** n cuarto de los invitados; **spare time** n tiempo libre; **spare tyre** (US **spare tire**) n (Aut) neumático or llanta (LAM) de recambio; **spare wheel** n (Aut) rueda de recambio
spark [spɑːk] n chispa; (fig) chispazo; **spark(ing) plug** n bujía
sparkle ['spɑːkl] n centelleo, destello ▷ vi (shine) relucir, brillar
sparrow ['spærəʊ] n gorrión m
sparse [spɑːs] adj esparcido, escaso
spasm ['spæzəm] n (Med) espasmo
spat [spæt] pt, pp of **spit**
spate [speɪt] n (fig): **a ~ of** un

torrente de
spatula ['spætjulə] n espátula
speak [spi:k] (pt **spoke**, pp **spoken**)
vt (language) hablar; (truth) decir ▷ vi
hablar; (make a speech) intervenir; **to
~ to sb/of** or **about sth** hablar con
algn/de or sobre algo; **~ up!** ¡habla
fuerte!; **speaker** n (in public) orador(a)
m/f; (also: **loudspeaker**) altavoz m; (for
stereo etc) bafle m; (Pol): **the Speaker**
(BRIT) el Presidente de la Cámara de los
Comunes; (US) el Presidente del Congreso
spear [spɪə*] n lanza ▷ vt alancear
special ['spɛʃl] adj especial; (edition
etc) extraordinario; (delivery) urgente;
special delivery n (Post): **by special
delivery** por entrega urgente;
special effects npl (Cine) efectos mpl
especiales; **specialist** n especialista
mf; **speciality** [spɛʃɪˈælɪtɪ] (BRIT)
n especialidad f; **specialize** vi: **to
specialize (in)** especializarse
(en); **specially** adv sobre todo,
en particular; **special needs** npl
(BRIT) **children with special needs**
niños que requieren una atención
diferenciada; **special offer** n (Comm)
oferta especial; **special school** n
(BRIT) colegio m de educación especial;
specialty (US) n = **speciality**
species ['spi:ʃi:z] n inv especie f
specific [spəˈsɪfɪk] adj específico;
specifically adv específicamente
specify ['spɛsɪfaɪ] vt, vi especificar,
precisar
specimen ['spɛsɪmən] n ejemplar m;
(Med: of urine) espécimen m; (: of blood)
muestra
speck [spɛk] n grano, mota
spectacle ['spɛktəkl] n espectáculo;
spectacles npl (BRIT: glasses) gafas
fpl (SP), anteojos mpl; **spectacular**
[-'tækjulə*] adj espectacular; (success)
impresionante
spectator [spɛk'teɪtə*] n
espectador(a) m/f
spectrum ['spɛktrəm] (pl **spectra**)
n espectro

speculate ['spɛkjuleɪt] vi: **to ~ (on)**
especular (en)
sped [spɛd] pt, pp of **speed**
speech [spi:tʃ] n (faculty) habla;
(formal talk) discurso; (spoken language)
lenguaje m; **speechless** adj mudo,
estupefacto
speed [spi:d] n velocidad f; (haste)
prisa; (promptness) rapidez f; **at full** or
top ~ a máxima velocidad; **speed up** vi
acelerarse ▷ vt acelerar; **speedboat**
n lancha motora; **speeding** n (Aut)
exceso de velocidad; **speed limit** n
límite m de velocidad, velocidad f
máxima; **speedometer** [spɪ'dɔmɪtə*]
n velocímetro; **speedy** adj (fast) veloz,
rápido; (prompt) pronto
spell [spɛl] (pt, pp **spelt** (BRIT) or **~ed**)
n (also: **magic ~**) encanto, hechizo;
(period of time) rato, período ▷ vt
deletrear; (fig) anunciar, presagiar;
to cast a ~ on sb hechizar a algn;
he can't ~ pone faltas de ortografía;
spell out vt (explain): **to spell sth out
for sb** explicar algo a algn en detalle;
spellchecker ['spɛltʃekə*] n corrector
m ortográfico; **spelling** n ortografía
spelt [spɛlt] pt, pp of **spell**
spend [spɛnd] (pt, pp **spent**) vt
(money) gastar; (time) pasar; (life)
dedicar; **spending** n: **government
spending** gastos mpl del gobierno
spent [spɛnt] pt, pp of **spend** ▷ adj
(cartridge, bullets, match) usado
sperm [spə:m] n esperma
sphere [sfɪə*] n esfera
spice [spaɪs] n especia ▷ vt
condimentar
spicy ['spaɪsɪ] adj picante
spider ['spaɪdə*] n araña
spike [spaɪk] n (point) punta; (Bot)
espiga
spill [spɪl] (pt, pp **spilt** or **~ed**) vt
derramar, verter ▷ vi derramarse; **to ~
over** desbordarse
spin [spɪn] (pt, pp **spun**) n (Aviat)
barrena; (trip in car) paseo (en coche);
(on ball) efecto ▷ vt (wool etc) hilar; (ball

etc) hacer girar ▷ *vi* girar, dar vueltas

spinach ['spɪnɪtʃ] *n* espinaca; (*as food*) espinacas *fpl*

spinal ['spaɪnl] *adj* espinal

spin doctor *n* informador(a) parcial al servicio de un partido político *etc*

spin-dryer (BRIT) *n* secador *m* centrífugo

spine [spaɪn] *n* espinazo, columna vertebral; (*thorn*) espina

spiral ['spaɪərl] *n* espiral *f* ▷ *vi* (*fig: prices*) subir desorbitadamente

spire ['spaɪə*] *n* aguja, chapitel *m*

spirit ['spɪrɪt] *n* (*soul*) alma; (*ghost*) fantasma *m*; (*attitude, sense*) espíritu *m*; (*courage*) valor *m*, ánimo; **spirits** *npl* (*drink*) licor(es) *m(pl)*; **in good ~s** alegre, de buen ánimo

spiritual ['spɪrɪtjuəl] *adj* espiritual ▷ *n* espiritual *m*

spit [spɪt] (*pt, pp* **spat**) *n* (*for roasting*) asador *m*, espetón *m*; (*saliva*) saliva ▷ *vi* escupir; (*sound*) chisporrotear; (*rain*) lloviznar

spite [spaɪt] *n* rencor *m*, ojeriza ▷ *vt* causar pena a, mortificar; **in ~ of** a pesar de, pese a; **spiteful** *adj* rencoroso, malévolo

splash [splæʃ] *n* (*sound*) chapoteo; (*of colour*) mancha ▷ *vt* salpicar ▷ *vi* (*also: ~ about*) chapotear; **splash out** (*inf*) *vi* (BRIT) derrochar dinero

splendid ['splendɪd] *adj* espléndido

splinter ['splɪntə*] *n* (*of wood etc*) astilla; (*in finger*) espigón *m* ▷ *vi* astillarse, hacer astillas

split [splɪt] (*pt, pp* **~**) *n* hendedura, raja; (*fig*) división *f*; (*Pol*) escisión *f* ▷ *vt* partir, rajar; (*party*) dividir; (*share*) repartir ▷ *vi* dividirse, escindirse; **split up** *vi* (*couple*) separarse; (*meeting*) acabarse

spoil [spɔɪl] (*pt, pp* **~t** *or* **~ed**) *vt* (*damage*) dañar; (*mar*) estropear; (*child*) mimar, consentir

spoilt [spɔɪlt] *pt, pp of* **spoil** ▷ *adj* (*child*) mimado, consentido; (*ballot paper*) invalidado

spoke [spəuk] *pt of* **speak** ▷ *n* rayo, radio

spoken ['spəukn] *pp of* **speak**

spokesman ['spəuksmən] (*irreg*) *n* portavoz *m*

spokesperson ['spəukspɜːsn] (*irreg*) *n* portavoz *m/f*, vocero/a (LAM)

spokeswoman ['spəukswumən] (*irreg*) *n* portavoz *f*

sponge [spʌndʒ] *n* esponja; (*also: ~ cake*) bizcocho ▷ *vt* (*wash*) lavar con esponja ▷ *vi*: **to ~ off** *or* **on sb** vivir a costa de algn; **sponge bag** (BRIT) *n* esponjera

sponsor ['sponsə*] *n* patrocinador(a) *m/f* ▷ *vt* (*applicant, proposal etc*) proponer; **sponsorship** *n* patrocinio

spontaneous [spon'teɪnɪəs] *adj* espontáneo

spooky ['spuːkɪ] (*inf*) *adj* espeluznante, horripilante

spoon [spuːn] *n* cuchara; **spoonful** *n* cucharada

sport [spɔːt] *n* deporte *m*; (*person*): **to be a good ~** ser muy majo ▷ *vt* (*wear*) lucir, ostentar; **sport jacket** (US) *n* = **sports jacket**; **sports car** *n* coche *m* deportivo, **sports centre** (BRIT) *n* polideportivo; **sports jacket** (BRIT) *n* chaqueta deportiva; **sportsman** (*irreg*) *n* deportista *m*; **sports utility vehicle** *n* todoterreno *m inv*; **sportswear** *n* trajes *mpl* de deporte *or* sport; **sportswoman** (*irreg*) *n* deportista; **sporty** *adj* deportista

spot [spot] *n* sitio, lugar *m*; (*dot: on pattern*) punto, mancha; (*pimple*) grano; (*Radio*) cuña publicitaria; (*TV*) espacio publicitario; (*small amount*): **a ~ of** un poquito de ▷ *vt* (*notice*) notar, observar; **on the ~** allí mismo; **spotless** *adj* perfectamente limpio; **spotlight** *n* foco, reflector *m*; (*Aut*) faro auxiliar

spouse [spauz] *n* cónyuge *mf*

sprain [spreɪn] *n* torcedura ▷ *vt*: **to ~ one's ankle/wrist** torcerse el tobillo/la muñeca

sprang [spræŋ] *pt of* **spring**

sprawl [sprɔ:l] vi tumbarse
spray [spreɪ] n rociada; (of sea) espuma; (container) atomizador m; (for paint etc) pistola rociadora; (of flowers) ramita ▷ vt rociar; (crops) regar
spread [sprɛd] (pt, pp ~) n extensión f; (for bread etc) pasta para untar; (inf: food) comilona ▷ vt extender; (butter) untar; (wings, sails) desplegar; (work, wealth) repartir; (scatter) esparcir ▷ vi (also: ~ out: stain) extenderse; (news) diseminarse; **spread out** vi (move apart) separarse; **spreadsheet** n hoja electrónica or de cálculo
spree [spri:] n: **to go on a ~** ir de juerga
spring [sprɪŋ] (pt **sprang**, pp **sprung**) n (season) primavera; (leap) salto, brinco; (coiled metal) resorte m; (of water) fuente f, manantial m ▷ vi saltar, brincar; **spring up** vi (thing: appear) aparecer; (problem) surgir; **spring onion** n cebolleta
sprinkle ['sprɪŋkl] vt (pour: liquid) rociar; (: salt, sugar) espolvorear; **to ~ water** etc **on**, **~ with water** etc rociar or salpicar de agua etc
sprint [sprɪnt] n esprint m ▷ vi esprintar
sprung [sprʌŋ] pp of **spring**
spun [spʌn] pt, pp of **spin**
spur [spə:*] n espuela; (fig) estímulo, aguijón m ▷ vt (also: ~ **on**) estimular, incitar; **on the ~ of the moment** de improviso
spurt [spə:t] n chorro; (of energy) arrebato ▷ vi chorrear
spy [spaɪ] n espía mf ▷ vi: **to ~ on** espiar a ▷ vt (see) divisar, lograr ver
sq. abbr = **square**
squabble ['skwɔbl] vi reñir, pelear
squad [skwɔd] n (Mil) pelotón m; (Police) brigada; (Sport) equipo
squadron ['skwɔdrn] n (Mil) escuadrón m; (Aviat, Naut) escuadra
squander ['skwɔndə*] vt (money) derrochar, despilfarrar; (chances) desperdiciar

square [skwɛə*] n cuadro; (in town) plaza; (inf: person) carca m/f ▷ adj cuadrado; (inf: ideas, tastes) trasnochado ▷ vt (arrange) arreglar; (Math) cuadrar; (reconcile) compaginar; **all ~** igual(es); **to have a ~ meal** comer caliente; **2 metres ~** 2 metros en cuadro; **2 ~ metres** 2 metros cuadrados; **square root** n raíz f cuadrada
squash [skwɔʃ] n (BRIT: drink): **lemon/orange ~** zumo (SP) or jugo (LAM) de limón/naranja; (US Bot) calabacín m; (Sport) squash m ▷ vt aplastar
squat [skwɔt] adj achaparrado ▷ vi (also: ~ **down**) agacharse, sentarse en cuclillas; **squatter** n okupa mf (SP)
squeak [skwi:k] vi (hinge) chirriar, rechinar; (mouse) chillar
squeal [skwi:l] vi chillar, dar gritos agudos
squeeze [skwi:z] n presión f; (of hand) apretón m; (Comm) restricción f ▷ vt (hand, arm) apretar
squid [skwɪd] n inv calamar m; (Culin) calamares mpl
squint [skwɪnt] vi bizquear, ser bizco ▷ n (Med) estrabismo
squirm [skwə:m] vi retorcerse, revolverse
squirrel ['skwɪrəl] n ardilla
squirt [skwə:t] vi salir a chorros ▷ vt chiscar
Sr abbr = **senior**
Sri Lanka [srɪ'læŋkə] n Sri Lanka m
St abbr = **saint; street**
stab [stæb] n (with knife) puñalada; (of pain) pinchazo; (inf: try): **to have a ~ at (doing) sth** intentar (hacer) algo ▷ vt apuñalar
stability [stə'bɪlɪtɪ] n estabilidad f
stable ['steɪbl] adj estable ▷ n cuadra, caballeriza
stack [stæk] n montón m, pila ▷ vt amontonar, apilar
stadium ['steɪdɪəm] n estadio
staff [sta:f] n (work force) personal m,

plantilla; (*BRIT Scol*) cuerpo docente
▷ *vt* proveer de personal
stag [stæg] *n* ciervo, venado
stage [steɪdʒ] *n* escena; (*point*) etapa; (*platform*) plataforma; (*profession*): **the ~** el teatro ▷ *vt* (*play*) poner en escena, representar; (*organize*) montar, organizar; **in ~s** por etapas
stagger [ˈstægə*] *vi* tambalearse
▷ *vt* (*amaze*) asombrar; (*hours, holidays*) escalonar; **staggering** *adj* asombroso
stagnant [ˈstægnənt] *adj* estancado
stag night, stag party *n*
despedida de soltero
stain [steɪn] *n* mancha; (*colouring*) tintura ▷ *vt* manchar; (*wood*) teñir; **stained glass** *n* vidrio *m* de color; **stainless steel** *n* acero inoxidable
staircase [ˈstɛəkeɪs] *n* ~ **stairway**
stairs [stɛəz] *npl* escaleras *fpl*
stairway [ˈstɛəweɪ] *n* escalera
stake [steɪk] *n* estaca, poste *m*; (*Comm*) interés *m*, (*Betting*) apuesta ▷ *vt* (*money*) apostar; (*life*) arriesgar; (*reputation*) poner en juego; (*claim*) presentar una reclamación; **to be at ~** estar en juego
stale [steɪl] *adj* (*bread*) duro; (*food*) pasado; (*smell*) rancio; (*beer*) agrio
stalk [stɔːk] *n* tallo, caña ▷ *vt* acechar, cazar al acecho
stall [stɔːl] *n* (*in market*) puesto; (*in stable*) casilla (de establo) ▷ *vt* (*Aut*) calar; (*fig*) dar largas a ▷ *vi* (*Aut*) calarse; (*fig*) andarse con rodeos
stamina [ˈstæmɪnə] *n* resistencia
stammer [ˈstæmə*] *n* tartamudeo ▷ *vi* tartamudear
stamp [stæmp] *n* sello (*SP*), estampilla (*LAM*), timbre *m* (*MEX*); (*mark*) marca, huella; (*on document*) timbre *m* ▷ *vi* (*also*: **~ one's foot**) patear ▷ *vt* (*mark*) marcar; (*letter*) franquear; (*with rubber stamp*) sellar; **stamp out** *vt* (*fire*) apagar con el pie; (*crime, opposition*) acabar con; **stamped addressed envelope** *n* (*BRIT*) sobre *m* sellado con las señas propias

stampede [stæmˈpiːd] *n* estampida
stance [stæns] *n* postura
stand [stænd] (*pt, pp* **stood**) *n* (*position*) posición *f*, postura; (*for taxis*) parada; (*hall stand*) perchero; (*music stand*) atril *m*; (*Sport*) tribuna; (*at exhibition*) stand *m* ▷ *vi* (*be*) estar, encontrarse; (*be on foot*) estar de pie; (*rise*) levantarse; (*remain*) quedar en pie; (*in election*) presentar candidatura ▷ *vt* (*place*) poner, colocar; (*withstand*) aguantar, soportar; (*invite to*) invitar; **to make a ~** (*fig*) mantener una postura firme; **to ~ for parliament** (*BRIT*) presentarse (como candidato) a las elecciones; **stand back** *vi* retirarse; **stand by** *vi* (*be ready*) estar listo ▷ *vt fus* (*opinion*) aferrarse a; (*person*) apoyar; **stand down** *vi* (*withdraw*) ceder el puesto; **stand for** *vt fus* (*signify*) significar; (*tolerate*) aguantar, permitir; **stand in for** *vt fus* suplir a; **stand out** *vi* destacarse; **stand up** *vi* levantarse, ponerse de pie; **stand up for** *vt fus* defender; **stand up to** *vt fus* hacer frente a
standard [ˈstændəd] *n* patrón *m*, norma; (*level*) nivel *m*; (*flag*) estandarte *m* ▷ *adj* (*size etc*) normal, corriente; (*text*) básico; **standards** *npl* (*morals*) valores *mpl* morales; **standard of living** *n* nivel *m* de vida
standing [ˈstændɪŋ] *adj* (*on foot*) de pie, en pie; (*permanent*) permanente ▷ *n* reputación *f*; **of many years' ~** que lleva muchos años; **standing order** (*BRIT*) *n* (*at bank*) orden *f* de pago permanente
stand: standpoint *n* punto de vista; **standstill** *n*: **at a standstill** (*industry, traffic*) paralizado; (*car*) parado; **to come to a standstill** quedar paralizado; pararse
stank [stæŋk] *pt of* **stink**
staple [ˈsteɪpl] *n* (*for papers*) grapa ▷ *adj* (*food etc*) básico ▷ *vt* grapar
star [stɑː*] *n* estrella; (*celebrity*) estrella, astro ▷ *vt* (*Theatre, Cinema*)

s

ser el/la protagonista de; **the stars** npl
(Astrology) el horóscopo
starboard ['stɑːbəd] n estribor m
starch [stɑːtʃ] n almidón m
stardom ['stɑːdəm] n estrellato
stare [stɛə*] n mirada fija ▷ vi: **to ~
at** mirar fijo
stark [stɑːk] adj (bleak) severo,
escueto ▷ adv: **~ naked** en cueros
start [stɑːt] n principio, comienzo;
(departure) salida; (sudden movement)
salto, sobresalto; (advantage) ventaja
▷ vt empezar, comenzar; (cause)
causar; (found) fundar; (engine) poner
en marcha ▷ vi comenzar, empezar;
(with fright) asustarse, sobresaltarse;
(train etc) salir; **to ~ doing** or **to do
sth** empezar a hacer algo; **start off**
vi empezar, comenzar; (leave) salir,
ponerse en camino; **start out** vi
(begin) empezar; (set out) partir, salir;
start up vi comenzar; (car) ponerse
en marcha ▷ vt comenzar; poner en
marcha; **starter** n (Aut) botón m de
arranque; (Sport: official) juez mf de
salida; (BRIT Culin) entrante m; **starting
point** n punto de partida
startle ['stɑːtl] vt asustar,
sobrecoger; **startling** adj alarmante
starvation [stɑː'veɪʃən] n hambre f
starve [stɑːv] vi tener mucha
hambre; (to death) morir de hambre
▷ vt hacer pasar hambre
state [steɪt] n estado ▷ vt (say,
declare) afirmar; **the S~s** los Estados
Unidos; **to be in a ~** estar agitado;
statement n afirmación f; **state
school** n escuela or colegio estatal;
statesman (irreg) n estadista m
static ['stætɪk] n (Radio) parásitos mpl
▷ adj estático
station ['steɪʃən] n estación f; (Radio)
emisora; (rank) posición f social ▷ vt
colocar, situar; (Mil) apostar
stationary ['steɪʃnərɪ] adj
estacionario, fijo
stationer's (shop) (BRIT) n
papelería

stationery [-nərɪ] n papel m de
escribir, artículos mpl de escritorio
station wagon (US) n ranchera
statistic [stə'tɪstɪk] n estadística;
statistics n (science) estadística
statue ['stætjuː] n estatua
stature ['stætʃə*] n estatura; (fig)
talla
status ['steɪtəs] n estado; (reputation)
estatus m; **status quo** n (e)statu
quo m
statutory ['stætjutrɪ] adj
estatutario
staunch [stɔːntʃ] adj leal,
incondicional
stay [steɪ] n estancia ▷ vi quedar(se);
(as guest) hospedarse; **to ~ put** seguir
en el mismo sitio; **to ~ the night/5
days** pasar la noche/estar 5 días;
stay away vi (from person, building)
no acercarse; (from event) no acudir;
stay behind vi quedar atrás; **stay
in** vi quedarse en casa; **stay on** vi
quedarse; **stay out** vi (of house) no
volver a casa; (on strike) permanecer
en huelga; **stay up** vi (at night) velar,
no acostarse
steadily ['stɛdɪlɪ] adv
constantemente; (firmly) firmemente;
(work, walk) sin parar; (gaze) fijamente
steady ['stɛdɪ] adj (firm) firme;
(regular) regular; (person, character)
sensato, juicioso; (boyfriend) formal;
(look, voice) tranquilo ▷ vt (stabilize)
estabilizar; (nerves) calmar
steak [steɪk] n filete m; (beef) bistec m
steal [stiːl] (pt **stole**, pp **stolen**) vt
robar ▷ vi robar; (move secretly) andar
a hurtadillas
steam [stiːm] n vapor m; (mist) vaho,
humo ▷ vt (Culin) cocer al vapor ▷ vi
echar vapor; **steam up** vi (window)
empañarse; **to get steamed up
about sth** (fig) ponerse negro por algo;
steamy adj (room) lleno de vapor;
(window) empañado; (heat, atmosphere)
bochornoso
steel [stiːl] n acero ▷ adj de acero

steep [sti:p] *adj* escarpado, abrupto; (*stair*) empinado; (*price*) exorbitante, excesivo ▷ *vt* empapar, remojar
steeple ['sti:pl] *n* aguja
steer [stɪə*] *vt* (*car*) conducir (SP), manejar (LAM); (*person*) dirigir ▷ *vi* conducir, manejar; **steering** *n* (*Aut*) dirección *f*; **steering wheel** *n* volante *m*
stem [stɛm] *n* (*of plant*) tallo; (*of glass*) pie *m* ▷ *vt* detener; (*blood*) restañar
step [stɛp] *n* paso; (*on stair*) peldaño, escalón *m* ▷ *vi*: **to ~ forward/back** dar un paso adelante/hacia atrás; **steps** *npl* (BRIT) = **stepladder**; **in/out of ~ (with)** acorde/en disonancia (con); **step down** *vi* (*fig*) retirarse, **step in** *vi* entrar; (*fig*) intervenir; **step up** *vt* (*increase*) aumentar; **stepbrother** *n* hermanastro; **stepchild** (*pl* **stepchildren**) *n* hijastro/a *m/f*; **stepdaughter** *n* hijastra; **stepfather** *n* padrastro; **stepladder** *n* escalera doble *or* de tijera; **stepmother** *n* madrastra; **stepsister** *n* hermanastra; **stepson** *n* hijastro
stereo ['stɛrɪəu] *n* estéreo ▷ *adj* (*also:* **~phonic**) estéreo, estereofónico
stereotype ['stɪərɪətaɪp] *n* estereotipo ▷ *vt* estereotipar
sterile ['stɛraɪl] *adj* estéril; **sterilize** ['stɛrɪlaɪz] *vt* esterilizar
sterling ['stə:lɪŋ] *adj* (*silver*) de ley ▷ *n* (*Econ*) libras *fpl* esterlinas *fpl*; **one pound ~** una libra esterlina
stern [stə:n] *adj* severo, austero ▷ *n* (*Naut*) popa
steroid ['stɪərɔɪd] *n* esteroide *m*
stew [stju:] *n* estofado, guiso ▷ *vt* estofar, guisar; (*fruit*) cocer
steward ['stju:əd] *n* camarero; **stewardess** *n* (*esp on plane*) azafata
stick [stɪk] (*pt, pp* **stuck**) *n* palo; (*of dynamite*) barreno; (*as weapon*) porra; (*also:* **walking ~**) bastón *m* ▷ *vt* (*glue*) pegar; (*inf: put*) meter; (*: tolerate*) aguantar, soportar; (*thrust*): **to ~ sth into** clavar *or* hincar algo en ▷ *vi*

pegarse; (*be unmoveable*) quedarse parado; (*in mind*) quedarse grabado; ⌐
stick out *vi* sobresalir; **stick up** *vi* sobresalir; **stick up for** *vt fus* defender; **sticker** *n* (*label*) etiqueta engomada; (*with slogan*) pegatina; **sticking plaster** *n* esparadrapo; **stick insect** *n* insecto palo; **stick shift** (US) *n* (*Aut*) palanca de cambios
sticky ['stɪkɪ] *adj* pegajoso; (*label*) engomado; (*fig*) difícil
stiff [stɪf] *adj* rígido, tieso; (*hard*) duro; (*manner*) estirado; (*difficult*) difícil; (*person*) inflexible; (*price*) exorbitante ▷ *adv*: **scared/bored ~** muerto de miedo/aburrimiento
stifling ['staɪflɪŋ] *adj* (*heat*) sofocante, bochornoso
stigma ['stɪgmə] *n* (*fig*) estigma *m*
stiletto [stɪ'lɛtəu] (BRIT) *n* (*also:* **~ heel**) tacón *m* de aguja
still [stɪl] *adj* inmóvil, quieto ▷ *adv* todavía; (*even*) aun; (*nonetheless*) sin embargo, aun así
stimulate ['stɪmjuleɪt] *vt* estimular
stimulus ['stɪmjuləs] (*pl* **stimuli**) *n* estímulo, incentivo
sting [stɪŋ] (*pt, pp* **stung**) *n* picadura; (*pain*) escozor *m*, picazón *f*; (*organ*) aguijón *m* ▷ *vt, vi* picar
stink [stɪŋk] (*pt* **stank**, *pp* **stunk**) *n* hedor *m*, tufo ▷ *vi* heder, apestar
stir [stə:*] *n* (*fig: agitation*) conmoción *f* ▷ *vt* (*tea etc*) remover; (*fig: emotions*) provocar ▷ *vi* moverse; **stir up** *vt* (*trouble*) fomentar; **stir-fry** *vt* sofreír removiendo ▷ *n* plato preparado sofriendo y removiendo los ingredientes
stitch [stɪtʃ] *n* (*Sewing*) puntada; (*Knitting*) punto; (*Med*) punto (de sutura); (*pain*) punzada ▷ *vt* coser; (*Med*) suturar
stock [stɔk] *n* (*Comm: reserves*) existencias *fpl*, stock *m*; (*: selection*) surtido; (*Agr*) ganado, ganadería; (*Culin*) caldo; (*descent*) raza, estirpe *f*; (*Finance*) capital *m* ▷ *adj* (*fig: reply etc*) clásico ▷ *vt* (*have in stock*) tener existencias de; **~s and shares** acciones

y valores; **in ~** en existencia or almacén; **out of ~** agotado; **to take ~ of** (fig) asesorar, examinar; **stockbroker** ['stɔkbrəukə*] n agente mf or corredor mf de bolsa(a); **stock cube** (BRIT) n pastilla de caldo; **stock exchange** n bolsa; **stockholder** ['stɔkhəuldə*] (US) n accionista m/f

stocking ['stɔkɪŋ] n media

stock market n bolsa (de valores)

stole [stəul] pt of **steal** ▷ n estola

stolen ['stəuln] pp of **steal**

stomach ['stʌmək] n (Anat) estómago; (belly) vientre m ▷ vt tragar, aguantar; **stomachache** n dolor m de estómago

stone [stəun] n piedra; (in fruit) hueso (= 6.348 kg; 14 libras) ▷ adj de piedra ▷ vt apedrear; (fruit) deshuesar

stood [stud] pt, pp of **stand**

stool [stu:l] n taburete m

stoop [stu:p] vi (also: **~ down**) doblarse, agacharse; (also: **have a ~**) ser cargado de espaldas

stop [stɔp] n parada; (in punctuation) punto ▷ vt parar, detener; (break) suspender; (block: pay) suspender; (: cheque) invalidar; (also: **put a ~ to**) poner término a ▷ vi pararse, detenerse; (end) acabarse; **to ~ doing sth** dejar de hacer algo; **stop by** vi pasar por; **stop off** vi interrumpir el viaje; **stopover** n parada; (Aviat) escala; **stoppage** n (strike) paro; (blockage) obstrucción f

storage ['stɔːrɪdʒ] n almacenaje m

store [stɔː*] n (stock) provisión f; (depot (BRIT: large shop) almacén m; (US) tienda; (reserve) reserva, repuesto ▷ vt almacenar; **stores** npl víveres mpl; **to be in ~ for sb** (fig) esperarle a algn; **storekeeper** (US) n tendero/a

storey ['stɔːrɪ] (US **story**) n piso

storm [stɔːm] n tormenta; (fig: of applause) salva; (: of criticism) nube f ▷ vi (fig) rabiar. ▷ vt tomar por asalto; **stormy** adj tempestuoso

story ['stɔːrɪ] n historia; (lie) mentira;

(US) = **storey**

stout [staut] adj (strong) sólido; (fat) gordo, corpulento; (resolute) resuelto ▷ n cerveza negra

stove [stəuv] n (for cooking) cocina; (for heating) estufa

straight [streɪt] adj recto, derecho; (frank) franco, directo; (simple) sencillo ▷ adv derecho, directamente; (drink) sin mezcla; **to put** or **get sth ~** dejar algo en claro; **~ away**, **~ off** en seguida; **straighten** vt (also: **straighten out**) enderezar, poner derecho ▷ vi (also: **straighten up**) enderezarse, ponerse derecho; **straightforward** adj (simple) sencillo; (honest) honrado, franco

strain [streɪn] n tensión f; (Tech) presión f; (Med) torcedura; (breed) tipo, variedad f ▷ vt (back etc) torcerse; (resources) agotar; (stretch) estirar; (food, tea) colar; **strained** adj (muscle) torcido; (laugh) forzado; (relations) tenso; **strainer** n colador m

strait [streɪt] n (Geo) estrecho (fig): **to be in dire ~s** estar en un gran apuro

strand [strænd] n (of thread) hebra; (of hair) trenza; (of rope) ramal m; **stranded** adj (person: without money) desamparado; (: without transport) colgado

strange [streɪndʒ] adj (not known) desconocido; (odd) extraño, raro; **strangely** adv de un modo raro; **stranger** n desconocido/a; (from another area) forastero/a

▌ Be careful not to translate **stranger** by the Spanish word extranjero.

strangle ['stræŋgl] vt estrangular

strap [stræp] n correa; (of slip, dress) tirante m

strategic [strə'ti:dʒɪk] adj estratégico

strategy ['strætɪdʒɪ] n estrategia

straw [strɔː] n paja; (drinking straw) caña, pajita; **that's the last ~!** ¡eso es el colmo!

strawberry ['strɔːbərɪ] n fresa,

frutilla (SC)

stray [streɪ] adj (animal) extraviado; (bullet) perdido; (scattered) disperso ▷ vi extraviarse, perderse

streak [striːk] n raya; (in hair) raya ▷ vt rayar ▷ vi: **to ~ past** pasar como un rayo

stream [striːm] n riachuelo, arroyo; (of people, vehicles) riada, caravana; (of smoke, insults etc) chorro ▷ vt (Scol) dividir en grupos por habilidad ▷ vi correr, fluir; **to ~ in/out** (people) entrar/salir en tropel

street [striːt] n calle f; **streetcar** (US) n tranvía m; **street light** n farol m (LAM), farola (SP); **street map** n plano (de la ciudad); **street plan** n plano

strength [streŋθ] n fuerza; (of girder, knot etc) resistencia; (fig: power) poder m; **strengthen** vt fortalecer, reforzar

strenuous ['strenjuəs] adj (energetic, determined) enérgico

stress [stres] n presión f; (mental strain) estrés m; (accent) acento ▷ vt subrayar, recalcar; (syllable) acentuar; **stressed** adj (tense) estresado, agobiado; (syllable) acentuado; **stressful** adj (job) estresante

stretch [stretʃ] n (of sand etc) trecho ▷ vi estirarse; (extend): **to ~ to or as far as** extenderse hasta ▷ vt extender, estirar; (make demands) exigir el máximo esfuerzo a; **stretch out** vi tenderse ▷ vt (arm etc) extender; (spread) estirar

stretcher ['stretʃə*] n camilla

strict [strɪkt] adj severo; (exact) estricto; **strictly** adv severamente; estrictamente

stride [straɪd] (pt **strode**, pp **stridden**) n zancada, tranco ▷ vi dar zancadas, andar a trancos

strike [straɪk] (pt, pp **struck**) n huelga; (of oil etc) descubrimiento; (attack) ataque m ▷ vt golpear, pegar; (oil etc) descubrir; (bargain, deal) cerrar ▷ vi declarar la huelga; (attack) atacar; (clock) dar la hora; **on ~** (workers)

en huelga; **to ~ a match** encender un fósforo; **striker** n huelguista mf; (Sport) delantero; **striking** adj llamativo

string [strɪŋ] (pt, pp **strung**) n cuerda; (row) hilera ▷ vt: **to ~ together** ensartar; **to ~ out** extenderse; **the strings** npl (Mus) los instrumentos de cuerda; **to pull ~s** (fig) mover palancas

strip [strɪp] n tira; (of land) franja; (of metal) cinta, lámina ▷ vt desnudar; (paint) quitar; (also: ~ **down**: machine) desmontar ▷ vi desnudarse; **strip off** vt (paint etc) quitar ▷ vi (person) desnudarse

stripe [straɪp] n raya; (Mil) galón m; **striped** adj a rayas, rayado

stripper ['strɪpə*] n artista mf de striptease

strip-search ['strɪpsəːtʃ] vt: **to ~ sb** desnudar y registrar a algn

strive [straɪv] (pt **strove**, pp **striven**) vi: **to ~ for sth/to do sth** luchar por conseguir/hacer algo

strode [strəud] pt of **stride**

stroke [strəuk] n (blow) golpe m; (Swimming) brazada; (Med) apoplejía; (of paintbrush) toque m ▷ vt acariciar, **at a ~** de un solo golpe

stroll [strəul] n paseo, vuelta ▷ vi dar un paseo or una vuelta; **stroller** (US) n (for child) sillita de ruedas

strong [strɒŋ] adj fuerte; **they are 50 ~** son 50; **stronghold** n fortaleza; (fig) baluarte m; **strongly** adv fuertemente, con fuerza; (believe) firmemente

strove [strəuv] pt of **strive**

struck [strʌk] pt, pp of **strike**

structure ['strʌktʃə*] n estructura; (building) construcción f

struggle ['strʌgl] n lucha ▷ vi luchar

strung [strʌŋ] pt, pp of **string**

stub [stʌb] n (of ticket etc) talón m; (of cigarette) colilla; **to ~ one's toe on sth** dar con el dedo (del pie) contra algo; **stub out** vt apagar

stubble ['stʌbl] n rastrojo; (on chin)

barba (incipiente)

stubborn ['stʌbən] *adj* terco, testarudo

stuck [stʌk] *pt, pp of* **stick** ▷ *adj* (*jammed*) atascado

stud [stʌd] *n* (*shirt stud*) corchete *m*; (*of boot*) taco; (*earring*) pendiente *m* (de bolita); (*also:* **~ farm**) caballeriza; (*also:* **~ horse**) caballo semental ▷ *vt* (*fig*): **~ded with** salpicado de

student ['stjuːdənt] *n* estudiante *mf* ▷ *adj* estudiantil; **student driver** (*us*) *n* conductor(a) *mf* en prácticas; **students' union** *n* (*building*) centro de estudiantes; (*BRIT: association*) federación *f* de estudiantes

studio ['stjuːdɪəu] *n* estudio; (*artist's*) taller *m*; **studio flat** *n* estudio

study ['stʌdɪ] *n* estudio ▷ *vt* estudiar; (*examine*) examinar, investigar ▷ *vi* estudiar

stuff [stʌf] *n* materia; (*substance*) material *m*, sustancia; (*things*) cosas *fpl* ▷ *vt* llenar; (*Culin*) rellenar; (*animals*) disecar; (*inf: push*) meter; **stuffing** *n* relleno; **stuffy** *adj* (*room*) mal ventilado; (*person*) de miras estrechas

stumble ['stʌmbl] *vi* tropezar, dar un traspié; **to ~ across**, **~ on** (*fig*) tropezar con

stump [stʌmp] *n* (*of tree*) tocón *m*; (*of limb*) muñón *m* ▷ *vt*: **to be ~ed for an answer** no saber qué contestar

stun [stʌn] *vt* dejar sin sentido

stung [stʌŋ] *pt, pp of* **sting**

stunk [stʌŋk] *pp of* **stink**

stunned [stʌnd] *adj* (*dazed*) aturdido, atontado; (*amazed*) pasmado; (*shocked*) anonadado

stunning ['stʌnɪŋ] *adj* (*fig: news*) pasmoso; (: *outfit etc*) sensacional

stunt [stʌnt] *n* (*in film*) escena peligrosa; (*publicity stunt*) truco publicitario

stupid ['stjuːpɪd] *adj* estúpido, tonto; **stupidity** [-'pɪdɪtɪ] *n* estupidez *f*

sturdy ['stɔːdɪ] *adj* robusto, fuerte

stutter ['stʌtə*] *n* tartamudeo ▷ *vi*

tartamudear

style [staɪl] *n* estilo; **stylish** *adj* elegante, a la moda; **stylist** *n* (*hair stylist*) peluquero/a

sub... [sʌb] *prefix* sub...; **subconscious** *adj* subconsciente

subdued [səb'djuːd] *adj* (*light*) tenue; (*person*) sumiso, manso

subject [*n* 'sʌbdʒɪkt, *vb* səb'dʒɛkt] *n* súbdito; (*Scol*) asignatura; (*matter*) tema *m*; (*Grammar*) sujeto ▷ *vt*: **to ~ sb to sth** someter a algn a algo; **to be ~ to** (*law*) estar sujeto a; (*person*) ser propenso a; **subjective** [-'dʒɛktɪv] *adj* subjetivo; **subject matter** *n* (*content*) contenido

subjunctive [səb'dʒʌŋktɪv] *adj, n* subjuntivo

submarine [sʌbmə'riːn] *n* submarino

submission [səb'mɪʃən] *n* sumisión *f*

submit [səb'mɪt] *vt* someter ▷ *vi*: **to ~ to sth** someterse a algo

subordinate [sə'bɔːdɪnət] *adj, n* subordinado/a *m/f*

subscribe [səb'skraɪb] *vi* suscribir; **to ~ to** (*opinion, fund*) suscribir, aprobar; (*newspaper*) suscribirse a

subscription [səb'skrɪpʃən] *n* abono; (*to magazine*) subscripción *f*

subsequent ['sʌbsɪkwənt] *adj* subsiguiente, posterior; **subsequently** *adv* posteriormente, más tarde

subside [səb'saɪd] *vi* hundirse; (*flood*) bajar; (*wind*) amainar

subsidiary [səb'sɪdɪərɪ] *adj* secundario ▷ *n* sucursal *f*, filial *f*

subsidize ['sʌbsɪdaɪz] *vt* subvencionar

subsidy ['sʌbsɪdɪ] *n* subvención *f*

substance ['sʌbstəns] *n* sustancia

substantial [səb'stænʃl] *adj* sustancial, sustancioso; (*fig*) importante

substitute ['sʌbstɪtjuːt] *n* (*person*) suplente *mf*; (*thing*) sustituto ▷ *vt*: **to ~ A for B** sustituir A por B, reemplazar B por A; **substitution** *n* sustitución *f*

subtle ['sʌtl] *adj* sutil
subtract [səb'trækt] *vt* restar, sustraer
suburb ['sʌbə:b] *n* barrio residencial; **the ~s** las afueras (de la ciudad); **suburban** [sə'bə:bən] *adj* suburbano; (*train etc*) de cercanías
subway ['sʌbweɪ] *n* (BRIT) paso subterráneo or inferior; (US) metro
succeed [sək'si:d] *vi* (*person*) tener éxito; (*plan*) salir bien ▷ *vt* suceder a; **to ~ in doing** lograr hacer
success [sək'sɛs] *n* éxito

> Be careful not to translate **success** by the Spanish word *suceso*.

successful *adj* exitoso; (*business*) próspero; **to be successful (in doing)** lograr (hacer); **successfully** *adv* con éxito
succession [sək'sɛʃən] *n* sucesión *f*, serie *f*
successive [sək'sɛsɪv] *adj* sucesivo
successor [sək'sɛsə*] *n* sucesor(a) *m/f*
succumb [sə'kʌm] *vi* sucumbir
such [sʌtʃ] *adj* tal, semejante; (*of that kind*): **~ a book** tal libro; (*so much*): **~ courage** tanto valor ▷ *adv* tan; **~ a long trip** un viaje tan largo; **~ a lot of** tanto(s)/a(s); **~ as** (*like*) tal como; **as ~** como tal; **such-and-such** *adj* tal o cual
suck [sʌk] *vt* chupar; (*bottle*) sorber; (*breast*) mamar
Sudan [su'dæn] *n* Sudán *m*
sudden ['sʌdn] *adj* (*rapid*) repentino, súbito; (*unexpected*) imprevisto; **all of a ~** de repente; **suddenly** *adv* de repente
sudoku [su'dəuku:] sudoku *m*
sue [su:] *vt* demandar
suede [sweɪd] *n* ante *m*, gamuza
suffer ['sʌfə*] *vt* sufrir, padecer; (*tolerate*) aguantar, soportar ▷ *vi* sufrir; **to ~ from** (*illness etc*) padecer; **suffering** *n* sufrimiento
suffice [sə'faɪs] *vi* bastar, ser suficiente
sufficient [sə'fɪʃənt] *adj* suficiente, bastante

suffocate ['sʌfəkeɪt] *vi* ahogarse, asfixiarse
sugar ['ʃugə*] *n* azúcar *m* ▷ *vt* echar azúcar a, azucarar
suggest [sə'dʒɛst] *vt* sugerir; **suggestion** [-'dʒɛstʃən] *n* sugerencia
suicide ['suɪsaɪd] *n* suicidio; (*person*) suicida *mf*; *see also* **commit**; **suicide attack** *n* atentado suicida; **suicide bomber** *n* terrorista *mf* suicida; **suicide bombing** *n* atentado suicida
suit [su:t] *n* (*man's*) traje *m*; (*woman's*) conjunto; (*Law*) pleito; (*Cards*) palo ▷ *vt* convenir; (*clothes*) sentar a, ir bien a; (*adapt*): **to ~ sth to** adaptar or ajustar algo a; **well ~ed** (*well matched: couple*) hecho el uno para el otro; **suitable** *adj* conveniente; (*apt*) indicado; **suitcase** *n* maleta, valija (RPL)
suite [swi:t] *n* (*of rooms, Mus*) suite *f*; (*furniture*): **bedroom/dining room ~** (juego de) dormitorio/comedor; *see also* **three-piece suite**
sulfur ['sʌlfə*] (US) *n* = **sulphur**
sulk [sʌlk] *vi* estar de mal humor
sulphur ['sʌlfə*] (US **sulfur**) *n* azufre *m*
sultana [sʌl'tɑ:nə] *n* (*fruit*) pasa de Esmirna
sum [sʌm] *n* suma; (*total*) total *m*; **sum up** *vt* resumir ▷ *vi* hacer un resumen
summarize ['sʌməraɪz] *vt* resumir
summary ['sʌmərɪ] *n* resumen *m* ▷ *adj* (*justice*) sumario
summer ['sʌmə*] *n* verano ▷ *cpd* de verano; **in ~** en verano; **summer holidays** *npl* vacaciones *fpl* de verano; **summertime** *n* (*season*) verano
summit ['sʌmɪt] *n* cima, cumbre *f*; (*also*: **~ conference**, **~ meeting**) (conferencia) cumbre *f*
summon ['sʌmən] *vt* (*person*) llamar; (*meeting*) convocar; (*Law*) citar
Sun. *abbr* (= *Sunday*) dom
sun [sʌn] *n* sol *m*; **sunbathe** *vi* tomar el sol; **sunbed** *n* cama solar;

S

sunblock n filtro solar; **sunburn** n (painful) quemadura; (tan) bronceado; **sunburned, sunburnt** adj (painfully) quemado por el sol; (tanned) bronceado

Sunday ['sʌndɪ] n domingo

sunflower ['sʌnflauə*] n girasol m

sung [sʌŋ] pp of **sing**

sunglasses ['sʌnglɑ:sɪz] npl gafas fpl (SP) or anteojos fpl (LAM) de sol

sunk [sʌŋk] pp of **sink**

sun: sunlight n luz f del sol; **sun lounger** n tumbona, perezosa (LAM); **sunny** adj soleado; (day) de sol; (fig) alegre; **sunrise** n salida del sol; **sun roof** n (Aut) techo corredizo; **sunscreen** n protector m solar; **sunset** n puesta del sol; **sunshade** n (over table) sombrilla; **sunshine** n sol m; **sunstroke** n insolación f; **suntan** n bronceado; **suntan lotion** n bronceador m; **suntan oil** n aceite m bronceador

super ['su:pə*] (inf) adj genial

superb [su:'pə:b] adj magnífico, espléndido

superficial [su:pə'fɪʃəl] adj superficial

superintendent [su:pərɪn'tɛndənt] n director(a) m/f; (Police) subjefe/a m/f

superior [su'pɪərɪə*] adj superior; (smug) desdeñoso ▷ n superior m

superlative [su'pə:lətɪv] n superlativo

supermarket ['su:pəmɑ:kɪt] n supermercado

supernatural [su:pə'nætʃərəl] adj sobrenatural ▷ n lo sobrenatural

superpower ['su:pəpauə*] n (Pol) superpotencia

superstition [su:pə'stɪʃən] n superstición f

superstitious [su:pə'stɪʃəs] adj supersticioso

superstore ['su:pəstɔ:*] n (BRIT) hipermercado

supervise ['su:pəvaɪz] vt supervisar; **supervision** [-'vɪʒən] n supervisión f; **supervisor** n supervisor(a) m/f

supper ['sʌpə*] n cena

supple ['sʌpl] adj flexible

supplement [n 'sʌplɪmənt, vb sʌplɪ'mɛnt] n suplemento ▷ vt suplir

supplier [sə'plaɪə*] n (Comm) distribuidor(a) m/f

supply [sə'plaɪ] vt (provide) suministrar; (equip): **to ~ (with)** proveer (de) ▷ n provisión f; (of gas, water etc) suministro; **supplies** npl (food) víveres mpl; (Mil) pertrechos mpl

support [sə'pɔ:t] n apoyo; (Tech) soporte m ▷ vt apoyar; (financially) mantener; (uphold, Tech) sostener

Be careful not to translate **support** by the Spanish word soportar.

supporter n (Pol etc) partidario/a; (Sport) aficionado/a

suppose [sə'pəuz] vt suponer; (imagine) imaginarse; (duty): **to be ~d to do sth** deber hacer algo; **supposedly** [sə'pəuzɪdlɪ] adv según cabe suponer; **supposing** conj en caso de que

suppress [sə'prɛs] vt suprimir; (yawn) ahogar

supreme [su'pri:m] adj supremo

surcharge ['sə:tʃɑ:dʒ] n sobretasa, recargo

sure [ʃuə*] adj seguro; (definite, convinced) cierto; **to make ~ of sth/that** asegurarse de algo/asegurar que; **~!** (of course) ¡claro!, ¡por supuesto!; **~ enough** efectivamente; **surely** adv (certainly) seguramente

surf [sə:f] n olas fpl ▷ vt: **to ~ the Net** navegar por Internet

surface ['sə:fɪs] n superficie f ▷ vt (road) revestir ▷ vi salir a la superficie; **by ~ mail** por vía terrestre

surfboard ['sə:fbɔ:d] n tabla (de surf)

surfer ['sə:fə*] n (in sea) surfista mf; **web** or **net ~** internauta mf

surfing ['sə:fɪŋ] n surf m

surge [sə:dʒ] n oleada, oleaje m ▷ vi (wave) romper; (people) avanzar en tropel

surgeon ['sə:dʒən] n cirujano/a

surgery ['sə:dʒərɪ] n cirugía; (BRIT: room) consultorio

surname ['sə:neɪm] n apellido

surpass [sə:'pɑːs] vt superar, exceder

surplus ['sə:pləs] n excedente m; (Comm) superávit m ▷ adj excedente, sobrante

surprise [sə'praɪz] n sorpresa ▷ vt sorprender; **surprised** adj (look, smile) de sorpresa; **to be surprised** sorprenderse; **surprising** adj sorprendente; **surprisingly** adv: **it was surprisingly easy** me etc sorprendió lo fácil que fue

surrender [sə'rɛndə*] n rendición f, entrega ▷ vi rendirse, entregarse

surround [sə'raund] vt rodear, circundar; (Mil etc) cercar; **surrounding** adj circundante; **surroundings** npl alrededores mpl, cercanías fpl

surveillance [sə:'veɪləns] n vigilancia

survey [n 'sə:veɪ, vb sə:'veɪ] n inspección f, reconocimiento; (inquiry) encuesta ▷ vt examinar, inspeccionar; (look at) mirar, contemplar; **surveyor** n agrimensor(a) m/f

survival [sə'vaɪvl] n supervivencia

survive [sə'vaɪv] vi sobrevivir; (custom etc) perdurar ▷ vt sobrevivir a; **survivor** n superviviente mf

suspect [adj, n 'sʌspɛkt, vb səs'pɛkt] adj, n sospechoso/a m/f ▷ vt (person) sospechar de; (think) sospechar

suspend [səs'pɛnd] vt suspender; **suspended sentence** n (Law) libertad f condicional; **suspenders** npl (BRIT) ligas fpl; (US) tirantes mpl

suspense [səs'pɛns] n incertidumbre f, duda; (in film etc) suspense m; **to keep sb in ~** mantener a algn en suspense

suspension [səs'pɛnʃən] n (gen, Aut) suspensión f; (of driving licence) privación f; **suspension bridge** n puente m colgante

suspicion [səs'pɪʃən] n sospecha; (distrust) recelo; **suspicious** adj

receloso; (causing suspicion) sospechoso

sustain [səs'teɪn] vt sostener, apoyar; (suffer) sufrir, padecer

SUV (esp US) n abbr (= sports utility vehicle) todoterreno m inv, 4x4 m

swallow ['swɔləu] n (bird) golondrina ▷ vt tragar; (fig.: pride) tragarse

swam [swæm] pt of **swim**

swamp [swɔmp] n pantano, ciénaga ▷ vt (with water etc) inundar; (fig) abrumar, agobiar

swan [swɔn] n cisne m

swap [swɔp] n canje m, intercambio ▷ vt: **to ~ (for)** cambiar (por)

swarm [swɔ:m] n (of bees) enjambre m; (fig) multitud f ▷ vi (bees) formar un enjambre; (people) pulular; **to be ~ing with** ser un hervidero de

sway [sweɪ] vi mecerse, balancearse ▷ vt (influence) mover, influir en

swear [swɛə*] (pt **swore**, pp **sworn**) vi (curse) maldecir; (promise) jurar ▷ vt jurar; **swear in** vt: **to be sworn in** prestar juramento; **swearword** n taco, palabrota

sweat [swɛt] n sudor m ▷ vi sudar

sweater ['swɛtə*] n suéter m

sweatshirt ['swɛtʃə:t] n suéter m

sweaty ['swɛtɪ] adj sudoroso

Swede [swi:d] n sueco/a

swede [swi:d] (BRIT) n nabo

Sweden ['swi:dn] n Suecia; **Swedish** ['swi:dɪʃ] adj sueco ▷ n (Ling) sueco

sweep [swi:p] (pt, pp **swept**) n (act) barrido; (also: **chimney ~**) deshollinador(a) m/f ▷ vt barrer; (with arm) empujar; (current) arrastrar ▷ vi barrer; (arm etc) moverse rápidamente; (wind) soplar con violencia

sweet [swi:t] n (BRIT: candy) dulce m, caramelo; (BRIT: pudding) postre m ▷ adj dulce; (fig: kind) dulce, amable; (: attractive) mono; **sweetcorn** n maíz m; **sweetener** ['swi:tnə*] n (Culin) edulcorante m; **sweetheart** n novio/a; **sweetshop** n (BRIT) confitería, bombonería

swell [swɛl] (pt **~ed**, pp **swollen** or **~ed**)

n (of sea) marejada, oleaje *m* ▷ *adj (us: inf: excellent)* estupendo, fenomenal ▷ *vt* hinchar, inflar ▷ *vi (also:* **~ up**) hincharse; *(numbers)* aumentar; *(sound, feeling)* ir aumentando; **swelling** *n (Med)* hinchazón *f*

swept [swɛpt] *pt, pp of* **sweep**

swerve [swəːv] *vi* desviarse bruscamente

swift [swɪft] *n (bird)* vencejo ▷ *adj* rápido, veloz

swim [swɪm] *(pt* **swam**, *pp* **swum**) *n*: **to go for a ~** ir a nadar or a bañarse ▷ *vi* nadar; *(head, room)* dar vueltas ▷ *vt* nadar; *(the Channel etc)* cruzar a nado; **swimmer** *n* nadador(a) *m/f*; **swimming** *n* natación *f*; **swimming costume** *(BRIT)* bañador *m*, traje *m* de baño; **swimming pool** *n* piscina, alberca *(MEX)*, pileta *(RPL)*; **swimming trunks** *npl* bañador *m (de hombre)*; **swimsuit** *n* = **swimming costume**

swing [swɪŋ] *(pt, pp* **swung**) *n (in playground)* columpio; *(movement)* balanceo, vaivén *m*; *(change of direction)* viraje *m*; *(rhythm)* ritmo ▷ *vt* balancear; *(also:* **~ round**) voltear, girar ▷ *vi* balancearse, columpiarse; *(also:* **~ round**) dar media vuelta; **to be in full ~** estar en plena marcha

swipe card [swaɪp-] *n* tarjeta magnética deslizante, tarjeta swipe

swirl [swəːl] *vi* arremolinarse

Swiss [swɪs] *adj, n inv* suizo/a *m/f*

switch [swɪtʃ] *n (for light etc)* interruptor *m*; *(change)* cambio ▷ *vt (change)* cambiar de; **switch off** *vt* apagar; *(engine)* parar; **switch on** *vt* encender *(SP)*, prender *(LAM)*; *(engine, machine)* arrancar; **switchboard** *n (Tel)* centralita *(SP)*, conmutador *m (LAM)*

Switzerland ['swɪtsələnd] *n* Suiza

swivel ['swɪvl] *vi (also:* **~ round**) girar

swollen ['swəulən] *pp of* **swell**

swoop [swuːp] *n (by police etc)* redada ▷ *vi (also:* **~ down**) calarse

swop [swɔp] = **swap**

sword [sɔːd] *n* espada; **swordfish** *n*

pez *m* espada

swore [swɔː*] *pt of* **swear**

sworn [swɔːn] *pp of* **swear** ▷ *adj (statement)* bajo juramento; *(enemy)* implacable

swum [swʌm] *pp of* **swim**

swung [swʌŋ] *pt, pp of* **swing**

syllable ['sɪləbl] *n* sílaba

syllabus ['sɪləbəs] *n* programa *m* de estudios

symbol ['sɪmbl] *n* símbolo; **symbolic(al)** [sɪm'bɔlɪk(l)] *adj* simbólico; **to be symbolic(al) of sth** simbolizar algo

symmetrical [sɪ'mɛtrɪkl] *adj* simétrico

symmetry ['sɪmɪtrɪ] *n* simetría

sympathetic [sɪmpə'θɛtɪk] *adj (understanding)* comprensivo; *(showing support)*: **~ to(wards)** bien dispuesto hacia

> Be careful not to translate **sympathetic** by the Spanish word *simpático*.

sympathize ['sɪmpəθaɪz] *vi*: **to ~ with** *(person)* compadecerse de; *(feelings)* comprender; *(cause)* apoyar

sympathy ['sɪmpəθɪ] *n (pity)* compasión *f*

symphony ['sɪmfənɪ] *n* sinfonía

symptom ['sɪmptəm] *n* síntoma *m*, indicio

synagogue ['sɪnəgɔg] *n* sinagoga

syndicate ['sɪndɪkɪt] *n* sindicato; *(of newspapers)* agencia (de noticias)

syndrome ['sɪndrəum] *n* síndrome *m*

synonym ['sɪnənɪm] *n* sinónimo

synthetic [sɪn'θɛtɪk] *adj* sintético

Syria ['sɪrɪə] *n* Siria

syringe [sɪ'rɪndʒ] *n* jeringa

syrup ['sɪrəp] *n* jarabe *m*; *(also:* **golden ~)** almíbar *m*

system ['sɪstəm] *n* sistema *m*; *(Anat)* organismo; **systematic** [-'mætɪk] *adj* sistemático, metódico; **systems analyst** *n* analista *mf* de sistemas

t

la prensa popular británica, por el tamaño más pequeño de los periódicos. A diferencia de los de la llamada **quality press**, estas publicaciones se caracterizan por un lenguaje sencillo, una presentación llamativa y un contenido sensacionalista, centrado a veces en los escándalos financieros y sexuales de los famosos, por lo que también reciben el nombre peyorativo de "gutter press".

taboo [tə'bu:] *adj, n* tabú *m*

tack [tæk] *n (nail)* tachuela; *(fig)* rumbo ▷ *vt (nail)* clavar con tachuelas; *(stitch)* hilvanar ▷ *vi* virar

tackle ['tækl] *n (fishing tackle)* aparejo (de pescar); *(for lifting)* aparejo ▷ *vt (difficulty)* enfrentarse con; *(challenge: person)* hacer frente a; *(grapple with)* agarrar; *(Football)* cargar; *(Rugby)* placar

tacky ['tækɪ] *adj* pegajoso; *(pej)* cutre

tact [tækt] *n* tacto, discreción *f*; **tactful** *adj* discreto, diplomático

tactics ['tæktɪks] *npl* táctica

tactless ['tæktlɪs] *adj* indiscreto

tadpole ['tædpəʊl] *n* renacuajo

taffy ['tæfɪ] *(US) n* melcocha

tag [tæg] *n (label)* etiqueta

tail [teɪl] *n* cola; *(of shirt, coat)* faldón *m* ▷ *vt (follow)* vigilar a; **tails** *npl (formal suit)* levita

tailor ['teɪlə*] *n* sastre *m*

Taiwan [taɪ'wɑ:n] *n* Taiwán *m*; **Taiwanese** [taɪwə'ni:z] *adj, n* taiwanés/esa *m/f*

take [teɪk] *(pt* **took***, pp* **taken***) vt* tomar; *(grab)* coger (SP), agarrar (LAM); *(gain: prize)* ganar; *(require: effort, courage)* exigir; *(tolerate: pain etc)* aguantar; *(hold: passengers etc)* tener cabida para; *(accompany, bring, carry)* llevar; *(exam)* presentarse a; **to ~ sth from** *(drawer etc)* sacar algo de; *(person)* quitar algo a; **I ~ it that ...** supongo

ta [tɑ:] *(BRIT: inf) excl* ¡gracias!

tab [tæb] *n* lengüeta; *(label)* etiqueta; **to keep ~s on** *(fig)* vigilar

table ['teɪbl] *n* mesa; *(of statistics etc)* cuadro, tabla ▷ *vt (BRIT: motion etc)* presentar; **to lay** *or* **set the ~** poner la mesa; **tablecloth** *n* mantel *m*; **table d'hôte** [tɑ:bl'dəʊt] *adj* del menú; **table lamp** *n* lámpara de mesa, **tablemat** *n (for plate)* posaplatos *m inv*; *(for hot dish)* salvamantel *m*; **tablespoon** *n* cuchara de servir; *(also:* **tablespoonful***: as measurement)* cucharada

tablet ['tæblɪt] *n (Med)* pastilla, comprimido; *(of stone)* lápida

table tennis *n* ping-pong *m*, tenis *m* de mesa

tabloid ['tæblɔɪd] *n* periódico popular sensacionalista

● **TABLOID PRESS**
●
● El término **tabloid press** o **tabloids** se usa para referirse a

que ...; **take after** vt fus parecerse a;
take apart vt desmontar; **take away**
vt (remove) quitar; (carry) llevar; (Math)
restar; **take back** vt (return) devolver;
(one's words) retractarse de; **take
down** vt (building) derribar; (letter etc)
apuntar; **take in** vt (deceive) engañar;
(understand) entender; (include) abarcar;
(lodger) acoger, recibir; **take off** vi
(Aviat) despegar ▷ vt (remove) quitar;
take on vt (work) aceptar; (employee)
contratar; (opponent) desafiar; **take out**
vt sacar; **take over** vt (business) tomar
posesión de; (country) tomar el poder
▷ vi: **to take over from sb** reemplazar
a algn; **take up** vt (a dress) acortar;
(occupy: time, space) ocupar; (engage
in: hobby etc) dedicarse a; (accept): **to
take sb up on** aceptar algo de algn;
takeaway (BRIT) adj (food) para llevar
▷ n tienda o restaurante m de comida
para llevar; **taken** pp of **take**; **takeoff**
n (Aviat) despegue m; **takeout** (US)
n = **takeaway**; **takeover** n (Comm)
absorción f; **takings** npl (Comm)
ingresos mpl
talc [tælk] n (also: **~um powder**)
(polvos de) talco
tale [teɪl] n (story) cuento; (account)
relación f; **to tell ~s** (fig) chivarse
talent ['tælnt] n talento; **talented**
adj de talento
talk [tɔːk] n charla; (conversation)
conversación f; (gossip) habladurías
fpl, chismes mpl ▷ vi hablar; **talks** npl
(Pol etc) conversaciones fpl; **to ~ about**
hablar de; **to ~ sb into doing sth**
convencer a algn para que haga algo;
to ~ sb out of doing sth disuadir a
algn de que haga algo; **to ~ shop** hablar
del trabajo; **talk over** vt discutir; **talk
show** n programa m de entrevistas
tall [tɔːl] adj alto; (object) grande; **to
be 6 feet ~** (person) ≈ medir 1 metro 80
tambourine [tæmbə'riːn] n
pandereta
tame [teɪm] adj domesticado; (fig)
mediocre

tamper ['tæmpə*] vi: **to ~ with** tocar,
andar con
tampon ['tæmpən] n tampón m
tan [tæn] n (also: **sun~**) bronceado
▷ vi ponerse moreno ▷ adj (colour)
marrón
tandem ['tændəm] n tándem m
tangerine [tændʒə'riːn] n
mandarina
tangle ['tæŋgl] n enredo; **to get
in(to) a ~** enredarse
tank [tæŋk] n (water tank) depósito,
tanque m; (for fish) acuario; (Mil)
tanque m
tanker ['tæŋkə*] n (ship) buque m,
cisterna; (truck) camión m cisterna
tanned [tænd] adj (skin) moreno
tantrum ['tæntrəm] n rabieta
Tanzania [tænzə'nɪə] n Tanzania
tap [tæp] n (BRIT: on sink etc) grifo (SP),
llave f, canilla (RPL); (gas tap) llave f;
(gentle blow) golpecito ▷ vt (hit gently)
dar golpecitos en; (resources) utilizar,
explotar; (telephone) intervenir; **on ~**
(fig: resources) a mano; **tap dancing**
n claqué m
tape [teɪp] n (also: **magnetic ~**)
cinta magnética; (cassette) cassette
f, cinta; (sticky tape) cinta adhesiva;
(for tying) cinta ▷ vt (record) grabar
(en cinta); (stick with tape) pegar con
cinta adhesiva; **tape measure** n cinta
métrica, metro; **tape recorder** n
grabadora
tapestry ['tæpɪstrɪ] n (object) tapiz
m; (art) tapicería
tar [tɑː] n alquitrán m, brea
target ['tɑːgɪt] n blanco
tariff ['tærɪf] n (on goods) arancel m;
(BRIT: in hotels etc) tarifa
tarmac ['tɑːmæk] n (BRIT: on road)
asfaltado; (Aviat) pista (de aterrizaje)
tarpaulin [tɑː'pɔːlɪn] n lona
impermeabilizada
tarragon ['tærəgən] n estragón m
tart [tɑːt] n (Culin) tarta;
(BRIT: inf: prostitute) puta ▷ adj agrio,
ácido

tartan ['tɑːtn] n tejido escocés m
tartar(e) sauce ['tɑːtə-] n salsa tártara
task [tɑːsk] n tarea; **to take to ~** reprender
taste [teɪst] n (sense) gusto; (flavour) sabor m; (sample): **have a ~!** ¡prueba un poquito!; (fig) muestra, idea ▷ vt probar ▷ vi: **to ~ of** or **like** (fish, garlic etc) saber a; **you can ~ the garlic (in it)** se nota el sabor a ajo; **in good/bad ~** de buen/mal gusto; **tasteful** adj de buen gusto; **tasteless** adj (food) soso; (remark etc) de mal gusto; **tasty** adj sabroso, rico
tatters ['tætəz] npl: **in ~** hecho jirones
tattoo [tə'tuː] n tatuaje m; (spectacle) espectáculo militar ▷ vt tatuar
taught [tɔːt] pt, pp of **teach**
taunt [tɔːnt] n burla ▷ vt burlarse de
Taurus ['tɔːrəs] n Tauro
taut [tɔːt] adj tirante, tenso
tax [tæks] n impuesto ▷ vt gravar (con un impuesto); (fig: memory) poner a prueba; (: patience) agotar; **tax-free** adj libre de impuestos
taxi ['tæksɪ] n taxi m ▷ vi (Aviat) rodar por la pista; **taxi driver** n taxista mf; **taxi rank** (BRIT) n = **taxi stand**; **taxi stand** n parada de taxis
tax payer n contribuyente mf
TB n abbr = **tuberculosis**
tea [tiː] n té m; (BRIT: meal) ≈ merienda (SP); cena; **high ~** (BRIT) merienda-cena (SP); **tea bag** n bolsita de té; **tea break** (BRIT) n descanso para el té
teach [tiːtʃ] (pt, pp **taught**) vt: **to ~ sb sth, ~ sth to sb** enseñar algo a algn ▷ vi (be a teacher) ser profesor(a), enseñar; **teacher** n (in secondary school) profesor(a) m/f; (in primary school) maestro/a, profesor(a) de EGB; **teaching** n enseñanza
tea: tea cloth n (BRIT) paño de cocina, trapo de cocina (LAM); **teacup** n taza para el té
tea leaves npl hojas de té
team [tiːm] n equipo; (of horses) tiro;

team up vi asociarse
teapot ['tiːpɒt] n tetera
tear¹ [tɪə*] n lágrima; **in ~s** llorando
tear² [tɛə*] (pt **tore**, pp **torn**) n rasgón m, desgarrón m ▷ vt romper, rasgar ▷ vi rasgarse; **tear apart** vt (also fig) hacer pedazos; **tear down** vt +adv (building, statue) derribar; (poster, flag) arrancar; **tear off** vt (sheet of paper etc) arrancar; (one's clothes) quitarse a tirones; **tear up** vt (sheet of paper etc) romper
tearful ['tɪəfəl] adj lloroso
tear gas ['tɪə-] n gas m lacrimógeno
tearoom ['tiːruːm] n salón m de té
tease [tiːz] vt tomar el pelo a
tea: teaspoon n cucharita; (also: **teaspoonful**: as measurement) cucharadita; **teatime** n hora del té; **tea towel** (BRIT) n paño de cocina
technical ['tɛknɪkl] adj técnico
technician [tɛk'nɪʃn] n técnico/a
technique [tɛk'niːk] n técnica
technology [tɛk'nɒlədʒɪ] n tecnología
teddy (bear) ['tɛdɪ-] n osito de felpa
tedious ['tiːdɪəs] adj pesado, aburrido
tee [tiː] n (Golf) tee m
teen [tiːn] adj = **teenage** ▷ n (US) = **teenager**
teenage ['tiːneɪdʒ] adj (fashions etc) juvenil; (children) quinceañero; **teenager** n adolescente mf
teens [tiːnz] npl: **to be in one's ~** ser adolescente
teeth [tiːθ] npl of **tooth**
teetotal ['tiː'təutl] adj abstemio
telecommunications [tɛlɪkəmjuː-nɪ'keɪʃənz] n telecomunicaciones fpl
telegram ['tɛlɪɡræm] n telegrama m
telegraph pole ['tɛlɪɡrɑːf-] n poste m telegráfico
telephone ['tɛlɪfəun] n teléfono ▷ vt llamar por teléfono, telefonear; (message) dar por teléfono; **to be on the ~** (talking) hablar por teléfono; (possessing telephone) tener teléfono;

telephone book n guía f telefónica; **telephone booth, telephone box** (BRIT) n cabina telefónica; **telephone call** n llamada (telefónica); **telephone directory** n guía (telefónica); **telephone number** n número de teléfono

telesales ['tɛlɪseɪlz] npl televenta(s) (f(pl))

telescope ['tɛlɪskəup] n telescopio

televise ['tɛlɪvaɪz] vt televisar

television ['tɛlɪvɪʒən] n televisión f; **on ~** en la televisión; **television programme** n programa m de televisión

tell [tɛl] (pt, pp **told**) vt decir; (relate: story) contar; (distinguish): **to ~ sth from** distinguir algo de ▷ vi (talk): **to ~ (of)** contar; (have effect) tener efecto; **to ~ sb to do sth** mandar a algn hacer algo; **tell off** vt: **to tell sb off** regañar a algn; **teller** n (in bank) cajero/a

telly ['tɛlɪ] (BRIT: inf) n abbr (= television) tele f

temp [tɛmp] n abbr (BRIT) (= temporary) temporero/a

temper ['tɛmpə*] n (nature) carácter m; (mood) humor m; (bad temper) (mal) genio; (fit of anger) acceso de ira ▷ vt (moderate) moderar; **to be in a ~** estar furioso; **to lose one's ~** enfadarse, enojarse

temperament ['tɛmprəmənt] n (nature) temperamento; **temperamental** [tɛmprə'mɛntl] adj temperamental

temperature ['tɛmprətʃə*] n temperatura; **to have** or **run a ~** tener fiebre

temple ['tɛmpl] n (building) templo; (Anat) sien f

temporary ['tɛmpərərɪ] adj provisional; (passing) transitorio; (worker) temporero; (job) temporal

tempt [tɛmpt] vt tentar; **to ~ sb into doing sth** tentar or inducir a algn a hacer algo; **temptation** n tentación

f; **tempting** adj tentador(a); (food) apetitoso/a

ten [tɛn] num diez

tenant ['tɛnənt] n inquilino/a

tend [tɛnd] vt cuidar ▷ vi: **to ~ to do sth** tener tendencia a hacer algo; **tendency** ['tɛndənsɪ] n tendencia

tender ['tɛndə*] adj (person, care) tierno, cariñoso; (meat) tierno; (sore) sensible ▷ n (Comm: offer) oferta; (money): **legal ~** moneda de curso legal ▷ vt ofrecer

tendon ['tɛndən] n tendón m

tenner ['tɛnə*] n (inf) (billete m de) diez libras m

tennis ['tɛnɪs] n tenis m; **tennis ball** n pelota de tenis; **tennis court** n cancha de tenis; **tennis match** n partido de tenis; **tennis player** n tenista mf; **tennis racket** n raqueta de tenis

tenor ['tɛnə*] n (Mus) tenor m

tenpin bowling ['tɛnpɪn-] n (juego de los) bolos

tense [tɛns] adj (person) nervioso; (moment, atmosphere) tenso; (muscle) tenso, en tensión ▷ n (Ling) tiempo

tension ['tɛnʃən] n tensión f

tent [tɛnt] n tienda (de campaña) (SP), carpa (LAM)

tentative ['tɛntətɪv] adj (person, smile) indeciso; (conclusion, plans) provisional

tenth [tɛnθ] num décimo

tent: tent peg n clavija, estaca; **tent pole** n mástil m

tepid ['tɛpɪd] adj tibio

term [tə:m] n (word) término; (period) período; (Scol) trimestre m ▷ vt llamar; **terms** npl (conditions, Comm) condiciones fpl; **in the short/long ~** a corto/largo plazo; **to be on good ~s with sb** llevarse bien con algn; **to come to ~s with** (problem) aceptar

terminal ['tə:mɪnl] adj (disease) mortal; (patient) terminal ▷ n (Elec) borne m; (Comput) terminal m; (also: **air ~**) terminal f; (BRIT: also: **coach ~**)

estación f terminal f

terminate ['tə:mɪneɪt] vt terminar

termini ['tə:mɪnaɪ] npl of **terminus**

terminology [tə:mɪ'nɔlədʒɪ] n terminología

terminus ['tə:mɪnəs] (pl **termini**) n término, (estación f) terminal f

terrace ['terəs] n terraza; (BRIT: row of houses) hilera de casas adosadas; **the ~s** (BRIT Sport) las gradas fpl; **terraced** adj (garden) en terrazas; (house) adosado

terrain [te'reɪn] n terreno

terrestrial [tɪ'restrɪəl] adj (life) terrestre; (BRIT: channel) de transmisión (por) vía terrestre

terrible ['terɪbl] adj terrible, horrible; (inf) atroz; **terribly** adv terriblemente; (very badly) malísimamente

terrier ['terɪə*] n terrier m

terrific [tə'rɪfɪk] adj (very great) tremendo; (wonderful) fantástico, fenomenal

terrified ['terɪfaɪd] adj aterrorizado

terrify ['terɪfaɪ] vt aterrorizar; **terrifying** adj aterrador(a)

territorial [terɪ'tɔ:rɪəl] adj territorial

territory ['terɪtərɪ] n territorio

terror ['terə*] n terror m; **terrorism** n terrorismo; **terrorist** n terrorista mf; **terrorist attack** n atentado (terrorista)

test [test] n (gen, Chem) prueba; (Med) examen m; (Scol) examen m, test m; (also: **driving ~**) examen m de conducir ▷ vt probar, poner a prueba; (Med, Scol) examinar

testicle ['testɪkl] n testículo

testify ['testɪfaɪ] vi (Law) prestar declaración; **to ~ to sth** atestiguar algo

testimony ['testɪmənɪ] n (Law) testimonio

test: test match n (Cricket, Rugby) partido internacional; **test tube** n probeta

tetanus ['tetənəs] n tétano

text [tekst] n texto; (on mobile phone)

mensaje m (de texto) ▷ vt: **to ~ sb** (inf) enviar un mensaje (de texto) or un SMS a algn; **textbook** n libro de texto

textile ['tekstaɪl] n textil m, tejido

text message n mensaje m de texto

text messaging [-'mesɪdʒɪŋ] n (envío de) mensajes mpl de texto

texture ['tekstʃə*] n textura

Thai [taɪ] adj, n tailandés/esa m/f

Thailand ['taɪlænd] n Tailandia

than [ðæn] conj (in comparisons): **more ~ 10/once** más de 10/una vez; **I have more/less ~ you/Paul** tengo más/menos que tú/Paul; **she is older ~ you think** es mayor de lo que piensas

thank [θæŋk] vt dar las gracias a, agradecer; **~ you (very much)** muchas gracias; **~ God!** ¡gracias a Dios! ▷ excl (also: **many ~s, ~s a lot**) ¡gracias! ▷ **~s to** prep gracias a; **thanks** npl gracias fpl; **thankfully** adv (fortunately) afortunadamente; **Thanksgiving (Day)** n día m de Acción de Gracias

⬤ **THANKSGIVING (DAY)**
⬤
⬤ En Estados Unidos el cuarto jueves
⬤ de noviembre es **Thanksgiving**
⬤ **Day**, fiesta oficial en la que se
⬤ recuerda la celebración que
⬤ hicieron los primeros colonos
⬤ norteamericanos ("Pilgrims"
⬤ o "Pilgrim Fathers") tras la
⬤ estupenda cosecha de 1621, por
⬤ la que se dan gracias a Dios. En
⬤ Canadá se celebra una fiesta
⬤ semejante el segundo lunes
⬤ de octubre, aunque no está
⬤ relacionada con dicha fecha
⬤ histórica.

○ **KEYWORD**

that [ðæt] (pl **those**) adj (demonstrative) ese/a; (pl) esos/as; (more remote) aquel(aquella); (pl) aquellos/as; **leave those books on the table** deja

esos libros sobre la mesa; **that one**
ése(ésa); (*more remote*) aquél(aquélla);
that one over there ése(ésa) de ahí;
aquél(aquélla) de allí
▷ *pron* **1**(*demonstrative*) ése/a; (*pl*)
ésos/as; (*neuter*) eso; (*more remote*)
aquél(aquélla); (*pl*) aquéllos/as; (*neuter*)
aquello; **what's that?** ¿qué es eso (*or*
aquello)?; **who's that?** ¿quién es ése/a
(*or* aquél (aquella))?; **is that you?** ¿eres
tú?; **will you eat all that?** ¿vas a comer
todo eso?; **that's my house** ésa es mi
casa; **that's what she said** eso es lo que
dijo; **that is (to say)** es decir
2 (*relative: subject, object*) que; (*with
preposition*) (el (la)) que *etc*, el(la) cual
etc; **the book (that) I read** el libro que
leí; **the books that are in the library**
los libros que están en la biblioteca; **all
(that) I have** todo lo que tengo; **the
box (that) I put it in** la caja en la que
or donde lo puse; **the people (that) I
spoke to** la gente con la que hablé
3 (*relative: of time*) que; **the day (that)
he came** el día (en) que vino
▷ *conj* que; **he thought that I was ill**
creyó que yo estaba enfermo
▷ *adv* (*demonstrative*): **I can't work that
much** no puedo trabajar tanto; **I didn't
realise it was that bad** no creí que
fuera tan malo; **that high** así de alto

thatched [θætʃt] *adj* (*roof*) de paja;
(*cottage*) con tejado de paja
thaw [θɔ:] *n* deshielo ▷ *vi* (*ice*)
derretirse; (*food*) descongelarse ▷ *vt*
(*food*) descongelar

○ **KEYWORD**

the [ði:, ðə] *def art* **1**(*gen*) el *f*, la *pl*,
los *fpl*, las (NB 'el' immediately before f n
beginning with stressed (h)a; a+ el =al; de +
el = del); **the boy/girl** el chico/la chica;
the books/flowers los libros/las
flores; **to the postman/from
the drawer** al cartero/del cajón; **I
haven't the time/money** no tengo

tiempo/dinero
2 (+*adj to form n*) los; lo; **the rich and
the poor** los ricos y los pobres; **to
attempt the impossible** intentar lo
imposible
3 (*in titles*): **Elizabeth the First** Isabel
primera; **Peter the Great** Pedro el
Grande
4 (*in comparisons*): **the more he works
the more he earns** cuanto más
trabaja más gana

theatre ['θɪətə*] (*us* **theater**) *n*
teatro; (*also:* **lecture ~**) aula; (*Med: also:*
operating ~) quirófano
theft [θɛft] *n* robo
their [ðɛə*] *adj* su; **theirs** *pron* (el)
suyo((la) suya etc); *see also* **my; mine¹**
them [ðɛm, ðəm] *pron* (*direct*)
los/las; (*indirect*) les; (*stressed, after prep*)
ellos(ellas); *see also* **me**
theme [θi:m] *n* tema *m*; **theme park**
n parque de atracciones (*en torno a un
tema central*)
themselves [ðəm'sɛlvz] *pl pron*
(*subject*) ellos mismos(ellas mismas);
(*complement*) se; (*after prep*) sí
(mismos(as)); *see also* **oneself**
then [ðɛn] *adv* (*at that time*) entonces;
(*next*) después; (*later*) luego, después;
(*and also*) además ▷ *conj* (*therefore*)
en ese caso, entonces ▷ *adj*: **the ~
president** el entonces presidente;
by ~ para entonces; **from ~ on** desde
entonces
theology [θɪˈɔlədʒɪ] *n* teología
theory ['θɪərɪ] *n* teoría
therapist ['θɛrəpɪst] *n* terapeuta *mf*
therapy ['θɛrəpɪ] *n* terapia

○ **KEYWORD**

there ['ðɛə*] *adv* **1 there is, there are**
hay; **there is no-one here/no bread
left** no hay nadie aquí/no queda pan;
there has been an accident ha habido
un accidente
2 (*referring to place*) ahí; (*distant*) allí; **it's**

there está ahí; **put it in/on/up/down there** ponlo ahí dentro/encima/arriba/abajo; **I want that book there** quiero ese libro de ahí; **there he is!** ¡ahí está!

3 there, there (esp to child) ea, ea

there: thereabouts adv por ahí; **thereafter** adv después; **thereby** adv así, de ese modo; **therefore** adv por lo tanto; **there's** = **there is**; **there has**

thermal ['θə:ml] adj (before n) termal; (paper) térmico

thermometer [θə'mɔmɪtə*] n termómetro

thermostat ['θə:məustæt] n termostato

these [ði:z] pl adj estos/as ▷ pl pron éstos/as

thesis ['θi:sɪs] (pl **theses**) n tesis f inv

they [ðeɪ] pl pron ellos(ellas); (stressed) ellos (mismos)(ellas mismas); **~ say that …** (it is said that) se dice que …; **they'd** = **they had**; **they would**; **they'll** = **they shall**; **they will**; **they're** = **they are**; **they've** = **they have**

thick [θɪk] adj (in consistency) espeso; (in size) grueso; (stupid) torpe ▷ n: **in the ~ of the battle** en lo más reñido de la batalla; **it's 20 cm ~** tiene 20 cm de espesor; **thicken** vi espesarse ▷ vt (sauce etc) espesar; **thickness** n espesor m; grueso

thief [θi:f] (pl **thieves**) n ladrón/ona m/f

thigh [θaɪ] n muslo

thin [θɪn] adj (person, animal) flaco; (in size) delgado; (in consistency) poco espeso; (hair, crowd) escaso ▷ vt: **to ~ (down)** diluir

thing [θɪŋ] n cosa; (object) objeto, artículo; (matter) asunto; (mania): **to have a ~ about sb/sth** estar obsesionado con algn/algo; **things** npl (belongings) efectos mpl (personales); **the best ~ would be to …** lo mejor sería …; **how are ~s?** ¿qué tal?

think [θɪŋk] (pt, pp **thought**) vi

pensar ▷ vt pensar, creer; **what did you ~ of them?** ¿qué te parecieron?; **to ~ about sth/sb** pensar en algo/algn; **I'll ~ about it** lo pensaré; **to ~ of doing sth** pensar en hacer algo; **I ~ so/not** creo que sí/no; **to ~ well of sb** tener buen concepto de algn; **think over** vt reflexionar sobre, meditar; **think up** vt (plan etc) idear

third [θə:d] adj (before n) tercer(a); (following n) tercero/a ▷ n tercero/a; (fraction) tercio; (BRIT Scol: degree) título de licenciado con calificación de aprobado; **thirdly** adv en tercer lugar; **third party insurance** (BRIT) n seguro contra terceros; **Third World** n Tercer Mundo

thirst [θə:st] n sed f; **thirsty** adj (person, animal) sediento; (work) que da sed; **to be thirsty** tener sed

thirteen ['θə:'ti:n] num trece; **thirteenth** [-'ti:nθ] adj decimotercero

thirtieth ['θə:tɪəθ] adj trigésimo

thirty ['θə:tɪ] num treinta

○ **KEYWORD**

this [ðɪs] (pl **these**) adj (demonstrative) este/a pl; estos/as; (neuter) esto; **this man/woman** este hombre(esta mujer); **these children/flowers** estos chicos/estas flores; **this one (here)** éste/a, esto (de aquí) ▷ pron (demonstrative) éste/a pl, éstos/as; (neuter) esto; **who is this?** ¿quién es éste/ésta?; **what is this?** ¿qué es esto?; **this is where I live** aquí vivo; **this is what he said** esto es lo que dijo; **this is Mr Brown** (in introductions) le presento al Sr. Brown; (photo) éste es el Sr. Brown; (on telephone) habla el Sr. Brown ▷ adv (demonstrative): **this high/long** etc así de alto/largo etc; **this far** hasta aquí

thistle ['θɪsl] n cardo

thorn [θɔːn] *n* espina
thorough ['θʌrə] *adj* (*search*)
minucioso; (*wash*) a fondo;
(*knowledge, research*) profundo;
(*person*) meticuloso; **thoroughly** *adv*
(*search*) minuciosamente; (*study*)
profundamente; (*wash*) a fondo;
(*utterly: bad, wet etc*) completamente,
totalmente
those [ðəuz] *pl adj* esos(esas); (*more
remote*) aquellos/as
though [ðəu] *conj* aunque ▷ *adv* sin
embargo
thought [θɔːt] *pt, pp of* **think** ▷ *n*
pensamiento; (*opinion*) opinión *f*;
thoughtful *adj* pensativo; (*serious*)
serio; (*considerate*) atento; **thoughtless**
adj desconsiderado
thousand ['θauzənd] *num* mil; **two
~** dos mil; **~s of** miles de; **thousandth**
num milésimo
thrash [θræʃ] *vt* azotar; (*defeat*)
derrotar
thread [θrɛd] *n* hilo; (*of screw*) rosca
▷ *vt* (*needle*) enhebrar
threat [θrɛt] *n* amenaza; **threaten** *vi*
amenazar ▷ *vt*: **to threaten sb with/
to do** amenazar a algn con/con hacer;
threatening *adj* amenazador(a),
amenazante
three [θriː] *num* tres; **three-
dimensional** *adj* tridimensional;
three-piece suite *n* tresillo; **three-
quarters** *npl* tres cuartas partes;
three-quarters full tres cuartas
partes lleno
threshold ['θrɛʃhəuld] *n* umbral *m*
threw [θruː] *pt of* **throw**
thrill [θrɪl] *n* (*excitement*) emoción
f; (*shudder*) estremecimiento ▷ *vt*
emocionar; **to be ~ed** (*with gift etc*)
estar encantado; **thrilled** *adj*: **I was
thrilled** Estaba emocionada; **thriller** *n*
novela (*or obra or película*) de suspense;
thrilling *adj* emocionante
thriving ['θraɪvɪŋ] *adj* próspero
throat [θrəut] *n* garganta; **to have a
sore ~** tener dolor de garganta

throb [θrɔb] *vi* latir; dar punzadas;
vibrar
throne [θrəun] *n* trono
through [θruː] *prep* por, a través
de; (*time*) durante; (*by means of*) por
medio de, mediante; (*owing to*) gracias
a ▷ *adj* (*ticket, train*) directo ▷ *adv*
completamente, de parte a parte; de
principio a fin; **to put sb ~ to sb** (*Tel*)
poner *or* pasar a algn con algn; **to be ~**
(*Tel*) tener comunicación; (*have finished*)
haber terminado; **"no ~ road"** (*BRIT*)
"calle sin salida"; **throughout** *prep*
(*place*) por todas partes de, por todo;
(*time*) durante todo ▷ *adv* por *or* en
todas partes
throw [θrəu] (*pt* **threw**, *pp* **thrown**)
n tiro; (*Sport*) lanzamiento ▷ *vt* tirar,
echar; (*Sport*) lanzar; (*rider*) derribar;
(*fig*) desconcertar; **to ~ a party** dar una
fiesta; **throw away** *vt* tirar; (*money*)
derrochar; **throw in** *vt* (*Sport: ball*)
sacar; (*include*) incluir; **throw off** *vt*
deshacerse de; **throw out** *vt* tirar;
(*person*) echar; expulsar; **throw up**
vi vomitar
thru [θruː] (*US*) = **through**
thrush [θrʌʃ] *n* zorzal *m*, tordo
thrust [θrʌst] (*pt, pp* **~**) *vt* empujar
con fuerza
thud [θʌd] *n* golpe *m* sordo
thug [θʌg] *n* gamberro/a
thumb [θʌm] *n* (*Anat*) pulgar *m*; **to ~
a lift** hacer autostop; **thumbtack** (*US*)
n chincheta (*SP*)
thump [θʌmp] *n* golpe *m*; (*sound*)
ruido seco *or* sordo ▷ *vt* golpear ▷ *vi*
(*heart etc*) palpitar
thunder ['θʌndə*] *n* trueno ▷ *vi*
tronar; (*train etc*): **to ~ past** pasar como
un trueno; **thunderstorm** *n* tormenta
Thur(s). *abbr* (= *Thursday*) juev
Thursday ['θəːzdɪ] *n* jueves *m inv*
thus [ðʌs] *adv* así, de este modo
thwart [θwɔːt] *vt* frustrar
thyme [taɪm] *n* tomillo
Tibet [tɪ'bɛt] *n* el Tibet
tick [tɪk] *n* (*sound: of clock*) tictac *m*;

(*mark*) palomita; (*Zool*) garrapata; (*BRIT: inf*): **in a ~** en un instante ▷ *vi* hacer tictac ▷ *vt* marcar; **tick off** *vt* marcar; (*person*) reñir

ticket ['tɪkɪt] *n* billete *m* (*SP*), boleto (*LAM*); (*for cinema etc*) entrada; (*in shop: on goods*) etiqueta; (*for raffle*) papeleta; (*for library*) tarjeta; (*parking ticket*) multa de aparcamiento (*SP*) or por estacionamiento (indebido) (*LAM*); **ticket barrier** *n* (*BRIT: Rail*) barrera más allá de la cual se necesita billete/boleto; **ticket collector** *n* revisor(a) *m/f*; **ticket inspector** *n* revisor(a) *m/f*, inspector(a) *m/f* de boletos (*LAM*); **ticket machine** *n* máquina de billetes (*SP*) or boletos (*LAM*); **ticket office** *n* (*Theatre*) taquilla (*SP*), boletería (*LAM*); (*Rail*) mostrador *m* de billetes (*SP*) or boletos (*LAM*)

tickle ['tɪkl] *vt* hacer cosquillas a ▷ *vi* hacer cosquillas; **ticklish** *adj* (*person*) cosquilloso; (*problem*) delicado

tide [taɪd] *n* marea; (*fig: of events etc*) curso, marcha

tidy ['taɪdɪ] *adj* (*room etc*) ordenado; (*dress, work*) limpio; (*person*) (bien) arreglado ▷ *vt* (*also: ~ up*) poner en orden

tie [taɪ] *n* (*string etc*) atadura; (*BRIT: also: neck~*) corbata; (*fig: link*) vínculo, lazo; (*Sport etc: draw*) empate *m* ▷ *vt* atar ▷ *vi* (*Sport etc*) empatar; **to ~ in a bow** atar con un lazo; **to ~ a knot in sth** hacer un nudo en algo; **tie down** *vt* (*fig: person: restrict*) atar; (*: to price, date etc*) obligar a; **tie up** *vt* (*dog, person*) atar; (*arrangements*) concluir; **to be tied up** (*busy*) estar ocupado

tier [tɪə*] *n* grada; (*of cake*) piso

tiger ['taɪgə*] *n* tigre *m*

tight [taɪt] *adj* (*rope*) tirante; (*money*) escaso; (*clothes*) ajustado; (*bend*) cerrado; (*shoes, schedule*) apretado; (*budget*) ajustado; (*security*) estricto; (*inf: drunk*) borracho ▷ *adv* (*squeeze*) muy fuerte; (*shut*) bien; **tighten** *vt* (*rope*) estirar; (*screw, grip*) apretar;

(*security*) reforzar ▷ *vi* estirarse; apretarse; **tightly** *adv* (*grasp*) muy fuerte; **tights** (*BRIT*) *npl* panti *mpl*

tile [taɪl] *n* (*on roof*) teja; (*on floor*) baldosa; (*on wall*) azulejo

till [tɪl] *n* caja (registradora) ▷ *vt* (*land*) cultivar ▷ *prep, conj* = **until**

tilt [tɪlt] *vt* inclinar ▷ *vi* inclinarse

timber ['tɪmbə*] *n* (*material*) madera

time [taɪm] *n* tiempo; (*epoch: often pl*) época; (*by clock*) hora; (*moment*) momento; (*occasion*) vez *f*; (*Mus*) compás *m* ▷ *vt* calcular or medir el tiempo de; (*race*) cronometrar; (*remark, visit etc*) elegir el momento para; **a long ~** mucho tiempo; **4 at a ~** de 4 en 4; **4 a la vez**; **for the ~ being** de momento, por ahora; **from ~ to ~** de vez en cuando; **at ~s** a veces; **in ~** (*soon enough*) a tiempo; (*after some time*) con el tiempo; (*Mus*) al compás; **in a week's ~** dentro de una semana; **in no ~** en un abrir y cerrar de ojos; **any ~** cuando sea; **on ~** a la hora; **5 ~s 5** 5 por 5; **what ~ is it?** ¿qué hora es?; **to have a good ~** pasarlo bien, divertirse; **time limit** *n* plazo; **timely** *adj* oportuno; **timer** *n* (*in kitchen etc*) programador *m* horario; **time-share** *n* apartamento (*or* casa) a tiempo compartido; **timetable** *n* horario; **time zone** *n* huso horario

timid ['tɪmɪd] *adj* tímido

timing ['taɪmɪŋ] *n* (*Sport*) cronometraje *m*; **the ~ of his resignation** el momento que eligió para dimitir

tin [tɪn] *n* estaño; (*also: ~ plate*) hojalata; (*BRIT: can*) lata; **tinfoil** *n* papel *m* de estaño

tingle ['tɪŋgl] *vi* (*person*): **to ~ (with)** estremecerse (de); (*hands etc*) hormiguear

tinker ['tɪŋkə*]: **~ with** *vt fus* jugar con, tocar

tinned [tɪnd] (*BRIT*) *adj* (*food*) en lata, en conserva

tin opener [-əupnə*] (*BRIT*) *n* abrelatas *m inv*

tint [tɪnt] n matiz m; (for hair) tinte m; **tinted** adj (hair) teñido; (glass, spectacles) ahumado

tiny ['taɪnɪ] adj minúsculo, pequeñito

tip [tɪp] n (end) punta; (gratuity) propina; (BRIT: for rubbish) vertedero; (advice) consejo ▷ vt (waiter) dar una propina a; (tilt) inclinar; (empty: also: ~ **out**) vaciar, echar; (overturn: also: ~ **over**) volcar; **tip off** vt avisar, poner sobreaviso a

tiptoe ['tɪptəʊ] n: **on ~** de puntillas

tire ['taɪə*] n (us) = **tyre** ▷ vt cansar ▷ vi cansarse; (become bored) aburrirse; **tired** adj cansado; **to be tired of sth** estar harto de algo; **tire pressure** (us) = **tyre pressure**; **tiring** adj cansado

tissue ['tɪʃuː] n tejido; (paper handkerchief) pañuelo de papel, kleenex® m; **tissue paper** n papel m de seda

tit [tɪt] n (bird) herrerillo común; **to give ~ for tat** dar ojo por ojo

title ['taɪtl] n título

T-junction ['tiːdʒʌŋkʃən] n cruce m en T

TM abbr = **trademark**

○ KEYWORD

to [tuː, tə] prep **1** (direction) a; **to go to France/London/school/the station** ir a Francia/Londres/al colegio/a la estación; **to go to Claude's/the doctor's** ir a casa de Claude/al médico; **the road to Edinburgh** la carretera de Edimburgo

2 (as far as) hasta, a; **from here to London** de aquí a or hasta Londres; **to count to 10** contar hasta 10; **from 40 to 50 people** entre 40 y 50 personas

3 (with expressions of time): **a quarter/ twenty to 5** las 5 menos cuarto/veinte

4 (for, of): **the key to the front door** la llave de la puerta principal; **she is secretary to the director** es la secretaría del director; **a letter to his wife** una carta a or para su mujer

5 (expressing indirect object) a; **to give sth to sb** darle algo a algn; **to talk to sb** hablar con algn; **to be a danger to sb** ser un peligro para algn; **to carry out repairs to sth** hacer reparaciones en algo

6 (in relation to): **3 goals to 2** 3 goles a 2; **30 miles to the gallon** ≈ 94 litros a los cien (kms)

7 (purpose, result): **to come to sb's aid** venir en auxilio or ayuda de algn; **to sentence sb to death** condenar a algn a muerte; **to my great surprise** con gran sorpresa mía

▷ with vb **1** (simple infin): **to go/eat** ir/comer

2 (following another vb): **to want/try/ start to do** querer/intentar/empezar a hacer

3 (with vb omitted): **I don't want to** no quiero

4 (purpose, result) para; **I did it to help you** lo hice para ayudarte; **he came to see you** vino a verte

5 (equivalent to relative clause): **I have things to do** tengo cosas que hacer; **the main thing is to try** lo principal es intentarlo

6 (after adj etc): **ready to go** listo para irse; **too old to ...** demasiado viejo (como) para ...

▷ adv: **pull/push the door to** tirar de/empujar la puerta

toad [təʊd] n sapo; **toadstool** n hongo venenoso

toast [təʊst] n (Culin) tostada; (drink, speech) brindis m ▷ vt (Culin) tostar; (drink to) brindar por; **toaster** n tostador m

tobacco [tə'bækəʊ] n tabaco

toboggan [tə'bɔgən] n tobogán m

today [tə'deɪ] adv, n (also fig) hoy m

toddler ['tɔdlə*] n niño/a (que empieza a andar)

toe [təʊ] n dedo (del pie); (of shoe) punta; **to ~ the line** (fig) conformarse;

toenail n uña del pie

toffee ['tɒfɪ] n toffee m

together [tə'gɛðə*] adv juntos; (at same time) al mismo tiempo, a la vez; ~ **with** junto con

toilet ['tɔɪlət] n inodoro; (BRIT: room) (cuarto de) baño, servicio ▷ cpd (soap etc) de aseo; **toilet bag** n neceser m, bolsa de aseo; **toilet paper** n papel m higiénico; **toiletries** npl artículos mpl de tocador; **toilet roll** n rollo de papel higiénico

token ['təukən] n (sign) señal f, muestra; (souvenir) recuerdo; (disc) ficha ▷ adj (strike, payment etc) simbólico; **book/record ~** (BRIT) vale m para comprar libros/discos; **gift ~** (BRIT) vale-regalo

Tokyo ['təukjəu] n Tokio, Tókio

told [təuld] pt, pp of **tell**

tolerant ['tɒlərnt] adj: ~ **of** tolerante con

tolerate ['tɒləreɪt] vt tolerar

toll [təul] n (of casualties) número de víctimas; (tax, charge) peaje m ▷ vi (bell) doblar; **toll call** n (US Tel) conferencia, llamada interurbana; **toll-free** (US) adj, adv gratis

tomato [tə'mɑːtəu] (pl ~**es**) n tomate m; **tomato sauce** n salsa de tomate

tomb [tuːm] n tumba; **tombstone** n lápida

tomorrow [tə'mɒrəu] adv, n (also: fig) mañana; **the day after ~** pasado mañana; ~ **morning** mañana por la mañana

ton [tʌn] n tonelada (BRIT = 1016 kg; US = 907 kg), (metric ton) tonelada métrica; ~**s of** (inf) montones de

tone [təun] n tono ▷ vi (also: ~ **in**) armonizar; **tone down** vt (criticism) suavizar; (colour) atenuar

tongs [tɒŋz] npl (for coal) tenazas fpl; (curling tongs) tenacillas fpl

tongue [tʌŋ] n lengua; ~ **in cheek** irónicamente

tonic ['tɒnɪk] n (Med) tónico; (also: ~ **water**) (agua) tónica

tonight [tə'naɪt] adv, n esta noche; esta tarde

tonne [tʌn] n tonelada (métrica) (1.000kg)

tonsil ['tɒnsl] n amígdala; **tonsillitis** [-'laɪtɪs] n amigdalitis f

too [tuː] adv (excessively) demasiado; (also) también; ~ **much** demasiado; ~ **many** demasiados/as

took [tuk] pt of **take**

tool [tuːl] n herramienta; **tool box** n caja de herramientas; **tool kit** n juego de herramientas

tooth [tuːθ] (pl **teeth**) n (Anat, Tech) diente m; (molar) muela; **toothache** n dolor m de muelas; **toothbrush** n cepillo de dientes; **toothpaste** n pasta de dientes; **toothpick** n palillo

top [tɒp] n (of mountain) cumbre f, cima; (of tree) copa; (of head) coronilla; (of ladder, page) lo alto; (of table) superficie f; (of cupboard) parte f de arriba; (lid: of box) tapa; (: of bottle, jar) tapón m; (of list etc) cabeza, (toy) peonza; (garment) blusa; camiseta ▷ adj de arriba; (in rank) principal, primero; (best) mejor ▷ vt (exceed) exceder; (be first in) encabezar; **on ~ of** (above) sobre, encima de; (in addition to) además de; **from ~ to bottom** de pies a cabeza; **top up** vt llenar; (mobile phone) recargar (el saldo de); **top floor** n último piso; **top hat** n sombrero de copa

topic ['tɒpɪk] n tema m; **topical** adj actual

topless ['tɒplɪs] adj (bather, bikini) topless inv

topping ['tɒpɪŋ] n (Culin): **with a ~ of cream** con nata por encima

topple ['tɒpl] vt derribar ▷ vi caerse

top-up card n (for mobile phone) tarjeta prepago

torch [tɔːtʃ] n antorcha; (BRIT: electric) linterna

tore [tɔː*] pt of **tear²**

torment [n 'tɔːmɛnt, vt tɔː'mɛnt] n tormento ▷ vt atormentar; (fig: annoy) fastidiar

torn [tɔːn] *pp of* **tear²**

tornado [tɔːˈneɪdəʊ] (*pl* ~**es**) *n* tornado

torpedo [tɔːˈpiːdəʊ] (*pl* ~**es**) *n* torpedo

torrent ['tɔrnt] *n* torrente *m*; **torrential** [tɔˈrɛnʃl] *adj* torrencial

tortoise ['tɔːtəs] *n* tortuga

torture ['tɔːtʃə*] *n* tortura ▷ *vt* torturar; (*fig*) atormentar

Tory ['tɔːrɪ] (*BRIT*) *adj, n* (*Pol*) conservador(a) *m/f*

toss [tɔs] *vt* tirar, echar; (*one's head*) sacudir; **to ~ a coin** echar a cara o cruz; **to ~ up for sth** jugar a cara o cruz algo; **to ~ and turn** (*in bed*) dar vueltas

total ['təʊtl] *adj* total, entero; (*emphatic: failure etc*) completo, total ▷ *n* total *m*, suma ▷ *vt* (*add up*) sumar; (*amount to*) ascender a

totalitarian [təʊtælɪˈtɛərɪən] *adj* totalitario

totally ['təʊtəlɪ] *adv* totalmente

touch [tʌtʃ] *n* tacto; (*contact*) contacto ▷ *vt* tocar; (*emotionally*) conmover; **a ~ of** (*fig*) un poquito de; **to get in ~ with sb** ponerse en contacto con algn; **to lose ~** (*friends*) perder contacto; **touch down** *vi* (*on land*) aterrizar; **touchdown** *n* aterrizaje *m*; (*on sea*) amerizaje *m*; (*US Football*) ensayo; **touched** *adj* (*moved*) conmovido; **touching** *adj* (*moving*) conmovedor(a); **touchline** *n* (*Sport*) línea de banda; **touch-sensitive** *adj* sensible al tacto

tough [tʌf] *adj* (*material*) resistente; (*meat*) duro; (*problem etc*) difícil; (*policy, stance*) inflexible; (*person*) fuerte

tour ['tuə*] *n* viaje *m*, vuelta; (*also:* **package ~**) viaje *m* todo comprendido; (*of town, museum*) visita; (*by band etc*) gira ▷ *vt* recorrer, visitar; **tour guide** *n* guía *mf* turístico/a

tourism ['tuərɪzm] *n* turismo

tourist ['tuərɪst] *n* turista *mf* ▷ *cpd* turístico; **tourist office** *n* oficina de turismo

tournament ['tuənəmənt] *n* torneo

tour operator *n* touroperador(a) *m/f*, operador(a) *m/f* turístico/a

tow [təʊ] *vt* remolcar; **"on** *or* **in** (*US*) **~"** (*Aut*) "a remolque"; **tow away** *vt* llevarse a remolque

toward(s) [təˈwɔːd(z)] *prep* hacia; (*attitude*) respecto a, con; (*purpose*) para

towel ['tauəl] *n* toalla; **towelling** *n* (*fabric*) felpa

tower ['tauə*] *n* torre *f*; **tower block** (*BRIT*) *n* torre *f* (de pisos)

town [taun] *n* ciudad *f*; **to go to ~** ir a la ciudad; (*fig*) echar la casa por la ventana; **town centre** (*BRIT*) *n* centro de la ciudad; **town hall** *n* ayuntamiento

tow truck (*US*) *n* camión *m* grúa

toxic ['tɔksɪk] *adj* tóxico

toy [tɔɪ] *n* juguete *m*; **toy with** *vt fus* jugar con; (*idea*) acariciar; **toyshop** *n* juguetería

trace [treɪs] *n* rastro ▷ *vt* (*draw*) trazar, delinear; (*locate*) encontrar; (*follow*) seguir la pista de

track [træk] *n* (*mark*) huella, pista; (*path: gen*) camino, senda; (: *of bullet etc*) trayectoria; (: *of suspect, animal*) pista, rastro; (*Rail*) vía; (*Sport*) pista; (*on tape, record*) canción *f* ▷ *vt* seguir la pista de; **to keep ~ of** mantenerse al tanto de, seguir; **track down** *vt* (*prey*) seguir el rastro de; (*sth lost*) encontrar; **tracksuit** *n* chandal *m*

tractor ['træktə*] *n* tractor *m*

trade [treɪd] *n* comercio; (*skill, job*) oficio ▷ *vi* negociar, comerciar ▷ *vt* (*exchange*): **to ~ sth (for sth)** cambiar algo (por algo); **trade in** *vt* (*old car etc*) ofrecer como parte del pago; **trademark** *n* marca de fábrica; **trader** *n* comerciante *mf*; **tradesman** (*irreg*) *n* (*shopkeeper*) tendero; **trade union** *n* sindicato

trading ['treɪdɪŋ] *n* comercio

tradition [trəˈdɪʃən] *n* tradición *f*; **traditional** *adj* tradicional

traffic ['træfɪk] *n* (*gen, Aut*) tráfico,

circulación f ▷ vi: **to ~ in** (pej: liquor, drugs) traficar en; **traffic circle** (US) n isleta; **traffic island** n refugio, isleta; **traffic jam** n embotellamiento; **traffic lights** npl semáforo; **traffic warden** n guardia mf de tráfico

tragedy ['trædʒədɪ] n tragedia

tragic ['trædʒɪk] adj trágico

trail [treɪl] n (tracks) rastro, pista; (path) camino, sendero; (dust, smoke) estela ▷ vt (drag) arrastrar; (follow) seguir la pista de ▷ vi arrastrar; (in contest etc) ir perdiendo; **trailer** n (Aut) remolque m; (caravan) caravana; (Cinema) trailer m, avance m

train [treɪn] n tren m; (of dress) cola; (series) serie f ▷ vt (educate, teach skills to) formar; (sportsman) entrenar; (dog) adiestrar; (point: gun etc): **to ~ on** apuntar a ▷ vi (Sport) entrenarse; (learn a skill): **to ~ as a teacher** etc estudiar para profesor etc; **one's ~ of thought** el razonamiento de algn; **trainee** [treɪ'niː] n aprendiz(a) m/f; **trainer** n (Sport: coach) entrenador(a) m/f; (of animals) domador(a) m/f; **trainers** npl (shoes) zapatillas fpl (de deporte); **training** n formación f, entrenamiento; **to be in training** (Sport) estar entrenando; **training course** n curso de formación; **training shoes** npl zapatillas fpl (de deporte)

trait [treɪt] n rasgo

traitor ['treɪtə*] n traidor(a) m/f

tram [træm] (BRIT) n (also: **~car**) tranvía m

tramp [træmp] n (person) vagabundo/a; (inf: pej: woman) puta

trample ['træmpl] vt: **to ~ (underfoot)** pisotear

trampoline ['træmpəliːn] n trampolín m

tranquil ['træŋkwɪl] adj tranquilo; **tranquillizer** (US **tranquilizer**) n (Med) tranquilizante m

transaction [træn'zækʃən] n transacción f, operación f

transatlantic ['trænzət'læntɪk] adj transatlántico

transcript ['trænskrɪpt] n copia

transfer [n 'trænsfə:*, vb træns'fə:*] n (of employees) traslado; (of money, power) transferencia; (Sport) traspaso; (picture, design) calcomanía ▷ vt trasladar; transferir; **to ~ the charges** (BRIT Tel) llamar a cobro revertido

transform [træns'fɔːm] vt transformar; **transformation** n transformación f

transfusion [træns'fjuːʒən] n transfusión f

transit ['trænzɪt] n: **in ~** en tránsito

transition [træn'zɪʃən] n transición f

transitive ['trænzɪtɪv] adj (Ling) transitivo

translate [trænz'leɪt] vt traducir; **translation** [-'leɪʃən] n traducción f; **translator** n traductor(a) m/f

transmission [trænz'mɪʃən] n transmisión f

transmit [trænz'mɪt] vt transmitir; **transmitter** n transmisor m

transparent [træns'pærnt] adj transparente

transplant ['trænsplɑːnt] n (Med) transplante m

transport [n 'trænspɔːt, vb træns'pɔːt] n transporte m; (car) coche m (SP), carro (LAM), automóvil m ▷ vt transportar; **transportation** [-'teɪʃən] n transporte m

transvestite [trænz'vestaɪt] n travestí mf

trap [træp] n (snare, trick) trampa; (carriage) cabriolé m ▷ vt coger (SP) or agarrar (LAM) (en una trampa); (trick) engañar; (confine) atrapar

trash [træʃ] n (rubbish) basura; (nonsense) tonterías fpl; (pej): **the book/ film is ~** el libro/la película no vale nada; **trash can** (US) n cubo or bote m (MEX) or tacho (SC) de la basura

trauma ['trɔːmə] n trauma m; **traumatic** [trɔː'mætɪk] adj traumático

t

travel ['trævl] n el viajar ▷ vi viajar ▷ vt (*distance*) recorrer; **travel agency** n agencia de viajes; **travel agent** n agente mf de viajes; **travel insurance** n seguro de viaje; **traveller** (us **traveler**) n viajero/a; **traveller's cheque** (us **traveler's check**) n cheque m de viajero; **travelling** (us **traveling**) n los viajes, el viajar; **travel-sick** adj: **to get travel-sick** marearse al viajar; **travel sickness** n mareo

tray [treɪ] n bandeja; (*on desk*) cajón m

treacherous ['tretʃərəs] adj traidor, traicionero; (*dangerous*) peligroso

treacle ['tri:kl] (BRIT) n melaza

tread [trɛd] (pt **trod**, pp **trodden**) n (*step*) paso, pisada; (*sound*) ruido de pasos; (*of stair*) escalón m; (*of tyre*) banda de rodadura ▷ vi pisar; **tread on** vt fus pisar

treasure ['trɛʒə*] n tesoro ▷ vt (*value: object, friendship*) apreciar; (: *memory*) guardar; **treasurer** n tesorero/a

treasury ['trɛʒəri] n: **the T~** el Ministerio de Hacienda

treat [tri:t] n (*present*) regalo ▷ vt tratar; **to ~ sb to sth** invitar a algn a algo; **treatment** n tratamiento

treaty ['tri:ti] n tratado

treble ['trɛbl] adj triple ▷ vt triplicar ▷ vi triplicarse

tree [tri:] n árbol m; **~ trunk** tronco (de árbol)

trek [trɛk] n (*long journey*) viaje m largo y difícil; (*tiring walk*) caminata

tremble ['trɛmbl] vi temblar

tremendous [trɪ'mɛndəs] adj tremendo, enorme; (*excellent*) estupendo

trench [trɛntʃ] n zanja

trend [trɛnd] n (*tendency*) tendencia; (*of events*) curso; (*fashion*) moda; **trendy** adj de moda

trespass ['trɛspəs] vi: **to ~ on** entrar sin permiso en; **"no ~ing"** "prohibido el paso"

trial ['traɪəl] n (*Law*) juicio, proceso; (*test: of machine etc*) prueba; **trial period** n periodo de prueba

triangle ['traɪæŋgl] n (*Math, Mus*) triángulo

triangular [traɪ'æŋgjulə*] adj triangular

tribe [traɪb] n tribu f

tribunal [traɪ'bju:nl] n tribunal m

tribute ['trɪbju:t] n homenaje m, tributo; **to pay ~ to** rendir homenaje a

trick [trɪk] n (*skill, knack*) tino, truco; (*conjuring trick*) truco; (*joke*) broma; (*Cards*) baza ▷ vt engañar; **to play a ~ on sb** gastar una broma a algn; **that should do the ~** a ver si funciona así

trickle ['trɪkl] n (*of water etc*) goteo ▷ vi gotear

tricky ['trɪkɪ] adj difícil; delicado

tricycle ['traɪsɪkl] n triciclo

trifle ['traɪfl] n bagatela; (*Culin*) dulce de bizcocho borracho, gelatina, fruta y natillas ▷ adv: **a ~ long** un poquito largo

trigger ['trɪgə*] n (*of gun*) gatillo

trim [trɪm] adj (*house, garden*) en buen estado; (*person, figure*) esbelto ▷ n (*haircut etc*) recorte m; (*on car*) guarnición f ▷ vt (*neaten*) arreglar; (*cut*) recortar; (*decorate*) adornar; (*Naut: a sail*) orientar

trio ['tri:əu] n trío

trip [trɪp] n viaje m; (*excursion*) excursión f; (*stumble*) traspié m ▷ vi (*stumble*) tropezar; (*go lightly*) andar a paso ligero; **on a ~** de viaje; **trip up** vi tropezar, caerse ▷ vt hacer tropezar or caer

triple ['trɪpl] adj triple

triplets ['trɪplɪts] npl trillizos/as mpl/fpl

tripod ['traɪpɔd] n trípode m

triumph ['traɪʌmf] n triunfo ▷ vi: **to ~ (over)** vencer; **triumphant** [traɪ'ʌmfənt] adj (*team etc*) vencedor(a); (*wave, return*) triunfal

trivial ['trɪvɪəl] adj insignificante; (*commonplace*) banal

trod [trɔd] pt of **tread**

trodden ['trɒdn] *pp of* **tread**

trolley ['trɒlɪ] *n* carrito; (*also:* **~ bus**) trolebús *m*

trombone [trɒm'bəʊn] *n* trombón *m*

troop [tru:p] *n* grupo, banda; **troops** *npl* (*Mil*) tropas *fpl*

trophy ['trəʊfɪ] *n* trofeo

tropical ['trɒpɪkl] *adj* tropical

trot [trɒt] *n* trote *m* ▷ *vi* trotar; **on the ~** (*BRIT: fig*) seguidos/as

trouble ['trʌbl] *n* problema *m*, dificultad *f*; (*worry*) preocupación *f*; (*bother, effort*) molestia, esfuerzo; (*unrest*) inquietud *f*; (*Med*): **stomach** *etc* **~** problemas *mpl* gástricos *etc* ▷ *vt* (*disturb*) molestar; (*worry*) preocupar, inquietar ▷ *vi*: **to ~ to do sth** molestarse en hacer algo; **troubles** *npl* (*Pol etc*) conflictos *mpl*; (*personal*) problemas *mpl*; **to be in ~** estar en un apuro; **it's no ~!** ¡no es molestia (ninguna)!; **what's the ~?** (*with broken TV etc*) ¿cuál es el problema?; (*doctor to patient*) ¿qué pasa?; **troubled** *adj* (*person*) preocupado; (*country, epoch, life*) agitado; **troublemaker** *n* agitador(a) *m/f*; (*child*) alborotador *m*; **troublesome** *adj* molesto

trough [trɒf] *n* (*also:* **drinking ~**) abrevadero; (*also:* **feeding ~**) comedero; (*depression*) depresión *f*

trousers ['traʊzəz] *npl* pantalones *mpl*; **short ~** pantalones *mpl* cortos

trout [traʊt] *n inv* trucha

trowel ['traʊəl] *n* (*of gardener*) palita; (*of builder*) paleta

truant ['truənt] *n*: **to play ~** (*BRIT*) hacer novillos

truce [tru:s] *n* tregua

truck [trʌk] *n* (*lorry*) camión *m*; (*Rail*) vagón *m*; **truck driver** *n* camionero

true [tru:] *adj* verdadero; (*accurate*) exacto; (*genuine*) auténtico; (*faithful*) fiel; **to come ~** realizarse

truly ['truːlɪ] *adv* (*really*) realmente; (*truthfully*) verdaderamente; (*faithfully*): **yours ~** (*in letter*) le saluda atentamente

trumpet ['trʌmpɪt] *n* trompeta

trunk [trʌŋk] *n* (*of tree, person*) tronco; (*of elephant*) trompa; (*case*) baúl *m*; (*US Aut*) maletero; **trunks** *npl* (*also:* **swimming ~s**) bañador *m* (de hombre)

trust [trʌst] *n* confianza; (*responsibility*) responsabilidad *f*; (*Law*) fideicomiso ▷ *vt* (*rely on*) tener confianza en; (*hope*) esperar; (*entrust*): **to ~ sth to sb** confiar algo a algn; **to take sth on ~** fiarse de algo; **trusted** *adj* de confianza; **trustworthy** *adj* digno de confianza

truth [tru:θ, *pl* tru:ðz] *n* verdad *f*; **truthful** *adj* veraz

try [traɪ] *n* tentativa, intento; (*Rugby*) ensayo ▷ *vt* (*attempt*) intentar; (*test: also:* **~ out**) probar, someter a prueba; (*Law*) juzgar, procesar; (*strain: patience*) hacer perder ▷ *vi* probar: **to have a ~** probar suerte; **to ~ to do sth** intentar hacer algo; **~ again!** ¡vuelve a probar!; **~ harder!** ¡esfuérzate más!; **well, I tried** al menos lo intenté; **try on** *vt* (*clothes*) probarse; **trying** *adj* (*experience*) cansado; (*person*) pesado

T-shirt ['ti:ʃɜ:t] *n* camiseta

tub [tʌb] *n* cubo (*SP*), cubeta (*SP, MEX*); balde *m* (*LAM*); (*bath*) bañera (*SP*), tina (*LAM*), bañadera (*RPL*)

tube [tju:b] *n* tubo; (*BRIT: underground*) metro; (*for tyre*) cámara de aire

tuberculosis [tjubɜ:kju'ləʊsɪs] *n* tuberculosis *f inv*

tube station (*BRIT*) *n* estación *f* de metro

tuck [tʌk] *vt* (*put*) poner; **tuck away** *vt* (*money*) guardar; (*building*): **to be tucked away** esconderse, ocultarse; **tuck in** *vt* meter dentro; (*child*) arropar ▷ *vi* (*eat*) comer con apetito; **tuck shop** *n* (*Scol*) tienda ≈ bar *m* (del colegio) (*SP*)

Tue(s). *abbr* (= *Tuesday*) mart

Tuesday ['tju:zdɪ] *n* martes *m inv*

tug [tʌg] *n* (*ship*) remolcador *m* ▷ *vt* tirar de

tuition [tju:'ɪʃən] *n* (*BRIT*) enseñanza;

(: *private tuition*) clases *fpl* particulares; (*US*: *school fees*) matrícula

tulip ['tjuːlɪp] *n* tulipán *m*

tumble ['tʌmbl] *n* (*fall*) caída ▷ *vi* caer; **to ~ to sth** (*inf*) caer en la cuenta de algo; **tumble dryer** (*BRIT*) *n* secadora

tumbler ['tʌmblə*] *n* (*glass*) vaso

tummy ['tʌmɪ] (*inf*) *n* barriga, tripa

tumour ['tjuːmə*] (*US* **tumor**) *n* tumor *m*

tuna ['tjuːnə] *n inv* (*also*: **~ fish**) atún *m*

tune [tjuːn] *n* melodía ▷ *vt* (*Mus*) afinar; (*Radio, TV, Aut*) sintonizar; **to be in/out of ~** (*instrument*) estar afinado/desafinado; (*singer*) cantar afinadamente/desafinar; **to be in/out of ~ with** (*fig*) estar de acuerdo/en desacuerdo con; **tune in** *vi*: **to tune in (to)** (*Radio, TV*) sintonizar (con); **tune up** *vi* (*musician*) afinar (su instrumento)

tunic ['tjuːnɪk] *n* túnica

Tunisia [tjuːˈnɪzɪə] *n* Túnez *m*

tunnel ['tʌnl] *n* túnel *m*; (*in mine*) galería ▷ *vi* construir un túnel/una galería

turbulence ['təːbjuləns] *n* (*Aviat*) turbulencia

turf [təːf] *n* césped *m*; (*clod*) tepe *m* ▷ *vt* cubrir con césped

Turk [təːk] *n* turco/a

Turkey ['təːkɪ] *n* Turquía

turkey ['təːkɪ] *n* pavo

Turkish ['təːkɪʃ] *adj, n* turco; (*Ling*) turco

turmoil ['təːmɔɪl] *n*: **in ~** revuelto

turn [təːn] *n* turno; (*in road*) curva; (*of mind, events*) rumbo; (*Theatre*) número; (*Med*) ataque *m* ▷ *vt* girar, volver; (*collar, steak*) dar la vuelta a; (*page*) pasar; (*change*): **to ~ sth into** convertir algo en ▷ *vi* volver; (*person*: *look back*) volverse; (*reverse direction*) dar la vuelta; (*milk*) cortarse; (*become*): **to ~ nasty/forty** ponerse feo/cumplir los cuarenta; **a good ~** un favor; **it gave me quite a ~** me dio un susto; **"no left ~"** (*Aut*) "prohibido girar a la izquierda"; **it's your ~** te toca a ti; **in ~** por turnos; **to take ~s (at)** turnarse (en); **turn around** *vi* (*person*) volverse, darse la vuelta ▷ *vt* (*object*) dar la vuelta a, voltear (*LAM*); **turn away** *vi* apartar la vista ▷ *vi* rechazar; **turn back** *vi* volverse atrás ▷ *vt* hacer retroceder; (*clock*) retrasar; **turn down** *vt* (*refuse*) rechazar; (*reduce*) bajar; (*fold*) doblar; **turn in** *vi* (*inf*: *go to bed*) acostarse ▷ *vt* (*fold*) doblar hacia dentro; **turn off** *vi* (*from road*) desviarse ▷ *vt* (*light, radio etc*) apagar; (*tap*) cerrar; (*engine*) parar; **turn on** (*light, radio etc*) encender (*SP*), prender (*LAM*); (*tap*) abrir; (*engine*) poner en marcha; **turn out** *vt* (*light, gas*) apagar; (*produce*) producir ▷ *vi* (*voters*) concurrir; **to turn out to be ...** resultar ser ...; **turn over** *vi* (*person*) volverse ▷ *vt* (*object*) dar la vuelta a; (*page*) volver; **turn round** *vi* volverse; (*rotate*) girar; **turn to** *vt fus*: **to turn to sb** acudir a algn; **turn up** *vi* (*person*) llegar, presentarse; (*lost object*) aparecer ▷ *vt* (*gen*) subir; **turning** *n* (*in road*) vuelta; **turning point** *n* (*fig*) momento decisivo

turnip ['təːnɪp] *n* nabo

turn: turnout *n* concurrencia; **turnover** *n* (*Comm*: *amount of money*) volumen *m* de ventas; (: *of goods*) movimiento; **turnstile** *n* torniquete *m*; **turn-up** (*BRIT*) *n* (*on trousers*) vuelta

turquoise ['təːkwɔɪz] *n* (*stone*) turquesa ▷ *adj* color turquesa

turtle ['təːtl] *n* galápago; **turtleneck (sweater)** *n* jersey *m* de cuello vuelto

tusk [tʌsk] *n* colmillo

tutor ['tjuːtə*] *n* profesor(a) *m/f*; **tutorial** [-ˈtɔːrɪəl] *n* (*Scol*) seminario

tuxedo [tʌkˈsiːdəu] (*US*) *n* smóking *m*, esmoquin *m*

TV [tiːˈviː] *n abbr* (= *television*) tele *f*

tweed [twiːd] *n* tweed *m*

tweezers ['twiːzəz] *npl* pinzas *fpl* (de depilar)

twelfth [twɛlfθ] *num* duodécimo
twelve [twɛlv] *num* doce; **at ~ o'clock** (*midday*) a mediodía; (*midnight*) a medianoche
twentieth ['twɛntɪɪθ] *adj* vigésimo
twenty ['twɛntɪ] *num* veinte
twice [twaɪs] *adv* dos veces; **~ as much** dos veces más
twig [twɪg] *n* ramita
twilight ['twaɪlaɪt] *n* crepúsculo
twin [twɪn] *adj, n* gemelo/a *m/f* ▷ *vt* hermanar; **twin(-bedded) room** *n* habitación *f* doble; **twin beds** *npl* camas *fpl* gemelas
twinkle ['twɪŋkl] *vi* centellear; (*eyes*) brillar
twist [twɪst] *n* (*action*) torsión *f*; (*in road, coil*) vuelta; (*in wire, flex*) doblez *f*; (*in story*) giro ▷ *vt* torcer; (*weave*) trenzar; (*roll around*) enrollar; (*fig*) deformar ▷ *vi* serpentear
twit [twɪt] (*inf*) *n* tonto
twitch [twɪtʃ] *n* (*pull*) tirón *m*; (*nervous*) tic *m* ▷ *vi* crisparse
two [tu:] *num* dos; **to put ~ and ~ together** (*fig*) atar cabos
type [taɪp] *n* (*category*) tipo, género; (*model*) tipo, (*Typ*) tipo, letra ▷ *vt* (*letter etc*) escribir a máquina; **typewriter** *n* máquina de escribir
typhoid ['taɪfɔɪd] *n* tifoidea
typhoon [taɪ'fu:n] *n* tifón *m*
typical ['tɪpɪkl] *adj* típico; **typically** *adv* típicamente
typing ['taɪpɪŋ] *n* mecanografía
typist ['taɪpɪst] *n* mecanógrafo/a
tyre ['taɪə*] (*us* **tire**) *n* neumático, llanta (*LAM*); **tyre pressure** (*BRIT*) *n* presión *f* de los neumáticos

UFO ['ju:fəu] *n abbr* (= *unidentified flying object*) OVNI *m*
Uganda [ju:'gændə] *n* Uganda
ugly ['ʌglɪ] *adj* feo; (*dangerous*) peligroso
UHT *abbr* (= *UHT milk*) leche *f* UHT, leche *f* uperizada
UK *n abbr* = **United Kingdom**
ulcer ['ʌlsə*] *n* úlcera; (*mouth ulcer*) llaga
ultimate ['ʌltɪmət] *adj* último, final; (*greatest*) máximo; **ultimately** *adv* (*in the end*) por último, al final; (*fundamentally*) a or en fin de cuentas
ultimatum [ʌltɪ'meɪtəm] (*pl* **~s** or **ultimata**) *n* ultimátum *m*
ultrasound ['ʌltrəsaund] *n* (*Med*) ultrasonido
ultraviolet ['ʌltrə'vaɪəlɪt] *adj* ultravioleta
umbrella [ʌm'brɛlə] *n* paraguas *m inv*; (*for sun*) sombrilla
umpire ['ʌmpaɪə*] *n* árbitro
UN *n abbr* (= *United Nations*) NN. UU.
unable [ʌn'eɪbl] *adj*: **to be ~ to do sth**

u

no poder hacer algo
unacceptable [ʌnək'sɛptəbl] *adj*
(*proposal, behaviour, price*) inaceptable;
it's ~ that no se puede aceptar que
unanimous [juː'nænɪməs] *adj*
unánime
unarmed [ʌn'ɑːmd] *adj* (*defenceless*)
inerme; (*without weapon*) desarmado
unattended [ʌnə'tɛndɪd] *adj*
desatendido
unattractive [ʌnə'træktɪv] *adj* poco
atractivo
unavailable [ʌnə'veɪləbl] *adj* (*article,
room, book*) no disponible; (*person*)
ocupado
unavoidable [ʌnə'vɔɪdəbl] *adj*
inevitable
unaware [ʌnə'wɛə*] *adj*: **to be ~ of**
ignorar; **unawares** *adv*: **to catch sb
unawares** pillar a algn desprevenido
unbearable [ʌn'bɛərəbl] *adj*
insoportable
unbeatable [ʌn'biːtəbl] *adj* (*team*)
invencible; (*price*) inmejorable; (*quality*)
insuperable
unbelievable [ʌnbɪ'liːvəbl] *adj*
increíble
unborn [ʌn'bɔːn] *adj* que va a nacer
unbutton [ʌn'bʌtn] *vt* desabrochar
uncalled-for [ʌn'kɔːldfɔː*] *adj*
gratuito, inmerecido
uncanny [ʌn'kænɪ] *adj* extraño
uncertain [ʌn'səːtn] *adj* incierto;
(*indecisive*) indeciso; **uncertainty** *n*
incertidumbre *f*
unchanged [ʌn'tʃeɪndʒd] *adj* igual,
sin cambios
uncle [ʌŋkl] *n* tío
unclear [ʌn'klɪə*] *adj* poco claro; **I'm
still ~ about what I'm supposed to
do** todavía no tengo muy claro lo que
tengo que hacer
uncomfortable [ʌn'kʌmfətəbl] *adj*
incómodo; (*uneasy*) inquieto
uncommon [ʌn'kɔmən] *adj* poco
común, raro
unconditional [ʌnkən'dɪʃənl] *adj*
incondicional

unconscious [ʌn'kɔnʃəs] *adj* sin
sentido; (*unaware*): **to be ~ of** no darse
cuenta de ▷ *n*: **the ~** el inconsciente
uncontrollable [ʌnkən'trəuləbl]
adj (*child etc*) incontrolable; (*temper*)
indomable; (*laughter*) incontenible
unconventional [ʌnkən'vɛnʃənl]
adj poco convencional
uncover [ʌn'kʌvə*] *vt* descubrir;
(*take lid off*) destapar
undecided [ʌndɪ'saɪdɪd] *adj*
(*character*) indeciso; (*question*) no
resuelto
undeniable [ʌndɪ'naɪəbl] *adj*
innegable
under ['ʌndə*] *prep* debajo de; (*less
than*) menos de; (*according to*) según,
de acuerdo con; (*sb's leadership*) bajo
▷ *adv* debajo, abajo; **~ there** allí abajo;
~ repair en reparación; **undercover**
adj clandestino; **underdone**
(*Culin*) poco hecho; **underestimate**
vt subestimar; **undergo** (*irreg*)
vt sufrir; (*treatment*) recibir;
undergraduate *n* estudiante *mf*;
underground *n* (*BRIT*: *railway*) metro;
(*Pol*) movimiento clandestino ▷ *adj*
(*car park*) subterráneo ▷ *adv* (*work*)
en la clandestinidad; **undergrowth**
n maleza; **underline** *vt* subrayar;
undermine *vt* socavar, minar;
underneath [ʌndə'niːθ] *adv* debajo
▷ *prep* debajo de, bajo; **underpants**
npl calzoncillos *mpl*; **underpass** (*BRIT*)
n paso subterráneo; **underprivileged**
adj desposeído; **underscore** *vt*
subrayar; **undershirt** (*US*) *n* camiseta;
underskirt (*BRIT*) *n* enaguas *fpl*
understand [ʌndə'stænd] *vt,
vi* entender, comprender; (*assume*)
tener entendido; **understandable**
adj comprensible; **understanding**
adj comprensivo ▷ *n* comprensión *f*,
entendimiento; (*agreement*) acuerdo
understatement ['ʌndəsteɪtmənt]
n modestia (excesiva); **that's an ~!**
¡eso es decir poco!
understood [ʌndə'stud] *pt, pp of*

understand ▷ adj (agreed) acordado; (implied): **it is ~ that** se sobreentiende que

undertake [ʌndə'teɪk] (irreg) vt emprender; **to ~ to do sth** comprometerse a hacer algo

undertaker ['ʌndəteɪkə*] n director(a) m/f de pompas fúnebres

undertaking ['ʌndəteɪkɪŋ] n empresa; (promise) promesa

under: underwater adv bajo el agua ▷ adj submarino; **underway** adj: **to be underway** (meeting) estar en marcha; (investigation) estar llevándose a cabo; **underwear** n ropa interior; **underwent** vb see **undergo**; **underworld** n (of crime) hampa, inframundo

undesirable [ʌndɪ'zaɪrəbl] adj (person) indeseable; (thing) poco aconsejable

undisputed [ʌndɪ'spjuːtɪd] adj incontestable

undo [ʌn'duː] (irreg) vt (laces) desatar; (button etc) desabrochar; (spoil) deshacer

undone [ʌn'dʌn] pp of **undo** ▷ adj: **to come ~** (clothes) desabrocharse; (parcel) desatarse

undoubtedly [ʌn'dautɪdlɪ] adv indudablemente, sin duda

undress [ʌn'drɛs] vi desnudarse

unearth [ʌn'ɜːθ] vt desenterrar

uneasy [ʌn'iːzɪ] adj intranquilo, preocupado; (feeling) desagradable; (peace) inseguro

unemployed [ʌnɪm'plɔɪd] adj parado, sin trabajo ▷ npl: **the ~** los parados

unemployment [ʌnɪm'plɔɪmənt] n paro, desempleo; **unemployment benefit** n (BRIT) subsidio de desempleo or paro

unequal [ʌn'iːkwəl] adj (unfair) desigual; (size, length) distinto

uneven [ʌn'iːvn] adj desigual; (road etc) lleno de baches

unexpected [ʌnɪk'spɛktɪd] adj inesperado; **unexpectedly** adv inesperadamente

unfair [ʌn'fɛə*] adj: **~ (to sb)** injusto (con algn)

unfaithful [ʌn'feɪθful] adj infiel

unfamiliar [ʌnfə'mɪlɪə*] adj extraño, desconocido; **to be ~ with** desconocer

unfashionable [ʌn'fæʃnəbl] adj pasado or fuera de moda

unfasten [ʌn'fɑːsn] vt (knot) desatar; (dress) desabrochar; (open) abrir

unfavourable [ʌn'feɪvərəbl] (us **unfavorable**) adj desfavorable

unfinished [ʌn'fɪnɪʃt] adj inacabado, sin terminar

unfit [ʌn'fɪt] adj bajo de forma; (incompetent). **~ (for)** incapaz (de); **~ for work** no apto para trabajar

unfold [ʌn'fəuld] vt desdoblar ▷ vi abrirse

unforgettable [ʌnfə'gɛtəbl] adj inolvidable

unfortunate [ʌn'fɔːtʃnət] adj desgraciado; (event, remark) inoportuno; **unfortunately** adv desgraciadamente

unfriendly [ʌn'frɛndlɪ] adj antipático; (behaviour, remark) hostil, poco amigable

unfurnished [ʌn'fɜːnɪʃt] adj sin amueblar

unhappiness [ʌn'hæpɪnɪs] n tristeza, desdicha

unhappy [ʌn'hæpɪ] adj (sad) triste; (unfortunate) desgraciado; (childhood) infeliz; **~ about/with** (arrangements etc) poco contento con, descontento de

unhealthy [ʌn'hɛlθɪ] adj (place) malsano; (person) enfermizo; (fig: interest) morboso

unheard-of [ʌn'hɜːdɔv] adj inaudito, sin precedente

unhelpful [ʌn'hɛlpful] adj (person) poco servicial; (advice) inútil

unhurt [ʌn'hɜːt] adj ileso

unidentified [ʌnaɪ'dɛntɪfaɪd] adj no identificado, sin identificar; see

u

also **UFO**

uniform ['ju:nɪfɔ:m] *n* uniforme *m*
▷ *adj* uniforme

unify ['ju:nɪfaɪ] *vt* unificar, unir

unimportant [ʌnɪm'pɔ:tənt] *adj* sin
importancia

uninhabited [ʌnɪn'hæbɪtɪd] *adj*
desierto

unintentional [ʌnɪn'tɛnʃənəl] *adj*
involuntario

union ['ju:njən] *n* unión *f*; (*also:* **trade
~**) sindicato ▷ *cpd* sindical; **Union Jack**
n bandera del Reino Unido

unique [ju:'ni:k] *adj* único

unisex ['ju:nɪsɛks] *adj* unisex

unit ['ju:nɪt] *n* unidad *f*; (*section: of
furniture etc*) elemento; (*team*) grupo;
kitchen ~ módulo de cocina

unite [ju:'naɪt] *vt* unir ▷ *vi* unirse;
united *adj* unido; (*effort*) conjunto;
United Kingdom *n* Reino Unido;
United Nations (Organization) *n*
Naciones *fpl* Unidas; **United States (of
America)** *n* Estados *mpl* Unidos

unity ['ju:nɪtɪ] *n* unidad *f*

universal [ju:nɪ'və:sl] *adj* universal

universe ['ju:nɪvə:s] *n* universo

university [ju:nɪ'və:sɪtɪ] *n*
universidad *f*

unjust [ʌn'dʒʌst] *adj* injusto

unkind [ʌn'kaɪnd] *adj* poco amable;
(*behaviour, comment*) cruel

unknown [ʌn'nəʊn] *adj*
desconocido

unlawful [ʌn'lɔ:ful] *adj* ilegal, ilícito

unleaded [ʌn'lɛdɪd] *adj* (*petrol, fuel*)
sin plomo

unleash [ʌn'li:ʃ] *vt* desatar

unless [ʌn'lɛs] *conj* a menos que;
~ he comes a menos que venga; **~
otherwise stated** salvo indicación
contraria

unlike [ʌn'laɪk] *adj* (*not alike*) distinto
de or a; (*not like*) poco propio de ▷ *prep*
a diferencia de

unlikely [ʌn'laɪklɪ] *adj* improbable;
(*unexpected*) inverosímil

unlimited [ʌn'lɪmɪtɪd] *adj* ilimitado

unlisted [ʌn'lɪstɪd] (*us*) *adj* (*Tel*) que
no consta en la guía

unload [ʌn'ləʊd] *vt* descargar

unlock [ʌn'lɔk] *vt* abrir (con llave)

unlucky [ʌn'lʌkɪ] *adj* desgraciado;
(*object, number*) que da mala suerte; **to
be ~** tener mala suerte

unmarried [ʌn'mærɪd] *adj* soltero

unmistak(e)able [ʌnmɪs'teɪkəbl]
adj inconfundible

unnatural [ʌn'nætʃrəl] *adj* (*gen*)
antinatural; (*manner*) afectado; (*habit*)
perverso

unnecessary [ʌn'nɛsəsərɪ] *adj*
innecesario, inútil

UNO ['ju:nəʊ] *n abbr* (= *United Nations
Organization*) ONU *f*

unofficial [ʌnə'fɪʃl] *adj* no oficial;
(*news*) sin confirmar

unpack [ʌn'pæk] *vi* deshacer las
maletas ▷ *vt* deshacer

unpaid [ʌn'peɪd] *adj* (*bill, debt*) sin
pagar, impagado; (*Comm*) pendiente;
(*holiday*) sin sueldo; (*work*) sin pago,
voluntario

unpleasant [ʌn'plɛznt] *adj*
(*disagreeable*) desagradable; (*person,
manner*) antipático

unplug [ʌn'plʌg] *vt* desenchufar,
desconectar

unpopular [ʌn'pɔpjulə*] *adj*
impopular, poco popular

unprecedented [ʌn'prɛsɪdəntɪd]
adj sin precedentes

unpredictable [ʌnprɪ'dɪktəbl] *adj*
imprevisible

unprotected ['ʌnprə'tɛktɪd] *adj* (*sex*)
sin protección

unqualified [ʌn'kwɔlɪfaɪd] *adj* sin
título, no cualificado; (*success*) total

unravel [ʌn'rævl] *vt* desenmarañar

unreal [ʌn'rɪəl] *adj* irreal;
(*extraordinary*) increíble

unrealistic [ʌnrɪə'lɪstɪk] *adj* poco
realista

unreasonable [ʌn'ri:znəbl] *adj*
irrazonable; (*demand*) excesivo

unrelated [ʌnrɪ'leɪtɪd] *adj* sin

relación; (*family*) no emparentado

unreliable [ʌnrɪˈlaɪəbl] *adj* (*person*) informal; (*machine*) poco fiable

unrest [ʌnˈrest] *n* inquietud *f*, malestar *m*; (*Pol*) disturbios *mpl*

unroll [ʌnˈrəul] *vt* desenrollar

unruly [ʌnˈruːlɪ] *adj* indisciplinado

unsafe [ʌnˈseɪf] *adj* peligroso

unsatisfactory [ˈʌnsætɪsˈfæktərɪ] *adj* poco satisfactorio

unscrew [ʌnˈskruː] *vt* destornillar

unsettled [ʌnˈsetld] *adj* inquieto, intranquilo; (*weather*) variable

unsettling [ʌnˈsetlɪŋ] *adj* perturbador(a), inquietante

unsightly [ʌnˈsaɪtlɪ] *adj* feo

unskilled [ʌnˈskɪld] *adj* (*work*) no especializado; (*worker*) no cualificado

unspoiled [ˈʌnˈspɔɪld], **unspoilt** [ˈʌnˈspɔɪlt] *adj* (*place*) que no ha perdido su belleza natural

unstable [ʌnˈsteɪbl] *adj* inestable

unsteady [ʌnˈstedɪ] *adj* inestable

unsuccessful [ʌnsəkˈsesful] *adj* (*attempt*) infructuoso; (*writer, proposal*) sin éxito; **to be ~** (*in attempting sth*) no tener éxito, fracasar

unsuitable [ʌnˈsuːtəbl] *adj* inapropiado; (*time*) inoportuno

unsure [ʌnˈʃuə*] *adj* inseguro, poco seguro

untidy [ʌnˈtaɪdɪ] *adj* (*room*) desordenado; (*appearance*) desaliñado

untie [ʌnˈtaɪ] *vt* desatar

until [ənˈtɪl] *prep* hasta ▷ *conj* hasta que; **~ he comes** hasta que venga; **~ now** hasta ahora; **~ then** hasta entonces

untrue [ʌnˈtruː] *adj* (*statement*) falso

unused [ʌnˈjuːzd] *adj* sin usar

unusual [ʌnˈjuːʒuəl] *adj* insólito, poco común; (*exceptional*) inusitado; **unusually** *adv* (*exceptionally*) excepcionalmente; **he arrived unusually early** llegó más temprano que de costumbre

unveil [ʌnˈveɪl] *vt* (*statue*) descubrir

unwanted [ʌnˈwɔntɪd] *adj* (*clothing*) viejo; (*pregnancy*) no deseado

unwell [ʌnˈwel] *adj*: **to be/feel ~** estar indispuesto/sentirse mal

unwilling [ʌnˈwɪlɪŋ] *adj*: **to be ~ to do sth** estar poco dispuesto a hacer algo

unwind [ʌnˈwaɪnd] (*irreg*) *vt* desenvolver ▷ *vi* (*relax*) relajarse

unwise [ʌnˈwaɪz] *adj* imprudente

unwittingly [ʌnˈwɪtɪŋlɪ] *adv* inconscientemente, sin darse cuenta

unwrap [ʌnˈræp] *vt* desenvolver

unzip [ʌnˈzɪp] *vt* abrir la cremallera de; (*Comput*) descomprimir

○ **KEYWORD**

up [ʌp] *prep*: **to go/be up sth** subir/estar subido en algo; **he went up the stairs/the hill** subió las escaleras/la colina; **we walked/climbed up the hill** subimos la colina; **they live further up the street** viven más arriba en la calle; **go up that road and turn left** sigue por esa calle y gira a la izquierda

▷ *adv* **1** (*upwards, higher*) más arriba; **up in the mountains** en lo alto (de la montaña); **put it a bit higher up** ponlo un poco más arriba *or* alto; **up there** ahí *or* allí arriba; **up above** en lo alto, por encima, arriba

2: **to be up** (*out of bed*) estar levantado; (*prices, level*) haber subido

3: **up to** (*as far as*) hasta; **up to now** hasta ahora *or* la fecha

4: **to be up to: it's up to you** (*depending on*) depende de ti; **he's not up to it** (*job, task etc*) no es capaz de hacerlo; **his work is not up to the required standard** su trabajo no da la talla; (*inf: be doing*): **what is he up to?** ¿que estará tramando?

▷ *n*: **ups and downs** altibajos *mpl*

up-and-coming [ʌpəndˈkʌmɪŋ] *adj* prometedor(a)

upbringing [ˈʌpbrɪŋɪŋ] *n* educación

f

update [ʌp'deɪt] *vt* poner al día

upfront [ʌp'frʌnt] *adj* claro, directo
▷ *adv* a las claras; (*pay*) por adelantado;
to be ~ about sth admitir algo
claramente

upgrade [ʌp'greɪd] *vt* (*house*)
modernizar; (*employee*) ascender

upheaval [ʌp'hi:vl] *n* trastornos *mpl*;
(*Pol*) agitación *f*

uphill [ʌp'hɪl] *adj* cuesta arriba;
(*fig: task*) penoso, difícil ▷ *adv*: **to go ~**
ir cuesta arriba

upholstery [ʌp'həulstəri] *n*
tapicería

upmarket [ʌp'mɑ:kɪt] *adj* (*product*)
de categoría

upon [ə'pɔn] *prep* sobre

upper ['ʌpə*] *adj* superior, de arriba
▷ *n* (*of shoe: also:* **~s**) empeine *m*; **upper-
class** *adj* de clase alta

upright ['ʌpraɪt] *adj* derecho;
(*vertical*) vertical; (*fig*) honrado

uprising ['ʌpraɪzɪŋ] *n* sublevación *f*

uproar ['ʌprɔ:*] *n* escándalo

upset [*n* 'ʌpsɛt, *vb, adj* ʌp'sɛt] *n* (*to
plan etc*) revés *m*, contratiempo; (*Med*)
trastorno ▷ *vt irreg* (*glass etc*) volcar;
(*plan*) alterar; (*person*) molestar,
disgustar ▷ *adj* molesto, disgustado;
(*stomach*) revuelto

upside-down [ʌpsaɪd'daun] *adv* al
revés; **to turn a place ~** (*fig*) revolverlo
todo

upstairs [ʌp'stɛəz] *adv* arriba ▷ *adj*
(*room*) de arriba ▷ *n* el piso superior

up-to-date ['ʌptə'deɪt] *adj* al día

uptown ['ʌptaun] (*US*) *adv* hacia las
afueras ▷ *adj* exterior, de las afueras

upward ['ʌpwəd] *adj* ascendente;
upward(s) *adv* hacia arriba; (*more
than*): **upward(s) of** más de

uranium [juə'reɪnɪəm] *n* uranio

Uranus [juə'reɪnəs] *n* Urano

urban ['ə:bən] *adj* urbano

urge [ə:dʒ] *n* (*desire*) deseo ▷ *vt*: **to ~
sb to do sth** animar a algn a hacer algo

urgency ['ə:dʒənsɪ] *n* urgencia

urgent ['ə:dʒənt] *adj* urgente; (*voice*)
perentorio

urinal ['juərɪnl] *n* (*building*) urinario;
(*vessel*) orinal *m*

urinate ['juərɪneɪt] *vi* orinar

urine ['juərɪn] *n* orina, orines *mpl*

US *n abbr* (= *United States*) EE. UU.

us [ʌs] *pron* nos; (*after prep*) nosotros/
as; *see also* **me**

USA *n abbr* (= *United States* (*of America*))
EE.UU.

use [*n* ju:s, *vb* ju:z] *n* uso, empleo;
(*usefulness*) utilidad *f* ▷ *vt* usar,
emplear; **she ~d to do it** (ella) solía *or*
acostumbraba hacerlo; **in ~** en uso; **out
of ~** en desuso; **to be of ~** servir; **it's
no ~** (*pointless*) es inútil; (*not useful*) no
sirve; **to be ~d to** estar acostumbrado
a, acostumbrar; **use up** *vt* (*food*)
consumir; (*money*) gastar; **used** [ju:zd]
adj (*car*) usado; **useful** *adj* útil;
useless *adj* (*unusable*) inservible;
(*pointless*) inútil; (*person*) inepto;
user *n* usuario/a; **user-friendly** *adj*
(*computer*) amistoso

usual ['ju:ʒuəl] *adj* normal, corriente;
as ~ como de costumbre; **usually** *adv*
normalmente

utensil [ju:'tɛnsl] *n* utensilio;
kitchen ~s batería de cocina

utility [ju:'tɪlɪtɪ] *n* utilidad *f*; (*public
utility*) (empresa de) servicio público

utilize ['ju:tɪlaɪz] *vt* utilizar

utmost ['ʌtməust] *adj* mayor ▷ *n*: **to
do one's ~** hacer todo lo posible

utter ['ʌtə*] *adj* total, completo
▷ *vt* pronunciar, proferir; **utterly** *adv*
completamente, totalmente

U-turn ['ju:'tə:n] *n* viraje *m* en
redondo

V

v. *abbr* = **verse; versus**; (= *volt*) v;
(= *vide*) véase

vacancy ['veɪkənsɪ] *n* (*BRIT: job*)
vacante *f*; (*room*) habitación *f* libre; **"no
vacancies"** "completo"

vacant ['veɪkənt] *adj* desocupado,
libre; (*expression*) distraído

vacate [və'keɪt] *vt* (*house, room*)
desocupar; (*job*) dejar (vacante)

vacation [və'keɪʃən] *n* vacaciones
fpl; **vacationer** (*us* **vacationist**) *n*
turista *m/f*

vaccination [væksɪ'neɪʃən] *n*
vacunación *f*

vaccine ['væksiːn] *n* vacuna

vacuum ['vækjum] *n* vacío; **vacuum
cleaner** *n* aspiradora

vagina [və'dʒaɪnə] *n* vagina

vague [veɪg] *adj* (*memory*)
borroso; (*ambiguous*) impreciso;
(*person: absent-minded*) distraído;
(: *evasive*): **to be ~** no decir las cosas
claramente

vain [veɪn] *adj* (*conceited*) presumido;
(*useless*) vano, inútil; **in ~** en vano

Valentine's Day ['væləntaɪnzdeɪ] *n*
día de los enamorados

valid ['vælɪd] *adj* válido; (*ticket*)
valedero; (*law*) vigente

valley ['vælɪ] *n* valle *m*

valuable ['væljuəbl] *adj* (*jewel*) de
valor; (*time*) valioso; **valuables** *npl*
objetos *mpl* de valor

value ['væljuː] *n* valor *m*; (*importance*)
importancia ▷ *vt* (*fix price of*) tasar,
valorar; (*esteem*) apreciar; **values** *npl*
(*principles*) principios *mpl*

valve [vælv] *n* válvula

vampire ['væmpaɪə*] *n* vampiro

van [væn] *n* (*Aut*) furgoneta,
camioneta

vandal ['vændl] *n* vándalo/a;
vandalism *n* vandalismo; **vandalize**
vt dañar, destruir

vanilla [və'nɪlə] *n* vainilla

vanish ['vænɪʃ] *vi* desaparecer

vanity ['vænɪtɪ] *n* vanidad *f*

vapour ['veɪpə*] (*us* **vapor**) *n* vapor
m; (*on breath, window*) vaho

variable ['vɛərɪəbl] *adj* variable

variant ['vɛərɪənt] *n* variante *f*

variation [vɛərɪ'eɪʃən] *n* variación *f*

varied ['vɛərɪd] *adj* variado

variety [və'raɪətɪ] *n* (*diversity*)
diversidad *f*; (*type*) variedad *f*

various ['vɛərɪəs] *adj* (*several: people*)
varios/as; (*reasons*) diversos/as

varnish ['vɑːnɪʃ] *n* barniz *m*; (*nail
varnish*) esmalte *m* ▷ *vt* barnizar; (*nails*)
pintar (con esmalte)

vary ['vɛərɪ] *vt* variar; (*change*)
cambiar ▷ *vi* variar

vase [vɑːz] *n* jarrón *m*

⎸ Be careful not to translate **vase** by
⎸ the Spanish word *vaso*.

Vaseline® ['væsɪliːn] *n* vaselina®

vast [vɑːst] *adj* enorme

VAT [væt] (*BRIT*) *n abbr* (= *value added
tax*) IVA *m*

vault [vɔːlt] *n* (*of roof*) bóveda;
(*tomb*) panteón *m*; (*in bank*) cámara
acorazada ▷ *vt* (*also*: **~ over**) saltar
(por encima de)

VCR *n abbr* = **video cassette recorder**

VDU *n abbr* (= *visual display unit*) UPV f

veal [viːl] *n* ternera

veer [vɪə*] *vi* (*vehicle*) virar; (*wind*) girar

vegan ['viːgən] *n* vegetariano/a estricto/a, vegetaliano/a

vegetable ['vɛdʒtəbl] *n* (*Bot*) vegetal *m*; (*edible plant*) legumbre f, hortaliza ▷ *adj* vegetal

vegetarian [vɛdʒɪ'tɛərɪən] *adj, n* vegetariano/a *m/f*

vegetation [vɛdʒɪ'teɪʃən] *n* vegetación f

vehicle ['viːɪkl] *n* vehículo; (*fig*) medio

veil [veɪl] *n* velo ▷ *vt* velar

vein [veɪn] *n* vena; (*of ore etc*) veta

Velcro® ['vɛlkrəu] *n* velcro® *m*

velvet ['vɛlvɪt] *n* terciopelo

vending machine ['vɛndɪŋ-] *n* distribuidor *m* automático

vendor ['vɛndə*] *n* vendedor(a) *m/f*; **street ~** vendedor(a) *m/f* callejero/a

vengeance ['vɛndʒəns] *n* venganza; **with a ~** (*fig*) con creces

venison ['vɛnɪsn] *n* carne f de venado

venom ['vɛnəm] *n* veneno; (*bitterness*) odio

vent [vɛnt] *n* (*in jacket*) respiradero; (*in wall*) rejilla (de ventilación) ▷ *vt* (*fig: feelings*) desahogar

ventilation [vɛntɪ'leɪʃən] *n* ventilación f

venture ['vɛntʃə*] *n* empresa ▷ *vt* (*opinion*) ofrecer ▷ *vi* arriesgarse, lanzarse; **business ~** empresa comercial

venue ['vɛnjuː] *n* lugar *m*

Venus ['viːnəs] *n* Venus *m*

verb [vəːb] *n* verbo; **verbal** *adj* verbal

verdict ['vəːdɪkt] *n* veredicto, fallo; (*fig*) opinión f, juicio

verge [vəːdʒ] (*BRIT*) *n* borde *m*; **"soft ~s"** (*Aut*) "arcén *m* no asfaltado"; **to be on the ~ of doing sth** estar a punto de hacer algo

verify ['vɛrɪfaɪ] *vt* comprobar, verificar

versatile ['vəːsətaɪl] *adj* (*person*) polifacético; (*machine, tool etc*) versátil

verse [vəːs] *n* poesía; (*stanza*) estrofa; (*in bible*) versículo

version ['vəːʃən] *n* versión f

versus ['vəːsəs] *prep* contra

vertical ['vəːtɪkl] *adj* vertical

very ['vɛrɪ] *adv* muy ▷ *adj*: **the ~ book which** el mismo libro que; **the ~ last** el último de todos; **at the ~ least** al menos; **~ much** muchísimo

vessel ['vɛsl] *n* (*ship*) barco; (*container*) vasija; *see* **blood**

vest [vɛst] *n* (*BRIT*) camiseta; (*US: waistcoat*) chaleco

vet [vɛt] *vt* (*candidate*) investigar ▷ *n abbr* (*BRIT*) = **veterinary surgeon**

veteran ['vɛtərn] *n* excombatiente *mf*, veterano/a

veterinary surgeon ['vɛtrɪnərɪ-] (*US* **veterinarian**) *n* veterinario/a *m/f*

veto ['viːtəu] (*pl* **-es**) *n* veto ▷ *vt* prohibir, poner el veto a

via ['vaɪə] *prep* por, por medio de

viable ['vaɪəbl] *adj* viable

vibrate [vaɪ'breɪt] *vi* vibrar

vibration [vaɪ'breɪʃən] *n* vibración f

vicar ['vɪkə*] *n* párroco (de la Iglesia Anglicana)

vice [vaɪs] *n* (*evil*) vicio; (*Tech*) torno de banco; **vice-chairman** (*irreg*) *n* vicepresidente *m*

vice versa ['vaɪsɪ'vəːsə] *adv* viceversa

vicinity [vɪ'sɪnɪtɪ] *n*: **in the ~ (of)** cercano (a)

vicious ['vɪʃəs] *adj* (*attack*) violento; (*words*) cruel; (*horse, dog*) resabido

victim ['vɪktɪm] *n* víctima

victor ['vɪktə*] *n* vencedor(a) *m/f*

Victorian [vɪk'tɔːrɪən] *adj* victoriano

victorious [vɪk'tɔːrɪəs] *adj* vencedor(a)

victory ['vɪktərɪ] *n* victoria

video ['vɪdɪəu] *n* vídeo (*SP*), video (*LAM*); **video call** *n* videollamada; **video camera** *n* videocámara, cámara de vídeo; **video (cassette) recorder** *n* vídeo (*SP*), video

(LAM); **video game** n videojuego;
videophone n videoteléfono; **video
shop** n videoclub m; **video tape** n
cinta de vídeo

vie [vaɪ] vi: **to ~ (with sb for sth)**
competir (con algn por algo)

Vienna [vɪ'ɛnə] n Viena

Vietnam [vjɛt'næm] n Vietnam
m; **Vietnamese** [-nə'miːz] n inv, adj
vietnamita mf

view [vjuː] n vista; (outlook)
perspectiva; (opinion) opinión f, criterio
▷ vt (look at) mirar; (fig) considerar;
on ~ (in museum etc) expuesto; **in full
~ (of)** en plena vista (de); **in ~ of the
weather/the fact that** en vista del
tiempo/del hecho de que; **in my ~** en
mi opinión; **viewer** n espectador(a)
m/f; (TV) telespectador(a) m/f;
viewpoint n (attitude) punto de vista;
(place) mirador m

vigilant [vɪdʒɪlənt] adj vigilante

vigorous ['vɪɡərəs] adj enérgico,
vigoroso

vile [vaɪl] adj vil, infame; (smell)
asqueroso; (temper) endemoniado

villa ['vɪlə] n (country house) casa de
campo; (suburban house) chalet m

village ['vɪlɪdʒ] n aldea; **villager** n
aldeano/a

villain ['vɪlən] n (scoundrel) malvado/
a; (in novel) malo; (BRIT: criminal)
maleante mf

vinaigrette [vɪneɪ'ɡrɛt] n vinagreta

vine [vaɪn] n vid f

vinegar ['vɪnɪɡə*] n vinagre m

vineyard ['vɪnjɑːd] n viña, viñedo

vintage ['vɪntɪdʒ] n (year) vendimia,
cosecha ▷ cpd de época

vinyl ['vaɪnl] n vinilo

viola [vɪ'əʊlə] n (Mus) viola

violate ['vaɪəleɪt] vt violar

violation [vaɪə'leɪʃən] n violación f;
in ~ of sth en violación de algo

violence ['vaɪələns] n violencia

violent ['vaɪələnt] adj violento;
(intense) intenso

violet ['vaɪələt] adj violado, violeta

▷ n (plant) violeta

violin [vaɪə'lɪn] n violín m

VIP n abbr (= very important person) VIP m

virgin ['vəːdʒɪn] n virgen f

Virgo ['vəːɡəʊ] n Virgo

virtual ['vəːtjuəl] adj virtual;
virtually adv prácticamente; **virtual
reality** n (Comput) mundo or realidad
f virtual

virtue ['vəːtjuː] n virtud f; (advantage)
ventaja; **by ~ of** en virtud de

virus ['vaɪərəs] n (also Comput)
virus m inv

visa ['viːzə] n visado (SP), visa (LAM)

vise [vaɪs] (US) n (Tech) = **vice**

visibility [vɪzɪ'bɪlɪtɪ] n visibilidad f

visible ['vɪzəbl] adj visible

vision ['vɪʒən] n (sight) vista;
(foresight, in dream) visión f

visit ['vɪzɪt] n visita ▷ vt (person
(US: also: ~ **with**)) visitar, hacer una
visita a; (place) ir a, (ir a) conocer;
visiting hours npl (in hospital etc)
horas fpl de visita; **visitor** n (in
museum) visitante mf; (invited to house)
visita; (tourist) turista mf; **visitor
centre** (US **visitor center**) n centro m
de información

visual ['vɪzjuəl] adj visual; **visualize**
vt imaginarse

vital ['vaɪtl] adj (essential) esencial,
imprescindible; (dynamic) dinámico;
(organ) vital

vitality [vaɪ'tælɪtɪ] n energía,
vitalidad f

vitamin ['vɪtəmɪn] n vitamina

vivid ['vɪvɪd] adj (account) gráfico;
(light) intenso; (imagination, memory)
vivo

V-neck ['viːnɛk] n cuello de pico

vocabulary [vəʊ'kæbjuləɪ] n
vocabulario

vocal ['vəʊkl] adj vocal; (articulate)
elocuente

vocational [vəʊ'keɪʃənl] adj
profesional

vodka ['vɒdkə] n vodka m

vogue [vəʊɡ] n: **in ~** en boga

voice [vɔɪs] *n* voz *f* ▷ *vt* expresar; **voice mail** *n* buzón de voz

void [vɔɪd] *n* vacío; (*hole*) hueco ▷ *adj* (*invalid*) nulo, inválido; (*empty*): **~ of** carente *or* desprovisto de

volatile ['vɔlətaɪl] *adj* (*situation*) inestable; (*person*) voluble; (*liquid*) volátil

volcano [vɔl'keɪnəu] (*pl* **~es**) *n* volcán *m*

volleyball ['vɔlibɔːl] *n* vol(e)ibol *m*

volt [vəult] *n* voltio; **voltage** *n* voltaje *m*

volume ['vɔljuːm] *n* (*gen*) volumen *m*; (*book*) tomo

voluntarily ['vɔləntrɪli] *adv* libremente, voluntariamente

voluntary ['vɔləntəri] *adj* voluntario

volunteer [vɔlən'tɪə*] *n* voluntario/a ▷ *vt* (*information*) ofrecer ▷ *vi* ofrecerse (de voluntario); **to ~ to do** ofrecerse a hacer

vomit ['vɔmɪt] *n* vómito ▷ *vt, vi* vomitar

vote [vəut] *n* voto; (*votes cast*) votación *f*; (*right to vote*) derecho de votar; (*franchise*) sufragio ▷ *vt* (*chairman*) elegir; (*propose*): **to ~ that** proponer que ▷ *vi* votar, ir a votar; **~ of thanks** voto de gracias; **voter** *n* votante *mf*; **voting** *n* votación *f*

voucher ['vautʃə*] *n* (*for meal, petrol*) vale *m*

vow [vau] *n* voto ▷ *vt*: **to ~ to do/ that** jurar hacer/que

vowel ['vauəl] *n* vocal *f*

voyage ['vɔɪɪdʒ] *n* viaje *m*

vulgar ['vʌlgə*] *adj* (*rude*) ordinario, grosero; (*in bad taste*) de mal gusto

vulnerable ['vʌlnərəbl] *adj* vulnerable

vulture ['vʌltʃə*] *n* buitre *m*

waddle ['wɔdl] *vi* anadear

wade [weɪd] *vi*: **to ~ through** (*water*) vadear; (*fig: book*) leer con dificultad

wafer ['weɪfə*] *n* galleta, barquillo

waffle ['wɔfl] *n* (*Culin*) gofre *m* ▷ *vi* dar el rollo

wag [wæg] *vt* menear, agitar ▷ *vi* moverse, menearse

wage [weɪdʒ] *n* (*also*: **~s**) sueldo, salario ▷ *vt*: **to ~ war** hacer la guerra

wag(g)on ['wægən] *n* (*horse-drawn*) carro; (*BRIT Rail*) vagón *m*

wail [weɪl] *n* gemido ▷ *vi* gemir

waist [weɪst] *n* cintura, talle *m*; **waistcoat** (*BRIT*) *n* chaleco

wait [weɪt] *n* (*interval*) pausa ▷ *vi* esperar; **to lie in ~ for** acechar a; **I can't ~ to** (*fig*) estoy deseando; **to ~ for** esperar (a); **wait on** *vt fus* servir a; **waiter** *n* camarero; **waiting list** *n* lista de espera; **waiting room** *n* sala de espera; **waitress** ['weɪtrɪs] *n* camarera

waive [weɪv] *vt* suspender

wake [weɪk] (*pt* **woke** *or* **~d**, *pp* **woken**

or **~d**) *vt* (*also:* **~ up**) despertar ▷ *vi*
(*also:* **~ up**) despertarse ▷ *n* (*for dead person*) vela, velatorio; (*Naut*) estela
Wales [weɪlz] *n* País *m* de Gales; **the Prince of ~** el príncipe de Gales
walk [wɔːk] *n* (*stroll*) paseo; (*hike*) excursión *f* a pie, caminata; (*gait*) paso, andar *m*; (*in park etc*) paseo, alameda ▷ *vi* andar, caminar; (*for pleasure, exercise*) pasear ▷ *vt* (*distance*) recorrer a pie, andar; (*dog*) pasear; **10 minutes' ~ from here** a 10 minutos de aquí andando; **people from all ~s of life** gente de todas las esferas; **walk out** *vi* (*audience*) salir; (*workers*) declararse en huelga; **walker** *n* (*person*) paseante *mf*, caminante *mf*; **walkie-talkie** [ˈwɔːkɪˈtɔːkɪ] *n* walkie-talkie *m*; **walking** *n* el andar; **walking shoes** *npl* zapatos *mpl* para andar; **walking stick** *n* bastón *m*; **Walkman®** *n* Walkman® *m*; **walkway** *n* paseo
wall [wɔːl] *n* pared *f*; (*exterior*) muro; (*city wall etc*) muralla
wallet [ˈwɔlɪt] *n* cartera, billetera
wallpaper [ˈwɔːlpeɪpə*] *n* papel *m* pintado ▷ *vt* empapelar
walnut [ˈwɔːlnʌt] *n* nuez *f*; (*tree*) nogal *m*
walrus [ˈwɔːlrəs] (*pl* **~** *or* **~es**) *n* morsa
waltz [wɔːlts] *n* vals *m* ▷ *vi* bailar el vals
wand [wɔnd] *n* (*also:* **magic ~**) varita (mágica)
wander [ˈwɔndə*] *vi* (*person*) vagar; deambular; (*thoughts*) divagar ▷ *vt* recorrer, vagar por
want [wɔnt] *vt* querer, desear; (*need*) necesitar ▷ *n*: **for ~ of** por falta de; **wanted** *adj* (*criminal*) buscado; **"wanted"** (*in advertisements*) "se busca"
war [wɔː*] *n* guerra; **to make ~ (on)** declarar la guerra (a)
ward [wɔːd] *n* (*in hospital*) sala; (*Pol*) distrito electoral; (*Law: child: also:* **~ of court**) pupilo/a
warden [ˈwɔːdn] *n* (BRIT: *of institution*) director(a) *m/f*; (*of park, game reserve*)

guardián/ana *m/f*; (BRIT: *also:* **traffic ~**) guardia *mf*
wardrobe [ˈwɔːdrəub] *n* armario, ropero; (*clothes*) vestuario
warehouse [ˈwɛəhaus] *n* almacén *m*, depósito
warfare [ˈwɔːfɛə*] *n* guerra
warhead [ˈwɔːhɛd] *n* cabeza armada
warm [wɔːm] *adj* caliente; (*thanks*) efusivo; (*clothes etc*) abrigado; (*welcome, day*) caluroso; **it's ~** hace calor; **I'm ~** tengo calor; **warm up** *vi* (*room*) calentarse; (*person*) entrar en calor; (*athlete*) hacer ejercicios de calentamiento ▷ *vt* calentar; **warmly** *adv* afectuosamente; **warmth** *n* calor *m*
warn [wɔːn] *vt* avisar, advertir; **warning** *n* aviso, advertencia; **warning light** *n* luz *f* de advertencia
warrant [ˈwɔrnt] *n* autorización *f*; (*Law: to arrest*) orden *f* de detención; (*: to search*) mandamiento de registro
warranty [ˈwɔrənti] *n* garantía
warrior [ˈwɔrɪə*] *n* guerrero/a
Warsaw [ˈwɔːsɔː] *n* Varsovia
warship [ˈwɔːʃɪp] *n* buque *m* *or* barco de guerra
wart [wɔːt] *n* verruga
wartime [ˈwɔːtaɪm] *n*: **in ~** en tiempos de guerra, en la guerra
wary [ˈwɛərɪ] *adj* cauteloso
was [wɔz] *pt of* **be**
wash [wɔʃ] *vt* lavar ▷ *vi* lavarse; (*sea etc*): **to ~ against/over sth** llegar hasta/cubrir algo ▷ *n* (*clothes etc*) lavado; (*of ship*) estela; **to have a ~** lavarse; **wash up** *vi* (BRIT) fregar los platos; (US) lavarse; **washbasin** (US) *n* lavabo; **wash cloth** (US) *n* manopla; **washer** *n* (*Tech*) arandela; **washing** *n* (*dirty*) ropa sucia; (*clean*) colada; **washing line** *n* cuerda de (colgar) la ropa; **washing machine** *n* lavadora; **washing powder** (BRIT) *n* detergente *m* (en polvo)
Washington [ˈwɔʃɪntən] *n* Washington *m*

W

wash: washing-up(*BRIT*) *n* fregado, platos *mpl* (para fregar); **washing-up liquid**(*BRIT*) *n* líquido lavavajillas; **washroom**(*US*) *n* servicios *mpl*

wasn't ['wɔznt] = **was not**

wasp [wɔsp] *n* avispa

waste [weɪst] *n* derroche *m*, despilfarro; (*of time*) pérdida; (*food*) sobras *fpl*; (*rubbish*) basura, desperdicios *mpl* ▷ *adj* (*material*) de desecho; (*left over*) sobrante; (*land*) baldío, descampado ▷ *vt* malgastar, derrochar; (*time*) perder; (*opportunity*) desperdiciar; **waste ground**(*BRIT*) terreno baldío; **wastepaper basket** *n* papelera

watch [wɔtʃ] *n* (*also:* **wrist ~**) reloj *m*; (*Mil: group of guards*) centinela *m*; (*act*) vigilancia; (*Naut: spell of duty*) guardia ▷ *vt* (*look at*) mirar, observar; (: *match, programme*) ver; (*spy on, guard*) vigilar; (*be careful of*) cuidarse de, tener cuidado de ▷ *vi* ver, mirar; (*keep guard*) montar guardia; **watch out** *vi* cuidarse, tener cuidado; **watchdog** *n* perro guardián; (*fig*) persona u organismo encargado de asegurarse de que las empresas actúan dentro de la legalidad; **watch strap** *n* pulsera (de reloj)

water ['wɔ:tə*] *n* agua ▷ *vt* (*plant*) regar ▷ *vi* (*eyes*) llorar; (*mouth*) hacerse la boca agua; **water down** *vt* (*milk etc*) aguar; (*fig: story*) dulcificar, diluir; **watercolour**(*US* **watercolor**) *n* acuarela; **watercress** *n* berro; **waterfall** *n* cascada, salto de agua; **watering can** *n* regadera; **watermelon** *n* sandía; **waterproof** *adj* impermeable; **water-skiing** *n* esquí *m* acuático

watt [wɔt] *n* vatio

wave [weɪv] *n* (*of hand*) señal *f* con la mano; (*on water*) ola; (*Radio, in hair*) onda; (*fig*) oleada ▷ *vi* agitar la mano; (*flag etc*) ondear ▷ *vt* (*handkerchief, gun*) agitar; **wavelength** *n* longitud *f* de onda

waver ['weɪvə*] *vi* (*voice, love etc*) flaquear; (*person*) vacilar

wavy ['weɪvɪ] *adj* ondulado

wax [wæks] *n* cera ▷ *vt* encerar ▷ *vi* (*moon*) crecer

way [weɪ] *n* camino; (*distance*) trayecto, recorrido; (*direction*) dirección *f*, sentido; (*manner*) modo, manera; (*habit*) costumbre *f*; **which ~? - this ~** ¿por dónde? *or* ¿en qué dirección? - por aquí; **on the ~** (*en route*) en (el) camino; **to be on one's ~** estar en camino; **to be in the ~** bloquear el camino; (*fig*) estorbar; **to go out of one's ~ to do sth** desvivirse por hacer algo; **under ~** en marcha; **to lose one's ~** extraviarse; **in a ~** en cierto modo *or* sentido; **no ~!** (*inf*) ¡de eso nada!; **by the ~ ...** a propósito ...; **"~ in"** (*BRIT*) "entrada"; **"~ out"** (*BRIT*) "salida"; **the ~ back** el camino de vuelta; **"give ~"** (*BRIT Aut*) "ceda el paso"

W.C. *n* (*BRIT*) wáter *m*

we [wi:] *pl pron* nosotros/as

weak [wi:k] *adj* débil, flojo; (*tea etc*) claro; **weaken** *vi* debilitarse; (*give way*) ceder ▷ *vt* debilitar; **weakness** *n* debilidad *f*; (*fault*) punto débil; **to have a weakness for** tener debilidad por

wealth [wɛlθ] *n* riqueza; (*of details*) abundancia; **wealthy** *adj* rico

weapon ['wɛpən] *n* arma; **~s of mass destruction** armas de destrucción masiva

wear [wɛə*] (*pt* **wore**, *pp* **worn**) *n* (*use*) uso; (*deterioration through use*) desgaste *m* ▷ *vt* (*clothes*) llevar; (*shoes*) calzar; (*damage: through use*) gastar, usar ▷ *vi* (*last*) durar; (*rub through etc*) desgastarse; **evening ~** ropa de etiqueta; **sports~/baby~** ropa de deportes/de niños; **wear off** *vi* (*pain etc*) pasar, desaparecer; **wear out** *vt* desgastar; (*person, strength*) agotar

weary ['wɪərɪ] *adj* cansado; (*dispirited*) abatido ▷ *vi*: **to ~ of** cansarse de

weasel ['wi:zl] *n* (*Zool*) comadreja

weather ['wɛðə*] *n* tiempo ▷ *vt* (*storm, crisis*) hacer frente a; **under**

the ~ (fig: ill) indispuesto, pachucho; **weather forecast** n boletín m meteorológico

weave [wiːv] (pt **wove**, pp **woven**) vt (cloth) tejer; (fig) entretejer

web [wɛb] n (of spider) telaraña; (on duck's foot) membrana; (network) red f; **the (World Wide) W~** la Red; **web address** n dirección f de Internet; **webcam** n webcam f; **web page** n (página) web m or f; **website** n sitio web

Wed. abbr (= Wednesday) miérc

wed [wɛd] (pt, pp **~ded**) vt casar ▷vi casarse

we'd [wiːd] = **we had**; **we would**

wedding ['wɛdɪŋ] n boda, casamiento; **silver/golden ~ (anniversary)** bodas fpl de plata/de oro; **wedding anniversary** n aniversario de boda; **wedding day** n día m de la boda; **wedding dress** n traje m de novia; **wedding ring** n alianza

wedge [wɛdʒ] n (of wood etc) cuña; (of cake) trozo ▷vt acuñar; (push) apretar

Wednesday ['wɛdnzdɪ] n miércoles m inv

wee [wiː] (SCOTTISH) adj pequeñito

weed [wiːd] n mala hierba, maleza ▷vt escardar, desherbar; **weedkiller** n herbicida m

week [wiːk] n semana; **a ~ today/on Friday** de hoy/del viernes en ocho días; **weekday** n día m laborable; **weekend** n fin m de semana; **weekly** adv semanalmente, cada semana ▷adj semanal ▷n semanario

weep [wiːp] (pt, pp **wept**) vi, vt llorar

weigh [weɪ] vt, vi pesar; **to ~ anchor** levar anclas; **weigh up** vt sopesar

weight [weɪt] n peso; (metal weight) pesa; **to lose/put on ~** adelgazar/engordar; **weightlifting** n levantamiento de pesas

weir [wɪə*] n presa

weird [wɪəd] adj raro, extraño

welcome ['wɛlkəm] adj bienvenido ▷n bienvenida ▷vt dar la bienvenida a; (be glad of) alegrarse de; **thank you – you're ~** gracias – de nada

weld [wɛld] n soldadura ▷vt soldar

welfare ['wɛlfɛə*] n bienestar m; (social aid) asistencia social; **welfare state** n estado del bienestar

well [wɛl] n fuente f, pozo ▷adv bien ▷ adj: **to be ~** estar bien (de salud) ▷excl ¡vaya!, ¡bueno!; **as ~** también; **as ~ as** además de; **~ done!** ¡bien hecho!; **get ~ soon!** ¡que te mejores pronto!; **to do ~** (business) ir bien; (person) tener éxito

we'll [wiːl] = **we will**; **we shall**

well: well-behaved adj bueno; **well-built** adj (person) fornido; **well-dressed** adj bien vestido

wellies ['wɛlɪz] (inf) npl (BRIT) botas de goma

well: well-known adj (person) conocido; **well-off** adj acomodado; **well-paid** [wɛl'peɪd] adj bien pagado, bien retribuido

Welsh [wɛlʃ] adj galés/esa ▷n (LING) galés m; **Welshman** (irreg) n galés m; **Welshwoman** (irreg) n galesa

went [wɛnt] pt of **go**

wept [wɛpt] pt, pp of **weep**

were [wə:*] pt of **be**

we're [wɪə*] = **we are**

weren't [wə:nt] = **were not**

west [wɛst] n oeste m ▷adj occidental, del oeste ▷adv al or hacia el oeste; **the W~** el Oeste, el Occidente; **westbound** ['wɛstbaund] adj (traffic, carriageway) con rumbo al oeste; **western** adj occidental ▷n (Cinema) película del oeste; **West Indian** adj, n antillano/a m/f

wet [wɛt] adj (damp) húmedo; (soaked) ▷adj mojado; (rainy) lluvioso ▷n (BRIT: Pol) conservador(a) m/f moderado/a; **to get ~** mojarse; **"~ paint"** "recién pintado"; **wetsuit** n traje m térmico

we've [wiːv] = **we have**

whack [wæk] vt dar un buen golpe a

whale [weɪl] n (Zool) ballena

W

wharf [wɔːf] (pl **wharves**) n muelle
m

○ **KEYWORD**

what [wɔt] adj **1** (in direct/indirect
questions) qué; **what size is he?** ¿qué
talla usa?; **what colour/shape is it?**
¿de qué color/forma es?
2 (in exclamations): **what a mess!** ¡qué
desastre!; **what a fool I am!** ¡qué
tonto soy!
▷ pron **1** (interrogative) qué; **what
are you doing?** ¿qué haces or estás
haciendo?; **what is happening?** ¿qué
pasa or está pasando?; **what is it
called?** ¿cómo se llama?; **what about
me?** ¿y yo qué?; **what about doing ...?**
¿qué tal si hacemos ...?
2 (relative) lo que; **I saw what you
did/was on the table** vi lo que hiciste/
había en la mesa
▷ excl (disbelieving) ¡cómo!; **what, no
coffee!** ¡que no hay café!

whatever [wɔtˈɛvə*] adj: **~ book
you choose** cualquier libro que elijas
▷ pron: **do ~ is necessary** haga lo que
sea necesario; **~ happens** pase lo que
pase; **no reason ~** or **whatsoever**
ninguna razón sea la que sea; **nothing
~** nada en absoluto
whatsoever [wɔtsəuˈɛvə*] adj see
whatever
wheat [wiːt] n trigo
wheel [wiːl] n rueda; (Aut: also:
steering ~) volante m; (Naut)
timón m ▷ vt (pram etc) empujar
▷ vi (also: **~ round**) dar la vuelta,
girar; **wheelbarrow** n carretilla;
wheelchair n silla de ruedas; **wheel
clamp** n (Aut) cepo
wheeze [wiːz] vi resollar

○ **KEYWORD**

when [wɛn] adv cuando; **when did
it happen?** ¿cuándo ocurrió?; **I know
when it happened** sé cuándo
ocurrió
▷ conj **1** (at, during, after the time that)
cuando; **be careful when you cross
the road** ten cuidado al cruzar la calle;
that was when I needed you fue
entonces que te necesité
2 (on, at which): **on the day when I met
him** el día en qué le conocí
3 (whereas) cuando

whenever [wɛnˈɛvə*] conj cuando;
(every time that) cada vez que ▷ adv
cuando sea
where [wɛə*] adv dónde ▷ conj
donde; **this is ~** aquí es donde;
whereabouts adv dónde ▷ n: **nobody
knows his whereabouts** nadie conoce
su paradero; **whereas** conj visto que,
mientras; **whereby** pron por lo cual;
wherever conj dondequiera que;
(interrogative) dónde
whether [ˈwɛðə*] conj si; **I don't
know ~ to accept or not** no sé si
aceptar o no; **~ you go or not** vayas
o no vayas

○ **KEYWORD**

which [wɪtʃ] adj **1** (interrogative: direct,
indirect) qué; **which picture(s) do you
want?** ¿qué cuadro(s) quieres?; **which
one?** ¿cuál?
2 in which case en cuyo caso; **we got
there at 8 pm, by which time the
cinema was full** llegamos allí a las 8,
cuando el cine estaba lleno
▷ pron **1** (interrogative) cual; **I don't
mind which** el/la que sea
2 (relative: replacing noun) que; (: replacing
clause) lo que; (: after preposition) (el(la))
que etc el/la cual etc; **the apple which
you ate/which is on the table** la
manzana que comiste/que está en
la mesa; **the chair on which you are
sitting** la silla en la que estás sentado;
**he said he knew, which is true/I
feared** dijo que lo sabía, lo cual or lo

que es cierto/me temía

whichever [wɪtʃˈɛvə*] *adj*: **take ~ book you prefer** coja (*SP*) el libro que prefiera; **~ book you take** cualquier libro que coja

while [waɪl] *n* rato, momento ▷ *conj* mientras; (*although*) aunque; **for a ~** durante algún tiempo

whilst [waɪlst] *conj* = **while**

whim [wɪm] *n* capricho

whine [waɪn] *n* (*of pain*) gemido; (*of engine*) zumbido; (*of siren*) aullido ▷ *vi* gemir; zumbar; (*fig: complain*) gimotear

whip [wɪp] *n* látigo; (*Pol: person*) encargado de la disciplina partidaria en el parlamento ▷ *vt* azotar; (*Culin*) batir; (*move quickly*): **to ~ sth out/off** sacar/quitar algo de un tirón; **whipped cream** *n* nata or crema montada

whirl [wə:l] *vt* hacer girar, dar vueltas a ▷ *vi* girar, dar vueltas; (*leaves etc*) arremolinarse

whisk [wɪsk] *n* (*Culin*) batidor *m* ▷ *vt* (*Culin*) batir; **to ~ sb away** or **off** llevar volando a algn

whiskers [ˈwɪskəz] *npl* (*of animal*) bigotes *mpl*; (*of man*) patillas *fpl*

whiskey [ˈwɪskɪ] (*US, IRELAND*) *n* = **whisky**

whisky [ˈwɪskɪ] *n* whisky *m*

whisper [ˈwɪspə*] *n* susurro ▷ *vi*, *vt* susurrar

whistle [ˈwɪsl] *n* (*sound*) silbido; (*object*) silbato ▷ *vi* silbar

white [waɪt] *adj* blanco; (*pale*) pálido ▷ *n* blanco; (*of egg*) clara; **whiteboard** *n* pizarra blanca; **interactive whiteboard** pizarra interactiva; **White House** (*US*) *n* Casa Blanca; **whitewash** *n* (*paint*) jalbegue *m*, cal *f* ▷ *vt* blanquear

whiting [ˈwaɪtɪŋ] *n inv* (*fish*) pescadilla

Whitsun [ˈwɪtsn] *n* pentecostés *m*

whittle [ˈwɪtl] *vt*: **to ~ away, ~ down** ir reduciendo

whizz [wɪz] *vi*: **to ~ past** or **by** pasar a toda velocidad

○ **KEYWORD**

who [hu:] *pron* **1** (*interrogative*) quién; **who is it?**, **who's there?** ¿quién es?; **who are you looking for?** ¿a quién buscas?; **I told her who I was** le dije quién era yo
2 (*relative*) que; **the man/woman who spoke to me** el hombre/la mujer que habló conmigo; **those who can swim** los que saben or sepan nadar

whoever [hu:ˈɛvə*] *pron*: **~ finds it** cualquiera or quienquiera que lo encuentre, **ask ~ you like** pregunta a quien quieras; **~ he marries** no importa con quién se case

whole [həul] *adj* (*entire*) todo, entero; (*not broken*) intacto ▷ *n* todo; (*all*): **the ~ of the town** toda la ciudad, la ciudad entera ▷ *n* (*total*) total *m*; (*sum*) conjunto; **on the ~, as a ~** en general; **wholefood(s)** *n(pl)* alimento(s) *m(pl)* integral(es); **wholeheartedly** [həulˈhɑːtɪdlɪ] *adv* con entusiasmo; **wholemeal** *adj* integral; **wholesale** *n* venta al por mayor ▷ *adj* al por mayor; (*fig: destruction*) sistemático; **wholewheat** *adj* = **wholemeal**; **wholly** *adv* totalmente, enteramente

○ **KEYWORD**

whom [hu:m] *pron* **1** (*interrogative*): **whom did you see?** ¿a quién viste?; **to whom did you give it?** ¿a quién se lo diste?; **tell me from whom you received it** dígame de quién lo recibí
2 (*relative*) que; **to whom** a quien(es); **of whom** de quien(es), del/de la que *etc*; **the man whom I saw/to whom I wrote** el hombre que vi/a quien escribí; **the lady about/with whom I was talking** la señora de (la) que/con

quien or (la) que hablaba

whore [hɔ:*] (inf, pej) n puta

○ **KEYWORD**

whose [hu:z] adj 1 (possessive: interrogative): **whose book is this?**, **whose is this book?** ¿de quién es este libro?; **whose pencil have you taken?** ¿de quién es el lápiz que has cogido?; **whose daughter are you?** ¿de quién eres hija?
2 (possessive: relative) cuyo/a, pl cuyos/as; **the man whose son you rescued** el hombre cuyo hijo rescataste; **those whose passports I have** aquellas personas cuyos pasaportes tengo; **the woman whose car was stolen** la mujer a quien le robaron el coche
▷ pron de quién; **whose is this?** ¿de quién es esto?; **I know whose it is** sé de quién es

○ **KEYWORD**

why [waɪ] adv por qué; **why not?** ¿por qué no?; **why not do it now?** ¿por qué no lo haces (or hacemos etc) ahora?
▷ conj: **I wonder why he said that** me pregunto por qué dijo eso; **that's not why I'm here** no es por eso (por lo) que estoy aquí; **the reason why** la razón por la que
▷ excl (expressing surprise, shock, annoyance) ¡hombre!, ¡vaya!; (explaining): **why, it's you!** ¡hombre, eres tú!; **why, that's impossible** ¡pero sí eso es imposible!

wicked ['wɪkɪd] adj malvado, cruel
wicket ['wɪkɪt] n (Cricket: stumps) palos mpl; (: grass area) terreno de juego
wide [waɪd] adj ancho; (area, knowledge) vasto, grande; (choice) amplio ▷ adv: **to open ~** abrir de par en par; **to shoot ~** errar el tiro; **widely** adv (travelled) mucho; (spaced) muy;

it is widely believed/known that ... mucha gente piensa/sabe que ...; **widen** vt ensanchar; (experience) ampliar ▷ vi ensancharse; **wide open** adj abierto de par en par; **widespread** adj extendido, general
widow ['wɪdəu] n viuda; **widower** n viudo
width [wɪdθ] n anchura; (of cloth) ancho
wield [wi:ld] vt (sword) blandir; (power) ejercer
wife [waɪf] (pl **wives**) n mujer f, esposa
Wi-Fi ['waɪfaɪ] n wifi m
wig [wɪg] n peluca
wild [waɪld] adj (animal) salvaje; (plant) silvestre; (person) furioso, violento; (idea) descabellado; (rough: sea) bravo; (: land) agreste; (: weather) muy revuelto; **wilderness** ['wɪldənɪs] n desierto; **wildlife** n fauna; **wildly** adv (behave) locamente; (lash out) a diestro y siniestro; (guess) a lo loco; (happy) a más no poder

○ **KEYWORD**

will [wɪl] aux vb 1 (forming future tense): **I will finish it tomorrow** lo terminaré or voy a terminar mañana; **I will have finished it by tomorrow** lo habré terminado para mañana; **will you do it? – yes I will/no I won't** ¿lo harás? – sí/no
2 (in conjectures, predictions): **he will** or **he'll be there by now** ya habrá or debe (de) haber llegado; **that will be the postman** será or debe ser el cartero
3 (in commands, requests, offers): **will you be quiet!** ¿quieres callarte?; **will you help me?** ¿quieres ayudarme?; **will you have a cup of tea?** ¿te apetece un té?; **I won't put up with it!** ¡no lo soporto!
▷ vt (pt, pp **willed**): **to will sb to do sth** desear que algn haga algo; **he willed himself to go on** con gran fuerza de voluntad, continuó

▷n voluntad f; (*testament*) testamento

willing ['wɪlɪŋ] *adj* (*with goodwill*) de buena voluntad; (*enthusiastic*) entusiasta; **he's ~ to do it** está dispuesto a hacerlo; **willingly** *adv* con mucho gusto

willow ['wɪləu] *n* sauce *m*

willpower ['wɪlpauə*] *n* fuerza de voluntad

wilt [wɪlt] *vi* marchitarse

win [wɪn] (*pt, pp* **won**) *n* victoria, triunfo ▷vt ganar; (*obtain*) conseguir, lograr ▷vi ganar; **win over** *vt* convencer a

wince [wɪns] *vi* encogerse

wind¹ [wɪnd] *n* viento; (*Med*) gases *mpl* ▷vt (*take breath away from*) dejar sin aliento a

wind² [waɪnd] (*pt, pp* **wound**) *vt* enrollar; (*wrap*) envolver; (*clock, toy*) dar cuerda a ▷vi (*road, river*) serpentear; **wind down** *vt* (*car window*) bajar; (*fig: production, business*) disminuir; **wind up** *vt* (*clock*) dar cuerda a; (*debate, meeting*) concluir, terminar

windfall ['wɪndfɔːl] *n* golpe *m* de suerte

wind farm *n* parque *m* eólico

winding ['waɪndɪŋ] *adj* (*road*) tortuoso; (*staircase*) de caracol

windmill ['wɪndmɪl] *n* molino de viento

window ['wɪndəu] *n* ventana; (*in car, train*) ventanilla; (*in shop etc*) escaparate *m* (*SP*), vidriera (*LAM*); **window box** *n* jardinera de ventana; **window cleaner** *n* (*person*) limpiacristales *mf inv*; **window pane** *n* cristal *m*; **window seat** *n* asiento junto a la ventana; **windowsill** *n* alféizar *m*, repisa

windscreen ['wɪndskriːn] (*US* **windshield**) *n* parabrisas *m inv*; **windscreen wiper** (*US* **windshield wiper**) *n* limpiaparabrisas *m inv*

windsurfing ['wɪndsəːfɪŋ] *n* windsurf *m*

windy ['wɪndɪ] *adj* de mucho viento;

it's ~ hace viento

wine [waɪn] *n* vino; **wine bar** *n* enoteca; **wine glass** *n* copa (para vino); **wine list** *n* lista de vinos; **wine tasting** *n* degustación f de vinos

wing [wɪŋ] *n* ala; (*Aut*) aleta; **wing mirror** *n* (espejo) retrovisor *m*

wink [wɪŋk] *n* guiño, pestañeo ▷vi guiñar, pestañear

winner ['wɪnə*] *n* ganador(a) *m/f*

winning ['wɪnɪŋ] *adj* (*team*) ganador(a); (*goal*) decisivo; (*smile*) encantador(a)

winter ['wɪntə*] *n* invierno ▷vi invernar; **winter sports** *npl* deportes *mpl* de invierno; **wintertime** *n* invierno

wipe [waɪp] *n*: **to give sth a ~** pasar un trapo sobre algo ▷vt limpiar; (*tape*) borrar; **wipe out** *vt* (*debt*) liquidar; (*memory*) borrar; (*destroy*) destruir; **wipe up** *vt* limpiar

wire ['waɪə*] *n* alambre *m*; (*Elec*) cable *m* (eléctrico); (*Tel*) telegrama *m* ▷vt (*house*) poner la instalación eléctrica en; (*also: ~ up*) conectar

wiring ['waɪərɪŋ] *n* instalación f eléctrica

wisdom ['wɪzdəm] *n* sabiduría, saber *m*; (*good sense*) cordura; **wisdom tooth** *n* muela del juicio

wise [waɪz] *adj* sabio; (*sensible*) juicioso

wish [wɪʃ] *n* deseo ▷vt querer; **best ~es** (*on birthday etc*) felicidades *fpl*; **with best ~es** (*in letter*) saludos *mpl*, recuerdos *mpl*; **to ~ sb goodbye** despedirse de algn; **he ~ed me well** me deseó mucha suerte; **to ~ to do/sb to do sth** querer hacer/que algn haga algo; **to ~ for** desear

wistful ['wɪstful] *adj* pensativo

wit [wɪt] *n* ingenio, gracia; (*also: ~s*) inteligencia; (*person*) chistoso/a

witch [wɪtʃ] *n* bruja

○ KEYWORD

with [wɪð, wɪθ] *prep* **1** (*accompanying, in the company of*) con (*con +mí, ti, sí =*

conmigo, contigo, consigo); **I was with him** estaba con él; **we stayed with friends** nos quedamos en casa de unos amigos; **I'm (not) with you** (*don't understand*) (no) te entiendo; **to be with it** (*inf: person: up-to-date*) estar al tanto; (: *alert*) ser despabilado **2** (*descriptive, indicating manner etc*) con; de; **a room with a view** una habitación con vistas; **the man with the grey hat/blue eyes** el hombre del sombrero gris/de los ojos azules; **red with anger** rojo de ira; **to shake with fear** temblar de miedo; **to fill sth with water** llenar algo de agua

withdraw [wɪθ'drɔ:] *vt* retirar, sacar ▷ *vi* retirarse; **to ~ money (from the bank)** retirar fondos (del banco); **withdrawal** *n* retirada; (*of money*) reintegro; **withdrawn** *pp of* **withdraw** ▷ *adj* (*person*) reservado, introvertido
withdrew [wɪθ'dru:] *pt of* **withdraw**
wither ['wɪðə*] *vi* marchitarse
withhold [wɪθ'həuld] *vt* (*money*) retener; (*decision*) aplazar; (*permission*) negar; (*information*) ocultar
within [wɪð'ɪn] *prep* dentro de ▷ *adv* dentro; **~ reach (of)** al alcance (de); **~ sight (of)** a la vista (de); **~ the week** antes de acabar la semana; **~ a mile (of)** a menos de una milla (de)
without [wɪð'aut] *prep* sin; **to go ~ sth** pasar sin algo
withstand [wɪθ'stænd] *vt* resistir a
witness ['wɪtnɪs] *n* testigo *mf* ▷ *vt* (*event*) presenciar; (*document*) atestiguar la veracidad de; **to bear ~ to** (*fig*) ser testimonio de
witty ['wɪtɪ] *adj* ingenioso
wives [waɪvz] *npl of* **wife**
wizard ['wɪzəd] *n* hechicero
wk *abbr* = **week**
wobble ['wɔbl] *vi* temblar; (*chair*) cojear
woe [wəu] *n* desgracia

woke [wəuk] *pt of* **wake**
woken ['wəukən] *pp of* **wake**
wolf [wulf] *n* lobo
woman ['wumən] (*pl* **women**) *n* mujer *f*
womb [wu:m] *n* matriz *f*, útero
women ['wɪmɪn] *npl of* **woman**
won [wʌn] *pt, pp of* **win**
wonder ['wʌndə*] *n* maravilla, prodigio; (*feeling*) asombro ▷ *vi*: **to ~ whether/why** preguntarse si/por qué; **to ~ at** asombrarse de; **to ~ about** pensar sobre or en; **it's no ~ (that)** no es de extrañarse (que +*subjun*); **wonderful** *adj* maravilloso
won't [wəunt] = **will not**
wood [wud] *n* (*timber*) madera; (*forest*) bosque *m*; **wooden** *adj* de madera; (*fig*) inexpresivo; **woodwind** *n* (*Mus*) instrumentos *mpl* de viento de madera; **woodwork** *n* carpintería
wool [wul] *n* lana; **to pull the ~ over sb's eyes** (*fig*) engatusar a algn; **woollen** (*US* **woolen**) *adj* de lana; **woolly** (*US* **wooly**) *adj* lanudo, de lana; (*fig: ideas*) confuso
word [wə:d] *n* palabra; (*news*) noticia; (*promise*) palabra (de honor) ▷ *vt* redactar; **in other ~s** en otras palabras; **to break/keep one's ~** faltar a la palabra/cumplir la promesa; **to have ~s with sb** reñir con algn; **wording** *n* redacción *f*; **word processing** *n* proceso de textos; **word processor** *n* procesador *m* de textos
wore [wɔ:*] *pt of* **wear**
work [wə:k] *n* trabajo; (*job*) empleo, trabajo; (*Art, Literature*) obra ▷ *vi* trabajar; (*mechanism*) funcionar, marchar; (*medicine*) ser eficaz, surtir efecto ▷ *vt* (*shape*) trabajar; (*stone etc*) tallar; (*mine etc*) explotar; (*machine*) manejar, hacer funcionar ▷ *npl* (*of clock, machine*) mecanismo; **to be out of ~** estar parado, no tener trabajo; **to ~ loose** (*part*) desprenderse; (*knot*) aflojarse; **works** *n* (*BRIT: factory*) fábrica; **work out** *vi* (*plans etc*) salir

bien, funcionar; **works** vt (problem) resolver; (plan) elaborar; **it works out at £100** suma 100 libras; **worker** n trabajador(a) m/f, obrero/a; **work experience** n: **I'm going to do my work experience in a factory** voy a hacer las prácticas en una fábrica; **workforce** n; **working class** n clase f obrera ▷ adj: **working-class** obrero; **working week** n semana laboral; **workman** (irreg) n obrero; **work of art** n obra de arte; **workout** n (Sport) sesión f de ejercicios; **work permit** n permiso de trabajo; **workplace** n lugar m de trabajo; **worksheet** n (Scol) hoja de ejercicios; **workshop** n taller m; **work station** n puesto or estación f de trabajo; **work surface** n encimera; **worktop** n encimera

world [wəːld] n mundo ▷ cpd (champion) del mundo; (power, war) mundial; **to think the ~ of sb** (fig) tener un concepto muy alto de algn; **World Cup** n (Football): **the World Cup** el Mundial, los Mundiales; **world-wide** adj mundial, universal; **World-Wide Web** n: **the World-Wide Web** el World Wide Web

worm [wəːm] n (also: **earth ~**) lombriz f

worn [wɔːn] pp of **wear** ▷ adj usado; **worn-out** adj (object) gastado; (person) rendido, agotado

worried ['wʌrɪd] adj preocupado

worry ['wʌrɪ] n preocupación f ▷ vt preocupar, inquietar ▷ vi preocuparse; **worrying** adj inquietante

worse [wəːs] adj, adv peor ▷ n lo peor; **a change for the ~** un empeoramiento; **worsen** vt, vi empeorar; **worse off** adj (financially): **to be worse off** tener menos dinero; (fig): **you'll be worse off this way** de esta forma estarás peor que nunca

worship ['wəːʃɪp] n adoración f ▷ vt adorar; **Your W~** (BRIT: to mayor) señor

alcalde; (: to judge) señor juez

worst [wəːst] adj, adv peor ▷ n lo peor; **at ~** en lo peor de los casos

worth [wəːθ] n valor m ▷ adj: **to be ~** valer; **it's ~ it** vale or merece la pena; **to be ~ one's while (to do)** merecer la pena (hacer); **worthless** adj sin valor; (useless) inútil; **worthwhile** adj (activity) que merece la pena; (cause) loable

worthy ['wəːðɪ] adj respetable; (motive) honesto; **~ of** digno de

○ **KEYWORD**

would [wud] aux vb **1** (conditional tense): **if you asked him he would do it** si se lo pidieras, lo haría; **if you had asked him he would have done it** si se lo hubieras pedido, lo habría or hubiera hecho

2 (in offers, invitations, requests): **would you like a biscuit?** ¿quieres una galleta?, (formal) ¿querría una galleta?; **would you ask him to come in?** ¿quiere hacerle pasar?; **would you open the window please?** ¿quiere or podría abrir la ventana, por favor?

3 (in indirect speech): **I said I would do it** dije que lo haría

4 (emphatic): **it WOULD have to snow today!** ¡tenía que nevar precisamente hoy!

5 (insistence): **she wouldn't behave** no quiso comportarse bien

6 (conjecture): **it would have been midnight** sería medianoche; **it would seem so** parece ser que sí

7 (indicating habit): **he would go there on Mondays** iba allí los lunes

wouldn't ['wudnt] = **would not**
wound¹ [wuːnd] n herida ▷ vt herir
wound² [waund] pt, pp of **wind²**
wove [wəuv] pt of **weave**
woven ['wəuvən] pp of **weave**
wrap [ræp] vt (also: **~ up**) envolver; (gift) envolver, abrigar ▷ vi (dress

w

warmly) abrigarse; **wrapper** n (*on chocolate*) papel m; (BRIT: *of book*) sobrecubierta; **wrapping** n envoltura, envase m; **wrapping paper** n papel m de envolver; (*fancy*) papel m de regalo
wreath [ri:θ, pl ri:ðz] n (*funeral wreath*) corona
wreck [rɛk] n (*ship: destruction*) naufragio; (: *remains*) restos mpl del barco; (*pej: person*) ruina ▷ vt (*car etc*) destrozar; (*chances*) arruinar; **wreckage** n restos mpl; (*of building*) escombros mpl
wren [rɛn] n (*Zool*) reyezuelo
wrench [rɛntʃ] n (*Tech*) llave f inglesa; (*tug*) tirón m; (*fig*) dolor m ▷ vt arrancar; **to ~ sth from sb** arrebatar algo violentamente a algn
wrestle ['rɛsl] vi: **to ~ (with sb)** luchar (con or contra algn); **wrestler** n luchador(a) m/f (de lucha libre); **wrestling** n lucha libre
wretched ['rɛtʃɪd] adj miserable
wriggle ['rɪgl] vi (*also:* **~ about**) menearse, retorcerse
wring [rɪŋ] (*pt, pp* **wrung**) vt retorcer; (*wet clothes*) escurrir; (*fig*): **to ~ sth out of sb** sacar algo por la fuerza a algn
wrinkle ['rɪŋkl] n arruga ▷ vt arrugar ▷ vi arrugarse
wrist [rɪst] n muñeca
writable ['raɪtəbl] adj (*CD, DVD*) escribible
write [raɪt] (*pt* **wrote**, *pp* **written**) vt escribir; (*cheque*) extender ▷ vi escribir; **write down** vt escribir; (*note*) apuntar; **write off** vt (*debt*) borrar (como incobrable); (*fig*) desechar por inútil; **write out** vt escribir; **write-off** n siniestro total; **writer** n escritor(a) m/f
writing ['raɪtɪŋ] n escritura; (*hand-writing*) letra; (*of author*) obras fpl; **in ~** por escrito; **writing paper** n papel m de escribir
written ['rɪtn] pp of **write**
wrong [rɔŋ] adj (*wicked*) malo; (*unfair*) injusto; (*incorrect*) equivocado,

incorrecto; (*not suitable*) inoportuno, inconveniente; (*reverse*) del revés ▷ adv equivocadamente ▷ n injusticia ▷ vt ser injusto con; **you are ~ to do it** haces mal en hacerlo; **you are ~ about that, you've got it ~** en eso estás equivocado; **to be in the ~** no tener razón, tener la culpa; **what's ~?** ¿qué pasa?; **to go ~** (*person*) equivocarse; (*plan*) salir mal; (*machine*) estropearse; **wrongly** adv mal, incorrectamente; (*by mistake*) por error; **wrong number** n (*Tel*): **you've got the wrong number** se ha equivocado de número
wrote [rəut] pt of **write**
wrung [rʌŋ] pt, pp of **wring**
WWW n abbr (= *World Wide Web*) WWW m

XL *abbr* = **extra large**

Xmas ['ɛksməs] *n abbr* = **Christmas**

X-ray ['ɛksreɪ] *n* radiografía ▷*vt* radiografiar, sacar radiografías de

xylophone ['zaɪləfəun] *n* xilófono

yacht [jɔt] *n* yate *m*; **yachting** *n* (*sport*) balandrismo

yard [jɑːd] *n* patio; (*measure*) yarda; **yard sale** (*us*) *n* venta de objetos usados (*en el jardín de una casa particular*)

yarn [jɑːn] *n* hilo; (*tale*) cuento, historia

yawn [jɔːn] *n* bostezo ▷*vi* bostezar

yd. *abbr* (=*yard*) yda

yeah [jɛə] (*inf*) *adv* sí

year [jɪə*] *n* año; **to be 8 ~s old** tener 8 años; **an eight-~-old child** un niño de ocho años (de edad); **yearly** *adj* anual ▷*adv* anualmente, cada año

yearn [jəːn] *vi*: **to ~ for sth** añorar algo, suspirar por algo

yeast [jiːst] *n* levadura

yell [jɛl] *n* grito, alarido ▷*vi* gritar

yellow ['jɛləu] *adj* amarillo; **Yellow Pages**® *npl* páginas *fpl* amarillas

yes [jɛs] *adv* sí ▷*n* sí *m*; **to say/ answer ~** decir/contestar que sí

yesterday ['jɛstədɪ] *adv* ayer ▷*n* ayer *m*; **~ morning/evening** ayer por la mañana/tarde; **all day ~** todo el día de ayer

yet [jɛt] *adv* ya; (*negative*) todavía ▷ *conj* sin embargo, a pesar de todo; **it is not finished ~** todavía no está acabado; **the best ~** el/la mejor hasta ahora; **as ~** hasta ahora, todavía

yew [juː] *n* tejo

Yiddish ['jɪdɪʃ] *n* yiddish *m*

yield [jiːld] *n* (*Agr*) cosecha; (*Comm*) rendimiento ▷ *vt* ceder; (*results*) producir, dar; (*profit*) rendir ▷ *vi* rendirse, ceder; (*us Aut*) ceder el paso

yob(bo) ['jɔb(bəʊ)] *n* (*BRIT inf*) gamberro

yoga ['jəʊgə] *n* yoga *m*

yog(h)ourt ['jəʊgət] *n* yogur *m*

yog(h)urt ['jəʊgət] *n* = **yog(h)ourt**

yolk [jəʊk] *n* yema (de huevo)

○ **KEYWORD**

you [juː] *pron* **1** (*subject: familiar*) tú; (*pl*) vosotros/as (*SP*), ustedes (*LAM*); (*polite*) usted; (*pl*) ustedes; **you are very kind** eres/es *etc* muy amable; **you Spanish enjoy your food** a vosotros (*or* ustedes) los españoles os (*or* les) gusta la comida; **you and I will go** iremos tú y yo

2 (*object: direct: familiar*) te; (*pl*) os (*SP*), les (*LAM*); (*polite*) le; (*pl*) les; (*f*) la; (*pl*) las; **I know you** te/le *etc* conozco

3 (*object: indirect: familiar*) te; (*pl*) os (*SP*), les (*LAM*); (*polite*) le; (*pl*) les; **I gave the letter to you yesterday** te/os *etc* di la carta ayer

4 (*stressed*): **I told you to do it** te dije a ti que lo hicieras, es a ti a quien dije que lo hicieras; *see also* **3; 5**

5 (*after prep: NB: con +ti = contigo: familiar*) ti; (*pl*) vosotros/as (*SP*), ustedes (*LAM*); (*: polite*) usted; (*pl*) ustedes; **it's for you** es para ti/vosotros *etc*

6 (*comparisons: familiar*) tú; (*pl*) vosotros/as (*SP*), ustedes (*LAM*); (*: polite*) usted; (*pl*) ustedes; **she's younger than you** es más joven que

tú/vosotros *etc*

7 (*impersonal one*): **fresh air does you good** el aire puro (te) hace bien; **you never know** nunca se sabe; **you can't do that!** ¡eso no se hace!

you'd [juːd] = **you had; you would**

you'll [juːl] = **you will; you shall**

young [jʌŋ] *adj* joven ▷ *npl* (*of animal*) cría; (*people*): **the ~** los jóvenes, la juventud; **youngster** *n* joven *mf*

your [jɔː*] *adj* tu; (*pl*) vuestro; (*formal*) su; *see also* **my**

you're [juə*] = **you are**

yours [jɔːz] *pron* tuyo (*pl*), vuestro; (*formal*) suyo; *see also* **faithfully; mine¹** *see also* **sincerely**

yourself [jɔː'sɛlf] *pron* tú mismo; (*complement*) te; (*after prep*) tí (mismo); (*formal*) usted mismo; (*: complement*) se; (*: after prep*) sí (mismo); **yourselves** *pl pron* vosotros mismos; (*after prep*) vosotros (mismos); (*formal*) ustedes (mismos); (*: complement*) se; (*: after prep*) sí mismos; *see also* **oneself**

youth [*pl* juːðz] *n* juventud *f*; (*young man*) joven *m*; **youth club** *n* club *m* juvenil; **youthful** *adj* juvenil; **youth hostel** *n* albergue *m* de juventud

you've [juːv] = **you have**

Z

zeal [ziːl] *n* celo, entusiasmo
zebra ['ziːbrə] *n* cebra; **zebra crossing** (*BRIT*) *n* paso de peatones
zero ['zɪərəu] *n* cero
zest [zɛst] *n* ánimo, vivacidad *f*; (*of orange*) piel *f*
zigzag ['zɪgzæg] *n* zigzag *m* ▷ *vi* zigzaguear, hacer eses
Zimbabwe [zɪm'bɑːbwɪ] *n* Zimbabwe *m*
zinc [zɪŋk] *n* cinc *m*, zinc *m*
zip [zɪp] *n* (*also:* **~ fastener,** (*US*) **~per**) cremallera (*SP*), cierre (*AM*) *m*, zíper *m* (*MEX, CAM*) ▷ *vt* (*also:* **~ up**) cerrar la cremallera de; (*file*) comprimir; **zip code** (*US*) *n* código postal; **zip file** *n* (*Comput*) archivo comprimido; **zipper** (*US*) *n* cremallera
zit [zɪt] *n* grano
zodiac ['zəudɪæk] *n* zodíaco
zone [zəun] *n* zona
zoo [zuː] *n* (jardín *m*) zoo *m*
zoology [zuːˈɔlədʒɪ] *n* zoología
zoom [zuːm] *vi*: **to ~ past** pasar zumbando; **zoom lens** *n* zoom *m*
zucchini [zuːˈkiːnɪ] (*US*) *n(pl)* calabacín(ines) *m(pl)*

z

Introduction

The **Verb Tables** in the following section contain 31 tables of the most common Spanish verbs (some regular, some irregular and some which change their stems) in alphabetical order. Each table shows you the following tenses and forms: **Present**, **Preterite**, **Future**, **Present Subjunctive**, **Imperfect**, **Conditional**, **Imperative**, **Past Participle** and **Gerund**.

In order to help you use the verbs shown in the Verb Tables correctly, there are also a number of example phrases at the bottom of each page to show the verb as it is used in context.

In Spanish there are **regular** verbs (their forms follow the normal rules); **irregular** verbs (their forms do not follow the normal rules); and verbs which change a vowel in their stem (the part that is left when you take off the ending) in fairly predictable ways. The regular verbs in these tables are:

hablar (regular -**ar** verb, Verb Table 12)
comer (regular -**er** verb, Verb Table 3)
vivir (regular -**ir** verb, Verb Table 31)
lavarse (regular -**ar** reflexive verb, Verb Table 15)

For a list of other Spanish irregular and stem-changing verb forms see pages 33-34.

The key at the top of page 33 explains which verb tenses or forms are shown on pages 33-34. For instance, **7** refers to the past participle. So, when you see abrir **7** abierto, you know that abrir has the irregular past participle *abierto*. Only irregular forms are listed. So, **4** busqué, at buscar, means that although *busqué* is irregular (the spelling changes to keep the [k] sound before the letter 'e'), the rest of the preterite tense behaves like any regular -**ar** verb: *busqué, buscaste, buscó, buscamos, buscasteis, buscaron*.

▶ **coger** (to take, to catch)

PRESENT

(yo)	cojo
(tú)	coges
(él/ella/usted)	coge
(nosotros/as)	cogemos
(vosotros/as)	cogéis
(ellos/ellas/ustedes)	cogen

PRESENT SUBJUNCTIVE

(yo)	coja
(tú)	cojas
(él/ella/usted)	coja
(nosotros/as)	cojamos
(vosotros/as)	cojáis
(ellos/ellas/ustedes)	cojan

PRETERITE

(yo)	cogí
(tú)	cogiste
(él/ella/usted)	cogió
(nosotros/as)	cogimos
(vosotros/as)	cogisteis
(ellos/ellas/ustedes)	cogieron

IMPERFECT

(yo)	cogía
(tú)	cogías
(él/ella/usted)	cogía
(nosotros/as)	cogíamos
(vosotros/as)	cogíais
(ellos/ellas/ustedes)	cogían

FUTURE

(yo)	cogeré
(tú)	cogerás
(él/ella/usted)	cogerá
(nosotros/as)	cogeremos
(vosotros/as)	cogeréis
(ellos/ellas/ustedes)	cogerán

CONDITIONAL

(yo)	cogería
(tú)	cogerías
(él/ella/usted)	cogería
(nosotros/as)	cogeríamos
(vosotros/as)	cogeríais
(ellos/ellas/ustedes)	cogerían

IMPERATIVE

coge / coged

PAST PARTICIPLE

cogido

GERUND

cogiendo

EXAMPLE PHRASES

La **cogí** entre mis brazos. I took her in my arms.
Estuvimos cogiendo setas. We were picking mushrooms.
¿Por qué no **coges** el tren de las seis? Why don't you get the six o'clock train?

Remember that subject pronouns are not used very often in Spanish.

▶ comer (to eat)

PRESENT

(yo)	como
(tú)	comes
(él/ella/usted)	come
(nosotros/as)	comemos
(vosotros/as)	coméis
(ellos/ellas/ustedes)	comen

PRESENT SUBJUNCTIVE

(yo)	coma
(tú)	comas
(él/ella/usted)	coma
(nosotros/as)	comamos
(vosotros/as)	comáis
(ellos/ellas/ustedes)	coman

PRETERITE

(yo)	comí
(tú)	comiste
(él/ella/usted)	comió
(nosotros/as)	comimos
(vosotros/as)	comisteis
(ellos/ellas/ustedes)	comieron

IMPERFECT

(yo)	comía
(tú)	comías
(él/ella/usted)	comía
(nosotros/as)	comíamos
(vosotros/as)	comíais
(ellos/ellas/ustedes)	comían

FUTURE

(yo)	comeré
(tú)	comerás
(él/ella/usted)	comerá
(nosotros/as)	comeremos
(vosotros/as)	comeréis
(ellos/ellas/ustedes)	comerán

CONDITIONAL

(yo)	comería
(tú)	comerías
(él/ella/usted)	comería
(nosotros/as)	comeríamos
(vosotros/as)	comeríais
(ellos/ellas/ustedes)	comerían

IMPERATIVE

come / comed

PAST PARTICIPLE

comido

GERUND

comiendo

EXAMPLE PHRASES

No **come** carne. He doesn't eat meat.
No **comas** tan deprisa. Don't eat so fast.
Se ha comido todo. He's eaten it all.

Remember that subject pronouns are not used very often in Spanish.

▶ **dar** (to give)

PRESENT

(yo)	doy
(tú)	das
(él/ella/usted)	da
(nosotros/as)	damos
(vosotros/as)	dais
(ellos/ellas/ustedes)	dan

PRESENT SUBJUNCTIVE

(yo)	dé
(tú)	des
(él/ella/usted)	dé
(nosotros/as)	demos
(vosotros/as)	deis
(ellos/ellas/ustedes)	den

PRETERITE

(yo)	di
(tú)	diste
(él/ella/usted)	dio
(nosotros/as)	dimos
(vosotros/as)	disteis
(ellos/ellas/ustedes)	dieron

IMPERFECT

(yo)	daba
(tú)	dabas
(él/ella/usted)	daba
(nosotros/as)	dábamos
(vosotros/as)	dabais
(ellos/ellas/ustedes)	daban

FUTURE

(yo)	daré
(tú)	darás
(él/ella/usted)	dará
(nosotros/as)	daremos
(vosotros/as)	daréis
(ellos/ellas/ustedes)	darán

CONDITIONAL

(yo)	daría
(tú)	darías
(él/ella/usted)	daría
(nosotros/as)	daríamos
(vosotros/as)	daríais
(ellos/ellas/ustedes)	darían

IMPERATIVE

da / dad

PAST PARTICIPLE

dado

GERUND

dando

EXAMPLE PHRASES

Me **da** miedo la oscuridad. I'm scared of the dark.
Nos **dieron** un par de entradas gratis. They gave us a couple of free tickets.
Te **daré** el número de mi móvil. I'll give you my mobile-phone number.

Remember that subject pronouns are not used very often in Spanish.

▶ **decir** (to say, to tell)

PRESENT

(yo)	digo
(tú)	dices
(él/ella/usted)	dice
(nosotros/as)	decimos
(vosotros/as)	decís
(ellos/ellas/ustedes)	dicen

PRESENT SUBJUNCTIVE

(yo)	diga
(tú)	digas
(él/ella/usted)	diga
(nosotros/as)	digamos
(vosotros/as)	digáis
(ellos/ellas/ustedes)	digan

PRETERITE

(yo)	dije
(tú)	dijiste
(él/ella/usted)	dijo
(nosotros/as)	dijimos
(vosotros/as)	dijisteis
(ellos/ellas/ustedes)	dijeron

IMPERFECT

(yo)	decía
(tú)	decías
(él/ella/usted)	decía
(nosotros/as)	decíamos
(vosotros/as)	decíais
(ellos/ellas/ustedes)	decían

FUTURE

(yo)	diré
(tú)	dirás
(él/ella/usted)	dirá
(nosotros/as)	diremos
(vosotros/as)	diréis
(ellos/ellas/ustedes)	dirán

CONDITIONAL

(yo)	diría
(tú)	dirias
(él/ella/usted)	diría
(nosotros/as)	diríamos
(vosotros/as)	diríais
(ellos/ellas/ustedes)	dirían

IMPERATIVE

di / decid

PAST PARTICIPLE

dicho

GERUND

diciendo

EXAMPLE PHRASES

¿Qué **dices**? What are you saying?
Me lo **dijo** ayer. He told me yesterday.
¿Te **ha dicho** lo de la boda? Has he told you about the wedding?

Remember that subject pronouns are not used very often in Spanish.

▶ **dormir** (to sleep)

PRESENT

(yo)	duermo
(tú)	duermes
(él/ella/usted)	duerme
(nosotros/as)	dormimos
(vosotros/as)	dormís
(ellos/ellas/ustedes)	duermen

PRESENT SUBJUNCTIVE

(yo)	duerma
(tú)	duermas
(él/ella/usted)	duerma
(nosotros/as)	durmamos
(vosotros/as)	durmáis
(ellos/ellas/ustedes)	duerman

PRETERITE

(yo)	dormí
(tú)	dormiste
(él/ella/usted)	durmió
(nosotros/as)	dormimos
(vosotros/as)	dormisteis
(ellos/ellas/ustedes)	durmieron

IMPERFECT

(yo)	dormía
(tú)	dormías
(él/ella/usted)	dormía
(nosotros/as)	dormíamos
(vosotros/as)	dormíais
(ellos/ellas/ustedes)	dormían

FUTURE

(yo)	dormiré
(tú)	dormirás
(él/ella/usted)	dormirá
(nosotros/as)	dormiremos
(vosotros/as)	dormiréis
(ellos/ellas/ustedes)	dormirán

CONDITIONAL

(yo)	dormiría
(tú)	dormirías
(él/ella/usted)	dormiría
(nosotros/as)	dormiríamos
(vosotros/as)	dormiríais
(ellos/ellas/ustedes)	dormirían

IMPERATIVE

duerme / dormid

PAST PARTICIPLE

dormido

GERUND

durmiendo

EXAMPLE PHRASES

No **duermo** muy bien. I don't sleep very well.
Nos dormimos en el cine. We fell asleep at the cinema.
Durmió durante doce horas. He slept for twelve hours.

Remember that subject pronouns are not used very often in Spanish.

▶ **empezar** (to begin, to start)

PRESENT

(yo)	empiezo
(tú)	empiezas
(él/ella/usted)	empieza
(nosotros/as)	empezamos
(vosotros/as)	empezáis
(ellos/ellas/ustedes)	empiezan

PRESENT SUBJUNCTIVE

(yo)	empiece
(tú)	empieces
(él/ella/usted)	empiece
(nosotros/as)	empecemos
(vosotros/as)	empecéis
(ellos/ellas/ustedes)	empiecen

PRETERITE

(yo)	empecé
(tú)	empezaste
(él/ella/usted)	empezó
(nosotros/as)	empezamos
(vosotros/as)	empezasteis
(ellos/ellas/ustedes)	empezaron

IMPERFECT

(yo)	empezaba
(tú)	empezabas
(él/ella/usted)	empezaba
(nosotros/as)	empezábamos
(vosotros/as)	empezabais
(ellos/ellas/ustedes)	empezaban

FUTURE

(yo)	empezaré
(tú)	empezarás
(él/ella/usted)	empezará
(nosotros/as)	empezaremos
(vosotros/as)	empezaréis
(ellos/ellas/ustedes)	empezarán

CONDITIONAL

(yo)	empezaría
(tú)	empezarías
(él/ella/usted)	empezaría
(nosotros/as)	empezaríamos
(vosotros/as)	empezaríais
(ellos/ellas/ustedes)	empezarían

IMPERATIVE

empieza / empezad

PAST PARTICIPLE

empezado

GERUND

empezando

EXAMPLE PHRASES

Empieza por aquí. Start here.
*¿Cuándo **empiezas** a trabajar en el sitio nuevo?* When do you start work at the new place?
*La semana que viene **empezaremos** un curso nuevo.* We'll start a new course next week.

Remember that subject pronouns are not used very often in Spanish.

▶ **entender** (to understand)

PRESENT

(yo)	entiendo
(tú)	entiendes
(él/ella/usted)	entiende
(nosotros/as)	entendemos
(vosotros/as)	entendéis
(ellos/ellas/ustedes)	entienden

PRESENT SUBJUNCTIVE

(yo)	entienda
(tú)	entiendas
(él/ella/usted)	entienda
(nosotros/as)	entendamos
(vosotros/as)	entendáis
(ellos/ellas/ustedes)	entiendan

PRETERITE

(yo)	entendí
(tú)	entendiste
(él/ella/usted)	entendió
(nosotros/as)	entendimos
(vosotros/as)	entendisteis
(ellos/ellas/ustedes)	entendieron

IMPERFECT

(yo)	entendía
(tú)	entendías
(él/ella/usted)	entendía
(nosotros/as)	entendíamos
(vosotros/as)	entendíais
(ellos/ellas/ustedes)	entendían

FUTURE

(yo)	entenderé
(tú)	entenderás
(él/ella/usted)	entenderá
(nosotros/as)	entenderemos
(vosotros/as)	entenderéis
(ellos/ellas/ustedes)	entenderán

CONDITIONAL

(yo)	entendería
(tú)	entenderías
(él/ella/usted)	entendería
(nosotros/as)	entenderíamos
(vosotros/as)	entenderíais
(ellos/ellas/ustedes)	entenderían

IMPERATIVE

entiende / entended

PAST PARTICIPLE

entendido

GERUND

entendiendo

EXAMPLE PHRASES

*No lo **entiendo**.* I don't understand.
*¿**Entendiste** lo que dijo?* Did you understand what she said?
*Con el tiempo lo **entenderás**.* You'll understand one day.

Remember that subject pronouns are not used very often in Spanish.

▶ **enviar** (to send)

PRESENT

(yo)	envío
(tú)	envías
(él/ella/usted)	envía
(nosotros/as)	enviamos
(vosotros/as)	enviáis
(ellos/ellas/ustedes)	envían

PRESENT SUBJUNCTIVE

(yo)	envíe
(tú)	envíes
(él/ella/usted)	envíe
(nosotros/as)	enviemos
(vosotros/as)	enviéis
(ellos/ellas/ustedes)	envíen

PRETERITE

(yo)	envié
(tú)	enviaste
(él/ella/usted)	envió
(nosotros/as)	enviamos
(vosotros/as)	enviasteis
(ellos/ellas/ustedes)	enviaron

IMPERFECT

(yo)	enviaba
(tú)	enviabas
(él/ella/usted)	enviaba
(nosotros/as)	enviábamos
(vosotros/as)	enviabais
(ellos/ellas/ustedes)	enviaban

FUTURE

(yo)	enviaré
(tú)	enviarás
(él/ella/usted)	enviará
(nosotros/as)	enviaremos
(vosotros/as)	enviaréis
(ellos/ellas/ustedes)	enviarán

CONDITIONAL

(yo)	enviaría
(tú)	enviarías
(él/ella/usted)	enviaría
(nosotros/as)	enviaríamos
(vosotros/as)	enviaríais
(ellos/ellas/ustedes)	enviarían

IMPERATIVE

envía / enviad

PAST PARTICIPLE

enviado

GERUND

enviando

EXAMPLE PHRASES

Envíe *todos sus datos personales*. Send all your personal details.
La han **enviado** *a Guatemala*. They've sent her to Guatemala.
Nos **enviarán** *más información*. They'll send us further information.

Remember that subject pronouns are not used very often in Spanish.

▶ **estar** (to be)

PRESENT

(yo)	estoy
(tú)	estás
(él/ella/usted)	está
(nosotros/as)	estamos
(vosotros/as)	estáis
(ellos/ellas/ustedes)	están

PRESENT SUBJUNCTIVE

(yo)	esté
(tú)	estés
(él/ella/usted)	esté
(nosotros/as)	estemos
(vosotros/as)	estéis
(ellos/ellas/ustedes)	estén

PRETERITE

(yo)	estuve
(tú)	estuviste
(él/ella/usted)	estuvo
(nosotros/as)	estuvimos
(vosotros/as)	estuvisteis
(ellos/ellas/ustedes)	estuvieron

IMPERFECT

(yo)	estaba
(tú)	estabas
(él/ella/usted)	estaba
(nosotros/as)	estábamos
(vosotros/as)	estabais
(ellos/ellas/ustedes)	estaban

FUTURE

(yo)	estaré
(tú)	estarás
(él/ella/usted)	estará
(nosotros/as)	estaremos
(vosotros/as)	estaréis
(ellos/ellas/ustedes)	estarán

CONDITIONAL

(yo)	estaría
(tú)	estarías
(él/ella/usted)	estaría
(nosotros/as)	estaríamos
(vosotros/as)	estaríais
(ellos/ellas/ustedes)	estarían

IMPERATIVE

está / estad

PAST PARTICIPLE

estado

GERUND

estando

EXAMPLE PHRASES

Estoy cansado. I'm tired.
Estuvimos en casa de mis padres. We were at my parents' place.
¿A qué hora **estarás** en casa? What time will you be home?

Remember that subject pronouns are not used very often in Spanish.

▶ **haber** (to have (auxiliary))

PRESENT

(yo)	he
(tú)	has
(él/ella/usted)	ha
(nosotros/as)	hemos
(vosotros/as)	habéis
(ellos/ellas/ustedes)	han

PRESENT SUBJUNCTIVE

(yo)	haya
(tú)	hayas
(él/ella/usted)	haya
(nosotros/as)	hayamos
(vosotros/as)	hayáis
(ellos/ellas/ustedes)	hayan

PRETERITE

(yo)	hube
(tú)	hubiste
(él/ella/usted)	hubo
(nosotros/as)	hubimos
(vosotros/as)	hubisteis
(ellos/ellas/ustedes)	hubieron

IMPERFECT

(yo)	había
(tú)	habías
(él/ella/usted)	había
(nosotros/as)	habíamos
(vosotros/as)	habíais
(ellos/ellas/ustedes)	habían

FUTURE

(yo)	habré
(tú)	habrás
(él/ella/usted)	habrá
(nosotros/as)	habremos
(vosotros/as)	habréis
(ellos/ellas/ustedes)	habrán

CONDITIONAL

(yo)	habría
(tú)	habrías
(él/ella/usted)	habría
(nosotros/as)	habríamos
(vosotros/as)	habríais
(ellos/ellas/ustedes)	habrían

IMPERATIVE

not used

PAST PARTICIPLE

habido

GERUND

habiendo

EXAMPLE PHRASES

¿**Has visto** eso? Did you see that?
Ya **hemos ido** a ver esa película. We've already been to see that film.
Eso nunca **había pasado** antes. That had never happened before.

Remember that subject pronouns are not used very often in Spanish.

▶ **hablar** (to speak, to talk)

PRESENT

(yo)	hablo
(tú)	hablas
(él/ella/usted)	habla
(nosotros/as)	hablamos
(vosotros/as)	habláis
(ellos/ellas/ustedes)	hablan

PRESENT SUBJUNCTIVE

(yo)	hable
(tú)	hables
(él/ella/usted)	hable
(nosotros/as)	hablemos
(vosotros/as)	habléis
(ellos/ellas/ustedes)	hablen

PRETERITE

(yo)	hablé
(tú)	hablaste
(él/ella/usted)	habló
(nosotros/as)	hablamos
(vosotros/as)	hablasteis
(ellos/ellas/ustedes)	hablaron

IMPERFECT

(yo)	hablaba
(tú)	hablabas
(él/ella/usted)	hablaba
(nosotros/as)	hablábamos
(vosotros/as)	hablabais
(ellos/ellas/ustedes)	hablaban

FUTURE

(yo)	hablaré
(tú)	hablarás
(él/ella/usted)	hablará
(nosotros/as)	hablaremos
(vosotros/as)	hablaréis
(ellos/ellas/ustedes)	hablarán

CONDITIONAL

(yo)	hablaría
(tú)	hablarías
(él/ella/usted)	hablaría
(nosotros/as)	hablaríamos
(vosotros/as)	hablaríais
(ellos/ellas/ustedes)	hablarían

IMPERATIVE

habla / hablad

PAST PARTICIPLE

hablado

GERUND

hablando

EXAMPLE PHRASES

Hoy **he hablado** con mi hermana. I've spoken to my sister today.
No **hables** tan alto. Don't talk so loud.
No **se hablan**. They don't talk to each other.

Remember that subject pronouns are not used very often in Spanish.

▶ **hacer** (to do, to make)

PRESENT

(yo)	hago
(tú)	haces
(él/ella/usted)	hace
(nosotros/as)	hacemos
(vosotros/as)	hacéis
(ellos/ellas/ustedes)	hacen

PRESENT SUBJUNCTIVE

(yo)	haga
(tú)	hagas
(él/ella/usted)	haga
(nosotros/as)	hagamos
(vosotros/as)	hagáis
(ellos/ellas/ustedes)	hagan

PRETERITE

(yo)	hice
(tú)	hiciste
(él/ella/usted)	hizo
(nosotros/as)	hicimos
(vosotros/as)	hicisteis
(ellos/ellas/ustedes)	hicieron

IMPERFECT

(yo)	hacía
(tú)	hacías
(él/ella/usted)	hacía
(nosotros/as)	hacíamos
(vosotros/as)	hacíais
(ellos/ellas/ustedes)	hacían

FUTURE

(yo)	haré
(tú)	harás
(él/ella/usted)	hará
(nosotros/as)	haremos
(vosotros/as)	haréis
(ellos/ellas/ustedes)	harán

CONDITIONAL

(yo)	haría
(tú)	harías
(él/ella/usted)	haría
(nosotros/as)	haríamos
(vosotros/as)	haríais
(ellos/ellas/ustedes)	harían

IMPERATIVE

haz / haced

PAST PARTICIPLE

hecho

GERUND

haciendo

EXAMPLE PHRASES

*Lo **haré** yo mismo.* I'll do it myself.
*¿Quién **hizo** eso?* Who did that?
*Quieres que **haga** las camas?* Do you want me to make the beds?

Remember that subject pronouns are not used very often in Spanish.

▶ **ir** (to go)

PRESENT

(yo)	voy
(tú)	vas
(él/ella/usted)	va
(nosotros/as)	vamos
(vosotros/as)	vais
(ellos/ellas/ustedes)	van

PRESENT SUBJUNCTIVE

(yo)	vaya
(tú)	vayas
(él/ella/usted)	vaya
(nosotros/as)	vayamos
(vosotros/as)	vayáis
(ellos/ellas/ustedes)	vayan

PRETERITE

(yo)	fui
(tú)	fuiste
(él/ella/usted)	fue
(nosotros/as)	fuimos
(vosotros/as)	fuisteis
(ellos/ellas/ustedes)	fueron

IMPERFECT

(yo)	iba
(tú)	ibas
(él/ella/usted)	iba
(nosotros/as)	íbamos
(vosotros/as)	ibais
(ellos/ellas/ustedes)	iban

FUTURE

(yo)	iré
(tú)	irás
(él/ella/usted)	irá
(nosotros/as)	iremos
(vosotros/as)	iréis
(ellos/ellas/ustedes)	irán

CONDITIONAL

(yo)	iría
(tú)	irías
(él/ella/usted)	iría
(nosotros/as)	iríamos
(vosotros/as)	iríais
(ellos/ellas/ustedes)	irían

IMPERATIVE

ve / id

PAST PARTICIPLE

ido

GERUND

yendo

EXAMPLE PHRASES

¿*Vamos* a comer al campo? Shall we have a picnic in the country?
El domingo *iré* a Edimburgo. I'll go to Edinburgh on Sunday.
Yo no *voy* con ellos. I'm not going with them.

Remember that subject pronouns are not used very often in Spanish.

▶ **lavarse** (to wash oneself)

PRESENT

(yo)	me lavo
(tú)	te lavas
(él/ella/usted)	se lava
(nosotros/as)	nos lavamos
(vosotros/as)	os laváis
(ellos/ellas/ustedes)	se lavan

PRESENT SUBJUNCTIVE

(yo)	me lave
(tú)	te laves
(él/ella/usted)	se lave
(nosotros/as)	nos lavemos
(vosotros/as)	os lavéis
(ellos/ellas/ustedes)	se laven

PRETERITE

(yo)	me lavé
(tú)	te lavaste
(él/ella/usted)	se lavó
(nosotros/as)	nos lavamos
(vosotros/as)	os lavasteis
(ellos/ellas/ustedes)	se lavaron

IMPERFECT

(yo)	me lavaba
(tú)	te lavabas
(él/ella/usted)	se lavaba
(nosotros/as)	nos lavábamos
(vosotros/as)	os lavabais
(ellos/ellas/ustedes)	se lavaban

FUTURE

(yo)	me lavaré
(tú)	te lavarás
(él/ella/usted)	se lavará
(nosotros/as)	nos lavaremos
(vosotros/as)	os lavaréis
(ellos/ellas/ustedes)	se lavarán

CONDITIONAL

(yo)	me lavaría
(tú)	te lavarías
(él/ella/usted)	se lavaría
(nosotros/as)	nos lavaríamos
(vosotros/as)	os lavaríais
(ellos/ellas/ustedes)	se lavarían

IMPERATIVE

lávate / lavaos

PAST PARTICIPLE

lavado

GERUND

lavándose

EXAMPLE PHRASES

Se lava todos los días. He washes every day.
Ayer **me lavé** el pelo. I washed my hair yesterday.
Nos lavaremos con agua fría. We'll wash in cold water.

Remember that subject pronouns are not used very often in Spanish.

▶ **leer** (to read)

PRESENT

(yo)	leo
(tú)	lees
(él/ella/usted)	lee
(nosotros/as)	leemos
(vosotros/as)	leéis
(ellos/ellas/ustedes)	leen

PRESENT SUBJUNCTIVE

(yo)	lea
(tú)	leas
(él/ella/usted)	lea
(nosotros/as)	leamos
(vosotros/as)	leáis
(ellos/ellas/ustedes)	lean

PRETERITE

(yo)	leí
(tú)	leíste
(él/ella/usted)	leyó
(nosotros/as)	leímos
(vosotros/as)	leísteis
(ellos/ellas/ustedes)	leyeron

IMPERFECT

(yo)	leía
(tú)	leías
(él/ella/usted)	leía
(nosotros/as)	leíamos
(vosotros/as)	leíais
(ellos/ellas/ustedes)	leían

FUTURE

(yo)	leeré
(tú)	leerás
(él/ella/usted)	leerá
(nosotros/as)	leeremos
(vosotros/as)	leeréis
(ellos/ellas/ustedes)	leerán

CONDITIONAL

(yo)	leería
(tú)	leerías
(él/ella/usted)	leería
(nosotros/as)	leeríamos
(vosotros/as)	leeríais
(ellos/ellas/ustedes)	leerían

IMPERATIVE

lee / leed

PAST PARTICIPLE

leído

GERUND

leyendo

EXAMPLE PHRASES

*Hace mucho tiempo que no **leo**.* I haven't read anything for ages.
*¿**Has leído** esta novela?* Have you read this novel?
*Lo **leí** hace tiempo.* I read it a while ago.

Remember that subject pronouns are not used very often in Spanish.

▶ **oír** (to hear)

PRESENT

(yo)	oigo
(tú)	oyes
(él/ella/usted)	oye
(nosotros/as)	oímos
(vosotros/as)	oís
(ellos/ellas/ustedes)	oyen

PRESENT SUBJUNCTIVE

(yo)	oiga
(tú)	oigas
(él/ella/usted)	oiga
(nosotros/as)	oigamos
(vosotros/as)	oigáis
(ellos/ellas/ustedes)	oigan

PRETERITE

(yo)	oí
(tú)	oíste
(él/ella/usted)	oyó
(nosotros/as)	oímos
(vosotros/as)	oísteis
(ellos/ellas/ustedes)	oyeron

IMPERFECT

(yo)	oía
(tú)	oías
(él/ella/usted)	oía
(nosotros/as)	oíamos
(vosotros/as)	oíais
(ellos/ellas/ustedes)	oían

FUTURE

(yo)	oiré
(tú)	oirás
(él/ella/usted)	oirá
(nosotros/as)	oiremos
(vosotros/as)	oiréis
(ellos/ellas/ustedes)	oirán

CONDITIONAL

(yo)	oiría
(tú)	oirías
(él/ella/usted)	oiría
(nosotros/as)	oiríamos
(vosotros/as)	oiríais
(ellos/ellas/ustedes)	oirían

IMPERATIVE

oye / oíd

PAST PARTICIPLE

oído

GERUND

oyendo

EXAMPLE PHRASES

*No **oigo** nada.* I can't hear anything.
*Si no **oyes** bien, ve al médico.* If you can't hear properly, go and see the doctor.
*¿**Has oído** eso?* Did you hear that?

Remember that subject pronouns are not used very often in Spanish.

▶ **pedir** (to ask for)

PRESENT

(yo)	pido
(tú)	pides
(él/ella/usted)	pide
(nosotros/as)	pedimos
(vosotros/as)	pedís
(ellos/ellas/ustedes)	piden

PRESENT SUBJUNCTIVE

(yo)	pida
(tú)	pidas
(él/ella/usted)	pida
(nosotros/as)	pidamos
(vosotros/as)	pidáis
(ellos/ellas/ustedes)	pidan

PRETERITE

(yo)	pedí
(tú)	pediste
(él/ella/usted)	pidió
(nosotros/as)	pedimos
(vosotros/as)	pedisteis
(ellos/ellas/ustedes)	pidieron

IMPERFECT

(yo)	pedía
(tú)	pedías
(él/ella/usted)	pedía
(nosotros/as)	pedíamos
(vosotros/as)	pedíais
(ellos/ellas/ustedes)	pedían

FUTURE

(yo)	pediré
(tú)	pedirás
(él/ella/usted)	pedirá
(nosotros/as)	pediremos
(vosotros/as)	pediréis
(ellos/ellas/ustedes)	pedirán

CONDITIONAL

(yo)	pediría
(tú)	pedirías
(él/ella/usted)	pediría
(nosotros/as)	pediríamos
(vosotros/as)	pediríais
(ellos/ellas/ustedes)	pedirían

IMPERATIVE

pide / pedid

PAST PARTICIPLE

pedido

GERUND

pidiendo

EXAMPLE PHRASES

*No nos **pidieron** el pasaporte.* They didn't ask us for our passports.
***Hemos pedido** dos cervezas.* We've ordered two beers.
***Pídele** el teléfono.* Ask her for her telephone number.

Remember that subject pronouns are not used very often in Spanish.

▶ **pensar** (to think)

PRESENT

(yo)	pienso
(tú)	piensas
(él/ella/usted)	piensa
(nosotros/as)	pensamos
(vosotros/as)	pensáis
(ellos/ellas/ustedes)	piensan

PRESENT SUBJUNCTIVE

(yo)	piense
(tú)	pienses
(él/ella/usted)	piense
(nosotros/as)	pensemos
(vosotros/as)	penséis
(ellos/ellas/ustedes)	piensen

PRETERITE

(yo)	pensé
(tú)	pensaste
(él/ella/usted)	pensó
(nosotros/as)	pensamos
(vosotros/as)	pensasteis
(ellos/ellas/ustedes)	pensaron

IMPERFECT

(yo)	pensaba
(tú)	pensabas
(él/ella/usted)	pensaba
(nosotros/as)	pensábamos
(vosotros/as)	pensabais
(ellos/ellas/ustedes)	pensaban

FUTURE

(yo)	pensaré
(tú)	pensarás
(él/ella/usted)	pensará
(nosotros/as)	pensaremos
(vosotros/as)	pensaréis
(ellos/ellas/ustedes)	pensarán

CONDITIONAL

(yo)	pensaría
(tu)	pensarias
(él/ella/usted)	pensaría
(nosotros/as)	pensaríamos
(vosotros/as)	pensaríais
(ellos/ellas/ustedes)	pensarían

IMPERATIVE

piensa / pensad

PAST PARTICIPLE

pensado

GERUND

pensando

EXAMPLE PHRASES

*No lo **pienses** más.* Don't think any more about it.
*Está **pensando** en comprarse un piso.* He's thinking of buying a flat.
***Pensaba** que vendrías.* I thought you'd come.

Remember that subject pronouns are not used very often in Spanish.

▶ **poder** (to be able to)

PRESENT

(yo)	puedo
(tú)	puedes
(él/ella/usted)	puede
(nosotros/as)	podemos
(vosotros/as)	podéis
(ellos/ellas/ustedes)	pueden

PRESENT SUBJUNCTIVE

(yo)	pueda
(tú)	puedas
(él/ella/usted)	pueda
(nosotros/as)	podamos
(vosotros/as)	podáis
(ellos/ellas/ustedes)	puedan

PRETERITE

(yo)	pude
(tú)	pudiste
(él/ella/usted)	pudo
(nosotros/as)	pudimos
(vosotros/as)	pudisteis
(ellos/ellas/ustedes)	pudieron

IMPERFECT

(yo)	podía
(tú)	podías
(él/ella/usted)	podía
(nosotros/as)	podíamos
(vosotros/as)	podíais
(ellos/ellas/ustedes)	podían

FUTURE

(yo)	podré
(tú)	podrás
(él/ella/usted)	podrá
(nosotros/as)	podremos
(vosotros/as)	podréis
(ellos/ellas/ustedes)	podrán

CONDITIONAL

(yo)	podría
(tú)	podrías
(él/ella/usted)	podría
(nosotros/as)	podríamos
(vosotros/as)	podríais
(ellos/ellas/ustedes)	podrían

IMPERATIVE

puede / poded

PAST PARTICIPLE

podido

GERUND

pudiendo

EXAMPLE PHRASES

¿**Puedo** entrar? Can I come in?
Puedes venir cuando quieras. You can come when you like.
¿**Podrías** ayudarme? Could you help me?

Remember that subject pronouns are not used very often in Spanish.

▶ **poner** (to put)

PRESENT

(yo)	pongo
(tú)	pones
(él/ella/usted)	pone
(nosotros/as)	ponemos
(vosotros/as)	ponéis
(ellos/ellas/ustedes)	ponen

PRESENT SUBJUNCTIVE

(yo)	ponga
(tú)	pongas
(él/ella/usted)	ponga
(nosotros/as)	pongamos
(vosotros/as)	pongáis
(ellos/ellas/ustedes)	pongan

PRETERITE

(yo)	puse
(tú)	pusiste
(él/ella/usted)	puso
(nosotros/as)	pusimos
(vosotros/as)	pusisteis
(ellos/ellas/ustedes)	pusieron

IMPERFECT

(yo)	ponía
(tú)	ponías
(él/ella/usted)	ponía
(nosotros/as)	poníamos
(vosotros/as)	poníais
(ellos/ellas/ustedes)	ponían

FUTURE

(yo)	pondré
(tú)	pondrás
(él/ella/usted)	pondrá
(nosotros/as)	pondremos
(vosotros/as)	pondréis
(ellos/ellas/ustedes)	pondrán

CONDITIONAL

(yo)	pondría
(tu)	pondrias
(él/ella/usted)	pondría
(nosotros/as)	pondríamos
(vosotros/as)	pondríais
(ellos/ellas/ustedes)	pondrían

IMPERATIVE

pon / poned

PAST PARTICIPLE

puesto

GERUND

poniendo

EXAMPLE PHRASES

Ponlo *ahí encima.* Put it on there.
Lo **pondré** *aquí.* I'll put it here.
Todos **nos pusimos** *de acuerdo.* We all agreed.

Remember that subject pronouns are not used very often in Spanish.

▶ **querer** (to want, to love)

PRESENT

(yo)	quiero
(tú)	quieres
(él/ella/usted)	quiere
(nosotros/as)	queremos
(vosotros/as)	queréis
(ellos/ellas/ustedes)	quieren

PRESENT SUBJUNCTIVE

(yo)	quiera
(tú)	quieras
(él/ella/usted)	quiera
(nosotros/as)	queramos
(vosotros/as)	queráis
(ellos/ellas/ustedes)	quieran

PRETERITE

(yo)	quise
(tú)	quisiste
(él/ella/usted)	quiso
(nosotros/as)	quisimos
(vosotros/as)	quisisteis
(ellos/ellas/ustedes)	quisieron

IMPERFECT

(yo)	quería
(tú)	querías
(él/ella/usted)	quería
(nosotros/as)	queríamos
(vosotros/as)	queríais
(ellos/ellas/ustedes)	querían

FUTURE

(yo)	querré
(tú)	querrás
(él/ella/usted)	querrá
(nosotros/as)	querremos
(vosotros/as)	querréis
(ellos/ellas/ustedes)	querrán

CONDITIONAL

(yo)	querría
(tú)	querrías
(él/ella/usted)	querría
(nosotros/as)	querríamos
(vosotros/as)	querríais
(ellos/ellas/ustedes)	querrían

IMPERATIVE

quiere / quered

PAST PARTICIPLE

querido

GERUND

queriendo

EXAMPLE PHRASES

Te **quiero**. I love you.
Quisiera preguntar una cosa. I'd like to ask something.
No **quería** decírmelo. She didn't want to tell me.

Remember that subject pronouns are not used very often in Spanish.

▶ **saber** (to know)

PRESENT

(yo)	sé
(tú)	sabes
(él/ella/usted)	sabe
(nosotros/as)	sabemos
(vosotros/as)	sabéis
(ellos/ellas/ustedes)	saben

PRESENT SUBJUNCTIVE

(yo)	sepa
(tú)	sepas
(él/ella/usted)	sepa
(nosotros/as)	sepamos
(vosotros/as)	sepáis
(ellos/ellas/ustedes)	sepan

PRETERITE

(yo)	supe
(tú)	supiste
(él/ella/usted)	supo
(nosotros/as)	supimos
(vosotros/as)	supisteis
(ellos/ellas/ustedes)	supieron

IMPERFECT

(yo)	sabía
(tú)	sabías
(él/ella/usted)	sabía
(nosotros/as)	sabíamos
(vosotros/as)	sabíais
(ellos/ellas/ustedes)	sabían

FUTURE

(yo)	sabré
(tú)	sabrás
(él/ella/usted)	sabrá
(nosotros/as)	sabremos
(vosotros/as)	sabréis
(ellos/ellas/ustedes)	sabrán

CONDITIONAL

(yo)	sabría
(tú)	sabrías
(él/ella/usted)	sabría
(nosotros/as)	sabríamos
(vosotros/as)	sabríais
(ellos/ellas/ustedes)	sabrían

IMPERATIVE

sabe / sabed

PAST PARTICIPLE

sabido

GERUND

sabiendo

EXAMPLE PHRASES

*No lo **sé**.* I don't know.
*¿**Sabes** una cosa?* Do you know what?
*Pensaba que lo **sabías**.* I thought you knew.

Remember that subject pronouns are not used very often in Spanish.

▶ **seguir** (to follow)

PRESENT

(yo)	sigo
(tú)	sigues
(él/ella/usted)	sigue
(nosotros/as)	seguimos
(vosotros/as)	seguís
(ellos/ellas/ustedes)	siguen

PRESENT SUBJUNCTIVE

(yo)	siga
(tú)	sigas
(él/ella/usted)	siga
(nosotros/as)	sigamos
(vosotros/as)	sigáis
(ellos/ellas/ustedes)	sigan

PRETERITE

(yo)	seguí
(tú)	seguiste
(él/ella/usted)	siguió
(nosotros/as)	seguimos
(vosotros/as)	seguisteis
(ellos/ellas/ustedes)	siguieron

IMPERFECT

(yo)	seguía
(tú)	seguías
(él/ella/usted)	seguía
(nosotros/as)	seguíamos
(vosotros/as)	seguíais
(ellos/ellas/ustedes)	seguían

FUTURE

(yo)	seguiré
(tú)	seguirás
(él/ella/usted)	seguirá
(nosotros/as)	seguiremos
(vosotros/as)	seguiréis
(ellos/ellas/ustedes)	seguirán

CONDITIONAL

(yo)	seguiría
(tú)	seguirías
(él/ella/usted)	seguiría
(nosotros/as)	seguiríamos
(vosotros/as)	seguiríais
(ellos/ellas/ustedes)	seguirían

IMPERATIVE

sigue / seguid

PAST PARTICIPLE

seguido

GERUND

siguiendo

EXAMPLE PHRASES

Siga *por esta calle hasta el final*. Go on till you get to the end of the street.
Nos seguiremos *viendo*. We will go on seeing each other.
Nos **siguió** *todo el camino*. He followed us all the way.

Remember that subject pronouns are not used very often in Spanish.

▶ **sentir** (to feel)

PRESENT

(yo)	siento
(tú)	sientes
(él/ella/usted)	siente
(nosotros/as)	sentimos
(vosotros/as)	sentís
(ellos/ellas/ustedes)	sienten

PRESENT SUBJUNCTIVE

(yo)	sienta
(tú)	sientas
(él/ella/usted)	sienta
(nosotros/as)	sintamos
(vosotros/as)	sintáis
(ellos/ellas/ustedes)	sientan

PRETERITE

(yo)	sentí
(tú)	sentiste
(él/ella/usted)	sintió
(nosotros/as)	sentimos
(vosotros/as)	sentisteis
(ellos/ellas/ustedes)	sintieron

IMPERFECT

(yo)	sentía
(tú)	sentías
(él/ella/usted)	sentía
(nosotros/as)	sentíamos
(vosotros/as)	sentíais
(ellos/ellas/ustedes)	sentían

FUTURE

(yo)	sentiré
(tú)	sentirás
(él/ella/usted)	sentirá
(nosotros/as)	sentiremos
(vosotros/as)	sentiréis
(ellos/ellas/ustedes)	sentirán

CONDITIONAL

(yo)	sentiría
(tú)	sentirías
(él/ella/usted)	sentiría
(nosotros/as)	sentiríamos
(vosotros/as)	sentiríais
(ellos/ellas/ustedes)	sentirían

IMPERATIVE

siente / sentid

PAST PARTICIPLE

sentido

GERUND

sintiendo

EXAMPLE PHRASES

Siento *mucho lo que pasó*. I'm really sorry about what happened.
Sentí *un pinchazo en la pierna*. I felt a sharp pain in my leg.
No creo que lo **sienta**. I don't think she's sorry.

Remember that subject pronouns are not used very often in Spanish.

▶ **ser** (to be)

PRESENT

(yo)	soy
(tú)	eres
(él/ella/usted)	es
(nosotros/as)	somos
(vosotros/as)	sois
(ellos/ellas/ustedes)	son

PRESENT SUBJUNCTIVE

(yo)	sea
(tú)	seas
(él/ella/usted)	sea
(nosotros/as)	seamos
(vosotros/as)	seáis
(ellos/ellas/ustedes)	sean

PRETERITE

(yo)	fui
(tú)	fuiste
(él/ella/usted)	fue
(nosotros/as)	fuimos
(vosotros/as)	fuisteis
(ellos/ellas/ustedes)	fueron

IMPERFECT

(yo)	era
(tú)	eras
(él/ella/usted)	era
(nosotros/as)	éramos
(vosotros/as)	erais
(ellos/ellas/ustedes)	eran

FUTURE

(yo)	seré
(tú)	serás
(él/ella/usted)	será
(nosotros/as)	seremos
(vosotros/as)	seréis
(ellos/ellas/ustedes)	serán

CONDITIONAL

(yo)	sería
(tú)	serías
(él/ella/usted)	sería
(nosotros/as)	seríamos
(vosotros/as)	seríais
(ellos/ellas/ustedes)	serían

IMPERATIVE

sé / sed

PAST PARTICIPLE

sido

GERUND

siendo

EXAMPLE PHRASES

Soy español. I'm Spanish.
¿**Fuiste** tú el que llamó? Was it you who phoned?
Era de noche. It was dark.

Remember that subject pronouns are not used very often in Spanish.

▶ **tener** (to have)

PRESENT

(yo)	tengo
(tú)	tienes
(él/ella/usted)	tiene
(nosotros/as)	tenemos
(vosotros/as)	tenéis
(ellos/ellas/ustedes)	tienen

PRESENT SUBJUNCTIVE

(yo)	tenga
(tú)	tengas
(él/ella/usted)	tenga
(nosotros/as)	tengamos
(vosotros/as)	tengáis
(ellos/ellas/ustedes)	tengan

PRETERITE

(yo)	tuve
(tú)	tuviste
(él/ella/usted)	tuvo
(nosotros/as)	tuvimos
(vosotros/as)	tuvisteis
(ellos/ellas/ustedes)	tuvieron

IMPERFECT

(yo)	tenía
(tú)	tenías
(él/ella/usted)	tenía
(nosotros/as)	teníamos
(vosotros/as)	teníais
(ellos/ellas/ustedes)	tenían

FUTURE

(yo)	tendré
(tú)	tendrás
(él/ella/usted)	tendrá
(nosotros/as)	tendremos
(vosotros/as)	tendréis
(ellos/ellas/ustedes)	tendrán

CONDITIONAL

(yo)	tendría
(tú)	tendrías
(él/ella/usted)	tendría
(nosotros/as)	tendríamos
(vosotros/as)	tendríais
(ellos/ellas/ustedes)	tendrían

IMPERATIVE

ten / tened

PAST PARTICIPLE

tenido

GERUND

teniendo

EXAMPLE PHRASES

Tengo sed. I'm thirsty.
No *tenía* suficiente dinero. She didn't have enough money.
Tuvimos que irnos. We had to leave.

Remember that subject pronouns are not used very often in Spanish.

▶ **traer** (to bring)

PRESENT

(yo)	traigo
(tú)	traes
(él/ella/usted)	trae
(nosotros/as)	traemos
(vosotros/as)	traéis
(ellos/ellas/ustedes)	traen

PRESENT SUBJUNCTIVE

(yo)	traiga
(tú)	traigas
(él/ella/usted)	traiga
(nosotros/as)	traigamos
(vosotros/as)	traigáis
(ellos/ellas/ustedes)	traigan

PRETERITE

(yo)	traje
(tú)	trajiste
(él/ella/usted)	trajo
(nosotros/as)	trajimos
(vosotros/as)	trajisteis
(ellos/ellas/ustedes)	trajeron

IMPERFECT

(yo)	traía
(tú)	traías
(él/ella/usted)	traía
(nosotros/as)	traíamos
(vosotros/as)	traíais
(ellos/ellas/ustedes)	traían

FUTURE

(yo)	traeré
(tú)	traerás
(él/ella/usted)	traerá
(nosotros/as)	traeremos
(vosotros/as)	traeréis
(ellos/ellas/ustedes)	traerán

CONDITIONAL

(yo)	traería
(tú)	traerías
(él/ella/usted)	traería
(nosotros/as)	traeríamos
(vosotros/as)	traeríais
(ellos/ellas/ustedes)	traerían

IMPERATIVE

trae / traed

PAST PARTICIPLE

traído

GERUND

trayendo

EXAMPLE PHRASES

*¿**Has traído** lo que te pedí?* Did you bring what I asked you to?
*No **trajo** el dinero.* He didn't bring the money.
***Trae** eso.* Give that here.

Remember that subject pronouns are not used very often in Spanish.

▶ **venir** (to come)

PRESENT

(yo)	vengo
(tú)	vienes
(él/ella/usted)	viene
(nosotros/as)	venimos
(vosotros/as)	venís
(ellos/ellas/ustedes)	vienen

PRESENT SUBJUNCTIVE

(yo)	venga
(tú)	vengas
(él/ella/usted)	venga
(nosotros/as)	vengamos
(vosotros/as)	vengáis
(ellos/ellas/ustedes)	vengan

PRETERITE

(yo)	vine
(tú)	viniste
(él/ella/usted)	vino
(nosotros/as)	vinimos
(vosotros/as)	vinisteis
(ellos/ellas/ustedes)	vinieron

IMPERFECT

(yo)	venía
(tú)	venías
(él/ella/usted)	venía
(nosotros/as)	veníamos
(vosotros/as)	veníais
(ellos/ellas/ustedes)	venían

FUTURE

(yo)	vendré
(tú)	vendrás
(él/ella/usted)	vendrá
(nosotros/as)	vendremos
(vosotros/as)	vendréis
(ellos/ellas/ustedes)	vendrán

CONDITIONAL

(yo)	vendría
(tú)	vendrías
(él/ella/usted)	vendría
(nosotros/as)	vendríamos
(vosotros/as)	vendríais
(ellos/ellas/ustedes)	vendrían

IMPERATIVE

ven / venid

PAST PARTICIPLE

venido

GERUND

viniendo

EXAMPLE PHRASES

Vengo andando desde la playa. I've walked all the way from the beach.
¿**Vendrás** conmigo al cine? Will you come to the cinema with me?
Prefiero que no **venga**. I'd rather he didn't come.

Remember that subject pronouns are not used very often in Spanish.

▶ **ver** (to see)

PRESENT

(yo)	veo
(tú)	ves
(él/ella/usted)	ve
(nosotros/as)	vemos
(vosotros/as)	veis
(ellos/ellas/ustedes)	ven

PRESENT SUBJUNCTIVE

(yo)	vea
(tú)	veas
(él/ella/usted)	vea
(nosotros/as)	veamos
(vosotros/as)	veáis
(ellos/ellas/ustedes)	vean

PRETERITE

(yo)	vi
(tú)	viste
(él/ella/usted)	vio
(nosotros/as)	vimos
(vosotros/as)	visteis
(ellos/ellas/ustedes)	vieron

IMPERFECT

(yo)	veía
(tú)	veías
(él/ella/usted)	veía
(nosotros/as)	veíamos
(vosotros/as)	veíais
(ellos/ellas/ustedes)	veían

FUTURE

(yo)	veré
(tú)	verás
(él/ella/usted)	verá
(nosotros/as)	veremos
(vosotros/as)	veréis
(ellos/ellas/ustedes)	verán

CONDITIONAL

(yo)	vería
(tú)	verías
(él/ella/usted)	vería
(nosotros/as)	veríamos
(vosotros/as)	veríais
(ellos/ellas/ustedes)	verían

IMPERATIVE

ve / ved

PAST PARTICIPLE

visto

GERUND

viendo

EXAMPLE PHRASES

No **veo** muy bien. I can't see very well.
Los **veía** a todos desde la ventana. I could see them all from the window.
¿**Viste** lo que pasó? Did you see what happened?

Remember that subject pronouns are not used very often in Spanish.

▶ **vivir** (to live)

PRESENT

(yo)	vivo
(tú)	vives
(él/ella/usted)	vive
(nosotros/as)	vivimos
(vosotros/as)	vivís
(ellos/ellas/ustedes)	viven

PRESENT SUBJUNCTIVE

(yo)	viva
(tú)	vivas
(él/ella/usted)	viva
(nosotros/as)	vivamos
(vosotros/as)	viváis
(ellos/ellas/ustedes)	vivan

PRETERITE

(yo)	viví
(tú)	viviste
(él/ella/usted)	vivió
(nosotros/as)	vivimos
(vosotros/as)	vivisteis
(ellos/ellas/ustedes)	vivieron

IMPERFECT

(yo)	vivía
(tú)	vivías
(él/ella/usted)	vivía
(nosotros/as)	vivíamos
(vosotros/as)	vivíais
(ellos/ellas/ustedes)	vivían

FUTURE

(yo)	viviré
(tú)	vivirás
(él/ella/usted)	vivirá
(nosotros/as)	viviremos
(vosotros/as)	viviréis
(ellos/ellas/ustedes)	vivirán

CONDITIONAL

(yo)	viviría
(tú)	vivirías
(él/ella/usted)	viviria
(nosotros/as)	viviríamos
(vosotros/as)	viviríais
(ellos/ellas/ustedes)	vivirían

IMPERATIVE

vive / vivid

PAST PARTICIPLE

vivido

GERUND

viviendo

EXAMPLE PHRASES

Vivo *en Valencia.* I live in Valencia.
Vivieron *juntos dos años.* They lived together for two years.
Hemos vivido *momentos difíciles.* We've had some difficult times.

Remember that subject pronouns are not used very often in Spanish.

▶ **volver** (to return)

PRESENT

(yo)	vuelvo
(tú)	vuelves
(él/ella/usted)	vuelve
(nosotros/as)	volvemos
(vosotros/as)	volvéis
(ellos/ellas/ustedes)	vuelven

PRESENT SUBJUNCTIVE

(yo)	vuelva
(tú)	vuelvas
(él/ella/usted)	vuelva
(nosotros/as)	volvamos
(vosotros/as)	volváis
(ellos/ellas/ustedes)	vuelvan

PRETERITE

(yo)	volví
(tú)	volviste
(él/ella/usted)	volvió
(nosotros/as)	volvimos
(vosotros/as)	volvisteis
(ellos/ellas/ustedes)	volvieron

IMPERFECT

(yo)	volvía
(tú)	volvías
(él/ella/usted)	volvía
(nosotros/as)	volvíamos
(vosotros/as)	volvíais
(ellos/ellas/ustedes)	volvían

FUTURE

(yo)	volveré
(tú)	volverás
(él/ella/usted)	volverá
(nosotros/as)	volveremos
(vosotros/as)	volveréis
(ellos/ellas/ustedes)	volverán

CONDITIONAL

(yo)	volvería
(tú)	volverías
(él/ella/usted)	volvería
(nosotros/as)	volveríamos
(vosotros/as)	volveríais
(ellos/ellas/ustedes)	volverían

IMPERATIVE

vuelve / volved

PAST PARTICIPLE

vuelto

GERUND

volviendo

EXAMPLE PHRASES

*Mi padre **vuelve** mañana.* My father's coming back tomorrow.
*No **vuelvas** por aquí.* Don't come back here.
*Ha **vuelto** a casa.* He's gone back home.

Remember that subject pronouns are not used very often in Spanish.

1 Gerund **2** Imperative **3** Present **4** Preterite **5** Future **6** Present subjunctive
7 Past participle **8** Imperfect

Etc indicates that the irregular root is used for all persons of the tense, e.g.
oír: **6** oiga, oigas, oiga, oigamos, oigáis, oigan

abrir 7 abierto
agradecer 3 agradezco **6** agradezca *etc*
almorzar 2 almuerza **3** almuerzo,
  almuerzas, almuerza, almuerzan
  4 almorcé **6** almuerce, almuerces,
  almuerce, almorcemos, almorcéis,
  almuercen
andar 4 anduve, anduviste, anduvo,
  anduvimos, anduvisteis, anduvieron
aprobar 2 aprueba **3** apruebo,
  apruebas, aprueba, aprueban
  6 apruebe, apruebes, apruebe,
  aprueben
atravesar 2 atraviesa **3** atravieso,
  atraviesas, atraviesa, atraviesan
  6 atraviese, atravieses, atraviese,
  atraviesen
buscar 4 busqué **6** busque *etc*
caber 3 quepo **4** cupe, cupiste, cupo,
  cupimos, cupisteis, cupieron **5** cabré
  etc **6** quepa *etc*
caer 1 cayendo **3** caigo **4** caí, caíste,
  cayó, caímos, caísteis, cayeron
  6 caiga *etc* **7** caído
cerrar 2 cierra **3** cierro, cierras, cierra,
  cierran **6** cierre, cierres, cierre, cierren
coger *see* Verb Table 2
colgar 2 cuelga **3** cuelgo, cuelgas,
  cuelga, cuelgan **4** colgué **6** cuelgue,
  cuelgues, cuelgue, colguemos,
  colguéis, cuelguen
comer (regular –er verb) *see* Verb Table 3
conducir 3 conduzco **4** conduje,
  condujiste condujo, condujimos,
  condujisteis, condujeron
  6 conduzca *etc*
conocer 3 conozco **6** conozca *etc*
construir 1 construyendo
  2 construye **3** construyo, construyes,
  construye, construyen **4** construyó,
  construyeron **6** construya *etc*

contar 2 cuenta **3** cuento, cuentas,
  cuenta, cuentan **6** cuente, cuentes,
  cuente, cuenten
continuar 2 continúa **3** continúo,
  continúas, continúa, continúan
  6 continúe, continúes, continúe,
  continúen
corregir 3 corrijo, corriges, corrige,
  corrigen **4** corrigió, corrigieron,
  6 corrija *etc*
creer 1 creyendo **4** creí, creíste, creyó,
  creímos, creísteis, creyeron **7** creído
cubrir 7 cubierto
dar *see* Verb Table 4
decir *see* Verb Table 5
descubrir 7 descubierto
despertar 2 despierta **3** despierto,
  despiertas, despierta, despiertan
  6 despierte, despiertes, despierte,
  despierten
dirigir 3 dirijo **6** dirija, dirijas, dirija,
  dirijamos, dirijáis, dirijan
divertir 1 divirtiendo **2** divierte
  3 divierto, diviertes, divierte,
  divierten **4** divirtió, divirtieron
  6 divierta, diviertas, divierta,
  divirtamos, divirtáis, diviertan
dormir *see* Verb Table 6
empezar *see* Verb Table 7
encontrar 2 encuentra **3** encuentro,
  encuentras, encuentra, encuentran
  6 encuentre, encuentres, encuentre,
  encuentren
entender *see* Verb Table 8
enviar *see* Verb Table 9
escribir 7 escrito
estar *see* Verb Table 10
freír 1 friendo **2** fríe, freíd **3** frío, fríes,
  fríe, freímos, freís, fríen **4** freí, freíste,
  frio, freímos, freísteis, frieron **5** freiré
  etc **6** fría, frías, fría, friamos, friais,
  frían **7** frito

haber *see* Verb Table 11

hablar (regular **–ar** verb) *see* Verb Table 12

hacer *see* Verb Table 13

imprimir 7 impreso

instruir 1 instruyendo **2** instruye **3** instruyo, instruyes, instruye, instruyen **4** instruyó, instruyeron **6** instruya *etc*

ir *see* Verb Table 14

jugar 2 juega **3** juego, juegas, juega, juegan **4** jugué **6** juegue *etc*

lavarse (regular **–ar** reflexive verb) *see* Verb Table 15

leer *see* Verb Table 16

marcar 4 marqué **6** marque *etc*

morir 1 muriendo **2** muere **3** muero, mueres, muere, mueren **4** murió, murieron **6** muera, mueras, muera, muramos, muráis, mueran **7** muerto

mover 2 mueve **3** muevo, mueves, mueve, mueven **6** mueva, muevas, mueva, muevan

negar 2 niega **3** niego, niegas, niega, niegan **4** negué **6** niegue, niegues, niegue, neguemos, neguéis, nieguen

oír *see* Verb Table 17

ofrecer 3 ofrezco **6** ofrezca *etc*

oler 2 huele **3** huelo, hueles, huele, huelen **6** huela, huelas, huela, huelan

pagar 4 pagué **6** pague *etc*

parecer 3 parezco **6** parezca *etc*

pedir *see* Verb Table 18

pensar *see* Verb Table 19

perder 2 pierde **3** pierdo, pierdes, pierde, pierden **6** pierda, pierdas, pierda, pierdan

poder *see* Verb Table 20

poner *see* Verb Table 21

preferir 1 prefiriendo **2** prefiere **3** prefiero, prefieres, prefiere, prefieren **4** prefirió, prefirieron **6** prefiera, prefieras, prefiera, prefiramos, prefiráis, prefieran

producir 3 produzco **4** produje, produjiste produjo, produjimos, produjisteis, produjeron **6** produzca *etc*

prohibir 2 prohíbe **3** prohíbo, prohíbes, prohíbe, prohíben **6** prohíba, prohíbas, prohíba, prohíban

querer *see* Verb Table 22

reír 2 ríe **3** río, ríes, ríe, reímos, reís, ríen **4** reí, reíste, rio, reímos, reísteis, rieron **6** ría, rías, ría, riamos, riais, rían

repetir 1 repitiendo **2** repite **3** repito, repites, repite, repiten **4** repitió, repitieron **6** repita etc

reunir 2 reúne **3** reúno, reúnes, reúne, reúnen, **6** reúna, reúnas, reúna, reúnan

rogar 2 ruega **3** ruego, ruegas, ruega, ruegan **4** rogué **6** ruegue, ruegues, ruegue, roguemos, roguéis, rueguen

romper 7 roto

saber *see* Verb Table 23

sacar 4 saqué **6** saque *etc*

salir 2 sal **3** salgo **5** saldré etc **6** salga *etc*

seguir *see* Verb Table 24

sentar 2 sienta **3** siento, sientas, sienta, sientan **6** siente, sientes, siente, sienten

sentir *see* Verb Table 25

ser *see* Verb Table 26

servir 3 sirviendo **2** sirve **3** sirvo, sirves, sirve, sirven **4** sirvió, sirvieron **6** sirva *etc*

soñar 2 sueña **3** sueño, sueñas, sueña, sueñan **6** sueñe, sueñes, sueñe, sueñen

tener *see* Verb Table 27

torcer 2 tuerce **3** tuerzo, tuerces, tuerce, tuercen **6** tuerza, tuerzas, tuerza, torzamos, torzáis, tuerzan

traer *see* Verb Table 28

valer 2 vale **3** valgo **5** valdré etc **6** valga *etc*

vencer 3 venzo **6** venza *etc*

venir *see* Verb Table 29

ver *see* Verb Table 30

vestir 1 vistiendo **2** viste **3** visto, vistes, viste, visten **4** vistió, vistieron **6** vista *etc*

vivir (regular **–ir** verb) *see* Verb Table 31

volver *see* Verb Table 32